EDUCATIONAL IDEAS IN AMERICA:

A Documentary History

EDUCATIONAL IDEAS IN AMERICA:

A Documentary History

Edited by

S. ALEXANDER RIPPA
UNIVERSITY OF VERMONT

DAVID McKAY COMPANY, INC.
New York

EDUCATIONAL IDEAS IN AMERICA

LIBRARY OF CONGRESS CATALOG CARD NUMBER: 69–12127

MANUFACTURED IN THE UNITED STATES OF AMERICA

To
Barbara

ACKNOWLEDGMENT

The cover photograph pictures the "Talking Typewriter," a computer-based, multi-sensory learning system that is used primarily for the teaching of reading. It is shown through courtesy of Responsive Environments Corporation, Englewood Cliffs, New Jersey.

Preface

My aim is to provide a source book of materials that will help bring educational history to life. The richness and diversity of America's heritage are represented by the works of educators, historians, political theorists, theologians, and essayists, in order to portray vividly the modes of educational thought characteristic of each period. Within a chronological framework, the book is topically arranged in a way that relates educational ideas to the development of American intellectual and social history.

I have avoided short, disjointed excerpts. Instead of presenting a great many snippets, I have tried to include the whole, or at least a major part, of each document selected. Wherever possible I have reproduced material from its primary source and in its original form.

The ideas which stirred the minds and hearts of Americans in the past should provoke serious thought today. In my introductions, I have highlighted some key issues; but at the same time, I have deliberately avoided digesting in advance the author's message. Analyses of the various selections I have left for each reader. I hope that this will retain the thrill of discovery and pave the way for some stimulating discussions.

I wish to thank my colleagues and fellow historians whose warm response to my earlier work, *Education in a Free Society,* encouraged the preparation of this new volume. Many have suggested collateral readings for inclusion in this anthology. Several libraries have extended their special courtesies to me, particularly the Houghton and Widener libraries of Harvard University, where I continuously sought, and have always obtained, patient and helpful assistance with my researches. I am grateful, too, to my editor, Gordon G. Hill, of David McKay Company, Inc., for his wise counsel during my years of research.

I also wish to express my deep gratitude to those authors, publishers, and owners of copyright, who have so kindly permitted me to use materials from their works.

As always, I am forever indebted to my wife, Barbara Frogel Rippa, and to our children, Diane and Joel, without whose forbearance and encouragement this book might never have been possible.

S. ALEXANDER RIPPA
April 15, 1969
Oxford, England

Table of Contents

Part Two

AN ERA OF TRANSITION: 1865–1919

Part Three

EDUCATION IN MODERN SOCIETY: 1919 to the Present

PART ONE

EDUCATIONAL THOUGHT: THE FORMATIVE YEARS

"There is inborn in human nature a love of liberty."

JOHN AMOS COMENIUS, *The Way of Light,* 1668

"Justice, when it has developed simply and soberly in the depths of a man's soul, is his best safeguard against the chief and most deadly consequences of prejudice."

JOHANN HEINRICH PESTALOZZI, Letter to Heinrich Gessner, 1799

"A plan of universal education ought to be adopted in the United States."

GEORGE WASHINGTON, Letter to Robert Brooke, March 16, 1795

"We must remember that ever since the days of Socrates, and especially after the establishment of Christianity, the dice of thought have been loaded. Certain pledges have preceded inquiry and divided the possible conclusions beforehand into the acceptable and the inacceptable, the edifying and the shocking, the noble and the base."

GEORGE SANTAYANA, "The Moral Background," 1920

Introduction

We begin with a look at the rich cultural heritage which the Old World bequeathed to the New. The clusters of values, the patterns of thought—indeed, all the agencies of American intellectual life—developed in the New World in relation to their European counterparts. America borrowed extensively from Europe. Each generation of immigrants who settled on American shores brought with them bodies of knowledge and concepts of good and evil. This transmission of thought was a vital force in the growth of educational ideas in America.

Because American culture came to differ from European life, educational ideas also changed. Emigrating from an English society of which they disapproved, the Puritans, for example, sought to build a better world in New England during the early seventeenth century. Class distinctions were sharp, and religious freedom and political democracy were not the general rule. But compared with that of the Old World, the evolving social order in America was open and fluid. As successive generations of Americans matured, educational ideas were gradually modified. This interrelationship between a changing social milieu and developing patterns of educational thought is an important theme which should not be overlooked.

I

Few topics have been discussed more fervently than America's religious tradition in education. In the legal sense, religion has meant sectarian teaching—a definition which connotes the inculcation of ideas and values. Assuming a more "neutral" position, educators sometimes seek to teach *about* religion. Still the basic issues remain unresolved: sectarian discussions of any nature in a *public* school trouble thoughtful citizens, for the religious tradition has deeply affected our most cherished beliefs. The accelerated trend toward secularism—toward a public school devoid of religious teaching and yet charged with a growing responsibility to inculcate ethics and morals—poses problems and issues that will certainly spark new controversies in the years ahead.

II

Desiderius Erasmus (1466?–1536) was an outstanding scholar of the Humanist movement. This era, which extends from about the beginning of the fifteenth to the end of the sixteenth centuries, was characterized by a revival of interest in ancient classical literature. Some Renaissance thinkers were called *Humanists* because they were interested in the humanities or the great literary classics of the past; indeed, some developed such an intense love for the Latin and Greek languages and literature that they tended to scorn all other authority. Many found a new interest in the nature of man and in the joys of this world.

Thus the spirit of Humanism was marked by an endeavor to enjoy life more fully and to make the educative process more attractive and rewarding. Of all the Humanist teachers of this period, Erasmus of Rotterdam has left the clearest instructions on how to accomplish these ends.

Erasmus traveled widely and taught at universities throughout England and France, espousing a Humanist point of view. Like other Renaissance scholars, he expressed an

3

interest in human nature. He wanted to free the individual from demands imposed by such authoritative institutions as the guilds, the monasteries, and the Church. He urged that exploitation and class differences be abolished and that every citizen be permitted to live with decency and a sense of honor.

A great proponent of Humanist learning, Erasmus advocated the study of the classics for the purpose of expanding the horizons of knowledge and of developing in men the ability to make decisions. "Sound education," he declared in 1529, "is the condition of real wisdom." His emphasis on individuality in learning was welcomed in an age accustomed to rote memory and slavish imitations of the Greek and Roman masters, especially Cicero.

A generation later, the French essayist Michel Eyquem de Montaigne (1533–1592) also deprecated instructors who proceeded as though teaching were merely a process of pouring knowledge into a funnel, into the pupil's ear. In seeking greater independence for the learner, both Erasmus and Montaigne were ahead of their times. Montaigne's views represent a secular form of Humanism which leads directly toward the scientific movement of the European Enlightenment.

III

The remarkable educational achievement of the Puritans was their success in preserving the heritage of Western thought amid barbaric conditions of a new and courageous venture. Puritan assumptions about life on earth, about literacy and learning, are so tightly interwoven into the fabric of Puritan theology that we are apt to overlook the real significance of education in colonial New England if we study only the external "system" of schools established in the Massachusetts Bay Colony in the seventeenth century. In the Puritan mind, everyday behavior, all knowledge and thought, were deemed education according to God's will. And in the eyes of God, the Puritan leaders sought to build in their Bible Commonwealth a city upon a hill, a mecca for saints, indeed a model for the whole Christian world to emulate. We fail to understand the spirit of Puritanism unless we realize that the founders of the Massachusetts Bay Colony in the sixteen-thirties viewed themselves as a chosen people whom God had led to the New World away from the sins of the Old.

The Puritans were Calvinists in the sense that they agreed with the theologian of Geneva. Both held that man had fallen into a state of sin and that in order to be saved, he must receive from God a special infusion of grace given to some but not to others. In Puritan thought, certain souls were "predestined" to heaven and others sentenced to eternal damnation. The Puritans accepted the doctrine, not because John Calvin taught it, but because they believed it. Their studies of Scripture and their observations of men seemed to confirm this belief in the sinfulness of man.

Thus Puritan theology, in its most elementary form, governed a whole way of life: God, who is omniscient and outside time, knows who will and who will not achieve salvation. There is no other reason except that God ordained it. This is the rule of Puritan existence: some are saved, and others are not; some are born wealthy, and others destitute; some bright, and others dull. While man must live by reason and abide by justice, he must not expect God's will to be confined by human conceptions of what is just and what is reasonable. The Puritan mission in the New World was fraught with anxiety because God's will was so unpredictable, so unlikely to conform to human ideas of mercy and justice. Only when viewed in this light does the idea of predestination assume real meaning and force in the Puritan's own world.

The closing years of the seventeenth century witnessed the gradual decline of the Bible Commonwealth. The experiment had lost its hold on the minds and hearts of the people. During the half-century of its supremacy, the theocracy passed through a succession of crises: the struggle for representative government, the outcry of Anne Hutchinson, the witchcraft hysteria in Salem. Stronger than any other force in its eventual defeat was the impact of the Enlightenment, of powerful ideas and new points of view which reshaped the minds of men and changed the process of education.

IV

Born in Zurich, Swtizerland, in 1746, Johann Heinrich Pestalozzi wrote several stories, but none surpassed *Leonard and Gertrude* in so beautifully stating its author's own pedagogic beliefs. It is a tale of deep love, not for an individual, but for children, for the homeless, the destitute, and the weak. It depicts Pestalozzi's hope and strivings for a better world for children everywhere.

Like Jean Jacques Rousseau, Pestalozzi rejected the religious aim in teaching and conceived of education as an organic process, as the "harmonious development of all the child's powers and faculties." But education, Pestalozzi insisted, is for everyone, not just the privileged few. And unlike Rousseau's, Pestalozzi's goal was to uplift all children—indeed, to reform society through education.

Leonard and Gertrude portrays a picture of village life that was as real to Pestalozzi as it is strange to us. Most important, of course, is the story's symbolic message: Bonnal, the dismal hamlet, is the world; the wicked bailiff stands for intrigue, for the evils which degrade society; and Gertrude is the noble and devoted woman—above all, the children's teacher whose successful "home-school" becomes the means for regeneration, for improving the world, if indeed it is to be improved. Note that social regeneration is effected, not by laws and money (important as these are), but by a new methodology used with skill and devotion by a master teacher whose "key-words"

made Pestalozzi's name immortal on two continents.

V

A symbol of the American Enlightenment, Benjamin Franklin (1706–1790) was successful in a number of ventures, ranging from science to public affairs and the business world. What distinguishes Franklin's writings is the secularization of his ideas. He expounds a humanitarianism coincident with Enlightenment ideals. Self-educated and intellectually curious, Franklin tried to retain some Puritan virtues devoid of theological meaning.

In his plan for an academy, for a new type of secondary education, Franklin brought into focus the issue of social mobility through the school. His "Proposals" were designed to meet the needs of a new middle class, "of *a rising* people," to use Franklin's own words. He not only prescribed a complete curriculum but also aimed toward an education which included more than the transmission of the cultural heritage. "Youth will come out of this School," Franklin concluded in 1751, "fitted for learning any Business, Calling, or Profession."

VI

In the history of American education, the most significant development from 1775 to 1829 was the emergence of ideas vital for a new republic. Especially important was a belief in the close relationship between freedom and education. The fact that education was not mentioned in the Constitution of the United States never meant that it was considered unessential. For the Founding Fathers, liberty without enlightenment was a contradiction in concepts. Clearly expressed in the writings of Thomas Jefferson (1743–1826), such ideas as freedom, equality, and individual rights were topics for lively discussions in letters, pamphlets, and town meetings throughout the colonies.

These ideas gained strength during the Enlightenment and found in young America a fertile soil, an atmosphere conducive to growth.

VII

The concern for equality of opportunity was an important element in the movement for free schools. Active in support of public education, for example, were the newly formed workingmen's associations which in the eighteen-thirties viewed tax-supported schools as gateways to opportunity in the United States. Spirited and vigorous, the campaign was led by some dedicated reformers whose crusading zeal has seldom, if ever, been surpassed in American history. Two of the ablest spokesmen in support of tax-supported systems of education were Thaddeus Stevens (1792–1868) and Horace Mann (1796–1859).

A contemporary of Mann, Ralph Waldo Emerson (1803–1882) thought of education as development from within, not as an external "system" of formal schooling. In his essay on "Education," he wisely urges self-trust and self-respect: respect the child, he tells the teacher over and over again, and help the child to respect himself. "The great object of Education should be commensurate with the object of life," Emerson states. "It should be a moral one; to teach self-trust." Emerson also argues repeatedly for individualism, for a certain inner strength that would provide each of us with the necessary fortitude to work for and keep our cherished ideals. "Trust thyself," he writes in his most famous essay; "every heart beats to that iron string." Those who object to conformity, to transforming modern society into a computerized number system, will find plenty of ammunition in Emerson's writings.

CHAPTER ONE

Intellectual Currents from the Old World

THE RELIGIOUS TRADITION

THE BIBLE *

Isaiah i, 16–18:

Cease to do evil;
Learn to do well;
Seek justice, relieve the oppressed,
Judge the fatherless, plead for the widow.
Come now, and let us reason together. . . .

Exodus xxiii, 1–2; xxiv, 12:

Thou shalt not utter a false report; put not thy hand with the wicked to be an unrighteous witness.

Thou shalt not follow a multitude to do evil; neither shalt thou bear witness in a cause to turn aside after a multitude to pervert justice.

. . . . .

And the Lord said unto Moses: "Come up to Me into the mount, and be there; and I will give thee the tables of stone, and the law and the commandment, which I have written, that thou mayest teach them."

Deuteronomy v, 16–22; vi, 5–7:

Honour thy father and thy mother, as the Lord thy God commanded thee; that thy days may be long, and that it may go well with thee, upon the land which the Lord thy God giveth thee.

Thou shalt not murder.

Neither shalt thou commit adultery.

Neither shalt thou steal.

* From the Old Testament, translated according to the Masoretic text.

Neither shalt thou bear false witness against thy neighbour.

Neither shalt thou covet thy neighbour's wife; neither shalt thou desire thy neighbour's house, his field, or his man-servant, or his maid-servant, his ox, or his ass, or any thing that is thy neighbour's.

These words the Lord spoke unto all your assembly in the mount out of the midst of the fire, of the cloud, and of the thick darkness, with a great voice, and it went on no more. And He wrote them upon two tables of stone, and gave them unto me.

. . . . .

And thou shalt love the Lord thy God with all thy heart, and with all thy soul, and with all thy might.

And these words, which I command thee this day, shall be upon thy heart;

And thou shalt teach them diligently unto thy children, and shalt talk of them when thou sittest in thy house, and when thou walkest by the way, and when thou liest down, and when thou risest up.

MOSES MAIMONIDES
"On True Wisdom" (1190) *

The ancient and the modern philosophers have shown that man can acquire four kinds
* Moses Maimonides. *The Guide of the Perplexed* (1190) (New York: Hebrew Publishing Co., [1881]; translated from the original and annotated by M. Friedländer), Book III, Chapter 54, "On True Wisdom," pp. 300–302. At the conclusion of his great book, in a tender and beseeching tone, Maimonides (1135–

7

of perfection. The first kind, the lowest, in the acquisition of which people spend their days, is perfection as regards property; the possession of money, garments, furniture, servants, land, and the like; the possession of the title of a great king belongs to this class. There is no close connection between this possession and its possessor; it is a perfectly imaginary relation when on account of the great advantage a person derives from these possessions, he says, This is my house, this is my servant, this is my money, and these are my hosts and armies. For when he examines himself he will find that all these things are external, and their qualities are entirely independent of the possessor. When, therefore, that relation ceases, he that has been a great king may one morning find that there is no difference between him and the lowest person, and yet no change has taken place in the things which were ascribed to him. The philosophers have shown that he whose sole aim in all his exertions and endeavours is the possession of this kind of perfection, only seeks perfectly imaginary and transient things; and even if these remain his property all his lifetime, they do not give him any perfection.

The second kind is more closely related to man's body than the first. It includes the perfection of the shape, constitution, and form of man's body; the utmost evenness of temperaments, and the proper order and strength of his limbs. This kind of perfection must likewise be excluded from forming our chief aim; because it is a perfection of the body, and man does not possess it as man, but as a living being; he has this property besides in common with the lowest animal; and even if a person possesses the

greatest possible strength, he could not be as strong as a mule, much less can he be as strong as a lion or an elephant; he, therefore, can at the utmost have strength that might enable him to carry a heavy burden, or break a thick substance, or do similar things, in which there is no great profit for the body. The soul derives no profit whatever from this kind of perfection.

The third kind of perfection is more closely connected with man himself than the second perfection. It includes moral perfection; the highest degree of excellency in man's character. Most of the precepts aim at producing this perfection; but even this kind is only a preparation for another perfection, and is not sought for its own sake. For all moral principles concern the relation of man to his neighbour; the perfection of man's moral principles is, as it were, given to man for the benefit of mankind. Imagine a person being alone, and having no connection whatever with any other person, all his good moral principles are at rest, they are not required, and give man no perfection whatever. These principles are only necessary and useful when man comes in contact with others.

The fourth kind of perfection is the true perfection of man; the possession of the highest intellectual faculties; the possession of such notions which lead to true metaphysical opinions as regards God. With this perfection man has obtained his final object; it gives him true human perfection; it remains to him alone; it gives him immortality, and on its account he is called man. Examine the first three kinds of perfection, you will find that, if you possess them, they are not your property, but the property of others, although, according to the ordinary view, they belong to you and to others. But the last kind of perfection is exclusively yours; no one else owns any part of it, "They shall be only thine own, and not strangers, with thee" (Prov. v. 17). Your aim must therefore be to attain this [fourth] perfection that is exclusively yours, and you ought not to continue to work and weary yourself for

---

1204) addresses the reader to the purpose and meaning of life. The whole drama of man's longings and ambitions—the achievements of character, health, and wisdom—unfolds. Here, then, in one of the first selections is an educational ideal formulated almost two thousand years ago. It is given classic expression in the words of the great Jewish thinker who reconciled Aristotle with Judaism.

that which belongs to others, whilst neglecting your soul till it has lost entirely its original purity through the dominion of the bodily powers over it. . . .

MARTIN LUTHER,
"Letter to the Mayors and Aldermen of All the Cities of Germany in Behalf of Christian Schools" (1524) *

Grace and peace from God our Father and the Lord Jesus Christ. Honored and dear Sirs: Having three years ago been put under the ban and outlawed, I should have kept silent, had I regarded the command of men more than that of God. Many persons in Germany both of high and low estate assail my discourses and writings on that account, and shed much blood over them. But God who has opened my mouth and bidden me speak, stands firmly by me, and without any counsel or effort of mine strengthens and extends my cause the more, the more they rage, and seems, as the second Psalm says, to "have them in derision." By this alone any one not blinded by prejudice may see that the work is of God; for it exhibits the divine method, according to which God's cause spreads most rapidly when men exert themselves most to oppose and suppress it. . . .

First of all we see how the schools are deteriorating throughout Germany. The universities are becoming weak, the monasteries are declining, and, as Isaiah says, "The grass withereth, the flower fadeth, because the spirit of the Lord bloweth upon it," through the Gospel. For through the word of God the unchristian and sensual character of these institutions is becoming known. And because selfish parents see that they

* Martin Luther, "Letter to the Mayors and Aldermen of All the Cities of Germany in Behalf of Christian Schools" (Wittenberg, 1524), as reprinted in F. V. N. Painter, *Luther on Education, including a Historical Introduction and a Translation of the Reformer's Two Most Important Educational Treatises* (Philadelphia: Lutheran Publication Society, 1889), pp. 169–171, 173–174, 177–187, 194–204, 206–209.

can no longer place their children upon the bounty of monasteries and cathedrals, they refuse to educate them. "Why should we educate our children," they say, "if they are not to become priests, monks, and nuns, and thus earn a support?"

. . . I beg you all, in the name of God and of our neglected youth, not to think of this subject lightly, as many do who see not what the prince of this world intends. For the right instruction of youth is a matter in which Christ and all the world are concerned. Thereby are we all aided. And consider that great Christian zeal is needed to overcome the silent, secret, and artful machinations of the devil. If we must annually expend large sums on muskets, roads, bridges, dams, and the like, in order that the city may have temporal peace and comfort, why should we not apply as much to our poor, neglected youth, in order that we may have a skillful school-master or two?

There is one consideration that should move every citizen, with devout gratitude to God, to contribute a part of his means to the support of schools—the consideration that if divine grace had not released him from exactions and robbery, he would still have to give large sums of money for indulgences, masses, vigils, endowments, anniversaries, mendicant friars, brotherhoods, and other similar impositions. And let him be sure that where turmoil and strife exist, there the devil is present, who did not writhe and struggle so long as men blindly contributed to convents and masses. For Satan feels that his cause is suffering injury. Let this, then, be the first consideration to move you,—that in this work we are fighting against the devil, the most artful and dangerous enemy of men. . . .

It is indeed a sin and shame that we must be aroused and incited to the duty of educating our children and of considering their highest interests, whereas nature itself should move us thereto, and the example of the heathen affords us varied instruction. There is no irrational animal that does not care for and instruct its young in what they should know, except the ostrich, of which God says; "She leaveth her eggs in the earth, and warmeth them in the dust; and is hardened against her young ones, as though they were not hers." And what would it avail if we possessed and performed all else, and became perfect saints, if we neglect that for which we chiefly live, namely, to care for the young? In my judgment there is no other outward offense that in the sight of God so heavily burdens the world, and deserves such heavy chastisement, as the neglect to educate children. . . .

But all that, you say, is addressed to parents; what does it concern the members of the council and the mayors? That is true; but how, if parents neglect it? Who shall attend to it then? Shall we therefore let it alone, and suffer the children to be neglected? How will the mayors and council excuse themselves, and prove that such a duty does not belong to them?

Parents neglect this duty from various causes.

In the first place, there are some who are so lacking in piety and uprightness that they would not do it if they could, but like the ostrich, harden themselves against their own offspring, and do nothing for them. Nevertheless these children must live among us and with us. How then can reason and, above all, Christian charity, suffer them to grow up ill-bred, and to infect other children, till at last the whole city be destroyed, like Sodom, Gomorrah, and some other cities?

In the second place, the great majority of parents are unqualified for it, and do not understand how children should be brought up and taught. For they have learned nothing but to provide for their bodily wants; and in order to teach and train children thoroughly, a separate class is needed.

In the third place, even if parents were qualified and willing to do it themselves, yet on account of other employments and household duties they have no time for it, so that necessity requires us to have teachers for public schools, unless each parent employ a private instructor. But that would be too expensive for persons of ordinary means, and many a bright boy, on account of poverty, would be neglected. Besides, many parents die and leave orphans; and how they are usually cared for by guardians, we might learn, even if observation were not enough, from the sixty-eighth Psalm, where God calls himself the "Father of the fatherless," as of those who are neglected by all others. Also there are some who have no children, and therefore feel no interest in them.

Therefore it will be the duty of the mayors and council to exercise the greatest care over the young. For since the happiness, honor, and life of the city are committed to their hands, they would be held recreant before God and the world, if they did not, day and night, with all their power, seek its welfare and improvement. Now the welfare of a city does not consist alone in great treasures, firm walls, beautiful houses, and munitions of war; indeed, where all these are found, and reckless fools come into power, the city sustains the greater injury. But the highest welfare, safety, and power of a city consists in able, learned, wise, upright, cultivated citizens, who can secure, preserve, and utilize every treasure and advantage. . . .

Since, then, a city must have well-trained people, and since the greatest need, lack, and lament is that such are not to be found, we must not wait till they grow up of themselves; neither can they be hewed out of stones nor cut out of wood; nor will God work miracles, so long as men can attain their object through means within their reach. Therefore we must see to it, and spare no trouble or expense to educate and form them ourselves. For whose fault is it that in all cities there are at present so few skillful people except the rulers, who have allowed the young to grow up like trees in the forest, and have not cared how they were reared and taught? The growth, consequently, has been so irregular that the forest furnishes no timber for building purposes, but like a useless hedge, is good only for fuel.

Yet there must be civil government. For us, then, to permit ignoramuses and blockheads to rule when we can prevent it, is irrational and barbarous. Let us rather make rulers out of swine and wolves, and set them over people who are indifferent to the manner in which they are governed. It is barbarous for men to think thus: "We will now rule; and what does it concern us how those fare who shall come after us?" Not over human beings, but over swine and dogs should such people rule, who think only of their own interests and honor in governing. Even if we exercise the greatest care to educate able, learned and skilled rulers, yet much care and effort are necessary in order to secure prosperity. How can a city prosper, when no effort is made?

But, you say again, if we shall and must have schools, what is the use to teach Latin, Greek, Hebrew, and the other liberal arts? Is it not enough to teach the Scriptures, which are necessary to salvation, in the mother tongue? To which I answer: I know, alas! that we Germans must always remain irrational brutes, as we are deservedly called by surrounding nations. But I wonder why we do not also say: of what use to us are silk, wine, spices, and other foreign articles, since we ourselves have an abundance of wine, corn, wool, flax, wood, and stone in the German states, not only for our necessities, but also for embellishment and ornament? The languages and other liberal arts, which are not only harmless, but even a greater ornament, benefit, and honor than these things, both for understanding the Holy Scriptures and carrying on the civil government, we are disposed to despise; and the foreign articles which are neither necessary nor useful, and which besides greatly impoverish us, we are unwilling to dispense with. Are we not rightly called German dunces and brutes?

Indeed, if the languages were of no practical benefit, we ought still to feel an interest in them as a wonderful gift of God, with which he has now blessed Germany almost beyond all other lands. We do not find many instances in which Satan has fostered them through the universities and cloisters; on the contrary, these institutions have fiercely inveighed and continue to inveigh against them. For the devil scented the danger that would threaten his kingdom, if the languages should be generally studied. But since he could not wholly prevent their cultivation, he aims at least to confine them within such narrow limits, that they will of themselves decline and fall into disuse. They are to him no welcome guest, and consequently he shows them scant courtesy in order that they may not remain long. This malicious trick of Satan is perceived by very few.

Therefore, my beloved countrymen, let us open our eyes, thank God for this precious treasure, and take pains to preserve it, and to frustrate the design of Satan. For we cannot deny that, although the Gospel has come and daily comes through the Holy Spirit, it has come by means of the languages, and through them must increase and be preserved. . . .

In the same measure that the Gospel is dear to us, should we zealously cherish the languages. For God had a purpose in giving the Scriptures only in two languages, the Old Testament in the Hebrew, and the New Testament in the Greek. What God did not despise, but chose before all others for His Word, we should likewise esteem above all others. . . .

And let this be kept in mind, that we will not preserve the Gospel without the languages. The languages are the scabbard in which the Word of God is sheathed. They are the casket in which this jewel is enshrined; the cask in which this wine is kept; the chamber in which this food is stored. And, to borrow a figure from the Gospel itself, they are the baskets in which this bread, and fish, and fragments are preserved. If through neglect we lose the languages (which may God forbid), we will not only lose the Gospel, but it will finally come to pass that we will lose also the ability to speak and write either Latin or German. Of this let us take as proof and warning the miserable and shocking example presented in the universities and cloisters, in which not only the Gospel has been perverted, but also the Latin and German languages have been corrupted, so that the wretched inmates have become like brutes, unable to speak and write German or Latin, and have almost lost their natural reason.

The apostles considered it necessary to embody the New Testament in the Greek language, in order, no doubt, that it might be securely preserved unto us as in a sacred shrine. For they foresaw what has since taken place, namely, that when the divine revelation is left to oral tradition, much disorder and confusion arise from conflicting opinions and doctrines. And there would be no way to prevent this evil and to protect the simple-minded, if the New Testament was not definitely recorded in writing. Therefore it is evident that where the languages are not preserved, there the Gospel will become corrupted.

. . . . .

So much for the utility and necessity of the languages, and of Christian schools for our spiritual interests and the salvation of the soul. Let us now consider the body and inquire: though there were no soul, nor heaven, nor hell, but only the civil government, would not this require good schools and learned men more than do our spiritual interests?

. . . We know, or ought to know, how necessary and useful a thing it is, and how acceptable to God, when a prince, lord, counsellor, or other ruler, is well-trained and skillful in discharging, in a Christian way, the functions of his office.

Even if there were no soul, (as I have already said,) and men did not need schools and the languages for the sake of Christianity and the Scriptures, still, for the establishment of the best schools everywhere, both for boys and girls, this consideration is of itself sufficient, namely, that society, for the maintenance of civil order and the proper regulation of the household, needs accomplished and well-trained men and women. Now such men are to come from boys, and such women from girls; hence it is necessary that boys and girls be properly taught and brought up. As I have before said, the ordinary man is not qualified for this task, and can not, and will not do it. Princes and lords ought to do it; but they spend their time in pleasure-driving, drinking, and folly, and are burdened with the weighty duties of the cellar, kitchen and bedchamber. And though some would be glad to do it, they must stand in fear of the rest, lest they be taken for fools or heretics. Therefore, honored members of the city councils, this work must remain in your hands; you have more time and better opportunity for it than princes and lords.

But each one, you say, may educate and discipline his own sons and daughters. To which I reply: We see indeed how it goes with this teaching and training. And where it is carried to the highest point, and is attended with success, it results in nothing more than that the learners, in some measure, acquire a forced external propriety of manner; in other respects they remain dunces, knowing nothing, and incapable of giving aid or advice. But were they instructed in schools or elsewhere by thoroughly qualified male or female teachers, who taught the languages, other arts, and history, then the pupils would hear the history and maxims of the world, and see how things went with each city, kingdom, prince, man, and woman; and thus, in a short time, they would be able to comprehend, as in a mirror, the character, life, counsels, undertakings, successes, and failures, of the whole world from the beginning. From this knowledge they could regulate their views, and order their course of life in the fear of God, having become wise in judging what is to be sought and what avoided in this outward life, and capable of advising and directing others. But the training which is given at home is expected to make us wise through our own experience. Before that can take place, we shall die a hundred times, and all through life act injudiciously; for much time is needed to give experience.

Now since the young must leap and jump, or have something to do, because they have a natural desire for it which should not be restrained, (for it is not well to check them in everything,) why should we not provide for them such schools, and lay before them such studies? By the gracious arrangement of God, children take delight in acquiring knowledge, whether languages, mathematics, or history. And our schools are no longer a hell or purgatory, in which children are tortured over cases and tenses, and in which with much flogging, trembling, anguish and wretchedness they learn nothing. If we take so much time and pains to teach our children to play cards, sing, and dance, why should we not take as much time to teach them reading and other branches of knowledge, while they are young and at leisure, are quick at learning, and take delight in it? As for myself,[1] if I had children and were able, I would have them learn not only the languages and history, but also singing, instrumental music, and the whole course of mathematics. For what is all this but mere child's play, in which the Greeks in former ages trained their children, and by this means became wonderfully skillful people, capable for every undertaking? How I regret that I did not read more poetry and history, and that no one taught me in these branches. Instead of these I was obliged with great cost, labor, and injury, to read Satanic filth, the Aristotelian and Scholastic philosophy, so that I have enough to do to get rid of it.

But you say, who can do without his children and bring them up, in this manner, to be young gentlemen? I reply: it is not my idea that we should establish schools as they have been heretofore, where a boy has studied Donatus and Alexander [2] twenty or

thirty years, and yet has learned nothing. The world has changed, and things go differently. My idea is that boys should spend an hour or two a day in school, and the rest of the time work at home, learn some trade and do whatever is desired, so that study and work may go on together, while the children are young and can attend to both. They now spend tenfold as much time in shooting with crossbows, playing ball, running, and tumbling about.

In like manner, a girl has time to go to school an hour a day, and yet attend to her work at home; for she sleeps, dances, and plays away more than that. The real difficulty is found alone in the absence of an earnest desire to educate the young, and to aid and benefit mankind with accomplished citizens. The devil much prefers blockheads and drones, that men may have more abundant trials and sorrows in the world.

But the brightest pupils, who give promise of becoming accomplished teachers, preachers, and workers, should be kept longer at school, or set apart wholly for study, as we read of the holy martyrs, who brought up St. Agnes, St. Agatha, St. Lucian, and others. For this purpose also the cloisters and cathedral schools were founded, but they have been perverted into another and accursed use. There is great need for such instruction; for the tonsured crowd is rapidly decreasing, and besides, for the most part, the monks are unskilled to teach and rule, since they know nothing but to care for their stomachs, the only thing they have been taught. Hence we must have persons qualified to dispense the Word of God and the Sacraments, and to be pastors of the people. But where will we obtain them, if schools are not established on a more Christian basis, since those hitherto maintained, even if they do not go down, can produce nothing but depraved and dangerous corrupters of youth?

There is consequently an urgent necessity, not only for the sake of the young, but also for the maintenance of Christianity and of civil government, that this matter be im-

[1] Luther was not yet married.
[2] Donatus wrote a Latin grammar used as a text-book during the Middle Ages. Alexander was the author of a commentary on Aristotle.

mediately and earnestly taken hold of, lest afterwards, although we would gladly attend to it, we shall find it impossible to do so, and be obliged to feel in vain the pangs of remorse forever.

. . . Let us use our reason, that God may observe in us gratitude for His mercies, and that other lands may see that we are human beings, capable both of learning and of teaching, in order that through us, also, the world may be made better. . . .

Finally, this must be taken into consideration by all who earnestly desire to see such schools established and the languages preserved in the German states: that no cost nor pains should be spared to procure good libraries in suitable buildings, especially in the large cities, which are able to afford it. For if a knowledge of the Gospel and of every kind of learning is to be preserved, it must be embodied in books, as the prophets and apostles did, as I have already shown. This should be done, not only that our spiritual and civil leaders may have something to read and study, but also that good books may not be lost, and that the arts and languages may be preserved, with which God has graciously favored us. St. Paul was diligent in this matter, since he lays the injunction upon Timothy: "Give attendance to reading;" and directs him to bring the books, but especially the parchments left at Troas.

All the kingdoms that have been distinguished in the world have bestowed care upon this matter, and particularly the Israelites, among whom Moses was the first to begin the work, who commanded them to preserve the book of the law in the ark of God, and put it under the care of the Levites, that any one might procure copies from them. He even commanded the king to make a copy of this book in the hands of the Levites. Among other duties, God directed the Levitical priesthood to preserve and attend to the books. Afterwards Joshua increased and improved this library, as did subsequently Samuel, David, Solomon, Isaiah, and many kings and prophets. Hence

have come to us the Holy Scriptures of the Old Testament, which would not otherwise have been collected and preserved, if God had not required such diligence in regard to it. . . .

Has it not been a grievous misfortune that a boy has hitherto been obliged to study twenty years or longer, in order to learn enough miserable Latin to become a priest and to read the mass? And whoever has succeeded in this, has been called blessed, and blessed the mother that has borne such a child! And yet he has remained a poor ignorant man all through life, and has been of no real service whatever. Everywhere we have had such teachers and masters, who have known nothing themselves, who have been able to teach nothing useful, and who have been ignorant even of the right methods of learning and teaching. How has it come about? No books have been accessible but the senseless trash of the monks and sophists. How could the pupils and teachers differ from the books they studied? A jackdaw does not hatch a dove, nor a fool make a man wise. That is the recompense of our ingratitude, in that we did not use diligence in the formation of libraries, but allowed good books to perish, and bad ones to survive.

But my advice is, not to collect all sorts of books indiscriminately, thinking only of getting a vast number together. I would have discrimination used, because it is not necessary to collect the commentaries of all the jurists, the productions of all the theologians, the discussions of all the philosophers, and the sermons of all the monks. Such trash I would reject altogether, and provide my library only with useful books; and in making the selection, I would advise with learned men.

In the first place, a library should contain the Holy Scriptures in Latin, Greek, Hebrew, German, and other languages. Then the best and most ancient commentators in Greek, Hebrew, and Latin.

Secondly, such books as are useful in acquiring the languages, as the poets and orators, without considering whether they are heathen or Christian, Greek or Latin. For it is from such works that grammar must be learned.

Thirdly, books treating of all the arts and sciences.

Lastly, books on jurisprudence and medicine, though here discrimination is necessary.

A prominent place should be given to chronicles and histories, in whatever languages they may be obtained; for they are wonderfully useful in understanding and regulating the course of the world, and in disclosing the marvelous works of God. O how many noble deeds and wise maxims produced on German soil have been forgotten and lost, because no one at the time wrote them down; or if they were written, no one preserved the books: hence we Germans are unknown in other lands, and are called brutes that know only how to fight, eat, and drink. But the Greeks and Romans, and even the Hebrews, have recorded their history with such particularity, that even if a woman or child did any thing noteworthy, all the world was obliged to read and know it; but we Germans are always Germans, and will remain Germans.

Since God has so graciously and abundantly provided us with art, scholars, and books, it is time for us to reap the harvest and gather for future use the treasures of these golden years. For it is to be feared, (and even now it is beginning to take place,) that new and different books will be produced, until at last, through the agency of the devil, the good books which are being printed will be crowded out by the multitude of ill-considered, senseless, and noxious works. For Satan certainly designs that we should torture ourselves again with Catholicons, Floristas, Modernists, and other trash of the accursed monks and sophists, always learning, yet never acquiring knowledge.

Therefore, my dear Sirs, I beg you to let my labor bear fruit with you. And though there be some who think me too insignificant to follow my advice, or who look down upon me as one condemned by tyrants: still let them consider that I am not seeking my own interest, but that of all Germany. And even if I were a fool, and should yet hit upon something good, no wise man should think it a disgrace to follow me. And even if I were a Turk and heathen, and it should yet appear that my advice was advantageous, not for myself, but for Christianity, no reasonable person would despise my counsel. Sometimes a fool has given better advice than a whole company of wise men. Moses received instruction from Jethro.

Herewith I commend you all to the grace of God. May He soften your hearts, and kindle therein a deep interest in behalf of the poor, wretched, and neglected youth; and through the blessing of God may you so counsel and aid them as to attain to a happy Christian social order in respect to both body and soul, with all fullness and abounding plenty, to the praise and honor of God the Father, through Jesus Christ our Saviour. Amen.

Wittenberg, 1524.

JOHN CALVIN
Institutes of the Christian Religion (1536)*

Book III, Chapter 21

.   .   .   .   .

Human curiosity renders the discussion of predestination, already somewhat difficult of itself, very confusing and even dangerous. No restraints can hold it back from wandering in forbidden bypaths and thrusting upward to the heights. If allowed, it will leave no secret to God that it will not search out and unravel. Since we see so many on all sides rushing into this audacity and impudence, among them certain men not otherwise bad, they should in due season be re-

* From *Calvin: Institutes of the Christian Religion,* II, LCC, Vol. XXI (Philadelphia: Westminster, 1960; edited by John T. McNeill and translated by Ford Lewis Battles). Copyright © 1960, W. L. Jenkins. Used by permission.

minded of the measure of their duty in this regard.

First, then, let them remember that when they inquire into predestination they are penetrating the sacred precincts of divine wisdom. If anyone with carefree assurance breaks into this place, he will not succeed in satisfying his curiosity and he will enter a labyrinth from which he can find no exit. For it is not right for man unrestrainedly to search out things that the Lord has willed to be hid in himself, and to unfold from eternity itself the sublimest wisdom, which he would have us revere but not understand that through this also he should fill us with wonder. He has set forth by his Word the secrets of his will that he has decided to reveal to us. These he decided to reveal in so far as he foresaw that they would concern us and benefit us.

. . . For we shall know that the moment we exceed the bounds of the Word, our course is outside the pathway and in darkness, and that there we must repeatedly wander, slip, and stumble. Let this, therefore, first of all be before our eyes: to seek any other knowledge of predestination than what the Word of God discloses is not less insane than if one should purpose to walk in a pathless waste, or to see in darkness. And let us not be ashamed to be ignorant of something in this matter, wherein there is a certain learned ignorance. Rather, let us willingly refrain from inquiring into a kind of knowledge, the ardent desire for which is both foolish and dangerous, nay, even deadly.

. . . . .

Predestination and foreknowledge of God

No one who wishes to be thought religious dares simply deny predestination, by which God adopts some to hope of life, and sentences others to eternal death. . . . We call predestination God's eternal decree, by which he determined with himself what he willed to become of each man. For all are not created in equal condition; rather, eternal life is foreordained for some, eternal

damnation for others. Therefore, as any man has been created to one or the other of these ends, we speak of him as predestined to life or to death.

. . . . .

Summary survey of the doctrine of election

As Scripture, then, clearly shows, we say that God once established by his eternal and unchangeable plan those whom he long before determined once for all to receive into salvation, and those whom, on the other hand, he would devote to destruction. We assert that, with respect to the elect, this plan was founded upon his freely given mercy, without regard to human worth; but by his just and irreprehensible but incomprehensible judgment he has barred the door of life to those whom he has given over to damnation. Now among the elect we regard the call as a testimony of election. Then we hold justification another sign of its manifestation, until they come into the glory in which the fulfillment of that election lies. But as the Lord seals his elect by call and justification, so, by shutting off the reprobate from knowledge of his name or from the sanctification of his Spirit, he, as it were, reveals by these marks what sort of judgment awaits them. Here I shall pass over many fictions that stupid men have invented to overthrow predestination. They need no refutation, for as soon as they are brought forth they abundantly prove their own falsity.

Book IV, Chapter 1

. . . . .

Education through the church, its value and its obligation

But let us proceed to set forth what pertains to this topic. Paul writes that Christ, "that he might fill all things," appointed some to be "apostles, some prophets, some evangelists, some pastors and teachers, for the equipment of the saints, for the work of the ministry, for the building up of the body of Christ, until we all reach the unity of the faith and of the knowledge of the Son of God, to perfect manhood, to the measure of the fully mature age of Christ." We see how God, who could in a moment perfect his own, nevertheless desires them to grow up into manhood solely under the education of the church. We see the way set for it: the preaching of the heavenly doctrine has been enjoined upon the pastors. We see that all are brought under the same regulation, that with a gentle and teachable spirit they may allow themselves to be governed by teachers appointed to this function. . . . From this it follows that all those who spurn the spiritual food, divinely extended to them through the hand of the church, deserve to perish in famine and hunger. God breathes faith into us only by the instrument of his gospel. . . .

By this plan He willed of old that holy assemblies be held at the sanctuary in order that the doctrine taught by the mouth of the priest might foster agreement in faith. The Temple is called God's "resting place"; the sanctuary, his "dwelling," where he is said to sit among the cherubim. Glorious titles, they are used solely to bring esteem, love, reverence, and dignity to the ministry of the heavenly doctrine. Otherwise, the appearance of a mortal and despised man would much detract from them. To make us aware, then, that an inestimable treasure is given us in earthen vessels, God himself appears in our midst, and, as Author of this order, would have men recognize him as present in his institution.

Accordingly, after he forbade his people to devote themselves to auguries, divinations, magic arts, necromancy, and other superstitions, he added that he would give what ought to suffice for all: that they should never be destitute of prophets. But as he did not entrust the ancient folk to angels but raised up teachers from the earth truly to perform the angelic office, so also today it is his will to teach us through human means. As he was of old not content with the law alone, but added priests as interpreters from whose lips the people might ask its true meaning, so today he not only desires us to be attentive to its reading, but also appoints instructors to help us by their effort. This is doubly useful. On the one hand, he proves our obedience by a very good test when we hear his ministers speaking just as if he himself spoke. On the other, he also provides for our weakness in that he prefers to address us in human fashion through interpreters in order to draw us to himself, rather than to thunder at us and drive us away. Indeed, from the dread with which God's majesty justly overwhelms them, all the pious truly feel how much this familiar sort of teaching is needed.

Those who think the authority of the Word is dragged down by the baseness of the men called to teach it disclose their own ungratefulness. For, among the many excellent gifts with which God has adorned the human race, it is a singular privilege that he deigns to consecrate to himself the mouths and tongues of men in order that his voice may resound in them. Let us accordingly not in turn dislike to embrace obediently the doctrine of salvation put forth by his command and by his own mouth. For, although God's power is not bound to outward means, he has nonetheless bound us to this ordinary manner of teaching. Fanatical men, refusing to hold fast to it, entangle themselves in many deadly snares. Many are led either by pride, dislike, or rivalry to the conviction that they can profit enough from private reading and meditation; hence they despise public assemblies and deem preaching superfluous. But, since they do their utmost to sever or break the sacred bond of unity, no one escapes the just penalty of this unholy separation without bewitching himself with pestilent errors and foulest delusions. In order, then, that pure simplicity of faith may flourish among us, let us not be reluctant to use this exercise of religion which God, by ordaining it, has shown us to be necessary and highly approved. No one —not even a fanatical beast—ever existed who would tell us to close our ears to God. But in every age the prophets and godly teachers have had a difficult struggle with the ungodly, who in their stubbornness can never submit to the yoke of being taught by human word and ministry. This is like blotting out the face of God which shines upon us in teaching.

RENAISSANCE IDEALS

DESIDERIUS ERASMUS
The Education of a Christian Prince (1516)*

Nature created all men equal, and slavery was superimposed on nature, which fact the laws of even the pagans recognized. Now stop and think how out of proportion it is for a Christian to usurp full power over other Christians, whom the laws did not design to be slaves, and whom Christ redeemed from all slavery. Recall the instance when Paul called Onesimus (who was born a slave) the brother of his former master Philemon, from the time of his baptism. How incongruous it is to consider them slaves whom Christ redeemed with the same blood [as He did you]; whom He declared free along with all others; whom He fostered with the same sacraments as He did you; whom He calls to the same heritage of immortality! And over them, who have the same Master as you, the Prince, Jesus Christ, will you impose the yoke of slavery?

There is only one Master of Christian men. Why, then, do those who assume His functions, prefer to take their pattern of government from anyone except Him, who alone is in all ways to be imitated? It is proper enough to gather from others whatever virtues they have; but in Him is the perfect example of all virtue and wisdom. This seems the [essence of] foolishness to those outside the faith, but to us, if we are really faithful, He is the goodness of God and the wisdom of God. Now I do not want you to think that this means that you should be a slave, not a ruler. On the contrary, it illustrates the finest way to rule, unless, of

* Desiderius Erasmus, *The Education of a Christian Prince* (New York: Columbia University Press, 1936; translated by Lester K. Born), pp. 177–178, 187, 212–214, and 256–257. Used by permission.

course, you think God is only a bondsman because He governs the whole universe without recompense, because everyone and everything has felt His kindness, although they give Him nothing in return, and unless the mind seems a slave because it looks out so zealously for the welfare of the body, which it does not need, or unless you think the eye is a slave to all the other parts of the body because it sees for them all. You may well consider this: if someone should turn all these men whom you call your own into swine and asses by the art of Circe, would you not say your ruling power had been reduced to a lower level? I think you would. And yet you may exercise more authority over swine and asses than over men. You may treat them as you please, divide them off as you will, and even kill them. Surely he who has reduced his free subjects to slaves has put his power on a meaner level. The loftier the ideal to which you fashion your authority, the more magnificently and splendidly will you rule. Whoever protects the liberty and standing of your subjects is the one that helps your sovereign power. God gave the angels and men free will so that He would not be ruling over bondsmen, and so that He might glorify and add further grandeur to His kingdom. And who, now, would swell with pride because he rules over men cowed down by fear, like so many cattle?

. . . . .

The first duty of a good prince is to desire the best things possible. The second duty, to see by what means all things that are evil can be avoided or removed; and on the other hand, how good conditions can be gained, developed, and strengthened.

. . . . .

A prince who is about to assume control of the state must be advised at once that the main hope of a state lies in the proper education of its youth. This Xenophon wisely taught in his *Cyropaedia*. Pliable youth is amenable to any system of training. Therefore the greatest care should be exercised over public and private schools and over the education of the girls, so that the children may be placed under the best and most trustworthy instructors and may learn the teachings of Christ and that good literature which is beneficial to the state. As a result of this scheme of things, there will be no need for many laws or punishments, for the people will of their own free will follow the course of right.

Education exerts such a powerful influence, as Plato says, that a man who has been trained in the right develops into a sort of divine creature, while on the other hand, a person who has received a perverted training degenerates into a monstrous sort of savage beast. Nothing is of more importance to a prince than to have the best possible subjects.

The first effort, then, is to get them accustomed to the best influences, because any music has a soothing effect to the accustomed ear, and there is nothing harder than to rid people of those traits which have become second nature to them through habit. None of those tasks will be too difficult if the prince himself adheres to the best manners. It is the essence of tyranny, or rather trickery, to treat the common citizen as animal trainers are accustomed to treat a savage beast: first they carefully study the way in which these creatures are quieted or aroused, and then they anger them or quiet them at their pleasure. This Plato has painstakingly pointed out. Such a course is an abuse of the emotions of the masses and is no help to them. However, if the people prove intractable and rebel against what is good for them, then you must bide your time and gradually lead them over to your end, either by some subterfuge or by some helpful pretence. This works just as

wine does, for when that is first taken it has no effect, but when it has gradually flowed through every vein it captivates the whole man and holds him in its power.

If sometimes the whirling course of events and public opinion beat the prince from his course, and he is forced to obey the [exigencies of the] time, yet he must not cease his efforts as long as he is able to renew his fight, and what he has not accomplished by one method he should try to effect by another.

. . . . .

We have written elsewhere more extensively on the evils of war and should not repeat here. I will only urge princes of Christian faith to put aside all feigned excuses and all false pretexts and with wholehearted seriousness to work for the ending of that madness for war which has persisted so long and disgracefully among Christians, that among those whom so many ties unite there may arise a peace and concord. Let them develop their genius to this end, and for this let them show their strength, combine their plans, and strain every nerve. Whoever desires to appear great, let him prove himself great in this way. If any one accomplishes this, he will have done a deed far more magnificent than if he had subdued the whole of Africa by arms. It would not be so difficult to do, if everyone would cease to favor his own cause, if we could set aside all personal feelings and carry out the common aim, if Christ, not the world, was in our plans. Now, while everyone is looking out for his own interests, while popes and bishops are deeply concerned over power and wealth, while princes are driven headlong by ambition or anger, while all follow after them for the sake of their own gain, it is not surprising that we run straight into a whirlwind of affairs under the guidance of folly. But if, after common counsel, we should carry out our common task, even those things which are purely personal to each one would be more prosperous. Now even that for which alone we are fighting is lost.

I have no doubt, most illustrious of princes, but that you are of this mind; for you were born in that atmosphere and have been trained by the best and most honorable men along those lines. For the rest, I pray that Christ, who is all good and supreme, may continue to bless your worthy efforts. He gave you a kingdom untainted by blood; He would have it always so. He rejoices to be called the Prince of Peace; may you do the same, that by your goodness and your wisdom, at last there may be a respite from the maddest of mad wars. The memory of the misfortunes we have passed through will also commend peace to us, and the calamities of earlier times will render two-fold the favor of your kindness.

MICHEL DE MONTAIGNE
"Of the Education of Children" (1580) *

To Madame Diana de Foix, Countess of Gurson:

. . . . .

A friend of mine, the . . . other day, told me that I should have enlarged a little more upon the education of children. Now, madam, were my abilities equal to the subject, I could not possibly employ them better than in presenting them to the little gentleman that threatens you shortly with a happy birth, and your friends are in daily hopes of (you are too generous to begin otherwise than with a male); for having had so great a hand in your marriage, I have a sort of right and interest in the greatness and prosperity of all that shall proceed from it; besides, as you have been so long in possession of a title to the best of my services, I am obliged to desire the honour and advantage of every thing that concerns you.

* Michel de Montaigne, *Essays, Letters and Journey through Germany and Italy* (Philadelphia: J. W. Moore, 1850; edited by William Hazlitt and translated by Charles Cotton), Book I, Chapter XXV, "Of the Education of Children," pp. 85–102.

But, in truth, all I understand, as to this particular, is only this, that the greatest and most important difficulty of human science is the nurture and education of children. For, as in agriculture, all that precedes planting, as also planting itself, is certain, plain, and easy; but, after that which is planted takes life and shoots up, there is a great deal more to be done, and much more difficulty to be got over to cultivate and bring it to perfection; so it is with men; it is no hard matter to plant them, but after they are born then begins the trouble, solicitude, and care, to train and bring them up.

. . . . .

'Tis the custom of schoolmasters to be eternally thundering in their pupils' ears, as they were pouring into a funnel, whilst the business of these is only to repeat what the others have said before. Now I would have a tutor to correct this error: and that, at the very first outset, he should, according to the capacity he has to deal with, put it to the test, permitting his pupil himself to taste and relish things, and of himself to choose and discern them, sometimes opening the way to him, and sometimes making him break the ice himself; that is, I would not have him alone to invent and speak, but that he should also hear his pupil speak in turn. . . .

The tutor should make his pupil, like a young horse, trot before him, that he may judge of his going, and how much he is to abate of his own speed to accommodate himself to the vigour and capacity of the other. For want of which due proportion we spoil all: yet to know how to adjust it, and to keep within an exact and due measure, is one of the hardest things I know, and 'tis the effect of a strong and well-tempered mind to know how to condescend to his puerile motions and to govern and direct them. I walked firmer and more secure up hill than down.

Let the master not only examine him about the bare words of his lesson, but also as to the sense and meaning of them, and let him judge of the profit he has made, not by the testimony of his memory, but by that of his understanding. Let him make him put what he hath learned into a hundred several forms, and accommodate it to so many several subjects, to see if he yet rightly comprehend it, and has made it his own; taking instruction by his progress from the institutions of Plato. 'Tis a sign of crudity and indigestion to throw up what we have eaten in the same condition it was swallowed down; the stomach has not performed its office unless it hath altered the form and condition of what was committed to it to concoct. Our minds work only upon trust, being bound and compelled to follow the appetite of another's fancy; enslaved and captive under the authority of another's instruction, we have been so subjected to the trammels that we have no free nor natural pace of our own, our own vigour and liberty is extinct and gone.

. . . . .

Let the tutor make his pupil examine and thoroughly sift every thing he reads, and lodge nothing in his head upon simple authority and upon trust. . . . Let him, at least, know that he does know. 'Tis for him to imbibe their knowledge, but not to adopt their dogmas; and no matter if he forgets where he had his learning, provided he knows how to apply it to his own use: truth and reason are common to every one, and are no more his who spoke them first than his who spake them after.

. . . . .

The advantages of our study are to become better and wiser. 'Tis, says Epicharmus, the understanding that sees and hears, the understanding that improves everything, that orders everything, and that acts, rules, and reigns. All other faculties are blind and deaf, and without soul; and certainly we

render it timorous and servile in not allowing it the liberty and privilege to do anything of itself. Who ever asked his pupil what he thought of grammar and rhetoric, or of such and such a sentence of Cicero? Our pedagogues stick them full feathered in our memories, and there establish them like oracles, of which the very letters and syllables are the substance of the thing. To know by rote is no knowledge, 'tis no more than only to retain what one has intrusted to his memory. That which a man rightly knows and understands he is the free disposer of at his own full liberty, without any regard to the author from whom he had it, or fumbling over the leaves of his book. A mere bookish learning is a poor stock to go upon: though it may serve for some kind of ornament, there is yet no foundation for any superstructure to be built upon it. . . .

And for this very reason acquaintance with the world is of very great use, and travel into foreign countries of singular advantage; not to bring back (as most of our young Monsieurs do) an account only of how many paces Santa Rotonda is in circuit; or of the richness of Signiora Livia's attire; or, as some others, how much Nero's face, in a statue in such an old ruin, is longer and broader than that made for him in such an old medal; but to be able to give an account of the humours, manners, customs, and laws of those nations where he has been. And, that we may whet and sharpen our wits, by rubbing them upon those of others, I would that a boy should be sent abroad very young and, in order to kill two birds with one stone, into those neighbouring nations whose language differs most from our own, and to which, if it be not formed betimes, the tongue will be grown too stiff to bend.

. . . . .

Let conscience and virtue be eminently manifest in his speech, and have only reason for their guide. Make him understand that to acknowledge the error he shall discover in his own argument, though only found out by himself, it is an effect of judgment and sincerity, which are the principal things he is to seek after. . . .

Let him examine every man's talent; a peasant, a bricklayer, or any casual passenger, a man may learn something from every one of these in their several capacities, and something will be picked out of their discourse, whereof some use may be made at one time or another; nay, even the folly and weakness of others will contribute to his instruction. By observing the graces and manners of all he sees, he will create to himself an emulation of the good, and a contempt of the bad.

Let an honest curiosity be planted in him to enquire after every thing, and whatever there is of singular and rare near the place where he shall reside, let him go and see it; a fine house, a fountain, an eminent man, the place where a battle was anciently fought. . . .

Let him inquire into the manners, revenues, and alliances of princes, things in themselves very pleasant to learn and very useful to know. In thus conversing with men, I mean, and principally, those who only live in the records of history; let him, by reading those books, converse with the great and heroic souls of better ages.

. . . . .

Human understanding is marvellously enlightened by daily conversation with men, for we are otherwise in ourselves stupid and dull, and have our sight limited to the length of our own noses.

. . . . .

The first doctrine with which one should season his understanding ought to be that which regulates his manners and his sense; that teaches him to know himself, and how both well to die and well to live. Amongst the liberal sciences, let us begin with that which makes us free.

. . . . .

As to the rest, this method of education ought to be carried on with a firm gentleness, quite contrary to the practice of our pedants, who instead of tempting and alluring children to letters, present nothing before them but rods and ferules, horror and cruelty. Away with this violence! away with this compulsion! than which, I certainly believe nothing more dulls and degenerates a well-born nature. If you would have him fear shame and chastisement, do not harden him to them. Inure him to heat and cold, to wind and sun, and to dangers that he ought to despise. Wean him from all effeminacy in clothes and lodging, eating and drinking; accustom him to every thing, that he may not be a Sir Paris, a carpet-knight, but a sinewy, hardy, and vigorous young man. I have ever, from a child to the age wherein I now am, been of this opinion, and am still constant to it. But, amongst other things, the strict government of most of our colleges has always displeased me, and peradventure they might have erred less perniciously on the indulgent side. They are mere gaols, where imprisoned youths are taught to be debauched, by being punished for it before they are so. Do but come in when they are about their lesson, and you shall hear nothing but the outcries of boys under execution, and the thundering of pedagogues, drunk with fury. A very pretty way this to tempt these tender and timorous souls to love their book! leading them on with a furious countenance, and a rod in hand! a wretched and pernicious way!

. . . How much more decent would it be to see their classes strewed with leaves and flowers, than with bloody stumps of birch! Were it left to my ordering, I should paint the school with pictures of joy and gladness. . . .

THE ENGLISH HERITAGE

THE REGULATIONS OF WESTMINSTER SCHOOL IN ENGLAND (1560) *

The two Masters of the Boys and their Duty.
. . . There shall be two masters, one of whom shall be called Head Master. The one shall be a master of grammar or of arts, the other a bachelor of arts at least, if this can conveniently be done. All the scholars shall be under their government, both of them shall be religious, learned, honourable and painstaking, so that they may make their pupils pious, learned, gentlemanly and industrious. The Dean of Christ Church, Oxford, and the Master of Trinity College, Cambridge, shall in turn elect these masters, with the consent of the Dean of Westminster. Their duty shall be not only to teach Latin, Greek and Hebrew Grammar, and the humanities, poets and orators, and diligently to examine in them, but also to build up and correct the boys' conduct, to see that they behave themselves properly in church, school, hall and chamber, as well as in all walks and games, that their faces and hands are washed, their heads combed, their hair and nails cut, their clothes both linen and woollen, gowns, stockings and shoes kept clean, neat, and like a gentleman's, and so that lice or other dirt may not infect or offend themselves or their companions, and that they never go out of the college precincts without leave. They shall further appoint various monitors from the gravest scholars to oversee and note the behaviour of the rest everywhere and prevent anything improper or dirty being done. If any monitor commits an offence or neglects to perform his duty he shall be severely flogged as an example to others. . . .

* "Elizabethan Statutes of Westminster School. 1560," as reprinted in *Educational Charters and Documents, 598 to 1909* (Cambridge, England: Cambridge University Press, 1911; edited by Arthur D. Leach), pp. 497–499, 505–517. Used by permission.

The Grammar Boys.

The grammar boys shall daily at 5 a.m., before they leave their chamber, and at 8 p.m. before they go to bed, kneeling in their chamber, clearly and devoutly say in turns morning and evening prayers. . . .

[The prayers are set out in Latin. The General Confession, the Lord's Prayer, O come let us sing unto the Lord, the hymn "Jam lucis orto sidere" etc., and the Graces before and after meals are also set out. They are the same as those in use at Winchester.]

The Teaching and Ordering of the Scholars.

All the scholars shall spend the night in one or two chambers, two in a bed.

At 5 o'clock that one of the Monitors of Chamber (who shall be four in number) who shall be in course for that week, shall intone "Get up." They shall immediately all get up and, kneeling down, say Morning Prayers, which each shall begin in turn, and all the rest follow, in alternate verses, saying, "O Lord, holy father, almighty, everlasting God," as in Chapter 10 On Divine worship.

Prayers finished they shall make their beds. Then each shall take any dust or dirt there may be under his bed into the middle of the chamber, which, after being placed in various parts of the chamber, shall then be swept up into a heap by four boys, appointed by the Monitor, and carried out.

Then two and two in a long line they shall all go down to wash their hands; when they come back from washing they shall go into school and each take his place.

Prayers To Be Said in School.

At 6 o'clock the Master shall come in and, kneeling at the top of the school, begin the following prayers, the boys following in alternate verses. [Ps. 67 and responses after.]

Prayers finished, the Master shall go down to the First or lowest class and hear a part of speech and of a verb in its turn. He shall pass on from the First class to the Second, from the Second to the Third, from the Third, if he thinks fit, to the Fourth, which sits in his part of the school till 7 o'clock, to examine if any obscurity arises.

Meanwhile one of the Prefects of School goes to the head of each form in the Head Master's as well as in the Usher's part, and gets from them in writing the names of those absent from morning prayers and hands them to the Usher. Another Prefect (who always performs this duty by himself) carefully inspects each boy's hands and face, to see if they have come with unwashed hands to school, and when the Head Master comes in immediately presents them to him. This order shall be kept every day.

At 7 o'clock the Fourth Form shall transfer itself from the Usher's part to the Head Master's. He shall come into school, and all the heads of each form shall after 7 o'clock hand him the names of their absents. And one of the Prefects of School shall hand the names of those who were absent from school after 6 and 7 o'clock in the evening on the day before to the Head Master and Usher respectively. Then all the classes shall say by heart what has been read to them in this order; viz. the Custos shall always begin and shall carefully observe the rest saying it afterwards.

At 8 o'clock the Head Master shall set some sentence to the Fourth Class to translate, to the Fifth to vary, and to the Sixth and Seventh to turn into verse. The Custos shall take it from his lips and translate it first. The Usher too shall set some sentence to the Third and Second Form to translate, and to the First also, but for them it shall be very short.

The vulguses shown up by each shall be written on the same morning, and next day they shall say it in order by heart, before or about 9 o'clock. The Custos of each of the

upper forms shall first say by heart the lesson of the form next to him and explain it. Then the Head Master shall read the same lesson to his boys as the Usher to his.

On Mondays and Wednesdays the four highest forms shall write a prose on a theme set them; in the Second, Third, and First Form each shall set himself a sentence and translate it into Latin.

On Tuesdays and Thursdays the higher forms shall round off the themes set them in verse, the other two shall write them in prose.

On Mondays and Tuesdays the Schoolmaster shall read

To Form
{
Fourth, Terence, Sallust, and Greek Grammar.
Fifth, Justin, Cicero on Friendship, and Isocrates.
Sixth and Seventh, Caesar's Commentaries, Livy, Demosthenes and Homer.
}

On those days the Usher shall read

To Form
{
Third, Terence, Sallust.
Second, Terence or Aesop's Fables.
First, Ludovico Vives or Cato.
}

On Wednesdays and Thursdays the Schoolmaster shall read to the

Fourth, Ovid's Tristia, Cicero on Duty, and Lucian's Dialogues in Greek.
Fifth, Ovid's Metamorphoses, or Plutarch in Greek.
Sixth and Seventh, Virgil and Homer.

On those days the Usher shall read to the

Third, Sturmius' Select Epistles of Cicero.
Second, Sacred Dialogues, Erasmus' Conversations.
First, Ludovico Vives, Corderius' Dialogues, or Boys' Talks.

From these lessons the boys shall gather the flowers, phrases or idioms, also antitheses, epithets, synonyms, proverbs, similes, comparisons, stories, descriptions of seasons, places, persons, fables, sayings, figures of speech, apophthegms.

At 9, when they have read the lesson to their forms, an interval should be given to the pupils to think over the lessons. Then they, standing upright in either part of the school, shall follow one who leads, appointed at the discretion of the Monitor. The prayers to be said in school before dinner, supper and play. . . .

Then two and two in a long line they shall go quietly to Hall and stand on either side of Hall till grace before meat [*sic*] is said.

Three or more of the scholars appointed by the Schoolmaster shall stand before the table in the middle of Hall, one of whom, at the selection of the Dean or Sub-dean or his vice-gerent, or the Schoolmaster, shall begin to say grace and consecrate the table, and all the rest then present shall say the responses together as above in Chapter 10 Of Divine worship.

Dinner done and grace said as above-written the scholars shall return to school in the same way as they left it. And the same order shall be observed wherever they go.

At 1 o'clock the Usher shall come in, and shall ask the Fourth Form, who are there until one, sitting in his part, what the Master read before dinner, and discuss each part of speech with them; the heads of the first four classes shall, when he comes in, show him the names of those absent.

At 2 o'clock the Fourth Form shall go to their own seats, and, the Master now coming in, the heads of each class shall hand him the names of those absent. The Head Master shall spend the time between 2 and 4 o'clock in examining the Fifth, Sixth and Seventh Forms, and shall make some vulguses out of the lesson set to exercise them in Latin, so however that half an hour before four the heads of the three upper forms shall bring up their own and the other boys' themes, which he shall examine carefully.

As a knowledge of singing is found to be of the greatest use for a clear and distinct elocution, we will that all the pupils in the Grammar School shall spend two hours each week, viz. from 2 to 3 p.m. on Wednesdays and Fridays, in the art of music, and for their better instruction in that art we

will that the choristers' master shall carefully teach the pupils of the Grammar School, and the same master shall receive from each of them (except those who have been choristers) 6*d.* for each term from their tutors.

At 4 o'clock the Head Master may, if he wishes, go out of school, returning before 5 o'clock.

At 5 or before, when the Head Master comes into school, the Usher may go out for half an hour.

During this time they shall say out of these authors as much as the Master has set them, one of the Monitors of School asking for it;

Form Fourth: from figures of speech and the method of verse-making.

Form Fifth: Valerius Maximus, Flowers of Lucian, Cicero's Epistles, Susenbrotus.

Form Sixth, Greek; Seventh, Hebrew Grammar, with a lesson in the Psalms in both languages, viz. Greek and Hebrew.

To the Usher the absences of his forms shall be shown; the themes of the Third Form; and the Sentences of the Second Form which each has set himself and turned into Latin.

Then every boy shall say by heart such part of the rules as has been prescribed for him, then too vulguses shall be made by the boys so that they may better understand the rules of grammar, and so the Latin language become familiar in every way.

At 6 o'clock they shall go out and return in the same order as before dinner and observe the same order in Hall.

At 7 o'clock two of the highest form who have been appointed by the Schoolmaster to teach the rest of the forms shall get their subjects together and practise those committed to their charge for half-an-hour in explaining what has been read to them and in turning sentences from English into Latin. Also they shall read aloud and put in order what has been dictated that day by the Usher. The heads of each class shall perform this duty, but the Monitors of the School shall pay attention to all so as to render them perfect in learning and behaviour.

Then when prayers are over they shall be dismissed to Hall to drink.

At 8 o'clock they shall always go to bed, after they have said prayers.

Evening Prayers to be said in chamber before going to bed.

[Prayers set out.]

Punishments on Friday.

On Fridays, after saying the lesson which they had set the day before, those who have committed any grave crime are accused; for it is right that they should pay the penalties of evil-doers. Then everyone is to repeat with the greatest diligence the lessons which have been read to them that week, partly before dinner up to 11, partly from 1 to 2, leaving out nothing of what they have read in the morning during the whole week.

After 3 they shall say to their teachers whatever they have learnt during the same week, between 4 and 5.

Before 5 the master shall read to the

Fourth, Apophthegms, Epigrams of Martial, Catullus or others.

Fifth, Horace.

Sixth and Seventh, Lucan, Silius Italicus.

For 7 o'clock next day the Master shall set a theme for the Sixth and Seventh Form on which to do varyings in verse, for the Fifth in prose: and for 1 p.m. the same day to be explained again by them more at length, and to the Fourth in prose.

Before 5 the Usher shall read

To the Third and Second, Aesop's Fables, and to the First Cato.

Saturday.

At 7 all the Forms shall say what had been read to them the day before. Varyings shall be given up to the Schoolmaster. The Usher shall examine in all he read the day before.

At 1 they shall hear the boys say the dictation of the week.

At 2 on the 7th day, two or three ap-

pointed by the Schoolmaster, shall declaim on a set theme, publicly in Hall before the whole College, a bell being rung beforehand when the Master orders it.

Things to be observed every day.

Before 7 no leave out of school shall be given except as nature may require, and not even in that case to more than three at a time, and then it is allowed to go out with the club, which they use for the purpose.

That boy shall be made custos in each class who has spoken in English, or who cannot repeat one of the rules he has learnt without making more than three mistakes, or through neglect of writing perfectly has made three mistakes in spelling in his notes.

THE CURRICULUM AND METHODOLOGY OF A GRAMMAR SCHOOL IN LONDON, ENGLAND (1637–1660) *

Hoole's Grammar School Curriculum.

1637–60.

A NEW

DISCOVERY

of the old Art of

TEACHING SCHOOLE,

In four small

TREATISES.

1		A Petty-Schoole	
2	concerning	The Usher's Duty	In a
3		The Master's Method	Grammar
4		Scholastick Discipline	Schoole.

Showing how Children in their
playing years may
grammatically attain to a
firm groundedness and
exercise of the Latine, Greek
and Hebrew Tongues.

Written about Twenty-three yeares ago, for the benefit of *Rotherham* School, where

* "Hoole's Grammar School Curriculum. 1637–60," as reprinted in *Educational Charters and Documents, 598 to 1909* (Cambridge, England: Cambridge University Press, 1911; edited by Arthur D. Leach), pp. 530–534. Used by permission.

it was first used; and after 14 years' trial by diligent practise in London in many particulars enlarged, and now at last published for the general profit, especially of young Schoole-Masters. By *Charles Hoole,* Master of Arts, and Teacher of a Private Grammar School in Lothbury Gardens, London.
London: Printed by *J. T.,* for Andrew Crook, at the *Green Dragon,* in Paul's Churchyard, 1660.

The Usher's Duty, or a Plat-forme of Teaching Lilie's Grammar, by C. H.

. . . . .

But because their wits are now ripened for the better understanding of Grammar, and it is necessary for them to be made wholly acquainted with it before they proceed to the exact reading of Authors, and making School-exercises, I would have them spend one quarter of a yeare chiefly in getting *Figurae* and *Prosodia* and making daily repetition of the whole Accidents and Common-Grammars, so that this third year will be well bestowed in teaching children of between nine and ten years of age the whole *Grammar,* and the right use of it, in a method answerable to their capacities, and not much differing from the common rode [*sic*] of teaching.

The Master's Method, or the Exercising of Scholars in Grammars, Authours, and Exercises; Greek, Latine, and Hebrew.

Chap. I.

p. 129. *How to make the Scholars of the fourth Form very perfect in the* Art of Grammar *and* Elements of Rhetorick; *and how to enter them upon Greek in an easy way. How to practise them (as they read* Terence *and* Ovid de Tristibus *and his* Metamorphosis, *and* Janua Latinae linguae *and* Sturmius, *and* Textor's Epistles) *in getting* Copy of words, *and learning their* Derivations *and* Differences, *and in* varying phrases. *How to show them the right way*

of double translating *and* writing a most pure Latine style. *How to acquaint them with all sorts of* English *and* Latine verses *and to make them to write* familiar *and* elegant Epistles, *either in English or Latine,* upon all occasions.

Chap. II.

p. 167. *How to teach Scholars in the fifth form to keep and improve the Latine and Greek Grammars, and Rhetorick, and how to acquaint them with an Oratory, stile and pronunciation. How to help them to translate Latine into Greek, and to make Greek verses as they read* Isocrates *and* Theognis. *How they may profit well in reading Virgil, and easily learn to make good Theams and elegant Verses with delight and certainty. And what Catechismes they may learn in Greek.*

V Form.

I have experienced it to be a most effectual mean to draw on my Scholars to emulate one another, who could make the best exercises of their own in the most Rhetoricall style, and have often seen the most bashfull and least promising boyes to outstrip their fellowes in pronouncing with a courage and comely gesture; and for bringing up this use first in my School I must here thank that modest and ingenious gentleman, Mr Edward Perkins, who was then my Usher, for advising me to set upon it. For I found nothing that I did formerly to put such a spirit into my Scholars, and make them like so many Nightingales, to contend who could most melodiously tune his voice and frame style to pronounce and imitate the prementioned orations. . . .

On Tuesdaies and Thursdaies in the afternoons, after other tasks ended, to collect Short Histories out of Plutarch, &c.; Apologues out of Æsop, Hieroglyphicks out of Pierius and Causinus, Emblems and Symbols out of Alciat, Bega, Quarles, &c.; Ancient Laws and Customs out of Diodorus Siculus, &c. Witty Sentences out of Golden Grove, Moral Philosophie, &c. Rhetorical exornations out of Vossius, Farnabie, Butler, &c. Topical pieces out of Caussinus, &c. Descriptions of things natural and artificial out of Orbis Pictus, &c., which, together with all that can be got of this nature, should be laid up in the Schoole Library for Scholars to pick what they can . . . out of these they are to write on a Theme set.

Chapter III.

How to enter Scholars of the Sixth Forme in Hebrew; How to employ them in reading the best and most difficult Authours in Latine and Greeke, and how to acquaint them with all manner of Schoole Exercises, Latine, Greek or Hebrew.

p. 193. Though it be found a thing very rare, and is by some adjudged to be of little use for School boyes to make exercises in Hebrew; yet it is no small ornament and commendation to a Schoole (as Westminster Schoole at present can evidence) that Scholars are able to make orations and verses in Hebrew, Arabick or other Oriental Tongues, to the amazement of most of their hearers, who are angry at their own ignorance, because they knew not well what is then said or written.

p. 202. The constant employment of this Sixth Form is:—

1. To read twelve verses out of the Greek Testament every morning before Parts.

2. To repeat Latine and Greek Grammar Parts and Elementa Rhetorices every Thursday morning.

3. To learn the Hebrew Tongue on Mondaies, Tuesdaies and Wednesdaies for morning Parts.

4. To read Hesiod, Homer, Pindar and Lycophron for forenoon lessons on Mondaies and Wednesdaies.

5. Zenophon, Sophocles, Euripides and Aristophanes on Tuesdaies and Thursdaies.

6. Laubegeois Breviarium Graecae linguae for afternoon Parts on Mondaies and Wednesdaies.

7. Lucian's Select Dialogues and Pontani Progymnasmata Latinitatis on Tuesday afternoons; and

8. Tullie's orations, Plinie's Panegyricos, Quintilian's Declamations on Thursdaye afternoons, and Goodwin's Antiquities at leisure times.

9. Their exercises for oratory should be to make Themes, Orations and Declamations, Latine, Greek and Hebrew; and for Poetry to make Verses upon such Themes as are appointed them every week.

10. And to exercise themselves in Anagrams, Epigrams, Epitaphs, Epithalamias, Eclogues and Acrosticks, English, Latine, Greek and Hebrew.

11. Their Catechismes are Nowell and Birket in Greek and the Church Catechisme in Hebrew.

So that in six, or at the most seven, yeares time (which children commonly squander away, if they be not continued at the Schoole after they can read English and write well) they may easily attaine to such knowledge in the Latine, Greek and Hebrew Tongues as is requisite to furnish them for future studies in the Universities, or to enable them for any ingenuous profession or employments which their friends shall think fit to put them upon in other places.

BERNARD BAILYN
Family Life in Sixteenth- and Early Seventeenth-Century England (1960) *

The most important agency in the transfer of culture was not formal institutions of instruction or public instruments of communication, but the family; and the character of family life in late sixteenth- and early seventeenth-century England is critical for understanding the history of education in colonial America.

The family familiar to the early colonists was a patrilineal group of extended kinship gathered into a single household. By modern standards it was large. Besides children, who often remained in the home well into

* Bernard Bailyn, *Education in the Forming of American Society: Needs and Opportunities for Study* (Chapel Hill: University of North Carolina Press, 1960), pp. 15–22. Used by permission.

maturity, it included a wide range of other dependents: nieces and nephews, cousins, and, except for families at the lowest rung of society, servants in filial discipline. In the Elizabethan family the conjugal unit was only the nucleus of a broad kinship community whose outer edges merged almost imperceptibly into the society at large.

The organization of this group reflected and reinforced the general structure of social authority. Control rested with the male head to whom all others were subordinate. His sanctions were powerful; they were rooted deep in the cultural soil. They rested upon tradition that went back beyond the memory of man; on the instinctive sense of order as hierarchy, whether in the cosmic chain of being or in human society; on the processes of law that reduced the female to perpetual dependency and calibrated a detailed scale of male subordination and servitude; and, above all, on the restrictions of the economy, which made the establishment of independent households a difficult enterprise.

It was these patriarchal kinship communities that shouldered most of the burden of education. They were, in the first place, the primary agencies in the socialization of the child. Not only did the family introduce him to the basic forms of civilized living, but it shaped his attitudes, formed his patterns of behavior, endowed him with manners and morals. It introduced him to the world; and in so doing reinforced the structure of its authority. For the world to the child was an intricate, mysterious contrivance in controlling which untutored skills, raw nature, mere vigor counted for less than knowledge and experience. The child's dependence on his elders was not an arbitrary decree of fate; it was not only biologically but socially functional.

But the family's educational role was not restricted to elementary socialization. Within these kinship groupings, skills that provided at least the first step in vocational training were taught and practiced. In a great many cases, as among the agricultural laboring population and small tradesmen who together comprised the overwhelming majority of the population, all the vocational instruction necessary for mature life was provided by the family.

The family's role in vocational training was extended and formalized in a most important institution of education, apprenticeship. Apprenticeship was the contractual exchange of vocational training in an atmosphere of family nurture for absolute personal service over a stated period of years. Like other forms of bonded servitude, it was a condition of dependency, a childlike state of legal incompetence, in which the master's role, and responsibilities, was indistinguishable from the father's, and the servant's obligations were as total, as moral, and as personal as the son's. Servants of almost every degree were included within the family, and it was the family's discipline that most directly enforced the condition of bondage. The master's parental concern for his servants, and especially for apprentices, included care for their moral welfare as well as for their material condition. He was expected and required by law to bring them up in good Christian cultivation, and to see to their proper deportment.

What the family left undone by way of informal education the local community most often completed. It did so in entirely natural ways, for so elaborate was the architecture of family organization and so deeply founded was it in the soil of stable, slowly changing village and town communities in which intermarriage among the same groups had taken place generation after generation, that it was at times difficult for the child to know where the family left off and the greater society began. The external community, comprising with the family a continous world, naturally extended instruction and discipline in work and in the conduct of life. And it introduced the youth in a most significant way to a further discipline, that of government and the state. So extensive and intricate were the community's involvements with the family and yet so important was its function as a public agency that the youth moved naturally and gradually across the border line that separates the personal from the impersonal world of authority.

More explicit in its educational function than either family or community was the church. Aside from its role as formal educator exercised through institutions of pedagogy which it supported and staffed, in its primary purpose of serving the spiritual welfare and guarding the morals of the community it performed other less obvious but not less important educational functions. It furthered the introduction of the child to society by instructing him in the system of thought and imagery which underlay the culture's values and aims. It provided the highest sanctions for the accepted forms of behavior, and brought the child into close relationship with the intangible loyalties, the ethos and highest principles, of the society in which he lived. In this educational role, organized religion had a powerfully unifying influence. Indistinguishable at the parish level from the local community, agent and ward of the state, it served as a mechanism of social integration. In all its functions, and especially in those that may be called educational, its force was centripetal.

Family, community, and church together accounted for the greater part of the mechanism by which English culture transferred itself across the generations. The instruments of deliberate pedagogy, of explicit, literate education, accounted for a smaller, though indispensable, portion of the process. For all the interest in formal instruction shown in the century after the Reformation in England, and for all the extension of explicitly educational agencies, the span of pedagogy in the entire spectrum of education remained small. The cultural burdens it bore were relatively slight. Formal instruction in elementary and grammar schools, and in the university, was highly utilitarian. Its avowed purpose was the training of the individual for specific social roles. Of the love of letters, knowledge, and science for their own sakes in Elizabethan and Stuart England there was, needless to say, no lack; but the justification for formal education was not phrased in terms of the enrichment of the personality and the satisfactions of knowledge. Literacy had its uses required for the daily tasks of an increasing part of the population. Latin grammar and classical literature, far from being then the cultural ornaments they have since become, were practical subjects of instruction: as necessary for the physician as for the architect, as useful to the local functionary as to the statesman. Even the middle classes, for whom classical education had acquired a special meaning as a symbol of social ascent, justified their interest in grammar school training by reference to its moral and social utility. And the universities' function as professional schools had not been transformed by the influx of sons of gentle and noble families; it had merely been broadened to include training for public responsibility.

The sense of utility that dominated formal education was related in a significant way to the occupational structure of the society. Despite a considerable amount of occupational mobility, the normal expectation was that the child would develop along familiar lines, that the divergence of his career from that of his parents' and grandparents' would be limited, and that he could proceed with confidence and security along a well-worn path whose turnings and inclines had long been known and could be dealt with by measures specified by tradition.

Whatever their limitations by modern standards, formal institutions of instruction occupied a strategic place in English life, and they therefore fell within the concern of the state. But the role of the state in formal education, though forceful, was indirect. It was exhortatory, empowering, supervisory, regulatory; it was, with rare exceptions, neither initiating nor sustaining. Support for schools and universities was almost universally from private benefaction.

usually in the form of land endowments; public taxation was rare and where it existed, local and temporary. The reliable support from endowment funds gave educational institutions above the elementary level a measure of autonomy, an independence from passing influences which allowed them to function conservatively, retarding rather than furthering change in their freedom from all but the most urgent pressures.

Of these characteristics of education as it existed in late sixteenth- and early seventeenth-century England prospective emigrants to America would hardly have been aware, and not simply because they were not habituated to think in such terms. They had little cause to probe the assumptions and circumstances that underlay their culture's self-perpetuation. The rapid expansion of instructional facilities of which they were witness had not sprung from dissatisfaction with the traditional modes of education, but from the opposite, from confidence, from satisfaction, and from the desire and the capacity to deal more fully, in familiar ways, with familiar social needs. The basis of education lay secure within the continuing traditions of an integrated, unified culture. The future might be uncertain, but the uncertainties were limited. Nothing disturbed the confident expectation that the world of the child's maturity would be the same as that of the parents' youth, and that the past would continue to be an effective guide to the future.

None of the early settlers in English America, not even those who hoped to create in the New World a utopian improvement on the Old, contemplated changes in this configuration of educational processes, this cluster of assumptions, traditions, and institutions. Yet by the end of the colonial period it had been radically transformed. Education had been dislodged from its ancient position in the social order, wrenched loose from the automatic, instinctive workings of society, and cast as a matter for deliberation into the forefront of consciousness. Its functionings had become problematic and controversial. Many were transferred from informal to formal institutions, from agencies to whose major purpose they had been incidental to those, for the most part schools, to which they were primary. Schools and formal schooling had acquired a new importance. They had assumed cultural burdens they had not borne before. Where there had been deeply ingrained habits, unquestioned tradition, automatic responses, security, and confidence there was now awareness, doubt, formality, will, and decision. The whole range of education had become an instrument of deliberate social purpose.

In many ways the most important changes, and certainly the most dramatic, were those that overtook the family in colonial America. In the course of these changes the family's traditional role as the primary agency of cultural transfer was jeopardized, reduced, and partly superseded.

CHAPTER TWO

Colonial Views on Education

THE TRANSMISSION OF A RENAISSANCE CULTURE

PHILIP VICKERS FITHIAN
Journal and Letters (1773–1774) *

[JOURNAL]

Monday Novemr 1st

We began School—The School consists of eight—Two of Mr Carters Sons—One Nephew—And five Daughters—The endest Son is reading Salust; Gramatical Exercises, and latin Grammer—The second Son is reading english Grammar Reading English: Writing, and Cyphering in Subtraction— The Nephew is Reading and Writing as above; and Cyphering in Reduction—The eldest daughter is Reading the Spectator; Writing; & beginning to Cypher—The second is reading next out of the Spelling-Book, and begining to write—The next is reading in the Spelling-Book—The fourth is Spelling in the beginning of the Spelling-Book—And the last is beginning her letters—

Teusday 2.

Busy in School—begun to read Pictete—

[LETTER OF PHILIP V. FITHIAN TO THE REVEREND ENOCH GREEN]

Westmoreland. Novr 2d 1773.

REVD SIR.

According as I appointed I take this early oppertunity of acquainting you that I am

* *Journal and Letters of Philip Vickers Fithian, 1773–1774: A Plantation Tutor of the Old Dominion* (Williamsburg, Va.: Colonial Williamsburg, Inc., 1957; New Edition, edited by Hunter Dickinson Farish), pp. 20–21, 26–27, 31–32, 45–47, and 159–168. Used by permission.

arrived safe; and I am to assure you that I find the place fully equal to my highest expectations—I am situated in the *Northern-Neck,* in a most delightful Country; in a civil, polite neighbourhood; and in a family remarkable for regularity, and oeconomy, tho' confessedly of the highest quality and greatest worth of any in *Virginia.* I teach only Mr Carters children, and only one of them is to learn Languages, and he is reading Salust and the Greek grammer, is seventeen years old, and seems to be a Boy of Genius—the other two learn writing and Arithmetic—But he has four Daughters, young Misses that are at times to be taught writing and English—I have the terms as I expected, and find the place wholly agreeable—and am strongly solicited to stay many years—But money nor conveniency shall detain me long from my most important connections at home—You may expect me in may at the *Synod.* Please to have my compliments to Mrs Green, to Miss Betsy if at Deerfield, and to my acquaintances that shall enquire and accept to yourself the

Respect of your humble Servt

PHILIP V FITHIAN

[JOURNAL]

Wednesday 3.

Busy in School—

Thursday 4.

Busy in School—To day the two eldest Daughters, and second Son attended the Dancing School.

Fryday 5.

Busy in School—

. . . . .

[LETTER OF PHILIP V. FITHIAN TO THE REVEREND ENOCH GREEN]

Decemr 1st 1773.

REVD SIR.

As you desired I may not omit to inform you, so far as I can by a letter, of the business in which I am now engaged, it would indeed be vastly agreeable to me if it was in my power to give you particular intelligence concerning the state and plan of my employment here.

I set out from home the 20th of Octr and arrived at the Hon: Robert Carters, of Nominy, in Westmorland County, the 28th I began to teach his children the first of November. He has two sons, and one Nephew; the oldest Son is turned of seventeen, and is reading Salust and the greek grammer; the others are about fourteen, and in english grammer, and Arithmetic. He has besides five daughters which I am to teach english, the eldest is turned of fifteen, and is reading the spectator; she is employed two days in every week in learning to play the Forte-Piana, and Harpsicord—The others are smaller, and learning to read and spell. Mr Carter is one of the Councellors in the general court at Williamsburg, and possest of as great, perhaps the clearest fortune according to the estimation of people here, of any man in Virginia: He seems to be a good scholar, even in classical learning, and is remarkable one in english grammar; and notwithstanding his rank, which in general seems to countenance indulgence to children, both himself and Mrs Carter have a manner of instructing and dealing with children far superior, I may say it with confidence, to any I have ever seen, in any place, or in any family. They keep them in perfect subjection to themselves, and never pass over an occasion of reproof; and I blush for many of my acquaintances when I say

that the children are more kind and complaisant to the servants who constantly attend them than we are to our superiors in age and condition. Mr Carter has an overgrown library of Books of which he allows me the free use. It consists of a general collection of law books, all the Latin and Greek Classicks, vast number of Books on Divinity chiefly by writers who are of the established Religion; he has the works of almost all the late famous writers, as Locke, Addison, Young, Pope, Swift, Dryden, &c. in Short, Sir, to speak moderately, he has more than eight times your number—His eldest Son, who seems to be a Boy of Genius and application is to be sent to Cambridge University, but I believe will go through a course either in Philadelphia or Princeton College first. As to what is commonly said concerning Virginia that it is difficult to avoid being corrupted with the manners of the people, I believe it is founded wholly in a mistaken notion that persons must, when here frequent all promiscuous assemblies; but this is so far from truth that any one who does practise it, tho' he is accused of no crime, loses at once his character; so that either the manners have been lately changed, or the report is false, for he seems now to be best esteemed and most applauded who attends to his business, whatever it be, with the greatest diligence. I believe the virginians have of late altered their manner very much, for they begin to find that their estates by even small extravagance, decline, and grow involved with debt, this seems to be the spring which induces the People of fortune who are the pattern of all behaviour here, to be frugal, and moderate. You may expect me at home by the permission of Providence the latter end of april next, or the beginning of May; and as I proposed I shall present my exercises for the examination of the Presbytery; and if they think proper I shall gladly accept of a license in the fall: I must beg your favour to mention me to such of my acquaintances in Deerfield as you think proper, but especially to Mrs Green, Miss *Betsy,* your family, and Mrs Pecks—I must also beg you to transmit so much of this intelligence to Mr Hunter as that my relations in Greenwich may know that I am through the mercy of heaven in good health. I beg, Sir, you will not fail to write, and let it be known to Mr Hunter, that a letter will come as secure by the Post as from Cohansie to Philadelphia; the Letters are to be directed to me thus, To Mr Philip V. Fithian at Mr *Carters* of Nominy, to be left at Hobes Hole

> I am, Sir, yours
> PHILIP V FITHIAN

. . . . .

[JOURNAL]

Wednesday 15.

Busy in School—To day Dined with us Mrs Turburville, & her Daughter Miss Letty Miss Jenny Corbin, & Mr Blain. We dined at three. The manner here is different from our way of living in Cohansie—In the morning so soon as it is light a Boy knocks at my Door to make a fire; after the Fire is kindled, I rise which now in the winter is commonly by Seven, or a little after, By the time I am drest the Children commonly enter the School-Room, which is under the Room I sleep in; I hear them round one lesson, when the Bell rings for eight o-Clock (for Mr Carter has a large good Bell of upwards of 60 Lb. which may be heard some miles, & this is always rung at meal Times;) the Children then go out; and at half after eight the Bell rings for Breakfast, we then repair to the Dining-Room; after Breakfast, which is generally about half after nine, we go into School, and sit til twelve, when the Bell rings, & they go out for noon; the dinner-Bell rings commonly about half after two, often at three, but never before two.—After dinner is over, which in common, when we have no Company, is about half after three we go into School, & sit til the Bell rings at five, when they separate til the next morning; I have to myself in the Evening, a neat Chamber, a large Fire, Books, & Candle & my Liberty, either to continue in the school room, in my own Room or to sit over at the great House with Mr & Mrs Carter—We go into Supper commonly about half after eight or at nine & I usually go to Bed between ten and Eleven. Altho the family in which I live, is certainly under as good political Regulations, and every way as suitable & agreeable as I can expect, or even could desire; & though the Neighbourhood is polite, & the Country pleasant, yet I cannot help reflecting on my situation last winter, which was near the lovely *Laura* for whom I cannot but have the truest, and the warmest Esteem! possibly, If Heaven shall preserve my life, in some future time, I may again enjoy her good society.

Mr Carter heard this Evening that Captain *Walker* cannot go to Maryland, he is thus stop'd.

. . . . .

Sunday [January] 2. 1774.

The weather warm and Damp—The Family rode to Church today and are to dine out. Mr Carter at my request, gave me the Keys of his Book-Cases and allowed me to spend the Day alone in his Library.

The place seems suitable for Study, & the Day ought to be spent in serious contemplation; therefore, as I proposed Yesterday, I shall collect together and write down what I have been doing in the last Year. But will my Life bear the review? Can I look upon my Actions and Blush! And shall I be no less careful, or have no better Success, in the prosecution of my Duty the Year to come, if I shall be kept alive to the Close of it?—

In the Beginning of the last year I was in Deerfield, in Cumberland County New-Jersey, with Rev'd Mr Green; Under him I studied the Hebrew-Language and Divinity. I left the college the last of September 1772. After having setled my business at Home, I entered upon the Study of Divinity with the Rev'd Andrew Hunter; I was with him about a Month, and on the first of December I went to Mr *Green* with a design to acquaint myself with the Hebrew Tongue; he put me to the Grammar, which I learn'd through, and read some Chapters in the Psalter in the Course of the Winter: In Divinity, he advised me to read Ridgeleys body of Divinity for a System: And he gave me several separate treatisses on Repentance, Regeneration, Faith, &c, & towards spring gave me subjects to consider in the Sermon-Way. Yet how barren am I still? It is an arduous task to bring the Mind to close application; & still greater to lay up and retain useful Knowledge. I continued with Mr *Green* & pursued my studies, I hope with some Success till August 1773. when I was solicited by Dr *Witherspoon* to go into *Virginia* & teach in a Gentlemans Family—The Offer seem'd profitable; I was encouraged by the Dr and was to have his Recommendation—I had likewise myself a strong inclination to go—Yet I was in great Doubt, & Wholly undetermined for some Weeks, because many of my friends, and some of my near Relations opposed my leaving Home, and all seem'd utterly unwilling to advise to go—It is time, according to the Course of my Life they said that I was settling to some constant Employment, and they told me I ought especially to enter with as great speed as convenient into that plan of Life for which I have in particular had my Education—That Virginia is sickly—That the People there are profane, and exceeding wicked—That I shall read there no Calvinistic Books, nor hear any Presbyterian Sermons—That I must keep much Company, and therefore spend as much, very probably much more Money than my Salary—These considerations unsettled for a while my mind—On the other hand I proposed to myself the following advantages by going—A longer opportunity for Study than my friends would willingly allow me If I should remain at home—A more general acquaintance with the manners of Mankind; and a better Knowledge of the Soil, & Commerce of these neighbouring Provinces—And a more perfect acquaintance with the Doctrines, & method of Worship in the established Church in these Colonies, & especially

with the Conduct of the Clergy of which there have been so many bad reports—All these however when I had laid them together, seem'd to overbear the others, so that I determined at last to break through and go!—Here now I am in a strange Province; But I am under no more nor stronger temptations to any kind of vice, perhaps not so great as at Cohansie,—unless sometimes when I am solicited to dance I am forc'd to blush, for my Inability—I have the opportunity of living with Credit perfectly retired—in a well regulated family—With a man of Sense—May God help me to walk in his fear & Gloryfy his Name!—

. . . . .

[LETTER OF PHILIP V. FITHIAN TO JOHN PECK]

Nomini Hall August 12th 1774.

"Si bene moneo [Maneo], attende."—

SIR.

I never reflect, but with secret, and peculiar pleasure, on the time when I studied in *Deerfield* with you, & several other pleasant Companions, under our common, & much respected instructor, Mr *Green.* And I acknowledge now, with a thankful heart, the many favours, which I received from your family while I was a member of it. This sense of obligation to your Family. And personal friendship for you, have excited me, when it was in my power, to introduce you to the business which I now occupy; into a family, where, if you be prudent and industrious, I am confident you will speedily acquire to yourself both Honour & Profit—But inasmuch as you are wholly a stranger to this Province; & have had little or no Experience in the business which you ar[e] shortly to enter upon; & lest, from common Fame, which is often erroneous, you shall have entertained other notions of the manners of the People here, & of your business as a Tutor, than you will find, when you come, to be actually true; I hope you will not think it *vain* or *untimely,* if I venture to lay before you some Rules for your direction which I have collected from a year's observation. I shall class what I have to say in the following order. First. I shall attempt to give you some direction for the plan of your Conduct among your neighbours, & the People in General here, so long as you sustain the character of a Tutor. Then I shall advise you concerning the rules which I think will be most profitable & convenient in the management of your little lovely charge, the School. Last of all. I shall mention several Rules for your personal conduct. I choose to proceed in the order I have laid down, as well that you may more fully & speedily receive my mind, as that you may also the more readily select out and apply what you shall find to be most necessary.

First. . . . You come here, it is true, with an intention to teach, but you ought likewise to have an inclination to learn. At any rate I solemnly injoin it upon you, that you never suffer the spirit of a Pedagogue to attend you without the walls of your little Seminary. In all promiscuous Company be as silent & attentive as Decency will allow you, for you have nothing to communicate, which such company, will hear with pleasure, but you may learn many things which, in after life, will do you singular service.— In regard to Company in general, if you think it worth the while to attend to my example, I can easily instruct you in the manner of my Conduct in this respect. I commonly attend Church; and often, at the request of Gentlemen, after Service according to the custom, dine abroad on Sunday— I seldom fail, when invited by Mr or Mrs *Carter,* of going out with them; but I make it a point, however strongly solicited to the contrary, to return home with them too— Except in one of these cases, I seldom go out, but with a valuable variety of books I live according to Horace's direction, & love "Secretum Iter et fallentis Semita Vitae." Close retirement and a life by Stealth. The last direction I shall venture to mention on this head, is, that you abstain totally from Women. What I would have you under-

stand from this, is, that by a train of faultless conduct in the whole course of your tutorship, you make every Lady within the Sphere of your acquaintance, who is between twelve & forty years of age, so much pleased with your person, & so fully satisfied as to your abilities in the capacity of—a Teacher; & in short, fully convinced, that, from a principle of Duty, you have, both by night & by day endeavoured to acquit yourself honourably, in the Character of a Tutor; & that, on this account, you have their free & hearty consent, without making any manner of demand upon you, either to stay longer in the County with them, which they would choose, or whenever your business calls you away, that they may not have it in their Power either by charms or Justice to detain you, & when you must leave them, have their sincere wishes & constant prayrs for Length of days & much prosperity, I therefore beg that you will attend literally to this advice, & abstain totally from Women. But this last precaution, which I have been at some pains to dress in the plainest language, I am much inclined to think, will be wholly useless in regard to you, notwithstanding it is founded in that *Honour* and *Equity* which is on all hands allow'd to be due from one Sex to the other, & to many of your *age,* & *Standing* no doubt would be entirely salutary. Because the necessary connections which you have had with the Fair, from your Puberty upwards have been so unfavourable & ill-fated, that instead of apprehending any danger on the score of over fondness, I am fearful your rancour has grown so inveterate at length, as, not only to preserve you, in thought & practice, pure of every Fleshly foible, but has carried you so far towards the other extream, as that you will need many persuasions, when your circumstances shall seem to require it, to bring you back to a rational & manly habit of thinking & acting with respect to the Sex; which yet, after all (& eternally will continue to be, tho it is so much courted & whined after) if considered in the fullest manner, & set forth to the best advantage, never rises above its divine definition viz "The weaker Vessel." But without detaining you any longer with a matter merely depending on accident or Circumstance I pass on to the second General Head; in which "Ludis atque Jocis amotis [amatis]" I shall offer to your consideration & recommend for your practice several Rules concerning the management of the School. 2. You will act wisely, if, from the begining, you convince all your Scholars which you may easily do, of your abilities in the several branches, which you shall profess to teach; you are not to tell them, totidem Verbis, "that you understand, perhaps as well as any man on the Continent both the Latin & Greek Classicks;" "& have gone through the usual Course in the noted College of New-Jersey, under Dr Witherspoon, so universally known & admired, where you have studied Criticism, Oratory, History, not to mention Mathematical & philosophical Studies, & dipt a good way into the French-Language, & that you have learn'd a smattering of Dancing, Cards &c. &c. &c." For Dun-p or Hack---n or the most profound dunce in your College or School would have too much sense to pass such impudence by, & not despise and reproach it; but you may speedily & certainly make them think you a "Clever Fellow" (which is a phrase in use here for a good Scholar) if you never mention any thing before them, only what you seem to be wholly master of—This will teach them never to dispute your determination, & always to rely upon your Judgment; two things which are most essential for your peace, & their advantage. That you may avoid yourself of this with certainty I shall recommend for your practice the following method, as useful at least, if not intirely necessary. Read over carefully, the lessons in Latin & Greek, in your leisure hours, that the story & Language be fresh in your memory, when you are hearing the respective lessons; for your memory is treacherous, & I am pretty certain it would confound you if you should be accosted by a pert School-Boy, in the midst of a blunder, with "Physi-

cian heal thyself"!—You ought likewise to do this with those who are working Figures; probably you may think that because the highest Cypherer is only in decimal arithmetic, it is not there fore worth your critical attention to be looking previously into the several Sums. But you are to consider that a sum in the Square-Root, or even in the Single Rule of three direct, is to your Pupils of as great importance, as the most abstruse problem in the Mathematicks to an able artist; & you may lay this down for a Maxim, that they will reckon upon your abilities, according as they find you acquainted & expert in what they themselves are studying. If therefore you have resolution (as I do not question your ability) to carry this plan which I have laid down into execution; you will thereby convince them of the propriety of their Subordination to you, & obedience to your instructions, so that you may lead them, without any resistance, and fix them to the Study of whatever Science you think proper, in which they will rise according to their respective Capacities. I have said that you ought to strive "from the beginning" in fixing this very material article in the minds of your Scholars, Viz a Sense of your authority; for one error of Judgment, or false determination will diminish your Ability with them more than doing forty things with truth would increase your authority—They act in this case as you would do in the company of a number of Strangers—A whole evenings conversation, if it was tolerable good Sense, would perhaps make little or no impression on you; But if through hast[e] in speaking, or inattention, any one should let fall a sentence either remarkably foolish, or grossly wicked, it would be difficult if not impossible to persuade you presently that the author was not either a *thick-Scull,* or a *Villain!*—The education of children requires constant unremitting attention. The meanest qualification you can mention in a useful teacher is *diligence* And without diligence no possible abilities or qualifications can bring children on either with speed or profit. There must be a Combination of qualifications whicn must all operate strongly & uniformly. In short, give this said Pedagogizing the softest name you will, it is still a "difficult Task." You will meet with numberless difficulties, in your new imployment, which you never dreamt had yet existence. All these you must endeavour to resist & Subdue. This I have seen compared to a Man swimming against a current of Water. But I am mistaken if you will agree, after having six months practice, that the comparison be strong as the truth: You will add to the figure, I am certain, & throw into the Current sharp fragments of *Ice*, & *Blocks,* which would make swimming not only difficult but dangerous! I am not urging these things to discourage you; they are hints for your direction, which, if you will attend to, tho' at first the practice seem rough & unpleasant, shall yet make the remainder of your task pleasing, & the whole of it useful, I will mention several of these Obstacles that you may the more easily guard against them. You will, in the first place, be often solicited, probably oftner than you would wish, to ride abroad; this, however, if you do it moderately, & in seasonable time, & go to proper company, I recommend as conducive to health to one in your sedentary manner of living. But if you go much into company, you will find it extremely difficulty to break away with any manner of credit till very late at night or in most cases for several days, & if you are wanting to your School, you do manifest injury to your Imployer. In this case, I advise you to copy Mr *Carter.* Whenever he invites you, ride. You may *stay,* and talk, & drink, & ride to as great excess as he; & may with safety associate yourself with those whom you find to be his intimates. In all other Cases, except when you ride to Church, at least till you are very intimate in the Colony, you had better ride to a certain Stump, or to some noted plantation, or pretty landscape; you will have in this every advantage of exercise, the additional advantage of undisturbed Meditation, & you will be under no Jealous apprehension in

point of behaviour, nor any restraint as to the time of your return.

Another current difficulty will be petitions for holidays. You must have good deal of steadiness if you are able to evade cleverly this practice which has grown so habitual to your little charge from a false method in their early education that they absolutely claim it as a necessary right.

You must also as much as you can, avoid visible partiality. At least you must never suffer your fondness for one Scholar to grow so manifest, as that all your School shall see you look over a fault in him or her which same fault, if commited by another, you severely chastise. This will certainly produce in the others hatred & contempt. A fourth difficulty, and the last I shall mention, consists in knowing when, & in what measure to give the Boys Liberty to go from Home. The two younger Boys are wholly under your inspection; so that not only the progress they make in learning, but their moral Conduct (for both of these are critically observed & examined) either justifies or condemns your management to the World. If you keep them much at home, & close to business, they themselves will call you unfeeling and cruel; & refuse to be industrious; if you suffer them to go much abroad they are certainly out of the way of improvement by Study, probably, by discovering their gross Ignorance, they will expose to ridicule both themselves & all their former instructors, & possibly they may commit actual Crimes so as very much to injure themselves; & scandalize their family; but in each of these you will have a large share of blame, perhaps more than the parents, or even the Boys themselves—It will be said that the parents gave them no licence relying wholly on your judgment & prudence, this will in good measure justify them to the world. And as to the Boys they are full of youthful impetuosity & vigour, & these compel them, when they are free of restraint, to commit actions which with proper management they had surely avoided. I say, when you lay these things together, & view them on every side you will find so many perplexities arising in your mind, from a sense of ignorance of your duty, that you will proceed with caution & moderation, & will be careful to examine with some precision into the circumstances of *time, company, & Business* when you license them to go out entirely at the risk of your Reputation—But the practice of three or four Weeks will give you a more full notion of these & many other incidents than I am able now either to recollect or express; I shall have gained my End if these hints prevent you from setting off wrong, & doing inadvertantly at first what your Scholars will assert to be precedents for your after conduct. I go on, therefore, in the third place as I proposed,

3. To mention several Rules for your personal conduct. The happy Education which you have had in point of religion, you ought to consider as an important and distinguishing Blessing of Heaven. That train of useful *Instruction, Advice & Example* to which you have been accustomed from your infancy is a more perfect, & will be a safer guide in your future walk, than any directions I am able to give you. You have taken notice of a method for Assistance in Composition, which Longinus recommends. Place, says he, in imagination, several eminent ancient Authors before your Eyes, & suppose that they inspect your Work, a Sense of inferiority would make you diligent, & your composition accurate. Perhaps the same advice when transferr'd to Morality, would be equally salutary. Unless it be objected that a Belief of Gods presence at all times in every place is the strongest possible restraint against committing Sin. This I constantly admit; but when I consider how easily our minds are put in motion, & how strongly they are sometimes agitated merely by the senses, & that the senses are affected most by things which fall under their immediate notice, I am fully convinced that if some such plan as I have just mentioned should be fallen upon, & practised, it would make a visible and useful change in our behaviour— In this place I think it needful to caution

you against hasty & ill founded prejudices. When you enter among a people, & find that their manner of living, their *Eating, Drinking, Diversions, Exercise* &c, are in many respects different from any thing you have been accustomed to, you will be apt to fix your opinion in an instant, & (as some divines deal with poor Sinners) you will condemn all before you without any meaning or distinction what seems in your Judgment disagreable at first view, when you are smitten with the novelty. You will be making ten thousand Comparisons. The face of the Country, The *Soil,* the *Buildings,* the *Slaves,* the *Tobacco,* the method of spending *Sunday* among Christians; *Ditto* among the Negroes; the three grand divisions of time at the Church on Sundays, Viz. before Service giving & receiving letters of business, reading Advertisements, consulting about the price of Tobacco, Grain &c. & settling either the lineage, Age, or qualities of favourite Horses 2. In the Church at Service, prayrs read over in haste, a Sermon seldom under & never over twenty minutes, but always made up of sound morality, or deep studied Metaphysicks. 3. After Service is over three quarters of an hour spent in strolling round the Church among the Crowd, in which time you will be invited by several different Gentlemen home with them to dinner. The Balls, the Fish-Feasts, the Dancing-Schools, the Christnings, the Cock fights, the Horse-Races, the Chariots, the Ladies Masked, for it is a custom among the Westmorland Ladies whenever they go from home, to muffle up their heads, & Necks, leaving only a narrow passage for the Eyes, in Cotton or silk handkerchiefs; I was in distress for them when I first came into the Colony, for every Woman that I saw abroad, I looked upon as ill either with the *Mumps* or Tooth-Ach!—I say, you will be often observing & comparing these things which I have enumerated, & many more that now escape me, with the manner of spending Money time & credit at Cohansie: You are young, &, (you will allow me the Expression) in the morning of Life. But I hope you have plann'd off, and entered upon the work which is necessary to be performed in the course of your Day; if not, I think it my duty to acquaint you, that a combination of the amusements which I have just now mentioned, being always before your Eyes, & inviting your Compliance will have a strong tendency to keep you doubtful & unsetled, in your notions of Morality & Religion, or else will fix you in a false & dangerous habit of *thinking & acting,* which must terminate at length in Sorrow & despair. You are therefore, if you count any thing upon the value of my advice, to fix the plan in which you would spend your life; let this be done with deliberation, Candour, & precission, looking to him for direction, by fervent Prayr, who is the "Wonderful Counsellor;" & when you have done this, let no importunity of whatever kind prevail over you, & cause you to transgress your own Limitations. I have already exceeded the usual bounds of an Epistle. But you will easily pardon a little prolixity, when I assure you it flows from a heart deeply impressed with a sense of the many difficulties which you must encounter, & the dangers which will surround you when you come first out from the peaceful recess of Contemplation, & enter, young and unexperienced, into the tumultuous undiscerning World. I submit these hints to your consideration, & have nothing more than sincere & ardent wishes for your present & perpetual Felicity.

I am, Sir,

yours.

PHILIP. V FITHIAN.

To MR JOHN PECK.
On going to Virginia in
Character of a Tutor.

QUAKER IDEAS

WILLIAM PENN,
"Some Fruits of Solitude in Reflections and Maxims" (1693)*

IGNORANCE

It is admirable to consider how many Millions of People come into, and go out of the World, Ignorant of themselves, and of the World they have lived in.

2. If one went to see Windsor-Castle, or Hampton-Court, it would be strange not to observe and remember the Situation, the Building, the Gardens, Fountains, &c. that make up the Beauty and Pleasure of such a Seat? And yet few People know themselves; No, not their own Bodies, the Houses of their Minds, the most curious Structure of the World; a living walking Tabernacle: Nor the World of which it was made, and out of which it is fed; which would be so much our Benefit, as well as our Pleasure, to know. We cannot doubt of this when we are told that the Invisible Things of God are brought to light by the Things that are seen; and consequently we read our Duty in them as often as we look upon them, to him that is the Great and Wise Author of them, if we look as we should do.

3. The World is certainly a great and stately Volume of natural Things; and may be not improperly styled the Hieroglyphicks of a better: But, alas! how very few Leaves of it do we seriously turn over! This ought to be the Subject of the Education of our Youth, who, at Twenty, when they should be fit for Business, know little or nothing of it.

EDUCATION

4. We are in Pain to make them Scholars, but not Men! To talk, rather than to know, which is true Canting.

* William Penn, "Some Fruits of Solitude in Reflections and Maxims, Relating to the Conduct of Human Life," Part I (1693), from *Select Works of William Penn To Which Is Prefixed a Journal of His Life* (London: Printed in 1771), pp. 723–724, 730–731.

5. The first Thing obvious to Children is what is sensible; and that we make no Part of their rudiments.

6. We press their Memory too soon, and puzzle, strain, and load them with Words and Rules; to know Grammer and Rhetorick, and a strange Tongue or two, that it is ten to one may never be useful to them; Leaving their natural Genius to Mechanical and Physical, or natural Knowledge uncultivated and neglected; which would be of exceeding Use and Pleasure to them through the whole Course of their Life.

7. To be sure, Languages are not to be despised or neglected. But Things are still to be preferred.

8. Children had rather be making of Tools and Instruments of Play; Shaping, Drawing, Framing, and Building, &c. than getting some Rules of Propriety of Speech by Heart: And those also would follow with more Judgment, and less Trouble and Time.

9. It were Happy if we studied Nature more in natural Things; and acted according to Nature; whose rules are few, plain and most reasonable.

10. Let us begin where she begins, go her Pace, and close always where she ends, and we cannot miss of being good Naturalists.

11. The Creation would not be longer a Riddle to us: The Heavens, Earth, and Waters, with their respective, various and numerous Inhabitants: Their Productions, Natures, Seasons, Sympathies and Antipathies; their Use, Benefit and Pleasure, would be better understood by us: And an eternal Wisdom, Power, Majesty, and Goodness, very conspicuous to us, thro' those sensible and passing Forms: The World wearing the Mark of its Maker, whose Stamp is everywhere visible, and the Characters very legible to the Children of Wisdom.

12. And it would go a great way to caution and direct People in their Use of the World, that they were better studied and known in the Creation of it.

13. For how could Man find the Confidence to abuse it, while they should see the Great Creator stare them in the Face, in all and every part thereof?

14. Their Ignorance makes them insensible, and that Insensibility hardy in misusing this noble Creation, that has the Stamp and Voice of a Deity every where, and in every Thing to the Observing.

15. It is pity therefore that Books have not been composed for Youth, by some curious and careful Naturalists, and also Mechanicks, in the Latin Tongue, to be used in Schools, that they might learn Things with Words: Things obvious and familiar to them, and which would make the Tongue easier to be obtained by them.

16. Many able Gardiners and Husbandmen are yet Ignorant of the Reason of their Calling; as most Artificers are of the Reason of their own Rules that govern their excellent Workmanship. But a Naturalist and Mechanick of this sort is Master of the Reason of both, and might be of the Practice too, if his Industry kept pace with his Speculation; which were very commendable; and without which he cannot be said to be a complete Naturalist or Mechanick.

17. Finally, if Man be the Index or Epitomy of the World, as Philosophers tell us, we have only to read our selves well to be learned in it. But because there is nothing we less regard than the Characters of the Power that made us, which are so clearly written upon us and the World he has given us, and can best tell us what we are and should be, we are even Strangers to our own Genius: The Glass in which we should see that true instructing and agreeable Variety, which is to be observed in Nature, to the Admiration of that Wisdom and Adoration of that Power which made us all.

. . . . .

KNOWLEDGE

162. Knowledge is the Treasure, but Judgment the Treasurer of a Wise Man.

163. He that has more Knowledge than Judgment, is made for another Man's use more than his own.

164. It cannot be a good Constitution, where the Appetite is great and the Digestion is weak.

165. There are some Men like Dictionaries; to be lookt into upon occasions, but have no Connection, and are little entertaining.

166. Less Knowledge than Judgment will always have the advantage upon the Injudicious knowing Man.

167. A Wise Man makes what he learns his own, 'tother shows he's but a Copy, or a Collection at most.

WIT

168. Wit is an happy and striking way of expressing a Thought.

169. 'Tis not often tho' it be lively and mantling, that it carries a great Body with it.

170. Wit therefore is fitter for Diversion than Business, being more grateful to Fancy than Judgment.

171. Less Judgment than Wit, is more Sale than Ballast.

172. Yet it must be confessed, that Wit gives an Edge to Sense, and recommends it extreamly.

173. Where Judgment has Wit to express it, there's the best Orator.

OBEDIENCE TO PARENTS

174. If thou wouldest be obeyed, being a Father; being a Son, be Obedient.

175. He that begets thee, owes thee; and has a natural Right over thee.

176. Next to God, thy Parents; next them, the Magistrate.

177. Remember that thou are not more indebted to thy Parents for thy Nature, than for thy Love and Care.

178. Rebellion therefore in Children, was made Death by God's Law, and the next Sin to Idolatry, in the People; which is renouncing of God, the Parent of all.

179. Obedience to Parents is not only our Duty, but our Interest. If we received our Life from them, We prolong it by obeying them: For Obedience is the first Commandment with Promise.

180. The Obligation is as indissolvable as the Relation.

181. If we must not disobey God to obey them; at least we must let them see, that there is nothing else in our refusal. For some unjust commands cannot excuse the general Neglect of our Duty. They will be our Parents and we must be their Children still: And if we cannot act for them against God, neither can we act against them for ourselves or anything else.

PURITAN THOUGHT

JOHN WINTHROP
"A Modell of Christian Charity" (1630)*

A MODELL OF CHRISTIAN CHARITY.

Written
On Boarde the Arrabella,
On the Attlantick Ocean.

By the Honorable JOHN WINTHROP Esquire.

In His passage, (with the great Company of Religious people, of which Christian

* John Winthrop, "A Modell of Christian Charity," *The Winthrop Papers* (Boston: Massachusetts Historical Society, 1931), II, 282–284, 292–295. Used by permission.

Tribes he was the Brave Leader and famous Governor;) from the Island of Great Brittaine, to New-England in the North America.

Anno 1630.

CHRISTIAN CHARITIE.

A MODELL HEREOF.

God Almightie in his most holy and wise providence hath soe disposed of the Condicion of mankinde, as in all times some must be rich some poore, some highe and eminent in power and dignitie; others meane and in subieccion.

THE REASON HEREOF.

1. REAS: *First,* to hold conformity with the rest of his workes, being delighted to shewe forthe the glory of his wisdome in the variety and differance of the Creatures and the glory of his power, in ordering all these differences for the preservacion and good of the whole, and the glory of his greatnes that as it is the glory of princes to haue many officers, soe this great King will haue many Stewards counting himselfe more honoured in dispenceing his guifts to man by man, then if hee did it by his owne immediate hand.

2. REAS: *Secondly,* That he might haue the more occasion to manifest the worke of his Spirit: first, vpon the wicked in moderateing and restraineing them: soe that the riche and mighty should not eate vpp the poore, nor the poore, and dispised rise vpp against theire superiours, and shake off theire yoake; 2ly in the regenerate in exerciseing his graces in them, as in the greate ones, theire loue mercy, gentlenes, temperance etc., in the poore and inferiour sorte, theire faithe patience, obedience etc:

3. REAS: Thirdly, That every man might haue need of other, and from hence they might be all knitt more nearly together in the Bond of brotherly affeccion: from hence it appears plainely that noe man is made more honourable then another or more wealthy etc., out of any perticuler and singuler respect to himselfe but for the glory of his Creator and the Common good of the Creature, Man; Therefore God still reserues the propperty of these guifts to himselfe as Ezek: 16. 17. he there calls wealthe his gold and his silver etc. Prov: 3. 9. he claimes theire seruice as his due honour the Lord with thy riches etc. All men being thus (by divine providence) rancked into two sortes, riche and poore; vnder the first, are comprehended all such as are able to liue comfortably by theire owne meanes duely improued; and all others are poore according to the former distribution. There are two rules whereby wee are to walke one towards another: JUSTICE and MERCY. These are allwayes distinguished in theire Act and in theire obiect, yet may they both concurre in the same Subiect in eache respect; as sometimes there may be an occasion of shewing mercy to a rich man, in some sudden danger of distresse, and allsoe doeing of meere Justice to a poor man in regard of some perticuler contract etc. There is likewise a double Lawe by which wee are regulated in our conversacion one towardes another: in both the former respects, the lawe of nature and the lawe of grace, or the morrall lawe or the lawe of the gospell, to omitt the rule of Justice as not properly belonging to this purpose otherwise then it may fall into consideracion in some perticuler Cases: By the first of these lawes man as he was enabled soe withall [is] commaunded to loue his neighbour as himselfe vpon this ground stands all the precepts of the morrall lawe, which concernes our dealings with men. To apply this to the works of mercy this lawe requires two things first that every man afford his help to another in every want or distresse Secondly, That hee performe this out of the same affeccion, which makes him carefull of his owne good according to that of our Saviour Math: [7.12] Whatsoever ye would that men should doe to you. This was practised by Abraham and Lott in entertaineing the Angells and the old man of Gibea.

The Lawe of Grace or the Gospell hath some differance from the former as in these respectes first the lawe of nature was giuen to man in the estate of innocency; this of the gospell in the estate of regeneracy: 2ly, the former propounds one man to another, as the same fleshe and Image of god, this as a brother in Christ allsoe, and in the Communion of the same spirit and soe teacheth vs to put a difference betweene Christians and others. Doe good to all especially to the household of faith; vpon this ground the Israelites were to putt a difference betweene the brethren of such as were strangers though not of the Canaanites. 3ly. The Lawe of nature could giue noe rules for dealeing with enemies for all are to be considered as freinds in the estate of innocency, but the Gospell commaunds loue to an enemy. proofe. If thine Enemie hunger feede him; Loue your Enemies doe good to them that hate you Math: 5. 44.

This Lawe of the Gospell propoundes likewise a difference of seasons and occasions there is a time when a christian must sell all and giue to the poore as they did in the Apostles times. There is a tyme allsoe when a christian (though they giue not all yet) must giue beyond theire abillity, as they of Macedonia. Cor: 2. 6. likewise communi'y of perills calls for extraordinary liberallity and soe doth Community in some speciall seruice for the Churche. Lastly, when there is noe other meanes whereby our Christian brother may be releiued in this distresse, wee must help him beyond our ability, rather then tempt God, in putting him vpon help by miraculous or extraordinary meanes.

. . . . .

It rests now to make some applicacion of this discourse by the present designe which gaue the occasion of writeing of it. Herein are 4 things to be propounded: first the persons, 2ly, the worke, 3ly, the end, 4ly the meanes.

1. For the persons, wee are a Company professing our selues fellow members of Christ, In which respect onely though wee were absent from eache other many miles, and had our imploymentes as farre distant, yet wee ought to account our selues knitt together by this bond of loue, and liue in the exercise of it, if wee would haue comforte of our being in Christ, this was notorious in the practise of the Christians in former times, as is testified of the Waldenses from the mouth of one of the adversaries Aeneas Syluius, mutuo [solent amare] penè antequam norint, they vse to loue any of theire owne religion even before they were acquainted with them.

2ly. for the worke wee haue in hand, it is by a mutuall consent through a speciall overruleing providence, and a more then an ordinary approbation of the Churches of Christ to seeke out a place of Cohabitation and Consorteshipp vnder a due forme of Government both ciuill and ecclesiasticall. In such cases as this the care of the publique must oversway all private respects, by which not onely conscience, but meare Ciuill pollicy doth binde vs; for it is a true rule that perticuler estates cannott subsist in the ruine of the publique.

3ly. The end is to improue our liues to doe more seruice to the Lord the comforte and encrease of the body of christe whereof wee are members that our selues and posterity may be the better preserued from the Common corrupcions of this euill world to serue the Lord and worke out our Salvacion vnder the power and purity of his holy Ordinances.

4ly for the meanes whereby this must bee effected, they are 2fold, a Conformity with the worke and end wee aime at, these wee see are extraordinary, therefore wee must not content our selues with vsuall ordinary meanes whatsoever wee did or ought to haue done when wee liued in England, the same must wee doe and more allsoe where wee goe: That which the most in theire Churches maineteine as a truthe in profession onely, wee must bring into familiar and constant practise, as in this duty of loue wee must loue brotherly without dissimulation, wee must loue one another with a pure hearte feruently wee must beare one anothers burthens, wee must not looke onely on our owne things, but allsoe on the things of our brethren, neither must wee think that the lord will beare with such faileings at our hands as hee dothe from those among whome wee haue lived. . . . Thus stands the cause betweene God and vs, wee are entered into Covenant with him for this worke, wee haue taken out a Commission, the Lord hath giuen vs leaue to drawe our owne Articles wee haue professed to enterprise these Accions vpon these and these ends, wee haue herevpon besought him of favour and blessing: Now if the Lord shall please to heare vs, and bring vs in peace to the place wee desire, then hath hee ratified this Covenant and sealed our Commission, [and] will expect a strickt performance of the Articles contained in it, but if wee shall neglect the observacion of these Articles which are the ends wee haue propounded, and dissembling with our God, shall fall to embrace this present world and prosecute our carnall intencions, seekeing greate things for our selues and our posterity, the Lord will surely breake out in wrathe against vs be revenged of such a periured people and make vs knowe the price of the breache of such a Covenant.

Now the onely way to avoyde this shipwracke and to provide for our posterity is to followe the Counsell of Micah, to doe Justly, to loue mercy, to walke humbly with our God, for this end, wee must be knitt together in this worke as one man, wee must entertaine each other in brotherly Afeccion, wee must be willing to abridge our selues of our superfluities, for the supply of others necessities, wee must vphold a familiar Commerce together in all meekenes, gentlenes, patience and liberallity, wee must delight in eache other, make others Condicions our owne reioyce together, mourne together, labour, and suffer together, allwayes haueing before our eyes our Commission and Community in the worke, our Community as members of the same body, soe shall wee keepe the vnitie of the spirit in the bond of peace, the Lord will be our God and delight to dwell among vs, as his owne people and will commaund a blessing vpon vs in all our wayes, soe that wee shall see much more of his wisdome power goodnes and truthe then formerly wee haue beene acquainted with, wee shall finde that the God of Israell is among vs, when tenn of vs shall be able to resist a thousand of our enemies, when hee shall make vs a prayse and glory, that men shall say of succeeding plantacions: the lord make it like that of New England: for wee must Consider that wee shall be as a Citty vpon a Hill, the eies of all people are vppon vs; soe that if wee shall deale falsely with our god in this worke wee haue vndertaken and soe cause him to withdrawe his present help from vs, wee shall be made a story and a by-word through the world, wee shall open the mouthes of enemies to speake euill of the wayes of god and all professours for Gods sake; wee shall shame the faces of many of gods worthy seruants, and cause theire prayers to be turned into Cursses vpon vs till wee be consumed out of the good land whether wee are goeing: And to shutt vpp this discourse with that exhortacion of Moses that faithfull seruant of the Lord in his last farewell to Israell Deut. 30. Beloued there is now sett before vs life, and good, deathe and euill in that wee are Commaunded this day to loue the Lord our God, and to loue one another to walke in his wayes and to keepe his Commaundements and his Ordinance, and his lawes, and the Articles of our Covenant with him that wee may liue and be multiplyed, and that the Lord our God may blesse vs in the land whether wee goe to possesse it: But if our heartes shall turne away soe that wee will not obey, but shall be seduced and worshipp [serue cancelled] other Gods our pleasures, and proffitts, and serue them; it is propounded vnto vs this day, wee shall surely perishe out of the good Land whether wee passe over this vast Sea to possesse it;

> Therefore lett vs choose life,
> that wee, and our Seede,
> may liue; by obeyeing his
> voyce, and cleaueing to him,
> for hee is our life, and
> our prosperity.

MICHAEL WIGGLESWORTH
The Day of Doom (1662) *

. . . . .

* Michael Wigglesworth, *The Day of Doom: or A Description of the Great and Last Judgment, with A Short Discourse about Eternity* (London: Printed by W. G. for John Sims, at the Kings-Head at Sweetings-Alley-end in Cornhill, . . . 1673).

XXXVIII.

All silence keep both Goats and Sheep
  before the Judge's Throne;
With mild aspect to his Elect
  then speaks the Holy One:
"My Sheep draw near, your Sentence hear,
  which is to you no dread,
Who clearly now discern and know
  your sins are pardonéd.

. . . . .

XLIII.

"My grace to one is wrong to none;
  none can Election claim;
Amongst all those their souls that lose,
  none can Rejection blame.
He that may choose, or else refuse,
  all men to save or spill,
May this Man choose, and that refuse,
  redeeming whom he will.

XLIV.

"But as for those whom I have chose
  Salvation's heirs to be,
I underwent their punishment,
  and therefore set them free.
I bore their grief, and their relief
  by suffering procur'd,
That they of bliss and happiness
  might firmly be assur'd.

. . . . .

CXLIV.

Then at the Bar arraignéd are
  an impudenter sort,
Who to evade the guilt that's laid
  Upon them, thus retort:
"How could we cease thus to transgress?
  How could we Hell avoid,
Whom God's Decree shut out from thee,
  and sign'd to be destroy'd?

. . . . .

CXLVII.

Christ readily makes this Reply:
  "I damn you not because
You are rejected, nor yet elected;
  but you have broke my Laws.

It is in vain your wits to strain
  the end and means to sever;
Men fondly seek to part or break
  what God hath link'd together.

CXLVIII.

"Whom God will save, such he will have
  the means of life to use;
Whom he'll pass by shall choose to die,
  and ways of life refuse.
He that fore-sees and fore-decrees,
  in wisdom order'd has,
That man's free-will, electing ill,
  shall bring his Will to pass.

CXLIX.

"High God's Decree, as it is free,
  so doth it none compel
Against their will to good or ill;
  it forceth none to Hell.
They have their wish whose Souls perish
  with Torments in Hell-fire,
Who rather choose their souls to lose,
  than leave a loose desire.

. . . . .

CLXVI.

Then to the Bar all they drew near
  Who died in infancy,
And never had or good or bad
  effected pers'nally;
But from the womb unto the tomb
  were straightway carriéd,
(Or at the least ere they transgress'd)
  who thus began to plead:

CLXVII.

"If for our own transgressi-on,
  or disobedience,
We here did stand at thy left hand,
  just were the Recompense;
But Adam's guilt our souls hath spilt,
  his fault is charg'd upon us;
And that alone hath overthrown
  and utterly undone us.

CLXVIII.

"Not we, but he ate of the Tree,
  whose fruit was interdicted;

Yet on us all of his sad Fall
    the punishment's inflicted.
How could we sin that had not been,
    or how is his sin our,
Without consent, which to prevent
    we never had the pow'r?

CLXIX.

"O great Creator why was our Nature
    depravéd and forlorn?
Why so defil'd, and made so vil'd,
    whilst we were yet unborn?
If it be just, and needs we must
    transgressors reckon'd be,
Thy Mercy, Lord, to us afford,
    which sinners hath set free.

CLXX.

"Behold we see Adam set free,
    and sav'd from his trespass,
Whose sinful Fall hath split us all,
    and brought us to this pass.
Canst thou deny us once to try,
    or Grace to us to tender,
When he finds grace before thy face,
    who was the chief offender?"

CLXXI.

Then answeréd the Judge most dread:
    "God doth such doom forbid,
That men should die eternally
    for what they never did.
But what you call old Adam's Fall,
    and only his Trespass,
You call amiss to call it his,
    both his and yours it was.

CLXXII.

"He was design'd of all Mankind
    to be a public Head;
A common Root, whence all should shoot,
    and stood in all their stead.
He stood and fell, did ill or well,
    not for himself alone,
But for you all, who now his Fall
    and trespass would disown.

CLXXIII.

"If he had stood, then all his brood
    had been establishéd

In God's true love never to move,
    nor once awry to tread;
Then all his Race my Father's Grace
    should have enjoy'd for ever,
And wicked Sprites by subtile sleights
    could them have harméd never.

CLXXIV.

Would you have griev'd to have receiv'd
    through Adam so much good,
As had been your for evermore,
    if he at first had stood?
Would you have said, 'We ne'er obey'd
    nor did thy laws regard;
It ill befits with benefits,
    us, Lord, to so reward?'

CLXXV.

"Since then to share in his welfare,
    you could have been content,
You may with reason share in his treason,
    and in the punishment.
Hence you were born in state forlorn,
    with Natures so depravéd;
Death was your due because that you
    had thus yourselves behavéd.

CLXXVI.

"You think 'If we had been as he,
    whom God did so betrust,
We to our cost would ne'er have lost
    all for a paltry lust.'
Had you been made in Adam's stead,
    you would like things have wrought,
And so into the self-same woe,
    yourselves and yours have brought.

CLXXVII.

"I may deny you once to try,
    or Grace to you to tender,
Though he finds Grace before my face
    who was the chief offender;
Else should my Grace cease to be Grace,
    for it would not be free,
If to release whom I should please
    I have no liberty.

CLXXVIII.

"If upon one what's due to none
    I frankly shall bestow,

And on the rest shall not think best
  compassion's skirt to throw,
Whom injure I? will you envy
  and grudge at others' weal?
Or me accuse, who do refuse
  yourselves to help and heal?

CLXXIX.

"Am I alone of what's my own,
  no Master or no Lord?
And if I am, how can you claim
  what I to some afford?
Will you demand Grace at my hand,
  and challenge what is mine?
Will you teach me whom to set free,
  and thus my Grace confine?

CLXXX.

"You sinners are, and such a share
  as sinners, may expect
Such you shall have, for I do save
  none but mine own Elect.
Yet to compare your sin with their
  who liv'd a longer time,
I do confess yours is much less,
  though every sin's a crime.

CLXXXI.

"A crime it is, therefore in bliss
  you may not hope to dwell;
But unto you I shall allow
  the easiest room in Hell."

. . . . .

CCII.

Oh piercing words, more sharp than swords!
  What! to depart from Thee,
Whose face before for evermore
  the best of Pleasures be!
What! to depart (unto our smart),
  from thee *Eternally!*
To be for aye banish'd away
  with Devil's company!

CCIII.

What! to be sent to Punishment,
  and flames of burning Fire!
To be surrounded, and eke confounded
  with God's revengeful Ire!

What! to abide, not for a tide,
  these Torments, but for Ever!
To be releas'd, or to be eas'd,
  not after years, but Never!

CCIV.

Oh fearful Doom! now there's no room
  for hope or help at all;
Sentence is past which aye shall last;
  Christ will not it recall.
Then might you hear them rend and tear
  the Air with their out-cries;
The hideous noise of their sad voice
  ascendeth to the Skies.

CCV.

They wring their hands, their caitiff-hands,
  and gnash their teeth for terror;
They cry, they roar for anguish sore,
  and gnaw their tongues for horror.
But get away without delay,
  Christ pities not your cry;
Depart to Hell, there may you yell,
  and roar Eternally.

COTTON MATHER
Essays to Do Good (1710) *

Reader, suppose thyself standing before the judgment seat of Christ! a necessary, a prudent supposition: it ought to be a very frequent one. The Judge demands, "What hast thou to plead for a portion in the blessedness of the righteous?" The plea must be, "O my glorious Judge, thou hast been my sacrifice. O thou Judge of all the earth, permit dust and ashes to say, my righteousness is on the bench. Surely, in the Lord have I righteousness. O my Savior, I have received it, I have secured it on thy own gracious offer of it." The Judge proceeds: "But what hast thou to plead that thy faith should not be rejected as the faith of the hypocrite?" Here the plea must be, "O Lord, my faith was thy work. It was a faith

* Cotton Mather, *Essays to Do Good; Addressed to All Christians, Whether in Public or Private Capacities* (New York: American Tract Society, n.d.; first published in 1710), pp. 20, 32–33, 36, 39, 40, 46–47, 51, 75–79.

which disposed me to all the good works of thy holy religion. It sanctified me. It brought me to thee, my Savior, for grace to perform the works of righteousness: it embraced thee for my Lord as well as Savior: it caused me, with sincerity, to love and keep thy commandments, and with assiduity to serve the interests of thy kingdom in the world."

. . . . .

PARENTS! how much ought you to be devising for the good of your *children!* Often consider how to make them "wise children;" how to give them a desirable education, an education that may render them desirable; how to render them lovely and polite, and serviceable to their generation. Often consider how to enrich their minds with valuable knowledge; how to instil into their minds generous, gracious, and heavenly principles; how to restrain and rescue them from the "paths of the destroyer," and fortify them against their peculiar temptations. There is a world of good that you have to do for them. You are without the natural feelings of humanity, if you are not in a continual agony to do for them all the good that lies in your power. It was no mistake of an ancient writer, in saying, "Nature teaches us to love our children as ourselves."

. . . . .

I would be solicitous to have my children expert, not only at reading with propriety, but also at writing a fair hand. I will then assign them such books to read, as I may judge most agreeable and profitable, obliging them to give me some account of what they read; but will keep a strict eye on what they read, lest they should stumble on the devil's library, and poison themselves with foolish romances, novels, plays, songs, or jests, "that are not convenient."

. . . . .

I would be very watchful and cautious about the companions of my children. I would be very inquisitive to learn what company they keep. If they are in danger of being ensnared by vicious company, I will earnestly pull them out of it, as "brands out of the burning;" and will try to procure for them fit and useful associates.

. . . . .

When the children are in any trouble, whether by sickness or otherwise, I will take advantage of the occasion to set before them the evil of sin, the cause of all our trouble; and will represent to them, how fearful a thing it will be to be cast among the damned, who are in unceasing and endless trouble. I will set before them the benefit of an interest in Christ, by which their trouble will be sanctified to them, and they be prepared for death, and for fulness of joy in a happy eternity after death.

. . . . .

If you will but remember four words, and attempt all that is comprised in them, OBEDIENCE, HONESTY, INDUSTRY, AND PIETY, you will be the *blessings* and the *Josephs* of the families in which you live. Let these four words be distinctly and frequently recollected, and cheerfully perform all your business on this consideration, that it is an obedience to heaven, and from thence will have a recompense.

. . . . .

If any poor children in the neighborhood are totally destitute of education, do not suffer them to remain in that state. Let care be taken that they may be taught to read, to learn their catechism, and the truths and ways of their only Savior.

. . . . .

THE DUTIES OF SCHOOL TEACHERS.

The SCHOOL TEACHER has many opportunities of doing good. God make him sensible of his obligations! We read, that "the little ones have their angels." It is hard work to keep a school; but it is God's work, and it may be so managed as to be like the work of angels. Melchior Adams properly styled it "An office most laborious, yet to God most pleasing."

Teachers! will you not regard the children under your care, as committed to you by the glorious Lord, with such a charge as this: "Take them, and bring them up for me, and I will pay you your wages!" Whenever a new scholar comes under your care, you may say, "Here my Lord sends me another object, for whom I may do something, that he may be useful in the world." Suffer little children to come unto you, and consider what you may do, instrumentally, that of such may be the kingdom of heaven.

Let it be your grand design, to instill into their minds the documents of piety. Consider it as their chief interest, and yours also, that they may so know the Holy Scriptures as to become wise to salvation. Embrace every opportunity of dropping some honey from the rock upon them. Happy the children, and as happy the teacher, where they who relate the history of their conversion may say, "There was a school-teacher who brought us to Christ." You have been told, "Certainly, it is a nobler work to make the little ones know their Savior than know their letters." The lessons of Jesus are nobler than the lessons of Cato.

CATECHISING should be a *frequent,* at least a *weekly* exercise in the school; and it should be conducted in the most edifying, applicatory, and admonitory manner. . . . Let it be proposed, that you not only pray with your scholars daily, but also take occasion, from the public sermons, and from remarkable occurrences in your neighborhood, frequently to inculcate the lessons of piety on the children.

Instructors in colleges may do well to converse with each of their pupils alone, with all possible solemnity and affection, concerning their internal state, concerning repentance for sin, and faith in Jesus Christ, and to bring them to express resolutions of serious piety. You may do a thousand things to render your pupils orthodox in sentiment, regular in practice, and qualified for public service.

I have read of a teacher who made it his constant practice, in every recitation, to take occasion from something or other that occurred, to drop at least one sentence that had a tendency to promote the fear of God in their hearts. This method sometimes cost him a good deal of study, but the good effect sufficiently recompensed him for it. . . .

Among the occasions for promoting religion in the scholars, one in the *writing schools* deserves peculiar notice. I have read of an atrocious sinner who was converted to God by accidentally reading the following sentence of Austin written in a window: "He who has promised pardon to the penitent sinner, has not promised repentance to the presumptuous one." Who can tell what good may be done to the young scholar by a sentence in his copy-book? Let their copies be composed of sentences worthy to be had in everlasting remembrance—of sentences which shall contain the brightest maxims of wisdom, worthy to be written on the fleshly tables of their hearts, to be graven with the point of a diamond there. God has blessed such sentences to many scholars; they have been useful to them all their days.

In the grammar school, also, the scholars may be directed, for their exercises, to turn into Latin such passages as may be useful for their instruction in the principles of Christianity, and furnish them with supplies from "the tower of David." Their letters also may be on the subjects which may be friendly to the interests of virtue.

I will add, it is very desirable to manage the *discipline* of the school by means of rewards, rather than of punishments. Many methods of rewarding the diligent and deserving may be invented; and a boy of an ingenious temper, by the expectation of reward, will do his best. You esteem Quintillian. Hear him: "Use stripes sparingly; rather let the youth be stimulated by praise, and by the distinctions conferred on his classmates." If a fault must be punished, let instruction, both to the delinquent and to the spectator, accompany the correction. Let the odious name of the sin which enforced the correction be declared; and let nothing be done in anger, but with every mark of tenderness and concern.

THE NEW ENGLAND PRIMER
[1727 and 1737 editions] *

A   In *Adam's* Fall
   We Sinned all.

B   Thy Life to Mend
   This *Book* Attend.

C   The *Cat* doth play
   And after slay.

D   A *Dog* will bite
   A Thief at night.

E   An *Eagles* flight
   Is out of sight.

F   The Idle *Fool*
   Is whipt at School.

G   As runs the *Glass*
   Mans life doth pass.

H   My *Book* and *Heart*
   Shall never part.

J   *Job* feels the Rod
   Yet blesses GOD.

K   Our *KING* the good
   No man of blood.

L   The *Lion* bold
   The *Lamb* doth hold.

M   The *Moon* gives light
   In time of night.

N   *Nightingales* sing
   In Time of Spring.

* *The New England Primer: A History of its Origin and Development, with a Reprint of the Unique Copy of the Earliest Known Edition and Many Fac-simile Illustrations and Reproductions* (New York: Dodd, Mead, 1897; edited by Paul Leicester Ford; Limited Edition No. 386), [1727 edition:] pp. 65–70; [1737 edition:] pp. 329–330.

O   The *Royal Oak* it was the Tree
   That sav'd His Royal Majestie.

P   *Peter* denies
   His Lord and cries.

Q   Queen *Esther* comes in Royal State
   To Save the JEWS from dismal Fate.

R   *Rachol* doth mourn
   For her first born.

S   *Samuel* anoints
   Whom God appoints.

T   *Time* cuts down all
   Both great and small.

U   *Uriah's* beauteous Wife
   Made *David* seek his Life.

W   *Whales* in the Sea
   God's Voice obey.

X   *Xerxes* the great did die,
   And so must you & I.

Y   *Youth* forward slips
   Death soonest nips.

Z   *Zacheus* he
   Did climb the Tree
   His Lord to see.

Now the Child being entred in his Letters and Spelling, let him learn these and such like Sentences by Heart, whereby he will be both instructed in his Duty, and encouroged in his Learning.

The Dutiful Child's Promises,

I Will fear GOD, and honour the KING.
I will honour my Father & Mother.
I will Obey my Superiours.
I will Submit to my Elders.
I will Love my Friends.
I will hate no Man.
I will forgive my Enemies, and pray to God
   for them.

I will as much as in me lies keen all God's
  Holy Commandments.
I will learn my Catechism.
I will keep the Lord's Day Holy.
I will Reverence God's Sanctuary,
  For our GOD is a consuming Fire.

VERSES *for Children.*

THOUGH I am but a little one,
If I can speak and go alone,
Then I must learn to know the Lord,
And learn to read his holy word.
'Tis time to seek to God and pray
For what I want for every day:
I have a precious soul to save,
And I a mortal body have,
Tho' I am young yet I may die,
And hasten to eternity:
There is a dreadful fiery hell,
Where wicked ones must always dwell; . . .
I must not sin as others do,
Lest I lie down in sorrow too:
For God is angry every day,
With wicked ones who go astray.

All sinful words I must restrain:
I must not take God's name in vain.
I must not work, I must not play,
Upon God's holy sabbath day.
And if my parents speak the word,
I must obey them in the Lord.
Nor steal, nor lie, nor spend my days,
In idle tales and foolish plays.
I must obey my Lord's commands,
Do something with my little hands:
Remember my creator now,
In youth while time will it allow.
Young SAMUEL that little child,
He served the Lord, liv'd undefil'd;
Him in his service God employ'd,
While ELI's wicked children dy'd.
When wicked children mocking said,
To a good man, *Go up bald head,*
God was displeas'd with them and sent
Two bears which them in pieces rent.
I must not like these children vile,
Displease my God, myself defile
Like young ABIJAH, I must see,
That good things may be found in me.

TOWARD A MORE HUMANE CONCEPTION OF THE CHILD

CHRISTOPHER DOCK
The Schul-Ordnung (1770) *

A

Simple and Thoroughly Prepared

SCHOOL-MANAGEMENT

Clearly setting forth not only in what
  manner children may best be taught
  in the branches usually given at
  school, but also how they may
  be well instructed in the
  knowledge of godliness.

* Martin G. Brumbaugh, "Translation of *The
Schul-Ordnung,*" in *The Life and Works of
Christopher Dock: America's Pioneer Writer
on Education, with a translation of his works
into the English language* (Philadelphia and
London: Lippincott, 1908), pp. 19–20, 89, 91,
93–97, 99, 104–111, 122–124. Used by permission.

Prepared out of love for mankind by the
  skilful schoolmaster of many
  years experience,

CHRISTOPHER DOCK

And through the efforts of several friends
  of the common good authorized
  to be printed.

Germantown:
Printed by, and to be had of,

Christopher Saur, 1770

PUBLISHER'S PREFACE

BELOVED READER:

. . . Parents should be especially careful
of the company into which they send their
children, and especially what teachers they
choose for them; for what they see and hear
of these impresses itself deeply upon their
tender spirits.

This my beloved father saw clearly, and already almost twenty years ago he felt a desire to meet our wants, as far as possible, in this respect, and as he knew of a man whose whole desire was to seek the children's best advantage in body and soul, to teach godliness as well as the ordinary branches, and in accordance with the advice of the Apostle Paul (Tit. ii, 7), always showed himself a good example, and was also blessed with a natural gift, he was desirous of obtaining a written statement of his school management that he might print and publish it, that other teachers who are anxious to instruct their children well and are not so richly gifted might find something in it to improve themselves. And for others, who care not whether the children learn anything or not, so long as they receive their pay, it should serve as a means of shaming them, when they see that parents too know how a well-planned school should be kept, and finally it is to teach the parents themselves what to do with children whom they earnestly wish to teach something good, for many parents in this country are obliged to teach their children themselves, (and others should do so rather than send them to teachers whose lives are stained with vice). These and other considerations have induced my beloved father to write to one of his good friends, as may be seen from the following letter.

Thus our good friend Dock was willing to write such a work, but when it was completed, he could not make up his mind to have it printed, because of a certain modesty, fearing that it would be looked upon as a monument to himself and thus be taken amiss. For this reason he was unwilling for it to be published during his lifetime, and it therefore lay nineteen years, until a few friends of the common good begged him persistently to have it published. Finally he yielded, and in the year just passed it was given me to publish. . . .

That this little work may serve the purpose for which it was first written and compiled by the author, and having been de-layed so long may be received with the greater attention, is the sincere wish of your faithful friend who has at heart the welfare of all men.

CHRISTOPHER SAUR.
GERMANTOWN, March 27, 1770.

OCCASION FOR WRITING THIS LITTLE BOOK

FRIEND DIELMAN KOLB:

The thought has frequently occurred to me, gone and returned, that you should (if you have the time in the future) some time write down for me the art and method employed in keeping school by our friend Dock. How he receives the children into school. How he manages various children in different ways. How he treats them kindly and lovingly that they both fear and love him. That they love one another. Also of their letter-writing. How he trains them to maintain silence. How he uses shame as an incentive to teach diligence. Also how he draws childlike pictures for them to practice. In fine, I should like to have you describe it to me briefly or at length, in such a manner that if he should depart this life we could give a just description of him, partly for the glory of God and partly for the instruction of other schoolmasters and of their successors, how it is possible to educate the youth. This I think would be well worth printing, during his life-time if he be willing, or afterward.

. . . I send my heartiest regards to you and your wife and remain indebted to you in love and service.

CHRISTOPHER SAUR
GERMANTOWN, Aug. 3, 1750.

AUTHOR'S PREFACE
SOLLFORD, Aug. 8, 1750.

SALUTEM, ESTEEMED FRIEND:

. . . Concerning Friend Saur's first question, how I receive the children at school, I proceed as follows: the child is first given a welcome by the other children, who extend their hands to him. Then I ask him if he will be diligent and obedient. If he promises this, he is told how to behave; and when he can say his A B C's and point out each letter with his index finger, he is put into the Ab. When he reaches this class his father owes him a penny, and his mother must fry him two eggs for his diligence, and the same reward is due him with each advance; for instance, when he enters the word class. But when he enters the reading class, I owe him a present, if he reaches the class in the required time and has been diligent, and the first day this child comes to school he receives a note stating: "Diligent. One pence." This means that he has been admitted to the school; but it is also explained to him that if he is lazy or disobedient his note is taken from him. Continued disinclination to learn and stubbornness causes the pupil to be proclaimed lazy and inefficient before the whole class, and he is told that he belongs in a school for incorrigibles. Then I ask the child again if he will be diligent and obedient. Answering yes, he is shown his place. If it is a boy, I ask the other boys, if a girl, I ask the girls, who among them will take care of this new child and teach it. According to the extent to which the child is known, or its pleasant or unpleasant appearance, more or less children express their willingness. If none apply, I ask who will teach this child for a certain time for a bird or a writing-copy. Then it is seldom difficult to get a response. This is a description of my way of receiving the child into school.

Further report concerning the assembling of the children at school:

The children arrive as they do because some have a great distance to school, others a short distance, so that the children cannot assemble as punctually as they can in a city. Therefore, when a few children are present, those who can read their Testament sit together on one bench; but the boys and girls occupy separate benches. They are given a chapter which they read at sight consecutively. Meanwhile I write copies for them. Those who have read their passage of Scripture without error take their places at the table and write. Those who fail have to sit at the end of the bench, and each new arrival the same; as each one is thus released in order he takes up his slate. This process continues until they have all assembled. The last one left on the bench is a "lazy pupil."

When all are together, and examined, whether they are washed and combed, they sing a psalm or a morning hymn, and I sing and pray with them. As much as they can understand of the Lord's Prayer and the ten commandments (according to the gift God has given them), I exhort and admonish them accordingly. This much concerning the assembling of pupils. But regarding prayer I will add this additional explanation. Children say the prayers taught them at home half articulately, and too fast, especially the "Our Father" which the Lord Himself taught His disciples and which contains all that we need. I therefore make a practice of saying it for them kneeling, and they kneeling repeat it after me. After these devotional exercises those who can write resume their work. Those who cannot read the Testament have had time during the assemblage to study their lesson. These are heard recite immediately after prayer. Those who know their lesson receive an O on the hand, traced with crayon. This is a mark of excellence. Those who fail more than three times are sent back to study their lesson again. When all the little ones have recited, these are asked again, and any one having failed in more than three trials a second time, is called "Lazy" by the entire class and his name is written down. Whether such a child fear the rod or not, I know from experience that this denunciation of the children hurts more than if I were constantly to wield and flourish the rod. If then such a child has friends in school who are able to instruct him and desire to do so, he will visit more frequently than before. For this reason: if the pupil's name has not been erased before dismissal the pupils are at liberty to write down the names of those who have been lazy, and take them along home. But if the child learns his lesson well in the future, his name is again presented to the other pupils, and they are told that he knew his lesson well and failed in no respect. Then all the pupils call "Diligent" to him. When this has taken place his name is erased from the slate of lazy pupils, and the former transgression is forgiven.

The children who are in the spelling class are daily examined in pronunciation. In spelling, when a word has more than one syllable, they must repeat the whole word, but some, while they can say the letters, cannot pronounce the word, and so cannot be put to reading. For improvement a child must repeat the lesson, and in this way: The child gives me the book, I spell the word and he pronounces it. If he is slow, another pupil pronounces it for him, and in this way he hears how it should be done, and knows that he must follow the letters and not his own fancy.

Concerning A B C pupils, it would be best, having but one child, to let it learn one row of letters at a time, to say forward and backward. But with many, I let them learn the alphabet first, and then ask a child to point out a letter that I name. If a child is backward or ignorant, I ask another, or the whole class, and the first one that points to the right letter, I grasp his finger and hold it until I have put a mark opposite his name. I then ask for another letter, &c. Whichever child has during the day received the greatest number of marks, has pointed out the greatest number of letters. To him I owe something—a flower drawn on paper or a bird. But if several have the same number, we draw lots; this causes less annoyance. In this way not only are the very timid cured of their shyness (which is a great hindrance in learning), but a fondness for school is increased. Thus much in answer to his question, how I take the children into school, how school proceeds before and after prayers, and how the inattentive and careless are made attentive and careful, and how the timid are assisted.

Further I will state that when the little ones have recited for the first time, I give the Testament pupils a verse to learn. Those reading newspapers and letters sit separately, and those doing sums sit separately. But when I find that the little ones are good enough at their reading to be fit to read the Testament, I offer them to good Testament readers for instruction. The willing teacher takes the pupil by the hand and leads him to his seat. I give them two verses to try upon. But if I find that another exercise is necessary after this (such as finding a passage in Scripture, or learning a passage, in which case each reads a verse), I give only one verse, which is not too hard for those trying to read in the Testament. If pupils are diligent and able, they are given a week's trial, in which time they must learn their lesson in the speller with the small pupils and also their lesson with the Testament pupil. If they stand the test they are advanced the next week from the spelling to the Testament class, and they are also allowed to write. But those who fail in the Testament remain a stated time in the A B C class before they are tested again. After the Testament pupils have recited, the little ones are taken again. This done they are reminded of the chapter read them, and asked to consider the teaching therein. As it is the case that this thought is also expressed in other passages of Holy Writ, these are found and read, and then a hymn is given containing the same teaching. If time remains, all are given a short passage of Scripture to learn. This done, they must show their writing exercises. These are examined and numbered, and then the first in turn is given a hard word to spell. If he fails the next must spell it and so on. The one to spell correctly receives his exercise. Then the first is given another hard word, and so each receives his exercise by spelling a word correctly.

As the children carry their dinner, an hour's liberty is given them after dinner. But as they are usually inclined to misapply their time if one is not constantly with them, one or two of them must read a story of the Old Testament (either from Moses and the Prophets, or from Solomon's or Sirach's Proverbs), while I write copies for them. This exercise continues during the noon hour.

It is also to be noted that children find it necessary to ask to leave the room, and one must permit them to do this, not wishing the uncleanness and odor in the school. But the clamor to go out would continue all day, and sometimes without need, so that occasionally two or three are out at the same time, playing. To prevent this I have driven a nail in the door-post, on which hangs a wooden tag. Any one needing to leave the room looks for the tag. If it is on the nail, this is his permit to go out without asking. He takes the tag out with him. If another wishes to leave, he does not ask either, but stands by the door until the first returns, from whom he takes the tag and goes. If the tag is out too long, the one wishing to go inquires who was out last, and from him it can be ascertained to whom he gave the tag, so that none can remain out too long.

To teach the uninitiated numbers and figures, I write on the blackboard (which hangs where all can see) these figures 1 2 3 4 5 6 7 8 9 0 far apart, that other figures can be put before and behind them. Then I put an 0 before the 1 and explain that this does not increase the number. Then I erase the 0 and put it after the 1, so that it makes 10. If two ciphers follow it makes 100, if three follow, 1000, & c. This I show them through all the digits. This done I affix to the 1 another 1, making 11. But if an 0 is put between it makes 101, but if it be placed after, it makes 110. In a similar manner I go through all the digits. When this is done I give them something to find in the Testament or hymnal. Those who are quickest have something to claim for their diligence, from me or at home.

As it is desirable for intelligent reading to take note of commas, but as the inexperienced find this difficult, I have this rule: If one of the Testament pupils does not read

on, but stops before he reaches a comma or period, this counts one-fourth failure. Similarly if one reads over a comma, it is one-fourth failure. Repeating a word counts one-half. Then all failures are noted, and especially where each one has failed. When all have read, all those who have failed must step forward and according to the number of errors stand in a row. Those who have not failed move up, and the others take the lowest positions.

Regarding the correspondence, I may say that for twelve years I kept two schools, as already said, and for four summers (during the three months that I had free owing to the harvest) I taught school at Germantown. Then the pupils in Skippack, when I went to Sollford, gave me letters, and when I returned, the Sollford pupils did likewise. It was so arranged that pupils of equal ability corresponded. When one became his correspondent's superior, he wrote to another whose equal he tried to be.

The superscription was only this: My friendly greeting to N. N. The contents of the letter consisted of a short rhyme, or a passage from Scripture, and they told something of their school exercises (their motto for the week and where it is described, &c.). Sometimes one would give the other a question to be answered by a passage of Scripture. I doubt not, if two schoolmasters (dwelling in one place or not) loving one another and desiring their pupils to love one another, were to do this in the love of God, it would bear fruit.

This is a piecemeal description of how children are taught letters, and how their steps are led from one degree to the next.

. . . . .

Now experience teaches that a timid child is harmed rather than benefited by harsh words or much application of the rod, and to improve it, other means must be employed. Likewise a stupid child is only harmed. A child that is treated to too much flogging at home is not benefited by it at school, but it is made still worse. If such children are to be helped, it must happen through other means.

. . . . .

My colleagues will agree with me that the souls put in our keeping are very precious. We will be called to account for them by our God, and though we have the power to punish they would, I think, agree with me in saying that it is preferable to bring the children to do things from a love of doing than to force them by the rod.

. . . . .

Regarding my friend's question, how I treat the children with love that they both love and fear me, I will say that in this respect I cannot take the least credit upon myself, if I am at all successful with children, either in teaching or in performing religious duties. First I owe God particular thanks, because besides calling me to this profession He has given me an extreme love of children. For if it were not for love it would be an unbearable burden to live among children. But love bears and never tires. If a natural mother did not love her children all the little incidents in the education of a child would be unbearably wearisome, but her love makes this burden light.

. . . . .

". . . Out of the love of God, [Christopher Dock] loved his pupils as if they all were his own children. They, in turn, loved him dearly. Whenever he was obliged to reprove the children for ill-behavior, he did so with grievous words coming from his wounded heart, so that he frequently softened their hearts; and when they were about to cry, tears crept into his eyes. He studied out many plans so that he might not need to resort to the rod. On going to and from school the children went quietly and orderly without stopping to play, loiter and quarrel. The children of the poor he taught as willingly without pay as he taught others for pay. Those who learned to write, he induced to correspond with one another. The pupils were required to show him the letters and he pointed out for them the places where improvements should be made. He also told them that this was no ordinary matter. For those who could not compose a letter, he set copies so that they might apply their minds to good thoughts for the improvement of their souls. He regarded it indifferently whether he received the tuition fees or not and did not treasure up for himself anything but a good name and a clear conscience."

CHRISTOPHER SAUER, 1752

CHAPTER THREE

The Mind of the Enlightenment

THE EMERGENCE OF A SCIENTIFIC METHODOLOGY

FRANCIS BACON
Novum Organum (1620) *

APHORISMS
CONCERNING
THE INTERPRETATION OF NATURE
AND
THE KINGDOM OF MAN.
APHORISM

I.

MAN, being the servant and interpreter of Nature, can do and understand so much and so much only as he has observed in fact or in thought of the course of nature: beyond this he neither knows anything nor can do anything.

. . . . .

III.

Human knowledge and human power meet in one; for where the cause is not known the effect cannot be produced. Nature to be commanded must be obeyed; and that which in contemplation is as the cause is in operation as the rule.

IV.

Towards the effecting of works, all that man can do is to put together or put asunder

* Francis Bacon, *Novum Organum* (1620), *The Works of Francis Bacon* (New York: Hurd and Houghton, 1878), Vol. I, Part 2, "Aphorisms Concerning the Interpretation of Nature and the Kingdom of Man," pp. 67–72, 75–80, 126–127, 145–146.

natural bodies. The rest is done by nature working within.

. . . . .

IX.

The cause and root of nearly all evils in the sciences is this—that while we falsely admire and extol the powers of the human mind we neglect to seek for its true helps.

. . . . .

XI.

As the sciences which we now have do not help us in finding out new works, so neither does the logic which we now have help us in finding out new sciences.

XII.

The logic now in use serves rather to fix and give stability to the errors which have their foundation in commonly received notions than to help the search after truth. So it does more harm than good.

XIII.

The syllogism is not applied to the first principles of sciences, and is applied in vain to intermediate axioms; being no match for the subtlety of nature. It commands assent therefore to the proposition, but does not take hold of the thing.

XIV.

The syllogism consists of propositions, propositions consist of words, words are

58

symbols of notions. Therefore if the notions themselves (which is the root of the matter) are confused and over-hastily abstracted from the facts, there can be no firmness in the superstructure. Our only hope therefore lies in a true induction.

. . . . .

XIX.

There are and can be only two ways of searching into and discovering truth. The one flies from the senses and particulars to the most general axioms, and from these principles, the truth of which it takes for settled and immoveable, proceeds to judgment and to the discovery of middle axioms. And this way is now in fashion. The other derives axioms from the senses and particulars, rising by a gradual and unbroken ascent, so that it arrives at the most general axioms last of all. This is the true way, but as yet untried.

. . . . .

XXIV.

It cannot be that axioms established by argumentation should avail for the discovery of new works; since the subtlety of nature is greater many times over than the subtlety of argument. But axioms duly and orderly formed from particulars easily discover the way to new particulars, and thus render sciences active.

. . . . .

XXXVI.

One method of delivery alone remains to us; which is simply this: we must lead men to the particulars themselves, and their series and order; while men on their side must force themselves for awhile to lay their notions by and begin to familiarise themselves with facts.

XXXVII.

The doctrine of those who have denied that certainty could be attained at all, has some agreement with my way of proceeding at the first setting out; but they end in being infinitely separated and opposed. For the holders of that doctrine assert simply that nothing can be known; I also assert that not much can be known in nature by the way which is now in use. But then they go on to destroy the authority of the senses and understanding; whereas I proceed to devise and supply helps for the same.

XXXVIII.

The idols and false notions which are now in possession of the human understanding, and have taken deep root therein, not only so beset men's minds that truth can hardly find entrance, but even after entrance obtained, they will again in the very instauration of the sciences meet and trouble us, unless men being forewarned of the danger fortify themselves as far as may be against their assaults.

XXXIX.

There are four classes of Idols which beset men's minds. To these for distinction's sake I have assigned names,—calling the first class *Idols of the Tribe;* the second, *Idols of the Cave;* the third, *Idols of the Marketplace;* the fourth, *Idols of the Theatre.*

XL.

The formation of ideas and axioms by true induction is no doubt the proper remedy to be applied for the keeping off and clearing away of idols. To point them out, however, is of great use; for the doctrine of Idols is to the Interpretation of Nature what the doctrine of the refutation of Sophisms is to common Logic.

XLI.

The Idols of the Tribe have their foundation in human nature itself, and in the tribe or race of men. For it is a false assertion that the sense of man is the measure of things. On the contrary, all perceptions as well of the sense as of the mind are according to the measure of the individual and not according to the measure of the universe.

And the human understanding is like a false mirror, which, receiving rays irregularly, distorts and discolours the nature of things by mingling its own nature with it.

XLII.

The Idols of the Cave are the idols of the individual man. For every one (besides the errors common to human nature in general) has a cave or den of his own, which refracts and discolours the light of nature; owing either to his own proper and peculiar nature; or to his education and conversation with others; or to the reading of books, and the authority of those whom he esteems and admires; or to the differences of impressions, accordingly as they take place in a mind preoccupied and predisposed or in a mind indifferent and settled; or the like. So that the spirit of man (according as it is meted out to different individuals) is in fact a thing variable and full of perturbation, and governed as it were by chance. Whence it was well observed by Heraclitus that men look for sciences in their own lesser worlds, and not in the greater or common world.

XLIII.

There are also Idols formed by the intercourse and association of men with each other, which I call Idols of the Market-place, on account of the commerce and consort of men there. For it is by discourse that men associate; and words are imposed according to the apprehension of the vulgar. And therefore the ill and unfit choice of words wonderfully obstructs the understanding. Nor do the definitions or explanations wherewith in some things learned men are wont to guard and defend themselves, by any means set the matter right. But words plainly force and overrule the understanding, and throw all into confusion, and lead men away into numberless empty controversies and idle fancies.

XLIV.

Lastly, there are Idols which have immigrated into men's minds from the various dogmas of philosophies, and also from wrong laws of demonstration. These I call Idols of the Theatre; because in my judgment all the received systems are but so many stage-plays, representing worlds of their own creation after an unreal and scenic fashion. Nor is it only of the systems now in vogue, or only of the ancient sects and philosophies, that I speak; for many more plays of the same kind may yet be composed and in like artificial manner set forth; seeing that errors the most widely different have nevertheless causes for the most part alike. Neither again do I mean this only of entire systems, but also of many principles and axioms in science, which by tradition, credulity, and negligence have come to be received.

. . . . .

XLVI.

The human understanding when it has once adopted an opinion (either as being the received opinion or as being agreeable to itself) draws all things else to support and agree with it. And though there be a greater number and weight of instances to be found on the other side, yet these it either neglects and despises, or else by some distinction sets aside and rejects; in order that by this great and pernicious predetermination the authority of its former conclusions may remain inviolate. And therefore it was a good answer that was made by one who when they showed him hanging in a temple a picture of those who had paid their vows as having escaped shipwreck, and would have him say whether he did not now acknowledge the power of the gods,—"Aye," asked he again, "but where are they painted that were drowned after their vows?" And such is the way of all superstition, whether in astrology, dreams, omens, divine judgments, or the like; wherein men, having a delight in such vanities, mark the events where they are fulfilled, but where they fail, though this happen much oftener, neglect and pass them by. But with far more subtlety does this mischief insinuate itself into philosophy and the sciences; in which the first conclusion colours and brings into conformity with itself all that come after, though far sounder and better. Besides, independently of that delight and vanity which I have described, it is the peculiar and perpetual error of the human intellect to be more moved and excited by affirmatives than by negatives; whereas it ought properly to hold itself indifferently disposed towards both alike. Indeed in the establishment of any true axiom, the negative instance is the more forcible of the two.

. . . . .

XC.

Again, in the customs and institutions of schools, academies, colleges, and similar bodies destined for the abode of learned men and the cultivation of learning, everything is found adverse to the progress of science. For the lectures and exercises there are so ordered, that to think or speculate on anything out of the common way can hardly occur to any man. And if one or two have the boldness to use any liberty of judgment, they must undertake the task all by themselves, they can have no advantage from the company of others. And if they can endure this also, they will find their industry and largeness of mind no slight hindrance to their fortune. For the studies of men in these places are confined and as it were imprisoned in the writings of certain authors,

from whom if any man dissent he is straightway arraigned as a turbulent person and an innovator. But surely there is a great distinction between matters of state and the arts; for the danger from new motion and from new light is not the same. In matters of state a change even for the better is distrusted, because it unsettles what is established; these things resting on authority, consent, fame and opinion, not on demonstration. But arts and sciences should be like mines, where the noise of new works and further advances is heard on every side.

. . . . .

CXIV.

Lastly, even if the breath of hope which blows on us from that New Continent were fainter than it is and harder to perceive; yet the trial (if we would not bear a spirit altogether abject) must by all means be made. For there is no comparison between that which we may lose by not trying and by not succeeding; since by not trying we throw away the chance of an immense good; by not succeeding we only incur the loss of a little human labour. But as it is, it appears to me from what has been said, and also from what has been left unsaid, that there is hope enough and to spare, not only to make a bold man try, but also to make a soberminded and wise man believe.

THE DOCTRINE OF EMPIRICISM

JOHN LOCKE
An Essay Concerning Human Understanding (1690)*

* John Locke, *An Essay Concerning Human Understanding and a Treatise on the Conduct of the Understanding* (Philadelphia: Troutman and Hayes, and Pittsburgh: Kay and Co., 1853; "Complete, in one volume, with the author's last additions and corrections"), Book I, pp. 41–42, 62; Book II, pp. 75–76, 82–83.

BOOK I.

OF INNATE NOTIONS.

CHAPTER II.

NO INNATE PRINCIPLES IN THE MIND.

SECT. 1. *The way shown how we come by any knowledge, sufficient to prove it not innate.*—It is an established opinion among some men, that there are in the understanding certain innate principles; some primary notions; Κοιναὶ ἔννοιαι, characters as it were, stamped upon the mind of man, which the soul receives in its very first being, and brings into the world with it. It would be sufficient to convince unprejudiced readers of the falseness of this supposition, if I should only show (as I hope I shall in the following parts of this discourse) how men, barely by the use of their natural faculties, may attain to all the knowledge they have, without the help of any innate impressions; and may arrive at certainty, without any such original notions or principles. For I imagine any one will easily grant, that it would be impertinent to suppose the ideas of colour innate in a creature, to whom God hath given sight and a power to receive them by the eyes, from external objects: and no less unreasonable would it be to attribute several truths to the impressions of nature, and innate characters, when we may observe in ourselves faculties fit to attain as easy and certain knowledge of them, as if they were originally imprinted on the mind.

But because a man is not permitted, without censure, to follow his own thoughts in the search of truth, when they lead him ever so little out of the common road, I shall set down the reasons that made me doubt of the truth of that opinion, as an excuse for my mistake, if I be in one; which I leave to be considered by those, who, with me, dispose themselves to embrace truth, wherever they find it.

. . . . .

SECT. 5. *Not on the mind naturally imprinted, because not known to children, ideots, &c.*—For, first, it is evident, that all children and ideots have not the least apprehension or thought of them; and the want of that is enough to destroy that universal assent, which must needs be the necessary concomitant of all innate truths; it seeming to me near a contradiction to say, that there are truths imprinted on the soul, which it perceives or understands not; imprinting, if it signify any thing, being nothing else but, the making certain truths to be perceived. For,

to imprint any thing on the mind, without the mind's perceiving it, seems to me hardly intelligible. If, therefore, children and ideots have souls, have minds, with those impressions upon them, they must unavoidably perceive them, and necessarily know and assent to these truths; which, since they do not, it is evident that there are no such impressions: for if they are not notions naturally imprinted, how can they be innate? and if they are notions imprinted, how can they be unknown?

. . . . .

CHAPTER IV.

OTHER CONSIDERATIONS CONCERNING INNATE PRINCIPLES BOTH SPECULATIVE AND PRACTICAL.

. . . SECT. 2. *Ideas, especially those belonging to principles, not born with children.* —If we will attentively consider new-born children, we shall have little reason to think that they bring many ideas into the world with them. For bating perhaps some faint ideas of hunger and thirst, and warmth, and some pains which they may have felt in the womb, there is not the least appearance of any settled ideas at all in them; especially of ideas answering the terms which make up those universal propositions that are esteemed innate principles. One may perceive how, by degrees, afterward, ideas come into their minds; and that they get no more, nor no other than what experience, and the observation of things that come in their way, furnish them with: which might be enough to satisfy us that they are not original characters stamped on the mind.

BOOK II.

OF IDEAS.

CHAPTER I.

OF IDEAS IN GENERAL, AND THEIR ORIGINAL.

SECT. 1. *Idea is the object of thinking.*— Every man being conscious to himself that he thinks, and that which his mind is applied about whilst thinking, being the ideas that are there, it is past doubt, that men have in their minds several ideas, such as are those expressed by the words whiteness, hardness, sweetness, thinking, motion, man, elephant, army, drunkenness, and others. It is in the first place then to be inquired, how he comes by them. I know it is a received doctrine, that men have native ideas and original characters stamped upon their minds in their very first being. This opinion I have, at large, examined already; and I suppose, what I have said, in the foregoing book, will be much more easily admitted, when I have shown whence the understanding may get all the ideas it has, and by what ways and degrees they may come into the mind; for which I shall appeal to every one's own observation and experience.

SECT. 2. *All ideas come from sensation or reflection.*—Let us then suppose the mind to be, as we say, white paper, void of all characters, without any ideas; how comes it to be furnished? Whence comes it by that vast store which the busy and boundless fancy of man has painted on it, with an almost endless variety? Whence has it all the materials of reason and knowledge? To this I answer in one word, from experience; in that all our knowledge is founded, and from that it ultimately derives itself. Our observation employed either about external sensible objects, or about the internal operations of our minds, perceived and reflected on by ourselves, is that which supplies our understandings with all the materials of thinking. These two are the fountains of knowledge, from whence all the ideas we have, or can naturally have, do spring.

SECT. 3. *The objects of sensation one source of ideas.*—First, Our senses, conversant about particular sensible objects, do convey into the mind several distinct perceptions of things, according to those various ways wherein those objects do affect them: and thus we come by those ideas we have of yellow, white, heat, cold, soft, hard, bitter, sweet, and all those which we call sensible qualities; which, when I say the senses convey into the mind, I mean, they, from external objects, convey into the mind what produces there those perceptions. This great source of most of the ideas we have, depending wholly upon our senses, and derived by them to the understanding, I call SENSATION.

SECT. 4. *The operations of our minds the other source of them.*—Secondly, The other fountain from which experience furnisheth the understanding with ideas, is the perception of the operations of our own mind within us, as it is employed about the ideas it has got, which operations, when the soul comes to reflect on and consider, do furnish the understanding with another set of idea, which could not be had from things without; and such are preception, thinking, doubting, believing, reasoning, knowing, willing, and all the different actings of our own minds; which we being conscious of and observing in ourselves, do from these receive into our understandings as distinct ideas, as we do from bodies affecting our senses.

This source of ideas every man has wholly in himself; and though it be not sense, as having nothing to do with external objects, yet it is very like it, and might properly enough be called internal sense. But as I call the other sensation, so I call this, REFLECTION, the ideas it affords being such only as the mind gets by reflecting on its own operations within itself. By reflection, then, in the following part of this discourse, I would be understood to mean that notice which the mind takes of its own operations, and the manner of them; by reason whereof there come to be ideas of these operations in the understanding. These two, I say, viz. external material things, as the objects of sensation and the operations of our own minds within, as the objects of reflection; are to me the only originals from whence all our ideas take their beginnings. The term operations here I use in a large sense, as comprehending not barely the actions of the mind about its ideas, but some sort of passions arising sometimes from them, such as is the satisfaction or uneasiness arising from any thought.

SECT. 5. *All our ideas are of the one or the other of these.*—The understanding seems to me not to have the least glimmering of any ideas, which it doth not receive from one of these two. External objects furnish the mind with the ideas of sensible qualities, which are all those different perceptions they produce in us: and the mind furnishes the understanding with ideas of its own operations.

These, when we have taken a full survey of them and their several modes, combinations, and relations, we shall find to contain all our whole stock of ideas; and that we have nothing in our minds which did not come in one of these two ways. Let any one examine his own thoughts, and thoroughly search into his understanding; and then let him tell me, whether all the original ideas he has there are any other than of the objects of his senses, or of the operations of his mind, considered as objects of his reflection; and how great a mass of knowledge soever he imagines to be lodged there, he will, upon taking a strict view, see that he has not any idea in his mind, but what one of these two have imprinted; though perhaps with infinite variety compounded and enlarged by the understanding, as we shall see hereafter.

. . . . .

SECT. 24. *The original of all our knowledge.*—In time the mind comes to reflect on its own operations, about the ideas got by sensation, and thereby stores itself with a new set of ideas, which I call ideas of reflection. These are the impressions that are made on our senses by outward objects, that are extrinsical to the mind, and its own operations, proceeding from powers intrinsical and proper to itself: which, when reflected on by itself, becoming also objects of its contemplation, are, as I have said, the original of all knowledge. Thus, the first capacity of human intellect is that the mind is fitted to receive the impressions made on it, either through the senses, by outward objects, or by its own operations, when it reflects on them. This is the first step a man makes towards the discovery of any thing, and the ground work whereon to build all those notions which ever he shall have naturally in this world. All those sublime thoughts which tower above the clouds, and reach as high as heaven itself, take their rise and footing here: in all that good extent wherein the mind wanders, in those remote speculations it may seem to be elevated with, it stirs not one jot beyond those ideas which sense or reflection have offered for its contemplation. . . .

A NEW VIEW OF HUMAN NATURE

JEAN JACQUES ROUSSEAU,
Émile, ou Traité de l'Éducation (1762)*

* From *Emilius; or an Essay on Education,* by John James Rousseau, Citizen of Geneva (London: Printed for J. Nourse and P. Vaillant, in the Strand, 1763; in two volumes), Book I, pp. 1–5, 7–12, 20, 22–23, 25, 27, 31, 59–60; Book II, pp. 71–73, 75–76, 88–89, 93, 94–95, 99; Book III, pp. 231–232, 236–237, 239, 256, 266–267, 309–311; Book IV, pp. 313, 315–316, 323–325, 333, 354, 362, 400–401, 403. The Latin form Emilius, which was used in the 1763 translation, was replaced in later editions by the original word Émile.

BOOK I

Every thing is perfect, coming from the hands of the Creator; every thing degenerates in the hands of man. He forces a spot of ground to nourish the productions of a foreign soil; or a tree to bear fruit by the insition of another: he mixes and confounds climates, elements, seasons: he mutilates his dog, his horse, his slave: he inverts the nature of things, only to disfigure them: he is fond of deformity, and monstrous productions: he is pleased with nothing, as it is framed by nature, not even with man: we must break him to his mind, like a managed horse; we must fashion him to his taste, like the trees or plants of his garden.

Were it not for this culture, things would still be worse; for our species will not bear being fashioned by halves. In the present constitution of things, man abandoned from his birth to his own guidance among the rest of society, would be a most monstrous animal. Prejudices, authority, necessity, example, and all the social institutions with which we are surrounded, would stifle the voice of nature, and substitute nothing else in its place. Nature would be to him like a plant or shrub, that shoots up spontaneously in the highway, but is soon trodden down and destroyed by travellers. . . .

We are all brought into the world feeble and weak, yet we stand in need of strength; we are destitute of every thing, yet we want assistance; we are senseless and stupid, yet we have occasion for judgment. All that we have not at our birth, and that we stand in need of at the years of maturity, is the gift of education.

Education is either from nature, from men, or from things. The developing of our faculties and organs, is the education of nature; that of men is the application we learn to make of this very developing; and that of things is the experience we acquire in regard to the different objects by which we are affected.

Mankind are all formed by three sorts of masters. The pupil, in whom their instructions contradict each other, is ill-educated, and will never be self-consistent. He, in whom they all coincide on the same point, and tend to the same end, he alone may be said to hit his aim, and to live consistently. In short, he alone is well-educated.

Now, of those three different educations, that of nature is independent on us: that of things depends on us only in particular respects: that of men is the only one really in our power, and this in a hypothetical sense; for who can pretend to direct every word and action of those who have the care of an infant?

No sooner therefore does education become an art, than it is almost impossible it should succeed; since the concurrence of circumstances necessary for its success, is in no man's power. All that we can possibly do, by dint of care, is, to come near the mark, more or less; but he must be very fortunate indeed who hits it.

But what mark is this? you will say: the very same that nature has in view. This we have just now proved; for since the concurrence of the three educations is necessary for their completion, the other two must be directed towards that which is no way subject to our control. But perhaps the word *nature* may bear, on this occasion, too indeterminate a sense; we shall therefore endeavour to fix it.

Nature, you will say, is nothing more than an habit. But what do you mean by that? Are not there habits contracted by mere force, which cannot be said, however, to stifle nature? Such, for instance, is the habit of plants, constrained in their vertical direction. Restored to their liberty, they still retain the direction they have been forced to assume; yet the sap has not changed its original impression; and if the plant continues to vegetate, its prolongation once more becomes vertical. It is the same in regard to human inclinations. So long as we continue in the same state, we may retain such inclinations as result from habit, and are least natural to us; but as soon as the situation changes, the habit ceases, and nature revives. Education surely is nothing more than habit. And yet are there not some people, who altogether forget, and others, who retain their education? Whence this difference? If we are to confine the word *nature* to habits conformable to nature, surely we may spare ourselves the trouble of this nonsensical expression. . . .

In order to be something, to be one's self, and always the same, we should act as we speak; we should ever be determined in regard to the cause or part we are to espouse; we should espouse it warmly, and follow it closely. I want to see this prodigy. I want to know whether he is a man or a citizen, or how he goes to work, in order to become both at the same time.

From these objects, necessarily opposite, two contrary forms of institutions arise; the one public and common, the other particular and domestic. . . .

Those ridiculous establishments, known by the name of colleges, cannot be considered as a public institution. Neither do I look upon a secular education in that light, because this, by tending to two contrary ends, misses both: it is fit only to render men double and deceitful; as it seems to refer every thing to public good, and yet calculates every thing for private emolument. Now these appearances being practised by all the world, impose upon no body; therefore they are so much time and trouble lost.

From these contradictions arises that which we incessantly feel within ourselves. Dragged by nature, and by man, into contrary pursuits, and constrained to divide ourselves between these different impulses, we follow one of a compound nature, which leads us to neither end. Thus contending and fluctuating the whole course of our lives, we conclude the scene without having been ever self-consistent, and without being of the least utility either to ourselves or to our neighbours.

There remains lastly the domestic education, or that of nature. But of what service can a man be to others, who is solely educated for himself? Perhaps, if the twofold object which we have in view could be reunited in a single point, by removing the contradictions of man, we should remove a great impediment to his happiness. In order to judge of him, we should see him quite formed; we should observe his inclinations, view his movements, and trace his footsteps; in a word, we should be acquainted with man in his natural state. I am apt to flatter myself, that some progress will be made in this research, after the perusal of these papers.

In order to form this extraordinary man, what have we to do? A great deal, without doubt; we are to hinder any thing from being done. When we are only to sail against the wind, the whole business is to laveer; but if the sea runs high, and we want to tarry in a place, we must cast anchor. Take care, young pilot, that thy cable does not break, or, before thou art aware, thy vessel drags her anchor.

In the social order, where all places are marked down, each man ought to be brought up to his station. If a private person, formed for his own condition of life, attempts to get out of it, he is no longer of any service. Education is of no use any farther, than as people's fortune agrees with the vocation of their parents; in every other case, it is prejudicial to the young pupil; if on no other account, because of the prejudices which he imbibes from thence. In Egypt, where the son was obliged to follow his father's profession, there was at least a certain aim or design in their education; but in Europe, where the ranks alone are continued, and the men keep continually changing, you cannot tell whether, in bringing up your son to your own calling, you do not act counter to his interest.

Mankind being all upon an equality in the natural state, their common vocation is the state of man; and whoever has had a proper education for the former, cannot misbehave in the different circumstances relative to that state. Whether our pupil be brought up to the army, to the church, or to the bar, little does it import; before the vocation received from his parents, nature has designed him for human life. To live is the trade I want him to learn. . . .

Our real study is that of the human condition. He who knows best how to bear the prosperous and adverse turns of fortune, is, in my opinion, the best educated. Whence it follows, that real education consists less in theory than in practice. We begin to gain instruction upon our first coming into the world; our education commences with our existence; and our first preceptor is our nurse. . . .

We think no more than of the preservation of our infant, but that is not sufficient. We ought to learn him how to preserve himself as a man, to defy the unprosperous strokes of fortune, to live, if there should be occasion, on the snows of Iceland, or on the burning rock of Malta. In vain do you use precautions to save him from dying, for die he must: and were his death not to be forwarded by your too great care of his health, it would still be misapplied. The point is not so much to keep him from dying, as to make him live. Life is not confined to respiration, it implies also to act; it implies the use of our organs, of our senses, of our faculties, and of every part of ourselves, by which we are rendered sensible of our existence. The man who has lived the longest, is not he who has told the greatest number of years; but he who has had the greatest sensibility of life. Such a one is interred at a hundred years of age, who died at his nativity. He would have been a gainer in dying young; at least he would have lived till the day of his death.

The whole sum of human wisdom consists in servile prejudices: our customs are nothing more than subjection and restraint. The member of the civil state is born, lives, and dies in slavery; at his birth he is sown up in swaddling cloaths, at his death he is nailed in a coffin; so long as he preserves the human form, he is fettered by different institutions.

. . . . .

Observe nature, and follow the steps pointed out by that prudent dame. She trains up children to constant exercise; she hardens their constitution by every kind of trial; she initiates them by times into the school of adversity. The cutting of their teeth throws them into fevers; colic pains fling them into convulsions; hooping coughs almost suffocate them; worms torment them; plethories corrupt their blood; fermentations arise in the whole mass, and are productive of divers eruptions. Almost the intire stage of infancy consists of dangerous maladies; and one half of the children that come into the world, depart this life before they attain their eighth year. The infant, after he has undergone these trials, acquires strength; and as soon as he is in a capacity to make a proper use of life, the vital principle is consolidated.

Such is the rule of nature; and why should you act counter to her? . . .

The fate of man is to suffer at all times. The very care of his preservation is attended with trouble and pain. How happy are we in our infancy in knowing none but physical evils! Evils by far less severe, and less painful than the others; and more rarely the cause of renouncing our existence. People do not kill themselves in a fit of the gout; none but the tortures of the mind produce despair. We pity the state of infants, while it is our own we ought to pity. Our greatest evils flow from ourselves.

An infant squalls the moment he comes into life; and his early days are spent in crying. One time he is dandled and wheedled; another time he is huffed and beaten to make him quiet. Either we do what is agreeable to him, or we require of him what is agreeable to us: either we subject ourselves to his fancy, or we make him submit to ours: there is no medium; he must either give or receive orders. Hence his first ideas are those of empire and servitude. Before he knows how to speak, he commands; before he is able to act, he obeys; and sometimes he is chastised, before he is capable of knowing, or rather of committing an error. Hence his young breast is early imbued with passions, which are afterwards imputed to nature; and when we have been at the trouble of making him vicious, we complain of his vices.

Thus does a child pass six or seven years of life in the hands of women, a victim to their caprice and his own: and after they have learnt him a few trifles, that is, after charging his memory with words which he is incapable of understanding, or with things that are of no manner of use to him; after stifling nature by passions, which we ourselves have raised in his little breast; this factitious being is consigned into the hands of a preceptor, who unfolds the artificial shoots, which he finds already quite formed, and teaches him every thing, except to know himself, to draw from his own fountain, to understand life, and to be happy. The child becomes a slave, and a tyrant, replete with knowledge, but devoid of sense, and alike infirm in body and mind: being thus introduced into life, he exhibits his weakness, his insolence, and vices, so as to excite our commiseration of his folly and of human perversity. But we are mistaken; this is a man framed according to our own fancy: man is otherwise formed by nature. . . .

Who then is to educate my child? Already have I said it, thyself. I cannot do it. Thou canst not! Get then a friend to do it for thee. I see no other resource.

A governor! O what sublimity of soul is requisite for this office! In truth, to form a man, you must either be a father, or more than a man. Yet this is an employment generally committed to mercenary tutors.

The more we reflect, the more difficulties will arise in regard to this article. The governor ought to be educated on purpose for his pupil, the servants ought to be trained for their master, every one that comes near him ought to receive such impressions as are proper to be communicated by them to him; in short, there should be a scale of educations, mounting God knows how high. How is it possible for a child to be properly educated by a person, who has not had a proper education himself?

Is this rare mortal no where to be found? I cannot tell. In this degenerate age, who knows to what point of virtue a human soul is still capable of attaining? But let us suppose this prodigy has been found. . . .

Hence have I thought proper to pitch upon an imaginary pupil; to suppose myself to have the age, state of health, knowledge, and other abilities, requisite for the care of his education; to be entrusted with that employ from the very instant of his birth, to the years of maturity, when he will no longer have occasion for any other guide

than himself. This method appears to be of some use, to prevent an author, diffident of his abilities, from losing himself in visionary schemes: for whenever he deviates from the beaten road, he has only to make a trial of his own practice upon his pupil, and he will soon perceive, or the reader will perceive for him, whether he follows the natural progress of childhood, and the beaten path of humanity.

Such is the method which, amidst innumerable difficulties, I have thought fit to pursue. To prevent the book from swelling to no purpose, I have been satisfied with laying down principles, the truth of which should be obvious to all the world. But in regard to the rules, which might stand in need of proofs, I have applied them all to my Emilius, or to other examples, and have particularly pointed out in what manner those rules were capable of being reduced to practice. Such at least is the plan I proposed to follow; it is the reader's business to judge whether I have succeeded. . . .

Emilius is an orphan: for it little imports whether his father and mother be living. Entrusted with their duties, I succeed to their rights. He ought to honour his parents, but to obey me only. This is my first, or rather only agreement.

·　·　·　·　·

Children, as they grow up, acquire strength, become less troublesome, less active, and are more confined within their own center. The soul and the body place themselves, as it were, in an equilibrium, and nature requires nothing more of us than the motion necessary for our preservation. But the desire of command is not extinguished at the same time, as the want which gave it birth; power awakes, and flatters self-love, while habit strengthens it; fancy succeeds to want; and thus prejudices and opinions are first rooted.

When once the principle is known, we clearly see the point where we turned out of nature's path; let us see what is proper to be done, to prevent our losing our way.

So far from being endued with too much strength, children have not even the force sufficient for every thing that nature requires of them; we must therefore let them have the full enjoyment of the vigour they received from nature, so long as they can do no harm or mischief with it. This is the first maxim.

A second maxim is, that we ought to assist them, and supply their wants, whether as to understanding, strength, or any other physical defect.

A third maxim is, that whatever aid or assistance we grant them, we should always confine ourselves to real utility, without allowing any indulgence to fancy or unreasonable desire; for fancy will not torment them, when they have not been the cause of it themselves, since it never proceeds from nature.

The fourth maxim is, that we should carefully study their language and signs, to the end that during a stage of life, in which they are incapable of dissembling, we may be able to distinguish their desires; which of them, for instance, are derived immediately from nature, and which from opinion.

The intent of these rules is, that children shall enjoy more real liberty, and less command; that they shall do more of themselves, and require less of others. Thus being accustomed to measure their desires by their strength, they will scarcely feel the privation of what is not in their power.

The above is a new, and indeed a very important reason, for leaving children to the free use of their limbs: only with the precaution of keeping them out of all danger of falling, and letting nothing approach their hands, by which they can possibly be hurt. . . .

BOOK II

We are now entered upon the second stage of life, and here it is, that infancy properly terminates. . . .

Far am I from desiring that Emilius should never receive any hurt; on the con-trary, I should be very much concerned, were he never to have a cut or wound, or not to experience the nature of pain. To suffer is the first and most useful knowledge he can acquire. Infants seem to have been framed with infirm little bodies, only to learn those useful lessons without danger. If a child falls down, he does not break his leg; if he hits himself a blow with a stick, he does not dislocate an arm; if he takes up a knife, he does not grasp it fast, nor cut himself too deep. I never heard an instance of a child, left alone, that killed, maimed, or did himself any other considerable harm, unless he were indiscreetly exposed on some high place, or left near the fire, or some dangerous tools were laid within his reach. What shall we say of those numerous machines, which are put round a child, in order to arm him at all points against pain? When he comes of age, he is void of courage and experience, he thinks himself dead at the prick of a pin, and faints away upon seeing the least drop of blood.

Such is our pedantic folly in regard to children, that we are continually teaching them what they would learn much better of themselves, while we neglect to direct them, where they are in absolute want of our assistance. Can any thing be more absurd than the pains people take, to learn them to walk, as if ever there had been an instance of a child, who, through the carelessness of his nurse, was incapable of this motion, when he came to a proper age? On the contrary, how many do we see walk very ill during their whole lives, because they had been ill taught in their infancy.

. . . . .

You that are men, feel like men; this is your first duty: be humane to every state, to every age, to every thing not foreign to your species. What wisdom or philosophy can you be said to have without humanity? Be fond of infants; encourage their sports, their pleasures, their amiable inclinations. . . . Humanity has its place in the order of things; infancy has also its place in the order of human life: we must consider humanity in man, and infancy in infants.

. . . . .

There are two excesses; one of rigour, the other of indulgence, both equally to be avoided. If you let children suffer, you endanger their healths and their lives, and you moreover render them actually miserable: if you are over solicitous to guard them against every the least hurt or inconveniency, you only expose them to future misery; by rendering them too delicate, you divest them of the human state, to which they will one day or other return, in spite of all your endeavours. To prevent their being exposed to a few natural evils, you give them such as are merely artificial. You will tell me, that I am fallen into the case of those bad fathers, whom I rebuked for sacrificing the present happiness of their children to the consideration of a distant and uncertain advantage.

Not at all: the liberty I allow my pupil is an ample indemnity for the slight inconveniencies, to which I leave him exposed. I see a parcel of little boys playing in the snow, their faces livid, quite benumbed with cold, and hardly able to move their fingers. They have it in their power to warm themselves, whenever they list; and yet they go on with their play: were they to be compelled to it, they would be infinitely more sensible of the severity of the constraint, than they are of the cold. Why then do you complain? Shall I render your child miserable, by exposing him only to inconveniencies, which he is rejoiced to suffer? I study his present good, by leaving him at his liberty; and his future good, by arming him against evils, to which he must be hereafter subject. Had he his option to be your pupil or mine, do you think he would hesitate a moment?

Is there a possibility of enjoying any real happiness beyond the limits of our natural constitution? And is it not exceeding the limits of a child's situation, to attempt exempting him alike from all the evils, to which his species is subject? I maintain, it is:

to be sensible of great advantages, he must feel little hardships; such is his natural frame. If too much care is taken of his health, his manners are vitiated. The man who is an utter stranger to pain, knows no tender sentiment of humanity, no tear of compassion; were his heart insensible to every affection, he would be unfit for society; he would be a monster in nature. . . .

I return now to the practice. Already have I observed, that your child should obtain nothing, because he asks it, but because of his wants; and let him do nothing from a motive of obedience, but through necessity: thus the words *obey* and *command* will be expunged from his dictionary, and much more those of duty and obligation; but those of force, necessity, impotency, and constraint, are to be ranked in the first order. . . .

The lectures of morality usually made to children may be reduced to the present form.

Master. You must not do that.

Child. And why so?

Master. Because it is wrong.

Child. Wrong! what do you mean by wrong?

Master. That which you are forbid to do.

Child. What harm is there in doing what I am forbid?

Master. You will be chastised for disobeying.

Child. I shall take care it shall not be known.

Master. You will be carefully watched.

Child. I intend to conceal myself.

Master. You will be examined.

Child. I will tell a lie.

Master. You must not tell a lie.

Child. Why must not I tell a lie?

Master. Because it is wrong, &c.

Here is a circle unavoidable. Get out of it, if you can; the child knows not what to make of you. Are not these very fine instructions? I should be glad to hear what you could substitute in the room of this dialogue. Mr. Locke himself would, I make no doubt, be greatly puzzled. To distinguish moral good and evil, to know the reason of social duties, is much above a child's capacity.

Nature requires we should be children, before we arrive to the state of manhood. Should we attempt to invert this order, our fruit would be too forward; it would have neither flavour nor taste, and would quickly spoil; we should have young doctors, and old children. Infants have their own peculiar ways of seeing, thinking, and acting; nothing can be more absurd than to substitute ours in the room of theirs; I should be as well pleased to see a child five feet high, as to have maturity of judgment at the age of ten. And of what use would this reason be at that age? It is a restraint to force, and a child has no need of that restraint.

. . . . .

Let us establish it as an incontestable maxim, that the first movements of nature are always right: there is no original perversity in the human breast.

. . . . .

BOOK III

Although the course of human life till the age of puberty be a period of weakness, yet there is a point in this early stage, at which the progress of force having exceeded that of want, the growing animal, still absolutely weak, becomes relatively strong. His wants not being all displayed, his actual strength is more than sufficient to answer his present necessities. Considered as man, he would be undoubtedly feeble; as an infant, he is possessed of a considerable force.

Whence arises this weakness in man? From the disproportion between his abilities and his desires. It is our passions that render us feeble, because it requires greater powers to satisfy them, than we have received from nature. Diminish your desires, and it will be the same as if you had increased your force; he, whose power is superior to his desires, has some to spare; and is certainly a powerful being. Here commences the third state of infancy, of which

I am now about to treat. I continue to call it infancy, for want of a more proper term; for this is not yet the stage of puberty, though bordering upon it.

At twelve or thirteen years of age, a child's powers increase much faster than his wants. The most impetuous, the most terrible of them all, is not yet felt; the organ itself remains in an imperfect state, and seems to wait for the exertion of the will, to enter upon action. Almost insensible to the injuries of air and seasons, his natural heat supplies the warmth of apparel, and his appetite the provocations of sauce; whatever is but nourishing suits his age; if he is drowsy, he lays himself on the ground, and falls asleep; he is supplied on every side with necessaries; no imaginary want torments his mind; he is influenced by no opinion; his desires go no farther than his arms can reach; he is not only capable of providing for himself, but is possessed of powers that exceed his wants; and this is the only time of life, in which he will be so circumstanced. . . .

This earth is the island designed for the human species: the object most striking to the eye is the sun. As soon as our thoughts begin to be diverted from ourselves, our first considerations are directed to both those subjects. Hence the philosophy of most savage nations is entirely confined to the imaginary divisions of the earth, and the divinity of the sun.

Some perhaps will say, what a strange digression! Just now our thoughts were employed about what immediately affects and surrounds us: and now, on a sudden, we are traversing the globe, and making excursions to the further extremity of the universe! This digression, however, is owing to the progress of our abilities, and to the bent of our understanding. During the state of weakness and insufficiency, the care of our preservation confines us within ourselves: in the state of power and strength, the desire of extending our existence carries us out of ourselves, and makes us launch out as far as we can possibly reach; but the intellectual world being yet unknown to us, our thought can pierce no further than the eye, and our understanding is enlarged only in proportion to the space it measures.

Let us transform our sensations into ideas, without making a sudden transition from sensible to intellectual objects. It is by the former we are to arrive at the knowledge of the latter. Let the mind, in its first operations, be always guided by the senses. Let there be no other book but the world, no other instruction than facts. The boy that reads, does not think, nor gain instruction, he only learns a parcel of words.

Endeavour to make your pupil attentive to the phænomena of nature, and you will soon excite his curiosity; but to keep it alive, be not in a hurry to satisfy it. Put some queries to him, suited to his capacity, and let him solve them himself. Let his knowledge be not founded in your authority, but in his own investigation; let him not learn, but invent the sciences. If ever you substitute authority in the place of reason, he will reason no more, but be a dupe to the opinions of others. . . .

Never talk to your pupil in a language he does not understand. Make use of no pompous descriptions, no flowers of rhetoric, no figures, nor poetry. At present, taste and sentiment are out of the question. Continue to be plain and intelligible; the time will come but too soon, when you must have recourse to another language.

Your pupil being educated according to the principles here laid down, and accustomed to draw all his knowledge from himself, and never to apply for assistance, but when he was convinced of his own inabilities, every new object he beholds, he examines it a long time in thoughtful silence. He meditates, but does not ask many questions. You must therefore be satisfied with representing the objects to him at a proper time; and when you have seen his curiosity sufficiently excited, propose some laconic question to him, which shall put him in the way of resolving his doubts.

. . . . .

Let a child do nothing upon trust; nothing is good in regard to him but what he perceives to be such. By anticipating his natural knowledge, you imagine you are acting with forecast; but you are mistaken. To supply him with a few idle instruments, for which perhaps he will never have occasion, you deprive him of the most universal and useful of all others, that of good sense; you accustom him to suffer himself to be always conducted, and to be a mere machine in the hands of others. You are willing he should be docile while he is young; this is desiring he should be a credulous fool when he is ripened in years. You are continually making use of these words: *All I desire of you, is for your own good, but you are not as yet capable of knowing it. What is it to me, whether you do what I require of you or not? It is for yourself only you are doing it.* With these fine speeches you intend at present to make him wise, but you only pave the way for the artful discourses of some projector, conjurer, false prophet, or any other kind of knave; who will endeavour to catch him in their snare, or persuade him to adopt their folly.

It is very fit a man should be acquainted with a variety of things, the utility of which is above a child's comprehension? but is it necessary, or even possible, a child should learn every thing it behoves a man to know? Endeavour to teach a boy whatever is useful to one of his years, and you will find him full employment. Why should you, in prejudice to the studies fit for his present state, make him apply himself to such as are suitable only to an age, which he is so uncertain of ever attaining? But will it be time, you say, to learn what is proper for him to know, just when he has occasion to make use of his knowledge? I cannot tell, but I am very certain, it is impossible for him to learn it sooner; for our real masters are experience and sensation. . . .

Never point out any thing to a child, which it is impossible for him to comprehend. While he is yet almost a stranger to humanity, as you cannot raise him to a state of manhood, level this state to his capacity. When your thoughts are employed about what may be useful to him at another period of life, talk to him only of what he sees attended with present utility. But above all, never draw any comparisons between him and other children; let him have no rivals nor competitors, not even at running. When he begins to reason, I had much rather he never learned any knowledge at all, than acquire it by means of jealousy or vanity. I should only take notice to him annually of the progress he had made that year, and compare it to what I expect from him the year following; I should tell him, you are grown so much; there is the ditch you jumped over, the load you carried, the distance you flung a stone, or the ground you run over without fetching your breath; let us see what you are able to do at present. Thus would I encourage him, without raising his jealousy; he would desire, and he ought, to surpass himself; and I see no inconveniency in his being his own rival.

I have an aversion to books; they only instruct us to talk beyond our knowledge. Hermes is said to have engraved the elements of the sciences on columns, in order to secure his discoveries from being lost in a deluge. Had he imprinted them in the minds of men, they would have been preserved by tradition. The brain, duly prepared, is the monument, in which all human knowledge is best engraved.

Is there no possibility of collecting the great variety of instructions diffused through such a multitude of volumes? No means of uniting them under one common head, which may be viewed with ease, pursued with profit, and even serve as a spur and encouragement to youth? Could we imagine a situation in life, in which all the natural wants of man were represented in a manner obvious to the capacity of a child, and the means of providing against those wants were successively displayed with the same facility, a lively and ingenuous description of that state should be the first thing in which we ought to exercise his fancy.

Impetuous philosopher! I see your imagination already upon the wing: give yourself no trouble; such a situation has been found out already; a description of it has been published, and without any disparagement to your abilities, much better than you would have done it, at least with more exactness and simplicity. Since we must have books, there is one, which, in my opinion, is a most excellent treatise on natural education. This is the first my Emilius shall read; his whole library shall long consist of this work only, which shall preserve an eminent rank to the very last. It shall be the text, to which all our conversations on natural science are to serve only as a comment. It shall be a guide during our progress to maturity of judgment; and so long as our taste is not adulterated, the perusal of this book will afford us pleasure. And what surprizing book is this? Is it Aristotle, is it Pliny, is it Buffon? No, it is Robinson Crusoe.

Robinson Crusoe, cast away upon a desart island, destitute of human assistance, and of mechanic instruments, yet providing for his subsistence and preservation, and even procuring to himself a comfortable sort of being, is an object interesting to every age, and may be rendered a thousand ways agreeable to children.

．　．　．　．　．

Emilius has but little knowledge, but that little is really his own; he knows nothing by halves. Among the few things he knows, and which he fully understands, the most important is, that there are many things, of which he is ignorant, but which he is likely to know some time or other; a great many that other people know, but with which he will never be acquainted; and an infinite number that will never be known by any mortal whatever. He is an universal genius, not by his present knowledge, but by his extensive capacity; his mind is open, intelligent, disposed to receive every communication, and, as Montaigne says, if not instructed, at least capable of receiving instruction. It is sufficient for me, that he knows the utility of whatever he does, and the reason of whatever he believes. Once more I say, my intention is not to furnish him with learning, but to teach him how to acquire it, when it may be of use to him; to shew him how to set a just value on it; and, above all things, to inspire him with the love of truth. Pursuing this method, he advances slowly, but he never takes an useless step, nor is he obliged to go retrograde.

My pupil understands no other science, but that of nature. He does not so much as know the name of history, nor the meaning of the words metaphysics and morality. He is acquainted with the essential relations of man to things, but with none of the moral relations between man and man. He knows but very little of general ideas, or abstract notions of things. He observes the general qualities of certain bodies, without reasoning on those qualities themselves. He is acquainted with abstract extension, by the aid of geometrical figures; and with abstract quantity, by means of algebraical signs. These figures and signs are the support of those abstractions, on which his senses depend. He has no curiosity of investigating the nature of things, but only of discovering those relations in which he is interested. He estimates outward objects in regard to himself only; but then this estimation is just and exact. Fancy or general agreement have no weight with him. He sets the greatest value on what is most useful to him; and never deviating from this manner of estimating, he pays no regard at all to human opinion.

Emilius is fond of exercise, temperate in his diet, patient under difficulties, of great firmness of mind, and of invincible courage. His imagination is never so heightened, as to magnify dangers; he is affected with very few hardships, and capable of suffering with constancy, because he never learnt to repine against fate. With regard to death, he does not rightly know the nature of it as yet; but being used to submit to the law of necessity without reluctance, when it is his turn to go off the stage, he will do it with a

good grace; this is the utmost that nature will admit of in that critical minute, abhorred by all. To live free and independent, and to have very little connexion with the world, is the best way of learning to die.

In a word, Emilius is possessed of every virtue that has a relation to himself. In order to possess the social virtues, he only wants to be made acquainted with the relations on which they subsist; he only stands in need of those instructions, which his mind is prepared to receive.

He considers himself without any connexion with others. He requires nothing of any man, and believes no man has a right to require any thing of him. He is single in the midst of society, and depends upon himself alone. He has indeed a greater right than any body else to this independency, because he is possessed of every real accomplishment that a person of his age is capable of attaining. He is subject to no errors, but only such as are inseparable from humanity; he has no vices, or those only, from which no man living can be exempt. He has a sound constitution, an active body, a clear understanding, with a free and dispassionate heart. Self-love, the first and most natural of all passions, has scarcely made itself known to him. Without disturbing any body's repose, he has hitherto lived content, happy, and as free as the condition of humanity would permit. Do you think that a youth, who with these accomplishments has attained his fifteenth year, can be said to have mispent the foregoing part of his life.

BOOK IV

How swiftly our life passes upon this earth! The first quarter is elapsed before we know its use; the last quarter still running out, after we have ceased to enjoy it. At first we know not how to live; soon we are no longer in a capacity for it; and during the space which separates these two useless extremities, three fourths of the time are spent in sleep, labour, pain, constraint, and every kind of uneasiness. Life is short, not so much on account of the brevity of its duration, as of the little time we have to enjoy it. . . .

Our passions are the chief instruments of our preservation; it is therefore a vain as well as ridiculous attempt to destroy them; it is controlling nature, and reforming the handy-work of God. If the Deity wanted man to annihilate the passions which are given him, he would not know his own mind, he would be inconsistent with himself. But never did he issue out so absurd an order; never was any thing like it imprinted on the heart of man; and what God is willing man should do, he does not tell him by the mouth of another, but reveals it to him himself, and stamps it in indelible characters on his heart.

Now to attempt to suppress the passions, seems to be almost as weak, as if you endeavoured to destroy them: and whoever imagines that this has been my design, is certainly mistaken.

But would it be reasoning justly, if from its being in the nature of man to be endowed with passions, we were to conclude, that all the passions we feel, and observe in others, are natural? Their source is natural, I grant you, but it has been swelled by a thousand rivulets; it is a great river, whose bed is continually inlarging, and in which you would scarce find a few drops of the original spring. Our natural passions are very much limited; yet they are the instruments of our liberty, and tend to our preservation. Those which enslave and destroy us, come from another quarter; they are not the gift of nature, we adopt them to her prejudice.

. . . . .

If the period at which man becomes conscious of his sex, differs as much by education as by nature, it follows from thence, that this period may be either forwarded or retarded, according to the manner in which children are educated; and if the body acquires or loses its consistency, in proportion

as this progress is encouraged or delayed, the consequence also is, that the more backward we endeavour to render it, the more a youth will improve in vigour and strength. I speak as yet only of physical effects, we shall presently see they do not stop here.

From these reflections, I draw the solution of a question so often debated, whether it be proper to instruct children betimes in regard to objects of their curiosity, or whether it be more advisable to put them off by some modest deceit? In my opinion, we should do neither. In the first place, this curiosity never rises in their minds, without being occasioned by ourselves; and therefore we should endeavour to prevent it. Secondly, in regard to questions which we are not obliged to answer, it is not at all necessary we should deceive the child who proposes them; it is far preferable to silence him, than to answer him with a lie. He will not be much surprized at this law, if you have taken care to subject him to it in matters of indifference. In fine, if you are determined to answer, let it be with the greatest simplicity, without any mystery or embarrassment, and even without a smile. For there is not so much danger in satisfying, as in raising the curiosity of children.

Let your answers be always grave, concise, and steady, without seeming to have the least hesitation. I have no need to add, that they ought always to be true. It is impossible to make children sensible of the danger of telling lies to men, without being sensible ourselves of the much greater danger for men to tell lies to children. A single untruth affirmed by a master to his pupil, is enough to destroy the whole fruit of his education.

An absolute ignorance in regard to certain matters, is perhaps the most proper for children; but let them learn betimes what you cannot possibly conceal from them for ever. Either their curiosity must never be excited at all; or it should be satisfied before the time of life, in which it is attended with danger. Your behaviour towards your pupil in this respect, must depend on his particular situation, on the people that are about him, and on the different circumstances of life. It is of the utmost importance to leave nothing to hazard, and unless you are certain of keeping him in ignorance of the difference of sex till he is sixteen, let him learn it before he is ten.

I do not approve the affecting too refined a language in the presence of children, nor of long circumlocutions perceptible by them, to avoid calling things by their right name. In these matters, people of real virtue behave with great simplicity; but the imagination corrupted by vice, renders the ear delicate, and obliges us to a continual refinement of expression. Indelicate terms are of no manner of consequence; lascivious ideas are what we should endeavour to prevent.

Though modesty be natural to the human species, yet it is not natural to children. It proceeds only from the knowledge of evil; and as children neither have, nor can be supposed to have that knowledge, how should they have the sensation it produces? To give them lessons on shame and modesty, is telling them that there are shameful and immodest actions; it is inspiring them with a secret desire of knowing those things. Sooner or later they compass their end and the first spark that reaches the imagination, sets all the senses immediately on fire. Whoever blushes, is already guilty; true innocence is ashamed of nothing.

. . . . .

Let him not see the glittering outside of polite society, till he is capable of estimating its intrinsic value. To shew him the world before he knows human nature, is not forming, but corrupting his mind; is not giving him instruction, but leading him into error.

Men are not by nature kings, grandees, courtiers, nor possessed of opulence; we are all born poor, and naked; all subject to the miseries of life, to vexations, misfortunes, necessities, and pain of every kind; in short, we are all condemned to die. This is the real state of man; from this no body living can plead an exemption. Begin therefore with studying that part of our nature, which most essentially constitutes humanity.

At sixteen, a youth knows what it is to suffer, for he has suffered himself; but he is scarcely sensible that other beings also suffer. To see without feeling it, is no knowledge; for as I have often said before, a child having no idea of what others feel, knows no evils except his own.

. . . . .

Tutors are apt to complain, that the natural fire of this age renders youth intractable. I grant it does; but is it not their own fault? When once they have suffered this fire to vent itself through the senses, can they be ignorant that it will take no other course? Will the tedious insipid sermons of a pedant be able to cancel the ideas of pleasure in the mind of his pupil? Will they banish from his heart those insatiable desires? Will they extinguish that fire of constitution, with the use of which he is so well acquainted? Will he not be irritated against the obstacles that oppose the only felicity of which he has any idea? And while he finds himself restrained by a severe law, without being convinced of its reasonableness, in what other light shall he be able to consider it, but as the capricious aversion of a man, who only seeks to torment him? Is it therefore in the least surprizing, that he should mutiny and shew the same aversion towards his master?

I can easily conceive, that by treating your pupil with indulgence, you may render your situation more tolerable, and preserve the appearance of authority. But I do not understand the use of that authority, which is preserved only by encouraging the vices it ought to repress; it is just as if a riding-master, in order to tame an unruly horse, were to make him leap down a precipice.

This fire of youth, instead of being a bar to education, is the very thing by which it is compleatly finished; it is that which gives you hold of a young man's heart, when he ceases to be weaker than yourself.

. . . . .

Let him know, that man is naturally good; let him feel it in his own heart; let him judge of his neighbour by himself; but, at the same time, let him perceive in what manner mankind are corrupted and ruined by society; let him see that all their vices are derived from their prejudices, as their real source. Let him esteem each individual, but despise the multitude; let him observe, that all mankind wear nearly the same mask; but let him also know, that there are faces much handsomer than the masks by which they are disguised.

. . . . .

I am aware the reader will be surprized to find me attending my pupil throughout the first stage of life, without mentioning a word of religion. At fifteen he was ignorant that he had a soul, and perhaps at eighteen it will not be yet time for him to be informed of it; for if he learns it too soon, he runs a risk of never knowing it at all.

Were I to exhibit a scene of disagreeable stupidity, it would be that of a pedant teaching children the articles of religion; and if I intended to puzzle a child, I would oblige him to explain his meaning, when he repeats his catechism. I shall be told, that most of the dogmas of Christianity being religious mysteries, to wait till the human understanding is capable of conceiving them, is not waiting till the child grows, but till he is no more. To this I answer, in the first place, that there are mysteries, which it is not only impossible for men to conceive, but to believe; and I see no advantage in teaching them betime to children, except it be to learn them to tell lies. Further, I say, that before we admit of mysteries, we must at least conceive them to be incomprehensible; and children are incapable even of that idea. At an age in which every thing is mysterious, there are no mysteries properly so called.

We must believe in God, in order to be saved. The misapprehension of this dogma, is the source of the bloody doctrine of persecution, and the cause of all those idle instructions, which endeavour to subvert human reason, by accustoming it to be satisfied with words. No doubt but we ought not to hesitate a moment about working out our eternal salvation; but if to obtain this end, it is sufficient to repeat a certain form of words, I do not see what can hinder us from peopling heaven with perroquets and magpies, as well as with children. . . .

Let us avoid divulging the truth to those, who are incapable of understanding it; for this would be to substitute an error in its place. It would be much better to have no idea at all of God, than to entertain such notions as are mean, fantastical, injurious and unworthy of the divine Majesty. . . .

TOWARD AN ENLIGHTENED PEDAGOGY

JOHANN HEINRICH PESTALOZZI
Leonard and Gertrude (1781–1787) *

* Johann Heinrich Pestalozzi, *Leonard and Gertrude* (Boston: Heath, 1907; translated by Eva Channing), pp. 1–5, 42–47, 52–55, 84, 87–89, 116–119, 129–132, 134–135, 139, 152–157, 159. *Leonard and Gertrude* was first printed in 1781, when about one-fourth of the total work appeared; three more volumes were published in 1783, 1785, and 1787. Used by permission.

CHAPTER I.

A WEAK MAN, A BRAVE WOMAN, AND A
FATHERLY RULER.

In the village of Bonnal there lived a mason named Leonard. His trade would have enabled him to support his family of a wife and seven children, if he could have resisted the temptation to frequent the tavern, where there were always enough idle loafers to entice him in, and induce the good-natured, easy-going man to squander his earnings in drink and gambling. Leonard always repented his weakness when he saw his children want for bread, yet was not strong enough to reform. He was blest with a good, pious wife, who was overwhelmed with sorrow at the ruin which seemed to stare them in the face.

"Take courage, dear," she repeated, "and trust in your Father in heaven. I would not willingly grieve you, and you well know that I do not ask for more than bread and water at your side; and that I often work uncomplainingly till long past midnight for you and the children. But, husband, I should not feel I was true to you or our dear ones if I concealed my cares from you. Our children are loving and dutiful now; but they will not remain so if we do not fulfil our obligation as parents. Think how you would feel if all our little ones should lose their gratitude and respect for us through our fault! And could you bear to see your Nicholas, your Jonas, your Lizzie and Annie, homeless and forced to seek their bread among strangers? It would kill me!" and her tears flowed as she spoke.

Leonard wept also. "O Gertrude, what shall I do? It breaks my heart to make you miserable, but I cannot help it. I owe the Bailiff Hummel thirty florins, and if I stay away from his tavern, he threatens me with the law; yet if I go, he gets possession of all my wages."

"Can you not go to Arner, the people's father? All the widows and orphans praise him, and I think he would give you advice and protection."

"Gertrude, I dare not! How could I, a poor miserable drunkard, complain of the Bailiff, who has a thousand ways of blackening me in the eyes of his superior? And think how he would revenge himself if I should try it and fail!"

"But he will ruin you in any case. Leonard, think of your children, and go. If you do not, I shall!"

"I dare not! But, Gertrude, if you have the courage, go to Arner in Heaven's name, and tell him all."

"I will!" she answered. She prayed throughout the sleepless night, and the next morning took her blooming baby and walked two long hours to the Castle.

The nobleman was sitting under a linden-tree at the gate, and saw her as she approached, with tears in her eyes and the infant on her arm. "Who are you, my daughter, and what do you wish?" he asked, in so kind a tone that she took heart to answer: "I am Gertrude, wife of the mason Leonard in Bonnal."

"You are a good woman," said Arner. "I have noticed that your children behave better than all the others in the village, and they seem better fed, although I hear you are very poor. What can I do for you, my daughter?"

"O gracious Sir, for a long time my husband has owed thirty florins to the Bailiff Hummel, a hard man, who leads him into all sorts of temptation. Leonard is in his power: so he dares not keep away from the tavern, where day after day he spends the wages which ought to buy bread for his family. We have seven little children, Sir, and unless something is done we shall all be beggars. I ventured to come to you for help, because I know that you have compassion for the widowed and fatherless. I have brought the money I have laid aside for my children, to deposit with you, if you will be so good as to make some arrangement so that the Bailiff shall not torment my husband any more until he is paid."

Arner took up a cup which stood near, and said to Gertrude: "Drink this tea, and give your pretty baby some of this milk." She blushed, and was moved even to tears by his fatherly kindness.

The nobleman now requested her to relate her causes of complaint against the Bailiff, and listened attentively to her story of the cares and troubles of many years. Suddenly he asked her how it had been possible to lay aside money for her children in the midst of her distress.

"It was very hard, gracious Sir; yet I could not help feeling as if the money were not mine, but had been given me by a dying man on his death-bed, in trust for his children. So when in the hardest times I had to borrow from it to buy bread for the family, I gave myself no rest till by working late and early I had paid it back again."

Gertrude laid seven neat packages on the table, each of which had a ticket attached, saying whose it was; and if she had taken anything from it, the fact was noted, and likewise when she had replaced it. She saw him read these tickets through attentively, and said blushing: "I ought to have taken those papers away, gracious Sir."

Arner only smiled, and admired the modesty which shrank from even merited praise. He added something to each parcel, saying: "Carry back your children's money, Gertrude; I will lay aside thirty florins until the Bailiff is paid. Now go home; I shall be in the village to-morrow, at all events, and will settle the matter with Hummel."

"God reward you, gracious Sir!" she faltered; and started joyfully with her baby on the long homeward way. Leonard saw her as she approached the house. "Already back again?" he cried. "You have been successful with Arner."

"How do you know?"

"I can see it in your face, my dear wife, —you cannot deceive me."

From this time forward, when the mason's children said their prayers at morning and evening, they prayed not only for their father and mother, but also for Arner, the people's father.

．　．　．　．　．

CHAPTER VIII.

A GOOD MOTHER'S SATURDAY EVENING.

Gertrude, meanwhile, was at home alone with her children. Thoughtful and silent, she prepared the supper, and then took from the chest the Sunday clothes of all the family, so that on the morrow no petty cares might distract her thoughts from better things. When all was ready, she gathered the children about her, for it was her custom every Saturday to call their attention to their faults, and inculcate any lessons which the events of the week might bring home to their minds. To-day she was especially anxious to impress their young hearts with a sense of the goodness of God, as manifested during the past week; and when the little hands were all folded, Gertrude thus spoke: "Children, I have something joyful to tell you. Your dear father has the promise of such good work that he will be able to earn much more than before, and we may hope in future to have less trouble and anxiety about getting our daily bread. Thank the dear God, my children, for being so good to us, and do not forget the time when every mouthful of bread had to be counted! Think always of those who suffer from hunger and want, as you did once, and if you have a trifle more than you really need, do not grudge giving it to them. Will you do this, children?"

"Oh, yes indeed, mother!" they all cried with one voice. Gertrude now asked the children whether they would not sometimes like to give away their afternoon bread to those poorer than themselves, and on meeting with an eager response, she told each one to think of some hungry child who might be gladdened by the gift. Nicholas mentioned their neighbor, little Rudy; Lizzie spoke of Marx's daughter Betty; and so with the others in turn. They were all so full of the idea that they resolved, with one accord, to carry out the plan on the following day.

Then Gertrude spoke of Arner's presents to the children, and promising to show them the money after their evening prayer, she began: "Well, my dears, how has it been about doing right this week?" The children looked at each other, and were silent. "Annie, have you been good this week?"

Casting down her eyes in shame, the child replied: "No, mother; you know how it was with my little brother"—

"Annie, something might have happened to the child,—and just think how *you* would like it, if you should be shut up in a room all alone without food or amusement! Little children who are left alone in that way sometimes scream so that they injure themselves for life. Why, Annie, I could never feel easy about going away from home, if I thought you would not take good care of the child."

"Indeed, mother, I will never leave him alone again!"

"And, Nicholas," said Gertrude, turning to her oldest son; "how is it with you this week?"

"I don't remember anything wrong."

"Have you forgotten that you knocked down litle Peggy on Monday?"

"I didn't mean to, mother."

"I should hope not, Nicholas! Aren't you ashamed of talking so? If you grow up without considering the comfort of those about you, you will have to learn the lesson through bitter experience. Remember that, and be careful, my dear boy.—And Lizzie, how have you behaved this week?"

"I can't think of anything out of the way this week, mother."

"Are you sure?"

"I really can't, mother, think as hard as I can; if I could, I would willingly tell you of it, mother."

"How you do manage to use as many words, even when you have nothing to say, as any one else who says a great deal!"

"What did I say now, mother?"

"Nothing at all, and yet a great deal. It is just what we have told you a thousand times,—you never think beforehand of what you are going to say, and yet must be always talking. What business was it of yours to tell the Bailiff, day before yesterday, that you knew Arner would come soon? Suppose your father had not wished him to know that he knew it, and your chattering had brought him into trouble?"

"I should be very sorry, mother. But neither of you said a word about its being a secret."

"Very well, I will tell your father when he comes home, that, whenever we are talking together, we must take care to add after each sentence: 'Lizzie may tell that to the neighbors, and talk about it at the well; but this she must not mention outside the house.' So then you will know precisely what you may chatter about."

"O mother, forgive me! That was not what I meant."

Gertrude talked similarly with all the other children about their faults, even saying to little Peggy: "You mustn't be so impatient for your soup, or I shall make you wait longer another time, and give it to one of the others."

After this was over, the children folded their hands and said their usual evening prayer, followed by a special prayer for Saturday night, which Gertrude had taught them. When the mother had uttered a final benediction, all sat quiet for a little while, until Lizzie broke the silence. "Now will you show us the new money, mother?"

"Yes. But, Lizzie, you are always the first to speak!"

Nicholas sprang from his seat, and in pressing forward to the light, gave little Peggy such a violent push that she cried aloud.

"Nicholas!" said his mother, "that is not right. It is not a quarter of an hour since you promised to be more careful. You are not in earnest."

"O mother, I never will do so again as long as I live! I am really in earnest, and very sorry."

"So am I, dear boy; but you will forget it all unless I punish you. You must go to bed without your supper."

She led the boy to his room, while the other children stood sadly by. "Do let him out again, just this once!" they entreated.

"No, my dears; he must be cured of his carelessness."

"Then we'll not look at our money till to-morrow, so that he can see it with us," proposed Annie.

"That is right, Annie!"—and after giving

the children their supper, Gertrude went with them to the bedroom, where Nicholas was still crying. "My dear, dear boy," she said, "do be careful another time!"

"Forgive me, dear mother!" he cried, throwing his arms about her neck. "Only forgive me and kiss me, and I don't mind losing my supper at all."

Gertrude kissed him, and a warm tear fell upon his face. She blessed the other children, and returned alone to the dimly lighted room. A solemn stillness filled her heart; she was penetrated with a consciousness of God's goodness, and the happiness of those who place their trust in him. She was so deeply moved that she sank upon her knees and wept. Her eyes were still moist when her husband returned home. "Why are you weeping, Gertrude?" he inquired.

"My dear husband, these are no tears of sorrow; I wanted to thank God for the blessings of this week, but my heart was so full that I could not speak for weeping."

Leonard leaned his head upon her breast, and his eyes were also filled with tears. Neither spoke for a short time; but at last Gertrude asked if he did not wish any supper. "No," he replied; "my heart is too full; I cannot eat."

"Neither can I, dear. But I will tell you what we will do. We will carry our supper to poor Rudy, whose mother died to-day."

When they reached the house, Rudy was sitting weeping beside the corpse, and his little boy called from the adjoining room, begging for bread, or raw roots, or anything to eat. "Alas! I have nothing," answered the father. "For Heaven's sake, be quiet till morning!"

"But I am so hungry, father!" moaned the child. "I am so hungry I cannot sleep."

Leonard and Gertrude heard the words, and opening the door, set down the food, and bade them eat quickly, before it was cold. Deeply affected, the mourner called to the boy: "Rudy, these are the people from whom you stole potatoes,—and alas! I too, have eaten some!"

"Say no more about that," said Gertrude, "but eat."

"Do let us eat, father!" begged the child.

"Well, then, say your grace."

The boy obeyed, then took up the spoon, trembled, wept and ate. They put aside a part of the food for the sleeping children, and the afflicted father attempted once more to thank his benefactors. As he did so, a sigh escaped him.

"Is anything the matter, Rudy? Is there anything we can do for you?" asked Leonard and Gertrude.

"No, nothing, thank you," he replied, with difficulty repressing another deep sigh.

The two looked at him compassionately. "But you sigh; you certainly have some trouble at heart."

"Do tell them, father, they are so good!" besought little Rudy.

"May I?" said the poor man reluctantly. "I have neither shoes nor stockings, and to-morrow I must follow my mother to the grave, and the day after go to the Castle."

"The idea of tormenting yourself so about that!" cried Leonard. "Why didn't you say so at first? I shall be very glad to provide you with them."

"And can you believe," said Rudy humbly, "that, after all that has happened, I will return them to you uninjured and with thanks?"

"Hush, Rudy! I would trust you yet further than that. Your poverty and distress have made you too distrustful."

As Gertrude expressed a wish to look upon the dead, they all went with a feeble light to the bedside, and stood with tears in their eyes, gazing down upon the peaceful face. Then they covered up the lifeless form, and took leave of each other warmly, although without words.

．　．　．　．　．

CHAPTER X.

SUNDAY JOYS AND CHILDISH CHARACTER.

Meanwhile, the Sunday had been very differently spent in the humble dwelling of the mason. While Leonard and Gertrude were at church, the children prayed, sang, and reviewed what they had learned during the week, so as to be ready to repeat it to their mother in the evening. Lizzie, the oldest, had the care of baby Peggy during Gertrude's absence, and it was her greatest delight to dress, feed, and tend the little one. It was pretty to see her motherly airs as she dandled and kissed and played with her charge. How pleased she was when the baby laughed back at her with outstretched arms, and kicked with its tiny feet! Then it would grasp Lizzie's cap, or her pig-tails, or her nose, and crow over her bright Sunday neckerchief, until Nicholas and Annie would come up behind and crow in imitation; then the little one would turn at the sound, and laugh at the merry Nicholas, who would spring forward to kiss his baby sister. This would arouse Lizzie's jealousy, and she would exert herself to the utmost to make the little darling laugh at her. She devoted herself to the amusement of her charge, lifting the child in her arms almost to the ceiling, and then letting it down carefully to the very ground, until it screamed aloud with delight. Then she would hold it close to the looking-glass, so that it laughed at the baby within; but the most joyful moment of all was when the little one espied its mother far down the street, crowed, stretched out its tiny hands, and nearly sprang out of Lizzie's arms.

Gertrude was satisfied with her children to-day, for they had done everything as she had told them. They now had their reward in a frolic with their parents, for climbing joyfully into the laps of father and mother, the children possessed themselves of their hands, and clasped their necks tightly with small arms. Ever since Gertrude had been a mother, this was her Sunday delight; but to-day Leonard's eyes filled with tears at the thought that he had often deprived himself of these home joys. The happy parents talked with the children of their Father in heaven, and the sufferings of their Saviour, while the little ones listened attentively. The noon hour passed as swiftly and happily as a wedding feast, and the peal of bells again summoned Leonard and Gertrude to church.

When they returned home in the afternoon, the children ran down the steps to meet them, crying: "Oh, do hurry, mother! We want to repeat what we have learned this week, and get through as soon as possible."

"Why are you in such desperate haste, my dears?" asked Gertrude smiling.

"Why, when we are through, mother, you know what you promised us yesterday about the bread. We may, mother, mayn't we?"

"First I will see how well you know what you have learned," was the reply.

The lesson was soon satisfactorily concluded, whereupon Gertrude brought out the bread, and two dishes of milk from which she had not removed the cream, because it was a holiday. Not one of the children touched the bread, but each rejoiced over his or her piece, maintaining that it was the largest. When the milk had disappeared, Nicholas crept up to his mother's side, and taking her hand, whispered: "You will give me just one mouthful of bread for myself, will you not, mother?"

"You have your piece, Nicholas."

"But I must give it to Rudy."

"I haven't told you to give it to him," said his mother. "You can eat it if you like."

"I don't want to eat it; but you will give me just one mouthful?"

"Certainly not, my boy."

"Why not?"

"So that you needn't imagine we are only to think of the poor after our own hunger is satisfied. And now will you give him the whole of it?"

"Yes, mother, every bit. I know he is frightfully hungry, and we have supper at six."

"Yes, Nicholas, and I hardly think he will have anything to eat then."

The mother now turned to the other children, and asked if they, too, had quite decided to give their bread away, receiving in each case an affirmative answer. "That is right, children," she said. "But now, how will you set about it?—Nicholas, how are you going to manage with your bread?"

"I'll run as fast as I can, and call Rudy. I shall not put it in my pocket, so that he may have it all the quicker. Let me go, mother!"

"Stop a minute, Nicholas!—Lizzie, what are you going to do?"

"I am not going to do like Nicholas. I shall call Betty into a corner, and hide the bread under my apron, so that nobody will see it, not even her father."

"And Annie?"

"I can't tell where I shall find Harry—I shall give it to him just as it happens."

"And Jonas, you little rogue, you have some mischief in your head; how are you planning to do it?"

"I shall stick my bread into his mouth, mother, as you do to me in fun. 'Open your mouth and shut your eyes,' I shall say, and then put it between his teeth. Don't you think he'll laugh?"

"That is all very well, children," said Gertrude. "But I must tell you one thing: you must give away the bread quietly, so no one may see, that people needn't think you want to show off your generosity."

"Whew! mother," cried Nicholas; "then I must put my bread in my pocket?"

"Of course, Nicholas."

"That is just what occurred to me, mother," said Lizzie. "You know I said just now that I wouldn't do like him."

"You are always the wisest, Lizzie. I forgot to praise you for it, and you do well to remind me of it yourself." Lizzie colored, and was silent.

The children departed on their several missions. . . .

·　·　·　·　·

CHAPTER XVI.

DOMESTIC ORDER AND DISORDER.

. . . The mason's children were all at their spinning-wheels, and although they greeted their guests joyfully, they did not stop working for a moment. "Hurry and get through, and then you can play with your little friends till six o'clock," said Gertrude. Rudy's children stood in open-mouthed wonder at the beautiful work and the cheerful aspect of the room. "Can you spin?" she asked.

"No," they answered.

"Then you must learn, my dears. My children wouldn't sell their knowledge of it at any price, and are happy enough on Saturday, when they each get their few kreutzers. The year is long, my dears, and if we earn something every week, at the end of the year there is a lot of money, without our knowing how we came by it."

"Oh, please teach us!" implored the children, nestling close to the good woman.

"Willingly," Gertrude replied; "come every day, if you like, and you will soon learn."

Meanwhile, the others had finished their work, and put away their yarn and wheels; they took their visitors by the hand, and all the children sprang merrily about in the meadow under the trees. Gertrude's children were more careful than their companions to avoid the mud and the thorns, and took heed to their clothes. They tied up their stockings and shoes when they became undone, and would often say to Rudy's children: "You are losing your garter," or "You are getting dirty," or "You will tear your dress on the thorns." Their playfellows took it all in good part, for they saw that the mason's children did everything themselves which they prescribed, and were not putting on airs.

On the stroke of six, Gertrude's children ran into the house, like birds to their nests at sundown. "Will you come with us? We are going to pray now," they said to their visitors; and as they were playing the game called "cat's tail," they led the long procession through the meadow, up the steps, and to the very table where they seated themselves. "Must you not go home to prayers, my dears?" inquired Gertrude of the little strangers.

"We don't pray till we go to bed," replied the eldest.

"And when must you go to bed?"

"How do I know?" said the child; and another answered: "When it begins to grow dark."

"Well, then, you can pray with us, and then it will be time for you to go home." Gertrude heard her own children pray in turn, and then, after letting Rudy's children repeat the prayers they knew, she accompanied them to the corner of the house with a cheery parting, bidding them come again soon.

. . . . .

CHAPTER XXII.

PLANS OF REGENERATION IN BONNAL.

As the Sunday approached when Arner had decreed that Hummel should be exposed to the view of the whole congregation, while the pastor held up his previous life as a warning to those present, the prisoner expressed the utmost horror of this penalty, declaring that he would rather have his punishment at the gallows repeated, than stand under the pulpit to be the laughing-stock of the town. He represented that such a ceremony could neither dispose him to thoughts of repentance, nor have a beneficial effect upon the spectators. The pastor was finally so moved by his entreaties, as well as convinced of the reasonableness of his plea, that he interceded with Arner, and induced him to remit the sentence. Accordingly, the clergyman merely took Hummel's life as a text, preaching a stirring sermon against the wickedness and corruption which had been fostered so long in their midst, and which were still rife, in almost equal measure, in the hearts of many of his listeners.

This discourse everywhere made a profound impression; the peasants could talk of nothing else on the way home, and Arner, pressing the good pastor's hand, thanked him heartily for his edifying words. He expressed, at the same time, an earnest desire to labor for the improvement of the village, and asked the clergyman if he could recom-

mend an upright, able man from among the people, who could help him in furthering his designs. The parson mentioned at once the spinner known as Cotton Meyer, and proposed they should visit him and his sister that afternoon. They were accompanied by the Lieutenant Glülphi, one of Arner's aids in regulating the economic conditions of his government.

Cotton Meyer was sitting at his door with a child in his lap, when the three gentlemen approached, and had no suspicion that they were seeking him, until they paused before his garden gate. Then he went to meet them with so calm and dignified a bearing that Glülphi did not give him his hand, as he usually did to the peasants, and Arner addressed him less familiarly than was his wont when speaking to his dependants.

The visitors were about to seat themselves on the bench under the apple-tree; but Meyer led them into the parlor, where his sister was sitting by the table, nodding over the open Bible, as was her custom on Sunday afternoons. She started up with a cry as the door opened, and straightening her cap, closed the Bible; then, taking a sponge, she moistened it in a tin hand-basin which shone like silver, and erased the chalk figures with which her brother had covered the table, despite the remonstrance of the strangers, who feared that Meyer might have further use for his reckoning. After wiping the table carefully, she brought a large fine linen table-cloth, and laid new tin plates, with knives, forks and heavy silver spoons upon it.

"What are you doing?" inquired her guests; "we have already dined."

"I suppose so," answered Maria; "but since you have come into a peasant's house, you must take kindly to our peasant ways." Running into the kitchen, she returned with two plates of little cakes and a fine large ham, and Arner, Glülphi and the pastor seated themselves good-naturedly before the shining dishes.

When the visitors began to praise the

house, the garden and the whole establishment, Maria remarked that twenty years ago they had been among the poorest in the village. "I know it," said Arner, "and I wonder at your prosperity the more, as the weavers and spinners have usually turned out the most good-for-nothing people in the country."

Meyer was forced to admit that this was true, but denied that the cause lay in the industry itself. The trouble was, he said, that these poor people were not in the habit of laying up anything from their earnings, and led wretched, aimless lives. He felt sure that Arner might find many ways of winning the hearts of the people, so as to lead them into better paths, and suggested, as one expedient, that he should promise to every child, which up to its twentieth year should annually lay aside ten florins from its earnings, a field free from tithes. "But," went on Meyer, "after all, we can do very little with the people, unless the next generation is to have a very different training from that our schools furnish. The school ought really to stand in the closest connection with life of the home, instead of, as now, in strong contradiction to it."

Glülphi joined in the conversation with eagnerness, and argued that a true school should develop to the fullest extent all the faculties of the child's nature. The question next arose, how such a school could be established in Bonnal. Cotton Meyer, when appealed to, rejoined: "I know a spinning-woman in the village who understands it far better than I"; and he went on to tell the others such things of Gertrude's little school and its effects upon her children, that they resolved to visit her and examine her method for themselves. They also spoke of the corruption prevailing in the village, and discussed the best method of choosing a good bailiff. Cotton Meyer showed himself through it all a man of such clear judgment and practical common sense, that his guests left him with a feeling of respect almost approaching veneration.

. . . . .

CHAPTER XXV.

GERTRUDE'S METHOD OF INSTRUCTION.

It was quite early in the morning when Arner, Glülphi and the pastor went to the mason's cottage. The room was not in order when they entered, for the family had just finished breakfast, and the dirty plates and spoons still lay upon the table. Gertrude was at first somewhat disconcerted, but the visitors reassured her, saying kindly: "This is as it should be; it is impossible to clear the table before breakfast is eaten!"

The children all helped wash the dishes, and then seated themselves in their customary places before their work. The gentlemen begged Gertrude to let everything go on as usual, and after the first half hour, during which she was a little embarrassed, all proceeded as if no stranger were present. First the children sang their morning hymns, and then Gertrude read a chapter of the Bible aloud, which they repeated after her while they were spinning, rehearsing the most instructive passages until they knew them by heart. In the mean time, the oldest girl had been making the children's beds in the adjoining room, and the visitors noticed through the open door that she silently repeated what the others were reciting. When this task was completed, she went into the garden and returned with vegetables for dinner, which she cleaned while repeating Bible-verses with the rest.

It was something new for the children to see three gentlemen in the room, and they often looked up from their spinning toward the corner where the strangers sat. Gertrude noticed this, and said to them: "Seems to me you look more at these gentlemen than at your yarn." But Harry answered: "No, indeed! We are working hard, and you'll have finer yarn to-day than usual."

Whenever Gertrude saw that anything was amiss with the wheels or cotton, she rose from her work, and put it in order. The smallest children, who were not old enough to spin, picked over the cotton for carding, with a skill which excited the admiration of the visitors.

Although Gertrude thus exerted herself to develop very early the manual dexterity of her children, she was in no haste for them to learn to read and write. But she took pains to teach them early how to speak; for, as she said, "of what use is it for a person to be able to read and write, if he cannot speak? —since reading and writing are only an artificial sort of speech." To this end she used to make the children pronounce syllables after her in regular succession, taking them from an old A-B-C book she had. This exercise in correct and distinct articulation was, however, only a subordinate object in her whole scheme of education, which embraced a true comprehension of life itself. Yet she never adopted the tone of instructor toward her children; she did not say to them: "Child, this is your head, your nose, your hand, your finger;" or: "Where is your eye, your ear?"—but instead, she would say: "Come here,—child, I will wash your little hands," "I will comb your hair," or: "I will cut your finger-nails." Her verbal instruction seemed to vanish in the spirit of her real activity, in which it always had its source. The result of her system was that each child was skilful, intelligent and active to the full extent that its age and development allowed.

The instruction she gave them in the rudiments of arithmetic was intimately connected with the realities of life. She taught them to count the number of steps from one end of the room to the other, and two of the rows of five panes each, in one of the windows, gave her an opportunity to unfold the decimal relations of numbers. She also made them count their threads while spinning, and the number of turns on the reel, when they wound the yarn into skeins. Above all, in every occupation of life she taught them an accurate and intelligent observation of common objects and the forces of nature.

All that Gertrude's children knew, they knew so thoroughly that they were able to teach it to the younger ones; and this they often begged permission to do. On this day,

while the visitors were present, Jonas sat with each arm around the neck of a smaller child, and made the little ones pronounce the syllables of the A-B-C book after him; while Lizzie placed herself with her wheel between two of the others, and while all three spun, taught them the words of a hymn with the utmost patience.

When the guests took their departure, they told Gertrude they would come again on the morrow. "Why?" she returned; "You will only see the same thing over again." But Glülphi said: "That is the best praise you could possibly give yourself." Gertrude blushed at this compliment, and stood confused when the gentlemen kindly pressed her hand in taking leave.

The three could not sufficiently admire what they had seen at the mason's house, and Glülphi was so overcome by the powerful impression made upon him, that he longed to be alone and seek counsel of his own thoughts. He hastened to his room, and as he crossed the threshold, the words broke from his lips: "*I must be schoolmaster in Bonnal!*" All night visions of Gertrude's schoolroom floated through his mind, and he only fell asleep toward morning. Before his eyes were fairly open, he murmured: "I will be schoolmaster!"—and hastened to Arner to acquaint him with his resolution.

CHAPTER XXVI.

MATCH-MAKING AND SCHOOL-MAKING.

Arner rejoiced greatly over Glülphi's determination, and calling for the good pastor on their way, the two friends turned their steps for the second time to Gertrude's door. She had expected them, but had made no change in her usual programme. As they entered, at the close of the Bible reading, the morning sun shone brightly into the room, and the children, of their own accord, struck up the song beginning:

> "With what a fair and radiant gleam
> The sun's mild rays upon us beam,
> Bringing refreshment to the eye,
> And filling all our souls with joy!"

. . . Glülphi had been waiting impatiently to speak to Gertrude of his own plans, and he now asked her whether she thought it would be possible to introduce into a regular school the same method she pursued at home with her children. "I am not sure," she replied; "although I am inclined to think that what is possible with ten children would be possible with forty. But it would be difficult to find a schoolmaster who would tolerate such an arrangement in his school."

"But supposing one could be found," said the lieutenant, "who would be willing to introduce it, would you help him?"

"To be sure,—*if* one could be found," she returned with a laugh.

"And if I were he?"

"Were *who*?"

"The man who is ready to establish such a school as you have in your room."

"You are no schoolmaster!"

"But I will be."

"Yes, in some great city, perhaps, and in things village people know nothing about!"

"No, in a village, and in things all village people ought to understand."

"That must be a queer sort of village, where a gentleman like you wants to be schoolmaster! Such a gentleman as you doesn't take a fancy to teach children like these here."

"That you don't know."

"But I have an idea that it is so."

"So I perceive. But if I really wanted to be such a schoolmaster, what then? Would you help me?"

"To be sure," said Gertrude again, still under the impression he was joking; "I will help you all I can."

Glülphi turned to Arner and the pastor, saying: "You have heard, she has promised twice to help me."

"That's fine!" they said laughing.

Gertrude began to be confused, and when she found they were actually in earnest, she stoutly declared herself incapable of showing the lieutenant the least thing in the world, although she would gladly send her children

to school to him, and come herself if she were only younger. But they answered that her help would be indispensable, and when she pleaded her lack of time and the cares of her household, and named another excellent housekeeper whose aid might be of service, Glülphi replied: "She will doubtless be useful, too, but there can be no substitute for your mother's heart, which I must have for my school."

"My mother's heart is hardly large enough for my own room," said Gertrude; "and if you are really to be our schoolmaster, I know you will bring a father's heart and a father's strength into the work, such as will make my little mother's heart quite superfluous."

"It is very true," remarked the other gentlemen, "that our lieutenant will bring a great father's heart with him; but that will not render the coöperation of your mother's heart unnecessary." Then they explained to her that they regarded the proper education of the youthful population as the only means of elevating the condition of the corrupt village; and full of emotion, Gertrude promised them she would do anything in her power to forward the good cause.

·　·　·　·　·

CHAPTER XXVIII.

HOW SLANDER IS PUNISHED AND THE COMMON DIVIDED.

After his visit to Gertrude's school, Arner sat down and wrote a long letter to his intimate friend Bylifsky, now minister of the Duke, describing the impression made upon him by what he had just seen, and stating the views of Cotton Meyer with regard to the means of bettering the condition of the corrupt village. "These views," he concluded, "can be summed up under the following heads:

1. A school shall be organized which can be brought into harmony with the developing influence of domestic life, as is the case with that in Gertrude's house.

2. The better portion of the people of Bonnal shall unite with the Castle and the parsonage, for the purpose of gaining a sure and active influence over the various households of the village.

3. A new method of choosing the overseers shall be adopted, whereby the evil influence exerted by bad overseers may in future be removed."

.   .   .   .   .

CHAPTER XXXI.

THE ORGANIZATION OF A NEW SCHOOL.

Glülphi was full of the idea of his school, and could speak of nothing else with Arner and the pastor. He used all his spare time in visiting Gertrude, in order to talk it over with her; but she seemed quite unable to explain her method in words, and usually deprecated the idea of her advice being necessary. Occasionally, however, she would let drop some significant remark which the lieutenant felt went to the root of the whole matter of education. For example, she said to him one day: "You should do for your children what their parents fail to do for them. The reading, writing and arithmetic are not, after all, what they most need; it is all well and good for them to learn something, but the really important thing is for them to *be* something,—for them to become what they are meant to be, and in becoming which they so often have no guidance or help at home."

Finally, the day arrived on which the new schoolmaster was to be formally presented to the village. Arner and the pastor led him solemnly between them to the church, which was crowded with the inhabitants of Bonnal. The good clergyman preached a sermon on the ideal function of the school in its relation to the home, and to the moral development of the community; after which Arner led Glülphi forward to the railing of the choir, and introducing him to the people, made a short but earnest plea in his behalf. The lieutenant was much affected, but mastered his emotion sufficiently to express in a few words his sense of the responsibility conferred upon him, and his hope that the parents would coöperate with him in his undertaking.

Arner was anxious to make the occasion of Glülphi's installation a festival for the school-children, so after the services at the church, he invited all the little folks to the parsonage, where, with the help of the pastor's wife, preparations had been made to receive them. It was a time-honored custom that every year, at Christmas and Easter, eggs and rolls should be distributed among the children of Bonnal. On this day, on entering the parsonage, the young people beheld even more beautifully painted eggs than they had seen at Easter; and beside each child's portion lay a bright nosegay.

The lieutenant, who knew nothing of the whole matter, was in an adjoining room, when suddenly the door was thrown open, and the children, at a sign from Theresa, struck up with one accord their prettiest song, and Glülphi found himself surrounded by the lively throng of his future charges. He was much moved, and when the song was concluded, he greeted them kindly, shaking many of them by the hand, and chatting pleasantly with them. Arner ordered some of his own wine to be brought, and the children drank the health of their new schoolmaster.

On the following morning the lieutenant began his school, and Gertrude helped him in the arrangement of it. They examined the children with regard to their previous studies, and seated those together who were equally advanced. First there were those who had not learned their letters, then those who could read separate words, and finally, those who already knew how to read. Beside reading, all were to learn writing and arithmetic, which previously had only been taught to the more wealthy, in private lessons.

At first Glülphi found it harder than he had expected; but every day, as he gained in experience, his task became easier and more delightful. A good and capable woman, named Margaret, who came to take charge of the sewing, spinning etc., proved a most valuable and conscientious helper in the work. Whenever a child's hand or wheel stopped, she would step up and restore things to their former condition. If the children's hair was in disorder, she would braid it up while they studied and worked; if there was a hole in their clothes, she would take a needle and thread, and mend it; and she showed them how to fasten their shoes and stockings properly, beside many other things they did not understand.

The new master was anxious, above all, to accustom his charges to strict order, and thus lead them to the true wisdom of life. He began school punctually on the stroke of the clock, and did not allow any one to come in late. He also laid great stress on good habits and behavior. The children were obliged to come to school clean in person and apparel, and with their hair combed. While standing, sitting, writing and working, they always were taught to keep the body erect as a candle. Glülphi's schoolroom must be clean as a church, and he would not suffer a pane of glass to be missing from the window, or a nail to be driven crooked in the floor. Still less did he allow the children to throw the smallest thing upon the floor, or to eat while they were studying; and it was even arranged that in getting up and sitting down they should not hit against each other.

Before school began, the children came up to their teacher one by one, and said: "God be with you!" He looked them over from head to foot, so that they knew by his eye if anything was wrong. If this glance was not sufficient, he spoke to them, or sent a message to their parents. A child would not infrequently come home with the word: "The schoolmaster sends greeting, and wants to know whether you have no needles and thread," or "whether water is dear," etc. At the close of school, those who had done well went up to him first, and said: "God be with you!" He held out his hand to each

one, replying: "God be with you, my dear child!" Then came those who had only done partly well, and to these he merely said: "God be with you!" without giving them his hand. Finally, those who had not done well at all had to leave the room without even going to him.

The lieutenant's punishments were designed to remedy the faults for which they were inflicted. An idle scholar was made to cut fire-wood, or to carry stones for the wall which some of the older boys were constructing under the master's charge; a forgetful child was made school-messenger, and for several days was obliged to take charge of all the teacher's business in the village. Disobedience and impertinence he punished by not speaking publicly to the child in question for a number of days, talking with him only in private, after school. Wickedness and lying were punished with the rod, and any child thus chastised was not allowed to play with the others for a whole week; his name was registered in a special record-book of offences, from which it was not erased until plain evidence of improvement was given. The schoolmaster was kind to the children while punishing them, talking with them more then than at any other time, and trying to help them correct their faults.

CHAPTER XXXII.

A GOOD PASTOR AND SCHOOLMASTER; THE OPENING OF A NEW ERA.

In his instruction, Glülphi constantly sought to lay the foundation of that equanimity and repose which man can possess in all circumstances of life, provided the hardships of his lot have early become a second nature to him. The success of this attempt soon convinced the pastor that all verbal instruction, in so far as it aims at true human wisdom, and at the highest goal of this wisdom, true religion, ought to be subordinated to a constant training in practical domestic labor. The good man, at the same time, became aware that a single word of the lieutenant's could accomplish more than hours of his preaching. With true humility, he profited by the superior wisdom of the schoolmaster, and remodelled his method of religious instruction. He united his efforts to those of Glülphi and Margaret, striving to lead the children, without many words, to a quiet, industrious life, and thus to lay the foundations of a silent worship of God and love of humanity. To this end, he connected every word of his brief religious teachings with their actual, every-day experience, so that when he spoke of God and eternity, it seemed to them as if he were speaking of father and mother, house and home, in short, of the things with which they were most familiar. He pointed out to them in their books the few wise and pious passages which he still desired them to learn by heart, and completely ignored all questions involving doctrinal differences. He no longer allowed the children to learn any long prayers by rote, saying that this was contrary to the spirit of Christianity, and the express injunctions of their Saviour.

The lieutenant often declared that the pastor was quite unable to make a lasting impression on men, because he spoiled them by his kindness. Glülphi's own principles in regard to education were very strict, and were founded on an accurate knowledge of the world. He maintained that love was only useful in the education of men when in conjunction with fear; for they must learn to root out thorns and thistles, which they never do of their own accord, but only under compulsion, and in consequence of training.

He knew his children better in eight days than their parents did in eight years, and employed this knowledge to render deception difficult, and to keep their hearts open before his eyes. He cared for their heads as he did for their hearts, demanding that whatever entered them should be plain and clear as the silent moon in the sky. To insure this, he taught them to see and hear with accuracy, and cultivated their powers of attention. Above all, he sought to give them a thorough training in arithmetic; for he was convinced that arithmetic is the natural

safeguard against error in the pursuit of truth. . . .

The condition of the poor people of the village was much improved in various ways. The prospect of tithe-free land brought order and thrift into the houses of many of the spinners, and the poor in general were no longer so servile in their obedience to the whims and exactions of the rich. Renold's wife, who had always been noted for her charity, began to see that more good could be done by leading the people to help themselves, than by all her alms-giving. . . .

JOHANN HEINRICH PESTALOZZI
Letter to a Friend about His Orphanage at Stanz, Switzerland (1799)*

My friend, once more I awake from a dream; once more I see my work destroyed, and my failing strength wasted.

But, however weak and unfortunate my attempt may have been, a friend of humanity will not grudge a few moments to consider the reasons which convince me that some day a more fortunate posterity will certainly take up the thread of my hopes at the place where it is now broken.

From its very beginning I looked on the Revolution as a simple consequence of the corruption of human nature, and on the evils which it produced as a necessary means of bringing men back to a sense of the conditions which are essential to their happiness.

Although I was by no means prepared to accept all the political forms that a body of such men as the revolutionists might make for themselves, I was inclined to look upon certain points of their Constitution not only as useful measures protecting important interests, but as suggesting the principles upon

* Letter dated 1799 from Pestalozzi to Heinrich Gessner, a bookseller, concerning his orphanage at Stanz, Switzerland, as reprinted in Roger de Guimps, *Pestalozzi: His Life and Work* (New York and London: Appleton, 1890; authorized translation from the second French edition by J. Russell), pp. 149–163, 165–171.

which all true progress of humanity must be based.

I once more made known, therefore, as well as I could, my old wishes for the education of the people. In particular, I laid my whole scheme before Legrand (then one of the directors), who not only took a warm interest in it, but agreed with me that the Republic stood in urgent need of a reform of public education. . . .

As I have explained my plan for the public education of the poor in the third and fourth parts of *Leonard and Gertrude,* I need not repeat it here. I submitted it to the director Stapfer, with all the enthusiasm of a man who felt that his hopes were about to be realized, and he encouraged me with an earnestness which showed how thoroughly he understood the needs of popular education. It was the same with the minister Rengger.

It was my intention to try to find near Zurich or in Aargau a place where I should be able to join industry and agriculture to the other means of instruction, and so give my establishment all the development necessary to its complete success. But the Unterwalden disaster (September, 1798) left me no further choice in the matter. The Government felt the urgent need of sending help to this unfortunate district, and begged me for this once to make an attempt to put my plans into execution in a place where almost everything that could have made it a success was wanting.

I went there gladly. I felt that the innocence of the people would make up for what was wanting, and that their distress would, at any rate, make them grateful.

My eagerness to realize at last the great dream of my life would have led me to work on the very highest peaks of the Alps, and, so to speak, without fire or water.

For a house, the Government made over to me the new part of the Ursuline convent at Stanz, but when I arrived it was still uncompleted, and not in any way fitted to receive a large number of children. Before anything else could be done, then, the house itself had to be got ready. The Government gave the necessary orders, and Rengger pushed on the work with much zeal and useful activity. I was never indeed allowed to want for money.

In spite, however, of the admirable support I received, all this preparation took time, and time was precisely what we could least afford, since it was of the highest importance that a number of children, whom the war had left homeless and destitute, should be received at once.

I was still without everything but money when the children arrived; neither kitchen, rooms, nor beds were ready to receive them. At first this was a source of inconceivable confusion. For the first few weeks I was shut up in a very small room; the weather was bad, and the alterations, which made a great dust and filled the corridors with rubbish, rendered the air very unhealthy.

The want of beds compelled me at first to send some of the poor children home at night; these children generally came back the next day covered with vermin. Most of them on their arrival were very degenerated specimens of humanity. Many of them had a sort of chronic skin-disease, which almost prevented their walking, or sores on their heads, or rags full of vermin; many were almost skeletons, with haggard, careworn faces, and shrinking looks; some brazen, accustomed to begging, hypocrisy, and all sorts of deceit; others broken by misfortune, patient. suspicious, timid, and entirely devoid of affection. There were also some spoilt children amongst them who had known the sweets of comfort, and were therefore full of pretensions. These kept to themselves, affected to despise the little beggars their comrades, and to suffer from this equality, and seemed to find it impossible to adapt themselves to the ways of the house, which differed too much from their old habits. But what was common to them all was a persistent idleness, resulting from their want of physical and mental activity. Out of every ten children there was hardly one who knew his A B C; as for any other knowledge, it was, of course, out of the question.

This complete ignorance was what troubled me least, for I trusted in the natural powers that God bestows on even the poorest and most neglected children. I had observed for a long time that behind their coarseness, shyness, and apparent incapacity, are hidden the finest faculties, the most precious powers; and now, even amongst these poor creatures by whom I was surrounded at Stanz, marked natural abilities soon began to show themselves. I knew how useful the common needs of life are in teaching men the relations of things, in bringing out their natural intelligence, in forming their judgment, and in arousing faculties which, buried, as it were, beneath the coarser elements of their nature, cannot become active and useful till they are set free. It was my object then to arouse these faculties, and bring them to bear on the pure and simple circumstances of domestic life, for I was convinced that in this way I should be able to form the hearts and minds of children almost as I wished.

Now that I had an opportunity of carrying out this object, I felt sure that my affection would change the nature of my children as quickly as the sun changes the frozen earth in spring; nor was I wrong, for before the snow of our mountains had melted the children were no longer the same.

But I must not anticipate. Just as in the evening I often mark the quick growth of the gourd by the side of the house, so I want you to mark the growth of my plant; and, my friend, I will not hide from you the worm which sometimes eats into its leaves, sometimes even into its heart.

I opened the establishment with no other helper but a woman-servant. I had not only to teach the children, but to look after their physical needs. I preferred being alone, and, indeed, it was the only way to reach my end. No one in the world would have cared to fall in with my views for the education of children, and at that time I knew scarcely any one capable even of understanding them. The better the education of the men who might have helped me, the less their power of understanding me and of confining themselves, even in theory, to the simple beginnings to which I sought to return. All their views as to the organization and needs of the enterprise were entirely different from mine. What they especially disagreed with was the idea that such an undertaking could be carried out without the help of any artificial means, but simply by the influence exercised on the children by Nature, and by the activity to which they were aroused by the needs of their daily life.

And yet it was precisely upon this idea that I based my chief hope of success; it was, as it were, a basis for innumerable other points of view.

Experienced teachers, then, could not help me; still less boorish, ignorant men. I had nothing to put into the hands of assistants to guide them, nor any results or apparatus by which I could make my ideas clearer to them.

Thus, whether I would or no, I had first to make my experiment alone, and collect facts to illustrate the essential features of my system before I could venture to look for outside help. Indeed, in my then position, nobody could help me. I knew that I must help myself and shaped my plans accordingly.

I wanted to prove by my experiment that if public education is to have any real value, it must imitate the methods which make the merit of domestic education; for it is my opinion that if public education does not take into consideration the circumstances of family life, and everything else that bears on a man's general education, it can only lead to an artificial and methodical dwarfing of humanity.

In any good education, the mother must be able to judge daily, nay hourly, from the child's eyes, lips, and face, of the slightest change in his soul. The power of the educator, too, must be that of a father, quickened by the general circumstances of domestic life.

Such was the foundation upon which I

built. I determined that there should not be a minute in the day when my children should not be aware from my face and my lips that my heart was theirs, that their happiness was my happiness, and their pleasures my pleasures.

Man readily accepts what is good, and the child readily listens to it; but it is not for you that he wants it, master and educator, but for himself. The good to which you would lead him must not depend on your capricious humour or passion; it must be a good which is good in itself and by the nature of things, and which the child can recognize as good. He must feel the necessity of your will in things which concern his comfort before he can be expected to obey it.

Whenever he does anything gladly, anything that brings him honour, anything that helps to realize any of his great hopes, or stimulates his powers, and enables him to say with truth, *I can,* then he is exercising his will.

The will, however, cannot be stimulated by mere words; its action must depend upon those feelings and powers which are the result of general culture. Words alone cannot give us a knowledge of things; they are only useful for giving expression to what we have in our mind.

The first thing to be done was to win the confidence and affection of the children. I was sure that if I succeeded in doing that, all the rest would follow of itself. Think for a moment of the prejudices of the people, and even of the children, and you will understand the difficulties with which I had to contend.

The unfortunate country had suffered all the horrors of war. Most of the inhabitants detested the new constitution, and were not only exasperated with the Government, but suspicious of its offered help. Opposed by the natural melancholy of their character to anything new coming from outside, they held fast, with bitter and defiant obstinacy, to everything connected with their former condition, wretched as it was in many re-

spects. To these people I was simply an agent of the new order of things. They looked on me as a mere instrument, working not for them, but for the men who were the cause of their misfortunes, and whose opinions, views, and plans were entirely opposed to their own. This political distrust was strengthened by a no less deep religious distrust. I was a heretic, and so all my efforts to do good could only imperil their children's souls. Amongst them no Protestant had ever held the smallest public office; what must they have felt, then, on seeing one made a teacher of children? To make matters worse, religious and political passion in Stanz was just then excited to an unusually high degree.

Think, my friend, of this temper of the people, of my weakness, of my poor appearance, of the ill-will to which I was almost publicly exposed, and then judge how much I had to endure for the sake of carrying on my work.

And yet, however painful this want of help and support was to me, it was favourable to the success of my undertaking, for it compelled me to be always everything for my children. I was alone with them from morning till night. It was my hand that supplied all their wants, both of body and soul. All needful help, consolation, and instruction they received direct from me. Their hands were in mine, my eyes were fixed on theirs.

We wept and smiled together. They forgot the world and Stanz; they only knew that they were with me and I with them. We shared our food and drink. I had neither family, friends, nor servants; nothing but them. I was with them in sickness, and in health, and when they slept, I was the last to go to bed, and the first to get up. In the bedroom I prayed with them, and, at their own request, taught them till they fell asleep. Their clothes and bodies were intolerably filthy, but I looked after both myself, and was thus constantly exposed to the risk of contagion.

This is how it was that these children

gradually became so attached to me, some indeed so deeply that they contradicted their parents and friends when they heard evil things said about me. They felt that I was being treated unfairly, and loved me, I think, the more for it. But of what avail is it for the young nestlings to love their mother when the bird of prey that is bent on destroying them is constantly hovering near?

However, the first results of these principles and of this line of action were not always satisfactory, nor, indeed, could they be so. The children did not always understand my love. Accustomed to idleness, unbounded liberty, and the fortuitous and lawless pleasures of an almost wild life, they had come to the convent in the expectation of being well fed, and of having nothing to do. Some of them soon discovered that they had been there long enough, and wanted to go away again; they talked of the school fever that attacks children when they are kept employed all day long. This dissatisfaction, which showed itself during the first months, resulted principally from the fact that many of them were ill, the consequence either of the sudden change of diet and habits, or of the severity of the weather and the dampness of the building in which we lived. We all coughed a great deal, and several children were seized with a peculiar sort of fever.

This fever, which always began with sickness, was very general in the district. Cases of sickness, however, not followed by fever, were not at all rare, and were an almost natural consequence of the change of food. Many people attributed the fever to bad food, but the facts soon showed them to be wrong, for not a single child succumbed.

On the return of spring it was evident to everybody that the children were all doing well, growing rapidly, and gaining colour. Certain magistrates and ecclesiastics, who saw them some time afterwards, stated that they had improved almost beyond recognition.

A few of the children, however, continued in ill-health for some time, and the influence of the parents was not favourable to their recovery. "Poor child, how ill you look! I am sure I could look after you at home as well as you are looked after here. Come away with me." That was the sort of thing said by women who were in the habit of begging from door to door. On Sundays, especially, numbers of parents used to come and openly pity their children till they made them cry, and then urge them to go away. I lost a great many in this way; and though their places were soon filled by others, you can understand how bad these constant changes were for an establishment that was only just beginning.

Many parents thought they were doing me a personal favour by leaving the children with me, and even asked the Capuchins [friars at a nearby monastery] whether it was because I had no other means of subsistence that I was so anxious to have pupils. It was the general opinion amongst these people that poverty alone could have induced me to give myself so much trouble, an opinion which came out in their behaviour towards me.

Some asked me for money to make up for what they had lost by their children being no longer able to beg; others, hat on head, informed me that they did not mind trying a few days longer; others, again, laid down their own conditions.

Months passed in this way before I had the satisfaction of having my hand grasped by a single grateful parent. But the children were won over much sooner. They even wept sometimes when their parents met me or left me without a word of salutation. Several of them were perfectly happy, and used to say to their mothers: "I am more comfortable here than at home." At home, indeed, as they readily told me when we talked alone, they had been ill-used and beaten, and had often had neither bread to eat nor bed to lie down upon. And yet these same children would sometimes go off with their mothers the very next morning.

A good many others, however, soon saw that by staying with me they might both learn something and become something, and these never failed in their zeal and attachment. Before very long their conduct was imitated by others, though not always from the same considerations.

Those who ran away were the worst in character and the least capable. But they were not incited to go till they were free of their vermin and their rags. Several were sent to me with no other purpose than that of being taken away again as soon as they were clean and well clothed.

But after a time their better judgment overcame the defiant hostility with which they arrived. In 1799 I had nearly eighty children. Most of them were bright and intelligent, some even remarkably so.

For most of them study was something entirely new. As soon as they found that they could learn, their zeal was indefatigable, and in a few weeks children who had never before opened a book, and could hardly repeat a *Pater Noster* or an *Ave,* would study the whole day long with the keenest interest. Even after supper, when I used to say to them, "Children, will you go to bed, or learn something?" they would generally answer, especially in the first month or two, "Learn something." It is true that afterwards, when they had to get up very early, it was not quite the same.

But this first eagerness did much towards starting the establishment on the right lines, and making the studies the success they ultimately were, a success, indeed, which far surpassed my expectations. And yet the difficulties in the way of introducing a well-ordered system of studies were at that time almost insurmountable.

Neither my trust nor my zeal had as yet been able to overcome either the intractability of individuals or the want of coherence in the whole experiment. The general order of the establishment, I felt, must be based upon order of a higher character. As this higher order did not yet exist, I had to attempt to create it; for without this foundation I could not hope to organize properly either the teaching or the general management of the place, nor should I have wished

to do so. I wanted everything to result not from a preconceived plan, but from my relations with the children. The high principles and educating forces I was seeking, I looked for from the harmonious common life of my children, from their attention, activity, and needs. It was not, then, from any external organization that I looked for the regeneration of which they stood so much in need. If I had employed constraint, regulations and lectures, I should, instead of winning and ennobling my children's hearts, have repelled them and made them bitter, and thus been farther than ever from my aim. First of all, I had to arouse in them pure, moral, and noble feelings, so that afterwards, in external things, I might be sure of their ready attention, activity, and obedience. I had, in short, to follow the high precept of Jesus Christ, "Cleanse first that which is within, that the outside may be clean also"; and if ever the truth of this precept was made manifest, it was made manifest then.

My one aim was to make their new life in common, and their new powers, awaken a feeling of brotherhood amongst the children, and make them affectionate, just, and considerate.

I reached this end without much difficulty. Amongst these seventy wild beggar-children there soon existed such peace, friendship, and cordial relations as are rare even between actual brothers and sisters.

The principle to which I endeavoured to conform all my conduct was as follows: Endeavour, first, to broaden your children's sympathies, and, by satisfying their daily needs, to bring love and kindness into such unceasing contact with their impressions and their activity, that these sentiments may be engrafted in their hearts; then try to give them such judgment and tact as will enable them to make a wise, sure, and abundant use of these virtues in the circle which surrounds them. In the last place, do not hesitate to touch on the difficult questions of good and evil, and the words connected with them. And you must do this especially in connection with the ordinary events of every day.

upon which your whole teaching in these matters must be founded, so that the children may be reminded of their own feelings, and supplied, as it were, with solid facts upon which to base their conception of the beauty and justice of the moral life. Even though you should have to spend whole nights in trying to express in two words what others say in twenty, never regret the loss of sleep.

I gave my children very few explanations; I taught them neither morality nor religion. But sometimes, when they were perfectly quiet, I used to say to them, "Do you not think that you are better and more reasonable when you are like this than when you are making a noise?" When they clung round my neck and called me their father, I used to say, "My children, would it be right to deceive your father? After kissing me like this, would you like to do anything behind my back to vex me?" When our talk turned on the misery of the country, and they were feeling glad at the thought of their own happier lot, I would say, "How good God is to have given man a compassionate heart!" Sometimes, too, I asked them if they did not see a great difference between a Government that cares for the poor and teaches them to earn a livelihood, and one that leaves them to their idleness and vice, with beggary and the workhouse for sole resource.

Often I drew them a picture of the happiness of a simple, peaceful household, that by economy and hard work has provided for all its wants, and put itself in a position to give advice to the ignorant, and help to the unfortunate. When they pressed round me, I used to ask the best of them, even during the first few months, whether they would not like to live like me, and have a number of unfortunate children about them to take care of and turn into useful men. The depth of their feelings would even bring tears to their eyes, as they answered, "Ah, if I could only do that!"

What encouraged them most was the thought of not always remaining poor, but of some day taking their place again amongst their fellows, with knowledge and talents that should make them useful, and win them the esteem of other men. They felt that, owing to my care, they made more progress in this respect than other children; they perfectly understood that all they did was but a preparation for their future activity, and they looked forward to happiness as the certain result of their perseverance. That is why steady application soon became easy to them, its object being in perfect accordance with their wishes and their hopes. Virtue, my friend, is developed by this agreement, just as the young plant thrives when the soil suits its nature, and supplies the needs of its tender shoots.

I witnessed the growth of an inward strength in my children, which, in its general development, far surpassed my expectations, and in its particular manifestations not only often surprised me, but touched me deeply.

When the neighbouring town of Altdorf was burnt down, I gathered the children round me, and said, "Altdorf has been burnt down; perhaps, at this very moment, there are a hundred children there without home, food, or clothes; will you not ask our good Government to let twenty of them come and live with us?" I still seem to see the emotion with which they answered, "Oh, yes, yes!" "But, my children," I said, "think well of what you are asking! Even now we have scarcely money enough, and it is not at all certain that if these poor children came to us, the Government would give us any more than they do at present, so that you might have to work harder, and share your clothes with these children, and sometimes perhaps go without food. Do not say, then, that you would like them to come unless you are quite prepared for all these consequences." After having spoken to them in this way as seriously as I could, I made them repeat all I had said, to be quite sure that they had thoroughly understood what the consequences of their request would be. But they were not in the least shaken in their decision, and all repeated, "Yes, yes, we are quite ready to work harder, eat less, and share our clothes, for we want them to come."

Some refugees from the Grisons having given me a few crowns for my poor children, I at once called them, and said, "These men are obliged to leave their country; they hardly know where they will find a home tomorrow, yet, in spite of their trouble, they have given me this for you. Come and thank them." The emotion of the children at these words brought tears to the eyes of the refugees.

It was in this way that I strove to awaken the feeling of each virtue before talking about it, for I thought it unwise to talk to children on subjects which would compel them to speak without thoroughly understanding what they were saying.

I followed up this awakening of the sentiments by exercises intended to teach the children self-control, and interest the best natures amongst them in the practical questions of every-day life.

It will easily be understood that, in this respect, it was not possible to organize any system of discipline for the establishment; that could only come slowly, as the general work developed.

Silence, as an aid to application, is perhaps the great secret of such an institution. I found it very useful to insist on silence when I was teaching, and also to pay particular attention to the attitude of my children. The result was that the moment I asked for silence, I could teach in quite a low voice. The children repeated my words all together; and as there was no other sound, I was able to detect the slightest mistakes of pronunciation. It is true that this was not always so. Sometimes, whilst they repeated sentences after me, I would ask them half in fun to keep their eyes fixed on their middle fingers. It is hardly credible how useful simple things of this sort sometimes are as means to the very highest ends.

One young girl, for instance, who had been little better than a savage, by keeping her head and body upright, and not looking about, made more progress in her moral education than any one would have believed possible.

These experiences have shown me that the mere habit of carrying oneself well does much more for the education of the moral sentiments than any amount of teaching and lectures in which this simple fact is ignored.

Thanks to the application of these principles, my children soon became more open, more contented and more susceptible to every good and noble influence than any one could possibly have foreseen when they first came to me, so utterly devoid were they of ideas, good feelings, and moral principles. As a matter of fact, this lack of previous instruction was not a serious obstacle to me; indeed, it hardly troubled me at all. I am inclined even to say that, in the simple method I was following, it was often an advantage, for I had incomparably less trouble to develop those children whose minds were still blank, than those who had already acquired a few more or less correct ideas. The former, too, were much more open than the latter to the influence of all pure and simple sentiments.

But when the children were obdurate and churlish, then I was severe, and made use of corporal punishment.

My dear friend, the pedagogical principle which says that we must win the hearts and minds of our children by words alone, without having recourse to corporal punishment, is certainly good, and applicable under favourable conditions and circumstances; but with children of such widely different ages as mine, children for the most part beggars, and all full of deeply-rooted faults, a certain amount of corporal punishment was inevitable, especially as I was anxious to arrive surely, speedily, and by the simplest means, at gaining an influence over them all, for the sake of putting them all in the right road. I was compelled to punish them, but it would be a mistake to suppose that I thereby, in any way, lost the confidence of my pupils.

It is not the rare and isolated actions that form the opinions and feelings of children, but the impressions of every day and every hour. From such impressions they judge whether we are kindly disposed towards them or not, and this settles their general attitude towards us. Their judgment of isolated actions depends upon this general attitude.

This is how it is that punishments inflicted by parents rarely make a bad impression. But it is quite different with schoolmasters and teachers who are not with their children night and day, and have none of those relations with them which result from life in common.

My punishments never produced obstinacy; the children I had beaten were quite satisfied if a moment afterwards I gave them my hand and kissed them, and I could read in their eyes that the final effect of my blows was really joy. The following is a striking instance of the effect this sort of punishment sometimes had. One day one of the children I liked best, taking advantage of my affection, unjustly threatened one of his companions. I was very indignant, and my hand did not spare him. He seemed at first almost brokenhearted, and cried bitterly for at least a quarter of an hour. When I had gone out, however, he got up, and going to the boy he had ill-treated, begged his pardon, and thanked him for having spoken about his bad conduct. My friend, this was no comedy; the child had never seen anything like it before.

It was impossible that this sort of treatment should produce a bad impression on my children, because all day long I was giving them proofs of my affection and devotion. They could not misread my heart, and so they did not misjudge my actions. . . .

Many things that make no difference in a small household could not be tolerated where the numbers were so great. I tried to make my children feel this, always leaving them to decide what could or could not be allowed. It is true that, in my intercourse with them, I never spoke of liberty or equality; but, at the same time, I encouraged them as far as possible to be free and uncon-

strained in my presence, with the result that every day I marked more and more that clear, open look in their eyes which, in my experience, is the sign of a really liberal education. I could not bear the thought of betraying the trust I read in their faces, and was always seeking to encourage it, as well as the free development of their individuality, that nothing might cloud their angel eyes, the mere sight of which gave me such deep pleasure. . . .

I have generally found that great, noble, and high thoughts are indispensable for developing wisdom and firmness of character.

Such an instruction must be complete in the sense that it must take account of all our aptitudes and all our circumstances; it must be conducted, too, in a truly psychological spirit, that is to say, simply, lovingly, energetically, and calmly. . . .

I believe that the first development of thought in the child is very much disturbed by a wordy system of teaching, which is not adapted either to his faculties or the circumstances of his life.

According to my experience, success depends upon whether what is taught to children commends itself to them as true, through being closely connected with their own personal observation and experience.

Without this foundation, truth must seem to them to be little better than a plaything, which is beyond their comprehension, and therefore a burden. Truth and justice are certainly more than empty words to men, for they are the outcome of inward convictions, high views, noble aspirations, and sound judgment, to say nothing of the external signs by which their power may be made manifest.

And what is not less true is that this sentiment of truth and justice, when it has developed simply and soberly in the depths of a man's soul, is his best safeguard against the chief and most deadly consequences of prejudice; nor will it ever allow error, ignorance, or superstition, however bad they may be in themselves, to influence him as they do and always must influence those who, without a trace of love or justice in their hearts, are incessantly prating of religion and right.

These general principles of human instruction are like pieces of pure gold; the particular truths which depend upon them are but silver and copper. I cannot help comparing the swimmer, who loses himself in this sea, made up of so many thousand drops of truth, to a merchant who, after having amassed a fortune, penny by penny, should become so attached not only to the general principle of looking after the pence, but to each individual penny, that the loss of a single one would distress him as much as that of a golden guinea.

When the peaceful exercise of his duty produces a harmony between a man's powers and feelings, when the charm of pure relations between men is increased and ensured by the wider recognition of certain simple and lofty truths, there is nothing to be feared from prejudices; they will disappear before the natural development of these feelings and powers like darkness before the dawn.

Human knowledge derives its real advantages from the solidity of the foundations on which it rests. The man who knows a great deal must be stronger, and must work harder than others, if he is to bring his knowledge into harmony with his nature and with the circumstances of his life. If he does not do this, his knowledge is but a delusive will-o'-the-wisp, and will often rob him of such ordinary pleasures of life as even the most ignorant man, if he have but common sense, can make quite sure of. That, my dear friend, is why I felt it to be so important that this harmony of the soul's powers, the combined effect of our nature and first impressions, should not be disturbed by the errors of human art.

I have now put before you my views as to the family spirit which ought to prevail in an educational establishment, and I have told you of my attempts to carry them out. I have still to explain the essential principles upon which all my teaching was based.

I knew no other order, method, or art, but that which resulted naturally from my children's conviction of my love for them, nor did I care to know any other.

Thus I subordinated the instruction of my children to a higher aim, which was to arouse and strengthen their best sentiments by the relations of every-day life as they existed between themselves and me.

I had Gedicke's reading-book, but it was of no more use to me than any other school-book; for I felt that, with all these children of such different ages, I had an admirable opportunity for carrying out my own views on early education. I was well aware, too, how impossible it would be to organize my teaching according to the ordinary system in use in the best schools.

As a general rule I attached little importance to the study of words, even when explanations of the ideas they represented were given.

I tried to connect study with manual labour, the school with the workshop, and make one thing of them. . . .

I hold it to be extremely important that men should be encouraged to learn by themselves and allowed to develop freely. It is in this way alone that the diversity of individual talent is produced and made evident.

I always made the children learn perfectly even the least important things, and I never allowed them to lose ground; a word once learnt, for instance, was never to be forgotten, and a letter once well written never to be written badly again. I was very patient with all who were weak or slow, but very severe with those who did anything less well than they had done it before.

The number and inequality of my children rendered my task easier. Just as in a family the eldest and cleverest child readily shows what he knows to his younger brothers and sisters, and feels proud and happy to be able to take his mother's place for a moment, so my children were delighted when they knew something that they could teach others. A sentiment of honour awoke in them, and they learned twice as well by making the younger ones repeat their words. In this way I soon had helpers and collaborators amongst the children themselves. When I was teaching them to spell difficult words by heart, I used to allow any child who succeeded in saying one properly to teach it to the others. These child-helpers, whom I had formed from the very outset, and who had followed my method step by step, were certainly much more useful to me than any regular schoolmasters could have been.

I myself learned with the children. Our whole system was so simple and so natural that I should have had difficulty in finding a master who would not have thought it undignified to learn and teach as I was doing.

My aim was so to simplify the means of instruction that it should be quite possible for even the most ordinary man to teach his children himself; thus schools would gradually almost cease to be necessary, so far as the first elements are concerned. Just as the mother gives her child its first material food, so is she ordained by God to give it its first spiritual food, and I consider that very great harm is done to the child by taking it away from home too soon and submitting it to artificial school methods. The time is drawing near when methods of teaching will be so simplified that each mother will be able not only to teach her children without help, but continue her own education at the same time. And this opinion is justified by my experience, for I found that some of my children developed so well as to be able to follow in my footsteps. And I am more than ever convinced that as soon as we have educational establishments combined with workshops, and conducted on a truly psychological basis, a generation will necessarily be formed which, on the one hand, will show us by experience that our present studies do not require one tenth part of the time or trouble we now give to them, and on the other, that the time and strength this instruction demands, as well as the means of acquiring it, may be made to fit in so perfectly with the conditions of domestic life, that every parent will easily be able to supply it by a member or friend of the family, a result which will daily become easier, according as the method of instruction is simplified, and the number of educated people increased.

I have proved two things which will be of considerable use to us in bringing about this desirable improvement. The first is that it is possible and even easy to teach many children of different ages at once and well; the second, that many things can be taught to such children even whilst they are engaged in manual labour. This sort of teaching will appear little more than an exercise of memory, as indeed it is; but when the memory is applied to a series of psychologically graduated ideas, it brings all the other faculties into play. Thus, by making children learn at one time spelling, at another exercises on numbers, at another simple songs, we exercise not only their memory, but their power of combination, their judgment, their taste, and many of the best feelings of their hearts. In this way it is possible to stimulate all a child's faculties, even when one seems to be exercising his memory only.

These exercises not only gave my children an ever-increasing power of attention and discernment, but did very much for their general mental and moral development, and gave that balance to their natures which is the foundation of human wisdom. . . .

Such were my dreams; but at the very moment that I seemed to be on the point of realizing them, I had to leave Stanz.

JOHANN HEINRICH PESTALOZZI
In the Old Castle at Yverdun, Switzerland (1805–1807, 1809)*

[Reminiscence of L. Vuillemin, a historian, who entered Pestalozzi's Institute in

* Excerpts from autobiographies and commentaries, as reprinted in Roger de Guimps, *Pestalozzi: His Life and Work* (New York and London: Appleton, 1890; authorized translation from the second French edition by J. Russell), pp. 253–256, 261–262.

1805 at the age of eight and remained there until 1807:]

Imagine, my children, a very ugly man, with rough, bristling hair, his face scarred with small-pox and covered with freckles, a pointed, untidy beard, no neck-tie, ill-fitting trousers, stockings down, and enormous shoes; add to this a breathless, shuffling gait, eyes either large and flashing, or half-closed as though turned within, features expressing either a profound sadness or the most peaceful happiness, speech now slow and musical, now thundering and hurried, and you will have some idea of the man we called "Father Pestalozzi."

Such as I have described him to you, we loved him; yes, we all loved him, for he loved us all; we loved him so much that when we lost sight of him for a time we felt sad and lonely, and when he came back to us again we could not turn our eyes away from him.

We knew that at the time when the wars of the Swiss Revolution had so largely increased the number of poor and orphan children, he had taken a great number of them into his house and cared for them as a father, and we felt that he was the true friend of children, and of all who were in trouble or misfortune.

My fellow-citizens of Yverdun, my native town, had generously placed at his disposal the old Castle. It was built in the shape of a huge square, and its great rooms and courts were admirably adapted for the games as well as the studies of a large school. Within its walls were assembled from a hundred and fifty to two hundred children of all nations, who divided their time between lessons and happy play. It often happened that a game of prisoner's base, begun in the Castle court, would be finished on the grass near the lake. In winter we used to make a mighty snow-fortress, which was attacked and defended with equal heroism. Sickness was hardly known among us.

Early every morning we went in turns and had a shower of cold water thrown over us. We were generally bareheaded, but once, when a bitterly cold wind was blowing, my father took pity upon me, and gave me a hat. My companions had no sooner perceived it than a hue and cry was raised: "A hat, a hat!" It was soon knocked off my head and a hundred hands sent it flying about the playground and corridors, till at last it went spinning through a window, and fell into the river that flows under the walls of the Castle. It was carried away to the lake and I never saw it again.

Our masters were for the most part young men, and nearly all children of the revolutionary period, who had grown up round Pestalozzi, their father and ours. There were, indeed, a few educated men and scholars who had come to share his task; but, taken altogether, there was not much learning. I myself have heard Pestalozzi boast, when an old man, of not having read anything for forty years. Nor did our masters, his first pupils, read much more than Pestalozzi himself. Their teaching was addressed to the understanding rather than the memory, and had for its aim the harmonious cultivation of the germs implanted in us by Providence. "Make it your aim to develop the child," Pestalozzi was never tired of repeating, "and do not merely train him as you would train a dog, and as so many children in our schools often are trained."

Our studies were almost entirely based on number, form, and language. Language was taught us by the help of sense-impression; we were taught to see correctly, and in that way to form for ourselves a just idea of the relations of things. What we had thoroughly understood we had no trouble to express clearly.

The first elements of geography were taught us from the land itself. We were first taken to a narrow valley not far from Yverdun, where the river Buron runs. After taking a general view of the valley, we were made to examine the details, until we had obtained an exact and complete idea of it. We were then told to take some of the clay which lay in beds on one side of the valley, and fill the baskets which we had brought for the purpose. On our return to the Castle, we took our places at the long tables, and reproduced in relief the valley we had just studied, each one doing the part which had been allotted to him. In the course of the next few days more walks and more explorations, each day on higher ground and each time with a further extension of our work. Only when our relief was finished were we shown the map, which by this means we did not see till we were in a position to understand it.

We had to discover the truths of geometry for ourselves. After being once put in the way of it, the end to be reached was pointed out to us, and we were left to work alone. It was the same with arithmetic, which we did aloud, without paper. Some of us became wonderfully quick at this, and as charlatanism penetrates everywhere, these only were brought before the numerous strangers that the name of Pestalozzi daily attracted to Yverdun. We were told over and over again that a great work was going on in our midst, that the eyes of the world were upon us, and we readily believed it.

The Pestalozzian Method, as it was somewhat ostentatiously called, was, it is true, an enigma, not only to us but to our teachers, who, like the disciples of Socrates, each interpreted the master's doctrine in his own way. But we were still far from the time when these divergencies resulted in discord, and when the chief masters, after each claiming to be the only one who had understood Pestalozzi, ended by declaring that Pestalozzi had not understood himself.

[Remarks by Charles Ritter, a geographer, who visited Pestalozzi at Yverdun in 1807 and again in 1809:]

The noble old man, always a child in heart, was kept by his eager enthusiasm in an almost constant state of feverish activity; his wife was a model of unassuming virtue, delicacy and kind-heartedness. . . .

The work has grown to such proportions that its founder can no longer attend to the whole of it. There are more than a hundred and fifty pupils, and as many as forty student-teachers of various ages, some of whom are already engaged in active work outside the institute, and all of whom apply themselves diligently to the study of the "method." I have not been able to ascertain the number of masters. Add to all this a school for girls, two private establishments, and a number of teachers who live with their pupils in the town, but give and receive lessons in the institute, and you will have some idea of what is going on here.

Pestalozzi himself is unable to apply his own method in any of the simplest subjects of instruction. He is quick in grasping principles, but is helpless in matters of detail; he possesses the faculty, however, of putting his views with such force and clearness that he has no difficulty in getting them carried out. He was right, indeed, when he said to me, speaking of himself: "I cannot say that it is I who have created what you see before you. [John] Niederer, [Hermann] Krusi and [Joseph] Schmidt would laugh at me if I called myself their master; I am good neither at figures nor writing; I know nothing about grammar, mathematics, or any other science; the most ignorant of our pupils knows more of these things than I do; I am but the *initiator* of the institute, and depend on others to carry out my views."

He spoke the truth, and yet without him nothing that is here would exist. He has no gift for guiding or governing this great undertaking, and yet it continues. He has sacrificed everything he possessed to this end; even now he knows nothing of the value of money, and is as ignorant of accounts as a child. Even his speech, which is neither German nor French, is scarcely intelligible, and yet in everything he is the soul of this vast establishment. All his words, and more especially his religious utterances, sink deep into the hearts of his pupils, who love and venerate him as a father.

BENJAMIN FRANKLIN'S IDEAS ON EDUCATION

BENJAMIN FRANKLIN
"Advice to a Young Tradesman, Written by
an Old One" [1748]*

To my Friend A. B.

As you have desired it of me, I write the following Hints, which have been of Service to me, and may, if observed, be so to you.

Remember that TIME is Money. He that can earn Ten Shillings a Day by his Labour, and goes abroad, or sits idle one half of that Day, tho' he spends but Sixpence during his Diversion or Idleness, ought not to reckon That the only Expence; he has really spent or rather thrown away Five Shillings besides.

Remember that CREDIT is Money. If a Man lets his Money lie in my Hands after it is due, he gives me the Interest, or so much as I can make of it during that Time. This amounts to a considerable Sum where a Man has good and large Credit, and makes good Use of it.

Remember that Money is of a prolific generating Nature. Money can beget Money, and its Offspring can beget more, and so on. Five Shillings turn'd, is *Six:* Turn'd again, 'tis Seven and Three Pence; and so on 'til it becomes an Hundred Pound. The more there is of it, the more it produces every Turning, so that the Profits rise quicker and quicker. He that kills a breeding Sow, destroys all her Offspring to the thousandth Generation. He that murders a Crown, destroys all it might have produc'd, even Scores of Pounds.

Remember that Six Pounds a Year is but

a Groat a Day. For this little Sum (which may be daily wasted either in Time or Expence unperceiv'd) a Man of Credit may on his own Security have the constant Possession and Use of an Hundred Pounds. So much in Stock briskly turn'd by an industrious Man, produces great Advantage.

Remember this Saying, *That the good Paymaster is Lord of another Man's Purse.* He that is known to pay punctually and exactly to the Time he promises, may at any Time, and on any Occasion, raise all the Money his Friends can spare. This is sometimes of great Use: Therefore never keep borrow'd Money an Hour beyond the Time you promis'd, lest a Disappointment shuts up your Friends Purse forever.

The most trifling Actions that affect a Man's Credit, are to be regarded. The Sound of your Hammer at Five in the Morning or Nine at Night, heard by a Creditor, makes him easy Six Months longer. But if he sees you at a Billiard Table, or hears your Voice in a Tavern, when you should be at Work, he sends for his Money the next Day. Finer Cloaths than he or his Wife wears, or greater Expence in any particular than he affords himself, shocks his Pride, and he duns you to humble you. Creditors are a kind of People, that have the sharpest Eyes and Ears, as well as the best Memories of any in the World.

Good-natur'd Creditors (and such one would always chuse to deal with if one could) feel Pain when they are oblig'd to ask for Money. Spare 'em that Pain, and they will love you. When you receive a Sum of Money, divide it among 'em in Proportion to your Debts. Don't be asham'd of paying a small Sum because you owe a greater. Money, more or less, is always welcome; and your Creditor had rather be at the Trouble of receiving Ten Pounds voluntarily brought him, tho' at ten different Times or Payments, than be oblig'd to go ten Times to demand it before he can re-

---

* Benjamin Franklin, "Advice to a Young Tradesman, Written by an Old One" [July 21, 1748], *The Papers of Benjamin Franklin* (New Haven: Yale University Press, 1961; edited by Leonard W. Labaree *et al.*), III, 306–308. Used by permission. This selection is from the earliest known printing. In subsequent printings the title was usually omitted, and the "Advice" was concluded with a signature, "An old Tradesman."

ceive it in a Lump. It shews, besides, that you are mindful of what you owe; it makes you appear a careful as well as an honest Man; and that still encreases your Credit.

Beware of thinking all your own that you possess, and of living accordingly. 'Tis a Mistake that many People who have Credit fall into. To prevent this, keep an exact Account for some Time of both your Expences and your Incomes. If you take the Pains at first to mention Particulars, it will have this good Effect; you will discover how wonderfully small trifling Expences mount up to large Sums, and will discern what might have been, and may for the future be saved, without occasioning any great Inconvenience.

In short, the Way to Wealth, if you desire it, is as plain as the Way to Market. It depends chiefly on two Words, INDUSTRY and FRUGALITY; i.e. Waste neither Time nor Money, but make the best Use of both. He that gets all he can honestly, and saves all he gets (necessary Expences excepted) will certainly become RICH; If that Being who governs the World, to whom all should look for a Blessing on their honest Endeavours, doth not in his wise Providence otherwise determine.

BENJAMIN FRANKLIN
"Proposals Relating to the Education of Youth in Pensilvania" (1749)*

ADVERTISEMENT TO THE READER.

It has long been regretted as a Misfortune to the Youth of this Province, that we have no ACADEMY, in which they might receive the Accomplishments of a regular Education.

The following Paper of *Hints* towards forming a Plan for that Purpose, is so far approv'd by some publick-spirited Gentle-

* Benjamin Franklin, "Proposals Relating to the Education of Youth in Pensilvania" (1749), *The Papers of Benjamin Franklin* (New Haven: Yale University Press, 1961; edited by Leonard W. Labaree *et al.*), III, 397–419. Used by permission.

men, to whom it has been privately communicated, that they have directed a Number of Copies to be made by the Press, and properly distributed, in order to obtain the Sentiments and Advice of Men of Learning, Understanding, and Experience in these Matters; and have determin'd to use their Interest and best Endeavours, to have the Scheme, when compleated, carried gradually into Execution; in which they have Reason to believe they shall have the hearty Concurrence and Assistance of many who are Wellwishers to their Country.

Those who incline to favour the Design with their Advice, either as to the Parts of Learning to be taught, the Order of Study, the Method of Teaching, the Oeconomy of the School, or any other Matter of Importance to the Success of the Undertaking, are desired to communicate their Sentiments as soon as may be, by Letter directed to B. Franklin, Printer, in Philadephia.

AUTHORS quoted in this PAPER.[1]

1. The famous Milton, whose Learning and Abilities are well known and who had

[1] Benjamin Franklin's quotations are from the following: John Milton, *Paradise Regain'd . . . To which is added. Samson Agonistes. And Poems upon several Occasions. With a Tractate of Education* (5th edit., London, 1721); John Locke, *Some Thoughts concerning Education* (11th edit., London, 1745); [David Fordyce], *Dialogues concerning Education* (2 vols., London, 1745–48), which BF erred in attributing to Francis Hutcheson, as he recognized in a letter to James Logan, Dec. 17, 1749; Obadiah Walker, *Of Education. Especially of Young Gentlemen* (5th impression, Oxford, 1687); Charles Rollin, *The Method of Studying and Teaching the Belles Lettres* (4th edit., 4 vols., London, 1749); George Turnbull, *Observations upon Liberal Education, In all its Branches* (London, 1742).

BF characteristically quoted his authorities with casual accuracy, altering and telescoping sentences and paragraphs, italicizing and capitalizing to suit his mood and promote his purpose, rather than to make a display of pedantic literalness. No attempt has been made to collate his versions with the originals, but in a few practised some Time the Education of Youth, so could speak from Experience.

2. The great Mr. Locke, who wrote a Treatise on Education, well known, and much esteemed, being translated into most of the modern Languages of Europe.

3. *Dialogues on Education,* 2 Vols. Octavo, that are much esteem'd, having had two Editions in 3 Years. Suppos'd to be wrote by the ingenious Mr. Hutcheson (Author of *A Treatise on the Passions,* and another on the *Ideas of Beauty and Virtue*) who has had much Experience in Educating of Youth, being a Professor in the College at Glasgow, &c.

4. The learned Mr. Obadiah Walker, who had been many Years a Tutor to young Noblemen, and wrote a Treatise *on the Education of a young Gentleman;* of which the Fifth Edition was printed 1687.

5. The much admired Mons. Rollin, whose whole Life was spent in a College; and wrote 4 Vols. on Education, under the Title of, *The Method of Teaching and Studying the Belles Lettres;* which are translated into English, Italian, and most of the modern Languages.

6. The learned and ingenious Dr. George Turnbull, Chaplain to the present Prince of Wales; who has had much Experience in the Educating of Youth, and publish'd a Book, Octavo, intituled, *Observations on Liberal Education, in all its Branches,* 1742.

With some others.

The good Education of Youth has been esteemed by wise Men in all Ages, as the surest Foundation of the Happiness both of private Families and of Common-wealths. Almost all Governments have therefore made it a principal Object of their Attention, to establish and endow with proper Revenues, such Seminaries of Learning, as might

---

instances the editors have clarified his citations by inserting missing volume numbers, and they have regularly italicized the titles of books mentioned in his text and notes, and have inserted opening and closing quotation marks that BF occasionally overlooked.

supply the succeeding Age with Men qualified to serve the Publick with Honour to themselves, and to their Country.

Many of the first Settlers of these Provinces, were Men who had received a good Education in Europe, and to their Wisdom and good Management we owe much of our present Prosperity. But their Hands were full, and they could not do all Things. The present Race are not thought to be generally of equal Ability: For though the American Youth are allow'd not to want Capacity; yet the best Capacities require Cultivation, it being truly with them, as with the best Ground, which unless well tilled and sowed with profitable Seed, produces only ranker Weeds.

That we may obtain the Advantages arising from an Increase of Knowledge, and prevent as much as may be the mischievous Consequences that would attend a general Ignorance among us, the following *Hints* are offered towards forming a Plan for the Education of the Youth of Pennsylvania, viz.

It is propos'd,

THAT some Persons of Leisure and publick Spirit, apply for a CHARTER, by which they may be incorporated, with Power to erect an ACADEMY for the Education of Youth, to govern the same, provide Masters, make Rules, receive Donations, purchase Lands, &c. and to add to their Number, from Time to Time such other Persons as they shall judge suitable.

That the Members of the Corporation make it their Pleasure, and in some Degree their Business, to visit the Academy often, encourage and countenance the Youth, countenance and assist the Masters, and by all Means in their Power advance the Usefulness and Reputation of the Design; that they look on the Students as in some Sort their Children, treat them with Familiarity and Affection, and when they have behav'd well, and gone through their Studies, and are to enter the World, zealously unite, and make all the Interest that can be made to establish them, whether in Business, Offices,

Marriages, or any other Thing for their Advantage, preferably to all other Persons whatsoever even of equal Merit.

And if Men may, and frequently do, catch such a Taste for cultivating Flowers, for Planting, Grafting, Inoculating, and the like, as to despise all other Amusements for their Sake, why may not we expect they should acquire a Relish for that *more useful* Culture of young Minds. Thompson says,

'Tis Joy to see the human Blossoms blow,
When infant Reason grows apace, and calls
For the kind Hand of an assiduous Care;
Delightful Task! to rear the tender Thought,
To teach the young Idea how to shoot,
To pour the fresh Instruction o'er the Mind,
To breathe th' enliv'ning Spirit, and to fix
The generous Purpose in the glowing Breast.

That a House be provided for the ACADEMY, if not in the Town, not many Miles from it; the Situation high and dry, and if it may be, not far from a River, having a Garden, Orchard, Meadow, and a Field or two.

That the House be furnished with a Library (if in the Country, if in the Town, the Town Libraries may serve) with Maps of all Countries, Globes, some mathematical Instruments, an Apparatus for Experiments in Natural Philosophy, and for Mechanics; Prints, of all Kinds, Prospects, Buildings, Machines, &c.

That the RECTOR be a Man of good Understanding, good Morals, diligent and patient, learn'd in the Languages and Sciences, and a correct pure Speaker and Writer of the English Tongue; to have such Tutors under him as shall be necessary.

That the boarding Scholars diet together, plainly, temperately, and frugally.

That to keep them in Health, and to strengthen and render active their Bodies, they be frequently exercis'd in Running, Leaping, Wrestling, and Swimming, &c.

That they have peculiar Habits to distinguish them from other Youth, if the Academy be in or near the Town; for this, among other Reasons, that their Behaviour may be the better observed.

As to their STUDIES, it would be well if they could be taught *every Thing* that is useful, and *every Thing* that is ornamental: But Art is long, and their Time is short. It is therefore propos'd that they learn those Things that are likely to be *most useful* and *most ornamental*, Regard being had to the several Professions for which they are intended.

All should be taught to write a *fair Hand*, and swift, as that is useful to All. And with it may be learnt something of *Drawing*, by Imitation of Prints, and some of the first Principles of Perspective.

Arithmetick, Accounts, and some of the first Principles of *Geometry* and *Astronomy*.

The English Language might be taught by Grammar; in which some of our best Writers, as Tillotson, Addison, Pope, Algernon Sidney, Cato's Letters, &c. should be Classicks: The *Stiles* principally to be cultivated, being the *clear* and the *concise*. Reading should also be taught, and pronouncing, properly, distinctly, emphatically; not with an even Tone, which *under-does,* nor a theatrical, which *over-does* Nature.

To form their Stile, they should be put on Writing Letters to each other, making Abstracts of what they read; or writing the same Things in their own Words; telling or writing Stories lately read, in their own Expressions. All to be revis'd and corrected by the Tutor, who should give his Reasons, explain the Force and Import of Words, &c.

To form their Pronunciation, they may be put on making Declamations, repeating Speeches, delivering Orations, &c. The Tutor assisting at the Rehearsals, teaching, advising, correcting their Accent, &c.

But if HISTORY be made a constant Part of their Reading, such as the Translations of the Greek and Roman Historians, and the modern Histories of antient Greece and Rome, &c. may not almost all Kinds of useful Knowledge be that Way introduc'd to

Advantage, and with Pleasure to the Student? As

GEOGRAPHY, by reading with Maps, and being required to point out the Places *where* the greatest Actions were done, to give their old and new Names, with the Bounds, Situation, Extent of the Countries concern'd &c.

CHRONOLOGY, by the Help of Helvicus or some other Writer of the Kind, who will enable them to tell *when* those Events happened; what Princes were Cotemporaries, what States or famous Men flourish'd about that Time, &c. The several principal Epochas to be first well fix'd in their Memories.

ANTIENT CUSTOMS, religious and civil, being frequently mentioned in History, will give Occasion for explaining them; in which the Prints of Medals, Basso Relievo's, and antient Monuments will greatly assist.

MORALITY, by descanting and making continual Observations on the Causes of the Rise or Fall of any Man's Character, Fortune, Power, &c. mention'd in History; the Advantages of Temperance, Order, Frugality, Industry, Perseverance, &c. &c. Indeed the general natural Tendency of Reading good History, must be, to fix in the Minds of Youth deep Impressions of the Beauty and Usefulness of Virtue of all Kinds, Publick Spirit, Fortitude, &c.

History will show the wonderful Effects of ORATORY, in governing, turning and leading great Bodies of Mankind, Armies, Cities, Nations. When the Minds of Youth are struck with Admiration at this, then is the Time to give them the Principles of that Art, which they will study with Taste and Application. Then they may be made acquainted with the best Models among the Antients, their Beauties being particularly pointed out to them. Modern Political Oratory being chiefly performed by the Pen and Press, its Advantages over the Antient in some Respects are to be shown; as that its Effects are more extensive, more lasting, &c.

History will also afford frequent Opportunities of showing the Necessity of a *Publick Religion,* from its Usefulness to the Publick; the Advantage of a Religious Character among private Persons; the Mischiefs of Superstition, &c. and the Excellency of the CHRISTIAN RELIGION above all others antient or modern.

History will also give Occasion to expatiate on the Advantage of Civil Orders and Constitutions, how Men and their Properties are protected by joining in Societies and establishing Government; their Industry encouraged and rewarded, Arts invented, and Life made more comfortable: The Advantages of *Liberty,* Mischiefs of *Licentiousness,* Benefits arising from good Laws and a due Execution of Justice, &c. Thus may the first Principles of sound *Politicks* be fix'd in the Minds of Youth.

On *Historical* Occasions, Questions of Right and Wrong, Justice and Injustice, will naturally arise, and may be put to Youth, which they may debate in Conversation and in Writing. When they ardently desire Victory, for the Sake of the Praise attending it, they will begin to feel the Want, and be sensible of the Use of *Logic,* or the Art of Reasoning to *discover* Truth, and of Arguing to *defend* it, and *convince* Adversaries. This would be the Time to acquaint them with the Principles of that Art. Grotius, Puffendorff, and some other Writers of the same Kind, may be used on these Occasions to decide their Disputes. Publick Disputes warm the Imagination, whet the Industry, and strengthen the natural Abilities.

When Youth are told, that the Great Men whose Lives and Actions they read in History, spoke two of the best Languages that ever were, the most expressive, copious, beautiful; and that the finest Writings, the most correct Compositions, the most perfect Productions of human Wit and Wisdom, are in those Languages, which have endured Ages, and will endure while there are Men; that no Translation can do them Justice, or give the Pleasure found in Reading the Originals; that those Languages contain all Science; that one of them is become almost universal, being the Language of Learned

Men in all Countries; that to understand them is a distinguishing Ornament, &c. they may be thereby made desirous of learning those Languages, and their Industry sharpen'd in the Acquisition of them. All intended for Divinity should be taught the Latin and Greek; for Physick, the Latin, Greek and French; for Law, the Latin and French; Merchants, the French, German, and Spanish: And though all should not be compell'd to learn Latin, Greek, or the modern foreign Languages; yet none that have an ardent Desire to learn them should be refused; their English, Arithmetick, and other Studies absolutely necessary, being at the same Time not neglected.

If the new *Universal History* were also read, it would give a *connected* Idea of human Affairs, so far as it goes, which should be follow'd by the best modern Histories, particularly of our Mother Country; then of these Colonies; which should be accompanied with Observations on their Rise, Encrease, Use to Great-Britain, Encouragements, Discouragements, &c. the Means to make them flourish, secure their Liberties, &c.

With the History of Men, Times and Nations, should be read at proper Hours or Days, some of the best *Histories of Nature,* which would not only be delightful to Youth, and furnish them with Matter for their Letters, &c. as well as other History; but afterwards of great Use to them, whether they are Merchants, Handicrafts, or Divines; enabling the first the better to understand many Commodities, Drugs, &c. the second to improve his Trade or Handicraft by new Mixtures, Materials, &c. and the last to adorn his Discourses by beautiful Comparisons, and strengthen them by new Proofs of Divine Providence. The Conversation of all will be improved by it, as Occasions frequently occur of making Natural Observations, which are instructive, agreeable, and entertaining in almost all Companies. *Natural History* will also afford Opportunities of introducing many Observations, relating to the Preservation of Health, which may be afterwards of great Use. Arbuthnot on Air and Aliment, Sanctorius on Perspiration, Lemery on Foods, and some others, may now be read, and a very little Explanation will make them sufficiently intelligible to Youth.

While they are reading Natural History, might not a little *Gardening, Planting, Grafting, Inoculating,* &c. be taught and practised; and now and then Excursions made to the neighbouring Plantations of the best Farmers, their Methods observ'd and reason'd upon for the Information of Youth. The Improvement of Agriculture being useful to all, and Skill in it no Disparagement to any.

The History of *Commerce,* of the Invention of Arts, Rise of Manufactures, Progress of Trade, Change of its Seats, with the Reasons, Causes, &c. may also be made entertaining to Youth, and will be useful to all. And this, with the Accounts in other History of the prodigious Force and Effect of Engines and Machines used in War, will naturally introduce a Desire to be instructed in *Mechanicks,* and to be inform'd of the Principles of that Art by which weak Men perform such Wonders, Labour is sav'd, Manufactures expedited, &c. &c. This will be the Time to show them Prints of antient and modern Machines, to explain them, to let them be copied, and to give Lectures in Mechanical Philosophy.

With the whole should be constantly inculcated and cultivated, that *Benignity of Mind,* which shows itself in *searching for* and *seizing* every Opportunity *to serve* and *to oblige;* and is the Foundation of what is called GOOD BREEDING; highly useful to the Possessor, and most agreeable to all.

The Idea of what is *true Merit,* should also be often presented to Youth, explain'd and impress'd on their Minds, as consisting in an *Inclination* join'd with an *Ability* to serve Mankind, one's Country, Friends and Family; which *Ability* is (with the Blessing of God) to be acquir'd or greatly encreas'd by *true Learning;* and should indeed be the great *Aim* and *End* of all Learning.

BENJAMIN FRANKLIN
"Idea of the English School" (1751) *

It is expected that every Scholar to be admitted into this School, be at least able to pronounce and divide the Syllables in Reading, and to write a legible Hand. None to be receiv'd that are under [   ]¹ Years of Age.

First or lowest CLASS.

Let the first Class learn the *English Grammar* Rules, and at the same time let particular Care be taken to improve them in *Orthography*. Perhaps the latter is best done by *Pairing* the Scholars, two of those nearest equal in their Spelling to be put together; let these strive for Victory, each propounding Ten Words every Day to the other to be spelt. He that spells truly most of the other's Words, is Victor for that Day; he that is Victor most Days in a Month, to obtain a Prize, a pretty neat Book of some Kind useful in their future Studies. This Method fixes the Attention of Children extreamly to the Orthography of Words, and makes them good Spellers very early. 'Tis a Shame for a Man to be so ignorant of this little Art, in his own Language, as to be perpetually confounding Words of like Sound and different Significations; the Consciousness of which Defect, makes some Men, otherwise of good Learning and Understanding, averse to Writing even a common Letter.

Let the Pieces read by the Scholars in this Class be short, such as Croxall's Fables, and little Stories. In giving the Lesson, let it be

* Benjamin Franklin, "Idea of the English School, Sketch'd out for the Consideration of the Trustees of the Philadelphia Academy" (1751), *The Papers of Benjamin Franklin* (New Haven: Yale University Press, 1961; edited by Leonard W. Labaree *et al.*), IV, 102–108. Used by permission.
¹ Left bank in the original manuscript. Benjamin Franklin told Samuel Johnson he thought the boys in the English School would be between eight and sixteen years old; and to Jared Eliot, he spoke of "little boys under 7" who were already in the Academy.

read to them; let the Meaning of the difficult Words in it be explained to them, and let them con it over by themselves before they are called to read to the Master, or Usher; who is to take particular Care that they do not read too fast, and that they duly observe the Stops and Pauses. A Vocabulary of the most usual difficult Words might be formed for their Use, with Explanations; and they might daily get a few of those Words and Explanations by Heart, which would a little exercise their Memories; or at least they might write a Number of them in a small Book for the Purpose, which would help to fix the Meaning of those Words in their Minds, and at the same Time furnish every one with a little Dictionary for his future Use.

The Second CLASS to be taught

Reading with Attention, and with proper Modulations of the Voice according to the Sentiments and Subject.

Some short Pieces, not exceeding the Length of a *Spectator,* to be given this Class as Lessons (and some of the easier *Spectators* would be very suitable for the Purpose.) These Lessons might be given over Night as Tasks, the Scholars to study them against the Morning. Let it then be required of them to give an Account, first of the Parts of Speech, and Construction of one or two Sentences; this will oblige them to recur frequently to their Grammar, and fix its principal Rules in their Memory. Next of the *Intention* of the Writer, or the *Scope* of the Piece; the Meaning of each Sentence, and of every uncommon Word. This would early acquaint them with the Meaning and Force of Words, and give them that most necessary Habit, of Reading with Attention.

The Master then to read the Piece with the proper Modulations of Voice, due Emphasis, and suitable Action, where Action is required; and put the Youth on imitating his Manner.

Where the Author has us'd an Expression not the best, let it be pointed out; and let his Beauties be particularly remarked to the Youth.

Let the Lessons for Reading be varied, that the Youth may be made acquainted with good Stiles of all Kinds in Prose and Verse, and the proper Manner of reading each Kind. Sometimes a well-told Story, a Piece of a Sermon, a General's Speech to his Soldiers, a Speech in a Tragedy, some Part of a Comedy, an Ode, a Satyr, a Letter, Blank Verse, Hudibrastick, Heroic, &c. But let such Lessons for Reading be chosen, as contain some useful Instruction, whereby the Understandings or Morals of the Youth, may at the same Time be improv'd.

It is requir'd that they should first study and understand the Lessons, before they are put upon reading them properly, to which End each Boy should have an English Dictionary to help him over Difficulties. When our Boys read English to us, we are apt to imagine *they* understand what *they* read because *we* do, and because 'tis their Mother Tongue. But they often read as Parrots speak, knowing little or nothing of the Meaning. And it is impossible a Reader should give the due Modulation to his Voice, and pronounce properly, unless his Understanding goes before his Tongue, and makes him Master of the Sentiment. Accustoming Boys to read aloud what they do not first understand, is the Cause of those even set Tones so common among Readers, which when they have once got a Habit of using, they find so difficult to correct: By which Means, among Fifty Readers we scarcely find a good One. For want of good Reading, Pieces publish'd with a View to influence the Minds of Men for their own or the publick Benefit, lose Half their Force. Were there but one good Reader in a Neighbourhood, a publick Orator might be heard throughout a Nation with the same Advantages, and have the same Effect on his Audience, as if they stood within the Reach of his Voice.

The Third CLASS to be taught

Speaking properly and gracefully, which is near of Kin to good Reading, and natu-rally follows it in the Studies of Youth. Let the Scholars of this Class begin with learning the Elements of Rhetoric from some short System, so as to be able to give an Account of the most usual Tropes and Figures. Let all their bad Habits of Speaking, all Offences against good Grammar, all corrupt or foreign Accents, and all improper Phrases, be pointed out to them. Short Speechs from the Roman or other History, or from our *Parliamentary Debates,* might be got by heart, and deliver'd with the proper Action, &c. Speeches and Scenes in our best Tragedies and Comedies (avoiding every Thing that could injure the Morals of Youth) might likewise be got by Rote, and the Boys exercis'd in delivering or acting them; great Care being taken to form their Manner after the truest Models.

For their farther Improvement, and a little to vary their Studies, let them now begin to read *History,* after having got by Heart a short Table of the principal Epochas in Chronology. They may begin with Rollin's *Antient and Roman Histories,* and proceed at proper Hours as they go thro' the subsequent Classes, with the best Histories of our own Nation and Colonies. Let Emulation be excited among the Boys by giving, Weekly, little Prizes, or other small Encouragements to those who are able to give the best Account of what they have read, as to Times, Places, Names of Persons, &c. This will make them read with Attention, and imprint the History well in their Memories. In remarking on the History, the Master will have fine Opportunities of instilling Instruction of various Kinds, and improving the Morals as well as the Understandings of Youth.

The Natural and Mechanic History contain'd in *Spectacle de la Nature,* might also be begun in this Class, and continued thro' the subsequent Classes by other Books of the same Kind: For next to the Knowledge of *Duty,* this Kind of Knowledge is certainly the most useful, as well as the most entertaining. The Merchant may thereby be enabled better to understand many Commodities in Trade; the Handicraftsman to improve his Business by new Instruments, Mixtures and Materials; and frequently Hints are given of new Manufactures, or new Methods of improving Land, that may be set on foot greatly to the Advantage of a Country.

The Fourth CLASS to be taught

Composition. Writing one's own Language well, is the next necessary Accomplishment after good Speaking. 'Tis the Writing-Master's Business to take Care that the Boys make fair Characters, and place them straight and even in the Lines: But to *form their Stile,* and even to take Care that the Stops and Capitals are properly disposed, is the Part of the English Master. The Boys should be put on Writing Letters to each other on any common Occurrences, and on various Subjects, imaginary Business, &c. containing little Stories, Accounts of their late Reading, what Parts of Authors please them, and why. Letters of Congratulation, of Compliment, of Request, of Thanks, of Recommendation, of Admonition, of Consolation, of Expostulation, Excuse, &c. In these they should be taught to express themselves clearly, concisely, and naturally, without affected Words, or high-flown Phrases. All their Letters to pass through the Master's Hand, who is to point out the Faults, advise the Corrections, and commend what he finds right. Some of the best Letters published in our own Language, as Sir William Temple's, those of Pope, and h's Friends, and some others, might be set before the Youth as Models, their Beauties pointed out and explained by the Master, the Letters themselves transcrib'd by the Scholar.

Dr. Johnson's *Ethices Elementa,* or first Principles of Morality, may now be read by the Scholars, and explain'd by the Master, to lay a solid Foundation of Virtue and Piety in their Minds. And as this Class continues the Reading of History, let them now at proper Hours receive some farther Instructions in Chronology, and in that Part of Geography (from the Mathematical Master) which is necessary to understand the Maps and Globes. They should also be acquainted with the modern Names of the Places they find mention'd in antient Writers. The Exercises of good Reading and proper Speaking still continued at suitable Times.

Fifth CLASS.

To improve the Youth in *Composition,* they may now, besides continuing to write Letters, begin to write little Essays in Prose; and sometimes in Verse, not to make them Poets, but for this Reason, that nothing acquaints a Lad so speedily with Variety of Expression, as the Necessity of finding such Words and Phrases as will suit with the Measure, Sound and Rhime of Verse, and at the same Time well express the Sentiment. These Essays should all pass under the Master's Eye, who will point out their Faults, and put the Writer on correcting them. Where the Judgment is not ripe enough for forming new Essays, let the Sentiments of a *Spectator* be given, and requir'd to be cloath'd in a Scholar's own Words; or the Circumstances of some good Story, the Scholar to find Expression. Let them be put sometimes on abridging a Paragraph of a diffuse Author, sometimes on dilating or amplifying what is wrote more closely. And now let Dr. Johnson's *Noetica,* or first Principles of human Knowledge, containing a Logic, or Art of Reasoning, &c. be read by the Youth, and the Difficulties that may occur to them be explained by the Master. The Reading of History, and the Exercises of good Reading and just Speaking still continued.

Sixth CLASS.

In this Class, besides continuing the Studies of the preceding, in History, Rhetoric, Logic, Moral and Natural Philosophy, the best English Authors may be read and explain'd; as Tillotson, Milton, Locke, Addison, Pope, Swift, the higher Papers in the *Spectator* and *Guardian,* the best Translations of Homer, Virgil and Horace, of *Telemachus, Travels of Cyrus,* &c.

Once a Year, let there be publick Exercises in the Hall, the Trustees and Citizens present. Then let fine gilt Books be given as Prizes to such Boys as distinguish themselves, and excel the others in any Branch of Learning; making three Degrees of Comparison; giving the best Prize to him that performs best; a less valuable One to him that comes up next to the best; and another to the third. Commendations, Encouragement and Advice to the rest; keeping up their Hopes that by Industry they may excel another Time. The Names of those that obtain the Prizes, to be yearly printed in a List.

The Hours of each Day are to be divided and dispos'd in such a Manner, as that some Classes may be with the Writing-Master, improving their Hands, others with the Mathematical Master, learning Arithmetick, Accompts, Geography, Use of the Globes, Drawing, Mechanicks, &c. while the rest are in the English School, under the English Master's Care.

Thus instructed, Youth will come out of this School fitted for learning any Business, Calling or Profession, except such wherein Languages are required; and tho' unaquainted with any antient or foreign Tongue, they will be Masters of their own, which is of more immediate and general Use; and withal will have attain'd many other valuable Accomplishments; the Time usually spent in acquiring those Languages, often without Success, being here employ'd in laying such a Foundation of Knowledge and Ability, as, properly improv'd, may qualify them to pass thro' and execute the several Offices of civil Life, with Advantage and Reputation to themselves and Country.

B. F.

BENJAMIN FRANKLIN

"Preface" to *Poor Richard Improved* (1758) *

* Benjamin Franklin, *Poor Richard Improved: Being an Almanack and Ephemeris . . . for*

Courteous Reader,

I have heard that nothing gives an Author so great Pleasure, as to find his Works respectfully quoted by other learned Authors. This Pleasure I have seldom enjoyed; for tho' I have been, if I may say it without Vanity, an *eminent Author* of Almanacks annually now a full Quarter of a Century, my Brother Authors in the same Way, for what Reason I know not, have ever been very sparing in their Applauses; and no other Author has taken the least Notice of me, so that did not my Writings produce me some solid *Pudding,* the great Deficiency of *Praise* would have quite discouraged me.

I concluded at length, that the People were the best Judges of my Merit; for they buy my Works; and besides, in my Rambles, where I am not personally known, I have frequently heard one or other of my Adages repeated, with, *as Poor Richard says,* at the End on't; this gave me some Satisfaction, as it showed not only that my Instructions were regarded, but discovered likewise some Respect for my Authority; and I own, that to encourage the Practice of remembering and repeating those wise Sentences, I have sometimes *quoted myself* with great Gravity.

Judge then how much I must have been gratified by an Incident I am going to relate to you. I stopt my Horse lately where a great Number of People were collected at a Vendue of Merchant Goods. The Hour of Sale not being come, they were conversing on the Badness of the Times, and one of the

the Year of Our Lord 1758 . . . , "Preface," *The Papers of Benjamin Franklin* (New Haven and London: Yale University Press, 1963; edited by Leonard W. Labaree *et al.*), VII, 340–350. Used by permission. In this pamphlet, Franklin created a new *persona,* called Father Abraham, "a plain clean old Man, with white Locks." At a public "vendue" the assembled crowd asked Father Abraham to comment on "the Times" and for advice on how to meet the "heavy Taxes" now in force. His speech in response to this request comprises the main theme of this extended "Preface."

Company call'd to a plain clean old Man, with white Locks, *Pray, Father Abraham, what think you of the Times? Won't these heavy Taxes quite ruin the Country? How shall we be ever able to pay them? What would you advise us to?*—Father Abraham stood up, and reply'd, If you'd have my Advice, I'll give it you in short, for a *Word to the Wise is enough,* and *many Words won't fill a Bushel,* as *Poor Richard says.* They join'd in desiring him to speak his Mind, and gathering round him, he proceeded as follows;

"Friends, says he, and Neighbours, the Taxes are indeed very heavy, and if those laid on by the Government were the only Ones we had to pay, we might more easily discharge them; but we have many others, and much more grievous to some of us. We are taxed twice as much by our *Idleness,* three times as much by our *Pride,* and four times as much by our *Folly,* and from these Taxes the Commissioners cannot ease or deliver us by allowing an Abatement. However let us hearken to good Advice, and something may be done for us; *God helps them that help themselves,* as Poor Richard says, in his Almanack of 1733.

It would be thought a hard Government that should tax its People one tenth Part of their *Time,* to be employed in its Service. But *Idleness* taxes many of us much more, if we reckon all that is spent in absolute *Sloth,* or doing of nothing, with that which is spent in idle Employments or Amusements, that amount to nothing. *Sloth,* by bringing on Diseases, absolutely shortens Life. *Sloth, like Rust, consumes faster than Labour wears, while the used Key is always bright,* as Poor Richard says. But *dost thou love Life, then do not squander Time, for that's the Stuff Life is made of,* as Poor Richard says. How much more than is necessary do we spend in Sleep! forgetting that *The sleeping Fox catches no Poultry,* and that *there will be sleeping enough in the Grave,* as Poor Richard says. If Time be of all Things the most precious, *wasting Time* must be, as Poor Richard says, *the greatest Prodigality,*

since, as he elsewhere tells us, *Lost Time is never found again;* and what we call *Time-enough, always proves little enough:* Let us then be up and be doing, and doing to the Purpose; so by Diligence shall we do more with less Perplexity. *Sloth makes all Things difficult, but Industry all easy,* as Poor Richard says; and *He that riseth late, must trot all Day, and shall scarce overtake his Business at Night.* While *Laziness travels so slowly, that Poverty soon overtakes him,* as we read in Poor Richard, who adds, *Drive thy Business, let not that drive thee;* and *Early to Bed, and early to rise, makes a Man healthy, wealthy and wise. . . .*

Methinks I hear some of you say, *Must a Man afford himself no Leisure?* I will tell thee, my Friend, what Poor Richard says, *Employ thy Time well if thou meanest to gain Leisure;* and, *since thou art not sure of a Minute, throw not away an Hour.* Leisure, is Time for doing something useful; this Leisure the diligent Man will obtain, but the lazy Man never; so that, as Poor Richard says, a *Life of Leisure and a Life of Laziness are two Things.* Do you imagine that Sloth will afford you more Comfort than Labour? No, for as Poor Richard says, *Trouble springs from Idleness, and grievous Toil from needless Ease. Many without Labour, would live by their* WITS *only, but they break for want of Stock.* Whereas Industry gives Comfort, and Plenty, and Respect: *Fly Pleasures, and they'll follow you. The diligent Spinner has a large Shift;* and *now I have a Sheep and a Cow, every Body bids me Good morrow;* all which is well said by Poor Richard.

But with our Industry, we must likewise be *steady, settled* and *careful,* and oversee our own Affairs *with our own Eyes,* and not trust too much to others; for, as Poor Richard says,

> I never saw an oft removed Tree,
> Nor yet an oft removed Family,
> That throve so well as those that settled
> be.

And again, *Three Removes is as bad as a Fire;* and again, *Keep thy Shop, and thy*

Shop will keep thee; and again, *If you would have your Business done, go; If not, send.* And again,

> *He that by the Plough would thrive,*
> *Himself must either hold or drive.*

. . . So much for Industry, my Friends, and Attention to one's own Business; but to these we must add *Frugality*, if we would make our *Industry* more certainly successful. A Man may, if he knows not how to save as he gets, *keep his Nose all his Life to the Grindstone*, and die not worth a *Groat* at last. *A fat Kitchen makes a lean Will*, as Poor Richard says; and,

> *Many Estates are spent in the Getting,*
> *Since Women for Tea forsook Spinning*
> *and Knitting,*
> *And Men for Punch forsook Hewing*
> *and Splitting.*

If you would be wealthy, says he, in another Almanack, *think of Saving as well as of Getting: The Indies have not made Spain rich, because her* Outgoes *are greater than her* Incomes. Away then with your expensive Follies, and you will not have so much Cause to complain of hard Times, heavy Taxes, and chargeable Families; for, as Poor Dick says,

> *Women and Wine, Game and Deceit,*
> *Make the Wealth small, and the Wants*
> *great.*

And farther, *What maintains one Vice, would bring up two Children.* You may think perhaps, That a *little* Tea, or a *little* Punch now and then, Diet a *little* more costly, Clothes a *little* finer, and a *little* Entertainment now and then, can be no *great* Matter; but remember what Poor Richard says, *Many a* Little *makes a Mickle;* and farther, *Beware of* little *Expences; a small Leak will sink a great Ship;* and again, *Who Dainties love, shall Beggars prove;* and moreover, *Fools make Feasts, and wise Men eat them.*

. . . Be *industrious* and *free;* be *frugal* and *free.* At present, perhaps, you may think yourself in thriving Circumstances, and that you can bear a little Extravagance without Injury; but,

> *For Age and Want, save while you*
> *may;*
> *No Morning Sun lasts a whole Day,*

as Poor Richard says. Gain may be temporary and uncertain, but ever while you live, Expence is constant and certain; and *'tis easier to build two Chimneys than to keep one in Fuel,* as Poor Richard says. So *rather go to Bed supperless than rise in Debt.*

> *Get what you can, and what you get*
> *hold;*
> *'Tis the Stone that will turn all your*
> *Lead into Gold,*

as Poor Richard says. And when you have got the Philosopher's Stone, sure you will no longer complain of bad Times, or the Difficulty of paying Taxes.

This Doctrine, my Friends, is *Reason* and *Wisdom;* but after all, do not depend too much upon your own *Industry*, and *Frugality*, and *Prudence*, though excellent Things, for they may all be blasted without the Blessing of Heaven; and therefore ask that Blessing humbly, and be not uncharitable to those that at present seem to want it, but comfort and help them. Remember Job suffered, and was afterwards prosperous.

And now to conclude, *Experience keeps a dear School, but Fools will learn in no other, and scarce in that;* for it is true, *we may give Advice, but we cannot give Conduct,* as Poor Richard says: However, remember this, *They that won't be counselled, can't be helped,* as Poor Richard says: And farther, That *if you will not hear Reason, she'll surely rap your Knuckles.*

Thus the old Gentleman ended his Harangue. The People heard it, and approved the Doctrine, and immediately practised the contrary, just as if it had been a common Sermon; for the Vendue opened, and they began to buy extravagantly, not withstanding all his Cautions, and their own Fear of Taxes. I found the good Man had thoroughly studied my Almanacks, and digested all I had dropt on those Topicks during the Course of Five-and-twenty Years. The frequent Mention he made of me must have tired any one else, but my Vanity was wonderfully delighted with it, though I was conscious that not a tenth Part of the Wisdom was my own which he ascribed to me, but rather the *Gleanings* I had made of the Sense of all Ages and Nations. However, I resolved to be the better for the Echo of it; and though I had at first determined to buy Stuff for a new Coat, I went away resolved to wear my old One a little longer. *Reader,* if thou wilt do the same, thy Profit will be as great as mine. I am, as ever, Thine to serve thee,   RICHARD SAUNDERS. July 7, 1757.

CHAPTER FOUR

Education for a New Republic

THE IDEAS OF BENJAMIN RUSH

BENJAMIN RUSH
A Plan for the Establishment of Public Schools (1786)*

Before I proceed to suggest a Plan for the establishment of public schools in Pennsylvania, I shall point out, in a few words, the influence and advantages of learning upon mankind.

I. It is friendly to religion, inasmuch as it assists in removing prejudice, superstition and enthusiasm, in promoting just notions of the Deity, and in enlarging our knowledge of his works.

II. It is favourable to liberty. A free government can only exist in an equal diffusion of literature. Without learning men become Savages or Barbarians, and where learning is confined to a *few* people, we always find monarchy, aristocracy and slavery.

III. It promotes just ideas of laws and government. "When the clouds of ignorance are dispelled (says the Marquis of Beccaria) by the radiance of knowledge, power trembles, but the authority of laws remains immoveable."

IV. It is friendly to manners. Learning, in all countries, promotes civilization, and the pleasures of society and conversation.

V. It promotes agriculture, the great basis

* Benjamin Rush, *A Plan for the Establishment of Public Schools and the Diffusion of Knowledge in Pennsylvania; to which are added Thoughts upon the Mode of Education, Proper in a Republic. Addressed to the Legislature and Citizens of the State* (Philadelphia: Printed for Thomas Dobson, 1786), pp. 3–12.

of national wealth and happiness. Agriculture is as much a science as hydraulics, or optics, and has been equally indebted to the experiments and researches of learned men. The highly cultivated state, and the immense profits of the farms in England, are derived wholly from the patronage which agriculture has received in that country, from learned men and learned societies.

VI. Manufactures of all kinds owe their perfection, chiefly to learning—hence the nations of Europe advance in manufactures and commerce, only in proportion as they cultivate the arts and sciences.

For the purpose of diffusing knowledge through every part of the state, I beg leave to propose the following simple plan.

I. Let there be one university in the state, and let this be established in the capital. Let law, physic, divinity, the law of nature and nations, œconomy, &c. be taught in it by public lectures in the winter season, after the manner of the European universities, and let the professors receive such salaries from the state as will enable them to deliver their lectures at a moderate price.

II. Let there be four colleges. One in Philadelphia,—one at Carlisle—a third, for the benefit of our German fellow citizens, at Manheim,—and a fourth, some years hence, at Pittsburgh. In these colleges, let young men be instructed in mathematics and in the higher branches of science, in the same manner that they are now taught in our American colleges. After they have taken a degree in one of these colleges, let them, if they can afford it, complete their studies by spending a season or two in attending the lectures in the university. I prefer four colleges in the state to one or two, for there is a certain size of colleges as there is of towns and armies, that is most favourable to morals and good government. Oxford and Cambridge in England are the seats of dissipation, while the more numerous, and less crouded universities and colleges in Scotland, are remarkable for the order, diligence, and decent behaviour of their students.

III. Let there be an academy established in each county, for the purpose of instructing youth in the [learned] languages, and thereby preparing them to enter college.[1]

IV. Let there be free schools established in every township, or in districts consisting of one hundred families. In these schools, let children be taught to read and write the English and German languages, and the use of figures. Such of them as have parents that can afford to send them from home, and are disposed to extend their educations, may remove their children from the free school to the county academy.

By this plan, the whole state will be tied together by one system of education. The university will in time furnish masters for the colleges, and the colleges will furnish masters for the academies and free schools, while the free Schools, in their turns, will supply the academies—the colleges, and the university, with scholars—students, and pupils. The same systems of grammar, oratory and philosophy will be taught in every part of the state, and the literary features of Pennsylvania will thus designate one great, and equally enlightened family.

A question now rises, and that is, How shall this plan be carried into execution?—I answer——

The funds of the university of Pennsylvania (if the English and other schools were separated from it) are nearly equal to the purpose of supporting able professors in all

[1] In the original manuscript the statement is printed: "learned youth in the languages." This is undoubtedly an erroneous transposition.

the arts and sciences that are taught in the European universities.

A small addition to the funds of Dickinson college, will enable it to exist without any further aid from government.

Twenty thousand acres of good land in the late Indian purchase, will probably afford a revenue large enough to support a college at Manheim, and another on the banks of the Ohio, in the course of twenty years.

Five thousand acres of land, appropriated to each county academy, will probably afford a revenue sufficient to support them in twenty years. In the mean while let a tax from £200 to £400 a year be laid on each county for that purpose, according to the number and wealth of its inhabitants.

Let sixty thousand acres of land be set apart, to be divided, twenty years hence, among the free schools. In the mean while let a tax from £30 to £60 a year be levied upon each district of one hundred families, for the support of the schoolmaster, and to prompt him to industry in increasing his school, let each scholar pay him from 1∫6 to 2∫6 every quarter.

But, how shall we bear the expence of these literary institutions under the present weight of our taxes?—I answer—These institutions are designed to *lessen* our taxes. They will enlighten us in the great business of finance—they will teach us to encrease the ability of the state to support government, by encreasing the profits of agriculture, and by promoting manufactures. They will teach us all the modern improvements and advantages of inland navigation. They will defend us from hasty and expensive experiments in government, by unfolding to us the experience and folly of past ages, and thus, instead of adding to our taxes and debts, they will furnish us with the true secret of lessening and discharging both of them.

But, shall the estates of orphans, batchelors and persons who have no children be taxed to pay for the support of schools from which they can derive no benefit? I answer in the affirmative, to the first part of the objection, and I deny the truth of the latter part of it. Every member of the community is interested in the propagation of virtue and knowledge in the state. But I will go further, and add, it will be true œconomy in individuals to support public schools. The batchelor will in time save his tax for this purpose, by being able to sleep with fewer bolts and locks to his doors,—the estates of orphans will in time be benefited, by being protected from the ravages of unprincipled and idle boys, and the children of wealthy parents will be less tempted, by bad company, to extravagance. Fewer pillories and whipping posts, and smaller jails, with their usual expences and taxes, will be necessary when our youth are properly educated, than at present. I believe it could be proved, that the expences of confining, trying and executing criminals amount every year, in most of the counties, to more money than would be sufficient to maintain all the schools that would be necessary in each county. The confessions of these criminals generally show us, that their vices and punishments are the fatal consequences of the want of a proper education in early life.

I submit these detatched hints to the consideration of the legislature and of the citizens of Pennsylvania. The plan for the free schools is taken chiefly from the plans which have long been used with success in Scotland, and in the Eastern states of America, where the influence of learning in promoting religion, morals, manners, government, &c. has never been exceeded in any country.

The manner in which these academies and schools, should be supported and governed,—the modes of determining the characters and qualifications of schoolmasters, and the arrangement of families in each district, so that children of the same religious sect and nation, may be educated as much as possible together, will form a proper part of a LAW for the establishment of schools, and therefore, does not come within the limits of this plan.

I shall conclude this part of the plan, by submitting it to the wisdom of the legislature, whether in granting charters for colleges in future, they should not confine them to giving degrees only in the *arts,* especially while they teach neither law, physic nor divinity. It is a folly peculiar to our American colleges, to confer literary honours in professions that are not taught by them, and which, if not speedily checked, will render degrees so cheap, that they will cease to be the honourable badges of industry and learning.

I have said nothing of the utility of public libraries in each college, academy and free school. Upon this subject, I shall only remark, that they will tend to diffuse knowledge more generally, if the farmers and tradesmen in the neighbourhood of them, (upon paying a moderate sum yearly) are permitted to have access to them.

The establishment of news papers, in a few of the most populous county towns, will contribute very much to diffuse knowledge of all kinds through the state. To accomplish this, the means of conveying the papers should be made easy, by the assistance of the legislature. The effects of a news paper, upon the state of knowledge and opinions, appear already in several of the counties beyond the Susquehannah. The passion for this useful species of instruction, is strongly marked in Pennsylvania, by the great encouragement this paper has received in those counties. In the space of eight months the number of subscribers to the Carlisle Gazette, have amounted to above 700. Henry the IVth of France, used to say, he hoped to live to see the time, when every peasant in his kingdom would dine on a turkey every Sundays. I have not a wish for the extension of literature in the state, that would not be gratified, by living to see a weekly news paper in every farm house in Pennsylvania. Part of the effects of this universal diffusion of knowledge, would probably be, to produce turkies and poultry of all kinds on the tables of our farmers, not only on Sundays, but on every day of the week.

By multiplying villages and county towns,

we encrease the means of diffusing knowledge. Villages are favourable to schools and public worship, and county towns, besides possessing these two advantages, are favourable to the propagation of political and legal information. The public officers of the county, by being obliged to maintain a connection with the capital of the government, often become repositories and vehicles of news and useful publications, while the judges and lawyers, who attend the courts that are held in these towns, seldom fail of leaving a large portion of knowledge behind them.

BENJAMIN RUSH
Thoughts upon the Mode of Education Proper in a Republic (1786)*

The business of education has acquired a new complexion by the independence of our country. The form of government we have assumed, has created a new class of duties to every American. It becomes us, therefore, to examine our former habits upon this subject, and in laying the foundations for nurseries of wise and good men, to adapt our modes of teaching to the peculiar form of our government.

The first remark that I shall make upon this subject is, that an education in our own, is to be preferred to an education in a foreign country. The principle of patriotism stands in need of the reinforcement of *prejudice,* and it is well known that our strongest prejudices in favour of our country are formed in the first one and twenty years of our lives. The policy of the Lacedamonians is well worthy of our imitation. When Antipater demanded fifty of their children as hostages for the fulfilment of a distant engagement, those wise republicans refused to comply with his demand, but readily offered

* Benjamin Rush, *A Plan for the Establishment of Public Schools and the Diffusion of Knowledge in Pennsylvania; to which are added Thoughts upon the Mode of Education, Proper in a Republic. Addressed to the Legislature and Citizens of the State* (Philadelphia: Printed for Thomas Dobson, 1786), pp. 13–36.

him double the number of their adult citizens, whose habits and prejudices could not be shaken by residing in a foreign country. Passing by, in this place, the advantages to the community from the early attachment of youth to the laws and constitution of their country, I shall only remark, that young men who have trodden the paths of science together, or have joined in the same sports, whether of swimming, scating, fishing, or hunting, generally feel, thro' life, such ties to each other, as add greatly to the obligations of mutual benevolence.

I conceive the education of our youth in this country to be peculiarly necessary in Pennsylvania, while our citizens are composed of the natives of so many different kingdoms in Europe. Our Schools of learning, by producing one general, and uniform system of education, will render the mass of the people more homogeneous, and thereby fit them more easily for uniform and peaceable government.

I proceed, in the next place, to enquire, what mode of education we shall adopt so as to secure to the state all the advantages that are to be derived from the proper instruction of youth; and here I beg leave to remark that the only foundation for a useful education in a republic is to be laid in RELIGION. Without this, there can be no virtue, and without virtue there can be no liberty, and liberty is the object and life of all republican governments.

Such is my veneration for every religion that reveals the attributes of the Deity, or a future state of rewards and punishments, that I had rather see the opinions of Confucius or Mahomed inculcated upon our youth, than see them grow up wholly devoid of a system of religious principles. But the religion I mean to recommend in this place, is the religion of JESUS CHRIST.

It is foreign to my purpose to hint at the arguments which establish the truth of the Christian revelation. My only business is to declare, that all its doctrines and precepts are calculated to promote the happiness of society, and the safety and well being of civil government. A Christian cannot fail of being a republican. The history of the creation of man, and of the relation of our species to each other by birth, which is recorded in the Old Testament, is the best refutation that can be given to the divine right of kings, and the strongest argument that can be used in favour of the original and natural equality of all mankind. A Christian, I say again, cannot fail of being a republican, for every precept of the Gospel inculcates those degrees of humility, self-denial, and brotherly kindness, which are directly opposed to the pride of monarchy and the pageantry of a court. A Christian cannot fail of being useful to the republic, for his religion teacheth him that no man "liveth to himself." And lastly, a Christian cannot fail of being wholly inoffensive, for his religion teacheth him, in all things to do to others what he would wish, in like circumstances, they should do to him.

I am aware that I dissent from one of those paradoxical opinions with which modern times abound; that it is improper to fill the minds of youth with religious prejudices of any kind, and that they should be left to choose their own principles, after they have arrived at an age in which they are capable of judging for themselves. Could we preserve the mind in childhood and youth a perfect blank, this plan of education would have more to recommend it; but this we know to be impossible. The human mind runs as naturally into principles as it does after facts. It submits with difficulty to those restraints or partial discoveries which are imposed upon it in the infancy of reason. Hence the impatience of children to be informed upon all subjects that relate to the invisible world. But I beg leave to ask, Why should we pursue a different plan of education with respect to religion from that which we pursue in teaching the arts and sciences? Do we leave our youth to acquire systems of geography, philosophy, or politics, till they have arrived at an age in which they are capable of judgeing for themselves? We do not. I claim no more then for reli-

gion, than for the other sciences, and I add further, that if our youth are disposed after they are of age to think for themselves, a knowledge of *one* system will be the best means of conducting them in a free enquiry into other systems of religion, just as an acquaintance with one system of philosophy is the best introduction to the study of all the other systems in the world.

I must beg leave upon this subject to go one step further. In order more effectually to secure to our youth the advantages of a religious education, it is necessary to impose upon them the doctrines and discipline of a particular church. Man is naturally an ungovernable animal, and observations on particular societies and countries will teach us, that when we add the restraints of eclesiastical, to those of domestic and civil government, we produce, in him, the highest degrees of order and virtue. That fashionable liberality which refuses to associate with any one sect of Christians is seldom useful to itself, or to society, and may fitly be compared to the unprofitable bravery of a soldier, who wastes his valour in solitary enterprizes, without the aid or effect of military associations. Far be it from me to recommend the doctrines or modes of worship of any one denomination of Christians. I only recommend to the persons entrusted with the education of youth, to inculcate upon them a strict conformity to that mode of worship which is most agreeable to their consciences, or the inclinations of their parents.

Under this head, I must be excused in not agreeing with those modern writers who have opposed the use of the Bible as a school book. The only objection I know to it is, its division into chapters and verses, and its improper punctuation, which render it a more difficult book to read *well*, than many others; but these defects may easily be corrected; and the disadvantages of them are not to be mentioned with the immense advantages of making children early, and intimately acquainted with the means of acquiring happiness both here and hereafter.

How great is the difference between making young people acquainted with the interesting and entertaining truths contained in the Bible, and the fables of Moore and Croxall, or the doubtful histories of antiquity! I maintain that there is no book of its size in the whole world, that contains half so much useful knowledge for the government of states, or the direction of the affairs of individuals as the bible. To object to the practice of having it read in schools, because it tends to destroy our veneration for it, is an argument that applies with equal force, against the frequency of public worship, and all other religious exercises. The first impressions upon the mind are the most durable. They survive the wreck of the memory, and exist in old age after the ideas acquired in middle life have been obliterated. Of how much consequence then must it be to the human mind in the evening of life, to be able to recal those ideas which are most essential to its happiness; and these are to be found chiefly in the Bible. The great delight which old people take in reading the Bible, I am persuaded is derived chiefly from its histories and precepts being *associated* with the events of childhood and youth, the recollection of which forms a material part of their pleasures.

I do not mean to exclude books of history, poetry or even fables from our schools. They may, and should be read frequently by our young people, but if the Bible is made to give way to them altogether, I foresee that it will be read, in a short time, only in churches, and in a few years will probably be found only in the offices of magistrates, and in courts of justice.[1]

[1] In a republic where all votes for public officers are given by *ballot,* should not a knowledge of reading and writing be considered as essential qualifications for an elector? and when a man, who is of a doubtful character, offers his vote, would it not be more consistent with sound policy and wise government to oblige him to read a few verses in the Bible to prove his qualifications, than simply to compel him to kiss the *outside* of it?

NEXT to the duty which young men owe to their Creator, I wish to see a SUPREME REGARD TO THEIR COUNTRY, inculcated upon them. When the Duke of Sully became prime minister to Henry the IVth of France, the first thing he did, he tells us, "Was to subdue and forget his own heart." The same duty is incumbent upon every citizen of a republic. Our country includes family, friends and property, and should be preferred to them all. Let our pupil be taught that he does not belong to himself, but that he is public property. Let him be taught to love his family, but let him be taught, at the same time, that he must forsake and even forget them, when the welfare of his country requires it. He must watch for the state as if its liberties depended upon his vigilance alone, but he must do this in such a manner as not to defraud his creditors, or neglect his family. He must love private life, but he must decline no station, however public or responsable it may be, when called to it by the suffrages of his fellow-citizens. He must love popularity, but he must despise it when set in competition with the dictates of his judgement, or the real interest of his country. He must love character, and have a due sense of injuries, but he must be taught to appeal only to the laws of the state, to defend the one, and punish the other. He must love family honour, but he must be taught that neither the rank nor antiquity of his ancestors can command respect, without personal merit. He must avoid neutrality in all questions that divide the state, but he must shun the rage, and acrimony of party spirit. He must be taught to love his fellow creatures in every part of the world, but he must cherish with a more intense and peculiar affection, the citizens of Pennsylvania and of the United States. I do not wish to see our youth educated with a single prejudice against any nation or country; but we impose a task upon human nature, repugnant alike to reason, revelation and the ordinary dimensions of the human heart, when we require him to embrace, with equal affection, the whole family of mankind. He must be taught to amass wealth, but it must be only to encrease his power of contributing to the wants and demands of the state. He must be indulged occasionally in amusements, but he must be taught that study and business should be his principal pursuits in life. Above all he must love life, and endeavour to acquire as many of its conveniences as possible by industry and œconomy, but he must be taught that this life "Is not his own," when the safety of his country requires it. These are practicable lessons, and the history of the commonwealths of Greece and Rome show, that human nature, without the aids of Christianity, has attained these degrees of perfection.

While we inculcate these republican duties upon our pupil, we must not neglect, at the same time, to inspire him with republican principles. He must be taught that there can be no durable liberty but in a republic, and that government, like all other sciences, is of a progressive nature. The chains which have bound this science in Europe are happily unloosed in America. *Here* it is open to investigation and improvement. While philosophy has protected us by its discoveries from a thousand natural evils, government has unhappily followed with an unequal pace. It would be to dishonour human genius only to name the many defects which still exist in the best systems of legislation. We daily see matter of a perishable nature rendered durable by certain chemical operations. In like manner, I conceive, that it is possible to analyze and combine power in such a manner as not only to encrease the happiness, but to promote the duration of republican forms of government far beyond the terms limited for them by history, or the common opinions of mankind.

To assist in rendering religious, moral and political instruction more effectual upon the minds of our youth, it will be necessary to subject their bodies to physical discipline. To obviate the inconveniences of their studious and sedantary mode of life, they should live upon a temperate diet, consisting chiefly of broths, milk and vegetables. The black broth of Sparta, and the barley broth of Scotland, have been alike celebrated for their beneficial effects upon the minds of young people. They should avoid tasting spirituous liquors. They should also be accustomed occasionally to work with their hands, in the intervals of study, and in the busy seasons of the year in the country. Moderate sleep, silence, occasional solitude, and cleanliness, should be inculcated upon them, and the utmost advantage should be taken of a proper direction of those great principles in human conduct,—sensibility, habit, imitation, and association.

The influence [of] these physical causes will be powerful upon the intellects, as well as upon the principles and morals of young people.

To those who have studied human nature, it will not appear paradoxical to recommend, in this essay, a particular attention to vocal music. Its mechanical effects in civilizing the mind, and thereby preparing it for the influence of religion and government, have been so often felt and recorded, that it will be unnecessary to mention facts in favour of its usefulness in order to excite a proper attention to it.

In the education of youth, let the authority of our masters be as *absolute* as possible. The government of schools like the government of private families, should be *arbitrary,* that it may not be *severe.* By this mode of education, we prepare our youth for the subordination of laws, and thereby qualify them for becoming good citizens of the republic. I am satisfied that the most useful citizens have been formed from those youth who have never known or felt their own wills till they were one and twenty years of age, and I have often thought that society owes a great deal of its order and happiness to the deficiencies of parental government, being supplied by those habits of obedience and subordination which are contracted at schools.

I cannot help bearing a testimony, in this place, against the custom, which prevails in some parts of America, (but which is daily falling into disuse in Europe) of crouding boys together under one roof for the purpose of education. The practice is the gloomy remains of monkish ignorance, and is as unfavourable to the improvements of the mind in useful learning, as monasteries are to the spirit of religion. I grant this mode of secluding boys from the intercourse of private families, has a tendency to make them scholars, but our business is to make them men, citizens and christians. The vices of young people are generally learned from each other. The vices of adults seldom infect them. By separating them from each other, therefore, in their hours of relaxation from study, we secure their morals from a principal source of corruption, while we improve their manners, by subjecting them to those restraints, which the difference of age and sex, naturally produce in private families.

I have hitherto said nothing of the AMUSEMENTS that are proper for young people in a republic. Those which promote health and good humour, will have a happy effect upon morals and government. To encrease this influence, let the persons who direct these amusements, be admitted into good company, and subjected, by that means, to restraints in behaviour and moral conduct. Taverns which in most countries are exposed to riot and vice, in Connecticut are places of business and innocent pleasure, because the tavern-keepers in that country are generally men of sober and respectable characters. The theatre will never be perfectly reformed till players are treated with the same respect as persons of other ornamental professions. It is to no purpose to attempt to write or preach down an amusement, which seizes so forcibly upon all the powers of the mind. Let ministers preach *to* players, instead of *against* them; let them open their churches and the ordinances of religion to them and their families, and, I am persuaded, we shall soon see such a reformation in the theatre as can never be effected by all the means that have hitherto been employed for that purpose. It is pos-

sible to render the stage, by these means, subsurvient to the purposes of virtue and even religion. Why should the minister of the gospel exclude the player from his visits, or from his public or private instructions? The Author of Christianity knew no difference in the occupations of men. He eat and drank daily with publicans and sinners.

From the observations that have been made it is plain, that I consider it as possible to convert men into republican machines. This must be done, if we expect them to perform their parts properly, in the great machine of the government of the state. That republic is sophisticated with monarchy or aristocracy that does not revolve upon the wills of the people, and these must be fitted to each other by means of education before they can be made to produce regularity and unison in government.

Having pointed out those general principles, which should be inculcated alike in all the schools of the state, I proceed now to make a few remarks upon the method of conducting, what is commonly called, a liberal or learned education in a republic.

I shall begin this part of my subject by bearing a testimony against the common practice of attempting to teach boys the learned languages, and the arts and sciences too early in life. The first twelve years of life are barely sufficient to instruct a boy in reading, writing and arithmetic. With these, he may be taught those modern languages which are necessary for him to *speak*. The state of the memory, in early life, is favourable to the acquisition of languages, especially when they are conveyed to the mind through the ear. It is, moreover, in early life only, that the organs of speech yield in such a manner as to favour the just pronounciation of foreign languages.

I do not wish the LEARNED OR DEAD LANGUAGES, as they are commonly called, to be reduced below their present just rank in the universities of Europe, especially as I consider an acquaintance with them as the best foundation for a correct and extensive knowledge of the language of our country.

Too much pains cannot be taken to teach our youth to read and write our American language with propriety and elegance. The study of the Greek language constituted a material part of the literature of the Athenians, hence the sublimity, purity and immortality of so many of their writings. The advantages of a perfect knowledge of our language to young men intended for the professions of law, physic or divinity are too obvious to be mentioned, but in a state which boasts of the first commercial city in America, I wish to see it cultivated by young men, who are intended for the compting house, for many such, I hope, will be educated in our colleges. The time is past when an academical education was thought to be unnecessary to qualify a young man for merchandize. I conceive no profession is capable of receiving more embellishments from it.

Connected with the study of our own language is the study of ELOQUENCE. It is well known how great a part it constituted of the Roman education. It is the first accomplishment in a republic, and often sets the whole machine of government in motion. Let our youth, therefore, be instructed in this art. We do not extol it too highly when we attribute as much to the power of eloquence as to the sword in bringing about the American revolution.

With the usual arts and sciences that are taught in our American colleges, I wish to see a regular course of lectures given upon HISTORY and CHRONOLOGY. The science of government, whether it relates to constitutions or laws, can only be advanced by a careful selection of facts, and these are to be found chiefly in history. Above all, let our youth be instructed in the history of the ancient republics, and the progress of liberty and tyranny in the different states of Europe. I wish likewise to see the numerous facts that relate to the origin and present state of COMMERCE, together with the nature and principles of MONEY, reduced to such a system as to be intelligible and agreeable to a young man. If we consider the commerce of our metropolis only as the avenue of the wealth of the state, the study of it merits a place in a young man's education; but, I consider commerce in a much higher light when I recommend the study of it in republican seminaries. I view it as the best security against the influence of hereditary monopolies of land, and, therefore, the surest protection against aristocracy. I consider its effects as next to those of religion in humanizing mankind, and lastly, I view it as the means of uniting the different nations of the world together by the ties of mutual wants and obligations.

CHEMISTRY by unfolding to us the effects of heat and mixture, enlarges our acquaintance with the wonders of nature, and the mysteries of art, hence it has become, in most of the universities of Europe, a necessary branch of a gentleman's education. In a young country, where improvements in agriculture and manufactures are so much to be desired, the cultivation of this science, which explains the principles of both of them, should be considered as an object of the utmost importance.

In a state where every citizen is liable to be a soldier and a legislator, it will be necessary to have some regular instruction given upon the ART OF WAR and upon PRACTICAL LEGISLATION. These branches of knowledge are of too much importance in a republic to be trusted to solitary study, or to a fortuitous acquaintance with books. Let mathematical learning, therefore, be carefully applied, in our colleges, to gunnery and fortification, and let philosophy be applied to the history of those compositions which have been made use of for the terrible purposes of destroying human life. These branches of knowledge will be indispensably necessary in our republic, if unfortunately war should continue hereafter to be the unchristian mode of arbitrating disputes between Christian nations. Again, let our youth be instructed in all the means of promoting national prosperity and independence, whether they relate to improvements in agriculture, manufactures, or inland navigation. Let him be instructed further in the general principles of legislation, whether they relate to revenue, or to the preservation of life, liberty or property. Let him be directed frequently to attend the courts of justice, where he will have the best opportunities of acquiring habits of arranging and comparing his ideas by observing the secretion of truth, in the examination of witnesses, and where he will hear the laws of the state explained, with all the advantages of that species of eloquence which belongs to the bar. Of so much importance do I conceive it to be, to a young man, to attend occasionally to the decisions of our courts of law, that I wish to see our colleges and academies established, only in county towns.

But further, considering the nature of our connection with the United States it will be necessary to make our pupil acquainted with all the prerogatives of the federal government. He must be instructed in the nature and variety of treaties. He must know the difference in the powers and duties of the several species of ambassadors. He must be taught wherein the obligations of individuals and of states are the same, and wherein they differ. In short, he must acquire a general knowledge of all those laws and forms, which unite the sovereigns of the earth, or separate them from each other.

I have only to add that it will be to no purpose to adopt this, or any other mode of education, unless we make choice of suitable masters to carry our plans into execution. Let our teachers be distinguished for their abilities and knowledge. Let them be grave in their manners,—gentle in their tempers, —exemplary in their morals, and of sound principles in religion and government. Let us not leave their support to the precarious resources to be derived from their pupils, but let such funds be provided for our schools and colleges as will enable us to allow them liberal salaries. By these means we shall render the chairs,—the professorships and rectorships of our colleges and academies objects of competition among learned men. By conferring upon our mas-

ters that independence, which is the companion of competency, we shall, moreover, strengthen their authority over the youth committed to their care. Let us remember that a great part of the divines, lawyers, physicians, legislators, soldiers, generals, delegates, counsellors, and governors of the state will probably hereafter pass through their hands. How great then should be the wisdom!—how honourable the rank! and how generous the reward of those men who are to form these necessary and leading members of the republic!

I beg pardon for having delayed so long, to say any thing of the separate and peculiar mode of education proper for WOMEN in a republic. I am sensible that they must concur in all our plans of education for young men, or no laws will ever render them effectual. To qualify our women for this purpose, they should not only be instructed in the usual branches of female education, but they should be instructed in the principles of liberty and government; and the obligations of patriotism, should be inculcated upon them. The opinions and conduct of men are often regulated by the women in the most arduous enterprizes of life; and their approbation is frequently the principal reward of the hero's dangers, and the patriot's toils. Besides, the *first* impressions upon the minds of children are generally derived from the women. Of how much consequence, therefore, is it in a republic, that they should think justly upon the great subjects of liberty and government!

The complaints that have been made against religion, liberty and learning, have been made against each of them in a *separate* state. Perhaps like certain liquors, they should only be used in a state of mixture. They mutually assist in correcting the abuses, and in improving the good effects of each other. From the combined and reciprocal influence of religion, liberty and learning upon the morals, manners and knowledge of individuals, of these, upon government, and of government, upon individuals, it is impossible to measure the degrees of happiness and perfection to which mankind may be raised. For my part, I can form no ideas of the golden age, so much celebrated by the poets, more delightful, than the contemplation of that happiness which it is now in the power of the legislature of Pennsylvania to confer upon her citizens, by establishing proper modes and places of education in every part of the state.

The *present time* is peculiarly favourable to the establishment of these benevolent and necessary institutions in Pennsylvania. The minds of our people have not as yet lost the yielding texture they acquired by the heat of the late revolution. They will *now* receive more readily, than five or even three years hence, new impressions and habits of all kinds. The spirit of liberty *now* pervades every part of the state. The influence of error and deception are *now* of short duration. Seven years hence, the affairs of our state may assume a new complexion. We may be rivetted to a criminal indifference for the safety and happiness of ourselves and our posterity. An aristocratic or democratic junto may arise, that shall find its despotic views connected with the prevalence of ignorance and vice in the state; or a few artful pedagogues who consider learning as useful only in proportion as it favours their pride or avarice, may prevent all new literary establishments from taking place, by raising a hue and cry against them, as the offspring of improper rivalship, or the nurseries of party spirit.

But in vain shall we lavish pains and expence, in establishing nurseries of virtue and knowledge in every part of the state. In vain shall we attempt to give the minds of our citizens a virtuous and uniform bias in early life, while the arms of our state are opened alike to receive into its bosom, and to confer equal priviledges upon, the virtuous emigrant, and the annual refuse of the jails of Britain, Ireland and our sister states. Of the many criminals that have been executed within these seven years, four out of five of them have been foreigners, who have arrived here during the war and since the peace. We are yet, perhaps, to see, and deplore the tracks of the enormous vices and crimes these men have left behind them. Legislators of Pennsylvania!—Stewards of the justice and virtue of heaven!—Fathers of children, who may be corrupted and disgraced by bad examples; say—can nothing be done to preserve our morals, manners, and government, from the infection of European vices?

GEORGE WASHINGTON'S THOUGHTS ON EDUCATION

GEORGE WASHINGTON
Letter to Robert Brooke (March 16, 1795) *

Philadelphia, 16 March, 1795.

Sir,

Ever since the General Assembly of Virginia were pleased to submit to my disposal

* Letter dated March 16, 1795, from George Washington to Robert Brooke, Governor of Virginia, *The Writings of George Washington; Being his Correspondence, Addresses, Messages, and Other Papers, Official and Private, Selected and Published from the Original Manuscripts* (Boston: Russell, Shattuck, and Williams, and Hilliard, Gray, and Co., 1836; edited by Jared Sparks), XI, 22–24.

fifty shares in the Potomac, and one hundred in the James River Company, it has been my anxious desire to appropriate them to an object most worthy of public regard.

It is with indescribable regret, that I have seen the youth of the United States migrating to foreign countries, in order to acquire the higher branches of erudition, and to obtain a knowledge of the sciences. Although it would be injustice to many to pronounce the certainty of their imbibing maxims not congenial with republicanism, it must nevertheless be admitted, that a serious danger is encountered by sending abroad among other political systems those, who have not well learned the value of their own.

The time is therefore come, when a plan of universal education ought to be adopted in the United States. Not only do the exigencies of public and private life demand it, but, if it should ever be apprehended, that prejudice would be entertained in one part of the Union against another, an efficacious remedy will be, to assemble the youth of every part under such circumstances as will, by the freedom of intercourse and collision of sentiment, give to their minds the direction of truth, philanthropy, and mutual conciliation.

It has been represented, that a university corresponding with these ideas is contemplated to be built in the Federal City, and that it will receive considerable endowments. This position is so eligible from its centrality, so convenient to Virginia, by whose legislature the shares were granted and in which part of the Federal District stands, and combines so many other conveniences, that I have determined to vest the Potomac shares in that university.

Presuming it to be more agreeable to the General Assembly of Virginia, that the shares in the James River Company should be reserved for a similar object in some part of that State, I intend to allot them for a seminary to be erected at such place as they shall deem most proper. I am disposed to believe, that a seminary of learning upon an enlarged plan, but yet not coming up to the full idea of a university, is an institution to be preferred for the position which is to be chosen. The students, who wish to pursue the whole range of science, may pass with advantage from the seminary to the university, and the former by a due relation may be rendered coöperative with the latter.

I cannot however dissemble my opinion, that if all the shares were conferred on a university, it would become far more important, than when they are divided; and I have been constrained from concentring them in the same place, merely by my anxiety to reconcile a particular attention to Virginia with a great good, in which she will abundantly share in common with the rest of the United States.

I must beg the favor of your Excellency to lay this letter before that honorable body, at their next session, in order that I may appropriate the James River shares to the place which they may prefer. They will at the same time again accept my acknowledgments for the opportunity, with which they have favored me, of attempting to supply so important a desideratum in the United States as a university adequate to our necessity, and a preparatory seminary. With great consideration and respect, I am, Sir, &c.[1]

[1] This letter was accordingly communicated by the Governor of Virginia to the Assembly at their next session, when the following resolves were passed:

"In the House of Delegates,
1 December, 1795.

"Whereas the migration of American youth to foreign countries, for the completion of their education, exposes them to the danger of imbibing political prejudices disadvantageous to their own republican forms of government, and ought therefore to be rendered unnecessary and avoided;

"Resolved, that the plan contemplated of erecting a university in the Federal City, where the youth of the several States may be assembled, and their course of education finished, deserves the countenance and support of each State.

"And whereas, when the General Assembly presented sundry shares in the James River and Potomac Companies to George Washington, as a small token of their gratitude for the great, eminent, and unrivalled services he had rendered to this commonwealth, to the United States, and the world at large, in support of the principles of liberty and equal government, it was their wish and desire that he should appropriate them as he might think best; and whereas, the present General Assembly retain the same high sense of his virtues, wisdom, and patriotism;

"Resolved, therefore, that the appropriation by the said George Washington of the aforesaid shares in the Potomac Company to the university, intended to be erected in the Federal City, is made in a manner most worthy of pub-

GEORGE WASHINGTON,
Letter to Alexander Hamilton (September 1, 1796)*

(Private)

Philadelphia, September 1, 1796.

My dear Sir: About the middle of last Week I wrote to you; and that it might escape the eye of the Inquisitive (for some of my letters have lately been pried into) I took the liberty of putting it under a cover to Mr. Jay.

Since then, revolving on the Paper [1] that was enclosed therein; on the various matters it contained; and on the first expression of the advice or recommendation which was given in it, I have regretted that another subject (which in my estimation is of interesting concern to the well-being of this country) was not touched upon also: I mean Education *generally* as one of the surest means of enlightening and givg. just ways of thinkg to our Citizens, but particularly the establishment of a University; where the Youth from *all parts* of the United States might receive the polish of Erudition in the Arts, Sciences and Belle Letters; and where those who were disposed to run a political course, might not only be instructed in the theory and principles, but (this Semi-

nary being at the Seat of the General Government) where the Legislature wd. be in Session half the year, and the Interests and politics of the Nation of course would be discussed, they would lay the surest foundation for the practical part also.

But that which would render it of the highest importance, in my opinion, is, that the Juvenal period of life, when friendships are formed, and habits established that will stick by one; the youth, or young men from different parts of the United States would be assembled together, and would by degrees discover that there was not that cause for those jealousies and prejudices which one part of the Union had imbibed against another part: of course, sentiments of more liberality in the general policy of the Country would result from it. What, but the mixing of people from different parts of the United States during the War rubbed off these impressions? A century in the ordinary intercourse, would not have accomplished what the Seven years association in Arms did: but that ceasing, prejudices are beginning to revive again, and never will be eradicated so effectually by any other means as the intimate intercourse of characters in early life, who, in all probability, will be at the head of the councils of this country in a more advanced stage of it.

To shew that this is no *new* idea of mine, I may appeal to my early communications to Congress; and to prove how seriously I have reflected on it since, and how well disposed I have been, and still am, to contribute my aid towards carrying the measure into effect, I enclose you the extract of a letter from me to the Governor of Virginia on this Subject, and a copy of the resolves of the Legislature of that State in consequence thereof.

I have not the smallest doubt that this donation (when the Navigation is in complete operation, which it certainly will be in less than two years), will amount to twelve or £1500 Sterlg a year, and become a rapidly increasing fund. The Proprietors of the Federal City have talked of doing something handsome towards it likewise; and if Con-

lic regard, and of the approbation of this commonwealth.

"Resolved, also, that he be requested to appropriate the aforesaid shares in the James River Company to a seminary at such place in the upper country, as he may deem most convenient to a majority of the inhabitants thereof."

* Letter dated September 1, 1796, from George Washington to Alexander Hamilton, *The Writings of George Washington from the Original Manuscript Sources,* 1745-1799 (Washington, D.C.: U.S. Government Printing Office, 1940; Prepared under the direction of the United States George Washington Bicentennial Commission and published by authority of Congress; edited by John C. Fitzpatrick), XXXV, 198-201.

[1] The Farewell Address.

gress would appropriate some of the Western lands to the same uses, funds sufficient, and of the most permanent and increasing sort might be so established as to envite the ablest Professors in Europe, to conduct it.

Let me pray you, therefore, to introduce a Section in the Address expressive of these sentiments, and recommendatory of the measure; without any mention, however, of my proposed personal contribution to the plan.[2]

Such a Section would come in very properly after the one which relates to our religious obligations, or in a preceeding part, as one of the recommendatory measures to counteract the evils arising from Geographical discriminations. With Affecte. regard etc.

EQUALITY AND EXCELLENCE: THE JEFFERSONIAN CONCEPTION

THOMAS JEFFERSON
"A Bill for Establishing Religious Freedom" (1779)*

Well aware that the opinions and belief of men depend not on their own will, but follow involuntarily the evidence proposed to their minds; that Almighty God hath created the mind free, *and manifested his supreme will that free it shall remain by making it altogether insusceptible of restraint;* that all attempts to influence it by temporal punishments, or burthens, or by civil incapacitations, tend only to beget habits of hypocrisy and meanness, and are a departure from the plan of the holy author of our religion, who being lord both of body and mind, yet chose not to propagate it by coercions on either, as was in his Almighty power to do, *but to extend it by its influence on reason alone;* that the impious presumption of legislators and rulers, civil as well as ecclesiastical, who, being themselves but fallible and uninspired men, have assumed dominion over the faith of others, setting up their own opinions and modes of thinking as the only true and infallible, and as such endeavoring to impose them on others, hath established and maintained false religions over the greatest part of the world and through all time: That to compel a man to furnish contributions of money for the propagation of opinions which he disbelieves *and abhors,* is sinful and tyrannical; that even the forcing him to support this or that teacher of his own religious persuasion, is depriving him of the comfortable liberty of giving his contributions to the particular pastor whose morals he would make his pattern, and whose powers he feels most persuasive to righteousness; and is withdrawing from the ministry those temporary rewards, which proceeding from an approbation of their personal conduct, are an additional incitement to earnest and unremitting labours for the instruction of mankind; that our civil rights have no dependance on our religious opinions, any more than our opinions in physics or geometry; that therefore the proscribing any citizen as unworthy the public confidence by laying upon him an incapacity of being called to offices of trust and emolument, unless he profess or renounce this or that religious opinion, is depriving him injuriously of those privileges and advantages to which, in common with his fellow citizens, he has a natural right; that it tends also to corrupt the principles of that *very* religion it is meant to encourage,

* Thomas Jefferson, "A Bill for Establishing Religious Freedom" (1779), *The Papers of Thomas Jefferson* (Princeton: Princeton University Press, 1950; edited by Julian P. Boyd), II, 545–547. Used by permission.

[2] Hamilton answered (September 4), that "The idea of the university is one of those which I think will be most properly reserved for your speech at the opening of the session. A general suggestion respecting education will very fitly come into the address."

by bribing, with a monopoly of worldly honours and emoluments, those who will externally profess and conform to it; that though indeed these are criminal who do not withstand such temptation, yet neither are those innocent who lay the bait in their way; *that the opinions of men are not the object of civil government, nor under its jurisdiction;* that to suffer the civil magistrate to intrude his powers into the field of opinion and to restrain the profession or propagation of principles on supposition of their ill tendency is a dangerous falacy, which at once destroys all religious liberty, because he being of course judge of that tendency will make his opinions the rule of judgment, and approve or condemn the sentiments of others only as they shall square with or differ from his own; that it is time enough for the rightful purposes of civil government for its officers to interfere when principles break out into overt acts against peace and good order; and finally, that truth is great and will prevail if left to herself; that she is the proper and sufficient antagonist to error, and has nothing to fear from the conflict unless by human interposition disarmed of her natural weapons, free argument and debate; errors ceasing to be dangerous when it is permitted freely to contradict them.

We the General Assembly of Virginia do enact that no man shall be compelled to frequent or support any religious worship, place, or ministry whatsoever, nor shall be enforced, restrained, molested, or burthened in his body or goods, nor shall otherwise suffer, on account of his religious opinions or belief; but that all men shall be free to profess, and by argument to maintain, their opinions in matters of religion, and that the same shall in no wise diminish, enlarge, or affect their civil capacities.

And though we well know that this Assembly, elected by the people for the ordinary purposes of legislation only, have no power to restrain the acts of succeeding Assemblies, constituted with powers equal to our own, and that therefore to declare this act irrevocable would be of no effect in law;

yet we are free to declare, and do declare, that the rights hereby asserted are of the natural rights of mankind, and that if any act shall be hereafter passed to repeal the present or to narrow its operation, such act will be an infringement of natural right.

THOMAS JEFFERSON
Notes on the State of Virginia (1781–1782)*

QUERY XIV.

The administration of justice and the description of the laws?

. . . Many of the laws which were in force during the monarchy being relative merely to that form of government, or inculcating principles inconsistent with republicanism, the first assembly which met after the establishment of the commonwealth appointed a committee to revise the whole code, to reduce it into proper form and volume, and report it to the assembly. This work has been executed by three gentlemen, and reported; but probably will not be taken up till a restoration of peace shall leave to the legislature leisure to go through such a work.

The plan of the revisal was this. The common law of England, by which is meant, that part of the English law which was anterior to the date of the oldest statutes extant, is made the basis of the work. It was thought dangerous to attempt to reduce it to a text: it was therefore left to be collected from the usual monuments of it. Necessary alterations in that, and so much of the whole body of the British statutes, and of acts of assembly, as were thought proper to be retained, were digested into 126 new acts, in which simplicity of style was aimed at, as far as was safe. The following are the most remarkable alterations proposed:

* Thomas Jefferson, *Notes on the State of Virginia, with an Appendix* (Newark: Printed by Pennington & Gould, 1801; Third American Edition), Query XIV, pp. 202–203, 216–221; Query XVII, pp. 233–239; Query XVIII, pp. 240–242.

To change the rules of descent, so as that the lands of any person dying intestate shall be divisible equally among all his children, or other representatives, in equal degree.

To make slaves distributable among the next of kin, as other moveables.

To have all public expenses, whether of the general treasury, or of a parish or county, (as for the maintenance of the poor, building bridges, court-houses, &c.) supplied by assessments on the citizens, in proportion to their property.

To hire undertakers for keeping the public roads in repair, and indemnify individuals through whose lands new roads shall be opened.

To define with precision the rules whereby aliens should become citizens, and citizens make themselves aliens.

To establish religious freedom on the broadest bottom.

To emancipate all slaves born after passing the act. . . .

Another object of the revisal is, to diffuse knowledge more generally through the mass of the people. This bill proposes to lay off every county into small districts of five or six miles square, called hundreds, and in each of them to establish a school for teaching reading, writing, and arithmetic. The tutor to be supported by the hundred and every person in it entitled to send their children three years gratis, and as much longer as they please, paying for it. These schools to be under a visitor who is annually to chuse the boy, of best genius in the school, of those whose parents are too poor to give them further education, and to send him forward to one of the grammar schools, of which twenty are proposed to be erected in different parts of the country, for teaching Greek, Latin, geography, and the higher branches of numerical arithmetic. Of the boys thus sent in one year, trial is to be made at the grammar schools one or two years, and the best genius of the whole selected, and continued six years, and the residue dismissed. By this means twenty of the best geniusses will be raked from the rubbish annually, and be instructed, at the public expence, so far as the grammar schools go. At the end of six years instruction, one half are to be discontinued (from among whom the grammar schools will probably be supplied with future masters;) and the other half, who are to be chosen for the superiority of their parts and disposition, are to be sent and continued three years in the study of such sciences as they shall chuse, at William and Mary college, the plan of which is proposed to be enlarged, as will be hereafter explained, and extended to all the useful sciences. The ultimate result of the whole scheme of education would be the teaching all the children of the state reading, writing, and common arithmetic: turning out ten annually of superior genius, well taught in Greek, Latin, geography, and the higher branches of arithmetic: turning out ten others annually, of still superior parts, who, to those branches of learning, shall have added such of the sciences as their genius shall have led them to; the furnishing to the wealthier part of the people convenient schools, at which their children may be educated at their own expence.—The general objects of this law are to provide an education adapted to the years, to the capacity, and the condition of every one, and directed to their freedom and happiness. Specific details were not proper for the law. These must be the business of the visitors entrusted with its execution. The first stage of this education being the schools of the hundreds wherein the great mass of the people will receive their instruction, the principle foundations of future order will be laid here. Instead therefore of putting the Bible and Testament into the hands of the children at an age when their judgments are not sufficiently matured for religious inquiries, their memories may here be stored with the most useful facts from Grecian, Roman, European and American history. The first elements of morality too may be instilled into their minds; such as, when further developed as their judgements advance in strength, may teach them how to work out their own greatest happiness, by shewing them that it does not depend on the condition of life in which chance has placed them, but is always the result of a good conscience, good health, occupation, and freedom in all just pursuits.—Those whom either the wealth of their parents or the adoption of the state shall destine to higher degrees of learning, will go on to the grammar schools, which constitute the next stage, there to be instructed in the languages. The learning Greek and Latin, I am told, is going into disuse in Europe. I know not what their manners and occupations may call for: but it would be very ill-judged in us to follow their example in this instance. There is a certain period of life, say from eight to fifteen or sixteen years of age, when the mind like the body is not yet firm enough for laborious and close operations. If applied to such, it falls an early victim to premature exertion: exhibiting indeed at first, in these young and tender subjects, the flattering appearance of their being men while they are yet children, but ending in reducing them to be children when they should be men. The memory is then most susceptible and tenacious of impressions; and the learning of languages being chiefly a work of memory, it seems precisely fitted to the powers of this period, which is long enough too for acquiring the most useful languages ancient and modern. I do not pretend that language is science. It is only an instrument for the attainment of science. But that time is not lost which is employed in providing tools for future operation: more especially as in this case the books put into the hands of the youth for this purpose may be such as will at the same time impress their minds with useful facts and good principles. If this period be suffered to pass in idleness, the mind becomes lethargic and impotent, as would the body it inhabits if unexercised during the same time. The sympathy between body and mind during their rise, progress and decline, is too strict and obvious to endanger our being misled while we reason from one to the other.—As soon as they are

of sufficient age, it is supposed they will be sent on from the grammar schools to the university, which constitutes our third and last stage, there to study those sciences which may be adapted to their views.—By that part of our plan which prescribes the selection of the youths of genius from among the classes of the poor, we hope to avail the state of those talents which nature has sown as liberally among the poor as the rich, but which perish without use, if not sought for and cultivated. But of the views of this law none is more important, none more legitimate, than that of rendering the people the safe, as they are the ultimate guardians of their own liberty. For this purpose the reading in the first stage, where *they* will receive their whole education, is proposed, as has been said, to be chiefly historical. History by apprising them of the past will enable them to judge of the future; it will avail them of the experience of other times and other nations; it will qualify them as judges of the actions and designs of men; it will enable them to know ambition under every disguise it may assume; and knowing it, to defeat its views. In every government on earth is some traces of human weakness, some germ of corruption and degeneracy, which cunning will discover, and wickedness insensibly open, cultivate and improve. Every government degenerates when trusted to the rulers of the people alone. The people themselves then are its only safe depositories. And to render them safe their minds must be improved to a certain degree. This indeed is not all that is necessary, though it be essentially necessary. An amendment of our constitution must here come in aid of the public education. The influence over government must be shared among all the people. If every individual which composes their mass participates of the ultimate authority, the government will be safe; because the corrupting the whole mass will exceed any private resources of wealth: and public ones cannot be provided but by levies on the people. In this case every man would have to pay his own price. The government of

Great-Britain has been corrupted, because but one man in ten has a right to vote for members of parliament. The sellers of the government therefore get nine-tenths of their price clear. It has been thought that corruption is restrained by confining the right of suffrage to a few of the wealthier of the people: but it would be more effectually restrained by an extension of that right to such numbers as would bid defiance to the means of corruption.

Lastly, it is proposed, by a bill in this revisal, to begin a public library and gallery, by laying out a certain sum annually in books, paintings, and statues.

QUERY XVII.

The different religions received into that state?

. . . The present state of our laws on the subject of religion is this. The convention of May 1776, in their declaration of rights, declared it to be a truth, and a natural right, that the exercise of religion should be free; but when they proceeded to form on that declaration the ordinance of government, instead of taking up every principle declared in the bill of rights, and guarding it by legislative sanction, they passed over that which asserted our religious rights, leaving them as they found them. The same convention, however, when they met as a member of the general assembly in October, 1776, repealed all *acts of parliament* which had rendered criminal the maintaining any opinions in matters of religion, the forbearing to repair to church, and the exercising any mode of worship; and suspended the laws giving salaries to the clergy, which suspension was made perpetual in October 1779. Statutory oppressions being thus wiped away, we remain at present under those only imposed by the common law, or by our own acts of assembly. At the common law, *heresy* was a capital offence, punishable by burning. Its definition was left to the ecclesiastical judges, before whom the conviction was, till the statute of the 1 El. c. 1. circumscribed it, by declaring, that nothing should be deemed heresy, but what had been so determined by authority of the canonical scriptures, or by one of the four first general councils, or by some other council having for the grounds of their declaration the express and plain words of the scriptures. Heresy, thus circumscribed, being an offence at the common law, our act of assembly of October, 1777, c. 17. gives cognisance of it to the general court, by declaring, that the jurisdiction of that court shall be general in all matters at the common law. The execution is by the writ *De hæretico cumburendo*. By our own act of assembly of 1705, c. 30. if a person brought up in the Christian religion denies the being of a God, or the Trinity, or asserts there are more gods than one, or denies the christian religion to be true, or the scriptures to be of divine authority, he is punishable on the first offence by incapacity to hold any office or employment ecclesiastical, civil, or military; on the second by disability to sue, to take any gift or legacy, to be guardian, executor, or administrator, and by three years imprisonment without bail. A father's right to the custody of his own children being founded in law on his right of guardianship, this being taken away, they may of course be severed from him, and put by the authority of the court, into more orthodox hands. This is a summary view of that religious slavery, under which a people have been willing to remain, who have lavished their lives and fortunes for the establishment of their civil freedom. The error seems not sufficiently eradicated, that the operations of the mind, as well as the acts of the body, are subject to the coercion of the laws. But our rulers can have no authority over such natural rights only as we have submitted to them. The rights of conscience we never submitted, we could not submit. We are answerable for them to our God. The legitimate powers of government extend to such acts only as are injurious to others. But it does me no injury for my neighbor to say there are twenty Gods, or no God. It neither picks my pocket nor breaks by leg. If it be said, his testimony in a court of justice cannot be relied on, reject it then, and be the stigma on him. Constraint may make him worse by making him a hypocrite, but it will never make him a truer man. It may fix him obstinately in his errors, but will not cure them. Reason and free inquiry are the only effectual agents against error. Give a loose to them, they will support the true religion, by bringing every false one to their tribunal, to the test of their investigation. They are the natural enemies of error, and of error only. Had not the Roman government permitted free inquiry, Christianity could never have been introduced.—Had not free inquiry been indulged at the æra of the reformation, the corruptions of Christianity could not have been purged away. If it be restrained now, the present corruptions will be protected and new ones encouraged. Was the government to prescribe to us our medicine and diet, our bodies would be in such keeping as our souls are now. Thus in France the emetic was once forbidden as a medicine, and the potatoe as an article of food. Government is just as infallible too when it fixes systems in physics. Galileo was sent to the inquisition for affirming that the earth was a sphere: the government had declared it to be as flat as a trencher, and Galileo was obliged to abjure his error. This error however at length prevailed, the earth became a globe, and Descartes declared it was whirled round its axis by a vortex. The government in which he lived was wise enough to see that this was no question of civil jurisdiction, or we should all have been involved by authority in vortices. In fact, the vortices have been explored, and the Newtonian principle of gravitation is now more firmly established, on the basis of reason, than it would be were the government to step in, and make it an article of necessary faith. Reason and experiment have been indulged, and error has fled before them. It is error alone which needs the support of government. Truth can stand by itself. Subject opinion to coercion: whom will you make your inquisitors? Fallible men; men governed by bad passions, by private as well as public reasons. And why subject it to coercion? To produce uniformity. But is uniformity of opinion desirable? No more than of face and stature. Introduce the bed of Procrustes then, and as there is danger that the great men may beat the small, make us all of a size, by lopping the former and stretching the latter. Difference of opinion is advantageous in religion. The several sects perform the office of a censor morum over each other. Is uniformity attainable? Millions of innocent men, women, and children, since the introduction of Christianity, have been burnt, tortured, fined, imprisoned; yet we have not advanced one inch toward uniformity. What has been the effect of coercion? to make one half the world fools, and the other half hypocrites. To support roguery and error all over the earth. Let us reflect that it is inhabited by a thousand millions of people. That these profess probably a thousand different systems of religion. That ours is but one of that thousand. That if there be but one right, and ours that one, we should wish to see the 999 wandering sects gathered into the fold of truth. But against such a majority we cannot effect this by force. Reason and persuasion are the only practicable instruments. To make way for these, free inquiry must be indulged; how can we wish others to indulge it while we refuse it ourselves. But every state, says an inquisitor, has established some religion. No two, say I, have established the same. Is this a proof of the infallibility of establishments? Our sister states of Pennsylvania and New-York, however, have long subsisted without any establishment at all. The experiment was new and doubtful when they made it. It has answered beyond conception. They flourish infinitely. Religion is well supported; of various kinds, indeed, but all good enough; all sufficient to preserve peace and order: or if a sect arises, whose tenets would subvert morals, good sense has fair play, and reasons and laughs it out of doors, without suffering the state to be troubled with it. They do not hang more malefactors than we do. They are not more disturbed with religious dissensions than we are. On the contrary, their harmony is unparalleled, and can be ascribed to nothing but their unbounded tolerance, because there is no other circumstance in which they differ from every nation on earth. They have made the happy discovery, that the way to silence religious disputes, is to take no notice of them. Let us too give this experiment fair play, and get rid, while we may, of those tyrannical laws. It is true, we are as yet secured against them by the spirit of the times. I doubt whether the people of this country would suffer an execution for heresy, or a three years imprisonment for not comprehending the mysteries of the Trinity. But is the spirit of the people an infalliable, a permanent reliance? Is it government? Is this the kind of protection we receive in return for the rights we give up? Besides, the spirit of the times may alter, will alter. Our rulers will become corrupt, our people careless. A single zealot may commence persecutor, and better men be his victims. It can never be too often repeated, that the time for fixing every essential right on a legal basis is while our rulers are honest, and ourselves united. From the conclusion of this war we shall be going down hill. It will not then be necessary to resort every moment to the people for support. They will be forgotten, therefore, and their rights disregarded. They will forget themselves, but in the sole faculty of making money, and will never think of uniting to effect a due respect for their rights. The shackles, therefore, which shall not be nocked off at the conclusion of this war, will remain on us long, will be made heavier and heavier, till our rights shall revive or expire in a convulsion.

QUERY XVIII.

The *particular* customs and manners that may happen to be received in that state?

It is difficult to determine on the standard by which the manners of a nation may be tried, whether *catholic,* or *particular.* It is

more difficult for a native to bring to that standard the manners of his own nation, familiarized to him by habit. There must doubtless be an unhappy influence on the manners of our people produced by the existence of slavery among us. The whole commerce between master and slave is a perpetual exercise of the most boisterous passions, the most unremitting despotism on the one part, and degrading submissions on the other. Our children see this, and learn to imitate it; for man is an imitative animal. This quality is the germ of all education in him. From his cradle to his grave he is learning to do what he sees others do. If a parent could find no motive either in his philanthropy or his self-love, for restraining the intemperance of passion towards his slave, it should always be a sufficient one that his child is present. But generally it is not sufficient. The parent storms, the child looks on, catches the lineaments of wrath, puts on the same airs in the circle of smaller slaves, gives a loose to the worst of his passions, and thus nursed, educated, and daily exercised in tyranny, cannot but be stamped by it with odious peculiarities. The man must be a prodigy who can retain his manners and morals undepraved by such circumstances. And with what execration should the statesman be loaded, who permitting one half the citizens thus to trample on the rights of the other, transforms those into despots, and these into enemies, destroys the morals of the one part, and the amor patriæ of the other. For if a slave can have a country in this world, it must be any other in preference to that in which he is born to live and labor for another: in which he must lock up the faculties of his nature, contribute as far as depends on his individual endeavors to the evanishment of the human race, or entail his own miserable condition on the endless generations proceeding from him. With the morals of the people, their industry also is destroyed. For in a warm climate, no man will labor for himself who can make another labor for him. This is so true, that of the proprietors of slaves a very small proportion indeed are ever seen to labor. And can the liberties of a nation be thought secure when we have removed their only firm basis, a conviction in the minds of the people that these liberties are of the gift of God? That they are not to be violated but with his wrath? Indeed I tremble for my country when I reflect that God is just; that his justice cannot sleep for ever: that considering numbers, nature and natural means only, a revolution of the wheel of fortune, an exchange of situation is among possible events: that it may become probable by supernatural interference! The Almighty has no attribute which can take side with us in such a contest.—But it is impossible to be temperate and to pursue this subject through the various considerations of policy, of morals, of history natural and civil. We must be contented to hope they will force their way into every one's mind. I think a change already perceptible, since the origin of the present revolution. The spirit of the master is abating, that of the slave is rising from the dust, his condition mollifying, the way I hope preparing, under the auspices of heaven, for a total emancipation, and that this is disposed, in the order of events, to be with the consent of the masters, rather than by their extirpation.

THOMAS JEFFERSON

Letter to George Wythe (August 13, 1786) *

DEAR SIR   Paris Aug. 13. 1786.

Your favors of Jan. 10. and Feb. 10. came to hand on the 20th. and 23d of May. I availed myself of the first opportunity which occurred, by a gentleman going to England, of sending to Mr. Joddrel a copy of the Notes on our country, with a line informing him that it was you who had emboldened me to take that liberty. Madison, no doubt, informed you of the reason

* Letter dated August 13, 1786, from Thomas Jefferson to George Wythe, *The Papers of Thomas Jefferson* (Princeton: Princeton University Press, 1954; edited by Julian P. Boyd), X, 243–245. Used by permission.

why I had sent only a single copy to Virginia. Being assured by him that they will not do the harm I had apprehended, but on the contrary may do some good, I propose to send thither the copies remaining on hand, which are fewer than I had intended, but of the numerous corrections they need, there are one or two so essential that I must have them made, by printing a few new leaves and substituting them for the old. This will be done while they are engraving a map which I have constructed of the country from Albemarle sound to Lake Erie, and which will be inserted in the book. A bad French translation which is getting out here, will probably oblige me to publish the original more freely, which it neither deserved nor was ever intended. Your wishes, which are laws to me, will justify my destining a copy for you. Otherwise I should as soon have thought of sending you a hornbook; for there is no truth there that is not familiar to you, and it's errors I should hardly have proposed to treat you with.

Immediately on the receipt of your letter, I wrote to a correspondent at Florence to enquire after the family of Tagliaferro as you desired. I received his answer two days ago, a copy of which I now inclose. The original shall be sent by some other occasion. I will have the copper plate immediately engraved. This may be ready within a few days, but the probability is that I shall be long getting an opportunity of sending it to you, as these rarely occur. You do not mention the size of the plate but, presuming it is intended for labels for the inside of books, I shall have it made of a proper size for that. I shall omit the word αριϛος, according to the license you allow me, because I think the beauty of a motto is to condense much matter in as few words as possible. The word omitted will be supplied by every reader.

The European papers have announced that the assembly of Virginia were occupied on the revisal of their Code of laws. This, with some other similar intelligence, has contributed much to convince the people of

Europe, that what the English papers are constantly publishing of our anarchy, is false; as they are sensible that such a work is that of a people only who are in perfect tranquillity. Our act for freedom of religion is extremely applauded. The Ambassadors and ministers of the several nations of Europe resident at this court have asked of me copies of it to send to their sovereigns, and it is inserted at full length in several books now in the press; among others, in the new Encyclopedie. I think it will produce considerable good even in these countries where ignorance, superstition, poverty and oppression of body and mind in every form, are so firmly settled on the mass of the people, that their redemption from them can never be hoped. If the almighty had begotten a thousand sons, instead of one, they would not have sufficed for this task. If all the sovereigns of Europe were to set themselves to work to emancipate the minds of their subjects from their present ignorance and prejudices, and that as zealously as they now endeavor the contrary, a thousand years would not place them on that high ground on which our common people are now setting out. Ours could not have been so fairly put into the hands of their own common sense, had they not been separated from their parent stock and been kept from contamination, either from them, or the other people of the old world, by the intervention of so wide an ocean. To know the worth of this, one must see the want of it here. I think by far the most important bill in our whole code is that for the diffusion of knowledge among the people. No other sure foundation can be devised for the preservation of freedom, and happiness. If any body thinks that kings, nobles, or priests are good conservators of the public happiness, send them here. It is the best school in the universe to cure them of that folly. They will see here with their own eyes that these descriptions of men are an abandoned confederacy against the happiness of the mass of people. The omnipotence of their effect cannot be better proved than in this country

particularly, where notwithstanding the finest soil upon earth, the finest climate under heaven, and a people of the most benevolent, the most gay, and amiable character of which the human form is susceptible, where such a people I say, surrounded by so many blessings from nature, are yet loaded with misery by kings, nobles and priests, and by them alone. Preach, my dear Sir, a crusade against ignorance; establish and improve the law for educating the common people. Let our countrymen know that the people alone can protect us against these evils, and that the tax which will be paid for this purpose is not more than the thousandth part of what will be paid to kings, priests and nobles who will rise up among us if we leave the people in ignorance.—The people of England, I think, are less oppressed than here. But it needs but half an eye to see, when among them, that the foundation is laid in their dispositions, for the establishment of a despotism. Nobility, wealth, and pomp are the objects of their adoration. They are by no means the free-minded people we suppose them in America. Their learned men too are few in number, and are less learned and infinitely less emancipated from prejudice than those of this country. An event too seems to be prospering, in the order of things, which will probably decide the fate of that country. It is no longer doubtful that the harbour of Cherbourg will be completed, that it will be a most excellent one, and capacious enough to hold the whole navy of France. Nothing has ever been wanting to enable this country to invade that, but a naval force conveniently stationed to protect the transports. This change of situation, must oblige the English to keep up a great standing army, and there is no king, who, with a sufficient force, is not always ready to make himself absolute. —My paper warns me it is time to recommend myself to the friendly recollection of Mrs. Wythe, of Colo. Taliaferro and his family and particularly of Mr. R. T. and to assure you of the affectionate esteem with which I am Dear Sir your friend & servt.,

TH: JEFFERSON

THOMAS JEFFERSON

Letter to John Adams (October 28, 1813)*

MONTICELLO, October 28, 1813.

DEAR SIR,—According to the reservation between us, of taking up one of the subjects of our correspondence at a time, I turn to your letters of August the 16th and September the 2d.

The passage you quote from Theognis, I think has an ethical rather than a political object. The whole piece is a moral *exhortation, παραινεσις*, and this passage particularly seems to be a reproof to man, who, while with his domestic animals he is curious to improve the race, by employing always the finest male, pays no attention to the improvement of his own race, but intermarries with the vicious, the ugly, or the old, for considerations of wealth or ambition. It is in conformity with the principle adopted afterwards by the Pythagoreans, and expressed by Ocellus in another form; περι δε τῆς 'εκ τῶν αλληλων ανθρωπων γενεσεως etc.,—ουχ ηδονης ενεκα η μιξις· which, as literally as intelligibility will admit, may be thus translated: "concerning the interprocreation of men, how, and of whom it shall be, in a perfect manner, and according to the laws of modesty and sanctity, conjointly, this is what I think right. First to lay it down that we do not commix for the sake of pleasure, but of the procreation of children. For the powers, the organs and desires for coition have not been given by God to man for the sake of pleasure, but for the procreation of the race. For as it were incongruous, for a mortal born to partake of divine life, the immortality of the race being taken away, God fulfilled the purpose by making the generations uninterrupted and continuous. This, therefore, we are especially to lay down as a

* Letter dated October 28, 1813, from Thomas Jefferson to John Adams, *The Writings of Thomas Jefferson* (Washington, D.C.: The Thomas Jefferson Memorial Association of the U.S., 1905; "Definitive Edition, containing his Autobiography, Notes on Virginia . . . ," edited by Albert Ellery Bergh), XIII, 394–403.

principle, that coition is not for the sake of pleasure." But nature, not trusting to this moral and abstract motive, seems to have provided more securely for the perpetuation of the species, by making it the effect of the *oestrum* implanted in the constitution of both sexes. And not only has the commerce of love been indulged on this unhallowed impulse, but made subservient also to wealth and ambition by marriage, without regard to the beauty, the healthiness, the understanding, or virtue of the subject from which we are to breed. The selecting the best male for a harem of well-chosen females also, which Theognis seems to recommend from the example of our sheep and asses, would doubtless improve the human, as it does the brute animal, and produce a race of veritable αριστοι. For experience proves, that the moral and physical qualities of man, whether good or evil, are transmissible in a certain degree from father to son. But I suspect that the equal rights of men will rise up against this privileged Solomon and his harem, and oblige us to continue acquiescence under the "Αμαυρωσις γενεος αστων" which Theognis complains of, and to content ourselves with the accidental aristoi produced by the fortuitous concourse of breeders. For I agree with you that there is a natural aristocracy among men. The grounds of this are virtue and talents. Formerly, bodily powers gave place among the aristoi. But since the invention of gunpowder has armed the weak as well as the strong with missile death, bodily strength, like beauty, good humor, politeness and other accomplishments, has become but an auxiliary ground of distinction. There is also an artificial aristocracy, founded on wealth and birth, without either virtue or talents; for with these it would belong to the first class. The natural aristocracy I consider as the most precious gift of nature, for the instruction, the trusts, and government of society. And indeed, it would have been inconsistent in creation to have formed man for the social state, and not to have provided virtue and wisdom enough to manage the concerns of the society. May we not even say, that that form of government is the best, which provides the most effectually for a pure selection of these natural aristoi into the offices of government? The artificial aristocracy is a mischievous ingredient in government, and provision should be made to prevent its ascendency. On the question, what is the best provision, you and I differ; but we differ as rational friends, using the free exercise of our own reason, and mutually indulging its errors. You think it best to put the pseudo-aristoi into a separate chamber of legislation, where they may be hindered from doing mischief by their co-ordinate branches, and where, also, they may be a protection to wealth against the agrarian and plundering enterprises of the majority of the people. I think that to give them power in order to prevent them from doing mischief, is arming them for it, and increasing instead of remedying the evil. For if the co-ordinate branches can arrest their action, so may they that of the co-ordinates. Mischief may be done negatively as well as positively. Of this, a cabal in the Senate of the United States has furnished many proofs. Nor do I believe them necessary to protect the wealthy; because enough of these will find their way into every branch of the legislation, to protect themselves. From fifteen to twenty legislatures of our own, in action for thirty years past, have proved that no fears of an equalization of property are to be apprehended from them. I think the best remedy is exactly that provided by all our constitutions, to leave to the citizens the free election and separation of the aristoi from the pseudo-aristoi, of the wheat from the chaff. In general they will elect the really good and wise. In some instances, wealth may corrupt, and birth blind them; but not in sufficient degree to endanger the society.

It is probable that our difference of opinion may, in some measure, be produced by a difference of character in those among whom we live. From what I have seen of Massachusetts and Connecticut myself, and still more from what I have heard, and the character given of the former by yourself, (volume I, page III,) who know them so much better, there seems to be in those two States a traditionary reverence for certain families, which has rendered the offices of the government nearly hereditary in those families. I presume that from an early period of your history, members of those families happening to possess virtue and talents, have honestly exercised them for the good of the people, and by their services have endeared their names to them. In coupling Connecticut with you, I mean it politically only, not morally. For having made the Bible the common law of their land, they seem to have modeled their morality on the story of Jacob and Laban. But although this hereditary succession to office with you, may, in some degree, be founded in real family merit, yet in a much higher degree, it has proceeded from your strict alliance of Church and State. These families are canonized in the eyes of the people on common principles, "you tickle me, and I will tickle you." In Virginia we have nothing of this. Our clergy, before the revolution, having been secured against rivalship by fixed salaries, did not give themselves the trouble of acquiring influence over the people. Of wealth, there were great accumulations in particular families, handed down from generation to generation, under the English law of entails. But the only object of ambition for the wealthy was a seat in the King's Council. All their court then was paid to the crown and its creatures; and they Philipized in all collisions between the King and the people. Hence they were unpopular; and that unpopularity continues attached to their names. A Randolph, a Carter, or a Burwell must have great personal superiority over a common competitor to be elected by the people even at this day. At the first session of our legislature after the Declaration of Independence, we passed a law abolishing entails. And this was followed by one abolishing the privilege of primogeniture, and dividing the lands of intestates equally among all their children, or other representatives. These laws, drawn by myself, laid the axe to the foot of pseudo-aristocracy. And had another which I prepared been adopted by the legislature, our work would have been complete. It was a bill for the more general diffusion of learning. This proposed to divide every county into wards of five or six miles square, like your townships; to establish in each ward a free school for reading, writing and common arithmetic; to provide for the annual selection of the best subjects from these schools, who might receive, at the public expense, a higher degree of education at a district school; and from these district schools to select a certain number of the most promising subjects, to be completed at an university, where all the useful sciences should be taught. Worth and genius would thus have been sought out from every condition of life, and completely prepared by education for defeating the competition of wealth and birth for public trusts. My proposition had, for a further object, to impart to these wards those portions of self-government for which they are best qualified, by confiding to them the care of their poor, their roads, police, elections, the nomination of jurors, administration of justice in small cases, elementary exercises of militia; in short, to have made them little republics, with a warden at the head of each, for all those concerns which, being under their eye, they would better manage than the larger republics of the county or State. A general call of ward meetings by their wardens on the same day through the State, would at any time produce the genuine sense of the people on any required point, and would enable the State to act in mass, as your people have so often done, and with so much effect by their town meetings. The law for religious freedom, which made a part of this system, having put down the aristocracy of the clergy, and restored to the citizen the freedom of the mind, and those of entails and descents nurturing an equality of condition among them, this on education would have raised the mass of the people to

the high ground of moral respectability necessary to their own safety, and to orderly government; and would have completed the great object of qualifying them to select the veritable aristoi, for the trusts of government, to the exclusion of the pseudalists; and the same Theognis who has furnished the epigraphs of your two letters, assures us that "Ουδεμιαν πω, Κυρν', αγαθοι πολιν ωλεσαν ανδρες." [Not any state, Cyrnus, have good men yet destroyed.] Although this law has not yet been acted on but in a small and inefficient degree, it is still considered as before the legislature, with other bills of the revised code, not yet taken up, and I have great hope that some patriotic spirit will, at a favorable moment, call it up, and make it the keystone of the arch of our government.

With respect to aristocracy, we should further consider, that before the establishment of the American States, nothing was known to history but the man of the old world, crowded within limits either small or overcharged, and steeped in the vices which that situation generates. A government adapted to such men would be one thing; but a very different one, that for the man of these States. Here every one may have land to labor for himself, if he chooses; or, preferring the exercise of any other industry, may exact for it such compensation as not only to afford a comfortable subsistence, but wherewith to provide for a cessation from labor in old age. Every one, by his property, or by his satisfactory situation, is interested in the support of law and order. And such men may safely and advantageously reserve to themselves a wholesome control over their public affairs, and a degree of freedom, which, in the hands of the *canaille* of the cities of Europe, would be instantly perverted to the demolition and destruction of everything public and private. The history of the last twenty-five years of France, and of the last forty years in America, nay of its last two hundred years, proves the truth of both parts of this observation.

But even in Europe a change has sensibly taken place in the mind of man. Science had liberated the ideas of those who read and reflect, and the American example had kindled feelings of right in the people. An insurrection has consequently begun, of science, talents, and courage, against rank and birth, which have fallen into contempt. It has failed in its first effort, because the mobs of the cities, the instrument used for its accomplishment, debased by ignorance, poverty, and vice, could not be restrained to rational action. But the world will recover from the panic of this first catastrophe. Science is progressive, and talents and enterprise on the alert. Resort may be had to the people of the country, a more governable power from their principles and subordination; and rank, and birth, and tinsel-aristocracy will finally shrink into insignificance, even there. This, however, we have no right to meddle with. It suffices for us, if the moral and physical condition of our own citizens qualifies them to select the able and good for the direction of their government, with a recurrence of elections at such short periods as will enable them to displace an unfaithful servant, before the mischief he meditates may be irremediable.

I have thus stated my opinion on a point on which we differ, not with a view to controversy, for we are both too old to change opinions which are the result of a long life of inquiry and reflection; but on the suggestions of a former letter of yours, that we ought not to die before we have explained ourselves to each other. We acted in perfect harmony, through a long and perilous contest for our liberty and independence. A constitution has been acquired, which, though neither of us thinks perfect, yet both consider as competent to render our fellow citizens the happiest and the securest on whom the sun has ever shone. If we do not think exactly alike as to its imperfections, it matters little to our country, which, after devoting to it long lives of disinterested labor, we have delivered over to our successors in life, who will be able to take care of it and of themselves.

Of the pamphlet on aristocracy which has been sent to you, or who may be its author, I have heard nothing but through your letter. If the person you suspect, it may be known from the quaint, mystical, and hyperbolical ideas, involved in affected, new-fangled and pedantic terms which stamp his writings. Whatever it be, I hope your quiet is not to be affected at this day by the rudeness or intemperance of scribblers; but that you may continue in tranquillity to live and to rejoice in the prosperity of our country, until it shall be your own wish to take your seat among the aristoi who have gone before you. Ever and affectionately yours.

THOMAS JEFFERSON
Letter to Roger C. Weightman (June 24, 1826)*

MONTICELLO, June 24, 1826.

RESPECTED SIR,—The kind invitation I receive from you, on the part of the citizens of the city of Washington, to be present with them at their celebration on the fiftieth anniversary of American Independence, as one of the surviving signers of an instrument pregnant with our own, and the fate of the world, is most flattering to myself, and heightened by the honorable accompaniment proposed for the comfort of such a journey. It adds sensibly to the sufferings of sickness, to be deprived by it of a personal participation in the rejoicings of that day. But acquiescence is a duty, under circumstances not placed among those we are permitted to control. I should, indeed, with peculiar delight, have met and exchanged there congratulations personally with the small band, the remnant of that host of worthies, who joined with us on that day, in the bold and doubtful election we were to make for our country, between submission or the sword; and to have enjoyed with them the consolatory

* Letter dated June 24, 1826, from Thomas Jefferson to Roger C. Weightman, *The Writings of Thomas Jefferson* (Washington, D.C.: The Thomas Jefferson Memorial Association of the U.S., 1905; "Definitive Edition, containing his Autobiography, Notes on Virginia . . . ," edited by Albert Ellery Bergh), XVI, 181–182.

fact, that our fellow citizens, after half a century of experience and prosperity, continue to approve the choice we made. May it be to the world, what I believe it will be, (to some parts sooner, to others later, but finally to all,) the signal of arousing men to burst the chains under which monkish ignorance and superstition had persuaded them to bind themselves, and to assume the blessings and security of self-government. That form which we have substituted, restores the free right to the unbounded exercise of reason and freedom of opinion. All eyes are opened, or opening, to the rights of man. The general spread of the light of science has already laid open to every view the palpable truth, that the mass of mankind has not been born with saddles on their backs, nor a favored few booted and spurred, ready to ride them

legitimately, by the grace of God. These are grounds of hope for others. For ourselves, let the annual return of this day forever refresh our recollections of these rights, and an undiminished devotion to them.

I will ask permission here to express the pleasure with which I should have met my ancient neighbors of the city of Washington and its vicinities, with whom I passed so many years of a pleasing social intercourse; an intercourse which so much relieved the anxieties of the public cares, and left impressions so deeply engraved in my affections, as never to be forgotten. With my regret that ill health forbids me the gratification of an acceptance, be pleased to receive for yourself and those for whom you write, the assurance of my highest respect and friendly attachments.

RESISTANCE TO ACCULTURATION: THE DUTCH SCENE

WASHINGTON IRVING
"Sleepy Hollow" (1819)*

[FOUND AMONG THE PAPERS OF THE LATE
DIEDRICH KNICKERBOCKER.]

A pleasing land of drowsy head it was,
    Of dreams that wave before the half-shut
        eye,
And of gay castles in the clouds that pass,
    For ever flushing round a summer sky.
                    Castle of Indolence.

In the bosom of one of those spacious coves which indent the eastern shore of the Hudson, at that broad expansion of the river denominated by the ancient Dutch navigators the Tappan Zee, and where they always prudently shortened sail, and implored the protection of St. Nicholas when they crossed, there lies a small market-town or rural port,

* Washington Irving, "The Legend of Sleepy Hollow," from *The Sketch Book of Geoffrey Crayon, Gent.* (Paris, France: Baudry, Bookseller in Foreign Languages, 1831; One Volume Edition, originally published in 1819), pp. 437–448, 458–462, 465–468.

which by some is called Greensburgh, but which is more generally and properly known by the name of Tarry Town. This name was given, we are told, in former days, by the good housewives of the adjacent country, from the inveterate propensity of their husbands to linger about the village tavern on market-days. Be that as it may, I do not vouch for the fact, but merely advert to it for the sake of being precise and authentic. Not far from this village, perhaps about two miles, there is a little valley, or rather lap of land, among high hills, which is one of the quietest places in the whole world. A small brook glides through it, with just murmur enough to lull one to repose; and the occasional whistle of a quail, or tapping of a woodpecker, is almost the only sound that ever breaks in upon the uniform tranquillity.

I recollect that, when a stripling, my first exploit in squirrel-shooting was in a grove of tall walnut-trees that shades one side of the valley. I had wandered into it at noon-time, when all nature is particularly quiet, and was startled by the roar of my own gun, as it broke the Sabbath stillness around, and was prolonged and reverberated by the angry echoes. If ever I should wish for a retreat, whither I might steal from the world and its distractions, and dream quietly away the remnant of a troubled life, I know of none more promising than this little valley.

From the listless repose of the place, and the peculiar character of its inhabitants, who are descendants from the original Dutch settlers, this sequestered glen has long been known by the name of SLEEPY HOLLOW, and its rustic lads are called the Sleepy Hollow Boys throughout all the neighboring country. A drowsy, dreamy influence seems to hang over the land, and to pervade the very atmosphere. Some say that the place was bewitched by a high German doctor, during the early days of the settlement; others, that an old Indian chief, the prophet or wizard of his tribe, held his pow-wows there before the country was discovered by Master Hendrick Hudson. Certain it is, the place still continues under the sway of some bewitching power, that holds a spell over the minds of the good people, causing them to walk in a continual reverie. They are given to all kinds of marvellous beliefs; are subject to trances and visions; and frequently see strange sights, and hear music and voices in the air. The whole neighborhood abounds with local tales, haunted spots, and twilight superstitions; stars shoot and meteors glare oftener across the valley than in any other part of the country, and the nightmare, with her whole ninefold, seems to make it the favorite scene of her gambols. . . .

I mention this peaceful spot with all possible laud; for it is in such little retired Dutch valleys, found here and there embosomed in the great State of New York, that population, manners, and customs remain fixed; while the great torrent of migration and improvement, which is making such incessant changes in other parts of this restless country, sweeps by them unobserved. They are like those little nooks of still water which border a rapid stream; where we may see the straw and bubble riding quietly at anchor, or slowly revolving in their mimic harbor, un-

disturbed by the rush of the passing current. Though many years have elapsed since I trod the drowsy shades of Sleepy Hollow, yet I question whether I should not still find the same trees and the same families vegetating in its sheltered bosom.

In this by-place of nature, there abode, in a remote period of American history, that is to say, some thirty years since, a worthy wight of the name of Ichabod Crane; who sojourned, or, as he expressed it, "tarried," in Sleepy Hollow, for the purpose of instructing the children of the vicinity. He was a native of Connecticut, a State which supplies the Union with pioneers for the mind as well as for the forest, and sends forth yearly its legions of frontier woodsmen and country schoolmasters. The cognomen of Crane was not inapplicable to his person. He was tall, but exceedingly lank, with narrow shoulders, long arms and legs, hands that dangled a mile out of his sleeves, feet that might have served for shovels, and his whole frame most loosely hung together. His head was small, and flat at top, with huge ears, large green glassy eyes, and a long snipe nose, so that it looked like a weathercock perched upon his spindle neck, to tell which way the wind blew. To see him striding along the profile of a hill on a windy day, with his clothes bagging and fluttering about him, one might have mistaken him for the genius of famine descending upon the earth, or some scarecrow eloped from a corn-field.

His school-house was a low building of one large room, rudely constructed of logs; the windows partly glazed, and partly patched with leaves of old copy-books. It was most ingeniously secured at vacant hours by a withe twisted in the handle of the door, and stakes set against the window-shutters; so that, though a thief might get in with perfect ease, he would find some embarrassment in getting out: an idea most probably borrowed by the architect, Yost Van Houten, from the mystery of an eel-pot. The school-house stood in a rather lonely but pleasant situation, just at the foot of a woody hill, with a brook running close by, and a formidable birch-tree growing at one end of it. From hence the low murmur of his pupils' voices, conning over their lessons, might be heard on a drowsy summer's day, like the hum of a bee-hive; interrupted now and then by the authoritative voice of the master, in the tone of menace or command; or, peradventure, by the appalling sound of the birch, as he urged some tardy loiterer along the flowery path of knowledge. Truth to say, he was a conscientious man, and ever bore in mind the golden maxim, "Spare the rod and spoil the child."—Ichabod Crane's scholars certainly were not spoiled.

I would not have it imagined, however, that he was one of those cruel potentates of the school, who joy in the smart of their subjects; on the contrary, he administered justice with discrimination rather than severity, taking the burden off the backs of the weak, and laying it on those of the strong. Your mere puny stripling, that winced at the least flourish of the rod, was passed by with indulgence; but the claims of justice were satisfied by inflicting a double portion on some little, tough, wrong-headed, broad-skirted Dutch urchin, who sulked and swelled and grew dogged and sullen beneath the birch. All this he called "doing his duty" by their parents; and he never inflicted a chastisement without following it by the assurance, so consolatory to the smarting urchin, that "he would remember it, and thank him for it the longest day he had to live."

When school-hours were over, he was even the companion and playmate of the larger boys; and on holiday afternoons would convoy some of the smaller ones home, who happened to have pretty sisters, or good housewives for mothers, noted for the comforts of the cupboard. Indeed it behooved him to keep on good terms with his pupils. The revenue arising from his school was small, and would have been scarcely sufficient to furnish him with daily bread, for he was a huge feeder, and, though lank, had the dilating powers of an anaconda; but to help out his maintenance, he was, according to country custom in those parts, boarded and lodged at the houses of the farmers, whose children he instructed. With these he lived successively a week at a time; thus going the rounds of the neighborhood, with all his worldly effects tied up in a cotton handkerchief.

That all this might not be too onerous on the purses of his rustic patrons, who are apt to consider the costs of schooling a grievous burden, and schoolmasters as mere drones, he had various ways of rendering himself both useful and agreeable. He assisted the farmers occasionally in the lighter labors of their farms; helped to make hay; mended the fences; took the horses to water; drove the cows from pasture; and cut wood for the winter fire. He laid aside, too, all the dominant dignity and absolute sway with which he lorded it in his little empire, the school, and became wonderfully gentle and ingratiating. He found favor in the eyes of the mothers, by petting the children, particularly the youngest; and like the lion bold, which whilom so magnanimously the lamb did hold, he would sit with a child on one knee, and rock a cradle with his foot for whole hours together.

In addition to his other vocations, he was the singing-master of the neighborhood, and picked up many bright shillings by instructing the young folks in psalmody. It was a matter of no little vanity to him, on Sundays, to take his station in front of the church-gallery, with a band of chosen singers; where, in his own mind, he completely carried away the palm from the parson. Certain it is, his voice resounded far above all the rest of the congregation; and there are peculiar quavers still to be heard in that church, and which may even be heard half a mile off, quite to the opposite side of the mill-pond, on a still Sunday morning, which are said to be legitimately descended from the nose of Ichabod Crane. Thus, by divers little makeshifts in that ingenious way which is commonly denominated "by hook and by crook," the worthy pedagogue got on tolerably enough, and was thought, by all who understood nothing of the labor of headwork, to have a wonderfully easy life of it.

The schoolmaster is generally a man of some importance in the female circle of a rural neighborhood; being considered a kind of idle, gentleman-like personage, of vastly superior taste and accomplishments to the rough country swains, and, indeed, inferior in learning only to the parson. His appearance, therefore, is apt to occasion some little stir at the tea-table of a farm-house, and the addition of a supernumerary dish of cakes or sweet-meats, or, peradventure, the parade of a silver tea-pot. Our man of letters, therefore, was peculiarly happy in the smiles of all the country damsels. How he would figure among them in the churchyard, between services on Sundays! gathering grapes for them from the wild vines that overrun the surrounding trees; reciting for their amusement all the epitaphs on the tombstones; or sauntering, with a whole bevy of them, along the banks of the adjacent mill-pond; while the more bashful country bumpkins hung sheepishly back, envying his superior elegance and address.

From his half itinerant life, also, he was a kind of travelling gazette, carrying the whole budget of local gossip from house to house: so that his appearance was always greeted with satisfaction. He was, moreover, esteemed by the women as a man of great erudition, for he had read several books quite through, and was a perfect master of Cotton Mather's *History of New England Witchcraft,* in which, by the way, he most firmly and potently believed.

He was, in fact, an odd mixture of small shrewdness and simple credulity. His appetite for the marvellous, and his powers of digesting it, were equally extraordinary; and both had been increased by his residence in this spellbound region. No tale was too gross or monstrous for his capacious swallow. It was often his delight, after his school was dismissed in the afternoon, to stretch himself on the rich bed of clover bordering the little brook that whimpered by his schoolhouse, and there con over old Mather's direful tales, until the gathering dusk of the evening made the printed page a mere mist before his eyes. Then, as he wended his way, by swamp and stream, and awful woodland, to the farm-house where he happened to be quartered, every sound of nature, at that witching hour, fluttered his excited imagination; the moan of the whippoorwill from the hill-side; the boding cry of the tree-toad, that harbinger of storm; the dreary hooting of the screech-owl, or the sudden rustling in the thicket of birds frightened from their roost. The fire-flies, too, which sparkled most vividly in the darkest places, now and then startled him, as one of uncommon brightness would stream across his path; and if, by chance, a huge blockhead of a beetle came winging his blundering flight against him, the poor varlet was ready to give up the ghost, with the idea that he was struck with a witch's token. His only resource on such occasions, either to drown thought or drive away evil spirits, was to sing psalm-tunes; and the good people of Sleepy Hollow, as they sat by their doors of an evening, were often filled with awe, at hearing his nasal melody, "in linkèd sweetness long drawn out," floating from the distant hill, or along the dusky road.

Another of his sources of fearful pleasure was, to pass long winter evenings with the old Dutch wives, as they sat spinning by the fire, with a row of apples roasting and spluttering along the hearth, and listen to their marvellous tales of ghosts and goblins, and haunted fields, and haunted brooks, and haunted bridges, and haunted houses, and particularly of the headless horseman, or Galloping Hessian of the Hollow, as they sometimes called him. He would delight them equally by his anecdotes of witchcraft, and of the direful omens and portentous sights and sounds in the air, which prevailed in the earlier times of Connecticut; and would frighten them wofully with speculations upon comets and shooting-stars, and with the alarming fact that the world did absolutely turn round, and that they were half the time topsy-turvy!

But if there was a pleasure in all this, while snugly cuddling in the chimney-corner of a chamber that was all of a ruddy glow from the crackling wood-fire, and where, of course, no spectre dared to show his face, it was dearly purchased by the terrors of his subsequent walk homewards. What fearful shapes and shadows beset his path amidst the dim and ghastly glare of a snowy night! —With what wistful look did he eye every trembling ray of light streaming across the waste fields from some distant window!— How often was he appalled by some shrub covered with snow, which, like a sheeted spectre, beset his very path!—How often did he shrink with curdling awe at the sound of his own steps on a frosty crust beneath his feet; and dread to look over his shoulder, lest he should behold some uncouth being tramping close behind him!—and how often was he thrown into complete dismay by some rushing blast, howling among the trees, in the idea that it was the Galloping Hessian on one of his nightly scourings! . . .

On a fine autumnal afternoon, Ichabod, in pensive mood, sat enthroned on the lofty stool whence he usually watched all the concerns of his little literary realm. In his hand he swayed a ferule, that sceptre of despotic power; the birch of justice reposed on three nails, behind the throne, a constant terror to evil-doers; while on the desk before him might be seen sundry contraband articles and prohibited weapons, detected upon the persons of idle urchins; such as half-munched apples, popguns, whirligigs, fly-cages, and whole legions of rampant little paper game-cocks. Apparently there had been some appalling act of justice recently inflicted, for his scholars were all busily intent upon their books, or slyly whispering behind them with one eye kept upon the master; and a kind of buzzing stillness reigned throughout the school-room. It was

suddenly interrupted by the appearance of a negro, in tow-cloth jacket and trousers, a round-crowned fragment of a hat, like the cap of Mercury, and mounted on the back of a ragged, wild, half-broken colt, which he managed with a rope by way of halter. He came clattering up to the school-door with an invitation to Ichabod to attend a merry-making or "quilting frolic," to be held that evening at Mynheer Van Tassel's; and having delivered his message with that air of importance, and effort at fine language, which a negro is apt to display on petty embassies of the kind, he dashed over the brook, and was seen scampering away up the Hollow, full of the importance and hurry of his mission.

All was now bustle and hubbub in the late quiet school-room. The scholars were hurried through their lessons, without stopping at trifles; those who were nimble skipped over half with impunity, and those who were tardy had a smart application now and then in the rear, to quicken their speed, or help them over a tall word. Books were flung aside without being put away on the shelves, inkstands were overturned, benches thrown down, and the whole school was turned loose an hour before the usual time, bursting forth like a legion of young imps, yelping and racketing about the green, in joy at their early emancipation. . . .

It was, as I have said, a fine autumnal day, the sky was clear and serene, and nature wore that rich and golden livery which we always associate with the idea of abundance. The forests had put on their sober brown and yellow, while some trees of the tenderer kind had been nipped by the frosts into brilliant dyes of orange, purple, and scarlet. Streaming files of wild ducks began to make their appearance high in the air; the bark of the squirrel might be heard from the groves of beech and hickory nuts, and the pensive whistle of the quail at intervals from the neighboring stubble-field.

The small birds were taking their farewell banquets. In the fulness of their revelry, they fluttered, chirping and frolicking, from bush to bush, and tree to tree, capricious from the very profusion and variety around them. There was the honest cockrobin, the favorite game of stripling sportsmen, with its loud querulous notes; and the twittering blackbirds flying in sable clouds; and the golden-winged woodpecker, with his crimson crest, his broad black gorget, and splendid plumage; and the cedarbird, with its red-tipt wings and yellow-tipt tail, and its little monteiro cap of feathers; and the blue jay, that noisy coxcomb, in his gay light-blue coat and white under-clothes, screaming and chattering, nodding and bobbing and bowing, and pretending to be on good terms with every songster of the grove.

As Ichabod jogged slowly on his way, his eye, ever open to every symptom of culinary abundance, ranged with delight over the treasures of jolly autumn. On all sides he beheld vast store of apples; some hanging in oppressive opulence on the trees; some gathered into baskets and barrels for the market; others heaped up in rich piles for the cider-press. Farther on he beheld great fields of Indian corn, with its golden ears peeping from their leafy coverts, and holding out the promise of cakes and hasty-pudding; and the yellow pumpkins lying beneath them, turning up their fair round bellies to the sun, and giving ample prospects of the most luxurious of pies. . . .

Ichabod prided himself upon his dancing as much as upon his vocal powers. Not a limb, not a fibre about him was idle; and to have seen his loosely hung frame in full motion, and clattering about the room, you would have thought Saint Vitus himself, that blessed patron of the dance, was figuring before you in person. He was the admiration of all the negroes; who, having gathered, of all ages and sizes, from the farm and the neighborhood, stood forming a pyramid of shining black faces at every door and window, gazing with delight at the scene, rolling their white eyeballs, and showing grinning rows of ivory from ear to ear. How could the flogger of urchins be otherwise than animated and joyous? the lady of his heart was his partner in the dance, and smiling graciously in reply to all his amorous oglings; while Brom Bones, sorely smitten with love and jealousy, sat brooding by himself in one corner.

When the dance was at an end, Ichabod was attracted to a knot of the sager folks, who, with old Van Tassel, sat smoking at one end of the piazza, gossiping over former times, and drawing out long stories about the war.

This neighborhood, at the time of which I am speaking, was one of those highly favored places which abound with chronicle and great men. The British and American line had run near it during the war; it had, therefore, been the scene of marauding, and infested with refugees, cow-boys, and all kinds of border chivalry. Just sufficient time has elapsed to enable each story-teller to dress up his tale with a little becoming fiction, and, in the indistinctness of his recollection, to make himself the hero of every exploit. . . .

But all these were nothing to the tales of ghosts and apparitions that succeeded. The neighborhood is rich in legendary treasures of the kind. Local tales and superstitions thrive best in these sheltered long-settled retreats; but are trampled underfoot by the shifting throng that forms the population of most of our country places. Besides, there is no encouragement for ghosts in most of our villages, for they have scarcely had time to finish their first nap, and turn themselves in their graves before their surviving friends have travelled away from the neighborhood; so that when they turn out at night to walk their rounds, they have no acquaintance left to call upon. This is perhaps the reason why we so seldom hear of ghosts, except in our long-established Dutch communities.

The immediate cause, however, of the prevalence of supernatural stories in these parts was doubtless owing to the vicinity of Sleepy Hollow. There was a contagion in the very air that blew from that haunted region; it breathed forth an atmosphere of dreams and fancies infecting all the land. . . .

THE CHANGING CONTENT OF AMERICAN TEXTBOOKS

NOAH WEBSTER,
The Reforming of Spelling (1789)*

IT has been observed by all writers on the English language, that the orthography or spelling of words is very irregular; the same letters often representing different sounds, and the same sounds often expressed by different letters. For this irregularity, two principal causes may be assigned:

1. THE changes to which the pronunciation of a language is liable, from the progress of science and civilization.

2. THE mixture of different languages, occasioned by revolutions in England, or by a predilection of the learned, for words of foreign growth and ancient origin. . . .

THE question now occurs; ought the Americans to retain these faults which produce innumerable inconveniencies in the acquisition and use of the language, or ought they at once to reform these abuses, and introduce order and regularity into the orthography of the AMERICAN TONGUE?

LET us consider this subject with some attention.

SEVERAL attempts were formerly made in England to rectify the orthography of the language. But I apprehend their schemes failed of success, rather on account of their intrinsic difficulties, than on account of any necessary impracticability of a reform. It was proposed, in most of these schemes, not merely to throw out superfluous and silent letters, but to introduce a number of new characters. Any attempt on such a plan must

* Noah Webster, "An Essay on the Necessity, Advantages, and Practicality of Reforming the MODE of SPELLING and of Rendering the Orthography of Words Correspondent to Pronunciation," *Dissertations on the English Language: with Notes, Historical and Critical, to which is added, by way of Appendix, an Essay on a Reformed Mode of Spelling, with Dr. Franklin's Arguments on that subject* (Boston: Isaiah Thomas and Co., 1789), pp. 391, 393–398, 405–406.

undoubtedly prove unsuccessful. It is not to be expected that an orthography, perfectly regular and simple, such as would be formed by a "Synod of Grammarians on principles of science," will ever be substituted for that confused mode of spelling which is now established. But it is apprehended that great improvements may be made, and an orthography almost regular, or such as shall obviate most of the present difficulties which occur in learning our language, may be introduced and established with little trouble and opposition.

THE principal alterations, necessary to render our orthography sufficiently regular and easy, are these:

1. THE omission of all superfluous or silent letters; as *a* in *bread.* Thus *bread, head, give, breast, built, meant, realm, friend,* would be spelt, *bred, hed, giv, brest, bilt, ment, relm, frend.* Would this alteration produce any inconvenience, any embarrassment or expense? By no means. On the other hand, it would lessen the trouble of writing, and much more, of learning the language; it would reduce the true pronunciation to a certainty; and while it would assist foreigners and our own children in acquiring the language, it would render the pronunciation uniform, in different parts of the country, and almost prevent the possibility of changes.

2. A SUBSTITUTION of a character that has a certain definite sound, for one that is more vague and indeterminate. Thus by putting *ee* instead of *ea* or *ie*, the words *mean, near, speak, grieve, zeal,* would become *meen, neer, speek, greev, zeel.* This alteration could not occasion a moments trouble; at the same time it would prevent a doubt respecting the pronunciation; whereas the *ea* and *ie* having different sounds, may give a learner much difficulty. Thus *greef* should be substituted for *grief;* *kee* for *key;* *beleev* for *believe; laf* for *laugh; dawter* for *daughter; plow* for *plough; tuf* for *tough; proov* for *prove; blud* for *blood;* and *draft* for *draught.* In this

manner *ch* in Greek derivatives, should be changed into *k;* for the English *ch* has a soft sound, as in *cherish;* but *k* always a hard sound. Therefore *character, chorus, cholic, architecture,* should be written *karacter, korus, kolic, arkitecture;* and were they thus written, no person could mistake their true pronunciation.

THUS *ch* in French derivatives should be changed into *sh; machine, chaise, chevalier,* should be written *masheen, shaze, shevaleer;* and *pique, tour, oblique,* should be written *peek, toor, obleek.*

3. A TRIFLING alteration in a character, or the addition of a point would distinguish different sounds, without the substitution of a new character. Thus a very small stroke across *th* would distinguish its two sounds. A point over a vowel, in this manner, *à,* or *û,* or *ī,* might answer all the purposes of different letters. And for the dipthong *ow,* let the two letters be united by a small stroke, or both engraven on the same piece of metal, with the left hand line of the *w* united to the *o.*

THESE, with a few other inconsiderable alterations, would answer every purpose, and render the orthography sufficiently correct and regular.

THE advantages to be derived from these alterations are numerous, great and permanent.

1. THE simplicity of the orthography would facilitate the learning of the language. It is now the work of years for children to learn to spell; and after all, the business is rarely accomplished. A few men, who are bred to some business that requires constant exercise in writing, finally learn to spell most words without hesitation; but most people remain, all their lives, imperfect masters of spelling, and liable to make mistakes, whenever they take up a pen to write a short note. Nay, many people, even of education and fashion, never attempt to write a letter, without frequently consulting a dictionary.

BUT with the proposed orthography, a child would learn to spell, without trouble, in a very short time, and the orthography

being very regular, he would ever afterwards find it difficult to make a mistake. It would, in that case, be as difficult to spell *wrong,* as it is now to spell *right.*

BESIDES this advantage, foreigners would be able to acquire the pronunciation of English, which is now so difficult and embarrassing, that they are either wholly discouraged on the first attempt, or obliged, after many years labor, to rest contented with an imperfect knowledge of the subject.

2. A CORRECT orthography would render the pronunciation of the language, as uniform as the spelling in books. A general uniformity thro the United States, would be the event of such a reformation as I am here recommending. All persons, of every rank, would speak with some degree of precision and uniformity.[1] Such a uniformity in these states is very desireable; it would remove prejudice, and conciliate mutual affection and respect.

3. SUCH a reform would diminish the number of letters about one sixteenth or eighteenth. This would save a page in eighteen; and a saving of an eighteenth in the expense of books, is an advantage that should not be overlooked.

4. BUT a capital advantage of this reform in these states would be, that it would make a difference between the English orthography and the American. This will startle those who have not attended to the subject; but I am confident that such an event is an object of vast political consequence. For,

THE alteration, however small, would encourage the publication of books in our own country. It would render it, in some measure, necessary that all books should be printed in America. The English would never copy our orthography for their own use; and consequently the same impressions of books would not answer for both countries. The inhabit-

[1] I once heard Dr. Franklin remark, "that those people spell best, who do not know how to spell;" that is, they spell as their ears dictate, without being guided by rules, and thus fall into a regular orthography.

ants of the present generation would read the English impressions; but posterity, being taught a different spelling, would prefer the American orthography.

BESIDES this, a *national language* is a band of *national union*. Every engine should be employed to render the people of this country *national;* to call their attachments home to their own country; and to inspire them with the pride of national character. However they may boast of Independence, and the freedom of their government, yet their *opinions* are not sufficiently independent; an astonishing respect for the arts and literature of their parent country, and a blind imitation of its manners, are still prevalent among the Americans. Thus an habitual respect for another country, deserved indeed and once laudable, turns their attention from their own interests, and prevents their respecting themselves. . . .

SENSIBLE I am how much easier it is to *propose* improvements, than to *introduce* them. Every thing *new* starts the idea of difficulty; and yet it is often mere novelty that excites the appearance; for on a slight examination of the proposal, the difficulty vanishes. When we firmly *believe* a scheme to be practicable, the work is *half* accomplished. We are more frequently deterred by fear from making an attack, than repulsed in the encounter.

HABIT also is opposed to changes; for it renders even our errors dear to us. Having surmounted all difficulties in childhood, we forget the labor, the fatigue, and the perplexity we suffered in the attempt, and imagin[e] the progress of our studies to have been smooth and easy.[2] What seems intrinsically right, is so merely thro habit.

[2] Thus most people suppose the present mode of spelling to be really the *easiest* and *best*. This opinion is derived from habit; the new mode of spelling proposed would save three fourths of the labor now bestowed in learning to write our language. A child would learn to spell as well in one year, as he can now in four. This is not a supposition—it is an assertion capable of

INDOLENCE is another obstacle to improvements. The most arduous task a reformer has to execute, is to make people *think;* to rouse them from that lethargy, which, like the mantle of sleep, covers them in repose and contentment.

BUT America is in a situation the most favorable for great reformations; and the present time is, in a singular degree, auspicious. The minds of men in this country have been awakened. New scenes have been, for many years, presenting new occasions for exertion; unexpected distresses have called forth the powers of invention; and the application of new expedients has demanded every possible exercise of wisdom and talents. Attention is roused; the mind expanded; and the intellectual faculties invigorated. Here men are prepared to receive improvements, which would be rejected by nations, whose habits have not been shaken by similar events.

NOW is the time, and *this* the country, in which we may expect success, in attempting changes favorable to language, science and government. Delay, in the plan here proposed, may be fatal; under a tranquil general government, the minds of men may again sink into indolence; a national acquiescence in error will follow; and posterity be doomed to struggle with difficulties, which time and accident will perpetually multiply.

LET us then seize the present moment, and establish a *national language,* as well as a national government. Let us remember that there is a certain respect due to the opinions of other nations. As an independent people, our reputation abroad demands that, in all things, we should be federal; be *national;* for if we do not respect *ourselves,* we may be assured that *other nations* will not respect us. In short, let it be impressed upon

proof; and yet people, never knowing, or having forgot the labor of learning, suppose the present mode to be the easiest. No person, but one who has taught children, has any idea of the difficulty of learning to spell and pronounce our language in its present form.

the mind of every American, that to neglect the means of commanding respect abroad, is treason against the character and dignity of a brave independent people. . . .

WILLIAM HOLMES McGUFFEY
The Eclectic Third Reader (1837)*

SUGGESTIONS TO TEACHERS.

IT is recommended that the pupil be required to *master* every thing as he goes along. He should remember that reading is a *study,* requiring much time and attention.

THE REMARKS on the subject of reading need not, as a general thing, be committed to memory, but only well studied, so as to be understood. They are designed to assist the learner in acquiring correct habits of reading, are generally short and simple, and have a direct, though not *exclusive* reference to the lesson which immediately follows.

THE EXERCISES IN SPELLING, will, it is believed, be found eminently beneficial in fixing in the memory the *orthographical form of words,* not only as they appear in the columns of a spelling-book or dictionary, but in all the variety of their different numbers, oblique cases, degrees of comparison, modes, tenses, and other forms in which they are found in a reading lesson.

THE EXERCISE OF DEFINING produces a similar effect in regard to the meaning of the terms employed. It must be recollected, however, that it is the connection alone, that can convey to the mind, the true meaning of words. No two words in the language are exactly alike in signification. How then can definition, *merely,* be made to convey their import?

THE EXERCISES IN ARTICULATION in the Introduction and between the Reading Lessons, form a new feature in this edition, to which the attention of teachers is particularly invited.

* William Holmes McGuffey, *The Eclectic Reader; consisting of Progressive Lessons in Reading and Spelling* (Cincinnati: Truman and Smith, [1853]; "McGuffey's Third Reader of the Eclectic Series"), pp. 22, 27–31, 55–61.

THE EXERCISES IN ARTICULATION AND PRONUNCIATION, prefixed to each lesson, refer to those errors which are most commonly observed among the imperfectly educated, although they are by no means confined to that class. In marking these errors, it is frequently impossible to express, by *any* combination of letters, the faulty sounds. All that can be accomplished is an indication of the error. The Teacher is requested to use the labors of the compiler here, as in all other particulars, as *hints* rather than *rules,* and thus to exercise his own judgment and good sense in giving extension to the principles involved [here].

THE QUESTIONS appended to each lesson, are, as in the preceding volume, designed to *suggest,* rather than to *direct,* the *interrogative* method of *oral* instruction. The Teacher will frequently find questions the answers to which are not contained in the antecedent lesson, but only suggested by it. This is calculated to awaken inquiry on the part of the pupil, and to lay the instructor under a kind of obligation to read the lesson over carefully, before he attempts to hear it recited by the learner; a plan which the author can not too earnestly recommend in regard to *every possible kind* of teaching.

THIRD READER

. . . . .

LESSON II.

WORDS TO BE SPELLED AND DEFINED.

2. Awk'-ward, clumsy, unhandy.
4. En-tan'-gled, disordered, twisted up.
5. Ex-claim'-ed, cried out.
   As-sist'-ance, aid, help.
   Dis-en-ga'-ged, loosened, made free.
6. Pre-par'-ed, made ready.
   Dig'-ni-ty, majestic manner.
7. Dis-ap-point'-ment, the not obtaining what was expected.
   Dis-cour'-age, to take away courage.
10. Ob-jec'-tion, reason against a measure.
11. Per-se-ver'-ance, continuing in any thing begun.

Mot'-to, a word or short sentence expressing much.

PERSEVERANCE.

UTTER distinctly the *t* and *d*. Lift, not *lif:* kind-ly, not *kine-ly:* chil-dren, not *chil-ren:* hand, not *han:* wind, not *win:* found, not *foun:* stand, not *stan:* de-pends, not *de-pen's.*

1. "Will you give my kite a lift?" said my little nephew to his sister, after trying in vain to make it fly by dragging it along the ground. Lucy very kindly took it up and threw it into the air, but, her brother neglecting to run off at the same moment, the kite fell down again.

2. "Ah! now, how awkward you are!" said the little fellow. "It was your fault entirely," answered his sister. "TRY AGAIN, children," said I.

3. "Lucy once more took up the kite; but now John was in too great a hurry; he ran off so suddenly that he twitched it out of her hand; and the kite fell flat as before. "Well, who is to blame now?" asked Lucy. "TRY AGAIN," said I.

4. They did, and with more care; but a side-wind coming suddenly, as Lucy let go the kite, it was blown against some shrubs, and the tail got entangled in a moment, leaving the poor kite hanging with its head downward.

5. "There, there!" exclaimed John, "that comes of your throwing it all to one side." "As if I could make the wind blow straight," said Lucy. In the mean time, I went to the kite's assistance, and having disengaged the long tail, I rolled it up, saying, "Come, children, there are too many trees here; let us find a more open space, and then TRY AGAIN."

6. We presently found a nice grass plot, at one side of which I took my stand; and all things being prepared, I tossed the kite up just as little John ran off. It rose with all the dignity of a balloon, and promised a lofty flight; but John, delighted to find it pulling so hard at the string, stopped short to look upward and admire. The string slack-

ened, the kite tottered, and, the wind not being very favorable, down came the kite to the grass. "Oh, John, you should not have stopped," said I. "However, TRY AGAIN."

7. "I won't try any more," replied he, rather sullenly. "It is of no use, you see. The kite won't fly, and I do n't want to be plagued with it any longer." "Oh fie, my little man! would you give up the sport, after all the pains we have taken both to make and to fly the kite? A few disappointments ought not to discourage us. Come, I have wound up your string, and now, TRY AGAIN."

8. And he did try, and succeeded, for the kite was carried up on the breeze as lightly as a feather; and when the string was all out, John stood in great delight, holding fast the stick, and gazing on the kite, which now seemed as a little white speck in the blue sky. "Look, look, aunt, how high it flies! and it pulls like a team of horses, so that I can hardly hold it. I wish I had a mile of string; I am sure it would go to the end of it."

"After enjoying the sight as long as he pleased, little John proceeded to roll up the string slowly; and when the kite fell, he took it up with great glee, saying that it was not at all hurt, and that it had behaved very well. "Shall we come out tomorrow, aunt, after lessons, and TRY AGAIN?"

10. "I have no objection, my dear, if the weather is fine. And now, as we walk home, tell me what you have learned from your morning's sport." "I have learned to fly my kite properly." "You may thank aunt for it, brother," said Lucy, "for you would have given it up long ago, if she had not persuaded you to TRY AGAIN."

11. "Yes, my dear children, I wish to teach you the value of PERSEVERANCE, even when nothing more depends upon it than the flying of a kite. Whenever you fail in your attempts to do any good thing, let your motto be, TRY AGAIN."

CHARLOTTE ELIZABETH.

QUESTIONS.—What is the subject of this lesson? Why was John discouraged in his attempts to raise his kite? What did his aunt say to him? What may we learn from this? What should be our motto if we expect to be successful in any undertaking? What note is after the word "lift," in the first sentence? What after the word "are," in the second paragraph? What word can you substitute for "awkward," in the second paragraph? What mark is that over "do n't," in the 7th paragraph and what is its use?

LESSON III.

1. Suc-ceed', to gain the thing desired.
   Cour'-age, resolution.
   Con'quer, to gain the victory.
2. Pre-vail', to overcome.
   Dis-grace', shame.
3. Re-ward', any thing given in return for good or bad conduct.
   Pa'-tience, constancy in labor.

TRY, TRY AGAIN.

REMARK.—To read well is, to convey with the voice fully the meaning contained in the passage which is read. To do this, it is necessary to *understand* what is read.

UTTER each sound *distinctly*. First, not *firss:* ap-pear, not *'pear:* last, not *lass:* task, not *tass:* your re-ward, not *youreward.*

1. 'T is a lesson you should heed,
       Try, try again;
    If at first you do n't succeed,
       Try, try again;
    Then your courage should appear,
    For, if you will persevere,
    You will conquer, never fear;
       Try, try again.

2. Once or twice though you should fail,
       Try, try again;
    If you would, at last, prevail,
       Try, try again;
    If we strive, 't is no disgrace,
    Though we may not win the race;
    What should you do in the case?
       Try, try again.

3. If you find your task is hard,
       Try, try again;

Time will bring you your reward,
   Try, try again;
All that other folks can do,
Why, with patience, should not you?
Only keep this rule in view;
   TRY, TRY AGAIN.
                              T. H. PALMER.

QUESTIONS.—What is the advice contained in this lesson? How many different stops are there in this lesson, and what are they? What mark is that before " 'Tis," in the first line, and what does it here indicate?

TO TEACHERS.

That the pupil may *understand* what he reads, he must know the meaning of all the words that he uses. To aid him in this, some of the more difficult are defined at the head of each lesson. It is recommended, however, that the teacher should examine the class upon the definition of *all* the unusual or difficult words, and that the pupil should be accustomed to discover their meaning from their connection.

ARTICULATION.

To secure the benefit of these exercises, *each sound* composing a syllable, must be dwelt upon, and *carefully, forcibly,* and *distinctly* uttered. Silent letters are sometimes omitted, that they may not mislead with regard to the real sounds, as the *e* in riddle, huddle, &c.

Dr. Drum, drug, drink, droll, dry, hydra.
Dl. Riddl', huddl', ladl' cradl', needl', idl'.

. . . . .

LESSON XIV.

1. Con'-se-quence, importance, influence.
   Dis-grace'-ful, shameful.
2. A-cad'-e-my, a school of high order.
   Col'-lege, a seminary of learning of the highest order.
   Pre-cep'-tor, a teacher.
3. Prep-a-ra'-tion, a making ready.
4. In'-do-lent, lazy.

5. Vig'-or-ous, strong, active.
6. A-lac'-ri-ty, cheerfulness, sprightliness.
8. Pro-fess'-or, a teacher in a college.
9. Lu'-di-crous, adapted to raise laughter.
Ap-plaus'-es, praises.
Dis'-si-pa-ted, given up to vicious habits.
10. Im-prove'-ment, increase of knowledge.

THE CONSEQUENCES
OF IDLENESS.

REMARK.—You will derive interest and instruction from reflecting much upon what you have *read*, and making it, as opportunity offers, the subject of conversation.

ARTICULATE carefully all the consonants in such words as the following: *disgraceful, perception, preparation, recollection, fresh, blunders, professor, trembling, ludicrous, improvement, effects, expecting, persons, prepare, diligently, present, proper, alacrity, frightened, neglected, suspend, reward, industry.*

1. MANY young persons seem to think it of not much consequence if they do not improve their time well in youth, vainly expecting that they can make it up by diligence, when they are older. They also think it is disgraceful for *men* and *women* to be idle, but that there can be no harm for persons who are *young,* to spend their time in any manner they please.

2. George Jones thought so. When he was twelve years old, he went to an academy to prepare to enter college. His father was at great expense in obtaining books for him, clothing him, and paying his tuition. But George was idle. The preceptor of the academy would often tell him, that if he did not study diligently when young, he would never succeed well.

3. But George thought of nothing but present pleasure. He would often go to school without having made any preparation for his morning lesson; and, when called to recite with his class, he would stammer and make such blunders, that the rest of the class could not help laughing at him. He was one of the poorest scholars in the school, because he was one of the most idle.

4. When recess came, and all the boys ran out of the academy upon the play ground, idle George would come moping along. Instead of studying diligently while in school, he was indolent and half asleep. When the proper time for play came, he had no relish for it. I recollect very well, that, when *tossing up* for a game of ball, we used to choose every body on the play ground, before we chose George. And if there were enough without him, we used to leave him out. Thus was he unhappy in school, and out of school.

5. There is nothing which makes a person enjoy play so well, as to study hard. When recess was over, and the rest of the boys returned, fresh and vigorous, to their studies, George might be seen lagging and moping along to his seat. Sometimes he would be asleep in school; sometimes he would pass his time in catching flies, and penning them up in little holes, which he cut in his seat. And sometimes, when the preceptor's back was turned, he would throw a paper ball across the room.

6. When the class was called up to recite, George would come drowsily along, looking as mean and ashamed as though he were going to be whipped. The rest of the class stepped up to the recitation with alacrity, and appeared happy and contented. When it came George's turn to recite, he would be so long in doing it, and make such blunders, that all, most heartily, wished him out of the class.

7. At last George went with his class to enter college. Though he passed a very poor examination, he was admitted with the rest; for those who examined him thought it was possible, that the reason why he did not answer questions better, was because he was frightened. Now came hard times for poor George. In college there is not much mercy shown to bad scholars; and George had neglected his studies so long, that he could not now keep up with his class, let him try ever so hard.

8. He could, without much difficulty, get along in the academy where there were only two or three boys of his own class to laugh at him. But now he had to go into a large recitation room, filled with students from all parts of the country. In the presence of all these, he must rise and recite to a professor. Poor fellow! He paid dearly for his idleness.

9. You would have pitied him, if you could have seen him trembling in his seat, every moment expecting to be called upon to recite. And when he was called upon, he would stand up, and take what the class called a *dead set;* that is, he could not recite at all. Sometimes he would make such ludicrous blunders, that the whole class would burst into a laugh. Such are the applauses an idler gets. He was wretched, of course. He had been idle so long, that he hardly knew how to apply his mind to study. All the good scholars avoided him; they were ashamed to be seen in his company. He became discouraged, and gradually grew dissipated.

10. The officers of the college were soon compelled to suspend him. He returned in a few months, but did no better; and his father was then advised to take him from college. He left college, despised by every one. A few months ago, I met him a poor wanderer, without money and without friends. Such are the wages of idleness. I hope every reader will, from this history, take warning, and "stamp improvement on the wings of time."

11. This story of George Jones, which is a true one, shows how sinful and ruinous it is to be idle. Every child, who would be a Christian, and have a home in heaven, must guard against this sin. But as I have given you one story, which shows the sad effects of indolence, I will now present you with another, more pleasing, which shows the reward of industry.

ABBOTT.

QUESTIONS.—What is this story about? What did George Jones think most about? Was this wise? What gives new pleasure to our sports? Where did George go after he left school? How did he get along in college? What must we do to escape the disgrace which fell upon George? Do you think there is any idleness in heaven?

LESSON XV.

1. His'-to-ry, a description or a narration of events.
2. Con'-science, our own knowledge of right and wrong.
   Game, play, sport.
4. Re-com-mend-a'-tion, speaking in praise of any one.
5. Re-view', to examine again.
   Tran'-quil, quiet, calm.
6. Con-fer'-red, given, bestowed.
7. Grad'-u-a-ted, received a degree from a college.
8. U-ni-vers'-al-ly, by all, without exception.
9. In-va'-ri-a-bly, always, uniformly.
10. Ev'-i-den-ces, proofs.
    Ad-van'-ta-ges, opportunities for getting good.

ADVANTAGES OF INDUSTRY.

REMARK.—In order to read with ease and force, stand erect, hold the head up, and throw the shoulders back.

UTTER each sound *distinctly* and *correctly.* His-to-ry, not *his-t'ry:* dil-i-gent, not *dil'-gent:* gen-er-al-ly, not *gen'r'lly:* of-fi-cers, not *of'cers:* de-liv-er, not *d'liv-er:* in-ter-est-ing, not *in-t'rest-ing:* mis-er-a-ble, not *mis' ra-ble:* ev-i-den-ces, not *ev'den-ces.*

1. I GAVE you the history of George Jones, an idle boy, and showed you the consequences of his idleness. I shall now give you the history of Charles Bullard, a class mate of George. Charles was about the same age with George, and did not possess superior talents. Indeed, I doubt whether he was equal to him, in natural powers of mind.

2. But Charles was a hard student. When quite young, he was always careful and diligent in school. Sometimes, when there was

a *very hard* lesson, instead of going out to play during recess, he would stay in to study. He had resolved that his first object should be to get his lessons well, and then he could play with a good conscience. He loved play as well as any body, and was one of the best players on the ground. I hardly ever saw any boy catch a ball better than he could. When playing any game, every one was glad to get Charles on his side.

3. I have said, that Charles would sometimes stay in, at recess. This, however, was very seldom; it was only when the lessons were very hard indeed. Generally, he was among the first on the play ground, and he was also among the first to go into school, when called. Hard study gave him a relish for play, and play again gave him a relish for hard study, so he was happy both in school and out. The preceptor could not help liking him, for he always had his lessons well committed, and never gave him any trouble.

4. When he went to enter college, the preceptor gave him a good recommendation. He was able to answer all the questions, which were put to him when he was examined. He had studied so well, when he was in the academy, and was so thoroughly prepared for college, that he found it very easy to keep up with his class, and had much time for reading interesting books.

5. But he would always get his lesson well, before he did any thing else, and would review it just before recitation. When called upon to recite, he rose tranquil and happy, and very seldom made mistakes. The officers of the college had a high opinion of him, and he was respected by all the students.

6. There was in the college, a society made up of all the best scholars. Charles was chosen a member of that society. It was the custom to choose some one of the society, to deliver a public address every year. This honor was conferred on Charles; and he had studied so diligently, and read so much, that he delivered an address, which was very interesting to all who heard it.

7. At last he *graduated,* as it is called; that is, he finished his collegiate course, and received his degree. It was known by all that he was a good scholar, and by all that he was respected. His father and mother, brothers and sisters came, on the commencement day, to hear him speak.

8. They all felt gratified, and loved Charles more than ever. Many situations of usefulness and profit were opened to him, for Charles was now an intelligent man, and universally respected. He is still a useful and a happy man. He has a cheerful home, and is esteemed by all who know him.

9. Such are the rewards of industry. How strange it is, that any person should be willing to live in idleness, when it will certainly make him unhappy! The idle boy is almost invariably poor and miserable; the industrious boy is happy and prosperous.

10. But perhaps some child who reads this, asks, "Does God notice little children in school?" He certainly does. And if you are not diligent in the improvement of your time, it is one of the surest evidences that your heart is not right with God. You are placed in this world to improve your time. In youth, you must be preparing for future usefulness. And if you do not improve the advantages you enjoy, you sin against your Maker.

"With books, or work, or healthful play,
  Let your first years be past,
That you may give, for every day,
  Some good account at last."

ABBOTT.

QUESTIONS.—What is the subject of this lesson? In what respect was Charles Bullard different from George Jones? Which of them do you think most worthy of imitation? For what are we placed in this world? Should you not then be diligent in your studies? How should you sit or stand when you read? What word can you put in the place of "conferred," in the 6th paragraph? Why does the word "Maker" commence with a capital letter?

In the last paragraph what part of speech is *child? God? school? time? heart? little?*

diligent? future? healthful? How are adjectives compared? What adjective of the superlative degree is there in the last paragraph? Compare it. What does the word *superlative* mean?

ARTICULATION.

Nt. Point, oint, joint, blunt[2], hunt[2], front[6].

Nj. Hinge[2], cringe[2], singe[2], twinge[2], tinge[2], plunge[2].

Nch. Bunch[2], punch[2], branch[2], stanch[3], bench[2], wench[2].

CHAPTER FIVE

New Foundations for Public Education

THE RISE OF THE COMMON MAN

MARGARET BAYARD SMITH
"The People's President": An Eyewitness Account of Andrew Jackson's Inauguration (March, 1829)*

[Washington] March 11th, Sunday [1829.] . . . Thursday morning. I left the rest of this sheet for an account of the inauguration. It was not a thing of detail of a succession of small incidents. No, it was one grand whole, an imposing and majestic spectacle and to a reflective mind one of moral sublimity. Thousands and thousands of people, without distinction of rank, collected in an immense mass round the Capitol, silent, orderly and tranquil, with their eyes fixed on the front of that edifice, waiting the appearance of the President in the portico. The door from the Rotunda opens, preceded by the marshals, surrounded by the Judges of the Supreme Court, the old man with his grey locks, that crown of glory, advances, bows to the people, who greet him with a shout that rends the air, the Cannons, from the heights around, from Alexandria and Fort Warburton proclaim the oath he has taken and all the hills reverberate the sound.

* Letter dated March 11, 1829, from Mrs. Margaret Bayard Smith to her sister, Mrs. Jane Kirkpatrick, as reprinted in *The First Forty Years of Washington Society Portrayed by the Family Letters of Mrs. Samuel Harrison Smith* (*Margaret Bayard*) (New York: Scribner, 1906; edited by Gaillard Hunt), pp. 290–297. Mrs. Smith's husband was president of the Washington branch of the Bank of the United States until the office was abolished in 1835.

It was grand,—it was sublime! An almost breathless silence, succeeded and the multitude was still,—listening to catch the sound of his voice, tho' it was so low, as to be heard only by those nearest to him. After reading his speech, the oath was administered to him by the Chief Justice. The Marshal presented the Bible. The President took it from his hands, pressed his lips to it, laid it reverently down, then bowed again to the people—Yes, to the people in all their majesty. And had the spectacle closed here, even Europeans must have acknowledged that a free people, collected in their might, silent and tranquil, restrained solely by a moral power, without a shadow around of military force, was majesty, rising to sublimity, and far surpassing the majesty of Kings and Princes, surrounded with armies and glittering in gold. But I will not anticipate, but will give you an account of the inauguration in mere detail. The whole of the preceding day, immense crowds were coming into the city from all parts, lodgings could not be obtained, and the newcomers had to go to George Town, which soon overflowed and others had to go to Alexandria. I was told the Avenue and adjoining streets were so crowded on Tuesday afternoon that it was difficult to pass.

A national salute was fired early in the morning, and ushered in the 4th of March. By ten oclock the Avenue was crowded with carriages of every description, from the splendid Barronet and coach, down to waggons and carts, filled with women and children, some in finery and some in rags, for it was the peoples President, and all would see him; the men all walked. . . . We stood on the South steps of the terrace; when the appointed hour came saw the General and his company advancing up the Avenue, slow, very slow, so impeded was his march by the crowds thronging around him. Even from a distance, he could be discerned from those who accompanied him, for he only was uncovered, (the Servant in presence of his Sovereign, the People). The south side of the Capitol hill was literally alive with the multitude, who stood ready to receive the hero and the multitude who attended him. "There, there, that is he," exlaimed different voices. "Which?" asked others. "He with the white head," was the reply. "Ah," exclaimed others, "there is the old man and his gray hair, there is the old veteran, there is Jackson." At last he enters the gate at the foot of the hill and turns to the road that leads round to the front of the Capitol. In a moment every one who until then had stood like statues gazing on the scene below them, rushed onward, to right, to left, to be ready to receive him in the front. Our party, of course, were more deliberate, we waited until the multitude had rushed past us and then left the terrace and walked round to the furthest side of the square, where there were no carriages to impede us, and entered it by the gate fronting the Capitol. Here was a clear space, and stationing ourselves on the central gravel walk we stood so as to have a clear, full view of the whole scene. The Capitol in all its grandeur and beauty. The Portico and grand steps leading to it, were filled with ladies. Scarlet, purple, blue, yellow, white draperies and waving plumes of every kind and colour, among the white marble pillars, had a fine effect. In the centre of the portico was a table covered with scarlet, behind it the closed door leading into the rotunda, below the Capitol and all around, a mass of living beings, not a ragged mob, but well dressed and well behaved respectable and worthy citizens. Mr. Frank Key, whose arm I had, and an old and frequent witness of great spectacles, often exclaimed, as well as myself, a mere novice, "It is beautiful, it is sublime!" The sun had been obscured through the morning by a mist, or haziness. But the concussion in the air, produced by the discharge of the cannon, dispersed it and the sun shone forth in all his brightness. At the moment the General entered the Portico and advanced to the table, the shout that rent the air, still resounds in my ears. When the speech was over, and the President made his parting bow, the barrier that had separated the people from him was broken down and they rushed up the steps all eager to shake hands with him. It was with difficulty he made his way through the Capitol and down the hill to the gateway that opens on the avenue. Here for a moment he was stopped. The living mass was impenetrable. After a while a passage was opened, and he mounted his horse which had been provided for his return (for he had walked to the Capitol) then such a cortege as followed him! Country men, farmers, gentlemen, mounted and dismounted, boys, women and children, black and white. Carriages, wagons and carts all pursuing him to the President's house. . . .

The day was delightful, the scene animating, so we walked backward and forward at every turn meeting some new acquaintance and stopping to talk and shake hands. Among others we met Zavr. Dickinson with Mr. Frelinghuysen and Dr. Elmendorf, and Mr. Saml Bradford. We continued promenading here, until near three, returned home unable to stand and threw ourselves on the sopha. Some one came and informed us the crowd before the President's house, was so far lessen'd, that they thought we might enter. This time we effected our purpose. But what a scene did we witness! The *Majesty of the People* had disappeared, and a rabble, a mob, of boys, negros, women, children, scrambling fighting, romping. What a pity what a pity! No arrangements had been made no police officers placed on duty and the whole house had been inundated by the rabble mob. We came too late. The President, after having been *literally* nearly pressed to death and almost suffocated and torn to pieces by the people in their eagerness to shake hands with Old Hickory, had retreated through the back way or south front and had escaped to his lodgings at Gadsby's. Cut glass and china to the amount of several thousand dollars had been broken in the struggle to get the refreshments, punch and other articles had been carried out in tubs and buckets, but had it been in hogsheads it would have been insufficient, ice-creams, and cake and lemonade, for 20,000 people, for it is said that number were there, tho' I think the estimate exaggerated. Ladies fainted, men were seen with bloody noses and such a scene of confusion took place as is impossible to describe,—those who got in could not get out by the door again, but had to scramble out of windows. At one time, the President who had retreated and retreated until he was pressed against the wall, could only be secured by a number of gentlemen forming round him and making a kind of barrier of their own bodies, and the pressure was so great that Col Bomford who was one said that at one time he was afraid they should have been pushed down, or on the President. It was then the windows were thrown open, and the torrent found an outlet, which otherwise might have proved fatal.

This concourse had not been anticipated and therefore not provided against. Ladies and gentlemen, only had been expected at this Levee, not the people en masse. But it was the People's day, and the People's President and the People would rule. God grant that one day or other, the People, do not put down all rule and rulers. I fear, enlightened Freemen as they are, they will be found, as they have been found in all ages and countries where they get the Power in their hands, that of all tyrants, they are the most ferocious, cruel and despotic. The no[is]y and disorderly rabble in the President's House brought to my mind descriptions I had read, of the mobs in the Tuileries and at Versailles, I expect to hear the carpets and furniture are ruined, the streets were muddy, and these guests all went thither on foot.

The rest of the day, overcome with fatigue I lay upon the sopha. . . .

INDIVIDUALISM AND REFORM: THE EMERSONIAN CONCEPTION

RALPH WALDO EMERSON
"Self-Reliance" (1841)*

> "Ne te quæsiveris extra."

MAN is his own star; and the soul that can
Render an honest and a perfect man,
Commands all light, all influence, all fate;
Nothing to him falls early or too late.
Our acts our angels are, or good or ill,
Our fatal shadows that walk by us still.
*Epilogue to Beaumont and Fletcher's
Honest Man's Fortune.*

* Ralph Waldo Emerson, "Self-Reliance" (1841), *Essays: First Series* (Boston and New York: Houghton Mifflin, 1865; Centenary Edition of *The Complete Works of Ralph Waldo Emerson*, Vol. II), pp. 43–90.

Cast the bantling on the rocks,
Suckle him with the she-wolf's teat,
Wintered with the hawk and fox,
Power and speed be hands and feet.

I read the other day some verses written by an eminent painter which were original and not conventional. The soul always hears an admonition in such lines, let the subject be what it may. The sentiment they instil is of more value than any thought they may contain. To believe your own thought, to believe that what is true for you in your private heart is true for all men,—that is genius. Speak your latent conviction, and it shall be the universal sense; for the inmost in due time becomes the outmost, and our first thought is rendered back to us by the trumpets of the Last Judgment. Familiar as the voice of the mind is to each, the highest merit we ascribe to Moses, Plato and Milton is that they set at naught books and traditions, and spoke not what men, but what *they* thought. A man should learn to detect and watch that gleam of light which flashes across his mind from within, more than the lustre of the firmament of bards and sages. Yet he dismisses without notice his thought, because it is his. In every work of genius we recognize our own rejected thoughts; they come back to us with a certain alienated majesty. Great works of art have no more affecting lesson for us than this. They teach us to abide by our spontaneous impression with good-humored inflexibility then most when the whole cry of voices is on the other side. Else to-morrow a stranger will say with masterly good sense precisely what we have thought and felt all the time, and we shall be forced to take with shame our own opinion from another.

There is a time in every man's education when he arrives at the conviction that envy is ignorance; that imitation is suicide; that he must take himself for better for worse as his portion; that though the wide universe is full of good, no kernel of nourishing corn can come to him but through his toil bestowed on that plot of ground which is given to him to till. The power which resides in him is new in nature, and none but he knows what that is which he can do, nor does he know until he has tried. Not for nothing one face, one character, one fact, makes much impression on him, and another none. This sculpture in the memory is not without preëstablished harmony. The eye was placed where one ray should fall, that it might testify of that particular ray. We but half express ourselves, and are ashamed of that divine idea which each of us represents. It may be safely trusted as proportionate and of good issues, so it be faithfully imparted, but God will not have his work made manifest by cowards. A man is relieved and gay when he has put his heart into his work and

done his best; but what he has said or done otherwise shall give him no peace. It is a deliverance which does not deliver. In the attempt his genius deserts him; no muse befriends; no invention, no hope.

Trust thyself: every heart vibrates to that iron string. Accept the place the divine providence has found for you, the society of your contemporaries, the connection of events. Great men have always done so, and confided themselves childlike to the genius of their age, betraying their perception that the absolutely trustworthy was seated at their heart, working through their hands, predominating in all their being. And we are now men, and must accept in the highest mind the same transcendent destiny; and not minors and invalids in a protected corner, not cowards fleeing before a revolution, but guides, redeemers and benefactors, obeying the Almighty effort and advancing on Chaos and the Dark.

What pretty oracles nature yields us on this text in the face and behavior of children, babes, and even brutes! That divided and rebel mind, that distrust of a sentiment because our arithmetic has computed the strength and means opposed to our purpose, these have not. Their mind being whole, their eye is as yet unconquered, and when we look in their faces we are disconcerted. Infancy conforms to nobody; all conform to it; so that one babe commonly makes four or five out of the adults who prattle and play to it. So God has armed youth and puberty and manhood no less with its own piquancy and charm, and made it enviable and gracious and its claims not to be put by, if it will stand by itself. Do not think the youth has no force, because he cannot speak to you and me. Hark! in the next room his voice is sufficiently clear and emphatic. It seems he knows how to speak to his contemporaries. Bashful or bold then, he will know how to make us seniors very unnecessary.

The nonchalance of boys who are sure of a dinner, and would disdain as much as a lord to do or say aught to conciliate one, is the healthy attitude of human nature. A boy is in the parlor what the pit is in the play-house; independent, irresponsible, looking out from his corner on such people and facts as pass by, he tries and sentences them on their merits, in the swift, summary way of boys, as good, bad, interesting, silly, eloquent, troublesome. He cumbers himself never about consequences, about interests; he gives an independent, genuine verdict. You must court him; he does not court you. But the man is as it were clapped into jail by his consciousness. As soon as he has once acted or spoken with *éclat* he is a committed person, watched by the sympathy or the hatred of hundreds, whose affections must now enter into his account. There is no Lethe for this. Ah, that he could pass again into his neutrality! Who can thus avoid all pledges and, having observed, observe again from the same unaffected, unbiased, unbribable, unaffrighted innocence,—must always be formidable. He would utter opinions on all passing affairs, which being seen to be not private but necessary, would sink like darts into the ear of men and put them in fear.

These are the voices which we hear in solitude, but they grow faint and inaudible as we enter into the world. Society everywhere is in conspiracy against the manhood of every one of its members. Society is a joint-stock company, in which the members agree, for the better securing of his bread to each shareholder, to surrender the liberty and culture of the eater. The virtue in most request is conformity. Self-reliance is its aversion. It loves not realities and creators, but names and customs.

Whoso would be a man, must be a non-conformist. He who would gather immortal palms must not be hindered by the name of goodness, but must explore if it be goodness. Nothing is at last sacred but the integrity of your own mind. Absolve you to yourself, and you shall have the suffrage of the world. I remember an answer which when quite young I was prompted to make to a valued adviser who was wont to importune me with the dear old doctrines of the church. On my

saying, "What have I to do with the sacredness of traditions, if I live wholly from within?" my friend suggested,—"But these impulses may be from below, not from above." I replied, "They do not seem to me to be such; but if I am the Devil's child, I will live then from the Devil." No law can be sacred to me but that of my nature. Good and bad are but names very readily transferable to that or this; the only right is what is after my constitution; the only wrong what is against it. A man is to carry himself in the presence of all opposition as if every thing were titular and ephemeral but he. I am ashamed to think how easily we capitulate to badges and names, to large societies and dead institutions. Every decent and well-spoken individual affects and sways me more than is right. I ought to go upright and vital, and speak the rude truth in all ways. If malice and vanity wear the coat of philanthropy, shall that pass? If an angry bigot assumes this bountiful cause of Abolition, and comes to me with his last news from Barbadoes, why should I not say to him, 'Go love thy infant; love thy wood-chopper; be good-natured and modest; have that grace; and never varnish your hard, uncharitable ambition with this incredible tenderness for black folk a thousand miles off. Thy love afar is spite at home.' Rough and graceless would be such greeting, but truth is handsomer than the affectation of love. Your goodness must have some edge to it,—else it is none. The doctrine of hatred must be preached, as the counteraction of the doctrine of love, when that pules and whines. I shun father and mother and wife and brother when my genius calls me. I would write on the lintels of the door-post, *Whim*. I hope it is somewhat better than whim at last, but we cannot spend the day in explanation. Expect me not to show cause why I seek or why I exclude company. Then again, do not tell me, as a good man did to-day, of my obligation to put all poor men in good situations. Are they *my* poor? I tell thee, thou foolish philanthropist, that I grudge the dollar, the dime, the cent I give to such men as do not belong to me and to whom I do not belong. There is a class of persons to whom by all spiritual affinity I am bought and sold; for them I will go to prison if need be; but your miscellaneous popular charities; the education at college of fools; the building of meeting-houses to the vain end to which many now stand; alms to sots, and the thousand-fold Relief Societies;—though I confess with shame I sometimes succumb and give the dollar, it is a wicked dollar, which by and by I shall have the manhood to withhold.

Virtues are, in the popular estimate, rather the exception than the rule. There is the man *and* his virtues. Men do what is called a good action, as some piece of courage or charity, much as they would pay a fine in expiation of daily non-appearance on parade. Their works are done as an apology or extenuation of their living in the world,—as invalids and the insane pay a high board. Their virtues are penances. I do not wish to expiate, but to live. My life is for itself and not for a spectacle. I much prefer that it should be of a lower strain, so it be genuine and equal, than that it should be glittering and unsteady. I wish it to be sound and sweet, and not to need diet and bleeding. I ask primary evidence that you are a man, and refuse this appeal from the man to his actions. I know that for myself it makes no difference whether I do or forbear those actions which are reckoned excellent. I cannot consent to pay for a privilege where I have intrinsic right. Few and mean as my gifts may be, I actually am, and do not need for my own assurance or the assurance of my fellows any secondary testimony.

What I must do is all that concerns me, not what the people think. This rule, equally arduous in actual and in intellectual life, may serve for the whole distinction between greatness and meanness. It is the harder because you will always find those who think they know what is your duty better than you know it. It is easy in the world to live after the world's opinion; it is easy in solitude to live after our own; but the great man is he who in the midst of the crowd keeps with perfect sweetness the independence of solitude.

The objection to conforming to usages that have become dead to you is that it scatters your force. It loses your time and blurs the impression of your character. If you maintain a dead church, contribute to a dead Bible-society, vote with a great party either for the government or against it, spread your table like base housekeepers,—under all these screens I have difficulty to detect the precise man you are: and of course so much force is withdrawn from your proper life. But do your work, and I shall know you. Do your work, and you shall reinforce yourself. A man must consider what a blindman's-buff is this game of conformity. If I know your sect I anticipate your argument. I hear a preacher announce for his text and topic the expediency of one of the institutions of his church. Do I not know beforehand that not possibly can he say a new and spontaneous word? Do I not know that with all this ostentation of examining the grounds of the institution he will do no such thing? Do I not know that he is pledged to himself not to look but at one side, the permitted side, not as a man, but as a parish minister? He is a retained attorney, and these airs of the bench are the emptiest affectation. Well, most men have bound their eyes with one or another handkerchief, and attached themselves to some one of these communities of opinion. This conformity makes them not false in a few particulars, authors of a few lies, but false in all particulars. Their every truth is not quite true. Their two is not the real two, their four not the real four; so that every word they say chagrins us and we know not where to begin to set them right. Meantime nature is not slow to equip us in the prison-uniform of the party to which we adhere. We come to wear one cut of face and figure, and acquire by degrees the gentlest asinine expression. There is a mortifying experience in particular, which does not fail to wreak itself also in the general history; I mean "the foolish face of praise," the forced smile which we put on in company where we do not feel at ease, in answer to conversation which does not interest us. The muscles, not spontaneously moved but moved by a low usurping wilfulness, grow tight about the outline of the face, with the most disagreeable sensation.

For nonconformity the world whips you with its displeasure. And therefore a man must know how to estimate a sour face. The by-standers look askance on him in the public street or in the friend's parlor. If this aversion had its origin in contempt and resistance like his own he might well go home with a sad countenance; but the sour faces of the multitude, like their sweet faces, have no deep cause, but are put on and off as the wind blows and a newspaper directs. Yet is the discontent of the multitude more formidable than that of the senate and the college. It is easy enough for a firm man who knows the world to brook the rage of the cultivated classes. Their rage is decorous and prudent, for they are timid, as being very vulnerable themselves. But when to their feminine rage the indignation of the people is added, when the ignorant and the poor are aroused, when the unintelligent brute force that lies at the bottom of society is made to growl and mow, it needs the habit of magnanimity and religion to treat it godlike as a trifle of no concernment.

The other terror that scares us from self-trust is our consistency; a reverence for our past act or word because the eyes of others have no other data for computing our orbit than our past acts, and we are loth to disappoint them.

But why should you keep your head over your shoulder? Why drag about this corpse of your memory, lest you contradict somewhat you have stated in this or that public place? Suppose you should contradict yourself; what then? It seems to be a rule of wisdom never to rely on your memory alone, scarcely even in acts of pure memory, but to bring the past for judgment into the thousand-eyed present, and live ever in a new day. In your metaphysics you have denied personality to the Deity, yet when the devout motions of the soul come, yield to them heart and life, though they should clothe God with shape and color. Leave your theory, as Joseph his coat in the hand of the harlot, and flee.

A foolish consistency is the hobgoblin of little minds, adored by little statesmen and philosophers and divines. With consistency a great soul has simply nothing to do. He may as well concern himself with his shadow on the wall. Speak what you think now in hard words and to-morrow speak what to-morrow thinks in hard words again, though it contradict every thing you said to-day.— 'Ah, so you shall be sure to be misunderstood.'—Is it so bad then to be misunderstood? Pythagoras was misunderstood, and Socrates, and Jesus, and Luther, and Copernicus, and Galileo, and Newton, and every pure and wise spirit that ever took flesh. To be great is to be misunderstood.

I suppose no man can violate his nature. All the sallies of his will are rounded in by the law of his being, as the inequalties of Andes and Himmaleh are insignificant in the curve of the sphere. Nor does it matter how you gauge and try him. A character is like an acrostic or Alexandrian stanza;— read it forward, backward, or across, it still spells the same thing. In this pleasing contrite wood-life which God allows me, let me record day by day my honest thought without prospect or retrospect, and, I cannot doubt, it will be found symmetrical, though I mean it not and see it not. My book should smell of pines and resound with the hum of insects. The swallow over my window should interweave that thread or straw he carries in his bill into my web also. We pass for what we are. Character teaches above our wills. Men imagine that they communicate their virtue or vice only by overt actions, and do not see that virtue or vice emit a breath every moment.

There will be an agreement in whatever variety of actions, so they be each honest and natural in their hour. For of one will, the actions will be harmonious, however unlike they seem. These varieties are lost sight of at a little distance, at a little height of thought. One tendency unites them all. The voyage of the best ship is a zigzag line of a hundred tacks. See the line from a sufficient distance, and it straightens itself to the average tendency. Your genuine action will explain itself and will explain your other genuine actions. Your conformity explains nothing. Act singly, and what you have already done singly will justify you now. Greatness appeals to the future. If I can be firm enough to-day to do right and scorn eyes, I must have done so much right before as to defend me now. Be it how it will, do right now. Always scorn appearances and you always may. The force of character is cumulative. All the foregone days of virtue work their health into this. What makes the majesty of the heroes of the senate and the field, which so fills the imagination? The consciousness of a train of great days and victories behind. They shed a united light on the advancing actor. He is attended as by a visible escort of angels. That is it which throws thunder into Chatham's voice, and dignity into Washington's port, and America into Adams's eye. Honor is venerable to us because it is no ephemera. It is always ancient virtue. We worship it to-day because it is not of to-day. We love it and pay it homage because it is not a trap for our love and homage, but is self-dependent, self-derived, and therefore of an old immaculate pedigree, even if shown in a young person.

I hope in these days we have heard the last of conformity and consistency. Let the words be gazetted and ridiculous henceforward. Instead of the gong for dinner, let us hear a whistle from the Spartan fife. Let us never bow and apologize more. A great man is coming to eat at my house. I do not wish to please him; I wish that he should wish to please me. I will stand here for humanity, and though I would make it kind, I would make it true. Let us affront and reprimand the smooth mediocrity and squalid contentment of the times, and hurl in the face of custom and trade and office, the fact which

is the upshot of all history, that there is a great responsible Thinker and Actor working wherever a man works; that a true man belongs to no other time or place, but is the centre of things. Where he is, there is nature. He measures you and and all men and all events. Ordinarily, every body in society reminds us of somewhat else, or of some other person. Character, reality, reminds you of nothing else; it takes place of the whole creation. The man must be so much that he must make all circumstances indifferent. Every true man is a cause, a country, and an age; requires infinite spaces and numbers and time fully to accomplish his design; —and posterity seem to follow his steps as a train of clients. A man Cæsar is born, and for ages after we have a Roman Empire. Christ is born, and millions of minds so grow and cleave to his genius that he is confounded with virtue and the possible of man. An institution is the lengthened shadow of one man; as, Monachism, of the Hermit Antony; the Reformation, of Luther; Quakerism, of Fox; Methodism, of Wesley; Abolition, of Clarkson. Scipio, Milton called "the height of Rome;" and all history resolves itself very easily into the biography of a few stout and earnest persons.

Let a man then know his worth, and keep things under his feet. Let him not peep or steal, or skulk up and down with the air of a charity-boy, a bastard, or an interloper in the world which exists for him. But the man in the street, finding no worth in himself which corresponds to the force which built a tower or sculptured a marble god, feels poor when he looks on these. To him a palace, a statue, or a costly book have an alien and forbidding air, much like a gay equipage, and seem to say like that, "Who are you, Sir?" Yet they all are his, suitors for his notice, petitioners to his faculties that they will come out and take possession. The picture waits for my verdict; it is not to command me, but I am to settle its claims to praise. That popular fable of the sot who was picked up dead-drunk in the street, carried to the duke's house, washed and dressed and laid in the duke's bed, and, on his waking, treated with all obsequious ceremony like the duke, and assured that he had been insane, owes its popularity to the fact that it symbolizes so well the state of man, who is in the world a sort of sot, but now and then wakes up, exercises his reason and finds himself a true prince.

Our reading is mendicant and sycophantic. In history our imagination plays us false. Kingdom and lordship, power and estate, are a gaudier vocabulary than private John and Edward in a small house and common day's work; but the things of life are the same to both; the sum total of both is the same. Why all this deference to Alfred and Scanderbeg and Gustavus? Suppose they were virtuous; did they wear out virtue? As great a stake depends on your private act to-day as followed their public and renowned steps. When private men shall act with original views, the lustre will be transferred from the actions of kings to those of gentlemen.

The world has been instructed by its kings, who have so magnetized the eyes of nations. It has been taught by this colossal symbol the mutual reverence that is due from man to man. The joyful loyalty with which men have everywhere suffered the king, the noble, or the great proprietor to walk among them by a law of his own, make his own scale of men and things and reverse theirs, pay for benefits not with money but with honor, and represent the law in his person, was the hieroglyphic by which they obscurely signified their consciousness of their own right and comeliness, the right of every man.

The magnetism which all original action exerts is explained when we inquire the reason of self-trust. Who is the Trustee? What is the aboriginal Self, on which a universal reliance may be grounded? What is the nature and power of that science-baffling star, without parallax, without calculable elements, which shoots a ray of beauty even into trivial and impure actions, if the least mark of independence appear? The inquiry leads us to that source, at once the essence of genius, of virtue, and of life, which we call Spontaneity or Instinct. We denote this primary wisdom as Intuition, whilst all later teachings are tuitions. In that deep force, the last fact behind which analysis cannot go, all things find their common origin. For the sense of being which in calm hours rises, we know not how, in the soul, is not diverse from things, from space, from light, from time, from man, but one with them and proceeds obviously from the same source whence their life and being also proceed. We first share the life by which things exist and afterwards see them as appearances in nature and forget that we have shared their cause. Here is the fountain of action and of thought. Here are the lungs of that inspiration which giveth man wisdom and which cannot be denied without impiety and atheism. We lie in the lap of immense intelligence, which makes us receivers of its truth and organs of its activity. When we discern justice, when we discern truth, we do nothing of ourselves, but allow a passage to its beams. If we ask whence this comes, if we seek to pry into the soul that causes, all philosophy is at fault. Its presence or its absence is all we can affirm. Every man discriminates between the voluntary acts of his mind and his involuntary perceptions, and knows that to his involuntary perceptions a perfect faith is due. He may err in the expression of them, but he knows that these things are so, like day and night, not to be disputed. My wilful actions and acquisitions are but roving;—the idlest reverie, the faintest native emotion, command my curiosity and respect. Thoughtless people contradict as readily the statement of perceptions as of opinions, or rather much more readily; for they do not distinguish between perception and notion. They fancy that I choose to see this or that thing. But perception is not whimsical, but fatal. If I see a trait, my children will see it after me, and in course of time all mankind,—although it may chance that no one has seen it before me. For my perception of it is as much a fact as the sun.

The relations of the soul to the divine

spirit are so pure that it is profane to seek to interpose helps. It must be that when God speaketh he should communicate, not one thing, but all things; should fill the world with his voice; should scatter forth light, nature, time, souls, from the centre of the present thought; and new date and new create the whole. Whenever a mind is simple and receives a divine wisdom, old things pass away,—means, teachers, texts, temples fall; it lives now, and absorbs past and future into the present hour. All things are made sacred by relation to it,—one as much as another. All things are dissolved to their centre by their cause, and in the universal miracle petty and particular miracles disappear. If therefore a man claims to know and speak of God and carries you backward to the phraseology of some old mouldered nation in another country, in another world, believe him not. Is the acorn better than the oak which is its fulness and completion? Is the parent better than the child into whom he has cast his ripened being? Whence then this worship of the past? The centuries are conspirators against the sanity and authority of the soul. Time and space are but physiological colors which the eye makes, but the soul is light: where it is, is day; where it was, is night; and history is an impertinence and an injury if it be any thing more than a cheerful apologue or parable of my being and becoming.

Man is timid and apologetic; he is no longer upright; he dares not say 'I think,' 'I am,' but quotes some saint or sage. He is ashamed before the blade of grass or the blowing rose. These roses under my window make no reference to former roses or to better ones; they are for what they are; they exist with God to-day. There is no time to them. There is simply the rose; it is perfect in every moment of its existence. Before a leaf-bud has burst, its whole life acts; in the full-blown flower there is no more; in the leafless root there is no less. Its nature is satisfied and it satisfies nature in all moments alike. But man postpones or remembers; he does not live in the present, but with reverted eye laments the past, or, heedless of the riches that surround him, stands on tiptoe to foresee the future. He cannot be happy and strong until he too lives with nature in the present, above time.

This should be plain enough. Yet see what strong intellects dare not yet hear God himself unless he speak the phraseology of I know not what David, or Jeremiah, or Paul. We shall not always set so great a price on a few texts, on a few lives. We are like children who repeat by rote the sentences of grandames and tutors, and, as they grow older, of the men of talents and character they chance to see,—painfully recollecting the exact words they spoke; afterwards, when they come into the point of view which those had who uttered these sayings, they understand them and are willing to let the words go; for at any time they can use words as good when occasion comes. If we live truly, we shall see truly. It is as easy for the strong man to be strong, as it is for the weak to be weak. When we have new perception, we shall gladly disburden the memory of its hoarded treasures as old rubbish. When a man lives with God, his voice shall be as sweet as the murmur of the brook and the rustle of the corn.

And now at last the highest truth on this subject remains unsaid; probably cannot be said; for all that we say is the far-off remembering of the intuition. That thought by what I can now nearest approach to say it, is this. When good is near you, when you have life in yourself, it is not by any known or accustomed way; you shall not discern the footprints of any other; you shall not see the face of man; you shall not hear any name;—the way, the thought, the good, shall be wholly strange and new. It shall exclude example and experience. You take the way from man, not to man. All persons that ever existed are its forgotten ministers. Fear and hope are alike beneath it. There is somewhat low even in hope. In the hour of vision there is nothing that can be called gratitude, nor properly joy. The soul raised over passion beholds identity and eternal causation, perceives the self-existence of Truth and Right, and calms itself with knowing that all things go well. Vast spaces of nature, the Atlantic Ocean, the South Sea; long intervals of time, years, centuries, are of no account. This which I think and feel underlay every former state of life and circumstances, as it does underlie my present, and what is called life and what is called death.

Life only avails, not the having lived. Power ceases in the instant of repose; it resides in the moment of transition from a past to a new state, in the shooting of the gulf, in the darting to an aim. This one fact the world hates; that the soul *becomes;* for that forever degrades the past, turns all riches to poverty, all reputation to a shame, confounds the saint with the rogue, shoves Jesus and Judas equally aside. Why then do we prate of self-reliance? Inasmuch as the soul is present there will be power not confident but agent. To talk of reliance is a poor external way of speaking. Speak rather of that which relies because it works and is. Who has more obedience than I masters me, though he should not raise his finger. Round him I must revolve by the gravitation of spirits. We fancy it rhetoric when we speak of eminent virtue. We do not yet see that virtue is Height, and that a man or a company of men, plastic and permeable to principles, by the law of nature must overpower and ride all cities, nations, kings, rich men, poets, who are not.

This is the ultimate fact which we so quickly reach on this, as on every topic, the resolution of all into the ever-blessed ONE. Self-existence is the attribute of the Supreme Cause, and it constitutes the measure of good by the degree in which it enters into all lower forms. All things real are so by so much virtue as they contain. Commerce, husbandry, hunting, whaling, war, eloquence, personal weight, are somewhat, and engage my respect as examples of its presence and impure action. I see the same law working in nature for conservation and growth. Power is, in nature, the essential measure of right. Nature suffers nothing to remain in her

kingdoms which cannot help itself. The genesis and maturation of a planet, its poise and orbit, the bended tree recovering itself from the strong wind, the vital resources of every animal and vegetable, are demonstrations of the self-sufficing and therefore self-relying soul.

Thus all concentrates: let us not rove; let us sit at home with the cause. Let us stun and astonish the intruding rabble of men and books and institutions by a simple declaration of the divine fact. Bid the invaders take the shoes from off their feet, for God is here within. Let our simplicity judge them, and our docility to our own law demonstrate the poverty of nature and fortune beside our native riches.

But now we are a mob. Man does not stand in awe of man, nor is his genius admonished to stay at home, to put itself in communication with the internal ocean, but it goes abroad to beg a cup of water of the urns of other men. We must go alone. I like the silent church before the service begins, better than any preaching. How far off, how cool, how chaste the persons look, begirt each one with a precinct or sanctuary! So let us always sit. Why should we assume the faults of our friend, or wife, or father, or child, because they sit around our hearth, or are said to have the same blood? All men have my blood and I all men's. Not for that will I adopt their petulance or folly, even to the extent of being ashamed of it. But your isolation must not be mechanical, but spiritual, that is, must be elevation. At times the whole world seems to be in conspiracy to importune you with emphatic trifles. Friend, client, child, sickness, fear, want, charity, all knock at once at thy closet door and say,— 'Come out unto us.' But keep thy state; come not into their confusion. The power men possess to annoy me I give them by a weak curiosity. No man can come near me but through my act. "What we love that we have, but by desire we bereave ourselves of the love."

If we cannot at once rise to the sanctities of obedience and faith, let us at least resist our temptations; let us enter into the state of war and wake Thor and Woden, courage and constancy, in our Saxon breasts. This is to be done in our smooth times by speaking the truth. Check this lying hospitality and lying affection. Live no longer to the expectation of these deceived and deceiving people with whom we converse. Say to them, 'O father, O mother, O wife, O brother, O friend, I have lived with you after appearances hitherto. Henceforward I am the truth's. Be it known unto you that henceforward I obey no law less than the external law. I will have no covenants but proximities. I shall endeavor to nourish my parents, to support my family, to be the chaste husband of one wife,—but these relations I must fill after a new and unprecedented way. I appeal from your customs. I must be myself. I cannot break myself any longer for you, or you. If you can love me for what I am, we shall be the happier. If you cannot, I will still seek to deserve that you should. I will not hide my tastes or aversions. I will so trust that what is deep is holy, that I will do strongly before the sun and moon whatever inly rejoices me and the heart appoints. If you are noble, I will love you; if you are not, I will not hurt you and myself by hypocritical attentions. If you are true, but not in the same truth with me, cleave to your companions; I will seek my own. I do this not selfishly but humbly and truly. It is alike your interest, and mine, and all men's, however long we have dwelt in lies, to live in truth. Does this sound harsh to-day? You will soon love what is dictated by your nature as well as mine, and if we follow the truth it will bring us out safe at last.'—But so may you give these friends pain. Yes, but I cannot sell my liberty and my power, to save their sensibility. Besides, all persons have their moments of reason, when they look out into the region of absolute truth; then will they justify me and do the same thing.

The populace think that your rejection of popular standards is a rejection of all standard, and mere antinomianism; and the bold sensualist will use the name of philosophy to gild his crimes. But the law of consciousness abides. There are two confessionals, in one or the other of which we must be shriven. You may fulfil your round of duties by clearing yourself in the *direct,* or in the *reflex* way. Consider whether you have satisfied your relations to father, mother, cousin, neighbor, town, cat and dog—whether any of these can upbraid you. But I may also neglect this reflex standard and absolve me to myself. I have my own stern claims and perfect circle. It denies the name of duty to many offices that are called duties. But if I can discharge its debts it enables me to dispense with the popular code. If any one imagines that this law is lax, let him keep its commandment one day.

And truly it demands something godlike in him who has cast off the common motives of humanity and has ventured to trust himself for a taskmaster. High be his heart, faithful his will, clear his sight, that he may in good earnest be doctrine, society, law, to himself, that a simple purpose may be to him as strong as iron necessity is to others!

If any man consider the present aspects of what is called by distinction *society,* he will see the need of these ethics. The sinew and heart of man seem to be drawn out, and we are become timorous, desponding whimperers. We are afraid of truth, afraid of fortune, afraid of death, and afraid of each other. Our age yields no great and perfect persons. We want men and women who shall renovate life and our social state, but we see that most natures are insolvent, cannot satisfy their own wants, have an ambition out of all proportion to their practical force and do lean and beg day and night continually. Our housekeeping is mendicant, our arts, our occupations, our marriages, our religion we have not chosen, but society has chosen for us. We are parlor soldiers. We shun the rugged battle of fate, where strength is born.

If our young men miscarry in their first enterprises they lose all heart. If the young merchant fails, men say he is *ruined.* If the finest genius studies at one of our colleges and is not installed in an office within one year afterwards in the cities or suburbs of Boston or New York, it seems to his friends and to himself that he is right in being disheartened and in complaining the rest of his life. A sturdy lad from New Hampshire or Vermont, who in turn tries all the professions, who *teams it, farms it, peddles,* keeps a school, preaches, edits a newspaper, goes to Congress, buys a township, and so forth, in successive years, and always like a cat falls on his feet, is worth a hundred of these city dolls. He walks abreast with his days and feels no shame in not 'studying a profession,' for he does not postpone his life, but lives already. He has not one chance, but a hundred chances. Let a Stoic open the resources of man and tell men they are not leaning willows, but can and must detach themselves; that with the exercise of self-trust, new powers shall appear; that a man is the word made flesh, born to shed healing to the nations; that he should be ashamed of our compassion, and that the moment he acts from himself, tossing the laws, the books, idolatries and customs out of the window, we pity him no more but thank and revere him;—and that teacher shall restore the life of man to splendor and make his name dear to all history.

It is easy to see that a greater self-reliance must work a revolution in all the offices and relations of men; in their religion; in their education; in their pursuits; their modes of living; their association; in their property; in their speculative views.

1. In what prayers do men allow themselves! That which they call a holy office is not so much as brave and manly. Prayer looks abroad and asks for some foreign addition to come through some foreign virtue, and loses itself in endless mazes of natural and supernatural, and mediatorial and miraculous. Prayer that craves a particular commodity, anything less than all good, is vicious. Prayer is the contemplation of the facts of life from the highest point of view. It is the soliloquy of a beholding and jubilant soul. It is the spirit of God pronouncing his works good. But prayer as a means to effect a private end is meanness and theft. It supposes dualism and not unity in nature and consciousness. As soon as the man is at one with God, he will not beg. He will then see prayer in all action. The prayer of the farmer kneeling in his field to weed it, the prayer of the rower kneeling with the stroke of his oar, are true prayers heard throughout nature, though for cheap ends. Caratach, in Fletcher's "Bonduca," when admonished to inquire the mind of the god Audate, replies,—

His hidden meaning lies in our endeavors;
Our valors are our best gods.

Another sort of false prayers are our regrets. Discontent is the want of self-reliance: it is infirmity of will. Regret calamities if you can thereby help the sufferer; if not, attend your own work and already the evil begins to be repaired. Our sympathy is just as base. We come to them who weep foolishly and sit down and cry for company, instead of imparting to them truth and health in rough electric shocks, putting them once more in communication with their own reason. The secret of fortune is joy in our hands. Welcome evermore to gods and men is the self-helping man. For him all doors are flung wide; him all tongues greet, all honors crown, all eyes follow with desire. Our love goes out to him and embraces him because he did not need it. We solicitously and apologetically caress and celebrate him because he held on his way and scorned our disapprobation. The gods love him because men hated him. "To the persevering mortal," said Zoroaster, "the blessed Immortals are swift."

As men's prayers are a disease of the will, so are their creeds a disease of the intellect. They say with those foolish Israelites, 'Let not God speak to us, lest we die. Speak thou, speak any man with us, and we will obey.' Everywhere I am hindered of meeting God in my brother, because he has shut his own temple doors and recites fables merely of his brother's, or his brother's brother's God.

Every new mind is a new classification. If it prove a mind of uncommon activity and power, a Locke, a Lavoisier, a Hutton, a Bentham, a Fourier, it imposes its classification on other men, and lo! a new system. In proportion to the depth of the thought, and so to the number of the objects it touches and brings within reach of the pupil, is his complacency. But chiefly is this apparent in creeds and churches, which are also classifications of some powerful mind acting on the elemental thought of duty and man's relation to the Highest. Such is Calvinism, Quakerism, Swedenborgism. The pupil takes the same delight in subordinating every thing to the new terminology as a girl who has just learned botany in seeing a new earth and new seasons thereby. It will happen for a time that the pupil will find his intellectual power has grown by the study of his master's mind. But in all unbalanced minds the classification is idolized, passes for the end and not for a speedily exhaustible means, so that the walls of the system blend to their eye in the remote horizon with the walls of the universe; the luminaries of heaven seem to them hung on the arch their master built. They cannot imagine how you aliens have any right to see,—how you can see; 'It must be somehow that you stole the light from us.' They do not yet perceive that light, unsystematic, indomitable, will break into any cabin, even into theirs. Let them chirp awhile and call it their own. If they are honest and do well, presently their neat new pinfold will be too strait and low, will crack, will lean, will rot and vanish, and the immortal light, all young and joyful, million-orbed, million-colored, will beam over the universe as on the first morning.

2. It is for want of self-culture that the superstition of Travelling, whose idols are Italy, England, Egypt, retains its fascination for all educated Americans. They who made England, Italy, or Greece venerable in the imagination, did so by sticking fast where they were, like an axis of the earth. In manly hours we feel that duty is our place. The soul is no traveller; the wise man stays at home, and when his necessities, his duties, on any occasion call him from his house, or into foreign lands, he is at home still and shall make men sensible by the expression of his countenance that he goes, the missionary of wisdom and virtue, and visits cities and men like a sovereign and not like an interloper or a valet.

I have no churlish objection to the circumnavigation of the globe for the purposes of art, of study, and benevolence, so that the man is first domesticated, or does not go abroad with the hope of finding somewhat greater than he knows. He who travels to be amused, or to get somewhat which he does not carry, travels away from himself, and grows old even in youth among old things. In Thebes, in Palmyra, his will and mind have become old and dilapidated as they. He carries ruins to ruins.

Travelling is a fool's paradise. Our first journeys discover to us the indifference of places. At home I dream that at Naples, at Rome, I can be intoxicated with beauty and lose my sadness. I pack my trunk, embrace my friends, embark on the sea and at last wake up in Naples, and there beside me is the stern fact, the sad self, unrelenting, identical, that I fled from. I seek the Vatican and the palaces. I affect to be intoxicated with sights and suggestions, but I am not intoxicated. My giant goes with me wherever I go.

3. But the rage of travelling is a symptom of a deeper unsoundness affecting the whole intellectual action. The intellect is vagabond, and our system of education fosters restlessness. Our minds travel when our bodies are forced to stay at home. We imitate; and what is imitation but the travelling of the mind? Our houses are built with foreign taste; our shelves are garnished with foreign ornaments; our opinions, our tastes, our faculties, lean, and follow the Past and the Distant. The soul created the arts wherever they have flourished. It was in his own mind that the artist sought his model. It was an application of his own thought to the thing to be done and the conditions to be observed.

And why need we copy the Doric or the Gothic model? Beauty, convenience, grandeur of thought and quaint expression are as near to us as to any, and if the American artist will study with hope and love the precise thing to be done by him, considering the climate, the soil, the length of the day, the wants of the people, the habit and form of the government, he will create a house in which all these will find themselves fitted, and taste and sentiment will be satisfied also.

Insist on yourself; never imitate. Your own gift you can present every moment with the cumulative force of a whole life's cultivation; but of the adopted talent of another you have only an extemporaneous half possession. That which each can do best, none but his Maker can teach him. No man yet knows what it is, nor can, till that person has exhibited it. Where is the master who could have taught Shak[e]speare? Where is the master who could have instructed Franklin, or Washington, or Bacon, or Newton? Every great man is a unique. The Scipionism of Scipio is precisely that part he could not borrow. Shak[e]speare will never be made by the study of Shak[e]speare. Do that which is assigned you, and you cannot hope too much or dare too much. There is at this moment for you an utterance brave and grand as that of the colossal chisel of Phidias, or trowel of the Egyptians, or the pen of Moses or Dante, but different from all these. Not possibly will the soul, all rich, all eloquent, with thousand-cloven tongue, deign to repeat itself; but if you can hear what these patriarchs say, surely you can reply to them in the same pitch of voice; for the ear and the tongue are two organs of one nature. Abide in the simple and noble regions of thy life, obey thy heart, and thou shalt reproduce the Foreworld again.

4. As our Religion, our Education, our Art look abroad, so does our spirit of society. All men plume themselves on the improvement of society, and no man improves.

Society never advances. It recedes as fast on one side as it gains on the other. It undergoes continual changes; it is barbarous, it is civilized, it is christianized, it is rich, it is scientific; but this change is not amelioration. For every thing that is given something is taken. Society acquires new arts and loses old instincts. What a contrast between the well-clad, reading, writing, thinking American, with a watch, a pencil and a bill of exchange in his pocket, and the naked New Zealander, whose property is a club, a spear, a mat and an undivided twentieth of a shed to sleep under! But compare the health of the two men and you shall see that the white man has lost his aboriginal strength. If the traveller tell us truly, strike the savage with a broad-axe and in a day or two the flesh shall unite and heal as if you struck the blow into soft pitch, and the same blow shall send the white to his grave.

The civilized man has built a coach, but has lost the use of his feet. He is supported on crutches, but lacks so much support of muscle. He has a fine Geneva watch, but he fails of the skill to tell the hour by the sun. A Greenwich nautical almanac he has, and so being sure of the information when he wants it, the man in the street does not know a star in the sky. The solstice he does not observe; the equinox he knows as little; and the whole bright calendar of the year is without a dial in his mind. His note-books impair his memory; his libraries overload his wit; the insurance-office increases the number of accidents; and it may be a question whether machinery does not encumber; whether we have not lost by refinement some energy, by a Christianity, entrenched in establishments and forms, some vigor of wild virtue. For every Stoic was a Stoic; but in Christendom where is the Christian?

There is no more deviation in the moral standard than in the standard of height or bulk. No greater men are now than ever were. A singular equality may be observed between the great men of the first and of the last ages; nor can all the science, art, religion, and philosophy of the nineteenth century avail to educate greater men than Plutarch's heroes, three or four and twenty centuries ago. Not in time is the race progressive. Phocion, Socrates, Anaxagoras, Diogenes, are great men, but they leave no class. He who is really of their class will not be called by their name, but will be his own man, and in his turn the founder of a sect. The arts and inventions of each period are only its costume and do not invigorate men. The harm of the improved machinery may compensate its good. Hudson and Behring accomplished so much in their fishing-boats as to astonish Parry and Franklin, whose equipment exhausted the resources of science and art. Galileo, with an opera-glass, discovered a more splendid series of celestial phenomena than any one since. Columbus found the New World in an undecked boat. It is curious to see the periodical disuse and perishing of means and machinery which were introduced with loud laudation a few years or centuries before. The great genius returns to essential man. We reckoned the improvements of the art of war among the triumphs of science, and yet Napoleon conquered Europe by the bivouac, which consisted of falling back on naked valor and disencumbering it of all aids. The Emperor held it impossible to make a perfect army, says Las Casas, "without abolishing our arms, magazines, commissaries and carriages, until, in imitation of the Roman custom, the soldier should receive his supply of corn, grind it in his hand-mill and bake his bread himself."

Society is a wave. The wave moves onward, but the water of which it is composed does not. The same particle does not rise from the valley to the ridge. Its unity is only phenomenal. The persons who make up a nation to-day, next year die, and their experience dies with them.

And so the reliance on Property, including the reliance on governments which protect it, is the want of self-reliance. Men have looked away from themselves and at things so long that they have come to esteem the religious, learned and civil institutions as guards of property, and they deprecate assaults on these, because they feel them to be assaults on property. They measure their esteem of each other by what each has, and not by what each is. But a cultivated man becomes ashamed of his property, out of new respect for his nature. Especially he hates what he has if he see that it is accidental,—came to him by inheritance, or gift, or crime; then he feels that it is not having; it does not belong to him, has no root in him and merely lies there because no revolution or no robber takes it away. But that which a man is, does always by necessity acquire; and what the man acquires, is living property, which does not wait the beck of rulers, or mobs, or revolutions, or fire, or storm, or bankruptcies, but perpetually renews itself wherever the man breathes. "Thy lot or portion of life," said the Caliph Ali, "is seeking after thee; therefore be at rest from seeking after it." Our dependence on these foreign goods leads us to our slavish respect for numbers. The political parties meet in numerous conventions; the greater the concourse and with each new uproar of announcement, The delegation from Essex! The Democrats from New Hampshire! The Whigs of Maine! the young patriot feels himself stronger than before by a new thousand of eyes and arms. In like manner the reformers summon conventions and vote and resolve in multitude. Not so, O friends! will the God deign to enter and inhabit you, but by a method precisely the reverse. It is only as a man puts off all foreign support and stands alone that I see him to be strong and to prevail. He is weaker by every recruit to his banner. Is not a man better than a town? Ask nothing of men, and, in the endless mutation, thou only firm column must presently appear the upholder of all that surrounds thee. He who knows that power is inborn, that he is weak because he has looked for good out of him and elsewhere, and, so perceiving, throws himself unhesitatingly on his thought, instantly rights himself, stands in the erect position, commands his limbs, works miracles; just as a man who stands on his feet is stronger than a man who stands on his head.

So use all that is called Fortune. Most men

gamble with her, and gain all, and lose all, as her wheel rolls. But do thou leave as unlawful these winnings, and deal with Cause and Effect, the chancellors of God. In the Will work and acquire, and thou hast chained the wheel of Chance, and shall sit hereafter out of fear from her rotations. A political victory, a rise of rents, the recovery of your sick or the return of your absent friend, or some other favorable event raises your spirits, and you think good days are preparing for you. Do not believe it. Nothing can bring you peace but yourself. Nothing can bring you peace but the triumph of principles.

RALPH WALDO EMERSON
"Man the Reformer" (1841)*

MR. PRESIDENT, AND GENTLEMEN:

I wish to offer to your consideration some thoughts on the particular and general relations of man as a reformer. I shall assume that the aim of each young man in this association is the very highest that belongs to a rational mind. Let it be granted that our life, as we lead it, is common and mean; that some of those offices and functions for which we were mainly created are grown so rare in society that the memory of them is only kept alive in old books and in dim traditions; that prophets and poets, that beautiful and perfect men we are not now, no, nor have even seen such; that some sources of human instruction are almost unnamed and unknown among us; that the community in which we live will hardly bear to be told that every man should be open to ecsta[s]y or a divine illumination, and his daily walk elevated by intercourse with the spiritual world. Grant all this, as we must, yet I suppose none of my auditors will deny that we ought

* Ralph Waldo Emerson, "Man the Reformer" (A lecture read before the Mechanics' Apprentices' Library Association in Boston on January 25, 1841), *Nature: Addresses and Lectures* (Boston and New York: Houghton Mifflin, 1876; Centenary Edition of *The Complete Works of Ralph Waldo Emerson*, Vol. I), pp. 227–229, 247–254.

to seek to establish ourselves in such disciplines and courses as will deserve that guidance and clearer communication with the spiritual nature. And further, I will not dissemble my hope that each person whom I address has felt his own call to cast aside all evil customs, timidities, and limitations, and to be in his place a free and helpful man, a reformer, a benefactor, not content to slip along through the world like a footman or a spy, escaping by his nimbleness and apologies as many knocks as he can, but a brave and upright man, who must find or cut a straight road to everything excellent in the earth, and not only go honorably himself, but make it easier for all who follow him to go in honor and with benefit.

In the history of the world the doctrine of Reform had never such scope as at the present hour. Lutherans, Herrnhutters, Jesuits, Monks, Quakers, Knox, Wesley, Swedenborg, Bentham, in their accusations of society, all respected something,—church or state, literature or history, domestic usages, the market town, the dinner table, coined money. But now all these and all things else hear the trumpet, and must rush to judgment,—Christianity, the laws, commerce, schools, the farm, the laboratory; and not a kingdom, town, statute, rite, calling, man, or woman, but is threatened by the new spirit.

What if some of the objections whereby our institutions are assailed are extreme and speculative, and the reformers tend to idealism? That only shows the extravagance of the abuses which have driven the mind into the opposite extreme. It is when your facts and persons grow unreal and fantastic by too much falsehood, that the scholar flies for refuge to the world of ideas, and aims to recruit and replenish nature from that source. Let ideas establish their legitimate sway again in society, let life be fair and poetic, and the scholars will gladly be lovers, citizens, and philanthropists.

. . . . .

The idea which now begins to agitate society has a wider scope than our daily employments, our households, and the institutions of property. We are to revise the whole of our social structure, the State, the school, religion, marriage, trade, science, and explore their foundations in our own nature; we are to see that the world not only fitted the former men, but fits us, and to clear ourselves of every usage which has not its roots in our own mind. What is a man born for but to be a Reformer, a Remaker of what man has made; a renouncer of lies; a restorer of truth and good, imitating that great Nature which embosoms us all, and which sleeps no moment on an old past, but every hour repairs herself, yielding us every morning a new day, and with every pulsation a new life? Let him renounce everything which is not true to him, and put all his practices back on their first thoughts, and do nothing for which he has not the whole world for his reason. If there are inconveniences and what is called ruin in the way, because we have so enervated and maimed ourselves, yet it would be like dying of perfumes to sink in the effort to re-attach the deeds of every day to the holy and mysterious recesses of life.

The power which is at once spring and regulator in all efforts of reform is the conviction that there is an infinite worthiness in man, which will appear at the call of worth, and that all particular reforms are the removing of some impediment. Is it not the highest duty that man should be honored in us? I ought not to allow any man, because he has broad lands, to feel that he is rich in my presence. I ought to make him feel that I can do without his riches, that I cannot be bought,—neither by comfort, neither by pride,—and though I be utterly penniless, and receiving bread from him, that he is the poor man beside me. And if, at the same time, a woman or a child discovers a sentiment of piety, or a juster way of thinking than mine, I ought to confess it by my respect and obedience, though it go to alter my whole way of life.

The Americans have many virtues, but they have not Faith and Hope. I know no two words whose meaning is more lost sight of. We use these words as if they were as obsolete as Selah and Amen. And yet they have the broadest meaning, and the most cogent application to Boston in this year. The Americans have little faith. They rely on the power of a dollar; they are deaf to a sentiment. They think you may talk the north wind down as easily as raise society; and no class more faithless than the scholars or intellectual men. Now if I talk with a sincere wise man, and my friend, with a poet, with a conscientious youth who is still under the dominion of his own wild thoughts, and not yet harnessed in the team of society to drag with us all in the ruts of custom, I see at once how paltry is all this generation of unbelievers, and what a house of cards their institutions are, and I see what one brave man, what one great thought executed might effect. I see that the reason of the distrust of the practical man in all theory, is his inability to perceive the means whereby we work. Look, he says, at the tools with which this world of yours is to be built. As we cannot make a planet, with atmosphere, rivers, and forests, by means of the best carpenters' or engineers' tools, with chemist's laboratory and smith's forge to boot,—so neither can we ever construct that heavenly society you prate of out of foolish, sick, selfish men and women, such as we know them to be. But the believer not only beholds his heaven to be possible, but already to begin to exist,—not by the men or materials the statesman uses, but by men transfigured and raised above themselves by the power of principles. To principles something else is possible that transcends all the power of expedients. . . .

But there will dawn ere long on our politics, on our modes of living, a nobler morning than that Arabian faith, in the sentiment of love. This is the one remedy for all ills, the panacea of nature. We must be lovers, and at once the impossible becomes possible. Our age and history, for these thousand years, has not been the history of kindness, but of selfishness. Our distrust is very expensive. The money we spend for courts and prisons is very ill laid out. We make, by distrust, the thief, and burglar, and incendiary, and by our court and jail we keep him so. An acceptance of the sentiment of love throughout Christendom for a season would bring the felon and the outcast to our side in tears, with the devotion of his faculties to our service. See this wide society of laboring men and women. We allow ourselves to be served by them, we live apart from them, and meet them without a salute in the streets. We do not greet their talents, nor rejoice in their good fortune, nor foster their hopes, nor in the assembly of the people vote for what is dear to them. Thus we enact the part of the selfish noble and king from the foundation of the world. . . .

Let our affection flow out to our fellows; it would operate in a day the greatest of all revolutions. It is better to work on institutions by the sun than by the wind. The State must consider the poor man, and all voices must speak for him. Every child that is born must have a just chance for his bread. Let the amelioration in our laws of property proceed from the concession of the rich, not from the grasping of the poor. Let us begin by habitual imparting. Let us understand that the equitable rule is, that no one should take more than his share, let him be ever so rich. . . .

RALPH WALDO EMERSON
"Education" (1876)*

EDUCATION.

With the key of the secret he marches faster
From strength to strength, and for night
  brings day,
While classes or tribes too weak to master
The flowing conditions of life, give way.

A new degree of intellectual power seems cheap at any price. The use of the world

* Ralph Waldo Emerson, "Education" (1876), *Lectures and Biographical Sketches* (Boston: Houghton Mifflin, 1884; Riverside Edition of *Emerson's Complete Works*, Vol. X), pp. 123–156.

is that man may learn its laws. And the human race have wisely signified their sense of this, by calling wealth, means,—Man being the end. Language is always wise.

Therefore I praise New England because it is the country in the world where is the freest expenditure for education. We have already taken, at the planting of the Colonies, (for aught I know for the first time in the world,) the initial step, which for its importance might have been resisted as the most radical of revolutions, thus deciding at the start the destiny of this country,—this, namely, that the poor man, whom the law does not allow to take an ear of corn when starving, nor a pair of shoes for his freezing feet, is allowed to put his hand into the pocket of the rich, and say, You shall educate me, not as you will, but as I will: not alone in the elements, but, by further provision, in the languages, in sciences, in the useful and in elegant arts. The child shall be taken up by the State, and taught, at the public cost, the rudiments of knowledge, and, at last, the ripest results of art and science.

Humanly speaking, the school, the college, society, make the difference between men. All the fairy tales of Aladdin or the invisible Gyges or the talisman that opens kings' palaces or the enchanted halls under-ground or in the sea, are only fictions to indicate the one miracle of intellectual enlargement. When a man stupid becomes a man inspired, when one and the same man passes out of the torpid into the perceiving state, leaves the din of trifles, the stupor of the senses, to enter into the quasi-omniscience of high thought,—up and down, around, all limits disappear. No horizon shuts down. He sees things in their causes, all facts in their connection.

One of the problems of history is the beginning of civilization. The animals that accompany and serve man make no progress as races. Those called domestic are capable of learning of man a few tricks of utility or amusement, but they cannot communicate the skill to their race. Each individual must be taught anew. The trained dog cannot train another dog. And Man himself in many races retains almost the unteachableness of the beast. For a thousand years the islands and forests of a great part of the world have been filled with savages who made no steps of advance in art or skill beyond the necessity of being fed and warmed. Certain nations with a better brain and usually in more temperate climates, have made such progress as to compare with these as these compare with the bear and the wolf.

Victory over things is the office of man. Of course, until it is accomplished, it is the war and insult of things over him. His continual tendency, his great danger, is to overlook the fact that the world is only his teacher, and the nature of sun and moon, plant and animal only means of arousing his interior activity. Enamored of their beauty, comforted by their convenience, he seeks them as ends, and fast loses sight of the fact that they have worse than no values, that they become noxious, when he becomes their slave.

This apparatus of wants and faculties, this craving body, whose organs ask all the elements and all the functions of Nature for their satisfaction, educate the wondrous creature which they satisfy with light, with heat, with water, with wood, with bread, with wool. The necessities imposed by this most irritable and all-related texture have taught Man hunting, pasturage, agriculture, commerce, weaving, joining, masonry, geometry, astronomy. Here is a world pierced and belted with natural laws, and fenced and planted with civil partitions and properties, which all put new restraints on the young inhabitant. He too must come into this magic circle of relations, and know health and sickness, the fear of injury, the desire of external good, the charm of riches, the charm of power. The household is a school of power. There, within the door, learn the tragi-comedy of human life. Here is the sincere thing, the wondrous composition for which day and night go round. In that routine are the sacred relations, the passions that bind and sever. Here is poverty and all the wisdom its hated necessities can teach, here labor drudges, here affections glow, here the secrets of character are told, the guards of man, the guards of woman, the compensations which, like angels of justice, pay every debt: the opium of custom, whereof all drink and many go mad. Here is Economy, and Glee, and Hospitality, and Ceremony, and Frankness, and Calamity, and Death, and Hope.

Every one has a trust of power,—every man, every boy a jurisdiction, whether it be over a cow or a rood of a potato-field, or a fleet of ships, or the laws of a state. And what activity the desire of power inspires! What toils it sustains! How it sharpens the perceptions and stores the memory with facts. Thus a man may well spend many years of life in trade. It is a constant teaching of the laws of matter and of mind. No dollar of property can be created without some direct communication with nature, and of course some acquisition of knowledge and practical force. It is a constant contest with the active faculties of men, a study of the issues of one and another course of action, an accumulation of power, and, if the higher faculties of the individual be from time to time quickened, he will gain wisdom and virtue from his business.

As every wind draws music out of the Æolian harp, so doth every object in Nature draw music out of his mind. Is it not true that every landscape I behold, every friend I meet, every act I perform, every pain I suffer, leaves me a different being from that they found me? That poverty, love, authority, anger, sickness, sorrow, success, all work actively upon our being and unlock for us the concealed faculties of the mind? Whatever private or petty ends are frustrated, this end is always answered. Whatever the man does, or whatever befalls him, opens another chamber in his soul,—that is, he has got a new feeling, a new thought, a new organ. Do we not see how amazingly for this end man is fitted to the world?

What leads him to science? Why does he

track in the midnight heaven a pure spark, a luminous patch wandering from age to age, but because he acquires thereby a majestic sense of power; learning that in his own constitution he can set the shining maze in order, and finding and carrying their law in his mind, can, as it were, see his simple idea realized up yonder in giddy distances and frightful periods of duration. If Newton come and first of men perceive that not alone certain bodies fall to the ground at a certain rate, but that all bodies in the Universe, the universe of bodies, fall always, and at one rate; that every atom in nature draws to every other atom,—he extends the power of his mind not only over every cubic atom of his native planet, but he reports the condition of millions of worlds which his eye never saw. And what is the charm which every ore, every new plant, every new fact touching winds, clouds, ocean currents, the secrets of chemical composition and decomposition possess for Humboldt? What but that much revolving of similar facts in his mind has shown him that always the mind contains in its transparent chambers the means of classifying the most refractory phenomena, of depriving them of all casual and chaotic aspect, and subordinating them to a bright reason of its own, and so giving to man a sort of property,—yea, the very highest property in every district and particle of the globe.

By the permanence of Nature, minds are trained alike, and made intelligible to each other. In our condition are the roots of language and communication, and these instructions we never exhaust.

In some sort the end of life is that the man should take up the universe into himself, or out of that quarry leave nothing unrepresented. Yonder mountain must migrate into his mind. Yonder magnificent astronomy he is at last to import, fetching away moon, and planet, solstice, period, comet and binal star, by comprehending their relation and law. Instead of the timid stripling he was, he is to be the stalwart Archimedes, Pythagoras, Columbus, Newton, of the physic,

metaphysic and ethics of the design of the world.

For truly the population of the globe has its origin in the aims which their existence is to serve; and so with every portion of them. The truth takes flesh in forms that can express it; and thus in history an idea always overhangs, like the moon, and rules the tide which rises simultaneously in all the souls of a generation.

Whilst thus the world exists for the mind; whilst thus the man is ever invited inward into shining realms of knowledge and power by the shows of the world, which interpret to him the infinitude of his own consciousness,—it becomes the office of a just education to awaken him to the knowledge of this fact.

We learn nothing rightly until we learn the symbolical character of life. Day creeps after day, each full of facts, dull, strange, despised things, that we cannot enough despise,—call heavy, prosaic, and desert. The time we seek to kill: the attention it is elegant to divert from things around us. And presently the aroused intellect finds gold and gems in one of these scorned facts, —then finds that the day of facts is a rock of diamonds; that a fact is an Epiphany of God.

We have our theory of life, our religion, our philosophy; and the event of each moment, the shower, the steamboat disaster, the passing of a beautiful face, the apoplexy of our neighbor, are all tests to try our theory, the approximate result we call truth, and reveal its defects. If I have renounced the search of truth, if I have come into the port of some pretending dogmatism, some new church or old church, some Schelling or Cousin, I have died to all use of these new events that are born out of prolific time into multitude of life every hour. I am as a bankrupt to whom brilliant opportunities offer in vain. He has just foreclosed his freedom, tied his hands, locked himself up and given the key to another to keep.

When I see the doors by which God enters into the mind; that there is no sot or fop, ruffian or pedant into whom thoughts do not enter by passages which the individual never left open, I can expect any revolution in character. "I have hope," said the great Leibnitz, "that society may be reformed, when I see how much education may be reformed."

It is ominous, a presumption of crime, that this word Education has so cold, so hopeless a sound. A treatise on education, a convention for education, a lecture, a system, affects us with slight paralysis and a certain yawning of the jaws. We are not encouraged when the law touches it with its fingers. Education should be as broad as man. Whatever elements are in him that should foster and demonstrate. If he be dexterous, his tuition should make it appear; if he be capable of dividing men by the trenchant sword of his thought, education should unsheathe and sharpen it; if he is one to cement society by his all-reconciling affinities, oh! hasten their action! If he is jovial, if he is mercurial, if he is great-hearted, a cunning artificer, a strong commander, a potent ally, ingenious, useful, elegant, witty, prophet, diviner,—society has need of all these. The imagination must be addressed. Why always coast on the surface and never open the interior of nature, not by science, which is surface still, but by poetry? Is not the Vast an element of the mind? Yet what teaching, what book of this day appeals to the Vast?

Our culture has truckled to the times,—to the senses. It is not manworthy. If the vast and the spiritual are omitted, so are the practical and the moral. It does not make us brave or free. We teach boys to be such men as we are. We do not teach them to aspire to be all they can. We do not give them a training as if we believed in their noble nature. We scarce educate their bodies. We do not train the eye and the hand. We exercise their understandings to the apprehension and comparison of some facts, to a skill in numbers, in words; we aim to make accountants, attorneys, engineers; but not to make able, earnest, greathearted men. The great object of Education should be commensurate with the object of life. It should be a moral one; to teach self-trust: to inspire the youthful man with an interest in himself; with a curiosity touching his own nature; to acquaint him with the resources of his mind, and to teach him that there is all his strength, and to inflame him with a piety towards the Grand Mind in which he lives. Thus would education conspire with the Divine Providence. A man is a little thing whilst he works by and for himself, but, when he gives voice to the rules of love and justice, is godlike, his word is current in all countries; and all men, though his enemies, are made his friends and obey it as their own.

In affirming that the moral nature of man is the predominant element and should therefore be mainly consulted in the arrangements of a school, I am very far from wishing that it should swallow up all the other instincts and faculties of man. It should be enthroned in his mind, but if it monopolize the man he is not yet sound, he does not yet know his wealth. He is in danger of becoming merely devout, and wearisome through the monotony of his thought. It is not less necessary that the intellectual and the active faculties should be nourished and matured. Let us apply to this subject the light of the same torch by which we have looked at all the phenomena of the time; the infinitude, namely, of every man. Everything teaches that.

One fact constitutes all my satisfaction, inspires all my trust, viz., this perpetual youth, which, as long as there is any good in us, we cannot get rid of. It is very certain that the coming age and the departing age seldom understand each other. The old man thinks the young man has no distinct purpose, for he could never get anything intelligible and earnest out of him. Perhaps the young man does not think it worth his while to explain himself to so hard and inapprehensive a confessor. Let him be led up with a long-sighted forbearance, and let not the sallies of his petulance or folly be checked with disgust or indignation or despair.

I call our system a system of despair, and

I find all the correction, all the revolution that is needed and that the best spirits of this age promise, in one word, in Hope. Nature, when she sends a new mind into the world, fills it beforehand with a desire for that which she wishes it to know and do. Let us wait and see what is this new creation, of what new organ the great Spirit had need when it incarnated this new Will. A new Adam in the garden, he is to name all the beasts in the field, all the gods in the sky. And jealous provision seems to have been made in his constitution that you shall not invade and contaminate him with the worn weeds of your language and opinions. The charm of life is this variety of genius, these contrasts and flavors by which Heaven has modulated the identity of truth, and there is a perpetual hankering to violate this individuality, to warp his ways of thinking and behavior to resemble or reflect your thinking and behavior. A low self-love in the parent desires that his child should repeat his character and fortune; an expectation which the child, if justice is done him, will nobly disappoint. By working on the theory that this resemblance exists, we shall do what in us lies to defeat his proper promise and produce the ordinary and mediocre. I suffer whenever I see that common sight of a parent or senior imposing his opinion and way of thinking and being on a young soul to which they are totally unfit. Cannot we let people be themselves, and enjoy life in their own way? You are trying to make that man another *you*. One's enough.

Or we sacrifice the genius of the pupil, the unknown possibilities of his nature, to a neat and safe uniformity, as the Turks whitewash the costly mosaics of ancient art which the Greeks left on their temple walls. Rather let us have men whose manhood is only the continuation of their boyhood, natural characters still; such are able and fertile for heroic action; and not that sad spectacle with which we are too familiar, educated eyes in uneducated bodies.

I like boys, the masters of the playground and of the street,—boys, who have the same liberal ticket of admission to all shops, factories, armories, town-meetings, caucuses, mobs, target-shootings, as flies have; quite unsuspected, coming in as naturally as the janitor,—known to have no money in their pockets, and themselves not suspecting the value of this poverty; putting nobody on his guard, but seeing the inside of the show,—hearing all the asides. There are no secrets from them, they know everything that befalls in the fire-company, the merits of every engine and of every man at the brakes, how to work it, and are swift to try their hand at every part; so too the merits of every locomotive on the rails, and will coax the engineer to let them ride with him and pull the handles when it goes to the engine-house. They are there only for fun, and not knowing that they are at school, in the court-house, or the cattle-show, quite as much and more than they were, an hour ago, in the arithmetic class.

They know truth from counterfeit as quick as the chemist does. They detect weakness in your eye and behavior a week before you open your mouth, and have given you the benefit of their opinion quick as a wink. They make no mistakes, have no pedantry, but entire belief on experience. Their elections at base-ball or cricket are founded on merit, and are right. They don't pass for swimmers until they can swim, nor for stroke-oar until they can row: and I desire to be saved from their contempt. If I can pass with them, I can manage well enough with their fathers.

Everybody delights in the energy with which boys deal and talk with each other; the mixture of fun and earnest, reproach and coaxing, love and wrath, with which the game is played;—the good-natured yet defiant independence of a leading boy's behavior in the school-yard. How we envy in later life the happy youths to whom their boisterous games and rough exercise furnish the precise element which frames and sets off their school and college tasks, and teaches them, when least they think it, the use and meaning of these. In their fun and extreme freak they hit on the topmost sense of Horace. The young giant, brown from his hunting-tramp, tells his story well, interlarded with lucky allusions to Homer, to Virgil, to college-songs, to Walter Scott; and Jove and Achilles, partridge and trout, opera and binomial theorem, Cæsar in Gaul, Sherman in Savannah, and hazing in Holworthy, dance through the narrative in merry confusion, yet the logic is good. If he can turn his books to such picturesque account in his fishing and hunting, it is easy to see how his reading and experience, as he has more of both, will interpenetrate each other. And every one desires that this pure vigor of action and wealth of narrative, cheered with so much humor and street rhetoric, should be carried into the habit of the young man, purged of its uproar and rudeness, but with all its vivacity entire. His hunting and campings-out have given him an indispensable base: I wish to add a taste for good company through his impatience of bad. That stormy genius of his needs a little direction to games, charades, verses of society, song, and a correspondence year by year with his wisest and best friends. Friendship is an order of nobility; from its revelations we come more worthily into nature. Society he must have or he is poor indeed; he gladly enters a school which forbids conceit, affectation, emphasis and dulness, and requires of each only the flower of his nature and experience; requires good-will, beauty, wit, and select information; teaches by practice the law of conversation, namely, to hear as well as to speak.

Meantime, if circumstances do not permit the high social advantages, solitude has also its lessons. The obscure youth learns there the practice instead of the literature of his virtues; and, because of the disturbing effect of passion and sense, which by a multitude of trifles impede the mind's eye from the quiet search of that fine horizon-line which truth keeps,—the way to knowledge and power has ever been an escape from too much engagement with affairs and possessions; a way, not through plenty and superfluity, but by denial and renunciation, into solitude and privation; and, the more is taken away, the more real and inevitable wealth of being is made known to us. The solitary knows the essence of the thought, the scholar in society only its fair face. There is no want of example of great men, great benefactors, who have been monks and hermits in habit. The bias of mind is sometimes irresistible in that direction. The man is, as it were, born deaf and dumb, and dedicated to a narrow and lonely life. Let him study the art of solitude, yield as gracefully as he can to his destiny. Why cannot he get the good of his doom, and if it is from eternity a settled fact that he and society shall be nothing to each other, why need he blush so, and make wry faces to keep up a freshman's seat in the fine world? Heaven often protects valuable souls charged with great secrets, great ideas, by long shutting them up with their own thoughts. And the most genial and amiable of men must alternate society with solitude, and learn its severe lessons.

There comes the period of the imagination to each, a later youth; the power of beauty, the power of books, of poetry. Culture makes his books realities to him, their characters more brilliant, more effective on his mind, than his actual mates. Do not spare to put novels into the hands of young people as an occasional holiday and experiment; but, above all, good poetry in all kinds, epic, tragedy, lyric. If we can touch the imagination, we serve them, they will never forget it. Let him read "Tom Brown at Rugby," read "Tom Brown at Oxford,"—better yet, read "Hodson's Life"—Hodson who took prisoner the king of Delhi. They teach the same truth,—a trust, against all appearances, against all privations, in your own worth, and not in tricks, plotting, or patronage.

I believe that our own experience instructs us that the secret of Education lies in respecting the pupil. It is not for you to choose what he shall know, what he shall do. It is chosen and foreordained, and he only holds the key to his own secret. By your tampering and thwarting and too much governing he may be hindered from his end and kept out of his own. Respect the child. Wait and see the new product of Nature. Nature loves analogies, but not repetitions. Respect the child. Be not too much his parent. Trespass not on his solitude.

But I hear the outcry which replies to this suggestion:—Would you verily throw up the reins of public and private discipline; would you leave the young child to the mad career of his own passions and whimsies, and call this anarchy a respect for the child's nature? I answer,—Respect the child, respect him to the end, but also respect yourself. Be the companion of his thought, the friend of his friendship, the lover of his virtue,—but no kinsman of his sin. Let him find you so true to yourself that you are the irreconcilable hater of his vice and the imperturbable slighter of his trifling.

The two points in a boy's training are, to keep his *naturel* and train off all but that:— to keep his *naturel*, but stop off his uproar, fooling and horse-play;—keep his nature and arm it with knowledge in the very direction in which it points. Here are the two capital facts, Genius and Drill. The first is the inspiration in the well-born healthy child, the new perception he has of nature. Somewhat he sees in forms or hears in music or apprehends in mathematics, or believes practicable in mechanics or possible in political society, which no one else sees or hears or believes. This is the perpetual romance of new life, the invasion of God into the old dead world, when he sends into quiet houses a young soul with a thought which is not met, looking for something which is not there, but which ought to be there: the thought is dim but it is sure, and he casts about restless for means and masters to verify it; he makes wild attempts to explain himself and invoke the aid and consent of the bystanders. Baffled for want of language and methods to convey his meaning, not yet clear to himself, he conceives that though not in this house or town, yet in some other house or town is the wise master who can put him in possession of the rules and instruments to execute his will. Happy this child with a bias, with a thought which entrances him, leads him, now into deserts now into cities, the fool of an idea. Let him follow it in good and in evil report, in good or bad company; it will justify itself; it will lead him at last into the illustrious society of the lovers of truth.

In London, in a private company, I became acquainted with a gentleman, Sir Charles Fellowes, who, being at Xanthus, in the Ægean Sea, had seen a Turk point with his staff to some carved work on the corner of a stone almost buried in the soil. Fellowes scraped away the dirt, was struck with the beauty of the sculptured ornaments, and, looking about him, observed more blocks and fragments like this. He returned to the spot, procured laborers and uncovered many blocks. He went back to England, bought a Greek grammar and learned the language; he read history and studied ancient art to explain his stones; he interested Gibson the sculptor; he invoked the assistance of the English Government; he called in the succor of Sir Humphry Davy to analyze the pigments; of experts in coins, of scholars and connoisseurs; and at last in his third visit brought home to England such statues and marble reliefs and such careful plans that he was able to reconstruct, in the British Museum where it now stands, the perfect model of the Ionic trophy-monument, fifty years older than the Parthenon of Athens, and which had been destroyed by earthquakes, then by iconoclast Christians, then by savage Turks. But mark that in the task he had achieved an excellent education, and become associated with distinguished scholars whom he had interested in his pursuit; in short, had formed a college for himself; the enthusiast had found the master, the masters, whom he sought. Always genius seeks genius, desires nothing so much as to be a pupil and to find those who can lend it aid to perfect itself.

Nor are the two elements, enthusiasm and drill, incompatible. Accuracy is essential to beauty. The very definition of the intellect is Aristotle's: "that by which we know terms or boundaries." Give a boy accurate perceptions. Teach him the difference between the similar and the same. Make him call things by their right names. Pardon in him no blunder. Then he will give you solid satisfaction as long as he lives. It is better to teach the child arithmetic and Latin grammar than rhetoric or moral philosophy, because they require exactitude of performance; it is made certain that the lesson is mastered, and that power of performance is worth more than the knowledge. He can learn anything which is important to him now that the power to learn is secured: as mechanics say, when one has learned the use of tools, it is easy to work at a new craft.

Letter by letter, syllable by syllable, the child learns to read, and in good time can convey to all the domestic circle the sense of Shak[e]speare. By many steps each just as short, the stammering boy and the hesitating collegian, in the school debate, in college clubs, in mock court, comes at last to full, secure, triumphant unfolding of his thought in the popular assembly, with a fullness of power that makes all the steps forgotten.

But this function of opening and feeding the human mind is not to be fulfilled by any mechanical or military method; is not to be trusted to any skill less large than Nature itself. You must not neglect the form, but you must secure the essentials. It is curious how perverse and intermeddling we are, and what vast pains and cost we incur to do wrong. Whilst we all know in our own experience and apply natural methods in our own business,—in education our common sense fails us, and we are continually trying costly machinery against nature, in patent schools and academies and in great colleges and universities.

The natural method forever confutes our experiments, and we must still come back to it. The whole theory of the school is on the nurse's or mother's knee. The child is as hot to learn as the mother is to impart. There is mutual delight. The joy of our childhood in hearing beautiful stories from some skilful aunt who loves to tell them, must be repeated in youth. The boy wishes to learn to skate, to coast, to catch a fish in the brook, to hit a mark with a snowball or a stone; and a boy a little older is just as well pleased to teach him these sciences. Not less delightful is the mutual pleasure of teaching and learning the secret of algebra, or of chemistry, or of good reading and good recitation of poetry or of prose, or of chosen facts in history or in biography.

Nature provided for the communication of thought, by planting with it in the receiving mind a fury to impart it. 'T is so in every art, in every science. One burns to tell the new fact, the other burns to hear it. See how far a young doctor will ride or walk to witness a new surgical operation. I have seen a carriage-maker's shop emptied of all its workmen into the street, to scrutinize a new pattern from New York. So in literature, the young man who has taste for poetry, for fine images, for noble thoughts, is insatiable for this nourishment, and forgets all the world for the more learned friend,—who finds equal joy in dealing out his treasures.

Happy the natural college thus self-instituted around every natural teacher; the young men of Athens around Socrates; of Alexandria around Plotinus; of Paris around Abelard; of Germany around Fichte, or Niebuhr, or Goethe: in short the natural sphere of every leading mind. But the moment this is organized, difficulties begin. The college was to be the nurse and home of genius; but, though every young man is born with some determination in his nature, and is a potential genius; is at last to be one; it is, in the most, obstructed and delayed, and, whatever they may hereafter be, their senses are now opened in advance of their minds. They are more sensual than intellectual. Appetite and indolence they have, but no enthusiasm. These come in numbers to the college: few geniuses: and the teaching comes to be arranged for these many, and not for those few. Hence the instruction seems to require skilful tutors, of accurate and systematic mind, rather than ardent and inventive masters. Besides, the youth of genius are eccentric, won't drill, are irritable, uncertain, explosive, solitary, not men of the world, not good for every-day association. You have to work for large classes instead of individuals; you must lower your flag and reef your sails to wait for the dull sailors; you grow departmental, routinary, military almost with your discipline and college police. But what doth such a school to form a great and heroic character? What abiding Hope can it inspire? What Reformer will it nurse? What poet will it breed to sing to the human race? What discoverer of Nature's laws will it prompt to enrich us by disclosing in the mind the statute which all matter must obey? What fiery soul will it send out to warm a nation with his charity? What tranquil mind will it have fortified to walk with meekness in private and obscure duties, to wait and to suffer? Is it not manifest that our academic institutions should have a wider scope; that they should not be timid and keep the ruts of the last generation, but that wise men thinking for themselves and heartily seeking the good of mankind, and counting the cost of innovation, should dare to arouse the young to a just and heroic life; that the moral nature should be addressed in the school-room, and children should be treated as the high-born candidates of truth and virtue?

So to regard the young child, the young man, requires, no doubt, rare patience: a patience that nothing but faith in the remedial forces of the soul can give. You see his sensualism; you see his want of those tastes and perceptions which make the power and safety of your character. Very likely. But he has something else. If he has his own vice, he has its correlative virtue. Every mind should be allowed to make its own statement in action, and its balance will appear. In these judgments one needs that foresight which was attributed to an eminent reformer, of whom it was said "his patience could see in the bud of the aloe the blossom

at the end of a hundred years." Alas for the cripple Practice when it seeks to come up with the bird Theory, which flies before it. Try your design on the best school. The scholars are of all ages and temperaments and capacities. It is difficult to class them, some are too young, some are slow, some perverse. Each requires so much consideration, that the morning hope of the teacher, of a day of love and progress, is often closed at evening by despair. Each single case, the more it is considered, shows more to be done; and the strict conditions of the hours, on one side, and the number of tasks, on the other. Whatever becomes of our method, the conditions stand fast,—six hours, and thirty, fifty, or a hundred and fifty pupils. Something must be done, and done speedily, and in this distress the wisest are tempted to adopt violent means, to proclaim martial law, corporal punishment, mechanical arrangement, bribes, spies, wrath, main strength and ignorance, in lieu of that wise genial providential influence they had hoped, and yet hope at some future day to adopt. Of course the devotion to details reacts injuriously on the teacher. He cannot indulge his genius, he cannot delight in personal relations with young friends, when his eye is always on the clock, and twenty classes are to be dealt with before the day is done. Besides, how can he please himself with genius, and foster modest virtue? A sure proportion of rogue and dunce finds its way into every school and requires a cruel share of time, and the gentle teacher, who wished to be a Providence to youth, is grown a martinet, sore with suspicions; knows as much vice as the judge of a police court, and his love of learning is lost in the routine of grammars and books of elements.

A rule is so easy that it does not need a man to apply it; an automaton, a machine, can be made to keep a school so. It facilitates labor and thought so much that there is always the temptation in large schools to omit the endless task of meeting the wants of each single mind, and to govern by steam. But it is at frightful cost. Our modes of

Education aim to expedite, to save labor; to do for masses what cannot be done for masses, what must be done reverently, one by one: say rather, the whole world is needed for the tuition of each pupil. The advantages of this system of emulation and display are so prompt and obvious, it is such a time-saver, it is so energetic on slow and on bad natures, and is of so easy application, needing no sage or poet, but any tutor or schoolmaster in his first term can apply it,—that it is not strange that this calomel of culture should be a popular medicine. On the other hand, total abstinence from this drug, and the adoption of simple discipline and the following of nature, involves at once immense claims on the time, the thoughts, on the life of the teacher. It requires time, use, insight, event, all the great lessons and assistances of God; and only to think of using it implies character and profoundness; to enter on this course of discipline is to be good and great. It is precisely analogous to the difference between the use of corporal punishment and the methods of love. It is so easy to bestow on a bad boy a blow, overpower him, and get obedience without words, that in this world of hurry and distraction, who can wait for the returns of reason and the conquest of self; in the uncertainty too whether that will ever come? And yet the familiar observation of the universal compensations might suggest the fear that so summary a stop of a bad humor was more jeopardous than its continuance.

Now the correction of this quack practice is to import into Education the wisdom of life. Leave this military hurry and adopt the pace of Nature. Her secret is patience. Do you know how the naturalist learns all the secrets of the forest, of plants, of birds, of beasts, of reptiles, of fishes, of the rivers and the sea? When he goes into the woods the birds fly before him and he finds none; when he goes to the river bank, the fish and the reptile swim away and leave him alone. His secret is patience; he sits down, and sits still; he is a statue; he is a log. These creatures have no value for their time, and he must put as low a rate on his. By dint of obstinate sitting still, reptile, fish, bird and beast, which all wish to return to their haunts, begin to return. He sits still; if they approach, he remains passive as the stone he sits upon. They lose their fear. They have curiosity too about him. By and by the curiosity masters the fear, and they come swimming, creeping and flying towards him; and as he is still immovable, they not only resume their haunts and their ordinary labors and manners, show themselves to him in their work-day trim, but also volunteer some degree of advances towards fellowship and good understanding with a biped who behaves so civilly and well. Can you not baffle the impatience and passion of the child by your tranquillity? Can you not wait for him, as Nature and Providence do? Can you not keep for his mind and ways, for his secret, the same curiosity you give to the squirrel, snake, rabbit, and the sheldrake and the deer? He has a secret; wonderful methods in him; he is,—every child,—a new style of man; give him time and opportunity. Talk of Columbus and Newton! I tell you the child just born in yonder hovel is the beginning of a revolution as great as theirs. But you must have the believing and prophetic eye. Have the self-command you wish to inspire. Your teaching and discipline must have the reserve and taciturnity of Nature. Teach them to hold their tongues by holding your own. Say little; do not snarl; do not chide; but govern by the eye. See what they need, and that the right thing is done.

I confess myself utterly at a loss in suggesting particular reforms in our ways of teaching. No discretion that can be lodged with a school-committee, with the overseers or visitors of an academy, of a college, can at all avail to reach these difficulties and perplexities, but they solve themselves when we leave institutions and address individuals. The will, the male power, organizes, imposes its own thought and wish on others, and makes that military eye which controls boys as it controls men; admirable in its results, a fortune to him who has it, and only dangerous when it leads the workman to overvalue and overuse it and precludes him from finer means. Sympathy, the female force,—which they must use who have not the first, —deficient in instant control and the breaking down of resistance, is more subtle and lasting and creative. I advise teachers to cherish mother-wit. I assume that you will keep the grammar, reading, writing and arithmetic in order; 't is easy and of course you will. But smuggle in a little contraband wit, fancy, imagination, thought. If you have a taste which you have suppressed because it is not shared by those about you, tell them that. Set this law up, whatever becomes of the rules of the school: they must not whisper, much less talk; but if one of the young people says a wise thing, greet it, and let all the children clap their hands. They shall have no book but school-books in the room; but if one has brought in a Plutarch or Shak[e]speare or Don Quixote or Goldsmith or any other good book, and understands what he reads, put him at once at the head of the class. Nobody shall be disorderly, or leave his desk without permission, but if a boy runs from his bench, or a girl, because the fire falls, or to check some injury that a little dastard is inflicting behind his desk on some helpless sufferer, take away the medal from the head of the class and give it on the instant to the brave rescuer. If a child happens to show that he knows any fact about astronomy, or plants, or birds, or rocks, or history, that interests him and you, hush all the classes and encourage him to tell it so that all may hear. Then you have made your school-room like the world. Of course you will insist on modesty in the children, and respect to their teachers, but if the boy stops you in your speech, cries out that you are wrong and sets you right, hug him!

To whatsover upright mind, to whatsoever beating heart I speak, to you it is committed to educate men. By simple living, by an illimitable soul, you inspire, you correct, you instruct, you raise, you embellish all. By your own act you teach the beholder how to do the practicable. According to the depth from which you draw your life, such is the depth not only of your strenuous effort, but of your manners and presence.

The beautiful nature of the world has here blended your happiness with your power. Work straight on in absolute duty, and you lend an arm and an encouragement to all the youth of the universe. Consent yourself to be an organ of your highest thought, and lo! suddenly you put all men in your debt, and are the fountain of an energy that goes pulsing on with waves of benefit to the borders of society, to the circumference of things.

THE IDEOLOGY OF THE COMMON SCHOOL CRUSADE

THADDEUS STEVENS
A Plea for Free Schools (April 11, 1835)*

Mr. Speaker,—I will briefly give you the reasons why I shall oppose the repeal of the school law. This law was passed at the last

* Thaddeus Stevens' plea for free schools is reprinted under the heading, "General Education—Remarks of Mr. Stevens" [before the Pennsylvania House of Representatives], in *Hazard's Register of Pennsylvania*, Vol. XV, No. 18 (Philadelphia: Printed by Wm. F. Geddes and edited by Samuel Hazard, May 2, 1835), pp. 283–287,

session of the legislature with unexampled unanimity, but one member of this house voting against it. It has not yet come into operation, and none of its effects have been tested by experience in Pennsylvania. The passage of such a law is enjoined by the constitution; and has been recommended by every governor since its adoption. Much to his credit, it has been warmly urged by the present executive in all his annual messages delivered at the opening of the legislature. To repeal it now, before its practical effects have been discovered, would argue that it contained some glaring and pernicious defect; and that the last legislature acted under some strong and fatal delusion, which blinded every man of them, to the interests of the commonwealth. I will attempt to show that the law is salutary, useful and important; and that consequently, the last legislature acted wisely in passing, and the present would act unwisely in repealing it.—That instead of being oppressive to the people, it will lighten their burthens, while it elevates them in the scale of human intellect.

It would seem to be humiliating to be under the necessity, in the nineteenth century, of entering into a formal argument to prove the utility, and to free governments, the absolute necessity of education. More than two thousand years ago the Deity who presided over intellectual endowments, ranked highest for dignity, chastity and virtue, among the goddesses worshipped by cultivated pagans. And I will not insult this House or our constituents by supposing any course of reasoning necessary to convince *them* of its high importance. Such necessity would be degrading to a Christian age and a free republic!

If then, education be of admitted importance to the people under all forms of governments; and of unquestioned *necessity* when they govern themselves, it follows, of cou[r]se, that its cultivation and diffusion is a matter of *public* concern; and a duty which every government owes to its people. In accordance with this principle, the ancient republics, who were most renowned for their wisdom and success, considered every child born subject to their control, as the property of the state, so far as its education was concerned; and during the proper period of instruction, they were withdrawn from the control of their parents, and placed under the guardianship of the commonwealth. There all were instructed at the same school; all were placed on perfect equality, the rich and the poor man's sons, for all were deemed children of the same common parent—of the commonwealth. Indeed, where *all* have the means of knowledge

placed within their reach, and meet at common schools on equal terms, the *forms* of government seem of less importance to the happiness of the people than is generally supposed; or rather, such a people are seldom in danger of having their rights invaded by their rulers. They would not long be invaded with impunity. Prussia, whose form of government is absolute monarchy extends the blessing of free schools into every corner of the kingdom,—to the lowest and poorest of the people. With a population equal to our whole Union, she has not more than 20,000 children who do not enjoy its advantages. And the consequence is, that Prussia, although governed by an absolute monarch, enjoys more happiness and the rights of the people are better respected than in any other government in Europe.

If an elective republic is to endure for any great length of time, *every* elector must have sufficient information, not only to accumulate wealth, and take care of his pecuniary concerns, but to direct wisely the legislatures, the ambassadors, and the executive of the nation—for *some* part of all these things, *some* agency in approving or disapproving of them, falls to every freeman. If then, the permanency of our government depends upon such knowledge, it is the duty of government to see that the means of information be diffused to every citizen. This is a sufficient answer to those who deem education a private and not a public duty— who argue that they are willing to educate their *own* children, but not their *neighbor's* children.

But while but few are found ignorant and shameless enough to deny the advantages of general education, many are alarmed at its supposed burthensome operation. A little judicious reflection, or a single year's experience, would show that education, under the free school system will cost more than one one-half less, and afford better and more permanent instruction than the present disgraceful plan pursued by Pennsylvania.— Take a township of six miles square and make the estimate—such townships, on an average, will contain about 200 children to be schooled. The present rate of tuition generally (in the country) is two dollars per quarter. If the children attend school two quarters each year, such township would pay $800 per annum. Take the free school system—lay the township off into districts three miles square; the farthest scholars would then have one mile and a half to go, which would not be too far. It would require four schools. These will be taught I presume, as in other states, three months in the winter by male, and three months in the summer by female teachers; good male teachers can be had at from sixteen to eighteen dollars per month and board themselves; females at nine dollars per month—Take the highest price, eighteen dollars for three months,

would be	$54 00
And then for females at $9 for three months,	27 00
Each school would cost	81 00
Four to a township	4
	324 00
The price now paid for the same is	800 00

Saving for each township of six miles square, $476 00 per annum.

If the instruction of 200 scholars will save by the free school law $476, the 500,000 children in Pennsylvania will save [$]1,190,-000! Very few men are aware of the immense amount of money which the present expensive and partial mode of education costs the people. Pennsylvania has half a million of children, who either do, or ought to go to school six months in the year. If they *do* go, at two dollars per quarter, their schooling costs two millions of dollars per annum! If they do *not* go when they are able, their parents deserve to be held in disgrace. Where they are unable, if the state does not furnish the means, she is criminally negligent. But by the free school law, that same amount of education, which would now cost two millions of dollars, could be supplied at less than one-third of this amount. The amendment which is now proposed as a substitute for the school law

of last session, is, in my opinion, of a most hateful and degrading character. It is a reenactment of the pauper law of 1809. It proposes that the assessors shall take a census, and make a record of the *poor;* This shall be revised, and a new record made by the county commissioners, so that the names of those who have the misfortune to be poor men's children shall be forever preserved, as a distinct class, in the archives of the county! The teacher, too, is to keep in his school a *pauper* book, and register the names and attendance of poor scholars. Thus pointing out and recording their poverty in the midst of their companions. Sir, hereditary distinctions of rank are sufficiently odious; but that which is founded on poverty is infinitely more so. Such a law should be entitled "an act for branding and marking the poor, so that they may be known from the rich and proud."—Many complain of this tax, not so much on account of its amount, as because it is for the benefit of others and not themselves. This is a mistake. It is for *their own* benefit, inasmuch as it perpetuates the government, and ensures the due administration of the laws under which they live, and by which their lives and property are protected. Why do they not urge the same objection against all other taxes? The industrious, thrifty, rich farmer pays a heavy county tax to support criminal courts, build jails, and pay sheriffs and jail keepers, and yet probably he never has and never will have any direct personal use of either. He never gets the worth of his money by being tried for a crime before the court, allowed the privilege of the jail on conviction; or receiving an equivalent from the sheriff or his hangman officers! He cheerfully pays the tax which is necessary to support and punish convicts; but loudly complains of that which goes to prevent his fellow being from becoming criminal, and to obviate the necessity of those humiliating institutions.

This law is often objected to, because its benefits are shared by the children of the profligate spendthrift equally with those of the most industrious and economical habits.

It ought to be remembered, that the benefit is bestowed, not upon the erring parents, but the innocent children. Carry out this objection and you punish children for the crimes or misfortunes of their parents. You virtually establish castes and grades founded on no merit of the particular generation, but on the demerits of their ancestors; An aristocracy of the most odious and insolent kind—the aristocracy of wealth and pride.

It is said that its advantages will be unjustly and unequally enjoyed, because the industrious, money-making man keeps his whole family *constantly* employed, and has but little time for them to spend at school; while the idle man has but little employment for his family and they will constantly attend school. I know sir, that there are some men, whose whole souls are so completely absorbed in the accumulation of wealth; and whose avarice so increases with success that they look upon their very children in no other light than as instruments of gain—that they, as well as the ox and the ass within their gates, are valuable only in proportion to their annual earnings. And according to the present system, the children of such men are reduced almost to an intellectual level with their co-laborers of the brute creation. This law will be of vast advantage to the offspring of such misers. If they are compelled to pay their taxes to support schools, their very meanness will induce them to send their children to them to get the worth of their money. Thus it will extract good out of the very penuriousness of the miser. Surely a system, which will work such wonders, ought to be as greedily sought for, and more highly prized than that coveted alchymy, which was to produce gold and silver out of the blood and entrails of vipers, lizards and other filthy vermin!

Why, sir, are the colleges and literary institutions of Pennsylvania now, and ever have been, in a languishing, sickly condition? Why, with a fertile soil and genial climate, has she, in proportion to her population, scarcely one-third as many collegiate students, as cold, barren, New England? The answer is obvious—She has no free schools. Until she shall have, you may in vain endow college after college, they will never be filled; or filled only by students from other states. In New England free schools plant the seeds and the desire of knowledge in *every* mind, without regard to the wealth of the parent or the texture of the pupil's garments. When the seed thus universally sown, happens to fall on fertile soil, it springs up and is fostered by a generous public, until it produces its glorious fruit.— Those who have but scanty means and are pursuing a collegiate education, find it necessary to spend a portion of the year in teaching common schools; thus imparting the knowledge which they acquire, they raise the dignity of the employment to a rank which it should always hold, honorable in proportion to the high qualifications necessary for its discharge. Thus devoting a portion of their time to acquiring the means of subsistence, industrious habits are forced upon them, and their minds and bodies become disciplined to a regularity and energy which is seldom the lot of the rich. It is no uncommon occurrence to see the poor man's son, thus encouraged by wise legislation, far outstrip and bear off the laurels from the less industrious heirs of wealth. Some of the ablest men of the present and past days never could have been educated except for that benevolent system. Not to mention any of the living, it is well known that that architect of an immortal name, who "plucked the lightnings from heaven, and the sceptre from tyrants," was the child of free schools. Why shall Pennsylvania now repudiate a system, which is calculated to elevate her to that rank in the intellectual, which, by the blessing of Providence, she holds in the natural world? To be the key-stone of the arch, the "very first among her equals?" I am aware, sir, how difficult it is for the great mass of the people who have never seen it in operation, to understand its advantages. But is it not wise to let it go into full operation, and learn its results from experience? Then if it prove useless or burthensome, how easy to repeal it? I know how large a portion of the community can scarcely feel any sympathy with, or understand the necessities of the poor; or appreciate the exqu'site feelings which they enjoy when they see their children receiving the boon of education, and rising in intellectual superiority, above the clogs which hereditary poverty had cast upon them. It is not wonderful that he whose fat acres have descended to him from father to son in unbroken succession, should never have become familiar with misery, and therefore should never have sought for the surest means of alleviating it. Sir, when I reflect how apt hereditary wealth, hereditary influence, and perhaps as a consequence hereditary pride are to close the avenues and steel the heart against the wants and the rights of the poor, I am induced to thank my Creator for having from early life, bestowed upon me the blessing of poverty. Sir, it *is* a blessing—for if there be any human sensation more ethereal and divine than all others, it is that which feelingly sympathises with misfortune.

But we are told that this law is unpopular; that the people desire its repeal. Has it not always been so with every new reform in the condition of man? Old habits, and old prejudices are hard to be removed from the mind. Every new improvement, which has been gradually leading man from the savage through the civilized up to a highly cultivated state, has required the most strenuous, and often perilous exertions of the wise and the good. But, sir, much of its unpopularity is chargeable upon the vile arts of unprincipled demagogues. Instead of attempting to remove the honest misapprehensions of the people, they cater to their prejudices, and take advantage of them, to gain low, dirty, temporary, local triumphs. I do not charge this on any particular party. Unfortunately, almost the only spot on which all parties meet in union, is this ground of common infamy! I have seen the present chief magistrate of this commonwealth violently assailed as the projector and father of this law. I am not the eulogist of that gentleman;

he has been guilty of many deep political sins. But he deserves the undying gratitude of the people, for the steady untiring zeal, which he has manifested in favor of common schools. I will not say that his exertions in that cause have covered all, but they have atoned for many of his errors. I trust that the people of this state will never be called on to choose between a supporter and an opposer of free schools. But if it should come to that; if that should be made the turning point on which we are to cast our suffrages; if the opponent of education were my most intimate personal and political friend; and the free school candidate my most obnoxious enemy, I should deem it my duty as a patriot, at this moment of our intellectual crisis, to forget all other considerations, and I should place myself unhesitatingly, and cordially, in the ranks of him, whose banner streams in light. I would not foster nor flatter ignorance, to gain political victories, which however they might profit individuals, must prove disastrous to our country. Let it not be supposed from these remarks, that because I deem this a paramount object, that I think less highly than heretofore of those great, important cardinal principles, which for years past have controlled my political action. They are, and ever shall be, deeply cherished in my inmost heart. But I must be allowed to exercise my own judgment as to the best means of effectuating that and every other object which I think beneficial to the community. And according to that judgment, the light of general information, will as surely counteract the pernicious influence of secret, oath-bound, murderous institutions, as the sun in heaven dispels the darkness and damp vapours of the night.

It is said that some gentlemen here owe their election to their hostility to general education. That it was placed distinctly on that ground, and that others lost their election by being in favor of it, and that they consented to supercede the regularly nominated candidates of their own party, who had voted for this law—it may be so. I believe that two highly respectable members of the last legislature, from Union county, who voted for the school law, did fail of re-election on that ground only. They were summoned before a county meeting, and requested to pledge themselves to vote for its repeal, as the price of their re-election. But they were too high-minded and honorable men to consent to such degradation. The people, incapable for the moment of appreciating their worth, dismissed them from their service. But I venture to predict that they have passed them by only for the moment. Those gentlemen have earned the approbation of all good and intelligent men more effectually by their retirement, than they could ever have done by retaining popular favor at the expense of self humiliation. They fell, it is true, in this great struggle between the powers of light and darkness; but they fell as every Roman mother wished her sons to fall—facing the enemy, with all their wounds in front.

True it is, also, that two other gentlemen, and I believe two only, lost their election on account of their vote on that question. I refer to the late members from Berks, who were candidates for re-election; and I regret that gentlemen, whom I so highly respect, and whom I take pleasure in ranking among my personal friends, had not possessed a little more nerve to enable them to withstand the assaults which were made upon them; or if they must be overpowered, to wrap their mantles gracefully around them and yield with dignity. But this, I am aware, requires a high degree of fortitude; and those respected gentlemen distracted and faltering between the dictates of conscience, and the clamor of the populace, at length turned and fled: but duty had detained them so long that they fled too late; and the shaft, which had already been winged by ignorance, overtook and pierced them from behind. I am happy to say, sir, that a more fortunate fate awaited our friends from York. Possessing a keener insight into futurity, and a sharper instinct of danger, they saw the peril at a greater distance, and retreated in time to escape the fury of the storm; and can now safely boast that "discretion is the better part of valor," and that "they fought, and run away," "and live to fight—on 'tother side."

Sir, it is to be regretted that any gentleman should have consented to place his election on hostility to general education. If honest ambition were his object, he will ere long lament that he attempted to raise his monument of glory on so muddy a foundation. But if it be so that they were placed here to obstruct the diffusion of knowledge, it is but justice to say that they fitly and faithfully represent the spirit which sent them here, when they attempt to sacrifice this law on the altars, which at home, among their constituents they have raised and consecrated to Intellectual darkness; and on which they are pouring out oblations to send forth their foetid and noxious odours over the ten miles square of their ambition! But will this legislature—will the wise guardians of the dearest interests of a great commonwealth, consent to surrender the high advantages and brilliant prospects which this law promises, because it is desired by worthy gentlemen, who in a moment of causeless panic and popular delusion, sailed into power on a Tartarean flood? A flood of ignorance, darker, and to the intelligent mind, more dreadful, than that accursed Stygean pool, at which mortals and immortals tremble! Sir, it seems to me that the liberal and enlightened proceedings of the last legislature have aroused the demon of ignorance from his slumber; and, maddened at the threatened loss of his murky empire, his discordant howlings are heard in every part of our land!

Gentlemen will hardly contend for the doctrine of cherishing and obeying the prejudices and errors of their constituents. Instead of prophecying smooth things, and flattering the people with the belief of their present perfection, and thus retarding the mind in its onward progress, it is the duty of faithful legislators to create and sustain such laws and institutions, as shall teach us our wants—foster our cravings after knowledge, and urge us forward in the march of intellect.—The barbarous and disgraceful cry, which we hear abroad in some parts of our land, "that learning makes us worse —that education makes men rogues," should find no echo within these walls. Those who hold such doctrines any where, would be the objects of bitter detestation, if they were not rather the pitiable subjects of commiseration. For even voluntary fools require our compassion as well as natural idiots!

Those who would repeal this law because it is obnoxious to a portion of the people, would seem to found their justification on a desire of popularity. That is not an unworthy object, when they seek that enduring fame, which is constructed of imperishable materials.—But have these gentlemen looked back and consulted the history of their race, to learn on what foundation, and on what materials that popularity is built which outlives its possessor—which is not buried in the same grave which covers his mortal remains? Sir, I believe that kind of fame may be acquired either by deep learning, or even the love of it, by mild philanthropy, or unconquerable courage. And it seems to me, that in the present state of feeling in Pennsylvania, those who will heartily and successively support the cause of general education, can acquire, at least some portion of the honor of all these qualities combined; while those who oppose it will be remembered without pleasure, and soon pass away with the things that perish. In giving this law to posterity, you act the part of the philanthropist, by bestowing upon the poor as well as the rich the greatest earthly boon, which they are capable of receiving: you act the part of the philosopher by pointing, if you do not lead them up the hill of science: you act the part of the hero, if it be true as you say, that popular vengeance follows close upon your footsteps. Here then, if you wish true popularity, is a theatre on which you may acquire it. What renders the name of Socrates immortal, but his love of the human family, exhibited under all circumstances and in contempt of every

danger? But courage, even with but little benevolence, may confer lasting renown. It is this which makes us bow with involuntary respect, at the names of Napole[o]n, of Caesar and of Richard of the Lion heart. But what earthly glory is there equal in lustre and duration to that conferred by education?— What else could have bestowed such renown upon the Philosophers, the Poets, the Statesmen, and Orators of antiquity? What else could have conferred such undisputed applause upon Aristotle, Demosthenes, and Homer; on Virgil, Horace, and Cicero? And is learning less interesting and important now than it was in centuries past, when those statesmen and orators charmed and ruled empires with their eloquence?

Sir, let it not be thought that those great men acquired a higher fame than is within the reach of the present age. Pennsylvania's sons possess as high native talents as any other nation of ancient or modern time! Many of the poorest of her children possess as bright intellectual gems, if they were as highly polished, as did the proudest scholars of Greece or Rome.—But too long— too disgracefully long, has coward, trembling, procrastinating legislation permitted them to lie buried in "dark unfathomed caves."

If you wish to acquire popularity, how often have you been admonished to build not your monuments of brass or marble, but make them of ever-living mind!—Although the period of yours, or your children's renown, cannot be as long as that of the ancients, because you start from a later period, yet it may be no less brilliant. Equal attention to the same learning; equal ardor in pursuing the same arts and liberal studies, which has rescued their names from the rust of corroding time, and handed them down to us untarnished from remote antiquity, would transmit the names of your children, and your children's children in the green undying fame down through the long vista of succeeding ages, until time shall mingle with eternity.

Let all, therefore, who would sustain the character of the philosopher or philanthropist, sustain this law.—Those who would add thereto the glory of the hero, can acquire it here; for in the present state of feeling in Pennsylvania, I am willing to admit, that but little less dangerous to the public man is the war-club and battle-axe of savage ignorance, than to the Lion Hearted Richard was the keen scim[i]tar of the Saracen. He, who would oppose it, either through inability to comprehend the advantages of general education; or from unwillingness to bestow them on all his fellow citizens, even to the lowest and the poorest; or from dread of popular vengeance, seems to me to want either the head of the philosopher, the heart of the philanthropist or the nerve of the hero.

All these things would be easily admitted by almost every man, were it not for the supposed cost. I have endeavored to show that it is not expensive; but admit that it were somewhat so, why do you cling so closely to your gold? The trophies which it can purchase; the idols which it sets up, will scarcely survive their purchaser. No name, no honor can long be perpetuated by mere matter. Of this, Egypt furnishes melancholy proof. Look at her stupendous pyramids, which were raised at such immense expenses of toil and treasure.—As mere masses of matter they seem as durable as the everlasting hills, yet the deeds, and the names which they were intended to perpetuate, are no longer known on earth. That ingenious people attempted to give immortality to matter, by embalming their great

men and monarchs. Instead of doing deeds worthy to be recorded in history, their very names are unknown, and nothing is left to posterity but their disgusting mortal frames for idle curiosity to stare at. What rational being can view such soulless, material perpetuation with pleasure? If you can enjoy it, go, sir, to the foot of Vesuvius; to Herculaneum, and Pompeii, those eternal monuments of human weakness. There, if you set such value on material monuments of riches, may you see all the glory of art, the magnificence of wealth, the gold of Ophir, and the rubies of the East preserved in indestructible lava along with their haughty wearers, the cold, smooth, petrified, lifeless, beauties of the "Cities of the Dead."

Who would not shudder at the idea of such prolonged material identity? Who would not rather do one living deed, than to have his ashes forever enshrined in ever-burnished gold. Sir, I trust, that when we come to act on this question we shall all take lofty ground—look beyond the narrow space which now circumscribes our vision—beyond the passing, fleeting point of time on which we stand; and so cast our votes that the blessing of education shall be conferred on every son of Pennsylvania—shall be carried home to the poorest child of the poorest inhabitant of the meanest hut of your mountains, so that even he may be prepared to act well his part in this land of freemen, and lay on earth, a broad and a solid foundation for that enduring knowledge, which goes on increasing through increasing eternity.

EDUCATION FOR A FREE SOCIETY:
THE IDEAS OF HORACE MANN

HORACE MANN
Ninth Annual Report (December 10, 1845) *

Essential requisites in a teacher's character are, a love of children, and a love of his

* Horace Mann, *Ninth Annual Report of the Secretary of the Board of Education, Boston, December 10, 1845* (Boston: Dutton and Wentworth, State Printers, 1846), pp. 83–85, 94–96.

work. He must not be a hireling. It is right that he should have a regard for his compensation; but, his compensation being provided for, it should be forgotten. To exclude the feeling of monotony and irksomeness, he must look upon his work, as ever a new one; for such it really is. The school teacher is not, as it sometimes seems to be supposed, placed upon a perpetually revolving wheel, and carried through a daily round of the same labors and duties. Such a view of his office is essentially a low and false one. What if he does turn over the leaves of the same book from day to day, and hear the same lessons recited from year to year? What if he is required to explain the same principles, and to reiterate the same illustrations, until his path, in the accustomed exercises of the schoolroom, is as worn and beaten, as the one by which, morning and night, he travels to and from it. Still, in the truest and highest sense, his labor is always a new one; *because the subject upon which he operates, is constantly changing.* Every day he is developing new faculties, or carrying forward the old, through new stages of their course. Though the books which he uses, and the instruction which he imparts, may be the same, yet his real work consists in his taking up class after class, and conducting them onward through new portions of their progress. The charge committed to his care is weak, ignorant, immature, and constitutionally subject to error. He imparts vigor; he supplies knowledge; he ripens judgment; he establishes principle; and he then sends them on their way, to fulfil the great duties of earth, and to be more and more prepared for another life. But so soon as he has fulfilled his duty to one company of the ever-onward moving procession of young life, another company steps in to occupy the place of the former. Their need of guidance, their capacities of improvement, are as great as those which have gone before them. They too, are bound on the same perilous journey of life, and for the same goal of an immortal existence. He is to guide their steps aright; he is to see that before they pass from under his hands, they have some adequate conception of the great objects at which they are to aim, of the glorious destiny at which they may arrive; and that they are endued with the energy and the perseverance which will make their triumph certain. As soon as this labor is done to one company, he bids them a hasty farewell, that he may turn, with glad welcome, to hail another, more lately arrived upon the confines of existence, who ask his guidance as they are crossing the narrow isthmus of time, on their way to eternity. Such is the teacher's duty,—to welcome each new group, to prepare them for the journey of life, and to speed them on their way; and again to welcome, to prepare, and to speed; and, I repeat it, it is, and forever must be, a new work, while new beings emerge into existence, to be benefited by him,—to be rescued from what is wrong, to be consecrated to what is right. No teacher, therefore, who regards his duties in the light of reason and religion, can look upon them as repulsive, or monotonous, or irksome. The angel that unlocks the gates of heaven, might as well become weary of the service, though, with every opening of the door, a new spirit is ushered into the mansions of bliss.

Let the teacher, then, who cannot draw exhaustless energies from a contemplation of the nature of his calling; let the teacher, whose heart is not exhilarated, as he looks round upon the groups of children committed to his care; let the teacher who can ever consciously speak of the "tedium of school keeping," or the "irksome task of instruction," either renovate his spirit, or abandon his occupation. The repining teacher may be useful in some other sphere; he may be fit to work upon the perishable materials of wood, or iron, or stone, but he is unfit to work upon the imperishable mind.

The teacher should enter the schoolroom as the friend and benefactor of his scholars. He is supposed to possess more knowledge, than they, by the utmost diligence and stretch of faculty, can receive from him; but yet no fact is more certain, or law more universal, than that they will make no valuable and abiding acquisition, without their own consent and coöperation. The teacher can neither transfuse knowledge by any process of decanting, nor inject it by any force, into the mind of a child; but the law of the relation subsisting between them is, that he must have the child's conscious assent and concurrence, before he can impart it. He cannot impart, unless the child consents to receive. What then is the state of mind most receptive of knowledge, and most coöperative in acquiring it? Surely, it is a state of confidence, of trustfulness, of respect, of affection. Hence it follows that the first great duty of a teacher is to awaken these sentiments in the breasts of his pupils. For this end, he can do more, the first half day he enters the schoolroom, than in any week afterwards. But if a teacher presents himself before his pupils with a haughty or a contemptuous air; if he introduces himself by beginning to speak of *his* power and *his* authority, he will soon create the occasion for using them.

. . . . .

One of the highest and most valuable objects, to which the influences of a school can be made conducive, consists in training our children to self-government. The doctrine of No-government, even if all forms of violence did not meet, the first day, to celebrate its introduction by a jubilee, would forfeit all the power that originates in concert and union. So tremendous, too, are the evils of anarchy and lawlessness, that a government by mere force, however arbitrary and cruel, has been held preferable to no-government. But self-government, self-control, a voluntary compliance with the laws of reason and duty, have been justly considered as the highest point of excellence attainable by a human being. No one, however, can consciously obey the laws of reason and duty, until he understands them. Hence the preliminary necessity of their being clearly explained, of their being made to stand out, broad, lofty, and as conspicuous as a mountain against a clear sky. There may be blind obedience without a knowledge of the law, but only of the will of the lawgiver; but the first step towards rational obedience is a knowledge of the rule to be obeyed, and of the reasons on which it is founded.

The above doctrine acquires extraordinary force, in view of our political institutions,—founded, as they are, upon the great idea of the capacity of man for self-government,—an idea so long denounced by the state as treasonable, and by the church as heretical. In order that men may be prepared for self-government, their apprenticeship must commence in childhood. The great moral attribute of self-government cannot be born and matured in a day; and if school children are not trained to it, we only prepare ourselves for disappointment, if we expect it from grown men. Every body acknowledges the justness of the declaration, that a foreign people, born and bred and dwarfed under the despotisms of the Old World, cannot be transformed into the full stature of American citizens, merely by a voyage across the Atlantic, or by subscribing the oath of naturalization. If they retain the servility in which they have been trained, some self-appointed lord or priest, on this side of the water, will succeed to the authority of the master, they have left behind them. If, on the other hand, they identify liberty with an absence from restraint, and an immunity from punishment, then they are liable to become intoxicated and delirious with the highly stimulating properties of the air of freedom; and thus, in either case, they remain unfitted, until they have become morally acclimated to our institutions, to exercise the rights of a freeman. But can it make any substantial difference, whether a man is suddenly translated into all the independence and prerogatives of an American citizen, from the bondage of an Irish lord or an English manufacturer, or from the equally rigorous bondage of a parent, guardian or school teacher? He who has been a serf until the day before he is twenty-one years of age, cannot be an independent citizen the day after; and it makes no difference whether he has been a serf in Austria or in America. As the fitting apprenticeship for despotism consists in being trained to despotism, so the fitting apprenticeship for self-government consists in being trained to self-government; and liberty and self-imposed law are as appropriate a preparation for the subjects of an arbitrary power, as the law of force and authority is for developing and maturing those sentiments of self-respect, of honor and of dignity, which belong to a truly republican citizen. Were we hereafter to govern irresponsibly, then our being forced to yield implicit obedience to an irresponsible governor would prepare us to play the tyrant in our turn; but if we are to govern by virtue of a law which embraces all, which overlies all, which includes the governor as well as the governed, then lessons of obedience should be inculcated upon childhood, in reference to that sacred law. If there are no two things wider asunder than freedom and slavery, then must the course of training which fits children for these two opposite conditions of life be as diverse as the points to which they lead. Now, for the high purpose of training an American child to become an American citizen,—a constituent part of a self-governing people,—is it not obvious that, in all cases, the law by which he is to be bound should be made intelligible to him; and, as soon as his capacity will permit, that the reasons on which it is founded, should be made as intelligible as the law itself?

HORACE MANN
Twelfth Annual Report (November 24, 1848) *

Without undervaluing any other human agency, it may be safely affirmed that the Common School, improved and energized, as it can easily be, may become the most effective and benignant of all the forces of civilization. Two reasons sustain this position. In the first place, there is a universality in its operation, which can be affirmed of no other institution whatever. If adminis-

* Horace Mann, *Twelfth Annual Report of the Secretary of the Board of Education, West Newton [Massachusetts], November 24, 1848* (Boston: Dutton and Wentworth, State Printers, 1849), pp. 42–45, 52–56, 59–60, 67–68, 76, 84–85, 90–91, 94, 103–105, 117, 138–142.

tered in the spirit of justice and conciliation, all the rising generation may be brought within the circle of its reformatory and elevating influences. And, in the second place, the materials upon which it operates are so pliant and ductile as to be susceptible of assuming a greater variety of forms than any other earthly work of the Creator. The inflexibility and ruggedness of the oak, when compared with the lithe sapling or the tender germ, are but feeble emblems to typify the docility of childhood, when contrasted with the obduracy and intractableness of man. It is these inherent advantages of the Common School, which, in our own State, have produced results so striking, from a system so imperfect, and an administration so feeble. In teaching the blind, and the deaf and dumb, in kindling the latent spark of intelligence that lurks in an idiot's mind, and in the more holy work of reforming abandoned and outcast children, education has proved what it can do, by glorious experiments. These wonders, it has done in its infancy, and with the lights of a limited experience; but, when its faculties shall be fully developed, when it shall be trained to wield its mighty energies for the protection of society against the giant vices which now invade and torment it;—against intemperance, avarice, war, slavery, bigotry, the woes of want and the wickedness of waste,— then, there will not be a height to which these enemies of the race can escape, which it will not scale, nor a Titan among them all, whom it will not slay.

I proceed, then, in endeavoring to show how the true business of the schoolroom connects itself, and becomes identical, with the great interests of society. The former is the infant, immature state of those interests; the latter, their developed, adult state. As "the child is father to the man," so may the training of the schoolroom expand into the institutions and fortunes of the State.

PHYSICAL EDUCATION.

In the worldly prosperity of mankind, Health and Strength are indispensable ingredients. Reflect, for a moment, what an inroad upon the comfort of a family and its means of support, is a case of chronic sickness or debility, in a single one of its members. Should a farmer contract to support, and to continue to pay, his laborer, or a manufacturer his operative, whether able or unable to work, they would demand a serious abatement of wages, as a premium for the risk. But, whatever drawback a sick member would be to the pecuniary prosperity of a family, or a sick laborer to that of an employer bound to support him, just such a drawback is a sick or disabled member of the community to the financial prosperity of the State to which he belongs. The amount of loss consequent upon such sickness or disability may not be drawn out of the public treasury, but it is subtracted from the common property of the State, in a way still more injurious than if the same amount of gold were taken from the public coffers by warrant of the executive. Money, so taken, would be transferred to another hand. It would still exist. But the want of health and strength is a dead loss to the community; and, whenever the next valuation is taken, there will be a corresponding deficit in the aggregate of national property. Hence, every citizen, as such, is pecuniarily interested in the health and strength of all his fellow-citizens. . . .

Now modern science has made nothing more certain, than that both good and ill health are the direct result of causes, mainly within our own control. In other words, the health of the race is dependent upon the conduct of the race. The health of the individual is determined primarily by his parents; secondarily, by himself. The vigorous growth of the body, its strength and its activity, its powers of endurance, and its length of life, on the one hand; and dwarfishness, sluggishness, infirmity, and premature death, on the other, are all the subjects of unchangeable laws. These laws are ordained of God; but the knowledge of them is left to our diligence, and the observance of them to our free agency. These laws are very few;

they are so simple that all can understand them, and so beautiful that the pleasure of contemplating them, even independent of their utility, is a tenfold reward for all the labor of their acquisition. The laws, I repeat, are few. The circumstances, however, under which they are to be applied, are exceedingly various and complicated. These circumstances embrace the almost infinite varieties of our daily life;—exercise and rest; sleeping and watching; eating, drinking, and abstinence; the affections and passions; exposure to vicissitudes of temperature, to dryness and humidity, to the effluvia and exhalations of dead animal or decaying vegetable matter;—in fine, they embrace all cases where excesses, indiscretions, or exposures, may induce disease; or where exercise, temperance, cleanliness, and pure air, may avert it. Hence it would be wholly impossible to write out any code of "Rules and Regulations," applicable to all cases. So, too, the occasions for applying the laws to new circumstances recur so continually that no man can have a Mentor at his side, in the form of a physician or physiologist, to direct his conduct in new emergencies. Even the most favored individual, in ninety-nine cases in a hundred, must prescribe for himself. And hence the uncompromising necessity that all children should be instructed in these laws; and not only instructed, but that they should receive such a *training,* during the whole course of pupilage, as to enlist the mighty forces of habit on the side of obedience; and that their judgment also should be so developed and matured that they will be able to discriminate between different combinations of circumstances, and to adapt, in each case, the regimen to the exigency. . . .

My general conclusion, then, under this head, is, that it is the duty of all the governing minds in society,—whether in office or out of it,—to diffuse a knowledge of these beautiful and beneficent laws of health and life, throughout the length and breadth of the State;—to popularize them; to make them, in the first place, the common acquisition of all, and, through education and custom, the common inheritance of all; so that the healthful habits naturally growing out of their observance, shall be inbred in the people; exemplified in the personal regimen of each individual; incorporated into the economy of every household; observable in all private dwellings, and in all public edifices, especially in those buildings which are erected by capitalists for the residence of their work-people, or for renting to the poorer classes; obeyed, by supplying cities with pure water; by providing public baths, public walks, and public squares; by rural cemeteries; by the drainage and sewerage of populous towns, and in whatever else may promote the general salubrity of the atmosphere;—in fine, by a religious observance of all those sanitary regulations with which modern science has blessed the world.

For this thorough diffusion of sanitary intelligence, the Common School is the only agency.

·   ·   ·   ·   ·

INTELLECTUAL EDUCATION, AS A MEANS OF REMOVING POVERTY, AND SECURING ABUNDANCE.

Another cardinal object which the government of Massachusetts, and all the influential men in the State should propose to themselves, is the physical well-being of all the people,—the sufficiency, comfort, competence, of every individual, in regard to food, raiment, and shelter. And these necessaries and conveniences of life should be obtained by each individual for himself, or by each family for themselves, rather than accepted from the hand of charity, or extorted by poor-laws. It is not averred that this most desirable result can, in all instances, be obtained; but it is, nevertheless, the end to be aimed at. True statesmanship and true political economy, not less than true philanthropy, present this perfect theory as the goal, to be more and more closely approximated by our imperfect practice. The desire to achieve such a result cannot be re-

garded as an unreasonable ambition; for, though all mankind were well-fed, well-clothed, and well-housed, they might still be but half-civilized.

Poverty is a public as well as a private evil. There is no physical law necessitating its existence. The earth contains abundant resources for ten times,—doubtless for twenty times,—its present inhabitants. Cold, hunger, and nakedness, are not, like death, an inevitable lot. . . .

According to the European theory, men are divided into classes,—some to toil and earn, others to seize and enjoy. According to the Massachusetts theory, all are to have an equal chance for earning, and equal security in the enjoyment of what they earn. The latter tends to equality of condition; the former to the grossest inequalities. Tried by any Christian standard of morals, or even by any of the better sort of heathen standards, can any one hesitate, for a moment, in declaring which of the two will produce the greater amount of human welfare; and which, therefore, is the more conformable to the Divine will? The European theory is blind to what constitutes the highest glory, as well as the highest duty, of a State. Its advocates and admirers are forgetful of that which should be their highest ambition, and proud of that which constitutes their shame. How can any one, possessed of the attributes of humanity, look with satisfaction upon the splendid treasures, the golden regalia, deposited in the Tower of London, or in Windsor Palace, each "an India in itself," while thousands around are dying of starvation; or have been made criminals by the combined forces of temptation and neglect? The present condition of Ireland cancels all the glories of the British crown. The brilliant conception which symbolizes the nationality of Great Britain as a superb temple, whose massive and grand proportions are upheld and adorned by the four hundred and thirty Corinthian columns of the aristocracy, is turned into a loathing and a scorn, when we behold the five millions of paupers that cower and shiver at its base.

The galleries and fountains of Versailles, the Louvre of Paris, her Notre Dame, and her Madeleine, though multiplied by thousands in number and in brilliancy, would be no atonement for the hundred thousand Parisian *ouvriers*, without bread and without work. The galleries of painting and of sculpture, at Rome, at Munich, or at Dresden, which body forth the divinest ideals ever executed or ever conceived, are but an abomination in the sight of Heaven and of all good men, while actual, living beings,— beings that have hearts to palpitate, and nerves to agonize, and affections to be crushed or corrupted,—are experimenting, all around them, upon the capacities of human nature for suffering and for sin. . . .

If one class possesses all the wealth and the education, while the residue of society is ignorant and poor, it matters not by what name the relation between them may be called; the latter, in fact and in truth, will be the servile dependants and subjects of the former. But if education be equally diffused, it will draw property after it, by the strongest of all attractions; for such a thing never did happen, and never can happen, as that an intelligent and practical body of men should be permanently poor. Property and labor, in different classes, are essentially antagonistic; but property and labor, in the same class, are essentially fraternal. The people of Massachusetts have, in some degree, appreciated the truth, that the unexampled prosperity of the State,—its comfort, its competence, its general intelligence and virtue,—is attributable to the education, more or less perfect, which all its people have received; but are they sensible of a fact equally important?—namely, that it is to this same education that two thirds of the people are indebted for not being, to-day, the vassals of as severe a tyranny, in the form of capital, as the lower classes of Europe are bound to in the form of brute force.

Education, then, beyond all other devices of human origin, is the great equalizer of the conditions of men—the balance-wheel of the social machinery. I do not here mean that it so elevates the moral nature as to make men disdain and abhor the oppression of their fellow-men. This idea pertains to another of its attributes. But I mean that it gives each man the independence and the means, by which he can resist the selfishness of other men. It does better than to disarm the poor of their hostility towards the rich; it prevents being poor. Agrarianism is the revenge of poverty against wealth. The wanton destruction of the property of others,— the burning of hay-ricks and corn-ricks, the demolition of machinery, because it supersedes hand-labor, the sprinkling of vitriol on rich dresses,—is only agrarianism run mad. Education prevents both the revenge and the madness. On the other hand, a fellow-feeling for one's class or caste is the common instinct of hearts not wholly sunk in selfish regards for person, or for family. The spread of education, by enlarging the cultivated class or caste, will open a wider area over which the social feelings will expand; and, if this education should be universal and complete, it would do more than all things else to obliterate factitious distinctions in society.

The main idea set forth in the creeds of some political reformers, or revolutionizers, is, that some people are poor *because* others are rich. This idea supposes a fixed amount of property in the community, which, by fraud or force, or arbitrary law, is unequally divided among men; and the problem presented for solution is, how to transfer a portion of this property from those who are supposed to have too much, to those who feel and know that they have too little. At this point, both their theory and their expectation of reform stop. But the beneficent power of education would not be exhausted, even though it should peaceably abolish all the miseries that spring from the coëxistence, side by side, of enormous wealth and squalid want. It has a higher function. Beyond the power of diffusing old wealth, it has the prerogative of creating new. It is a thousand times more lucrative than fraud; and adds a thousand fold more to a nation's resources than the most successful conquests. Knaves and robbers can obtain only what was before possessed by others. But education creates or develops new treasures,—treasures not before possessed or dreamed of by any one. . . .

For the creation of wealth, then,—for the existence of a wealthy people and a wealthy nation,—intelligence is the grand condition. The number of improvers will increase, as the intellectual constituency, if I may so call it, increases. In former times, and in most parts of the world even at the present day, not one man in a million has ever had such a development of mind, as made it possible for him to become a contributor to art or science. Let this development precede, and contributions, numberless, and of inestimable value, will be sure to follow. That Political Economy, therefore, which busies itself about capital and labor, supply and demand, interest and rents, favorable and unfavorable balances of trade; but leaves out of account the element of a wide-spread mental development, is nought but stupendous folly. The greatest of all the arts in political economy is, to change a consumer into a producer; and the next greatest is, to increase the producer's producing power;—an end to be directly attained, by increasing his intelligence.

.   .   .   .   .

POLITICAL EDUCATION.

The necessity of general intelligence,—that is, of education, (for I use the terms as substantially synonymous; because general intelligence can never exist without general education, and general education will be sure to produce general intelligence,)—the necessity of general intelligence, under a republican form of government, like most other very important truths, has become a very trite one. It is so trite, indeed, as to have lost much of its force by its familiarity.

Almost all the champions of education seize upon this argument, first of all; because it is so simple as to be understood by the ignorant, and so strong as to convince the sceptical. Nothing would be easier than to follow in the train of so many writers, and to demonstrate, by logic, by history, and by the nature of the case, that a republican form of government, without intelligence in the people, must be, on a vast scale, what a mad-house, without superintendent or keepers, would be, on a small one. . . .

However elevated the moral character of a constituency may be; however well informed in matters of general science or history, yet they must, if citizens of a Republic, understand something of the true nature and functions of the government under which they live. That any one who is to participate in the government of a country, when he becomes a man, should receive no instruction respecting the nature and functions of the government he is afterwards to administer, is a political solecism. In all nations, hardly excepting the most rude and barbarous, the future sovereign receives some training which is supposed to fit him for the exercise of the powers and duties of his anticipated station. . . . Hence, the constitution of the United States, and of our own State, should be made a study in our Public Schools. The partition of the powers of government into the three co-ordinate branches,—legislative, judicial, and executive,—with the duties appropriately devolving upon each; the mode of electing or of appointing all officers, with the reasons on which it was founded; and, especially, the duty of every citizen, in a government of laws, to appeal to the courts for redress, in all cases of alleged wrong, instead of undertaking to vindicate his own rights by his own arm; and, in a government where the people are the acknowledged sources of power, the duty of changing laws and rulers by an appeal to the ballot, and not by rebellion, should be taught to all the children until they are fully understood.

.   .   .   .   .

MORAL EDUCATION.

Moral education is a primal necessity of social existence. The unrestrained passions of men are not only homicidal, but suicidal; and a community without a conscience would soon extinguish itself. Even with a natural conscience, how often has Evil triumphed over Good! From the beginning of time, Wrong has followed Right, as the shadow the substance. . . . The government sees the evils that come from the use of intoxicating drinks, and prohibits their sale; but unprincipled men pander to depraved appetites, and gather a harvest of dishonest profits. Instead of licensing lotteries, and deriving a revenue from the sale of tickets, the State forbids the mischievous traffic; but while law-abiding men disdain to practise an illicit trade, knavish brokers, by means of the prohibition itself, secure a monopoly of the sales, and pocket the infamous gain. The government imposes duties on imported goods; smugglers evade the law, and bring goods into the country clandestinely; or perjurers swear to false invoices, and escape the payment of duty, and thus secure to themselves the double advantage of increased sales, and enhanced profits upon what is sold. Science prepares a new medicine to heal or alleviate the diseases of men; crime adulterates it, or prepares, as a substitute, some cheap poison that resembles it, and can be sold instead of it. A benefactor of the race discovers an agent which has the marvellous power to suspend consciousness, and take away the susceptibility of pain; a villain uses it to rob men or pollute women. Houses are built; the incendiary burns them, that he may purloin the smallest portion of their goods. The press is invented to spread intelligence; but libellers use it to give wings to slander. And, so, throughout all the infinitely complex and ramified relations of society, wherever there is a right there may be a wrong; and wherever a law is made to repress the wrong, it may be evaded by artifice or overborne by violence. In fine, all means and laws designed to repress injustice and crime, give occasion to new injustice and crime. For every lock that is made, a false key is made to pick it; and for every Paradise that is created, there is a Satan who would scale its walls. . . .

Education has never yet been brought to bear with one hundredth part of its potential force, upon the natures of children, and, through them, upon the character of men, and of the race. In all the attempts to reform mankind which have hitherto been made, whether by changing the frame of government, by aggravating or softening the severity of the penal code, or by substituting a government-created, for a God-created religion;—in all these attempts, the infantile and youthful mind, its amenability to influences, and the enduring and self-operating character of the influences it receives, have been almost wholly unrecognized. Here, then, is a new agency, whose powers are but just beginning to be understood, and whose mighty energies, hitherto, have been but feebly invoked; and yet, from our experience, limited and imperfect as it is, we do know that, far beyond any other earthly instrumentality, it is comprehensive and decisive.

.   .   .   .   .

RELIGIOUS EDUCATION.

. . . On this subject, I propose to speak with freedom and plainness, and more at length than I should feel required to do, but for the peculiar circumstances in which I have been placed. It is matter of notoriety, that the views of the Board of Education,—and my own, perhaps still more than those of the Board,—on the subject of religious instruction in our Public Schools, have been subjected to animadversion. Grave charges have been made against us, that our purpose was to exclude religion; and to exclude that, too, which is the common exponent of religion,—the Bible,—from the Common Schools of the State; or, at least, to derogate from its authority, and destroy its influence in them. Whatever prevalence a suspicion of the truth of these imputations may have heretofore had, I have reason to believe that further inquiry and examination have done much to disabuse the too credulous recipients of so groundless a charge. Still, amongst a people so commendably sensitive on the subject of religion, as are the people of Massachusetts, any suspicion of irreligious tendencies, will greatly prejudice any cause, and, so far as any cause may otherwise have the power of doing good, will greatly impair that power.

It is known, too, that our noble system of Free Schools for the whole people, is strenuously opposed;—by a few persons in our own State, and by no inconsiderable numbers in some of the other states of this Union;—and that a rival system of "Parochial" or "Sectarian Schools," is now urged upon the public by a numerous, a powerful, and a well-organized body of men. It has pleased the advocates of this rival system, in various public addresses, in reports, and through periodicals devoted to their cause, to denounce our system as irreligious and anti-Christian. They do not trouble themselves to describe what our system is, but adopt a more summary way to forestall public opinion against it, by using general epithets of reproach, and signals of alarm. . . .

All the schemes ever devised by governments, to secure the prevalence and permanence of religion among the people, however variant in form they may have been, are substantially resolvable into two systems. One of these systems holds the regulation and control of the religious belief of the people to be one of the functions of government, like the command of the army or the navy, or the establishment of courts, or the collection of revenues. According to the other system, religious belief is a matter of individual and parental concern; and, while the government furnishes all practicable facilities for the independent formation of that belief, it exercises no authority to prescribe, or coercion to enforce it. The former is the system, which, with very few exceptions, has prevailed throughout Christendom, for fifteen hundred years. Our own government is almost a solitary example among the nations of the earth, where freedom of opinion, and the inviolability of conscience, have been even theoretically recognized by the law. . . .

The very terms, *Public School,* and *Common School,* bear upon their face, that they are schools which the children of the entire community may attend. Every man, not on the pauper list, is taxed for their support. But he is not taxed to support them as special religious institutions; if he were, it would satisfy, at once, the largest definition of a Religious Establishment. But he is taxed to support them, as a *preventive* means against dishonesty, against fraud, and against violence; on the same principle that he is taxed to support criminal courts as a *punitive* means against the same offences. He is taxed to support schools, on the same principle that he is taxed to support paupers; because a child without education is poorer and more wretched than a man without bread. He is taxed to support schools, on the same principle that he would be taxed to defend the nation against foreign invasion, or against rapine committed by a foreign foe; because the general prevalence of ignorance, superstition, and vice, will breed Goth and Vandal at home, more fatal to the public well-being, than any Goth or Vandal from abroad. And, finally, he is taxed to support schools, because they are the most effective means of developing and training those powers and faculties in a child, by which, when he becomes a man, he may understand what his highest interests and his highest duties are; and may be, in fact, and not in name only, a free agent. . . .

If, then, a government would recognize and protect the rights of religious freedom, it must abstain from subjugating the capacities of its children to any legal standard of religious faith, with as great fidelity as it abstains from controlling the opinions of men. It must meet the unquestionable fact, that the old spirit of religious domination is adopting new measures to accomplish its work,—measures, which, if successful, will be as fatal to the liberties of mankind, as those which were practised in by-gone days of violence and terror. These new measures are aimed at children instead of men. They propose to supersede the necessity of subduing free thought, *in the mind of the adult,* by forestalling the development of any capacity of free thought, *in the mind of the child.* They expect to find it easier to subdue the free agency of children, by binding them in fetters of bigotry, than to subdue the free agency of men, by binding them in fetters of iron. For this purpose, some are attempting to deprive children of their right to labor, and, of course, of their daily bread, unless they will attend a government school, and receive its sectarian instruction. Some are attempting to withhold all means, even of secular education, from the poor, and thus punish them with ignorance, unless, with the secular knowledge which they desire, they will accept theological knowledge which they condemn. Others, still, are striving to break down all free Public School systems, where they exist, and to prevent their establishment, where they do not exist, in the hope, that on the downfall of these, their system will succeed. The sovereign antidote against these machinations, is, Free Schools for all, and the right of every parent to determine the religious education of his children.

This topic invites far more extended exposition; but this must suffice. In bidding an official Farewell to a system, with which I have been so long connected, to which I have devoted my means, my strength, my health, twelve years of time, and, doubtless, twice that number of years from what might otherwise have been my term of life, I have felt bound to submit these brief views in its defence. In justice to my own name and memory; in justice to the Board of which I was originally a member, and from which I have always sought counsel and guidance; and in justice to thousands of the most wise, upright, and religious-minded men in Massa-chusetts, who have been my fellow-laborers in advancing the great cause of Popular Education, under the auspices of this system, I have felt bound to vindicate it from the aspersions cast upon it, and to show its consonance with the eternal principles of equity and justice. I have felt bound to show, that, so far from its being an irreligious, an anti-Christian, or an un-Christian system, it is a system which recognizes religious obligations in their fullest extent; that it is a system which invokes a religious spirit, and can never be fitly administered without such a spirit; that it inculcates the great commands, upon which hang all the law and the prophets; that it welcomes the Bible, and therefore welcomes all the doctrines which the Bible really contains, and that it listens to these doctrines so reverently, that, for the time being, it will not suffer any rash mortal to thrust in his interpolations of their meaning, or overlay the text with any of the "many inventions" which the heart of man has sought out. It is a system, however, which leaves open all other means of instruction,—the pulpits, the Sunday schools, the Bible classes, the catechisms, of all denominations,—to be employed according to the preferences of individual parents. It is a system which restrains itself from teaching, that what it does teach is all that needs to be taught, or that should be taught; but leaves this to be decided by each man for himself, according to the light of his reason and conscience; and on his responsibility to that Great Being, who, in holding him to an account for the things done in the body, will hold him to the strictest account for the manner in which he has "trained up" his children.

Such, then, in a religious point of view, is the Massachusetts system of Common Schools. Reverently, it recognizes and affirms the sovereign rights of the Creator; sedulously and sacredly it guards the religious rights of the creature; while it seeks to remove all hinderances, and to supply all furtherances to a filial and paternal communion between man and his Maker. In a social and political sense, it is a *Free* school system. It knows no distinction of rich and poor, of bond and free, or between those who, in the imperfect light of this world, are seeking, through different avenues, to reach the gate of heaven. Without money and without price, it throws open its doors, and spreads the table of its bounty, for all the children of the State. Like the sun, it shines, not only upon the good, but upon the evil, that they may become good; and, like the rain, its blessings descend, not only upon the just, but upon the unjust, that their injustice may depart from them and be known no more.

To the great founders of this system, we look back with filial reverence and love. Amid the barrenness of the land, and in utter destitution of wealth, they coined the rude comforts, and even the necessaries of life, into means for its generous support. Though, as laborers by day, they subdued the wilderness, and, as sentinels by night, they guarded the camp, yet they found time for the vigilant administration and oversight of the schools, in the day of their infancy and weakness. But for this single institution, into which they transfused so much of their means and of their strength, and of which they have made us the inheritors, how different would our lot and our life have been! Upon us, its accumulated blessings have descended. It has saved us from innumerable pains and perils, that would otherwise have been our fate;—from the physical wretchedness, that is impotent to work out its own relief; from the darkness of the intellect, whose wanderings after light so often plunge it into deeper gloom; and from the moral debasement, whose pleasures are vices and crimes. It has surrounded us with a profusion of comforts and blessings, of which the most poetic imagination would never otherwise have conceived. It has found, not mythologic goddesses, but gigantic and tireless laborers in every stream; not evil and vindictive spirits, but beneficent and helping ones, in all the elements; and, by a profounder alchemy than the schoolmen ever dreamed of, it transmutes quarries and icefields into gold. It has given cunning to the hand of the mechanic, keenness to the artisan's eye, and made a sterile soil grow grateful beneath the skill of the husbandman. Hence, the absence of poverty among our native population; hence, a competency for the whole people, the means for mental and moral improvement, and for giving embellishment and dignity to life, such as the world has never known before, and such as no where else can be found upon the face of the earth. . . .

But not the fortunes of our children alone, or of our children's children, are dependant upon us. The influences of our conduct extend outward in space, as well as onward in time. We are part of a mighty nation, which has just embarked upon the grandest experiment ever yet attempted upon earth;— the experiment of the capacity of mankind for the wise and righteous government of themselves.

PART TWO

AN ERA OF TRANSITION: 1865–1919

"We here highly resolve that the dead shall not have died in vain, that the nation shall, under God, have a new birth of freedom."

ABRAHAM LINCOLN, The Gettysburg Address, November 19, 1863

"There is no way to lift up life that is on so low a level except by the free education of all the people."

WALTER HINES PAGE, Letter to a friend in North Carolina, April, 1902

"Try to think of the deep upheaval of the human soul, pulled up by the roots from its ancient, precious soil, cast abroad among you here, withering for a space. . . . Oh, if I could show you America as we of the oppressed peoples see it!"

MARCUS E. RAVAGE, *An American in the Making,* 1917

"The school must permit the *free, natural manifestations* of the *child* if in the school scientific pedagogy is to be born. This is the essential reform."

MARIA MONTESSORI, "A Critical Consideration of the New Pedagogy in Its Relation to Modern Science," 1912

Introduction

I

Booker T. Washington (1856–1915) was born a plantation slave. After emancipation, he moved with his mother to a village near Charleston, West Virginia, where he worked in a coal mine to help support the family and studied in the evening with a teacher from a Negro school. At seventeen, he walked three hundred miles to enroll at Hampton Institute. He learned how to be a brickmason and earned his board by working as a janitor. After favorably impressing General Samuel C. Armstrong, Hampton's principal, Washington was recommended in 1881 to head Tuskegee Institute in Alabama.

From 1881 to 1915, Washington was the most important figure in American Negro history. At Tuskegee he helped to transform a backward community, subsisting mainly on corn bread and fat pork, into a progressive town. "All the industries at Tuskegee [were] started in natural and logical order, growing out of the needs of a community settlement," explained Washington in *Up from Slavery* (1901). "We started with farming, because we wanted something to eat." Beginning with his own idea of "learn by doing," always linking academic subjects with practical work, he educated thousands of Negro teachers and craftsmen for positions in the rural South.

Sometimes overlooked is the rationale for Washington's advocacy of industrial education: his whole program was based on the hope that economic stability would ease tensions and gradually rectify social injustices. He stressed vocational training *first*, believing that Negroes would become so economically indispensable to the South that white citizens would eventually lower the barriers to racial equality. His first aim, then, was to prepare good workmen; and he did, in fact, instill in Tuskegee graduates a strong spirit of craftsmanship.

Washington rejected a militant abolitionist strategy. An exponent of "gradualism," he sought to prepare Negroes for citizenship rather than seek it directly for them. "Cast down your bucket where you are," he told his people in September, 1895, in a widely publicized address before the Cotton States' Exposition in Atlanta, Georgia. Washington proclaimed that the two races could be separate socially but united on all matters essential to progress. His words aroused great enthusiasm among white citizens. An eloquent speaker, seemingly prudent and constructive, he was quite successful in his appeals to northern philanthropists. By the turn of the century, he was a nationally recognized leader of his race, and he seemed to speak for all Negro Americans.

But this was not the case. Before he died in 1915, Washington was being harshly criticized for his conciliatory approach to the racial dilemma. Militants doubted seriously from the very beginning whether Washington really understood the growing crisis: the terroristic Ku Klux Klan, the lynchings in the South, the legalized schemes for disfranchisement of Negro citizens. Chief among the critics was W. E. Burghardt Du Bois (1868–1963).

Educated at Berlin and Harvard, intensely proud of his Negro ancestry, Du Bois challenged Washington's program of concession and compromise. He deplored the neglect of higher education for Negro teachers and potential leaders, the "Talented Tenth" (Du Bois's favorite phrase). In 1905 he and his militant young followers met at Niagara

Falls to launch what later became known as the Niagara Movement. Its platform was a bold manifesto calling for an end to racial restrictions in education and civil rights. Four years later Du Bois and the Niagara group, supported by such leaders as Jane Addams and John Dewey, formed the bi-racial National Association for the Advancement of Colored People.

By 1919, then, Negro Americans were free but not yet equal. In the South, as well as in the North, they were still viewed as second-class citizens. However, they had firmly established a tradition of protest and strategy: under Booker T. Washington, Negro leadership was acquiescent and co-operative; under W. E. Burghardt Du Bois, articulate and defiant.

II

From 1880 to 1914, about ten million people from southern and eastern Europe entered the United States. Bewildered by a strange environment, the new immigrants succumbed to the squalor of the slums into which poverty forced them.

This influx into a free society of non-English-speaking people with diverse customs and values added new dimensions to the old issue of Americanization. Most native-born citizens favored an assimilative process which would erase ethnic differences. Thus acculturation meant shedding old values and accepting instead certain "American" ways.

Some, however, viewed the issue from another vantage point. Horace M. Kallen, for example, urged America to conserve and encourage "individuality." Cultural pluralism, argued Kallen in 1915, is preferable to the "melting pot" concept. He envisioned a free America where it would be respectable to be different, where ethnic diversity would enrich the main stream.

As a "neighbourhood social station," the settlement house tried to bridge the gap between the ethnic island of the ghetto and a surrounding world whose customs and demands carried little meaning in the hearts of immigrant families. "We looked upon the settlement as a moving, living force whose idea was one of service and not of power," recalled Angelo Patri, a school principal, in 1923. ". . . It gave us the hope that some day the school itself would be a bigger thing than it had ever been before." Settlement-house workers helped to ease the conflicts of cultures by encouraging a respect for the ethnic traditions of the Old World.

III

For almost half a century, the followers of John Dewey (1859–1952) led their students to believe that the ideology of progressive education was so universally true, so exclusively adequate, that a democracy had no need to consider other systems of thought. Such leadership was persuasive among those who were not philosophically oriented. It was easy to experience vicariously with the original mind the creative process of an unfolding organization of ideas.

The unqualified acceptance of one system of thought is fraught with real danger. What is often overlooked is that the power of discipleship stems from a commitment to the master; and this commitment denies a follower the privilege of substantially changing his philosophic stance.

Yet it was this privilege that kept a brilliant thinker like John Dewey free. By not committing himself to any extant philosophy in his own heritage, he was free to question his own basic premises, to wonder about the adequacy of his ideas, to rebuild or abandon. This freedom a disciple jeopardizes in his unqualified commitment to a single system of thought.

Ideally, a teacher's commitment should be unlike that of any disciple: in a democracy the commitment is to a never-ending search for truth in which the path is enlightened by all systems of thought and not directed by any one of them. Hopefully such knowledge leads to wisdom, not to dogma. With wisdom the teacher discovers that, despite all knowledge, one does not finally know. Here, then, is the spirit of liberal learning in which the teacher not only knows more than his students but also learns with them in a distinctive way. And the students' awareness of this fact sets them at one with their teacher in a ceaseless quest. It is the spirit of this never-ending search for truth that encourages the creative thinking in which a free society must place its ultimate faith.

IV

Since the early nineteen-fifties, there has been a renewed interest in the ideas of Jean Piaget (1896–   ) and Maria Montessori (1870–1952). Piaget, who obtained his doctorate in biology from the University of Lausanne, is interested in the study of the child as a means to answering certain key questions about the nature and origin of knowledge.

From about 1922 to 1930 Piaget began his research by exploring the depth and extent of the child's reasoning powers. He recorded the spontaneous talk of three- to ten-year-old children while they played alone or with others and their conversations with him and his assistant. Using this *méthode clinique,* Piaget collected those childish sayings which some parents find nonsensical and amusing. He systematized the forms of verbal expression according to age levels and revealed an interesting sequence governing the development of the child's mental processes.

The Language and Thought of the Child (1926) traces the use of language from the "egocentric stage," when speech is merely the vocal accompaniment of the child's solipsistic thoughts, actions, and games, to the period of socialization, when it becomes a comprehensible and purposeful tool for communication. *The Child's Conception of Physical Causality* (1930) deals with children's explanations of physical phenomena, of the origins of names and things, and the causes which underlie physical and social happenings. From these and other studies, Piaget concluded that the thought of the child gradually passes through a series of

stages, from early animism through magic and artificialism to rational thinking; at each level the child constructs a systematic "cosmology" of the world according to the modes of reasoning available to him at that stage.

Thus Piaget discovered that children not only reason differently from adults but also have implicit philosophies or world-views. His research and penetrating insights are adding new dimensions to the understanding of child development.

Maria Montessori, from the very beginning of her professional career, was deeply concerned with the education of children. In fact, most of her long life was devoted to freeing the child from a pedagogy which she considered harmful to physical and mental growth. Through lectures and personal demonstrations, she tried to reorient the thinking of teachers and parents along the lines of her own "Method," to develop, in brief, a new philosophy of education.

Born near Ancona, Italy, Mrs. Montessori was the first woman to earn a medical degree from the University of Rome. After graduation in 1894, she worked among retarded and feeble-minded children. Her "Method" originated from this work and from her experiences as director of a *Casa dei Bambini* (Children's House), a school for so-called normal children.

Mrs. Montessori's greatest achievement was her success with culturally different children from the slums. In an area of Rome where no woman dared walk alone at night, she demonstrated how undisciplined boys and girls who had previously run wild in the streets could learn to read, write, compute, and develop "the power of spontaneous reasoning." The children learned this in an atmosphere of freedom, but they were taught in a carefully "prepared environment." This "prepared environment" was a strong force in the acquisition of new skills, attitudes, and values.

For Mrs. Montessori some form of environmental "nourishment" was deemed essential to mental growth. "The sole problem," she wrote in 1917, "is that of offering the child the necessary nourishment." The power of her learning tools (for example, the sandpaper letters and the form and weight inset boards) stemmed from the fact that they "nourished" the development of mental structures through the use of relevant classroom materials. Note, however, that she did not advocate the *acceleration* of mental growth. (This point is frequently misunderstood by her American followers.)

What Mrs. Montessori emphasized was the necessity of providing an atmosphere which freed each child for mental and physical growth, for self-realization *at one's own pace*.

We should take a fresh look at the ideas of this remarkable woman. Her contribution to the history of educational thought is so relevant to the process of early childhood education, so pertinent to the needs of all children.

CHAPTER SIX

Evolving Patterns of Educational Thought

TOWARD UNIVERSAL EDUCATION

THE SUPREME COURT OF MICHIGAN
The Kalamazoo Decision (July 21, 1874) *

Charles E. Stuart and others v. School District No. 1 of the Village of Kalamazoo and others.

*Heard July 10 and 15.
Decided July 21. [1874]*

Appeal in Chancery from Kalamazoo
Circuit.

Edwards & Sherwood and *G. V. N. Lothrop,*
for complainants.
Dwight May and *D. Darwin Hughes,* for
defendants.

COOLEY, J.:

The bill in this case is filed to restrain the collection of such portion of the school taxes assessed against complainants for the year 1872, as have been voted for the support of the high school in that village, and for the payment of the salary of the superintendent. While, nominally, this is the end sought to be attained by the bill, the real purpose of the suit is wider and vastly more comprehensive than this brief statement would indicate, inasmuch as it seeks a judicial determination of the right of school authorities, in what are called union school districts of the state, to levy taxes upon the general public for the support of what in this state are known as high schools, and to make free by such taxation the instruction of children

* *Stuart v. School District No. 1 of the Village of Kalamazoo et al.,* 30 Mich. 69–85 (1874).

in other languages than the English. The bill is, consequently, of no small interest to all the people of the state, and to a large number of very flourishing schools, it is of the very highest interest, as their prosperity and usefulness, in a large degree, depend upon the method in which they are supported, so that a blow at this method seems a blow at the schools themselves. . . .

The more general question which the record presents we shall endeav[o]r to state in our own language, but so as to make it stand out distinctly as a naked question of law, disconnected from all considerations of policy or expediency; in which light alone are we at liberty to consider it. It is, as we understand it, that there is no authority in this state to make the high schools free by taxation levied on the people at large. The argument is that while there may be no constitutional provision expressly prohibiting such taxation, the general course of legislation in the state and the general understanding of the people have been such as to require us to regard the instruction in the classics and in living modern languages in these schools as in the nature not of practical and therefore necessary instruction for the benefit of the people at large, but rather as accomplishments for the few, to be sought after in the main by those best able to pay for them, and to be paid for by those who seek them, and not by general tax. And not only has this been the general state policy, but this higher learning of itself, when supplied by the state, is so far a matter of

211

private concern to those who receive it that the courts ought to declare it incompetent to supply it wholly at the public expense. This is in substance, as we understand it, the position of the complainants in this suit.

When this doctrine was broached to us, we must confess to no little surprise that the legislation and policy of our state were appealed to against the right of the state to furnish a liberal education to the youth of the state in schools brought within the reach of all classes. We supposed it had always been understood in this state that education, not merely in the rudiments, but in an enlarged sense, was regarded as an important practical advantage to be supplied at their option to rich and poor alike, and not as something pertaining merely to culture and accomplishment to be brought as such within the reach of those whose accumulated wealth enabled them to pay for it. As this, however, is now so seriously disputed, it may be necessary, perhaps, to take a brief survey of the legislation and general course, not only of the state, but of the antecedent territory, on the subject. . . .

In 1827 the educational system was supplemented by "an act for the establishment of common schools," which is also worthy of special attention and reflection, as indicating what was understood at that day by the common schools which were proposed to be established.

The first section of that act provided "that every township within this territory, containing fifty families or householders, shall be provided with a good schoolmaster or schoolmasters, of good morals, to teach children to read and write, and to instruct them in the English or French language, as well as in arithmetic, orthography, and decent behavior, for such term of time as shall be equivalent to six months for one school in each year. And every township containing one hundred families or householders, shall be provided with such schoolmaster or teacher for such term of time as shall be equivalent to twelve months for one school in each year. And every township containing

one hundred and fifty families or householders shall be provided with such schoolmaster or teacher for such term of time as shall be equivalent to six months in each year, and shall, in addition thereto, be provided with a schoolmaster or teacher, as above described, to instruct children in the English language for such term of time as shall be equivalent to twelve months for one school in each year. And every township containing two hundred families or householders shall be provided with a grammar schoolmaster, of good morals, *well instructed in the Latin, French and English languages,* and shall, in addition thereto, be provided with a schoolmaster or teacher, as above described, to instruct children in the English language, for such term of time as shall be equivalent to twelve months for each of said schools in each year." And the townships respectively were required under a heavy penalty, to be levied in case of default on the inhabitants generally, to keep and maintain the schools so provided for.—*Code of 1827, p. 448; Territorial Laws, Vol. 2, p. 472.*

Here, then, was a general law, which, under the name of common schools, required not only schools for elementary instruction, but also grammar schools to be maintained. The qualifications required in teachers of grammar schools were such as to leave it open to no doubt that grammar schools in the sense understood in England and the Eastern states were intended, in which instruction in the classics should be given, as well as in such higher branches of learning as would not usually be taught in the schools of lowest grade. How is it possible, then, to say, as the exigencies of complainants' case require them to do, that the term common or primary schools, as made use of in our legislation, has a known and definite meaning which limits it to the ordinary district schools, and that consequently the legislative authority to levy taxes for the primary schools cannot be held to embrace taxation for the schools supported by village and city districts in which a higher grade of learning is imparted.

It is probable that this act, like that of 1817, was found in advance of the demands of the people of the territory, or of their ability to support high schools, and it was repealed in 1833, and another passed which did not expressly require the establishment or support of schools of secondary grade, but which provided only for school directors, who must maintain a district school at least three months in each year.—*Code of 1833, p. 129.* The act contains no express limitations upon their powers, but it is not important now to consider whether or not they extended to the establishment of grammar schools as district schools, where, in their judgment, they might be required. Such schools would certainly not be out of harmony with any territorial policy that as yet had been developed or indicated.

Thus stood the law when the constitution of 1835 was adopted. The article on education in that instrument contained the following provisions:

"2. The legislature shall encourage by all suitable means the promotion of intellectual, scientifical and agricultural improvement. The proceeds of all lands that have been, or hereafter may be, granted by the United States to this state for the support of schools, which shall hereafter be sold or disposed of, shall be and remain a perpetual fund, the interest of which, together with the rents of all such unsold lands, shall be inviolably appropriated to the support of schools throughout the state.

"3. The legislature shall provide for a system of common schools, by which a school shall be kept up and supported in each school district at least three months in every year; and any school district neglecting to keep up and support such a school may be deprived of its equal proportion of the interest of the public fund."

The fifth section provided for the support of the university, "with such branches as the public convenience may hereafter demand for the promotion of literature, the arts and sciences," etc. Two things are specially noticeable in these provisions: *first,* that they contemplated provision by the state for a complete system of instruction, beginning with that of the primary school and ending with that of the university; *second,* that while the legislature was required to make provision for district schools for at least three months in each year, no restriction was imposed upon its power to establish schools intermediate the common district school and the university, and we find nothing to indicate an intent to limit their discretion as to the class or grade of schools to which the proceeds of school lands might be devoted, or as to the range of studies or grade of instruction which might be provided for in the district schools.

In the very first executive message after the constitution went into effect, the governor, in view of the fact that "our institutions have leveled the artificial distinctions existing in the societies of other countries, and have left open to every one the avenues to distinction and honor," admonished the legislature that it was their "imperious duty to secure to the state a general diffusion of knowledge," and that "this can in no wise be so certainly effected as by the perfect organization of a uniform and liberal system of common schools." Their "attention was therefore called to the effectuation of a perfect school system, open to all classes, as the surest basis of public happiness and prosperity." In his second message he repeated his admonitions, advising that provision be made for ample compensation to teachers, that those of the highest character, both moral and intellectual, might be secured, and urging that the "youth be taught the first principles in morals, in science, and in government, commencing their studies in the primary schools, elevating its grades as you approach the district seminary, and continue its progress till you arrive at the university." This message indicated no plan, but referred the legislature to the report of the superintendent, who would recommend a general system.

The system reported by superintendent Pierce contemplated a university, with branches in different parts of the state as preparatory schools, and district schools. This is the parent of our present system, and though its author did not find the legislature prepared to accept all his views, the result has demonstrated that he was only a few years in advance of his generation, and that the changes in our school system which have since been adopted have been in the direction of the views which he then held and urged upon the public. And an examination of his official report for 1837 will show that the free schools he then favored were schools which taught something more than the rudiments of a common education; which were to give to the poor the advantages of the rich, and enable both alike to obtain within the state an education broad and liberal, as well as practical.

It would be instructive to make liberal extracts from this report did time and space permit. The superintendent would have teachers thoroughly trained, and he would have the great object of common schools "to furnish good instruction in all the elementary and common branches of knowledge, for all classes of community, *as good, indeed, for the poorest boy of the state as the rich man can furnish for his children with all his wealth.*" The context shows that he had the systems of Prussia and of New England in view, and that he proposed by a free school system to fit the children of the poor as well as of the rich for the highest spheres of activity and influence.

It might also be useful in this connection to show that the Prussian system and that "of the Puritans," of which he speaks in such terms of praise, resemble in their main features, so far as bringing within the reach of all a regular gradation of schools is concerned, the system of public instruction as it prevails in this state to-day. But it is not necessary for the purposes of the present case to enter upon this subject. It must suffice to say that the law of 1827, which provided for grammar schools as a grade of common schools, was adopted from laws which from a very early period had been in

existence in Massachusetts, and which in like manner, under heavy penalties, compelled the support of these grammar schools in every considerable town.—See *Mass. Laws, 1789, p. 39;* compare *General Stat., 1860, p. 215, § 2.*

The system adopted by the legislature, and which embraced a university and branches, and a common or primary school in every school district of the state, was put into successful operation, and so continued, with one important exception, until the adoption of the constitution of 1850. The exception relates to the branches of the university, which the funds of the university did not warrant keeping up, and which were consequently abandoned. Private schools to some extent took their place; but when the convention met to frame a constitution in 1850, there were already in existence, in a number of the leading towns, schools belonging to the general public system, which were furnishing instruction which fitted young men for the university. These schools for the most part had been organized under special laws, which, while leaving the primary school laws in general applicable, gave the districts a larger board of officers and larger powers of taxation for buildings and the payment of teachers. As the establishment and support of such schools were optional with the people, they encountered in some localities considerable opposition, which, however, is believed to have been always overcome, and the authority of the districts to provide instruction in the languages in these union schools was not, so far as we are aware, seriously contested. The superintendent of public instruction devotes a considerable portion of his annual report for 1848 to these schools, and in that of 1849 he says: "This class of institutions, which may be made to constitute a connecting link between the ordinary common school and the state university, is fast gaining upon the confidence of the public. Those already established have generally surpassed the expectations of their founders. Some of them have already attained a standing rarely equaled by the academical institutions of the older states. Large, commodious, and beautiful edifices have been erected in quite a number of villages for the accommodation of these schools. These school-houses frequently occupy the most eligible sites in the villages where they are located. I am happy in being able to state in this connection that the late capitol of our state, having been fitted up at much expense, was, in June last, opened as a *common school-house;* and that in that house is maintained a free school which constitutes the pride and ornament of the city of the straits." This *common* free school was a union school equivalent in its instruction to the ordinary high school in most matters, and the report furnishes very clear evidence that the superintendent believed schools of that grade to be entirely competent under the primary school law.

It now becomes important to see whether the constitutional convention and the people, in 1850, did any thing to undo what previously had been accomplished towards furnishing high schools as a part of the primary school system. The convention certainly did nothing to that end. On the contrary, they demonstrated in the most unmistakable manner that they cherished no such desire or purpose. The article on education as originally reported, while providing for free schools to be kept in each district at least three months in every year, added that "the English language and no other shall be taught in such schools." Attention was called to this provision, and it was amended so as to read that instruction should be "conducted in the English language." The reason for the change was fully given, that as it was reported it might be understood to prohibit the teaching of other languages than the English in the primary schools; a result that was not desired. Judge Whipple stated in the convention that, in the section from which he came, French and German were taught, and "it is a most valuable improvement of the common school system." The late superintendent Pierce said

that in some schools Latin was taught, and that he himself had taught Latin in a common school. He would not adopt any provision by which any knowledge would be excluded. "All that we ought to do is this: we should say the legislature shall establish primary schools." This, in his opinion, would give full power, and the details could be left to legislation.—See *Debates of the Convention, 269, 549.*

The instrument submitted by the convention to the people and adopted by them provided for the establishment of free schools in every school district for at least three months in each year, and for the university. By the aid of these we have every reason to believe the people expected a complete collegiate education might be obtained. The branches of the university had ceased to exist; the university had no preparatory department, and it must either have been understood that young men were to be prepared for the university in the common schools, or else that they should go abroad for the purpose, or be prepared in private schools. Private schools adapted to the purpose were almost unknown in the state, and comparatively a very few persons were at that time of sufficient pecuniary ability to educate their children abroad. The inference seems irresistible that the people expected the tendency towards the establishment of high schools in the primary school districts would continue until every locality capable of supporting one was supplied. And this inference is strengthened by the fact that a considerable number of our union schools date their establishment from the year 1850 and the two or three years following.

If these facts do not demonstrate clearly and conclusively a general state policy, beginning in 1817 and continuing until after the adoption of the present constitution, in the direction of free schools in which education, and at their option the elements of classical education, might be brought within the reach of all the children of the state, then, as it seems to us, nothing can demonstrate it. We might follow the subject further, and show that the subsequent legislation has all concurred with this policy, but it would be a waste of time and labor. We content ourselves with the statement that neither in our state policy, in our constitution, or in our laws, do we find the primary school districts restricted in the branches of knowledge which their officers may cause to be taught, or the grade of instruction that may be given, if their voters consent in regular form to bear the expense and raise the taxes for the purpose.

Having reached this conclusion, we shall spend no time upon the objection that the district in question had no authority to appoint a superintendent of schools, and that the duties of superintendency should be performed by the district board. We think the power to make the appointment was incident to the full control which by law the board had over the schools of the district, and that the board and the people of the district have been wisely left by the legislature to follow their own judgment in the premises.

It follows that the decree dismissing the bill was right, and should be affirmed.

The other Justices concurred.

THE QUEST OF THE NEGRO

WHITELAW REID
After the War: A Southern Tour (1866) *

Among the Negro Schools.

In the good old times, before the advent of Farragut and Butler, the statutes of Louisiana declared teaching slaves to read and write a "crime, having a tendency to excite insubordination among the servile class, and punishable by imprisonment at hard labor for not more than twenty-one years, or by death, at the discretion of the court." When asked, therefore, to visit the negro schools of New Orleans, I was not unduly sanguine in my expectations. Reverend and Lieutenant Wheelock, a keen, practical Yankee preacher, acting as secretary to the "Board of Education for Freedmen," instituted by General Banks, was guide.

The first school-house to which we were conducted was an old store-room, the second story of which had been used as a hall for the Knights of the Golden Circle, and still bore on its walls the symbols of that hollowest and most insolent of Southern

* Whitelaw Reid, *After the War: A Southern Tour. May 1, 1865, to May 1, 1866* (New York: Moore, Wilstach & Baldwin, and London: Sampson Low, Son & Co., 1866), Chapter XXV, "Among the Negro Schools," pp. 246–258.

humbugs. Rude partitions divided the store-room, and separated the three different grades of the primary school.

In the first we were received by a coarse, ill-dressed, rude-looking man, who evidently sprang from the poor white trash. Ranged along the wall as we entered were a dozen or more boys, reading as boys do read, in the Third Reader—with many a pause and many a tracing of hard words with a great fore-finger that blurs everything it touches. Among the class was a bright, fair-haired boy, who would have been called handsome anywhere. Seated behind the little desks were some large, coarse girls, seemingly eighteen or twenty years of age, conning their spelling-books. The hot air was languidly stirred by the hot breeze from the street windows, which brought in with it the sound of boys at play on the pavement; and one did not wonder at the noise and general inattention that prevailed.

The next room was ruled by a woman as coarse and slatternly as became the neighbor of the man whose school we had just left. A little fellow made some noise to displease her as we entered, and she bowled him against the wall as one would bowl a ball down a ten-pin alley. Children were at work mumbling over charts hung against the wall, and professing, with much noisy show of industry, to be spelling out simple sentences. But their zeal did not prevent surreptitious pinches, when the slatternly school-mistress's back was turned, nor a trade of "five alleys for a bright-colored glass one," on the sly. I think such scenes are not unknown even in model Northern schools.

The teacher in the third room was as great a contrast to the two we had just seen as was her school to theirs. She was smart, bright, looking for all the world like a Lowell factory girl of the better class; and her pupils, though by no means quiet as lambs, were in fine order. Their faces had evidently been washed systematically; long labors had forced upon their comprehension the advantages of clean aprons and pinafores; and they appeared attentive and noisily anxious to learn. This teacher seemed capable of giving an intelligent opinion as to the capacities of her scholars. She had taught at the North, and she saw no difference in the rapidity with which whites and blacks learned to spell and read. There were dull scholars and bright scholars everywhere. Some here were as dull as any she ever saw; others were bright as the brightest. And she called out a little coal-black creature, who had been in school eight days, and was apparently not more than as many years old. The eyes of the little thing sparkled as she began to spell! Eight days ago she had not known her letters. From spelling she went to reading, and was soon found to have mastered every sentence on the charts hung about the walls.

The more advanced scholars were found in the old hall of the K. G. C., up stairs. Here, where once schemes for taking Cuba, or perpetuating slavery in the South, were discussed, forty or fifty boys and girls, lately slaves, stood before the platform where the knights had ranged themselves for initiation, and peacefully recited their lesson in the Fourth Reader! Where once the Knight Commander sat, stalked now a loose-jointed, angular oddity from one of the Middle States—narrow-headed, and with ideas in proportion, which he seemed in nowise fitted to impart. Nigger school-teaching was manifestly not the respectable thing to do in New Orleans; and the Board seemed to have been put to sad straits sometimes for teachers. The reading was bunglingly done, but the teacher didn't read so very much better himself. On spelling the class did better. In geography they had learned by rote the answers to the common questions; and they could point out with considerable accuracy, on the outline maps, New Orleans and Louisiana, and the Mississippi River and the Gulf of Mexico. But one woolly-headed urchin brought his teacher to grief and wrath, by selecting Cuba as the proper location for Iceland; matters were nowise improved by the further transfer of Asia to the exact latitude and longitude of San Francisco. Yet, with all the allowances, it was a fair average school. Boys and girls, ranging in age from twelve to twenty, read the Fourth Reader passably; some of them had a fair conception of geography, and they had even made an entrance on the mysteries of grammar. Arithmetic seemed to be all plain sailing till they reached long division. Here the process became too complicated, and they were sure to blunder in the multiplication of the divisor by the dividend, or to add where they should subtract, or to bring down the wrong figures at the wrong time. Was it the fault of the stupid teacher? or was their previous progress due to their imitative faculties, and did they fail now simply because they had reached a point where reasoning powers of their own were needed? It is the question which touches the marrow of the whole discussion about the average negro capacity; but the time has been too short and the experiments have been too incomplete as yet to furnish satisfactory data for its solution.

The next school to which we were conducted was kept by a middle-aged negro, in gold spectacles, and with amusingly consequential air. His assistant—what would not the Opposition journals have given for such a fact during the late political campaign?—

was an English girl, young and lame, who seemed to have gone to work here, "among the niggers," very much as she would have gone to work among the pots and kettles, simply because a living was to be earned, and this way to earn it happened to offer. The negro principal had a short, sharp way of dealing with his pupils; and strap and ferule lay convenient for immediate use beside the books upon his table. He explained that many of his pupils were "contrabans," from the plantations, or negroes that had been "refugeed" from the Red River country; and their experiences in slavery had been such that they knew no motive for obedience but the fear of punishment. "Coax 'em and they'll laugh at you; you've got to knock 'em about, or they won't think you've got any power over 'em." The theory seemed to have made a pretty good school, whether by virtue of the ferule or in spite of it.

The children were having their noon recess when we entered, and the school-room was perfectly quiet. At the sound of the bell they came trooping noisily to the door, and in a few moments the black tide had overflowed all the desks. A Fourth Reader class was called up, which read well—quite as well as the average of such classes anywhere. Now and then one noticed a curious mouthing of the words and a quaint mispronunciation that the forms of the ordinary negro dialect would not account for. In these cases the children were of French parentage, and were learning a language as well as the art of reading. "The children are taught exclusively in English," the Board of Education say sententiously in their report. "Bound by the strong ligament of a common tongue, they will never foster the subtle enmity to national unity that lurks in diversity of speech."

The exercises in arithmetic that followed disclosed the same slower progress in this than in other branches, which had already been observed in the schools previously visited. A few questions of a miscellaneous nature showed that the scholars were by no means destitute of general intelligence; and

especially that they had a very keen appreciation of the fact that they had once been slaves, but were so no longer.

We were treated to a special performance before we left—reserved for the closing of the school, except upon grand occasions. An astonishing youth, with wool growing down almost to his eyebrows, beneath which gleamed cunning eyes that alone relieved the face from an expression of utter stupidity, took his place in the aisle in front of the teacher's desk. The hum of the school suddenly hushed, and all eyes were fastened on the droll figure. The woolly head gave a bob forward, while the body seemed to go through contortions caused by some inward pain. As the head ducked down the second time and came up with snapping eyes, the opening of the song was ejected, and the shrill voice was soon drowned in the roar that joined in from the whole open-throated throng.

Such singing may never be heard elsewhere. The nearest approach a Northern reader is ever likely to make to it is when he hears the enthusiastic chorus at some noisy camp-meeting about the time the "power" is supposed to be "coming down, coming down." The song was nothing—a rhyming effort of the gold-spectacled teacher himself, I believe, rudely setting forth the joy of the slaves at the great deliverance, and ending in a refrain of thanks and prayer for "Honest Abe." But the negroes, too, have learned to worship the rising rather than the setting sun. "Honest Abe" was very well in his way; but if the schools were to be continued and the teachers paid, there would be more present need of help from his successor. And so the song had been already patched; and the refrain came thundering in for "Andie J." After all, there is a good deal of human nature in negroes!

Some rickety, tumble-down buildings on an out-of-the-way corner had been secured for another school, which we next visited. A motherly old negress here had her brood of little ones gathered about her, learning in concert the alphabet from the chart which she held in her lap. Up the row and down it she led them with the little pointer, which looked as if it might be chosen a double duty to perform. Now one was singled out to name a letter selected at random from some other chart; then the pointer flitted from top to bottom and back to middle of the alphabet, and the shiny-faced urchins eagerly shouted the responses, or winced as the pointer descended threateningly near some naughty hand that was wandering into foreign pockets.

In another room, a bright, lady-like young quadroon, who was similarly occupied, smiled a pleasant greeting as we entered. She had been at the fair at Pierre Soulé's. With ample means and a pleasant home, she volunteered to do this work of duty to her race; and the neat, orderly school-room, with the quiet ways and clean faces of her little charge[s], not less than their prompt answers, told her success.

In one of the rooms in this building a row of picaninnies, ranging from four to fourteen, stood up to recite in the First Reader. At their head, painfully spelling his way through a sentence as we entered, was an old man of sixty, with white wool and a wrinkled face. He wore a pair of huge brass-rimmed spectacles; but they would not stick on his bullet-shaped head without further contrivance, and so he had tied a bit of packing-cord into the ends of the brass temples, and around his head. I asked the old man what he wanted to learn to read for.

"Reckon if it's good for white folks, good for me too."

"But you're so old, uncle, one would think you wouldn't care for such things any more."

"Reckon if it's good for chil'en, can't be bad for old folks."

Subsequent talk showed that the old man had a Bible, and wanted to learn to read it, and, further, that he believed, as soon as he could read, he would be entitled to vote. Precisely what good that would do him he did not seem to understand; but he worked away industriously over his well-thumbed

First Reader, and scarcely gave a second look to the visitors, at whom the children were staring with all their eyes. It was a trifling thing, doubtless, and the old man may have been very silly to be thus setting himself to children's tasks, in the simplicity of his desire to learn what he knew white folks had found good for them; but to me there seemed nothing more touching or suggestive in all the sights of New Orleans.

We saw no other old men in the schools, and few young ones beyond the age of twenty; but the teachers said the cases were quite numerous in which the more intelligent scholars were instructing their parents at home. In all such instances the parents were sure to enforce regular attendance on the part of their children, and the influence of the school became reflex, first on the scholars, from them to the families, thence back to the school again.

The few schools spoken of above may be taken as a fair specimen of the system in operation in New Orleans in June, 1865. It was soon destined to give way to the reaction of public feeling, which already began to influence the affairs of the department. But it had now been carried on for fourteen months. Few, even of the most advanced, had, at the beginning, been able to read the simplest sentence. Now there were classes in geography, grammar, and arithmetic, and a very fair proportion of the fourteen thousand seven hundred and forty-one scholars could read quite intelligently. The gate of knowledge had been opened to them; there was little likelihood that hereafter a General commanding would be able to stop the spread of these dangerous arts of reading and writing, by an official notification that the opening of schools for negro children would be very hazardous and unwise.[1]

[1] General Emory so admonished Rev. Thomas Conway, months after our occupation of the city. The idea seemed to be, that the Rebel population could not have their feelings agitated by efforts to teach their negroes, without great danger of popular disturbances!

So rapid was the progress that, on the 1st of January, 1865, the scholars had advanced so far as to be thus classified:

Writing on slates, 3,883; writing in copy-books, 1,108; studying grammar, 283; studying geography, 1,338; studying practical arithmetic, 1,223; studying mental arithmetic, 4,628; reading, 7,623; spelling, 8,301; learning the alphabet, 2,103.

And from the beginning of the experiment down to the 1st of June, 1865, there had been a regular increase of eleven hundred and fourteen scholars and fourteen teachers per month. Two thousand new scholars had come into the schools in May alone; in April there had been fifteen hundred. The expense of this entire system was about one-half what it cost to support a single regiment in the field. This expense was to be met by a tax on the property within the lines of military occupation; General Banks's order explaining, for the comfort of dissatisfied tax-payers, that henceforth labor must be educated in the South in order to be valuable, and that if they didn't support the negro schools, they would find it hard to secure negro labor.

Judging, both from personal observation and from the testimony of the teachers and the Board of Education, I should say that the negro pupils are as orderly and as easily governed as any corresponding number of white children, under similar circumstances. There is, I think, a more earnest desire to learn, and a more general opinion that it is a great favor to have the opportunity. There is less destruction of books, less whittling of school furniture, less disposition to set up petty revolts against the teacher's authority. The progress in learning to read is exceptionally rapid. I do not believe that in the best schools at the North they learn the alphabet and First Reader quicker than do the average of these slave children. The negroes are not quicker-witted, but they are more anxious to learn. In writing they make equally rapid progress, and where the teachers are competent they do well in geography.

Arithmetic presents the first real obstacles, and arouses painful inquiries as to the actual mental capacity of this long-neglected race.

But, up to this point, the question of negro education is no longer an experiment. In reading and writing I do not hesitate to say that the average progress of the children of plantation hands, as shown in every negro school from Fortress Monroe around to New Orleans, is fully equal to the average progress of white children at the North.

The experiment of high schools is about to be tried among them, under the auspices of a voluntary organization, mainly made up and sustained by themselves. Its constitution was adopted a fortnight or more before our visit, and such men as Thomas J. Durant were uniting with the negroes in an effort to get the enterprise properly started.

On the Sunday after our visit to these schools, we were taken to see a Sunday-school, made up largely of the same scholars, although conducted under the auspices of Mr. Conway, a business-like preacher, in charge of the Freedmen's Bureau in the city. The building into which we were conducted had been, in former times, a medical college. Ranged upon the seats, which arose, amphitheater-like, half-way to the ceiling, sat row after row of closely-crowded, smiling, black-faced, but bright-eyed, Sunday-school scholars, as clean, as smiling, and as prettily dressed as one would see almost anywhere in our Northern rural districts. On the higher benches, where the larger scholars sat, were a few young ladies, tastefully attired in white. At that distance, one had difficulty in seeing that their faces were not of the pure Anglo-Saxon tinge; but, neat and pretty as they looked, they were only niggers, and nigger Sunday-school teachers at that.

A graduate of Amherst met us as we mounted the platform once occupied by the demonstrator of anatomy. He was a sober, sedate figure, in professional black, and, with his dignified ways, might have been taken for a Southern Doctor of Divinity, if you did not look at his face. That was as black as his coat. His son, a handsome, graceful young fellow (always barring the black face and the kinky wool), took his seat at the piano. The sober representative of Amherst rapped on the table, and tapped the little bell, till the children slowly and gradually mastered the almost irrepressible torrent of whispers and laughter. But the bell-taps sounded clearer and clearer; silence at last reigned. A hymn was read; the young negro at the piano softly touched the keys for a moment, and then the whole rich, joyous nature of the children gushed into a volume of melody that rose and swelled till the very air of the old lecture-room was vocal with praise. It was like listening to the grand peals of Plymouth Church itself.

There followed a little address, with, perhaps, a trifle too much of talk about their liberty, and too little of how it should be made profitable; too much about the prejudices against them, and too little about the means for an improvement which should conquer prejudices; too much about the faults of their masters, and too little about their own. But this seems to be the general strain; and perhaps, after all, it may be necessary, in some such way, to gain the confidence of the children before you can instruct them. Occasional questions kept alive the interest, and the lustily shouted answers showed an intelligence that plainly took in the full meaning of the speech.

"What great man freed you all, and was then taken home?"

Surely, if the murdered President could but have been present, beside his old associate, at that scene, he would have thought the shouts that brought back his name the sweetest praise the lips of mortals ever bore him.

"Are you really free now?"

"Yes, yes."

"What would you do if anybody should now try to take your freedom away?"

It was fine to watch the play of surprise and apprehension across the animated faces. "We'd fight," exclaimed a sturdy fellow,

twelve or fourteen years old. "We would n't let them," said many more. "The soldiers would stop it," murmured the most. That, alas! seemed still the main hope of these submissive, long-enslaved people. They had not reached—not even the oldest of them— the conception of organized effort to protect themselves. "The soldiers would stop it." That was all.

SAMUEL C. ARMSTRONG
"The Founding of the Hampton Institute" (April, 1868) *

Two and a half years' service [from 1863 to 1866] with the Negro soldiers (after a year as Captain and Major in the One Hundred and Twenty-fifth New York Volunteers), as Lieutenant Colonel and Colonel of the Ninth and Eighth Regiments of United States Colored Troops, convinced me of the excellent qualities and capacities of the freedmen. Their quick response to good treatment and to discipline was a constant surprise. Their tidiness, devotion to their duty and their leaders, their dash and daring in battle, and ambition to improve,—often studying their spelling books under fire,— showed that slavery was a false though doubtless, for the time being, an educative condition, and that they deserved as good a chance as any people.

In March, 1866, I was placed by General O. O. Howard, Commissioner of the Freedmen's Bureau, in charge of ten counties in Eastern Virginia, with headquarters at Hampton, the great "contraband" camp, to manage Negro affairs and adjust, if possible, the relation of the races. Colored squatters by thousands, and General Lee's disbanded soldiers returning to their families, came together in my district on hundreds of "abandoned" farms which government had seized and allowed the freedmen to occupy. There

* From an autobiographical statement written in 1890 by General Samuel C. Armstrong, as reprinted in *Old South Leaflets*, Vol. VI (General Series), No. 149 (Boston: Directors of the Old South Work, [1904]), pp. 523–529, 534–535.

was irritation, but both classes were ready to do the fair thing. It was about a two years' task to settle matters by making terms with the land-owners, who employed many laborers on their restored homes. Swarms went back on passes to the "old plantations" with thirty days' rations, and nearly a thousand were placed in families in Massachusetts as servants, through the agency of a Home in Cambridgeport, under charge of a committee of Boston ladies.

Hardest of all was to settle the ration question: about two thousand, having been fed for years, were demoralized and seemed hopeless. Notice was given that in three months, on Oct. 1, 1866, all rations would be stopped, except to those in hospital, for whom full provision was made. Trouble was expected, but there was not a ripple of it or a complaint that day. Their resource was surprising: the Negro in a tight place is a genius.

It was my duty, every three months, to personally visit and report upon the condition of the ten counties; to inspect the Bureau office in each, in charge of an army officer, to investigate troubles, and to study the relations of the races. The better class of whites were well disposed, but inactive in suppressing any misconduct of the lower class. Friendliness between the races was general, broken only by political excitement, and was due, I think, to the fact that they had been brought up together, often in the most intimate way, from childhood,—a surprise to me; for, on missionary ground, parents, with the spirit of martyrs, take every pains to prevent contact of their children with the natives around them.

Martial law prevailed. There were no civil courts, and for many months the Bureau officer in each county acted on all kinds of cases, gaining generally the confidence of both races. When martial law was over, the Military Court at Hampton was kept up by common consent for about six months. Scattered families were reunited. Even from Louisiana—for the whole South was mapped out, each county officered, and, as a rule,

wisely administered—would come inquiries about the relatives and friends of those who had been sold to traders years before; and great justice and humanity were shown in bringing together broken households.

General Howard and the Freedmen's Bureau did for the ex-slaves, from 1865 to 1870, a marvellous work, for which due credit has not been given,—among other things, granting three and a half millions of dollars for school-houses, salaries, etc., thereby giving an impulse and foundation to the education of about a million colored children. The principal Negro educational institutions of to-day, then starting, were liberally aided at a time of vital need. Hampton received over $50,000 through General Howard for buildings and improvements.

On relieving my predecessor, Captain C. B. Wilder, of Boston, at the Hampton headquarters, I found an active, excellent educational work going on under the American Missionary Association of New York. This society in 1862 had opened in the vicinity the first school for freedmen in the South, in charge of an ex-slave, Mrs. Mary Peake. Over fifteen hundred children were gathered daily,—some in old hospital barracks; for here was Camp Hamilton, the base hospital of the Army of the James, where during the war thousands of sick and wounded soldiers had been cared for, and now where over six thousand lie buried in a beautiful national cemetery. The largest class was held in the "Butler School" building, since replaced by the "John G. Whittier School-house."

Close at hand the pioneer settlers of America and the first slaves landed on this continent. Here Powhatan reigned, here the Indian was first met, here the first Indian child was baptized, here freedom was first given the slaves by General Butler's famous "contraband" order. In sight of this shore the battle of the "Monitor" and "Merrimac" saved the Union and revolutionized naval warfare. Here General Grant based the operations of his final campaign. The place was easily accessible by railroad and water routes to the North, and to a population of two millions of Negroes. The centre of prospective great commercial and maritime development—of which Newport News, soon to have the largest and finest ship-yard in the world, is beginning the grand fulfilment—and, withal, a place most healthful and beautiful for situation.

I soon felt the fitness of this historic and strategic spot for a permanent and great educational work. The suggestion was cordially received by the American Missionary Association, which authorized the purchase, in June, 1867, of "Little Scotland," an estate of 125 acres on Hampton River, looking out over Hampton Roads. Not expecting to have charge, but only to help, I was surprised, one day, by a letter from Secretary E. P. Smith, of the A. M. A., stating that the man selected for the place had declined, and asking me if I could take it. I replied, "Yes." Till then my own future had been blind: it had only been clear that there was a work to be done for the ex-slaves and where and how it should be done.

A day-dream of the Hampton School, nearly as it is, had come to me during the war a few times,—once in camp during the siege of Richmond, and once one beautiful evening on the Gulf of Mexico, while on the wheel-house of the transport steamship "Illinois," *en-route* for Texas with the Twenty-fifth Army Corps (Negro) for frontier duty on the Rio Grande River, whither it had been ordered under General Sheridan, to watch and, if necessary, defeat Maximilian in his attempted conquest of Mexico.

The thing to be done was clear: to train selected Negro youth who should go out and teach and lead their people, first by example by getting land and homes; to give them not a dollar that they could earn for themselves; to teach respect for labor; to replace stupid drudgery with skilled hands; and, to these ends, to build up an industrial system, for the sake not only of self-support and intelligent labor, but also for the sake of character. And it seemed equally clear that the people of the country would support a wise work for the freedmen. I think so still.

The missionary plan in Hawaii had not, I thought, considered enough the real needs and weaknesses of the people, whose ignorance alone was not half the trouble. The chief difficulty with them was deficient character, as it is with the Negro. He is what his past has made him. The true basis of work for him and all men is the scientific one,—one recognizing the facts of heredity and surrounding all the facts of the case.

There was no enthusiasm for the manual labor plan. People said, "It has been tried at Oberlin and elsewhere and given up: it won't pay." "Of course," said I, "it cannot pay in a *money* way, but it will pay in a *moral* way, especially with the freedmen. It will make them men and women as nothing else will. It is the only way to make them good Christians."

The school has had, from the first, the good fortune of liberal-minded trustees. They accepted its unformulated, practical plan, when it opened in April, 1868, with two teachers and fifteen pupils, and adopted my formal report of 1870, the year of its incorporation under a special Act of the Assembly of Virginia. By this Act of Incorporation the school became independent of any association or sect and of the government. It does work for the state and general government, for which it receives aid, but is not controlled or supported by them.

From the first it has been true to the idea of education by self-help, and I hope it will remain so. Nothing is asked for the student that he can provide by his own labor; but the system that gives him this chance is costly. The student gets nothing but an opportunity to work his way. While the workshops must be made to pay as far as possible, instruction is as important as production.

The Slater Fund has been a great stimulus to technical training. The Negro girl has proved a great success as a teacher. The women of the race deserve as good a chance as the men. So far it has been impossible to supply the demand for Negro teachers. School-houses and salaries, such as they are

are ready; but competent teachers are the great and pressing need, and there is no better work for the country than to supply them. But the short public school sessions, of from three to seven months, do not give full support, and skilled labor is the only resource of many teachers for over half the year. As farmers and mechanics, they are nearly as useful as in the school-room. Hence the importance of industrial training.

Hampton's thousand graduates (discounting ten per cent. as disappointing), with half that number of undergraduates, are a working force for Negro and Indian civilization.

It was not in the original plan of the school that any but Negroes should be received, though the liberal State charter made no limit as to color; but when, in April, 1878, a "Macedonian cry" came from some Indian ex-prisoners of war in Florida —once the worst of savages—through Captain R. H. Pratt, seventeen were accepted at private expense, Bishop Whipple providing for five of them.

A few weeks after the arrival of the Indian ex-prisoners, I called on the Hon. Carl Schurz, then Secretary of the Interior, to suggest that the so far very encouraging experiment in Indian civilization be tried more fully by bringing some younger material, girls especially. He called in Mr. E. A. Hayt, Commissioner, who stated, in effect, that the education of Indian girls had been a failure, and threw cold water on the plan. I urged that there is no civilization without educated women, and begged the Secretary to let us try. He decided to do so, and gave the necessary orders, and at my request sent Captain Pratt—whom Secretary of War Robert Lincoln had, on my application, detailed temporarily to help us in our Hampton experiment—to Dakota, whence he brought back to Hampton, in November, 1878, forty boys and nine girls, chiefly Sioux. I wish to give Mr. Carl Schurz the credit of creating, on the government side, the work of Eastern Indian schools. This action of his was a turning-point. The work then became

routine, though not without difficulties, and our Indian contingent soon reached its limit of one hundred and twenty, aided by government, and from fifteen to twenty by charity, occasionally an able-bodied young man working out his entire expenses.

The old homesickness of Indians at Eastern schools is over. The three years' period at school, which was formerly too much like a prison term, is more and more ignored; and the idea of fitting for life, whatever time it takes, gains strength. Indians are no longer coaxed to come. Twice as many as we can take wish to come, yet the really desirable ones are not very many, and we do not care to increase our numbers. Our Indian work is illustrative rather than exhaustive. Hampton's work for the "despised races" of our country, while chiefly for the Negro, is really for all who need it. Till our limit is reached, any youth in the land, however poor, can come here and work his way.

In this review I cannot but refer to my associates, without whom this work could not have been what it is. Too little credit has been given them,—the men and women who have labored with noblest zeal, have enjoyed the privileges of such work, and are thankful for it. The present efficient force of officers and teachers could manage successfully every department of the school, should its head be taken away. In twenty-two years it has attained a life of its own: it would be poor organization and development that would not in that time have reached this point. It might once have been, but is not now, run by "one-man power." The change will come, and the school will be ready for it.

We have been fortunate in our neighbors, who from the first have been most friendly. The wide-awake town of Hampton, with an enterprising white community, has a Negro population of about three thousand, and illustrates as well as any place in the South the formation of two classes among the freedmen, the progressive and non-progressive. For miles around the country is dotted with their hard-earned homesteads; yet the "shiftless" class is large. There is little race friction, and steady improvement. Adjoining our grounds is the National Soldiers' Home, with its three thousand army veterans, and two miles distant is the United States Artillery School at Fort Monroe.

Full of resources, this famous peninsula, comparatively dormant for two hundred and fifty years, is awakening to a wonderful development, especially along its magnificent harbor front on Hampton Roads and James River. From historic Yorktown, Old Point Comfort, Newport News, and up to Jamestown Island, where stands the oldest ruin of English civilization on this continent, have already sprung large commercial, national, and educational enterprises and institutions. Thousands flock to these shores, winter and summer, for rest and recreation. The growth has only begun.

This new life and energy but typifies the awakening of the whole South under the idea which won in the war. The "Boys in Blue" did a fearful but necessary work of destruction. "It is for us to finish the work which they so nobly began," said Lincoln at Gettysburg. The duty of the hour is construction, to build up. With all credit to the pluck and heroic self-help of the Southern people and to Northern enterprise for railroad, mineral and other commercial development, the great constructive force in the South and everywhere is the Christian teacher. *"In hoc signo vinces,"* is as true now as in the days of Constantine. Let us make the teachers, and we will make the people.

The Hampton Institute should be pushed steadily, not to larger but to better, more thorough effort, and placed on a solid foundation. It is big enough, but its work is only begun. Its work, with that of other like schools, is on the line of Providential purpose in ending the great struggle as it did,— the redemption of both races from the evils of slavery, which, while to the Negro educative up to a certain point, was a curse to the country. God said, "Let my people go," and it had to be done.

[Statements found among General Armstrong's papers after his death at Hampton, Virginia, on May 11, 1893:]

Now that all is bright, the family together, and there is nothing to alarm and very much to be thankful for, it is well to look ahead and, perhaps, to say the things that I should wish known should I suddenly die.

I wish to be buried in the school graveyard, among the students, where one of them would have been put had he died next.

.   .   .   .   .

In the school the great thing is not to quarrel; to pull all together; to refrain from hasty, unwise words and actions; to unselfishly and wisely seek the best good of all; and to get rid of workers whose temperaments are unfortunate—whose heads are not level; no matter how much knowledge or culture they may have. Cantankerousness is worse than heterodoxy.

.   .   .   .   .

Hampton must not go down. See to it, you who are true to the black and red children of the land and to just ideas of education.

The loyalty of old soldiers and of my students has been an unspeakable comfort.

It pays to follow one's best light—to put God and country first, ourselves afterward.

Taps has just sounded.

S. C. ARMSTRONG.
HAMPTON, VIRGINIA, New Year's Eve, 1890.

W. E. BURGHARDT DU BOIS
"Strivings of the Negro People" (1897)*

Between me and the other world there is ever an unasked question: unasked by some through feelings of delicacy; by others

* W. E. Burghardt Du Bois, "Strivings of the Negro People," *Atlantic Monthly,* LXXX (August, 1897), 194–198.

through the difficulty of rightly framing it. All, nevertheless, flutter round it. They approach me in a half-hesitant sort of way, eye me curiously or compassionately, and then, instead of saying directly, How does it feel to be a problem? they say, I know an excellent colored man in my town; or, I fought at Mechanicsville; or, Do not these Southern outrages make your blood boil? At these I smile, or am interested, or reduce the boiling to a simmer, as the occasion may require. To the real question, How does it feel to be a problem? I answer seldom a word.

And yet, being a problem is a strange experience,—peculiar even for one who has never been anything else, save perhaps in babyhood and in Europe. It is in the early days of rollicking boyhood that the revelation first bursts upon one, all in a day, as it were. I remember well when the shadow swept across me. I was a little thing, away up in the hills of New England, where the dark Housatonic winds between Hoosac and Taghanic to the sea. In a wee wooden schoolhouse, something put it into the boys' and girls' heads to buy gorgeous visiting-cards—ten cents a package—and exchange. The exchange was merry, till one girl, a tall newcomer, refused my card,—refused it peremptorily, with a glance. Then it dawned upon me with a certain suddenness that I was different from the others; or like, mayhap, in heart and life and longing, but shut out from their world by a vast veil. I had thereafter no desire to tear down that veil, to creep through; I held all beyond it in common contempt, and lived above it in a region of blue sky and great wandering shadows. That sky was bluest when I could beat my mates at examination-time, or beat them at a foot-race, or even beat their stringy heads. Alas, with the years all this fine contempt began to fade; for the world I longed for, and all its dazzling opportunities, were theirs, not mine. But they should not keep these prizes, I said; some, all, I would wrest from them. Just how I would do it I could never decide: by reading law, by healing the sick, by telling the wonderful tales that swam in my head,—some way. With other black boys the strife was not so fiercely sunny: their youth shrunk into tasteless sycophancy, or into silent hatred of the pale world about them and mocking distrust of everything white; or wasted itself in a bitter cry, Why did God make me an outcast and a stranger in mine own house? The "shades of the prisonhouse" closed round about us all: walls strait and stubborn to the whitest, but relentlessly narrow, tall, and unscalable to sons of night who must plod darkly on in resignation, or beat unavailing palms against the stone, or steadily, half hopelessly watch the streak of blue above.

After the Egyptian and Indian, the Greek and Roman, the Teuton and Mongolian, the Negro is a sort of seventh son, born with a veil, and gifted with second-sight in this American world,—a world which yields him no self-consciousness, but only lets him see himself through the revelation of the other world. It is a peculiar sensation, this double-consciousness, this sense of always looking at one's self through the eyes of others, of measuring one's soul by the tape of a world that looks on in amused contempt and pity. One ever feels his two-ness,—an American, a Negro; two souls, two thoughts, two unreconciled strivings; two warring ideals in one dark body, whose dogged strength alone keeps it from being torn asunder. The history of the American Negro is the history of this strife,—this longing to attain self-conscious manhood, to merge his double self into a better and truer self. In this merging he wishes neither of the older selves to be lost. He does not wish to Africanize America, for America has too much to teach the world and Africa; he does not wish to bleach his Negro blood in a flood of white Americanism, for he believes—foolishly, perhaps, but fervently—that Negro blood has yet a message for the world. He simply wishes to make it possible for a man to be both a Negro and an American without being cursed and spit upon by his fellows, without losing the opportunity of self-development.

This is the end of his striving: to be a co-worker in the kingdom of culture, to escape both death and isolation, and to husband and use his best powers. These powers, of body and of mind, have in the past been so wasted and dispersed as to lose all effectiveness, and to seem like absence of all power, like weakness. The double-aimed struggle of the black artisan, on the one hand to escape white contempt for a nation of mere hewers of wood and drawers of water, and on the other hand to plough and nail and dig for a poverty-stricken horde, could only result in making him a poor craftsman, for he had but half a heart in either cause. By the poverty and ignorance of his people the Negro lawyer or doctor was pushed toward quackery and demagogism, and by the criticism of the other world toward an elaborate preparation that overfitted him for his lowly tasks. The would-be black savant was confronted by the paradox that the knowledge his people needed was a twice-told tale to his white neighbors, while the knowledge which would teach the white world was Greek to his own flesh and blood. The innate love of harmony and beauty that set the ruder souls of his people a-dancing, a-singing, and a-laughing raised but confusion and doubt in the soul of the black artist; for the beauty revealed to him was the soul-beauty of a race which his larger audience despised, and he could not articulate the message of another people.

This waste of double aims, this seeking to satisfy two unreconciled ideals, has wrought sad havoc with the courage and faith and deeds of eight thousand thousand people, has sent them often wooing false gods and invoking false means of salvation, and has even at times seemed destined to make them ashamed of themselves. In the days of bondage they thought to see in one divine event the end of all doubt and disappointment; eighteenth-century Rousseauism never worshiped freedom with half the unquestioning faith that the American Negro did for two centuries. To him slavery was, indeed, the sum of all villainies, the cause of all sorrow, the root of all prejudice; emancipation was the key to a promised land of sweeter beauty than ever stretched before the eyes of wearied Israelites. In his songs and exhortations swelled one refrain, liberty; in his tears and curses the god he implored had freedom in his right hand. At last it came,—suddenly, fearfully, like a dream. With one wild carnival of blood and passion came the message in his own plaintive cadences:—

> "Shout, O children!
>   Shout, you're free!
>   The Lord has bought your liberty!"

Years have passed away, ten, twenty, thirty. Thirty years of national life, thirty years of renewal and development, and yet the swarthy ghost of Banquo sits in its old place at the national feast. In vain does the nation cry to its vastest problem,—

> "Take any shape but that, and my firm nerves
> Shall never tremble!"

The freedman has not yet found in freedom his promised land. Whatever of lesser good may have come in these years of change, the shadow of a deep disappointment rests upon the Negro people,—a disappointment all the more bitter because the unattained ideal was unbounded save by the simple ignorance of a lowly folk.

The first decade was merely a prolongation of the vain search for freedom, the boon that seemed ever barely to elude their grasp,—like a tantalizing will-o'-the-wisp, maddening and misleading the headless host. The holocaust of war, the terrors of the Kuklux Klan, the lies of carpet-baggers, the disorganization of industry, and the contradictory advice of friends and foes left the bewildered serf with no new watchword beyond the old cry for freedom. As the decade closed, however, he began to grasp a new idea. The ideal of liberty demanded for its attainment powerful means, and these the Fifteenth Amendment gave him. The ballot, which before he had looked upon as a visible sign of freedom, he now regarded as the chief means of gaining and perfecting the liberty with which war had partially endowed him. And why not? Had not votes made war and emancipated millions? Had not votes enfranchised the freedmen? Was anything impossible to a power that had done all this? A million black men started with renewed zeal to vote themselves into the kingdom. The decade fled away,—a decade containing, to the freedman's mind, nothing but suppressed votes, stuffed ballot-boxes, and election outrages that nullified his vaunted right of suffrage. And yet that decade from 1875 to 1885 held another powerful movement, the rise of another ideal to guide the unguided, another pillar of fire by night after a clouded day. It was the ideal of "book-learning;" the curiosity, born of compulsory ignorance, to know and test the power of the cabalistic letters of the white man, the longing to know. Mission and night schools began in the smoke of battle, ran the gauntlet of reconstruction, and at last developed into permanent foundations. Here at last seemed to have been discovered the mountain path to Canaan; longer than the highway of emancipation and law, steep and rugged, but straight, leading to heights high enough to overlook life.

Up the new path the advance guard toiled, slowly, heavily, doggedly; only those who have watched and guided the faltering feet, the misty minds, the dull understandings, of the dark pupils of these schools know how faithfully, how piteously, this people strove to learn. It was weary work. The cold statistician wrote down the inches of progress here and there, noted also where here and there a foot had slipped or some one had fallen. To the tired climbers, the horizon was ever dark, the mists were often cold, the Canaan was always dim and far away. If, however, the vistas disclosed as yet no goal, no resting-place, little but flattery and criticism, the journey at least gave leisure for reflection and self-examination; it changed the child of emancipation to the youth with dawning self-consciousness, self-realization, self-respect.

In those sombre forests of his striving his own soul rose before him, and he saw himself,—darkly as through a veil; and yet he saw in himself some faint revelation of his power, of his mission. He began to have a dim feeling that, to attain his place in the world, he must be himself, and not another. For the first time he sought to analyze the burden he bore upon his back, that dead-weight of social degradation partially masked behind a half-named Negro problem. He felt his poverty; without a cent, without a home, without land, tools, or savings, he had entered into competition with rich, landed, skilled neighbors. To be a poor man is hard, but to be a poor race in a land of dollars is the very bottom of hardships. He felt the weight of his ignorance,—not simply of letters, but of life, of business, of the humanities; the accumulated sloth and shirking and awkwardness of decades and centuries shackled his hands and feet. Nor was his burden all poverty and ignorance. The red stain of bastardy, which two centuries of systematic legal defilement of Negro women had stamped upon his race, meant not only the loss of ancient African chastity, but also the hereditary weight of a mass of filth from white whoremongers and adulterers, threatening almost the obliteration of the Negro home.

A people thus handicapped ought not to be asked to race with the world, but rather allowed to give all its time and thought to its own social problems. But alas! while sociologists gleefully count his bastards and his prostitutes, the very soul of the toiling, sweating black man is darkened by the shadow of a vast despair. Men call the shadow prejudice, and learnedly explain it as the natural defense of culture against barbarism, learning against ignorance, purity against crime, the "higher" against the "lower" races. To which the Negro cries Amen! and swears that to so much of this strange prejudice as is founded on just homage to civilization, culture, righteousness, and progress he humbly bows and meekly does obeisance. But before that nameless prejudice that leaps beyond all this he stands helpless, dismayed, and well-nigh speechless; before that personal disrespect and mockery, the ridicule and systematic humiliation, the distortion of fact and wanton license of fancy, the cynical ignoring of the better and boisterous welcoming of the worse, the all-pervading desire to inculcate disdain for everything black, from Toussaint to the devil,—before this there rises a sickening despair that would disarm and discourage any nation save that black host to whom "discouragement" is an unwritten word.

They still press on, they still nurse the dogged hope,—not a hope of nauseating patronage, not a hope of reception into charmed social circles of stock-jobbers, pork-packers, and earl-hunters, but the hope of a higher synthesis of civilization and humanity, a true progress, with which the chorus "Peace, good will to men,"

> "May make one music as before,
> But vaster."

Thus the second decade of the American Negro's freedom was a period of conflict, of inspiration and doubt, of faith and vain questionings, of *Sturm und Drang*. The ideals of physical freedom, of political power, of school training, as separate all-sufficient panaceas for social ills, became in the third decade dim and overcast. They were the vain dreams of credulous race childhood; not wrong, but incomplete and over-simple. The training of the schools we need to-day more than ever,—the training of deft hands, quick eyes and ears, and the broader, deeper, higher culture of gifted minds. The power of the ballot we need in sheer self-defense, and as a guarantee of good faith. We may misuse it, but we can scarce do worse in this respect than our whilom masters. Freedom, too, the long-sought, we still seek,—the freedom of life and limb, the freedom to work and think. Work, culture, and liberty,—all these we need, not singly, but together; for to-day these ideals among the Negro people are gradually coalescing, and finding a higher

meaning in the unifying ideal of race,—the ideal of fostering the traits and talents of the Negro, not in opposition to, but in conformity with, the greater ideals of the American republic, in order that some day, on American soil, two world races may give each to each those characteristics which both so sadly lack. Already we come not altogether empty-handed: there is to-day no true American music but the sweet wild melodies of the Negro slave; the American fairy tales are Indian and African; we are the sole oasis of simple faith and reverence in a dusty desert of dollars and smartness. Will America be poorer if she replace her brutal, dyspeptic blundering with the light-hearted but determined Negro humility; or her coarse, cruel wit with loving, jovial good humor; or her Annie Rooney with Steal Away?

Merely a stern concrete test of the underlying principles of the great republic is the Negro problem, and the spiritual striving of the freedmen's sons is the travail of souls whose burden is almost beyond the measure of their strength, but who bear it in the name of an historic race, in the name of this the land of their fathers' fathers, and in the name of human opportunity.

W. E. BURGHARDT DU BOIS
"Of the Training of Black Men" (1902) *

. . . The one panacea of Education leaps to the lips of all: such human training as will best use the labor of all men without enslaving or brutalizing; such training as will give us poise to encourage the prejudices that bulwark society, and stamp out those that in sheer barbarity deafen us to the wail of prisoned souls within the Veil, and the mounting fury of shackled men.

But when we have vaguely said Education will set this tangle straight, what have we uttered but a truism? Training for life teaches living; but what training for the

* W. E. Burghardt Du Bois, "Of the Training of Black Men," *Atlantic Monthly,* XC (September, 1902), 290, 296–297.

profitable living together of black men and white?

·   ·   ·   ·   ·

We ought not to forget that despite the pressure of poverty, and despite the active discouragement and even ridicule of friends, the demand for higher training steadily increases among Negro youth: there were, in the years from 1875 to 1880, twenty-two Negro graduates from Northern colleges; from 1885 to 1890 there were forty-three, and from 1895 to 1900, nearly 100 graduates. From Southern Negro colleges there were, in the same three periods, 143, 413, and over 500 graduates. Here, then, is the plain thirst for training; by refusing to give this Talented Tenth the key to knowledge can any sane man imagine that they will lightly lay aside their yearning and contentedly become hewers of wood and drawers of water?

·   ·   ·   ·   ·

I sit with Shakespeare and he winces not. Across the color line I move arm in arm with Balzac and Dumas, where smiling men and welcoming women glide in gilded halls. From out the caves of Evening that swing between the strong-limbed earth and the tracery of the stars, I summon Aristotle and Aurelius and what soul I will, and they come all graciously with no scorn nor condescension. So, wed with Truth, I dwell above the Veil. Is this the life you grudge us, O knightly America? Is this the life you long to change into the dull red hideousness of Georgia? Are you so afraid lest peering from this high Pisgah, between Philistine and Amalekite, we sight the Promised Land?

W. E. BURGHARDT DU BOIS
"The Training of Negroes for Social Power" (1903) *

. . . We believe that a rationally arranged college course of study for men and women

* W. E. Burghardt Du Bois, "The Training of Negroes for Social Power," *Outlook,* Vol. LXXV, No. 7 (October 17, 1903), pp. 413–414.

able to pursue it is the best and only method of putting into the world negroes with ability to use the social forces of their race so as to stamp out crime, strengthen the home, eliminate degenerates, and inspire and encourage the higher tendencies of the race not only in thought and aspiration but in every-day toil. And we believe this, not simply because we have argued that such training ought to have these effects, or merely because we hope for such results in some dim future, but because already for years we have seen in the work of our graduates precisely such results as I have mentioned: successful teachers of teachers, intelligent and upright ministers, skilled physicians, principals of industrial schools, business men, and, above all, makers of model homes and leaders of social groups, out from which radiate subtle but tangible forces of uplift and inspiration. The proof of this lies scattered in every State of the South, and, above all, in the half-unwilling testimony of men disposed to decry our work.

Between the negro college and industrial school there are the strongest grounds for co-operation and unity. It is not a matter of mere emphasis, for we would be glad to see ten industrial schools to every college. It is not a fact that there are to-day too few negro colleges, but rather that there are too many institutions attempting to do college work. But the danger lies in the fact that the best of the negro colleges are poorly equipped and are to-day losing support and countenance, and that, unless the Nation awakens to its duty, ten years will see the annihilation of higher negro training in the South. We need a few strong, well-equipped negro colleges, and we need them now, not tomorrow; unless we can have them and have them decently supported, negro education in the South, both common-school and industrial, is doomed to failure, and the forces of social regeneration will be fatally weakened, for the college to-day among negroes is, just as truly as it was yesterday among whites, the beginning and not the end of human training, the foundation and not the capstone of popular education.

Strange, is it not, my brothers, how often in America those great watchwords of human energy—"Be strong!" "Know thyself!" "Hitch your wagon to a star!"—how often these die away into dim whispers when we face these seething millions of black men? And yet do they not belong to them? Are they not their heritage as well as yours? Can they bear burdens without strength, know without learning, and aspire without ideals? Are you afraid to let them try? Fear rather, in this our common fatherland, lest we live to lose those great watchwords of Liberty and Opportunity which yonder in the eternal hills their fathers fought with your fathers to preserve.

BOOKER T. WASHINGTON
"Industrial Education for the Negro" (1903) *

One of the most fundamental and far-reaching deeds that has been accomplished during the last quarter of a century has been that by which the Negro has been helped to find himself and to learn the secrets of civilization—to learn that there are a few simple, cardinal principles upon which a race must start its upward course, unless it would fail, and its last estate be worse than its first.

It has been necessary for the Negro to learn the difference between being worked and working—to learn that being worked meant degradation, while working means civilization; that all forms of labor are honorable, and all forms of idleness disgraceful. It has been necessary for him to learn that all races that have got upon their feet have done so largely by laying an economic foundation, and, in general, by beginning in a proper cultivation and ownership of the soil.

Forty years ago my race emerged from slavery into freedom. If, in too many cases,

* Booker T. Washington, "Industrial Education for the Negro," from *The Negro Problem: A Series of Articles by Representative American Negroes To-day* (New York: James Pott and Co., 1903), pp. 9–19, 28–29.

the Negro race began development at the wrong end, it was largely because neither white nor black properly understood the case. Nor is it any wonder that this was so, for never before in the history of the world had just such a problem been presented as that of the two races at the coming of freedom in this country.

For two hundred and fifty years, I believe the way for the redemption of the Negro was being prepared through industrial development. Through all those years the Southern white man did business with the Negro in a way that no one else has done business with him. In most cases if a Southern white man wanted a house built he consulted a Negro mechanic about the plan and about the actual building of the structure. If he wanted a suit of clothes made he went to a Negro tailor, and for shoes he went to a shoemaker of the same race. In a certain way every slave plantation in the South was an industrial school. On these plantations young colored men and women were constantly being trained not only as farmers but as carpenters, blacksmiths, wheelwrights, brick masons, engineers, cooks, laundresses, sewing women and housekeepers.

I do not mean in any way to apologize for the curse of slavery, which was a curse to both races, but in what I say about industrial training in slavery I am simply stating facts. This training was crude, and was given for selfish purposes. It did not answer the highest ends, because there was an absence of mental training in connection with the training of the hand. To a large degree, though, this business contact with the Southern white man, and the industrial training on the plantations, left the Negro at the close of the war in possession of nearly all the common and skilled labor in the South. The industries that gave the South its power, prominence and wealth prior to the Civil War were mainly the raising of cotton, sugar cane, rice and tobacco. Before the way could be prepared for the proper growing and marketing of these crops forests had to be cleared, houses to be built, public roads and railroads constructed. In all these works the Negro did most of the heavy work. In the planting, cultivating and marketing of the crops not only was the Negro the chief dependence, but in the manufacture of tobacco he became a skilled and proficient workman, and in this, up to the present time, in the South, holds the lead in the large tobacco manufactories.

In most of the industries, though, what happened? For nearly twenty years after the war, except in a few instances, the value of the industrial training given by the plantations was overlooked. Negro men and women were educated in literature, in mathematics and in the sciences, with little thought of what had been taking place during the preceding two hunded and fifty years, except, perhaps, as something to be escaped, to be got as far away from as possible. As a generation began to pass, those who had been trained as mechanics in slavery began to disappear by death, and gradually it began to be realized that there were few to take their places. There were young men educated in foreign tongues, but few in carpentry or in mechanical or architectural drawing. Many were trained in Latin, but few as engineers and blacksmiths. Too many were taken from the farm and educated, but educated in everything but farming. For this reason they had no interest in farming and did not return to it. And yet eighty-five per cent. of the Negro population of the Southern states lives and for a considerable time will continue to live in the country districts. The charge is often brought against the members of my race— and too often justly, I confess—that they are found leaving the country districts and flocking into the great cities where temptations are more frequent and harder to resist, and where the Negro people too often become demoralized. Think, though, how frequently it is the case that from the first day that a pupil begins to go to school his books teach him much about the cities of the world and city life, and almost nothing about the country. How natural it is, then, that when he has

the ordering of his life he wants to live it in the city. . . .

Some years ago, when we decided to make tailoring a part of our training at the Tuskegee Institute, I was amazed to find that it was almost impossible to find in the whole country an educated colored man who could teach the making of clothing. We could find numbers of them who could teach astronomy, theology, Latin or grammar, but almost none who could instruct in the making of clothing, something that has to be used by every one of us every day in the year. How often have I been discouraged as I have gone through the South, and into the homes of the people of my race, and have found women who could converse intelligently upon abstruse subjects, and yet could not tell how to improve the condition of the poorly cooked and still more poorly served bread and meat which they and their families were eating three times a day. It is discouraging to find a girl who can tell you the geographical location of any country on the globe and who does not know where to place the dishes upon a common dinner table. It is discouraging to find a woman who knows much about theoretical chemistry, and who cannot properly wash and iron a shirt.

In what I say here I would not by any means have it understood that I would limit or circumscribe the mental development of the Negro student. No race can be lifted until its mind is awakened and strengthened. By the side of industrial training should always go mental and moral training, but the pushing of mere abstract knowledge into the head means little. We want more than the mere performance of mental gymnastics. Our knowledge must be harnessed to the things of real life. I would encourage the Negro to secure all the mental strength, all the mental culture—whether gleaned from science, mathematics, history, language or literature that his circumstances will allow, but I believe most earnestly that for years to come the education of the people of my race should be so directed that the greatest proportion of the mental strength of the masses will be brought to bear upon the every-day practical things of life, upon something that is needed to be done, and something which they will be permitted to do in the community in which they reside. And just the same with the professional class which the race needs and must have, I would say give the men and women of that class, too, the training which will best fit them to perform in the most successful manner the service which the race demands.

I would not confine the race to industrial life, not even to agriculture, for example, although I believe that by far the greater part of the Negro race is best off in the country districts and must and should continue to live there, but I would teach the race that in industry the foundation must be laid—that the very best service which any one can render to what is called the higher education is to teach the present generation to provide a material or industrial foundation. On such a foundation as this will grow habits of thrift, a love of work, economy, ownership of property, bank accounts. Out of it in the future will grow practical education, professional education, positions of public responsibility. Out of it will grow moral and religious strength. Out of it will grow wealth from which alone can come leisure and the opportunity for the enjoyment of literature and the fine arts. . . .

I would set no limits to the attainments of the Negro in arts, in letters or statesmanship, but I believe the surest way to reach those ends is by laying the foundation in the little things of life that lie immediately about one's door. I plead for industrial education and development for the Negro not because I want to cramp him, but because I want to free him. . . .

I close, then, as I began, by saying that as a slave the Negro was worked, and that as a freeman he must learn to work. There is still doubt in many quarters as to the ability of the Negro unguided, unsupported, to hew his own path and put into visible, tangible, indisputable form, products and

signs of civilization. This doubt cannot be much affected by abstract arguments, no matter how delicately and convincingly woven together. Patiently, quietly, doggedly, persistently, through summer and winter, sunshine and shadow, by self-sacrifice, by foresight, by honesty and industry, we must re-enforce argument with results. One farm bought, one house built, one home sweetly and intelligently kept, one man who is the largest tax payer or has the largest bank account, one school or church maintained, one factory running successfully, one truck garden profitably cultivated, one patient cured by a Negro doctor, one sermon well preached, one office well filled, one life cleanly lived—these will tell more in our favor than all the abstract eloquence that can be summoned to plead our cause. Our pathway must be up through the soil, up through swamps, up through forests, up through the streams, the rocks, up through commerce, education and religion!

BOOKER T. WASHINGTON
My Larger Education (1911) *

My own early experience was, I suppose, like that of most other teachers; I picked up quite naturally those methods of teaching that were in vogue around me or that seemed to be prescribed by the textbooks. My method consisted in asking pupils to learn what was in the book, and then requiring them to recite it.

I shall long remember the time when the folly and uselessness of much of the old-time method of teaching first fairly dawned upon me. I was teaching a country school near my old home in West Virginia. This school was located near a piece of land that was wet and marshy, but nevertheless beautiful in appearance. It was June and the day was hot and sultry; when the usual recess or playtime came, I was as anxious as the

* Booker T. Washington, *My Larger Education: Being Chapters from My Experience* (Garden City, N.Y.: Doubleday, Page, 1911), pp. 131–143. Used by permission of Mrs. Portia Washington Pittman.

children were to get outside of the close and stuffy school room into the open air. That day I prolonged the playtime to more than twice the usual period.

The hour previous to recess had been employed by me in trying to get a class of children interested in what proved to be a rather stupid geography lesson. I had been asking my pupils a lot of dull and tiresome questions, getting them to define and name lakes, capes, peninsulas, islands, and so forth. Naturally the answers of the children were quite as dull and stupid as the questions.

As soon as the children were out of doors at playtime, however, they all, as if by common instinct, scampered off into the marshes. In a few seconds they were wading in the cool water, jumping about in the fragrant grass, and enjoying themselves in a way that was in striking contrast to the dull labour of the geography lesson. I soon became infected with the general fever; and in a few minutes I found myself following the children at a rapid rate and entering into the full enjoyment of the contrast between the dull, dead atmosphere of the school room and the vivid tingling sense of the living out-doors.

We had not been out of the school house and away from the old geography lesson long before one of the boys who had been among the dullest in his recitation in the school room became the leader of a sort of exploring party. Under his leadership we began to discover, as we waded along the stream, dozens of islands, capes, and peninsulas, with here and there a little lake or bay, which, as some of the pupils pointed out, would furnish a safe harbour for ships if the stream were only large enough. Soon every one of the children was busy pointing out and naming the natural divisions of land and water. And then, after a few days, we got pieces of wood and bark and let them float down the stream; we imagined them to be great ships carrying their cargoes of merchandise from one part of the world to another. We studied the way the stream wandered about in the level land, and noticed how the little sand bars and the corresponding harbours were formed by the particles of sand and earth which were rolled down by the stream. We located cities on these harbours, and tried to find water-power where we might build up manufacturing centres.

Before long I discovered that, quite unconsciously, we had taken up again the lessons in the school room and were studying geography after a new fashion. This time, however, we found a real joy and zest in the work, and I think both teacher and pupils learned more geography in that short period than they ever learned in the same space of time before or since.

For the first time the real difference between studying about things through the medium of books, and studying things themselves without the medium of books, was revealed to me. The children in this recess period had gained more ideas in regard to the natural divisions of the earth than they would have gained in several days by merely studying geography inside the school room. To be sure, they had not learned the names, the locations, nor the definitions of the capes, bays, and islands, but they had learned what was more important—to *think* capes, islands, and peninsulas. From that time on they found no difficulty and were really greatly interested in recognizing the natural divisions of land and water wherever they met them.

The lesson that I learned thus early in my experience as a teacher I have never forgotten. In all my work at Tuskegee Institute I have lost no opportunity to impress upon our teachers the importance of training their students to study, analyze, and compare actual things, and to use what they have learned in the school room and in the text-book, to enable them to observe, think about, and deal with the objects and situations of actual life.

Not long ago I visited the class room of a new teacher at Tuskegee, who was conducting a class in measurements. This teacher had insisted that each member of the class should commit to memory the tables of measurement, and when I came in they were engaged in reciting, singsong, something that sounded like a sort of litany composed of feet, yards, rods, acres, gills, pints, quarts, ounces, pounds, and the rest. I looked on at this proceeding for a few minutes; then a happy thought occurred to me and I asked the teacher to let me take the class in hand. I began by asking if any one in the class had ever measured the class room in which they were sitting. There was a dumb silence. Then I asked if any one had ever marked off an acre of actual land, had ever measured a gill of water, or had ever weighed an ounce or a pound of sugar. Not a hand was raised in reply.

Then I told the teacher that I would like to take charge of the class for a few days. Before the week was over I had seen to it that every member of the class had supplied himself with a rule or a measure of some sort. Under my direction the students measured the class room and found what it would cost to paint the walls of the room.

From the class room we went to a part of the farm where the students were engaged in planting sweet potatoes. Soon we had an acre of sweet potatoes measured off. We computed the number of bushels raised on that acre and calculated the cost and profit of raising them.

Before the week was over the whole class had been through the boarding department, where they had an opportunity to weigh actual sugar. From the steward we obtained some interesting figures as to how much sugar was used a day; then we computed how much was used by each student. We went to the farm again and weighed a live pig, and I had the class find out the selling price of pork on that particular day, not in Chicago, but in Alabama. I had them calculate the amount that—not an imaginary pig or a pig in Chicago—the pig that they had weighed would bring that day in the local market. It took some time to go through all these operations, but I think that it paid

to do so. Besides, it was fun. It was fun for me, and it was a great deal more fun for the students. Incidentally the teacher got an awakening and learned a lesson that I dare say he has never forgotten.

At the present time all teachers in the academic studies are expected to make a careful study of the work carried on by the students in the industries. Nearly every day, for example, some class in mathematics, goes under the charge of a teacher, into the shops or the dairy or out on the farm to get its problems in mathematics at first hand. Students are sent from the English classes to look up the history of some trade, or some single operation performed by students in the shop, and to write out an account of that trade or that operation for the benefit of the other members of the class. In such cases attention is paid not merely to the form in which the report is written, but more especially to the accuracy and clearness of the statement. The student who prepares that kind of paper is writing something in which other students have a practical interest, and if students are not accurate there are always one or more students in the class who know enough about the subject to criticise and correct the statements made. The student in this case finds himself dealing with live matters, and he naturally feels responsibility for the statements that he makes—a responsibility that he would not feel if he were merely putting together facts that he had gathered from some encyclopædia or other second-hand source of information.

In emphasizing the importance of studying things rather than books, I do not mean to underrate the importance of studying history, general literature, or any of the other so-called cultural studies. I do think, however, that it is important that young men and young women should first of all get clear and definite ideas of things right about them, because these are the ideas by which they are going to measure and interpret things farther removed from their practical interests. To young, inexperienced minds there seems to be a kind of fatal charm about the vague, the distant, and the mysterious.

In the early days of freedom, when education was a new thing, the boy who went away to school had a very natural human ambition to be able to come back home in order to delight and astonish the old folks with the new and strange things that he had learned. If he could speak a few words in some strange tongue that his parents had never heard before, or read a few sentences out of a book with strange and mysterious characters, he was able to make them very proud and happy. There was a constant temptation therefore for schools and teachers to keep everything connected with education in a sort of twilight realm of the mysterious and supernatural. Quite unconsciously they created in the minds of their pupils the impression that a boy or a girl who had passed through certain educational forms and ceremonies had been initiated into some sort of secret knowledge that was inaccessible to the rest of the world. Connected with this was the notion that because a man had passed through these educational forms and ceremonies he had somehow become a sort of superior being set apart from the rest of the world—a member of the "Talented Tenth" or some other ill-defined and exclusive caste.

Nothing, in my opinion, could be more fatal to the success of a student or to the cause of education than the general acceptance of any such ideas. In the long run it will be found that neither black people nor white people want such an education for their children, and they will not support schools that give it.

My experience has taught me that the surest way to success in education, and in any other line for that matter, is to stick close to the common and familiar things— things that concern the greater part of the people the greater part of the time.

I want to see education as common as grass, and as free for all as sunshine and rain.

The way to open opportunities of education for every one, however, is to teach things that every one needs to know. I venture to say that anything in any school, taught with the object of fitting students to produce and serve food, for example, will win approval and popularity for the school. The reason is simple: every human being is interested, several times a day, in the subject of food; and a large part of the world is interested, either directly or indirectly, in its production and sale.

Not long ago I attended the closing exercises of a high school in a community composed mainly of people in the humble walks of life. The general theme of the graduating addresses was "An Imaginary Trip to Europe." Of course the audience was bored, and I was not surprised that a number of people went to sleep. As a matter of fact, I do not think that the parents of a single student who delivered one of these addresses had ever been to Europe or will have an opportunity to go at any time in the near future. The thing did not touch a common chord. It was too far removed from all the practical, human interests of which they had any experience. The average family in America is not ordinarily engaged in travelling through Europe for any large part of the time. Besides that, none of the members of this graduating class had ever been to Europe; consequently they were not writing about something of which they had any real knowledge.

Some years ago, in an effort to bring our rhetorical and commencement exercises into a little closer touch with real things, we tried the experiment at Tuskegee of having students write papers on some subject of which they had first-hand knowledge. As a matter of fact, I believe that Tuskegee was the first institution that attempted to reform its commencement exercises in this particular direction.

Ordinarily, at the closing exercises of a high school, graduates are expected to stand up on the platform and, out of all their inexperience, instruct their elders how to succeed in life. We were fortunate at Tuskegee, in the thirty-seven industries carried on there and in the thousand acres of land that are cultivated, to be able to give our students, in addition to their general education, a pretty good knowledge of some one of the familiar trades or vocations. They have, therefore, something to talk about in their essays in which all of the audience are interested and with which all are more or less familiar.

Instead of having a boy or girl read a paper on some subject like "Beyond the Alps Lies Italy," we have them explain and demonstrate to the audience how to build a roof, or the proper way to make cheese, or how to hatch chickens with an incubator. Perhaps one of the graduates in the nurses' training school will show how to lend "first aid to the injured." If a girl is taking the course in dairying, she will not only describe what she has learned but will go through, on the platform, the various methods of operating a modern dairy.

Instead of letting a boy tell why one ought to do right, we ask him to tell what he has learned about the feeding of pigs, about their diseases, and the care of them when they are sick. In such a case the student will have the pig on the platform, in order to illustrate the methods of caring for it, and demonstrate to the audience the points that he is trying to make.

One of our students, in his commencement oration last May, gave a description of how he planted and raised an acre of cabbages. Piled high upon the platform by his side were some of the largest and finest cabbages that I have ever seen. He told how and where he had obtained the seed; he described his method of preparing and enriching the soil, of working the land, and harvesting the crop; and he summed up by giving the cost of the whole operation. In the course of his account of this comparatively simple operation, this student had made use of much that he had learned in composition, grammar, mathematics, chemistry, and agriculture. He had not merely woven into his narrative all these various elements that I have referred to, but he had given the audience (which was made up largely of coloured farmers from the surrounding country) some useful and practical information in regard to a subject which they understood and were interested in. I wish that any one who does not believe it possible to make a subject like cabbages interesting in a commencement oration could have heard the hearty cheers which greeted the speaker when, at the close of his speech, he held up one of the largest cabbages on the platform for the audience to look at and admire. As a matter of fact, there is just as much that is interesting, strange, mysterious, and wonderful; just as much to be learned that is edifying, broadening, and refining in a cabbage as there is in a page of Latin. There is, however, this distinction: it will make very little difference to the world whether one Negro boy, more or less, learns to construe a page of Latin. On the other hand, as soon as one Negro boy has been taught to apply thought and study and ideas to the growing of cabbages, he has started a process which, if it goes on and continues, will eventually transform the whole face of things as they exist in the South to-day.

I have spoken hitherto about industrial education as a means of connecting education with life. The mere fact that a boy has learned in school to handle a plane or that he has learned something about the chemistry of the soil does not of itself insure that he has gained any new and vital grip upon the life about him. He must at the same time learn to use the knowledge and the training that he has received to change and improve the conditions about him. . . .

BOOKER T. WASHINGTON
"The Highest Education" (1902) *

* Booker T. Washington, *Character Building: Being Addresses Delivered on Sunday Evenings to the Students of Tuskegee Institute* (New York: Doubleday, Page, 1902), "The Highest Education," pp. 111–117.

It may seem to some of you that I am continually talking to you about education —the right kind of education, how to get an education, and such kindred subjects— but surely no subject could be more pertinent, since the object for which you all are here is to get an education; and if you are to do this, you wish to get the best kind possible.

You will understand, then, I am sure, if I speak often about this, or refer to the subject frequently, that it is because I am very anxious that all of you go out from here with a definite and correct idea of what is meant by education, of what an education is meant to accomplish, what it may be expected to do for one.

We are very apt to get the idea that education means the memorizing of a number of dates, of being able to state when a certain battle took place, of being able to recall with accuracy this event or that event. We are likely to get the impression that education consists in being able to commit to memory a certain number of rules in grammar, a certain number of rules in arithmetic, and in being able to locate correctly on the earth's surface this mountain or that river, and to name this lake and that gulf.

Now I do not mean to disparage the value of this kind of training, because among the things that education should do for us is to give us strong, orderly and well developed minds. I do not wish to have you get the idea that I undervalue or overlook the strengthening of the mind. If there is one person more than another who is to be pitied, it is the individual who is all heart and no head. You will see numbers of persons going through the world whose hearts are full of good things—running over with the wish to do something to make somebody better, or the desire to make somebody happier—but they have made the sad mistake of being absolutely without development of mind to go with this willingness of heart. We want development of mind and we want strengthening of the mind.

I have often said to you that one of the best things that education can do for an individual is to teach that individual to get hold of what he wants, rather than to teach him how to commit to memory a number of facts in history or a number of names in geography. I wish you to feel that we can give you here orderliness of mind—I mean a trained mind—that will enable you to find dates in history or to put your finger on names in geography when you want them. I wish to give you an education that will enable you to construct rules in grammar and arithmetic for yourselves. That is the highest kind of training.

But, after all, this kind of thing is not the end of education. What, then, do we mean by education? I would say that education is meant to give us an idea of truth. Whatever we get out of text books, whatever we get out of industry, whatever we get here and there from any sources, if we do not get the idea of truth at the end, we do not get education. I do not care how much you get out of history, or geography, or algebra, or literature, I do not care how much you have got out of all your text books:—unless you have got truth, you have failed in your purpose to be educated. Unless you get the idea of truth so pure that you cannot be false in anything, your education is a failure.

Then education is meant to make us just in our dealings with our fellow men. The man or woman who has learned to be absolutely just, so far as he can interpret, has, in that degree, an education, is to that degree an educated man or woman. Education is meant to make us change for the better, to make us more thoughtful, to make us so broad that we will not seek to help one man because he belongs to this race or that race of people, and seek to hinder another man because he does not belong to this race or that race of people.

Education in the broadest and truest sense will make an individual seek to help all people, regardless of race, regardless of colour, regardless of condition. And you will find that the person who is most truly educated is the one who is going to be kindest, and is going to act in the gentlest manner toward persons who are unfortunate, toward the race or the individual that is most despised. The highly educated person is the one who is the most considerate of those individuals who are less fortunate. I hope that when you go out from here, and meet persons who are afflicted by poverty, whether of mind or body, or persons who are unfortunate in any way, that you will show your education by being just as kind and just as considerate toward those persons as it is possible for you to be. That is the way to test a person with education. You may see ignorant persons, who, perhaps, think themselves educated, going about the street, who, when they meet an individual who is unfortunate—lame, or with a defect of body, mind or speech—are inclined to laugh at and make sport of that individual. But the highly educated person, the one who is really cultivated, is gentle and sympathetic to everyone.

Education is meant to make us absolutely honest in dealing with our fellows. I don't care how much arithmetic we have, or how many cities we can locate;—it all is useless unless we have an education that makes us absolutely honest.

Education is meant to make us give satisfaction, and to get satisfaction out of giving it. It is meant to make us get happiness out of service for our fellows. And until we get to the point where we can get happiness and supreme satisfaction out of helping our fellows, we are not truly educated. Education is meant to make us generous. In this connection let me say that I very much hope that when you go out from here you will show that you have learned this lesson of being generous in all charitable objects, in the support of your churches, your Sunday schools, your hospitals, and in being generous in giving help to the poor.

I hope, for instance, that a large proportion of you—in fact all of you—will make it a practice to give something yearly to this institution. If you cannot give but twenty-five cents, fifty cents, or a dollar a year, I hope you will put it down as a thing that you will not forget, to give something to this institution every year. We want to show to our friends who have done so much for us, who have supported this school so generously, how much interest we take in the institution that has given us so nearly all that we possess. I hope that every senior, in particular, will keep this in mind. I am glad to say that we have many graduates who send us such sums, even if small, and one graduate who for the last eight or ten years has sent us ten dollars annually. I hope a number of you in the senior class that I see before me will do the same thing.

Education is meant to make us appreciate the things that are beautiful in nature. A person is never educated until he is able to go into the swamps and woods and see something that is beautiful in the trees and shrubs there, is able to see something beautiful in the grass and flowers that surround him, is, in short, able to see something beautiful, elevating and inspiring in everything that God has created. Not only should education enable us to see the beauty in these objects which God has put about us, but it is meant to influence us to bring beautiful objects about us. I hope that each one of you, after you graduate, will surround himself at home with what is beautiful, inspiring and elevating. I do not believe that any person is educated so long as he lives in a dirty, miserable shanty. I do not believe that any person is educated until he has learned to want to live in a clean room made attractive with pictures and books, and with such surroundings as are elevating.

In a word, I wish to say again, that education is meant to give us that culture, that refinement, that taste which will make us deal truthfully with our fellow men, and will make us see what is beautiful, elevating and inspiring in what God has created. I want you to bear in mind that your text books, with all their contents, are not an end, but a means to an end, a means to help us get the highest, the best, the purest and the most beautiful things out of life.

EDUCATING THE IMMIGRANT: THE ISSUE OF AMERICANIZATION

JOHN SPARGO
"The School Child" (1906)*

" 'It is good when it happens,' say the children,
'That we die before our time.' "
—MRS. BROWNING.

In a New York kindergarten one winter's morning a frail, dark-eyed girl stood by the radiator warming her tiny blue and benumbed hands. She was poorly and scantily clad, and her wan, pinched face was unutterably sad with the sadness that shadows the children of poverty and comes from cares which only maturer years should know. When she had warmed her little hands back to life again, the child looked wistfully up into the teacher's face and asked:—

"Teacher, do you love God?"

"Why, yes, dearie, of course I love God," answered the wondering teacher.

"Well, I don't—I hate Him!" was the fierce rejoinder. "He makes the wind blow, and I haven't any warm clothes—He makes it snow, and my shoes have holes in them—He makes it cold, and we haven't any fire at home—He makes us hungry, and mamma hadn't any bread for our breakfast—Oh, I hate Him!"

This story, widely published in the newspapers two or three years ago and vouched for by the teacher, is remarkable no less for its graphic description of the thing called poverty than for the child's passionate revolt against the supposed author of her misery. Poor, scanty clothing, cheerless homes, hunger day by day,—these are the main characteristics of that heritage of poverty to which so many thousands of children are born. Tens of thousands of baby lives

* John Spargo, *The Bitter Cry of the Children* (New York: Macmillan, 1906), Chapter II, "The School Child," pp. 57–60, 117–124.

are extinguished by its blasts every year as though they were so many candles swept by angry winds. But their fate is far more merciful and enviable than the fate of those who survive.

For the children who survive the struggle with poverty in their infant years, and those who do not encounter that struggle until they have reached school age, not only feel the anguish and shame which comes with developed consciousness, but society imposes upon them the added burden of mental effort. Regarding education as the only safe anchorage for a Democracy, we make it compulsory and boast that it is one of the fundamental principles of our economy that every child shall be given a certain amount of elementary instruction. This is our safeguard against those evils which other generations regarded as being inherent in popular, representative government. The modern public school, with its splendid equipment devised to promote the mental and physical development of our future citizens, is based upon motives and instincts of self-preservation as distinct and clearly defined as those underlying our systems of naval and military defences against armed invasion, or the systems of public sanitation and hygiene through which we seek to protect ourselves from devastating plagues within.

The past fifty or sixty years have been attended with a wonderful development of the science of education, as remarkable and important in its way as anything of which we may boast. We are proud, and justly so, of the admirable machinery of instruction which we have created, the fine buldings, laboratories, curricula, highly trained teachers, and so on, but there is a growing conviction that all this represents only so much mechanical, rather than human, progress. We have created a vast network of means, there is no lack of equipment, but we have largely neglected the human and most important factor, the child. The futility of expecting efficient education when the teacher is handicapped by poor and inadequate means is generally recognized, but not so as yet the futility of expecting it when the teacher has poor material to work upon in the form of chronically underfed children, too weak in mind and body to do the work required of them. We are forever seeking the explanation of the large percentage of educational failures in the machinery of instruction rather than in the human material, the children themselves.

The nervous, irritable, half-ill children to be found in such large numbers in our public schools represent poor material. They are largely drawn from the homes of poverty, and constitute an overwhelming majority of those children for whom we have found it necessary to make special provision,—the backward, dull pupils found year after year in the same grades with much younger children. In a measure the relation of a child's educability to its physical health and comfort has been recognized by the correlation of physical and mental exercises in most up-to-date schools, but its larger social and economic significance has been almost wholly ignored. And yet it is quite certain that poverty exercises the same retarding influences upon the physical training as upon mental education. There are certain conditions precedent to successful education, whether physical or mental. Chief of these are a reasonable amount of good, nourishing food and a healthy home. Deprived of these, physical or mental development must necessarily be hindered. And poverty means just that to the child. It denies its victim these very necessities with the inevitable result, physical and mental weakness and inefficiency.

. . . . .

Summarizing, briefly, the results of this investigation, the problem of poverty as it affects school children may be stated in a few lines. All the data available tend to show that not less than 2,000,000 children of school age in the United States are the victims of poverty which denies them common necessities, particularly adequate nourishment. As a result of this privation they are far inferior in physical development to their more fortunate fellows. This inferiority of physique, in turn, is responsible for much mental and moral degeneration. Such children are in very many cases incapable of successful mental effort, and much of our national expenditure for education is in consequence an absolute waste. With their enfeebled bodies and minds we turn these children adrift unfitted for the struggle of life, which tends to become keener with every advance in our industrial development, and because of their lack of physical and mental training they are found to be inefficient industrially and dangerous socially. They become dependent, paupers, and the procreators of a pauper and dependent race.

Here, then, is a problem of awful magnitude. In the richest country on earth hundreds of thousands of children are literally damned to lifelong, helpless, and debasing poverty. They are plunged in the earliest and most important years of character formation into that terrible maelstrom of poverty which casts so many thousands, ay, millions, of physical, mental, and moral wrecks upon the shores of our social life. For them there is little or no hope of escape from the blight and curse of pauperism unless the nation, pursuing a policy of enlightened self-interest and protection, decides to save them. In the main, this vast sum of poverty is due to causes of a purely impersonal nature which the victims cannot control, such as sickness, accident, low wages, and unemployment. Personal causes, such as ignorance, thriftlessness, gambling, intemperance, indolence, wife-desertion, and other vices or weaknesses, are also responsible for a good deal of poverty, though by no means most of it as is sometimes urged by superficial observers. There are many thousands of temperate and industrious workers who are miserably poor, and many of those who are thriftless or intemperate are the victims of poverty's degenerating influences. But whether a child's hunger and privation is due to some fault of its parents or to causes beyond their control, the fact of its suffering remains, and its impaired physical and mental strength tends almost irresistibly to make it inefficient as a citizen. Whatever the cause, therefore, of its privation, society must, as a measure of self-protection, take upon itself the responsibility of caring for the child.

There can be no compromise upon this vital point. Those who say that society should refuse to do anything for those children who are the victims of their parents' vices or weaknesses adopt a singularly indefensible attitude. In the first place it is barbarously unjust to allow the sins of the parents to bring punishment and suffering upon the child, to damn the innocent and unoffending. No more vicious doctrine than this, which so many excellent and well-intentioned persons are fond of preaching, has ever been formulated by human perversity. Carried to its logical end, it would destroy all legislation for the protection of children from cruel parents or guardians. It is strange that the doctrinaire advocates of this brutal gospel should overlook its practical consequences. If discrimination were to be made at all, it should be in favor of, rather than against, the children of drunken and profligate parents. For these children have a special claim upon society for protection from wrongs in the shape of influences injurious to their physical and moral well-being, and tending to lead them into evil and degrading ways. The half-starved child of the inebriate is not less entitled to the protection of society than the victim of inhuman physical torture.

Should these children be excluded from any system of feeding adopted by the state upon the ground that their parents have not fulfilled their parental responsibilities, society joins in a conspiracy against their very lives. And that conspiracy ultimately and inevitably involves retribution. In the interests and name of a beguiling economy, fearful that if it assumes responsibility for the care of the child of inebriate parents, it will foster and encourage their inebriety and neglect, society leaves the children surrounded by circumstances which practically force them to become drunkards, physical and moral wrecks, and procreators of a like degenerate progeny. *Then* it is forced to accept the responsibility of their support, either as paupers or criminals. That is the stern Nemesis of retribution. Where an enlightened system of child saving has been followed, this principle has been clearly recognized. In Minnesota, for example, the state assumes the responsibility for the care of such children as a matter of self-protection. To quote the language of a report of the State Public School at Owatonna: "It is for economic as well as for humane reasons that this work is done. The state is thus protecting itself from dangers to which it would be exposed in a very few years if these children were reared in the conditions which so injuriously affect them." Whatever steps may be taken to punish, or make responsible to the state, those parents who by their vice and neglect bring suffering and want upon their children, the children themselves should be saved.

To the contention that society, having assumed the responsibility of insisting that every child shall be educated, and providing the means of education, is necessarily bound to assume the responsibility of seeing that they are made fit to receive that education, so far as possible, there does not seem to be any convincing answer. It will be objected that for society to do this would mean the destruction of the responsibility of the parents. That is obviously true. But it is equally true of education itself, the responsibility for which society has assumed. Some individualists there are who contend that society is wrong in doing this, and their opposition to the proposal that it should undertake to provide the children with food is far more logical than that of those who believe that society should assume the responsibility of educating the child, but not that of equipping it with the necessary physical basis for that education. The fact is that society insists upon the education of the children, not, primarily, in their interests nor in the interests of the parents, but in its own. All legislation upon child labor, education, child guardianship in general, is based upon a denial of proprietary rights to children by their parents. The child belongs to society rather than to its parents.

Further, private charity, which is the only alternative suggestion offered for the solution of this problem, equally removes responsibility from the parents and is open to other weightier objections. In the first place, where it succeeds, it is far more demoralizing than such a system of public support provided at the public cost, as the child's birthright, could possibly be. Still more important is the fact that private charity does not succeed in the vast majority of instances. To their credit, it must be remembered that the poor as a class refuse to beg or to parade their poverty. They suffer in silence and never seek alms. Pride and the shame of begging seal their lips. Here, too, the question of the children of inebriate, dissolute, worthless parents enters. Every one who has had the least experience of charitable work knows that these are the persons who are most relieved by charity. They do not hesitate to plead for charity. "I have not strength to dig; to beg I am ashamed," is the motto of the self-respecting, silent, suffering poor. The failure of charity is incontestable. As some witty Frenchman has well said, "Charity creates one-half the misery she relieves, but cannot relieve one-half the misery she creates."

It is impossible to enter here into a discussion of the question of cost, but the argument that society could not afford to undertake this further responsibility must be briefly considered. In view of our well-nigh boundless resources there is small reason for the belief that we cannot provide for the needs of all our children. If it were true that we could not provide for their necessities, then wholesale death would be merciful and

desirable. At any rate, it would be far better to feed them first, neglecting their education altogether, than to waste our substance in the brutally senseless endeavor to educate them while they starve and pine for bread. There can be little doubt that the economic waste involved in fruitless charity, and the still vaster waste involved in the maintenance of the dependent and criminal classes whose degeneracy is mainly attributable to underfeeding in childhood, amount to a sum far exceeding the cost of providing adequate nutrition for every child. It is essentially a question of the proper adjustment of our means to our needs. Otherwise we must admit the utter failure of our civilization and confess that, in the language of Sophocles, it is

> "Happiest beyond compare
>   Never to taste of life;
> Happiest in order next,
>   Being born, with quickest speed
> Thither again to turn
>   From whence we came." [1]

JANE ADDAMS
"Educational Methods" (1902)*

As democracy modifies our conception of life, it constantly raises the value and function of each member of the community, however humble he may be. We have come to believe that the most "brutish man" has a value in our common life, a function to perform which can be fulfilled by no one else. We are gradually requiring of the educator that he shall free the powers of each man and connect him with the rest of life. We ask this not merely because it is the man's right to be thus connected, but because we have become convinced that the social order cannot afford to get along without his special contribution. Just as we have come to resent all hindrances which keep us

* Jane Addams, *Democracy and Social Ethics* (New York: Macmillan, 1902), Chapter VI, "Educational Methods," pp. 178–192, 208–216, 218–220.

[1] *Œdipus Coloneus.*

from untrammelled comradeship with our fellows, and as we throw down unnatural divisions, not in the spirit of the eighteenth-century reformers, but in the spirit of those to whom social equality has become a necessity for further social development, so we are impatient to use the dynamic power residing in the mass of men, and demand that the educator free that power. We believe that man's moral idealism is the constructive force of progress, as it has always been; but because every human being is a creative agent and a possible generator of fine enthusiasm, we are sceptical of the moral idealism of the few and demand the education of the many, that there may be greater freedom, strength, and subtilty of intercourse and hence an increase of dynamic power. We are not content to include all men in our hopes, but have become conscious that all men are hoping and are part of the same movement of which we are a part.

Many people impelled by these ideas have become impatient with the slow recognition on the part of the educators of their manifest obligation to prepare and nourish the child and the citizen for social relations. The educators should certainly conserve the learning and training necessary for the successful individual and family life, but should add to that a preparation for the enlarged social efforts which our increasing democracy requires. The democratic ideal demands of the school that it shall give the child's own experience a social value; that it shall teach him to direct his own activities and adjust them to those of other people. We are not willing that thousands of industrial workers shall put all of their activity and toil into services from which the community as a whole reaps the benefit, while their mental conceptions and code of morals are narrow and untouched by any uplift which the consciousness of social value might give them.

We are impatient with the schools which lay all stress on reading and writing, suspecting them to rest upon the assumption that the ordinary experience of life is worth little, and that all knowledge and interest must be brought to the children through the medium of books. Such an assumption fails to give the child any clew to the life about him, or any power to usefully or intelligently connect himself with it. This may be illustrated by observations made in a large Italian colony situated in Chicago, the children from which are, for the most part, sent to the public schools.

The members of the Italian colony are largely from South Italy,—Calabrian and Sicilian peasants, or Neapolitans from the workingmen's quarters of that city. They have come to America with the distinct aim of earning money, and finding more room for the energies of themselves and their children. In almost all cases they mean to go back again, simply because their imaginations cannot picture a continuous life away from the old surroundings. Their experiences in Italy have been those of simple outdoor activity, and their ideas have come directly to them from their struggle with Nature,—such a hand-to-hand struggle as takes place when each man gets his living largely through his own cultivation of the soil, or with tools simply fashioned by his own hands. The women, as in all primitive life, have had more diversified activities than the men. They have cooked, spun, and knitted, in addition to their almost equal work in the fields. Very few of the peasant men or women can either read or write. They are devoted to their children, strong in their family feeling, even to remote relationships, and clannish in their community life.

The entire family has been upheaved, and is striving to adjust itself to its new surroundings. The men, for the most part, work on railroad extensions through the summer, under the direction of a *padrone,* who finds the work for them, regulates the amount of their wages, and supplies them with food. The first effect of immigration upon the women is that of idleness. They no longer work in the fields, nor milk the goats, nor pick up faggots. The mother of the family buys all the clothing, not only already spun and woven but made up into garments, of a cut and fashion beyond her powers. It is, indeed, the most economical thing for her to do. Her house-cleaning and cooking are of the simplest; the bread is usually baked outside of the house, and the macaroni bought prepared for boiling. All of those outdoor and domestic activities, which she would naturally have handed on to her daughters, have slipped away from her. The domestic arts are gone, with their absorbing interests for the children, their educational value, and incentive to activity. A household in a tenement receives almost no raw material. For the hundreds of children who have never seen wheat grow, there are dozens who have never seen bread baked. The occasional washings and scrubbings are associated only with discomfort. The child of such a family receives constant stimulus of most exciting sort from his city street life, but he has little or no opportunity to use his energies in domestic manufacture, or, indeed, constructively in any direction. No activity is supplied to take the place of that which, in Italy, he would naturally have found in his own surroundings, and no new union with wholesome life is made for him.

Italian parents count upon the fact that their children learn the English language and American customs before they do themselves, and the children act not only as interpreters of the language, but as buffers between them and Chicago, resulting in a certain almost pathetic dependence of the family upon the child. When a child of the family, therefore, first goes to school, the event is fraught with much significance to all the others. The family has no social life in any structural form and can supply none to the child. He ought to get it in the school and give it to his family, the school thus becoming the connector with the organized society about them. It is the children aged six, eight, and ten, who go to school, entering, of course, the primary grades. If a boy is twelve or thirteen on his arrival in America, his parents see in him a wage-earning

factor, and the girl of the same age is already looking toward her marriage.

Let us take one of these boys, who has learned in his six or eight years to speak his native language, and to feel himself strongly identified with the fortunes of his family. Whatever interest has come to the minds of his ancestors has come through the use of their hands in the open air; and open air and activity of body have been the inevitable accompaniments of all their experiences. Yet the first thing that the boy must do when he reaches school is to sit still, at least part of the time, and he must learn to listen to what is said to him, with all the perplexity of listening to a foreign tongue. He does not find this very stimulating, and is slow to respond to the more subtle incentives of the schoolroom. The peasant child is perfectly indifferent to showing off and making a good recitation. He leaves all that to his schoolfellows, who are more sophisticated and equipped with better English. His parents are not deeply interested in keeping him in school, and will not hold him there against his inclination. Their experience does not point to the good American tradition that it is the educated man who finally succeeds. The richest man in the Italian colony can neither read nor write—even Italian. His cunning and acquisitiveness, combined with the credulity and ignorance of his countrymen, have slowly brought about his large fortune. The child himself may feel the stirring of a vague ambition to go on until he is as the other children are; but he is not popular with his schoolfellows, and he sadly feels the lack of dramatic interest. Even the pictures and objects presented to him, as well as the language, are strange.

If we admit that in education it is necessary to begin with the experiences which the child already has and to use his spontaneous and social activity, then the city streets begin this education for him in a more natural way than does the school. The South Italian peasant comes from a life of picking olives and oranges, and he easily sends his children out to pick up coal from railroad tracks, or wood from buildings which have been burned down. Unfortunately, this process leads by easy transition to petty thieving. It is easy to go from the coal on the railroad track to the coal and wood which stand before a dealer's shop; from the potatoes which have rolled from a rumbling wagon to the vegetables displayed by the grocer. This is apt to be the record of the boy who responds constantly to the stimulus and temptations of the street, although in the beginning his search for bits of food and fuel was prompted by the best of motives.

The school has to compete with a great deal from the outside in addition to the distractions of the neighborhood. Nothing is more fascinating than that mysterious "down town," whither the boy longs to go to sell papers and black boots, to attend theatres, and, if possible, to stay all night on the pretence of waiting for the early edition of the great dailies. If a boy is once thoroughly caught in these excitements, nothing can save him from over-stimulation and consequent debility and worthlessness; he arrives at maturity with no habits of regular work and with a distaste for its dulness.

On the other hand, there are hundreds of boys of various nationalities who conscientiously remain in school and fulfil all the requirements of the early grades, and at the age of fourteen are found in factories, painstakingly performing their work year after year. These later are the men who form the mass of the population in every industrial neighborhood of every large city; but they carry on the industrial processes year after year without in the least knowing what it is all about. The one fixed habit which the boy carries away with him from the school to the factory is the feeling that his work is merely provisional. In school the next grade was continually held before him as an object of attainment, and it resulted in the conviction that the sole object of present effort is to get ready for something else. This tentative attitude takes the last bit of social stimulus out of his factory work; he pursues it merely as a necessity, and his very mental

attitude destroys his chance for a realization of its social value. As the boy in school contracted the habit of doing his work in certain hours and taking his pleasure in certain other hours, so in the factory he earns his money by ten hours of dull work and spends it in three hours of lurid and unprofitable pleasure in the evening. Both in the school and in the factory, in proportion as his work grows dull and monotonous, his recreation must become more exciting and stimulating. The hopelessness of adding evening classes and social entertainments as a mere frill to a day filled with monotonous and deadening drudgery constantly becomes more apparent to those who are endeavoring to bring a fuller life to the industrial members of the community, and who are looking forward to a time when work shall cease to be senseless drudgery with no self-expression on the part of the worker. It sometimes seems that the public schools should contribute much more than they do to the consummation of this time. If the army of school children who enter the factories every year possessed thoroughly vitalized faculties, they might do much to lighten this incubus of dull factory work which presses so heavily upon so large a number of our fellow-citizens. Has our commercialism been so strong that our schools have become insensibly commercialized, whereas we supposed that our industrial life was receiving the broadening and illuminating effects of the schools? The training of these children, so far as it has been vocational at all, has been in the direction of clerical work. It is possible that the business men, whom we in America so tremendously admire, have really been dictating the curriculum of our public schools, in spite of the conventions of educators and the suggestions of university professors. The business man, of course, has not said, "I will have the public schools train office boys and clerks so that I may have them easily and cheaply," but he has sometimes said, "Teach the children to write legibly and to figure accurately and quickly; to acquire habits of punctuality and order; to be prompt to obey;

and you will fit them to make their way in the world as I have made mine." Has the workingman been silent as to what he desires for his children, and allowed the business man to decide for him there, as he has allowed the politician to manage his municipal affairs, or has the workingman so far shared our universal optimism that he has really believed that his children would never need to go into industrial life at all, but that all of his sons would become bankers and merchants?

Certain it is that no sufficient study has been made of the child who enters into industrial life early and stays there permanently, to give him some offset to its monotony and dulness, some historic significance of the part he is taking in the life of the community.

.　.　.　.　.

We constantly hear it said in educational circles, that a child learns only by "doing," and that education must proceed "through the eyes and hands to the brain"; and yet for the vast number of people all around us who do not need to have activities artificially provided, and who use their hands and eyes all the time, we do not seem able to reverse the process. We quote the dictum, "What is learned in the schoolroom must be applied in the workshop," and yet the skill and handicraft constantly used in the workshop have no relevance or meaning given to them by the school; and when we do try to help the workingman in an educational way, we completely ignore his everyday occupation. Yet the task is merely one of adaptation. It is to take actual conditions and to make them the basis for a large and generous method of education, to perform a difficult idealization doubtless, but not an impossible one.

We apparently believe that the workingman has no chance to realize life through his vocation. We easily recognize the historic association in regard to ancient buildings. We say that "generation after generation have stamped their mark upon them,

have recorded their thoughts in them, until they have become the property of all." And yet this is even more true of the instruments of labor, which have constantly been held in human hands. A machine really represents the "seasoned life of man" preserved and treasured up within itself, quite as much as an ancient building does. At present, workmen are brought in contact with the machinery with which they work as abruptly as if the present set of industrial implements had been newly created. They handle the machinery day by day, without any notion of its gradual evolution and growth. Few of the men who perform the mechanical work in the great factories have any comprehension of the fact that the inventions upon which the factory depends, the instruments which they use, have been slowly worked out, each generation using the gifts of the last and transmitting the inheritance until it has become a social possession. This can only be understood by a man who has obtained some idea of social progress. We are still childishly pleased when we see the further subdivision of labor going on, because the quantity of the output is increased thereby, and we apparently are unable to take our attention away from the product long enough to really focus it upon the producer. Theoretically, "the division of labor" makes men more interdependent and human by drawing them together into a unity of purpose. "If a number of people decide to build a road, and one digs, and one brings stones, and another breaks them, they are quite inevitably united by their interest in the road. But this naturally presupposes that they know where the road is going to, that they have some curiosity and interest about it, and perhaps a chance to travel upon it." If the division of labor robs them of interest in any part of it, the mere mechanical fact of interdependence amounts to nothing.

The man in the factory, as well as the man with the hoe, has a grievance beyond being overworked and disinherited, in that he does not know what it is all about. We may well regret the passing of the time when the variety of work performed in the unspecialized workshop naturally stimulated the intelligence of the workingmen and brought them into contact both with the raw material and the finished product. But the problem of education, as any advanced educator will tell us, is to supply the essentials of experience by a short cut, as it were. If the shop constantly tends to make the workman a specialist, then the problem of the educator in regard to him is quite clear: it is to give him what may be an offset from the over-specialization of his daily work, to supply him with general information and to insist that he shall be a cultivated member of society with a consciousness of his industrial and social value.

As sad a sight as an old hand-loom worker in a factory attempting to make his clumsy machine compete with the flying shuttles about him, is a workingman equipped with knowledge so meagre that he can get no meaning into his life nor sequence between his acts and the far-off results.

Manufacturers, as a whole, however, when they attempt educational institutions in connection with their factories, are prone to follow conventional lines, and to exhibit the weakness of imitation. We find, indeed, that the middle-class educator constantly makes the mistakes of the middle-class moralist when he attempts to aid working people. The latter has constantly and traditionally urged upon the workingman the specialized virtues of thrift, industry, and sobriety— all virtues pertaining to the individual. When each man had his own shop, it was perhaps wise to lay almost exclusive stress upon the industrial virtues of diligence and thrift; but as industry has become more highly organized, life becomes incredibly complex and interdependent. If a workingman is to have a conception of his value at all, he must see industry in its unity and entirety; he must have a conception that will include not only himself and his immediate family and community, but the industrial organization as a whole. It is doubtless true that dexterity of hand becomes less and less imperative as the

invention of machinery and subdivision of labor proceeds; but it becomes all the more necessary, if the workman is to save his life at all, that he should get a sense of his individual relation to the system. Feeding a machine with a material of which he has no knowledge, producing a product, totally unrelated to the rest of his life, without in the least knowing what becomes of it, or its connection with the community, is, of course, unquestionably deadening to his intellectual and moral life. To make the moral connection it would be necessary to give him a social consciousness of the value of his work, and at least a sense of participation and a certain joy in its ultimate use; to make the intellectual connection it would be essential to create in him some historic conception of the development of industry and the relation of his individual work to it.

Workingmen themselves have made attempts in both directions, which it would be well for moralists and educators to study. It is a striking fact that when workingmen formulate their own moral code, and try to inspire and encourage each other, it is always a large and general doctrine which they preach. They were the first class of men to organize an international association, and the constant talk at a modern labor meeting is of solidarity and of the identity of the interests of workingmen the world over. It is difficult to secure a successful organization of men into the simplest trades organization without an appeal to the most abstract principles of justice and brotherhood. As they have formulated their own morals by laying the greatest stress upon the largest morality, so if they could found their own schools, it is doubtful whether they would be of the mechanic institute type. Courses of study arranged by a group of workingmen are most naïve in their breadth and generality. They will select the history of the world in preference to that of any period or nation. The "wonders of science" or "the story of evolution" will attract workingmen to a lecture when zoölogy or chemistry will drive them away. The "outlines of literature" or "the best in literature" will draw an audience when a lecturer in English poetry will be solitary. This results partly from a wholesome desire to have general knowledge before special knowledge, and is partly a rebound from the specialization of labor to which the workingman is subjected. When he is free from work and can direct his own mind, he tends to roam, to dwell upon large themes. . . .

It is easy to indict the educator, to say that he has gotten entangled in his own material, and has fallen a victim to his own methods; but granting this, what has the artist done about it—he who is supposed to have a more intimate insight into the needs of his contemporaries, and to minister to them as none other can?

It is quite true that a few writers are insisting that the growing desire for labor, on the part of many people of leisure, has its counterpart in the increasing desire for general knowledge on the part of many laborers. They point to the fact that the same duality of conscience which seems to stifle the noblest effort in the individual because his intellectual conception and his achievement are so difficult to bring together, is found on a large scale in society itself, when we have the separation of the people who think from those who work. And yet, since Ruskin ceased, no one has really formulated this in a convincing form. And even Ruskin's famous dictum, that labor without art brutalizes, has always been interpreted as if art could only be a sense of beauty or joy in one's own work, and not a sense of companionship with all other workers. The situation demands the consciousness of participation and well-being which comes to the individual when he is able to see himself "in connection and co-operation with the whole"; it needs the solace of collective art inherent in collective labor.

As the poet bathes the outer world for us in the hues of human feeling, so the workman needs some one to bathe his surroundings with a human significance—some one who shall teach him to find that which will give a potency to his life. His education, however simple, should tend to make him widely at home in the world, and to give him a sense of simplicity and peace in the midst of the triviality and noise to which he is constantly subjected. He, like other men, can learn to be content to see but a part, although it must be a part of something.

It is because of a lack of democracy that we do not really incorporate him in the hopes and advantages of society, and give him the place which is his by simple right. We have learned to say that the good must be extended to all of society before it can be held secure by any one person or any one class; but we have not yet learned to add to that statement, that unless all men and all classes contribute to a good, we cannot even be sure that it is worth having. In spite of many attempts we do not really act upon either statement.

EDWARD BOK
Autobiography (1920)*

THE FIRST DAYS IN AMERICA

The leviathan of the Atlantic Ocean, in 1870, was *The Queen,* and when she was warped into her dock on September 20 of that year, she discharged, among her passengers, a family of four from the Netherlands who were to make an experiment of Americanization.

The father, a man bearing one of the most respected names in the Netherlands, had acquired wealth and position for himself; unwise investments, however, had swept away his fortune, and in preference to a new start in his own land, he had decided to make the new beginning in the United States, where a favorite brother-in-law had gone several years before. But that, never a simple matter for a man who has reached forty-two, is particularly difficult for a foreigner in a strange land. This fact he and

* *The Americanization of Edward Bok: The Autobiography of a Dutch Boy Fifty Years After* (New York: Scribner, 1920), pp. 1–5, 434–452. Used by permission of Cary W. Bok.

his wife were to find out. The wife, also carefully reared, had been accustomed to a scale of living which she had now to abandon. Her Americanization experiment was to compel her, for the first time in her life, to become a housekeeper without domestic help. There were two boys: the elder, William, was eight and a half years of age; the younger, in nineteen days from his landing-date, was to celebrate his seventh birthday.

This younger boy was Edward William Bok. He had, according to the Dutch custom, two other names, but he had decided to leave those in the Netherlands. And the American public was, in later years, to omit for him the "William."

Edward's first six days in the United States were spent in New York, and then he was taken to Brooklyn, where he was destined to live for nearly twenty years.

Thanks to the linguistic sense inherent in the Dutch, and to an educational system that compels the study of languages, English was already familiar to the father and mother. But to the two sons, who had barely learned the beginnings of their native tongue, the English language was as a closed book. It seemed a cruel decision of the father to put his two boys into a public school in Brooklyn, but he argued that if they were to become Americans, the sooner they became part of the life of the country and learned its language for themselves, the better. And so, without the ability to make known the slightest want or to understand a single word, the morning after their removal to Brooklyn, the two boys were taken by their father to a public school.

The American public-school teacher was perhaps even less well equipped in those days than she is to-day to meet the needs of two Dutch boys who could not understand a word she said, and who could only wonder what it was all about. The brothers did not even have the comfort of each other's company, for, graded by age, they were placed in separate classes.

Nor was the American boy of 1870 a whit less cruel than is the American boy of 1920;

and he was none the less loath to show that cruelty. This trait was evident at the first recess of the first day at school. At the dismissal, the brothers naturally sought each other, only to find themselves surrounded by a group of tormentors who were delighted to have such promising objects for their fun. And of this opportunity they made the most. There was no form of petty cruelty boys' minds could devise that was not inflicted upon the two helpless strangers. Edward seemed to look particularly inviting, and nicknaming him "Dutchy" they devoted themselves at each noon recess and after school to inflicting their cruelties upon him.

Louis XIV may have been right when he said that "every new language requires a new soul," but Edward Bok knew that while spoken languages might differ, there is one language understood by boys the world over. And with this language Edward decided to do some experimenting. After a few days at school, he cast his eyes over the group of his tormenters, picked out one who seemed to him the ringleader, and before the boy was aware of what had happened, Edward Bok was in the full swing of his first real experiment with Americanization. Of course the American boy retaliated. But the boy from the Netherlands had not been born and brought up in the muscle-building air of the Dutch dikes for nothing, and after a few moments he found himself looking down on his tormentor and into the eyes of a crowd of very respectful boys and giggling girls who readily made a passageway for his brother and himself when they indicated a desire to leave the schoolyard and go home.

Edward now felt that his Americanization had begun; but, always believing that a thing begun must be carried to a finish, he took, or gave—it depends upon the point of view —two or three more lessons in this particular phase of Americanization before he convinced these American schoolboys that it might be best for them to call a halt upon further excursions in torment.

At the best, they were difficult days at school for a boy of six without the language.

But the national linguistic gift inherent in the Dutch race came to the boy's rescue, and as the roots of the Anglo-Saxon lie in the Frisian tongue, and thus in the language of his native country, Edward soon found that with a change of vowel here and there the English language was not so difficult of conquest. At all events, he set out to master it.

But his fatal gift of editing, although its possession was unknown to him, began to assert itself when, just as he seemed to be getting along fairly well, he balked at following the Spencerian style of writing in his copy-books. Instinctively he rebelled at the flourishes which embellished that form of handwriting. He seemed to divine somehow that such penmanship could not be useful or practicable for after life, and so, with that Dutch stolidity that, once fixed, knows no altering, he refused to copy his writing lessons. Of course trouble immediately ensued between Edward and his teacher. Finding herself against a literal blank wall—for Edward simply refused, but had not the gift of English with which to explain his refusal—the teacher decided to take the matter to the male principal of the school. She explained that she had kept Edward after school for as long as two hours to compel him to copy his Spencerian lesson, but that the boy simply sat quiet. He was perfectly well-behaved, she explained, but as to his lesson, he would attempt absolutely nothing.

It was the prevailing custom in the public schools of 1870 to punish boys by making them hold out the palms of their hands, upon which the principal would inflict blows with a rattan. The first time Edward was punished in this way, his hand became so swollen he wondered at a system of punishment which rendered him incapable of writing, particularly as the discerning principal had chosen the boy's right hand upon which to rain the blows. Edward was told to sit down at the principal's own desk and copy the lesson. He sat, but he did not write. He would not for one thing, and he could not if he would. After half an hour of purposeless

sitting, the principal ordered Edward again to stand up and hold out his hand; and once more the rattan fell in repeated blows. Of course it did no good, and as it was then five o'clock, and the principal had inflicted all the punishment that the law allowed, and as he probably wanted to go home as much as Edward did, he dismissed the sore-handed but more-than-ever-determined Dutch boy.

.   .   .   .   .

WHERE AMERICA FELL SHORT WITH ME

When I came to the United States as a lad of six, the most needful lesson for me, as a boy, was the necessity for thrift. I had been taught in my home across the sea that thrift was one of the fundamentals in a successful life. My family had come from a land (the Netherlands) noted for its thrift; but we had been in the United States only a few days before the realization came home strongly to my father and mother that they had brought their children to a land of waste.

Where the Dutchman saved, the American wasted. There was waste, and the most prodigal waste, on every hand. In every street-car and on every ferry-boat the floors and seats were littered with newspapers that had been read and thrown away or left behind. If I went to a grocery store to buy a peck of potatoes, and a potato rolled off the heaping measure, the groceryman, instead of picking it up, kicked it into the gutter for the wheels of his wagon to run over. The butcher's waste filled my mother's soul with dismay. If I bought a scuttle of coal at the corner grocery, the coal that missed the scuttle, instead of being shovelled up and put back into the bin, was swept into the street. My young eyes quickly saw this; in the evening I gathered up the coal thus swept away, and during the course of a week I collected a scuttleful. The first time my mother saw the garbage pail of a family almost as poor as our own, with the wife and husband constantly complaining that they could not get along, she could scarcely believe her eyes. A half pan of hominy of the preceding day's breakfast lay in the pail next to a third of a loaf of bread. In later years, when I saw, daily, a scow loaded with the garbage of Brooklyn householders being towed through New York harbor out to sea, it was an easy calculation that what was thrown away in a week's time from Brooklyn homes would feed the poor of the Netherlands.

At school, I quickly learned that to "save money" was to be "stingy"; as a young man, I soon found that the American disliked the word "economy," and on every hand as plenty grew spending grew. There was literally nothing in American life to teach me thrift or economy; everything to teach me to spend and to waste.

I saw men who had earned good salaries in their prime, reach the years of incapacity as dependents. I saw families on every hand either living quite up to their means or beyond them; rarely within them. The more a man earned, the more he—or his wife— spent. I saw fathers and mothers and their children dressed beyond their incomes. The proportion of families who ran into debt was far greater than those who saved. When a panic came, the families "pulled in"; when the panic was over, they "let out." But the end of one year found them precisely where they were at the close of the previous year, unless they were deeper in debt.

It was in this atmosphere of prodigal expenditure and culpable waste that I was to practise thrift: a fundamental in life! And it is into this atmosphere that the foreign-born comes now, with every inducement to spend and no encouragement to save. For as it was in the days of my boyhood, so it is to-day—only worse. One need only go over the experiences of the past two years, to compare the receipts of merchants who cater to the working-classes and the statements of savings-banks throughout the country, to read the story of how the foreign-born are learning the habit of criminal wastefulness as taught them by the American.

Is it any wonder, then, that in this, one of the essentials in life and in all success, America fell short with me, as it is continuing to fall short with every foreign-born who comes to its shores?

As a Dutch boy, one of the cardinal truths taught me was that whatever was worth doing was worth doing well: that next to honesty came thoroughness as a factor in success. It was not enough that anything should be done: it was not done at all if it was not done well. I came to America to be taught exactly the opposite. The two infernal Americanisms "That's good enough" and "That will do" were early taught me, together with the maxim of quantity rather than quality.

It was not the boy at school who could write the words in his copy-book best who received the praise of the teacher; it was the boy who could write the largest number of words in a given time. The acid test in arithmetic was not the mastery of the method, but the number of minutes required to work out an example. If a boy abbreviated the month January to "Jan." and the word Company to "Co." he received a hundred per cent mark, as did the boy who spelled out the words and who could not make the teacher see that "Co." did not spell "Company."

As I grew into young manhood, and went into business, I found on every hand that quantity counted for more than quality. The emphasis was almost always placed on how much work one could do in a day, rather than upon how well the work was done. Thoroughness was at a discount on every hand; production at a premium. It made no difference in what direction I went, the result was the same: the cry was always for quantity, quantity! And into this atmosphere of almost utter disregard for quality I brought my ideas of Dutch thoroughness and my conviction that doing well whatever I did was to count as a cardinal principle in life.

During my years of editorship, save in one or two conspicuous instances, I was never able to assign to an American writer, work which called for painstaking research. In every instance, the work came back to me either incorrect in statement, or otherwise obviously lacking in careful preparation.

One of the most successful departments I ever conducted in *The Ladies' Home Journal* called for infinite reading and patient digging, with the actual results sometimes almost negligible. I made a study of my associates by turning the department over to one after another, and always with the same result: absolute lack of a capacity for patient research. As one of my editors, typically American, said to me: "It isn't worth all the trouble that you put into it." Yet no single department ever repaid the searcher more for his pains. Save for assistance derived from a single person, I had to do the work myself for all the years that the department continued. It was apparently impossible for the American to work with sufficient patience and care to achieve a result.

We all have our pet notions as to the particular evil which is "the curse of America," but I always think that Theodore Roosevelt came closest to the real curse when he classed it as a lack of thoroughness.

Here again, in one of the most important matters in life, did America fall short with me; and, what is more important, she is falling short with every foreigner that comes to her shores.

In the matter of education, America fell far short in what should be the strongest of all her institutions: the public school. A more inadequate, incompetent method of teaching, as I look back over my seven years of attendance at three different public schools, it is difficult to conceive. If there is one thing that I, as a foreign-born child, should have been carefully taught, it is the English language. The individual effort to teach this, if effort there was, and I remember none, was negligible. It was left for my father to teach me, or for me to dig it out for myself. There was absolutely no indication on the part of teacher or principal of responsibility

for seeing that a foreign-born boy should acquire the English language correctly. I was taught as if I were American-born, and, of course, I was left dangling in the air, with no conception of what I was trying to do.

My father worked with me evening after evening; I plunged my young mind deep into the bewildering confusions of the language—and no one realizes the confusions of the English language as does the foreign-born—and got what I could through these joint efforts. But I gained nothing from the much-vaunted public-school system which the United States had borrowed from my own country, and then had rendered incompetent—either by a sheer disregard for the thoroughness that makes the Dutch public schools the admiration of the world, or by too close a regard for politics.

Thus, in her most important institution to the foreign-born, America fell short. And while I am ready to believe that the public school may have increased in efficiency since that day, it is, indeed, a question for the American to ponder, just how far the system is efficient for the education of the child who comes to its school without a knowledge of the first word in the English language. Without a detailed knowledge of the subject, I know enough of conditions in the average public school to-day to warrant at least the suspicion that Americans would not be particularly proud of the system, and of what it gives for which annually they pay millions of dollars in taxes.

I am aware in making this statement that I shall be met with convincing instances of intelligent effort being made with the foreign-born children in special classes. No one has a higher respect for those efforts than I have—few, other than educators, know of them better than I do, since I did not make my five-year study of the American public school system for naught. But I am not referring to the exceptional instance here and there. I merely ask of the American, interested as he is or should be in the Americanization of the strangers within his gates, how far the public school system, as a whole, urban and rural, adapts itself, with any true efficiency, to the foreign-born child. I venture to color his opinion in no wise; I simply ask that he will inquire and ascertain for himself, as he should do if he is interested in the future welfare of his country and his institutions; for what happens in America in the years to come depends, in large measure, on what is happening to-day in the public schools of this country.

As a Dutch boy I was taught a wholesome respect for law and for authority. The fact was impressed upon me that laws of themselves were futile unless the people for whom they were made respected them, and obeyed them in spirit more even than in the letter. I came to America to feel, on every hand, that exactly the opposite was true. Laws were passed, but were not enforced; the spirit to enforce them was lacking in the people. There was little respect for the law; there was scarcely any for those appointed to enforce it.

The nearest that a boy gets to the law is through the policeman. In the Netherlands a boy is taught that a policeman is for the protection of life and property; that he is the natural friend of every boy and man who behaves himself. The Dutch boy and the policeman are, naturally, friendly in their relations. I came to America to be told that a policeman is a boy's natural enemy; that he is eager to arrest him if he can find the slightest reason for doing so. A policeman, I was informed, was a being to hold in fear, not in respect. He was to be avoided, not to be made friends with. The result was that, as did all boys, I came to regard the policeman on our beat as a distinct enemy. His presence meant that we should "stiffen up"; his disappearance was the signal for us to "let loose."

So long as one was not caught, it did not matter. I heard mothers tell their little children that if they did not behave themselves, the policeman would put them into a bag and carry them off, or cut their ears off. Of course, the policeman became to them an object of terror; the law he represented, a cruel thing that stood for punishment. Not a note of respect did I ever hear for the law in my boyhood days. A law was something to be broken, to be evaded, to call down upon others as a source of punishment, but never to be regarded in the light of a safeguard.

And as I grew into manhood, the newspapers rang on every side with disrespect for those in authority. Under the special dispensation of the liberty of the press, which was construed into the license of the press, no man was too high to escape editorial vituperation if his politics did not happen to suit the management, or if his action ran counter to what the proprietors believed it should be. It was not criticism of his acts, it was personal attack upon the official; whether supervisor, mayor, governor, or president, it mattered not.

It is a very unfortunate impression that this American lack of respect for those in authority makes upon the foreign-born mind. It is difficult for the foreigner to square up the arrest and deportation of a man who, through an incendiary address, seeks to overthrow governmental authority, with the ignoring of an expression of exactly the same sentiments by the editor of his next morning's newspaper. In other words, the man who writes is immune, but the man who reads, imbibes, and translates the editor's words into action is immediately marked as a culprit, and America will not harbor him. But why harbor the original cause? Is the man who speaks with type less dangerous than he who speaks with his mouth or with a bomb?

At the most vital part of my life, when I was to become an American citizen and exercise the right of suffrage, America fell entirely short. It reached out not even the suggestion of a hand.

When the Presidential Conventions had been held in the year I reached my legal majority, and I knew I could vote, I endeavored to find out whether, being foreign-born, I was entitled to the suffrage. No one could tell me; and not until I had visited six different municipal departments, being referred from one to another, was it explained that, through my father's naturalization, I became, automatically, as his son, an American citizen. I decided to read up on the platforms of the Republican and Democratic parties, but I could not secure copies anywhere, although a week had passed since they had been adopted in convention.

I was told the newspapers had printed them. It occurred to me there must be many others besides myself who were anxious to secure the platforms of the two parties in some more convenient form. With the eye of necessity ever upon a chance to earn an honest penny, I went to a newspaper office, cut out from its files the two platforms, had them printed in a small pocket edition, sold one edition to the American News Company and another to the News Company controlling the Elevated Railroad bookstands in New York City, where they sold at ten cents each. So great was the demand which I had only partially guessed, that within three weeks I had sold such huge editions of the little books that I had cleared over a thousand dollars.

But it seemed to me strange that it should depend on a foreign-born American to supply an eager public with what should have been supplied through the agency of the political parties or through some educational source.

I now tried to find out what a vote actually meant. It must be recalled that I was only twenty-one years old, with scant education, and with no civic agency offering me the information I was seeking. I went to the headquarters of each of the political parties and put my query. I was regarded with puzzled looks.

"What does it mean to vote?" asked one chairman. "Why, on Election Day you go up to the ballot-box and put your ballot in, and that's all there is to it."

But I knew very well that that was not all there was to it, and was determined to find out the significance of the franchise. I met with dense ignorance on every hand.

I went to the Brooklyn Library, and was frankly told by the librarian that he did not know of a book that would tell me what I wanted to know. This was in 1884.

As the campaign increased in intensity, I found myself a desired person in the eyes of the local campaign managers, but not one of them could tell me the significance and meaning of the privilege I was for the first time to exercise.

Finally, I spent an evening with Seth Low, and, of course, got the desired information.

But fancy the quest I had been compelled to make to acquire the simple information that should have been placed in my hands or made readily accessible to me. And how many foreign-born would take equal pains to ascertain what I was determined to find out?

Surely America fell short here at the moment most sacred to me: that of my first vote!

Is it any easier to-day for the foreign citizen to acquire this information when he approaches his first vote? I wonder! Not that I do not believe there are agencies for this purpose. You know there are, and so do I. But how about the foreign-born? Does he know it? Is it not perhaps like the owner of the bulldog who assured the friend calling on him that it never attacked friends of the family? "Yes," said the friend, "that's all right. You know and I know that I am a friend of the family; but does the dog know?"

Is it to-day made known to the foreign-born, about to exercise his privilege of suffrage for the first time, where he can be told what that privilege means: is the means to know made readily accessible to him: is it, in fact, as it should be, brought to him?

It was not to me; is it to him?

One fundamental trouble with the present desire for Americanization is that the American is anxious to Americanize two classes —if he is a reformer, the foreign-born; if he is an employer, his employees. It never occurs to him that he himself may be in need of Americanization. He seems to take it for granted that because he is American-born, he is an American in spirit and has a right understanding of American ideals. But that, by no means, always follows. There are thousands of the American-born who need Americanization just as much as do the foreign-born. There are hundreds of American employers who know far less of American ideals than do some of their employees. In fact, there are those actually engaged to-day in the work of Americanization, men at the top of the movement, who sadly need a better conception of true Americanism.

An excellent illustration of this came to my knowledge when I attended a large Americanization Conference in Washington. One of the principal speakers was an educator of high standing and considerable influence in one of the most important sections of the United States. In a speech setting forth his ideas of Americanization, he dwelt with much emphasis and at considerable length upon instilling into the mind of the foreign-born the highest respect for American institutions.

After the Conference he asked me whether he could see me that afternoon at my hotel; he wanted to talk about contributing to the magazine. When he came, before approaching the object of his talk, he launched out on a tirade against the President of the United States; the weakness of the Cabinet, the inefficiency of the Congress, and the stupidity of the Senate. If words could have killed, there would have not remained a single living member of the Administration at Washington.

After fifteen minutes of this, I reminded him of his speech and the emphasis which he had placed upon the necessity of inculcating in the foreign-born respect for American institutions.

Yet this man was a power in his community, a strong influence upon others; he believed he could Americanize others, when he himself, according to his own statements, lacked the fundamental principle of Americanization. What is true of this man is, in lesser or greater degree, true of hundreds of others. Their Americanization consists of lip-service; the real spirit, the only factor which counts in the successful teaching of any doctrine, is absolutely missing. We certainly cannot teach anything approaching a true Americanism until we ourselves feel and believe and practise in our own lives what we are teaching to others. No law, no lip-service, no effort, however well-intentioned, will amount to anything worth while in inculcating the true American spirit in our foreign-born citizens until we are sure that the American spirit is understood by ourselves and is warp and woof of our own being.

To the American, part and parcel of his country, these particulars in which his country falls short with the foreign-born are, perhaps, not so evident; they may even seem not so very important. But to the foreign-born they seem distinct lacks; they loom large; they form serious handicaps which, in many cases, are never surmounted; they are a menace to that Americanization which is, to-day, more than ever our fondest dream, and which we now realize more keenly than before is our most vital need.

It is for this reason that I have put them down here as a concrete instance of where and how America fell short in my own Americanization, and, what is far more serious to me, where she is falling short in her Americanization of thousands of other foreign-born.

"Yet you succeeded," it will be argued.

That may be; but you, on the other hand, must admit that I did not succeed by reason of these shortcomings: it was in spite of them, by overcoming them—a result that all might not achieve.

WHAT I OWE TO AMERICA

Whatever shortcomings I may have found during my fifty-year period of Americanization; however America may have failed to help my transition from a foreigner into an American, I owe to her the most priceless gift that any nation can offer, and that is opportunity.

As the world stands to-day, no nation offers opportunity in the degree that America does to the foreign-born. Russia may, in the future, as I like to believe she will, prove a second United States of America in this respect. She has the same limitless area; her people the same potentialities. But, as things are to-day, the United States offers, as does no other nation, a limitless opportunity: here a man can go as far as his abilities will carry him. It may be that the foreign-born, as in my own case, must hold on to some of the ideals and ideas of the land of his birth; it may be that he must develop and mould his character by overcoming the habits resulting from national shortcomings. But into the best that the foreign-born can retain, America can graft such a wealth of inspiration, so high a national idealism, so great an opportunity for the highest endeavor, as to make him the fortunate man of the earth to-day.

He can go where he will: no traditions hamper him; no limitations are set except those within himself. The larger the area he chooses in which to work, the larger the vision he demonstrates, the more eager the people are to give support to his undertakings if they are convinced that he has their best welfare as his goal. There is no public confidence equal to that of the American public, once it is obtained. It is fickle, of course, as are all publics, but fickle only toward the man who cannot maintain an achieved success.

A man in America cannot complacently lean back upon victories won, as he can in the older European countries, and depend upon the glamour of the past to sustain him or the momentum of success to carry him. Probably the most alert public in the world, it requires of its leaders that they be alert. Its appetite for variety is insatiable, but its appreciation, when given, is full-handed and whole-hearted. The American public never holds back from the man to whom it gives; it never bestows in a niggardly way; it gives all or nothing.

What is not generally understood of the American people is their wonderful idealism. Nothing so completely surprises the foreign-born as the discovery of this trait in the American character. The impression is current in European countries—perhaps less generally since the war—that America is given over solely to a worship of the American dollar. While between nations as between individuals, comparisons are valueless, it may not be amiss to say, from personal knowledge, that the Dutch worship the gulden infinitely more than do the Americans the dollar.

I do not claim that the American is always conscious of this idealism; often he is not. But let a great convulsion touching moral questions occur, and the result always shows how close to the surface is his idealism. And the fact that so frequently he puts over it a thick veneer of materialism does not affect its quality. The truest approach, the only approach in fact, to the American character is, as Viscount Bryce has so well said, through its idealism.

It is this quality which gives the truest inspiration to the foreign-born in his endeavor to serve the people of his adopted country. He is mentally sluggish, indeed, who does not discover that America will make good with him if he makes good with her.

But he must play fair. It is essentially the straight game that the true American plays, and he insists that you shall play it too. Evidence there is, of course, to the contrary in American life, experiences that seem to give ground for the belief that the man succeeds who is not scrupulous in playing his cards. But never is this true in the long run. Sooner or later—sometimes, unfortunately, later than sooner—the public discovers the trickery. In no other country in the world is the moral conception so clear and true as in America, and no people will give a larger and more permanent reward to the man whose effort for that public has its roots in honor and truth.

"The sky is the limit" to the foreign-born who comes to America endowed with honest endeavor, ceaseless industry, and the ability to carry through. In any honest endeavor, the way is wide open to the will to succeed. Every path beckons, every vista invites, every talent is called forth, and every efficient effort finds its due reward. In no land is the way so clear and so free.

How good an American has the process of Americanization made me? That I cannot say. Who *can* say that of himself? But when I look around me at the American-born I have come to know as my close friends, I wonder whether, after all, the foreign-born does not make in some sense a better American—whether he is not able to get a truer perspective; whether his is not the deeper desire to see America greater; whether he is not less content to let its faulty institutions be as they are; whether in seeing faults more clearly he does not make a more decided effort to have America reach those ideals or those fundamentals of his own land which he feels are in his nature, and the best of which he is anxious to graft into the character of his adopted land?

It is naturally with a feeling of deep satisfaction that I remember two Presidents of the United States considered me a sufficiently typical American to wish to send me to my native land as the accredited minister of my adopted country. And yet when I analyze the reasons for my choice in both these instances, I derive a deeper satisfaction from the fact that my strong desire to work in America for America led me to ask to be permitted to remain here.

It is this strong impulse that my Americanization has made the driving power of my life. And I ask no greater privilege than to be allowed to live to see my potential America become actual: the America that I like to think of as the America of Abraham Lincoln and of Theodore Roosevelt—not faultless, but less faulty. It is a part in trying to shape that America, and an opportunity to work in that America when it comes, that I ask in return for what I owe to her. A greater privilege no man could have.

CHAPTER SEVEN

Toward a New Synthesis of Educational Theory

THE INFLUX OF EDUCATIONAL IDEAS FROM ABROAD

JOHANN FRIEDRICH HERBART
The Science of Education (1806) *

GENERAL PRINCIPLES OF THE SCIENCE OF EDUCATION PSYCHOLOGICALLY DEDUCED FROM ITS AIM.

The aim of all those who educate and demand education is determined by the range of thought they bring to the subject.

The majority of those who teach have entirely neglected in the first instance to construct for themselves their own range of thought in view of this work; it opens out gradually as the work progresses, and is formed partly by their own characteristics, partly by the individuality and environment of the pupil. If the teachers possess originality, they will utilize all that comes to hand to provide stimulus and occupation for the objects of their care; if they have foresight, they exclude all which may be harmful to health, disposition, or manners. Thus a boy grows to manhood, who is tested in everything that is not dangerous, practised in the consideration and treatment of the common things of daily life, and with all the sensibilities which the narrow circle wherein

* Johann Friedrich Herbart, *The Science of Education: Its General Principles Deduced from Its Aim* (Boston: Heath, 1895; translated from the German by Henry M. and Emmie Felkin; first published in 1806), pp. 78, 81–83, 111–112.

he lives can arouse in him. If he has really grown up thus, he may be congratulated on the result. But educators complain unceasingly of the harmful influence of surrounding circumstances—of servants, relatives, playmates, the natural instincts and the university. And it is no wonder, when the mental diet is determined more by chance than by human skill, that a robust health, which can bid defiance to unfavourable influences, cannot always flourish on fare that is often so meagre. . . .

Let us all consider the proposition—each but experiences, what he attempts. A non-[a]genarian village schoolmaster has the experience of his ninety years' routine course; he has the consciousness of his long toils, but has he also the criticism of his work and his methods? Much that is new has prospered with our modern educators; they have found their reward in the gratitude of men, and they can inwardly rejoice over it. But whether they can determine from *their* experience all that can be attained by means of education, and all that can be done with children, is a question.

It is much to be desired that those who wish to base education on experience *alone,* would for once attentively consider other experimental sciences; that they would condescend to inquire, in the case of physics or chemistry, how much is really involved in the demonstration of one single proposition in the sphere of empiricism, with all the exactness that empiricism admits of. They would then *experience,* that nothing is learned from *one* experience, and just as little from scattered observations; but that one must repeat the experiment twenty times with twenty variations before a result is obtained, which even then opposing theories can explain each in its own way. They would experience then, that no one has a right to speak of experience until the experiment is completed, until, above all things, the *residuum* has been accurately weighed and tested. In the case of educational experiments, this residuum is represented by the faults of the pupil when he has attained to manhood. Thus the time required for one such experiment is at least half a human life. When then does any one become an experienced teacher? And of how many experiences, with how many variations is the experience of each to consist? How infinitely greater than this is the experience of the empirical doctor, and for how many centuries have the experiences of great men been recorded for him! Nevertheless the science of medicine is so weak, that it is just a swampy ground on which new sophistries so rankly grow.

Is this to be the fate of education also? Is it to become the shuttlecock of factions, which, themselves a sport of the time, have long ago carried everything of importance with them, and only left the apparently lowly realm of childhood untouched. It has already come to pass, that nothing is more natural to the younger and more philosophical teachers, who now see that thinking ought not to be divorced from education, than to test the perfect adaptability or pliancy of what is truly a very versatile wisdom in educating, in order to form, to synthetically improve, and mystically teach upon *a priori* principles, those intrusted to their care—and when patience fails, to reject them as incapable of preparation for initiation. The rejected ones will pass no longer with the same fresh natures into other, and what other hands?

It would be better if the science of educa-

tion remained as true as possible to its intrinsic conceptions, and cultivated more an independent mode of thought, by which it would become the centre of a sphere of exploration, and be no longer exposed to the danger of government by a stranger as a remote tributary province. Only when each science seeks to teach in its own way, and also with the same force as its neighbours, can a beneficial intercourse take place between them. Surely philosophy must rejoice when other sciences approach her thoughtfully, and at any rate the philosophic public of the day, though not philosophy itself, sadly needs the chance of more numerous, more varied points of view, from which it can survey all sides.

I have required science and mental force from the teacher. To others, science may be a pair of spectacles, to me it is an eye, and the best of eyes too, which human beings possess for the contemplation of their environment. It is true, that the teachings of all the sciences are not free from error, but this is the very reason why they disagree one with another; the error betrays itself, or at least one learns to be careful about doubtful points. On the other hand, he who considers himself clever without scientific knowledge, fosters errors in his opinions, as great and even greater, without the consciousness, or perhaps even the possibility of consciousness of them, for his points of contact with the world are blunted. The errors of science are originally the errors of men, but only of the best minds.

The first, though by no means the complete science of the educator, would be a psychology in which the total possibilities of human activity were sketched out *a priori.* I think I recognise the difficulty as well as the possibility of such a science. Long will it be before we have it, longer still before we can expect it from teachers. Never, however, can it be a substitute for observation of the pupil; the individual can only be discovered, not deduced. The construction of the pupil on *a priori* principles is therefore a misleading expression in itself, and is also at present an empty idea which the science of education cannot handle for a long time.

. . . . .

I look at life, and find very many upon whom morality is a stunted growth, very few with whom it is the principle of life itself. Most men possess a character independent of goodness, and a plan of life formed only according to their own inclination; they do the good when convenient, and gladly avoid the evil, when the better leads to the same goal. Moral principles are wearisome to them, because for them nothing follows from those principles, except now and again a limitation of their course of thought—indeed everything adverse to this limitation is welcome to them. The young poacher has their sympathy, if he sins with some boldness, and they pardon at the bottom of their heart everything which is neither ridiculous nor malicious. If it be the object of moral education to lead the pupil into the ranks of these, we have an easy task; we need only take care that he grows up, without being teased or insulted, in the consciousness of his power, and receives certain principles of honour, which are easily impressed, because they treat of honour not as a wearisome acquisition, but as a possession which nature makes a present of, and which must be protected and put in force on certain occasions according to conventional forms. But who will warrant us that the future man will not himself search out the good, to make it the object of his willing, the aim of his life, the standard of his self-criticism? Who will protect us against the severe judgment which will then overtake us? How will it be, if he calls us to account, because we presumed to anticipate the chance, which yet, perhaps, might have brought about better opportunities of genuine elevation of spirit, and would certainly not have caused the delusion that education for him is already a thing accomplished. There are instances of the kind; and it is never safe to set up as business manager for another if we have no mind to do the

work well. No one at any rate would like to lie under so severe a condemnation from a man of strict moral sense, as he would who has arrogated to himself an influence over any one which might have made him worse.

Therefore that the ideas of the right and good in all their clearness and purity may become the essential objects of the will, that the innermost intrinsic contents of the character—the very heart of the personality —shall determine itself according to these ideas, putting back all arbitrary impulses— this and nothing less is the aim of moral culture.

FRIEDRICH FROEBEL
The Education of Man (1826)*

GROUNDWORK OF THE WHOLE.

§ 1. In all things there lives and reigns an eternal law. To him whose mind, through disposition and faith, is filled, penetrated, and quickened with the necessity that this can not possibly be otherwise, as well as to him whose clear, calm mental vision beholds the inner in the outer and through the outer, and sees the outer proceeding with logical necessity from the essence of the inner, this law has been and is enounced with equal clearness and distinctness in nature (the external), in the spirit (the internal), and in life which unites the two. This all-controlling law is necessarily based on an all-pervading, energetic, living, self-conscious, and hence eternal Unity. This fact, as well as the Unity itself, is again vividly recognized, either through faith or through insight, with equal clearness and comprehensiveness; therefore, a quietly observant human mind, a thoughtful, clear human intellect, has never failed, and will never fail, to recognize this Unity.

This Unity is God. All things have come from the Divine Unity, from God, and have

* Friedrich Froebel, The Education of Man (New York: Appleton, 1887; translated from the German and annotated by W. N. Hailman; first published in 1826), pp. 1–5, 8–9, 21, 27– 30, 36, 54–56, 89, 94–96, 98–101, 113–119.

their origin in the Divine Unity, in God alone. God is the sole source of all things. In all things there lives and reigns the Divine Unity, God. All things live and have their being in and through the Divine Unity, in and through God. All things are only through the divine effluence that lives in them. The divine effluence that lives in each thing is the essence of each thing.

§ 2. It is the destiny and life-work of all things to unfold their essence, hence their divine being, and, therefore, the Divine Unity itself—to reveal God in their external and transient being. It is the special destiny and life-work of man, as an intelligent and rational being, to become fully, vividly, and clearly conscious of his essence, of the divine effluence in him, and, therefore, of God; to become fully, vividly, and clearly conscious of his destiny and life-work; and to accomplish this, to render it (his essence) active, to reveal it in his own life with self-determination and freedom.

Education consists in leading man, as a thinking, intelligent being, growing into self-consciousness, to a pure and unsullied, conscious and free representation of the inner law of Divine Unity, and in teaching him ways and means thereto.[1]

[1] In his educational work this principle of life-unity was ever uppermost in Froebel's mind. The full, clear, consistent translation of this principle into life, and into the work of education, constitutes the chief characteristic, as well as the chief merit, of his work. Viewed in its light, education becomes a process of unification; therefore, Froebel frequently called his educational method "developing, or human culture for all-sided unification of life." In his letter to the Duke of Meiningen he characterizes his tendency in these words: "I would educate human beings who with their feet stand rooted in God's earth, in nature, whose heads reach even into heaven and there behold truth, in whose hearts are united both earth and heaven, the varied life of earth and nature, and the glory and peace of heaven, God's earth and God's heaven." Still later he said, in the same vein: "There is no other power but that of the idea; the identity of the cosmic laws with the

§ 3. The knowledge of that eternal law, the insight into its origin, into its essence, into the totality, the connection, and intensity of its effects, the knowledge of life in its totality, constitute *science, the science of life;* and, referred by the self-conscious, thinking, intelligent being to representation and practice through and in himself, this becomes *science of education.*

The system of directions, derived from the knowledge and study of that law, to guide thinking, intelligent beings in the apprehension of their life-work and in the accomplishment of their destiny, is *the theory of education.*

laws of our mind must be recognized, all things must be seen as the embodiments of *one* idea." With reference to the individual human being, this *unification of life* means to Froebel harmony in feeling, thinking, willing, and doing; with reference to humanity, it means subordination of self to the common welfare and to the progressive development of mankind; with reference to nature, it means a thoughtful subordination to her laws of development; with reference to God, it means perfect faith as Froebel finds it realized in Christianity.

It may not be amiss to point out at the very start the essential agreement between Froebel and Herbert Spencer in this fundamental principle of unification. Of course, it will be necessary in this comparison to keep in mind that Froebel applies the principle to education in its practical bearings as an interpretation of thought in life, whereas Spencer applies it to philosophy, as the interpretation of life in thought. To Spencer "knowledge of the lowest kind is *ununified* knowledge; science is *partially-unified* knowledge; philosophy is *completely-unified* knowledge." In the concluding paragraphs of "First Principles" he sets forth the "power of which no limit in time or space can be conceived" as the "inexpugnable consciousness in which religion and philosophy are at one with common sense," and as "likewise that on which all exact science is based." He designates "unification" as the "characteristic of developing thought," just as Froebel finds in it the characteristic of developing life; and Spencer's faith in the "eventual arrival at unity" in thought is as firm as Froebel's faith in the eventual arrival at unity in life.—*Translator.*

The self-active application of this knowledge in the direct development and cultivation of rational beings toward the attainment of their destiny, is *the practice of education.*

The object of education is the realization of a faithful, pure, inviolate, and hence holy life.

Knowledge and application, consciousness and realization in life, united in the service of a faithful, pure, holy life, constitute the *wisdom of life,* pure wisdom.

§ 4. *To be wise is the highest aim of man,* is the most exalted achievement of human self-determination.

To educate one's self and others, with consciousness, freedom, and self-determination, is a twofold achievement of wisdom: it *began* with the first appearance of man upon the earth; it *was manifest* with the first appearance of full self-consciousness in man; it *begins now* to proclaim itself as a necessary, universal requirement of humanity, and to be heard and heeded as such. With this achievement man enters upon the path which alone leads to life; which surely tends to the fulfillment of the inner, and thereby also to the fulfillment of the outer, requirement of humanity; which, through a faithful, pure, holy life, attains beatitude.

§ 5. By education, then, the divine essence of man should be unfolded, brought out, lifted into consciousness, and man himself raised into free, conscious obedience to the divine principle that lives in him, and to a free representation of this principle in his life.

Education, in instruction, should lead man to see and know the divine, spiritual, and eternal principle which animates surrounding nature, constitutes the essence of nature, and is permanently manifested in nature; and, in living reciprocity and united with training, it should express and demonstrate the fact that the same law rules both (the divine principle and nature), as it does nature and man.

Education as a whole, by means of instruction and training, should bring to man's consciousness, and render efficient in his life, the fact that man and nature proceed from God and are conditioned by him—that both have their being in God.

Education should lead and guide man to clearness concerning himself and in himself, to peace with nature, and to unity with God; hence, it should lift him to a knowledge of himself and of mankind, to a knowledge of God and of nature, and to the pure and holy life to which such knowledge leads.

. . . . .

§ 8. We grant space and time to young plants and animals because we know that, in accordance with the laws that live in them, they will develop properly and grow well; young animals and plants are given rest, and arbitrary interference with their growth is avoided, because it is known that the opposite practice would disturb their pure unfolding and sound development; but the young human being is looked upon as a piece of wax, a lump of clay, which man can mold into what he pleases. O man, who roamest through garden and field, through meadow and grove, why dost thou close thy mind to the silent teaching of nature? Behold even the weed, which, grown up amid hindrances and constraint, scarcely yields an indication of inner law; behold it in nature, in field or garden, and see how perfectly it conforms to law—what a pure inner life it shows, harmonious in all parts and features: a beautiful sun, a radiant star, it has burst from the earth! Thus, O parents, could your children, on whom you force in tender years forms and aims against their nature, and who, therefore, walk with you in morbid and unnatural deformity—thus could your children, too, unfold in beauty and develop in all-sided harmony!

. . . . .

§ 19. Therefore the child should, from the very time of his birth, be viewed in accordance with his nature, treated correctly, and given the free, all-sided use of his powers. By no means should the use of certain powers and members be enhanced at the expense of others, and these hindered in their development; the child should neither be partly chained, fettered, nor swathed; nor, later on, spoiled by too much assistance. The child should learn early how to find in himself the center and fulcrum of all his powers and members, to seek his support in this, and, resting therein, to move freely and be active, to grasp and hold with his own hands, to stand and walk on his own feet, to find and observe with his own eyes, to use his members symmetrically and equally. At an early period the child should learn, apply, and practice the most difficult of all arts— to hold fast the center and fulcrum of his life in spite of all digressions, disturbances, and hindrances.

. . . . .

§ 22. Not only in regard to the cultivation of the divine and religious elements in man, but in his entire cultivation, it is highly important that his development should proceed continuously from *one* point, and that this *continuous* progress be seen and ever guarded. Sharp limits and definite subdivisions within the continuous series of the years of development, withdrawing from attention the permanent continuity, the living connection, the inner living essence, are therefore highly pernicious, and even destructive in their influence. Thus, it is highly pernicious to consider the stages of human development—infant, child, boy or girl, youth or maiden, man or woman, old man or matron—as really distinct, and not, as life shows them, as continuous in themselves, in unbroken transitions; highly pernicious to consider the child or boy as something wholly different from the youth or man, and as something so distinct that the common foundation (*human being*) is seen but vaguely in the idea and word, and scarcely at all considered in life and for life. And yet this is the actual condition of affairs; for, if we consider common speech and life *as it actually is,* how wholly distinct do the child and the boy appear! Especially do the later

stages speak of the earlier ones as something quite foreign, wholly different from them; the boy has ceased to see in himself the child, and fails to see in the child the boy; the youth no longer sees in himself the boy and the child, nor does he see in these the youth—with affected superiority he scorns them; and, most pernicious of all, the adult man no longer finds in himself the infant, the child, the boy, the youth, the earlier stages of development, nor in these the coming adult man, but speaks of the child, the boy, and the youth as of wholly different beings, with wholly different natures and tendencies.

These definite subdivisions and sharp limitations have their origin in the want of early and continuously growing attention to the development and self-observation of his own life. It is possible only to indicate, but not to point out in their full extent, the unspeakable mischief, disturbance, and hindrance in the development and advancement of the human race, arising from these subdivisions and limitations. Suffice it to say that only rare inner force can break through the limits set up around the human being by those who influence him. Even this can be accomplished only by a violent effort that threatens to destroy, or, at least, to check and disturb, other phases of development. Therefore, there is throughout life somewhat of violence in the actions of a man who has done this at any stage of his development.

How different could this be in every respect, if parents were to view and treat the child with reference to all stages of development and age, without breaks and omissions; if, particularly, they were to consider the fact that the vigorous and complete development and cultivation of each successive stage depends on the vigorous, complete, and characteristic development of each and all preceding stages of life! Parents are especially prone to overlook and disregard this. When the human being has reached the age of boyhood, they look upon him as a boy; when he has reached the age of youth or manhood, they take him to be a youth or a man. Yet the boy has not become a boy, nor has the youth become a youth, by reaching a certain age, but only by having lived through childhood, and, further on, through boyhood, true to the requirements of his mind, his feelings, and his body; similarly, adult man has not become an adult man by reaching a certain age, but only by faithfully satisfying the requirements of his childhood, boyhood, and youth. Parents and fathers, in other respects quite sensible and efficient, expect not only that the child should begin to show himself a boy or a youth, but, more particularly, that the boy, at least, should show himself a man, that in all his conduct he should be a man, thus jumping the stages of boyhood and youth. To see and respect *in* the child and boy the germ and promise of the coming youth and man is very different from considering and treating him as if he were already a man; very different from asking the child or boy to show himself a youth or man; to feel, to think, and to conduct himself as a youth or a man. Parents who ask this overlook and forget that they themselves became mature and efficient only in so far as they lived through the various stages in natural succession and in certain relationships which they would have their child to forego.

This disregard of the value of earlier, and particularly of the earliest, stages of development with reference to later ones, prepares for the future teacher and educator of the boy difficulties which it will be scarcely possible to overcome. In the first place, the boy so conditioned has also a notion that it is possible for him to do wholly without the instruction and training of the preceding stage of development; in the second place, he is much injured and weakened by having placed before himself, at an early period, an extraneous aim for imitation and exertion, such as preparation for a certain calling or sphere of activity. *The child, the boy, man, indeed, should know no other endeavor but to be at every stage of development wholly what this stage calls for.* Then

will each successive stage spring like a new shoot from a healthy bud; and, at each successive stage, he will with the same endeavor again accomplish the requirements of this stage: for only the adequate development of man at each preceding stage can effect and bring about adequate development at each succeeding later stage.

.   .   .   .   .

§ 23. Thus is seen in the child man as a whole; thus the unity of humanity and of man appears in childhood; thus the whole future activity of man has its germs in the child. And it can not be otherwise. If we would develop man and in him humanity as a whole, we must view him even in the child as a unit and in all his earthly relations. Now, since unity in the finite manifestations implies diversity, and since all all-sidedness in the finite manifestations implies a succession in time, the world and life are unfolded for the child and in the child in diversity and succession. Similarly, powers and tendencies, the activities of the senses and limbs, should be developed in the order in which they appear in the child.

.   .   .   .   .

§ 30. *Play.—Play* is the highest phase of child-development—of human development at this period; for *it is self-active representation of the inner—representation of the inner from inner necessity and impulse.*

Play is the purest, most spiritual activity of man at this stage, and, at the same time, typical of human life as a whole—of the inner hidden natural life in man and all things. It gives, therefore, joy, freedom, contentment, inner and outer rest, peace with the world. It holds the sources of all that is good. A child that plays thoroughly, with self-active determination, perseveringly until physical fatigue forbids, will surely be a thorough, determined man, capable of self-sacrifice for the promotion of the welfare of himself and others. Is not the most beautiful expression of child-life at this time a playing child?—a child wholly absorbed in his play? —a child that has fallen asleep while so absorbed?

As already indicated, play at this time is not trivial, it is highly serious and of deep significance. Cultivate and foster it, O mother; protect and guard it, O father! To the calm, keen vision of one who truly knows human nature, the spontaneous play of the child discloses the future inner life of the man.

The plays of childhood are the germinal leaves of all later life; for the whole man is developed and shown in these, in his tenderest dispositions, in his innermost tendencies. The whole later life of man, even to the moment when he shall leave it again, has its source in the period of childhood—be this later life pure or impure, gentle or violent, quiet or impulsive, industrious or indolent, rich or poor in deeds, passed in dull stupor or in keen creativeness, in stupid wonder or intelligent insight, producing or destroying, the bringer of harmony or discord, of war or peace. His future relations to father and mother, to the members of the family, to society and mankind, to nature and God— in accordance with the natural and individual disposition and tendencies of the child —depend chiefly upon his mode of life at this period; for the child's life in and with himself, his family, nature, and God, is as yet a unit. Thus, at this age, the child can scarcely tell which is to him dearer—the flowers, or his joy about them, or the joy he gives to the mother when he brings or shows them to her, or the vague presentiment of the dear Giver of them.

Who can analyze these joys in which this period is so rich?

If the child is injured at this period, if the germinal leaves of the future tree of his life are marred at this time, he will only with the greatest difficulty and the utmost effort grow into strong manhood; he will only with the greatest difficulty escape in his further development the stunting effects of the injury or the onesidedness it entails.

. . . . .

§ 42. Let us learn from our children, let us give heed to the gentle admonitions of their life, to the silent demands of their minds.

Let us live with our children: then will the life of our children bring us peace and joy, then shall we begin to grow wise, to be wise.

. . . . .

THE BOYHOOD OF MAN.

§ 45. As the preceding period of human development, the *period of childhood,* was predominantly that of *life* for the sake merely of living, for making the internal external, so the *period of boyhood* is predominantly the period for *learning,* for making the external internal.

On the part of parents and educators the period of infancy demanded chiefly *fostering care.* During the succeeding period of childhood, which looks upon man predominantly as a unit, and would lead him to unity, *training* prevails. The period of boyhood leads man chiefly to the consideration of particular relationships and individual things, in order to enable him later on to discover their inner unity. The inner tendencies and relationships of individual things and conditions are sought and established.

Now, the consideration and treatment of individual and particular things, as such, and in their inner bearings and relationships, constitute the essential character and work of instruction; therefore, *boyhood is the period in which instruction predominates.*

This instruction is conducted not so much in accordance with the nature of man as in accordance with the fixed, definite, clear *laws* that lie in the nature of things, and more particularly the laws to which man and things are equally subject. It is conducted not so much in the method in which the universal, eternal law finds peculiar expression in man as rather in the method in which this law finds peculiar expression in each external thing, or simultaneous expression in both man and thing. It is conducted, then, in accordance with fixed and definite conditions lying *outside* the human being; and this implies knowledge, insight, a conscious and comprehensive survey of the field.

Such a process constitutes the *school* in the widest sense of the word. The school, then, leads man to a knowledge of external things, and of their nature in accordance with the particular and general laws that lie in them; by the presentation of the external, the individual, the particular, it leads man to a knowledge of the internal, of unity, of the universal. Therefore, on entering the period of boyhood, man becomes at the same time a *school-boy*. With this period school begins for him, be it in the home or out of it, and taught by the father, the members of the family, or a teacher. School, then, means here by no means the school-room, nor school-keeping, but *the conscious communication of knowledge, for a definite purpose and in definite inner connection.*

§ 46. On the other hand, as it has appeared and continues to appear in every aspect, the development and cultivation of man, for the attainment of his destiny and fulfillment of his mission, constitute an unbroken whole, steadily and continuously progressing, gradually ascending. The feeling of community, awakened in the infant, becomes in the child impulse, inclination; these lead to the formation of the disposition and of the heart, and arouse in the boy his intellect and will.

To give firmness to the will, to quicken it, and to make it pure, strong, and enduring, in a life of pure humanity, is the chief concern, the main object in the guidance of the boy, in instruction and the school.

.   .   .   .   .

§ 49. Now, in the family, the child sees the parents and other members of the family at work, producing, doing something; the same he notices with adults generally in life and in those active interests with which his family is concerned. Consequently the child, at this stage, would like himself to represent what he sees. He would like to represent—

and tries to do so—all he sees his parents and other adults do and represent in work, all which he thus sees represented by human power and human skill.

What formerly the child did only *for the sake of the activity,* the boy now does *for the sake of the result* or product of his activity; the child's instinct of activity has in the boy become a *formative instinct,* and this occupies the whole outward life, the outward manifestation of boy-life at this period.

How cheerfully and eagerly the boy and the girl at this age begin to share the work of father and mother—not the easy work, indeed, but the difficult work, calling for strength and labor!

Be cautious, be careful and thoughtful, at this point, O parents! You can here at one blow destroy, at least for a long time, the instinct of formative activity in your children, if you repel their help as childish, useless, of little avail, or even as a hindrance.

Do not let the urgency of your business tempt you to say, "Go away, you only hinder me," or, "I am in a hurry, leave me alone."

Boys and girls are thus disturbed in their inner activity; they see themselves shut out from the whole with which they felt themselves so intimately united; their inner power is aroused, but they see themselves alone, and do not know what to do with the aroused power; nay, it becomes a burden to them, and they become fretful and indolent.

After a third rebuff of this character, scarcely any child will again propose to help and share the work. He becomes fretful and dull, even when he sees his parents engaged in work which he might share. Who has not later on heard the parents of such children complain: "When this boy (or girl) was small and could not help, he busied himself about everything; now that he knows something and is strong enough, he does not want to do anything"?

Just so! In accordance with the nature of the spiritual principle working in man, as yet unconsciously and unrecognized, the first utterances of the instinct of activity, of the formative instinct, come without any effort on his part, and even against his will, as indeed happens to him even in later life. Now, if this inner impulse to formative activity in man, particularly in early youth, is met by an external obstacle, especially by one like the will of parents, which can not be set aside, the inner power itself is weakened, and a frequent repetition of this forces it back into complete inactivity.

When the child has been thus disturbed, he does not consider why his help was permissible at one time and not at another time; he chooses that which is more agreeable to his physical nature. He abstains from the activity the more readily and willingly, because the will of his parents seems to make it his duty to do so.

The child becomes indolent—i. e., spirit and life cease to animate his physical being; the latter becomes a mere body to him, which now he must carry as a burden; whereas, formerly, the sense of power led him to feel his body, not as such, but as the mighty source of the power that filled him.

Therefore, O parents, if you wish your children eventually to help you, foster in them at an early period the instinct of activity, and especially the formative instinct of boyhood, even though it should involve some effort, some sacrifice on your part. It will repay a hundred-fold, as does good wheat planted in good soil. . . .

How the serene, happy boy of this age rejoices in song! He feels, as it were, a new, true life in song. It is the sense of growing power that in his wanderings from the valley to the hill, and from hill to hill, pours forth the joyous song from his throat.

The intense desire to understand himself holds the boy; therefore he seeks the clear, pure, living water in lake or brook. In his play he ever returns to this, because in it he sees himself, the image of his soul, and because in and through it he hopes to get a knowledge of his spiritual nature.

What the water in brook and lake, what the pure air and wide expanse on the mountain-top are to the boy's soul, that, too, play

is to him—a mirror of the life-struggles that await him; therefore, in order to gain strength for these, boys and youth seek obstacles, difficulties, and strife in their play.

The desire to gain a knowledge of the past and of nature attracts the boy again and again to flowers and to old walls and ruined vaults. The desire to express what fills his innermost heart and mind urges him to sing. Thus it is certain that very many of the external phenomena, very many things in the boy's conduct and actions, have an inner, spiritual significance; that they indicate his inner, spiritual life and tendency, and are, therefore, symbolic.

How salutary would it be for parents and child, for their present and future, if parents believed in this symbolism of childhood and boyhood, if they heeded the child's life in reference to this! It would unite parents and children by a new living tie; it would establish a new living connection between their present and their future life.

§ 50. Such is pure boy-life at this period. From this description of inner and outer pure boy-life and child-life, which fortunately for man we still meet occasionally— where natural views of education prevail in actual life possibly in greater beauty, richness, and intensity than has been represented —from this description let us cast a glance upon boy-life and child-life as we generally meet it more or less pronounced in actual life. Let us look particularly upon the life of the child and boy in his filial, brotherly, domestic relations, in his activity and work as a pupil and companion. We shall be compelled to confess frankly that many things are very different: that we meet stubbornness, obstinacy, supineness, mental and physical indolence, sensuality, vanity and self-conceit, dogmatism and despotism, an unbrotherly and unfilial spirit, emptiness and superficiality, aversion to work and even to play, disobedience and ungodliness, etc.

When we look for the sources of these and many other undeniable shortcomings in the life of children and boys, we are confronted ultimately by a double reason: in the first place, the complete neglect of the development of certain sides of full human life; secondly, the early faulty tendency—the early faulty and unnatural steps of development and distortion of the originally good human powers and tendencies by arbitrary and willful interference with the original orderly and logical course of human development.

HERBERT SPENCER
Education: Intellectual, Moral and Physical (1860) *

WHAT KNOWLEDGE IS OF MOST WORTH?

How to live?—that is the essential question for us. Not how to live in the mere material sense only, but in the widest sense. The general problem which comprehends every special problem is—the right ruling of conduct in all directions under all circumstances. In what way to treat the body; in what way to treat the mind; in what way to manage our affairs; in what way to bring up a family; in what way to behave as a citizen; in what way to utilize all those sources of happiness which nature supplies —how to use all our faculties to the greatest advantage of ourselves and others—how to live completely? And this being the great thing needful for us to learn, is, by consequence, the great thing which education has to teach. To prepare us for complete living is the function which education has to discharge; and the only rational mode of judging of any educational course is, to judge in what degree it discharges such function.

This test, never used in its entirety, but rarely even partially used, and used then in a vague, half conscious way, has to be applied consciously, methodically, and

* Herbert Spencer, *Education: Intellectual, Moral and Physical* (New York: Appleton, 1860), Chapter I, "What Knowledge Is of Most Worth?" pp. 30–33, 35–95; Chapter II, "Intellectual Education," pp. 124–126; Chapter III, "Moral Education," pp. 166–168; and Chapter IV, "Physical Education," pp. 276–277, 281–282.

throughout all cases. It behoves us to set before ourselves, and ever to keep clearly in view, complete living as the end to be achieved; so that in bringing up our children we may choose subjects and methods of instruction, with deliberate reference to this end. Not only ought we to cease from the mere unthinking adoption of the current fashion in education, which has no better warrant than any other fashion; but we must also rise above that rude, empirical style of judging displayed by those more intelligent people who do bestow some care in overseeing the cultivation of their children's minds. It must not suffice simply to *think* that such or such information will be useful in after life, or that this kind of knowledge is of more practical value than that; but we must seek out some process of estimating their respective values, so that as far as possible we may positively *know* which are most deserving of attention.

Doubtless the task is difficult—perhaps never to be more than approximately achieved. But, considering the vastness of the interests at stake, its difficulty is no reason for pusillanimously passing it by; but rather for devoting every energy to its mastery. And if we only proceed systematically, we may very soon get at results of no small moment.

Our first step must obviously be to classify, in the order of their importance, the leading kinds of activity which constitute human life. They may be naturally arranged into:—1. Those activities which directly minister to self-preservation; 2. Those activities which, by securing the necessaries of life, indirectly minister to self-preservation; 3. Those activities which have for their end the rearing and discipline of offspring; 4. Those activities which are involved in the maintenance of proper social and political relations; 5. Those miscellaneous activities which make up the leisure part of life, devoted to the gratification of the tastes and feelings.

That these stand in something like their true order of subordination, it needs no long consideration to show. The actions and precautions by which, from moment to moment, we secure personal safety, must clearly take precedence of all others. Could there be a man, ignorant as an infant of all surrounding objects and movements, or how to guide himself among them, he would pretty certainly lose his life the first time he went into the street: notwithstanding any amount of learning he might have on other matters. And as entire ignorance in all other directions would be less promptly fatal than entire ignorance in this direction, it must be admitted that knowledge immediately conducive to self-preservation is of primary importance. . . .

Of course the ideal of education is—complete preparation in all these divisions. But failing this ideal, as in our phase of civilization every one must do more or less, the aim should be to maintain *a due proportion* between the degrees of preparation in each. Not exhaustive cultivation in any one, supremely important though it may be—not even an exclusive attention to the two, three, or four divisions of greatest importance; but an attention to all,—greatest where the value is greatest, less where the value is less, least where the value is least. For the average man (not to forget the cases in which peculiar aptitude for some one department of knowledge rightly makes that one the breadwinning occupation)—for the average man, we say, the desideratum is, a training that approaches nearest to perfection in the things which most subserve complete living, and falls more and more below perfection in the things that have more and more remote bearings on complete living.

In regulating education by this standard, there are some general considerations that should be ever present to us. The worth of any kind of culture, as aiding complete living, may be either necessary or more or less contingent. There is knowledge of intrinsic value; knowledge of quasi-intrinsic value; and knowledge of conventional value. Such facts as that sensations of numbness and tingling commonly precede paralysis, that the resistance of water to a body moving through it varies as the square of the velocity, that chlorine is a disinfectant,—these, and the truths of Science in general, are of intrinsic value: they will bear on human conduct ten thousand years hence as they do now. The extra knowledge of our own language, which is given by an acquaintance with Latin and Greek, may be considered to have a value that is quasi-intrinsic: it must exist for us and for other races whose languages owe much to these sources; but will last only as long as our languages last. While that kind of information which, in our schools, usurps the name History—the mere tissue of names and dates and dead unmeaning events—has a conventional value only: it has not the remotest bearing upon any of our actions; and is of use only for the avoidance of those unpleasant criticisms which current opinion passes upon its absence. Of course, as those facts which concern all mankind throughout all time must be held of greater moment than those which concern only a portion of them during a limited era, and of far greater moment than those which concern only a portion of them during the continuance of a fashion; it follows that in a rational estimate, knowledge of intrinsic worth must, other things equal, take precedence of knowledge that is of quasi-intrinsic or conventional worth.

One further preliminary. Acquirement of every kind has two values—value as *knowledge* and value as *discipline*. Besides its use for guidance in conduct, the acquisition of each order of facts has also its use as mental exercise; and its effects as a preparative for complete living have to be considered under both these heads.

These, then, are the general ideas with which we must set out in discussing a *curriculum:*—Life as divided into several kinds of activity of successively decreasing importance; the worth of each order of facts as regulating these several kinds of activity, intrinsically, quasi-intrinsically, and conventionally; and their regulative influences estimated both as knowledge and discipline.

Happily, that all-important part of education which goes to secure direct self-preservation, is in great part already provided for. Too momentous to be left to our blundering, Nature takes it into her own hands. While yet in its nurse's arms, the infant, by hiding its face and crying at the sight of a stranger, shows the dawning instinct to attain safety by flying from that which is unknown and may be dangerous; and when it can walk, the terror it manifests if an unfamiliar dog comes near, or the screams with which it runs to its mother after any startling sight or sound, shows this instinct further developed. Moreover, knowledge subserving direct self-preservation is that which it is chiefly busied in acquiring from hour to hour. How to balance its body; how to control its movements so as to avoid collisions; what objects are hard, and will hurt if struck; what objects are heavy, and injure if they fall on the limbs; which things will bear the weight of the body, and which not; the pains inflicted by fire, by missiles, by sharp instruments—these, and various other pieces of information needful for the avoidance of death or accident, it is ever learning. And when, a few years later, the energies go out in running, climbing, and jumping, in games of strength and games of skill, we see in all these actions by which the muscles are developed, the perceptions sharpened, and the judgment quickened, a preparation for the safe conduct of the body among surrounding objects and movements; and for meeting those greater dangers that occasionally occur in the lives of all. Being thus, as we say, so well cared for by Nature, this fundamental education needs comparatively little care from us. What we are chiefly called upon to see, is, that there shall be free scope for gaining this experience, and receiving this discipline,—that there shall be no such thwarting of Nature as that by which stupid schoolmistresses commonly prevent the girls in their charge from the spontaneous physical activities they would indulge in; and so render them comparatively incapable of taking care of themselves in circumstances of peril.

This, however, is by no means all that is comprehended in the education that prepares for direct self-preservation. Besides guarding the body against mechanical damage or destruction, it has to be guarded against injury from other causes—against the disease and death that follow breaches of physiologic law. For complete living it is necessary, not only that sudden annihilations of life shall be warded off; but also that there shall be escaped the incapacities and the slow annihilation which unwise habits entail. As, without health and energy, the industrial, the parental, the social, and all other activities become more or less impossible; it is clear that this secondary kind of direct self-preservation is only less important than the primary kind; and that knowledge tending to secure it should rank very high.

It is true that here, too, guidance is in some measure ready supplied. By our various physical sensations and desires, Nature has insured a tolerable conformity to the chief requirements. Fortunately for us, want of food, great heat, extreme cold, produce promptings too peremptory to be disregarded. And would men habitually obey these and all like promptings when less strong, comparatively few evils would arise. If fatigue of body or brain were in every case followed by desistance; if the oppression produced by a close atmosphere always led to ventilation; if there were no eating without hunger, or drinking without thirst; then would the system be but seldom out of working order. But so profound an ignorance is there of the laws of life, that men do not even know that their sensations are their natural guides, and (when not rendered morbid by long-continued disobedience) their trustworthy guides. So that though, to speak teleologically, Nature has provided efficient safeguards to health, lack of knowledge makes them in a great measure useless.

If any one doubts the importance of an acquaintance with the fundamental principles of physiology as a means to complete living, let him look around and see how many men and women he can find in middle or later life who are thoroughly well. Occasionally only do we meet with an example of vigorous health continued to old age; hourly do we meet with examples of acute disorder, chronic ailment, general debility, premature decrepitude. Scarcely is there one to whom you put the question, who has not, in the course of his life, brought upon himself illnesses which a little knowledge would have saved him from. Here is a case of heart disease consequent on a rheumatic fever that followed reckless exposure. There is a case of eyes spoiled for life by over-study. Yesterday the account was of one whose long-enduring lameness was brought on by continuing, spite of the pain, to use a knee after it had been slightly injured. And today we are told of another who has had to lie by for years, because he did not know that the palpitation he suffered from resulted from overtaxed brain. Now we hear of an irremediable injury that followed some silly feat of strength; and, again, of a constitution that has never recovered from the effects of excessive work needlessly undertaken. While on all sides we see the perpetual minor ailments which accompany feebleness. Not to dwell on the natural pain, the weariness, the gloom, the waste of time and money thus entailed, only consider how greatly ill-health hinders the discharge of all duties—makes business often impossible, and always more difficult; produces an irritability fatal to the right management of children; puts the functions of citizenship out of the question; and makes amusement a bore. Is it not clear that the physical sins—partly our forefathers' and partly our own—which produce this ill-health, deduct more from complete living than anything else? and to a great extent make life a failure and a burden instead of a benefaction and a pleasure?

To all which add the fact, that life, besides being thus immensely deteriorated, is also cut short. It is not true, as we commonly suppose, that a disorder or disease from which we have recovered leaves us as before. No disturbance of the normal course of the functions can pass away and leave things exactly as they were. In all cases a permanent damage is done—not immediately appreciable, it may be, but still there; and along with other such items which Nature in her strict account-keeping never drops, will tell against us to the inevitable shortening of our days. Through the accumulation of small injuries it is that constitutions are commonly undermined, and break down, long before their time. And if we call to mind how far the average duration of life falls below the possible duration, we see how immense is the loss. When, to the numerous partial deductions which bad health entails, we add this great final deduction, it results that ordinarily more than one-half of life is thrown away.

Hence, knowledge which subserves direct self-preservation by preventing this loss of health, is of primary importance. We do not contend that possession of such knowledge would by any means wholly remedy the evil. For it is clear that in our present phase of civilization men's necessities often compel them to transgress. And it is further clear that, even in the absence of such compulsion, their inclinations would frequently lead them, spite of their knowledge, to sacrifice future good to present gratification. But we do contend that the right knowledge impressed in the right way would effect much; and we further contend that as the laws of health must be recognised before they can be fully conformed to, the imparting of such knowledge must precede a more rational living—come when that may. We infer that as vigorous health and its accompanying high spirits are larger elements of happiness than any other things whatever, the teaching how to maintain them is a teaching that yields in moment to no other whatever. And therefore we assert that such a course of physiology as is needful for the comprehension of its general truths, and their bearings on daily conduct, is an all-essential part of a rational education.

Strange that the assertion should need making! Stranger still that it should need defending! Yet are there not a few by whom such a proposition will be received with something approaching to derision. Men who would blush if caught saying Iphigénia instead of Iphigenía, or would resent as an insult any imputation of ignorance respecting the fabled labours of a fabled demi-god, show not the slightest shame in confessing that they do not know where the Eustachian tubes are, what are the actions of the spinal cord, what is the normal rate of pulsation, or how the lungs are inflated. While anxious that their sons should be well up in the superstitions of two thousand years ago, they care not that they should be taught anything about the structure and functions of their own bodies—nay, would even disapprove such instruction. So overwhelming is the influence of established routine! So terribly in our education does the ornamental override the useful!

We need not insist on the value of that knowledge which aids indirect self-preservation by facilitating the gaining of a livelihood. This is admitted by all; and, indeed, by the mass is perhaps too exclusively regarded as the end of education. But while every one is ready to endorse the abstract proposition that instruction fitting youths for the business of life is of high importance, or even to consider it of supreme importance; yet scarcely any inquire what instruction will so fit them. It is true that reading, writing, and arithmetic are taught with an intelligent appreciation of their uses; but when we have said this we have said nearly all. While the great bulk of what else is acquired has no bearing on the industrial activities, an immensity of information that has a direct bearing on the industrial activities is entirely passed over.

For, leaving out only some very small classes, what are all men employed in? They are employed in the production, preparation, and distribution of commodities. And on what does efficiency in the production, preparation, and distribution of commodities depend? It depends on the use of methods fitted to the respective natures of these commodities; it depends on an adequate knowledge of their physical, chemical, or vital properties, as the case may be; that is, it depends on Science. This order of knowledge, which is in great part ignored in our school courses, is the order of knowledge underlying the right performance of all those processes by which civilized life is made possible. Undeniable as is this truth, and thrust upon us as it is at every turn, there seems to be no living consciousness of it: its very familiarity makes it unregarded. To give due weight to our argument, we must, therefore, realize this truth to the reader by a rapid review of the facts.

For all the higher arts of construction, some acquaintance with Mathematics is indispensable. The village carpenter, who, lacking rational instruction, lays out his work by empirical rules learnt in his apprenticeship, equally with the builder of a Britannia Bridge, makes hourly reference to the laws of quantitative relations. The surveyor on whose survey the land is purchased; the architect in designing a mansion to be built on it; the builder in preparing his estimates; his foreman in laying out the foundations; the masons in cutting the stones; and the various artisans who put up the fittings; are all guided by geometrical truths. Railway-making is regulated from beginning to end by mathematics: alike in the preparation of plans and sections; in staking out the line; in the mensuration of cuttings and embankments; in the designing, estimating, and building of bridges, culverts, viaducts, tunnels, stations. And similarly with the harbours, docks, piers, and various engineering and architectural works that fringe the coasts and overspread the face of the country; as well as the mines that run underneath it. Out of geometry, too, as applied to astronomy, the art of navigation has grown; and so, by this science, has been made possible that enormous foreign commerce which supports a large part of our population, and supplies us with many necessaries and most of our luxuries. And now-a-days even the farmer, for the correct laying out of his drains, has recourse to the level—that is, to geometrical principles. When from those divisions of mathematics which deal with *space,* and *number,* some small smattering of which is given in schools, we turn to that other division which deals with *force,* of which even a smattering is scarcely ever given, we meet with another large class of activities which this science presides over. On the application of rational mechanics depends the success of nearly all modern manufacture. The properties of the lever, the wheel and axle, &c., are involved in every machine—every machine is a solidified mechanical theorem; and to machinery in these times we owe nearly all production. Trace the history of the breakfast-roll. The soil out of which it came was drained with machine-made tiles; the surface was turned over by a machine; the seed was put in by a machine; the wheat was reaped, thrashed, and winnowed by machines; by machinery it was ground and bolted; and had the flour been sent to Gosport, it might have been made into biscuits by a machine. Look round the room in which you sit. If modern, probably the bricks in its walls were machine-made; by machinery the flooring was sawn and planed, the mantel-shelf sawn and polished, the paper-hangings made and printed; the veneer on the table, the turned legs of the chairs, the carpet, the curtains, are all products of machinery. And your clothing—plain, figured, or printed—is it not wholly woven, nay, perhaps even sewed, by machinery? And the volume you are reading—are not its leaves fabricated by one machine and covered with these words by another? Add to which that for the means of distribution over both land and sea, we are similarly indebted. And then let it be remembered that according as the principles of mechanics are well or ill used to these ends, comes success or failure—individual and national. The engineer who misapplies his formulæ for the strength of materials, builds a bridge that breaks down. The manufacturer whose apparatus is badly devised, cannot compete with another whose apparatus wastes less in friction and inertia. The ship-builder adher-

ing to the old model, is outsailed by one who builds on the mechanically-justified wave-line principle. And as the ability of a nation to hold its own against other nations depends on the skilled activity of its units, we see that on such knowledge may turn the national fate. Judge then the worth of mathematics.

Pass next to Physics. Joined with mathematics, it has given us the steam-engine, which does the work of millions of labourers. That section of physics which deals with the laws of heat, has taught us how to economise fuel in our various industries; how to increase the produce of our smelting furnaces by substituting the hot for the cold blast; how to ventilate our mines; how to prevent explosions by using the safety-lamp; and, through the thermometer, how to regulate innumerable processes. That division which has the phenomena of light for its subject, gives eyes to the old and the myopic; aids through the microscope in detecting diseases and adulterations; and by improved lighthouses prevents shipwrecks. Researches in electricity and magnetism have saved incalculable life and property by the compass; have subserved sundry arts by the electrotype; and now, in the telegraph, have supplied us with the agency by which for the future all mercantile transactions will be regulated, political intercourse carried on, and perhaps national quarrels often avoided. While in the details of indoor life, from the improved kitchen-range up to the stereoscope on the drawing-room table, the applications of advanced physics underlie our comforts and gratifications.

Still more numerous are the bearings of Chemistry on those activities by which men obtain the means of living. The bleacher, the dyer, the calico-printer, are severally occupied in processes that are well or ill done according as they do or do not conform to chemical laws. The economical reduction from their ores of copper, tin, zinc, lead, silver, iron, are in a great measure questions of chemistry. Sugar-refining, gas-making, soap-boiling, gunpowder manufacture, are operations all partly chemical; as are also those by which are produced glass and porcelain. Whether the distiller's wort stops at the alcoholic fermentation or passes into the acetous, is a chemical question on which hangs his profit or loss; and the brewer, if his business is sufficiently large, finds it pay[s] to keep a chemist on his premises. Glance through a work on technology, and it becomes at once apparent that there is now scarcely any process in the arts or manufactures over some part of which chemistry does not preside. And then, lastly, we come to the fact that in these times, agriculture, to be profitably carried on, must have like guidance. The analysis of manures and soils; their adaptations to each other; the use of gypsum or other substance for fixing ammonia; the utilization of coprolites; the production of artificial manures—all these are boons of chemistry which it behoves the farmer to acquaint himself with. Be it in the lucifer match, or in disinfected sewage, or in photographs—in bread made without fermentation, or perfumes extracted from refuse, we may perceive that chemistry affects all our industries; and that, by consequence, knowledge of it concerns every one who is directly or indirectly connected with our industries.

And then the science of life—Biology: does not this, too, bear fundamentally upon these processes of indirect self-preservation? With what we ordinarily call manufactures, it has, indeed, little connexion; but with the all-essential manufacture—that of food—it is inseparably connected. As agriculture must conform its methods to the phenomena of vegetable and animal life, it follows necessarily that the science of these phenomena is the rational basis of agriculture. Various biological truths have indeed been empirically established and acted upon by farmers while yet there has been no conception of them as science: such as that particular manures are suited to particular plants; that crops of certain kinds unfit the soil for other crops; that horses cannot do good work on poor food; that such and such diseases of

cattle and sheep are caused by such and such conditions. These, and the everyday knowledge which the agriculturist gains by experience respecting the right management of plants and animals, constitute his stock of biological facts; on the largeness of which greatly depends his success. And as these biological facts, scanty, indefinite, rudimentary, though they are, aid him so essentially; judge what must be the value to him of such facts when they become positive, definite, and exhaustive. Indeed, even now we may see the benefits that rational biology is conferring on him. The truth that the production of animal heat implies waste of substance, and that, therefore, preventing loss of heat prevents the need for extra food—a purely theoretical conclusion—now guides the fattening of cattle: it is found that by keeping cattle warm, fodder is saved. Similarly with respect to variety of food. The experiments of physiologists have shown that not only is change of diet beneficial, but that digestion is facilitated by a mixture of ingredients in each meal: both which truths are now influencing cattle-feeding. The discovery that a disorder known as "the staggers," of which many thousands of sheep have died annually, is caused by an entozoon which presses on the brain; and that if the creature is extracted through the softened place in the skull which marks its position, the sheep usually recovers; is another debt which agriculture owes to biology. When we observe the marked contrast between our farming and farming on the Continent, and remember that this contrast is mainly due to the far greater influence science has had upon farming here than there; and when we see how, daily, competition is making the adoption of scientific methods more general and necessary; we shall rightly infer that very soon, agricultural success in England will be impossible without a competent knowledge of animal and vegetable physiology.

Yet one more science have we to note as bearing directly on industrial success—the Science of Society. Without knowing it, men who daily look at the state of the money-market, glance over prices current, discuss the probable crops of corn, cotton, sugar, wool, silk, weigh the chances of war, and from all those data decide on their mercantile operations, are students of social science: empirical and blundering students it may be; but still, students who gain the prizes or are plucked of their profits, according as they do or do not reach the right conclusion. Not only the manufacturer and the merchant must guide their transactions by calculations of supply and demand, based on numerous facts, and tacitly recognising sundry general principles of social action; but even the retailer must do the like: his prosperity very greatly depending upon the correctness of his judgments respecting the future wholesale prices and the future rates of consumption. Manifestly, all who take part in the entangled commercial activities of a community, are vitally interested in understanding the laws according to which those activities vary.

Thus, to all such as are occupied in the production, exchange, or distribution of commodities, acquaintance with science in some of its departments, is of fundamental importance. Whoever is immediately or remotely implicated in any form of industry (and few are not) has a direct interest in understanding something of the mathematical, physical, and chemical properties of things; perhaps, also, has a direct interest in biology; and certainly has in sociology. Whether he does or does not succeed well in that indirect self-preservation which we call getting a good livelihood, depends in a great degree on his knowledge of one or more of these sciences: not, it may be, a rational knowledge; but still a knowledge, though empirical. For what we call learning a business, really implies learning the science involved in it; though not perhaps under the name of science. And hence a grounding in science is of great importance, both because it prepares for all this, and because rational knowledge has an immense superiority over empirical knowledge. Moreover, not only is it that scientific culture is

requisite for each, that he may understand the *how* and the *why* of the things and processes with which he is concerned as maker or distributor; but it is often of much moment that he should understand the *how* and the *why* of various other things and processes. In this age of joint-stock undertakings, nearly every man above the labourer is interested as capitalist in some other occupation than his own; and, as thus interested, his profit or loss often depends on his knowledge of the sciences bearing on this other occupation. Here is a mine, in the sinking of which many shareholders ruined themselves, from not knowing that a certain fossil belonged to the old red sandstone, below which no coal is found. Not many years ago, 20,000*l*. was lost in the prosecution of a scheme for collecting the alcohol that distils from bread in baking: all which would have been saved to the subscribers, had they known that less than a hundredth part by weight of the flour is changed in fermentation. Numerous attempts have been made to construct electromagnetic engines, in the hope of superseding steam; but had those who supplied the money, understood the general law of the correlation and equivalence of forces, they might have had better balances at their bankers. Daily are men induced to aid in carrying out inventions which a mere tyro in science could show to be futile. Scarcely a locality but has its history of fortunes thrown away over some impossible project.

And if already the loss from want of science is so frequent and so great, still greater and more frequent will it be to those who hereafter lack science. Just as fast as productive processes become more scientific, which competition will inevitably make them do; and just as fast as joint-stock undertakings spread, which they certainly will; so fast will scientific knowledge grow necessary to every one.

That which our school courses leave almost entirely out, we thus find to be that which most nearly concerns the business of life. All our industries would cease, were it not for that information which men begin to acquire as they best may after their education is said to be finished. And were it not for this information, that has been from age to age accumulated and spread by unofficial means, these industries would never have existed. Had there been no teaching but such as is given in our public schools, England would now be what it was in feudal times. That increasing acquaintance with the laws of phenomena which has through successive ages enabled us to subjugate Nature to our needs, and in these days gives the common labourer comforts which a few centuries ago kings could not purchase, is scarcely in any degree owed to the appointed means of instructing our youth. The vital knowledge—that by which we have grown as a nation to what we are, and which now underlies our whole existence, is a knowledge that has got itself taught in nooks and corners; while the ordained agencies for teaching have been mumbling little else but dead formulas.

We come now to the third great division of human activities—a division for which no preparation whatever is made. If by some strange chance not a vestige of us descended to the remote future save a pile of our school-books or some college examination papers, we may imagine how puzzled an antiquary of the period would be on finding in them no indication that the learners were ever likely to be parents. "This must have been the *curriculum* for their celibates," we may fancy him concluding. "I perceive here an elaborate preparation for many things: especially for reading the books of extinct nations and of co-existing nations (from which indeed it seems clear that these people had very little worth reading in their own tongue); but I find no reference whatever to the bringing up of children. They could not have been so absurd as to omit all training for this gravest of responsibilities. Evidently then, this was the school course of one of their monastic orders."

Seriously, is it not an astonishing fact, that though on the treatment of offspring depend their lives or deaths, and

their moral welfare or ruin; yet not one word of instruction on the treatment of offspring is ever given to those who will hereafter be parents? Is it not monstrous that the fate of a new generation should be left to the chances of unreasoning custom, impulse, fancy—joined with the suggestions of ignorant nurses and the prejudiced counsel of grandmothers? If a merchant commenced business without any knowledge of arithmetic and book-keeping, we should exclaim at his folly, and look for disastrous consequences. Or if, before studying anatomy, a man set up as a surgical operator, we should wonder at his audacity and pity his patients. But that parents should begin the difficult task of rearing children without ever having given a thought to the principles —physical, moral, or intellectual—which ought to guide them, excites neither surprise at the actors nor pity for their victims.

To tens of thousands that are killed, add hundreds of thousands that survive with feeble constitutions, and millions that grow up with constitutions not so strong as they should be; and you will have some idea of the curse inflicted on their offspring by parents ignorant of the laws of life. Do but consider for a moment that the regimen to which children are subject is hourly telling upon them to their life-long injury or benfit; and that there are twenty ways of going wrong to one way of going right; and you will get some idea of the enormous mischief that is almost everywhere inflicted by the thoughtless, haphazard system in common use. Is it decided that a boy shall be clothed in some flimsy short dress, and be allowed to go playing about with limbs reddened by cold? The decision will tell on his whole future existence—either in illnesses; or in stunted growth; or in deficient energy; or in a maturity less vigorous than it ought to have been, and consequent hindrances to success and happiness. Are children doomed to a monotonous dietary, or a dietary that is deficient in nutritiveness? Their ultimate physical power and their efficiency as men and women, will inevitably be more or less diminished by it. Are they forbidden vociferous play, or (being too ill-clothed to bear exposure), are they kept in-doors in cold weather? They are certain to fall below that measure of health and strength to which they would else have attained. When sons and daughters grow up sickly and feeble, parents commonly regard the event as a misfortune—as a visitation of Providence. Thinking after the prevalent chaotic fashion, they assume that these evils come without causes; or that the causes are supernatural. Nothing of the kind. In some cases the causes are doubtless inherited; but in most cases foolish regulations are the causes. Very generally parents themselves are responsible for all this pain, this debility, this depression, this misery. They have undertaken to control the lives of their offspring from hour to hour; with cruel carelessness they have neglected to learn anything about these vital processes which they are unceasingly affecting by their commands and prohibitions; in utter ignorance of the simplest physiologic laws, they have been year by year undermining the constitutions of their children; and have so inflicted disease and premature death, not only on them but on their descendants.

Equally great are the ignorance and the consequent injury, when we turn from physical training to moral training. Consider the young mother and her nursery legislation. But a few years ago she was at school, where her memory was crammed with words, and names, and dates, and her reflective faculties scarcely in the slightest degree exercised—where not one idea was given her respecting the methods of dealing with the opening mind of childhood; and where her discipline did not in the least fit her for thinking out methods of her own. The intervening years have been passed in practising music, in fancy-work, in novel-reading, and in party-going: no thought having yet been given to the grave responsibilities of maternity; and scarcely any of that solid intellectual culture obtained which would be some preparation for such responsibilities. And now see her with an unfolding human character committed to her charge— see her profoundly ignorant of the phenomena with which she has to deal, undertaking to do that which can be done but imperfectly even with the aid of the profoundest knowledge. She knows nothing about the nature of the emotions, their order of evolution, their functions, or where use ends and abuse begins. She is under the impression that some of the feelings are wholly bad, which is not true of any one of them; and that others are good, however far they may be carried, which is also not true of any one of them. And then, ignorant as she is of that with which she has to deal, she is equally ignorant of the effects that will be produced on it by this or that treatment. What can be more inevitable than the disastrous results we see hourly arising? Lacking knowledge of mental phenomena, with their causes and consequences, her interference is frequently more mischievous than absolute passivity would have been. This and that kind of action, which are quite normal and beneficial, she perpetually thwarts; and so diminishes the child's happiness and profit, injures its temper and her own, and produces estrangement. Deeds which she thinks it desirable to encourage, she gets performed by threats and bribes, or by exciting a desire for applause: considering little what the inward motive may be, so long as the outward conduct conforms; and thus cultivating hypocrisy, and fear, and selfishness, in place of good feeling. While insisting on truthfulness, she constantly sets an example of untruth, by threatening penalties which she does not inflict. While inculcating self-control, she hourly visits on her little ones angry scoldings for acts that do not call for them. She has not the remotest idea that in the nursery, as in the world, that alone is the truly salutary discipline which visits on all conduct, good and bad, the natural consequences—the consequences, pleasurable or painful, which in the nature of things such conduct tends to bring. Being thus without theoretic guidance, and quite incapable of guiding herself by tracing the mental processes going on in her children, her rule is impulsive, inconsistent, mischievous, often, in the highest degree; and would indeed be generally ruinous, were it not that the overwhelming tendency of the growing mind to assume the moral type of the race, usually subordinates all minor influences.

And then the culture of the intellect—is not this, too, mismanaged in a similar manner? Grant that the phenomena of intelligence conform to laws; grant that the evolution of intelligence in a child also conforms to laws; and it follows inevitably that education can be rightly guided only by a knowledge of these laws. To suppose that you can properly regulate this process of forming and accumulating ideas, without understanding the nature of the process, is absurd. How widely, then, must teaching as it is, differ from teaching as it should be; when hardly any parents, and but few teachers, know anything about psychology. As might be expected, the system is grievously at fault, alike in matter and in manner. While the right class of facts is withheld, the wrong class is forcibly administered in the wrong way and in the wrong order. With that common limited idea of education which confines it to knowledge gained from books, parents thrust primers into the hands of their little ones years too soon, to their great injury. Not recognising the truth that the function of books is supplementary—that they form an indirect means to knowlerge when direct means fail—a means of seeing through other men what you cannot see for yourself; they are eager to give second-hand facts in place of first-hand facts. Not perceiving the enormous value of that spontaneous education which goes on in early years—not perceiving that a child's restless observation, instead of being ignored or checked, should be diligently administered to, and made as accurate and complete as possible; they insist on occupying its eyes and thoughts with things that are, for the time being, inconprehensible and repugnant. Possessed by a superstition which worships the symbols of knowledge instead of the knowledge itself, they do not see that only when his acquaintance with the objects and processes of the household, the streets, and the fields, is becoming tolerably exhaustive—only then should a child be introduced to the new sources of information which books supply: and this, not only because immediate cognition is of far greater value than mediate cognition; but also, because the words contained in books can be rightly interpreted into ideas, only in proportion to the antecedent experience of things. Observe next, that this formal instruction, far too soon commenced, is carried on with but little reference to the laws of mental development. Intellectual progress is of necessity from the concrete to the abstract. But regardless of this, highly abstract subjects, such as grammar, which should come quite late, are begun quite early. Political geography, dead and uninteresting to a child, and which should be an appendage of sociological studies, is commenced betimes; while physical geography, comprehensible and comparatively attractive to a child, is in great part passed over. Nearly every subject dealt with is arranged in abnormal order: definitions, and rules, and principles being put first, instead of being disclosed, as they are in the order of nature, through the study of cases. And then, pervading the whole, is the vicious system of rote learning —a system of sacrificing the spirit to the letter. See the results. What with perceptions unnaturally dulled by early thwarting, and a coerced attention to books—what with the mental confusion produced by teaching subjects before they can be understood, and in each of them giving generalizations before the facts of which these are the generalizations—what with making the pupil a mere passive recipient of other's ideas, and not in the least leading him to be an active inquirer or self-instructor—and what with taxing the faculties to excess; there are very few minds that become as efficient as they might be. Examinations being once passed, books are laid aside; the greater part of what has been acquired, being unorganized, soon drops out of recollection; what remains is mostly inert —the art of applying knowledge not having been cultivated; and there is but little power either of accurate observation or independent thinking. To all which add, that while much of the information gained is of relatively small value, an immense mass of information of transcendent value is entirely passed over.

Thus we find the facts to be such as might have been inferred *à priori*. The training of children—physical, moral, and intellectual—is dreadfully defective. And in great measure it is so, because parents are devoid of that knowledge by which this training can alone be rightly guided. What is to be expected when one of the most intricate of problems is undertaken by those who have given scarcely a thought to the principles on which its solution depends? For shoe-making or house-building, for the management of a ship or a locomotive-engine, a long apprenticeship is needful. Is it, then, that the unfolding of a human being in body and mind, is so comparatively simple a process, that any one may superintend and regulate it with no preparation whatever? If not—if the process is with one exception more complex than any in Nature, and the task of administering to it one of surpassing difficulty; is it not madness to make no provision for such a task? Better sacrifice accomplishments than omit this all-essential instruction. When a father, acting on false dogmas adopted without examination, has alienated his sons, driven them into rebellion by his harsh treatment, ruined them, and made himself miserable; he might reflect that the study of Ethology would have been worth pursuing, even at the cost of knowing nothing about Æschylus. When a mother is mourning over a first-born that has sunk under the sequelæ of scarlet-fever—when perhaps a candid medical man has confirmed her suspicion that her child would have recovered had not its system been enfeebled by over-study—when she is prostrate under the pangs of combined grief and remorse; it is but a small consolation that she can read Dante in the original.

Thus we see that for regulating the third great division of human activities, a knowledge of the laws of life is the one thing needful. Some acquaintance with the first principles of physiology and the elementary truths of psychology is indispensable for the right bringing up of children. We doubt not that this assertion will by many be read with a smile. That parents in general should be expected to acquire a knowledge of subjects so abstruse, will seem to them an absurdity. And if we proposed that an exhaustive knowledge of these subjects should be obtained by all fathers and mothers, the absurdity would indeed be glaring enough. But we do not. General principles only, accompanied by such detailed illustrations as may be needed to make them understood, would suffice. And these might be readily taught—if not rationally, then dogmatically. Be this as it may, however, here are the indisputable facts:—that the development of children in mind and body rigorously obeys certain laws; that unless these laws are in some degree conformed to by parents, death is inevitable; that unless they are in a great degree conformed to, there must result serious physical and mental defects; and that only when they are completely conformed to, can a perfect maturity be reached. Judge, then, whether all who may one day be parents, should not strive with some anxiety to learn what these laws are.

From the parental functions let us pass now to the functions of the citizen. We have here to inquire what knowledge best fits a man for the discharge of these functions. It cannot be alleged, as in the last case, that the need for knowledge fitting him for these functions is wholly overlooked; for our school courses contain certain studies which, nominally at least, bear upon political and social duties. Of these the only one that occupies a prominent place is History.

But, as already more than once hinted, the historic information commonly given is almost valueless for purposes of guidance.

Scarcely any of the facts set down in our school-histories, and very few even of those contained in the more elaborate works written for adults, give any clue to the right principles of political action. The biographies of monarchs (and our children commonly learn little else) throw scarcely any light upon the science of society. Familiarity with court intrigues, plots, usurpations, or the like, and with all the personalities accompanying them, aids very little in elucidating the principles on which national welfare depends. We read of some squabble for power, that it led to a pitched battle; that such and such were the names of the generals and their leading subordinates; that they had each so many thousand infantry and cavalry, and so many cannon; that they arranged their forces in this and that order; that they manœuvred, attacked, and fell back in certain ways; that at this part of the day such disasters were sustained, and at that such advantages gained; that in one particular movement some leading officer fell, while in another a certain regiment was decimated; that after all the changing fortunes of the fight, the victory was gained by this or that army; and that so many were killed and wounded on each side, and so many captured by the conquerors. And now, out of the accumulated details which make up the narrative, say which it is that helps you in deciding on your conduct as a citizen. Supposing even that you had diligently read, not only "The Fifteen Decisive Battles of the World," but accounts of all other battles that history mentions; how much more judicious would your vote be at the next election? "But these are facts—interesting facts," you say. Without doubt they are facts (such, at least, as are not wholly or partially fictions); and to many they may be interesting facts. But this by no means implies that they are valuable. Factitious or morbid opinion often gives seeming value to things that have scarcely any. A tulipomaniac will not part with a choice bulb for its weight in gold. To another man an ugly piece of cracked old china seems his most desirable possession. And there are those who give high prices for the relics of celebrated murderers. Will it be contended that these tastes are any measures of value in the things that gratify them? If not, then it must be admitted that the liking felt for certain classes of historical facts is no proof of their worth; and that we must test their worth as we test the worth of other facts, by asking to what uses they are applicable. Were some one to tell you that your neighbour's cat kittened yesterday, you would say the information was worthless. Fact though it might be, you would say it was an utterly useless fact—a fact that could in no way influence your actions in life—a fact that would not help you in learning how to live completely. Well, apply the same test to the great mass of historical facts, and you will get the same result. They are facts from which no conclusions can be drawn—*unorganizable* facts; and therefore facts which can be of no service in establishing principles of conduct, which is the chief use of facts. Read them, if you like, for amusement; but do not flatter yourself they are instructive.

That which constitutes History, properly so called, is in great part omitted from works on the subject. Only of late years have historians commenced giving us, in any considerable quantity, the truly valuable information. As in past ages the king was every thing and the people nothing; so, in past histories the doings of the king fill the entire picture, to which the national life forms but an obscure background. While only now, when the welfare of nations rather than of rulers is becoming the dominant idea, are historians beginning to occupy themselves with the phenomena of social progress. That which it really concerns us to know, is the natural history of society. We want all facts which help us to understand how a nation has grown and organized itself. Among these, let us of course have an account of its government; with as little as may be of gossip about the men who officered it, and as much as possible about the structure, principles, methods, prejudices, corruptions, &c., which it exhibited: and let this account not only include the nature and actions of the central government, but also those of local governments, down to their minutest ramifications. Let us of course also have a parallel description of the ecclesiastical government—its organization, its conduct, its power, its relations to the State: and accompanying this, the ceremonial, creed, and religious ideas—not only those nominally believed, but those really believed and acted upon. Let us at the same time be informed of the control exercised by class over class, as displayed in all social observances—in titles, salutations, and forms of address. Let us know, too, what were all the other customs which regulated the popular life out of doors and in-doors: including those which concern the relations of the sexes, and the relations of parents to children. The superstitions, also, from the more important myths down to the charms in common use, should be indicated. Next should come a delineation of the industrial system: showing to what extent the division of labour was carried; how trades were regulated, whether by caste, guilds, or otherwise; what was the connection between employers and employed; what were the agencies for distributing commodities, what were the means of communication; what was the circulating medium. Accompanying all which should come an account of the indusutrial arts technically considered: stating the processes in use, and the quality of the products. Further, the intellectual condition of the nation in its various grades should be depicted: not only with respect to the kind and amount of education, but with respect to the progress made in science, and the prevailing manner of thinking. The degree of æsthetic culture, as displayed in architecture, sculpture, painting, dress, music, poetry, and fiction, should be described. Nor should there be omitted a sketch of the daily lives of the people—their food, their homes, and their amusements. And lastly, to connect the whole, should be exhibited the morals, theoretical and practical, of all classes: as indicated in their laws, habits, proverbs, deeds. All these facts, given with as much brevity as consists with clearness and accuracy, should be so grouped and arranged that they may be comprehended in their *ensemble;* and thus may be contemplated as mutually dependent parts of one great whole. The aim should be so to present them that we may readily trace the *consensus* subsisting among them; with the view of learning what social phenomena co-exist with what others. And then the corresponding delineations of succeeding ages should be so managed as to show us, as clearly as may be, how each belief, institution, custom, and arrangement was modified; and how the *consensus* of preceding structures and functions was developed into the *consensus* of succeeding ones. Such alone is the kind of information respecting past times, which can be of service to the citizen for the regulation of his conduct. The only history that is of practical value, is what may be called Descriptive Sociology. And the highest office which the historian can discharge, is that of so narrating the lives of nations, as to furnish materials for a Comparative Sociology; and for the subsequent determination of the ultimate laws to which social phenomena conform.

But now mark, that even supposing an adequate stock of this truly valuable historical knowledge has been acquired, it is of comparatively little use without the key. And the key is to be found only in Science. Without an acquaintance with the general truths of biology and psychology, rational interpretation of social phenomena is impossible. Only in proportion as men obtain a certain rude, empirical knowledge of human nature, are they enabled to understand even the simplest facts of social life: as, for instance, the relation between supply and demand. And if not even the most elementary truths of sociology can be reached until some knowledge is obtained of how men generally think, feel, and act under given circumstances; then it is manifest that there can be nothing like a wide comprehension of sociology, unless through a competent knowledge of man in all his faculties, bodily and mental. Consider the matter in the abstract, and this conclusion is self-evident. Thus:—Society is made up of individuals; all that is done in society is done by the combined actions of individuals; and therefore, in individual actions only can be found the solutions of social phenomena. But the actions of individuals depend on the laws of their natures; and their actions cannot be understood until these laws are understood. These laws, however, when reduced to their simplest expression, are found to depend on the laws of body and mind in general. Hence it necessarily follows, that biology and psychology are indispensable as interpreters of sociology. Or, to state the conclusions still more simply:—all social phenomena are phenomena of life—are the most complex manifestations of life—are ultimately dependent on the laws of life—and can be understood only when the laws of life are understood. Thus, then, we see that for the regulation of this fourth division of human activities, we are, as before, dependent on Science. Of the knowledge commonly imparted in educational courses, very little is of any service in guiding a man in his conduct as a citizen. Only a small part of the history he reads is of practical value; and of this small part he is not prepared to make proper use. He commonly lacks not only the materials for, but the very conception of, descriptive sociology; and he also lacks that knowledge of the organic sciences, without which even descriptive sociology can give him but little aid.

And now we come to that remaining division of human life which includes the relaxations, pleasures, and amusements filling leisure hours. After considering what training best fits for self-preservation, for the obtainment of sustenance, for the discharge of parental duties, and for the regulation of social and political conduct; we have now to consider what training best fits for the miscellaneous ends not included in

these—for the enjoyments of Nature, of Literature, and of the Fine Arts, in all their forms. Postponing them as we do to things that bear more vitally upon human welfare; and bringing everything, as we have, to the test of actual value; it will perhaps be inferred that we are inclined to slight these less essential things. No greater mistake could be made, however. We yield to none in the value we attach to æsthetic culture and its pleasures. Without painting, sculpture, music, poetry, and the emotions produced by natural beauty of every kind, life would lose half its charm. So far from thinking that the training and gratification of the tastes are unimportant, we believe the time will come when they will occupy a much larger share of human life than now. When the forces of Nature have been fully conquered to man's use—when the means of production have been brought to perfection—when labour has been economized to the highest degree—when education has been so systematized that a preparation for the more essential activities may be made with comparative rapidity—and when, consequently, there is a great increase of spare time; then will the poetry, both of Art and Nature, rightly fill a large space in the minds of all.

But it is one thing to admit that æsthetic culture is in a high degree conducive to human happiness; and another thing to admit that it is a fundamental requisite to human happiness. However important it may be, it must yield precedence to those kinds of culture which bear more directly upon the duties of life. As before hinted, literature and the fine arts are made possible by those activities which make individual and social life possible; and manifestly, that which is made possible, must be postponed to that which makes it possible. A florist cultivates a plant for the sake of its flower; and regards the roots and leaves as of value, chiefly because they are instrumental in producing the flower. But while, as an ultimate product, the flower is the thing to which everything else is subordinate, the florist very well knows that the root and leaves are intrinsically of greater importance; because on them the evolution of the flower depends. He bestows every care in rearing a healthy plant; and knows it would be folly if, in his anxiety to obtain the flower, he were to neglect the plant. Similarly in the case before us. Architecture, sculpture, painting, music, poetry, &c., may be truly called the efflorescence of civilized life. But even supposing them to be of such transcendent worth as to subordinate the civilized life out of which they grow (which can hardly be asserted), it will still be admitted that the production of a healthy civilized life must be the first consideration; and that the knowledge conducing to this must occupy the highest place.

And here we see most distinctly the vice of our educational system. It neglects the plant for the sake of the flower. In anxiety for elegance, it forgets substance. While it gives no knowledge conducive to self-preservation—while of knowledge that facilitates gaining a livelihood it gives but the rudiments, and leaves the greater part to be picked up any how in after life—while for the discharge of parental functions it makes not the slightest provision—and while for the duties of citizenship it prepares by imparting a mass of facts, most of which are irrelevant, and the rest without a key; it is diligent in teaching every thing that adds to refinement, polish, éclat. However fully we may admit that extensive acquaintance with modern languages is a valuable accomplishment, which, through reading, conversation, and travel, aids in giving a certain finish; it by no means follows that this result is rightly purchased at the cost of that vitally important knowledge sacrificed to it. Supposing it true that classical education conduces to elegance and correctness of style; it cannot be said that elegance and correctness of style are comparable in importance to a familiarity with the principles that should guide the rearing of children. Grant that the taste may be greatly improved by reading all the poetry written in extinct lan-

guages; yet it is not to be inferred that such improvement of taste is equivalent in value to an acquaintance with the laws of health. Accomplishments, the fine arts, *belles-lettres*, and all those things which, as we say, constitute the efflorescence of civilization, should be wholly subordinate to that knowledge and discipline in which civilization rests. *As they occupy the leisure part of life, so should they occupy the leisure part of education.*

Recognising thus the true position of æsthetics, and holding that while the cultivation of them should form a part of education from its commencement, such cultivation should be subsidiary; we have now to inquire what knowledge is of most use to this end—what knowledge best fits for this remaining sphere of activity. To this question the answer is still the same as heretofore. Unexpected as the assertion may be, it is nevertheless true, that the highest Art of every kind is based upon Science—that without Science there can be neither perfect production nor full appreciation. Science, in that limited technical acceptation current in society, may not have been possessed by many artists of high repute; but acute observers as they have been, they have always possessed a stock of those empirical generalizations which constitute science in its lowest phase; and they have habitually fallen far below perfection, partly because their generalizations were comparatively few and inaccurate. That science necessarily underlies the fine arts, becomes manifest, à priori, when we remember that art-products are all more or less representative of objective or subjective phenomena; that they can be true only in proportion as they conform to the laws of these phenomena; and that before they can thus conform the artist must know what these laws are. That this à priori conclusion tallies with experience we shall soon see.

Youths preparing for the practice of sculpture, have to acquaint themselves with the bones and muscles of the human frame in their distribution, attachments, and movements. This is a portion of science; and it has been found needful to impart it for the prevention of those many errors which sculptors who do not possess it commit. For the prevention of other mistakes, a knowledge of mechanical principles is requisite; and such knowledge not being usually possessed, grave mechanical mistakes are frequently made. Take an instance. For the stability of a figure it is needful that the perpendicular from the centre of gravity—"the line of direction," as it is called—should fall within the base of support; and hence it happens, that when a man assumes the attitude known as "standing at ease," in which one leg is straightened and the other relaxed, the line of direction falls within the foot of the straightened leg. But sculptors unfamiliar with the theory of equilibrium, not uncommonly so represent this attitude, that the line of direction falls midway between the feet. Ignorance of the laws of momentum leads to analogous errors: as witness the admired Discobolus, which, as it is posed, must inevitably fall forward the moment the quoit is delivered.

In painting, the necessity for scientific knowledge, empirical if not rational, is still more conspicuous. In what consists the grotesqueness of Chinese pictures, unless in their utter disregard of the laws of appearances—in their absurd linear perspective, and their want of aerial perspective? In what are the drawings of a child so faulty, if not in a similar absence of truth—an absence arising, in great part, from ignorance of the way in which the aspects of things vary with the conditions? Do but remember the books and lectures by which students are instructed; or consider the criticisms of Ruskin; or look at the doings of the Pre-Raffaelites; and you will see that progress in painting implies increasing knowledge of how effects in Nature are produced. The most diligent observation, if not aided by science, fails to preserve from error. Every painter will indorse the assertion that unless it is known what appearances must exist under given circumstances, they often will not be perceived; and to know what ap-

pearances must exist, is, in so far, to understand the science of appearances. From want of science Mr. J. Lewis, careful painter as he is, casts the shadow of a lattice-window in sharply-defined lines upon an opposite wall; which he would not have done, had he been familiar with the phenomena of penumbræ. From want of science, Mr. Rosetti, catching sight of a peculiar iridescence displayed by certain hairy surfaces under particular lights (an iridescence caused by the diffraction of light in passing the hairs), commits the error of showing this iridescence on surfaces and in positions where it could not occur.

To say that music, too, has need of scientific aid will seem still more surprising. Yet it is demonstrable that music is but an idealization of the natural language of emotion; and that consequently, music must be good or bad according as it conforms to the laws of this natural language. The various inflections of voice which accompany feelings of different kinds and intensities, have been shown to be the germs out of which music is developed. It has been further shown, that these inflections and cadences are not accidental or arbitrary; but that they are determined by certain general principles of vital action; and that their expressiveness depends on this. Whence it follows that musical phrases and the melodies built of them, can be effective only when they are in harmony with these general principles. It is difficult here properly to illustrate this position. But perhaps it will suffice to instance the swarms of worthless ballads that infest drawing-rooms, as compositions which science would forbid. They sin against science by setting to music ideas that are not emotional enough to prompt musical expression; and they also sin against science by using musical phrases that have no natural relation to the ideas expressed: even where these are emotional. They are bad because they are untrue. And to say they are untrue, is to say they are unscientific.

Even in poetry the same thing holds. Like music, poetry has its root in those natural modes of expression which accompany deep feeling. Its rhythm, its strong and numerous metaphors, its hyperboles, its violent inversions, are simply exaggerations of the traits of excited speech. To be good, therefore, poetry must pay respect to those laws of nervous action which excited speech obeys. In intensifying and combining the traits of excited speech, it must have due regard to proportion—must not use its appliances without restriction; but, where the ideas are least emotional, must use the forms of poetical expression sparingly; must use them more freely as the emotion rises; and must carry them all to their greatest extent only where the emotion reaches a climax. The entire contravention of these principles results in bombast or doggerel. The insufficient respect for them is seen in didactic poetry. And it is because they are rarely fully obeyed, that we have so much poetry that is inartistic.

Not only is it that the artist, of whatever kind, cannot produce a truthful work without he understands the laws of the phenomena he represents; but it is that he must also understand how the minds of spectators or listeners will be affected by the several peculiarities of his work—a question in psychology. What impression any given art-product generates, manifestly depends upon the mental natures of those to whom it is presented; and as all mental natures have certain general principles in common, there must result certain corresponding general principles on which alone art-products can be successfully framed. These general principles cannot be fully understood and applied, unless the artist sees how they follow from the laws of mind. To ask whether the composition of a picture is good, is really to ask how the perceptions and feelings of observers will be affected by it. To ask whether a drama is well constructed, is to ask whether its situations are so arranged as duly to consult the power of attention of an audience, and duly to avoid overtaxing any one class of feelings. Equally in arranging the leading divisions of a poem or fiction, and in combining the words of a single sentence,

the goodness of the effect depends upon the skill with which the mental energies and susceptibilities of the reader are economized. Every artist, in the course of his education and after-life, accumulates a stock of maxims by which his practice is regulated. Trace such maxims to their roots, and you find they inevitably lead you down to psychological principles. And only when the artist rationally understands these psychological principles and their various corollaries, can he work in harmony with them.

We do not for a moment believe that science will make an artist. While we contend that the leading laws both of objective and subjective phenomena must be understood by him, we by no means contend that knowledge of such laws will serve in place of natural perception. Not only the poet, but also the artist of every type, is born, not made. What we assert is, that innate faculty alone will not suffice; but must have the aid of organized knowledge. Intuition will do much, but it will not do all. Only when Genius is married to Science can the highest results be produced.

As we have above asserted, Science is necessary not only for the most successful production, but also for the full appreciation of the fine arts. In what consists the greater ability of a man than of a child to perceive the beauties of a picture; unless it is in his more extended knowledge of those truths in nature or life which the picture renders? How happens the cultivated gentleman to enjoy a fine poem so much more than a boor does; if it is not because his wider acquaintance with objects and actions enables him to see in the poem much that the boor cannot see? And if, as is here so obvious, there must be some familiarity with the things represented, before the representation can be appreciated; then the representation can be completely appreciated, only in proportion as the things represented are completely understood. The fact is, that every additional truth which a work of art expresses, gives an additional pleasure to the percipient mind— a pleasure that is missed by those ignorant of this truth. The more realities an artist indicates in any given amount of work, the more faculties does he appeal to; the more numerous associated ideas does he suggest; the more gratification does he afford. But to receive this gratification the spectator, listener, or reader, must know the realities which the artist has indicated; and to know these realities is to know so much science.

And now let us not overlook the further great fact, that not only does science underlie sculpture, painting, music, poetry, but that science is itself poetic. The current opinion that science and poetry are opposed is a delusion. It is doubtless true that as states of consciousness, cognition and emotion tend to exclude each other. And it is doubtless also true that an extreme activity of the reflective powers tends to deaden the feelings; while an extreme activity of the feelings tends to deaden the reflective powers: in which sense, indeed, all orders of activity are antagonistic to each other. But it is not true that the facts of science are unpoetical; or that the cultivation of science is necessarily unfriendly to the exercise of imagination or the love of the beautiful. On the contrary science opens up realms of poetry where to the unscientific all is a blank. Those engaged in scientific researches constantly show us that they realize not less vividly, but more vividly, than others, the poetry of their subjects. Whoever will dip into Hugh Miller's works on geology, or read Mr. Lewes's "Seaside Studies," will perceive that science excites poetry rather than extinguishes it. And whoever will contemplate the life of Goethe will see that the poet and the man of science can co-exist in equal activity. Is it not, indeed, an absurd and almost a sacrilegious belief that the more a man studies Nature the less he reveres it? Think you that a drop of water, which to the vulgar eye is but a drop of water, loses anything in the eye of the physicist who knows that its elements are held together by a force which, if suddenly liberated, would produce a flash of lightning? Think you that what is carelessly looked upon by the uninitiated as a

mere snow-flake, does not suggest higher associations to one who has seen through a microscope the wondrously varied and elegant forms of snow-crystals? Think you that the rounded rock marked with parallel scratches calls up as much poetry in an ignorant mind as in the mind of a geologist, who knows that over this rock a glacier slid a million years ago? The truth is, that those who have never entered upon scientific pursuits know not a tithe of the poetry by which they are surrounded. Whoever has not in youth collected plants and insects, knows not half the halo of interest which lanes and hedge-rows can assume. Whoever has not sought for fossils, has little idea of the poetical associations that surround the places where imbedded treasures were found. Whoever at the seaside has not had a microscope and aquarium, has yet to learn what the highest pleasures of the seaside are. Sad, indeed, is it to see how men occupy themselves with trivialities, and are indifferent to the grandest phenomena—care not to understand the architecture of the Heavens, but are deeply interested in some contemptible controversy about the intrigues of Mary Queen of Scots!—are learnedly critical over a Greek ode, and pass by without a glance that grand epic written by the finger of God upon the strata of the Earth!

We find, then, that even for this remaining division of human activities, scientific culture is the proper preparation. We find that æsthetics in general are necessarily based upon scientific principles; and can be pursued with complete success only through an acquaintance with these principles. We find that for the criticism and due appreciation of works of art, a knowledge of the constitution of things, or in other words, a knowledge of science, is requisite. And we not only find that science is the handmaid to all forms of art and poetry, but that, rightly regarded, science is itself poetic.

Thus far our question has been, the worth of knowledge of this or that kind for purposes of guidance. We have now to judge the relative values of different kinds of knowledge for purposes of discipline. This division of our subject we are obliged to treat with comparative brevity; and happily, no very lengthened treatment of it is needed. Having found what is best for the one end, we have by implication found what is best for the other. We may be quite sure that the acquirement of those classes of facts which are most useful for regulating conduct, involves a mental exercise best fitted for strengthening the faculties. It would be utterly contrary to the beautiful economy of Nature, if one kind of culture were needed for the gaining of information and another kind were needed as a mental gymnastic. Everywhere throughout creation we find faculties developed through the performance of those functions which it is their office to perform; not through the performance of artificial exercises devised to fit them for these functions. The Red Indian acquires the swiftness and agility which make him a successful hunter, by the actual pursuit of animals; and by the miscellaneous activities of his life, he gains a better balance of physical powers than gymnastics ever give. That skill in tracking enemies and prey which he has reached by long practice, implies a subtlety of perception far exceeding anything produced by artificial training. And similarly throughout. From the Bushman whose eye, which being habitually employed in identifying distant objects that are to be pursued or fled from, has acquired a quite telescopic range, to the accountant whose daily practice enables him to add up several columns of figures simultaneously, we find that the highest power of a faculty results from the discharge of those duties which the conditions of life require it to discharge. And we may be certain, *à priori,* that the same law holds throughout education. The education of most value for guidance, must at the same time be the education of most value for discipline. Let us consider the evidence.

One advantage claimed for that devotion to language-learning which forms so prominent a feature in the ordinary *curriculum,* is, that the memory is thereby strengthened.

And it is apparently assumed that this is an advantage peculiar to the study of words. But the truth is, that the sciences afford far wider fields for the exercise of memory. It is no slight task to remember all the facts ascertained respecting our solar system; much more to remember all that is known concerning the structure of our galaxy. The new compounds which chemistry daily accumulates, are so numerous that few, save professors, know the names of them all; and to recollect the atomic constitutions and affinities of all these compounds, is scarcely possible without making chemistry the occupation of life. In the enormous mass of phenomena presented by the Earth's crust, and in the still more enormous mass of phenomena presented by the fossils it contains, there is matter which it takes the geological student years of application to master. In each leading division of physics— sound, heat, light, electricity—the facts are numerous enough to alarm any one proposing to learn them all. And when we pass to the organic sciences, the effort of memory required becomes still greater. In human anatomy alone, the quantity of detail is so great, that the young surgeon has commonly to get it up half-a-dozen times before he can permanently retain it. The number of species of plants which botanists distinguish, amounts to some 320,000; while the varied forms of animal life with which the zoologist deals, are estimated at some two millions. So vast is the accumulation of facts which men of science have before them, that only by dividing and subdividing their labours can they deal with it. To a complete knowledge of his own division, each adds but a general knowledge of the rest. Surely, then, science, cultivated even to a very moderate extent, affords adequate exercise for memory. To say the very least, it involves quite as good a training for this faculty as language does.

But now mark that while for the training of mere memory, science is as good as, if not better than, language; it has an immense superiority in the kind of memory it cultivates. In the acquirement of a language, the connexions of ideas to be established in the mind correspond to facts that are in great measure accidental; whereas, in the acquirement of science, the connexions of ideas to be established in the mind correspond to facts that are mostly necessary. It is true that the relations of words to their meaning is in one sense natural, and that the genesis of these relations may be traced back a certain distance; though very rarely to the beginning; (to which let us add the remark that the laws of this genesis form a branch of mental science—the science of philology.) But since it will not be contended that in the acquisition of languages, as ordinarily carried on, these natural relations between words and their meanings are habitually traced, and the laws regulating them explained; it must be admitted that they are commonly learned as fortuitous relations. On the other hand, the relations which science presents are causal relations; and, when properly taught, are understood as such. Instead of being practically accidental, they are necessary; and as such, give exercise to the reasoning faculties. While language familiarizes with non-rational relations, science familiarizes with rational relations. While the one exercises memory only, the other exercises both memory and understanding.

Observe next that a great superiority of science over language as a means of discipline, is, that it cultivates the judgment. As, in a lecture on mental education delivered at the Royal Institution, Professor Faraday well remarks, the most common intellectual fault is deficiency of judgment. He contends that "society, speaking generally, is not only ignorant as respects education of the judgment, but it is also ignorant of its ignorance." And the cause to which he ascribes this state is want of scientific culture. The truth of his conclusion is obvious. Correct judgment with regard to all surrounding things, events, and consequences, becomes possible only through knowledge of the way in which surrounding phenomena depend on each other. No extent of acquaintance with the meanings of words, can give the power of forming correct inferences respecting causes and effects. The constant habit of drawing conclusions from data, and then of verifying those conclusions by observation and experiment, can alone give the power of judging correctly. And that it necessitates this habit is one of the immense advantages of science.

Not only, however, for intellectual discipline is science the best; but also for *moral* discipline. The learning of languages tends, if anything, further to increase the already undue respect for authority. Such and such are the meanings of these words, says the teacher or the dictionary. So and so is the rule in this case, says the grammar. By the pupil these dicta are received as unquestionable. His constant attitude of mind is that of submission to dogmatic teaching. And a necessary result is a tendency to accept without inquiry whatever is established. Quite opposite is the attitude of mind generated by the cultivation of science. By science, constant appeal is made to individual reason. Its truths are not accepted upon authority alone; but all are at liberty to test them—nay, in many cases, the pupil is required to think out his own conclusions. Every step in a scientific investigation is submitted to his judgment. He is not asked to admit it without seeing it to be true. And the trust in his own powers thus produced, is further increased by the constancy with which Nature justifies his conclusions when they are correctly drawn. From all which there flows that independence which is a most valuable element in character. Nor is this the only moral benefit bequeathed by scientific culture. When carried on, as it should always be, as much as possible under the form of independent research, it exercises perseverance and sincerity. . . .

Lastly we have to assert—and the assertion will, we doubt not, cause extreme surprise—that the discipline of science is superior to that of our ordinary education, because of the *religious* culture that it gives.

Of course we do not here use the words scientific and religious in their ordinary limited acceptations; but in their widest and highest acceptations. Doubtless, to the superstitions that pass under the name of religion, science is antagonistic; but not to the essential religion which these superstitions merely hide. Doubtless, too, in much of the science that is current, there is a pervading spirit of irreligion; but not in that true science which has passed beyond the superficial into the profound. . . .

So far from science being irreligious, as many think, it is the neglect of science that is irreligious—it is the refusal to study the surrounding creation that is irreligious. Take a humble simile. Suppose a writer were daily saluted with praises couched in superlative language. Suppose the wisdom, the grandeur, the beauty of his works, were the constant topics of the eulogies addressed to him. Suppose those who unceasingly uttered these eulogies on his works were content with looking at the outsides of them; and had never opened them, much less tried to understand them. What value should we put upon their praises? What should we think of their sincerity? Yet, comparing small things to great, such is the conduct of mankind in general, in reference to the Universe and its Cause. Nay, it is worse. Not only do they pass by without study, these things which they daily proclaim to be so wonderful; but very frequently they condemn as mere triflers those who give time to the observation of Nature—they actually scorn those who show any active interest in these marvels. We repeat, then, that not science, but the neglect of science, is irreligious. Devotion to science, is a tacit worship—a tacit recognition of worth in the things studied; and by implication in their Cause. It is not a mere lip-homage, but a homage expressed in actions—not a mere professed respect, but a respect proved by the sacrifice of time, thought, and labour.

Nor is it thus only that true science is essentially religious. It is religious, too, inasmuch as it generates a profound respect for, and an implicit faith in, those uniform laws which underlie all things. By accumulated experiences the man of science acquires a thorough belief in the unchanging relations of phenomena—in the invariable connexion of cause and consequence—in the necessity of good or evil results. Instead of the rewards and punishments of traditional belief, which men vaguely hope they may gain, or escape, spite of their disobedience; he finds that there are rewards and punishments in the ordained constitution of things, and that the evil results of disobedience are inevitable. He sees that the laws to which we must submit are not only inexorable but beneficent. He sees that in virtue of these laws, the process of things is ever towards a greater perfection and a higher happiness. Hence he is led constantly to insist on these laws, and is indignant when men disregard them. And thus does he, by asserting the eternal principles of things and the necessity of conforming to them, prove himself intrinsically religious.

To all which add the further religious aspect of science, that it alone can give us true conceptions of ourselves and our relation to the mysteries of existence. At the same time that it shows us all which can be known, it shows us the limits beyond which we can know nothing. Not by dogmatic assertion does it teach the impossibility of comprehending the ultimate cause of things; but it leads us clearly to recognise this impossibility by bringing us in every direction to boundaries we cannot cross. It realizes to us in a way which nothing else can, the littleness of human intelligence in the face of that which transcends human intelligence. While towards the traditions and authorities of men its attitude may be proud, before the impenetrable veil which hides the Absolute its attitude is humble—a true pride and a true humility. Only the sincere man of science (and by this title we do not mean the mere calculator of distances, or analyser of compounds, or labeller of species; but him who through lower truths seeks higher, and eventually the highest)—only the genuine man of science, we say, can truly know how utterly beyond, not only human knowledge, but human conception, is the Universal Power of which Nature, and Life, and Thought are manifestations.

We conclude, then, that for discipline, as well as for guidance, science is of chiefest value. In all its effects, learning the meanings of things, is better than learning the meanings of words. Whether for intellectual, moral, or religious training, the study of surrounding phenomena is immensely superior to the study of grammars and lexicons.

Thus to the question with which we set out—What knowledge is of most worth?—the uniform reply is—Science. This is the verdict on all the counts. For direct self-preservation, or the maintenance of life and health, the all-important knowledge is—Science. For that indirect self-preservation which we call gaining a livelihood, the knowledge of greatest value is—Science. For the due discharge of parental functions, the proper guidance is to be found only in—Science. For that interpretation of national life, past and present, without which the citizen cannot rightly regulate his conduct, the indispensable key is—Science. Alike for the most perfect production and highest enjoyment of art in all its forms, the needful preparation is still—Science. And for purposes of discipline—intellectual, moral, religious—the most efficient study is, once more—Science. The question which at first seemed so perplexed, has become, in the course of our inquiry, comparatively simple. We have not to estimate the degrees of importance of different orders of human activity, and different studies as severally fitting us for them; since we find that the study of Science, in its most comprehensive meaning, is the best preparation for all these orders of activity. We have not to decide between the claims of knowledge of great though conventional value, and knowledge of less though intrinsic value; seeing that the knowledge which we find to be of most value in all other respects, is intrinsically most valuable: its worth is not dependent upon opinion, but is as fixed as is the relation of man to the surrounding world. Necessary and eternal as are its truths, all Science concerns all mankind for all time. Equally at present, and in the remotest future, must it be of incalculable importance for the regulation of their conduct, that men should understand the science of life, physical, mental, and social; and that they should understand all other science as a key to the science of life.

. . . . .

INTELLECTUAL EDUCATION

In education the process of self-development should be encouraged to the fullest extent. Children should be led to make their own investigations, and to draw their own inferences. They should be *told* as little as possible, and induced to *discover* as much as possible. Humanity has progressed solely by self-instruction; and that to achieve the best results, each mind must progress somewhat after the same fashion, is continually proved by the marked success of self-made men. Those who have been brought up under the ordinary school-drill, and have carried away with them the idea that education is practicable only in that style, will think it hopeless to make children their own teachers. If, however, they will call to mind that the all-important knowledge of surrounding objects which a child gets in its early years is got without help—if they will remember that the child is self-taught in the use of its mother tongue—if they will estimate the amount of that experience of life, that out-of-school wisdom, which every boy gathers for himself—if they will mark the unusual intelligence of the uncared-for London *gamin,* as shewn in all the directions in which his faculties have been tasked—if further, they will think how many minds have struggled up unaided, not only through the mysteries of our irrationally-planned *curriculum,* but through hosts of other obstacles besides; they will find it a not unreasonable conclusion, that if the subjects be put before him in right order and right form, any pupil of ordinary capacity will surmount his successive difficulties with but little assistance. Who indeed can watch the ceaseless observation, and inquiry, and inference going on in a child's mind, or listen to its acute remarks on matters within the range of its faculties, without perceiving that these powers which it manifests, if brought to bear systematically upon any studies *within the same range,* would readily master them without help? This need for perpetual telling is the result of our stupidity, not of the child's.

.   .   .   .   .

MORAL EDUCATION

The current assumption respecting family government, as respecting national government, is, that the virtues are with the rulers and the vices with the ruled. Judging by educational theories, men and women are entirely transfigured in the domestic relation. The citizens we do business with, the people we meet in the world, we all know to be very imperfect creatures. In the daily scandals, in the quarrels of friends, in bankruptcy disclosures, in lawsuits, in police reports, we have constantly thrust before us the pervading selfishness, dishonesty, brutality. Yet when we criticise nursery management, and canvass the misbehaviour of juveniles, we habitually take for granted that these culpable men and women are free from moral delinquency in the treatment of their offspring! So far is this from the truth, that we do not hesitate to say that to parental misconduct is traceable a great part of the domestic disorder commonly ascribed to the perversity of children. We do not assert this of the more sympathetic and self-restrained, among whom we hope most of our readers may be classed, but we assert it of the mass. What kind of moral discipline is to be expected from a mother who, time after time, angrily shakes her infant because it will not suckle her, which we

once saw a mother do? How much love of justice and generosity is likely to be instilled by a father who, on having his attention drawn by his child's scream to the fact that its finger is jammed between the window sash and the sill, forthwith begins to beat the child instead of releasing it? Yet that there are such fathers is testified to us by an eye-witness. Or, to take a still stronger case, also vouched for by direct testimony—what are the educational prospects of the boy who, on being taken home with a dislocated thigh, is saluted with a castigation? It is true that these are extreme instances—instances exhibiting in human beings that blind instinct which impels brutes to destroy the weakly and injured of their own race. But extreme though they are, they typify feelings and conduct daily observable in many families. Who has not repeatedly seen a child slapped by nurse or parent for a fretfulness probably resulting from bodily derangement? Who, when watching a mother snatch up a fallen little one, has not often traced, both in the rough manner and in the sharply-uttered exclamation—'You stupid little thing!'—an irascibility foretelling endless future squabbles? Is there not in the harsh tones in which a father bids his children be quiet, evidence of a deficient fellow-feeling with them? Are not the constant, and often quite needless, thwartings that the young experience—the injunctions to sit still, which an active child cannot obey without suffering great nervous irritation, the commands not to look out of the window when travelling by railway, which on a child of any intelligence entails serious deprivation—are not these thwartings, we ask, signs of a terrible lack of sympathy? The truth is, that the difficulties of moral education are necessarily of dual origin—necessarily result from the combined faults of parents and children.

.   .   .   .   .

PHYSICAL EDUCATION

Those who, in eagerness to cultivate their pupils' minds, are reckless of their bodies, do not remember that success in the world depends much more upon energy than upon information; and that a policy which in cramming with information undermines energy, is self-defeating. The strong will and untiring activity which result from abundant animal vigour, go far to compensate even for great defects of education; and when joined with that quite adequate education which may be obtained without sacrificing health, they ensure an easy victory over competitors enfeebled by excessive study: prodigies of learning though they may be. A comparatively small and ill-made engine, worked at high-pressure, will do more than a larger and well-finished one worked at low-pressure. What folly is it, then, while finishing the engine, so to damage the boiler that it will not generate steam! . . .

Our general conclusion is, then, that the ordinary treatment of children is, in various ways, seriously prejudicial. It errs in deficient feeding; in deficient clothing; in deficient exercise (among girls at least); and in excessive mental application. Considering the *régime* as a whole, its tendency is too exacting: it asks too much and gives too little. In the extent to which it taxes the vital energies, it makes the juvenile life much more like the adult life than it should be.

It overlooks the truth that, as in the foetus the entire vitality is expended in the direction of growth—as in the infant, the expenditure of vitality in growth is so great as to leave extremely little for either physical or mental action; so throughout childhood and youth growth is the dominant requirement to which all others must be subordinated: a requirement which dictates the giving of much and the taking away of little—a requirement which, therefore, restricts the exertion of body and mind to a degree proportionate to the rapidity of growth—a requirement which permits the mental and physical activities to increase only as fast as the rate of growth diminishes. . . .

Our education has become almost exclusively mental. Instead of respecting the body and ignoring the mind, we now respect the mind and ignore the body. Both these attitudes are wrong. We do not yet sufficiently realize the truth that as, in this life of ours, the physical underlies the mental, the mental must not be developed at the expense of the physical. The ancient and modern conceptions must be combined.

Perhaps nothing will so much hasten the time when body and mind will both be adequately cared for, as a diffusion of the belief that the preservation of health is a *duty*.

THE CONSERVATIVE STANCE

WILLIAM TORREY HARRIS
Compulsory Education in Relation to Crime and Social Morals [1885] *

What is the training which develops in the child a respect for the social whole, a feeling that society embodies his substantial good,—a feeling of preference for the good of his fellow-man over his own whim or caprice?

Certainly, that training is the training

* William Torrey Harris, *Compulsory Education in Relation to Crime and Social Morals* (Washington, D.C.: privately printed, [1885]), pp. 4–9.

which is given by bringing up the child in the society of others, and causing him to practise perpetually those customs which respect persons and property. A due sense of public opinion, a respect for the ideal standard of right and wrong set up in the community, is the primary requisite.

It is clear that man can live in society and constitute a social whole only so far as individuals are educated out of their natural animal condition, and made to respect social forms more highly than mere animal impulses. Hence, it is clear that society itself rests upon education, in this broad sense of the word.

But what has this to do with school education? Much of the education into a respect for social forms and usages is given by the family, and before the age proper for schooling. Then, again, it must be admitted that another part of this education comes later, and is learned in the pursuit of one's vocation in life,—the education that comes from bending one's energies into a special channel for the purpose of earning a living. Another form of education is to be found in the part that one bears in politics, within one's party, or in the exercise of functions conferred by the State, or still farther in the exercise of patriotic feeling. Lastly, there is the Church, which furnishes a form of education most important, because it lays fullest stress on human duty, basing it on divine commands. The Church educates the individual into the sense of his existence as a mere unsubstantial creature when living in neglect of the divine ideal manhood, but as a substantial and eternally blessed life when lived according to the forms prescribed in religion. These forms are forms that respect the welfare of the whole, and measure the conduct of the individual by his preference of that welfare over his own selfish impulses.

The family, the vocation, the State, the Church, are the four great cardinal institutions of education. The school is only a device brought in to re-enforce these substantial institutions; but it is a very important device, notwithstanding its supplementary character. It may re-enforce the family by giving to the youth the command of such conventionalities as reading and writing and moral behavior; or it may re-enforce the vocation by giving instruction in arts and trades or professions; or it may re-enforce the Church as a Sunday-school, giving instruction in religion; the military school or the naval school may re-enforce the education of the State.

Our question deals directly with the education of the school; but we must carefully bear in mind the several educational functions of these institutions, so as not to overestimate the functions of the school or in any way confound its province with what belongs to the great social institutions.

Family education must furnish that indispensable preliminary education in personal habits, such as cleanliness, care of the person and clothing, respectful treatment of elders and superiors, obedience to authority, the sense of shame, religious observances, and the use of the mother tongue. The school must presuppose that these are already taught by the family; but the school must not neglect them, although it does not make them its special aim. The family does more, in fact, than educate the child in those indispensable things just recited. It builds up within the child's mind the structure of his moral character, making for him a second nature of moral habit and custom, whose limits and boundaries he regards as of supreme moment. This second nature, or moral nature, is secured by daily sacrifice; and all forms of education lay stress upon self-sacrifice as the foundation of their disciplines.

This process which we call education is, in short, essentially the shaping of man by habit into an ideal or spiritual type of being,—a realization of what we call human nature in contradistinction to mere animal nature. It is an artificial life, a conventional form of living; but it is far more substantial and divine than the life of the mere animal man. Man as an animal is a savage: as civilized, he is an ethical being, who has set up within himself a system of duties and obligations which he observes at the expense of neglecting the impulses of his merely animal nature.

To what end is all this? Is it not because man, as an individual, wills to combine with his fellow-men in such a way as to avail himself of the united endeavor of all? By the organization of social institutions, he converts a multitude of atomic individuals into a social unity. The individuals do not get lost in this social unity, like the waves of the sea. But the social unity is of that wonderful character that it re-enforces the might of each individual by the might of the whole.

Speaking technically, the individual becomes the species; or, in giving up by self-sacrifice his selfish peculiarities and devoting himself to the service of others, he gains for himself the service of all mankind. The individuals are transmuted into one grand individual, of which each individual is the head, and each individual is also the foot. According to Kant's definition, a living organism is such that every part of it is alike means and end to all the other parts. So, in this social body, every individual human being is alike the means and the end for all others. Hence there is a "Grand Man," as Swedenborgians say.

In the matter of food, clothing, and shelter, the individual toils in his vocation to produce a special product,—something useful to the rest, and demanded in the market of the world. In return for this gift of his day's labor, he is permitted to draw from the market of the world his share of all the productions collected from all climes, brought hither by the commerce of nations. This is a perpetual process of united human endeavor, in which by self-sacrifice the individual re-enforces himself by the race.

So, too, the family, the most embryonic of human institutions,—the family enables the elder to assist the younger, the mature the immature, the well and strong to assist the sick and weak. It equalizes age and bodily condition, re-enforcing each condition by the aid of all others.

The great object, then, of education is the preparation of the individual for a life in institutions, the preparation of each individual for social combination. Education inculcates sacrifice of animal proclivities, in order to secure a higher well-being in the life of the community.

Crime is, therefore, a reaction on the part of the individual against the very object of education. It attacks the necessary forms of social life, and asserts for itself the right to persist in the form of the non-social individual. Society must defend itself, and reduce the rebellious individual to harmony with itself. Inasmuch as the social form is such that the individual who puts it on and be-comes a member of the family, the community, or the State, does not act directly for himself, but works for others and accepts the service of others in return for his own deed, so, too, punishment for crime takes on the same form: the criminal is made to receive for his deed an equivalent reflected back from society. As his deed injures society, it is returned upon him by society and injures him. If he attacks his neighbors by personal violence, his deed is made to come back to him by physical constraint or even by violent death on the gallows. If he attacks the property of his fellow-men, he is made to suffer in property, in the possession of personal freedom and the right to the products of his own labor. Thus, society treats the criminal who rebels against it just as though he, the criminal, had intended to do a social deed, and not a selfish one. It is a piece of irony. The State says to the criminal: "Of course, you recognize society, and expect to reap what you sow. You have an undoubted right to possess and enjoy the fruits of your own deeds. I will see that they are returned upon you. Your deed of violence on your neighbor shall therefore return upon you. Whatever you do you shall do to yourself."

Turning now from this view of the general educative character of the institutions of society, and the end and aim of all society to aid the individual by the might of the whole, and from this study of crime, let us define for ourselves the place of the school in education, and try to discover its relation to the prevention of crime.

The school, as we have seen, is a means of education auxiliary to each of the four cardinal institutions; and, as such, the school in all of its forms is ethical and preventive of crime. The ordinary type of school—the so-called "common school"—receives the child from the family at the age of five or six years. It receives him into a social body (for the school is a community), and educates him by "discipline" and "instruction," as they are technically called. By "discipline" is meant the training in behavior, a training of the will, moral training. It consists in imposing upon the child a set of forms of behavior rendered necessary in order to secure concert of action,—such forms as regularity, punctuality, silence, and industry. These are the four cardinal duties of the school pupil. Without them, the school cannot act as a unit, instruction cannot be given in classes, and no good result achieved. We call these duties mechanical duties, but they underlie all higher ethics. Without silence in the school, without self-sacrifice on the part of each pupil, restraining his impulse to prate and chatter and occupy the attention of his fellow-pupils, there could be no work done. Each pupil would interfere with the work of every other pupil; and the result would be chaos or worse,—because anarchy is chaos made active and hostile to heaven's first law.

Order is not only the first celestial law, but it is the first law of all social combination. The school could not possibly undertake a more direct and efficient training of the child for social combination than it does undertake in its four cardinal phases of discipline,—regularity, punctuality, silence, and industry.

Its method of securing these items of discipline may be good, bad, or indifferent, according to the pains it takes to convert external constraint into willing obedience and unconscious habit. The good school unquestionably shows us the constant spectacle of good behavior become or becoming a second nature to the pupils, so that there is a maximum of regularity, punctuality, silence, and industry with a minimum of self-consciousness in regard to it, although there is an insight into the necessity of such conformity to rule, and a conscious conviction in favor of it whenever any untoward occasion brings up the question. Consequently there is a minimum of corporal punishment in the good school. Necessary as it is in dealing with crude depravity, the school must have got far beyond that stage of discipline before it can be called "good."

This training of the will, we observe, is a training of each pupil to behave in such a form of artificial or conventional restraint that he may combine in the best manner with his fellow-pupils, and be in a condition to give to and receive from them school instruction. Is it not clear that, once trained to observe set forms of behavior in the school, it becomes a second nature to observe such forms everywhere, and the individual has solved the problem of life so far as the prevention of crime is concerned?

WILLIAM GRAHAM SUMNER
"Integrity in Education" (circa 1885)*

In addressing you on the present occasion, I am naturally led to speak of matters connected with education. We are met here amid surroundings which, to the great majority of us, are unfamiliar, but we are assembled in the atmosphere of our school days and under the inspiration of school memories. Some of us are rapidly approaching, if we have not already reached, the time when our interest in education re-arises in behalf of the next generation. Many are engaged in the work of teaching. Others have only just finished a stage in their education. I therefore propose to speak for a few minutes about integrity in education, believing that it is a subject of great importance at the present time, and one which may justly command your interest.

By integrity in education, I mean the opposite of all sensationalism and humbug in education. I would include under it as objects to be aimed at in education, not only the pursuit of genuine and accurate information and wide knowledge of some technical branch of study, but also real discipline in the use of mental powers, sterling character, good manners, and high breeding.

* William Graham Sumner, "Integrity in Education," from *The Forgotten Man and Other Essays* (New Haven: Yale University Press, 1919; edited by Albert Galloway Keller), pp. 409–419. Copyright © 1919 by Yale University Press. Sumner delivered this address in Hartford, Connecticut, during the 1880's. Used by permission.

Modern sensationalism is conquering a wide field for itself. It is a sort of parasite on high civilization. Its motto is that seeming is as good as being. Its intrinsic fault is its hollowness, insincerity, and falsehood. It deals in dash, flourish, and meretricious pretense. It resides in the form, not in the substance; in the outward appearance, not in the reality. It arouses disgust whenever it is perceived; but the worst of it is that its forms are so various, its manifestations are sometimes so delicate, and it often lies so near to the real and the true, that [it is] difficult to distinguish it. Life hurries past us very rapidly. The interests which demand our attention are very numerous and important. We have not time to scrutinize them all. Then, too, the publicity of everything nowadays prevents modest retirement from being a sign of merit. We go on the principle that if anything is good, it is for the public. Publicity is honorable and proper recognition, and those who have charge of the public trumpets have not time, if they have the ability, to discriminate and criticize very closely.

These reflections account sufficiently for the growth of sensationalism in general. Probably each one sees the mischief which it does in his own circle or profession more distinctly than elsewhere. I have certainly been struck by its influence on education. I see it in common-school education as well as in the universities. It attaches to methods as well as to subjects. It develops a dogmatism of its own. Men without education, or experience as teachers, often take up the pitiful rôle of another class which has come to be called "educators." They start off with a whim or two which they elaborate into theories of education. These they propound with great gravity in speech and writing, producing long discussions as to plans and methods. They are continually searching for a patent method of teaching, or a royal road to learning, when, in fact, the only way to learn is by the labor of the mind in observing, comparing, and generalizing, and any patent method which avoids this irksome labor produces sham results and fails of producing the mental power and discipline of which education consists.

Persons of this class are generally impatient until they have attained some opportunity of putting their notions in practice, and then it is all over with any institution which becomes subject to their wild empiricism.

The saddest results of such proceedings are seen, of course, in the pupils. That a certain school should lose its pupils, or fall into debt, or be closed, is a comparatively small affair. The real mischief is that men should be produced who have no real education, but only a perverse training in putting forward plausible and meretricious appearances. Such education falls in with the outward phenomena of a sensational era and strengthens the impressions which a young and inexperienced observer gets from our modern society, that audacity is the chief of talents, that success or failure is the only measure of right or wrong, that the man to be admired is the one who invents clever tricks to circumvent a rival or opponent, or to skip over a troublesome principle. Young people are more acute in their observations, and they draw inferences and form generalizations more logically and consistently than their elders. They have not yet learned respect for dogmas, traditions, and conventionalities, and their "education" goes on silently but surely, developing a philosophy of life either of one kind or another. If, therefore, you have an educational system consisting of formal cram for recitation or examination, if there is a skimming of textbooks, an empty acquisition of terms, a memorizing of results only, you may pursue high-sounding studies and "cover a great deal of ground," you may have an elaborate curriculum and boast of your proficiency in difficult branches, but you will have no education. You may produce men who can spend a lifetime dawdling over trifles, or men who always scatter their force when they try to think, but you will not have intelligent men with minds well-disciplined and well under control, who are able to apply their full force to any new exigency, or any new problem, and to grasp and conquer it.

The fault here is plain enough. People forget, or do not perceive, that simplicity and modesty are the first requisites in scientific pursuits. We have to begin humbly and with small beginnings if we want to go far. Inflation and pretense only lead to vanity and dil[ett]antism, not to strength and fruitful activity. If we advance eagerly, we deceive ourselves by the notion that we are making grand progress. We are only leaving much undone which we shall have to go back and repair. If, on the other hand, we proceed slowly and with painstaking, every step of advance is sure and genuine. It forms a great vantage-ground for the next step. It strengthens and confirms the mental powers. They come to act with certainty by scientific processes, not by guesses, and this mental discipline enables us to apply our powers wherever we need them. A new task is not a dead wall which is impassable to us because we have never seen one like it before. It is only a new case for the application of old and familiar processes. I never see anything more pitiable than the helpless floundering in a new subject of a young man far on in his education who has never yet learned to use his mind.

In what I have already said about the philosophy of life which a young person forms during the process of education, I have suggested that education must exert a great influence on character. It is sometimes asserted that education ought to mold character—ought to have that object and work towards it, of set purpose. I do not deny this, but I beg you to observe that it obscures the truth. The truth is that education inevitably forms character one way or the other. The error is in speaking as if academical instruction could be carried on without training character, unless the set purpose were entertained. One might read many books on mathematics and the sciences without any very direct moral culture, but everything we learn about this world in which we live reacts in some sort of principle for the regulation of our conduct here. This, however, is not the most important thing. A school is a miniature society. Do we not all know how it forms an atmosphere of its own, how the members make a code of their own, and a public opinion of their own? And then, what a position the teacher holds in this little community. What a dangerous and responsible eminence he occupies. What criticism he undergoes. What an authority his example exerts. So, in this little society, general notions of conduct are unconsciously formed, principles are adopted, habits grow. Every member in his place gives to, and takes from, the common life. It may be well doubted whether there is any association of life which exerts greater influence on character than does the school, and its influence comes, too, just as the formative period, when impressions are most easily received and sink deepest.

Here then is where sensationalism may do its greatest harm, and where integrity of method is most important. The untruthfulness of sensationalism here becomes a germinal principle, which develops into manifold forms of untruthfulness in character. Young people cannot practice show and pretense and yet be taught to believe that the only important thing is what you are, and not at all what people think about you. They cannot practice the devices which give a semblance of learning, and yet be taught to believe that shams are disgraceful and that the frank honesty which owns the worst is a noble trait. They may learn to be ashamed when caught in a false pretense, but they will not learn shame at deceit. I do not say that they will lie or steal, but it is a pitiful code which defines honesty as refraining from seizing other people's property. Honesty is a far wider virtue than not-stealing. It embraces rectitude of motive and purpose, completeness and consistency of principle, and delicacy of responsibility. Truthfulness is the very cornerstone of character, and an instinct of dislike for whatever is false or meretricious is one of the feelings which all sound education must inculcate. It cannot do so, however, unless its *personnel* and its methods are all animated by unflinching integrity.

I mentioned also, at the outset, amongst those things which are embraced in education and to which I desire to see the principle of integrity applied, good manners. Some people make an ostentatious display of neglect for good manners. They think it democratic, or a sign of good fellowship, to be negligent in this respect. They think it something to be boasted of that they have no breeding. Some others make manners supersede education and training and even character. It is the latter error which most invades the sphere of education. We are familiar with its forms. It gives us the mock gentleman of the drawing-room under the same coat with the rowdy of the bar-room. When this system triumphs, it fits our young people out with a few fashionable phrases, which suffice for the persiflage of the drawing-room, when a scientific subject by chance comes up. Girls are the victims of this system far more than boys, but in "cultivated circles" cases are common of this kind, in which a smattering of books has been engrafted on the culture of the dancing school. Young men and young women who have tacked together a few miscellaneous phrases current amongst the learned will deliver you their opinions roundly on the gravest problems of philosophy and science. The phrases which stick in their minds the longest are those which are epigrammatic and paradoxical, whether true or not. In fact, they could not analyze or criticize their mental stock if they should try. They have never learned to consider a subject and form an opinion.

It does not follow, however, that boorishness is erudition, or that it does not belong to education to teach the good manners which are good simply because they are the spontaneous expression of a sound heart and a well-trained mind. Envy, malice, and selfishness are the usual springs of bad manners. They belong to the untrained and brutish man, and it is the province of true education to eradicate them. Hence it is that where true education is wanting we may often find the worst manners with the greatest social experience, and the truest courtesy where there has been genuine discipline, but little acquaintance with social forms.

I have not started this train of thought in order to tell you now that we have enjoyed the true method of education, and that others have not, but there are some things connected with this institution which we may remember with pleasure in view of the reflections which I have presented.

This school was founded so long ago that it already has a body of graduates who are useful and influential men in this city, and many others are scattered up and down the country, useful and honorable, if not celebrated citizens. It was not founded without some struggle, but the more enlightened views prevailed and the results have vindicated those views, I suppose to the satisfaction of everybody. The enterprise enjoyed at the outset the patronage of a body of men of remarkably broad views and sound public spirit. We who profited by its instruction in our time may properly remember those men on this occasion with gratitude and respect. One of them, surpassed by none in zeal to work for and intelligence to plan such an institution, has only just passed away. Your city has been fortunate in possessing such citizens.

The plan on which the school was founded was remarkably wise and farseeing. It has placed the highest education within the reach of every boy in your city who had sufficient industry and self-denial to seek it. Many of you are now in the position of active and responsible citizens. You must regard this institution as one of the boasts of your city. Guard it well. You may not boast of it only. You owe it a debt which you must pay. Every boy and girl who has graduated here owes a debt to the common school system of America. Every man for whom this school has opened a career which would otherwise have been beyond his reach, owes a tenfold debt, both to the common school system and to the class in which he was born. Sectarian interests, private school interests, property interests, and some cliques of "culture" falsely so called, are rallying against the system a force which people as yet underrate. There is no knowing how soon the struggle may open, and you may be called upon to pay the allegiance you owe.

This school has also been remarkably fortunate in the selection of the teachers who have presided over it. We cannot exaggerate the value of this selection. It is by the imperceptible influence of the teacher's character and example that the atmosphere of a school is created. It is from this that the pupils learn what to admire and what to abhor, what to seek and what to shun. It is from this that they learn what methods of action are honorable and what ones are unbecoming. They learn all this from methods of discipline as well as from methods of instruction. They may learn craft and intrigue, or they may learn candor and sincerity. They may learn to win success at any cost, or they may learn to accept failure with dignity, when success could only be won by dishonor.

You know well what has always been the tone impressed on this institution by the teachers we had here. We had many, both gentlemen and ladies, whom we remember with respect and affection. Our later experience of the world and of life has only served to show us more distinctly, in the retrospect, how elevated was their tone, how sincere their devotion, how simple and upright their methods of dealing with us. They were not taskmasters to us, and their work was not a harsh and ungrateful routine to them.

One figure will inevitably arise before the minds of all when these words are said, the figure of one who died with the harness on. I have never seen anywhere, in my experience, a man of more simple and unconscious high-breeding, one who combined more thoroughly the dignity of official authority with the suavity of unrestrained intercourse with his pupils. It is a part of the good fortune which came to us and to this city from this institution that so many young people here enjoyed his personal influence.

It follows, as a natural consequence, from these facts, that we enjoyed here to a high degree what I have described as integrity in education. Sensationalism of any kind has always been foreign to the system here. It must perish in such an atmosphere. We had instruction which was real and solid, which conceded nothing to show and sacrificed nothing to applause. We learned to work patiently for real and enduring results. We learned the faith that what is genuine must outlast and prevail over what is meretricious. We learned to despise empty display. We had also a discipline which was complete and sufficient, but which was attained without friction. There was no sentimentality, no petting, no affectation of free and easy manners. Discipline existed because it was necessary, and it was smooth because it was reasonable.

Now there is nothing to which people apply more severe criticism, as they grow old, than to their education. They find the need of it every day, and they have to ask whether it was sufficient and suited to the purpose or not. It is because we find, I think, that our education here does stand this test that we are able to meet here on an occasion like this with genuine interest and sympathy. The years in their flight have s[ca]ttered us and brought us weighty cares and new interests. We could not lay these aside to come back here for purposes of mere sentiment, or to repeat conventional phrases. We meet on the ground of grateful recollection of benefits received, benefits which we can specify and weigh and measure.

This school must be regarded as a local institution. It belongs to this city and its advantages are offered to the young people who grow up here. I have referred to the exceptional wisdom and enlightenment which presided over its foundation and have nourished its growth. In conclusion, let me refer to what concerns its present and its future. We are reminded by all we see about us here that its building and its appliances are far better than they were in our day. Its prosperity bears witness to its present good management. But, gentlemen, these good things are not to be preserved without vigilance and labor. The same wisdom and enlightenment must preside over the future as over the past. I doubt not that the value of this institution to your city is so fully appreciated, and the methods by which it has been developed are so well understood, that any peril to it or to them would arouse your earnest efforts for its defence. Keep it as it has been, devoted to correct objects by sound methods. Sacrifice nothing to the *éclat* of hasty and false success. Concede nothing to the modern quackery of education. Resist the specious schemes of reckless speculators on educational theories. It is not to be expected that you can escape these dangers any more than other people, and you have to be on your guard against them. You want here an educational institution which shall, in its measure, instruct your children in the best science and thought of the day. You want it to make them masters of themselves and of their powers. You want it to make them practical in the best and only true sense, by making them efficient in dealing intelligently with all the problems of life. The country needs such citizens to-day. The state needs them. Your city needs them. They are needed in all the trades and professions. You must look to such institutions as this to provide them, and you must keep it true to its methods and purpose if you want it to turn out men of moral courage, high principle, and devotion to duty.

AN AMERICAN SYNTHESIS: THE IDEOLOGY OF PROGRESSIVE EDUCATION

FRANCIS WAYLAND PARKER
Notes of Talks on Teaching (1882)*

TALK I.

PRELIMINARY.

I shall try in these lessons to help you learn more of the great art of teaching. We have come from widely different sections, and are, for the most part, strangers to each other, and may find it a little difficult at first to draw together. But a common interest will unite us in the bonds of sympathy and good-fellowship. We have all seen teachers who

* Francis Wayland Parker, *Notes of Talks on Teaching Given at the Martha's Vineyard Summer Institute, July 17 to August 19, 1882* (New York: E. L. Kellogg and Co., 1883; reported by Lelia E. Patridge), pp. 19–24, 157–160, 163–164, 166, 170, 179–182. Apparently these "Notes" are quite authentic. In a statement dated April 19, 1883, Parker wrote: "I have carefully examined the ms. of the 'Notes of Talks on Teaching' prepared by Miss Patridge, and find it substantially correct. /s/ Francis W. Parker"

were so self-satisfied that they seemed—to their own minds—to have rounded the circle of teaching, made the circuit of knowledge and skill complete, and closed their minds against the entrance of all further impressions. Such can never learn till the barriers of conceit behind which they have intrenched themselves are broken down. There are others, the opposite of those just described, who stand like empty pitchers waiting to be filled; they accept any and all methods which are popular, or have some show of authority. Such teachers are imitators merely, and will change when any novelty is brought to their notice. No one was ever great by imitation; imitative power never leads up to creative power. Just here let me say that I shall object quite as strongly to your taking the methods which I may present, unquestioned, as I should to your acceptance of others in which I do not believe.

Again, there are teachers who have some good ways, but who are so prejudiced that they have no regard for anything outside their own work; they cling to the old, have a ready-made objection to the new, and have ceased to examine. Facts are the eyes through which we see laws. There is no better founded pedagogical rule than that the facts must be known before generalizations can be. It follows, then, logically, first, that we cannot know which is the better of two methods without knowing both; second, that we cannot know which is the best without knowing all; and, third, that we cannot know any method without knowing the principles which the method applies. Finally, no one can fairly judge a method by seeing it in operation once or twice, because the application may not be correct, and that cannot be judged unless the foundation principles are known.

The great difficulty in the way is, that teachers are not willing to pay the price of genuine success—that is, untiring study in the most economical directions—hard labor. The demand for good teaching was never so great as now, and no matter where you are, if your work is good it will attract attention.

I have been often asked to explain the so-called Quincy system. So far as I have been able to understand this system, it does not consist of methods with certain fixed details, but rather presents the art of teaching as the greatest art in all the world; and because it is the greatest art, demands two things: first, an honest, earnest investigation of the truth as found in the learning mind and the subjects taught; and, second, the courageous application of the truth when found. In the talks which follow, the only real substantial help I can give you is to aid you in such investigation. All the truths that you may learn must be discovered by yourselves. In this way alone truth is made a living power. Nothing is farther from my present purpose than to have you take what I shall say without the most careful scrutiny. The great mass of teachers simply follow tradition, without questioning whether it be right or wrong, and it requires very little mental action to glide in the ruts of old ways.

The work of the next hundred years will be to break away from traditional forms and come back to natural methods.

Every act has a motive, and it is the motive which colors, directs, forms the action. Consequently, if we would understand the educational work of to-day, we must know its motive, bearing in mind the fact that due allowance must be made for the stupefying effects of long-established usage. The motive commonly held up is the acquisition of a certain degree of skill and an amount of knowledge. The quantity of skill and knowledge is generally fixed by courses of study and the conventional examinations. This is a mistake. In contrast with this false motive of education, to wit, the gaining of skill and knowledge, I place what I firmly believe to be the true motive of all education, which is the harmonious development of the human being, body, mind, and soul. This truth has come to us gradually and in fragments from the great teachers and thinkers of the past. It was two hundred years ago that Comenius said, "Let things that have to be done be learned by doing them." Following this, but broader and deeper in its significance, came Pestalozzi's declaration, "Education is the generation of power." Last of all, summing up the wisdom of those who had preceded him, and embodying it in one grand principle, Froebel announced the true end and aim of all our work—the harmonious growth of the whole being. This is the central point. Every act, thought, plan, method, and question should lead to this. . . .

TECHNICAL SKILL.

In order to train children how to do, we must be able to do ourselves; hence the great importance of that preparation on the part of a teacher which will result in skill in the technics of school work. First of all, the voice should be trained, for a clear musical voice is one of the teacher's most potent qualifications for success, and cannot be overrated. Drill in phonics is necessary, not only to gain the ability to give the slow pronunciation with ease and with natural inflections, but as an aid to perfect articulation and pronunciation. That every teacher should be an expressive reader is self-evident, but it might not occur to all that to be an eloquent talker is also one of the requisites demanded by the New Methods. Faults of tone, modulation, and manner are propagated by the teacher, as well as false syntax and incorrect pronunciation. Then, too, every teacher should be able to sing, and sing well. Music fills the air with beauty, and in the school-room everything should be quiet and musical, with never a harsh note. Failing in this the school lacks harmony. Writing is the second great means of language expression, and should follow immediately upon talking. A teacher who cannot write well, cannot teach writing well; for the copy on the blackboard should be well nigh perfect. Skill is the expression of power, and drawing is the second best way of expressing thought. Given the skill to draw, and a teacher is never helpless, for then he can teach, even if everything else is taken away. Besides, I see a future in drawing which I see in nothing else in the way of developing the mental powers; hence the demands made upon teachers for knowledge and skill in this art must increase with every year. Moulding in sand is one of the best possible ways to teach geography, and should precede map drawing. Moulding in clay is a valuable means of form teaching, and is also the best of preparations for drawing. Last of all, gymnastics—the training of the whole body—is of the utmost importance, not only to insure symmetrical physical development, but to aid in the establishment of good order. Mental action, as you know, depends largely upon physical conditions, and therefore we should train the body that the mind may act. Believing that the skill of the teacher in these directions measures in a great degree his power to do good work, I have endeavored in this course of lessons to provide you with the best of teachers for these different departments. Now, a word of caution: time and strength are both limited, therefore don't try too much; but that you may become experts in these technical matters, let me add, whatever you do try, be sure to follow it up.

· · · · ·

TALK XXIV.

SCHOOL GOVERNMENT.

. . . The highest motive of school government, is to give the child the power and necessary reason to control himself. The immediate and direct motive of school government is, the limitation of mental power to attention. That order is the best, which leads the child to withdraw attention from all other objects except the one in hand. Whether the purpose be thinking, or performing some act of skill, or both, the direct motive of order remains the same. Attention does not consist of the attitude of the body, but of the mind. Pupils may stare intently at a book, may be paying the strictest attention, to the eyes of the teacher, while their minds are "over the hills and far away." There is a vast difference between real and apparent attention. In the one, the thing attended to, fills and controls the consciousness; in the other, the body may be in correct attitude, the eye fixed upon the object, the picture of the object may be upon the retina, but the presence of other objects of thought in the consciousness, shuts out all perception of the object seen. Attention may be impelled by a desire springing from within, from the attractiveness of the object; or compelled from without, by the will of the teacher, who expresses her will by means of rewards and punishments. The first great question, then, for the teacher to decide, is, To what extent can the attractiveness of the object be made to control attention? That is, in what measure can the interest of the child, and the love of work, be excited and quickened, so as to reduce the amount of rewards and punishments?

. . . Play, is God's elementary method of training the child to work. The kindergarten is founded upon the child's intense love of play. Who ever saw anything but constant delight on the faces of the little children in a true kindergarten, where hands and heads and hearts, are in continual harmonious action? The secret lies in the fact that the child's life consists of building, weaving, drawing, taking apart and putting together, and at the same time feeding the imagination for higher flights. When should this delightful play and work stop? When the primary teacher meets him at the door of a castle, fetters his active limbs to a hard seat, and imprisons his expanding mind in a narrow cell walled by unmeaning hieroglyphics? No! A thousand times no! It is cruelty to stop the blessed work done in the kindergarten. Froebel said, that the principles he discovered and advocated, when thoroughly applied, would revolutionize the world; and he was right. In the kindergarten, is the seed-corn and germination of the New Education and the new life. The seed has been planted, the buds and flowers are turned toward the sun: let not the chilling frost of traditional teaching blight and wither them.

. . . One great reason why we continue unnatural teaching, may be found in the fact, that the strongest tendencies and impulses of beautiful child-nature are utterly ignored. Every child loves nature: the birds, flowers, and beasts are a source of exhaustless curiosity and wonder. Carry this love into the school-room, bring the child closer and closer to the thought of God and His creatures, and that implanted desire to know more and more of His works, will never cease.

Reading, writing, spelling, numbers, are simply the means of getting an education, and they may be all beautifully taught, under the delightful stimulus of that which a child loves. The child has a strong desire to express his thoughts in the concrete, by re-creating the forms that come into his mind. He makes mud-pies, hills and valleys, fences and houses, with childish glee. Carry this same impelling tendency into the school-room; lay the foundation of the grand science of geometry, by moulding in clay. Next to the child's love for making forms, comes the joy he finds in drawing; a child loves to draw, as well as if not better, than he loves to talk. Continue this love, by putting crayon or pencil in his hand as soon as he enters school, and give him free room to express all he can. These tendencies are the thrifty roots of true mental and moral growth; foster and nurture them by good teaching, and soon we will have a new and better race of men.

. . . I am aware that I have been painting an ideal school, under ideal teaching. Many of you, no doubt, are anxiously asking the question, "What shall we do, who are training children who have not had the benefits of the kindergarten and the best primary teaching"? I must refer you, for the answer to this important question, to the other means of limiting attention; i.e., your wills used in governing children, who are not attracted by their work. "Fear is the beginning of wisdom." The first important element on your part, necessary to govern a school well, is self-control; the second, courage. The children, after the innocence of the first year is past, have formed a habit that leads them to govern you, if you cannot govern them. They study you, as soldiers do a fortress that they intend to attack. If there is one weak point indicated by your presence, in movement, attitude, or expression, they will make the charge there. If you can be teased, irritated, or made angry they, will find, for want of better things, the greatest pleasure in sticking pins (figurative) into the weak places of your moral anatomy. If you threaten, they take great delight in listening to your threats. If you scold, they will invent ways of perpetuating the process. But if they see in you, a quiet, unalterable determination to control them, softened and strengthened by a great love for children, in most cases, their surrender will be complete and permanent; provided you have already at hand, some nutritious and tasteful food, in the way of good teaching and training. Give them something to do, the first moment you enter the schoolroom. Show them how skilful you are, in all points of technical training, without being ostentatious, and they will soon forget their desire to badger and control you, in the pleasure of doing.

But perfect courage and self-control are ideal again. "What if I haven't these qualities?" you ask. "How shall I meet a rebellious boy?" You see, I cannot avoid the great question of corporal punishment. Putting it in its right place, it is, at best, but a poor substitute for a teacher's lack of moral power and skill. If the choice between anarchy, misrule, and comparative order must be made, I am bound to recommend, in such cases, the judicious use of a good rattan. Corporal punishment is far preferable to scolding; that turns a schoolroom into a perpetual washing-day. It is preferable to many inventions that have been discovered to avoid straightforward punishment—such as shutting children up in dark closets, making them stand for hours in the floor, sending them home, or keeping them after school. If you punish in anger, you simply enhance the difficulty. Anger begets anger. The sting of the rod must be accompanied by the genuine sympathy of real love. This is one of the painful subjects which must be met by every teacher, until the kindergarten and true teaching, have done their effectual work with the little children. "Fear is the beginning of wisdom," but "Perfect love casteth out fear!"

TALK XXV.

MORAL TRAINING.

No matter how much educators may differ in regard to the means and methods of teaching, upon one point there is substantial agreement; viz. that the end and aim of all education, is the development of character. There is also, little or no difference of opinion, in regard to the elements that form the common ideal of character. Love of truth, justice, and mercy; benevolence, humility, energy, patience, and self-control, are recognized the world over, as some of the essentials that should govern human action. True character is recognized and felt, by all classes and conditions of society though they may be incapable of its analysis. Just as the lower types of intellect feel the power of the few masterpieces of art, without knowing its source.

All the knowledge and skill of an individual, all he thinks, knows, and does, is manifested in his character. Character is the summation of all these manifestations. . . . In the school, we find all the primary elements of society, but lacking the conventionalities of the grown-up world; and here, the child acts out his nature, freely. The eager, searching eye of the teacher, fixed upon the good of the child's soul, rather than the quantity of knowledge to be gained, sees through the mass of her little ones, into the weakness of each individual. The order, the writing, the reading, the number lessons, the play-ground, all furnish countless occasions, where the child may be led to act in the right way, from right motives. Selfishness may be turned to benevolence, cruelty to love, deceit to honesty, sullenness to cheerfulness, conceit to humility, and obstinacy to compliance, by the careful leading of the child's heart to the right emotion. But, in this work, the most responsible of all human undertakings, we cannot afford to experiment; there is one indispensable requirement,—*the teacher must know the child, and its nature.*

. . . The end and aim of school education, is to train a child to work, to work systematically, to love work, and to put his brains into work. The clearest expression of thought, is expression in the concrete. Working with the hands, is one great means of primary development. It is also one of the very best means of moral training. From the first, every child has an intense desire to express his thought in some other way, than in language. Froebel discovered this, and founded the Kindergarten. No one can deny, that true Kindergarten training is moral training. Ideas and thoughts come into the mind, demanding expression. The use of that which is expressed, to the child, is the means it gives him, to compare his thought, with its concrete expression. The expression of the form made, compared with the ideal, stimulates to further trials. In making and building, is found the best means of training attention.

I wish to make a sharp distinction here, between *real work,* and *drudgery.* Real work is done on real things, producing tangible results, results that are seen and felt. Real work is adapted at every step to the child's power to do. Every struggle brings success, and makes better work possible. Drudgery, on the other hand, is the forced action of the mind upon that which is beyond mental grasp, upon words that cannot be apprehended, upon lessons not understood. Drudgery, consists, mainly, of the monotonous use of the verbal memory. There is no variety; not a bush or shrub along the pathway. This is the kind of study that produces ill-health. It is the straining of the mind upon disliked subjects, with the single motive, to gain applause, rewards, and diplomas. Thousands of nervous, earnest, faithful girls, spurred on by unwise parents, yearly lose their lives, or become hopeless invalids, in this costly and useless struggle. Real work stimulates every activity of mind and body. It furnishes the variety so necessary to interest, and is like true physical development that exercises every muscle and strengthens the whole man. Real work is always interesting, like real play. No matter how earnest the striving may be, it is followed by a glow of genuine pleasurable emotion.

There is great outcry against our schools and colleges, caused by the suspicion that they educate children to be above manual labor. This suspicion is founded upon fact, I am sorry to say; but the statement of the fact is not correct. Children are educated *below* manual labor. The vague, meaningless things they learn are not adapted to real work; no effectual habits of labor are formed by rote-learning. The student's desire is too often, when he leaves school or college, to get a living by means of empty words. The world has little or no use for such rubbish. That man should gain his bread by the sweat of his brow, is a curse changed to the highest possible blessing. The clergyman, the lawyer, the physician, the teacher, need the benefit of an early training in manual labor, quite as much as the man who is to labor with his hands all his life. Manual labor is the foundation of clear thinking, sound imagination, and good health. There should be no real difference between the methods of our common schools, and the methods of training in manual labor schools. A great mistake has been made in separating them. All school work should be real work. We learn to do by doing. "Satan finds some mischief still, for idle hands to do." The direct influence of real work is, to absorb the attention in the things to be done; leaving no room in the consciousness for idleness, and its consequent vices. Out of real work, the child develops a motive, that directs his life work. Doing work thoroughly, has a great moral influence. One piece of work well done, one subject well mastered, makes the mind far stronger and better, than a smattering of all the branches taught in our schools. School work, and manual labor, have been for a long time divorced; I predict that the time is fast coming, when they will be joined in indissoluble bonds. The time too, is coming, when ministers will urge upon their hearers, the great importance of manual labor, as a means of spiritual growth. At no distant date, industrial rooms will become an indispensable part of every good school; the work of the head, and skill of the hand, will be joined in classroom, and workshop, into one comprehensive method of developing harmoniously the powers of body, mind, and soul. If you would develop morality in the child, train him to work.

In all that I have said, and whatever mistakes I have made, either in thought or expression, I have had but one motive in my heart, and that is, that the dear children of our common country, may receive at our hands, a development of intellectual, moral, and spiritual power, that will enable them to fight life's battle, to be thoughtful conscientious citizens, and prepare them for all that may come thereafter. Whatever we would have our pupils, we must be ourselves.

FRANCIS WAYLAND PARKER
"Democracy and Education" (July, 1891) *

The public school in a republic means that in their early life children of all classes, of all nationalities, of all sects, of rich and poor alike, children of both sexes, shall work together under the highest and best conditions in one community for from eight to twelve years; that they shall have teachers who are trained in the art of all arts—the art of teaching; that in the school, before prejudice has entered their childish souls, before hate has become fixed, before mistrust has become a habit, they shall have influences surrounding them that shall lead to the best work with the best motive of mutual assistance.

Why should boys and girls be taught together from the kindergarten to the university, inclusive? Because they are to live together, to help each other throughout life, and must understand each other. The isolation of sexes in school has begotten mistrust, misunderstanding, false—nay even impure—fancies. The separation of sexes in school is a crime against nature. It is often argued that the sexes differ in intellectual capacity and moral power, and therefore should be separated in education; if this be true, it is all the more reason why they should be together. The strongest factor in education is the reflected light of character upon character.

The social factor in school is the greatest factor of all; it stands higher than subjects of learning, than methods of teaching, than the teacher himself. That which children learn from each other in play or work,

* Francis Wayland Parker, *Talks on Pedagogics: An Outline of the Theory of Concentration* (New York and Chicago: E. L. Kellogg and Co., 1894; a "Talk" presented at the Teachers' Retreat, Chautauqua Assembly, New York, in July, 1891), "Democracy and Education," pp. 420-421, 435-436, 440-442, 446, 450-451.

though the work be drudgery, is the highest that is ever learned. The young man in the university learns more from his mates, of good or bad, than from his professors. This mingling, fusing, and blending give personal power, and make the public school a tremendous force for the upbuilding of democracy.

.   .   .   .   .

What stands in the way of the one precious thing on earth—the freedom of the soul, the advancement of civilization, the happiness of man? I answer, first of all, tradition and its methods. It is impossible to measure the tremendous influence of tradition. It is very difficult to draw the line between education and heredity, but it is far more difficult to draw it between tradition and original personal power. We are at best creatures of tradition, controlled by the past, often bound hand and foot by the fixed habits of mankind; and this influence is dominant to-day in our public schools.

The methods of the few, in their control of the many, still govern our public schools, and to a great degree determine their management: the method of the prison, torture, police, and standing army survives in corporal punishment; the method of bribery,—in reward and prize giving. Both of these immoral methods are absolutely useless; they are the outcome of quantity teaching and the makeshifts of unskilled teachers. Given devoted trained teachers, together with right surroundings and the right educative work, there is absolutely no necessity for either corporal punishment or the bribery of rewards.

The method of mystery still exercises its fearful power,—the inoculated belief that there is something occult and mysterious in knowledge. The height of art is its simplicity, and the same can be said of the art of teaching. What I mean by the control of mystery is illustrated by the attitude of the people toward education. Let a teacher in a country school teach that which a farmer most needs upon the farm,—practical chemistry; let him teach soil, physics, meteorology, zoology of the insects that infest his crops; let him teach arithmetic sensibly by measuring and weighing,—and the farmers would call an indignation meeting and put out a man holding and teaching such new-fangled notions. By learning they mean some mysterious process foreign to them. It does not readily enter their minds that that which is most practical is most logical, and that the old teaching of quantity, the mysterious pedantry of the school-teacher, who is supposed to know so much, is a relic of barbarism, and should hold the same place in the world of affairs as the sickle and the scythe.

.   .   .   .   .

The strongest indication that quantity teaching is in the ascendancy is the profound disbelief of the people in anything like a science of education. I have not time to prove that there is a science of education. If, however, there is no such science, then all the other sciences are myths and delusions. Science is organized knowledge of law; and to deny that there is a science of education is to deny that the development of human beings is governed by law.

Robert Lowe (Lord Sherbrooke), while at the head of the English Privy Council, and Chairman of the Education Committee, was asked to support a movement for the establishment of chairs of pedagogics in universities. "There are no principles of education," said this child of tradition. Less than fifteen years ago a distinguished head of a great university declared that all there is to pedagogics could be learned in an hour and a half! It is well for me to say here, that the gentleman has changed his mind most decidedly; indeed, he is a prominent leader in the so-called new education. Colleges did not recognize this science until within a few years. The first Professor of Pedagogics in America, Miss Bibb, was appointed in the University of Missouri within a few years.

The substantial disbelief in a science of education, and the almost universal indiffer-

ence in regard to it, has one cause, and that cause is quantity teaching; the stimulus to the drudgery is the strap, or, worse, rewards and prizes. A teacher with a conscience, an artist teacher, cannot do such menial service: it would be like requiring a Raphael to paint a board fence. If quantity teaching is ideal teaching, then the plainest deduction is, there is no science of education.

By far the greatest barrier to making the common school what it should and can be, by no means springs from active opposition to the system or from the patronage and pulls of pot-house politicians: *the greatest barrier is the profound indifference of the most intelligent people in regard to the possibilities of radical improvement.* This indifference has been enhanced until within a few years by the influence of colleges and universities, in which quantity instruction has had full swing. The average member of a school board often fancies that he knows all there is to be known about teaching; his measure is the quantity standard, acquired in his own education, which he rigidly enforces, crushing every effort toward quality work.[1]

The social and political standing of teachers indicates the general depreciation of anything like a science of education or an art of teaching. When a discussion of an educational question is provoked, that of "fads," for instance, the opinions of educators are not generally invited; quantity teaching has instructed every citizen in the exact needs of the schools—quantity is the standard of judgment, and the "3 R's" *limit the education of freemen!!*

The people generally have never felt the quickening power of scientific teaching: they believe that their children must submit to the same process that they have endured; they judge teachers by their power to go over the most ground *thoroughly.* To them there is no need of a science of education,

[1] "We have excellent schools and no incompetent teachers" exposes the standard of education on the part of an incompetent member of a school board.

and from the quantity standpoint this judgment is perfectly logical. Scientific teaching means quality of mental action; it means the shortest line of resistance in the advance toward truth; it means the development of mental and moral power—a power that comprehends conditions and overcomes obstacles. I repeat, profound public indifference and an alarming ignorance in regard to the possibilities of education are the greatest obstacles to progress.

Quality is freedom. Let the quality of mental action be right, quantity will take care of itself. The principal cause of so many dullards is quantity teaching. Quantity teaching is strongly intrenched by incompetency. An imperative demand for scientific teaching would throw large numbers of present school incumbents out of business, or make them burn the midnight oil to an extent hitherto unheard of.

.   .   .   .   .

Further, whatever duties the body politic neglects become the prey and spoil of the pot-house politician. Many of the common schools in this republic are managed and controlled by a class of spoilmongers who do not have the faintest idea of education, who indeed do not care what becomes of the schools if their patronage is not touched. Their prey is the innocent little ones; they strike at the very heart of the republic.

If any business in the world, any railroad, bank, store, or manufactory, were conducted upon the same principles (?) that obtain in the management of schools in most of our large cities and in many small districts, hopeless bankruptcy would be the inevitable result. Superintendents are too seldom chosen for professional skill or executive ability, and when they are, the school boards take away from them every vital influence that would make them efficient managers. The vast majority of teachers have not the slightest professional training or the faintest idea of the science of education; thus quantity cram is the rule, and quality teaching the exception. Every other business in the world

requires experts but the care of immortal souls!!

.   .   .   .   .

The common school can be made the best school, in every respect, in the world. Everything is ready to this end, except one thing, and that is the introduction of scientific teaching. The organization is ready, the buildings have been erected, the money is paid: that which awaits is the method of democracy,—that education which shall set the souls of children free.

It is no dream or illusory vision, the realization of a common school, perfect in its appointments, with the means for the highest and best education at hand. All is ready when the people are ready to move, to demand that the methods of quantity shall go, and the methods of quality shall come. Unrealized possibilities of human growth are the infinite line of march.

A school should be a model home, a complete community and embryonic democracy. How? you ask. Again I answer, by putting into every schoolroom an educated, cultured, trained, devoted, child-loving teacher, a teacher imbued with a knowledge of the science of education, and a zealous, enthusiastic applicant of its principles. Where shall we find such teachers? They will spring from the earth and drop from the clouds when they *hear the demand*. We have asked for quantity teachers, and they have come by the tens of thousands. Now, let us demand the *artist teacher,* the teacher trained and skilled in the science of education—a genuine leader of little feet.

Nothing that is good is too good for the child; no thought too deep; no toil too great; no work too arduous: for the welfare of the child means happier homes, better society, a pure ballot and the perpetuity of republican institutions. Not only must the people demand the artist teacher with an authority which will admit no denial, they must also demand that the methods of aristocracy, which have degraded and debased mankind, be totally eliminated from the training of citizens; instead, let us have a doctrine of education which means freedom to every child.

WILLIAM JAMES
Pragmatism (1907) *

LECTURE II
"What Pragmatism Means"

The pragmatic method is primarily a method of settling metaphysical disputes that otherwise might be interminable. Is the world one or many?—fated or free?—material or spiritual?—here are notions either of which may or may not hold good of the world; and disputes over such notions are unending. The pragmatic method in such cases is to try to interpret each notion by tracing its respective practical consequences. What difference would it practically make to any one if this notion rather than that notion were true? If no practical difference whatever can be traced, then the alternatives mean practically the same thing, and all dispute is idle. Whenever a dispute is serious, we ought to be able to show some practical difference that must follow from one side or the other's being right.

A glance at the history of the idea will show you still better what pragmatism means. The term is derived from the same Greek word πράγμα, meaning action, from which our words "practice" and "practical" come. It was first introduced into philosophy by Mr. Charles Peirce in 1878. In an article entitled "How to Make Our Ideas Clear," in the "Popular Science Monthly" for January of that year Mr. Peirce, after pointing out that our beliefs are really rules for action, said that, to develop a thought's meaning, we need only determine what conduct it is fitted to produce: that conduct is for us its

* William James, *Pragmatism: A New Name for Some Old Ways of Thinking; Popular Lectures on Philosophy* (New York: Longmans, Green, 1907), Lecture II, "What Pragmatism Means," pp. 45–47, 49–51, 53, 54–58, 68, 75–76; Lecture VI, "Pragmatism's Conception of Truth," pp. 198–201, 224–225. By permission.

sole significance. And the tangible fact at the root of all our thought-distinctions, however subtle, is that there is no one of them so fine as to consist in anything but a possible difference of practice. To attain perfect clearness in our thoughts of an object, then, we need only consider what conceivable effects of a practical kind the object may involve—what sensations we are to expect from it, and what reactions we must prepare. Our conception of these effects, whether immediate or remote, is then for us the whole of our conception of the object, so far as that conception has positive significance at all.

This is the principle of Peirce, the principle of pragmatism. . . .

It is astonishing to see how many philosophical disputes collapse into insignificance the moment you subject them to this simple test of tracing a concrete consequence. There can *be* no difference anywhere that does n't *make* a difference elsewhere—no difference in abstract truth that does n't express itself in a difference in concrete fact and in conduct consequent upon that fact, imposed on somebody, somehow, somewhere, and somewhen. The whole function of philosophy ought to be to find out what definite difference it will make to you and me, at definite instants of our life, if this world-formula or that world-formula be the true one.

There is absolutely nothing new in the pragmatic method. Socrates was an adept at it. Aristotle used it methodically. Locke, Berkeley, and Hume made momentous contributions to truth by its means. Shadworth Hodgson keeps insisting that realities are only what they are "known as." But these forerunners of pragmatism used it in fragments: they were a prelude only. Not until in our time has it generalized itself, become conscious of a universal mission, pretended to a conquering destiny. I believe in that destiny, and I hope I may end by inspiring you with my belief.

Pragmatism represents a perfectly familiar attitude in philosophy, the empiricist attitude, but it represents it, as it seems to me, both in a more radical and in a less objectionable form than it has ever yet assumed. A pragmatist turns his back resolutely and once for all upon a lot of inveterate habits dear to professional philosophers. He turns away from abstraction and insufficiency, from verbal solutions, from bad *a priori* reasons, from fixed principles, closed systems, and pretended absolutes and origins. He turns towards concreteness and adequacy, towards facts, towards action and towards power. That means the empiricist temper regnant and the rationalist temper sincerely given up. It means the open air and possibilities of nature, as against dogma, artificiality, and the pretence of finality in truth.

At the same time it does not stand for any special results. It is a method only. . . .

If you follow the pragmatic method, you cannot look on any such word as closing your quest. You must bring out of each word its practical cash-value, set it at work within the stream of your experience. It appears less as a solution, then, than as a program for more work, and more particularly as an indication of the ways in which existing realities may be *changed*.

Theories thus become instruments, not answers to enigmas, in which we can rest. We don't lie back upon them, we move forward, and, on occasion, make nature over again by their aid. Pragmatism unstiffens all our theories, limbers them up and sets each one at work. . . .

No particular results then, so far, but only an attitude of orientation, is what the pragmatic method means. *The attitude of looking away from first things, principles, "categories," supposed necessities; and of looking towards last things, fruits, consequences, facts.*

So much for the pragmatic method! You may say that I have been praising it rather than explaining it to you, but I shall presently explain it abundantly enough by showing how it works on some familiar problems. Meanwhile the word pragmatism has come to be used in a still wider sense, as meaning

also a certain *theory of truth*. I mean to give a whole lecture to the statement of that theory, after first paving the way, so I can be very brief now. But brevity is hard to follow, so I ask for your redoubled attention for a quarter of an hour. If much remains obscure, I hope to make it clearer in the later lectures.

One of the most successfully cultivated branches of philosophy in our time is what is called inductive logic, the study of the conditions under which our sciences have evolved. Writers on this subject have begun to show a singular unanimity as to what the laws of nature and elements of fact mean, when formulated by mathematicians, physicists and chemists. When the first mathematical, logical, and natural uniformities, the first *laws*, were discovered, men were so carried away by the clearness, beauty and simplification that resulted, that they believed themselves to have deciphered authentically the eternal thoughts of the Almighty. His mind also thundered and reverberated in syllogisms. He also thought in conic sections, squares and roots and ratios, and geometrized like Euclid. He made Kepler's laws for the planets to follow; he made velocity increase proportionally to the time in falling bodies; he made the law of the sines for light to obey when refracted; he established the classes, orders, families and genera of plants and animals, and fixed the distances between them. He thought the archetypes of all things, and devised their variations; and when we rediscover any one of these his wondrous institutions, we seize his mind in its very literal intention.

But as the sciences have developed farther, the notion has gained ground that most, perhaps all, of our laws are only approximations. The laws themselves, moreover, have grown so numerous that there is no counting them; and so many rival formulations are proposed in all the branches of science that investigators have become accustomed to the notion that no theory is absolutely a transcript of reality, but that any one of them may from some point of view be useful. Their great use is to summarize old facts and to lead to new ones. They are only a man-made language, a conceptual shorthand, as some one calls them, in which we write our reports of nature; and languages, as is well known, tolerate much choice of expression and many dialects.

Thus human arbitrariness has driven divine necessity from scientific logic. If I mention the names of Sigwart, Mach, Ostwald, Pearson, Milhaud, Poincaré, Duhem, Heymans, those of you who are students will easily identify the tendency I speak of, and will think of additional names.

Riding now on the front of this wave of scientific logic Messrs. Schiller and Dewey appear with their pragmatistic account of what truth everywhere signifies. Everywhere, these teachers say, "truth" in our ideas and beliefs means the same thing that it means in science. It means, they say, nothing but this, *that ideas (which themselves are but parts of our experience) become true just in so far as they help us to get into satisfactory relation with other parts of our experience,* to summarize them and get about among them by conceptual short-cuts instead of following the interminable succession of particular phenomena. Any idea upon which we can ride, so to speak; any idea that will carry us prosperously from any one part of our experience to any other part, linking things satisfactorily, working securely, simplifying, saving labor; is true for just so much, true in so far forth, true *instrumentally.* This is the "instrumental" view of truth taught so successfully at Chicago, the view that truth in our ideas means their power to "work," promulgated so brilliantly at Oxford. . . .

See the exquisite contrast of the types of mind! The pragmatist clings to facts and concreteness, observes truth at its work in particular cases, and generalizes. Truth, for him, becomes a class-name for all sorts of definite working-values in experience. For the rationalist it remains a pure abstraction, to the bare name of which we must defer. When the pragmatist undertakes to show in detail just *why* we must defer, the rationalist is unable to recognize the concretes from which his own abstraction is taken. He accuses us of *denying* truth; whereas we have only sought to trace exactly why people follow it and always ought to follow it. Your typical ultra-abstractionist fairly shudders at concreteness: other things equal, he positively prefers the pale and spectral. If the two universes were offered, he would always choose the skinny outline rather than the rich thicket of reality. It is so much purer, clearer, nobler. . . .

I am well aware how odd it must seem to some of you to hear me say that an idea is "true" so long as to believe it is profitable to our lives. That it is *good,* for as much as it profits, you will gladly admit. If what we do by its aid is good, you will allow the idea itself to be good in so far forth, for we are the better for possessing it. But is it not a strange misuse of the word "truth," you will say, to call ideas also "true" for this reason?

To answer this difficulty fully is impossible at this stage of my account. You touch here upon the very central point of Messrs. Schiller's, Dewey's and my own doctrine of truth, which I can not discuss with detail until my sixth lecture. Let me now say only this, that truth is *one species of good,* and not, as is usually supposed, a category distinct from good, and co-ordinate with it. *The true is the name of whatever proves itself to be good in the way of belief, and good, too, for definite, assignable reasons.*

·   ·   ·   ·   ·

LECTURE VI

"Pragmatism's Conception of Truth"

Truth, as any dictionary will tell you, is a property of certain of our ideas. It means their "agreement," as falsity means their disagreement, with "reality." Pragmatists and intellectualists both accept this definition as a matter of course. They begin to quarrel only after the question is raised as to what may precisely be meant by the term "agreement," and what by the term "reality," when reality is taken as something for our ideas to agree with.

In answering these questions the pragmatists are more analytic and painstaking, the intellectualists more offhand and irreflective. The popular notion is that a true idea must copy its reality. Like other popular views, this one follows the analogy of the most usual experience. Our true ideas of sensible things do indeed copy them. Shut your eyes and think of yonder clock on the wall, and you get just such a true picture or copy of its dial. But your idea of its "works" (unless you are a clockmaker) is much less of a copy, yet it passes muster, for it in no way clashes with the reality. Even though it should shrink to the mere word "works," that word still serves you truly; and when you speak of the "time-keeping function" of the clock, or of its spring's "elasticity," it is hard to see exactly what your ideas can copy.

You perceive that there is a problem here. Where our ideas cannot copy definitely their object, what does agreement with that object mean? Some idealists seem to say that they are true whenever they are what God means that we ought to think about that object. Others hold the copy-view all through, and speak as if our ideas possessed truth just in proportion as they approach to being copies of the Absolute's eternal way of thinking.

These views, you see, invite pragmatistic discussion. But the great assumption of the intellectualists is that truth means essentially an inert static relation. When you've got your true idea of anything, there's an end of the matter. You're in possession; you *know;* you have fulfilled your thinking destiny. You are where you ought to be mentally; you have obeyed your categorical imperative; and nothing more need follow on that climax of your rational destiny. Epistemologically you are in stable equilibrium.

Pragmatism, on the other hand, asks its usual question. "Grant an idea or belief to be true," it says, "what concrete difference will its being true make in any one's actual life? How will the truth be realized? What experiences will be different from those which would obtain if the belief were false? What, in short, is the truth's cash-value in experiential terms?"

The moment pragmatism asks this question, it sees the answer: *True ideas are those that we can assimilate, validate, corroborate and verify. False ideas are those that we can not.* That is the practical difference it makes to us to have true ideas; that, therefore, is the meaning of truth, for it is all that truth is known-as.

This thesis is what I have to defend. The truth of an idea is not a stagnant property inherent in it. Truth *happens* to an idea. It *becomes* true, is *made* true by events. Its verity *is* in fact an event, a process: the process namely of its verifying itself, its veri-*fication.* Its validity is the process of its valid-*ation.* . . .

I have already insisted on the fact that truth is made largely out of previous truths. Men's beliefs at any time are so much experience *funded.* But the beliefs are themselves parts of the sum total of the world's experience, and become matter, therefore, for the next day's funding operations. So far as reality means experienceable reality, both it and the truths men gain about it are everlastingly in process of mutation—mutation towards a definite goal, it may be—but still mutation.

WILLIAM JAMES
The Meaning of Truth: A Sequel to "Pragmatism"—Author's Preface (1909) *

Most of the pragmatist and anti-pragmatist warfare is over what the word "truth" shall be held to signify, and not over any of the facts embodied in truth-situations; for both pragmatists and anti-pragmatists believe in existent objects, just as they believe in our ideas of them. The difference is that

* William James, *The Meaning of Truth: A Sequel to "Pragmatism"* (New York: Longmans, Green, 1909), Preface, pp. xi–xiv. By permission.

when the pragmatists speak of truth, they mean exclusively something about the ideas, namely their workableness; whereas when anti-pragmatists speak of truth they seem most often to mean something about the objects. Since the pragmatist, if he agrees that an idea is "really" true, also agrees to whatever it says about its object; and since most anti-pragmatists have already come round to agreeing that, if the object exists, the idea that it does so is workable; there would seem so little left to fight about that I might well be asked why instead of re-printing my share in so much verbal wrangling, I do not show my sense of "values" by burning it all up.

I understand the question and I will give my answer. I am interested in another doctrine in philosophy to which I give the name of radical empiricism, and it seems to me that the establishment of the pragmatist theory of truth is a step of first-rate importance in making radical empiricism prevail. Radical empiricism consists first of a postulate, next of a statement of fact, and finally of a generalized conclusion.

The postulate is that the only things that shall be debatable among philosophers shall be things definable in terms drawn from experience. (Things of an unexperienceable nature may exist ad libitum, but they form no part of the material for philosophic debate.)

The statement of fact is that the relations between things, conjunctive as well as disjunctive, are just as much matters of direct particular experience, neither more so nor less so, than the things themselves.

The generalized conclusion is that therefore the parts of experience hold together from next to next by relations that are themselves parts of experience. The directly apprehended universe needs, in short, no extraneous trans-empirical connective support, but possesses in its own right a concatenated or continuous structure.

The great obstacle to radical empiricism in the contemporary mind is the rooted rationalist belief that experience as immediately given is all disjunction and no conjunction, and that to make one world out of this separateness, a higher unifying agency must be there. In the prevalent idealism this agency is represented as the absolute all-witness which "relates" things together by throwing "categories" over them like a net. The most peculiar and unique, perhaps, of all these categories is supposed to be the truth-relation, which connects parts of reality in pairs, making of one of them a knower, and of the other a thing known, yet which is itself contentless experientially, neither describable, explicable, nor reduceable to lower terms, and denotable only by uttering the name "truth."

The pragmatist view, on the contrary, of the truth-relation is that it has a definite content, and that everything in it is experienceable. Its whole nature can be told in positive terms. The "workableness" which ideas must have, in order to be true, means particular workings, physical or intellectual, actual or possible, which they may set up from next to next inside of concrete experience.

JOHN DEWEY
"The Psychological Aspect of the School Curriculum" (1897) *

There is a rough and ready way, in current pedagogical writing, of discriminating between the consideration of the curriculum or subject-matter of instruction and the method. The former is taken to be objective in character, determined by social and logical considerations without any particular reference to the nature of the individual. It is supposed that we can discuss and define geography, mathematics, language, etc., as studies of the school course, without having recourse to principles which flow from the psychology of the individual. The standpoint of method is taken when we have to reckon with the adaptation of this objective given material to the processes, interests, and pow-

* John Dewey, "The Psychological Aspect of the School Curriculum," *Educational Review*, XIII (April, 1897), 356–369.

ers of the individual. The study is there ready-made; method inquires how the facts and truths supplied may be most easily and fruitfully assimilated by the pupil.

Taken as a convenient working distinction, no great harm is likely to arise from this parceling out of the two phases of instruction. When pressed, however, into a rigid principle, and made the basis for further inferences, or when regarded as a criterion by reference to which other educational questions may be decided, the view is open to grave objections.

On the philosophic side it sets up a dualism which, to my own mind, is indefensible; and which, from any point of view, is questionable. Moreover, many of the writers who hold this distinction on the practical or pedagogical side would certainly be the last to admit it if it were presented to them as a philosophic matter. This dualism is one between mental operation on one side, and intellectual content on the other—between mind and the material with which it operates; or, more technically, between subject and object in experience. The philosophic presupposition is that there is somehow a gap or chasm between the workings of the mind and the subject-matter upon which it works. In taking it for granted that the subject-matter may be selected, defined, and arranged without any reference to psychological consideration (that is, apart from the nature and mode of action of the individual), it is assumed that the facts and principles exist in an independent and external way, without organic relation to the methods and functions of mind. I do not see how those who refuse to accept this doctrine as good philosophy can possibly be content with the same doctrine when it presents itself in an educational garb.

This dualism reduces the psychological factor in education to an empty gymnastic. It makes it a mere formal training of certain distinct powers called perception, memory, judgment, which are assumed to exist and operate by themselves, without organic reference to the subject-matter. . . .

The doctrine, if logically carried out in practice, is even less attractive than upon the strictly theoretical side. The material, the stuff to be learned, is, from this point of view, inevitably something external, and therefore indifferent. There can be no native and intrinsic tendency of the mind toward it, nor can it have any essential quality which stimulates and calls out the mental powers. No wonder the upholders of this distinction are inclined to question the value of interest in instruction, and to throw all the emphasis upon the dead lift of effort. The externality of the material makes it more or less repulsive to the mind. The pupil, if left to himself, would, upon this assumption, necessarily engage himself upon something else. It requires a sheer effort of will power to carry the mind over from its own intrinsic workings and interests to this outside stuff.

On the other side, the mental operation being assumed to go on without any intrinsic connection with the material, the question of method is degraded to a very low plane. Of necessity it is concerned simply with the various devices which have been found empirically useful, or which the ingenuity of the individual teacher may invent. There is nothing fundamental or philosophical which may be used as a standard in deciding points in method. It is simply a question of discovering the temporary expedients and tricks which will reduce the natural friction between the mind and the external material. No wonder, once more, that those who hold even unconsciously to this dualism (when they do not find the theory of effort to work practically) seek an ally in the doctrine of interest interpreted to mean the amusing, and hold that the actual work of instruction is how to make studies which have no intrinsic interest interesting —how, that is, to clothe them with factitious attraction, so that the mind may swallow the repulsive dose unaware.

The fact that this dualistic assumption gives material on one hand such an external and indifferent character, while on the other it makes method trivial and arbitrary, is certainly a reason for questioning it. . . .

What, then, do we mean by a study in the curriculum? What does it stand for? What fixes the place which it occupies in the school work? What furnishes it its end? What gives it its limitations? By what standard do we measure its value? The ordinary schoolteacher is not, of course, called upon to raise such questions. He has certain subjects given to him. The curriculum is, as we say, laid out, and the individual teacher has to do the best he can with the studies as he finds them. But those who are concerned theoretically with the nature of education, or those who have to do practically with the organization of the course of study—those who "lay out" the course—cannot afford to ignore these questions. . . .

The primary point of concern in education is beyond question with the subject as a special mode of personal experience, rather than with the subject as a body of wrought-out facts and scientifically tested principles. To the child, simply because he is a child, geography is not, and cannot be, what it is to the one who writes the scientific treatise on geography. *The latter has had exactly the experience which it is the problem of instruction to induce on the part of the former.* To identify geography as it is to the pupil of seven or fifteen with geography as it is to Humboldt or Ritter is a flagrant case of putting the cart before the horse. With the child, instruction must take the standpoint not of the accomplished results, but of the crude beginnings. We must discover what there is lying within the child's present sphere of experience (or within the scope of experiences which he can easily get) which deserves to be called geographical. It is not the question of *how* to teach the child geography, but first of all the question *what* geography is for the child.

There is no fixed body of facts which, in itself, is eternally set off and labeled geography, natural history, or physics. Exactly the same objective reality will be one or other, or none of these three, according to the

interest and intellectual attitude from which it is surveyed. Take a square mile of territory, for example; if we view it from one interest, we may have trigonometry; from another standpoint we should label the facts regarding it botany; from still another, geology; from another, mineralogy; from another, geography; from still another standpoint it would become historical material. There is absolutely nothing in the fact, as an objective fact, which places it under any one head. Only as we ask what kind of an experience is going on, what attitude some individual is actually assuming, what purpose or end some individual has in view, do we find a basis for selecting and arranging the facts under the label of any particular study.

Even in the most logical and objective consideration, we do not, therefore, really escape from the psychological point of view. We do not get away from all reference to the person having an experience, and from the point of how and why he has it. We are simply taking the psychology of the adult (that is to say, of the one who has already gone through a certain series of experiences), of one who has, therefore, a certain background and course of growth, and substituting the mature and developed interest of such a person for the crude and more or less blind tendency which the child has. If we act upon this distinction in our educational work, it means that we substitute the adult's consciousness for the child's consciousness.

I repeat, therefore, that the first question regarding any subject of study is the psychological one, What is that study, considered as a form of living, immediate, personal experience? What is the interest in that experience? What is the motive or stimulus to it? How does it act and react with reference to other forms of experience? How does it gradually differentiate itself from others? And how does it function so as to give them additional definiteness and richness of meaning? We must ask these questions not only with reference to the child in general, but with reference to the specific child—the child of a certain age, of a certain degree of attainment, and of specific home and neighborhood contacts.

Until we ask such questions the consideration of the school curriculum is arbitrary and partial, because we have not the ultimate criterion for decision before us. The problem is not simply what facts a child is capable of grasping or what facts can be made interesting to him, but what experience does he himself have in a given direction. The subject must be differentiated out of that experience in accordance with its own laws. Unless we know what these laws are, what are the intrinsic stimuli, modes of operation and functions of a certain form of experience, we are practically helpless in dealing with it. We may follow routine, or we may follow abstract logical consideration, but we have no decisive educational criterion. It is the problem of psychology to answer these questions; and when we get them answered, we shall know how to clarify, build up, and put in order the content of experience, so that in time it will grow to include the systematic body of facts which the adult's consciousness already possesses.

This is a distinctly practical question—a question which concerns the actual work of the schoolroom and not simply the professorial chair. Upon the whole, I believe that the crying evil in instruction to-day is that the subject-matter of the curriculum, both as a whole and in its various stages, is selected and determined on the objective or logical basis instead of upon the psychological. The humble pedagogue stands with his mouth and his hands wide open, waiting to receive from the abstract scientific writers the complete system which the latter, after centuries of experience and toilsome reflection, have elaborated. Receiving in this trustful way the ready-made "subject," he proceeds to hand it over in an equally ready-made way to the pupil. The intervening medium of communication is simply certain external attachments in the way of de-

vices and tricks called "method," and certain sugar-coatings in the way of extrinsic inducements termed "arousing of interest."

All this procedure overlooks the point that the first pedagogical question is, How, out of the crude native experience which the child already has, the complete and systematic knowledge of the adult consciousness is gradually and systematically worked out. The first question is, How experience grows; not, What experience the adult has succeeded in getting together during his development from childhood to maturity. The scientific writer, having a background of original experience, and having passed through the whole period of growth, may safely assume them and not get lost; the subject-matter standing to him in its proper perspective and relation. But when this adult material is handed over ready-made to the child, the perspective is ignored, the subject is forced into false and arbitrary relations, the intrinsic interest is not appealed to, and the experience which the child already has, which might be made a vital instrument of learning, is left unutilized and to degenerate.

The genuine course of procedure may be stated as follows:

We have first to fix attention upon the child to find out what kind of experience is appropriate to him at the particular period selected; to discover, if possible, what it is that constitutes the special feature of the child's experience at this time; and why it is that his experience takes this form rather than another. This means that we observe in detail what experiences have most meaning and value to him, and what attitude he assumes toward them. We search for the point, or focus, of interest in these experiences. We ask where they get their hold upon him and how they make their appeal to him. We endeavor by observation and reflection to see what tastes and powers of the child are active in securing these experiences. We ask what habits are being formed; what ends and aims are being proposed. We inquire what the stimuli are and what responses the child is making. We ask what impulses are struggling for expression; in what characteristic ways they find an outlet; and what results inure to the child through their manifestation.

All this is a psychological inquiry. It may be summed up, if I am permitted to use the word, under the head of "interest." Our study is to find out what the actual interests of the child are; or, stated on the objective side, what it is in the world of objects and persons that attracts and holds the child's attention, and that constitutes for him the significance and worth of his life. . . .

In the second place, in saying that these psychical phenomena afford opportunities, give clews, and furnish leverages, we are virtually saying that they set problems. They need to be interpreted. They have the value of signs, and, like all signs, must be interpreted into the realities for which they stand. Now it is the province of the subject-matter on its logical and objective side to help us in this work of translation. We see the meaning of the beginning through reading it in terms of its outcome; of the crude in terms of the mature. We see, for example, what the first babbling instincts and impulses mean by contemplating the articulate structure of language as an instrument of social communication, of logical thought, and of artistic expression. We see what the interest of the child in counting and measuring represents, by viewing the developed system of arithmetic and geometry. The original phenomena are prophecy. To realize the full scope of the prophecy, its promise and potency, we must look at it not in its isolation, but in its fulfillment.

This doctrine is misconceived when taken to mean that these accomplished results of the adult experience may be made a substitute for the child's experience, or may be directly inserted into his consciousness through the medium of instruction, or, by any external device whatsoever, grafted upon him. Their value is not that of furnishing the immediate material or subject-matter of instruction, any more than the phenomena of interest furnish the final standards and goals of instruction. The function of this ordered and arranged experience is strictly interpretative or mediatory. We must bear it in mind in order to appreciate, to place, the value of the child's interests as he manifests them.

Thus we come, in the third place, to the selection and determination of the material of instruction, and to its adaptation to the process of learning. This involves the interaction of two points of view just considered. It is working back and forth from one to the other. The transitory and more or less superficial phenomena of child life must be viewed through their full fruitage. The objective attainments of the adult consciousness must be taken out of their abstract and logical quality and appreciated as living experiences of the concrete individual. Then we may see what both subject-matter and method of instruction stand for. The subject-matter is the present experience of the child, taken in the light of what it may lead to. The method is the subject-matter rendered into the actual life experience of some individual. The final problem of instruction is thus the reconstruction of the individual's experience, through the medium of what is seen to be involved in that experience as its matured outgrowth.

We have two counterpart errors: one is the appeal to the child's momentary and more or less transitory interest, as if it were final and complete, instead of a sign of nascent power; as if it were an end instead of an instrument; as if it furnished an ideal instead of setting a problem. The other is taking the studies from the scientific standpoint, and regarding them as affording the subject-matter of the curriculum. As the phenomena of interest need to be controlled by reference to their fullest possibility, so the scientific content of the studies needs to be made over by being "psychologized," seen as what some concrete individual may experience in virtue of his own impulses, interests, and powers. It is the element of control which takes us out of the region of arbitrary tricks and devices into the domain of orderly method. It is the making over and psychological translation of the studies which renders them a genuine part of the *Lehrstoff* of the pupil. It is because of the necessity of this operation, the transfiguring of the dead objective facts by seeing them as thoughts and feelings and acts of some individual, that we are justified in saying that there is a psychological aspect to the curriculum.

In applying this to the actual studies which make up the present curriculum, no one would deny, I suppose, that language, literature, history, and art, being manifestations of human nature, cannot be understood in their entirety, nor yet fully utilized in the work of instruction, until they are regarded as such manifestation. But we must go a point further, and recognize that in education we are not concerned with the language that has been spoken, the literature that has been created, the history that has been lived, but with them only as they become a part of what an individual reports, expresses, and lives. Even in the sciences, where we appear to be dealing with matters that are more remote from the individual, we need to remember that educationally our business is not with science as a body of fixed facts and truths, but with it as a method and attitude of experience. Science in the sense in which we can find it stated in books, or set forth in lectures, is not the subject-matter of instruction. Anything that can be found in these forms is simply an index and instrument. It sets before us our goal—the attitude of [m]ind and [k]ind of experience which we wish to induce; when it is read over, into psychological terms, it helps us reach our goal; but without the psychological rendering, it is inert, mechanical, and deadening.

Because the actual, as distinct from the abstract or possible, subject is a mode of personal experience, not simply an ordered collection of facts and principles, the curriculum as a whole, and every study in detail, has a psychological side whose neglect and denial lead to confusion in pedagogic theory; and in educational practice to the dead following of historic precedent and routine, or else to the substitution of the abstract and the formal for the vital and personal.

JOHN DEWEY
The School and Society (1899) *

It is useless to bemoan the departure of the good old days of children's modesty, reverence, and implicit obedience, if we expect merely by bemoaning and by exhortation to bring them back. It is radical conditions which have changed, and only an equally radical change in education suffices. We must recognize our compensations—the increase in toleration, in breadth of social judgment, the larger acquaintance with human nature, the sharpened alertness in reading signs of character and interpreting social situations, greater accuracy of adaptation to differing personalities, contact with greater commercial activities. These considerations mean much to the city-bred child of today. Yet there is a real problem: how shall we retain these advantages, and yet introduce into the school something representing the other side of life—occupations which exact personal responsibilities and which train the child with relation to the physical realities of life?

When we turn to the school, we find that one of the most striking tendencies at present is toward the introduction of so-called manual training, shop-work, and the household arts—sewing and cooking.

This has not been done "on purpose," with a full consciousness that the school must now supply that factor of training formerly taken care of in the home, but rather by instinct, by experimenting and finding that such work takes a vital hold of pupils and gives them something which was

* John Dewey, *The School and Society: Being Three Lectures* (Chicago: University of Chicago Press, 1899; supplemented by "A Statement of the University Elementary School"), Lecture I, "The School and Social Progress," pp. 25–32, 40–44; and Lecture III, "Waste in Education," pp. 89–90, 97, 106–107.

not to be got in any other way. Consciousness of its real import is still so weak that the work is often done in a half-hearted, confused, and unrelated way. The reasons assigned to justify it are painfully inadequate or sometimes even positively wrong.

If we were to cross-examine even those who are most favorably disposed to the introduction of this work into our school system, we should, I imagine, generally find the main reasons to be that such work engages the full spontaneous interest and attention of the children. It keeps them alert and active, instead of passive and receptive; it makes them more useful, more capable, and hence more inclined to be helpful at home; it prepares them to some extent for the practical duties of later life—the girls to be more efficient house managers, if not actually cooks and sempstresses; the boys (were our educational system only adequately rounded out into trade schools) for their future vocations. I do not underestimate the worth of these reasons. Of those indicated by the changed attitude of the children I shall indeed have something to say in my next talk, when speaking directly of the relationship of the school to the child. But the point of view is, upon the whole, unnecessarily narrow. We must conceive of work in wood and metal, of weaving, sewing, and cooking, as methods of life not as distinct studies.

We must conceive of them in their social significance, as types of the processes by which society keeps itself going, as agencies for bringing home to the child some of the primal necessities of community life, and as ways in which these needs have been met by the growing insight and ingenuity of man; in short, as instrumentalities through which the school itself shall be made a genuine form of active community life, instead of a place set apart in which to learn lessons.

A society is a number of people held together because they are working along common lines, in a common spirit, and with reference to common aims. The common needs and aims demand a growing interchange of thought and growing unity of sympathetic feeling. The radical reason that the present school cannot organize itself as a natural social unit is because just this element of common and productive activity is absent. Upon the playground, in game and sport, social organization takes place spontaneously and inevitably. There is something to do, some activity to be carried on, requiring natural divisions of labor, selection of leaders and followers, mutual coöperation and emulation. In the schoolroom the motive and the cement of social organization are alike wanting. Upon the ethical side, the tragic weakness of the present school is that it endeavors to prepare future members of the social order in a medium in which the conditions of the social spirit are eminently wanting.

The difference that appears when occupations are made the articulating centers of school life is not easy to describe in words; it is a difference in motive, of spirit and atmosphere. As one enters a busy kitchen in which a group of children are actively engaged in the preparation of food, the psychological difference, the change from more or less passive and inert recipiency and restraint to one of buoyant outgoing energy, is so obvious as fairly to strike one in the face. Indeed, to those whose image of the school is rigidly set the change is sure to give a shock. But the change in the social attitude is equally marked. The mere absorption of facts and truths is so exclusively individual an affair that it tends very naturally to pass into selfishness. There is no obvious social motive for the acquirement of mere learning, there is no clear social gain in success thereat. Indeed, almost the only measure for success is a competitive one, in the bad sense of that term—a comparison of results in the recitation or in the examination to see which child has succeeded in getting ahead of others in storing up, in accumulating the maximum of information. So thoroughly is this the prevalent atmosphere that for one child to help another in his task has become a school crime. Where the school work consists in simply learning lessons, mutual assistance, instead of being the most natural form of coöperation and association, becomes a clandestine effort to relieve one's neighbor of his proper duties. Where active work is going on all this is changed. Helping others, instead of being a form of charity which impoverishes the recipient, is simply an aid in setting free the powers and furthering the impulse of the one helped. A spirit of free communication, of interchange of ideas, suggestions, results, both successes and failures of previous experiences, becomes the dominating note of the recitation. So far as emulation enters in, it is in the comparison of individuals, not with regard to the quantity of information personally absorbed, but with reference to the quality of work done— the genuine community standard of value. In an informal but all the more pervasive way, the school life organizes itself on a social basis.

Within this organization is found the principle of school discipline or order. Of course, order is simply a thing which is relative to an end. If you have the end in view of forty or fifty children learning certain set lessons, to be recited to a teacher, your discipline must be devoted to securing that result. But if the end in view is the development of a spirit of social coöperation and community life, discipline must grow out of and be relative to this. There is little order of one sort where things are in process of construction; there is a certain disorder in any busy workshop; there is not silence; persons are not engaged in maintaining certain fixed physical postures; their arms are not folded; they are not holding their books thus and so. They are doing a variety of things, and there is the confusion, the bustle, that results from activity. But out of occupation, out of doing things that are to produce results, and out of doing these in a social and coöperative way, there is born a discipline of its own kind and type. Our whole conception of school discipline changes when we get this point of view. In critical moments we all realize that the only

discipline that stands by us, the only training that becomes intuition, is that got through life itself. That we learn from experience, and from books or the sayings of others *only* as they are related to experience, are not mere phrases. But the school has been so set apart, so isolated from the ordinary conditions and motives of life, that the place where children are sent for discipline is the one place in the world where it is most difficult to get experience—the mother of all discipline worth the name. It is only where a narrow and fixed image of traditional school discipline dominates, that one is in any danger of overlooking that deeper and infinitely wider discipline that comes from having a part to do in constructive work, in contributing to a result which, social in spirit, is none the less obvious and tangible in form—and hence in a form with reference to which responsibility may be exacted and accurate judgment passed.

The great thing to keep in mind, then, regarding the introduction into the school of various forms of active occupation, is that through them the entire spirit of the school is renewed. It has a chance to affiliate itself with life, to become the child's habitat, where he learns through directed living; instead of being only a place to learn lessons having an abstract and remote reference to some possible living to be done in the future. It gets a chance to be a miniature community, an embryonic society. This is the fundamental fact, and from this arise continuous and orderly sources of instruction. . . .

Our school methods, and to a very considerable extent our curriculum, are inherited from the period when learning and command of certain symbols, affording as they did the only access to learning, were all-important. The ideals of this period are still largely in control, even where the outward methods and studies have been changed. We sometimes hear the introduction of manual training, art and science into the elementary, and even the secondary schools, deprecated on the ground that they tend toward the production of specialists—that they detract from our present scheme of generous, liberal culture. The point of this objection would be ludicrous if it were not often so effective as to make it tragic. It is our present education which is highly specialized, one-sided and narrow. It is an education dominated almost entirely by the mediæval conception of learning. It is something which appeals for the most part simply to the intellectual aspect of our natures, our desire to learn, to accumulate information, and to get control of the symbols of learning; not to our impulses and tendencies to make, to do, to create, to produce, whether in the form of utility or of art. The very fact that manual training, art and science are objected to as technical, as tending toward mere specialism, is of itself as good testimony as could be offered to the specialized aim which controls current education. Unless education had been virtually identified with the exclusively intellectual pursuits, with learning as such, all these materials and methods would be welcome, would be greeted with the utmost hospitality.

While training for the profession of learning is regarded as the type of culture, as a liberal education, that of a mechanic, a musician, a lawyer, a doctor, a farmer, a merchant, or a railroad manager is regarded as purely technical and professional. The result is that which we see about us everywhere—the division into "cultured" people and "workers," the separation of theory and practice. . . . While our educational leaders are talking of culture, the development of personality, etc., as the end and aim of education, the great majority of those who pass under the tuition of the school regard it only as a narrowly practical tool with which to get bread and butter enough to eke out a restricted life. If we were to conceive our educational end and aim in a less exclusive way, if we were to introduce into educational processes the activities which appeal to those whose dominant interest is to do and to make, we should find the hold of the school upon its members to be more vital, more prolonged, containing more of culture.

But why should I make this labored presentation? The obvious fact is that our social life has undergone a thorough and radical change. If our education is to have any meaning for life, it must pass through an equally complete transformation. This transformation is not something to appear suddenly, to be executed in a day by conscious purpose. It is already in progress. Those modifications of our school system which often appear (even to those most actively concerned with them, to say nothing of their spectators) to be mere changes of detail, mere improvement within the school mechanism, are in reality signs and evidences of evolution. The introduction of active occupations, of nature study, of elementary science, of art, of history; the relegation of the merely symbolic and formal to a secondary position; the change in the moral school atmosphere, in the relation of pupils and teachers—of discipline; the introduction of more active, expressive, and self-directing factors—all these are not mere accidents, they are necessities of the larger social evolution. It remains but to organize all these factors, to appreciate them in their fullness of meaning, and to put the ideas and ideals involved into complete, uncompromising possession of our school system. To do this means to make each one of our schools an embryonic community life, active with types of occupations that reflect the life of the larger society, and permeated throughout with the spirit of art, history, and science. When the school introduces and trains each child of society into membership within such a little community, saturating him with the spirit of service, and providing him with the instruments of effective self-direction, we shall have the deepest and best guarantee of a larger society which is worthy, lovely, and harmonious.

.   .   .   .   .

From the standpoint of the child, the great waste in the school comes from his inability to utilize the experiences he gets outside the school in any complete and free way within the school itself; while, on the other hand, he is unable to apply in daily life what he is learning at school. That is the isolation of the school—its isolation from life. When the child gets into the schoolroom he has to put out of his mind a large part of the ideas, interests, and activities that predominate in his home and neighborhood. So the school, being unable to utilize this every day experience, sets painfully to work, on another tack and by a variety of means, to arouse in the child an interest in school studies. While I was visiting in the city of Moline a few years ago, the superintendent told me that they found many children every year, who were surprised to learn that the Mississippi river in the text-book had anything to do with the stream of water flowing past their homes. The geography being simply a matter of the schoolroom, it is more or less of an awakening to many children to find that the whole thing is nothing but a more formal and definite statement of the facts which they see, feel, and touch every day. When we think that we all live on the earth, that we live in an atmosphere, that our lives are touched at every point by the influences of the soil, flora, and fauna, by considerations of light and heat, and then think of what the school study of geography has been, we have a typical idea of the gap existing between the everyday experiences of the child, and the isolated material supplied in such large measure in the school. This is but an instance, and one upon which most of us may reflect long before we take the present artificiality of the school as other than a matter of course or necessity. . . .

The child can carry over what he learns in the home and utilize it in the school; and the things learned in the school he applies at home. These are the two great things in breaking down isolation, in getting connection—to have the child come to school with all the experience he has got outside the school, and to leave it with something to be immediately used in his everyday life. The child comes to the traditional school with a healthy body and a more or less unwilling mind, though, in fact, he does not bring both his body and mind with him; he has to leave his mind behind, because there is no way to use it in the school. If he had a purely abstract mind, he could bring it to school with him, but his is a concrete one, interested in concrete things, and unless these things get over into school life, he cannot take his mind with him. What we want is to have the child come to school with a whole mind and a whole body, and leave school with a fuller mind and an even healthier body.

.   .   .   .   .

Thus I have attempted to indicate how the school may be connected with life so that the experience gained by the child in a familiar, commonplace way is carried over and made use of there, and what the child learns in the school is carried back and applied in everyday life, making the school an organic whole, instead of a composite of isolated parts. The isolation of studies as well as of parts of the school system disappears. Experience has its geographical aspect, its artistic and its literary, its scientific and its historical sides. All studies arise from aspects of the one earth and the one life lived upon it. We do not have a series of stratified earths, one of which is mathematical, another physical, another historical, and so on. We should not live very long in any one taken by itself. We live in a world where all sides are bound together. All studies grow out of relations in the one great common world. When the child lives in varied but concrete and active relationship to this common world, his studies are naturally unified. It will no longer be a problem to correlate studies. The teacher will not have to resort to all sorts of devices to weave a little arithmetic into the history lesson, and the like. Relate the school to life, and all studies are of necessity correlated.

Moreover, if the school is related as a

whole to life as a whole, its various aims and ideals—culture, discipline, information, utility—cease to be variants, for one of which we must select one study and for another another. The growth of the child in the direction of social capacity and service, his larger and more vital union with life, becomes the unifying aim; and discipline, culture and information fall into place as phases of this growth.

CHAPTER EIGHT

Psychological Reorientations
in Educational Thought

THE IMPACT OF RESEARCH IN PSYCHOLOGY

GRANVILLE STANLEY HALL
"The Ideal School As Based On Child
Study" (1901)*

I shall try in this paper to break away
from all current practices, traditions, methods, and philosophies, for a brief moment,
and ask what education would be if based
solely upon a fresh and comprehensive view
of the nature and needs of childhood.
Hitherto the data for such a construction of
the ideal school have been insufficient, and
soon they will be too manifold for any one
mind to make the attempt; so the moment is
opportune. What follows is based almost
solely, point by point, upon the study of the
stages of child development, and might, perhaps, without presumption be called a first
attempt to formulate a practical programme
of this great movement. In my limited space
I can do little more than barely state the
conclusions that affect the practical work of
teachers.

The school I shall describe exists nowhere, but its methods, unless I err, are
valid everywhere. Although many of its features exist already, and could be pieced together in a mosaic from many lands and
ages, it is essentially the school invisible, not
made with hands. But, as there is nothing so
practical as the truly ideal, although my

* Granville Stanley Hall, "The Ideal School
As Based On Child Study," *Forum,* XXXII
(September, 1901), 24–39.

school to-day exists nowhere, it might be
organized anywhere to-morrow; and I hope
that the most and the least conservative will
agree that it is the true goal of all endeavor,
and will not differ except as to whether it
may be realized at once or only at the end
of a long period of labor. I confess that
something like this has from the first animated all my own feeble educational endeavors, and that without it I should be
without hope and without goal in the world
of pedagogy.

Beginning with the deep philosophy often
embedded in words, "school," or "schole,"
means leisure, exemption from work, the
perpetuation of the primeval paradise created before the struggle for existence began.
It stands for the prolongation of human infancy, and the no whit less important prolongation of adolescence. It is sacred to
health, growth, and heredity, a pound of
which is worth a ton of instruction. The
guardians of the young should strive first of
all to keep out of nature's way, and to prevent harm, and should merit the proud title
of defenders of the happiness and rights of
children. They should feel profoundly that
childhood, as it comes fresh from the hand
of God, is not corrupt, but illustrates the
survival of the most consummate thing in
the world; they should be convinced that
there is nothing else so worthy of love, reverence, and service as the body and soul of
the growing child.

325

Practically, this means that every invasion of this leisure, the provision of a right measure of which is our first duty to youth, has a certain presumption against it, and must justify itself by conclusive reasons. Before we let the pedagogue loose upon childhood, not only must each topic in his curriculum give an account of itself, but his inroads must be justified in the case of each child. We must overcome the fetishism of the alphabet, of the multiplication table, of grammars, of scales, and of bibliolatry, and must reflect that but a few generations ago the ancestors of all of us were illiterate. . . .

The child needs more mother, and less teacher; more of the educated nurse, and less of the metaphysician. We must largely eliminate, and partly reconstruct, the mother-plays, while transforming and vastly enlarging the repertory of the gifts and occupations. We must develop the ideal nursery, playgrounds, and rooms, where light, air, and water are at their best. The influences of the new hygiene have been felt least here, where they are needed most. The neglect of these basal principles suggests that we have still among us those whose practice implies a belief that any old place is good enough to hatch out beautiful souls, provided only Froebelian orthodoxy of doctrine and method is steadfastly maintained. In place of a magic mongering with them, the cubes, spheres, cylinder, and also the top, soap-bubble, doll, dances, marches, circus, and scores of other free plays and games; and in place of two or three fish, insects, animals, plants, several score must be provided, and a museum and *catalogue raisonné* of toys must be at hand. Eating bread, milk, fruit, with some simple table manners, and using paper napkins, sometimes do wonders for these human larvæ. Feeding brightens the mind and saves the disposition; a full stomach opens the mouth, and good courses of lessons could be derived from the viands themselves. . . .

We should lose no syllable of the precious positive philosophy of Froebel, the deepest of all modern educational thinkers; but we must profoundly reconstruct every practical expression that he attempted of his ideas, and must strive to induce at least a few college-trained men and women to turn their attention to the kindergarten, thus making the training schools feel, what they have hitherto known so little of, the real spirit and influence of modern science. Teachers should study every child, not necessarily by any of the current technical methods. They should learn far more than they can teach, and in place of the shallow mannikin child of books they should see, know, and love only the real thing. . . .

At eight or nine there begins a new period, which, for nearly four years, to the dawn of puberty, constitutes a unique stage of life, marked off by many important differences from the period which precedes and that which follows it. During these years there is a decreased rate of growth, so that the body relatively rests; but there is a striking increase of vitality, activity, and power to resist disease. Fatigue, too, is now best resisted, and it is amazing to see how much can be endured. The average child now plays more games and has more daily activity, in proportion to size and weight, than at any other stage. It would seem, as I have proposed elsewhere with ground for the theory, as though these four years represented, on the recapitulation theory, a long period in some remote age, well above the simian, but mainly before the historic, period, when our early forebears were well adjusted to their environment. Before a higher and much more modern story was added to human nature the young in warm climates, where most human traits were evolved, became independent of their parents, and broke away to subsist for themselves at an early age. In this age, which we will call the juvenile, the individual boy to-day is a precious key for the reconstruction of a stage in the history of the race otherwise very obscure.

However this may be, child nature suggests very plainly that this period should be mainly devoted to drill, habituation, and mechanism. The age of reason is only dawning, and is not yet much in order; but discipline should be the watchword here. Writing, and even reading, for instance, should be neglected in our system before eight, and previous school work should focus on stories, the study of nature, and education by play and other activities. Now writing and reading should be first taught with stress. Their nascent period is now beginning. If we teach them before, we are apt to make the average child a bad writer for life by precocious over-emphasis on the finer muscles. Modern studies show that the zigzag of the eye back and forth along the printed line is as dangerous as is the too early wigwag of the pen. At best the strain laid upon these tiny muscles is dangerous. Too early drill in read-writing is also enormously wasteful, because intensive effort gives facility now in an amazingly short time. Now first the smaller muscles in the average child, so important for mind and will training, can bear hard work and much strain. Accuracy, which when out of its season is fraught with so many dangers for mind and body, is now in order.

Verbal memory is now at its very best, and should be trained far more than it is. We are now educating the automatic bases of both mind and morals, and habits are never so easily formed or made stable. Manual training and games should be extremely diverse, manifold, and thorough. It is the time to break in the human colt, which is by nature in some sense the wildest of all wild animals. If the piano or any other musical instrument is to be learned, this is the time for drill, especially on scales and exercises. An instrumentalist's technique is rarely good if its foundations are not laid in this age. Names, even technical ones, come now. Drawing, too, should now come into prominence, beginning in its large and perfectly free form before writing, and only near the end of the period becoming severely methodic and accurate. Art training should not result in intimidation, but first everything should be drawn—battles, fires, shipwrecks, and railroad accidents, with plenty of human

figures and action, and no angles, straight lines, or regular curves, which have come very late in the history of the race. This would make drawing, as it should be, a real expression of the child's soul, and the child would copy what he, and not what the adult, sees.

The mother tongue will be the vehicle of nearly all the work of this period; but it will be on the short circuit from ear to mouth, which existed for unknown eons before writing or reading, and not chiefly on the long circuit and biologically very recent brain-path from eye to hand. Teachers praise written work in home and at school—compositions, essays, class work; but all these appeal to new and undeveloped powers of nerve and muscle. It is because we try to establish good English upon these foundations, so precarious at this stage, that we have so much and so just complaint of bad English. We ruin both handwriting and idiomatic speech by precocity. The child should live in a world of sonorous speech. He should hear and talk for hours each day; and then he would lay foundations for terse and correct English, and would keep read-writing, as it should forever be, subordinate to hearing and speaking. He would write as he speaks, and we should escape the abomination of bookish talk. At this stage written work should be required far less than at present.

Further, to secure these ends, we must first lay less stress upon correct spelling—which is, after all, of far less importance than we think—and also upon correct, adult Addisonian syntax. Good grammar is too much to expect yet. We must strive first for utterance and expression, which may be homely if only vigorous and adequate. Hence, much that we call slang has its place, and is really a revival of English in its most formative stage. The prim proprieties we idolize are not yet, but it is the hour of delight in cogency of expression. We do not yet know what slang to teach or how to teach it, but we ought to give the best of it an important place. The boy is not totally depraved because he loves the speech of Chimmie Fadden, of Mr. Ade, or of "The Charwoman," because such language is fresh from the mint where all words were made. Our end is the cultivation of expression, which must bring out clearly and strongly what is in the boy's soul. This expression must be of a kind at least no less effective for other boys than for us. A training that gives the power of writing or even talking upon any subject or upon none in particular is bad and vicious. Children have no right to write unless it is upon some subject that they know and upon which they feel strongly. Theme and composition should be strictly confined to the fields of interest, and then expression will find or make a vent for itself. Moreover, we should not teach language, as such, or apart from objects, acts, and concrete reality-truth. We must burn most of our language books. . . .

As to the dead languages, if they are to be taught, Latin should be begun not later than ten or eleven, and Greek never later than twelve or thirteen. Here both object and method are very different. These languages are taught through English, and the eye-hand circuit should have much more prominence. Word matching and translation are the goal. The chief reason why the German boy of fifteen or sixteen in *Unter Secunda* does so easily here what seems to us prodigious is because he is taught to study; and the teacher's chief business in class is not to hear recitations, but to study with the boys. One of the best of these teachers told me that the boy should never see a dictionary or even a vocabulary, but the teacher must be a "pony." The pupil should never be brought face to face with an unknown sentence, but everything must be carefully translated for him; he must note all the unknown words from the teacher's lips and all the special grammatical points, so that home study and the first part of the next lesson will be merely repetitions of what the teacher had told and done. . . .

The hand is in a sense never so near the brain as now; knowledge never so strongly

tends to become practical; muscular development never so conditions mental. Muscle training of every kind, from play up to manual work, must now begin. Instead of the Swedish or other curriculized and exactly finished objects made, we should have a curriculum of toys at first and of rude scientific apparatus later, where everything will focus more upon the ulterior use of the object than upon the process of making it. All these things will be chosen from the field of the child's interests. . . .

Lastly, the ideal teacher at this age will be the captain of the child's soul; will be able to do some things with his or her body that the child cannot; will be able to answer most of the questions suggested by the field, the forest, the beach, the street, and their denizens; will suggest plays and umpire games; will perhaps know a little of coaching, but will be a stern disciplinarian, genial withal, but rigorous and relentless in his exactions, and intolerant of all scamped work; will love occasional excursions and expeditions; will perhaps sing, play, and draw a little; will be able to do something expertly well; and, as perhaps the culminating quality, will have a repertory of the greatest stories the human race has ever told or heard. . . .

Adolescence is a term now applied to a pretty well-marked stage, beginning at about thirteen with girls and a year later with boys, and lasting about ten years, to the period of complete sexual maturity. It is subdivided into pubescence, the first two years; youth proper, from sixteen to twenty in boys and perhaps fifteen to nineteen in girls; and a finishing stage through the early twenties. The first stage is marked by a great increase in the rate of growth in both height and weight. It is a period of greater susceptibility to sickness for both sexes; but this vulnerability is due to the great changes, and the death rate is lower in the early teens than at any other age. It is the time when there is the most rapid development of the heart and all the feelings and emotions. Fear, anger, love, pity, jealousy, emulation, ambition, and sympathy are either now born or springing into their most intense life. Now young people are interested in adults, and one of their strong passions is to be treated as if they were mature. They desire to know, do, and be all that becomes a man or woman. Childhood is ending, and plans for future vocations now spring into existence, and slowly grow definite and controlling. . . .

In the ideal school system, the sexes will now, for a time at least, pretty much part company. They are beginning to differ in every cell and tissue, and girls for a time need some exemption from competition. They have more power than boys to draw upon their capital of physical energy and to take out of their system more than it can afford to lose, for the individuals of one generation can consume more than their share of vigor at the expense of posterity. In soul and body girls are more conservative; males vary, differentiate, and are more radical. Reproduction requires a far larger proportion of body and function in females. Now the leaders of the new education for girls recommend training them for self-support, assuming that if wifehood and motherhood come those who have received such a training can best take care of themselves. This assumption is radically wrong and vicious, and should be reversed. Every girl should be educated primarily to become a wife and mother, and, if this is done wisely and broadly, the small minority who remain single will with this training be best able to care for themselves.

A third conclusive and far-reaching principle is that at no stage of life is the power to appreciate and apprehend so very far ahead of the power to express. Hence we should let up on examinations; we should cast our bread upon the waters, knowing that it will be found after many days, because so sensitized is the soul now that nothing is lost. Mental and moral teaching and influences sink at once too deep to be reproduced in examinations of the present type without injury to both mind and will. There is nothing in the whole environment

to which the adolescent nature does not keenly respond. Neither you nor I, however specialized our knowledge, know anything really worth knowing the substance of which cannot be taught now if we have pedagogical tact; but, if we wait for its reproduction in the pupil, we starve and retard his soul. Hence facts, ideas, laws, and principles should be in the very atmosphere, for they are now the ingenuous youth's native breath, his vital air. He is all insight and receptivity; he has just entered the stage of apprenticeship to life; he has awakened to it as at a second birth, and has found all things new and glorious.

Yet another change is well defined. Whereas previously the pupil could work with some skill and accuracy, now body and mind are both again so plastic and unformed that they are clumsy, and precision and finish cannot be bought except at too great a price. The teacher's cue is now to graft the soul all over with buds and scions, and not to try to gather a harvest. The mind has laid aside its power to finish and elaborate. It can rudely assimilate everything by turns, but nothing well. The fundamental system of the body, which consists of the large muscles and not the small, and which therefore makes coarse massive movements and not exact ones, has now its innings; and the fundamentals of the soul, which are instinct and intuition, and not pure intellect, are now in season. We must lay new and larger foundations.

But, more specifically, what do these changes involve in the ideal school of the future? The transition from the grammar to the high school in this country corresponds far better than the European system to the need of changed environment at the age of fourteen; and this constitutes a rare opportunity which has, however, been thrown away. Although education, as we have seen, begins here, and many races have no other than a brief training at the dawn of the ephebic period, by a strange irony of fate secondary education has more or less lapsed to a mere link. Its functions are partly those of preparation for college, and are partly shaped by the mere momentum of the lower grades. The high school has lost its independence, and of all stages and grades has least interest in the large problems of education, namely, what to teach and how, in order to develop the nascent periods during the teens and to save powers now new-born in most profusion, but sure to be atrophied or perverted if not studied with tact and federated with individual adaptation. . . .

Few institutions of modern civilization so distrust human nature as does the modern, American high school, when under college domination. For lower grades the law of compulsory attendance is analogous to a high protective tariff, which removes the stimulus to better methods of manufacture, and interferes with the law of competition which is the mainspring of evolution. The high school is no less effectively protected against the currents of new ideas, and is left to be a victim of tradition, routine, the iron law of mechanism. It takes the easiest way by working under the shelter and dictation of the college above and on the momentum of the grammar school below. This, I believe, accounts for the rapidly decreasing numbers as we go up the high-school classes; for the decreasing proportion of high-school boys who go to college; for the preponderance of girls in the high school; and for the educational apathy of the high-school teacher, who is prone to all the narrowness and affectation of the specialist, without his redeeming virtue of productiveness in research.

The teacher must teach more, and know more; he must be a living fountain, not a stagnant pool. He should not be a dealer in desiccated, second-hand knowledge, a mere giver-out and hearer of lessons. . . .

I have spoken frankly, and have dealt only with general principles over a vast field, far too large to be adequately discussed here. I have carefully avoided all details, although I have fully worked them out on paper at great length, for each topic to the close of the high-school period or

the age of nineteen, when physical growth is essentially completed. This material will soon appear in a volume. The chief petition in my daily prayer now is for a millionaire. With the means at hand, I have no shadow of doubt or fear but that in five years from the date of any adequate gift, we shall be able to invite all interested to a system of education, covering this ground, which will be a practical realization of much present prophecy, and which will commend itself even to the most conservative defenders of things as they are and have been, because the best things established will be in it. But it will be essentially pedocentric rather than scholiocentric.

WILLIAM JAMES
Talks to Teachers on Psychology (1899) *

LECTURE I

"Psychology and the Teaching Art"

By all means let child-study go on,—it is refreshing all our sense of the child's life. There are teachers who take a spontaneous delight in filling syllabuses, inscribing observations, compiling statistics, and computing the per cent. Child-study will certainly enrich their lives. And, if its results, as treated statistically, would seem on the whole to have but trifling value, yet the anecdotes and observations of which it in part consist do certainly acquaint us more intimately with our pupils. Our eyes and ears grow quickened to discern in the child before us processes similar to those we have read of as noted in the children,—processes of which we might otherwise have remained inobservant. But, for Heaven's sake, let the rank and

* William James, *Talks to Teachers on Psychology: and to Students on Some of Life's Ideals* (New York: Holt, 1899), Lecture I, "Psychology and the Teaching Art," pp. 12–14; Lecture II, "The Stream of Consciousness," pp. 15–20; Lecture III, "The Child as a Behaving Organism," pp. 22–28; Lecture V, "The Necessity of Reactions," pp. 33–37; Lecture VII, "What the Native Reactions Are," pp. 54–55; and Lecture XI, "Attention," pp. 108–111.

file of teachers be passive readers if they so prefer, and feel free not to contribute to the accumulation. Let not the prosecution of it be preached as an imperative duty or imposed by regulation on those to whom it proves an exterminating bore, or who in any way whatever miss in themselves the appropriate vocation for it. I cannot too strongly agree with my colleague, Professor Münsterberg, when he says that the teacher's attitude toward the child, being concrete and ethical, is positively opposed to the psychological observer's, which is abstract and analytic. Although some of us may conjoin the attitudes successfully, in most of us they must conflict.

The worst thing that can happen to a good teacher is to get a bad conscience about her profession because she feels herself hopeless as a psychologist. Our teachers are overworked already. Every one who adds a jot or tittle of unnecessary weight to their burden is a foe of education. A bad conscience increases the weight of every other burden; yet I know that child-study, and other pieces of psychology as well, have been productive of bad conscience in many a really innocent pedagogic breast. I should indeed be glad if this passing word from me might tend to dispel such a bad conscience, if any of you have it; for it is certainly one of those fruits of more or less systematic mystification of which I have already complained. The best teacher may be the poorest contributor of child-study material, and the best contributor may be the poorest teacher. No fact is more palpable than this.

So much for what seems the most reasonable general attitude of the teacher toward the subject which is to occupy our attention.

LECTURE II

"The Stream of Consciousness"

I said a few minutes ago that the most general elements and workings of the mind are all that the teacher absolutely needs to be acquainted with for his purposes.

Now the *immediate* fact which psychol-ogy, the science of mind, has to study is also the most general fact. It is the fact that in each of us, when awake (and often when asleep), *some kind of consciousness is always going on.* There is a stream, a succession of states, or waves, or fields (or of whatever you please to call them), of knowledge, of feeling, of desire, of deliberation, etc., that constantly pass and repass, and that constitute our inner life. The existence of this stream is the primal fact, the nature and origin of it form the essential problem, of our science. So far as we class the states or fields of consciousness, write down their several natures, analyze their contents into elements, or trace their habits of succession, we are on the descriptive or analytic level. So far as we ask where they come from or why they are just what they are, we are on the explanatory level.

In these talks with you, I shall entirely neglect the questions that come up on the explanatory level. It must be frankly confessed that in no fundamental sense do we know where our successive fields of consciousness come from, or why they have the precise inner constitution which they do have. They certainly follow or accompany our brain states, and of course their special forms are determined by our past experiences and education. But, if we ask just *how* the brain conditions them, we have not the remotest inkling of an answer to give; and, if we ask just how the education moulds the brain, we can speak but in the most abstract, general, and conjectural terms. On the other hand, if we should say that they are due to a spiritual being called our Soul, which reacts on our brain states by these peculiar forms of spiritual energy, our words would be familiar enough, it is true; but I think you will agree that they would offer little genuine explanatory meaning. The truth is that we really *do not know* the answers to the problems on the explanatory level, even though in some directions of inquiry there may be promising speculations to be found. For our present purposes I shall therefore dismiss them entirely, and turn to mere description. This state of things was what I had in mind when, a moment ago, I said there was no "new psychology" worthy of the name.

We have thus fields of consciousness,—that is the first general fact; and the second general fact is that the concrete fields are always complex. They contain sensations of our bodies and of the objects around us, memories of past experiences and thoughts of distant things, feelings of satisfaction and dissatisfaction, desires and aversions, and other emotional conditions, together with determinations of the will, in every variety of permutation and combination.

In most of our concrete states of consciousness all these different classes of ingredients are found simultaneously present to some degree, though the relative proportion they bear to one another is very shifting. One state will seem to be composed of hardly anything but sensations, another of hardly anything but memories, etc. But around the sensation, if one consider carefully, there will always be some fringe of thought or will, and around the memory some margin or penumbra of emotion or sensation.

In most of our fields of consciousness there is a core of sensation that is very pronounced. You, for example, now, although you are also thinking and feeling, are getting through your eyes sensations of my face and figure, and through your ears sensations of my voice. The sensations are the *centre* or *focus,* the thoughts and feelings the *margin,* of your actually present conscious field.

On the other hand, some object of thought, some distant image, may have become the focus of your mental attention even while I am speaking,—your mind, in short, may have wandered from the lecture; and, in that case, the sensations of my face and voice, although not absolutely vanishing from your conscious field, may have taken up there a very faint and marginal place.

Again, to take another sort of variation, some feeling connected with your own body may have passed from a marginal to a focal place, even while I speak.

The expressions "focal object" and "marginal object," which we owe to Mr. Lloyd Morgan, require, I think, no further explanation. The distinction they embody is a very important one, and they are the first technical terms which I shall ask you to remember.

In the successive mutations of our fields of consciousness, the process by which one dissolves into another is often very gradual, and all sorts of inner rearrangements of contents occur. Sometimes the focus remains but little changed, while the margin alters rapidly. Sometimes the focus alters, and the margin stays. Sometimes focus and margin change places. Sometimes, again, abrupt alterations of the whole field occur. There can seldom be a sharp description. All we know is that, for the most part, each field has a sort of practical unity for its possessor, and that from this practical point of view we can class a field with other fields similar to it, by calling it a state of emotion, of perplexity, of sensation, of abstract thought, of volition, and the like.

Vague and hazy as such an account of our stream of consciousness may be, it is at least secure from positive error and free from admixture of conjecture or hypothesis. An influential school of psychology, seeking to avoid haziness of outline, has tried to make things appear more exact and scientific by making the analysis more sharp. The various fields of consciousness, according to this school, result from a definite number of perfectly definite elementary mental states, mechanically associated into a mosaic or chemically combined. According to some thinkers,—Spencer, for example, or Taine, —these resolve themselves at last into little elementary psychic particles or atoms of "mind-stuff," out of which all the more immediately known mental states are said to be built up. Locke introduced this theory in a somewhat vague form. Simple "ideas" of sensation and reflection, as he called them, were for him the bricks of which our mental architecture is built up. If I ever have to refer to this theory again, I shall refer to it as the theory of "ideas." But I shall try to steer clear of it altogether. Whether it be true or false, it is at any rate only conjectural; and, for your practical purposes as teachers, the more unpretending conception of the stream of consciousness, with its total waves or fields incessantly changing, will amply suffice.

LECTURE III

"The Child as a Behaving Organism"

I wish now to continue the description of the peculiarities of the stream of consciousness by asking whether we can in any intelligible way assign its *functions*.

It has two functions that are obvious: it leads to knowledge, and it leads to action.

Can we say which of these functions is the more essential?

An old historic divergence of opinion comes in here. Popular belief has always tended to estimate the worth of a man's mental processes by their effects upon his practical life. But philosophers have usually cherished a different view. "Man's supreme glory," they have said, "is to be a *rational* being, to know absolute and eternal and universal truth. The uses of his intellect for practical affairs are therefore subordinate matters. 'The theoretic life' is his soul's genuine concern." Nothing can be more different in its results for our personal attitude than to take sides with one or the other of these views, and emphasize the practical or the theoretical ideal. In the latter case, abstraction from the emotions and passions and withdrawal from the strife of human affairs would be not only pardonable, but praiseworthy; and all that makes for quiet and contemplation should be regarded as conducive to the highest human perfection. In the former, the man of contemplation would be treated as only half a human being, passion and practical resource would become once more glories of our race, a concrete victory over this earth's outward

powers of darkness would appear an equivalent for any amount of passive spiritual culture, and conduct would remain as the test of every education worthy of the name.

It is impossible to disguise the fact that in the psychology of our own day the emphasis is transferred from the mind's purely rational function, where Plato and Aristotle, and what one may call the whole classic tradition in philosophy had placed it, to the so long neglected practical side. The theory of evolution is mainly responsible for this. Man, we now have reason to believe, has been evolved from infra-human ancestors, in whom pure reason hardly existed, if at all, and whose mind, so far as it can have had any function, would appear to have been an organ for adapting their movements to the impressions received from the environment, so as to escape the better from destruction. Consciousness would thus seem in the first instance to be nothing but a sort of superadded biological perfection,—useless unless it prompted to useful conduct, and inexplicable apart from that consideration.

Deep in our own nature the biological foundations of our consciousness persist, undisguised and undiminished. Our sensations are here to attract us or to deter us, our memories to warn or encourage us, our feelings to impel, and our thoughts to restrain our behavior, so that on the whole we may prosper and our days be long in the land. Whatever of transmundane metaphysical insight or of practically inapplicable æsthetic perception or ethical sentiment we may carry in our interiors might at this rate be regarded as only part of the incidental excess of function that necessarily accompanies the working of every complex machine.

I shall ask you now—not meaning at all thereby to close the theoretic question, but merely because it seems to me the point of view likely to be of greatest practical use to you as teachers—to adopt with me, in this course of lectures, the biological conception, as thus expressed, and to lay your own emphasis on the fact that man, whatever else he may be, is primarily a practical being, whose mind is given him to aid in adapting him to this world's life.

In the learning of all matters, we have to start with some one deep aspect of the question, abstracting it as if it were the only aspect; and then we gradually correct ourselves by adding those neglected other features which complete the case. No one believes more strongly than I do that what our senses know as "this world" is only one portion of our mind's total environment and object. Yet, because it is the primal portion, it is the *sine qua non* of all the rest. If you grasp the facts about it firmly, you may proceed to higher regions undisturbed. As our time must be so short together, I prefer being elementary and fundamental to being complete, so I propose to you to hold fast to the ultra-simple point of view.

The reasons why I call it so fundamental can be easily told.

First, human and animal psychology thereby become less discontinuous. I know that to some of you this will hardly seem an attractive reason, but there are others whom it will affect.

Second, mental action is conditioned by brain action, and runs parallel therewith. But the brain, so far as we understand it, is given us for practical behavior. Every current that runs into it from skin or eye or ear runs out again into muscles, glands, or viscera, and helps to adapt the animal to the environment from which the current came. It therefore generalizes and simplifies our view to treat the brain life and the mental life as having one fundamental kind of purpose.

Third, those very functions of the mind that do not refer directly to this world's environment, the ethical utopias, æsthetic visions, insights into eternal truth, and fanciful logical combinations, could never be carried on at all by a human individual, unless the mind that produced them in him were also able to produce more practically useful products. The latter are thus the more essential, or at least the more primordial results.

Fourth, the inessential "unpractical" activities are themselves far more connected with our behavior and our adaptation to the environment than at first sight might appear. No truth, however abstract, is ever perceived, that will not probably at some time influence our earthly action. You must remember that, when I talk of action here, I mean action in the widest sense. I mean speech, I mean writing, I mean yeses and noes, and tendencies "from" things and tendencies "toward" things, and emotional determinations; and I mean them in the future as well as in the immediate present. As I talk here, and you listen, it might seem as if no action followed. You might call it a purely theoretic process, with no practical result. But it *must* have a practical result. It cannot take place at all and leave your conduct unaffected. If not to-day, then on some far future day, you will answer some question differently by reason of what you are thinking now. Some of you will be led by my words into new veins of inquiry, into reading special books. These will develop your opinion, whether for or against. That opinion will in turn be expressed, will receive criticism from others in your environment, and will affect your standing in their eyes. We cannot escape our destiny, which is practical; and even our most theoretic faculties contribute to its working out.

These few reasons will perhaps smooth the way for you to acquiescence in my proposal. As teachers, I sincerely think it will be a sufficient conception for you to adopt of the youthful psychological phenomena handed over to your inspection if you consider them from the point of view of their relation to the future conduct of their possessor. Sufficient at any rate as a first conception and as a main conception. You should regard your professional task as if it consisted chiefly and essentially in *training the pupil to behavior;* taking behavior, not in the narrow sense of his manners, but in the very widest possible sense, as including every possible sort of fit reaction on the circumstances into which he may find himself brought by the vicissitudes of life.

The reaction may, indeed, often be a negative reaction. *Not* to speak, *not* to move, is one of the most important of our duties, in certain practical emergencies. "Thou shalt refrain, renounce, abstain!" This often requires a great effort of will power, and, physiologically considered, is just as positive a nerve function as is motor discharge.

·   ·   ·   ·   ·

LECTURE V

"The Necessity of Reactions"

If all this be true, then immediately one general aphorism emerges which ought by logical right to dominate the entire conduct of the teacher in the classroom.

No reception without reaction, no impression without correlative expression,— this is the great maxim which the teacher ought never to forget.

An impression which simply flows in at the pupil's eyes or ears, and in no way modifies his active life, is an impression gone to waste. It is physiologically incomplete. It leaves no fruits behind it in the way of capacity acquired. Even as mere impression, it fails to produce its proper effect upon the memory; for, to remain fully among the acquisitions of this latter faculty, it must be wrought into the whole cycle of our operations. Its *motor consequences* are what clinch it. Some effect due to it in the way of an activity must return to the mind in the form of the *sensation of having acted,* and connect itself with the impression. The most durable impressions are those on account of which we speak or act, or else are inwardly convulsed.

The older pedagogic method of learning things by rote, and reciting them parrot-like in the schoolroom, rested on the truth that a thing merely read or heard, and never verbally reproduced, contracts the weakest possible adhesion in the mind. Verbal recitation or reproduction is thus a highly important kind of reactive behavior on our impressions; and it is to be feared that, in

the reaction against the old parrot-recitations as the beginning and end of instruction, the extreme value of verbal recitation as an element of complete training may nowadays be too much forgotten.

When we turn to modern pedagogics, we see how enormously the field of reactive conduct has been extended by the introduction of all those methods of concrete object teaching which are the glory of our contemporary schools. Verbal reactions, useful as they are, are insufficient. The pupil's words may be right, but the conceptions corresponding to them are often direfully wrong. In a modern school, therefore, they form only a small part of what the pupil is required to do. He must keep notebooks, make drawings, plans, and maps, take measurements, enter the laboratory and perform experiments, consult authorities, and write essays. He must do in his fashion what is often laughed at by outsiders when it appears in prospectuses under the title of "original work," but what is really the only possible training for the doing of original work thereafter. The most colossal improvement which recent years have seen in secondary education lies in the introduction of the manual training schools; not because they will give us a people more handy and practical for domestic life and better skilled in trades, but because they will give us citizens with an entirely different intellectual fibre. Laboratory work and shop work engender a habit of observation, a knowledge of the difference between accuracy and vagueness, and an insight into nature's complexity and into the inadequacy of all abstract verbal accounts of real phenomena, which once wrought into the mind, remain there as lifelong possessions. They confer precision; because, if you are *doing* a thing, you must do it definitely right or definitely wrong. They give honesty; for, when you express yourself by making things, and not by using words, it becomes impossible to dissimulate your vagueness or ignorance by ambiguity. They beget a habit of self-reliance; they keep the interest and attention always cheerfully engaged, and reduce the teacher's disciplinary functions to a minimum.

Of the various systems of manual training, so far as woodwork is concerned, the Swedish Sloyd system, if I may have an opinion on such matters, seems to me by far the best, psychologically considered. Manual training methods, fortunately, are being slowly but surely introduced into all our large cities. But there is still an immense distance to traverse before they shall have gained the extension which they are destined ultimately to possess.

No impression without expression, then, —that is the first pedagogic fruit of our evolutionary conception of the mind as something instrumental to adaptive behavior. But a word may be said in continuation. The expression itself comes back to us, as I intimated a moment ago, in the form of a still farther impression,—the impression, namely, of what we have done. We thus receive sensible news of our behavior and its results. We hear the words we have spoken, feel our own blow as we give it, or read in the bystander's eyes the success or failure of our conduct. Now this return wave of impression pertains to the completeness of the whole experience, and a word about its importance in the schoolroom may not be out of place.

It would seem only natural to say that, since after acting we normally get some return impression of result, it must be well to let the pupil get such a return impression in every possible case. Nevertheless, in schools where examination marks and "standing" and other returns of result are concealed, the pupil is frustrated of this natural termination of the cycle of his activities, and often suffers from the sense of incompleteness and uncertainty; and there are persons who defend this system as encouraging the pupil to work for the work's sake, and not for extraneous reward. Of course, here as elsewhere, concrete experience must prevail over psychological deduction. But, so far as our psychological deduction goes, it would

suggest that the pupil's eagerness to know how well he does is in the line of his normal completeness of function, and should never be balked except for very definite reasons indeed.

Acquaint them, therefore, with their marks and standing and prospects, unless in the individual case you have some special practical reason for not so doing.

.   .   .   .   .

LECTURE VII
"What the Native Reactions Are"

. . . We have of late been hearing much of the philosophy of tenderness in education; "interest" must be assiduously awakened in everything, difficulties must be smoothed away. *Soft* pedagogics have taken the place of the old steep and rocky path to learning. But from this lukewarm air the bracing oxygen of effort is left out. It is nonsense to suppose that every step in education *can* be interesting. The fighting impulse must often be appealed to. Make the pupil feel ashamed of being scared at fractions, of being "downed" by the law of falling bodies; rouse his pugnacity and pride, and he will rush at the difficult places with a sort of inner wrath at himself that is one of his best moral faculties. A victory scored under such conditions becomes a turning-point and crisis of his character. It represents the high-water mark of his powers, and serves thereafter as an ideal pattern for his self-imitation. The teacher who never rouses this sort of pugnacious excitement in his pupils falls short of one of his best forms of usefulness.

.   .   .   .   .

LECTURE XI
"Attention"

. . . The genius of the interesting teacher consists in sympathetic divination of the sort of material with which the pupil's mind is likely to be already spontaneously engaged, and in the ingenuity which discovers paths of connection from that material to the matters to be newly learned. The principle is easy to grasp, but the accomplishment is difficult in the extreme. And a knowledge of such psychology as this which I am recalling can no more make a good teacher than a knowledge of the laws of perspective can make a landscape painter of effective skill.

A certain doubt may now occur to some of you. A while ago, apropos of the pugnacious instinct, I spoke of our modern pedagogy as being possibly too "soft." You may perhaps here face me with my own words, and ask whether the exclusive effort on the teacher's part to keep the pupil's spontaneous interest going, and to avoid the more strenuous path of voluntary attention to repulsive work, does not savor also of sentimentalism. The greater part of schoolroom work, you say, must, in the nature of things, always be repulsive. To face uninteresting drudgery is a good part of life's work. Why seek to eliminate it from the schoolroom or minimize the sterner law?

A word or two will obviate what might perhaps become a serious misunderstanding here.

It is certain that most schoolroom work, till it has become habitual and automatic, is repulsive, and cannot be done without voluntarily jerking back the attention to it every now and then. This is inevitable, let the teacher do what he will. It flows from the inherent nature of the subjects and of the learning mind. The repulsive processes of verbal memorizing, of discovering steps of mathematical identity, and the like, must borrow their interest at first from purely external sources, mainly from the personal interests with which success in mastering them is associated, such as gaining of rank, avoiding punishment, not being beaten by a difficulty and the like. Without such borrowed interest, the child could not attend to them at all. But in these processes what becomes interesting enough to be attended to is not thereby attended to *without effort*. Effort always has to go on, derived interest, for the most part, not awakening attention that is *easy*, however spontaneous it may now have to be called. The interest which the teacher, by his utmost skill, can lend to the subject, proves over and over again to be only an interest sufficient *to let loose the effort*. The teacher, therefore, need never concern himself about *inventing* occasions where effort must be called into play. Let him still awaken whatever sources of interest in the subject he can by stirring up connections between it and the pupil's nature, whether in the line of theoretic curiosity, of personal interest, or of pugnacious impulse. The laws of mind will then bring enough pulses of effort into play to keep the pupil exercised in the direction of the subject. There is, in fact, no greater school of effort than the steady struggle to attend to immediately repulsive or difficult objects of thought which have grown to interest us through their association as means, with some remote ideal end.

NEW THEORIES OF LEARNING

EDWARD L. THORNDIKE
Animal Intelligence (1898) *

After considerable preliminary observation of animals' behavior under various con-

* Edward L. Thorndike, *Animal Intelligence: An Experimental Study of the Associative Processes in Animals* (New York, 1898; Psychological Monograph *Supplement*, Vol. II, No. 4), pp. 6–10, 12–15, 31, 39–40, 45–46, 65, 71, 97–99, 104–105, 108.

ditions, I chose for my general method one which, simple as it is, possesses several other marked advantages besides those which accompany experiment of any sort. It was merely to put animals when hungry in enclosures from which they could escape by some simple act, such as pulling at a loop of cord, pressing a lever, or stepping on a platform. (A detailed description of these boxes and pens will be given later.) The animal was put in the enclosure, food was left outside in sight, and his actions observed. Besides recording his general behavior, special notice was taken of how he succeeded in doing the necessary act (in case he did succeed), and a record was kept of the time that he was in the box before performing the successful pull, or clawing, or bite. This was repeated until the animal had formed a perfect association between the sense-impression of the interior of that box and the impulse leading to the successful movement. When the association was thus perfect, the time taken to escape was, of course, practically constant and very short.

If, on the other hand, after a certain time the animal did not succeed, he was taken out, but *not fed*. If, after a sufficient number of trials, he failed to get out, the case was recorded as one of complete failure. Enough different sorts of methods of escape were tried to make it fairly sure that association in general, not association of a particular sort of impulse, was being studied. Enough animals were taken with each box or pen to make it sure that the results were not due to individual peculiarities. None of the animals used had any previous acquaintance with any of the mechanical contrivances by which the doors were opened. So far as possible the animals were kept in a uniform state of hunger, which was practically utter hunger. That is, no cat or dog was experimented on when the experiment involved any important question of fact or theory, unless I was sure that his motive was of the standard strength. With chicks this is not practicable, on account of their delicacy. But with them dislike of loneliness acts as a uniform motive to get back to the other chicks. Cats (or rather kittens), dogs and chicks were the subjects of the experiments. All were apparently in excellent health, save an occasional chick.

By this method of experimentation the animals are put in situations which call into activity their mental functions and permit them to be carefully observed. One may, by following it, observe personally more intelligent acts than are included in any anecdotal collection. And this actual vision of animals in the act of using their minds is far more fruitful than any amount of histories of what animals have done without the history of how they did it. But besides affording this opportunity for purposeful and systematic observation, our method is valuable because it frees the animal from any influence of the observer. The animal's behavior is quite independent of any factors save its own hunger, the mechanism of the box it is in, the food outside, and such general matters as fatigue, indisposition, etc. Therefore the work done by one investigator may be repeated and verified or modified by another. No personal factor is present save in the observation and interpretation. Again, our method gives some very important results which are quite uninfluenced by *any* personal factor in any way. The curves showing the progress of the formation of associations, which are obtained from the records of the times taken by the animal in successive trials, are facts which may be obtained by any observer who can tell time. They are absolute, and whatever can be deduced from them is sure. So also the question of whether an animal does or does not form a certain association requires for an answer no higher qualification in the observer than a pair of eyes. The literature of animal psychology shows so uniformly and often so sadly the influence of the personal equation that any method which can partially eliminate it deserves a trial.

Furthermore, although the associations formed are such as could not have been previously experienced or provided for by heredity, they are still not too remote from the animal's ordinary course of life. They mean simply the connection of a certain act with a certain situation and resultant pleasure, and this general type of association is found throughout the animal's life normally. The muscular movements required are all such as might often be required of the animal. . . .

We may now start in with the description

of the apparatus and of the behavior of the animals.[1]

DESCRIPTION OF APPARATUS.

The shape and general apparatus of the boxes which were used for the cats is shown by the accompan[y]ing drawing of box **K**.

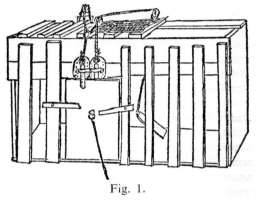

Fig. 1.

Unless special figures are given, it should be understood that each box is approximately 20 inches long by 15 broad by 12 high. Except where mention is made to the contrary, the door was pulled open by a weight attached to a string which ran over a pulley and was fastened to the door, just as soon as the animal loosened the bolt or bar which held it. Especial care was taken not to have the widest openings between the bars at all near the lever, or wire-loop, or what not, which governed the bolt on the door. For the animal instinctively attacks the large openings first, and if the mechanism which governs the opening of the door is situated near one of them the animal's task is rendered easier. You do not then get the association process so free from the helping hand of instinct as you do if you make the box without reference to the position of the mechanism to be set up within it. These

[1] The experiments now to be described were for the most part made in the Psychological Laboratory of Columbia University during the year '97–'98, but a few of them were made in connection with a general preliminary investigation of animal psychology undertaken at Harvard University in the previous year.

various mechanisms are so simple that a verbal description will suffice in most cases. The facts which the reader should note are the nature of the movement which the cat had to make, the nature of the object at which the movement was directed, and the position of the object in the box. In some special cases attention will also be called to the force required. In general, however, that was very slight (20 to 100 grams if applied directly). The various boxes will be designated by capital letters.

A. A string attached to the bolt which held the door ran up over a pulley on the front edge of the box, and was tied to a wire loop (2½ inches diameter) hanging 6 inches above the floor in front center of box. Clawing or biting it, or rubbing against it even, if in a certain way, opened the door. We may calls this box A *"O at front."*

B. A string attached to the bolt ran up over a pulley on the front edge of the door, then across the box to another pulley screwed into the inside of the back of the box 1¼ inches below the top, and passing over it ended in a wire loop (3 inches in diameter) 6 inches above the floor in back center of box. Force applied to the loop or *to the string* as it ran across the top of the box between two bars would open the door. We may call B *"O at back."*

B1. In B1 the string ran outside the box, coming down through a hole at the back, and was therefore inaccessible and invisible from within. Only by pulling the loop could the door be opened. B1 may be called *"O at back 2nd."*

C. A door of the usual position and size (as in Fig. 1) was kept closed by a wooden button 3½ inches long, ⅞ inch wide, ½ inch thick. This turned on a nail driven into the box ½ inch above the middle of the top edge of the door. The door would fall inward as soon as the button was turned from its vertical to a horizontal position. A pull of 125 grams would do this if applied sideways at the lowest point of the button 2¼ inches below its pivot. The cats usually clawed the button round by downward pressure on its top edge, which was 1¼ inches above the nail. Then, of course, more force was necessary. C may be called *"Button."* . . .

EXPERIMENTS WITH CATS.

In these various boxes were put cats from among the following. I give approximately their ages while under experiment.

No. 1. 8–10 months.
No. 2. 5–7 months.
No. 3. 5–11 months.
No. 4. 5–8 months.
No. 5. 5–7 months.
No. 6. 3–5 months.
No. 7. 3–5 months.
No. 8. 6–6½ months.
No. 10. 4–8 months.
No. 11. 7–8 months.
No. 12. 4–6 months.
No. 13. 18–19 months.

The behavior of all but 11 and 13 was practically the same. When put into the box the cat would show evident signs of discomfort and of an impulse to escape from confinement. It tries to squeeze through any opening; it claws and bites at the bars or wire; it thrusts its paws out through any opening and claws at everything it reaches; it continues its efforts when it strikes anything loose and shaky; it may claw at things within the box. It does not pay very much attention to the food outside, but seems simply to strive instinctively to escape from confinement. The vigor with which it struggles is extraordinary. For eight or ten minutes it will claw and bite and squeeze *incessantly.* With 13, *an old cat, and* 11, an uncommonly sluggish cat, the behavior was different. They did not struggle vigorously or continually. On some occasions they did not even struggle at all. It was therefore necessary to let them out of some box a few times, feeding them each time. After they thus associate climbing out of the box with getting food, they will try to get out whenever put in. They do not, even then, struggle so vigorously or get so excited as the rest. In either case, whether the impulse to struggle be due to an instinctive reaction to confinement or to an association, it is likely to succeed in letting the cat out of the box. The cat that is clawing all over the box in her impulsive struggle will probably claw the string or loop or button so as to open the door. And gradually all the other non-successful impulses will be stamped out and the particular impulse leading to the successful act will be stamped in by the resulting pleasure, until, after many trials, the cat will, when put in the box, immediately claw the button or loop in a definite way.

The starting point for the formation of any association in these cases, then, is the set of instinctive activities which are aroused when a cat feels discomfort in the box either because of confinement or a desire for food. This discomfort, plus the sense-impression of a surrounding, confining wall, expresses itself prior to any experience, in squeezings, clawings, bitings, etc. From among these movements one is selected by success. But this is the starting point only in the case of the first box experienced. After that the cat has associated with the feeling of confinement certain impulses which have led to success more than others and are thereby strengthened. A cat that has learned to escape from A by clawing has when put into C or G a greater tendency to claw at things than it instinctively had at the start, and a less tendency to squeeze through holes. A very pleasant form of this decrease in instinctive impulses was noticed in the gradual cessation of howling and mewing. However, the useless instinctive impulses die out slowly, and often play an important part even after the cat has had experience with six or eight boxes. And what is important in our previous statement, namely, that the activity of an animal when first put into a new box is not directed by any appreciation of *that* box's character, but by certain general impulses to acts, is not affected by this modification. Most of this activity is determined by heredity; some of it, by previous experience.

My use of the words *instinctive* and *im-*

pulse may cause some misunderstanding unless explained here. Let us, throughout this book, understand by instinct any reaction which an animal makes to a situation *without experience*. It thus includes unconscious as well as conscious acts. Any reaction, then, to totally new phenomena, when first experienced, will be called instinctive. Any impulse then felt will be called an instinctive impulse. Instincts include whatever the nervous system of an animal, as far as inherited, is capable of. My use of the word will, I hope, everywhere make clear what fact I mean. If the reader gets the fact meant in mind it does not in the least matter whether he would himself call such a fact instinct or not. Any one who objects to the word may substitute "hocus-pocus" for it wherever it occurs. The definition here made will not be used to prove or disprove any theory, but simply as a signal for the reader to imagine a certain sort of fact.

The word *impulse* is used against the writer's will, but there is no better. Its meaning will probably become clear as the reader finds it in actual use, but to avoid misconception at any time I will state now that *impulse* means the consciousness accompanying a muscular innervation *apart from that feeling of the act which comes from seeing oneself move, from feeling one's body in a different position, etc.* It is the *direct feeling of the doing* as distinguished from the *idea of the act done* gained through eye, etc. For this reason I say "impulse *and* act" instead of simply "act." Above all, it must be borne in mind that by impulse I never mean the *motive* to the act. In popular speech you may say that hunger is the impulse which makes the cat claw. That will never be the use here. The word *motive* will always denote that sort of consciousness. Any one who thinks that the act ought not to be thus subdivided into impulse and deed may feel free to use the word *act* for *impulse* or *impulse and act* throughout, if he will remember that the act in this aspect of being felt as to be done or as doing is in animals the important thing, is the thing which gets associated, while the act as done, as viewed from outside, is a secondary affair. I prefer to have a separate word, impulse, for the former, and keep the word act for the latter, which it commonly means.

Starting, then, with its store of instinctive impulses, the cat hits upon the successful movement, and gradually associates it with the sense-impression of the interior of the box until the connection is perfect, so that it performs the act as soon as confronted with the sense-impression.

⋅ ⋅ ⋅ ⋅

Surely every one must agree that no man now has a right to advance theories about what is in animals' minds or to deny previous theories unless he supports his thesis by systematic and extended experiments. My own theories, soon to be proclaimed, will doubtless be opposed by many. I sincerely hope they will, provided the denial is accompanied by actual experimental work. In fact I shall be tempted again and again in the course of this book to defend some theory, dubious enough to my own mind, in the hope of thereby inducing some one to oppose me and in opposing me to make the experiments I have myself had no opportunity to make yet. Probably there will be enough opposition if I confine myself to the theories I feel sure of.

⋅ ⋅ ⋅ ⋅

REASONING OR INFERENCE.

The first great question is whether or not animals are ever led to do any of their acts by reasoning. Do they ever conclude from inference that a certain act will produce a certain desired result, and so do it? The best opinion has been that they do not. The best interpretation of even the most extraordinary performances of animals has been that they were the result of accident and association or imitation. But it has after all been only opinion and interpretation, and the opposite theory persistently reappears in the literature of the subject. So, although it is in a way superfluous to give the *coup de grace* to the despised theory that animals reason, I think it is worth while to settle this question once for all.

The great support of those who do claim for animals the ability to infer has been their wonderful performances which resemble our own. These could not, they claim, have happened by accident. No animal could learn to open a latched gate by accident. The whole substance of the argument vanishes if, as a matter of fact, animals do learn those things by accident. *They certainly do.* . . .

The cat does not look over the situation, much less *think* it over, and then decide what to do. It bursts out at once into the activities which instinct and experience have settled on as suitable reactions to the situation *"confinement when hungry with food outside."* It does not ever in the course of its successes realize that such an act brings food and therefore decide to do it and thenceforth do it immediately from *decision* instead of from impulse. The one impulse, out of many accidental ones, which leads to pleasure, becomes strengthened and stamped in thereby, and more and more firmly associated with the sense-impression of that box's interior. Accordingly it is sooner and sooner fulfilled. Futile impulses are gradually stamped out. The gradual slope of the time-curve, then, shows the absence of reasoning. They represent the wearing smooth of a path in the brain, not the decisions of a rational consciousness. . . .

In all these experiments, where there was every motive for the use of any reasoning faculty, if such existed, where the animals literally lived by their intellectual powers, one finds no sign of abstraction, or inference, or judgment.

So far I have only given facts which are quite uninfl[u]enced by any possible incompetence or prejudice of the observer. These alone seem to disprove the existence of any rational faculty in the subjects experimented on. I may add that my observations of all the conduct of all these animals during the months spent with them, failed to find any act that even *seemed* due to reasoning. I should claim that this quarrel ought now to be dropped for good and all, that investigation ought to be directed along more sensible and profitable lines. I should claim that the psychologist who studies dogs and cats in order to defend this "reason" theory is on a level with a zoölogist who should study fishes with a view to supporting the thesis that they possessed clawed digits.

.　.　.　.　.

The Mental Fact in Association.

It is now time to put the question as to just what is in an animal's mind when, having profited by numerous experiences, he has formed the association and does the proper act when put in a certain box. The commonly accepted view of the mental fact then present is that the sight of the inside of the box reminds the animal of his *previous pleasant experience after escape* and *of the movements* which he made which were immediately followed by and so associated with that escape. It has been taken for granted that *if the animal remembered the pleasant experience and remembered the movement, he would make the movement.* It has been assumed that the association was *an association of ideas;* that when one of the ideas was of a movement the animal was capable of making the movement. . . .

But the animal can not form an association leading to an act unless the particular impulse to that act is present as an element of the association; he cannot supply it from a general stock. The groundwork of animal associations is not the association of *ideas,* but the association of idea or sense-impression with *impulse.*

.　.　.　.　.

The chief psychological interest of these data is that they show that permanence of associations *is not memory.* The fact that a cat, when after an interval she is put into box G, proceeds to immediately press the thumb-piece and push the door, does not at all mean that the cat feels the box to be the same from which she weeks ago freed herself by pushing down that thumb-piece, or thinks about ever having felt or done anything in that box. She does not refer the present situation to a situation of the past and realize that it is the same, but simply feels on being confronted with that situation the same impulse which she felt before. She does the thing now for just the same reason that she did it before, namely, because pleasure has connected that act above all others with that sense-impression, so that it is the one she feels like doing. Her condition is that of the swimmer who starts his summer season after a winter's deprivation. When he jumps off the pier and hits the water he swims, not because he remembers that this is the way he dealt with water last summer and so applies his remembrance to present use, but just because experience has taught him to feel like swimming when he hits the water. All talk about recognition and memory in animals, if it asserts the presence of anything more than this, is a gross mistake. . . . "Memory" in animals, if one still chooses to use the word, is *permanence of associations,* not the presence of an idea of an experience attributed to the past.

. . . . .

At least some of our results possess considerable pedagogical interest. The fundamental form of intellection, the association-process in animals, is one, we decided, which requires the personal experience of the animal in all its elements. The association cannot be taught by putting the animal through it or giving it a chance to imitate. Now every observant teacher realizes how often the cleverest explanation and the best models for imitation fail. Yet often, in such cases, a pupil, if somehow enticed to do the thing, even without comprehension of what it means, even without any real knowledge of what he is doing, will finally get hold of it. So, also, in very many kinds of knowl-

edge, the pupil who does anything from imitation, or who does anything from being put through it, fails to get a real and permanent mastery of the thing. I am sure that with a certain type of mind the only way to teach fractions in algebra, for example, is to get the pupil to do, do, do. I am inclined to think that in many individuals certain things cannot be learned save by actual performance. And I think it is often a fair question when explanation, imitation and actual performance are all possible methods, which is the best. We are here alongside the foundations of mental life, and this hitherto unsuspected law of animal mind may prevail in human mind to an extent hitherto unknown. The best way with children may often be in the pompous words of an animal trainer, "to arrange everything in connection with the trick so that the animal will be compelled by the laws of his own nature to perform it."

This does not at all imply that I think, as a present school of scientists seem to, that because a certain thing *has been* in phylogeny we ought to repeat it in ontogeny. Heaven knows that Dame Nature herself in ontogeny abbreviates and skips and distorts the order of the appearance of organs and functions, and for the best of reasons. We ought to make an effort, as she does, to omit the useless and antiquated and get to the best and most useful as soon as possible; we ought to change what *is* to what *ought to be,* as far as we can. And I would not advocate this animal-like method of learning in place of the later ones unless it does the same work better. I simply suggest that in many cases where at present its use is never dreamed of, it may be a good method. As the fundamental form of intellection every student of *theoretical* pedagogy ought to take it into account. . . .

If the reader cares here, at the end, to have the broadest possible statement of our conclusions and will take the pains to supply the right meaning, we might say that our work has described a method, crude but promising, and has made the beginning of an exact estimate of just what associations, simple and compound, an animal can form, how quickly he forms them, and how long he retains them. It has described the method of formation, and, on the condition that our subjects were representative, has rejected reason, comparison or inference, perception of similarity, and imitation.

JOHN B. WATSON
"Psychology as the Behaviorist Views It" (1913) *

Psychology as the behaviorist views it is a purely objective experimental branch of natural science. Its theoretical goal is the prediction and control of behavior. Introspection forms no essential part of its methods, nor is the scientific value of its data dependent upon the readiness with which they lend themselves to interpretation in terms of consciousness. The behaviorist, in his efforts to get a unitary scheme of animal response, recognizes no dividing line between man and brute. The behavior of man, with all of its refinement and complexity, forms only a part of the behaviorist's total scheme of investigation.

It has been maintained by its followers generally that psychology is a study of the science of the phenomena of consciousness. It has taken as its problem, on the one hand, the analysis of complex mental states (or processes) into simple elementary constituents, and on the other the construction of complex states when the elementary constituents are given. The world of physical objects (stimuli, including here anything which may excite activity in a receptor), which forms the total phenomena of the natural scientist, is looked upon merely as means to an end. That end is the production of mental states that may be "inspected" or "observed." The psychological object of observation in the case of an emotion, for example, is the mental state itself. The prob-

* John B. Watson, "Psychology as the Behaviorist Views It," *Psychological Review,* Vol. XX, No. 2 (March, 1913), pp. 158–159, 163, 167–177.

lem in emotion is the determination of the number and kind of elementary constituents present, their loci, intensity, order of appearance, etc. It is agreed that introspection is the method *par excellence* by means of which mental states may be manipulated for purposes of psychology. On this assumption, behavior data (including under this term everything which goes under the name of comparative psychology) have no value *per se.* They possess significance only in so far as they may throw light upon conscious states. Such data must have at least an analogical or indirect reference to belong to the realm of psychology.

Indeed, at times, one finds psychologists who are sceptical of even this analogical reference. Such scepticism is often shown by the question which is put to the student of behavior, "what is the bearing of animal work upon human psychology?" I used to have to study over this question. Indeed it always embarrassed me somewhat. I was interested in my own work and felt that it was important, and yet I could not trace any close connection between it and psychology as my questioner understood psychology. I hope that such a confession will clear the atmosphere to such an extent that we will no longer have to work under false pretences. We must frankly admit that the facts so important to us which we have been able to glean from extended work upon the senses of animals by the behavior method have contributed only in a fragmentary way to the general theory of human sense organ processes, nor have they suggested new points of experimental attack. The enormous number of experiments which we have carried out upon learning have likewise contributed little to human psychology. It seems reasonably clear that some kind of compromise must be effected: either psychology must change its viewpoint so as to take in facts of behavior, whether or not they have bearings upon the problems of "consciousness"; or else behavior must stand alone as a wholly separate and independent science. Should human psychologists fail to look with favor upon our overtures and refuse to modify their position, the behaviorists will be driven to using human beings as subjects and to employ methods of investigation which are exactly comparable to those now employed in the animal work. . . .

I do not wish unduly to criticize psychology. It has failed signally, I believe, during the fifty-odd years of its existence as an experimental discipline to make its place in the world as an undisputed natural science. Psychology, as it is generally thought of, has something esoteric in its methods. If you fail to reproduce my findings, it is not due to some fault in your apparatus or in the control of your stimulus, but it is due to the fact that your introspection is untrained. The attack is made upon the observer and not upon the experimental setting. In physics and in chemistry the attack is made upon the experimental conditions. The apparatus was not sensitive enough, impure chemicals were used, etc. In these sciences a better technique will give reproducible results. Psychology is otherwise. If you can't observe 3–9 states of clearness in attention, your introspection is poor. If, on the other hand, a feeling seems reasonably clear to you, your introspection is again faulty. You are seeing too much. Feelings are never clear.

The time seems to have come when psychology must discard all reference to consciousness; when it need no longer delude itself into thinking that it is making mental states the object of observation. . . .

The psychology which I should attempt to build up would take as a starting point, first, the observable fact that organisms, man and animal alike, do adjust themselves to their environment by means of hereditary and habit equipments. These adjustments may be very adequate or they may be so inadequate that the organism barely maintains its existence; secondly, that certain stimuli lead the organisms to make the responses. In a system of psychology completely worked out, given the response the stimuli can be predicted; given the stimuli the response can be predicted. Such a set

of statements is crass and raw in the extreme, as all such generalizations must be. Yet they are hardly more raw and less realizable than the ones which appear in the psychology texts of the day. I possibly might illustrate my point better by choosing an everyday problem which anyone is likely to meet in the course of his work. Some time ago I was called upon to make a study of certain species of birds. Until I went to Tortugas I had never seen these birds alive. When I reached there I found the animals doing certain things: some of the acts seemed to work peculiarly well in such an environment, while others seemed to be unsuited to their type of life. I first studied the responses of the group as a whole and later those of individuals. In order to understand more thoroughly the relation between what was habit and what was hereditary in these responses, I took the young birds and reared them. In this way I was able to study the order of appearance of hereditary adjustments and their complexity, and later the beginnings of habit formation. My efforts in determining the stimuli which called forth such adjustments were crude indeed. Consequently my attempts to control behavior and to produce responses at will did not meet with much success. Their food and water, sex and other social relations, light and temperature conditions were all beyond control in a field study. I did find it possible to control their reactions in a measure by using the nest and egg (or young) as stimuli. It is not necessary in this paper to develop further how such a study should be carried out and how work of this kind must be supplemented by carefully controlled laboratory experiments. Had I been called upon to examine the natives of some of the Australian tribes, I should have gone about my task in the same way. I should have found the problem more difficult: the types of responses called forth by physical stimuli would have been more varied, and the number of effective stimuli larger. I should have had to determine the social setting of their lives in a far more careful way. These savages would be more influenced by the responses of each other than was the case with the birds. Furthermore, habits would have been more complex and the influences of past habits upon the present responses would have appeared more clearly. Finally, if I had been called upon to work out the psychology of the educated European, my problem would have required several lifetimes. But in the one I have at my disposal I should have followed the same general line of attack. In the main, my desire in all such work is to gain an accurate knowledge of adjustments and the stimuli calling them forth. My final reason for this is to learn general and particular methods by which I may control behavior. My goal is not "the description and explanation of states of consciousness as such," nor that of obtaining such proficiency in mental gymnastics that I can immediately lay hold of a state of consciousness and say, "this, as a whole, consists of gray sensation number 350, of such and such extent, occurring in conjunction with the sensation of cold of a certain intensity; one of pressure of a certain intensity and extent," and so on *ad infinitum*. If psychology would follow the plan I suggest, the educator, the physician, the jurist and the business man could utilize our data in a practical way, as soon as we are able, experimentally, to obtain them. Those who have occasion to apply psychological principles practically would find no need to complain as they do at the present time. Ask any physician or jurist today whether scientific psychology plays a practical part in his daily routine and you will hear him deny that the psychology of the laboratories finds a place in his scheme of work. I think the criticism is extremely just. One of the earliest conditions which made me dissatisfied with psychology was the feeling that there was no realm of application for the principles which were being worked out in content terms.

What gives me hope that the behaviorist's position is a defensible one is the fact that those branches of psychology which have already partially withdrawn from the parent, experimental psychology, and which are consequently less dependent upon introspection are today in a most flourishing condition. Experimental pedagogy, the psychology of drugs, the psychology of advertising, legal psychology, the psychology of tests, and psychopathology are all vigorous growths. These are sometimes wrongly called "practical" or "applied" psychology. Surely there was never a worse misnomer. In the future there may grow up vocational bureaus which really apply psychology. At present these fields are truly scientific and are in search of broad generalizations which will lead to the control of human behavior. For example, we find out by experimentation whether a series of stanzas may be acquired more readily if the whole is learned at once, or whether it is more advantageous to learn each stanza separately and then pass to the succeeding. We do not attempt to apply our findings. The application of this principle is purely voluntary on the part of the teacher. In the psychology of drugs we may show the effect upon behavior of certain doses of caffeine. We may reach the conclusion that caffeine has a good effect upon the speed and accuracy of work. But these are general principles. We leave it to the individual as to whether the results of our tests shall be applied or not. Again, in legal testimony, we test the effects of recency upon the reliability of a witness's report. We test the accuracy of the report with respect to moving objects, stationary objects, color, etc. It depends upon the judicial machinery of the country to decide whether these facts are ever to be applied. For a "pure" psychologist to say that he is not interested in the questions raised in these divisions of the science because they relate indirectly to the application of psychology shows, in the first place, that he fails to understand the scientific aim in such problems, and secondly, that he is not interested in a psychology which concerns itself with human life. The only fault I have to find with these disciplines is that much of their material is stated in terms of introspection, whereas a statement in terms of objective results would be far more valuable. There is no reason why appeal should ever be made to consciousness in any of them. Or why introspective data should ever be sought during the experimentation, or published in the results. In experimental pedagogy especially one can see the desirability of keeping all of the results on a purely objective plane. If this is done, work there on the human being will be comparable directly with the work upon animals. For example, at Hopkins, Mr. Ulrich has obtained certain results upon the distribution of effort in learning—using rats as subjects. He is prepared to give comparative results upon the effect of having an animal work at the problem once per day, three times per day, and five times per day. Whether it is advisable to have the animal learn only one problem at a time or to learn three abreast. We need to have similar experiments made upon man, but we care as little about his "conscious processes" during the conduct of the experiment as we care about such processes in the rats. . . .

The man and the animal should be placed as nearly as possible under the same experimental conditions. Instead of feeding or punishing the human subject, we should ask him to respond by setting a second apparatus until standard and control offered no basis for a differential response. Do I lay myself open to the charge here that I am using introspection? My reply is not at all; that while I might very well feed my human subject for a right choice and punish him for a wrong one and thus produce the response if the subject could give it, there is no need of going to extremes even on the platform I suggest. But be it understood that I am merely using this second method as an abridged behavior method. We can go just as far and reach just as dependable results by the longer method as by the abridged. In many cases the direct and typically human method cannot be safely used. Suppose, for example, that I doubt the accuracy of the setting of the control instrument, in the above experiment, as I am very likely to do if I suspect a defect in vision? It is hopeless for me to get his introspective report. He will say: "There is no difference in sen-

sation, both are reds, identical in quality." But suppose I confront him with the standard and the control and so arrange conditions that he is punished if he responds to the "control" but not with the standard. I interchange the positions of the standard and the control at will and force him to attempt to differentiate the one from the other. If he can learn to make the adjustment even after a large number of trials it is evident that the two stimuli do afford the basis for a differential response. Such a method may sound nonsensical, but I firmly believe we will have to resort increasingly to just such method where we have reason to distrust the language method. . . .

The situation is somewhat different when we come to a study of the more complex forms of behavior, such as imagination, judgment, reasoning, and conception. At present the only statements we have of them are in content terms. Our minds have been so warped by the fifty-odd years which have been devoted to the study of states of consciousness that we can envisage these problems only in one way. We should meet the situation squarely and say that we are not able to carry forward investigations along all of these lines by the behavior methods which are in use at the present time. . . . As our methods become better developed it will be possible to undertake investigations of more and more complex forms of behavior. Problems which are now laid aside will again become imperative, but they can be viewed as they arise from a new angle and in more concrete settings. . . .

In concluding, I suppose I must confess to a deep bias on these questions. I have devoted nearly twelve years to experimentation on animals. It is natural that such a one should drift into a theoretical position which is in harmony with his experimental work. Possibly I have put up a straw man and have been fighting that. There may be no absolute lack of harmony between the position outlined here and that of functional psychology. I am inclined to think, however, that the two positions cannot be easily harmonized. Certainly the position I advocate is weak enough at present and can be attacked from many standpoints. Yet when all this is admitted I still feel that the considerations which I have urged should have a wide influence upon the type of psychology which is to be developed in the future. What we need to do is to start work upon psychology, making *behavior,* not *consciousness,* the objective point of our attack. Certainly there are enough problems in the control of behavior to keep us all working many lifetimes without ever allowing us time to think of consciousness *an sich.* Once launched in the undertaking, we will find ourselves in a short time as far divorced from an introspective psychology as the psychology of the present time is divorced from faculty psychology.

SUMMARY

1. Human psychology has failed to make good its claim as a natural science. Due to a mistaken notion that its fields of facts are conscious phenomena and that introspection is the only direct method of ascertaining these facts, it has enmeshed itself in a series of speculative questions which, while fundamental to its present tenets, are not open to experimental treatment. In the pursuit of answers to these questions, it has become further and further divorced from contact with problems which vitally concern human interest.

2. Psychology, as the behaviorist views it, is a purely objective, experimental branch of natural science which needs introspection as little as do the sciences of chemistry and physics. It is granted that the behavior of animals can be investigated without appeal to consciousness. Heretofore the viewpoint has been that such data have value only in so far as they can be interpreted by analogy in terms of consciousness. The position is taken here that the behavior of man and the behavior of animals must be considered on the same plane; as being equally essential to a general understanding of behavior. It can dispense with consciousness in a psychological sense. The separate observation of

"states of consciousness" is, on this assumption, no more a part of the task of the psychologist than of the physicist. We might call this the return to a non-reflective and naïve use of consciousness. In this sense consciousness may be said to be the instrument or tool with which all scientists work. Whether or not the tool is properly used at present by scientists is a problem for philosophy and not for psychology.

3. From the viewpoint here suggested the facts on the behavior of amœbæ have value in and for themselves without reference to the behavior of man. In biology studies on race differentiation and inheritance in amœbæ form a separate division of study which must be evaluated in terms of the laws found there. The conclusions so reached may not hold in any other form. Regardless of the possible lack of generality, such studies must be made if evolution as a whole is ever to be regulated and controlled. Similarly the laws of behavior in amœbæ, the range of responses, and the determination of effective stimuli, of habit formation, persistency of habits, interference and reinforcement of habits, must be determined and evaluated in and for themselves, regardless of their generality, or of their bearing upon such laws in other forms, if the phenomena of behavior are ever to be brought within the sphere of scientific control.

4. This suggested elimination of states of consciousness as proper objects of investigation in themselves will remove the barrier from psychology which exists between it and the other sciences. The findings of psychology become the functional correlates of structure and lend themselves to explanation in physico-chemical terms.

5. Psychology as behavior will, after all, have to neglect but few of the really essential problems with which psychology as an introspective science now concerns itself. In all probability even this residue of problems may be phrased in such a way that refined methods in behavior (which certainly must come) will lead to their solution.

B. F. SKINNER
The Behavior of Organisms (1938) *

A SYSTEM OF BEHAVIOR

The need for a science of behavior should be clear to anyone who looks about him at the rôle of behavior in human affairs. Indeed, the need is so obvious and so great that it has acted to discourage rather than to stimulate the establishment of such a science. It is largely because of its tremendous consequences that a rigorous treatment of behavior is still regarded in many quarters as impossible. The goal has seemed wholly inaccessible. What the eventual success of such a science might be, probably no one is now prepared to say; but the preliminary problems at least are not beyond the reach of existing scientific methods and practices, and they open up one of the most interesting prospects in modern science.

The two questions which immediately present themselves are: What will be the structure of a science of behavior? and How valid can its laws be made? . . . I am interested, first, in setting up a system of behavior in terms of which the facts of a science may be stated and, second, in testing the system experimentally at some of its more important points. . . .

A DEFINITION OF BEHAVIOR

It is necessary to begin with a definition. Behavior is only part of the total activity of an organism, and some formal delimitation is called for. The field might be defined historically by appeal to an established interest. As distinct from the other activities of the organism, the phenomena of behavior are held together by a common conspicuousness. Behavior is what an organism is *doing*—or more accurately what it is observed by another organism to be doing. . . .

* B. F. Skinner, *The Behavior of Organisms: An Experimental Analysis* (New York: Appleton-Century-Crofts, 1938), pp. 5–6, 19–21, 441–442. Reprinted by permission of Appleton-Century-Crofts, Division of Meredith Corporation.

By behavior, then, I mean simply the movement of an organism or of its parts in a frame of reference provided by the organism itself or by various external objects or fields of force. It is convenient to speak of this as the action of the organism upon the outside world, and it is often desirable to deal with an effect rather than with the movement itself, as in the case of the production of sounds.

. . . . .

OPERANT BEHAVIOR

With the discovery of the stimulus and the collection of a large number of specific relationships of stimulus and response, it came to be assumed by many writers that all behavior would be accounted for in this way as soon as the appropriate stimuli could be identified. Many elaborate attempts have been made to establish the plausibility of this assumption, but they have not, I believe, proved convincing. There is a large body of behavior that does not seem to be *elicited,* in the sense in which a cinder in the eye elicits closure of the lid, although it may eventually stand in a different kind of relation to external stimuli. The original "spontaneous" activity of the organism is chiefly of this sort, as is the greater part of the conditioned behavior of the adult organism, as I hope to show later. Merely to assert that there *must* be eliciting stimuli is an unsatisfactory appeal to ignorance. . . .

An event may occur without any observed antecedent event and still be dealt with adequately in a descriptive science. I do not mean that there are no originating forces in spontaneous behavior but simply that they are not located in the environment. We are not in a position to see them, and we have no need to. This kind of behavior might be said to be *emitted* by the organism, and there are appropriate techniques for dealing with it in that form. One important independent variable is time. In making use of it I am simply recognizing that the observed datum is the appearance of a given identifiable sample of behavior at some more or less orderly rate. The use of a rate is perhaps the outsanding characteristic of [this] general method . . . , where we shall be concerned very largely with behavior of this sort.

The attempt to force behavior into the simple stimulus-response formula has delayed the adequate treatment of that large part of behavior which cannot be shown to be under the control of eliciting stimuli. It will be highly important to recognize the existence of this separate field in the present work. Differences between the two kinds of behavior will accumulate throughout the book, and I shall not argue the distinction here at any length. The kind of behavior that is correlated with specific eliciting stimuli may be called *respondent* behavior and a given correlation *a respondent*. The term is intended to carry the sense of a relation to a prior event. Such behavior as is not under this kind of control I shall call *operant* and any specific example *an operant*. The term refers to a posterior event, to be noted shortly. The term reflex will be used to include both respondent and operant even though in its original meaning it applied to respondents only. A single term for both is convenient because both are topographical units of behavior and because an operant may and usually does acquire a relation to prior stimulation. In general, the notion of a reflex is to be emptied of any connotation of the active "push" of the stimulus. The terms refer here to correlated entities, and to nothing more. All implications of dynamism and all metaphorical and figurative definitions should be avoided as far as possible.

·   ·   ·   ·   ·

CONCLUSION

The traditional description and organization of behavior represented by the concepts of "will," "cognition," "intellect," and so on, cannot be accepted so long as it pretends to be dealing with a mental world, but the behavior to which these terms apply is natu-

rally part of the subject matter of a science of behavior. What is wanted in such a science is an alternative set of terms derived from an analysis of behavior and capable of doing the same work. No attempt has been made here to translate mentalistic or philosophical concepts into the terms of the present system. The only value of a translation would be pedagogical. Traditional concepts are based upon data at another level of analysis and cannot be expected to prove useful. They have no place in a system derived step by step from the behavior itself.

The reader will have noticed that almost no extension to human behavior is made or suggested. This does not mean that he is expected to be interested in the behavior of the rat for its own sake. The importance of a science of behavior derives largely from the possibility of an eventual extension to human affairs. . . .

Whether or not extrapolation is justified cannot at the present time be decided. It is possible that there are properties of human behavior which will require a different kind of treatment. But this can be ascertained only by closing in upon the problem in an orderly way and by following the customary procedures of an experimental science. We can neither assert nor deny discontinuity between the human and subhuman fields so long as we know so little about either. If, nevertheless, the author . . . is expected to hazard a guess publicly, I may say that the only differences I expect to see revealed between the behavior of rat and man (aside from enormous differences of complexity) lie in the field of verbal behavior.

WOLFGANG KÖHLER
The Mentality of Apes (1917)*

* Wolfgang Köhler, *The Mentality of Apes* (New York: Humanities Press, and London: Routledge & Kegan Paul, 1925; translated from the Second Revised Edition by Ella Winter; originally published in 1917), pp. 2–5, 130–134, 275–279. Used by permission of Humanities Press, Inc., and Routledge & Kegan Paul Ltd.

INTRODUCTION

There is probably no association psychologist who does not, in his own unprejudiced observations, distinguish, and, to a certain extent, contrast unintelligent behaviour and intelligent. For what is association psychology other than the theory that one can trace back to the phenomena of a generally-known simple association type even occurrences which, according to unbiassed observation, do not at first make the impression of being identical, above all so-called intelligence performances? In short, it is just these differences which are the starting-point of a strict association psychology; it is they which need to be theoretically accounted for; they are well known to the association psychologist. Thus for instance, we find a radical representative of this school (Thorndike) stating the conclusion, drawn from experiments on dogs and cats: "I failed to find any act that even *seemed* due to reasoning." To anyone who can formulate his results thus, other behaviour must already have seemed to be intelligent; he is already acquainted with the contrast in his observations, perhaps of human beings, even if he discards it afterwards in theory.

Accordingly, if we are to inquire whether the anthropoid ape behaves intelligently, this problem can for the present be treated quite independently of theoretical assumptions, particularly those for or against the association theory. It is true that it then becomes somewhat indefinite; we are not to inquire whether anthropoid apes show something well defined, but whether their behaviour approximates to a type rather superficially known by experience, and which we call "intelligence" in contrast to other behaviour— especially in animals. . . .

What seems to us "intelligence" tends to be called into play when circumstances block a course which seems obvious to us, leaving open a roundabout path which the human being or animal takes, so meeting the situation. In unexpressed agreement with this, nearly all those observers who heretofore have sought to solve the problem of animal intelligence, have done so by watching animals in just such predicaments. As in cases below the stage of development of anthropoid apes results are, in general, negative, there arose out of those experiments the view widely held at present, i.e. that there is very little intelligent behaviour in animals; only a small number of such experiments have been carried out on anthropoid apes, and they have not yet led to any very definite results. All the experiments described in the following pages are of one and the same kind: the experimenter sets up a situation in which the direct path to the objective is blocked, but a roundabout way left open. The animal is introduced into this situation, which can, potentially, be wholly surveyed, and so we shall be able to see up to which level of behaviour its capabilities take it, and, particularly, whether it can solve the problem in the possible "roundabout" way.

The experiments were at first applied to chimpanzees only, with the exception of a few cases taken for comparison, in which human beings, a dog, and hens were observed.

Seven of the animals belonged to the old branch of the anthropoid station which the Prussian Academy of Science maintained in Tenerife from 1912 to 1920. Of these seven the oldest, an adult female, was named Tschego, because of several characteristics which made us, perhaps wrongly, consider her a member of the Tschego species. (We are yet far from possessing a clear and systematized classification of the varieties of the chimpanzee.) The oldest of the smaller animals, called Grande, also differs considerably in several respects from its comrades. But as the differences concern its general character rather than the behaviour investigated in the intelligence tests, a detailed description of them would be out of place here. The other five, two males (Sultan and Konsul), three females (Tercera, Rana, and Chica), are of the usual chimpanzee type.

To the seven animals mentioned, two

others were added later, both of which led to valuable observations, but both of which, to our regret, soon died.

.   .   .   .   .

THE MAKING OF IMPLEMENTS

Are the two sticks ever combined so as to become technically useful? This time Sultan is the subject of experiment. His sticks are two hollow, but firm, bamboo rods, such as the animals often use for pulling along fruit. The one is so much smaller than the other, that it can be pushed in at either end quite easily. Beyond the bars lies the objective, just so far away that the animal cannot reach it with either rod. They are about the same length. Nevertheless, he takes great pains to try to reach it with one stick or the other, even pushing his right shoulder through the bars.[1] When everything proves futile, Sultan commits a "bad error," or, more clearly, a great stupidity, such as he made sometimes on other occasions. He pulls a box from the back of the room towards the bars; true, he pushes it away again at once as it is useless, or rather, actually in the way. Immediately afterwards, he does something which, although practically useless, must be counted among the "good errors": he pushes one of the sticks out as far as it will go, then takes the second, and with it pokes the first one cautiously towards the objective, pushing it carefully from the nearer end and thus slowly urging it towards the fruit. This does not always succeed, but if he has got pretty close in this way, he takes even greater precaution; he pushes very gently, watches the movements of the stick that is lying on the ground, and actually touches the objective with its tip. Thus, all of a sudden, for the first time, the contact "animal-objective" has been established, and Sultan visibly feels (we humans can sympathize) a certain satisfaction in having even so much power over the fruit that he can touch and slightly move it by pushing the stick. The proceeding is re-

peated; when the animal has pushed the stick on the ground so far out that he cannot possibly get it back by himself, it is given back to him. But although, in trying to steer it cautiously, he puts the stick in his hand exactly to the cut (i.e. the opening) of the stick on the ground, and although one might think that doing so would suggest the possibility of pushing one stick into the other, there is no indication whatever of such a practically valuable solution. Finally, the observer gives the animal some help by putting one finger into the opening of one stick under the animal's nose (without pointing to the other stick at all). This has no effect; Sultan, as before, pushes one stick with the other towards the objective, and as this pseudo-solution does not satisfy him any longer, he abandons his efforts altogether, and does not even pick up the sticks when they are both again thrown through the bars to him. The experiment has lasted over an hour, and is stopped for the present, as it seems hopeless, carried out like this. As we intend to take it up again after a while, Sultan is left in possession of his sticks; the keeper is left there to watch him.

Keeper's report: "Sultan first of all squats indifferently on the box, which has been left standing a little back from the railings; then he gets up, picks up the two sticks, sits down again on the box and plays carelessly with them. While doing this, it happens that he finds himself holding one rod in either hand in such a way that they lie in a straight line; he pushes the thinner one a little way into the opening of the thicker, jumps up and is already on the run towards the railings, to which he has up to now half turned his back, and begins to draw a banana towards him with the double stick. I call the master: meanwhile, one of the animal's rods has fallen out of the other, as he has pushed one of them only a little way into the other; whereupon he connects them again."[2]

[1] In order not to discourage the animal from the very beginning, I put the objective only just out of reach of the single stick.

[2] The keeper's tale seems acceptable to me, especially as, upon inquiries, he emphasized the fact that Sultan had first of all connected the sticks in play and without considering the ob-

The keeper's report covers a period of scarcely five minutes, which had elapsed since stopping the experiment. Called by the man, I continued observation myself: Sultan is squatting at the bars, holding out one stick, and, at its end, a second bigger one, which is on the point of falling off. It does fall. Sultan pulls it to him and forthwith, with the greatest assurance, pushes the thinner one in again, so that it is firmly wedged, and fetches a fruit with the lengthened implement. But the bigger tube selected is a little too big, and so it slips from the end of the thinner one several times; each time Sultan rejoins the tubes immediately by holding the bigger one towards himself in the left and the thinner one in his right hand and a little backwards, and then sliding one into the other. The proceeding seems to please him immensely; he is very lively, pulls all the fruit, one after the other, towards the railings, without taking time to eat it, and when I disconnect the double-stick he puts it together again at once, and draws any distant objects whatever to the bars.

The next day the test is repeated; Sultan begins with the proceeding which is in practice useless, but after he has pushed one of the tubes forward with the other for a few seconds, he again takes up both, quickly puts one into the other, and attains his objective with the double stick.

The objective lies in front of the railings, still farther away; Sultan has three tubes to resort to, the two bigger ones fitting over either end of the third. He tries to reach his objective with two tubes, as before; as the outer one keeps falling off, he takes distinct

pains to push the thinner stick farther into the bigger one. Contrary to expectation, he actually attains his objective with the double tube, and pulls it to him. The long tool sometimes get into his way when doing this, by its ings, when being moved obliquely, so the farther end getting caught between the rail-animal quickly separates it into its parts, and finishes the task with one tube only. From now on, he does this every time when the objective is so close that *one* stick is sufficient, and the double-stick awkward. The new objective is placed still farther away. In consequence, Sultan tries which of the bigger tubes is more useful when joined to the thin one; for they do not differ very much in length (64 and 70 cms.), and, of course, the animal does not lay them together in order to compare their lengths. *Sultan never tries to join the two bigger tubes;* once he puts them opposite to each other for a moment, not touching, and looks at the two openings, but puts one aside directly (without trying it) and picks up the third thinner one; the two wide tubes have openings of the same size.[3] The solution follows quite suddenly: Sultan fishes with a double-stick, consisting of the thinner one and one of the bigger ones, holding, as usual, the end of the smaller one in his hand. All of a sudden he pulls the double-stick in, turns it round, so that the thin end is before his eyes and the other towering up in the air behind him, seizes the third tube with his left hand, and introduces the tip of the double-stick into its opening. With the triple pole he reaches the objective easily; and when the long implement proves a hindrance in pulling the objective to him, it is disconnected as before.

. . . . .

CONCLUSION

The chimpanzees manifest intelligent behaviour of the general kind familiar in

---

jective (his task). The animals are constantly poking about with straws and small sticks in holes and cracks in their play, so that it would be more astonishing if Sultan had never done this, while playing about with the two sticks. There need be no suspicion that the keeper quickly "trained the animal"; the man would never dare it. If anybody continues to doubt, even that does not matter, for Sultan continually not only performs this act but shows that he realizes its meaning.

[3] It can be shown that when the chimpanzee connects the double-stick he is guided by the relation between the two thicknesses of the tubes.

human beings. Not all their intelligent acts are externally similar to human acts, but under well-chosen experimental conditions, the type of intelligent conduct can always be traced. This applies, in spite of very important differences between one animal and another, even to the least gifted specimens of the species that have been observed here, and, therefore, must hold good of every member of the species, as long as it is not mentally deficient, in the pathological sense of the word. With this exception, which is presumably rare, the success of the intelligence tests in general will be more likely endangered by the person making the experiment than by the animal. One must know and, if necessary, establish by preliminary observation, within which limits of difficulty and in which functions the chimpanzee *can possibly* show insight; negative or confused results from complicated and accidentally-chosen test-material, have obviously no bearing upon the fundamental question, and, in general, the experimenter should recognize that every intelligence test is a test, not only of the creature examined, but also of the experimenter himself. I have said that to myself quite often, and yet I have remained uncertain whether the experiments I performed may be considered "satisfactory" in this respect; without theoretical foundations, and in unknown territory, methodological mistakes may quite well have occurred; anyone who continues this work will be able to prevent them more easily.

At any rate, this remains true: Chimpanzees not only stand out against the rest of the animal world by several morphological and, in its narrower sense, physiological, characteristics, but they also behave in a way which counts as specifically human. As yet we know little of their neighbours on the other side, but according to the little we do know, with the results of this report, it is not impossible that, in this region of experimental research, the anthropoid is nearer to man *in intelligence too,* than to many of the lower ape-species. So far, observations agree well with the theories of evolution; in particular, the correlation between intelligence, and the development of the brain, is confirmed.

The positive result of the investigation requires a kind of boundary-line. It is, indeed, confirmed by experiments of a somewhat different nature, which will be recounted later; but a more complete picture should be formed when they are added, and, in so far, our judgment of the intelligence of apes is left some scope. Of much greater importance is the fact that the experiments in which we tested these animals brought them into situations in which all the factors were given, and the solution could be achieved. This method of experimentation is as well adapted to the chief problem of insight as are any which can bring about the decision "yes" or "no"; in fact, it may be the very best method possible at present, as it yields very many, and very clear, results. But we must not forget that it is just in these experimental circumstances that certain factors hardly appear, or appear not at all, which are rightly considered to be of the greatest importance for *human* intelligence. We do not test at all, or rather only once in passing, how far the chimpanzee is influenced by factors not present, whether things "merely thought about" occupy him noticeably at all. And most closely connected with this, is the following problem. In the method adopted so far we have not been able to tell how far back and forward stretches the time "in which the chimpanzee lives"; for we know that, though one can prove some effects of recognition and reproduction after considerable lapses of time—as is actually the case in anthropoids—this is not the same as "life for a longer space of time." A great deal of time spent with chimpanzees leads me to venture the opinion that, beside the lack of speech, it is in extremely narrow limits in *this* direction that the chief difference is to be found between anthropoids and even the most primitive human beings. The lack of an invaluable technical aid (speech) and a great limitation to those very important components of thought, so-called "images," would thus constitute the causes that prevent the chimpanzee from attaining even the smallest beginnings of cultural development. With special reference to the second fact, the chimpanzee, who is easily puzzled by the simplest optical complications, will indeed fare badly in "image-life," where even man has continually to be fighting against the running into one another, and melting together, of certain processes.

In the field of the experiments carried out here the insight of the chimpanzee shows itself to be principally determined by his optical apprehension of the situation; at times he even starts solving problems from a too visual point of view, and in many cases in which the chimpanzee *stops* acting with insight, it may have been simply that the lie of the land was too much for his visual grasp (relative "weakness of shape perception"). It is therefore difficult to give a satisfactory explanation of all his performances, so long as no detailed theory of shape (*Gestalt*) has been laid as a foundation. The need for such a theory will be felt the more, when one remembers that *solutions* showing insight in this field of intelligence necessarily take part in the nature of the structure of the situations, in so far as they arise in dynamic processes *co-ordinated with* the situation.

It would be less a boundary-line than a standard for the achievements of intelligence described here that would be arrived at by comparing with our experiments the performances of human beings (sick and well) and, above all, human children of different ages. As the results in this book have special reference to a particular method of testing and the special test-material of optically-given situations, it would be those psychological facts established in human beings (especially children), under the same conditions, which would have to be used. But such comparisons cannot be instituted, as, very much to the disadvantage of psychology, not even the most necessary of such facts have been ascertained. Preliminary experiments— some have been mentioned—have given me the impression that we are inclined to overestimate the capabilities of children of all ages up to maturity, and even adults, who have had no special technical training in this type of performance. We are in a region of *terra incognita*. Educational psychology, engaged on the well-known quantitative tests for some time, has not yet been able to test how far normal, and how far mentally-deficient, children can go in certain situations. As experiments of this kind can be performed at the very tenderest age, and are certainly as scientifically valuable as the intelligence tests usually employed, it can be forgiven if they do not become immediately practicable for school and other uses. M. Wertheimer has been expressing this view for some years in his lectures; in this place, where the lack of them makes itself so much felt, I should like to emphasize particularly the importance and—if the anthropoids do not deceive us—the fruitfulness of further work in this direction.

THE INFLUENCE OF EUROPEAN IDEAS

JEAN PIAGET
The Language and Thought of the Child (1926) *

* Jean Piaget, *The Language and Thought of the Child* (New York: Humanities Press, and London: Routledge & Kegan Paul, 1959; translated by Marjorie Gabain and originally published in 1926), pp. 267–274, 276–277. Used by permission of Humanities Press, Inc., and Routledge & Kegan Paul Ltd.

STUDIES IN CHILD LOGIC

THE CHILD'S INTELLECTUAL EGO-CENTRISM.—In our first studies of the child's thought, we used the word ego-centrism for lack of a better one, to denote an orientation of the mind, which seemed to us important at the outset of the individual's intellectual development, and which survives in adults in all circumstances where they are still

dominated by spontaneous, naïve and consequently infantile attitudes. Since our use of
this word has given rise to some misunderstanding,[1] we think it will be useful once
again to make its meaning clear before
determining how far verbal or social ego-
centrism is related to intellectual ego-centrism.

In the first place we must notice that what
specifically characterizes the child's ego-
centrism is not to be found in the social or
moral sphere nor in the child's awareness of
his own self, but definitely in the intellectual
field. Childish ego-centrism is a feature of
his knowledge; we might even say that it is
an epistemic phenomenon if one could speak
of comparative epistemology in regard to the
psychology of the child's intelligence. It is
undoubtedly because we began by describing the social and verbal ego-centrism of the
child before we described this epistemic ego-
centrism—the only important one from our
point of view—that people have objected to
some of our conclusions and shifted the dis-

cussion from its source to related but different ground.

What then is intellectual ego-centrism in
the child? It is the assemblage of all the different precritical and consequently pre-
objective cognitive attitudes of the child's
mind; whether these attitudes relate to nature, to others or to himself matters little.
Fundamentally, ego-centrism is thus neither
a conscious phenomenon (ego-centrism,
when self-conscious, is no longer ego-centrism), nor a phenomenon of social behaviour (behaviour is an indirect manifestation of ego-centrism but does not constitute
it) but a kind of systematic and unconscious
illusion, an illusion of perspective.

An illustration will help to make this
clear. Let us picture a simple ignorant man,
who has lived since his birth in a small
corner at the foot of mountains of which he
has a good view but which he has never explored. From the point of view of physical
knowledge, this observer will obviously fall
a prey to all sorts of illusions: he will not
only reckon that a neighbouring mountain is
higher than a more distant one but will
imagine that the source of a river is in a
mountain from which it appears to flow,
whereas this is not the case. He will see the
world as a system of which he occupies the
centre and all the mountains and valleys
grouped in relation to the place in which he
lives. Similar illusions will colour his knowledge of other people: the traveller coming
from a neighbouring town will be taken for
a foreigner from across the frontier; the intellectual, enjoying a holiday, will be
looked upon as a lazy *rentier*. Everybody
else's activity will thus be measured only in
terms of his own. Finally, as regards knowledge of his ego, the man we are considering,
who we suppose has never defined his physical position (because he has not travelled his
own country, is unable to locate it in relation
to others) nor his moral position (to judge
others objectively), will lack the necessary
systems of reference for knowing himself.
He will, of course, know that he is Joseph
and different from Peter, James or John.

[1] Because of the usual meaning of this word.
Practice does, however, override such ambiguity: there is, for instance, as much difference
between the meaning of what in common use
is called "realism" and that given to it in the
language of philosophy, as there is between
the generally accepted meaning of the word
"ego-centrism" and the one which we have
adopted by convention. "Realism" in ordinary
language signifies taking only facts into account, as opposed to the ideas or feelings of the
subject; philosophical realism, on the contrary,
consists in assuming the existence of things
such as they appear to be, *i.e.*, in confounding
the subjective with the objective. Similarly, in
daily speech, ego-centrism means referring
everything back to oneself, *i.e.*, to a conscious
self, whereas, when we use the term ego-centrism, we mean the inability to differentiate
between one's own point of view and other
people's or between one's own activity and
changes in the object. We adopted this word
by analogy with anthropocentrism, but the
child's anthropocentrism is as yet only adjusted
to his own individual activity as opposed to the
activity of men in general.

But in his own opinion he will be wiser than the foreigner visiting his country and more industrious than the writer who has come to it in order to describe it.

Now this man will not appear ego-centric to himself and perhaps not to others. So far as he himself is concerned, he has obviously no idea of how changed his outlook would be if it were broadened by gradually increasing his knowledge of the neighbourhood, especially if it went beyond the limits of his present horizon, just because this new outlook would not merely add to the type of knowledge he already possesses but would bring about a kind of readjustment, *i.e.*, a recasting of his system of perspectives and values. He is thus ego-centric without being aware of it and consciousness of his ego-centrism would either lessen or eliminate it. In his conversation with others he speaks of the same mountains, the same valleys, the same work and the same events as everyone else, which makes it difficult to detect the restricted and always personal way in which he makes use of ideas that are common property. Only a close observer will be able from time to time to discover, from some naïve remark, in what way his view of the world differs from that of the man who has been able to leave his small homestead and can see himself in relation to others.

To what then can the ego-centrism of the subject we have just described be attributed? In the first place, to a combination of external circumstances: absence of knowledge, the fact of being riveted to one particular small place and social group, etc. But does ignorance explain everything? Certainly not; for, should the subject go beyond his primitive horizon and gradually discover the surrounding country and get to know different kinds of men and social groups, he will be adding more than a few facts to those he already knows: he will be changing the system of his interpretation of things; what for him had been an absolute or a central group of ideas will become merely a point of view as against other points of view. There is thus a second factor to be considered in initial ego-centrism: as a mode of spontaneous apperception, which is common to every individual and as such needs no preliminary explanation, ego-centrism consists of a kind of primary adjustment of thought, an "intellectual simplicity of mind" in the sense of absence of all intellectual relativity and any rational system of reference. Now, such a mode of apperception cannot consist of a quality, susceptible of isolation, which can be observed either externally or by introspection; it remains nevertheless an essential feature of the intellect, conditioning a person's behaviour as well as his conscience, although it is on a different plane from them.

Let us now return to the child. From the double point of view of knowledge of the physical world and knowledge of others or of himself, the child's position is the same as that of the man whose case we have been considering. He finds himself in a physical and social universe, which he has never explored, he cannot therefore escape from making his own the particular view of things created by the circumstances in which he is placed. As to the epistemic attitude, which forms his response to this external situation, it could only be even more "innocent," since, during the first weeks of his existence, the child is unaware of himself as capable of thought or even as a living and conscious being, to such an extent that he is entirely absorbed in the things he sees, and knows nothing of critical distinction between the ego and the outside world.

What then is intellectual ego-centrism? It is a spontaneous attitude which, at the beginning, rules the child's psychical activity and which persists throughout life during periods of mental inertia. From a negative point of view, such an attitude runs counter to a comprehensive view of the universe and to the co-ordination of different points of view, in short, to any impersonal activity of the mind. From the positive point of view this attitude consists in the ego being absorbed in things and in the social group: but this absorption is such that the subject, while thinking that he has knowledge of people and things as they are, in reality attributes to them not only their objective characteristics but also qualities which come from his own ego or from the particular aspect of things of which he is aware at the time. For the subject, release from his ego-centrism will therefore consist not so much in acquiring new knowledge about things or his social group, nor even in turning more closely to the object qua external, but in un-centring himself and in being able to disso-ciate the subject or the object: in becoming aware of what is subjective in himself, in being able to find his true place in all pos-sible circumstances and thereby to establish between things, people and his own self a system of common and reciprocal relation-ship. Ego-centrism is thus in opposition with objectivity in so far as objectivity signifies relativity on the physical plane and reciproc-ity on the social plane.

To say that the child is ego-centric as re-gards knowledge of the physical world is thus merely to state that the child's concep-tion of things is at one and the same time what they appear to be (phenomenalism) and endowed with qualities similar to those which he possesses (intentionality, force and life, binding laws, etc.). For example, the moon is following us (phenomenalism) and it does so "in order to" give us light, watch us, or anything else you may choose (final-ism due to lack of dissociation between sub-jective and objective). How will the child correct this double illusion? In exactly the same way as when, during his first year, he ceased to believe in the changing size of things and attributed to them one that re-mained constant; just as Copernicus ceased to believe in geocentrism and Einstein in Newtonian absolutes; by seeing himself in relation to a system of objective relation-ships, which, as a complementary effect, eliminates phenomenalism in favour of a rational sense of reality and reduces previous subjective links (finality, force, intentional-ity, etc.) by dissociating subject from object. The example of the moon, however clear it may be, has no special privilege: in his in-terpretation of any movement, of any causal

relation, etc., the child has an opportunity of linking the phenomenalism of the immediate data with false absolutes of subjective origin. One can thus see what initial ego-centrism of physical knowledge is; it is not an over-developed consciousness of the ego, which would lead the child to lose interest in the experience of external things; it is, on the contrary, pure "realism," *i.e.*, an immediate taking possession of the object, but so im-mediate that the subject, who does not know himself, cannot manage to get outside him-self in order to see himself in a universe of relations freed from subjective accretions.

We are now in a position to understand what children's social ego-centrism is and, in the light of this knowledge, what their logical ego-centrism is. Social ego-centrism may be recognized as a particular form of epistemic ego-centrism, just as the latter can be deduced from the former. In other words, the child discovers people in exactly the same way as he discovers things and he knows them both in the same way. He is a prey to the same illusory lack of perspective in considering the social group and the ex-ternal world, and his ego is mingled with his picture of both people and material things.

In the first place, neither the child's social ego-centrism nor the ego-centrism of his knowledge of the physical world is a quality which can be observed within his self-con-sciousness or by watching his external be-haviour. Social ego-centrism, as much as purely intellectual ego-centrism, is an epis-temic attitude: it is a way of understanding others just as ego-centrism in general is a way of looking at things. A close watch on the child's language will no doubt show that it exists, as will careful observation of the child's spontaneous reactions to physical phenomena. But, considered as an epistemic attitude, ego-centrism can never be directly observed. Thus, as on the physical plane, the child turns entirely towards things and away from his own self as a subject of knowledge, so, on the social plane, the child turns completely towards others and thus finds himself at the antipodes of what in common language is called ego-centrism, *i.e.*, constant and conscious preoccupation with self. Nevertheless, just as on the physical plane he only sees things imbued with certain qualities which are personal to him, so, on the social plane, he sees others only in a symbiosis (unconscious of itself) between himself and those around him.

We can therefore from the start brush aside an objection often raised by the best of authors and which, to our mind, is due to a mere misunderstanding; ego-centrism would seem to be irreconcilable with the established fact that the child is a fundamentally sociable creature, "syntonizing" not only with human beings but with all living things and even with the entire universe. . . .

If we give the word ego-centrism its generally accepted meaning, that of conscious self-preoccupation, which precludes a feeling for the community, the word is clearly being given contradictory meanings. But if we use this word ego-centrism to describe something purely epistemic, to denote the confusion of subject with object during the act of acquiring knowledge, in which the subject does not know himself and, in turning towards the object, is unable to uncentre himself, then, ego-centrism and a sense of community are so little opposed to each other that they often constitute one and the same phenomenon. . . .

It may be briefly stated that in the make-up of childish ego-centrism, both on the social and on the physical plane, absence of knowledge is a factor of secondary importance. A factor of primary importance is that spontaneous attitude of the individual mind in which thought turns directly towards the object without first being aware of its own point of view. This is why sociability and ego-centrism in no way exclude each other. The ego-centric mind is, in fact, far more susceptible to suggestions from outside and to the influence of the group than a mind which has been disciplined by co-operation; in so far as it does not know itself, the ego-centric mind cannot become conscious of its own personality. Thus we find that the child shows a *maximum* of suggestibility at

the same ages as a *maximum* of ego-centrism and that these two characteristics diminish as the individual becomes truly socialized.

How does this socialization operate? We can see here again a striking parallel between the physical and social planes of the child's behaviour; in both cases the decrease in ego-centrism can be explained not by the acquisition of new knowledge or new feelings but by a change in the subject's point of view so that, although he does not abandon his original point of view, he merely places it among the mass of other possible points of view. In other words, this means that for the understanding of other people as well as for the understanding of the outside world, two conditions are necessary: (1) consciousness of oneself as a subject, and the ability to detach subject from object so as not to attribute to the second the characteristics of the first; (2) to cease to look upon one's own point of view as the only possible one, and to co-ordinate it with that of others. Expressed in other terms this means that to adapt oneself to a social setting as well as to particular physical surroundings is to construct a group of relations and by an effort of co-ordination, which itself involves adjustment and reciprocity of points of view, to give oneself a place in that group.

JEAN PIAGET
The Child's Conception of Physical Causality (1930) *

SUMMARY AND CONCLUSION

We propose in this final section [1] to enquire into the relations existing between the

* Jean Piaget, *The Child's Conception of Physical Causality* (New York: Humanities Press, and London: Routledge & Kegan Paul, 1930; translated by Marjorie Gabain), pp. 237, 241–252, 291–294, 301–304. Used by permission of Humanities Press, Inc., and Routledge & Kegan Paul Ltd.

[1] We shall summarise in this section the conclusions reached in the present volume and in our last book *The Child's Conception of the World.*

mind of the child and the external world. This should lead us into the very heart of the Problem of Knowledge. . . .

THE CHILD'S REALITY.—How does the idea of reality constitute itself in the child's mind? Any direct analysis of its origin is beyond our power; the earliest stages precede language or are contemporaneous with the first spoken words, and any effort to reach the child's consciousness during these stages is fruitless, if one claims to go beyond mere hypothesis. But if we can content ourselves with conjecture, then it is best to try and extricate the laws according to which the idea of reality develops between the ages of 3 and 11, and to extrapolate the guiding lines thus obtained so as to reconstruct the earliest stages. Moreover, as soon as we put this method into practice, we find that we can learn enough from the laws of evolution between 3 and 11 years, and that there is no need to attach any special importance to the original stage.

Three complementary processes seem to be at work in directing the evolution of reality as it is conceived by the child between the ages of 3 and 11. Child thought moves simultaneously: (1) *from realism to objectivity*, (2) *from realism to reciprocity*, and (3) *from realism to relativity*. By *objectivity* we mean the mental attitude of persons who are able to distinguish what comes from themselves and what forms part of external reality as it can be observed by everybody. We say that there is *reciprocity* when the same value is attributed to the point of view of other people as to one's own, and when the correspondence can be found between these two points of view. We say that there is *relativity* when no object and no quality or character is posited in the subject's mind with the claim to being an independent substance or attribute.

Let us examine these processes more closely. In order to be objective, one must have become conscious of one's "I." Objective knowledge can only be conceived in relation to subjective, and a mind that was ignorant of itself would inevitably tend to put into things its own pre-notions and prejudices, whether in the domain of reasoning, of immediate judgment, or even of perception. An objective intelligence in no way escapes from this law, but, being conscious of its own "I," it will be on its guard, it will be able to hold back and criticise, in short it will be able to say what, roughly, is fact and what is interpretation.

So that in stating that the child proceeds from realism to objectivity, all we are saying is that originally the child puts the whole content of consciousness on the same plane and draws no distinction between the "I" and the external world. Above all we mean that the constitution of the idea of reality presupposes a progressive splitting-up of this protoplasmic consciousness into two complementary universes—the objective universe and the subjective.

We have met with many examples of this realism of the first kind and of its progressive reduction. Children's ideas about thought may be taken as a first illustration of the phenomenon in question. The feeling of subjectivity and inwardness felt by the adult is, to a great extent, connected with the conviction of being the owner of a thought that is distinct from the things thought about, distinct from the physical world in general, and more internal and intimate than the body itself. This conviction only comes late in the child's development. During the earliest stages, the child believes that he thinks with his mouth, that thought consists in articulating words, and that these words themselves form part of the external things. The voice, being thus identified with thought itself, is regarded as a breath which participates with the surrounding air, and some children go so far as to say that it is identical with the wind in the trees, and that dreams are made of "wind." They are quite incapable of distinguishing between thought and the things thought about. To use the expression chosen by M. H. Delacroix, the sign "adheres" to the thing signified. Later on, the child gives up this realism and localises thought inside his mouth, then in a little voice placed in the head; he then gives up materialising thought and makes of it something *sui generis* which characterises the self as spirit.

The evolution of ideas about names is particularly suggestive from this same point of view. Word and name are about all that the child knows of thought, since he identifies thought with the voice. Now, names are, to begin with, situated in objects. They form part of things in the same way as do colour or form. Things have always had their names. It has always been sufficient to look at things in order to know their names. In some cases, this realism actually turns to magic: to deform the name is to deform the thing. Later on, names are situated in the adjoining air where the voice has uttered them, then in the voice, and finally in thought itself.

Dreams give rise to an equally definite realism. At first, they are thought to be pictures of air or light which come before our eyes from outside. At the earliest stage, the child thinks, naturally enough, that anyone could see the dream come into the room and go out again. Later on, the dream is believed to have an internal origin, but is conceived as coming out of the head or the stomach before appearing before the child. Finally, the child learns to distinguish between "being" and "seeming," and localises the dream, first in the eyes, then in the head.

All these facts show that the localisation of the objects of thought is not inborn. It is through a progressive differentiation that the internal world comes into being and is contrasted with the external. Neither of these two terms is given at the start. The initial realism is not due simply to ignorance of the internal world, it is due to confusion and absence of objectivity.

Consequently, during the gradual and slow differentiation of the initial protoplasmic reality into objective and subjective reality, it is clear that each of the two terms in process of differentiation will evolve in accordance with its own structure. In the case of every object there will be a displacement of values which will modify the character of the object. Take, for example, the notion of "air," or of "wind." During the earliest stages, air is conceived as participating with thought: the voice is air, and, in return, the wind takes notice of us, obeys us, is "good at making us grow," comes when we move our hands, and so on. When thought proper is localised in the self, and the participations between air and thought are broken, the nature of air changes by virtue of this fact alone. Air becomes independent of men, sufficient to itself, and living its own life. But owing to the fact that it is held to participate with the self, it retains at the very moment when it is severing these bonds, a certain number of purely human aspects: it still has consciousness, of a different kind perhaps than formerly, but its own nevertheless. Only very gradually will it be reduced to a mere thing.

This phenomenon is very general. During the early stages the world and the self are one; neither term is distinguished from the other. But when they become distinct, these two terms begin by remaining very close to each other: the world is still conscious and full of intentions, the self is still material, so to speak, and only slightly interiorised. At each step in the process of dissociation these two terms evolve in the sense of the greatest divergence, but they are never in the child (nor in the adult for that matter) entirely separate. From our present point of view, therefore, there is never complete objectivity: at every stage there remain in the conception of nature what we might call "adherences," fragments of internal experience which still cling to the external world.

We have distinguished at least five varieties of adherences defined in this way. There are, to begin with, during a very early stage, feelings of participation accompanied sometimes by magical beliefs; the sun and moon follow us, and if we walk, it is enough to make them move along; things around us notice us and obey us, like the wind, the clouds, the night, etc.; the moon, the street lamps, etc., send us dreams "to annoy us," etc., etc. In short, the world is filled with tendencies and intentions which are in participation with our own. This is what we have called dynamic participation, in contrast to substantial participation, to which, however, it may lead.

A second form of adherence, closely allied to the preceding, is that constituted by animism, which makes the child endow things with consciousness and life.

A third form is artificialism. The reader should be reminded at this point that artificialism in the child is not a theory which after reflection systematically takes man as the point of departure for everything. The terms must be reversed, and that is why artificialism has the same right to be classed among the adherences as animism. The child begins by thinking of things in terms of his own "I": the things around him take notice of man and are made for man; everything about them is willed and intentional, everything is organised for the good of men. If we ask the child, or if the child asks himself how things began, he has recourse to man to explain them. Thus artificialism is based on feelings of participation which constitute a very special and very important class of adherences in the sense that we have defined.

A fourth form is finalism: the starting-point and then the residuum both of animism and of artificialism, the deep and stubborn finalism of the child shows with what difficulty external reality frees itself from schemas due to internal and psychical experience.

A fifth form of adherence is constituted by the notion of force: things make efforts, and their powers imply an internal and substantial energy analogous to our own muscular force.

It is a striking fact that both the area of application and the strength of resistance of these adherences decrease progressively throughout the mental development of the child. And not only do these adherences lose ground little by little in correlation with each other, but their progressive disappearance seems to be proportional to the increasing clarity with which the child becomes conscious of his subjectivity. In other words, the better the child succeeds in dividing off the internal world from the external, the less stubborn are the adherences.

Three groups of facts may be mentioned in this connection. In the first place, as the child comes to notice the existence and the mechanism of his own thought, he separates signs from the things signified: thus, names cease to belong to the things named, thought is interiorised and ceases to participate with wind, dreams are no longer regarded as emanations of objects, and so on. Thus participations are loosened little by little, and even eliminated.

In the second place, in so far as the child discovers the existence and inwardness of his thought, animism, far from being strengthened is, through this alone, compromised and even completely destroyed. The decline of animism brings with it a progressive reduction of child dynamism. For so long as things seem to be alive and consequently active, the forces of nature are multiplied by the child; and the elimination of life leads to a mechanisation of force which means ultimately an impoverishment of the actual notion of force. This very general process of evolution which leads the child from a dynamic to a mechanical view has been dealt with at sufficient length in connection with the details of children's explanations to render any further comment [un]necessary.

Finally, as the child becomes conscious of his subjectivity, he rids himself of his egocentricity. For, after all, it is in so far as we fail to realise the personal nature of our own point of view that we regard this point of view as absolute and shared by all. Whereas, in so far as we discover this purely individual character, we learn to distinguish our own from the objective point of view. Egocentricity, in a word, diminishes as we become conscious of our subjectivity. Now the decrease of egocentricity means the decrease of anthropomorphic finalism, and consequently the decrease of all the feelings of participation that are at the bottom of artificialism.

Progressive separation of the outer from the inner world, and progressive reduction of the adherences, such, in brief, are the two fundamental aspects of the first process which we defined as a passage from realism to objectivity. What we have just said about the relations between egocentricity and artificialism takes us on to the analysis of the second process, for it goes without saying that all these processes are closely related to each other, so much so, indeed, that they may be said to be completely indissociable.

The second characteristic process in the evolution of the idea of reality is the passage *from realism to reciprocity*. This formula means that the child, after having regarded his own point of view as absolute, comes to discover the possibility of other points of view and to conceive of reality as constituted, no longer by what is immediately given, but by what is common to all points of view taken together.

One of the first aspects of this process is the passage from realism of perception to interpretation properly so called. All the younger children take their immediate perceptions as true, and then proceed to interpret them according to their egocentric pre-relations, instead of making allowance for their own perspective. The most striking example we have found is that of the clouds and the heavenly bodies, of which children believe that they follow us. The sun and moon are small globes travelling a little way above the level of the roofs of houses and following us about on our walks. Even the child of 6–8 years does not hesitate to take this perception as the expression of truth, and, curiously enough, he never thinks of asking himself whether these heavenly bodies do not also follow other people. When we ask the captious question as to which of two people walking in opposite directions the sun would prefer to follow, the child is taken aback and shows how new the question is to him. Children of 9–10 years, on the other hand, have discovered that the sun

follows everybody. From this they conclude that the truth lies in the reciprocity of the points of view: that the sun is very high up, that it follows no one, and that each sees it as just above him.

What we said just now about dreams is also to a certain extent germane to the present process: the child begins by regarding his own dreams as true, without asking himself whether every one dreams the same as he does.

Side by side with this realism of perception and images, there is a logical realism which is far more important. We met with numerous examples of it in the course of our studies on child logic. Before the age of 10, on the average, the child does not know that he is a brother in relation to his own brothers. The ideas of right and left, of dark and fair, of the points of the compass, etc., are all subject to the law which is occupying us at the moment. These conceptions are at first regarded as absolute, so long as the personal point of view is accepted as the only possible one; after that, the reciprocity of relations gradually begins to make itself felt. In the present volume (as also in *The Child's Conception of the World*) we have pointed to several fresh examples of this process, examples which were of importance in forming the structure of reality.

Such are, above all, the ideas of weight and density. During the earliest stages, an object is heavy or light according to the immediate judgment implied by the child's own point of view: a pebble is light, a boat is heavy. Later on, other points of view are taken into account, and the child will say, for example, that such and such a pebble is light for him but heavy for the water, and that a boat may be light for the lake while it remains heavy for the child.

These last examples bring us to the third process which marks the evolution of the child's idea of reality: thought evolves *from realism to relativity*. This process is closely related to the last, and yet differentiates itself from it on certain points. During the early stage, the child tends to think of everything under the form of absolute substance and quality; after that, bodies and their qualities seem to him more and more dependent upon each other and relative to us. Thus, substances become relations, on the one hand, because the mutual connection of phenomena has been seen, and on the other, because the relativity of our evaluations has been discovered. It would perhaps be as well to distinguish between these two aspects of "relativity," but the second is, as a matter of fact, nothing but a combination of the first with the "reciprocity" of which we spoke just now. It will therefore be enough to point to this connection without complicating our classification.

The most striking example of this process is undoubtedly the evolution of the conceptions about life and movement. During the early stages, every movement is regarded as singular, as the manifestation, that is, of a substantial and living activity. In other words, there is in every moving object a motor substance: the clouds, the heavenly bodies, water, and machines, etc., move by themselves. Even when the child succeeds in conceiving an external motor, which already takes away from the substantiality of movement, the internal motor continues to be regarded as necessary. Thus a leaf is alive, even though it moves with the wind, *i.e.* it retains its spontaneity even though the wind is needed to set it in motion. Similarly, a cloud or one of the heavenly bodies remains master of its movements, even though the wind is necessary to start it on its path. But later on, the movement of every body becomes the function of external movements, which are regarded no longer as necessary collaborators but as sufficient conditions. Thus the movement of clouds comes to be entirely explained by that of the wind. Then these external motors are conceived as themselves dependent upon other external motors, and so on. In this way there comes into being a universe of relations which takes the place of a universe of independent and spontaneous substances.

Closely analogous to this is the evolution of the idea of force, since it is, as we saw, intimately connected with the idea of life.

The idea of weight supplies us with an excellent example of this advance towards relativity, and the evolution in this particular case is closely bound up with the advance towards reciprocity which we spoke of just now. During the earliest stages, weight is synonymous with strength and activity. A pebble sunk in water weighs on the water, even when the latter is motionless, and produces a current towards the surface. An object floats because, being heavy, it has the strength to keep itself up. Weight is an absolute thing: it is a quality possessed by certain bodies, a variant of that life, or substantial force which we have described. Later on, weight is regarded as relative to the surrounding medium: bodies float because they are lighter than water, the clouds, because they are lighter than air, etc. But the relation is still vague: the child simply means that for the water in the lake, such and such a boat is light, but no comparison has been made which introduces proportional volumes. The wood of the boat is regarded as heavier than an equal volume of water. Finally, between the years of 9 and 10, "lighter than the water" begins to mean that the body in question is, taken at equal volume, lighter than water. Thus do the ideas of density and specific weight make their appearance: absolute weight is succeeded, in part at any rate, by relative weight.

The explanation of shadows and of night also offers an example of the progression from substantialism to an explanation founded on relations. During the earliest stages, night and shade are substances that emanate from clouds and bodies in general, and which come and go more or less intentionally. In the later stages, night and shade are nothing but the effects conditioned by the spatial relations which regulate the diffusion of light.

In every domain the substantialist realism of perception is succeeded by explanation through geometrical and cinematic relations.

Running parallel with this growing relativity of phenomena in relation to each other, can be seen a growing relativity of ideas and notions in relation to ourselves and our evaluations. Thus the establishment of relativity between phenomena leads to a relativity between the measurer and what is measured. The evolution of the notion of weight brings out very clearly this double development. On the one hand, as we have just seen, the weight of the body becomes relative to the medium constituted by the other bodies, and presupposes the establishment of a relation between weight and volume. On the other hand, the words "light" and "heavy" lose the absolute meaning they had during the earliest stages, and acquire a meaning that is relative to the units of measurement that have been chosen: the pebble is heavy for the water, light for us, etc. The absolute concept has become a relation. In such cases, the advance towards relativity ends by converging absolutely with the advance towards reciprocity of view-points; in other words, the second and third processes as we distinguished them, finally merge into one.

Such, then, is the evolution of the notion of reality in the child. Three processes help to make it emerge from its initial realism and to orientate it towards objectivity. In what relation do these three processes stand to one another? The first is of a purely social nature: the child replaces his own individual and egocentric point of view by the point of view of others and the reciprocity existing between them. The second of these three processes is of a purely intellectual order: substantialism of perception is replaced by the relativism of intelligence. The third process is both social and intellectual in character: in becoming conscious of his "I," the child clears external reality of all its subjective elements, and thus attains to objectivity; but it is, above all, social life that has forced the child to become conscious of his "ego." Are we then to conclude that social factors determine the progress in the understanding of reality, or does this prog-

ress itself explain the development of social life? Let us note, in the first place, that the three processes synchronise. All three begin very early, all three are very slow, they remain uncompleted at the close of childhood and survive throughout the intellectual development of the adult. There is therefore every reason to believe that they are interdependent.

As a matter of fact, we have here, as in the case of child logic, to suppose that social life is necessary to rational development, but that it is not sufficient to create the power of reasoning. Without collaboration between his own thought and that of others, the child would not become conscious of the divergences which separate his ego from that of others, and he would take each of his perceptions or conceptions as absolute. He would therefore never attain to objectivity, for lack of having ever discovered his own subjectivity. Without social life, he would never succeed in understanding the reciprocity of view-points, and, consequently, the existence of perspectives, whether geometrical or logical. He would never cease to believe that the sun follows him on his walks. He would be ignorant of the reciprocity of the notions of right and left, of dependence, in short, of relations in general. It is therefore highly probable that the relativity of ideas would elude him.

.   .   .   .   .

CHILD LOGIC.— . . . Let us remind the reader once again that in questioning the children about the phenomena of nature we did not reach their spontaneous thought, but a thought that was necessarily systematised and consequently deformed by the very fact of the interrogatory. Further, and this is the fundamental point, the most original and the most important part of the answers which the children gave us had never been communicated to anyone before it was given to us. Children do not talk amongst themselves about their conceptions of nature, and in so far as they put questions to adults upon the subject, these tend to annul the purely childish character of their conceptions. And yet these conceptions are constant in the towns where we were able to question children, and they are to be found amongst nearly all children of the same mental age. Nothing is more striking in this respect than the very simple experiments which are completely removed from anything that the children can have been taught. Such is, for example, the experiment of the pebble placed in a glass of water, so as to make the level of the water rise: all the younger children say that the water rises because the pebble is heavy, and all the older ones say that it rises because the pebble is big. The convergence here is extremely interesting.

This secret and yet constant character of childish views about the world shows very clearly that before the interrogatory the spontaneous thought of the subject must have been made up more of images and motor schemas than of conceptual thought, such as could be formulated in words. We have here a general confirmation of the hypothesis we put forward earlier, and according to which child thought is not social but egocentric, and consequently intermediate between autistic and logical thought. In autistic thought, intellectual work is carried on by means of images and motor schemas. In logical thought, word and concept replace these primitive instruments. These two processes mingle in the child's mind, the first retaining its power in so far as thought is secret and unformulated, the second undergoing development in so far as thought becomes socialised.

This explains why the thought of the children we questioned was so lacking in logic. We were able, within each sphere, to establish special stages, but it would be extremely difficult to establish inclusive stages for the reason that during these early years the child is still very incoherent. At the age when the child is still animistic, artificialist, or dynamic in his way of thinking on some points, he has already ceased to be so on others. He does not reap the benefits of a progress in

all the domains where this progress is bound eventually to make itself felt. Corresponding stages are at varying levels, because the influence of one belief upon another takes place unconsciously and not thanks to a conscious and deliberate generalisation. Thus child thought is in no way organised. There are, of course, certain remarkable correlations between one given achievement and another. But this is not the sign of discursive and reflective logic, it merely indicates the existence of a certain coherence between the warring parts of an organism which is unable as yet to release instantaneously such synergy as may exist. There is therefore not deduction, but juxtaposition, devoid of systematic logical multiplication and addition. The concepts of life, of weight, of force, of movement, etc., are not concepts properly so called, they are not defined by means of exact logical additions or multiplications, but they are those conglomerate concepts of which we have spoken elsewhere.

But leaving these more general considerations, let us see whether our present results tend to confirm the analysis which we formerly attempted to make of transduction, *i.e.* of the childish method of reasoning.

Childish transduction is opposed to adult deduction by the possession of three fundamental characteristics. (1) Transduction is, in the first place, purely a mental experiment, by which we mean that it begins by simply reproducing in imagination events such as they are or could be presented by immediate reality. For instance, having noticed that the presence of stones in a river produces tiny waves, the child explains the movement of the river by appealing to other stones which are supposed to have set it in motion. (2) Transduction is carried on by predicative judgments, or by certain simple judgments of relation. It might be better to say judgments of pre-relation, relations being conceived simply as properties: "the stone has force," etc. For to do no more than combine the data supplied by immediate perception is to forget the part played in perception by the self or by the personal point of view: it is, therefore, to take a false absolute instead of objective relations as a foundation for reasoning. Thus when a child says that a boat floats because it is heavy, he does so because, in his mind, the weight of the boat has not been compared to its volume nor to the weight of the water, but has been evaluated as a function of the subject's own point of view, taken as absolute. In the same way all those instances of reasoning which bear upon the concepts of force, life, and movement, will be found to contain false absolutes, mere pre-relations, simply because the laws of physics have not been desubjectified. (3) Owing to the fact that it does not reason by relations but is a simple combination of judgments, transduction does not attain to the strict generality of deduction but remains an irrational passage from particular to particular. When the child seems to be deducing, that is, to be applying the universal to the particular, or to be drawing the universal from the particular, he does so in appearance only, owing to the indeterminate character of the concepts employed. Here is an example: a boy tells us that large-sized or "big" bodies are heavier than small ones; yet a moment later he declares that a small pebble is heavier than a large cork. But he does not, for that matter, give up his first affirmation, he only declares that the stone is heavier than the cork "because some stones are bigger than corks." Thus the character "big" has not at all the same meaning as for us. It does not define a class, it is transmitted by syncretistic communication to analogous objects: since there are big stones, little stones participate in their bigness, and thus acquire weight. At other times, the child reasons only for special cases and does not generalise at all: one boat floats because it is heavy, another because it is light, and so on. In short, either we have a juxtaposition of special case reasonings without generalisation, or we have apparent generalisation, but generalisation by syncretism and not by correct logical addition and multiplication.

Our interpretation of transduction is therefore that it moves from particular to particular, regardless of contradictions, because it is ignorant of the logic of relations, and that there is mutual dependence between this ignorance of the logic of relations and the fact that reasoning occurs simply by mental experimentation.

.   .   .   .   .

LOGIC AND REALITY.— . . . Let us note the astonishing similarity of the general processes which condition the evolution of logic and that of the idea of reality. For the construction of the objective world and the elaboration of strict reasoning both consist in a gradual reduction of egocentricity in favour of the progressive socialisation of thought, in favour, that is to say, of objectivation and reciprocity of view-points. In both cases, the initial state is marked by the fact that the self is confused with the external world and with other people; the vision of the world is falsified by subjective adherences, and the vision of other people is falsified by the fact that the personal point of view predominates, almost to the exclusion of all others. Thus in both cases, truth —empirical truth or formal truth such as forms the subject-matter of argument—is obscured by the ego. Then, as the child discovers that others do not think as he does, he makes efforts to adapt himself to them, he bows to the exigencies of control and verification which are implied by discussion and argument, and thus comes to replace egocentric logic by the true logic created by social life. We saw that exactly the same process took place with regard to the idea of reality.

There is therefore an egocentric logic and an egocentric ontology, of which the consequences are parallel: they both falsify the perspective of logical relations and of things, because they both start from the assumption that other people understand us and agree with us from the first, and that things revolve around us with the sole purpose of serving us and resembling us.

Now, if we examine these parallel evolutions, logical and ontological, in greater detail, we shall distinguish three main stages in each. The first is that which precedes any clear consciousness of the self, and may be arbitrarily set down as lasting till the age of 2–3, that is, till the appearance of the first "whys," which symbolise in a way the first awareness of resistance in the external world. As far as we can conjecture, two phenomena characterise this first stage. From the point of view of logic, it is pure *autism,* or thought akin to dreams or day-dreams, thought in which truth is confused with desire. To every desire corresponds immediately an image or illusion which transforms this desire into reality, thanks to a sort of pseudo-hallucination or play. No objective observation or reasoning is possible: there is only a perpetual play which transforms perceptions and creates situations in accordance with the subject's pleasure. From the ontological view-point, what corresponds to this manner of thinking is primitive *psychological causality,* probably in a form that implies *magic* proper: the belief that any desire whatsoever can influence objects, the belief in the obedience of external things. Magic and autism are therefore two different sides of one and the same phenomenon —that confusion between the self and the world which destroys both logical truth and objective existence.

The second stage lasts from the age of 2–3 to the age of 7–8, and is characterised, from the logical point of view, by egocentricity: on the one hand, there is an absence of the desire to find logical justification for one's statements, and on the other, syncretism combines with juxtaposition to produce an excess of subjective and affective relations at the expense of genuine logical implications. To this egocentricity corresponds, in the ontological domain, *pre-causality,* in the widest sense, meaning all the forms of causality based on a confusion between psychological activity and physical mechanism. For pre-causality is to physical causality what syncretism is to logical implication.

Pre-causality confuses motive and cause, just as, in the sphere of logic, syncretism confuses subjective justification with verification.

Now among the various forms of pre-causality existing in this second period, two, of which one probably precedes the other, are particularly important: these are participation and dynamism. And each of these is dependent in its own way upon egocentric logic: participation is the ontological equivalent of transduction, and dynamism is closely connected with the predominance of conceptualism over the logic of relations, which predominance comes, as we saw, from the habits created by transduction.

With regard to transduction and participation, this is what we believe to be the truth: transduction passes from one singular or particular case to another, without bringing in any general laws or taking account of the reciprocity of relations. Thus to reason transductively about the formation of shadows is to dispense with laws altogether. To do so deductively, *i.e.* by means of generalisation or an appeal to already established laws, would mean saying: "This copy-book makes a shadow just like trees, houses, etc., etc. Now, what trees, houses, etc., have in common is that they block out the daylight. The shadow of the copy-book must therefore also come from the fact that it shuts out the daylight." In this way, we should bring in (1) analogy between individual cases, and (2) a law stating what all these individual cases had in common. The child, on the contrary, reasoning transductively, brings in no general law. He begins, indeed, as we do, by feeling the analogy of the shadow cast by the book with the shadows of trees, houses, etc. But this analogy does not lead him to abstract any relation: it simply leads him to identify the particular cases with one another. So that we have here, not analogy proper, but syncretism. The child argues as follows: "This copy-book makes a shadow; trees, houses, etc., make shadows. The copy-book's shadow (therefore) comes from the trees and the houses." Thus, from the point of view of the cause or of the structure of the object, there is participation.

MARIA MONTESSORI
The Montessori Method (1912) *

A Critical Consideration of the New Pedagogy in its Relation to Modern Science

. . . The school must permit the *free, natural manifestations* of the *child* if in the school scientific pedagogy is to be born. This is the essential reform.

No one may affirm that such a principle already exists in pedagogy and in the school. It is true that some pedagogues, led by Rousseau, have given voice to impracticable principles and vague aspirations for the liberty of the child, but the true concept of liberty is practically unknown to educators. . . . He who would say that the principle of liberty informs the pedagogy of to-day, would make us smile as at a child who, before the box of mounted butterflies, should insist that they were alive and could fly. The principle of slavery still pervades pedagogy, and, therefore, the same principle pervades the school. I need only give one proof—the stationary desks and chairs. . . .

I believe that it will not be many years before the public, scarcely believing the descriptions of these scientific benches, will come to touch with wondering hands the amazing seats that were constructed for the purpose of preventing among our school children curvature of the spine!

The development of these scientific benches means that the pupils were sub-

* Maria Montessori, *The Montessori Method: Scientific Pedagogy as Applied to Child Education in "The Children's Houses" with Additions and Revisions by the Author* (New York: Stokes, 1912; translated from the Italian by Anne E. George; Fourth Edition), pp. 15–21, 26–34, 36–39, 42–45, 70–72, 80–84, 86–88, 93, 95–98, 101, 167–169, 174–176, 209–214, 366–367, 371–372. Used by permission of Mario M. Montessori.

jected to a régime, which, even though they were born strong and straight, made it possible for them to become humpbacked! The vertebral column, biologically the most primitive, fundamental, and oldest part of the skeleton, the most fixed portion of our body, since the skeleton is the most solid portion of the organism—the vertebral column, which resisted and was strong through the desperate struggles of primitive man when he fought against the desert-lion, when he conquered the mammoth, when he quarried the solid rock and shaped the iron to his uses, bends, and cannot resist, under the yoke of the school.

It is incomprehensible that so-called *science* should have worked to perfect an instrument of slavery in the school. . . .

Some time ago a woman, believing me to be in sympathy with all scientific innovations concerning the school, showed me with evident satisfaction *a corset or brace for pupils*. She had invented this and felt that it would complete the work of the bench. . . .

It behooves us to think of what may happen to the *spirit* of the child who is condemned to grow in conditions so artificial that his very bones may become deformed. When we speak of the redemption of the workingman, it is always understood that beneath the most apparent form of suffering, such as poverty of the blood, or ruptures, there exists that other wound from which the soul of the man who is subjected to any form of slavery must suffer. It is at this deeper wrong that we aim when we say that the workman must be redeemed through liberty. We know only too well that when a man's very blood has been consumed or his intestines wasted away through his work, his soul must have lain oppressed in darkness, rendered insensible, or, it may be, killed within him. The *moral* degradation of the slave is, above all things, the weight that opposes the progress of humanity—humanity striving to rise and held back by this great burden. The cry of redemption speaks far more clearly for the souls of men than for their bodies.

What shall we say then, when the question before us is that of *educating children?*

We know only too well the sorry spectacle of the teacher who, in the ordinary schoolroom, must pour certain cut and dried facts into the heads of the scholars. In order to succeed in this barren task, she finds it necessary to discipline her pupils into immobility and to force their attention. Prizes and punishments are ever-ready and efficient aids to the master who must force into a given attitude of mind and body those who are condemned to be his listeners.

It is true that to-day it is deemed expedient to abolish official whippings and habitual blows, just as the awarding of prizes has become less ceremonious. These partial reforms are another prop approved of by science, and offered to the support of the decadent school. Such prizes and punishments are, if I may be allowed the expression, the *bench* of the soul, the instrument of slavery for the spirit. Here, however, these are not applied to lessen deformities, but to provoke them. The prize and the punishment are incentives toward unnatural or forced effort, and, therefore we certainly cannot speak of the natural development of the child in connection with them. The jockey offers a piece of sugar to his horse before jumping into the saddle, the coachman beats his horse that he may respond to the signs given by the reins; and, yet, neither of these runs so superbly as the free horse of the plains.

And here, in the case of education, shall man place the yoke upon man? . . .

To-day we hold the pupils in school, restricted by those instruments so degrading to body and spirit, the desk—and material prizes and punishments. Our aim in all this is to reduce them to the discipline of immobility and silence,—to lead them,—where? Far too often toward no definite end.

Often the education of children consists in pouring into their intelligence the intellectual content of school programmes. And often these programmes have been compiled in the official department of education, and their use is imposed by law upon the teacher and the child.

Ah, before such dense and wilful disregard of the life which is growing within these children, we should hide our heads in shame and cover our guilty faces with our hands!

Sergi says truly: "To-day an urgent need imposes itself upon society: the reconstruction of methods in education and instruction, and he who fights for this cause, fights for human regeneration."

HISTORY OF METHODS

If we are to develop a system of scientific pedagogy, we must, then, proceed along lines very different from those which have been followed up to the present time. The transformation of the school must be contemporaneous with the preparation of the teacher. For if we make of the teacher an observer, familiar with the experimental methods, then we must make it possible for her to observe and to experiment in the school. The fundamental principle of scientific pedagogy must be, indeed, the *liberty of the pupil;*—such liberty as shall permit a development of individual, spontaneous manifestations of the child's nature. If a new and scientific pedagogy is to arise from the *study of the individual,* such study must occupy itself with the observation of *free* children. In vain should we await a practical renewing of pedagogical methods from methodical examinations of pupils made under the guidance offered to-day by pedagogy, anthropology, and experimental psychology.

Every branch of experimental science has grown out of the application of a method peculiar to itself. Bacteriology owes its scientific content to the method of isolation and culture of microbes. Criminal, medical, and pedagogical anthropology owe their progress to the application of anthropological methods to individuals of various classes, such as criminals, the insane, the sick of the clinics, scholars. So experimental psychology needs as its starting point an exact definition of the technique to be used in making the experiment.

To put it broadly, it is important to define *the method, the technique,* and from its application to *await* the definite result, which must be gathered entirely from actual experience. One of the characteristics of experimental sciences is to proceed to the making of an experiment *without preconceptions of any sort* as to the final result of the experiment itself. For example, should we wish to make scientific observations concerning the developement of the head as related to varying degrees of intelligence, one of the conditions of such an experiment would be to ignore, in the taking of the measurements, which were the most intelligent and which the most backward among the scholars examined. And this because the preconceived idea that the most intelligent should have the head more fully developed will inevitably alter the results of the research.

He who experiments must, while doing so, divest himself of every preconception. It is clear then that if we wish to make use of a method of experimental psychology, the first thing necessary is to renounce all former creeds and to proceed by means of the *method* in the search for truth.

We must not start, for example, from any dogmatic ideas which we may happen to have held upon the subject of child psychology. Instead, we must proceed by a method which shall tend to make possible to the child complete liberty. This we must do if we are to draw from the observation of his spontaneous manifestations conclusions which shall lead to the establishment of a truly scientific child psychology. It may be that such a method holds for us great surprises, unexpected possibilities.

Child psychology and pedagogy must establish their content by successive conquests arrived at through the method of experimentation.

Our problem then, is this: to establish the *method peculiar* to experimental pedagogy. It cannot be that used in other experimental sciences. It is true that scientific pedagogy is rounded out by hygiene, anthropology, and psychology, and adopts in part the technical method characteristic of all three, although limiting itself to a special study of the individual to be educated. But in pedagogy this study of the individual, though it must accompany the very different work of *education,* is a limited and secondary part of the science as a whole.

This present study deals in part with the *method* used in experimental pedagogy, and is the result of my experiences during two years in the "Children's Houses." I offer only a beginning of the method, which I have applied to children between the ages of three and six. But I believe that these tentative experiments, because of the surprising results which they have given, will be the means of inspiring a continuation of the work thus undertaken.

Indeed, although our educational system, which experience has demonstrated to be excellent, is not yet entirely completed, it nevertheless constitutes a system well enough established to be practical in all institutions where young children are cared for, and in the first elementary classes.

Perhaps I am not exact when I say that the present work springs from two years of experience. I do not believe that these later attempts of mine could alone have rendered possible all that I set forth [here]. The origin of the educational system in use in the "Children's Houses" is much more remote, and if this experience with normal children seems indeed rather brief, it should be remembered that it sprang from preceding pedagogical experiences with abnormal children, and that considered in this way, it represents a long and thoughtful endeavour.

About fifteen years ago, being assistant doctor at the Psychiatric Clinic of the University of Rome, I had occasion to frequent the insane asylums to study the sick and to select subjects for the clinics. In this way I became interested in the idiot children who were at that time housed in the general insane asylums. In those days thyroid organotherapy was in full development, and this drew the attention of physicians to deficient children. I myself, having completed my regular hospital services, had already turned my attention to the study of children's diseases.

It was thus that, being interested in the idiot children, I became conversant with the special method of education devised for these unhappy little ones by Edward Séguin, and was led to study thoroughly the idea, then beginning to be prevalent among the physicians, of the efficacy of "pedagogical treatment" for various morbid forms of disease such as deafness, paralysis, idiocy, rickets, etc. The fact that pedagogy must join with medicine in the treatment of disease was the practical outcome of the thought of the time. And because of this tendency the method of treating disease by gymnastics became widely popular. I, however, differed from my colleagues in that I felt that mental deficiency presented chiefly a pedagogical, rather than mainly a medical, problem. Much was said in the medical congresses of the medico-pedagogic method for the treatment and education of the feeble minded, and I expressed my differing opinion in an address on *Moral Education* at the Pedagogical Congress of Turin in 1898. I believe that I touched a chord already vibrant, because the idea, making its way among the physicians and elementary teachers, spread in a flash as presenting a question of lively interest to the school.

In fact I was called upon by my master, Guido Baccelli, the great Minister of Education, to deliver to the teachers of Rome a course of lectures on the education of feeble-minded children. This course soon developed into the State Orthophrenic School, which I directed for more than two years.

In this school we had an all-day class of children composed of those who in the elementary schools were considered hopelessly deficient. Later on, through the help of a philanthropic organisation, there was founded a Medical Pedagogic Institute where, besides the children from the public schools, we brought together all of the idiot children from the insane asylums in Rome.

I spent these two years with the help of my colleagues in preparing the teachers of Rome for a special method of observation and education of feeble-minded children. Not only did I train teachers, but what was much more important, after I had been in London and Paris for the purpose of studying in a practical way the education of deficients, I gave myself over completely to the actual teaching of the children, directing at the same time the work of the other teachers in our institute.

I was more than an elementary teacher, for I was present, or directly taught the children, from eight in the morning to seven in the evening without interruption. These two years of practice are my first and indeed my true degree in pedagogy. From the very beginning of my work with deficient children (1898 to 1900) I felt that the methods which I used had in them nothing peculiarly limited to the instruction of idiots. I believed that they contained educational principles *more rational* than those in use, so much more so, indeed, that through their means an inferior mentality would be able to grow and develop. This feeling, so deep as to be in the nature of an intuition, became my controlling idea after I had left the school for deficients, and, little by little, I became convinced that similar methods applied to normal children would develop or set free their personality in a marvellous and surprising way.

It was then that I began a genuine and thorough study of what is known as remedial pedagogy, and, then, wishing to undertake the study of normal pedagogy and of the principles upon which it is based, I registered as a student of philosophy at the University. A great faith animated me, and although I did not know that I should ever be able to test the truth of my idea, I gave up every other occupation to deepen and broaden its conception. It was almost as if I prepared myself for an unknown mission. . . .

The pedagogic writings of Itard are most interesting and minute descriptions of educational efforts and experiences, and anyone reading them to-day must admit that they were practically the first attempts at experimental psychology. But the merit of having completed a genuine educational system for deficient children was due to Edward Séguin, first a teacher and then a physician. . . .

Guided by the work of these two men, I had manufactured a great variety of didactic material. These materials, which I have never seen complete in any institution, became in the hands of those who knew how to apply them, a most remarkable and efficient means, but unless rightly presented, they failed to attract the attention of the deficients.

I felt that I understood the discouragement of those working with feeble-minded children, and could see why they had, in so many cases, abandoned the method. The prejudice that the educator must place himself on a level with the one to be educated, sinks the teacher of deficients into a species of apathy. He accepts the fact that he is educating an inferior personality, and for that very reason he does not succeed. Even so those who teach little children too often have the idea that they are educating babies and seek to place themselves on the child's level by approaching him with games, and often with foolish stories. Instead of all this, we must know how to call to the *man* which lies dormant within the soul of the child. I felt this, intuitively, and believed that not the didactic material, but my voice which called to them, *awakened* the children, and encouraged them to use the didactic material, and through it, to educate themselves. I was guided in my work by the deep respect which I felt for their misfortune, and by the love which these unhappy children know how to awaken in those who are near them. . . .

This belief that we must act upon the spirit, served as a sort of *secret key,* opening to me the long series of didactic experiments so wonderfully analysed by Edward Séguin, —experiments which, properly understood, are really most efficacious in the education

of idiots. I myself obtained most surprising results through their application, but I must confess that, while my efforts showed themselves in the intellectual progress of my pupils, a peculiar form of exhaustion prostrated me. It was as if I gave to them some vital force from within me. Those things which we call encouragement, comfort, love, respect, are drawn from the soul of man, and the more freely we give of them, the more do we renew and reinvigorate the life about us.

Without such inspiration the most perfect *external stimulus* may pass unobserved. Thus the blind Saul, before the glory of the sun, exclaimed, "This?—It is the dense fog!"

Thus prepared, I was able to proceed to new experiments on my own account. This is not the place for a report of these experiments, and I will only note that at this time I attempted an original method for the teaching of reading and writing, a part of the education of the child which was most imperfectly treated in the works of both Itard and Séguin.

I succeeded in teaching a number of the idiots from the asylums both to read and to write so well that I was able to present them at a public school for an examination together with normal children. And they passed the examination successfully.

These results seemed almost miraculous to those who saw them. To me, however, the boys from the asylums had been able to compete with the normal children only because they had been taught in a different way. They had been helped in their psychic development, and the normal children had, instead, been suffocated, held back. I found myself thinking that if, some day, the special education which had developed these idiot children in such a marvellous fashion, could be applied to the development of normal children, the "miracle" of which my friends talked would no longer be possible. The abyss between the inferior mentality of the idiot and that of the normal brain can never be bridged if the normal child has reached his full development.

While everyone was admiring the progress of my idiots, I was searching for the reasons which could keep the happy healthy children of the common schools on so low a plane that they could be equalled in tests of intelligence by my unfortunate pupils! . . .

I had long wished to experiment with the methods for deficients in a first elementary class of normal children, but I had never thought of making use of the homes or institutions where very young children were cared for. It was pure chance that brought this new idea to my mind.

It was near the end of the year 1906, and I had just returned from Milan, where I had been one of a committee at the International Exhibition for the assignment of prizes in the subjects of Scientific Pedagogy and Experimental Psychology. A great opportunity came to me, for I was invited by Edoardo Talamo, the Director General of the Roman Association for Good Building, to undertake the organisation of infant schools in its model tenements. It was Signor Talamo's happy idea to gather together in a large room all the little ones between the ages of three and seven belonging to the families living in the tenement. The play and work of these children was to be carried on under the guidance of a teacher who should have her own apartment in the tenement house. It was intended that every house should have its school, and as the Association for Good Building already owned more than 400 tenements in Rome the work seemed to offer tremendous possibilities of development. The first school was to be established in January, 1907, in a large tenement house in the Quarter of San Lorenzo. In the same Quarter the Association already owned fifty-eight buildings, and according to Signor Talamo's plans we should soon be able to open sixteen of these "schools within the house."

This new kind of school was christened by Signora Olga Lodi, a mutual friend of Signor Talamo and myself, under the fortunate title of *Casa dei Bambini* or "The Children's House." Under this name the first

of our schools was opened on the sixth of January, 1907, at 58 Via dei Marsi. It was confided to the care of Candida Nuccitelli and was under my guidance and direction.

From the very first I perceived, in all its immensity, the social and pedagogical importance of such institutions, and while at that time my visions of a triumphant future seemed exaggerated, to-day many are beginning to understand that what I saw before was indeed the truth. . . .

The "Children's House" has a twofold importance: the social importance which it assumes through its peculiarity of being a school within the house, and its purely pedagogic importance gained through its methods for the education of very young children, of which I now made a trial.

As I have said, Signor Talamo's invitation gave me a wonderful opportunity for applying the methods used with deficients to normal children, not of the elementary school age, but of the age usual in infant asylums.

If a parallel between the deficient and the normal child is possible, this will be during the period of early infancy *when the child who has not the force to develop* and *he who is not yet developed* are in some ways alike.

The very young child has not yet acquired a secure co-ordination of muscular movements, and, therefore, walks imperfectly, and is not able to perform the ordinary acts of life, such as fastening and unfastening its garments. The sense organs, such as the power of accommodation of the eye, are not yet completely developed; the language is primordial and shows those defects common to the speech of the very young child. The difficulty of fixing the attention, the general instability, etc., are characteristics which the normal infant and the deficient child have in common. Preyer, also, in his psychological study of children has turned aside to illustrate the parallel between pathological linguistic defects, and those of normal children in the process of developing.

Methods which made growth possible to

the mental personality of the idiot ought, therefore, to *aid the development of young children,* and should be so adapted as to constitute a hygienic education of the entire personality of a normal human being. Many defects which become permanent, such as speech defects, the child acquires through being neglected during the most important period of his age, the period between three and six, at which time he forms and establishes his principal functions.

Here lies the significance of my pedagogical experiment in the "Children's Houses." It represents the results of a series of trials made by me, in the education of young children, with methods already used with deficients.

.   .   .   .   .

RULES AND REGULATIONS OF THE "CHILDREN'S HOUSES"

The Roman Association of Good Building hereby establishes within its tenement house number   , a "Children's House," in which may be gathered together all children under common school age, belonging to the families of the tenants.

The chief aim of the "Children's House" is to offer, free of charge, to the children of those parents who are obliged to absent themselves for their work, the personal care which the parents are not able to give.

In the "Children's House" attention is given to the education, the health, the physical and moral development of the children. This work is carried on in a way suited to the age of the children.

There shall be connected with the "Children's House" a Directress, a Physician, and a Caretaker.

The programme and hours of the "Children's House" shall be fixed by the Directress.

There may be admitted to the "Children's House" all the children in the tenement between the ages of three and seven.

The parents who wish to avail themselves of the advantages of the "Children's House" pay nothing. They must, however, assume these binding obligations:

(a) To send their children to the "Children's House" at the appointed time, clean in body and clothing, and provided with a suitable apron.

(b) To show the greatest respect and deference toward the Directress and toward all persons connected with the "Children's House," and to co-operate with the Directress herself in the education of the children. Once a week, at least, the mothers may talk with the Directress, giving her information concerning the home life of the child, and receiving helpful advice from her.

There shall be expelled from the "Children's House":

(a) Those children who present themselves unwashed, or in soiled clothing.

(b) Those who show themselves to be incorrigible.

(c) Those whose parents fail in respect to the persons connected with the "Children's House," or who destroy through bad conduct the educational work of the institution.

PEDAGOGICAL METHODS USED IN THE "CHILDREN'S HOUSES"

As soon as I knew that I had at my disposal a class of little children, it was my wish to make of this school a field for scientific experimental pedagogy and child psychology. . . .

The method of *observation* must undoubtedly include the *methodical observation* of the morphological growth of the pupils. But let me repeat that, while this element necessarily enters, it is not upon this particular kind of observation that the method is established.

The method of observation is established upon one fundamental base—*the liberty of the pupils in their spontaneous manifestations.*

With this in view, I first turned my attention to the question of environment, and this, of course, included the furnishing of the schoolroom. In considering an ample playground with space for a garden as an important part of this school environment, I am not suggesting anything new.

The novelty lies, perhaps, in my idea for the use of this open-air space, which is to be in direct communication with the schoolroom, so that the children may be free to go and come as they like, throughout the entire day. I shall speak of this more fully later on.

The principal modification in the matter of school furnishings is the abolition of desks, and benches or stationary chairs. I have had tables made with wide, solid, octagonal legs, spreading in such a way that the tables are at the same time solidly firm and very light, so light, indeed, that two four-year-old children can easily carry them about. These tables are rectangular and sufficiently large to accommodate two children on the long side, there being room for three if they sit rather close together. There are smaller tables at which one child may work alone.

I also designed and had manufactured little chairs. My first plan for these was to have them cane seated, but experience has shown the wear on these to be so great, that I now have chairs made entirely of wood. These are very light and of an attractive shape. In addition to these, I have in each schoolroom a number of comfortable little armchairs, some of wood and some of wicker.

Another piece of our school furniture consists of a little washstand, so low that it can be used by even a three-year-old child. This is painted with a white waterproof enamel and, besides the broad, upper and lower shelves which hold the little white enameled basins and pitchers, there are small side shelves for the soap-dishes, nail-brushes, towels, etc. There is also a receptacle into which the basins may be emptied. Wherever possible, a small cupboard provides each child with a space where he may keep his own soap, nail-brush, tooth-brush, etc.

In each of our schoolrooms we have provided a series of long low cupboards, especially designed for the reception of the didactic materials. The doors of these cupboards open easily, and the care of the materials is confided to the children. The tops of these cases furnish room for potted plants, small aquariums, or for the various toys with which the children are allowed to play freely. We have ample blackboard space, and these boards are so hung as to be easily used by the smallest child. Each blackboard is provided with a small case in which are kept the chalk, and the white cloths which we use instead of the ordinary erasers.

Above the blackboards are hung attractive pictures, chosen carefully, representing simple scenes in which children would naturally be interested. Among the pictures in our "Children's Houses" in Rome we have hung a copy of Raphael's "Madonna della Seggiola," and this picture we have chosen as the emblem of the "Children's Houses." For indeed, these "Children's Houses" represent not only social progress, but universal human progress, and are closely related to the elevation of the idea of motherhood, to the progress of woman and to the protection of her offspring. In this beautiful conception, Raphael has not only shown us the Madonna as a Divine Mother holding in her arms the babe who is greater than she, but by the side of this symbol of all motherhood, he has placed the figure of St. John, who represents humanity. So in Raphael's picture we see humanity rendering homage to maternity,—maternity, the sublime fact in the definite triumph of humanity. In addition to this beautiful symbolism, the picture has a value as being one of the greatest works of art of Italy's greatest artist. And if the day shall come when the "Children's Houses" shall be established throughout the world, it is our wish that this picture of Raphael's shall have its place in each of the schools, speaking eloquently of the country in which they originated.

The children, of course, cannot comprehend the symbolic significance of the "Madonna of the Chair," but they will see something more beautiful than that which they feel in more ordinary pictures, in which they see mother, father, and children. And the constant companionship with this picture will awaken in their heart a religious impression.

This, then, is the environment which I have selected for the children we wish to educate.

I know the first objection which will present itself to the minds of persons accustomed to the old-time methods of discipline; —the children in these schools, moving about, will overturn the little tables and chairs, producing noise and disorder; but this is a prejudice which has long existed in the minds of those dealing with little children, and for which there is no real foundation.

Swaddling clothes have for many centuries been considered necessary to the newborn babe, walking-chairs to the child who is learning to walk. So in the school, we still believe it necessary to have heavy desks and chairs fastened to the floor. All these things are based upon the idea that the child should grow in immobility, and upon the strange prejudice that, in order to execute any educational movement, we must maintain a special position of the body;—as we believe that we must assume a special position when we are about to pray.

Our little tables and our various types of chairs are all light and easily transported, and we permit the child to *select* the position which he finds most comfortable. He can *make himself comfortable* as well as seat himself in his own place. And this freedom is not only an external sign of liberty, but a means of education. If by an awkward movement a child upsets a chair, which falls noisily to the floor, he will have an evident proof of his own incapacity; the same movement had it taken place amid stationary benches would have passed unnoticed by him. Thus the child has some means by which he can correct himself, and having done so he will have before him the actual proof of the power he has gained: the little

tables and chairs remain firm and silent each in its own place. It is plainly seen that the *child has learned to command his movements.*

In the old method, the proof of discipline attained lay in a fact entirely contrary to this; that is, in the immobility and silence of the child himself. Immobility and silence which *hindered* the child from learning to move with grace and with discernment, and left him so untrained, that, when he found himself in an environment where the benches and chairs were not nailed to the floor, he was not able to move about without overturning the lighter pieces of furniture. In the "Children's Houses" the child will not only learn to move gracefully and properly, but will come to understand the reason for such deportment. The ability to move which he acquires here will be of use to him all his life. While he is still a child, he becomes capable of conducting himself correctly, and yet, with perfect freedom. . . .

DISCIPLINE

The pedagogical method of *observation* has for its base the *liberty* of the child; and *liberty is activity.*

Discipline must come through liberty. Here is a great principle which is difficult for followers of common-school methods to understand. How shall one obtain *discipline* in a class of free children? Certainly in our system, we have a concept of discipline very different from that commonly accepted. If discipline is founded upon liberty, the discipline itself must necessarily be *active.* We do not consider an individual disciplined only when he has been rendered as artificially silent as a mute and as immovable as a paralytic. He is an individual *annihilated,* not *disciplined.*

We call an individual disciplined when he is master of himself, and can, therefore, regulate his own conduct when it shall be necessary to follow some rule of life. Such a concept of *active discipline* is not easy either to comprehend or to apply. But certainly it contains a great *educational* prin-

ciple, very different from the old-time absolute and undiscussed coercion to immobility.

A special technique is necessary to the
teacher who is to lead the child along such
a path of discipline, if she is to make it possible for him to continue in this way all his
life, advancing indefinitely toward perfect
self-mastery. Since the child now learns to
move rather than to *sit still,* he prepares
himself not for the school, but for life; for
he becomes able, through habit and through
practice, to perform easily and correctly the
simple acts of social or community life. The
discipline to which the child habituates himself here is, in its character, not limited to
the school environment but extends to society.

The liberty of the child should have as its
limit the collective interest; as its *form,* what
we universally consider good breeding. We
must, therefore, check in the child whatever
offends or annoys others, or whatever tends
toward rough or ill-bred acts. But all the
rest,—every manifestation having a useful
scope,—whatever it be, and under whatever
form it expresses itself, must not only be
permitted, but must be *observed* by the
teacher. Here lies the essential point; from
her scientific preparation, the teacher must
bring not only the capacity, but the desire,
to observe natural phenomena. In our system, she must become a passive, much more
than an active, influence, and her passivity
shall be composed of anxious scientific curiosity, and of absolute *respect* for the phenomenon which she wishes to observe. The
teacher must understand and *feel* her position of *observer:* the *activity* must lie in the
phenomenon.

Such principles assuredly have a place in
schools for little children who are exhibiting
the first psychic manifestations of their lives.
We cannot know the consequences of suffo-
cating a *spontaneous action* at the time when
the child is just beginning to be active: perhaps we suffocate *life itself.* Humanity shows
itself in all its intellectual splendour during
this tender age as the sun shows itself at the
dawn, and the flower in the first unfolding

of the petals; and we must *respect* religiously,
reverently, these first indications of individuality. If any educational act is to be efficacious, it will be only that which tends to *help*
toward the complete unfolding of this life.
To be thus helpful it is necessary rigorously
to avoid the *arrest* of *spontaneous movements and the imposition of arbitrary tasks.*
It is of course understood, that here we do
not speak of useless or dangerous acts, for
these must be *suppressed, destroyed.* . . .

If discipline is to be lasting, its foundations must be laid in this way and these first
days are the most difficult for the directress.
The first idea that the child must acquire, in
order to be actively disciplined, is that of the
difference between *good* and *evil;* and the
task of the educator lies in seeing that the
child does not confound *good* with *immobility,* and *evil* with *activity,* as often happens
in the case of the old-time discipline. And
all this because our aim is to discipline *for
activity, for work, for good;* not for *immobility,* not for *passivity,* not for *obedience.*

A room in which all the children move
about usefully, intelligently, and voluntarily,
without committing any rough or rude act,
would seem to me a classroom very well disciplined indeed.

To seat the children in rows, as in the
common schools, to assign to each little one
a place, and to propose that they shall sit
thus quietly observant of the order of the
whole class as an assemblage—this can be
attained later, as *the starting place* of collective education. . . .

INDEPENDENCE

No one can be free unless he is independent: therefore, the first, active manifestations of the child's individual liberty must
be so guided that through this activity he
may arrive at independence. Little children,
from the moment in which they are weaned,
are making their way toward independence. . . .

Any pedagogical action, if it is to be efficacious in the training of little children,
must tend to *help* the children to advance

upon this road of independence. We must help them to learn to walk without assistance, to run, to go up and down stairs, to lift up fallen objects, to dress and undress themselves, to bathe themselves, to speak distinctly, and to express their own needs clearly. We must give such help as shall make it possible for children to achieve the satisfaction of their own individual aims and desires. All this is a part of education for independence.

We habitually *serve* children; and this is not only an act of servility toward them, but it is dangerous, since it tends to suffocate their useful, spontaneous activity. We are inclined to believe that children are like puppets, and we wash them and feed them as if they were dolls. We do not stop to think that the child *who does not do, does not know how to do*. He must, nevertheless, do these things, and nature has furnished him with the physical means for carrying on these various activities, and with the intellectual means for learning how to do them. And our duty toward him is, in every case, that of *helping him* to make a conquest of such useful acts as nature intended he should perform for himself. . . .

We must make of the future generation, *powerful men,* and by that we mean men who are independent and free.

ABOLITION OF PRIZES AND OF EXTERNAL FORMS OF PUNISHMENT

Once we have accepted and established such principles, the abolition of prizes and external forms of punishment will follow naturally. Man, disciplined through liberty, begins to desire the true and only prize which will never belittle or disappoint him, —the birth of human power and liberty within that inner life of his from which his activities must spring.

In my own experience I have often marvelled to see how true this is. . . .

EDUCATION OF THE SENSES

In a pedagogical method which is experimental the education of the senses must undoubtedly assume the greatest importance. . . .

The method used by me is that of making a pedagogical experiment with a didactic object and awaiting the spontaneous reaction of the child. . . .

With little children, we must proceed to the making of trials, and must select the didactic materials in which they show themselves to be interested.

This I did in the first year of the "Children's Houses" adopting a great variety of stimuli, with a number of which I had already experimented in the school for deficients.

Much of the material used for deficients is abandoned in the education of the normal child—and much that is used has been greatly modified. I believe, however, that I have arrived at a *selection of objects* (which I do not here wish to speak of in the technical language of psychology as stimuli) representing the minimum *necessary* to a practical sense education.

These objects constitute the *didactic system* (or set of didactic materials) used by me. They are manufactured by the House of Labour of the Humanitarian Society at Milan. . . .

Let me summarize briefly: Our didactic material renders auto-education possible, permits a methodical education of the senses. Not upon the ability of the teacher does such education rest, but upon the didactic system. This presents objects which, first, attract the spontaneous attention of the child, and, second, contain a rational gradation of stimuli.

We must not confuse the *education* of the senses, with the concrete ideas which may be gathered from our environment by means of the senses. Nor must this education of the senses be identical in our minds with the language through which is given the nomenclature corresponding to the concrete idea, nor with the acquisition of the abstract idea of the exercises.

Let us consider what the music master does in giving instruction in piano playing.

He teaches the pupil the correct position of the body, gives him the idea of the notes, shows him the correspondence between the written notes and the touch and the position of the fingers, and then he leaves the child to perform the exercise by himself. If a pianist is to be made of this child, there must, between the ideas given by the teacher and the musical exercises, intervene long and patient application to those exercises which serve to give agility to the articulation of the fingers and of the tendons, in order that the co-ordination of special muscular movements shall become automatic, and that the muscles of the hand shall become strong through their repeated use.

The pianist must, therefore, *act for himself,* and the more his natural tendencies lead him to *persist* in these exercises the greater will be his success. However, without the direction of the master the exercise will not suffice to develop the scholar into a true pianist.

The directress of the "Children's House" must have a clear idea of the two factors which enter into her work—the guidance of the child, and the individual exercise.

Only after she has this concept clearly fixed in her mind, may she proceed to the application of a *method* to *guide* the spontaneous education of the child and to impart necessary notions to him.

.   .   .   .   .

The only entirely successful experiments which we have made so far in the "Children's Houses" are those of the *clock,* and of the *lowered* or whispered *voice.* The trial is purely empirical, and does not lend itself to the measuring of the sensation, but it is, however, most useful in that it helps us to an approximate knowledge of the child's auditory acuteness.

The exercise consists in calling attention, when perfect silence has been established, to the ticking of the clock, and to all the little noises not commonly audible to the ear. Finally we call the little ones, one by one from an adjoining room, pronouncing

each name in a low voice. In preparing for such an exercise it is necessary to *teach* the children the real meaning of *silence.*

Toward this end I have several *games* of *silence,* which help in a surprising way to strengthen the remarkable discipline of our children.

I call the children's attention to myself, telling them to see how silent I can be. I assume different positions; standing, sitting, and maintain each pose *silently, without movement.* A finger moving can produce a noise, even though it be imperceptible. We may breathe so that we may be heard. But I maintain *absolute* silence, which is not an easy thing to do. I call a child, and ask him to do as I am doing. He adjusts his feet to a better position, and this makes a noise! He moves an arm, stretching it out upon the arm of his chair; it is a noise. His breathing is not altogether silent, it is not tranquil, absolutely unheard as mine is.

During these manœuvres on the part of the child, and while my brief comments are followed by intervals of immobility and silence, the other children are watching and listening. Many of them are interested in the fact, which they have never noticed before; namely, that we make so many noises of which we are not conscious, and that there are *degrees* of *silence.* There is an absolute silence where nothing, *absolutely nothing* moves. They watch me in amazement when I stand in the middle of the room, so quietly that it is really as if "I were not." Then they strive to imitate me, and to do even better. I call attention here and there to a foot that moves, almost inadvertently. The attention of the child is called to every part of his body in an anxious eagerness to attain to immobility.

When the children are trying in this way, there is established a silence very different from that which we carelessly call by that name.

It seems as if life gradually vanishes, and that the room becomes, little by little, empty, as if there were no longer anyone in it. Then we begin to hear the tick-tock of the clock, and this sound seems to grow in intensity as the silence becomes absolute. From without, from the court which before seemed silent, there come varied noises, a bird chirps, a child passes. The children sit fascinated by that silence as if by some conquest of their own. "Here," says the directress, "here there is no longer anyone; the children have all gone away."

Having arrived at that point, we darken the windows, and tell the children to close their eyes, resting their heads upon their hands. They assume this position, and in the darkness the absolute silence returns.

"Now listen," we say. "A soft voice is going to call your name." Then going to a room behind the children, and standing within the open door, I call in a low voice, lingering over the syllables as if I were calling from across the mountains. This voice, almost occult, seems to reach the heart and to call to the soul of the child. Each one as he is called, lifts his head, opens his eyes as if altogether happy, then rises, silently seeking not to move the chair, and walks on the tips of his toes, so quietly that he is scarcely heard. Nevertheless his step resounds in the silence, and amid the immobility which persists.

Having reached the door, with a joyous face, he leaps into the room, choking back soft outbursts of laughter. Another child may come to hide his face against my dress, another, turning, will watch his companions sitting like statues silent and waiting. The one who is called feels that he is privileged, that he has received a gift, a prize. And yet they know that all will be called, "beginning with the most silent one in all the room." So each one tries to merit by his perfect silence the certain call. I once saw a little one of three years try to suffocate a sneeze, and succeed! She held her breath in her little breast, and resisted, coming out victorious. A most surprising effort!

This game delights the little ones beyond measure. Their intent faces, their patient immobility, reveal the enjoyment of a great pleasure. In the beginning, when the soul of the child was unknown to me, I had thought of showing them sweetmeats and little toys, promising to give them to the ones who were *called*, supposing that the gifts would be necessary to persuade the child to make the necessary effort. But I soon found that this was unnecessary.

The children, after they had made the effort necessary to maintain silence, enjoyed the sensation, took pleasure in the *silence* itself. They were like ships safe in a tranquil harbour, happy in having experienced something new, and to have won a victory over themselves. This, indeed, was their recompense. They *forgot* the promise of sweets, and no longer cared to take the toys, which I had supposed would attract them. I therefore abandoned that useless means, and saw, with surprise, that the game became constantly more perfect, until even children of three years of age remained immovable in the silence throughout the time required to call the entire forty children out of the room!

It was then that I learned that the soul of the child has its own reward, and its peculiar spiritual pleasures. After such exercises it seemed to me that the children came closer to me, certainly they became more obedient, more gentle and sweet. We had, indeed, been isolated from the world, and had passed several minutes during which the communion between us was very close, I wishing for them and calling to them, and they receiving in the perfect silence the voice which was directed personally toward each one of them, crowning each in turn with happiness.

A Lesson in Silence

I am about to describe a lesson which *proved* most successful in teaching the perfect silence to which it is possible to attain. One day as I was about to enter one of the "Children's Houses," I met in the court a mother who held in her arms her little baby of four months. The little one was swaddled, as is still the custom among the people of Rome—an infant thus in the swaddling bands is called by us a *pupa*. This tranquil little one seemed the incarnation of peace.

I took her in my arms, where she lay quiet and good. Still holding her I went toward the schoolroom, from which the children now ran to meet me. They always welcomed me thus, throwing their arms about me, clinging to my skirts, and almost tumbling me over in their eagerness. I smiled at them, showing them the *"pupa."* They understood and skipped about me looking at me with eyes brilliant with pleasure, but did not touch me through respect for the little one that I held in my arms.

I went into the schoolroom with the children clustered about me. We sat down, I seating myself in a large chair instead of, as usual, in one of their little chairs. In other words, I seated myself solemnly. They looked at my little one with a mixture of tenderness and joy. None of us had yet spoken a word. Finally I said to them, "I have brought you a little teacher." Surprised glances and laughter. "A little teacher, yes, because none of you know how to be quiet as she does." At this all the children changed their positions and became quiet. "Yet no one holds his limbs and feet as quietly as she." Everyone gave closer attention to the position of limbs and feet. I looked at them smiling, "Yes, but they can never be as quiet as hers. You move a little bit, but she, not at all; none of you can be as quiet as she." The children looked serious. The idea of the superiority of the little teacher seemed to have reached them. Some of them smiled, and seemed to say with their eyes that the swaddling bands deserved all the merit. "Not one of you can be silent, voiceless as she." General silence. "It is not possible to be as silent as she, because,—listen to her breathing—how delicate it is; come near to her on your tiptoes."

Several children rose, and came slowly forward on tiptoe, bending toward the baby. Great silence. "None of you can breathe so silently as she." The children looked about amazed, they had never thought that even when sitting quietly they were making noises, and that the silence of a little babe is more profound than the silence of grown people.

They almost ceased to breathe. I rose. "Go out quietly, quietly," I said, "walk on the tips of your toes and make no noise." Following them I said, "And yet I still hear some sounds, but she, the baby, walks with me and makes no sound. She goes out silently!" The children smiled. They understood the truth and the jest of my words. I went to the open window, and placed the baby in the arms of the mother who stood watching us.

The little one seemed to have left behind her a subtle charm which enveloped the souls of the children. Indeed, there is in nature nothing more sweet than the silent breathing of a new-born babe. There is an indescribable majesty about this human life which in repose and silence gathers strength and newness of life. Compared to this, Wordsworth's description of the silent peace of nature seems to lose its force. "What calm, what quiet! The one sound the drip of the suspended oar." The children, too, felt the poetry and beauty in the peaceful silence of a newborn human life.

.   .   .   .   .

We often hear it said that a child's will should be "broken" that the best education for the will of the child is to learn to give it up to the will of adults. Leaving out of the question the injustice which is at the root of every act of tyranny, this idea is irrational because the child cannot give up what he does not possess. We prevent him in this way from forming his own will-power, and we commit the greatest and most blameworthy mistake. He never has time or opportunity to test himself, to estimate his own force and his own limitations because he is always interrupted and subjected to our tyranny, and languishes in injustice because he is always being bitterly reproached for not having what adults are perpetually destroying.

There springs up as a consequence of this, childish timidity, which is a moral malady acquired by a will which could not develop, and which with the usual calumny with which the tyrant consciously or not, covers up his own mistakes, we consider as an inherent trait of childhood. The children in our schools are never timid. One of their most fascinating qualities is the frankness with which they treat people, with which they go on working in the presence of others, and showing their work frankly, calling for sympathy. That moral monstrosity, a repressed and timid child, who is at his ease nowhere except alone with his playmates, or with street urchins, because his will-power was allowed to grow only in the shade, disappears in our schools. He presents an example of thoughtless barbarism, which resembles the artificial compression of the bodies of those children intended for "court dwarfs," museum monstrosities or buffoons. Yet this is the treatment under which nearly all the children of our time are growing up spiritually.

As a matter of fact in all the pedagogical congresses one hears that the great peril of our time is the lack of individual character in the scholars; yet these alarmists do not point out that this condition is due to the way in which education is managed, to scholastic slavery, which has for its specialty the repression of will-power and of force of character. The remedy is simply to enfranchise human development.

. . . . .

CONCLUSIONS AND IMPRESSIONS

In the "Children's Houses," the old-time teacher, who wore herself out maintaining discipline of immobility, and who wasted her breath in loud and continual discourse, has disappeared.

For this teacher we have substituted the *didactic material,* which contains within itself the control of errors and which makes auto-education possible to each child. The teacher has thus become a *director* of the spontaneous work of the children. She is not a *passive* force, a *silent* presence.

The children are occupied each one in a different way, and the directress, watching

them, can make psychological observations which, if collected in an orderly way and according to scientific standards, should do much toward the reconstruction of child psychology and the development of experimental psychology. I believe that I have by my method established the conditions necessary to the development of scientific pedagogy; and whoever adopts this method opens, in doing so, a laboratory of experimental pedagogy.

From such work, we must await the positive solution of all those pedagogical problems of which we talk to-day. For through such work there has already come the solution of some of these very questions: that of the liberty of the pupils; auto-education; the establishment of harmony between the work and activities of home life and school tasks, making both work together for the education of the child.

MARIA MONTESSORI
"The Teacher's Preparation" [1949] *

The first step an intending Montessori teacher must take is to prepare herself.[1] For one thing, she must keep her imagination alive; for while, in the traditional schools, the teacher sees the immediate behavior of her pupils, knowing that she must look after them and what she has to teach, the Montessori teacher is constantly looking for a child who is not yet there. This is the main point of difference. The teacher, when she begins work in our schools, must have a kind of faith that *the child will reveal himself* through work. She must free herself from all preconceived ideas concerning the levels at which the children may be. The many different types of children (meaning

* From *The Absorbent Mind* by Maria Montessori. Translated by Claude A. Claremont. All Rights Reserved. Reprinted by permission of Holt, Rinehart and Winston, Inc.
[1] The contents of this (address) were given by Dr. Montessori at the request of her Indian audience. . . . The simplicity and warmth of its advice to teachers, and its vivid human interest, justify its retention as a whole.—Translator.

they are more or less deviated) must not worry her. In her imagination she sees that single normalized type, which lives in a world of the spirit. The teacher must believe that this child before her will show his true nature when he finds a piece of work that attracts him. So what must she look out for? That one child or another will begin to concentrate. To this she must devote her energies, and her activities will change from stage to stage, as in a spiritual ascent. What she does will usually have three aspects.

First Stage. The teacher becomes the keeper and custodian of the environment. She attends to this instead of being distracted by the children's restlessness. From this will come healing, and the attraction that captures and polarizes the child's will. In our countries, where each wife has her own home, the wife tries to make the home as attractive as possible for herself and her husband. Instead of giving her whole attention to him, she gives much also to the house, so as to make surroundings in which a normal and constructive life can flourish. She tries to make the home a place of comfort and peace, with full and varied interests. The essential charm of a house is its cleanliness and order, with everything in its place, dusted, bright and cheerful. She makes this her first consideration. The teacher in the school must not do otherwise. All the apparatus is to be kept meticulously in order, beautiful and shining, in perfect condition. Nothing may be missing, so that to the child it always seems new, complete and ready for use. This means that the teacher also must be attractive, pleasing in appearance, tidy and clean, calm and dignified. These are ideals that each can realize in her own way, but let us always remember, when we present ourselves before children, that they are *"of the company of the elect."* The teacher's appearance is the first step to gaining the child's confidence and respect. The teacher should study her own movements, to make them as gentle and graceful as possible. The child of this age idealizes his mother. We

may not know what kind of woman she is, but we often hear a child say, when he sees a pretty woman, "How lovely she is—just like my mummy!" Quite possibly the mother is not at all beautiful, but she is so to the child, and everyone he admires is, to him, as beautiful as she. So, care for one's own person must form part of the environment in which the child lives; the teacher herself is the most vital part of his world.

The teacher's first duty is therefore to watch over the environment, and this takes precedence over all the rest. Its influence is indirect, but unless it be well done there will be no effective and permanent results of any kind, physical, intellectual or spiritual.

Second Stage. Having considered the environment, we must ask how the teacher shall behave toward the children. What can we do with these disorderly little people, with these confused and uncertain little minds that we hope to attract and cause to fasten upon work? Sometimes I use a word easily misunderstood: the teacher must be seductive, she must entice the children. Were the environment to be neglected, the furniture dusty, the apparatus broken and out of place, and if—above all—the teacher herself were slovenly, ill-mannered and harsh to the children, then the basic essentials would be lacking for the goal at which she aims. The teacher, in this first period, before concentration has shown itself, must be like the flame which heartens all by its warmth, enlivens and invites. There is no need to fear that she will interrupt some important psychic process, since these have not yet begun. Before concentration occurs, the directress may do more or less what she thinks best; she can interfere with the children's activities as much as she deems necessary.

I once read of a saint who tried to gather together some children whom he had found abandoned in the streets of a city in which the people's conduct was far from refined. What did he do? He tried to amuse them. This is what the teacher must do at this juncture. She can tell stories, have some games and singing, use nursery rhymes and poetry. The teacher who has a gift for charming the children can have them do various exercises, which, even if they have no great value educationally, are useful in calming them. Everyone knows that a lively teacher attracts more than a dull one, and we can all be lively if we try. Anyone, for example, can say cheerfully, "Let's move all the furniture today!" and work with the children, encouraging and praising them all in a bright and pleasing manner. Or she may say, "What about this brass water jug? It needs polishing." Or, again, "Let's go in the garden and pick some flowers." Every action of the teacher's can become a call and an invitation to the children.

This is the second phase of the teacher's work. If at this stage there is some child who persistently annoys the others, the most practical thing to do is to interrupt him. It is true that we have said, and repeated often enough, that when a child is absorbed in his work, one must refrain from interfering, so as not to interrupt his cycle of activity or prevent its free expansion; nevertheless, the right technique, now, is just the opposite; it is to break the flow of disturbing activity. The interruption may take the form of any kind of exclamation, or in showing a special and affectionate interest in the troublesome child. These distracting demonstrations of affection, which grow more numerous with the disturbing activities of the child, act on him like a series of electric shocks and they have their effect in time. Often a question will serve, such as, "How are you, Johnny? Come with me, I have something for you to do." Probably, he won't want to be shown, and the teacher will say, "All right, it doesn't matter. Let's go into the garden," and either she will go with him or send her assistant. In this way, he and his naughtiness will pass directly into the hands of the assistant, and the other children will cease to be disturbed by him.

Third Stage. Finally, the time comes in which the children begin to take an interest in something: usually, in the exercises of practical life, for experience shows that it is useless and harmful to give the children sensorial and cultural apparatus before they are ready to benefit from it.

Before introducing this kind of material, one must wait till the children have acquired the power to concentrate on something, and usually, as I say, this occurs with the exercises of practical life. When the child begins to show interest in one of these, the teacher must *not interrupt,* because this interest corresponds with natural laws and opens up a whole cycle of new activities. But the first step is so fragile, so delicate, that a touch can make it vanish again, like a soap bubble, and with it goes all the beauty of that moment.

The teacher, now, must be most careful. Not to interfere means not to interfere *in any way.* This is the moment at which the teacher most often goes wrong. The child, who up to that moment has been very difficult, finally concentrates on a piece of work. If, as she passes, the teacher merely says, "Good," it is enough to make the trouble break out all over again. Quite likely, it will be two weeks before the child takes an interest in anything else. If another child is finding it hard to do something, and the teacher goes to help him, he may leave it to her instead. The child's interest is not only focused on the operation itself, but more often it is based on his wish to *overcome the difficulty.* "If the teacher wants to overcome it instead of me, let her. I am no longer interested." That is his attitude. If the child is trying to lift something very heavy and the teacher tries to help him, it often happens that he leaves the object in her hands and runs away. Praise, help, or even a look, may be enough to interrupt him, or destroy the activity. It seems a strange thing to say, but this can happen even if the child merely becomes aware of being watched. After all, we too sometimes feel unable to go on working if someone comes to see what we are doing. The great principle which brings success to the teacher is this: *as soon as concentration has begun, act as if the child does not exist.*

Naturally, one can see what he is doing with a quick glance, but without his being aware of it. After this, the child who is no longer a prey to the boredom which made him go from one thing to another without ever fastening upon any, starts choosing his work purposefully, and this may produce problems in a class where many want the same thing at the same time. But even to solve these problems, one should not interfere unless asked; the children will solve them by themselves. The duty of the teacher is only to present new things when she knows that a child has exhausted all the possibilities of those he was using before.

The teacher's skill in not interfering comes with practice, like everything else, but it never comes very easily. It means rising to spiritual heights. True spirituality realizes that even to help can be a source of pride.

The real help that the teacher can give does not lie in obeying a sentimental impulse, but it comes from subjecting one's love to discipline, using it with discernment, because the doer of a kindness reaps greater happiness than the receiver. True kindness serves the needy without disclosing itself or, when it is discovered, it poses not as a help, but as something natural and spontaneous.

Although the relationship between child and teacher is in the spiritual field, the teacher can find a very good model for her behavior in the way a good valet looks after his master. He keeps his master's dressing table tidy, puts the brushes in place, but he does not tell his master when to use the brushes; he serves his meals, but does not oblige his master to eat; having served everything nicely, without a word, he discreetly disappears. So we must behave when the child's spirit is being forged. The master whom the teacher serves is the child's spirit; when it shows its needs she must hasten to respond to them. The valet never disturbs his master when alone, but if the latter calls, he hurries to find out what is wanted, and replies, "Yes, Sir." If he finds that admiration is expected, he expresses it, and may even say, "How lovely!" of something he does not find beautiful at all. In the same way, if a child does a piece of work with great concentration, we must keep out of the way, but if he shows a wish for our approval, we should give it generously.

In the psychological realm of relationship between teacher and child, the teacher's part and its techniques are analogous to those of the valet; they are to serve, and to serve well: to serve the spirit. This is something new, especially in the educational field. It is not a question of washing the child when he is dirty, of mending or cleaning his clothes. We do not serve the child's body, because we know that if he is to develop he must do these things for himself. The basis of our teaching is that he should *not* be served in this sense. The child has to acquire physical independence by being self-sufficient; he must become of independent will by using in freedom his own power of choice; he must become capable of independent thought by working alone without interruption. The child's development follows a path of successive stages of independence, and our knowledge of this must guide us in our behavior towards him. We have to help the child to act, will and think for himself. This is the art of serving the spirit, an art which can be practiced to perfection only when working among children.

If the teacher meets the needs of the group of children entrusted to her, she will see the qualities of social life burst surprisingly into flower, and will have the joy of watching these manifestations of the childish soul. It is a great privilege to be able to see them. It is the privilege of the traveler when he reaches an oasis and hears the water surging from the sandy breast of the desert which had seemed so arid, fiery and hopeless; for the higher qualities of the human soul are usually hidden in the deviated child, and when they appear, the teacher by whom they had been foreseen welcomes them with the joy of a faith rewarded. And in these qualities of the child, she sees man as he ought to be: the worker who never tires, because what drives him on is a perennial enthusiasm. She sees one who seeks out the greatest efforts because his constant aspiration is to make himself superior to difficulties; he is a person who really tries to help the weak, because in his heart there is the true charity which knows what is meant by respect for others, and that respect for a person's spiritual efforts is the water that nourishes the roots of his soul. In the possession of these characteristics, she will recognize the true child, who is father of the true man.

But this will only happen little by little. At first the teacher will say, "I have seen the child as he ought to be, and found him better than I could ever have supposed." This is what it means to understand infancy. It is not enough to know that this child is called John, that his father is a carpenter; the teacher must know and experience in her daily life the secret of childhood. Through this she arrives not only at a deeper knowledge, but at a new kind of love which does not become attached to the individual person, but to that which lies in the hidden darkness of this secret. When the children show her their real natures, she understands perhaps for the first time, what love really is. And this revelation transforms her also. It is a thing that touches the heart, and little by little it changes people. Once these facts have been seen, one cannot cease from writing and talking about them. The names of the children may become forgotten, but nothing can cancel the impression their spirits have made and the love they were able to awaken.

There are two levels of love. Often, when we speak of our love for children, we refer to the care we take of them, the caresses and affection we shower on those we know and who arouse our tender feelings, and if a spiritual relationship binds us to them, we show it by teaching them their prayers.

But I am speaking of something different. It is a level of love which is no longer personal or material. To serve the children is to feel one is serving the spirit of man, a spirit which has to free itself. The difference

of level has truly been set not by the teacher but by the child. It is the teacher who feels she has been lifted to a height she never knew before. The child has made her grow till she is brought within his sphere.

Before this, she used to feel that her task was a noble one, but she was glad when the holidays came and hoped, like all human beings who work for others, that her working hours would be reduced and her salary raised. Her satisfactions were, perhaps, to exert authority and to have the feeling of being an ideal to which the children looked up and tried to emulate. It would make her happy to become a headmistress, or even an inspectress. But to go from this level to the higher one is to understand that true happiness does not lie in these things. One who has drunk at the fountain of spiritual happiness says good-by of his own accord to the satisfactions that come from a higher professional status, and this is shown by the many heads of schools and inspectors who have abandoned their careers to dedicate themselves to small children, and to become what others call contemptuously "infant teachers."

I know two doctors of medicine in Paris who left their profession to devote themselves entirely to our work and to enter into the reality of these phenomena. They felt they had gone from a low level to a higher one.

What is the greatest sign of success for a teacher thus transformed? It is to be able to say, "The children are now working as if I did not exist."

Before the transformation, her feelings were just the contrary; she thought it was she who had taught the children, she who had raised them from a low level to a higher one. But now, with the manifestations before her of the child's spirit, the greatest value she can ascribe to her own contribution is expressed in the words: "I have helped this life to fulfill the tasks set for it by creation."

This is truly satisfying. The teacher of children up to six years of age knows that she has helped mankind in an essential part of its formation. She may know nothing of the children's circumstances, except what they have told her freely in conversation; possibly she takes no interest in their future: whether they will go on to secondary schools and the university, or end their studies sooner; but she is happy in the knowledge that in this formative period they were able to do what they had to do. She will be able to say: "I have served the spirits of those children, and they have fulfilled their development, and I kept them company in their experiences." The teacher, quite apart from the authority to whom she is responsible, feels the value of her work, and of what she has accomplished, in the form of a satisfied spiritual life, which is "life everlasting" and a prayer in itself from each morning to the next. This is hard to understand for one who has not adopted this life. Many think it is due to a virtue of self-sacrifice, and say, "How humble these teachers are, not to be interested even in their own authority over the children," and many say: "How can your method succeed if you ask your teachers to renounce all their most natural and spontaneous desires?" But what no one understands is that not sacrifice, but satisfaction, is in question; not renunciation, but a new life in which the values are different, where real life values, hitherto unknown, have come to exist.

Moreover, all the principles are different; justice, for example. In schools and in society, and in democratic countries, justice often means only that there is a single law for all; for the rich and powerful and for those dying of hunger. Justice is generally thought of in connection with lawsuits, with prisons and sentences. Courts of law are called Palaces of Justice, and to say, "I am an honest citizen," implies that one has nothing to do with legal administration (police or law courts). Even in the school, the teacher has to be careful about caressing a child, otherwise he might have to caress them all: he must be just. This is a kind of justice that puts everyone on the lowest level; as if, in a spiritual sense, we were to behead the tallest in order to have them all of the same height.

On this higher educational level justice is something truly spiritual; it tries to ensure that every child shall make the best of himself. Justice, here, is to give every human being the help he needs to bring about his fullest spiritual stature, and service of the spirit at every age means helping those energies that are at work to bring this about. This, perhaps, will be the basis on which society will be organized in the future. Nothing of these spiritual treasures should be lost. In comparison with these, economic treasures have no value. Whether I be rich or poor does not matter: if I can attain to the full measure of my powers, the economic problem solves itself. When mankind as a whole can fully perfect its spirit, it will become more productive, and the economic aspect of life will cease to preponderate. Men do not produce with their feet and their bodies, but with their spirit and intelligence, and when these shall have reached the level of development which is proper to them, then all our "insoluble problems" will have become solved.

Children unaided can construct an orderly society. For us adults, prisons, police, soldiers and guns are necessary. Children solve their problems peacefully; they have shown us that freedom and discipline are two faces of the same medal, because scientific freedom leads to discipline. Coins usually have two faces, one being more beautiful, finely chiseled, bearing a head or allegorical figure, while the other is less ornate, with nothing but a number or some writing. The plain side can be compared to freedom, and the finely chiseled side to discipline. This is so true that when her class becomes undisciplined, the teacher sees in the disorder merely an indication of some error that *she* has made; she seeks this out and corrects it. The teacher of the traditional school would feel this to be humiliating; but it is not humiliating, it is a part of the technique of the new education. In serving the child, one serves life; in helping nature one rises to the next stage, that of super-nature, for to go upward is a law of life. And it is the children who have made this beautiful staircase that mounts ever higher. The law of nature is order, and when order comes of itself, we know that we have re-entered the order of the universe. It is clear that nature includes among the missions she has entrusted to the child, the mission of arousing us adults to reach a higher level. The children take us to a higher plane of the spirit and material problems are thereby solved. Permit me to repeat, as a form of farewell, some words which have helped us to keep in mind all the things of which I have been speaking. It is not a prayer, but rather a reminder, and for our teachers, an invocation, a kind of syllabus, our only syllabus:

"HELP US, O GOD, TO ENTER INTO THE SECRET OF CHILDHOOD, SO THAT WE MAY KNOW, LOVE AND SERVE THE CHILD IN ACCORDANCE WITH THE LAWS OF THY JUSTICE AND FOLLOWING THY HOLY WILL."

PART THREE

EDUCATION IN
MODERN SOCIETY:
1919 TO THE PRESENT

"The making of money, the accumulation of material power, is not all there is to living. Life is something more than these, and the man who misses this truth misses the greatest joy and satisfaction that can come into his life—service for others."

EDWARD BOK, *Autobiography*, 1920

"Universities are social institutions, and should perform a social service. There is indeed no reason for the existence of Cornell, or of any university, or for maintaining the freedom of learning and teaching which they insist upon, except in so far as they serve to maintain and promote the humane and rational values which are essential to the preservation of democratic society, and of civilization as we understand it."

CARL L. BECKER, "The Cornell Tradition: Freedom and Responsibility," April 27, 1940

"This is a time in our national life more serious, more menacing, more crucial, than any I have ever experienced or ever hoped to experience."

GEORGE F. KENNAN, "Rebels Without a Program," January 21, 1968

Introduction

I

A dominant theme in American history has been the closing gap between human aspirations and educational opportunities. Noteworthy examples during the past century have been the demands of women for equality and the drive by Negro Americans for freedom and civil rights. At times, however, the quest for equality of opportunity has met with frustration and defeat.

By the late nineteen-sixties, the imbalance of opportunity had become a matter of grave national concern. In 1968, for example, at least fifty thousand American Indian families lived in unheated tents, shanties, and abandoned automobiles. A majority of their children did not complete high school. In terms of poverty, illness, and illiteracy, American Indians were the nation's most depressed minority group. As the findings of The Coleman Report (1966) revealed, there was an urgent need to implement fully America's ideals.

II

After 1919 American education developed into a giant enterprise. The common school had been extended upward to include the public high school. A legal basis for this extension was provided by the historic Kalamazoo decision of 1874, which affirmed a school board's power to levy taxes for the support of secondary education. Under the impact of industrialization, courses of instruction were oriented more toward vocational and technical aims. At the same time, the public schools were compelled to assume social roles previously expected of the family and the church or synagogue. By the end of World War I, no other nation had committed itself so completely to the idea of free public education for all children through the high-school years.

In quantitative terms, American education was becoming a mass system. From 1910 to 1930, public-school enrollments soared from about eighteen million to twenty-five million. On the college level, too, enrollments spiraled upward, and the number of courses offered was greatly increased.

Some of the most important changes occurred in elementary education. Not only did the schools expand numerically, but the atmosphere for learning was also different. New knowledge about child development was available, and classroom discipline became less severe. Most teachers were beginning to understand, as great educators have always known, that learning could be interesting and meaningful and still develop in children the ability to pursue intensive intellectual tasks.

These changes were partly due to the influence of John Dewey, who challenged sharply the practices of the conventional elementary school. "How many students were rendered callous to ideas, and how many lost the impetus to learn because of the way in which learning was experienced by them?" asked Dewey in *Experience and Education* (1938). In thirty-six books and more than eight hundred articles, Dewey expounded his views repeatedly and laid the basis for modern educational theory.

Today the individualization of instruction assumes new meaning and purpose. A modified view of the learning process and new roles for the teacher have literally transformed the classroom environment. Efforts to adapt programs to the needs and abilities of all children are leading to experimentation with team teaching, nongraded schools, and

393

other innovative practices. Multipurpose rooms, with movable furniture and educational media, are contributing to flexible procedures. Certainly these changes have not occurred in every school, but ideally, at least, the goal of American elementary education is to provide for each pupil a rich and rewarding learning experience.

III

In the secondary schools, the major emphasis after World War I was still on academic courses and preparation for college. In 1892 the Committee of Ten recognized the changing composition of the high-school population and then proceeded to recommend programs designed primarily for the college-bound youth. Most pupils enrolled in public high schools during the eighteen-nineties did not plan to attend college; over half, in fact, were girls with limited career aspirations. A large number dropped out before the twelfth grade. Yet, in spite of these revealing facts, the Committee held to the prevailing view that the studies which prepared a student for college admission also best prepared one for life. The report of the Committee of Ten, chaired by Charles W. Eliot (1834–1926), is a significant document in the history of American secondary education, because it determined the course of the public high school for at least a generation.

By mid-century secondary education had expanded to the point where most youth were actually attending classes and a vast majority remained to graduate. As enrollments increased at unprecedented rates, control by the precollege curriculum lessened. There was considerable growth not only in the number of subjects but also in the type and range of courses offered.

Meanwhile educators were reflecting seriously on the kind of secondary education that would best serve *all* boys and girls. The launching of Sputnik I in the fall of 1957 brought into focus the basic conflict over purpose. The ensuing dialogue was unrestrained as influential citizens and interest groups charged the public high schools with weakening academic standards. Certainly Russian space achievements have made Americans acutely aware of the need for quality education. Few critics approached the issues in a more constructive manner than did James Bryant Conant (1893–   ), whose studies of the comprehensive high school resulted in some practical, middle-of-the-road recommendations.

There is every indication that the decade ahead will be one of ferment and serious experimentation. Since the late nineteen-fifties, academic scholars in colleges and universities have joined the curriculum reform movement in growing numbers. All are concerned with modifying courses and instructional practices. Some of the most impressive trends are improved programs for culturally different students, expanded uses of new media and technology, increasing emphasis on the creative arts, greater provisions for independent study time, and better guidance services for all.

No one doubts America's capacity for innovation and change in secondary education; but the complex problems which lie ahead will demand from everyone a strong commitment to the ideals of a free society. Equality of opportunity calls for differentiation, not uniformity. The United States is a highly diversified nation and requires for its continued progress the talents and abilities of all citizens.

IV

Important changes also occurred in higher education. The first Morrill Act of 1862, along with another act of 1890, initiated a historic policy of federal aid to education and laid the basis for a new type of college curriculum at government expense. Justin S. Morrill (1810–1898), a self-educated Vermonter, believed strongly in a utilitarian training for the common man and sought to democratize the nation's colleges. The "land-grant" concept was a major factor in the rise of American state universities.

Within a decade after opening its doors

in 1876, Johns Hopkins University was being recognized as the most notable institution of its kind in the United States. President Daniel Coit Gilman (1831–1908), unrestricted in his plans, proposed a university modeled after the European pattern. He helped to establish a new foundation for graduate education in America.

The introduction of the elective principle, advocated by President Eliot of Harvard, elicited some lively discussions in college circles. By 1897 the only prescribed subject in the Harvard curriculum was rhetoric. President Noah Porter (1811–1892) of Yale vigorously opposed the idea, but Eliot's plan prevailed. By the turn of the century students at thirty-four leading colleges and universities could elect more than 70 per cent of their subjects.

A reaction against the extreme specialization fostered by the elective system has been the "general education" movement. But what is meant by "general education"? Proponents, for example, argue against separating labor from leisure, vocational aims from citizenship education. Nowhere is this idea more cogently analyzed than in the famous Harvard Report entitled *General Education in a Free Society* (1945).

Academic freedom is not a new concept. For Western man the idea probably had its first champion in Socrates, who, dedicated to the belief that the pursuit of truth has no boundaries, died rather than renounce this ideal. The issue of intellectual liberty has loomed ever larger since the beginnings of higher education. Incessantly the question arises: in the interest of social stability, how much difference of opinion is desirable, how much heterodoxy is permissible? Carl Becker's delightful commentary on "The Cornell Tradition" (1940) offers one answer: "a maximum of freedom" combined with a "sense of personal responsibility."

Like the elementary and secondary schools, American colleges and universities by the late nineteen-sixties were on a mass-production basis. Junior-college enrollments, in particular, climbed steadily. The number

of courses offered was increasing in many institutions. Student transfers and large classes further underscored the quantitative factor. And at no other level of the educational ladder was there more disorder and criticism. With insight and deep understanding, George F. Kennan (1904—   ) surveyed the contemporary scene in higher education. "Freedom, . . ." he declared in 1968, "is definable only in terms of the obligations and restraints and sacrifices it accepts. It exists, as a concept, only in relationship to something else which is by definition its opposite; and that means commitment, duty, self-restraint." In a troubled world, Kennan's words gave cause for reflection.

V

The use of technological aids in teaching has generated some heated debates. Those who argue for the use of programed materials, for example, often base their position on the hope that this type of instruction will greatly increase the efficiency of learning. The resistance has stemmed from a fear that teaching machines will tend to mechanize the teaching-learning process, will, it is argued, render the teacher obsolete; such an argument, of course, is without foundation. Almost everyone agrees that the human quality of teacher-pupil relationships must remain paramount when autoinstructional devices are used in the classroom.

The real cause for concern   has nothing at all to do with the so-called machine. In the use of programed instruction, the danger lies in a limited conception of the learning process.

The terms "situation," "response," and "reinforcement" led to a rather simple model of learning. In the use of programed materials, the pedagogical problem became one of arranging a schedule of reinforcements which modified or shaped the initial behavior until the specified terminal behavior had been produced.

Sometimes, however, this is not feasible. It is difficult, perhaps impossible, to identify elements in the learning of important tasks which correspond to the traditional definitions of situation, response, and reinforcement. Information stated in linguistic form, for instance, cannot be clearly translated into observable behavioral units. Behind any vocabulary are complex interpretations which escape this sort of reduction.

VI

Differences among teachers and pupils from the varied strata of American society sometimes lead to serious conflicts during classroom interactions. When teachers work with children from the inner city, for example, they are often dealing with boys and girls from a lower-class group. The teacher, however, usually comes from a different social class and expects behavior coincident with middle-class values. When such behavior is not evident in the classroom, the teacher attempts to reinforce middle-class expectations. Forced to comply with the teacher's demands, the children are pushed into patterns of behavior perceived as strange or even unnecessary. After all, why is classroom silence a sign of good behavior? Why are certain styles of dress expected in school (wearing a necktie, for instance)? When classroom behavior does not coincide with the teacher's expectations, the pupils are viewed as wrong or even hostile. And from this vantage point, they are frequently judged to be inferior—not inferior by the time they approach high school, but inferior by the time they leave the first grade.

It is important to keep in mind the complex phenomenon to which we apply descriptive labels. There is a tendency to categorize together under such labels as the "socially disadvantaged" or "culturally deprived" all pupils who come from different environments. Used instead of the clearer and often prejudicial words of the layman, such terms might perpetuate toward children from varied backgrounds an attitude of condescension or disdain. The term "culture" describes the ethos of any group of people: their beliefs, values, way of life. Of what, then, are children from ethnic groups deprived? Certainly not a "culture," for they are members of their own subcultures. Only if one believes that these children lack some other culture—for example, a middle-class culture—are they "socially disadvantaged" or "culturally deprived." And the only way in which they are deprived is in the absence of opportunities and material objects characteristic of middle-class America. The missing element, then, is a middle-class culture.

Too often American teachers assume that middle-class values reflect the ideal society. Anthropological research has sought to eliminate this ethnocentrism. Studies of kinship, for example, clearly indicate that children can be reared successfully in a variety of familial organizations and according to patterns defined by particular cultures. Through creative teaching and innovative procedures, we should try to reduce the pressures for conformity and aim instead for a greater understanding of the individual child's *own* world.

CHAPTER NINE

Social Currents of Equalitarianism

AMERICA IN PERSPECTIVE

GEORGE SANTAYANA
The American Image (1920) *

I have no axe to grind, only my thoughts to burnish, in the hope that some part of the truth of things may be reflected there; and I am confident of not giving serious offence to the judicious, because they will feel that it is affection for the American people that makes me wish that what is best and most beautiful should not be absent from their lives.

· · · · ·

In matters of morals, manners, and art, the danger of comparisons is not merely that they may prove invidious, by ranging qualities in an order of merit which might wound somebody's vanity; the danger is rather that comparisons may distort comprehension, because in truth good qualities are all different in kind, and free lives are different in spirit. Comparison is the expedient of those who cannot reach the heart of the things compared; and no philosophy is more external and egotistical than that which places the essence of a thing in its relation to something else. In reality, at the centre of every natural being there is something indi-

* George Santayana, *Character and Opinion in the United States, with Reminiscences of William James and Josiah Royce and Academic Life in America* (New York: Scribner, and London: Constable, 1920), Preface, p. vi, and Chapter 6, "Materialism and Idealism in American Life," pp. 166–191. Reprinted by permission of the publishers.

vidual and incommensurable, a seed with its native impulses and aspirations, shaping themselves as best they can in their given environment. Variation is a consequence of freedom, and the slight but radical diversity of souls in turn makes freedom requisite. Instead of instituting in his mind any comparisons between the United States and other nations, I would accordingly urge the reader to forget himself and, in so far as such a thing may be possible for him or for me, to transport himself ideally with me into the outer circumstances of American life, the better to feel its inner temper, and to see how inevitably the American shapes his feelings and judgements, honestly reporting all things as they appear from his new and unobstructed station.

I speak of the American in the singular, as if there were not millions of them, north and south, east and west, of both sexes, of all ages, and of various races, professions, and religions. Of course the one American I speak of is mythical; but to speak in parables is inevitable in such a subject, and it is perhaps as well to do so frankly. There is a sort of poetic ineptitude in all human discourse when it tries to deal with natural and existing things. Practical men may not notice it, but in fact human discourse is intrinsically addressed not to natural existing things but to ideal essences, poetic or logical terms which thought may define and play with. When fortune or necessity diverts our attention from this congenial ideal sport to crude facts and pressing issues, we turn our frail poetic ideas into symbols for those terrible irruptive things. In that paper money of our own stamping, the legal tender of the mind, we are obliged to reckon all the movements and values of the world. The universal American I speak of is one of these symbols; and I should be still speaking in symbols and creating moral units and a false simplicity, if I spoke of classes pedantically subdivided, or individuals ideally integrated and defined. As it happens, the symbolic American can be made largely adequate to the facts; because, if there are immense differences between individual Americans—for some Americans are black—yet there is a great uniformity in their environment, customs, temper, and thoughts. They have all been uprooted from their several soils and ancestries and plunged together into one vortex, whirling irresistibly in a space otherwise quite empty. To be an American is of itself almost a moral condition, an education, and a career. Hence a single ideal figment can cover a large part of what each American is in his character, and almost the whole of what most Americans are in their social outlook and political judgements.

The discovery of the new world exercised a sort of selection among the inhabitants of Europe. All the colonists, except the negroes, were voluntary exiles. The fortunate, the deeply rooted, and the lazy remained at home; the wilder instincts or dissatisfaction of others tempted them beyond the horizon. The American is accordingly the most adventurous, or the descendant of the most adventurous, of Europeans. It is in his blood to be socially a radical, though perhaps not intellectually. What has existed in the past, especially in the remote past, seems to him not only not authoritative, but irrelevant, inferior, and outworn. He finds it rather a sorry waste of time to think about the past at all. But his enthusiasm for the future is profound; he can conceive of no more decisive way of recommending an opinion or a practice than to say that it is what everybody is coming to adopt. This expectation of what he approves, or approval of what

he expects, makes up his optimism. It is the necessary faith of the pioneer.

Such a temperament is, of course, not maintained in the nation merely by inheritance. Inheritance notoriously tends to restore the average of a race, and plays incidentally many a trick of atavism. What maintains this temperament and makes it national is social contagion or pressure—something immensely strong in democracies. The luckless American who is born a conservative, or who is drawn to poetic subtlety, pious retreats, or gay passions, nevertheless has the categorical excellence of work, growth, enterprise, reform, and prosperity dinned into his ears: every door is open in this direction and shut in the other; so that he either folds up his heart and withers in a corner—in remote places you sometimes find such a solitary gaunt idealist—or else he flies to Oxford or Florence or Montmartre to save his soul—or perhaps not to save it.

The optimism of the pioneer is not limited to his view of himself and his own future: it starts from that; but feeling assured, safe, and cheery within, he looks with smiling and most kindly eyes on everything and everybody about him. Individualism, roughness, and self-trust are supposed to go with selfishness and a cold heart; but I suspect that is a prejudice. It is rather dependence, insecurity, and mutual jostling that poison our placid gregarious brotherhood; and fanciful passionate demands upon people's affections, when they are disappointed, as they soon must be, breed illwill and a final meanness. The milk of human kindness is less apt to turn sour if the vessel that holds it stands steady, cool, and separate, and is not too often uncorked. In his affections the American is seldom passionate, often deep, and always kindly. If it were given me to look into the depths of a man's heart, and I did not find goodwill at the bottom, I should say without any hesitation, You are not an American. But as the American is an individualist his goodwill is not officious. His instinct is to think well of everybody, and to wish everybody well, but in a spirit of rough comradeship, expecting every man to stand on his own legs and to be helpful in his turn. When he has given his neighbour a chance he thinks he has done enough for him; but he feels it is an absolute duty to do that. It will take some hammering to drive a coddling socialism into America.

As self-trust may pass into self-sufficiency, so optimism, kindness, and goodwill may grow into a habit of doting on everything. To the good American many subjects are sacred: sex is sacred, women are sacred, children are sacred, business is sacred, America is sacred, Masonic lodges and college clubs are sacred. This feeling grows out of the good opinion he wishes to have of these things, and serves to maintain it. If he did not regard all these things as sacred he might come to doubt sometimes if they were wholly good. Of this kind, too, is the idealism of single ladies in reduced circumstances who can see the soul of beauty in ugly things, and are perfectly happy because their old dog has such pathetic eyes, their minister is so eloquent, their garden with its three sunflowers is so pleasant, their dead friends were so devoted, and their distant relations are so rich.

Consider now the great emptiness of America: not merely the primitive physical emptiness, surviving in some regions, and the continental spacing of the chief natural features, but also the moral emptiness of a settlement where men and even houses are easily moved about, and no one, almost, lives where he was born or believes what he has been taught. Not that the American has jettisoned these impedimenta in anger; they have simply slipped from him as he moves. Great empty spaces bring a sort of freedom to both soul and body. You may pitch your tent where you will; or if ever you decide to build anything, it can be in a style of your own devising. You have room, fresh materials, few models, and no critics. You trust your own experience, not only because you must, but because you find you may do so safely and prosperously; the forces that determine fortune are not yet too complicated for one man to explore. Your detachable condition makes you lavish with money and cheerfully experimental; you lose little if you lose all, since you remain completely yourself. At the same time your absolute initiative gives you practice in coping with novel situations, and in being original; it teaches you shrewd management. Your life and mind will become dry and direct, with few decorative flourishes. In your works everything will be stark and pragmatic; you will not understand why anybody should make those little sacrifices to instinct or custom which we call grace. The fine arts will seem to you academic luxuries, fit to amuse the ladies, like Greek and Sanskrit; for while you will perfectly appreciate generosity in men's purposes, you will not admit that the execution of these purposes can be anything but business. Unfortunately the essence of the fine arts is that the execution should be generous too, and delightful in itself; therefore the fine arts will suffer, not so much in their express professional pursuit—for then they become practical tasks and a kind of business—as in that diffused charm which qualifies all human action when men are artists by nature. Elaboration, which is something to accomplish, will be preferred to simplicity, which is something to rest in; manners will suffer somewhat; speech will suffer horribly. For the American the urgency of his novel attack upon matter, his zeal in gathering its fruits, precludes meanderings in primrose paths; devices must be short cuts, and symbols must be mere symbols. If his wife wants luxuries, of course she may have them; and if he has vices, that can be provided for too; but they must all be set down under those headings in his ledgers.

At the same time, the American is imaginative; for where life is intense, imagination is intense also. Were he not imaginative he would not live so much in the future. But his imagination is practical, and the future it forecasts is immediate; it works with the clearest and least ambiguous terms known to his experience, in terms of number, measure, contrivance, economy, and speed. He is an idealist working on matter. Understanding as he does the material potentialities of things, he is successful in invention, conservative in reform, and quick in emergencies. All his life he jumps into the train after it has started and jumps out before it has stopped; and he never once gets left behind, or breaks a leg. There is an enthusiasm in his sympathetic handling of material forces which goes far to cancel the illiberal character which it might otherwise assume. The good workman hardly distinguishes his artistic intention from the potency in himself and in things which is about to realise that intention. Accordingly his ideals fall into the form of premonitions and prophecies; and his studious prophecies often come true. So do the happy workmanlike ideals of the American. When a poor boy, perhaps, he dreams of an education, and presently he gets an education, or at least a degree; he dreams of growing rich, and he grows rich—only more slowly and modestly, perhaps, than he expected; he dreams of marrying his Rebecca and, even if he marries a Leah instead, he ultimately finds in Leah his Rebecca after all. He dreams of helping to carry on and to accelerate the movement of a vast, seething, progressive society, and he actually does so. Ideals clinging so close to nature are almost sure of fulfilment; the American beams with a certain self-confidence and sense of mastery; he feels that God and nature are working with him.

Idealism in the American accordingly goes hand in hand with present contentment and with foresight of what the future very likely will actually bring. He is not a revolutionist; he believes he is already on the right track and moving towards an excellent destiny. In revolutionists, on the contrary, idealism is founded on dissatisfaction and expresses it. What exists seems to them an absurd jumble of irrational accidents and bad habits, and they want the future to be based

on reason and to be the pellucid embodiment of all their maxims. All their zeal is for something radically different from the actual and (if they only knew it) from the possible; it is ideally simple, and they love it and believe in it because their nature craves it. They think life would be set free by the destruction of all its organs. They are therefore extreme idealists in the region of hope, but not at all, as poets and artists are, in the region of perception and memory. In the atmosphere of civilised life they miss all the refraction and all the fragrance; so that in their conception of actual things they are apt to be crude realists; and their ignorance and inexperience of the moral world, unless it comes of ill-luck, indicates their incapacity for education. Now incapacity for education, when united with great inner vitality, is one root of idealism. It is what condemns us all, in the region of sense, to substitute perpetually what we are capable of imagining for what things may be in themselves; it is what condemns us, wherever it extends, to think *a priori;* it is what keeps us bravely and incorrigibly pursuing what we call the good— that is, what would fulfill the demands of our nature—however little provision the fates may have made for it. But the want of insight on the part of revolutionists touching the past and the present infects in an important particular their idealism about the future; it renders their dreams of the future unrealisable. For in human beings—this may not be true of other animals, more perfectly preformed—experience is necessary to pertinent and concrete thinking; even our primitive instincts are blind until they stumble upon some occasion that solicits them; and they can be much transformed or deranged by their first partial satisfactions. Therefore a man who does not idealise his experience, but idealises *a priori,* is incapable of true prophecy; when he dreams he raves, and the more he criticises the less he helps. American idealism, on the contrary, is nothing if not helpful, nothing if not pertinent to practicable transformations; and when the American frets, it is because whatever is useless and impertinent, be it idealism or inertia, irritates him; for it frustrates the good results which he sees might so easily have been obtained.

The American is wonderfully alive; and his vitality, not having often found a suitable outlet, makes him appear agitated on the surface; he is always letting off an unnecessarily loud blast of incidental steam. Yet his vitality is not superficial; it is inwardly prompted, and as sensitive and quick as a magnetic needle. He is inquisitive, and ready with an answer to any question that he may put to himself of his own accord; but if you try to pour instruction into him, on matters that do not touch his own spontaneous life, he shows the most extraordinary powers of resistance and oblivescence; so that he often is remarkably expert in some directions and surprisingly obtuse in others. He seems to bear lightly the sorrowful burden of human knowledge. In a word, he is young.

What sense is there in this feeling, which we all have, that the American is young? His country is blessed with as many elderly people as any other, and his descent from Adam, or from the Darwinian rival of Adam, cannot be shorter than that of his European cousins. Nor are his ideas always very fresh. Trite and rigid bits of morality and religion, with much seemly and antique political lore, remain axiomatic in him, as in the mind of a child; he may carry all this about with an unquestioning familiarity which does not comport understanding. To keep traditional sentiments in this way insulated and uncriticised is itself a sign of youth. A good young man is naturally conservative and loyal on all those subjects which his experience has not brought to a test; advanced opinions on politics, marriage, or literature are comparatively rare in America; they are left for the ladies to discuss, and usually to condemn, while the men get on with their work. In spite of what is old-fashioned in his more general ideas, the American is unmistakably young; and this, I should say, for two reasons: one, that he is chiefly occupied with his immediate environ-

ment, and the other, that his reactions upon it are inwardly prompted, spontaneous, and full of vivacity and self-trust. His views are not yet lengthened; his will is not yet broken or transformed. The present moment, however, in this, as in other things, may mark a great change in him; he is perhaps now reaching his majority, and all I say may hardly apply to-day, and may not apply at all to-morrow. I speak of him as I have known him; and whatever moral strength may accrue to him later, I am not sorry to have known him in his youth. The charm of youth, even when it is a little boisterous, lies in nearness to the impulses of nature, in a quicker and more obvious obedience to that pure, seminal principle which, having formed the body and its organs, always directs their movements, unless it is forced by vice or necessity to make them crooked, or to suspend them. Even under the inevitable crust of age the soul remains young, and, wherever it is able to break through, sprouts into something green and tender. We are all as young at heart as the most youthful American, but the seed in his case has fallen upon virgin soil, where it may spring up more bravely and with less respect for the giants of the wood. Peoples seem older when their perennial natural youth is encumbered with more possessions and prepossessions, and they are mindful of the many things they have lost or missed. The American is not mindful of them.

In America there is a tacit optimistic assumption about existence, to the effect that the more existence the better. The soulless critic might urge that quantity is only a physical category, implying no excellence, but at best an abundance of opportunities both for good and for evil. Yet the young soul, being curious and hungry, views existence *a priori* under the form of the good; its instinct to live implies a faith that most things it can become or see or do will be worth while. Respect for quantity is accordingly something more than the childish joy and wonder at bigness; it is the fisherman's joy in a big haul, the good uses of which he can take for granted. Such optimism is amiable. Nature cannot afford that we should begin by being too calculating or wise, and she encourages us by the pleasure she attaches to our functions in advance of their fruits, and often in excess of them; as the angler enjoys catching his fish more than eating it, and often, waiting patiently for the fish to bite, misses his own supper. The pioneer must devote himself to preparations; he must work for the future, and it is healthy and dutiful of him to love his work for its own sake. At the same time, unless reference to an ultimate purpose is at least virtual in all his activities, he runs the danger of becoming a living automaton, vain and ignominious in its mechanical constancy. Idealism about work can hide an intense materialism about life. Man, if he is a rational being, cannot live by bread alone nor be a labourer merely; he must eat and work in view of an ideal harmony which overarches all his days, and which is realised in the way they hang together, or in some ideal issue which they have in common. Otherwise, though his technical philosophy may call itself idealism, he is a materialist in morals; he esteems things, and esteems himself, for mechanical uses and energies. Even sensualists, artists, and pleasure-lovers are wiser than that, for though their idealism may be desultory or corrupt, they attain something ideal, and prize things only for their living effects, moral though perhaps fugitive. Sensation, when we do not take it as a signal for action, but arrest and peruse what it positively brings before us, reveals something ideal—a colour, shape, or sound; and to dwell on these presences, with no thought of their material significance, is an æsthetic or dreamful idealism. To pass from this idealism to the knowledge of matter is a great intellectual advance, and goes with dominion over the world; for in the practical arts the mind is adjusted to a larger object, with more depth and potentiality in it; which is what makes people feel that the material world is real, as they call it, and that the ideal world is not. Certainly the material

world is real; for the philosophers who deny the existence of matter are like the critics who deny the existence of Homer. If there was never any Homer, there must have been a lot of other poets no less Homeric than he; and if matter does not exist, a combination of other things exists which is just as material. But the intense reality of the material world would not prevent it from being a dreary waste in our eyes, or even an abyss of horror, if it brought forth no spiritual fruits. In fact, it does bring forth spiritual fruits, for otherwise we should not be here to find fault with it, and to set up our ideals over against it. Nature is material, but not materialistic; it issues in life, and breeds all sorts of warm passions and idle beauties. And just as sympathy with the mechanical travail and turmoil of nature, apart from its spiritual fruits, is moral materialism, so the continual perception and love of these fruits is moral idealism—happiness in the presence of immaterial objects and harmonies, such as we envisage in affection, speculation, religion, and all the forms of the beautiful.

The circumstances of his life hitherto have necessarily driven the American into moral materialism; for in his dealings with material things he can hardly stop to enjoy their sensible aspects, which are ideal, nor proceed at once to their ultimate uses, which are ideal too. He is practical as against the poet, and worldly as against the clear philosopher or the saint. The most striking expression of this materialism is usually supposed to be his love of the almighty dollar; but that is a foreign and unintelligent view. The American talks about money, because that is the symbol and measure he has at hand for success, intelligence, and power; but as to money itself he makes, loses, spends, and gives it away with a very light heart. To my mind the most striking expression of his materialism is his singular preoccupation with quantity. If, for instance, you visit Niagara Falls, you may expect to hear how many cubic feet or metric tons of water are precipitated per second over the cataract; how many cities and towns (with the number of their inhabitants) derive light and motive power from it; and the annual value of the further industries that might very well be carried on by the same means, without visibly depleting the world's greatest wonder or injuring the tourist trade. That is what I confidently expected to hear on arriving at the adjoining town of Buffalo; but I was deceived. The first thing I heard instead was that there are more miles of asphalt pavement in Buffalo than in any city in the world. Nor is this insistence on quantity confined to men of business. The President of Harvard College, seeing me once by chance soon after the beginning of a term, inquired how my classes were getting on; and when I replied that I thought they were getting on well, that my men seemed to be keen and intelligent, he stopped me as if I was about to waste his time. "I meant," said he, "*what is the number* of students in your classes."

Here I think we may perceive that this love of quantity often has a silent partner, which is diffidence as to quality. The democratic conscience recoils before anything that savours of privilege; and lest it should concede an unmerited privilege to any pursuit or person, it reduces all things as far as possible to the common denominator of quantity. Numbers cannot lie: but if it came to comparing the ideal beauties of philosophy with those of Anglo-Saxon, who should decide? All studies are good—why else have universities?—but those must be most encouraged which attract the greatest number of students. Hence the President's question. Democratic faith, in its diffidence about quality, throws the reins of education upon the pupil's neck, as Don Quixote threw the reins on the neck of Rocinante, and bids his divine instinct choose its own way.

The American has never yet had to face the trials of Job. Great crises, like the Civil War, he has known how to surmount victoriously; and now that he has surmounted a second great crisis victoriously, it is possible that he may relapse, as he did in the other case, into an apparently complete absorption in material enterprise and prosperity. But if serious and irremediable tribulation ever overtook him, what would his attitude be? It is then that we should be able to discover whether materialism or idealism lies at the base of his character. Meantime his working mind is not without its holiday. He spreads humour pretty thick and even over the surface of conversation, and humour is one form of moral emancipation. He loves landscape, he loves mankind, and he loves knowledge; and in music at least he finds an art which he unfeignedly enjoys. In music and landscape, in humour and kindness, he touches the ideal more truly, perhaps, than in his ponderous academic idealisms and busy religions; for it is astonishing how much even religion in America (can it possibly be so in England?) is a matter of meetings, building-funds, schools, charities, clubs, and picnics. To be poor in order to be simple, to produce less in order that the product may be more choice and beautiful, and may leave us less burdened with unnecessary duties and useless possessions—that is an ideal not articulate in the American mind; yet here and there I seem to have heard a sigh after it, a groan at the perpetual incubus of business and shrill society. Significant witness to such aspirations is borne by those new forms of popular religion, not mere variations on tradition, which have sprung up from the soil—revivalism, spiritualism, Christian Science, the New Thought. Whether or no we can tap, through these or other channels, some cosmic or inner energy not hitherto at the disposal of man (and there is nothing incredible in that), we certainly may try to remove friction and waste in the mere process of living; we may relax morbid strains, loosen suppressed instincts, iron out the creases of the soul, discipline ourselves into simplicity, sweetness, and peace. These religious movements are efforts toward such physiological economy and hygiene; and while they are thoroughly plebeian, with no great lights, and no idea of raising men from the most vulgar and humdrum worldly existence, yet they see the possibility of physical and moral health on that common plane, and pursue it. That is true morality. The dignities of various types of life or mind, like the gifts of various animals, are relative. The snob adores one type only, and the creatures supposed by him to illustrate it perfectly; or envies and hates them, which is just as snobbish. Veritable lovers of life, on the contrary, like Saint Francis or like Dickens, know that in every tenement of clay, with no matter what endowment or station, happiness and perfection are possible to the soul. There must be no brow-beating, with shouts of work or progress or revolution, any more than with threats of hell-fire. What does it profit a man to free the whole world if his soul is not free? Moral freedom is not an artificial con-

dition, because the ideal is the mother tongue of both the heart and the senses. All that is requisite is that we should pause in living to enjoy life, and should lift up our hearts to things that are pure goods in themselves, so that once to have found and loved them, whatever else may betide, may remain a happiness that nothing can sully. This natural idealism does not imply that we are immaterial, but only that we are animate and truly alive. When the senses are sharp, as they are in the American, they are already half liberated, already a joy in themselves; and when the heart is warm, like his, and eager to be just, its ideal destiny can hardly be doubtful. It will not be always merely pumping and working; time and its own pulses will lend it wings.

THE EDUCATION OF WOMEN

EMMA WILLARD
On the Education of Women (1819) *

The object of this Address, is to convince the public, that a reform, with respect to female education, is necessary; that it cannot be effected by individual exertion, but that it requires the aid of the legislature: and further, by shewing the justice, the policy, and the magnanimity of such an undertaking, to persuade that body, to endow a seminary for females, as the commencement of such reformation.

The idea of a college for males, will naturally be associated with that of a seminary, instituted and endowed by the public; and the absurdity of sending ladies to college, may, at first thought, strike every one, to

* Emma Willard, *An Address to the Public; particularly to the Members of the Legislature of New-York, proposing a Plan for Improving Female Education* (Middlebury, Vt.: Printed by J. W. Copeland, 1819), pp. 3–60. Mrs. Willard first delivered her famous *Address* before members of the New York Legislature in Albany at their request. When she returned to Middlebury, she published her manuscript in 1819 at her own expense.

whom this subject shall be proposed. I therefore hasten to observe, that the seminary here recommended, will be as different from those appropriated to the other sex, as the female character and duties are from the male.—The business of the husbandman is not to waste his endeavours, in seeking to make his orchard attain the strength and majesty of his forest, but to rear each, to the perfection of its nature.

That the improvement of female education will be considered by our enlightened citizens as a subject of importance, the liberality with which they part with their property to educate their daughters, is a sufficient evidence; and why should they not, when assembled in the legislature, act in concert to effect a noble object, which, though dear to them individually, cannot be accomplished by their unconnected exertions.

If the improvement of the American female character, and that alone, could be effected by public liberality, employed in giving better means of instruction; such improvement of one half of society, and that half, which barbarous and despotic nations have ever degraded, would of itself be an object, worthy of the most liberal government on earth; but if the female character be raised, it must inevitably raise that of the other sex: and thus does the plan proposed, offer, as the object of legislative bounty, to elevate the whole character of the community.

As evidence, that this statement does not exaggerate the female influence in society, our sex need but be considered, in the single relation of mothers. In this character, we have the charge of the whole mass of individuals, who are to compose the succeeding generation; during that period of youth, when the pliant mind takes any direction, to which it is steadily guided by a forming hand. How important a power is given by this charge! yet, little do too many of my sex know how, either to appreciate or improve it. Unprovided with the means of acquiring that knowledge, which flows liberally to the other sex—having our time of education devoted to frivolous acquirements, how should we understand the nature of the mind, so as to be aware of the importance of those early impressions, which we make upon the minds of our children?—or how should we be able to form enlarged and correct views, either of the character, to which we ought to mould them, or of the means most proper to form them aright?

Considered in this point of view, were the interests of male education alone to be consulted, that of females becomes of sufficient importance to engage the public attention. Would we rear the human plant to its perfection, we must first fertilize the soil which produces it. If it acquire its first bent and texture upon a barren plain, it will avail comparatively little, should it be afterwards transplanted to a garden.

In the arrangement of my remarks, I shall pursue the following order.

I. Treat of the defects of the present mode of female education, and their causes.

II. Consider the principles, by which education should be regulated.

III. Sketch a plan of a female seminary.

IV. Shew the benefits which society would receive from such seminaries.

DEFECTS IN THE PRESENT MODE OF FEMALE EDUCATION, AND THEIR CAUSES.

Civilized nations have long since been convinced, that education, as it respects males, will not, like trade, regulate itself; and hence, they have made it a prime object, to provide that sex with every thing requisite to facilitate their progress in learning: but female education has been left to the mercy of private adventurers; and the consequence has been to our sex, the same, as it would have been to the other, had legislatures left their accommodations, and means of instruction, to chance also.

Education cannot prosper in any community, unless, from the ordinary motives which actuate the human mind, the best and most cultivated talents of that community, can be brought into exercise in that way. Male education flourishes, because, from the guardian care of legislatures, the presidencies and professorships of our colleges, are some of the highest objects to which the eye of ambition is directed. Not so with female institutions. Preceptresses of these, are dependent on their pupils for support, and are consequently liable to become the victims of their caprice. In such a situation, it is not more desirable to be a preceptress, than it would be, to be a parent, invested with the care of children, and responsible for their behaviour, but yet, depending on them for subsistence, and destitute of power to enforce their obedience.

Feminine delicacy requires, that girls should be educated chiefly by their own sex. This is apparent from considerations, that regard their health and conveniences, the propriety of their dress and manners, and their domestic accomplishments.

Boarding schools, therefore, whatever may be their defects, furnish the best mode of education provided for females.

Concerning these schools it may be observed:

1. They are temporary institutions, formed

by individuals, whose object is present emolument. But they cannot be expected to be greatly lucrative; therefore, the individuals who establish them, cannot afford to provide suitable accommodations, as to room. At night, the pupils are frequently crowded in their lodging rooms; and during the day, they are generally placed together in one apartment, where there is a heterogeneous mixture of different kinds of business, accompanied with so much noise and confusion, as greatly to impede their progress in study.

2. As individuals cannot afford to provide suitable accommodations as to room, so neither can they afford libraries, and other apparatus, necessary to teach properly the various branches in which they pretend to instruct.

3. Neither can the individuals who establish these schools afford to provide suitable instruction. It not unfrequently happens, that one instructress teaches, at the same time, and in the same room, ten or twelve distinct branches. If assistants are provided, such are usually taken as can be procured for a small compensation. True, in our large cities, preceptresses provide their pupils with masters, though at an expense, which few can afford. Yet none of these masters, are responsible for the general proficiency, or demeanour of the pupils. Their only responsibility, is in the particular branch which they teach; and to a preceptress, who probably does not understand it herself, and who is, therefore incapable of judging, whether or not it is well taught.

4. It is impossible, that in these schools such systems should be adopted and enforced, as are requisite for properly classing the pupils. Institutions for young gentlemen are founded by public authority, and are permanent; they are endowed with funds, and their instructors and overseers, are invested with authority to make such laws, as they shall deem most salutary. From their permanency, their laws and rules are well known. With their funds they procure libraries, philosophical apparatus, and other advantages, superior to what can elsewhere be found; and to enjoy these, individuals are placed under their discipline, who would not else be subjected to it. Hence the directors of these institutions can enforce, among other regulations, those which enable them to make a perfect classification of their students. They regulate their qualifications for entrance, the kind and order of their studies, and the period of their remaining at the seminary. Female schools present the reverse of this. Wanting permanency, and dependent on individual patronage, had they the wisdom to make salutary regulations, they could neither enforce nor purchase compliance. The pupils are irregular in their times of entering and leaving school; and they are of various and dissimilar acquirements. Each scholar, of mature age, thinks she has a right to judge for herself respecting what she is to be taught; and the parents of those, who are not, consider, that they have the same right to judge for them. Under such disadvantages, a school cannot be classed, except in a very imperfect manner.

5. It is for the interest of instructresses of boarding schools, to teach their pupils showy accomplishments, rather than those, which are solid and useful. Their object in teaching is generally present profit. In order to realize this, they must contrive to give immediate celebrity to their schools. If they attend chiefly to the cultivation of the mind, their work may not be manifest at the first glance; but let the pupil return home, laden with fashionable toys, and her young companions, filled with envy and astonishment, are never satisfied till they are permitted to share the precious instruction. If it is true, with the turn of the fashion, the toys, which they are taught to make, will become obsolete; and no benefit remain to them, of perhaps the only money, that will ever be expended on their education; but the object of the instructress may be accomplished notwithstanding, if that is directed to her own, rather than her pupil's advantage.

6. As these schools are private establishments, their preceptresses are not account-

able to any particular persons. Any woman has a right to open a school in any place; and no one, either from law or custom, can prevent her. Hence the public are liable to be imposed upon, both with respect to the character and acquirements of preceptresses. I am far, however, from asserting that this is always the case. It has been before observed, that in the present state of things, the ordinary motives which actuate the human mind, would not induce ladies of the best and most cultivated talents, to engage in the business of instructing, from choice. But some have done it from necessity, and occasionally, an extraordinary female has occupied herself in instructing, because she felt that impulse to be active and useful, which is the characteristic of a vigorous and noble mind; and because she found few avenues to extensive usefulness open to her sex. But if such has been the fact, it has not been the consequence of any system, from which a similar result can be expected to recur with regularity; and it remains true, that the public are liable to imposition, both with regard to the character and acquirements of preceptresses.

Instances have lately occurred, in which women of bad reputation, at a distance from scenes of their former life, have been entrusted by our unsuspecting citizens with the instruction of their daughters.

But the moral reputation of individuals, is more a matter of public notoriety than their literary attainments; hence society are more liable to be deceived with regard to the acquirements of instructresses, than with respect to their characters.

Those women, however, who deceive society as to the advantages which they give their pupils, are not charged with any ill intention. They teach as they were taught, and believe that the public are benefitted by their labours. Acquiring, in their youth, a high value for their own superficial accomplishments, they regard all others as supernumerary, if not unbecoming. Although these considerations exculpate individuals, yet they do not diminish the injury which society receives; for they show, that the worst which is to be expected from such instruction, is not that the pupils will remain ignorant; but that, by adopting the views of their teachers, they will have their minds barred against future improvement, by acquiring a disrelish, if not a contempt for useful knowledge.

7. Although, from a want of public support, preceptresses of boarding schools have not the means of enforcing such a system as would lead to a perfect classification of their pupils; and although they are confined in other respects within narrow limits, yet, because these establishments are not depend[e]nt on any public body, within those limits, they have a power far more arbitrary and uncontrolled, than is allowed the learned and judicious instructors of our male seminaries.

They can, at their option, omit their own duties, and excuse their pupils from theirs.

They can make absurd and ridiculous regulations.

They can make improper and even wicked exactions of their pupils.

Thus the writer has endeavoured to point out the defects of the present mode of female education; chiefly in order to show, that the great cause of these defects consists in a state of things, in which legislatures, undervaluing the importance of women in society, neglect to provide for their education, and suffer it to become the sport of adventurers for fortune, who may be both ignorant and vicious.

OF THE PRINCIPLES BY WHICH EDUCATION SHOULD BE REGULATED.

To contemplate the principles which should regulate systems of instruction, and consider how little those principles have been regarded in educating our sex, will show the defects of female education in a still stronger point of light, and will also afford a standard, by which any plan for its improvement may be measured.

Education should seek to bring its subjects to the perfection of their moral, intellectual and physical nature: in order, that they may be of the greatest possible use to themselves and others: or, to use a different expression, that they may be the means of the greatest possible happiness of which they are capable, both as to what they enjoy, and what they communicate.

Those youth have the surest chance of enjoying and communicating happiness, who are best qualified, both by internal dispositions, and external habits, to perform with readiness, those duties, which their future life will most probably give them occasion to practice.

Studies and employments should, therefore, be selected, from one or both of the following considerations; either, because they are peculiarly fitted to improve the faculties; or, because they are such, as the pupil will most probably have occasion to practise in future life.

These are the principles, on which systems of male education are founded; but female education has not yet been systematized. Chance and confusion reign here. Not even is youth considered in our sex, as in the other, a season, which should be wholly devoted to improvement. Among families, so rich as to be entirely above labour, the daughters are hurried through the routine of boarding school instruction, and at an early period introduced into the gay world; and, thenceforth, their only object is amusement.—Mark the different treatment, which the sons of these families receive. While their sisters are gliding through the mazes of the midnight dance, they employ the lamp, to treasure up for future use the riches of ancient wisdom; or to gather strength and expansion of mind, in exploring the wonderful paths of philosophy. When the youth of the two sexes has been spent so differently, is it strange, or is nature in fault, if more mature age has brought such a difference of character, that our sex have been considered by the other, as the pampered, wayward babies of society, who must have some rattle put into our hands, to keep us from doing mischief to ourselves or others?

Another difference in the treatment of the sexes is made in our country, which, though not equally pernicious to society, is more pathetically unjust to our sex. How often have we seen a student, who, returning from his literary pursuits, finds a sister, who was his equal in acquirements, while their advantages were equal, of whom he is now ashamed. While his youth was devoted to study, and he was furnished with the means, she, without any object of improvement, drudged at home, to assist in the support of the father's family, and perhaps to contribute to her brother's subsistence abroad; and now, a being of a lower order, the rustic innocent wonders and weeps at his neglect.

Not only has there been a want of system concerning female education, but much of what has been done, has proceeded upon mistaken principles.

One of these is, that, without a regard to the different periods of life, proportionate to their importance, the education of females has been too exclusively directed, to fit them for displaying to advantage the charms of youth and beauty. Though it may be proper to adorn this period of life, yet, it is incomparably more important, to prepare for the serious duties of maturer years. Though well to decorate the blossom, it is far better to prepare for the harvest. In the vegetable creation, nature seems but to sport, when she embellishes the flower; while all her serious cares are directed to perfect the fruit.

Another errour is, that it has been made the first object in educating our sex, to prepare them to please the other. But reason and religion teach, that we too are primary existencies; that it is for us to move, in the orbit of our duty, around the Holy Centre of perfection, the companions, not the satellites of men; else, instead of shedding around us an influence, that may help to keep them in their proper course, we must accompany them in their wildest deviations.

I would not be understood to insinuate, that we are not, in particular situations, to yield obedience to the other sex. Submission and obedience belong to every being in the universe, except the great Master of the whole. Nor is it a degrading peculiarity to our sex, to be under human authority. Whenever one class of human beings, derive from another the benefits of support and protection, they must pay its equivalent, obedience. Thus, while we receive these benefits from our parents, we are all, without distinction of sex, under their authority; when we receive them from the government of our country, we must obey our rulers; and when our sex take the obligations of marriage, and receive protection and support from the other, it is reasonable, that we too should yield obedience. Yet is neither the child, nor the subject, nor the wife, under human authority, but in subservience to the divine. Our highest responsibility is to God, and our highest interest is to please him; therefore, to secure this interest, should our education be directed.

Neither would I be understood to mean, that our sex should not seek to make themselves agreeable to the other. The errour complained of, is that the taste of men, whatever it might happen to be, has been made a standard for the formation of the female character. In whatever we do, it is of the utmost importance, that the rule, by which we work, be perfect. For if otherwise, what is it, but to err upon principle? A system of education, which leads one class of human beings to consider the approbation of another, as their highest object, teaches, that the rule of their conduct should be the will of beings, imperfect and erring like themselves, rather than the will of God, which is the only standard of perfection.

Having now considered female education, both in theory and practice, and seen, that in its present state, it is in fact a thing "without form and void," the mind is naturally led to inquire after a remedy for the evils it has been contemplating. Can individuals furnish this remedy? It has heretofore been left to them, and we have seen the consequence. If education is a business, which might naturally prosper, if left to individual

exertion, why have legislatures intermeddled with it at all? if it is not, why do they make their daughters illegitimates, and bestow all their cares upon their sons?

It is the duty of a government, to do all in its power to promote the present and future prosperity of the nation, over which it is placed. This prosperity will depend on the character of its citizens. The characters of these will be formed by their mothers; and it is through the mothers, that the government can control the characters of its future citizens, to form them such as will ensure their country's prosperity. If this is the case, then it is the duty of our present legislators to begin now, to form the characters of the next generation, by controling that of the females, who are to be their mothers, while it is yet with them a season of improvement.

But should the conclusion be almost admitted, that our sex too are the legitimate children of the legislature; and, that it is their duty to afford us a share of their paternal bounty; the phantom of a college-learned lady, would be ready to rise up, and destroy every good resolution, which the admission of this truth would naturally produce in our favour.

To shew that it is not a masculine education which is here recommended, and to afford a definite view of the manner in which a female institution might possess the respectability, permanency, and uniformity of operation of those appropriated to males; and yet differ from them, so as to be adapted to that difference of character and duties, to which the softer sex should be formed, is the object of the following imperfect

SKETCH OF A FEMALE SEMINARY.

From considering the deficiencies in boarding schools, much may be learned, with regard to what would be needed, for the prosperity and usefulness of a public seminary for females.

I. There would be needed a building, with commodious rooms for lodging and recitation, apartments for the reception of apparatus, and for the accommodation of the domestic department.

II. A library, containing books on the various subjects in which the pupils were to receive instruction; musical instruments, some good paintings, to form the taste and serve as models for the execution of those who were to be instructed in that art; maps, globes, and a small collection of philosophical apparatus.

III. A judicious board of trust, competent and desirous to promote its interests, would in a female, as in a male literary institution, be the corner stone of its prosperity. On this board it would depend to provide,

IV. Suitable instruction. This article may be subdivided under four heads.

1. Religious and Moral.
2. Literary.
3. Domestic.
4. Ornamental.

1. RELIGIOUS AND MORAL. A regular attention to religious duties would, of course be required of the pupils by the laws of the institution. The trustees would be careful to appoint no instructors, who would not teach religion and morality, both by their example, and by leading the minds of the pupils to perceive, that these constitute the true end of all education. It would be desirable, that the young ladies should spend a part of their Sabbaths in hearing discourses relative to the peculiar duties of their sex. The evidences of Christianity, and moral philosophy, would constitute a part of their studies.

2. LITERARY INSTRUCTION. To make an exact enumeration of the branches of literature, which might be taught, would be impossible, unless the time of the pupils' continuance at the seminary, and the requisites for entrance, were previously fixed. Such an enumeration would be tedious, nor do I conceive that it would be at all promotive of my object. The difficulty complained of, is not, that we are at a loss what sciences we ought to learn, but that we have not proper advantages to learn any. Many writers have given us excellent advice with regard to what we should be taught, but no legislature has

provided us the means of instruction. Not however, to pass lightly over this fundamental part of education, I will mention one or two of the less obvious branches of science, which, I conceive should engage the youthful attention of my sex.

It is highly important, that females should be conversant with those studies, which will lead them to understand the operations of the human mind. The chief use to which the philosophy of the mind can be applied, is to regulate education by its rules. The ductile mind of the child is intrusted to the mother: and she ought to have every possible assistance, in acquiring a knowledge of this noble material, on which it is her business to operate, that she may best understand how to mould it to its most excellent form.

Natural philosophy has not often been taught to our sex. Yet why should we be kept in ignorance of the great machinery of nature, and left to the vulgar notion, that nothing is curious but what deviates from her common course? If mothers were acquainted with this science, they would communicate very many of its principles to their children in early youth. From the bursting of an egg buried in the fire, I have heard an intelligent mother, lead her prattling inquirer, to understand the cause of the earthquake. But how often does the mother, from ignorance on this subject, give her child the most erroneous and contracted views of the causes of natural phenomena; views, which, though he may afterwards learn to be false, are yet, from the laws of association, ever ready to return, unless the active powers of the mind are continually upon the alert to keep them out. A knowledge of natural philosophy is calculated to heighten the moral taste, by bringing to view the majesty and beauty of order and design; and to enliven piety, by enabling the mind more clearly to perceive, throughout the manifold works of God, that wisdom, in which he hath made them all.

In some of the sciences proper for our sex, the books, written for the other, would need alteration; because, in some they presuppose more knowledge than female pupils would possess; in others, they have parts not particularly interesting to our sex, and omit subjects immediately relating to their pursuits. There would likewise be needed, for a female seminary, some works, which I believe are no where extant, such as a systematic treatise on housewifery.

3. DOMESTIC INSTRUCTION should be considered important in a female seminary. It is the duty of our sex to regulate the internal concerns of every family; and unless they be properly qualified to discharge this duty, whatever may be their literary or ornamental attainments, they cannot be expected to make either good wives, good mothers, or good mistresses of families: and if they are none of these, they must be bad members of society; for it is by promoting or destroying the comfort and prosperity of their own families, that females serve or injure the community. To superintend the domestic department, there should be a respectable lady, experienced in the best methods of housewifery, and acquainted with propriety of dress and manners. Under her tuition the pupils ought to be placed for a certain length of time every morning. A spirit of neatness and order should here be treated as a virtue, and the contrary, if excessive and incorrigible, be punished with expulsion. There might be a gradation of employment in the domestic department, according to the length of time the pupils had remained at the institution. The older scholars might then assist the superintendent in instructing the younger, and the whole be so arranged, that each pupil might have advantages to become a good domestic manager by the time she has completed her studies.

This plan would afford a healthy exercise. It would prevent that estrangement from domestic duties, which would be likely to take place in a length of time devoted to study, with those, to whom they were previously familiar; and would accustom those to them, who, from ignorance, might otherwise put at hazard their own happiness, and the prosperity of their families.

These objects might doubtless be effected by a scheme of domestic instruction; and probably others of no inconsiderable importance. It is believed, that housewifery might be greatly improved, by being taught, not only in practice, but in theory. Why may it not be reduced to a system, as well as other arts? There are right ways of performing its various operations; and there are reasons why those ways are right; and why may not rules be formed, their reasons collected; and the whole be digested into a system to guide the learner's practice?

It is obvious, that theory alone, can never make a good artist; and it is equally obvious, that practice unaided by theory, can never correct errors, but must establish them. If I should perform any thing in a wrong manner all my life, and teach my children to perform it in the same manner, still, through my life and theirs, it would be wrong. Without alteration there can be no improvement; but how are we to alter, so as to improve, if we are ignorant of the principles of our art, with which we should compare our practice, and by which we should regulate it?

In the present state of things, it is not to be expected, that any material improvements in housewifery should be made. There being no uniformity of method, prevailing among different housewives, of course, the communications from one to another, are not much more likely to improve the art, than a communication, between two mechanics of different trades, would be, to improve each in his respective occupation. But should a system of principles be philosophically arranged, and taught, both in theory and by practice, to a large number of females, whose minds were expanded and strengthened by a course of literary instruction, those among them, of an investigating turn, would, when they commenced housekeepers, consider their domestic operations as a series of experiments, which either proved or refuted the system previously taught. They would then converse together like those, who practise a common art, and improve each other by their observations and experiments; and they would also be capable of improving the system, by detecting its errors, and by making additions of new priciples and better modes of practice.

4. The ORNAMENTAL branches, which I should recommend for a female seminary, are drawing and painting, elegant penmanship, music, and the grace of motion. Needlework is not here mentioned. The best style of useful needle-work should either be taught in the domestic department, or made a qualification for entrance; and I consider that useful, which may contribute to the decoration of a lady's person, or the convenience and neatness of her family. But the use of the needle, for other purposes than these, as it affords little to assist in the formation of the character, I should regard as a waste of time.

The grace of motion, must be learnt chiefly from instruction in dancing. Other advantages besides that of a graceful carriage, might be derived from such instruction, if the lessons were judiciously timed. Exercise is needful to the health, and recreation to the cheerfulness and contentment of youth. Female youth could not be allowed to range unrestrained, to seek amusement for themselves. If it was entirely prohibited, they would be driven to seek it by stealth; which would lead them to many improprieties of conduct, and would have a pernicious effect upon their general character, by inducing a habit of treading forbidden paths. The alternative that remains is to provide them with proper recreation, which, after the confinement of the day, they might enjoy under the eye of their instructors. Dancing is exactly suited to this purpose, as also to that of exercise; for perhaps in no way, can so much healthy exercise be taken in so short a time. It has besides, this advantage over other amusements, that it affords nothing to excite the bad passions; but, on the contrary, its effects are, to soften the mind, to banish its animosities, and to open it to social impressions.

It may be said, that dancing would dissipate the attention, and estrange it from study. Balls would doubtless have this effect; but let dancing be practised every day, by youth of the same sex, without change of place, dress, or company, and under the eye of those, whom they are accustomed to obey, and it would excite no more emotion, than any other exercise or amusement, but in degree, as it is of itself more pleasant. But it must ever be a grateful exercise to youth, as it is one, to which nature herself prompts them, at the sound of animating music.

It has been doubted, whether painting and music should be taught to young ladies, because much time is requisite to bring them to any considerable degree of perfection, and they are not immediately useful. Though these objections have weight, yet they are founded on too limited a view of the objects of education. They leave out the important consideration of forming the character. I should not consider it an essential point, that the music of a lady's piano should rival that of her master's; or that her drawing room should be decorated with her own paintings, rather than those of others; but it is the intrinsic advantage, which she might derive from the refinement of herself, that would induce me to recommend to her, an attention to these elegant pursuits. The harmony of sound, has a tendency to produce a correspondent harmony of soul; and that art, which obliges us to study nature, in order to imitate her, often enkindles the latent spark of taste—of sensibility for her beauties, till it glows to adoration for their author, and a refined love of all his works.

V. There would be needed, for a female, as well as for a male seminary, a system of laws and regulations, so arranged, that both the instructors and pupils would know their duty; and thus, the whole business, move with regularity and uniformity.

The laws of the institution would be chiefly directed, to regulate the pupil's qualifications for entrance, the kind and order of their studies, their behaviour while at the institution, the term allotted for the completion of their studies, the punishments to be inflicted on offenders, and the rewards or honours, to be bestowed on the virtuous and diligent.

The direct rewards or honors, used to stimulate the ambition of students in colleges, are first, the certificate or diploma, which each receives, who passes successfully through the term allotted to his collegiate studies; and secondly, the appointments to perform certain parts in public exhibitions, which are bestowed by the faculty, as rewards for superior scholarship. The first of these modes is admissible into a female seminary; the second is not; as public speaking forms no part of female education. The want of this mode, might, however, be supplied by examinations judiciously conducted. The leisure and inclination of both instructors and scholars, would combine to produce a thorough preparation for these; for neither would have any other public test of the success of their labors. Persons of both sexes would attend. The less entertaining parts, might be enlivened by interludes, where the pupils in painting and music, would display their several improvements. Such examinations, would stimulate the instructors to give their scholars more attention, by which the leading facts and principles of their studies, would be more clearly understood, and better remembered. The ambition excited among the pupils, would operate, without placing the instructors under the necessity of making distinctions among them, which are so apt to be considered as invidious; and which are, in our male seminaries, such fruitful sources of disaffection.

Perhaps the term allotted for the routine of study at the seminary, might be three years. The pupils, probably, would not be fitted to enter, till about the age of fourteen. Whether they attended to all, or any of the ornamental branches, should be left optional with the parents or guardians. Those who were to be instructed in them, should be entered for a longer term, but if this was a subject of previous calculation, no confusion would arise from it. The routine of the exer-

cises being established by the laws of the institution, would be uniform, and publicly known; and those who were previously acquainted with the branches first taught, might enter the higher classes; nor would those who entered the lowest, be obliged to remain during the three years. Thus the term of remaining at the institution, might be either one, two, three, four, or more years; and that, without interfering with the regularity and uniformity of its proceedings.

The writer has now given a sketch of her plan. She has by no means expressed all the ideas, which occurred to her concerning it. She wished to be as concise as possible, and yet afford conviction, that it is practicable, to organize a system of female education, which shall possess the permanency, uniformity of operation, and respectability of our male institutions; and yet differ from them, so as to be adapted, to that difference of character, and duties, to which early instruction should form the softer sex.

It now remains, to enquire more particularly, what would be the benefits resulting from such a system.

BENEFITS OF FEMALE SEMINARIES.

In inquiring, concerning the benefits of the plan proposed, I shall proceed upon the supposition, that female seminaries will be patronized throughout our country.

Nor is this altogether a visionary supposition. If one seminary should be well organized, its advantages would be found so great, that others would soon be instituted; and, that sufficient patronage can be found to put one in operation, may be presumed from its reasonableness, and from the public opinion, with regard to the present mode of female education. It is from an intimate acquaintance, with those parts of our country, whose education is said to flourish most, that the writer has drawn her picture of the present state of female instruction; and she knows, that she is not alone, in perceiving or deploring its faults. Her sentiments are shared by many an enlightened parent of a daughter, who has received a boarding school education. Counting on the promise of her childhood, the father had anticipated her maturity, as combining what is excellent in mind, with what is elegant in manners. He spared no expense that education might realize to him, the image of his imagination. His daughter returned from her boarding school,[1] improved in fashionable airs, and expert in manufacturing fashionable toys; but, in her conversation, he sought in vain, for that refined and fertile mind, which he had fondly expected. Aware that his disappointment has its source in a defective education, he looks with anxiety on his other daughters, whose minds, like lovely buds, are beginning to open. Where shall he find a genial soil, in which he may place them to expand? Shall he provide them male instructors?—Then the graces of their persons and manners, and whatever forms the distinguishing charm of the feminine character, they cannot be expected to acquire.—Shall he give them a private tutoress? She will have been educated at the boarding school, and his daughters will have the faults of its instruction second-handed. Such is now the dilemma of many parents; and it is one, from which they cannot be extricated by their individual exertions. May not then the only plan, which promises to relieve them, expect their vigorous support.

Let us now proceed to inquire, what benefits would result from the establishment of female seminaries.

They would constitute a grade of public education, superior to any yet known in the history of our sex; and through them, the lower grades of female instruction might be controlled. The influence of public seminaries, over these, would operate in two ways; first, by requiring certain qualifications for entrance; and secondly, by furnishing instructresses, initiated in their modes of teaching, and imbued with their maxims.

Female seminaries might be expected to have important and happy effects, on com-

[1] In the original printing, the word "her" preceded "school"—apparently a printer's transposition.

mon schools in general; and in the manner of operating on these, would probably place the business of teaching children, in hands now nearly useless to society; and take it from those, whose services the state wants in many other ways.

That nature designed for our sex the care of children, she has made manifest, by mental, as well as physical indications. She has given us, in a greater degree than men, the gentle arts of insinuation, to soften their minds, and fit them to receive impressions; a greater quickness of invention to vary modes of teaching to different dispositions; and more patience to make repeated efforts. There are many females of ability, to whom the business of instructing children is highly acceptable, and, who would devote all their faculties to their occupation. They would have no higher pecuniary object to engage their attention, and their reputation as instructors they would consider as important; whereas, whenever able and enterprizing men, engage in this business, they consider it, merely as a temporary employment, to further some other object, to the attainment of which, their best thoughts and calculations are all directed. If then women were properly fitted by instruction, they would be likely to teach children better than the other sex; they could afford to do it cheaper; and those men who would otherwise be engaged in this employment, might be at liberty to add to the wealth of the nation, by any of those thousand occupations, from which women are necessarily debarred.

But the females, who taught children, would have been themselves instructed either immediately or indirectly by the seminaries. Hence through these, the government might exercise an intimate, and most beneficial control over common schools. Any one, who has turned his attention to this subject, must be aware, that there is great room for improvement in these, both as to the modes of teaching, and the things taught; and what method could be devised so likely to effect this improvement, as to prepare by instruction, a class of individuals, whose interest, leisure, and natural talents, would combine to make them pursue it with ardour. Such a class of individuals would be raised up, by female seminaries. And therefore they would be likely to have highly important and happy effects on common schools.

It is believed, that such institutions, would tend to prolong, or perpetuate our excellent government.

An opinion too generally prevails, that our present form of government, though good, cannot be permanent. Other republics have failed, and the historian and philosopher have told us, that nations are like individuals; that, at their birth, they receive the seeds of their decline and dissolution. Here deceived by a false anal[o]gy, we receive an apt illustration of particular facts, for a general truth. The existence of nations, cannot, in strictness, be compared with the duration of animate life; for by the operation of physical causes, this, after a certain length of time, must cease: but the existence of nations, is prolonged by the succession of one generation to another, and there is no physical cause, to prevent this succession's going on, in a peaceable manner, under a good government, till the end of time. We must then look to other causes, than necessity, for the decline and fall of former republics. If we could discover these causes, and seasonably prevent their operation, then might our latest posterity enjoy the same happy government, with which we are blessed; or if but in part, then might the triumph of tyranny, be delayed, and a few more generations be free.

Permit me then to ask the enlightened politician of my country, whether amidst his researches for these causes, he cannot discover one, in the neglect, which free governments, in common with others, have shown, to whatever regarded the formation of the female character.

In those great republics, which have fallen of themselves, the loss of republican manners and virtues, has been the invariable precursor, of their loss of the republican form of government. But is it not in the power of our sex, to give society its tone, both as to manners and morals? And if such is the extent of female influence, it is wonderful, that republics have failed, when they calmly suffered that influence, to become enlisted in favour of luxuries and follies, wholly incompatible with the existence of freedom?

It may be said, that the depravation of morals and manners, can be traced to the introduction of wealth, as its cause. But wealth will be introduced; even the iron laws of Lycurgus could not prevent it. Let us then inquire, if means may not be devised, to prevent its bringing with it the destruction of public virtue. May not these means be found in education?—in implanting, in early youth, habits, that may counteract the temptations, to which, through the influence of wealth, mature age will be exposed? and in giving strength and expansion to the mind, that it may comprehend, and prize those principles, which teach the rigid performance of duty? Education, it may be said, has been tried as a preservative of national purity. But was it applied to every exposed part of the body politic? For if any part has been left within the pestilential atmosphere of wealth, without this preservative, then that part becoming corrupted, would communicate the contagion to the whole; and if so, then has the experiment, whether education may not preserve public virtue, never yet been fairly tried. Such a part has been left in all former experiments. Females have been exposed to the contagion of wealth without the preservative of a good education; and they constitute that part of the body politic, least endowed by nature to resist, most to communicate it. Nay, not merely have they been left without the defence of a good education, but their corruption has been accelerated by a bad one. The character of women of rank and wealth has been, and in the old governments of Europe now is, all that this statement would lead us to expect. Not content with doing nothing to promote their country's welfare, like pampered children, they revel in its prosperity, and scatter it to the winds, with a wanton profusion: and still worse,—they empoison its source, by diffusing a contempt for useful labour. To court pleasure their business,—within her temple, in defiance of the laws of God and man, they have erected the idol fashion; and upon her altar, they sacrifice, with shameless rites, whatever is sacred to virtue or religion. Not the strongest ties of nature,—not even maternal love can restrain them! Like the worshipper of Moloch, the mother while yet yearning over the new born babe, tears it from the bosom, which God has swelled with nutrition for its support, and casts it remorseless from her, the victim of her unhallowed devotion!

But while, with an anguished heart, I thus depict the crimes of my sex, let not the other stand by and smile. Reason declares, that you are guiltier than we. You are our natural guardians,—our brothers,—our fathers, and our rulers. You know that our ductile minds, readily take the impressions of education. Why then have you neglected our education? Why have you looked with lethargic indifference, on circumstances ruinous to the formation of our characters, which you might have controlled?

But it may be said, the observations here made, cannot be applied to any class of females in our country. True, they cannot yet; and if they could, it would be useless to make them; for when the females of any country have become thus debased, then, is that country so corrupted, that nothing, but the awful judgments of heaven, can arrest its career of vice. But it cannot be denied, that our manners are verging towards those described; and the change, though gradual, has not been slow: already do our daughters listen with surprise, when we tell them of the republican simplicity of our mothers. But our manners are not as yet so altered, but that, throughout our country, they are still marked with republican virtues.

The inquiry, to which these remarks have conducted us is this—What is offered by the plan of female education, here proposed, which may teach, or preserve, among females of wealthy families, that purity of manners, which is allowed, to be so essential to national prosperity, and so necessary, to the existence of a republican government.

1. Females, by having their understandings cultivated, their reasoning powers developed and strengthened, may be expected to act more from the dictates of reason, and less from those of fashion and caprice.

2. With minds thus strengthened they would be taught systems of morality, enforced by the sanctions of religion; and they might be expected to acquire juster and more enlarged views of their duty, and stronger and higher motives to its performance.

3. This plan of education, offers all that can be done to preserve female youth from a contempt of useful labour. The pupils would become accustomed to it, in conjunction with the high objects of literature, and the elegant pursuits of the fine arts; and it is to be hoped, that both from habit and association, they might in future life, regard it as respectable.

To this it may be added, that if housewifery could be raised to a regular art, and taught upon philosophical principles, it would become a higher and more interesting occupation; and ladies of fortune, like wealthy agriculturalists, might find, that to regulate their business, was an agreeable employment.

4. The pupils might be expected to acquire a taste for moral and intellectual pleasures, which would buoy them above a passion for show and parade, and which would make them seek to gratify the natural love of superiority, by endeavouring to excel others in intrinsic merit, rather than in the extrinsic frivolities of dress, furniture, and equipage.

5. By being enlightened in moral philosophy, and in that, which teaches the operations of the mind, females would be enabled to perceive the nature and extent, of that influence, which they possess over their children, and the obligation, which this lays them under, to watch the formation of their

characters with unceasing vigilance, to become their instructors, to devise plans for their improvement, to weed out the vices from their minds, and to implant and foster the virtues. And surely, there is that in the maternal bosom, which, when its pleadings shall be aided by education, will overcome the seductions of wealth and fashion, and will lead the mother, to seek her happiness in communing with her children, and promoting their welfare, rather than in a heartless intercourse, with the votaries of pleasure: especially, when with an expanded mind, she extends her views to futurity, and sees her care to her offspring rewarded by peace of conscience, the blessings of her family, the prosperity of her country, and finally with everlasting happiness to herself and them.

Thus, laudable objects and employments, would be furnished for the great body of females, who are not kept by poverty from excesses. But among these, as among the other sex, will be found master spirits, who must have pre-eminence, at whatever price they acquire it. Domestic life cannot hold these, because they prefer to be infamous, rather than obscure. To leave such, without any virtuous road to eminence, is unsafe to community; for not unfrequently, are the secret springs of revolution, set in motion by their intrigues. Such aspiring minds, we will regulate, by education, we will remove obstructions to the course of literature, which has heretofore been their only honorable way to distinction; and we offer them a new object, worthy of their ambition; to govern, and improve the seminaries for their sex.

In calling on my patriotic countrymen, to effect so noble an object, the consideration of national glory, should not be overlooked. Ages have rolled away;—barbarians have trodden the weaker sex beneath their feet;—tyrants have robbed us of the present light of heaven, and fain would take its future. Nations, calling themselves polite, have made us the fancied idols of a ridiculous worship, and we have repaid them with ruin for their folly. But where is that wise and heroic country, which has considered, that our rights are sacred, though we cannot defend them? that tho' a weaker, we are an essential part of the body politic, whose corruption or improvement must affect the whole? and which, having thus considered, has sought to give us by education, that rank in the scale of being, to which our importance entitles us? History shows not that country. It shows many, whose legislatures have sought to improve their various vegetable productions, and their breeds of useful brutes; but none, whose public councils have made it an object of their deliberations, to improve the character of their women. Yet though history lifts not her finger to such an one, anticipation does. She points to a nation, which, having thrown off the shackles of authority and precedent, shrinks not from schemes of improvement, because other nations have never attempted them; but which, in its pride of independence, would rather lead than follow, in the march of human improvement: a nation, wise and magnanimous to plan, enterprising to undertake, and rich in resources to execute. Does not every American exult that this country is his own? And who knows how great and good a race of men, may yet arise from the forming hand of mothers, enlightened by the bounty of that beloved country,—to defend her liberties,—to plan her future improvement,—and to raise her to unparalleled glory?

ELLEN AND KENNETH KENISTON
The Changing Image of the American Woman (1964) *

The most effective forms of oppression are those with which the victim covertly cooperates. So long as coercion is exercised from without and experienced as such by the coerced, revolt is possible and ultimately probable. As the rulers of Chinese thought-

* Ellen and Kenneth Keniston, "An American Anachronism: The Image of Women and Work," *American Scholar*, Vol. XXXIII, No. 3 (Summer, 1964). Copyright © 1964 by the United Chapters of Phi Beta Kappa. By permission of the publishers.

reform centers know, coercion is truly effective only when its targets assent to its justice, and, more than that, accept their servitude as a part of their view of themselves. As long as American Negroes consciously or unconsciously saw themselves as an inferior race, they inevitably collaborated in their own exploitation; only the awareness of their unwitting connivance with oppression has released their energies toward relieving their second-class citizenship.

The past few years have seen renewed concern about the problems, the continuing "oppression" and the "incomplete emancipation" of American women. We have been reminded that women attend college in smaller ratio to men than thirty years ago; that sex-linked wage differentials persist in most occupations; that other industrialized countries make far better provision for working mothers; that our mass media extol the virtues of home, family and children while deprecating the working woman; that feminism in America exhausted itself with the achievement of the vote for women. Although women work in greater numbers than ever before, many professions remain closed to any but the most resolute women, and most women's jobs are concentrated in underpaid and menial positions. Compared, say with Russian society, ours makes little use of the extrafamilial talents of women, and seems to "oppress" them by pushing them simultaneously away from work and toward home and family.[1]

In seeking to explain this apparent backwardness of our society, two interpretations are frequently given. One is largely conspiratorial: in its most extreme form, it holds that women are kept oppressed by a sinister junta of reactionary psychoanalysts, Madison Avenue hucksters, and insecure husbands;[2] in more moderate statement, it stresses the role of men's vanity, weakness, or need for an "Other."[3] The second common explanation of the "problem" of American women emphasizes the absence of "objective opportunities," such as equal employment regulations, subsidies for women's education, maternity benefits, community-supported day-care centers for children, more adequate domestic help, et cetera. Were such opportunities available, this argument runs, women would move easily outside the confines of kitchen, kaffee-klatsch and kindergarten.

Each of these explanations has something to be said for it. Advertisers clearly do have a vested interest in keeping women at home buying their products; psychoanalysts have often advanced theories of universal feminine "masochism" and "passivity" (which made it difficult to explain the undeniable intellectual talents and careers of many women psychoanalysts[4]); insecure men do frequently stand between their wives and "fulfillment" outside the home; and a majority of American (male) congressmen have shown little interest in legislation to equalize women's inferior economic position. So, too, the lack of adequate institutional support for women is clear, and clearly needs correction: the lot of working women, and especially of working mothers, could be vastly improved by changes in employment laws, by added social security benefits for maternity and by better facilities for child care. And the absence of such institutional support does indeed discourage women who might otherwise want to do something outside their own homes.

But both these interpretations overlook what seems to us the central "problem" for most American women: namely, that most not only accept but largely desire a homebound position, and the obstacles on which they founder are less often external conditions than internal ambivalences. The vast

[1] See, for example, Betty Friedan, *The Feminine Mystique* (New York: Norton, 1963); Simone de Beauvoir, *The Second Sex* (New York: Knopf, 1953); and the Spring, 1964, issue of *Dædalus*.
[2] Friedan, *op. cit.*

[3] de Beauvoir, *op. cit.*
[4] See Marie Bonaparte, *Female Sexuality* (New York: International Universities Press, 1956), for an extreme case.

majority of women in this country—even
the vast majority of middle-class college
graduates—give love, marriage and family
supreme priority over "career." If they are
indignant or resentful, it is most often over
the social or personal situation that requires
them to work, and far more rarely over
either the pressures that impede their working or the injustices of their situation in
work. Whether they work to supplement
their husbands' incomes (the reason given
by most working-class women), to relieve
the boredom of empty houses once children
are in school, or, as widowed, divorced, separated or unmarried women, simply to earn
a living, most women work because they
must, and would gladly exchange their
"careers" for the life of a happily-married,
financially-secure wife-and-mother. If working-class high school girls are asked about
their ideal life, they tell of a dream-cottage
with successful husband and many children:
there is no mention of work. And even in
elite women's colleges, many, and perhaps
most, girls consider any pressure to plan
seriously for a career an unwanted distraction from their main emotional concern—
finding husbands and beginning their lives
as wives-and-mothers. Despite the fact that
eight or nine out of every ten American
women will be employed at some time during their lives, probably the same proportion
in some part of themselves dislikes, even de-
tests, the thought of working.

Resentment and indignation at the social
barriers to complete emancipation are not
widespread. They tend to be concentrated
among a relatively small group of highly educated professional women, many of whom
have succeeded in overcoming these real
barriers and in finding interesting and even
"fulfilling" jobs because they were unam-
bivalently determined to do so. Indeed, if
anything like a majority of American women
felt a small part of their resentment and indignation, the social barriers would soon
crumble before the pressure. If even a quarter of the electorate (half of the women)
was willing to vote with some selectivity for

candidates who favored equal employment
opportunities for women, subsidies for
women's education, maternity benefits,
women's employment rights and community-
supported childcare centers, it would take
but a decade before these easily envisioned
goals were attained. But there is no consistent demand; these are rarely live political
issues; most women "fulfill their potential"
outside the home reluctantly, if at all. If
there is a "problem" for women in America
today, it is that they work only of necessity
or by default; if women remain unemanci-
pated, theirs is a largely voluntary servitude.

It is therefore an oversimplification to
trace the causes of women's homebound situation solely to masculine prejudice and to
seek a solution of the problem only in improvements in social opportunities. Behind
both masculine prejudice and women's homebound situation lie enormous historical
changes that have pushed the American
woman into an unprecedented social and
human situation; and behind the inability
of American women to create better social
conditions for themselves lie anachronistic
images of womanliness and work, defensively
reasserted by women themselves. How has
the situation of American women changed
in the past generations? And why do outmoded definitions of womanliness and work
persist despite these radical changes?

Consider the life-situation of the average
woman in all societies two hundred years
ago, and in most nonindustrial societies
today. None of the "problems of modern
woman" could possibly arise: to survive,
society had no choice but to require women
to spend their lives as guardians of the home
and of the next generation. In any community where the average life-span is thirty to
forty years and infant mortality approaches
fifty percent, mere maintenance of the population requires that adult women devote
all of their time to bearing children. Moreover, what to do with "the later years" is
hardly a problem: most women are dead
long before they reach the end of their fer-
tility, and those few who survive are usually

so exhausted from childbearing that they have little energy available for "a later career." And even if a singular woman wanted to have only a few children, knowledge of contraception was so limited that she had no way of doing it short of refusing all men.

Furthermore, high birth and death rates have usually gone hand in hand with a kind of family organization that gave a woman more than enough to do *within* her family. In most societies, the family, not the individual, was the basic unit of the economy, and women have had to work for and within families in order to survive. The peasant wife must share the tasks of the land with her husband; the wife of the hunter must clean and store her husband's game; the shepherd's wife must help to guard the herds. Even today on old-fashioned farms a wife is essential to care for domestic animals, can and store food for the winter, and maintain the domestic side of farm life. In a few complex and highly differentiated societies, of course, small groups of leisured aristocratic women have existed; but these women have often become, as Veblen pointed out, status symbols for their husbands; and much of their energy has traditionally gone toward maintaining the visible signs of leisure and affluence that would provide continual reminders of their husbands' wealth and power. Historically, then, women have always worked, but at the tasks of the family economy, not outside it.

The industrial revolution, however, brought a series of changes that created a "problem" where none could have existed before. Advances in medicine and public health have decreased the infant mortality rate and lengthened the life-span; changes in economic organization have all but destroyed the family as an economic unit. Women began to work outside the home primarily in response to these economic and social changes. Thoughts of self-fulfillment, always an aristocratic ideal, were far from the minds of the first women in the mills of England and Germany in the eighteenth and nineteenth centuries; for them factory labor was an unwanted economic necessity. To be sure, the physical conditions of life were probably better in the new mill towns than they had been for the peasantry; but the "alienated" labor of the woman factory worker was psychologically far more arduous than tilling fields that had been tended by the same family for generations. Working women in the early industrial period must have looked back with nostalgia to the lives of their own peasant mothers, for whom work and family were part of an unfragmented whole. For the vast majority of working women, work outside the family began as a deprivation, as a necessity, as part of the loss of peasant family life; and these meanings of work persist to the present.

The medical and technological advances made possible by the industrial revolution have of course borne full fruit only in the past two generations. Only now has infant mortality been sufficiently lowered and the life-span enough increased so that social survival is fully compatible with widespread family limitation. A modern American woman can rightly anticipate that her children will survive into adulthood, and that she herself will live into her mid-seventies. Modern medical care makes bearing children less dangerous, and modern conveniences make caring for them less onerous. Furthermore, any woman who wants to limit the size of her family has available a variety of contraceptive techniques; and the population explosion suggests that family limitation, formerly the route to social suicide, has on the contrary become a prerequisite for social survival. Technological advances have both freed and deprived women of the need to devote their lives to procreation and child care.

The impact on women of these technological advances has been shaped by equally unprecedented changes in the family.[5] Con-

[5] For a fuller account of American family structure, see Talcott Parsons, "The Kinship System of the Contemporary United States," Chap. XI in *Essays in Sociological Theory Pure*

sider the family's increasing sociological "isolation." Formerly, husband, wife and their children were embedded in a network of extended family relationships—cousins, aunts, uncles, grandparents and grandchildren who lived together and functioned as a social and economic unit. Now, increasingly, parents and their offspring live apart and separate, isolated both geographically and psychologically from wider family ties. In societies with extended family systems, surviving older women can be socially useful by caring for their grandchildren, nieces and nephews. But in our society a woman must anticipate that her adult children will leave her to establish new homes of their own, often far from her; and any older woman who assumes a maternal role with anyone but her own children is usually told, subtly or directly, that she is neither wanted nor needed. Furthermore, the isolation and the small size of American families mean that all emotional ties within the family are inevitably concentrated on a smaller number of people and, in that measure, intensified. The absence of aunts, grandmothers, female cousins and the like within the immediate family gives the mother an added centrality as the *only* female model available to her daughters during their early years—a point to which we will return.

In addition, the family's functions have been drastically reduced in the last century. The family is no longer the chief productive unit of society: only in a declining number of old-style farms or small retail stores do husband and wife share a family economic task; instead, for the vast majority of Americans of all classes, the "isolated" family is tied to the economic system solely through its breadwinner's work. To be sure, the older notion of husband and wife working "side by side" in a common task often recurs as a

and Applied (Glencoe: Free Press, 1949); and "The American Family: its Relations to Personality and to the Social Structure," Chap. I in T. Parsons and F. Bales, *Family, Socialization and Interaction Process* (Glencoe: Free Press, 1955).

dream or hope; but for most women it is a practical impossibility. Even those rare couples today who manage to work as a team usually do so outside the home; and most can testify how hard it is to maintain such a husband-wife team in a society that normally considers their marriage relationship detrimental to their objectivity, performance and achievement on the job. Work is no longer a family affair; the "home workshop" has become a place to play; both women and men sharply separate family and work.

What is left for a woman is of course her role as "homemaker," "wife-and-mother," nurturer and upbringer of her children. But even here her job has been drastically reduced. Laborsaving devices and modern homes, advances in the packaging and processing of food, the introduction of electricity, running water, bathrooms, refrigeration and telephones into American life, all mean that a woman's housework can be quickly done unless she is truly determined to make a full-time job of housecleaning and cooking. Nor can bringing up children be counted on to occupy a woman's life, for in the past two centuries the family has relinquished many of its child-rearing functions to schools. In a technological society, teaching children adult skills is too complex and essential a task to leave to idiosyncratic families; we therefore remove children from their parents for the better part of the day and "socialize" them in schools where more standardized learning is guaranteed. This approach again both frees women and deprives them of their traditional role as those who teach children the complex skills of adulthood; it leaves mothers responsible for the full-time care of their children for only five or six years.

Finally, new demands on men in their work directly increase the pressures on women. Over the past few generations, men's jobs have become increasingly specialized, increasingly distant from any visible relationship to a useful finished product, more and more demanding of technical skill, expertise, "rationality," and the suppression of emotion, fantasy and passion on the job. More and more, men work "to earn a living," and the real "living" for which they work is increasingly sought within the family, kept separate from the working world by physical distance and social convention. After marriage, the average woman sees nothing of her husband during the working-and-commuting day; and middle-class wives with "successful" husbands often do without their spouses evenings and weekends as well. To make a "career" of marriage is psychologically difficult when one's husband is away for eighty percent of one's waking hours.

And when men are with their wives, they usually need them to make up for what is lacking in their jobs. Like our ideals of recreation, our ideals of family life are defined by contrast with the demands of our working day. In home or recreation, women are expected to fill the emotional lacunae in their husbands' jobs and to relieve the pressures and tensions they come home with. In family or fun, the good wife should be spontaneous, warm, caring, emotionally responsive, not too practical or intellectual and somewhat passive, yet at the same time consoling and supportive when necessary. Above all, she should not be aggressive, initiating, intellectual, analytic, ambitious or in any other way encourage talents or qualities in herself that might remind her husband of the working world he comes home to forget.

In every nation with an advanced industrial technology, similar changes in medical care, family life and the demands of work have, as in America, begun to alter the situation of women and to create a "problem" where none could have existed two generations ago. But in most other industrial nations the impact of these social changes on women has been attenuated by strong centers of opposition to the new industrial order. Most often, opposition has sprung from traditional institutions and values that long antedated industrialism: in France, the Church and the peasantry; in Japan, "feudal" patterns of familial and social interdependence; in England, an entrenched class system. In each case, these traditional institutions have preserved competing models of family and woman, so that women who remained loyal to the Church, the extended family, or their social class could often be relatively unaffected by the new demands of industrialism. But in America, a nation without a "feudal" past, without an entrenched class system, without an established church or an aristocratic tradition, the impact of industrial society on women has been unusually thoroughgoing and intense.

The lack of an aristocratic tradition in this country is especially important in explaining the special stresses on American women. Traditionally, in Europe, women of the upper classes have had enough leisure and freedom from family needs to permit them, if they chose, to "work" outside their homes. Those who did choose to work gradually developed a positive definition of woman's work, at first concerned with matters charitable and educational, then artistic and intellectual, and finally even scientific or political—a model that in part counterbalanced the negative images of prostitutes, servants and factory workers. But in this country, where aristocratic traditions were weak and highly suspect and where most upper-class women devoted themselves not to intellectual attainment but to ostentatious display, no countervailing image of woman's work could develop. Most American women continue to view work as at best a necessity, to be avoided if possible and borne with resignation if required.

Countless other factors contribute to the special stresses on American women. Industrialization and specialization have been more thoroughgoing here than abroad, and the resulting pressures on the family, on women, and on men's demands on women, have been correspondingly more intense. Our national reverence for youth helps make it difficult for women (or men) to plan realistically for a time in life when neither they nor their children will be young. So, too, our traditional distrust of grand ideologies has inoculated most Americans against that continuing enthusiasm for feminist ideals that exists in other nations. Together, these factors have cooperated to push American women into the vanguard of social change; and it may always be the lot of those who must face an unprecedented historical situation without signposts, models or maps to suffer the most intensely and to blame themselves for their "problems." Without adequate signposts, a vanguard inevitably falls back on outdated guides. In this case, definitions of family, conceptions of womanliness and images of work left over from an era when they were necessary for social survival and congruent with family function have persisted into an era in which they are no longer viable. The result of this cultural lag is the "problem" of American women.

"Cultural lag" is of course not so much an explanation as a description, and only by examining the reasons why archaic definitions of womanliness have persisted can we understand the ambivalence and reluctance with which most American women confront the need for life outside the family. We cannot hope to deal here with all of the social, cultural and historical factors that have contributed to preserve more traditional ideals of woman's role, nor can we consider the enormous variety of outlooks on womanliness in different sectors of American society. Instead we will concentrate on the transmission of images of femininity and masculinity from generation to generation within the family.

The fundamental processes involved in learning the lessons of gender are fairly constant in American society. An American girl first learns what it means to be a woman at her mother's knee. She may decide to be like her mother, not to be like her mother, to be like her in some ways and not in other ways; or she may even believe she has completely forgotten her mother and set out on a new path of her own; but in the background

her conscious and unconscious assessment of her mother's life, of its joys, satisfactions, virtues and failings, almost always remains central. In determining this assessment, the mother's conception of her own adequacy as a woman is of enormous importance, but equally momentous is the father's conscious and unconscious conception of his wife. In most stable marriages, these two judgments are (or soon become) complementary; and in our small and "isolated" families where mother and father are the only two adults present to a small girl, their consensus is especially decisive in forming the daughter's view of her sex. So, too, from their parents American girls also learn the meanings of masculinity and, by repeated admonition and example, the precise boundaries between what is desirably "ladylike" and what is undesirably "boyish." Again, if the parents feel and act in concert, these early lessons become so deeply ingrained that they persist unconsciously even for adult women who consciously deny their validity.

Beyond these commonplaces of the learning of sex roles, there are vast differences among American families, differences related to individual idiosyncrasy, to ethnicity and social class, to region and religion. But, despite these differences, we know enough of how our society has changed in the last two generations to reconstruct a more or less "typical" pattern of development. Very few of the grandmothers of today's young women worked outside their families; rather, as did ninety percent of late Victorian women of all classes in America, they devoted themselves to the care of children, home and husband. In such a family, a daughter was likely to inherit from both mother and father an unambivalent definition of womanliness, which glorified domestic virtues and saw outside work as an unequivocal "fall" to menial status, factory exploitation, or—the ultimate fall—prostitution. The "outside world" was quintessentially masculine; and the sharp lines that separated male and female partly served to protect "innocent" women from a side of life and of themselves seen as potentially dangerous, wild and promiscuous.[6]

In our grandparents' day, this splitting of existence into a dangerous, masculine outside world and a sheltered, protected feminine domestic world was still workable. But for a woman born at the turn of the century and married in the 1920's, the situation began to change. Although she herself may have initially accepted her parents' view of womanhood, the rapid change in the objective conditions of women's lives—the dissipation of the extended family, the lengthening of the life-span, the introduction of laborsaving devices—all these meant that the definition of womanhood that satisfied her mother was less likely to satisfy her. New economic pressures, new job opportunities for women and her own lengthening life-span made it more likely that she would work at some point in her life—either to supplement the family income or to relieve her boredom in a spotless but empty house.

But the fact of working rarely meant joy in working. Given their upbringing, few women were psychologically prepared to enter a "man's world" without inner conflict. In the absence of any positive image of women's work, all ways of construing a job were fraught with difficulty; to find satisfaction in a job inevitably meant to find something heretofore defined as a male prerogative, and often resulted in a feeling of loss of

womanliness; not to find satisfaction in one's work—and still to work—meant to risk reduction to the role of a menial in one's own eyes. In either case, working seemed to mean not being as good as one's mother, who had "made a go" of a purely domestic life.

Furthermore, husbands of the last generation were rarely happy about wives who moved outside the family. Remembering their own mothers (who had stayed at home), they could seldom confront their wives' outside jobs without feelings of inadequacy. And should the wife work—whether as volunteer or as paid employee—in order to relieve her own frustration and boredom within an empty home, then the husband's guilt and fear would usually be even greater, for this suggested that he, compared to his father, was less able to "satisfy" his wife, to "provide for her" a marriage within which she felt "fulfilled"—with all the myriad sexual and economic implications of these terms. Men, like women, tended to see work as an exclusively male prerogative; and they felt easily unmanned by wives who entered any but a small number of traditionally feminine jobs, such as nursing.

Nor should we overlook the real elements of masculine identification and rivalry in women which were fostered by Victorian definitions of sex roles. The "outside world" of the Victorian male was seen as not only dangerous and wild, but intensely interesting, free and exciting; and the protected "inside world" of Victorian women had its custodial and even imprisoning side. Many a daughter of a Victorian family covertly scorned the domestic docility of her mother and, in her own quest for freedom and excitement, secretly envied and identified with men. Those few who acted on their envy had to accept society's explicit judgment that their demeanor was "mannish" and its unstated suspicion that their behavior was "loose." But most women guiltily suppressed whatever "mannish" and "loose" aspirations they had, and, by compulsive conscious attachment to a "homely" role, denied—even

[6] The "outside" male world was thus equated with two of the basic forces in instinctual life, aggression and sexuality; and its dangers and attractions for women grew partly out of the negative and positive aspects of these forces. Negatively, women feared the "aggressiveness" and the "promiscuity" in this world and themselves, as epitomized by the "aggressive" career woman, the "promiscuous" fallen woman, or as fused in the prostitute. But positively, they desired a right to be "active" in work and to end the double standard in sexual matters. It was, and still is, difficult for women (like men) not to fear that by seeking these legitimate goals they were also seeking illicit ones, and consequently to "solve" their dilemma by seeking neither.

to themselves—the existence of these aspirations.

A young woman of today is most likely to have grown up in a family in which her mother, if she worked, felt at some level inadequate or guilty about it, and if she did not work, felt frustration and resentment at the boredom of her homebound life. Her father was usually made subtly uneasy by whatever domestic discontents or career aspirations his wife had, and appreciated her most in her homely role. Such attitudes are of course rarely stated as such, but they are nonetheless expressed in countless indirect ways, and are the more powerful because, unstated, they are the harder to confront or oppose. A mother's look of remorse as she leaves for work, her fear of "neglecting" her children, her resentment of her need to work, her failure to discuss her work at home—these are far more expressive than any open discussion of her ambivalence. And a father's deprecation of "mannish" women, his praise for the "truly feminine," and his dislike of women in his own work more effectively tell his daughter what he desires from her than any lecture could. Most fathers and mothers of the last generation implicitly agreed in blaming women for their inability to be happy in a narrowly defined wife-and-mother role, and in seeing women who wanted to work as really wanting to wear the pants.

As often happens, the assumptions and conflicts of parents form the unconscious substratum of inner conflict in their children; the stage was thus set for a continuing, although often unconscious, ambivalence about the relationship between work and womanliness in this generation. But, ironically, both emulation of one's mother and rivalry with her have often led in practice to the same determination to excel in a homely role. The woman who strongly identifies with the best in her mother has usually come unconsciously to define the best as the domestic; the woman who seeks to avoid her mother's failings has usually learned to attribute women's failings to their inability

to find fulfillment within the family. And not least of all, many women who naturally enough envy and identify themselves with men's work and freedom cannot admit this envy to themselves because it seems a denial of their femininity; and they often devote themselves to home and family with a passion born partly from fear of their latent discontents.[7]

These same psychological themes can of course lead to very different outcomes in behavior.[8] But it is a rare working woman in whom inner conflict does *not* complicate the practical problems of combining marriage and career, for whom working is *not* accompanied by silent questions about her adequacy and by implicit apprehension about her "envy" of men, and who does *not* at some level consider a career a denial rather than an expression of femininity. On the other hand, few women are able to make a full and lifetime job from reduced family roles—and to remain satisfied and content in their later years. Not surprisingly, those who have escaped inner conflict have been most often recruited from atypical circumstances—from upper-class families or from European backgrounds [9] where a more posi-

[7] Even those women who sympathized with their mothers' plight and blamed their fathers for unduly constricting her, often resolved to avoid this plight merely by finding a husband who *would* provide the love (and/or money) to support a wife at home, thus continuing the basic pattern of domesticity.

[8] For excellent clinical descriptions of the varied solutions to the "problem" of femininity, see Helene Deutsch, *The Psychology of Women* (New York: Grune and Stratton, 1944-1945), esp. Vol. I, Chaps. V and VIII. Deutsch by and large interprets these solutions within an orthodox psychoanalytic framework. For an interpretation that stresses the importance of cultural factors, see Karen Horney, *New Ways in Psychoanalysis* (New York: Norton, 1939), esp. Chap. VI, "Feminine Psychology."

[9] For example, a remarkable number of women of outstanding scholarly achievement in this country were born in Europe.

tive conception of women's work prevails.

A woman's sense of what it is to be a woman, although founded on her relationships with her parents, is of course much more than this. But for most American girls the familistic lessons of their childhoods are merely reinforced by their later education. The curriculum of American schools is primarily oriented toward what are thought to be the special talents of boys, and this emphasis convinces girls that they are not "really good" at the things that matter in the world of men. So, too, girls soon learn that "popularity"—that peculiar American ecstasy from which all other goods flow—accrues to her who hides any intelligence she may have, flatters the often precarious maleness of adolescent boys, and devotes herself to activities that can in no way challenge their sex. The popular girls in high schools are seldom the brilliant girls; or if they are, it is only because they are so brilliant they can hide their brilliance from less brilliant boys.[10] Any girl whose parents support her in an early commitment to a career outside those few that are deemed unthreateningly feminine often spends many miserable years in a public school system. Indeed, most American public schools (like many private schools) make a girl with passionate intellectual interests feel a strong sense of her own inadequacy as a woman, feel guilty about these "masculine" outlooks, perhaps even wonder about her own normality.

At best, adolescence should provide a second chance in life, an opportunity to reassess childhood self-definitions, envies and identifications and to seek out new models of selfhood more appropriate to capacities and opportunities. But as we argued earlier, American society provides few models adequate to the situation of modern women. On the whole, mass media and popular fiction continue to portray career women as mannish, loose, or both; and the happy ending for working girls still involves abandoning work, marrying and having many children

[10] James S. Coleman, The Adolescent Society (Glencoe: Free Press, 1961), esp. Chap. VI.

—and there the story ends.[11] So, too, many of the potential models have been systematically debunked by the misapplication of psychiatric judgments; thus, few outstanding women have been spared the implication that their achievements spring primarily from neurosis.[12] And the most immediate models of working women available to girls during adolescence—their teachers—are too often unmarried women who have had to pay a high human price for their work. Thus, the selective reorganization and redefinition of childhood images of womanhood that could take place during adolescence rarely occur; and during her late teens and early twenties, many a girl who might otherwise be capable of more merely confirms her surrender to the pressures for popularity. Adequate models of adult identification can sustain one against strong internal and social pressure; when they are absent, one surrenders at the first push.

Paradoxically, then, the effect of new technology, of changes in family structure and function, has been to make many—probably most—women even more determined to make a go of a wife-and-mother role which objective conditions daily undermine more completely. Most young women in this country still cherish the fantasy of a marriage that will totally and automatically fulfill all emotional and intellectual needs, a fantasy that sets the stage for colossal disappointment, guilt and self-castigation when—as increasingly happens—marriage alone is not enough. So, too, most remain enormously ambivalent about the thought of working, to say nothing of finding a "vocation" in work; and even those who secretly enjoy their jobs often find it easier to blame their extrafamilial life on

[11] Friedan, op. cit., Chap. II, has an excellent analysis of the portrayal of working women in women's magazines.

[12] Cf. F. Lundberg and M. F. Farnham, Modern Woman: The Lost Sex (New York: Grosset's Universal Library, 1947), esp. Chap. VII, for an especially vicious treatment of feminists.

financial need than to admit, even to themselves, that they want or enjoy it. Although the dream-cottage with the built-in totally fulfilling wife-and-mother role has been destroyed by a changing society, most women cling tenaciously and sometimes defensively to this older image and blame themselves for the cracks in the picture window.

Assuming that our characterization is adequate, what can be done? Or, indeed, need anything be done? One rejoinder would be to argue that by freely choosing to devote themselves entirely to their husbands and families, women are merely expressing a deeply feminine outlook. But against this, recall that any American woman who has had a family of three children by the time she is thirty years old and who lives to the age of seventy-five will have forty years of her adult life that can*not* under any circumstances be spent primarily in child care. Furthermore, the disappearance of the family as a productive unit means that a woman has few economic functions to perform within the home. Cleaning, cooking, and caring for older children are, even for the most compulsive housewife and conscientious mother, at best part-time occupations. For a girl to dream only of being a happy wife-and-mother thus is a gross denial of reality, a motivated refusal to confront the kind of life she will actually lead.

Furthermore, the choice most women make can hardly be said to be "free" in the psychological sense. We have argued that identification, rivalry, emulation, fear and guilt often make it psychologically impossible for women to respond to changed social conditions, to seize the opportunities that do exist or to fight for those that do not. Thus we return to the proposition from which we began: the failure of most American women to exploit the potentials open to them or to struggle to create new opportunities stems in large part from their own inner conflicts, from archaic images of womanhood and from family patterns that subtly but effectively discourage commitment to vocation. If our society has not yet availed itself of the talents of women, it is largely because women themselves feel they must hide their talents under a bushel.

Nor can the choice of the wife-and-mother role to the exclusion of all else be seen as merely a "natural" expression of the "eternal feminine," of woman's biological role as bearer and nurturer of the next generation. To be sure, a woman's capacity for biological creativity is and must be central to many of her fundamental concerns, affecting her life-style, her personal relations, her conceptions of time, even her orientation to space. But women express their womanliness differently in every culture; and in our own culture they often express it in ways less than adequate to meet their unprecedented situation. Women need not abandon their distinguishing womanliness: even now, there are the many exceptions to these remarks who are sufficiently free of inner conflict to realize their womanliness both within their families and in useful work outside their homes. The problem is how to open this option to all women.

What, then, can be done to alter the prevailing outmoded definitions of the good life for women? We have already mentioned one major line of improvement—the development of social institutions to support and encourage those women who want or need to work. But if our analysis is correct, an even deeper problem than the lack of opportunities is the lack of unambivalent motivation. And the processes of generational identification, emulation and rivalry upon which such lack of motivation is based are difficult to change by direct social intervention. What parents communicate to their daughters about womanhood, work and femininity can only be affected indirectly, by changing other social agencies, ideologies and models, which may in turn affect patterns of family influence, interaction and identification.

This is not a small or simple task, but some of the ways it might be done can be anticipated. For one, the facts we have here emphasized should be continually reiterated to both young men and young women: that most women *will* work, that society has changed so as to make *impossible* the kind of fulfillment within the family that earlier generations found; that unless they work most women—single or married—will find themselves during the greater part of their adulthood with nothing to do. Educational authorities, mass media, schools, all can cooperate in emphasizing the difficulties in an older conception of womanhood and the objective possibilities open to women today.

Women's conceptions of their potentials might also be changed by altering the demands that men—their fathers and husbands—make upon them. Unlike all other "oppressed" groups, women live on terms of intimate interdependence with their alleged oppressors, and this interdependence means that if the lives of men are grossly lacking in some crucial quality, their women will be impelled to develop compensating and opposite qualities. Thus, as we argued earlier, many of the pressures that men exert on their wives and daughters ultimately spring from the lacks in their own work. Could we but make work more humane and more challenging for men, asking less of their patience and more of their imagination, it would be less necessary for women to compensate for what is missing on the job by being passively "feminine" in the home. As it is, a man whose work is essentially dull, monotonous and *un*fulfilling can be only threatened when his wife seeks "self-fulfillment" in her work.

But perhaps the greatest leverage for changing the image of women and their potential could be gained by providing more viable models of womanhood to girls in adolescence. In every community, there are some women who feel little inner conflict between their commitments to their families and their vocations, who manage both with equal womanliness. The existence of such women must be brought to the attention of adolescent girls searching for models for the future. At present, most adolescent girls are confronted with two equally un-

satisfactory models—spinster teachers, sometimes embittered, mannish and overly intellectual, and women like their mothers, who usually have the many conflicts about work and womanliness we have discussed. If a third model could be available as well—as housemothers, teachers, advisors and friends —a model that epitomizes marriage *and* career instead of marriage or career, more adolescent girls and young women might break out of these sterile alternatives. We Americans are not an ideological people, and our pragmatism demands visible proof of the possibility of what we advocate.[13] Such proof exists in every community, and were it consistently brought to the attention of girls in the process of defining their future lives as women, they might be better able to avoid the literally impossible alternatives in whose terms many now shape their futures.[14]

All this implies a vision of the possibilities available to women for the first time in history. We would hopefully envisage a society that was not an androgenous world in which men and women were as similar as anatomically possible,[15] but one in which

[13] Americans, habitually a nonideological and empirical people, have usually been more influenced by exemplary figures than by explicit ideologies, and we feel that adolescent girls who might be suspicious of ideological feminism could still admire women who embodied its virtues. See Carl N. Degler, "Revolution without Ideology: The Changing Place of Women in America," *Dædalus* (Spring, 1964).

[14] Although we have here stressed changing women's view of womanliness and work, it is equally important that men, who are after all the sons, husbands and fathers of women, should alter their conceptions as well. Any attack on the problem would fail unless it came to terms with the inevitable complementarity of expectations of men and women.

[15] Here we disagree with those who would push the social similarity of men and women as far as anatomically possible. This seems to us to ignore the many subtle nonanatomical differences between the sexes and to be potentially dangerous for the sexual identification of children, which largely depends on having parents

women could make what Erik Erikson calls their "inner space" [16] and their attitude toward their inner creativity felt in the outer world as well—and men could learn to enjoy it. We would hope that women who saw the need to extend their life-space beyond the family would become not less but more womanly in consequence; that in time they would evolve new ways of expressing, rather than denying, their womanliness in their work; and that the result would be a betterment of work for both men and women. We would hope that Americans of both sexes could gradually abandon outdated images of masculinity and femininity without ceasing to rejoice in the difference. And we would hope that women who were emancipated from voluntary servitude to anachronistic images of "femininity" could abandon outmoded alternatives for more appropriate alternations between the traditional inner world of children and family and new efforts to realize the virtues of this inner world outside the home. Thus, we would hope, the fruitful mutuality and interdependence of men and women that has always existed in love might be extended in the works of society.

CRISES AND RECURRING ISSUES

CHIEF JUSTICE EARL WARREN
Opinion of the United States Supreme Court (May 17, 1954) *

MR. CHIEF JUSTICE WARREN delivered the opinion of the Court.

These cases come to us from the States of Kansas, South Carolina, Virginia, and Delaware. They are premised on different facts and different local conditions, but a common legal question justifies their consideration together in this consolidated opinion.

In each of the cases, minors of the Negro race, through their legal representatives, seek the aid of the courts in obtaining admission to the public schools of their community on a nonsegregated basis. In each instance, they had been denied admission to schools attended by white children under laws requiring or permitting segregation according to race. This segregation was alleged to deprive the plaintiffs of the equal protection of the laws under the Fourteenth Amendment. In each of the cases other than the Delaware case, a three-judge federal district court denied relief to the plaintiffs on the so-called "separate but equal" doctrine announced by this Court in *Plessy* v. *Ferguson*, 163 U. S. 537. Under that doctrine, equality of treatment is accorded when the races are provided substantially equal facilities, even though these facilities be separate. In the Delaware case, the Supreme Court of Delaware adhered to that doctrine, but ordered that the plaintiffs be admitted to the white schools because of their superiority to the Negro schools.

The plaintiffs contend that segregated public schools are not "equal" and cannot be made "equal," and that hence they are deprived of the equal protection of the laws. Because of the obvious importance of the question presented, the Court took jurisdiction. Argument was heard in the 1952 Term, and reargument was heard this Term on certain questions propounded by the Court.

Reargument was largely devoted to the circumstances surrounding the adoption of

---

whose behavior is consistently gender-typed. And even if it were psychologically possible and harmless, a maximally androgenous world would seem to us an undesirably ugly one. Rather than attempt to become more similar, we feel men and women should learn to exploit and enjoy their complementarities in wider areas of life. For an able advocacy of androgeny, however, see Alice S. Rossi, "Equality between the Sexes: An Immodest Proposal," *Dædalus* (Spring, 1964).

[16] "Inner and Outer Space: Reflections on Womanhood," *Dædalus* (Spring, 1964).

* *Brown v. Board of Education of Topeka et al.*, 347 U.S. 486–496 (1954).

the Fourteenth Amendment in 1868. It covered exhaustively consideration of the Amendment in Congress, ratification by the states, then existing practices in racial segregation, and the views of proponents and opponents of the Amendment. This discussion and our own investigation convince us that, although these sources cast some light, it is not enough to resolve the problem with which we are faced. At best, they are inconclusive. The most avid proponents of the post-War Amendments undoubtedly intended them to remove all legal distinctions among "all persons born or naturalized in the United States." Their opponents, just as certainly, were antagonistic to both the letter and the spirit of the Amendments and wished them to have the most limited effect. What others in Congress and the state legislatures had in mind cannot be determined with any degree of certainty.

An additional reason for the inconclusive nature of the Amendment's history, with respect to segregated schools, is the status of public education at that time. In the South, the movement toward free common schools, supported by general taxation, had not yet taken hold. Education of white children was largely in the hands of private groups. Education of Negroes was almost nonexistent, and practically all of the race were illiterate. In fact, any education of Negroes was forbidden by law in some states. Today, in contrast, many Negroes have achieved outstanding success in the arts and sciences as well as in the business and professional world. It is true that public school education at the time of the Amendment had advanced further in the North, but the effect of the Amendment on Northern States was generally ignored in the congressional debates. Even in the North, the conditions of public education did not approximate those existing today. The curriculum was usually rudimentary; ungraded schools were common in rural areas; the school term was but three months a year in many states; and compulsory school attendance was virtually unknown. As a consequence, it is not surprising that there should be so little in the history of the Fourteenth Amendment relating to its intended effect on public education.

In the first cases in this Court construing the Fourteenth Amendment, decided shortly after its adoption, the Court interpreted it as proscribing all state-imposed discriminations against the Negro race. The doctrine of "separate but equal" did not make its appearance in this Court until 1896 in the case of *Plessy* v. *Ferguson, supra,* involving not education but transportation. American courts have since labored with the doctrine for over half a century. In this Court, there have been six cases involving the "separate but equal" doctrine in the field of public education. In *Cumming* v. *County Board of Education,* 175 U. S. 528, and *Gong Lum* v. *Rice,* 275 U. S. 78, the validity of the doctrine itself was not challenged.[1] In more recent cases, all on the graduate school level, inequality was found in that specific benefits enjoyed by white students were denied to Negro students of the same educational qualifications. *Missouri ex rel. Gaines* v. *Canada,* 305 U. S. 337; *Sipuel* v. *Oklahoma,* 332 U. S. 631; *Sweatt* v. *Painter,* 339 U. S. 629; *McLaurin* v. *Oklahoma State Regents,* 339 U. S. 637. In none of these cases was it necessary to re-examine the doctrine to grant relief to the Negro plaintiff. And in *Sweatt* v. *Painter, supra,* the Court expressly reserved decision on the question whether *Plessy* v. *Ferguson* should be held inapplicable to public education.

In the instant cases, that question is directly presented. Here, unlike *Sweatt* v. *Painter,* there are findings below that the Negro and white schools involved have been

[1] In the *Cumming* case, Negro taxpayers sought an injunction requiring the defendant school board to discontinue the operation of a high school for white children until the board resumed operation of a high school for Negro children. Similarly, in the *Gong Lum* case, the plaintiff, a child of Chinese descent, contended only that state authorities had misapplied the doctrine by classifying him with Negro children and requiring him to attend a Negro school.

equalized, or are being equalized, with respect to buildings, curricula, qualifications and salaries of teachers, and other "tangible" factors. Our decision, therefore, cannot turn on merely a comparison of these tangible factors in the Negro and white schools involved in each of the cases. We must look instead to the effect of segregation itself on public education.

In approaching this problem, we cannot turn the clock back to 1868 when the Amendment was adopted, or even to 1896 when *Plessy* v. *Ferguson* was written. We must consider public education in the light of its full development and its present place in American life throughout the Nation. Only in this way can it be determined if segregation in public schools deprives these plaintiffs of the equal protection of the laws.

Today, education is perhaps the most important function of state and local governments. Compulsory school attendance laws and the great expenditures for education both demonstrate our recognition of the importance of education to our democratic society. It is required in the performance of our most basic public responsibilities, even service in the armed forces. It is the very foundation of good citizenship. Today it is a principal instrument in awakening the child to cultural values, in preparing him for later professional training, and in helping him to adjust normally to his environment. In these days, it is doubtful that any child may reasonably be expected to succeed in life if he is denied the opportunity of an education. Such an opportunity, where the state has undertaken to provide it, is a right which must be made available to all on equal terms.

We come then to the question presented: Does segregation of children in public schools solely on the basis of race, even though the physical facilities and other "tangible" factors may be equal, deprive the children of the minority group of equal educational opportunities? We believe that it does.

In *Sweatt* v. *Painter, supra,* in finding that

a segregated law school for Negroes could not provide them equal educational opportunities, this Court relied in large part on "those qualities which are incapable of objective measurement but which make for greatness in a law school." In *McLaurin* v. *Oklahoma State Regents, supra,* the Court, in requiring that a Negro admitted to a white graduate school be treated like all other students, again resorted to intangible considerations: ". . . his ability to study, to engage in discussions and exchange views with other students, and, in general, to learn his profession." Such considerations apply with added force to children in grade and high schools. To separate them from others of similar age and qualifications solely because of their race generates a feeling of inferiority as to their status in the community that may affect their hearts and minds in a way unlikely ever to be undone. The effect of this separation on their educational opportunities was well stated by a finding in the Kansas case by a court which nevertheless felt compelled to rule against the Negro plaintiffs:

> Segregation of white and colored children in public schools has a detrimental effect upon the colored children. The impact is greater when it has the sanction of the law; for the policy of separating the races is usually interpreted as denoting the inferiority of the negro group. A sense of inferiority affects the motivation of a child to learn. Segregation with the sanction of law, therefore, has a tendency to [retard] the educational and mental development of negro children and to deprive them of some of the benefits they would receive in a racial[ly] integrated school system.

Whatever may have been the extent of psychological knowledge at the time of *Plessy* v. *Ferguson,* this finding is amply supported by modern authority. Any language in *Plessy* v. *Ferguson* contrary to this finding is rejected.

We conclude that in the field of public

education the doctrine of "separate but equal" has no place. Separate educational facilities are inherently unequal. Therefore, we hold that the plaintiffs and others similarly situated for whom the actions have been brought are, by reason of the segregation complained of, deprived of the equal protection of the laws guaranteed by the Fourteenth Amendment. This disposition makes unnecessary any discussion whether such segregation also violates the Due Process Clause of the Fourteenth Amendment.

Because these are class actions, because of the wide applicability of this decision, and because of the great variety of local conditions, the formulation of decrees in these cases presents problems of considerable complexity. On reargument, the consideration of appropriate relief was necessarily subordinated to the primary question—the constitutionality of segregation in public education. We have now announced that such segregation is a denial of the equal protection of the laws. In order that we may have the full assistance of the parties in formulating decrees, the cases will be restored to the docket, and the parties are requested to present further argument on Questions 4 and 5 previously propounded by the Court for the reargument this Term. The Attorney General of the United States is again invited to participate. The Attorneys General of the states requiring or permitting segregation in public education will also be permitted to appear as *amici curiae* upon request to do so by September 15, 1954, and submission of briefs by October 1, 1954.

It is so ordered.

EDWARD P. DOZIER

The American Indian: Acculturation under Duress (1965)*

* Edward P. Dozier, "The Adjustment Problems of Young American Indians (the Result of Cultural and Value Differences)," (Washington, D.C.: U.S. Department of the Interior, Bureau of Indian Affairs, Branch of Education [1965]; an address before the Bureauwide Guidance Workshop, Intermountain School,

A half century of cultural persecution [from 1880 to 1930] made an indelible mark on Indian society and personality. Bitterness, feelings of inadequacy and hostility to Government programs characterized all Indians, and these attitudes have been passed down to the present generation.

Sufficient deprivational factors have been indicated to account for the deep sense of inferiority and inadequacy from which the American Indian suffers—factors which in bulk and intensity would seem to exceed those to which other ethnic groups have been subjected. To all this must be added that American Indians share with other racially visible ethnic minority groups of low economic status discrimination, poverty, poor housing, lack of education, and other deprivational circumstances.

Both the positive and negative aspects of American Indian culture sketched above tend to affect young Indians adversely. The differences in culture and language are barriers to forming a single Indian pressure group which might make possible a united approach to common problems. Unlike other ethnic groups in the United States, American Indians come from small groups with distinctive languages and must communicate across these groups in an alien language—English. Reservation backgrounds where English is unfamiliar or poorly learned provide further handicaps. Since Indian culture, society, and the native language are undergoing change and disorganization, aspects of the cultural heritage also are transmitted ineffectively. Thus modern Indians are rarely masters of either their native language or English and the adjustment to either the Indian culture or the white one is a maze of confusion. Intra-Indian relations whether at school or off the

Brigham City, Utah, June 7–18, 1965), Vol. I, "General Assembly Addresses," pp. 58–60. Unpublished document used by permission of the Bureau of Indian Affairs and Edward P. Dozier, Professor of Anthropology, University of Arizona.

reservation are, therefore, rarely satisfying and rewarding experiences.

Those value orientations which Indians share also often act as deterrents to successful adjustment to American life and culture and to relations among other Indians. We have discussed these common denominators under two broad headings: (1) the equalitarian aspects of Indian society which emphasizes individualism, and (2) the legacy of bitterness, inferiority, and apathy inherited from the cultural deprivations suffered by parents and grandparents.

Taking first the individualism factor, it is a common experience of school teachers and school supervisors that initially young Indians seek answers to problems stubbornly on their own. But since such attempts are hampered by a narrow and often erroneous conception of the issues at hand and indeed of the white world generally, their efforts usually fail. Except for highly motivated Indians who very likely come from secure home backgrounds where social disorganization has not proceeded to extreme proportions, young Indians withdraw into themselves and live unhappily in school environments while seeking the first opportunity to drop out. Indian advisers in colleges and universities will amply document the cases of young Indians who try to wrestle [with] and solve the problem of school adjustment on their own. Even though the struggle is difficult and their grades attest to it, they will not seek help. At the University of Arizona we have a free tutorial program for Indians; yet out of a yearly enrollment of some thirty students, only about half-a-dozen students have ever taken advantage of the service. Yet, with one or two exceptions, all the Indian students do poorly; indeed, those who avail themselves of tutorial help are those who are less in need of it than the others.

Let us consider the second common denominator of Indian culture and society— the deprivation factor, which is perhaps the most serious of the handicaps suffered by Indian youngsters.

While the present school generation does not experience deprivation to the extent suffered by their parents and grandparents, they still have inherited the negative attitudes of their forefathers, and are living in a period of tremendous upheavals of their cultural, social, and linguistic heritage. Whether or not a student is able to verbalize the cause of his loneliness, his feeling of inadequacy, and his adjustment problems, it is clear that at the base of these difficulties lies the overpressing social and cultural deprivation he has suffered and is continuing to suffer.

The sense of inadequacy and the Indian's narrow conception of the white world also frequently make him a prey of dependency relationships. To a large extent this dependency condition was forced upon the Indians by placing them on reservations which were inadequate to supply their needs. The ration system of both food and clothing for many years intensified this condition. While the present Indian Bureau realizes the unfortunate consequences of the Indian's lack of self-reliance, unfortunately it cannot undo a hundred years or more of forced Americanization. Governmental policies in the late 1900's and early 1920's succeeded in pauperizing and making the Indian bitter and apathetic. The earlier system demoralized the Indian, for at the bottom of all the teaching was the feeling that an Indian should be ashamed to be what he was. The present policy of the Government is removing the sense of shame, letting the Indian move in the world as an equal, though different, citizen. Under the treatment he now is receiving he will probably give more to America and take more as well. But the dependency relationship persists and is evident in school environments as well as in other interrelations between Indians and whites.

The important question that confronts us now is: What can be done to help the young Indian? Unfortunately there is not a single answer to the many problems of adjustment to schools and to the dominant society and culture which the young Indian faces.

Understanding of the Indian's background is part of the answer. Where there is understanding of basic issues, both historical and contemporary, something can be done. Obviously as school teachers and school supervisors we all cannot be experts on Indian cultures—there are too many of them. Even the anthropologist who specializes in the study of societies all over the world cannot possibly absorb all knowledge of Indian cultures. Similarly distinct languages run into the hundreds and we cannot expect to learn all of their characteristics, much less learn to speak them. And the same thing applies to all the other facets of American Indian culture and society.

But we can learn about the sources of the basic adjustment problems of the Indians. Once we have this background we can proceed to approach the problems of the Indians with sympathy and patience. There are probably more approaches than one to attacking Indian adjustment problems, and perhaps several approaches will work better than one. But an understanding of the causes of resistance, apathy, and poor performance, as I have tried to outline them in this presentation, would appear to be the beginning for solutions.

JAMES S. COLEMAN ET AL.
Equality of Educational Opportunity (1966)*

THE SURVEY

In view of the fundamental significance of educational opportunity to many important social issues today, Congress requested the survey of educational opportunity reported in this document. The survey is, of course, only one small part of extensive and varied activities which numerous institutions and persons are pursuing in an effort to under-

* James S. Coleman *et al., Equality of Educational Opportunity* (Washington, D.C.: U.S. Government Printing Office, 1966; Superintendent of Documents Catalog No. FS5.238: 38001), pp. 1–3, 8–9, 12, 20–23, 25, 27–34. Used by permission.

stand the critical factors relating to the education of minority children and hence to build a sound basis for recommendations for improving their education. Probably the main contribution of the survey to this large and long-range effort will be in the fact that for the first time there is made available a comprehensive collection of data gathered on consistent specifications throughout the whole Nation. . . .

The survey was carried out by the National Center for Educational Statistics of the U.S. Office of Education. In addition to its own staff the Center used the services of outside consultants and contractors. James Coleman of Johns Hopkins University had major responsibility for the design, administration, and analysis of the survey. . . .

ALEXANDER M. MOOD,
*Assistant Commissioner
for Educational Statistics.*

1.0   SUMMARY REPORT

1.1   Segregation in the public schools

The great majority of American children attend schools that are largely segregated—that is, where almost all of their fellow students are of the same racial background as they are. Among minority groups, Negroes are by far the most segregated. Taking all groups, however, white children are most segregated. Almost 80 percent of all white pupils in 1st grade and 12th grade attend schools that are from 90 to 100 percent white. And 97 percent at grade 1, and 99 percent at grade 12, attend schools that are 50 percent or more white.

For Negro pupils, segregation is more nearly complete in the South (as it is for whites also), but it is extensive also in all the other regions where the Negro population is concentrated: the urban North, Midwest, and West.

More than 65 percent of all Negro pupils in the first grade attend schools that are between 90 and 100 percent Negro. And 87 percent at grade 1, and 66 percent at grade 12, attend schools that are 50 percent or more Negro. In the South most students attend schools that are 100 percent white or Negro.

The same pattern of segregation holds, though not quite so strongly, for the teachers of Negro and white students. For the Nation as a whole, the average Negro elementary pupil attends a school in which 65 percent of the teachers are Negro; the average white elementary pupil attends a school in which 97 percent of the teachers are white. White teachers are more predominant at the secondary level, where the corresponding figures are 59 and 97 percent. The racial matching of teachers is most pronounced in the South, where by tradition it has been complete. On a nationwide basis, in cases where the races of pupils and teachers are not matched, the trend is all in one direction: white teachers teach Negro children but Negro teachers seldom teach white children; just as, in the schools, integration consists primarily of a minority of Negro pupils in predominantly white schools but almost never of a few whites in largely Negro schools.

In its desegregation decision of 1954, the Supreme Court held that separate schools for Negro and white children are inherently unequal. This survey finds that, when measured by that yardstick, American public education remains largely unequal in most regions of the country, including all those where Negroes form any significant proportion of the population. Obviously, however, that is not the only yardstick. The next section of the summary describes other characteristics by means of which equality of educational opportunity may be appraised. . . .

1.2 The schools and their characteristics

The school environment of a child consists of many elements, ranging from the desk he sits at to the child who sits next to him, and including the teacher who stands at the front of his class. A statistical survey can give only fragmentary evidence of this environment.

Great collections of numbers such as are found in these pages—totals and averages and percentages—blur and obscure rather than sharpen and illuminate the range of variation they represent. If one reads, for example, that the average annual income per person in the State of Maryland is $3,000, there is a tendency to picture an average person living in moderate circumstances in a middle-class neighborhood holding an ordinary job. But that number represents at the upper end millionaires, and at the lower end the unemployed, the pensioners, the charwomen. Thus the $3,000 average income should somehow bring to mind the tycoon and the tramp, the showcase and the shack, as well as the average man in the average house.

So, too, in reading these statistics on education, one must picture the child whose school has every conceivable facility that is believed to enhance the educational process, whose teachers may be particularly gifted and well educated, and whose home and total neighborhood are themselves powerful contributors to his education and growth. And one must picture the child in a dismal tenement area who may come hungry to an ancient, dirty building that is badly ventilated, poorly lighted, overcrowded, understaffed, and without sufficient textbooks.

Statistics, too, must deal with one thing at a time, and cumulative effects tend to be lost in them. Having a teacher without a college degree indicates an element of disadvantage, but in the concrete situation, a child may be taught by a teacher who is not only without a degree but who has grown up and received his schooling in the local community, who has never been out of the State, who has a 10th-grade vocabulary, and who shares the local community's attitudes.

One must also be aware of the relative importance of a certain kind of thing to a certain kind of person. Just as a loaf of bread means more to a starving man than to a sated one, so one very fine textbook or, better, one very able teacher, may mean far more to a deprived child than to one who already has several of both.

Finally, it should be borne in mind that in cases where Negroes in the South receive unequal treatment, the significance in terms of actual numbers of individuals involved is very great, since 54 percent of the Negro population of school-going age, or approximately 3,200,000 children, live in that region.

All of the findings reported in this section of the summary are based on responses to questionnaires filled out by public school teachers, principals, district school superintendents, and pupils. The data were gathered in September and October of 1965 from 4,000 public schools. All teachers, principals, and district superintendents in these schools participated, as did all pupils in the 3d, 6th, 9th, and 12th grades. First-grade pupils in half the schools participated. More than 645,000 pupils in all were involved in the survey. About 30 percent of the schools selected for the survey did not participate; an analysis of the nonparticipating schools indicated that their inclusion would not have significantly altered the results of the survey. The participation rates were: in the metropolitan North and West, 72 percent; metropolitan South and Southwest, 65 percent; nonmetropolitan North and West, 82 percent; nonmetropolitan South and Southwest, 61 percent.

All the statistics on the physical facilities of the schools and the academic and extracurricular programs are based on information provided by the teachers and administrators. They also provided information about their own education, experience, and philosophy of education, and described as they see them the socioeconomic characteristics of the neighborhoods served by their schools.

The statistics having to do with the pupils' personal socioeconomic backgrounds, level of education of their parents, and certain items in their homes (such as encyclopedias, daily newspapers, etc.) are based on pupil responses to questionnaires. The pupils also answered questions about their academic aspirations and their attitudes toward staying in school.

All personal and school data were confidential and for statistical purposes only; the questionnaires were collected without the names or other personal identification of the respondents.

Data for Negro and white children are classified by whether the schools are in metropolitan areas or not. The definition of a metropolitan area is the one commonly used by government agencies: a city of over 50,000 inhabitants including its suburbs. All other schools in small cities, towns, or rural areas are referred to as nonmetropolitan schools. . . .

Facilities

Nationally, Negro pupils have fewer of some of the facilities that seem most related to academic achievement: They have less access to physics, chemistry, and language laboratories; there are fewer books per pupil in their libraries; their textbooks are less often in sufficient supply. To the extent that physical facilities are important to learning, such items appear to be more relevant than some others, such as cafeterias, in which minority groups are at an advantage. . . .

Programs

Just as minority groups tend to have less access to physical facilities that seem to be related to academic achievement, so too they have less access to curricular and extracurricular programs that would seem to have such a relationship.

Secondary school Negro students are less likely to attend schools that are regionally accredited; this is particularly pronounced in the South. Negro and Puerto Rican pupils have less access to college preparatory curriculums and to accelerated curriculums; Puerto Ricans have less access to vocational curriculums as well. Less intelligence testing is done in the schools attended by Negroes and Puerto Ricans. Finally, white students in general have more access to a more fully developed program of extracurricular activities, in particular those which might be related to academic matters (debate teams, for example, and student newspapers).

Again, regional differences are striking. For example, 100 percent of Negro high school students and 97 percent of whites in the metropolitan Far West attend schools having a remedial reading teacher (this does not mean, of course, that every student uses the services of that teacher, but simply that he has access to them) compared with 46 percent and 65 percent, respectively, in the metropolitan South—and 4 percent and 9 percent in the nonmetropolitan Southwest. . . .

Principals and Teachers

One percent of white elementary pupils attend a school with a Negro principal, and 56 percent of Negro children attend a school with a Negro principal. . . .

The average white student goes to an elementary school where 40 percent of the teachers spent most of their lives in the same city, town, or county; the average Negro pupil goes to a school where 53 percent of the teachers have lived in the same locality most of their lives. . . .

The average Negro pupil attends a school where a greater percentage of the teachers appears to be somewhat less able, as measured by these indicators, than those in the schools attended by the average white student. . . .

The average white pupil attends a school where 51 percent of the white teachers would not choose to move to another school, whereas the average Negro attends a school where 46 percent would not choose to move. . . .

Student Body Characteristics

Clear differences are found on these items [about characteristics of the student bodies attending various schools.] The average Negro has fewer classmates whose mothers graduated from high school; his classmates more frequently are members of large rather than small families; they are less often enrolled in a college preparatory curriculum; they have taken a smaller number of courses in English, mathematics, foreign language, and science.

On most items, the other minority groups fall between Negroes and whites, but closer to whites, in the extent to which each characteristic is typical of their classmates.

Again, there are substantial variations in the magnitude of the differences, with the difference usually being greater in the Southern States.

1.3   Achievement in the public schools

The schools bear many responsibilities. Among the most important is the teaching of certain intellectual skills such as reading, writing, calculating, and problem solving. One way of assessing the educational opportunity offered by the schools is to measure how well they perform this task. Standard achievement tests are available to measure these skills, and several such tests were administered in this survey to pupils at grades 1, 3, 6, 9, and 12.

These tests do not measure intelligence, nor attitudes, nor qualities of character. Furthermore, they are not, nor are they intended to be, "culture free." Quite the reverse: they are culture bound. What they measure are the skills which are among the most important in our society for getting a good job and moving up to a better one, and for full participation in an increasingly technical world. Consequently, a pupil's test results at the end of public school provide a good measure of the range of opportunities open to him as he finishes school—a wide range of choice of jobs or colleges if these skills are very high; a very narrow range that includes only the most menial jobs if these skills are very low. . . .

With some exceptions—notably Oriental Americans—the average minority pupil scores distinctly lower on these tests at every level than the average white pupil. The minority pupils' scores are as much as one standard deviation below the majority pupils' scores in the 1st grade. At the 12th grade, results of tests in the same verbal and non-verbal skills show that, in every case, the minority scores are farther below the majority than are the 1st-graders. For some groups, the relative decline is negligible; for others, it is large.

Furthermore, a constant difference in standard deviations over the various grades represents an increasing difference in grade level gap. For example, Negroes in the metropolitan Northeast are about 1.1 standard deviations below whites in the same region at grades 6, 9, and 12. But at grade 6 this represents 1.6 years behind; at grade 9, 2.4 years; and at grade 12, 3.3 years. Thus, by this measure, the deficiency in achievement is progressively greater for the minority pupils at progressively higher grade levels.

For most minority groups, then, and most particularly the Negro, schools provide little opportunity for them to overcome this initial deficiency; in fact they fall farther behind the white majority in the development of several skills which are critical to making a living and participating fully in modern society. Whatever may be the combination of nonschool factors—poverty, community attitudes, low educational level of parents—which put minority children at a disadvantage in verbal and nonverbal skills when they enter the first grade, the fact is the schools have not overcome it. . . .

1.4 Relation of achievement to school characteristics

If 100 students within a school take a certain test, there is likely to be great variation in their scores. One student may score 97 percent, another 13; several may score 78 percent. This represents variability in achievement within the particular school.

It is possible, however, to compute the average of the scores made by the students within that school and to compare it with the average score, or achievement, of pupils within another school, or many other schools. These comparisons then represent variations between schools.

When one sees that the average score on a verbal achievement test in school X is 55 and in school Y is 72, the natural question to ask is: What accounts for the difference?

There are many factors that may be associated with the difference. This analysis concentrates on one cluster of those factors. It attempts to describe what relationship the school's characteristics themselves (libraries, for example, and teachers and laboratories, and so on) seem to have to the achievement of majority and minority groups (separately for each group on a nationwide basis, and also for Negro and white pupils in the North and South).

The first finding is that the schools are remarkably similar in the way they relate to the achievement of their pupils when the socioeconomic background of the students is taken into account. It is known that socioeconomic factors bear a strong relation to academic achievement. When these factors are statistically controlled, however, it appears that differences between schools account for only a small fraction of differences in pupil achievement.

The schools do differ, however, in their relation to the various racial and ethnic groups. The average white student's achievement seems to be less affected by the strength or weakness of his school's facilities, curriculums, and teachers than is the average minority pupil's. To put it another way, the achievement of minority pupils depends more on the schools they attend than does the achievement of majority pupils. Thus, 20 percent of the achievement of Negroes in the South is associated with the particular schools they go to, whereas only 10 percent of the achievement of whites in the South is. Except for Oriental Americans, this general result is found for all minorities.

The inference might then be made that improving the school of a minority pupil may increase his achievement more than would improving the school of a white child increase his. Similarly, the average minority pupil's achievement may suffer more in a school of low quality than might the average white pupil's. In short, whites, and to a lesser extent Oriental Americans, are less affected one way or the other by the quality of their schools than are minority pupils. This indicates that it is for the most disadvantaged children that improvements in school quality will make the most difference in achievement.

All of these results suggest the next question: What are the school characteristics that are most related to achievement? In other words, what factors in the school seem to be most important in affecting achievement?

It appears that variations in the facilities and curriculums of the schools account for relatively little variation in pupil achievement insofar as this is measured by standard tests. Again, it is for majority whites that the variations make the least difference; for minorities, they make somewhat more difference. Among the facilities that show some relationship to achievement are several for which minority pupils' schools are less well equipped relative to whites. For example, the existence of science laboratories showed a small but consistent relationship to achievement, and . . . minorities, especially Negroes, are in schools with fewer of these laboratories.

The quality of teachers shows a stronger relationship to pupil achievement. Furthermore, it is progressively greater at higher grades, indicating a cumulative impact of the qualities of teachers in a school on the pupil's achievements. Again, teacher quality seems more important to minority achievement than to that of the majority.

It should be noted that many characteristics of teachers were not measured in this survey; therefore, the results are not at all conclusive regarding the specific characteristics of teachers that are most important. Among those measured in the survey, however, those that bear the highest relationship to pupil achievement are first, the teacher's score on the verbal skills test, and then his educational background—both his own level of education and that of his parents. On both

of these measures, the level of teachers of minority students, especially Negroes, is lower.

Finally, it appears that a pupil's achievement is strongly related to the educational backgrounds and aspirations of the other students in the school. Only crude measures of these variables were used (principally the proportion of pupils with encyclopedias in the home and the proportion planning to go to college). Analysis indicates, however, that children from a given family background, when put in schools of different social composition, will achieve at quite different levels. This effect is again less for white pupils than for any minority group other than Orientals. Thus, if a white pupil from a home that is strongly and effectively supportive of education is put in a school where most pupils do not come from such homes, his achievement will be little different than if he were in a school composed of others like himself. But if a minority pupil from a home without much educational strength is put with schoolmates with strong educational backgrounds, his achievement is likely to increase.

This general result, taken together with the earlier examinations of school differences, has important implications for equality of educational opportunity. . . . The principal way in which the school environments of Negroes and whites differ is in the composition of their student bodies, and it turns out that the composition of the student bodies has a strong relationship to the achievement of Negro and other minority pupils.

This analysis has concentrated on the educational opportunities offered by the schools in terms of their student body composition, facilities, curriculums, and teachers. This emphasis, while entirely appropriate as a response to the legislation calling for the survey, nevertheless neglects important factors in the variability between individual pupils within the same school; this variability is roughly four times as large as the variability between schools. For example, a pupil attitude factor, which appears to have a stronger relationship to achievement than do all the "school" factors together, is the extent to which an individual feels that he has some control over his own destiny. . . . The responses of pupils to questions in the survey show that minority pupils, except for Orientals, have far less conviction than whites that they can affect their own environments and futures. When they do, however, their achievement is higher than that of whites who lack that conviction.

Furthermore, while this characteristic shows little relationship to most school factors, it is related, for Negroes, to the proportion of whites in the schools. Those Negroes in schools with a higher proportion of whites have a greater sense of control. This finding suggests that the direction such an attitude takes may be associated with the pupil's school experience as well as his experience in the larger community. . . .

1.5   Other surveys and studies

Future Teachers

Since a number of investigations of teacher qualification in the past few years have indicated that teachers of Negro children are less qualified than those who teach primarily majority children, this survey investigated whether there might be some promise that the situation may be changed by college students now preparing to become teachers. To this end, questionnaire and achievement test data were secured from about 17,000 college freshmen and 5,500 college seniors in 32 teacher training colleges in 18 States that in 1960 included over 90 percent of the Nation's Negro population. Some of the findings of this survey are:

1. At both the freshman and senior levels, future teachers are very similar to students in their colleges who are following other career lines. (It should be remembered that these comparisons are limited to students in colleges that have a primary mission in the training of teachers, and is not, of course, a random sample of all colleges.)

2. Majority students being trained at the college level to enter teaching have a stronger preparation for college than have Negro students; that is, they had more courses in foreign languages, English, and mathematics, made better grades in high school, and more often were in the highest track in English.

3. Data from the senior students suggest that colleges do not narrow the gap in academic training between Negro and majority pupils; indeed, there is some evidence that the college curriculum increases this difference, at least in the South.

4. Substantial test score differences exist between Negro and white future teachers at both freshman and senior levels, with approximately 15 percent of Negroes exceeding the average score of majority students in the same region. (This figure varies considerably depending on the test, but in no case do as many as 25 percent of Negroes exceed the majority average.)

5. The test data indicate that the gap in test results widens in the South between the freshman and senior years. The significance of this finding lies in the fact that most Negro teachers are trained in the Southern States.

6. The preferences of future teachers for certain kinds of schools and certain kinds of pupils raise the question of the match between the expectations of teacher recruits and the characteristics of the employment opportunities.

The preferences of future teachers were also studied. Summarized in terms of market conditions, it seems apparent that far too many future teachers prefer to teach in an academic high school; that there is a far greater proportion of children of blue-collar workers than of teachers being produced who prefer to teach them; that there is a very substantial number of white teachers-in-training, even in the South, who prefer to teach in racially mixed schools; that very few future teachers of either race wish to teach in predominantly minority schools; and finally, that high-ability pupils are much more popular with future teachers than low-ability ones. The preferences of Negro future teachers are more compatible with the distribution of needs in the market than are those of the majority; too few of the latter, relative to the clientele requiring service, prefer blue-collar or low-ability children or prefer to teach in racially heterogeneous schools, or in special curriculum, vocational, or commercial schools. These data indicate that under the present organization of schools, relatively few of the best prepared future teachers will find their way into classrooms where they can offset some of the environmental disadvantage suffered by minority children.

School Enrollment and Dropouts

Another extensive study explored enrollment rates of children of various ages, races, and socioeconomic categories using 1960 census data. The study included also an investigation of school dropouts using the October 1965 Current Population Survey of the Bureau of the Census. This survey uses a carefully selected sample of 35,000 households. It was a large enough sample to justify reliable nationwide estimates for the Negro minority but not for other minorities. In this section the word "white" includes the Mexican American and Puerto Rican minorities.

According to the estimates of the Current Population Survey, approximately 6,960,000 persons of ages 16 and 17 were living in the United States in October 1965. Of this number 300,000 (5 percent) were enrolled in college, and therefore, were not considered by this Census Bureau study. Of the remaining, approximately 10 percent, or 681,000 youth of 16 and 17, had left school prior to completion of high school.

. . . About 17 percent of Negro adolescents (ages 16 and 17) [had] dropped out of school whereas the corresponding number for white adolescents [was] 9 percent. . . .

Relation of Integration to Achievement

An education in integrated schools can be expected to have major effects on attitudes toward members of other racial groups. At its best, it can develop attitudes appropriate to the integrated society these students will live in; at its worst, it can create hostile camps of Negroes and whites in the same school. Thus, there is more to "school integration" than merely putting Negroes and whites in the same building, and there may be more important consequences of integration than its effect on achievement.

Yet the analysis of school factors described earlier suggests that in the long run, integration should be expected to have a positive effect on Negro achievement as well. An analysis was carried out to seek such effects on achievement which might appear in the short run. This analysis of the test performance of Negro children in integrated schools indicates positive effects of integration, though rather small ones. . . .

Those pupils who first entered integrated schools in the early grades record consistently higher scores than the other groups, although the differences are again small. . . .

Although the differences are small, and although the degree of integration within the school is not known, there is evident, even in the short run, an effect of school integration on the reading and mathematics achievement of Negro pupils. . . .

Case Studies of School Integration

As part of the survey, two sets of case studies of school integration were commissioned. These case studies examine the progress of integration in individual cities and towns, and illustrate problems that have arisen not only in these communities but in many others as well. . . .

Compliance in a small community.—Many large metropolitan areas North and South are moving toward resegregation despite attempts by school boards and city administrations to reverse the trend. Racial housing concentration in large cities has reinforced neighborhood school patterns of racial isolation while, at the same time, many white families have moved to the suburbs and other families have taken their children out of the public school system, enrolling them instead in private and parochial schools. Small towns and medium-sized areas, North and South, on the other hand, are to some extent desegregating their schools.

In the Deep South, where there has been total school segregation for generations, there are signs of compliance within a number of school systems. The emphasis on open enrollment and freedom-of-choice plans, however, has tended to lead to token enrollment of Negroes in previously white schools. In school systems integrated at some grade levels but not at others, the choice of high school grades rather than elementary grades has tended further to cut down on the number of Negroes choosing to transfer because of the reluctance to take extra risks close to graduation. . . .

A voluntary transfer plan for racial balance in elementary schools.—The public schools are more rigidly segregated at the elementary level than in the higher grades. In the large cities, elementary schools have customarily made assignments in terms of neighborhood boundaries. Housing segregation has, therefore, tended to build a segregated elementary school system in most cities in the North and, increasingly, in the South as well, where *de facto* segregation is replacing *de jure* segregation.

Various communities have been struggling to find ways to achieve greater racial balance while retaining the neighborhood school. Bussing, pairing, redistricting, consolidating, and many other strategies have been tried. Many have failed; others have achieved at least partial success. In New Haven, Conn., considerable vigor has been applied to the problem: Whereas pairing was tried at the junior high level introducing compulsory integration, a voluntary transfer plan was implemented at the elementary level. Relief of overcrowding was given as the central intent of the transfer plan, but greater racial balance was achieved since it was the Negro schools that were overcrowded. With the provision of new school buildings, however, this indirect stimulus to desegregation will not be present. In New Haven the transfer plan was more effective than in many other communities because of commitment of school leadership, active solicitation of transfers by door-to-door visits, provision of transportation for those transferring, teacher cooperation, heterogeneous grouping in the classrooms, and other factors.

The original plan provided that a student could apply to any one of a cluster of several elementary schools within a designated "cluster district," and the application would be approved on the basis of availability of space, effect on racial balance and certain unspecified educational factors; that students "presently enrolled" at a particular school would be given priority; and that transportation would be provided where necessary.

Desegregation by redistricting at the junior high school level.—The junior high schools, customarily grades seven to nine, have been the focus of considerable effort and tension in desegregation plans in many communities. With most areas clinging to the neighborhood school at the elementary level with resultant patterns of racial concentration, and with high schools already more integrated because of their lesser reliance upon neighborhood boundaries and their prior consolidation to achieve maximum resources, junior high schools have been a natural place to start desegregation plans. Like the elementary schools, they have in the past been assigned students on the basis of geography; but on the other hand, they tend to represent some degree of consolidation in that children from several elementary schools feed one junior high school. Further, parental pressures have been less severe for the maintenance of rigid neighborhood boundaries than at the elementary level.

Pairing of two junior high schools to achieve greater racial balance has been tried in a number of communities. Redistricting or redrawing the boundaries of areas that feed the schools has been tried in other areas. In Berkeley, Calif., after considerable community tension and struggle, a plan was put into effect that desegregated all three junior high schools (one had been desegregated previously). All the ninth graders were sent to a single school, previously Negro, and the seventh and eighth graders were assigned to the other two schools. The new ninth grade school was given a new name to signal its new identity in the eyes of the community. . . .

A plan for racial balance at the high school level.—In a number of communities, students are assigned to high schools on the basis of area of residence and hence racial imbalance is continued. In Pasadena, Calif., a plan was initiated to redress this imbalance by opening places in the schools to allow the transfer of Negroes to the predominantly white high school. A measure of success was achieved but only after much resistance. Of interest particularly in this situation was the legal opinion that attempts to achieve racial balance were violations of the Constitution and that race could not be considered as a factor in school districting. Apparently previous racial concentration, aided by districting, had not been so regarded, yet attempts at desegregation were. The school board found its task made more difficult by such legal maneuvering. . . . The court . . . finally upheld the policy of transfers to achieve racial balance.

Segregation at a vocational school.—The Washburne Trade School in Chicago seems to be effectively segregated by virtue of the practices and customs of the trade unions, whose apprenticeship programs have been characterized by racial isolation. Washburne has presented the same picture since its founding in 1919 after the passage of the Smith-Hughes Act by Congress. That act provides for the creation of apprenticeship programs in which skilled workers are trained both in school and on the job. For example, a young man who wishes to be certified as a plumber may work at his job 4 days a week and attend a formal training program at least 1 day or more or evenings a week.

The apprenticeship programs are heavily financed and regulated by the Federal Government through the Department of Labor and the Department of Health, Education, and Welfare. In recent years the regulations have focused increasingly upon racial segregation within the union structures. One of the causes for this concern has been the rather discouraging racial pattern in the apprenticeship schools. Washburne seems to preserve that pattern. In 1960 an informal estimate showed that fewer than 1 percent of the 2,700 Washburne students were Negroes. Half of the apprenticeship programs conducted at the school had no Negroes whatsoever. . . .

Relation of a university to school desegregation.—Education is a continuum—from kindergarten through college—and increasingly public school desegregation plans are having an impact on colleges in the same area, particularly those colleges which are city or state supported. Free tuition, as in the New York City colleges, has no meaning for members of minority groups who have dropped out of school in high school and little meaning for those whose level of achievement is too low to permit work at the college level. A number of colleges, through summer tutorials and selective admittance of students whose grades would otherwise exclude them, are trying to redress this indirect form of racial imbalance.

JAMES S. COLEMAN

"The Coleman Report": A Commentary (1966) *

The Civil Rights Act of 1964 contains a section numbered 402, which went largely unnoticed at the time. This section instructs the Commissioner of Education to carry out a survey "concerning the lack of availability of equal educational opportunities" by reason of race, religion or national origin, and to report to Congress and the President within two years. The Congressional intent

* James S. Coleman, "Equal Schools or Equal Students?" *Public Interest*, No. 4 (Summer, 1966), pp. 70–75. © 1966 by National Affairs, Inc. Used by permission.

in this section is somewhat unclear. But if, as is probable, the survey was initially intended as a means of finding areas of continued intentional discrimination, the intent later became less punitive-oriented and more future-oriented: *i.e.,* to provide a basis for public policy, at the local, state, and national levels, which might overcome inequalities of educational opportunity.

[From 1964 to 1966] a remarkably vast and comprehensive survey was conducted, focussing principally on the inequalities of educational opportunity experienced by five racial and ethnic minorities: Negroes, Puerto Ricans, Mexican Americans, American Indians, and Oriental Americans. In the central and largest portion of the survey, nearly 600,000 children at grades 1, 3, 6, 9, and 12, in 4000 schools in all 50 states and the District of Columbia, were tested and questioned; 60,000 teachers in these schools were questioned and self-tested; and principals of these schools were also questioned about their schools. The tests and questionnaires (administered in the fall of 1965 by Educational Testing Service) raised a considerable controversy in public school circles and among some parents, with concern ranging from Federal encroachment on the local education system to the spectre of invasion of privacy. Nevertheless, with a participation rate of about 70% of all the schools sampled, the survey was conducted. . . .

The summary of the report [*Equality of Educational Opportunity,* 1966] has appeared to many who have read it to be curiously "flat," lacking in emphases and policy implications. Much of the same flatness can be found in the larger report. The seeming flatness probably derives from three sources: the research analyst's uneasiness in moving from description to implications; the government agency's uneasiness with survey findings that may have political repercussions; and, perhaps more important than either of these, the fact that the survey results do not lend themselves to the provision of simple answers. Nevertheless, the report is not so uncontroversial as it appears. And

some of its findings, though cautiously presented, have sharp implications.

Perhaps the greatest virtue of this survey —though it has many faults—is that it did not take a simple or politically expedient view of educational opportunity. To have done so would have meant to measure (a) the objective characteristics of schools— number of books in the library, age of buildings, educational level of teachers, accreditation of the schools, and so on; and (b) the actual extent of racial segregation in the schools. The survey did look into these matters (and found less inequity in school facilities and resources, more in the extent of segregation, than is commonly supposed); but its principal focus of attention was not on what resources go into education, but on what product comes out. It did this in a relatively uncomplicated way, which is probably adequate for the task at hand: by tests which measured those areas of achievement most necessary for further progress in school, in higher education, and in successful competition in the labor market—that is, verbal and reading skills, and analytical and mathematical skills. Such a criterion does not allow statements about absolute levels of inequality or equality of education provided by the schools, because obviously there are more influences than the school's on a child's level of achievement in school, and there are more effects of schools than in these areas of achievement. What it does do is to broaden the question beyond the school to all those educational influences that have their results in the level of verbal and mathematical skill a young person is equipped with when he or she enters the adult world. In effect, it takes the perspective of this young adult, and says that what matters to him is, not how "equal" his school is, but rather whether he is equipped at the end of school to compete on an equal basis with others, whatever his social origins. From the perspective of society, it assumes that what is important is not to "equalize the schools" in some formal sense, but to insure that children from all groups come into adult society so equipped as to insure their full participation in this society.

Another way of putting this is to say that the schools are successful only insofar as they reduce the dependence of a child's opportunities upon his social origins. We can think of a set of conditional probabilities: the probability of being prepared for a given occupation or for a given college at the end of high school, conditional upon the child's social origins. The effectiveness of the schools consists, in part, of making the conditional probabilities less conditional —that is, less dependent upon social origins. Thus, equality of educational opportunity implies, not merely "equal" schools, but equally effective schools, whose influences will overcome the differences in starting point of children from different social groups.

This approach to educational opportunity, using as it does achievement on standardized tests, treads on sensitive ground. Differences in average achievement between racial groups can lend themselves to racist arguments of genetic differences in intelligence; even apart from this, they can lead to invidious comparisons between groups which show different average levels of achievement. But it is precisely the avoidance of such sensitive areas that can perpetuate the educational deficiences with which some minorities are equipped at the end of schooling.

What, then, does the survey find with regard to effects of schooling on test achievement? Children were tested at the beginning of grades 1, 3, 6, 9, and 12. Achievement of the average American Indian, Mexican American, Puerto Rican, and Negro (in this descending order) was much lower than the average white or Oriental American, at all grade levels. The amount of difference ranges from about half a standard deviation to one standard deviation at early grade levels. At the 12th grade, it increases to beyond one standard deviation. (One standard deviation difference means that about 85% of the minority group children score below the aver-

age of the whites, while if the groups were equal only about 50% would score below this average.) The grade levels of difference range up to 5 years of deficiency (in math achievement) or 4 years (in reading skills) at the 12th grade. In short, the differences are large to begin with, and they are even larger at higher grades.

Two points, then, are clear: (1) *these minority children have a serious educational deficiency at the start of school, which is obviously not a result of school;* and (2) *they have an even more serious deficiency at the end of school, which is obviously in part a result of school.*

Thus, by the criterion stated earlier—that the effectiveness of schools in creating equality of educational opportunity lies in making the conditional probabilities of success less conditional—the schools appear to fail. At the end of school, the conditional probabilities of high achievement are even *more* conditional upon racial or ethnic background than they are at the beginning of school.

There are a number of results from the survey which give further evidence on this matter. First, within each racial group, the strong relation of family economic and educational background to achievement does not diminish over the period of school, and may even increase over the elementary years. Second, most of the variation in student achievement lies within the same school; very little of it is between schools. The implication of these last two results is clear: family background differences account for much more variation in achievement than do school differences.

Even the school-to-school variation in achievement, though relatively small, is itself almost wholly due to the *social* environment provided by the school: the educational backgrounds and aspirations of other students in the school, and the educational backgrounds and attainments of the teachers in the school. *Per pupil expenditure, books in the library, and a host of other facilities and curricular measures show virtually no relation to achievement if the "social" environ-*

ment of the school—the educational back-grounds of other students and teachers—is held constant.

The importance of this last result lies, of course, in the fact that schools, as currently organized, are quite culturally homogeneous as well as quite racially segregated: teachers tend to come from the same cultural groups (and especially from the same race) as their students, and the student bodies are themselves relatively homogeneous. Given this homogeneity, the principal agents of effectiveness in the schools—teachers and other students—act to maintain or reinforce the initial differences imposed by social origins.

One element illustrates well the way in which the current organization of schools maintains the differences over generations: a Negro prospective teacher leaves a Negro teacher's college with a much lower level of academic competence (as measured by the National Teacher's Examination) than does his white counterpart leaving his largely white college; then he teaches Negro children (in school with other Negro children, ordinarily from educationally deficient backgrounds), who learn at a lower level, in part because of his lesser competence; some of these students, in turn, go into teacher training institutions to become poorly-trained teachers of the next generation.

Altogether, *the sources of inequality of educational opportunity appear to lie first in the home itself and the cultural influences immediately surrounding the home; then they lie in the schools' ineffectiveness to free achievement from the impact of the home, and in the schools' cultural homogeneity which perpetuates the social influences of the home and its environs.*

Given these results, what do they suggest as to avenues to equality of educational opportunity? Several elements seem clear:

a) For those children whose family and neighborhood are educationally disadvantaged, it is important to replace this family environment as much as possible with an educational environment—by starting school at an earlier age, and by having a school which begins very early in the day and ends very late.

b) It is important to reduce the social and racial homogeneity of the school environment, so that those agents of education that do show some effectiveness—teachers and other students—are not mere replicas of the student himself. In the present organization of schools, it is the neighborhood school that most insures such homogeneity.

c) The educational program of the school should be made more effective than it is at present. The weakness of this program is apparent in its inability to overcome initial differences. It is hard to believe that we are so inept in educating our young that we can do no more than leave young adults in the same relative competitive positions we found them in as children.

Several points are obvious: It is not a solution simply to pour money into improvement of the physical plants, books, teaching aids, of schools attended by educationally disadvantaged children. For other reasons, it will not suffice merely to bus children or otherwise achieve pro forma integration. (One incidental effect of this would be to increase the segregation within schools, through an increase in tracking.)

The only kinds of policies that appear in any way viable are those which do not seek to improve the education of Negroes and other educationally disadvantaged at the expense of those who are educationally advantaged. This implies new kinds of educational institutions, with a vast increase in expenditures for education—not merely for the disadvantaged, but for all children. The solutions might be in the form of educational parks, or in the form of private schools paid by tuition grants (with Federal regulations to insure racial heterogeneity), public (or publicly-subsidized) boarding schools (like the North Carolina Advancement School), or still other innovations. This approach also implies reorganization of the curriculum within schools. One of the major reasons for "tracking" is the narrowness of our teaching methods—they can tolerate only a narrow range of skill in the same classroom. Methods which greatly widen the range are necessary to make possible racial and cultural integration within a school—and thus to make possible the informal learning that other students of higher educational levels can provide. Such curricular innovations are possible—but, again, only through the investment of vastly greater sums in education than currently occurs.

It should be recognized, of course, that the goal described here—of equality of educational opportunity through the schools—is far more ambitious than has ever been posed in our society before. The schools were once seen as a supplement to the family in bringing a child into his place in adult society, and they still function largely as such a supplement, merely perpetuating the inequalities of birth. Yet the conditions imposed by technological change, and by our postindustrial society, quite apart from any ideals of equal opportunity, require a far more primary role for the school, if society's children are to be equipped for adulthood.

One final result of the survey gives an indication of still another—and perhaps the most important—element necessary for equality of educational opportunity for Negroes. One attitude of students was measured at grades 9 and 12—an attitude which indicated the degree to which the student felt in control of his own fate. For example,

one question was: "Agree or disagree: good luck is more important than hard work for success." Another was: "Agree or disagree: every time I try to get ahead someone or something stops me." Negroes much less often than whites had such a sense of control of their fate—a difference which corresponds directly to reality, and which corresponds even more markedly to the Negro's historical position in American society. However, despite the very large achievement differences between whites and Negroes at the 9th and 12th grades, *those Negroes who gave responses indicating a sense of control of their own fate achieved higher on the tests than those whites who gave the opposite responses. This attitude was more highly related to achievement than any other factor in the student's background or school.*

This result suggests that internal changes in the Negro, changes in his conception of himself in relation to his environment, may have more effect on Negro achievement than any other single factor. The determination to overcome relevant obstacles, and the belief that he will overcome them—attitudes that have appeared in an organized way among Negroes only in recent years in some civil rights groups—may be the most crucial elements in achieving equality of opportunity —not because of changes they will create in the white community, but principally because of the changes they create in the Negro himself.

REDRESSING THE IMBALANCE OF OPPORTUNITY: PROGRESS TOWARD AN AMERICAN IDEAL

PAUL CONKLIN
A New Approach to Indian Education in America (1967) *

On the northern flank of Arizona's Black Mountain, an experiment has been started that could change the entire structure and

* Paul Conklin, "Good Day at Rough Rock," *American Education,* Vol. III, No. 2 (February, 1967), pp. 4–9. Used by permission.

philosophy of Indian education in America. Here, in a bleak setting of desert, rock, and sagebrush, near the center of the country's largest reservation—25,000 square miles—that is home to 105,000 Navajos, Robert A. Roessel, Jr., director of the Rough Rock Demonstration School, is applying a community control approach that could hold promise for poor, uneducated people everywhere. His method—to work with the Indians, not on them. His thesis—that Indians ought to be able to be Americans and Indians, too. "Education as the Indian knows it on the reservation can best be characterized as the Either-Or type," says Dr. Roessel, a vigorous man with an unruly, greying thatch of hair. "One is either an Indian or a white man, and the way we have traditionally weighted things, the good way is always the non-Indian way and the bad is always the Indian. We tell Indian children they are superstitious and primitive and that their hogans are dirty. We try to impose our values and tell them they should eat green, leafy vegetables and sleep on a bed and brush their teeth. In short, we try to make white men out of Indians. The Indian child listens and looks at himself and sees that he doesn't measure up. In his own eyes he is a failure. Education can be a shattering experience when one is taught nothing but negative things about himself for 12 years."

As he talks, Roessel occasionally squints through the window of his comfortable living room which, in keeping with his educational beliefs, is furnished in modern and Navajo. Outside, the wind blows incessantly, swirling sand against the panes and wearing away at the light-colored buildings that blend with the monochromatic landscape. In the far distance can be seen the looming red sandstone monoliths of Monument Valley.

"Now Indians have begun to question whether it is necessary for them to lose their heritage in order to become citizens of the United States," he continues. "And so the Both-And— both white and Indian—approach to Indian education was born."

Rough Rock Demonstration School is a self-contained community within a scattered population of about 600. It has to be. The nearest paved road is 16 miles away and the nearest sizable town, Gallup, N. Mex., 120 miles. The school has its own water system and fire engine, a spacious classroom-office building with a gymnasium, a separate kitchen-dining room, and a boys' dormitory and a girls' dormitory, each with a capacity of 165 children. The staff are quartered in 36 houses and 8 apartments. Roessel's expectations and hopes for the experiment come through clearly as he speaks of the school.

"Rough Rock is the first school to have the tools and resources to see whether this new approach can be effective. We want to instill in our youngsters a sense of pride in being Indian. We want to show them that they can be Indian and American at the same time, that they can take the best from each way of life and combine it into something viable. When I first came on the reservation as a teacher, I told children they had two legs, one being their Navajo heritage and the other the best part of the white world. They couldn't get along with just one leg, but needed both to be secure and whole."

The Rough Rock staff includes ten full-time classroom teachers, a remedial reading specialist, a speech therapist, an art teacher, a librarian, two TESL (Teaching English as a Second Language) specialists, and two recreation leaders. Fifteen members of the Volunteers in Service to America (VISTA) also work at the school. Of the 91 full-time people on the payroll, 46 are Indian, 35 of them from Rough Rock, a fact that illustrates a vital part of the Roessel philosophy —involving the local community in school life as much as possible.

The school laundry is a good example. Bureau of Indian Affairs schools typically contract their laundry out to private firms, which are usually located in towns many miles away. In the Rough Rock budget $5,000 was set aside for this purpose. Roessel spent $2,000 on washing machines and used the rest to hire two local women to operate them.

No opportunities are missed at the school to help the children understand themselves as Indians. Navajo motifs are freely mixed in with other classroom decorations. The library has a Navajo corner. Recordings of the Navajo music and rituals are played during the school day.

In the evening old men, the historians

and medicine men of the tribe, come to the dormitories and tell Navajo folk tales and legends. The staff is preparing biographies of successful Navajos to give the students something on which to pattern their own lives.

Each day, 35 minutes of class time are set aside in the preschool sections and lower three grades, and 45 minutes in grades three through six for "cultural identification" lessons. During the first six weeeks the lessons cover the Navajo hogan—its history, how it is built, the ceremonies that surround it, and how life is conducted in it. The second six weeks cover farming and caring for livestock. The third period deals with reservation facilities, the land and climate, Navajo history and tribal government.

A crucial part of "cultural identification" at Rough Rock is the adult arts and crafts program, which has a twofold purpose: to revive dying Navajo handicrafts so that the children of the school can observe the process, and to produce more local wage-earners.

This is the domain of Dr. Roessel's wife, Ruth, who is Navajo. A graduate of Arizona State University and a member of the Governor's Advisory Committee on Indian Education, Ruth is one of the reservation's most skilled weavers. She has also proved herself an able recruiter. Ambrose Roanhorse, renowned as the reservation's most skillful silversmith, came to Rough Rock at her invitation. His first apprentices have already reached the stage where they are ready to market their jewelry.

Sharing the school's arts and crafts center with the silversmiths are a weaver and a moccasin maker. They will soon be joined by basketmakers, potters, leather craftsmen, and rawhide workers.

"This is not art for art's sake, although the Navajo puts great store in creating beautiful things. These skills are extremely marketable and we are training people who otherwise would have no income," Roessel explains. The Indians now eke out a precarious existence herding sheep.

At one time in most Indian schools the children were punished if they spoke Navajo. At Rough Rock they are encouraged and even forced to use their own language. Navajo is taught in the fourth, fifth, and sixth grades for one hour three days a week. Also, for the first time on the reservation, portions of regular classes, such as arithmetic and social studies, are held in Navajo. The purpose is to see whether students find it easier to retain subject matter when taught in their native language, as research has suggested may be the case.

Roessel provides evening tutoring lessons in Navajo for his staff members who do not speak the language. They find it tough going, since Navajo—a harsh, gutt[u]ral tongue—is classified by linguists as the world's second most difficult language.

Because of the importance the Both-And philosophy places on mastery of both English and Navajo, Rough Rock's TESL department is highly active at the school. English is taught formally twice a day, informally at all times. For example, as the children pass through the cafeteria line at noon they must ask for their food in English.

A teaching aid which TESL director Virginia Hoffman has found invaluable is the school's closed-circuit TV system. Once a month she writes a simple play, using staff members and VISTA personnel in the cast. A recent drama, "The Zegafferelebra," took place in a painted jungle. The message, spoken by animals with papier-maché heads, dealt with correct intonation and the lengthening of vowels. Future productions will be concerned with gender, number, tense, "to be," and "is going to."

The idea for the Rough Rock experiment began to take shape at Arizona State University in 1959 and 1960 while Roessel studied for a doctor's degree. To gather raw material for his thesis, he visited over 100 Indian communities, talking to the elders about their needs and aspirations.

Much of what Roessel learned during that period was incorporated in a proposal which he and a number of Indian leaders later presented to the Office of Economic Opportunity (OEO) for the establishment of a different kind of Indian school. The result, in 1965, was the Lukachukai Navajo Demonstration School, which foundered after only one year, primarily because of an awkward administrative set-up. The school was funded by OEO, which superimposed a staff of academic and community development specialists on the existing staff of the Bureau of Indian Affairs (BIA) boarding school at Lukachukai, a hamlet not far from Rough Rock. The administrative dichotomy proved too much, and OEO reluctantly withdrew its support.

BIA and OEO, still mindful of the need for a new approach to Indian education and wary of repeating their mistakes at Lukachukai, put up money for another demonstration school that would be independent of them both. The funds, $335,000 from OEO and $307,000 from BIA, were awarded to a private, nonprofit corporation called Demonstration in Navajo Education, Inc.—whose Navajo acronym DINE means the Navajos, or "the people." Roessel was recruited as director and BIA turned over a brand new $3.5 million school which it had just built in Rough Rock.

At the time, Roessel was director of Arizona State University's Indian Community Action Center, one of three such centers established by OEO to provide technical assistance and training to reservation Indians under its Community Action Program.

His decision to go to Rough Rock was not easily made. "I was happy at Tempe, and felt important. I had real influence in the OEO Indian program and went to Washington every week. It wasn't easy to come out here where the roads are terrible and the phones never work. But I had been writing articles too long saying what was wrong with Indian education and Indian programs. Here was a chance to put into practice what I believed, or shut up."

Soon after Roessel's arrival, the people of Rough Rock elected one woman and four men to the school board. All were middle-aged Navajos and only one had ever had as

much as a day of formal education. In a move that must have raised eyebrows in many quarters, control of the demonstration school was immediately passed over to the board.

"At least 50 schools on the reservation have their own boards, so in this respect Rough Rock is not unique," Rosessel points out. "But the traditional Indian board has a housekeeping function: it builds roads, maintains buildings, and acts as a truant officer. It has no authority or decision-making power, and the superintendent really calls the shots. What we have here is local control in the true sense for the first time.

"The greatest need of Indian education today," he continues, "is to involve Indians. The belief persists that Indians have neither the desire nor the ability to manage their own affairs. It's the old 'father-knows-best' approach that says it's up to me, an expert sitting behind my desk, to make policy for them. But the Both-And philosophy says that Indians are eager for responsibility and, if given a chance, they'll act creatively and assume leadership."

Roessel takes the principle of local control seriously. Once a week he and a few of his senior staff discuss a part of the master program with the school board, explaining the reasons the staff consider it important. In each instance the board has accepted the proposal, modifying it, however, and adding a Navajo cast to it. Roessel sees the modifications as strengthening the demonstration program. So strong is his faith in the board members that he is willing to scrap completely any part that they oppose.

It is not simply rhetoric when Roessel says of Rough Rock, "This is a community-oriented school, rather than child-oriented. In the past, Indian schools have taken little interest in their communities, but here we want to involve adults and teenagers, dropouts, people who have never been to school."

Rough Rock's school facilities—gym, kitchen, dormitories, shower rooms, library —are open to anybody who wants to use them. School fairs, movies, basketball games, talent nights have drawn crowds that increase steadily.

Rough Rock parents are encouraged to come to the school for board meetings, to spend time in the classrooms, to eat in the cafeteria, and to stay overnight in the dormitories. They sometimes come in team-drawn wagons, the men with stiff-brimmed hats and, if they are of the old generation, their hair drawn into tight knots at the back. The women wear long velveteen skirts, silver jewelry, and strings of turquoise and coral. Quiet and grave, they flit shyly about the school like old-fashioned ghosts.

"Our school board has told the parents of this district that they can't use the school as a dumping ground where they can leave their children and forget them. We believe the kids belong to their parents and not to the school. Instead of limiting the child to two or three visits home a year, as is the case in most schools, we let parents take their children home any weekend they want," Roessel says.

To make the dormitories more homelike and to avoid the usual ratio in dormitory staffing of one adult for every 60 children, Roessel employs eight parents to mend clothes, tell stories, help with the twice-a-week shower, and do a variety of other chores that parents know how to do best. For this they receive a dollar an hour. The parents change every six weeks; the school board handles recruiting. With help from instructional aides, parents, and VISTA workers, the Rough Rock adult-child ratio has dropped to 1 to 15.

Just as most Navajo parents know virtually nothing about the way reservation schools are operated, so, too, is it rare to find a teacher in the system who has any first-hand knowledge about how life is lived in the Navajo hogan. In a study conducted in 1963, the Indian Education Center at Arizona State University found that only 15 of 100 reservation teachers had ever visited an Indian home.

One of the reasons for this failure was that the heavy daily routine makes escape from the classroom almost impossible for the teacher. And often the teacher is afraid he will be unwelcome in the hogan. Rough Rock teachers visit the homes of all their students at least twice a year. They are accompanied by the child, and an interpreter when necessary, and tell the parents about their children's progress.

Roessel would also like each of his non-Indian teachers to live in a Navajo hogan for a week. "I want them to see what it means to haul water five miles, to chop wood for heat, to go to bed at dark because there is no light, to eat bread and coffee for a meal," he says.

By giving his staff an awareness of the peculiar texture of Navajo life, Roessel hopes to avert a repetition of the small-scale tragedy that resulted from a teacher's inexperience at another reservation school. The teacher was from the East. Her credentials were excellent, but she had never taught Navajo children before. She noticed one morning that the face and arms of one of her third grade boys were covered by something that looked like soot. In his hair was a substance that resembled grease. With a normal respect for cleanliness, the teacher asked the boy to wash himself. When he refused she took him to the bathroom and washed him.

The boy never returned to school. It turned out that his family had conducted an important healing ceremony on his sick sister, the "soot" and "grease" being part of the ceremonial painting. With her soap and water the teacher destroyed the healing powers of the ceremony. The girl died and the parents could not be shaken in their belief that it was the teacher's fault. No member of the family has set foot in a school since.

Programs for adults have claimed only the peripheral attention of Indian education officials in the past. Through a canvass of the 600 Navajos who live in the area of Rough Rock, it was learned that the men are most interested in auto mechanics instruction. Women want classes in cooking and nutrition. Both are interested in classes in basic literacy. They want to gain a rudimentary knowledge of money and how to make change so they will not be cheated when they buy at the store. They want to acquire a basic English vocabulary of about 50 words that can carry them through their trips to the local trading post and to the outside world.

"It is here in our work with adults that the most significant thrust is being made at Rough Rock. It is an area to which other demonstrations have not been directed, an area of little prior activity," Roessel says. "At Rough Rock the BIA and OEO have said to the Indians in effect, 'This is your school. Make of it what you want. Develop a curriculum that will reflect what you think is important.' This is an isolated, illiterate community where 95 percent of the people are uneducated, but I am convinced that they have the necessary vision and concern for their future."

It would be hard to find a more disadvantaged community than Rough Rock, where the average family of six makes $500 a year and where cultural life is utterly threadbare. Roessel believes that if Rough Rock can succeed—if these uneducated people can determine the educational needs of their children and their community, then it cannot be said that impoverished, uneducated people any place are unable to provide self-leadership.

"This is why Rough Rock is the most exciting thing going on in Indian education anywhere in the country," says Roessel. "This is why our program has ramifications far outside the Indian world."

OSCAR HANDLIN
The Goals of American Minority Groups (1966)*

Since 1954, and even more so since 1960, Americans concerned with resolving the

* Oscar Handlin, "The Goals of Integration." Reprinted with permission from *Dædalus,* Journal of the American Academy of Arts and Sciences, Boston, Massachusetts. Winter, 1966, "The Negro American—2."

dilemma posed by the Negro's plight in a society committed to equal rights have lived in a state of crisis. The destruction of the concept of "separate but equal" in the Brown Case was the culmination of a quarter-century of re-examination of the premise that the colored men of the United States could be held permanently in a position that was actually separate but unequal. The implications of that decision were not immediately clear; nor have they been clarified in the intervening eleven years.[1]

Had the decision been immediately acceded to, it might have been possible to begin at once to explore its consequences. Instead, the necessity for fighting a succession of guerrilla actions behind the lines has delayed any consideration of long-range problems. Attention has been so narrowly focused on tactical issues that there has been no time to consider ultimate goals. The civil rights movement, which is actually a congeries of quite disparate efforts, maintains the pretense of unity only by a resolute determination not to think of long-term objectives.

However, we know all too well, from an earlier conflict a century ago, that battles and even wars can be won and yet the fruits of victory lost through men's haziness about what they are fighting for. In the present situation, the inability to define the ultimate goals of the civil rights struggle is an unacknowledged threat that complicates immediate tactics and that may deprive this momentous upheaval of its meaning.

In the absence of defined goals, it is difficult to estimate the character or pace of change or even to judge its direction. Under these circumstances, organizational controls and leadership weaken. There is confusion about which objectives are salient, and issues tend to crop up of their own accord. Action is sporadic, local, and discontinuous

[1] I have treated the background of this problem in greater detail in *The American People in the Twentieth Century* (Cambridge, Mass., 1954); *Race and Nationality in American Life* (Boston, 1957); and *Fire-Bell in the Night* (Boston, 1964).

and is not related to any general standard of importance. Explosive activists, always ready to precipitate conflict, find tactical opportunities to determine the questions to be fought over while the established leadership has to tag along to maintain its influence. At the same time, the atmosphere of continuous crisis generates the obligation of solidarity. Those who dissent must be silent or be counted as sympathizers of the antagonists. No one wishes to be known as an Uncle Tom or a white liberal.[2]

Recent demonstrations of solidarity on behalf of civil rights have been impressive. The march on Washington in 1963 and from Selma in 1965 showed the extent to which diverse elements in American society coalesced in support of a common cause. These occasions have ceremonial significance; they manifest the extent to which a variety of people affirm their dislike of brutality and their faith in the orderly methods of democracy. There is no difficulty in eliciting unanimity of support for the slogan of equal rights as man and citizen as long as the terms remain vague and undefined.

But it is erroneous to regard these events or professions of sentiment as expressions of unity with reference to a program of action. The calls for brotherly love sounded on the platforms do not reduce the intensity of the hatreds in Harlem. White resentment at black demands is also stiffening. It is a mistake to judge the extent of backlash by the refusal to commit suicide in 1964; the California vote on Proposition Fourteen that

[2] The civil rights movement is neither unified nor represented by a single spokesman. The attitudes here discussed reflect a trend expressed in statements of individuals. There are helpful collections of these views in Harold R. Isaacs, *The New World of Negro Americans* (New York, 1963); and Robert Penn Warren, *Who Speaks for the Negro?* (New York, 1965). For the background, see Richard Bardolph, *The Negro Vanguard* (New York, 1959); August Meier, *Negro Thought in America 1880–1915* (Ann Arbor, Mich., 1963). On the extremists, see Irving Howe, "New Styles in 'Leftism,'" *Dissent*, Vol. 12, No. 3 (Summer, 1965), pp. 312, 314, 318 ff.

year was more revealing than the national vote against Goldwater. Popular sentiment is still for tolerance and against prejudice; but the time is approaching for a test of the meaning of that preference.[3]

Insofar as the civil rights movement has proceeded beyond the call for brotherly love or for equality, it has ventured upon unsure ground. Civil rights demands in Alabama and Mississippi are comprehensible; the promises of personal security, the ballot, and decent schools are familiar and long overdue. But the issues blur in the newer context of New York or Chicago or Atlanta where these minimal gains are well on the way to attainment. There the failure to define appropriate goals has created future difficulties, the shape of which is already apparent. The new problems are important not only because an increasing percentage of American Negroes live in an urban environment, but also because the range of decisions involved will confront the nation long after the difficulties of the rural South are resolved.

In the earlier stages of the struggle for equality, it was enough to ask that the government be color-blind. The barriers that confined the Negro were the products of law, and it was necessary to demand only the equal treatment that the Constitution guaranteed. Desegregation was the response to segregation; and it was a response that attracted the support not only of other underprivileged minorities but also of many Americans who found it in accord with their own creed of individual dignity and equality of opportunity.

In the past decade, emphasis has gradually and imperceptibly shifted from desegregation to integration, but without adequate awareness of the consequences and often with a profound ambiguity about the nature of the desirable goal.

The term integration sometimes refers to the openness of society, to a condition in

[3] See, for example, *New York Times'* survey of whites' attitudes, September 21, 1964; Dean Harper, "Aftermath of a Long, Hot Summer," *Trans-action*, Vol. 2, No. 5 (July-August, 1965), pp. 9, 10.

which every individual can make the maximum number of voluntary contacts with others without regard to qualifications of ancestry. In that sense, the objective is a leveling of all barriers to association other than those based on ability, taste, and personal preference.

But integration sometimes also refers to a condition in which individuals of each racial or ethnic group are randomly distributed through the society so that every realm of activity contains a representative cross section of the population. In that sense, the object is the attainment, in every occupational, educational, and residential distribution, of a balance among the constituent elements in the society.

In crucial matters of public policy, antithetical consequences follow from the two positions. The one calls for improvements in the Negroes' opportunities for jobs, housing, and schooling even though the group may remain as separate as before; the other puts a primary emphasis upon racial balance.

The civil rights movement has never made a clear choice between these alternatives, nor has any spokesman fully articulated the implications of the two points of view. But increasingly in the past five years, the thrust has been in the latter direction, toward an organization in which every sector of society is racially balanced; and it is in that sense that the term integration will be used in the discussion which follows.

In part the change of recent years was due to the very intensity of the struggle against an intransigent opposition. More important, however, was the perception that the leveling of governmental barriers was in itself inadequate to remove the handicaps under which colored people labored. The vicious cycle of slum housing, poor schools, lack of skills, and low income trapped the urban Negro and widened rather than closed the gap between him and others in the society. Deprivation became a pattern of life that hopelessly handicapped him in the competition for desirable places. The simple neutrality

of government would not relieve him of these shackles; positive action to compensate was essential. The state was to intervene to assure the disadvantaged a due proportion of well-paying jobs and to balance the population of neighborhoods and schools in a thoroughly integrated pattern. That assurance was deemed necessary to restore equality to the disadvantaged. Hence the campaigns to destroy *de facto* segregation in the public schools, to secure preferential hiring and job quotas for Negroes in industry, and to manage housing in the interest of mixed residential neighborhoods.

This profound shift in the tactics of the civil rights movement during the past decade has come without any clear estimation of the consequences. To clarify those consequences, it is necessary to resolve the ambiguities in the goals of the civil rights movement. Is the ultimate objective to eliminate the differences that actually divide the population of the United States and thus dissolve its people into a single homogeneous and undifferentiated mass? Or will it be possible to reach toward equality while retaining the social subgroupings produced by a heritage of diversity and by the problems of managing a free population of almost 200 million? The answer, upon which the welfare of all Americans rests, should, to a greater degree than in the past, influence the tactics of the civil rights struggle.

The view of integration as racial balance rests on two fallacious assumptions—that the position of the Negro is absolutely unique in the American experience and that racist prejudice is so thoroughly ingrained in the people of the United States that only positive exertions by the government will assure the colored man his rights. Neither proposition conforms to the evidence.

The Negro is unique, it is argued, because his color sets him off from the majority more decisively than the traits of other ethnic groups did and because slavery crippled him so seriously that he cannot compete on equal terms and needs a crutch to help him along.

Certainly slavery was a more traumatic experience than the centuries of persecution, the hardships of migration, and the generations of depressed proletarian existence from which the Irish peasants suffered. But the argument slights the Negro's powers of recuperation and exaggerates the extent to which the damage caused more than a century ago remains a permanent part of his character. There has been a tendency to underestimate the extent of his achievements even in the fifty years immediately after emancipation, under conditions immensely more difficult than those of the present. When one considers the backwardness of the Southern economy after 1865, the exclusion from political power, the racist prejudices, and the bitterness left by a great war, it was a respectable accomplishment to have formed stable family units, to have developed productive skills, and to have created an array of churches, lodges, and media for cultural expression, with the limited resources the group possessed. Few people released from bondage in any society have performed as creditably.[4]

The disadvantages from which the Negro suffers in 1965 are less the products of the plantation than of the great migration to the city in the past fifty years; and that experience he shares with the other ethnic groups who have participated in American urbanization. Of course the Negroes are different from the Poles or Italians or Jews, just as those peoples differ among, and from, each other. The differences, however, are not of kind but of degree, and they are largely explained by the recency of arrival of the colored men, by their greater numbers, and by their dense concentration in a few cities. The problems of prejudice and acculturation from which the most recent newcomers suf-

[4] Reconstruction literature generally focuses on the failures and the missed opportunities rather than on the achievements. See E. Franklin Frazier, *The Negro in the United States* (New York, 1957), pp. 135, 142; W. E. B. Du Bois, *Black Reconstruction in America* (New York, 1935).

fer had their counterparts among the earlier arrivals.[5]

Nor is color the sole and unique sign of ethnic visibility. It is no doubt the most prominent mode of social recognition; but much depends upon the social assessment of this as of other physical traits. The Japanese-Americans are far less visible in 1965 than they were in 1940 although their color has not changed. And the Kennedys are still identified as Irish after five generations in the New World, and despite their wealth, prominence, and whiteness.

The assumption that color has a unique differentiating quality rests upon the argument that American society is inherently racist, its promise of equality reserved only for the white man. It has become fashionable in the past few years to sneer at Myrdal's statement of the American creed of equality and to urge that only forceful measures will restrain the propensity to prejudice.

There was a racist period in American history in the sixty years after the end of the Civil War; but the hatreds of that period were peculiar to the time and place. Much more significant is the deeper tradition of equality before and since that interlude. The agony with which slaveholders like Thomas Jefferson and George Mason considered their own situation, the tortured efforts of early scientists to understand color differences, and the torment the abolitionists caused in the North and the South were the results of the inability to square the existing labor system with the belief in the brotherhood of man and the commitment to equality. And the changes since 1945 have been the result not of fear either of the Negroes or of Africans but of the awareness that equality is a necessary ideal of the Republic.

Furthermore, the Negro, while the most prominent, was not the sole target even in the racist period. Prejudice was not limited by race, creed, national origin, or previous condition of servitude. The majority of the

[5] Oscar Handlin, *The Newcomers. Negroes and Puerto Ricans in a Changing Metropolis* (New York, 1959).

victims of lynchings in those years were Negroes; but there were 1,293 white victims of the rope and faggot as against 3,436 black. Italians in New Orleans, a Jew in Georgia, and Greeks in Omaha also met the fury of mob violence. The Ku Klux Klan of 1924 was more concerned with Catholics and Jews than with colored men.[6]

Above all, the response of Americans to the crisis of the past decade reveals the effectiveness of the appeal to the creed of equality. Even Bogalusa is not South Africa; and the inability of the open advocates of racism to attract support is the best evidence of the extent of commitment to that creed.

In estimating the meanings of integration, therefore, it is entirely appropriate to examine the analogous if not identical experience of other ethnic groups. Their process of acculturation will throw light on the need for defining the goals and the strategy of the civil rights movement.

Barring a major overturn of the American social system, which at the moment appears neither probable nor desirable, change will come within definable limits and will involve choices among alternatives. And decisions on this matter will be more effective if they come within an informed context that makes it possible to envision their results.

The inequities which survive from the past cannot be understood or remedied without a comprehension of the social order that produced them. They are the pathological manifestations of a mechanism of adjustment which permitted that order to function. Their successful removal requires a consideration of the function they serve; otherwise, the alternatives are grim. Either the order will collapse to the injury of everyone, white as well as black, or else uncontrolled alterna-

tive modes of adjustment will recreate and perpetuate the diseased condition.

This was the error of most of the abolitionists, who thought they could extirpate slavery without considering the effects upon Southern society. The result by 1900 was the restoration of the Negro's subordination in other forms than slavery.[7]

Hence, the importance, in any effort to foresee future developments, of an understanding of segregation, of its relationship to equality, and of the probable effects of integration.

Popularly speaking, segregation was a response to the dissolution of earlier forms of stratification. In a slave regime, the physical separation of the dominant and subordinate populations was superfluous and inconvenient. In other relatively static societies, where places were rigidly defined and the symbols of status clearly fixed by law or custom, groups could mingle with considerable promiscuity because there were no problems of recognition and no dangers to the established hierarchy of persons and groups.[8]

In the South, segregation was a response to the abolition of slavery and to the threat to white superiority posed by Reconstruction. The pattern that emerged in the last quarter of the nineteenth century used the law to fix the identity of the Negroes and to confine them to inferior social places. To those ends it established a rigid etiquette of behavior and separate institutions that restricted the opportunities of the former slaves for education and employment. Within the limits thus established, residential separateness was unnecessary. The measures that implemented segregation were deliberate on

[6] Walter White, *Rope & Faggot* (New York, 1929), pp. 20, 227, 230 ff.; James E. Cutler, *Lynch-Law* (New York, 1905), pp. 170 ff.; J. E. Coxe, "New Orleans Mafia Incident," *Louisiana Historical Quarterly*, Vol. 20, No. 4 (October, 1937), pp. 1067 ff.; Theodore Saloutos, *Greeks in the United States* (Cambridge, Mass., 1964), pp. 62–69.

[7] See Dwight L. Dumond, *Anti-Slavery* (Ann Arbor, Mich., 1961); Martin Duberman, *The Antislavery Vanguard* (Princeton, N.J., 1965), pp. 137 ff.; James M. McPherson, *The Struggle for Equality* (Princeton, N.J., 1964); Willie Lee Rose, *Rehearsal for Reconstruction* (Indianapolis, Ind., 1964).

[8] See Frank Tannenbaum, *Slave and Citizen* (New York, 1946); Stanley M. Elkins, *Slavery* (Chicago, 1959).

the part of the whites; the purposes were clearly understood at the time. As for the Negroes, their wishes were of no consequence; once they were excluded from political power, violence induced their acquiescence. The result was a kind of order, the price of which was inequality of rights.[9]

In the freer, more fluid, and more mobile sections of the country, segregation was achieved by withdrawal rather than by restraint and was voluntary rather than compulsory. As the Northern cities expanded with the influx of waves of heterogeneous newcomers, the old residents moved away, and the new arrivals sorted themselves out in neighborhoods that reflected their own sense of community. Education, employment, religious affiliation, and associational life fell within lines that were not imposed by law or by violence but were shaped by informal and largely spontaneous connections of kinship or community.

Although the Northern Negro suffered from prejudice as did the Southern, society was not polarized but fragmented; and he found himself but one of many groups comparably situated, some of which suffered from disabilities similar to his own. Negroes did not confront a homogeneous white community with a single chain of command leading up to a unified leadership. They found a place among numerous communities, each with its own power structure and its own leaders.[10]

The function of separateness in this context was not to establish or to perpetuate the inferiority of one group, but rather to accommodate diverse patterns of life that were the products of differences in ethnic and sectional heritage, or in economic and social background. By reducing contacts at the points of potential tension, this adjustment permitted each group to organize its own institutions without the oversight or interference of others, and yet was flexible enough to preserve some degree of order in a highly complex society. Furthermore, the expanding cities possessed enough free space and their organization was so loosely articulated that individuals who preferred not to affiliate could refrain from doing so and could get along in whatever degree of detachment they wished. The ghetto arrangement was therefore totally different in intention as well as in form from the segregation of the South.

Indeed the fact that the pluralistic order took account of actual differences within the population made it possible to preserve the *concept* of equality. Not every man was equally qualified in terms of inherited capital, cultural traits, personality, and intelligence to pursue equally the goals of success in American life. But the pursuit of happiness was not a single, unified scramble in which every individual sought the same prizes and in which only a few could be winners while the rest were doomed to frustration. In the stated beliefs of the society, every boy could grow up to be President— of the United States or at least a railroad. Americans could cling to faith in that useful proposition because they never subjected it to the test of practice. In reality the disparity of aspirations and career lines drew only a few persons into the competition for those lofty places while relatively independent subsystems, with their own values and rewards, provided satisfying alternatives to many more. The children of Irish or Italian parents did not count themselves failures if their lives did not follow a course identical with that of the children of the Yankees. They had their own criteria of achieve-

[9] C. Vann Woodward, *The Strange Career of Jim Crow* (New York, 1957) describes the process.

[10] See T. J. Woofter, *Negro Problem in Cities* (New York, 1928), pp. 177 ff.; Howard Brotz, *The Black Jews of Harlem* (New York, 1964); John Daniels, *In Freedom's Birthplace* (Boston, 1914), pp. 133 ff.; W. E. B. Du Bois, *The Philadelphia Negro* (Philadelphia, 1899), pp. 197 ff., 389 ff.; St. Clair Drake, *Churches and Voluntary Associations in the Chicago Negro Community* (Chicago, 1940); St. Clair Drake and Horace R. Cayton, *Black Metropolis* (New York, 1962), Vol. I, pp. 174 ff.

ment and their own sources of gratification.

The result was to take the edge off the harshly competitive psychological and social conditions of an open society. Pluralism permitted the deployment of the population in an intricate network of relationships and associations that facilitated cooperation at some points, but that left large areas free for the withdrawal of individuals and groups and that therefore minimized conflict-provoking contacts. There were manifestations of prejudice, discrimination, and occasional violence among many of the ethnic and occupational groups. Measured against the potential explosiveness of the situation, however, those were relatively minor. Until the migrations of the past half-century, Negro life in Northern cities was not essentially different from that of other ethnic groups. It had some distinctive problems as every other group did; but relatively small numbers and generally favorable conditions permitted an accommodation on essentially the same terms.

Neither in the North nor in the South is integration in the sense of racial balance a meaningful guide to proximate future action. Desegregation is likely soon to eliminate the vestiges of discrimination inherited from the Jim Crow era; and it may open the way to full participation by Negroes in the political and economic life of the nation, but it will do so within the terms of some approximation of the group life already developed. Integration, defined as the elimination of differences, on the other hand, demands of both Negroes and whites an impossible surrender of identity. The deletion of all memory of antecedents, the severance of all ties to the past, and the liquidation of all particularistic associations is not only unfeasible but undesirable. It would curtail the capacity of this society to deal with its problems under the conditions of freedom; and significantly some of its advocates are either altogether nihilistic or else do not flinch from the totalitarian methods and consequences that would be involved in achieving this version of integration.[11]

Only a small minority of Negroes, however, think in these terms. The vast majority understand that they are a group and will remain so; they seek an expansion of their rights and opportunities, but show neither a desire to merge with the whites nor any expectation that that will soon happen. Desegregation is a genuine issue; racial balance is a vague and confusing abstraction that turns their attention away from the genuine political, economic, and social problems they and other Americans confront.

The issue is perhaps clearest in the field of political action. No right is more basic than that to full and equal participation in the governmental process; and Negroes were quick to exercise the privileges of citizenship once they secured access to the ballot either through migration to the North or through the leveling of barriers in the South. Apathy was no more widespread among them than among other voters new to the suffrage. The colored people promptly assimilated the techniques of machine organization, and their power has increased steadily as their numbers have. With the appearance of a second generation, native to the city, they have begun to move into elective office at about the same pace as their predecessors did.

Three related factors continue to limit the effectiveness of their use of political power. The lack of competent leadership has enabled self-serving hacks and demagogues to push to the fore and has wasted on the quest for petty privilege the effort and energy that might have gone into improving the status of the whole group. The modes of collaboration with other blocs of voters have been slow to develop; and since the Negroes remain a minority, the ability to use their strength depends on alliances with others. Finally, Negroes have had difficulty in perceiving where their true interests lay when

[11] See, for example, Howard Zinn, *SNCC, The New Abolitionists* (Boston, 1964), pp. 216–241.

it came to such complex questions as education, urban renewal, and economic policy. In all three respects, they are repeating the experiences of earlier groups drawn into the processes of American democracy.

Nor is it to be expected that these people will be more enlightened in the use of power than their predecessors. Politics is not the cure-all that some naive observers consider it to be.[12] Post-Civil War Negroes in the South did not use their strength any more effectively than did the Irish of Boston in the first quarter of the twentieth century. The same sentimental temptation to idealize the underdog that once built up exaggerated expectations of the proletariat now sometimes leads to hopes for a panacea in the activities of the Negro citizen. There is no more reason to expect political wisdom from the black than from the white resident of a slum or from either than from the suburban commuter. The vote is not an abstract exercise in either intelligence or benevolence but a means of exercising influence on the processes that shape governmental decisions. For some time yet, Negroes will use it to serve narrowly defined group interests.

The removal of surviving restraints on the right to vote is obviously important; but integration is an irrelevant distraction which disperses energy and inhibits the development of responsible leadership which can take a full and active role in politics at every level. Political effectiveness will grow not through the weakening of the sense of identity but through the development of institutions that can clarify the group's interests, provide organized means of ascent to leadership, and retain the loyalties of the growing middle-class and professional elements in the colored population.

Integration in the sense of the elimination of distinctiveness is no more relevant to the economic plight than to the political plight of the mass of Negroes. The demands for preferential hiring, for assigned quotas

of desirable jobs, and for a Black Man's Marshall Plan are sometimes presented as if they were the means of attaining racial balance and therefore of furthering integration. Actually, they are calls for the recognition of the special character of the group; and to the extent that they are heeded, they strengthen identification with it.

Measurement of the rate of Negro progress is difficult because of the recency of this migration to the cities and because gross comparisons of whites and nonwhites distort the actual situation. A large proportion of urban Negroes have been where they are less than twenty years, almost all of them, less than fifty years. The analogous migration from Eastern and Southern Europe began in the 1890's and reached its peak between 1900 and 1910. The mass of Poles, Italians, and Russian Jews even in the prosperous 1920's, much less in the depression 1930's, had not made more rapid progress. Furthermore, the limitations of the census categories which recognize only whites and nonwhites obscure the genuine differences in occupation and income among the former and make comparisons invidious. Unfortunately, more refined data are difficult to come by.

It is undeniable, however, that a large percentage of American Negroes are confined to unskilled and poorly paid occupations at a time when technological changes reduce the demand for their labor. They therefore suffer more than do other sectors of the population from unemployment, low incomes, and the consequent social deprivations. Furthermore, the same economic forces that contract the demand for their services and their position as late arrivals prevent them from developing the protected trades through which other groups maintained quasi-monopolistic control of some employment opportunities.

The difficulty is that no occupation in the United States—hod-carrier, teamster, machinist, shopkeeper, physician, or banker— ever represented a cross-section of the whole population. The social and cultural condi-

[12] For example, Charles E. Silberman, *Crisis in Black and White* (New York, 1964).

tions that influenced recruitment to these callings did not prevail identically in all ethnic and sectional groups. Entirely apart from prejudice or discrimination, therefore, the chances that a given individual would follow one career line rather than another were likely to depend on an environment and on connections shaped by family influences.

Conceivably this pattern of recruitment could change. Since Jefferson's day, various utopians have dreamed of a mandarin system within which all infants start on equal terms and are directed by successive competitive tests of ability to their appropriate niches in life. This is the ultimate model of integration; and it would certainly put Negroes on terms of parity with all others. But, desirable or not, this solution is visionary. It is hardly necessary to attempt to estimate the social and psychological costs of such a system or even to speculate about the difficulty of defining ability (intelligence?) in that context. The dominant tendencies in American life have consistently broken down any effort to create the rigid controls upon which development in that direction depends. The likelihood is slim that those tendencies will change enough in the near future to offer any promise of relief to the Negroes' problems.

A general assault on the problems of poverty may, in time, mitigate the difficulties from which Negroes suffer along with the other unskilled and therefore superfluous elements in American society. But some Negroes at least are not content to wait for that happy outcome and are struggling now for better chances as a group. Pressure on employers to assign a quota of desirable places to colored people may result in a kind of tokenism, advantageous to a few without easing the hardships of the many. But such adjustments do help the few; and both the tactic and its outcome sustain and strengthen the sense of group solidarity. There are already contexts—in some levels of government employment, for instance—in which there is an advantage to being

black, a condition which puts a premium on affiliation with the group.

In the last analysis, the welfare of the Negroes depends upon the health of the whole economy and its capacity to produce and distribute goods according to an acceptable pattern. But the last analysis is remote indeed. In the interim, the Negroes will use what power they can muster as a group for their own advantage. Preferential treatment in some high-prestige forms of employment will be justified not because it will improve the lot of the great mass of the unskilled, but because it is a means of opening some avenues of escape for the most qualified. At relatively little cost in efficiency, this device can create a pool of potential leaders with a stake in social order and at the same time break the identification of the race with poverty.

Hence the importance of education upon which, increasingly, access to the more desirable places depends. The Negroes started with the initial disadvantage of dependence on the weakest schools in the country—those of the South. Migration compounded their difficulties, and the environment of poverty adds to their handicaps. The need for improvement is unarguable.

The methods of effecting that improvement are by no means clear, however. The pressure for integration has called attention to the problem; but it has also confused the solution. For some elements in the civil rights movement, integration in the form of racial balance has become an end in itself more important than the quality of the schools. Martin Luther King's hit-and-run involvement in this issue in Boston, Chicago, and Cleveland shows the danger of the thoughtless transference of the tactics of one kind of struggle to another.

Partly this outcome is the result of the historic development of the school issue in the South, where segregation was a means of perpetuating educational inequality and Negro inferiority. There desegregation was an essential step toward equality. However, the slogans of that effort were uncritically applied to the separateness of the Northern schools which had an altogether different function. The imbalance of the Northern schools was not designed to create or maintain Negro inferiority; and its result was not always to lower the quality of the education available to colored people.[13] Yet there was no forethought about the consequences of the attempt to end what came to be termed *de facto* segregation.

Furthermore, in this matter, there is a striking division of opinion among Negroes, covered up by the appearance of unity on such occasions as the school strikes. The most vocal persons in the civil rights movement are the most mobile, those whose aspirations reach furthest, those most irked by the identification of their color. Integration expresses their not fully understood desire to sever their ties with the past; and racial balance is a means toward that end.

This desire does not reach very far among the mass of Negroes. In such cities as New York and Boston, where open-enrollment plans offered parents an opportunity to send their children outside the districts of their residence, only a very small minority chose to do so. However the lack of response may be explained away, it reveals the limited scope of the appeal of racial balance.

Yet this issue in many places has overshadowed the far more important factors that enter into the Negroes' educational deprivation. And it is likely that time and energy will continue to be dissipated on the question of racial balance that might more usefully be expended on the quality of the schools and on the orientation of the educa-

tional process to the needs of the colored students.

The demand for racial balance has sometimes had a blackmail effect; it has forced concessions on municipal authorities willing to spend more heavily on slum schools than they might otherwise have in order to stave off the drive for bussing. But this tactic has also had the adverse effect of exaggerating the deficiences of schools in Negro neighborhoods and thus of frightening away experienced teachers, of hastening the flight to the suburbs and increasing the rate of withdrawal to private and parochial schools. The insistence upon integration is thus self-frustrating, as the experience of Washington, D.C., shows. Further pressure toward racial balance will certainly weaken the public schools and leave the Negroes the greatest sufferers.

The dilemma is unnecessary. There is no evidence that racial balance itself improves the capacity of the underprivileged to learn; nor that the *enforced* contact of dissimilar children has significant educational advantages. There is abundant evidence that deprived children have distinctive needs that require the special attention of the school. Yet the drive for integration has obscured, and sometimes actually impeded, the task of providing for those needs. Indeed the argument is now often being made that racial balance is desirable to meet the needs of white children.

Here, too, an awareness of the groups' identity and a determination to deal with its problems is the most promising path to equality. The Negro deserves preferential treatment in education because his needs are great. But to receive it calls for the recognition of the special character of his situation, not for costly efforts artificially to commingle his children with others in the interest of the ideal of balance.[14]

[13] A misleading impression is often the result of gross comparisons of selected Negro schools or school districts with a general white average. It is necessary to take account also of variables other than race that affect performance. An analysis of achievement in Boston district high schools, for instance, shows that schools in certain white neighborhoods are as deficient as those in Negro neighborhoods (reported in *Boston Globe,* December 14, 1964, pp. 1, 13).

[14] There is abundant evidence that significant improvement can come in the performance of Negroes in desegregated but racially unbalanced schools. The Banneker experiment in St. Louis, the experience of Washington, D.C., and

Since the desegregated, but unintegrated, school is a neighborhood school, there is a relationship between the range of residential choices and the conditions of education. The Negroes suffer from poverty, from their recency of arrival, and—in housing, more than in any other sphere—from prejudice. It remains unfortunately true that some whites willing to work side by side with the Negro or even to vote for him in an election will boggle at accepting him as a neighbor. That hesitation is connected with the fact that the residential district, especially in the middle-class areas of the city, is also the setting of a distinctive communal life, with group-derived values and activities of its own. The presence of any outsider is a potential threat, exaggerated in the case of the Negro by fears of a mass inundation.

Something has been done—by law and persuasion—to quiet these fears; a good deal more can be done by these methods. But it would help if the fearful were aware that there is no widespread desire among Negroes for residential intermixture as such. Colored people are primarily concerned with the quality of housing; they do not value highly propinquity to whites. Talk about racial balance not only distorts the actuality of Negro intentions, but it heightens the very fears that may limit the freedom of the occasional black family that wishes to move to a mixed neighborhood. A recent study of middle-income Negro families, for instance,

expressed surprise at the preference for ghetto residence and suggested that whites be moved in to encourage integration, as if that were a necessary and desirable end in itself. A state legislative committee on low-income housing uncritically adopted the same goal. These proposals repeat the errors of New York City's experiment with benign quotas which deprived Negroes of the quarters they needed in order to save room for whites, all out of the concern with balance.[15]

Integration is a false issue. The problem is housing—how can adequate space up to present-day standards of decency be made available to the poor? How can all other colored families get fair value up to the level of their incomes, without being penalized for their race? For most Negroes these are the primary issues. They are difficult enough without the complications of racial balance. The control of the urban renewal process, the role of government as entrepreneur, and problems of design and form will set the framework within which the character of the Negroes' future housing will be determined. And group cohesiveness will be of great importance in influencing decisions in these matters.

The development and strengthening of Negro communal institutions may also help normalize the situation of the colored family. The disorderly features of that position are well known—the absence of a male head, frequent illegitimacy and dependence —as well as their relationship to juvenile delinquency, crime, and narcotic addiction. But these characteristics have been too readily associated with the effects of the slave heritage. The servitude of the plantation may have left elements of weakness in the families of the freedmen; but the extent to which sound family life developed among

---

the results in Louisville, Kentucky, point to the same conclusion. Of course, improvement can also come in balanced schools. However, the essential element is not balance, but the allocation of adequate educational resources to compensate for the disadvantaged situation of the Negro. See also Frank G. Dickey, "A Frontal Attack on Cultural Deprivation," *Phi Delta Kappan*, Vol. 45, No. 8 (May, 1964), p. 398; *New York Times,* May 17, 1965. A good deal of the literature is summarized in T. F. Pettigrew, *A Profile of the Negro American* (Princeton, N.J., 1964), although the conclusions drawn are different.

[15] Lewis G. Watts *et al., The Middle-Income Negro Family Faces Urban Renewal* (Boston, 1964); Massachusetts Special Commission on Low-Income Housing, *Summary Report* (Boston, 1965), and *Final Report* (Boston, 1965), House Document 4040, p. 10.

the Negroes between 1865 and 1915 is impressive, as is the extent to which it still prevails in the rural South closest to the slave setting.

A more plausible source of disorder is the effect of rural-urban migration with low income and slum housing at its destination. That correlation conforms to what is known about the changes in family life in other societies in which slavery has not been a factor.[16] It conforms also to the experience of earlier groups of migrants to American cities. Less than a half-century ago, the foreign-born residents of Irish, Jewish, or Polish slums faced comparable problems of matriarchal households and delinquency.

It was not alone the tradition of solidarity and discipline that contained the damage among these peoples, but also the fact that their families were encased in social and cultural institutions which imposed restraints upon recalcitrant individuals, established norms of behavior, and disposed of weighty sanctions for conformity. Negroes have been slower to develop similar institutions, partly because this migration came at a moment when government absorbed some of these functions, but also because in their experience separation meant segregation and bore the imputation of inferiority. Yet those men who, in the name of integration, deny that there is a significant role for the Negro press, or for Negro churches, or for Negro associations are also denying the group of its media for understanding, for expression, and for action. They would thereby weaken the capacity of the people who need those media to act on their own behalf.[17]

It is the ultimate illogic of integration to deny the separateness of the Negro and

[16] See, for example, B. A. Pauw, *The Second Generation: A Study of the Family among the Urbanized Bantu in East London* (Cape Town, Union of South Africa, 1963); Raymond T. Smith, *The Negro Family in British Guiana* (London, 1956).

[17] See, for example, Louis E. Lomax, *The Negro Revolt* (New York, 1962), pp. 204, 205.

therefore to inhibit him from creating the communal institutions which can help cope with his problems. Delinquency, poverty, slums, and inadequate housing of course concern all Americans; and the attempt to eradicate them calls for common efforts from every part of the nation. But history has given the Negroes a special involvement in these matters; and to deny the actualities of the group's existence is to diminish its ability to deal with them. To confuse segregation, the function of which is to establish Negro inferiority, with the awareness of separate identity, the function of which is to generate the power for voluntary action, hopelessly confuses the struggle for equality.

Clarification of the goals of the civil rights movement has immediate tactical implications. Desegregation is not the same as integration; Selma is not Harlem, Bogalusa, not Chicago.

Where violence, exclusion from the ballot, or state power has deprived the Negro of his equal rights as a man and a citizen, it is his obligation and that of all other Americans to demand an immediate end to the discriminatory measures that aim at his subordination.

Desegregation will not solve any of the other important economic, social, and political problems of American life; it will only offer a starting point from which to confront them. The inadequacies of the political system, unemployment, inferior education, poor housing, and delinquency will still call for attention. In some of these matters the peculiarities of the Negroes' situation call for special treatment. But with reference to none of them is integration a meaningful mode of action; and the call for it which echoes from a different struggle on a different battleground only produces confusion.

Whatever may happen in the more distant future, Negroes will not merge into the rest of the population in the next few decades. Those who desire to eliminate every difference so that all Americans will more nearly resemble each other, those who imagine that there is a main stream into which every element in the society will be swept, are deceived about the character of the country in which they live. As long as common memories, experience, and interests make the Negroes a group, they will find it advantageous to organize and act as such. And the society will better be able to accommodate them as equals on those terms than it could under the pretense that integration could wipe out the past.

CHAPTER TEN

Crosscurrents in Educational Thought

THE AMERICAN SCHOOL IN TRANSITION

THE REPORT OF THE COMMITTEE OF TEN (December 4, 1893) *

A PROPOSED PROGRAM FOR SECONDARY SCHOOLS

To the National Council of Education:

The Committee of Ten appointed at the meeting of the National Educational Association at Saratoga on the 9th of July, 1892, have the honor to present the following report:—

At the meeting of the National Council of Education in 1891, a Committee appointed at a previous meeting made a valuable report through their Chairman, Mr. James H. Baker, then Principal of the Denver High School, on the general subject of uniformity in school programmes and in requirements for admission to college. The Committee was continued, and was authorized to procure a Conference on the subject of uniformity during the meeting of the National Council in 1892, the Conference to consist of representatives of leading colleges and secondary schools in different parts of the country. This Conference was duly summoned, and held meetings at Saratoga on

* National Education Association, *Report of the Committee on Secondary School Studies Appointed at the Meeting of the National Education Association, July 9, 1892; with the Reports of the Conferences arranged by this Committee and held December 28–30, 1892,* U.S. Bureau of Education, Document No. 205 (Washington: Government Printing Office, 1893), pp. 1–5, 16–17, 44–47, 51–53.

July 7th, 8th, and 9th, 1892. There were present between twenty and thirty delegates. Their discussions took a wide range, but resulted in the following specific recommendations, which the Conference sent to the National Council of Education then in session.

1. That it is expedient to hold a conference of school and college teachers of each principal subject which enters into the programmes of secondary schools in the United States and into the requirements for admission to college—as, for example, of Latin, of geometry, or of American history—each conference to consider the proper limits of its subject, the best methods of instruction, the most desirable allotment of time for the subject, and the best methods of testing the pupils' attainments therein, and each conference to represent fairly the different parts of the country.

2. That a Committee be appointed with authority to select the members of these conferences and to arrange their meetings, the results of all the conferences to be reported to this Committee for such action as it may deem appropriate, and to form the basis of a report to be presented to the Council by this Committee.

3. That this Committee consist of the following gentlemen:

CHARLES W. ELIOT, President of Harvard University, Cambridge, Mass., *Chairman.*

WILLIAM T. HARRIS, Commissioner of Education, Washington, D.C.

JAMES B. ANGELL, President of the University of Michigan, Ann Arbor, Mich.

465

JOHN TETLOW, Head Master of the Girls' High School and the Girls' Latin School, Boston, Mass.

JAMES M. TAYLOR, President of Vassar College, Poughkeepsie, N.Y.

OSCAR D. ROBINSON, Principal of the High School, Albany, N.Y.

JAMES H. BAKER, President of the University of Colorado, Boulder, Colo.

RICHARD H. JESSE, President of the University of Missouri, Columbia, Mo.

JAMES C. MACKENZIE, Head Master of the Lawrenceville School, Lawrenceville, N.J.

HENRY C. KING, Professor in Oberlin College, Oberlin, Ohio.

.   .   .   .   .

The Committee of Ten, after a preliminary discussion on November 9th, decided on November 10th to organize conferences on the following subjects:—1. Latin; 2. Greek; 3. English; 4. Other Modern Languages; 5. Mathematics; 6. Physics, Astronomy, and Chemistry; 7. Natural History (Biology, including Botany, Zoölogy, and Physiology); 8. History, Civil Government, and Political Economy; 9. Geography (Physical Geography, Geology, and Meteorology). . . .

On one very important question of general policy which affects profoundly the preparation of all school programmes, the Committee of Ten and all the Conferences are absolutely unanimous. Among the questions suggested for discussion in each Conference were the following:—

7. Should the subject be treated differently for pupils who are going to college, for those who are going to a scientific school, and for those who, presumably, are going to neither?

8. At what age should this differentiation begin, if any be recommended?

The 7th question is answered unanimously in the negative by the Conferences, and the 8th therefore needs no answer. The Committee of Ten unanimously agree with the Conferences. Ninety-eight teachers, intimately concerned either with the actual work of American secondary schools, or with the results of that work as they appear in students who come to college, unanimously declare that every subject which is taught at all in a secondary school should be taught in the same way and to the same extent to every pupil so long as he pursues it, no matter what the probable destination of the pupil may be, or at what point his education is to cease. Thus, for all pupils who study Latin, or history, or algebra, for example, the allotment of time and the method of instruction in a given school should be the same year by year. Not that all the pupils should pursue every subject for the same number of years; but so long as they do pursue it, they should all be treated alike. . . .

The Committee present the following working programmes, which they recommend for trial wherever the secondary school period is limited to four years. All four combined might, of course, be tabulated as one programme with options by subject.

All four programmes conform to the general recommendations of the Conferences, that is,—they treat each subject in the same way for all pupils with trifling exceptions; they give time enough to each subject to win from it the kind of mental training it is fitted to supply; they put the different principal subjects on an approximate equality so far as time-allotment is concerned; they omit all short information courses; and they make sufficiently continuous the instruction in each of the main lines, namely, language, science, history and mathematics. With slight modifications, they would prepare the pupils for admission to appropriate courses in any American college or university on the existing requirements; and they would also meet the new college requirements which are suggested below.

REQUIREMENTS FOR ADMISSION TO COLLEGE

One of the subjects which the Committee of Ten were directed to consider was requirements for admission to college; and

YEAR.	CLASSICAL. Three foreign languages (one modern).		LATIN-SCIENTIFIC. Two foreign languages (one modern).	
I.	Latin	5 p.	Latin	5 p.
	English	4 p.	English	4 p.
	Algebra	4 p.	Algebra	4 p.
	History	4 p.	History	4 p.
	Physical Geography	3 p.	Physical Geography	3 p.
		20 p.		20 p.
II.	Latin	5 p.	Latin	5 p.
	English	2 p.	English	2 p.
	* German [or French] begun . . .	4 p.	German [or French] begun	4 p.
	Geometry	3 p.	Geometry	3 p.
	Physics	3 p.	Physics	3 p.
	History	3 p.	Botany or Zoölogy	3 p.
		20 p.		20 p.
III.	Latin	4 p.	Latin	4 p.
	* Greek	5 p.	English	3 p.
	English	3 p.	German [or French]	4 p.
	German [or French]	4 p.	Mathematics {Algebra 2 / Geometry 2}	4 p.
	Mathematics {Algebra 2 / Geometry 2}	4 p.	Astronomy ½ yr. & Meteorology ½ yr.	3 p.
		20 p.	History	2 p.
				20 p.
IV.	Latin	4 p.	Latin	4 p.
	Greek	5 p.	English {as in Classical 2 / additional 2}	4 p.
	English	2 p.	German [or French]	3 p.
	German [or French]	3 p.	Chemistry	3 p.
	Chemistry	3 p.	Trigonometry & Higher Algebra / or / History } . .	3 p.
	Trigonometry & Higher Algebra / or / History } . .	3 p.	Geology or Physiography ½ yr. / and / Anatomy, Physiology, & Hygiene ½ yr. }	3 p.
		20 p.		20 p.

* In any school in which Greek can be better taught than a modern language, or in which local public opinion or the history of the school makes it desirable to teach Greek in an ample way, Greek may be substituted for German or French in the second year of the Classical programme.

(continued.)

YEAR.	MODERN LANGUAGES. Two foreign languages (both modern).		ENGLISH. One foreign language (ancient or modern).	
I.	French [*or* German] begun	5 p.	Latin, or German, or French . . .	5 p.
	English	4 p.	English	4 p.
	Algebra	4 p.	Algebra	4 p.
	History	4 p.	History	4 p.
	Physical Geography	3 p.	Physical Geography	3 p.
		20 p.		20 p.
II.	French [*or* German]	4 p.	Latin, or German, or French . .	5 or 4 p.
	English	2 p.	English	3 or 4 p.
	German [*or* French] begun	5 p.	Geometry	3 p.
	Geometry	3 p.	Physics	3 p.
	Physics	3 p.	History	3 p.
	Botany or Zoölogy	3 p.	Botany or Zoölogy	3 p.
		20 p.		20 p.
III.	French [*or* German]	4 p.	Latin, or German, or French . . .	4 p.
	English	3 p.	English { as in others 3 / additional 2 }	5 p.
	German [*or* French]	4 p.	
	Mathematics { Algebra 2 / Geometry 2 }	4 p.	Mathematics { Algebra 2 / Geometry 2 }	4 p.
	Astronomy ½ yr. & Meteorology ½ yr.	3 p.	Astronomy ½ yr. & Meteorology ½ yr.	3 p.
	History	2 p.	History { as in the Latin-Scientific 2 / additional 2 }	4 p.
		20 p.		20 p.
IV.	French [*or* German]	3 p.	Latin, or German, or French . . .	4 p.
	English { as in Classical 2 / additional 2 }	4 p.	English { as in Classical 2 / additional 2 }	4 p.
	German [*or* French]	4 p.	Chemistry	3 p.
	Chemistry	3 p.	Trigonometry & Higher Algebra . .	3 p.
	Trigonometry & Higher Algebra 3 / *or* / History }	3 p.	History	3 p.
	Geology or Physiography ½ yr. / and / Anatomy, Physiology, & Hygiene ½ yr. }	3 p.	Geology or Physiography ½ yr. / and / Anatomy, Physiology, & Hygiene ½ yr. }	3 p.
		20 p.		20 p.

particularly they were expected to report on uniform requirements for admission to colleges, as well as on a uniform secondary school programme. Almost all the Conferences have something to say about the best mode of testing the attainments of candidates at college admission examinations; and some of them, notably the Conferences on History and Geography, make very explicit declarations concerning the nature of college examinations. The improvements desired in the mode of testing the attainments of pupils who have pursued in the secondary schools the various subjects which enter into the course will be found clearly described under each subject in the several Conference reports; but there is a general principle concerning the relation of the secondary schools to colleges which the Committee of Ten, inspired and guided by the Conferences, feel it their duty to set forth with all possible distinctness.

The secondary schools of the United States, taken as a whole, do not exist for the purpose of preparing boys and girls for colleges. Only an insignificant percentage of the graduates of these schools go to colleges or scientific schools. Their main function is to prepare for the duties of life that small proportion of all the children in the country —a proportion small in number, but very important to the welfare of the nation—who show themselves able to profit by an education prolonged to the eighteenth year, and whose parents are able to support them while they remain so long at school. There are, to be sure, a few private or endowed secondary schools in the country, which make it their principal object to prepare students for the colleges and universities; but the number of these schools is relatively small. A secondary school programme intended for national use must therefore be made for those children whose education is not to be pursued beyond the secondary school. The preparation of a few pupils for college or scientific school should in the ordinary secondary school be the incidental, and not the principal object. At the same time, it is obviously

desirable that the colleges and scientific schools should be accessible to all boys or girls who have completed creditably the secondary school course. Their parents often do not decide for them, four years before the college age, that they shall go to college, and they themselves may not, perhaps, feel the desire to continue their education until near the end of their school course. In order that any successful graduate of a good secondary school should be free to present himself at the gates of the college or scientific school of his choice, it is necessary that the colleges and scientific schools of the country should accept for admission to appropriate courses of their instruction the attainments of any youth who has passed creditably through a good secondary school course, no matter to what group of subjects he may have mainly devoted himself in the secondary school. As secondary school courses are now too often arranged, this is not a reasonable request to prefer to the colleges and scientific schools; because the pupil may now go through a secondary school course of a very feeble and scrappy nature—studying a little of many subjects and not much of any one, getting, perhaps, a little information in a variety of fields, but nothing which can be called a thorough training. Now the recommendations of the nine Conferences, if well carried out, might fairly be held to make all the main subjects taught in the secondary schools of equal rank for the purposes of admission to college or scientific school. They would all be taught consecutively and thoroughly, and would all be carried on in the same spirit; they would all be used for training the powers of observation, memory, expression, and reasoning; and they would all be good to that end, although differing among themselves in quality and substance. In preparing the programmes, the Committee had in mind that the requirements for admission to colleges might, for schools which adopted a programme derived from [the above] table, be simplified to a considerable extent, though not reduced. A college might say,—We will accept for admission any groups of studies taken from the secondary school programme, provided that the sum of the studies in each of the four years amounts to sixteen, or eighteen, or twenty periods a week,—as may be thought best,—and provided, further, that in each year at least four of the subjects presented shall have been pursued at least three periods a week, and that at least three of the subjects shall have been pursued three years or more. For the purposes of this reckoning, natural history, geography, meteorology, and astronomy might be grouped together as one subject. Every youth who entered college would have spent four years in studying a few subjects thoroughly; and, on the theory that all the subjects are to be considered equivalent in educational rank for the purposes of admission to college, it would make no difference which subjects he had chosen from the programme—he would have had four years of strong and effective mental training. The Conferences on Geography and Modern Languages make the most explicit statement to the effect that college requirements for admission should coincide with high-school requirements for graduation. The Conference on English is of opinion "that no student should be admitted to college who shows in his English examination and his other examinations that he is very deficient in ability to write good English." This recommendation suggests that an ample English course in the secondary school should be required of all persons who intend to enter college. It would of course be possible for any college to require for admission any one subject, or any group of subjects, in the table, and the requirements of different colleges, while all kept within the table, might differ in many respects; but the Committee are of opinion that the satisfactory completion of any one of the four years' courses of study embodied in the foregoing programmes should admit to corresponding courses in colleges and scientific schools. They believe that this close articulation between the secondary schools and the higher institutions would be

advantageous alike for the schools, the colleges, and the country. . . .

> CHARLES W. ELIOT,
> WILLIAM T. HARRIS,
> JAMES B. ANGELL,
> JOHN TETLOW,
> JAMES M. TAYLOR,
> OSCAR D. ROBINSON,
> JAMES H. BAKER,
> RICHARD H. JESSE,
> JAMES C. MACKENZIE,
> HENRY C. KING.

4 December, 1893.

LETTER OF TRANSMITTAL

DEPARTMENT OF THE INTERIOR,
BUREAU OF EDUCATION,
Washington, D. C., December 8, 1893.

SIR: I have the honor to transmit herewith the Report of the Committee on Secondary School Studies appointed at the meeting of the National Educational Association, July 9, 1892, together with the reports of the conferences arranged by the committee and held December 28 to 30, 1892. This is in accordance with your expressed wish that this most important report should be printed as one of the documents of the Bureau of Education. . . .

It has been agreed on all hands that the most defective part of the education in this country is that of secondary schools. There is a wide divergence in the course of study, and the difference of opinion regarding what constitutes a secondary education works injury not only to the elementary schools by setting up an uncertain standard of admission, but also through a want of proper requirements for graduation prevents in thousands of cases the continuance of the course of education of youth in colleges and universities. The recommendations of this report will draw the attention of great numbers of teachers to the question of educational values, and this will lead to a better understanding of what the pupil should study to gain the most from his work in school. In this respect I consider this the most important educational document ever published in this country.

Respectfully submitted.

W. T. HARRIS,
Commissioner.

Hon. HOKE SMITH,
Secretary of the Interior.

JOHN W. GARDNER
The Challenge: Can a Democracy Be Equal and Excellent, Too? (1958) *

EXCELLENCE IN A DEMOCRACY

It is now widely recognized that our society has given too little attention to the individual of unusual talent or potentialities. To make such an assertion is not to deplore the unprecedented time and money we have devoted to raising the general level of achievement. It would serve no purpose to replace our neglect of the gifted by neglect of everyone else. We are all too prone to such wild swings of the pendulum in our national life. We must learn to view these matters in a perspective that will permit us to repair one omission without creating others.

It has not always been easy for Americans to think clearly about excellence. At the heart of the matter is a seeming paradox in democracy as we know it. On the one hand, ours is the form of society that says most convincingly, "Let the best man win," and rewards winners regardless of origin. On the other, it is the form of society that gives those who do not come out on top the widest latitude in rewriting the rules of the contest. It is cru-

* "Excellence in a Democracy" (pp. 355–357) and "Identification of Talent and the Uses of Diversity" (pp. 369–373), by John W. Gardner, Chairman of Panel V, from *The Pursuit of Excellence: Education and the Future of America,* by Rockefeller Brothers Fund, Inc. Copyright © 1958 by Rockefeller Brothers Fund, Inc. (As it appears in *Prospect for America,* © 1961). Reprinted by permission of Doubleday & Company, Inc.

cial to understand this tug of war between equality and excellence in a democracy. When the rewriting of the rules is prompted by the standards of fair play, by elementary considerations of justice, by basic value judgments as to what sort of a "best man" the society wants, democracy can have no quarrel with it. Indeed, it is the core process of a democracy. But when the rewriting of the rules is designed to banish excellence, to rule out distinguished attainment, to inhibit spirited individuals, then all who have a stake in the continued vitality of democracy must protest.

Every democracy *must* encourage high individual performance. If it does not, it closes itself off from the mainsprings of its dynamism and talent and imagination, and the traditional democratic invitation to the individual to realize his full potentialities becomes meaningless. More, perhaps, than any other form of government, a democracy must maintain what Ralph Barton Perry has called "an express insistence upon quality and distinction."

The eighteenth-century philosophers who made equality a central term in our political vocabulary never meant to imply that men are equal in all respects. Nor do Americans today take such a view. It is possible to state in fairly simple terms the views concerning equality that would receive most widespread endorsement in our country today. The fundamental view is that in the final matters of human existence all men are equally worthy of our care and concern. Further, we believe that men should be equal in enjoyment of certain familiar legal, civil, and political rights. They should, as the phrase goes, be equal before the law.

But men are unequal in their native capacities and their motivations, and therefore in their attainments. In elaborating our national views of equality, the most widely accepted means of dealing with this problem has been to emphasize *equality of opportunity*. The great advantage of the conception of equality of opportunity is that it candidly recognizes differences in endowment and motivation and accepts the certainty of differences in achievement. By allowing free play to these differences, it preserves the freedom to excel, which counts for so much in terms of individual aspirations and has produced so much of mankind's greatness.

Having committed ourselves to equality of opportunity, we must strive incessantly to make it a reality in our society. This is a task that will concern us at many points in the present report.

With respect to the pursuit of excellence, there are several considerations that we must keep firmly in mind.

First, we must not make the mistake of adopting a narrow or constricting view of excellence. *Our conception of excellence must embrace many kinds of achievement at many levels.* There is no single scale or simple set of categories in terms of which to measure excellence. There is excellence in abstract intellectual activity, in art, in music, in managerial activities, in craftsmanship, in human relations, in technical work.

Second, we must not assume that native capacity is the sole ingredient in superior performance. Excellence, as we shall later have occasion to note, is a product of ability and motivation and character. And the more one observes high performance in the dust and heat of daily life, the more one is likely to be impressed with the contribution made by the latter two ingredients.

Finally, we must recognize that judgments of differences in talent are not judgments of differences in human worth.

To sum up, it is possible for us to cultivate the ideal of excellence while retaining the moral values of equality. Whether we shall succeed in doing so is perhaps the fundamental issue in the development of our human resources. A challenge must be recognized before it can be met. Our society will have passed an important milestone of maturity when those who are the most enthusiastic proponents of a democratic way of life are also the most vigorous proponents of excellence.

. . . . .

IDENTIFICATION OF TALENT AND THE USES OF DIVERSITY

Any educational system is, among other things, a great sorting-out process. One of its most important goals is to identify and guide able students and to challenge each student to develop his capacities to the utmost.

There is overwhelming evidence of a determination on the part of the American people that the sorting-out process be carried out mercifully and generously rather than ruthlessly, rigidly, or mechanically. But it has sometimes seemed that rather than admit differences in talent—or at least taking responsibility for assessing it—we prefer to accept mediocrity.

In recent months there has been much discussion of large-scale testing programs for the purpose of identifying talent. Used with a sound understanding of their strengths and limitations, present testing procedures can contribute significantly to a program of talent identification. When large numbers are involved, tests may uncover talent that would otherwise go unnoticed. And even when large numbers are not involved, a particular youngster's aptitude may be such as to defy easy diagnosis and may escape the attention of all but the keenest of teachers.

But testing procedures unwisely used can do harm. A few basic considerations with respect to them must be understood.

First, tests are most effective in measuring academic aptitude and achievement. There are certain other kinds of aptitude and achievement that they can measure, but with less assurance. And there are many kinds of talent that must go unmeasured because no adequate measuring instruments exist. In short, the tests are effective on a limited front. Decisions based on test scores must be made with the awareness of the imponderables in human behavior. We cannot measure the rare qualities of character that are a necessary ingredient of great performance. We cannot measure aspiration or purpose. We cannot measure courage, vitality, or determination.

Second, no single test should become a basis for important decisions. A series of scores obtained over the years enables teachers to achieve a reliable perspective on the young person's aptitudes and minimizes the possibility of false diagnosis.

Third, test scores are one kind of data to be placed alongside other kinds of data. The test score is not to be worshiped as a datum so decisive that it alone can be used to settle an individual's fate; it is a highly useful addition to other data but should not replace them. Unfortunately, the most powerful influence making for excessive dependence on test scores is the willingness of adults to evade their responsibility for complex and difficult decisions concerning the child. The test score should be regarded as an aid in making—not a device for evading—such decisions.

The identification of talent is no more than the first step. It should be only part of a strong guidance program. The word *guidance* has a variety of meanings; we use it here to mean advice concerning the young person's educational problems and the most appropriate course of study for him. It cannot be emphasized too strongly that such guidance is essential to the success of our system. As many teachers as possible should be trained to take part in it. As many high schools as possible should have special guidance officers to supplement the teachers where greater technical knowledge is required.

The objective of all educational guidance should be to stimulate the individual to make the most of his potentialities. The fact that a substantial fraction of the top quarter of high school graduates fail to go on to college is a startling indictment of our guidance system. It is not surprising that teachers, trained as they are to deal protectively and helpfully toward young people, should focus a major portion of their guidance efforts on those who seem most in need of help, such as the retarded and the delinquents. But there are students at the high end of the scale who present an equally great problem as far as their own self-fulfillment is concerned and an even greater problem as far as society is concerned. Within the framework of concern for all, guidance should give particular attention to able students.

The general academic capacity of students should be at least tentatively identified by the eighth grade as the result of repeated testings and classroom performance in the elementary grades. An adequate guidance system would insure that each student would then be exposed to the sort of program that will develop to the full the gifts that he possesses.

But the schools cannot do full justice to each young person in developing what gifts he may possess until they face frankly the need to provide different programs for different types and levels of ability. Our schools have made far more progress in *identifying* different levels of talent than in the *development of programs* for these different levels. Adequate attention to individual differences means rejecting a rigid policy of promotion by age; and it means sensible experimentation with various kinds of flexibility in the curriculum to meet the varying needs of young people. And especially, it means providing unusually able boys and girls with rigorous and challenging experiences.

In courses in which there is a wide spread of student ability—in English and other courses required of all students—there should be sections arranged according to aptitude *in that subject*. It is important to note that a student might be in a fast-learning group in mathematics, in a second group for history, and a third group for French. This is a very different thing from arbitrarily separating all students with intelligence scores above a certain figure and placing them in a separate curriculum as a block.

Some critics of our schools have advocated the European pattern of two entirely separate school systems after approximately the sixth grade—one system college preparatory and the other vocational in character. Such separation would be unpalatable to most Americans, and in any case separate school systems are unnecessary. There is no reason why youngsters at all levels of scholastic ability should not sit in the same homeroom, play on the same teams, act in the same plays, attend the same dances, and share in the same student government. And there are many reasons why such a common experience is important.

The argument against two entirely separate school systems need not rule out the possibility that in our larger cities we may develop special schools to meet special purposes, for example, the famed Bronx High School of Science. Our best guide in these matters is to vary the rule to fit the circumstances.

We have referred repeatedly to that portion of the high school population capable of high caliber college work—roughly 15 to 20 per cent of the students. A more special problem is presented by the top *two* per cent of the high school population. From this highly selected group will come many of the young men and women who will reach the pinnacles of intellectual achievement and creativity in the years ahead. No effort should be spared to provide them with the opportunities for challenging study.

For this group particularly, the Advanced Placement Program is important. Under this program, now sponsored by the College Entrance Examination Board, an expanding number of secondary schools, both public and private, is offering college-level courses to their best juniors and seniors. Many colleges are prepared to permit such students to "leapfrog" freshman college courses and get credit for them. Another approach is represented by the experimental Program for Early Admission to College, under which about 1,000 able students have entered twelve different colleges over the last five years *before* completing the last year or two of high school. An evaluation of the first two groups to graduate from college under this experiment shows that, on the whole, they have far outperformed their classmates academically; and despite their lower age, their social and emotional adjustment to college compares favorably with that of students generally.

The important thing is to rid ourselves of the notion that either a flexible promotion policy or flexible curricular arrangements are undemocratic in spirit. We cannot escape the fact of individual differences, and we cannot escape the necessity for coping with them. Whether we like it or not, they are a central fact in any educational system —and in any society. The good society is not one that ignores them but one that deals with them wisely and compassionately.

If we are really serious about equality of opportunity, we shall be serious about individual differences because what constitutes opportunity for one man is a stone wall for the next. If we are to do justice to the individual, we must seek for him the level and kind of education that will open *his* eyes, stimulate *his* mind, and unlock *his* potentialities. We should seek to develop many educational patterns—each geared to the particular capacities of the student for whom it is designed.

But though the educational patterns may differ, the goals remain much the same for all: enabling each young person to go as far as his aptitude will permit in fundamental knowledge and skills, and motivating him to continue his own self-development to the full along similar lines.

If we recognize the necessity of diverse educational paths, it may then be easier to accept the fact that education in a four year college is not the only road to a full and useful life. Americans who honestly believe in the full realization of every man's potentialities find themselves engaged in a two-front war. On the one hand, they must fight to make college education more widely available to those who are fitted for it. On the other, they must deny that college is the only key to success and happiness.

We will do well to stress the many kinds of achievement of which a human being is capable. The sort of capacity measured by the conventional scholastic aptitude test is very important; but we should be wary of putting too monolithic an emphasis upon this particular talent. Instead, we should encourage all kinds of individuals to run on all kinds of tracks. In this way we can distribute very widely the rewards of self-esteem and self-respect, which are the healthiest preventives of leveling reactions. We can encourage on the broadest scale the release of individual energy and positive motivation that have traditionally been among the greatest strengths of our society. We can then insist, as we must, that democracy is not to be conceived as an invitation to share a common mediocrity but as a system that allows each to express and live up to the special excellence that is in him. We can then demand the best of our most gifted, most talented, and most spirited youngsters. And we can dedicate ourselves to the cultivation of distinction and a sense of quality.

JAMES BRYANT CONANT
The Comprehensive High School (1967) *

Let me attempt to summarize the results of our investigation and their implications for the financing of public secondary education.

[The following] Table, which is divided into two parts, summarizes [our findings] and, in addition, provides information on certain combinations of the criteria.

Since I am concerned with the comprehensive nature of the high schools we are examining, I attach particular significance to the combination of criteria of an academic type (first five, Table) and the offering of auto mechanics or building trades (item 7, Table). (It will be recalled that we chose those two headings as representing

* James Bryant Conant, *The Comprehensive High School: A Second Report to Interested Citizens* (New York: McGraw-Hill, 1967), pp. 65–70. Copyright © 1967 by James Bryant Conant. All rights reserved. Used by permission of the author.

vocational opportunities.) Anyone who challenges the offerings in these schools as not being widely comprehensive should note from [the] Table that over 90 per cent of the schools offer courses in business education and nearly 90 per cent in home economics. Perhaps one might say that if a school is going to be comprehensive it should offer, at the very least, a strong program in one subject on the academic side and one subject on the vocational side. With this in mind we asked questions that brought out the following fact: 60 per cent of the schools reporting offer auto mechanics, building trades, or closely related subjects *and* either calculus or four years of one modern foreign language.

[The] Table is essentially self-explanatory. It might be pointed out, however, that the larger the number of criteria applied in judging a school, the fewer the schools that will meet the standard. Although only 10.8 per cent of the schools meet all five criteria, nevertheless 31.8 per cent offer both four years of one modern foreign language and calculus. One additional fact not hitherto reported should be added—that 45.7 per cent of the schools reporting offer four years of two foreign languages. It seems quite certain that there is little connection between the spread of 1965 graduates entering post–high school institutions (25–74 per cent) and the vast improvement and extension in foreign language and mathematics offerings.

Because the comprehensive high school has so often been attacked as providing inadequate opportunities for the bright students, I have in both my first and second reports emphasized opportunities that should be available to those who are going on to college and, perhaps later, to professional school. One can conclude that in the ten years since I made my first study, considerable progress has been made in the teaching of mathematics, science, and foreign languages. Indeed, the situation regarding mathematics may be better than the findings in [the] Table indicate. Schools that offer advanced mathematics other than calculus may

TABLE: SUMMARY OF FINDINGS

A. Individual criteria and certain combinations

Criteria		Percentage of 2,000 schools
1. Instruction in calculus		40.0
2. Four years of one modern foreign language		65.0
3. School so organized that five academic subjects plus art or music and physical education may be studied in one day		74.2
4. Courses in the Advanced Placement Program available		30.2
*5. Ratio of English teachers to students studying English, 1 to 120 or less		25.8
Per cent of schools meeting all five of the above criteria	10.8	
Schools meeting first four of above criteria	13.2	
Schools meeting criteria 1, 2, 3, and 5	21.4	
Schools meeting first two criteria	31.8	
6. Three years of social studies required		43.4
7. Course in auto mechanics or building trades		52.2
Per cent of schools meeting criteria 1, 2, 6, and 7 (instruction in calculus, four years of one modern foreign language, three years of required social studies, course in auto mechanics or building trades)	15.3	
Per cent of schools meeting criteria 1, 2, and 7 (instruction in calculus, four years of one foreign language, auto mechanics or building trades)	21.7	
Per cent of schools meeting criteria 1 and 7 (instruction in calculus, auto mechanics or building trades)	27.9	

B. Summary of other findings

Criteria	Percentage of 2,000 schools
8. Ratio of certified professional staff to students of 1 to 20.4 or less	51.2
*9. Ratio of counselors to students of 1 to 349 or less	31.5
10. New physics, chemistry, or biology	64.9
11. Instruction in advanced mathematics other than calculus	22.6
12. Course in problems of democracy with heterogeneous classes	62.5
13. Course in distributive education	53.6
14. Summer school	80.1
15. Course for slow learners	91.9
16. Students grouped by ability in at least one course	96.5
17. Course in business education	92.4
18. Course in home economics	88.8
19. Instruction in music	98.8
20. Instruction in art	94.3

* These criteria represent a somewhat different standard from that set by the recommendations in *The American High School Today* [1959].

provide as satisfactorily for certain types of academically talented youth as those that offer calculus. Therefore, one might claim that something like 60 per cent of the schools are satisfactory in 12th-grade mathematics. Someone reading our findings with a critical eye might say, "Well, of course, the schools that provide so well for the ambitious and bright students are the schools among your 2,000 from which well over 50 per cent are going on to college." In order to examine this possible criticism, we divided our schools into three groups corresponding to the percentage of 1965 graduates proceeding with further education. One group included those schools from which 25–39 per cent proceeded, the next, 40–59 per cent, and the third, 60–75 per cent. We found that the middle group, which represents roughly 50 per cent going on to college, has as high a percentage of schools offering a strong academic program as does the group of schools from which 60 to 75 per cent proceeded. These results largely answer my hypothetical critic's objection. This is important. It might well have turned out that the good showing in foreign languages and calculus for the entire 2,000 schools was a consequence of a high percentage of academic offerings in those schools sending more than 60 per cent to college. But this is not the case. It seems quite certain that the vast improvement in foreign languages and mathematics is almost independent of the percentage of 1965 graduates who are continuing their education.

. . . Let me emphasize the significance of the data in [the] Table and our findings on the percentage of schools meeting different groups of my criteria. Whether one is encouraged or discouraged by contemplating these findings depends largely on one's expectation and one's judgment of what is important in secondary education. Had a similar compilation been possible ten years ago, [the] Table would show that American public education has been improving, but is yet far below the level I think it can reach before long.

ROBERT H. ANDERSON
Exemplars of Team Teaching (1965) *

Under the general heading of "cooperative teaching" may be found dozens of different patterns of school and staff organization. Some of these derive from, or are associated with, attempts to achieve greater flexibility in pupil grouping. Others are associated with efforts to eliminate the administrative and instructional characteristics of rigid, lockstep graded school structure. Still others involve the use of nonprofessional or paraprofessional assistants in the schools, and a few are the result of experimentation with mechanical devices, programed materials, and other technological resources. Most, however, have stemmed from a growing interdependence among teachers in the face of the increasing complexity of teaching responsibilities and the need for greater specialization in the professional ranks.

Woodring notes that team teaching might be more appropriately "called 'team organization and planning' because the teaching, at any given moment, usually is done by an individual rather than by a team." [1] Certainly this is often the case: a group of teachers may be joined together in a partnership concerned with instructional planning, coordination of schedules and resources, and general evaluation, but each teacher retains his essential sovereignty and performs teaching functions in privacy. If each teacher also deals primarily with "his own class" of pupils throughout the school week, and has a minimum of contact with

* Robert H. Anderson, "Some Types of Cooperative Teaching in Current Use," *National Elementary Principal*, XLIV (January, 1965), 22–26. Copyright 1965, Department of Elementary School Principals, National Education Association. All rights reserved. Used by permission.
[1] Woodring, Paul. "Reform Movements from the Point of View of Psychological Theory." *Theories of Learning and Instruction.* Sixty-Third Yearbook, Part I, National Society for the Study of Education. Chicago: University of Chicago Press, 1964. Chapter 12, p. 292.

the pupils of his teaching colleagues, then the label of "team teaching" would indeed be somewhat erroneous. Sometimes, however, the aforementioned teachers do in fact have a shared teaching responsibility for a good many children, so that many teaching decisions and outcomes are constantly examined by the total staff. It would seem that in such situations a more definite merging of sovereignties and an increase of side-by-side teaching activities may be expected to develop.

One model of cooperative teaching, then, requires an extensive co-involvement of a number of teachers (let us say between three and six) in the entire range of instructive-related functions: planning, actual work with the same children, and evaluation. In this model, which some regard as the ultimate or ideal, all team members (including the children when appropriate) share jointly in the formulation of broad, over-all instructional objectives and in the weekly or daily determination of the more immediate teaching goals. The model requires all team members to be at least minimally conversant with each other's specific daily plans and to be given at least periodic (e.g., weekly) opportunity to contribute to and criticize the plans of colleagues. Each team member, at least several times weekly, should carry on teaching functions in the actual presence of a colleague, whose own role at the moment might involve co-teaching, or assisting, or observing—it being the colleague's subsequent obligation to offer constructive advice or criticism in an evaluative session. This model, therefore, implies that arrangements can be made for extensive intra-team communication, and it obviously makes heavy demands upon the time, energies, and emotions of the teachers involved.

At this stage of development, this idealized model does not exist full-blown in any project known to the author. In all probability, hierarchically structured teams such as those in Lexington, Massachusetts, and Norwalk, Connecticut, come the closest to fulfilling the ideal model, yet even these have not yet solved all of the various problems that are involved.

Hierarchical structrure, in which leadership is formally assigned and in which the leader enjoys a salary supplement or equivalent recognition, has not yet become very widespread. However, it now seems that there is a trend toward the formal assignment of leadership to the best qualified person in the team. The relatively superior teacher, who also has a significant professional specialty and the talent and appetite for carrying leadership responsibility, can expect in a growing number of communities to be assigned as "team leader" with a salary supplement up to $1,000 or more. In the minds of some proponents, this feature of team teaching organization promises to attract and retain a greater number of outstanding persons in the teaching profession.

Formal hierarchical organization in some instances calls for more than one level of responsibility and competence above the regular role of teacher. The title of "senior teacher" or "specialist teacher" may be used, for example, to denote a professional with above average qualifications and an assigned leadership role under the team leader. This arrangement tends to be found chiefly where there are fairly large teams (e.g., five to eight members) or where an effort is being made to provide leadership experience for future team leaders.

Perhaps the most typical teaching teams pattern in current use is the semi-hierarchical structured team. Here, the members of the team are officially joined together in a close working relationship, the administration having designated various roles for the members (e.g., each member providing leadership in a given curriculum area) but all members having an essentially equal status. The person designated as "leader" is seen primarily as a parliamentary chairman or coordinator, without any unusual authority and without salary supplement or other tangible recognition of responsibilities carried. The leadership may actually rotate from member to member over a period of time, or the school principal may in effect be the team leader. An example of the latter is an outstanding project underway in the Hamilton School, a small elementary school in Newton, Massachusetts. Sometimes, the semi-hierarchical team is a good pattern to use in a school where there is apparent resistance to full-fledged hierarchy and/or where the administration is unsure as to which of the teachers have the talents and the temperament for leadership. In such situations, a gradual move can be made toward hierarchical structure as the staff becomes more accepting of the idea.

Many so-called team operations represent at best what might be called a voluntary federation of sovereign teachers. Membership in the team is not a formal obligation of the teacher, and his involvement in the professional planning and activities of his colleagues tends to be relatively minor. Nevertheless, this arrangement can be fruitful if the federated teachers take sufficient advantage of the flexibility and sharing that is possible. Leadership tends to be very informal, each teacher being in effect a free-lance participant.

In both the semi-structured and the federated patterns, examples can be found that are "departmental" in flavor. Although such arrangements are far more common in secondary schools, some elementary schools have lately turned to the use of subject matter specialists as one way of providing more competent instruction across the curriculum. Some schools have, in effect, discarded the self-contained classroom organization, wherein each teacher as a generalist taught in all curriculum areas, and rearranged teaching assignments along departmental or subject matter lines. Since departmentalization has for some time been in general disfavor in elementary education, it is therefore a source of concern in some circles that such a trend is discernible.

It may be helpful to point out that conventional departmentalization, with which the so-called "self-contained" classroom has long been contrasted, is itself a form of self-contained organization. That is to say, the teachers in conventional departmentalization are almost literally autonomous in their various roles, each as independent of the other as are "self-contained" classroom teachers. The chief difference between the two conventional patterns, then, is explained less by the meaning of the phrase "self-contained" than by the distinction between generalist and specialist. Most authorities would probably concede that more competent instruction *area by area* is characteristic of the departmentalized pattern, but it is generally believed that this advantage is countervailed by the uncoordinated, fragmentary experiences the child receives at the hands of independent teachers, each unaware of his colleagues' work and each seeing only a certain aspect of the child's growth and performance.

With the emergence of team teaching, a fresh impetus has been given to the idea of specialist teaching. A significant difference, however, may be found in some of the current plans involving the use of subject matter specialists in the elementary school: the team-oriented concept of communication, coordination, and cooperation. "Cooperative departmentalization," then, is a term we may use in cases where separate specialists join together in a federation under conditions somewhat resembling team organization.

By now the reader is aware of numerous variants of team organization and staff cooperation that may be found across the country at the present time. Some of these are primarily modifications of the old pattern of literal self-containment (generalist or specialist), while others are more valid examples of cooperative teaching ranging from loose federations all the way to formal, hierarchical team structure.

Two other trends in school organization may be identified, both having to do with the types of group memberships arranged in the school for children. The first of these is multi-age or inter-age grouping: the assignment of children to teams, classes, or instructional groups in which they associate with children of two or more age levels. One example is the multi-grade, multi-age grouping plan such as that developed about eight years ago in Torrance, California, where a primary class might include six-year-old, seven-year-old, and eight-year-old children, and an intermediate class might include nine-, ten-, and eleven-year-old youngsters. A second trend, closely related to the use of multi-age classes, is the abandonment of graded structure in favor of more flexible patterns of arranging and defining the vertical progress of pupils through the elementary school. It is not the purpose of this article to elaborate on multi-age and nongraded patterns, although this author is convinced of their merit and sees their acceptance and development as one of the important goals of American public schools in the years ahead.

One of the principal advantages of team teaching, and variants thereof, appears to be that it stimulates and fosters the further development of flexible grouping patterns and of the nongraded school itself. In many places where cooperative teaching has flourished, attitudes and practices associated with nongraded organization have tended also to flourish. Probably this is due to the more careful analysis that team teachers tend to make of their responsibilities and also to the increased flexibility they enjoy in responding to pupils' needs. We are tempted to argue, therefore, that experience with cooperative teaching is a useful strategic preparation for the adoption of a nongraded plan. Team teaching and nongradedness in combination, especially where multi-age groupings are also employed, appears to represent an ideal or ultimate form of elementary school organization.

In actual practice, at least twelve combinations of these organizational features and their opposites may be found at present in the United States:

POSSIBLE PATTERNS OF SCHOOL/CLASS ORGANIZATION

1	2	3	4	5	6
NG	NG	NG	NG	NG	NG
SC	SC	MSC	MSC	TT	TT
UA	MA	UA	MA	UA	MA

7	8	9	10	11	12
G	G	G	G	G	G
SC	SC	MSC	MSC	TT	TT
UA	MA	UA	MA	UA	MA

(Key)

G	Graded vertical organization (promotion/failure)
NG	Nongraded vertical organization (continuous progress)
UA	Unit age grouping (6-year-olds, 7-year-olds, etc.)
MA	Multi-age or inter-age groupings (6-7, 6-7-8, etc.)
SC	Self-contained horizontal organization (1 autonomous teacher)
MSC	Modified self-contained: cooperative departmentalization, semi-departmentalization, informal cooperation (several autonomous teachers)
TT	Team teaching horizontal organization

In our chart, boxes 1, 2, 7, and 8 refer to self-contained classes in which there is either graded or nongraded vertical organization and in which the children are either of the same age or of different ages. In boxes 3, 4, 9, and 10, the same factors exist except that there is some form of multiple-adult cooperative staff organization in effect. In boxes 5, 6, 11, and 12, the same variables are now combined with full-fledged team teaching organization.

Our previous argument in effect supports box 6 (nongrading combined with team teaching and inter-age grouping) as representing the theoretical ideal. By implication, box 7 represents the theoretically least desirable combination. Probably boxes 5 and 8 are, in turn, the next best and next worst, respectively, although both strategic and value considerations make this a very difficult judgment. As an interesting exercise, the reader might ask himself which boxes represent in fact the next best and the next worst arrangements.

If one believes with this author that nongradedness is the most precious and desirable of the organization forms we may consider, then boxes 12, 11, 10, and 9 seem to be useful avenues in the direction of box 6. Experience to date does not offer much advice as to how best to proceed from box 7 to the Utopia of box 6, although it may be that one or another form of cooperative teaching is easier to understand and to implement than is the more ambiguous and complicated concept of nongrading. If this is the case, perhaps a concerted effort to develop team teaching will be a useful step toward the eventual achievement of a workable nongraded structure.

Some team teaching projects involve the extensive use of teacher aides and clerical aides. The Norwalk model reserves a fairly major role for the aide, and the Lexington model calls for two full-time aides supplementing a full complement of six or seven teachers. Many projects call for a more limited use of aides, e.g., a half-time aide serving six teachers. In the new Granada Elementary School in Belvedere-Tiburon, California, the staff positions for a team serving 100 pupils include one team leader, one senior teacher (five or more years of experience), one junior teacher (little or no teaching experience), one full-time intern, two student teachers, a half-time teacher aide, and several volunteer instructional aides (parents who help with health, library, and various aide functions).

Perhaps the most prevalent pattern, for financial reasons, is the one involving *no* aides, or at most a small allotment of a school secretary's time. In fact, team teaching is not dependent upon the availability of nonprofessional assistants; but it is rather disappointing that American schools have been so slow to recognize the crying need for supporting services, and those teams fortunate enough to have aides seem to be making more rapid progress in improving instruction.

Team teaching is frequently associated with the use of varying sized instructional groupings, including large groups of 40, 75, 100 or more children on the one hand and small seminar groups (12–15 pupils) and working groups (5–8 pupils) on the other. Some critics have deplored large group instruction, especially for young children, and protested that teams seem not to arrange for seminar and working groups as often as would be desirable. This may well be a valid complaint, since most teams have been slow to develop small group instruction patterns. Regarding large groups, the critics have probably exaggerated both the extent to which large group instruction is actually carried on and the educational hazards of such instruction. Large group lessons, in part because they are usually prepared more carefully, are often superior in quality to lessons under conventional circumstances. It seems unlikely that teams will overindulge in this form of teaching, however, and in many existing team projects such lessons play only a minor role in the scheme of things. The great preponderance of team teaching is still done in class groupings of

20–30, although this may be due more to the habits of teachers and the influence of the architectural environment than to valid theories of educational grouping.[2]

Team teaching is not totally dependent upon flexibility in school design, although it is extremely helpful to have school spaces that lend themselves to various types of groupings. Existing school buildings usually have at least some flexibility, and sometimes they can be modified at reasonable cost. Especially urgent, it would seem, is alerting school boards and administrators to the need for flexibility in all *future* school construction.

Sub-groupings within the total team may be based upon some presumed similarity among the youngsters, so that the students tend to reinforce each other in the learning process, or upon some presumed dissimilarities as in the case of deliberate heterogeneous grouping. Academic history and potential, social or personal factors, age, interests, learning styles and personalities, and many other factors may serve to explain the various sub-groups that are formed. Increasingly, the varying talents and teaching styles of the adults in the team are also being taken into account.

Cooperative teaching in the 1965 setting finds its origins in century-old trends, yet it has a special currency in this time of fundamental ferment and change. That so many patterns exist is a reflection of the American system of decentralized schools, each community having the freedom to shape its educational program (within broad limits) along its own lines.

At the same time, certain team teaching models in particular have tended to influence the general trend to date because they were among the first to be widely described in the literature, both professional and popular. Whether the influence of these early pilot programs will diminish as research and theory become more highly developed is a matter for speculation. Suffice here to say that cooperative teaching is still in a formative, even primitive, stage. Yet despite its newness, most observers are agreed that cooperative teaching represents an extremely promising and challenging field for further exploration.

WILLIAM P. McLOUGHLIN
On the Concept of a Nongraded School (1968) *

Few propositions for educational change have generated and sustained as much interest as the nongraded school. It is discussed at nearly every major educational conference, and symposiums on the nongraded school are increasing in popularity. Furthermore, the body of available literature is increasing rapidly; most leading professional journals have published several articles on this topic. Through these and other means, educators have learned more of the promises of the nongraded school than they have of its accomplishments.

This is understandable, for nongrading appears to be preached more than practiced and practiced more than appraised. In fact, few dependable estimates on the present status and anticipated growth of the nongraded school are currently available and sound studies on its accomplishments are even more difficult to come by. From what is available one would be hard put to determine just how many schools have nongraded their instructional programs and how many are seriously contemplating the change. If findings in these areas are obscure, the outcomes of the evaluations of existing nongraded programs are even less definitive.

The available estimates of the number of schools with nongraded programs fluctuates

---

[2] Anderson, Robert H. "The Organization and Administration of Team Teaching." *Team Teaching.* (Edited by Judson T. Shaplin and Henry F. Olds, Jr.) New York: Harper & Row, 1964. Pp. 208–209.

* William P. McLoughlin, "The Phantom Nongraded School," *Phi Delta Kappan,* Vol. XLIX, No. 5 (January, 1968), pp. 248–250. Used by permission.

from 5.5 percent [1] to 30 percent.[2] These, it must be pointed out, are unqualified estimates; they do not consider the quality of the programs purporting to be nongraded. When this element is added, estimates of the number of schools with *truly* nongraded programs shrink considerably. Goodlad, in 1955, estimated that less than one percent of the schools in the country were nongraded [3] and in 1961 he felt there were probably fewer than 125 schools to be found with *truly* nongraded programs.[4]

If uncertainty marks present estimates of the number of schools operating nongraded programs, certainly forecasts for future growth are dubious. In 1958 the NEA reported 26.3 percent of the respondents to its survey saying they intended to nongrade their schools.[5] Five years later, however, this estimate had dwindled to 3.2 percent.[6] On the other hand, the USOE's pollings reverse this trend. Of schools queried in 1958, only 13.4 percent expected to become nongraded,[7] but two years later this estimate doubled and 26.3 percent of the respond-

ents reported considering nongrading their schools.[8] With these conflicting findings it is difficult to know if the nongraded school is coming into its own or passing out of existence.

One thing seems clear from these surveys, however: nongrading is related to district size. Nearly all available surveys confirm this; the larger the district, the more likely it is to have one or more nongraded units. Here we should stress that this does not mean that nongrading is the principal organizational pattern in large school districts. It simply means a nongraded unit is operating in one or more of the district's several elementary schools.[9]

Studies of the influence of nongrading on students are rare, too, and their composite findings somewhat bewildering. . . . Taken at face value, current research on the nongraded school seems to say that its contribution to the academic, social, and emotional development of children is marginal.

But should these findings be taken at face value? It might be naive to rest the fate of the nongraded school on past research. The validity of these studies should be rigorously tested, for they depend on one tacit but critical assumption: that the experimental schools, those purporting to be nongraded, are *truly* nongraded. If this assumption is not met and the experimental schools are not nongraded, then research has told us nothing about the efficacy of the nongraded school.

Too often, on close inspection, one finds that schools credited with operating nongraded programs are not nongraded at all. Homogeneous grouping and semi-departmentalization of instruction in reading and arithmetic are frequently passed off as nongraded programs. These techniques must be recognized for what they are. They are

[1] Lillian L. Gore and Rose E. Koury, *A Survey of Early Elementary Education in Public Schools, 1960–61*. Washington, D.C.: U.S. Department of Health, Education and Welfare, 1965.
[2] National Education Association, *Nongraded Schools*. Research Memo 1965–12. Washington, D.C.: Research Division, NEA, May, 1965.
[3] John I. Goodlad, "More About the Ungraded Plan," *NEA Journal*, May, 1955, pp. 295–96.
[4] National Education Association, *Nongrading: A Modern Practice in Elementary School Organization*. Research Memorandum 1961-37. Washington, D.C.: Research Division, NEA, October, 1961.
[5] National Education Association, *Administrative Practices in Urban School Districts, 1958–1959*. Research Report 1961-R10. Washington, D.C.: Research Division, NEA, May, 1961.
[6] NEA, *Nongraded Schools, op. cit.*
[7] Stuart E. Dean, *Elementary School Administration and Organization: A National Survey of Practices and Policies*. Washington, D.C.: U.S. Department of Health, Education and Welfare, 1963.

[8] Gore and Koury, *op. cit.*
[9] William P. McLoughlin, *The Nongraded School: A Critical Assessment*. Albany, N.Y.: The University of the State of New York, The New York State Education Department, 1967.

administrative expediencies developed to make the *graded* school work. They are not nongraded instructional programs.

If these are the "nongraded" programs represented in these studies, then researching their effectiveness is an exercise in futility, for the *experimental* schools are as graded as the control schools and no experimental treatment is being tested. Research has done nothing more than contrast the performances of children from graded schools called graded schools with the performance of children from graded schools called nongraded schools. Essentially, we have simply researched the age-old question: "What's in a name?"

The nongraded school is defensible only because the graded school is indefensible. Its justification flows from its efforts to correct the instructional errors of the graded school. It is reasonably unlikely that any amount of manipulation of the physical arrangements of schools will produce discernible differences in the academic or psychosocial development of children. Every grade label can be cleansed from every classroom door in the school without influencing the school's attainments with children as long as graded instructional practices prevail behind these doors.

Nongrading begins with significant alterations in instructional, not organizational, procedures. As long as schools seek practices designed to group away differences they are *not* nongraded. The nongraded school never held this as a goal, for it is impossible. Rather, nongrading says: "Accept children as they are, with all their differences, and teach to these differences. Don't try to eradicate them!" Until educators develop instructional programs that will meet this challenge they are not nongrading. They are simply masking their old egg-crate schools with a new facade.

INNOVATION AND REFORM

J. LLOYD TRUMP
On the "Ingredients of Change" (1963) *

You have an idea and you believe deeply in it. You want others to accept your belief. You are certain that results would be better if your idea were accepted in practice.

How do you change people? How do you change a school system? How do you change anything?

These questions are not new ones in the field of education or in other social enterprises. Finding answers to them has plagued educators and others for many years. Failure to discover better answers has resulted in the well-known time lag between the development of ideas, the try-out of experi-

mental approaches, and the production of effective changes in school systems. . . .

Ideas are powerful matters. Where did your idea originate? Did you hear it expressed, read about it, or see it in practice? Or did your mind generate the idea? Many ideas are logically developed from a complex of other persons' notions and experiences. Some appear to be new creations. Experimentation can lead to convincing results that need replication, dissemination, or revision. It is good, first of all, to analyze the sources of your ideas for change.

How do you know that your idea is worth the efforts you will make to change people and institutions? Those who purvey change have responsibility for the effects of change. How will you decide that the educational changes you suggest are good for students, teachers, and the community?

Of course, you may not be completely convinced yourself that your idea for change is good. Perhaps you want simply to dis-

* J. Lloyd Trump, "Rx Ingredients of Change," *Bulletin of the National Association of Secondary-School Principals,* XLVII (May, 1963), 11–20. Reprinted by permission of the National Association of Secondary School Principals, © Copyright: Washington, D.C.

cover whether the idea is worth investigation, or whether it has value for the school that you serve.

All of these concerns may be answered, and the appropriate decisions made, on the basis of a carefully developed prescription for effecting change. A prescription specifies ingredients. This statement identifies ten ingredients of change. Effective programs require attention to each of these elements. The rapidity of change will vary with the potency of these ten ingredients.

I. Related Dimensions

Three dimensions of school change need simultaneous attention. Ignoring any of these three facets inhibits the effectiveness of the other two. These three dimensions are: (1) selecting logical and sequential curricular content; (2) using more educational technology wisely; and (3) paying systematic attention to the institutional arrangements for learning.

Deciding what knowledge is of most worth, and how to organize it into a basic education curriculum required of all youth, are necessary components of change. Today's curriculum has too much unreasonable repetitiveness and too many unnatural termination points. The essential content in each subject discipline needs logical and sequential organization extending from the earliest years of childhood education through the time when a student ceases systematic contact with schools. Talented and interested students need supplementary depth education opportunities. Unless reasonable changes are sought in content and learning experiences for all children and youth, other types of changes will be relatively sterile.

However, improving curricular content and organization is not enough. This century has brought revolutionary developments in available instructional technology and more are coming. Proposed changes will be relatively less effective if students have available as aids to learning only the printed page and the physically present voices of their teacher and their student colleagues. Such questions as the following need consideration: If students at given stages in their development can learn better by listening and viewing than solely by reading, what recordings, films, television, and similar audiovisual materials should be available to them? What materials can different types of students learn with programmed instruction devices? What relationships should exist between books and other forms of technology? What tapes, records, films, slides, and the like should be used as integral parts of teaching and learning—just as textbooks and other reading materials are used today?

Reforms in curriculum content and organization, and in the use of technology, are not enough as ingredients of change. Different types of institutional arrangements also are essential. Three basic questions about content and technology need answering: (1) What instructional content and purposes can students of different ability levels learn and accomplish largely for themselves if they have the time, the space, the desire, and special assistants to help them do so? (2) What content and purposes require motivation, explanation, demonstration, or other types of presentations, by a competent teacher either physically present or by means of television, films or recordings, or programmed instruction devices? (3) What content and purposes require personal interaction among students and between students and a physically present teacher? The answers to these three questions suggest respectively programs of independent study, large-group instruction, and small-group discussion in student groupings different in size and composition than those found in conventional schools today. Other changes in institutional arrangements to facilitate improved conditions for learning include flexible use of time, team teaching, use of teacher assistants, individualized pupil programming, diversity of space, and monetary policies related more directly to the desired educational product.

Thus, the first ingredient of change requires planned relationships among curriculum content, instructional technology, and institutional arrangements. Emphasis on any one of these dimensions of change to the exclusion of, or limited attention to, the other one or two will limit the effectiveness of this first ingredient of change.

II. THE PRESENT SITUATION

Change rquires careful appraisal of forces that motivate the existing educational program. Alterations in the direction and the pressure of these forces condition resultant changes. Several illustrations can clarify this second ingredient of change.

Truly dedicated teachers feel deep emotional attachment to their personal responsibility for pupils' learning outcomes. Thus, they hesitate to allow instructional technology, teacher assistants, or other teachers to come between them and their students. Training and habit accustom teachers to certain patterns of teaching and evaluating. So they hesitate to change their methods, or the size of student groups they confront, for fear of personal inadequacy or, more important for them, the fear that their students may learn less. Some teachers are psychologically reinforced by the security of the self-contained classroom. Research studies show the influence of these personal values in creating resistance to change. Those who urge change in teaching arrangements must understand the power of the forces that cause teachers to conform to conventional practices. So, when changes are planned, specific efforts are needed to produce convincing evidence so that highly professional teachers are quite sure that the changes are good for them and their students.

Teachers bear heavy work loads. Quantitatively they average about 48 hours per week during the school year, more than most other workers. Also, theirs is an emotionally charged occupation. Those who propose change must not add to this work load if they expect sustained interest on the part of teachers. Research shows the importance of personal involvement in the changes— and that involvement takes time and energy.

So, time and proper conditions for personal involvement in the changes are needed.

Parents and their children feel reasonably secure in today's schools. Parents understand most school practices since those practices have remained quite constant. Whatever weaknesses in the schools appear are blamed largely on "Progressive Education," too many students, the teacher shortage, or lack of sufficient funds. Those who propose changes need to recognize those fears and simultaneously provide readily understood evidence that the students are learning more, passing examinations better, gaining admission to the colleges they wish and succeeding in them, or finding good jobs and doing well.

Although some taxpayers are interested only in tax reduction, most persons basically are concerned that their money is spent honestly and effectively. They are suspicious of frills, whatever meaning they ascribe to that term. They tend to resist educational change because their experience is that changes cost additional money. They know what they are getting now; they are uncertain about the effects of new approaches. The ingredient of change called for here is more attention to the relationships between financial input and product output. If the taxpayers' money is spent differently, the effects on what students know and do would also be different and demonstrable in terms that laymen can understand.

School administrators work hard to develop a smooth running machine. That result gives teachers and students confidence in administrative leadership and begets community acceptance. When they systematize as much of their job as possible, they can relax more and bask in the accompanying praise they receive. Change can upset all of that. If the school does not run so smoothly, or if there are more worries after the changes, there need to be some recognizable compensating factors: students learn more, teachers are more content, the community is enthusiastic.

So the second ingredient of change calls for clear analyses of all the forces that stabilize school practices in the present mold. Changing present practices requires altering the impact of those forces and substituting new outcomes that will produce another type of temporary stability—within the framework of the change that is sought.

III. EXPERIMENTAL STUDIES

Experimental approaches constitute a third basic ingredient in a program of change. Change based solely on opinion may be accepted because of the logic of the presentation or faith in the person urging the change. However, experimentation is more likely to produce change of a lasting nature.

Experimentation needs to be conducted in the local school setting. Although it is interesting and sometimes helpful to read about experimentation elsewhere, the findings will be more significant if they are replicated or discovered by local persons in the local school. Moreover, experimentation begets experimentation. Schools with a long-time reputation for high quality are schools that have constantly experimented over the years.

Three basic difficulties with experimentation need recognition. Some research is excellent in design, but what it signifies for school improvement is unclear. Other research touches very important matters, but it is done so poorly that few pay attention or accept it. And all research suffers from lack of impact on practices in schools.

There are essential ingredients in experimentation. Teachers involved in the studies need time to plan, conduct, and evaluate the results. Consultants can help them design studies so that adequate data are collected and other procedures followed to help all know what changes resulted from the experimentation.

It is unfortunate that many teachers and principals hesitate to conduct experimental studies. Some persons are overawed by technical statistical procedures and other characteristics of pure research. Most action research conducted in schools need not require such elaborate and difficult techniques. Experimentation and demonstration give

a local school something worth while to talk or write about. One rule in card playing is to "lead from strength." Those who experiment possess the essential ingredient of change.

IV. PREPARING AND DISTRIBUTING BROCHURES

Cleverly and honestly written, attractive brochures, describing the studies and demonstrations as well as the ideas growing out of them, need to be widely distributed periodically. The basic purpose of these publications is to acquaint staff members not immediately connected with these studies and the public in general with the nature of the projects under way.

These brochures should not be burdened with too much statistical material, nor should they be overly involved with historical backgrounds and quotations from authorities. The story should be told simply and directly. Simple line drawings and charts can be added to clarify and emphasize certain points. Photographs can be too complicated and actually detract from the story.

Professional help in developing these brochures is usually necessary. Unfortunately, the training of most teachers and principals has not included preparing effective materials of this nature. Someone with journalistic training often can take what others have written and remove excess or unclear verbiage. Such persons are often available on the local newspaper staff and can be obtained for a reasonable expenditure.

There is no magic length for these brochures. The number of pages usually will be in the range of 10–20 if they are widely read. The layout will include much "open space" so that the reader is not overwhelmed with printed material. It should be possible for the casual reader to complete the pamphlet in 15–20 minutes. The purpose of the pamphlet is not to tell the whole story, but rather to whet the appetite of the reader and to give him a general understanding of what is taking place at the school.

V. Speeches by Knowledgeable People

Innovations also need to be presented in an interesting manner by competent speakers. These speakers need to appear before as many organized groups in the community as possible. Women's organizations, service clubs, patriotic groups, church groups, and the like usually are looking for interesting programs. Too often, however, school speakers come seeking approval of a bond issue or a tax referendum, or they report in a somewhat dull manner on some aspects of the educational program. As was pointed out in the case of written materials, most teachers and principals have not had effective training in preparing and delivering speeches. They need professional help from speech teachers in the school or from competent persons in the community. The talks should be short, exciting, and, when possible, illustrated with overhead projector visuals or 2" by 2" slides.

The speeches basically aim to convey to varied audiences the notion that the school is constantly seeking better ways of doing things through research. Industry and other professions have capitalized heavily on this technique. It has not been sufficiently used by schools.

Speakers should always allow time for questions and comments by their audiences. These questions and comments can suggest ideas for future experimentation or revisions in programs now being studied.

VI. Demonstrations by Teachers and Students

Demonstrations of experimentation need to be much more dramatic than is usually the case today. Visiting class sessions in schools is in many cases a dull experience and a poor way for the person outside the school to learn something about the program. Watching a basketball game may be exciting, but watching a mathematics or history class often is an experience in slow motion.

Schools have sometimes sought to combat this lack of showmanship by placing demonstration classes in store windows downtown, or by conducting a class in front of a meeting of a woman's club. Neither of these methods has proved particularly effective for the same reasons that visiting a class in school is not for most people a stimulating experience. The action is too slow, and the purpose often is not clear to the viewer.

Demonstrations of experiments going on in the school should be presented in ways comparable with those used in a television or radio program. The program needs to provide a spirited explanation of the purposes and techniques, some tape recordings of student and teacher participants, some pictures and charts by means of 2" by 2" slides or other visuals, or some live demonstrations by teachers and students that have been carefully rehearsed to highlight what is going on in these studies. Be sure that the demonstration includes information and techniques on evaluation. The pacing of the demonstration should be carefully planned and the points of likely audience interest clearly and dramatically highlighted. The entire program ordinarily should not last more than 20–30 minutes. Professional help can enhance the program and produce more convincing results.

VII. Using Mass Media

What is going on in the experimentation should be described as effectively as possible in newspapers, on radio and television, by means of slide-tapes, and, if more funds are available, through professionally produced sound films. Persons using the mass media should study how these media are used effectively by commercial enterprises interested in selling products or changing the attitudes of people. School people should never forget that they have something tremendously interesting and vital to sell. They should work just as hard at it and as effectively as people who are selling products to make money.

VIII. Issuing Summary Reports of Changes

Periodically, the school should issue carefully written summaries of what is happening as a result of the experimental approaches and changes. These reports should contain statements by students and teachers giving their reactions to what is happening as well as provide illustrations and data showing the effects of the changes on students and teachers. The reports should be professionally prepared so they will be widely read and so that the message they convey will be understood by various groups.

This report differs from the one described under Ingredient IV in that the purpose here is to report progress, whereas the earlier document reports ideas and plans.

Parents, teachers, and others want assurances that the students are acquiring the knowledge and skills that colleges and employers expect. They also want to know about other learning outcomes for students, how teachers feel about the studies and the effects of the new procedures on them, and what consequences the changes produce on the school budget.

IX. Keeping Staff Members Informed

It is highly important that staff members not immediately involved in the experimentation be kept informed regarding what is going on and what is being accomplished. These staff members often are suspicious, and, in some cases, defensive about their own failure not to be involved in the studies. The kinds of reports described in the previous section are not enough for them. Staff members should receive memoranda from the principal of the school describing exactly what is taking place. The message should be written in such a way that those staff members not participating in the studies are encouraged and helped to conduct studies themselves. Obviously, staff members should not hear about experimentation from persons outside the school, or by means of gossip at faculty lunch tables. They should

receive very early in the planning stage information from official sources and continue to receive their information as long as the studies are being conducted.

X. Encourage Experimental Approaches

The central purpose of the administrative-supervisory hierarchy is to encourage and spearhead new ideas and searches for better ways of doing things. The tenth ingredient of change requires that officials work to develop a school environment in which change is possible, and where the chances of success are good.

Changes should be planned systematically. Appropriate persons should make priority decisions, writing out in detail what is to be done this year, next year, and by the end of five years. Such plans call for systematic evaluation since flexibility requires a willingness to change the plans when new evidence appears.

Truly professional educators do not fear change. Nor for them does insecurity result in defensive tactics against pressure groups which oppose change. Conversely, they find security in their eagerness to experiment with proposals from laymen or staff members who hypothesize that their ideas will serve better the individual needs of students, will increase the professional satisfactions and morale of teachers, and are logistically and financially feasible. Actually, the most secure and successful persons in the educational profession are those who understand the ingredients of change and are anxious to lead the way to better schools.

There are, of course, factors other than the foregoing ten that bear on educational change. Little is said here directly about laws, external events, and some personal factors that relate to these prescribed ingredients. However influential these other factors may be in a given situation, the fact remains that what results from the activities of educational researchers in their laboratories, the contacts of governmental or foundation officials, or what principals do in schools will be conditioned in a major manner by the wise use of these ten ingredients of change.

If you are the responsible person and have an idea you believe others should accept and follow, or if you wish to change a school, this is your prescription with the ingredients listed and the general directions given. The rest is up to you.

JEROME S. BRUNER
"The Spiral Curriculum" (1960) *

The curriculum of a subject should be determined by the most fundamental understanding that can be achieved of the underlying principles that give structure to that subject. Teaching specific topics or skills without making clear their context in the broader fundamental structure of a field of knowledge is uneconomical in several deep senses. In the first place, such teaching makes it exceedingly difficult for the student to generalize from what he has learned to what he will encounter later. In the second place, learning that has fallen short of a grasp of general principles has little reward in terms of intellectual excitement. The best way to create interest in a subject is to render it worth knowing, which means to make the knowledge gained usable in one's thinking beyond the situation in which the learning has occurred. Third, knowledge one has acquired without sufficient structure to tie it together is knowledge that is likely to be forgotten. An unconnected set of facts has a pitiably short half-life in memory. Organizing facts in terms of principles and ideas from which they may be inferred is the only known way of reducing the quick rate of loss of human memory.

Designing curricula in a way that reflects the basic structure of a field of knowledge requires the most fundamental understanding of that field. It is a task that cannot be

* Reprinted by permission of the publishers from Jerome S. Bruner, *The Process of Education* (Cambridge, Mass.: Harvard University Press, 1960). Copyright 1960 by the President and Fellows of Harvard College.

carried out without the active participation of the ablest scholars and scientists. The experience of the past several years has shown that such scholars and scientists, working in conjunction with experienced teachers and students of child development, can prepare curricula of the sort we have been considering. . . .

The "spiral curriculum." If one respects the ways of thought of the growing child, if one is courteous enough to translate material into his logical forms and challenging enough to tempt him to advance, then it is possible to introduce him at an early age to the ideas and styles that in later life make an educated man. We might ask, as a criterion for any subject taught in primary school, whether, when fully developed, it is worth an adult's knowing, and whether having known it as a child makes a person a better adult. If the answer to both questions is negative or ambiguous, then the material is cluttering the curriculum.

If the hypothesis . . . is true—that any subject can be taught to any child in some honest form—then it should follow that a curriculum ought to be built around the great issues, principles, and values that a society deems worthy of the continual concern of its members. Consider two examples—the teaching of literature and of science. If it is granted, for example, that it is desirable to give children an awareness of the meaning of human tragedy and a sense of compassion for it, is it not possible at the earliest appropriate age to teach the literature of tragedy in a manner that illuminates but does not threaten? There are many possible ways to begin: through a retelling of the great myths, through the use of children's classics, through presentation of and commentary on selected films that have proved themselves. Precisely what kinds of materials should be used at what age with what effect is a subject for research—research of several kinds. We may ask first about the child's conception of the the tragic, and here one might proceed in much the same way that Piaget and his colleagues have proceeded in studying the child's conception of physical causality, of morality, of number, and the rest. It is only when we are equipped with such knowledge that we will be in a position to know how the child will translate whatever we present to him into his own subjective terms. Nor need we wait for all the research findings to be in before proceeding, for a skillful teacher can also experiment by attempting to teach what seems to be intuitively right for children of different ages, correcting as he goes. In time, one goes beyond to more complex versions of the same kind of literature or simply revisits some of the same books used earlier. What matters is that later teaching build upon earlier reactions to literature, that it seek to create an ever more explicit and mature understanding of the literature of tragedy. Any of the great literary forms can be handled in the same way, or any of the great themes—be it the form of comedy or the theme of identity, personal loyalty, or what not.

So too in science. If the understanding of number, measure, and probability is judged crucial in the pursuit of science, then instruction in these subjects should begin as intellectually honestly and as early as possible in a manner consistent with the child's forms of thought. Let the topics be developed and redeveloped in later grades. Thus, if most children are to take a tenth-grade unit in biology, need they approach the subject cold? Is it not possible, with a minimum of formal laboratory work if necessary, to introduce them to some of the major biological ideas earlier, in a spirit perhaps less exact and more intuitive?

Many curricula are originally planned with a guiding idea much like the one set forth here. But as curricula are actually executed, as they grow and change, they often lose their original form and suffer a relapse into a certain shapelessness. It is not amiss to urge that actual curricula be reexamined with an eye to the issues of continuity and development. . . . One cannot predict the exact forms that revision might take; indeed, it is plain that there is now available too

little research to provide adequate answers. One can only propose that appropriate research be undertaken with the greatest vigor and as soon as possible.

BERNARD Z. FRIEDLANDER
On "Innovations in Teaching" (1966)*

The spirit of innovation is perhaps the most outstanding characteristic of today's educational scene. The rapid pace of change carries with it the danger that innovations may become new orthodoxies despite the absence of clear evidence that they can live up to the expectations for improvement that they arouse.

Of particular concern to both psychologists and teachers are the new and perhaps oversimplified views about how students think, learn, and remember. Though advances in recent research are often impressive, our knowledge about thinking, learning, and memory as they occur in everyday life is far from complete. This means that teachers will continue to face the responsibility and freedom to judge what and how to teach, with only limited means for discovering whether their judgments are correct.

I believe, therefore, that we must exercise our best critical faculties in order to identify new ideas which truly deserve serious attention. We must be prepared to discard proposals that represent no real advance, and rescue good ideas from the distortions of fad and fashion. I also believe that teachers must play an important role in the difficult task of selection.

If teachers are to maintain authority over their own enterprise under the stress of chronic change, they must seek and be granted a prominent part in evaluating the flood of new ideas. Classroom teachers are the only people in a school who have direct, daily contact with students at the level of thinking and learning. They would make a grave mistake to leave it entirely to others

* Bernard Z. Friedlander, "Today's Innovations in Teaching," *NEA Journal*, Vol. 55, No. 3 (March, 1966), pp. 11–14. Used by permission.

inside and outside the scholastic community to determine what innovations in curriculum and teaching practice should be accepted and what rejected.

What I would like to do here is to discuss three powerful ideas in education that I think are in danger of becoming seriously distorted as they acquire the status of general principles in a new, and possibly misshapen, orthodoxy. My purpose is not to assault or refute. I only wish to say a few words of caution that may prevent some excellent notions on teaching and learning from becoming unexamined fixtures of sacred ritual.

These three topics have to do with the roles of concepts, of curiosity, and of discovery in classroom learning.

Great attention is paid to the significance of emphasizing general principles in current teaching practices. Bruner has pointed out the importance of establishing "structures" of knowledge so that the student can find meaningful relationships among comprehensive ideas, rather than have to struggle with countless facts in isolation.

This is certainly a useful antidote to the old-fashioned teaching, in which feats of memory in a conceptual vacuum were often mistaken for successful learning. But in their healthy concern for trying to discover and teach underlying concepts, teachers may have become a bit cavalier and apologetic about the importance of having students acquire a firm command of rudimentary facts and skills.

What appears to be missing, especially in some of the new mathematics programs, is recognition that skill in performing routine operations may be the learner's key to comprehending concepts. In the quest for the communication of essential ideas, I think we in education have tended to forget that ideas grow best in minds well nourished with organized facts. One of the goals of teaching and learning is to have students accept the discipline of facts and skills as a prerequisite for true understanding.

I am not suggesting that teachers turn back the classroom clock and create new drudgeries for children to memorize; education must continue to be directed toward concepts and ideas. I am saying, however, that those of us who are concerned with teaching as a practical classroom art need to reexamine our attitudes toward some of the mechanics of language, numbers, science, history, and literature.

Where we conclude that certain mechanical skills and rote memory (dare I use the term?) are basic to the structure of what we want to teach, then we should go ahead and teach them without apology, making certain that we find effective ways to do the teaching so that the capable students really do learn what we deem important.

History teachers, for example, should not fear having students remember and recognize significant dates. How can they tell whether a student has any worthwhile comprehension of an historical trend if he cannot recall how many years elapsed between two related events, say between the Declaration of Independence and the signing of the Constitution? In short, from kindergarten through graduate school we ought to have serious reservations about a student's grasp of a concept unless he can exemplify it with a factual recitation or an able demonstration.

Another idea that has gained wide circulation is that children in their natural state possess a steady, all-consuming curiosity and that their desire to know new things compares almost to the insistence of the hunger drive. The early investigators of curiosity and of exploratory behavior as important psychological principles gave impetus to this view more than a decade ago. They spoke of curiosity motivation and curiosity behavior with the same terminology generally used in discussions of the primary drives based on body needs for survival.

From the statements that increasingly occur in the literature on children's motivation, the teacher may be led to infer that (a) children almost uniformly have powerful cravings to learn; (b) the teacher's real function is simply to get the children started in the right direction and then stand aside to avoid being trampled in the stampede to acquire knowledge; and (c) if otherwise "normal" children don't follow the above pattern, the teacher is doing something wrong.

I doubt whether the daily experience of most teachers matches this view of children's love of learning. Although many children certainly do show strong interest in learning new things at some times, in some places, and with some companions, curiosity may operate only marginally as an incentive for classroom learning. This is true for a number of reasons.

First of all, curiosity in older as well as in younger children is often unsystematic and noncumulative, whereas school learning must be systematic and cumulative if it is to have value.

Second, a child's curiosity may be immediately and easily satisfied; the child may try to avoid having it manipulated for any further learning.

For example, a bright eight-year-old acquaintance said to me recently: "I've got a question and I want you to answer it. Don't just give me back another question like you and the science teacher always do. I just want to know, Why doesn't an airplane fly sideways?"

The boy did not want a great learning experience or a Socratic dialogue. He wanted no more than an answer to a specific question, preferably fast and to the point. Teachers have told me his attitude is not uncommon. His was a curiosity that could not be manipulated for instructional purposes.

Third, children's curiosity may be most strongly aroused by matters that are frequently not part of the regular curriculum. Psychologists are in general agreement that children from kindergarten on upward have strong drives to learn about babies, love, marriage, and other sexual matters.

With increasing age, the pressure from this aspect of curiosity increases in an exponential manner, though not always visibly. This is especially so in a culture such as ours that suffers from acute ambivalence about sexuality, with notions of display and permissiveness at war with opposing notions of secretiveness and restriction.

These pressures and conflicts are often so great I sometimes wonder how many students, especially adolescents, can think or pretend to think seriously about any other topic. We should not be surprised that many children are not highly interested in or curious about academic topics when the questions that really concern and perturb them are left unanswered or, more likely, unasked.

A fourth problem in using curiosity incentives and rewards involves the difficulty of managing them for individual students in a group situation.

Below the level at which students are ready to work with considerable independence, spontaneous curiosity tends to arise in individualistic and fragmented ways that may contain few points of common contact in a class as a whole.

Although it is not impossible, it is quite difficult in a class with more than a half dozen students for even a skillful teacher to elicit and give appropriate responses to a heavy flow of spontaneous expressions of curiosity. Yet if inquiries prompted by curiosity are not rapidly refined and given appropriate responses, interest in a given topic quickly fades or turns elsewhere.

Finally, as a personal trait, curiosity is distinguished by a broad range of individual differences. Some children have lots of it and some have little. On these grounds alone, it is doubtful whether a comprehensive view of teaching and learning could be successfully based on the blanket assumption that children just naturally want to learn and can be easily induced to learn things teachers want to teach.

In fact, some children find new knowledge not only unrewarding, but also extremely threatening in ways teachers do not always perceive. It is not uncommon to find children who actively suppress an interest in learning new things, or who suppress showing on tests or in discussions what they actually have learned.

Such children—our underachievers—present perhaps the greatest frustration to even the most able teacher. When we recognize how large a portion of our student population falls into this category (including many who possess all the requisites for scholastic success) we can see how dangerous it is to depend upon the force of curiosity as a universal motivator for students.

To summarize this topic, I think we must view with extreme caution the notion that curiosity and the spontaneous desire to learn can, by themselves, generate the disciplined attention and motivation needed to master the increasing content of an expanding school curriculum. We are probably on safer ground for the time being if we continue to rely in the classroom on such extrinsic incentives as approval, the achievement motive, and possibly even the device of special privileges, in addition to the intrinsically rewarding effect of learning for its own sake.

Our third topic is the idea that having students "discover" for themselves the generalizations or inferences which the subject matter contains has to be superior to having the teacher present them.

There are two major reasons why discovery is thought of as an extremely powerful mode of learning. First, it capitalizes on the strong reward value of bringing order, clarity, and meaning to experiences that were previously muddled and confusing. Orderliness is gratifying; meaninglessness is distasteful.

Second, teaching by means of discovery techniques makes the student an active participant in his own learning. Because his learning is a product of his own thinking and manipulation of basic facts, the student is supposed to retain his new knowledge more completely than he would a system of facts and ideas presented to him by someone else.

Both of these reasons raise very specific problems. One problem involves the direction and correctness of discovery: Do discoveries necessarily lead to productive findings and resolutions? We know, of course, that some voyages of exploration are bound to fail and that failure can have its values. I doubt, however, that we are really prepared to face up to the frequency with which failures may occur—and the degree of confusion such failures can generate.

However well we structure the preliminary materials from which discoveries are to be launched, there remains an indefinitely large number of possibilities for derailing a productive train of thought. The student's thinking often may go off in directions that lead to needless complications of the learning process.

I once saw an excellent example of such a difficulty in a first grade reading class. A boy "discovered" that the phonetic value of the soft *c,* as in "cent," was determined by whether it was a capital or small letter, rather than by its relationship to the associated vowel as the teacher was leading the class to recognize.

In defending his mistake, the boy followed a common pattern of children's thinking by inventing an "explanation" when he could not find the right rule. The boy insisted that the letters on the chalkboard were capital and lower case, despite the fact that they were virtually identical in size and shape. Although the boy was wrong and had no objective basis for thinking the way he did, he clung to the propriety of his discovery even when the teacher offered him an "escape route" to the correct answer.

That brief episode alerted me to watch for other "discoveries" that lead to confusing outcomes. I soon found that it takes only a few hours of classroom observing to see frequent mistakes of this kind—mistakes, furthermore, that often go uncorrected. Errors of fact, of perception, or of association can lead to hopelessly chaotic chains of mistaken inferences and deductions when teachers seek to capitalize on the student's spontaneous reasoning.

I also found that the teacher often has understandable difficulty identifying the seemingly inscrutable logic that causes the student's primitive thoughts to jump the rail. When this happens, the consequence is likely to be discomfiture on the teacher's part and useless disruption of the lesson for the rest of the class. Such failures may be the price of progress, but we should not close our eyes to how high that price might be.

In addition to direction and correctness, a problem associated with discovery concerns the matter of retention—memory of what has been learned. Much of our faith in the discovery method of learning is based on the assumption that the student is more likely to retain insights he has developed on his own. I know of no extensive "hard" evidence to support this view. Findings relating discovery learning and self-directed study with memory are inconclusive.

Anecdotal evidence from teachers who have used discovery methods in their classrooms often bears out the inconclusiveness of research results. Teachers say that crucial notions are often "discovered" again and again by the same student—each time with just about the same naive glow of satisfaction, as if the thought had never occurred before, to him or to anyone else.

From all the criticisms presented thus far, one might conclude that I am somehow "against" teaching that searches for larger concepts, that seeks to stimulate and satisfy curiosity, and that attempts to provide structures within which students can find important facts and relationships. This is not my intent.

The purpose in raising these criticisms is to indicate the danger of having many important ideas about teaching and learning lose their potency because of oversimplification, misunderstanding, empty ritualistic application, and disappointment. By examining some of the unsettled problems, we can approach these ideas with greater clarity, using informed judgment to gain maximum advantage from them.

In using any of these ideas, the factor of judgment is crucial. When we recognize the complications of the teaching and learning process, with all its delicate balances between freedom and discipline, between concept and fact, and between memory and forgetting, we are not likely to find any one method or formula that fits all situations. Only the wise intervention of the teacher's judgment can hold these shifting stresses in equilibrium.

In order to fulfill his role, the modern teacher must play an active part in deciding how and what to teach, adapting each decision both to long-range objectives and to the needs of the moment as the learner comes to understand what he previously did not comprehend.

THE TECHNOLOGY OF EDUCATION

B. F. SKINNER
"The Science of Learning and the Art of Teaching" (1954)*

Some promising advances have recently been made in the field of learning. Special techniques have been designed to arrange what are called "contingencies of reinforcement"—the relations which prevail between

* B. F. Skinner, "The Science of Learning and the Art of Teaching," *Harvard Educational Review*, XXIV (Spring, 1954), 86–97. Copyright © 1954 by President and Fellows of Harvard College. Used by permission.

behavior on the one hand and the consequences of that behavior on the other—with the result that a much more effective control of behavior has been achieved. It has long been argued that an organism learns mainly by producing changes in its environment, but it is only recently that these changes have been carefully manipulated. In traditional devices for the study of learning—in the serial maze, for example, or in the T-maze, the problem box, or the familiar discrimination apparatus—the effects produced by the organism's behavior are left to many fluctuating circumstances. There is many a slip between the turn-to-the-right and the food-cup at the end of the alley. It is not surprising that techniques of this sort have yielded only very rough data from which the uniformities demanded by an experimental science can be extracted only by averaging many cases. In none of this work has the behavior of the individual organism been predicted in more than a statistical sense. The learning processes which are the presumed object of such research are reached only through a series of inferences. Current preoccupation with deductive systems reflects this state of the science.

Recent improvements in the conditions which control behavior in the field of learning are of two principal sorts. The Law of Effect has been taken seriously; we have made sure that effects *do* occur and that they occur under conditions which are optimal for producing the changes called learning. Once we have arranged the particular type of consequence called a reinforcement, our techniques permit us to shape up the behavior of an organism almost at will. It has become a routine exercise to demonstrate this in classes in elementary psychology by conditioning such an organism as a pigeon. Simply by presenting food to a hungry pigeon at the right time, it is possible to shape up three or four well-defined responses in a single demonstration period— such responses as turning around, pacing the floor in the pattern of a figure-8, standing still in a corner of the demonstration apparatus, stretching the neck, or stamping the foot. Extremely complex performances may be reached through successive stages in the shaping process, the contingencies of reinforcement being changed progressively in the direction of the required behavior. The results are often quite dramatic. In such a demonstration one can *see* learning take place. A significant change in behavior is often obvious as the result of a single reinforcement.

A second important advance in technique permits us to maintain behavior in given states of strength for long periods of time. Reinforcements continue to be important, of course, long after an organism has learned *how* to do something, long after it has acquired behavior. They are necessary to maintain the behavior in strength. Of special interest is the effect of various schedules of intermittent reinforcement. Charles B. Ferster and the author are currently preparing an extensive report of a five-year research program, sponsored by the Office of Naval Research, in which most of the important types of schedules have been investigated and in which the effects of schedules in general have been reduced to a few principles. On the theoretical side we now have a fairly good idea of why a given schedule produces its appropriate performance. On the practical side we have learned how to maintain any given level of activity for daily periods limited only by the physical exhaustion of the organism and from day to day without substantial change throughout its life. Many of these effects would be traditionally assigned to the field of motivation, although the principal operation is simply the arrangement of contingencies of reinforcement.

These new methods of shaping behavior and of maintaining it in strength are a great improvement over the traditional practices of professional animal trainers, and it is not surprising that our laboratory results are already being applied to the production of performing animals for commercial purposes. In a more academic environment they have been used for demonstration purposes which extend far beyond an interest in learning as such. For example, it is not too difficult to arrange the complex contingencies which produce many types of social behavior. Competition is exemplified by two pigeons playing a modified game of ping-pong. The pigeons drive the ball back and forth across a small table by pecking at it. When the ball gets by one pigeon, the other is reinforced. The task of constructing such a "social relation" is probably completely out of reach of the traditional animal trainer. It requires a carefully designed program of gradually changing contingencies and the skillful use of schedules to maintain the behavior in strength. Each pigeon is separately prepared for its part in the total performance, and the "social relation" is then arbitrarily constructed. The sequence of events leading up to this stable state are excellent material for the study of the factors important in nonsynthetic social behavior. It is instructive to consider how a similar series of contingencies could arise in the case of the human organism through the evolution of cultural patterns.

Cooperation can also be set up, perhaps more easily than competition. We have trained two pigeons to coordinate their behavior in a cooperative endeavor with a precision which equals that of the most skillful human dancers. In a more serious vein these techniques have permitted us to explore the complexities of the individual organism and to analyze some of the serial or coordinate behaviors involved in attention, problem solving, various types of self-control, and the subsidiary systems of responses within a single organism called "personalities." Some of these are exemplified in what we call multiple schedules of reinforcement. In general a given schedule has an effect upon the rate at which a response is emitted. Changes in the rate from moment to moment show a pattern typical of the schedule. The pattern may be as simple as a constant rate of responding at a given value, it may be a gradually accelerating rate between certain extremes, it may be an abrupt change from not responding at all to a given stable high rate, and so on. It has been shown that the performance characteristic of a given schedule can be brought under the control of a particular stimulus and that different performances can be brought under the control of different stimuli in the same organism. At a recent meeting of the American Psychological Association, Dr. Ferster and the author demonstrated a pigeon whose behavior showed the pattern typical of "fixed-interval" reinforcement in the presence of one stimulus and,

alternately, the pattern typical of the very different schedule called "fixed ratio" in the presence of a second stimulus. In the laboratory we have been able to obtain performances appropriate to *nine* different schedules in the presence of appropriate stimuli in random alternation. When Stimulus 1 is present, the pigeon executes the performance appropriate to Schedule 1. When Stimulus 2 is present, the pigeon executes the performance appropriate to Schedule 2. And so on. This result is important because it makes the extrapolation of our laboratory results to daily life much more plausible. We are all constantly shifting from schedule to schedule as our immediate environment changes, but the dynamics of the control exercised by reinforcement remain essentially unchanged.

It is also possible to construct very complex *sequences* of schedules. It is not easy to describe these in a few words, but two or three examples may be mentioned. In one experiment the pigeon generates a performance appropriate to Schedule A where the reinforcement is simply the production of the stimulus characteristic of Schedule B, to which the pigeon then responds appropriately. Under a third stimulus, the bird yields a performance appropriate to Schedule C where the reinforcement in this case is simply the production of the stimulus characteristic of Schedule D, to which the bird then responds appropriately. In a special case, first investigated by L. B. Wyckoff, Jr., the organism responds to one stimulus where the reinforcement consists of the *clarification* of the stimulus controlling another response. The first response becomes, so to speak, an objective form of "paying attention" to the second stimulus. In one important version of this experiment, as yet unpublished, we could say that the pigeon is telling us whether it is "paying attention" to the *shape* of a spot of light or to its *color*.

One of the most dramatic applications of these techniques has recently been made in the Harvard Psychological Laboratories by Floyd Ratliff and Donald S. Blough, who have skillfully used multiple and serial schedules of reinforcement to study complex perceptual processes in the infrahuman organism. They have achieved a sort of psychophysics without verbal instruction. In a recent experiment by Blough, for example, a pigeon draws a detailed dark-adaptation curve showing the characteristic breaks of rod and cone vision. The curve is recorded continuously in a single experimental period and is quite comparable with the curves of human subjects. The pigeon behaves in a way which, in the human case, we would not hesitate to describe by saying that it adjusts a very faint patch of light until it can just be seen.

In all this work, the species of the organism has made surprisingly little difference. It is true that the organisms studied have all been vertebrates, but they still cover a wide range. Comparable results have been obtained with pigeons, rats, dogs, monkeys, human children, and most recently, by the author in collaboration with Ogden R. Lindsley, human psychotic subjects. In spite of great phylogenetic differences, all these organisms show amazingly similar properties of the learning process. It should be emphasized that this has been achieved by analyzing the effects of reinforcement and by designing techniques which manipulate reinforcement with considerable precision. Only in this way can the behavior of the individual organism be brought under such precise control. It is also important to note that through a gradual advance to complex interrelations among responses, the same degree of rigor is being extended to behavior which would usually be assigned to such fields as perception, thinking, and personality dynamics.

From this exciting prospect of an advancing science of learning, it is a great shock to turn to that branch of technology which is most directly concerned with the learning process—education. Let us consider, for example, the teaching of arithmetic in the lower grades. The school is concerned with imparting to the child a large number of responses of a special sort. The responses are all verbal. They consist of speaking and writing certain words, figures, and signs which, to put it roughly, refer to numbers and to arithmetic operations. The first task is to shape up these responses—to get the child to pronounce and to write responses correctly, but the principal task is to bring this behavior under many sorts of stimulus control. This is what happens when the child learns to count, to recite tables, to count while ticking off the items in an assemblage of objects, to respond to spoken or written numbers by saying "odd," "even," "prime," and so on. Over and above this elaborate repertoire of numerical behavior, most of which is often dismissed as the product of rote learning, the teaching of arithmetic looks forward to those complex serial arrangements of responses involved in original mathematical thinking. The child must acquire responses of transposing, clearing fractions, and so on, which modify the order or pattern of the original material so that the response called a solution is eventually made possible.

Now, how is this extremely complicated verbal repertoire set up? In the first place, what reinforcements are used? Fifty years ago the answer would have been clear. At that time educational control was still frankly aversive. The child read numbers, copied numbers, memorized tables, and performed operations upon numbers to escape the threat of the birch rod or cane. Some positive reinforcements were perhaps eventually derived from the increased efficiency of the child in the field of arithmetic and in rare cases some automatic reinforcement may have resulted from the sheer manipulation of the medium—from the solution of problems or the discovery of the intricacies of the number system. But for the immediate purposes of education the child acted to avoid or escape punishment. It was part of the reform movement known as progressive education to make the positive consequences more immediately effective, but any one who visits the lower grades of the average school today will observe that a change has been made, not from aversive to positive control, but from one form of aversive stimulation to another. The child at his desk, filling in his workbook, is behaving primarily to escape from the threat of a series of minor aversive events—the teacher's displeasure, the criticism or ridicule of his classmates, an ignominious showing in a competition, low marks, a trip to the office "to be talked to" by the principal, or a word to the parent who may still resort to the birch rod. In this welter of aversive consequences, getting the right answer is in itself an insignificant event, any effect of which is lost amid the anxieties, the boredom, and the aggressions which are the inevitable by-products of aversive control.[1]

Secondly, we have to ask how the contingencies of reinforcement are arranged. When is a numerical operation reinforced as "right"? Eventually, of course, the pupil may be able to check his own answers and achieve some sort of automatic reinforcement, but in the early stages the reinforcement of being right is usually accorded by the teacher. The contingencies she provides are far from optimal. It can easily be demonstrated that, unless explicit mediating behavior has been set up, the lapse of only a few seconds between response and reinforcement destroys most of the effect. In a typical classroom, nevertheless, long periods of time customarily elapse. The teacher may walk up and down the aisle, for example, while the class is working on a sheet of problems, pausing here and there to say right or wrong. Many seconds or minutes intervene between the child's response and the teacher's reinforcement. In many cases —for example, when papers are taken home to be corrected—as much as 24 hours may intervene. It is surprising that this system has any effect whatsoever.

A third notable shortcoming is the lack of a skillful program which moves forward through a series of progressive approximations to the final complex behavior desired.

[1] Skinner, B. F. *Science and Human Behavior.* New York: Macmillan, 1953.

A long series of contingencies is necessary to bring the organism into the possession of mathematical behavior most efficiently. But the teacher is seldom able to reinforce at each step in such a series because she cannot deal with the pupil's responses one at a time. It is usually necessary to reinforce the behavior in blocks of responses—as in correcting a work sheet or page from a workbook. The responses within such a block must not be interrelated. The answer to one problem must not depend upon the answer to another. The number of stages through which one may progressively approach a complex pattern of behavior is therefore small, and the task so much the more difficult. Even the most modern workbook in beginning arithmetic is far from exemplifying an efficient program for shaping up mathematical behavior.

Perhaps the most serious criticism of the current classroom is the relative infrequency of reinforcement. Since the pupil is usually dependent upon the teacher for being right, and since many pupils are usually dependent upon the same teacher, the total number of contingencies which may be arranged during, say, the first four years, is of the order of only a few thousand. But a very rough estimate suggests that efficient mathematical behavior at this level requires something of the order of 25,000 contingencies. We may suppose that even in the brighter student a given contingency must be arranged several times to place the behavior well in hand. The responses to be set up are not simply the various items in tables of addition, subtraction, multiplication, and division; we have also to consider the alternative forms in which each item may be stated. To the learning of such material we should add hundreds of responses concerned with factoring, identifying primes, memorizing series, using short-cut techniques of calculation, constructing and using geometric representations or number forms, and so on. Over and above all this, the whole mathematical repertoire must be brought under the control of concrete problems of considerable variety.

Perhaps 50,000 contingencies is a more conservative estimate. In this frame of reference the daily assignment in arithmetic seems pitifully meagre.

The result of all this is, of course, well known. Even our best schools are under criticism for their inefficiency in the teaching of drill subjects such as arithmetic. The condition in the average school is a matter of wide-spread national concern. Modern children simply do not learn arithmetic quickly or well. Nor is the result simply incompetence. The very subjects in which modern techniques are weakest are those in which failure is most conspicuous, and in the wake of an ever-growing incompetence come the anxieties, uncertainties, and aggressions which in their turn present other problems to the school. Most pupils soon claim the asylum of not being "ready" for arithmetic at a given level or, eventually, of not having a mathematical mind. Such explanations are readily seized upon by defensive teachers and parents. Few pupils ever reach the stage at which automatic reinforcements follow as the natural consequences of mathematical behavior. On the contrary, the figures and symbols of mathematics have become standard emotional stimuli. The glimpse of a column of figures, not to say an algebraic symbol or an integral sign, is likely to set off —not mathematical behavior—but a reaction of anxiety, guilt, or fear.

The teacher is usually no happier about this than the pupil. Denied the opportunity to control via the birch rod, quite at sea as to the mode of operation of the few techniques at her disposal, she spends as little time as possible on drill subjects and eagerly subscribes to philosophies of education which emphasize material of greater inherent interest. A confession of weakness is her extraordinary concern lest the child be taught something unnecessary. The repertoire to be imparted is carefully reduced to an essential minimum. In the field of spelling, for example, a great deal of time and energy has gone into discovering just those words which the young child is going to use,

as if it were a crime to waste one's educational power in teaching an unnecessary word. Eventually, weakness of technique emerges in the disguise of a reformulation of the aims of education. Skills are minimized in favor of vague achievements— educating for democracy, educating the whole child, educating for life, and so on. And there the matter ends; for, unfortunately, these philosophies do not in turn suggest improvements in techniques. They offer little or no help in the design of better classroom practices.

There would be no point in urging these objections if improvement were impossible. But the advances which have recently been made in our control of the learning process suggest a thorough revision of classroom practices and, fortunately, they tell us how the revision can be brought about. This is not, of course, the first time that the results of an experimental science have been brought to bear upon the practical problems of education. The modern classroom does not, however, offer much evidence that research in the field of learning has been respected or used. This condition is no doubt partly due to the limitations of earlier research. But it has been encouraged by a too hasty conclusion that the laboratory study of learning is inherently limited because it cannot take into account the realities of the classroom. In the light of our increasing knowledge of the learning process we should, instead, insist upon dealing with those realities and forcing a substantial change in them. Education is perhaps the most important branch of scientific technology. It deeply affects the lives of all of us. We can no longer allow the exigencies of a practical situation to suppress the tremendous improvements which are within reach. The practical situation must be changed.

There are certain questions which have to be answered in turning to the study of any new organism. What behavior is to be set up? What reinforcers are at hand? What responses are available in embarking upon a program of progressive approximation which will lead to the final form of the behavior? How can reinforcements be most efficiently scheduled to maintain the behavior in strength? These questions are all relevant in considering the problem of the child in the lower grades.

In the first place, what reinforcements are available? What does the school have in its possession which will reinforce a child? We may look first to the material to be learned, for it is possible that this will provide considerable automatic reinforcement. Children play for hours with mechanical toys, paints, scissors and paper, noise-makers, puzzles—in short, with almost anything which feeds back significant changes in the environment and is reasonably free of aversive properties. The sheer control of nature is itself reinforcing. This effect is not evident in the modern school because it is masked by the emotional responses generated by aversive control. It is true that automatic reinforcement from the manipulation of the environment is probably only a mild reinforcer and may need to be carefully husbanded, but one of the most striking principles to emerge from recent research is that the *net* amount of reinforcement is of little significance. A very slight reinforcement may be tremendously effective in controlling behavior if it is wisely used.

If the natural reinforcement inherent in the subject matter is not enough, other reinforcers must be employed. Even in school the child is occasionally permitted to do "what he wants to do," and access to reinforcements of many sorts may be made contingent upon the more immediate consequences of the behavior to be established. Those who advocate competition as a useful social motive may wish to use the reinforcements which follow from excelling others, although there is the difficulty that in this case the reinforcement of one child is necessarily aversive to another. Next in order we might place the good will and affection of the teacher, and only when that has failed need we turn to the use of aversive stimulation.

In the second place, how are these reinforcements to be made contingent upon the desired behavior? There are two considerations here—the gradual elaboration of extremely complex patterns of behavior and the maintenance of the behavior in strength at each stage. The whole process of becoming competent in any field must be divided into a very large number of very small steps, and reinforcement must be contingent upon the accomplishment of each step. This solution to the problem of creating a complex repertoire of behavior also solves the problem of maintaining the behavior in strength. We could, of course, resort to the techniques of scheduling already developed in the study of other organisms but in the present state of our knowledge of educational practices, scheduling appears to be most effectively arranged through the design of the material to be learned. By making each successive step as small as possible, the frequency of reinforcement can be raised to a maximum, while the possibly aversive consequences of being wrong are reduced to a minimum. Other ways of designing material would yield other programs of reinforcement. Any supplementary reinforcement would probably have to be scheduled in the more traditional way.

These requirements are not excessive, but they are probably incompatible with the current realities of the classroom. In the experimental study of learning it has been found that the contingencies of reinforcement which are most efficient in controlling the organism cannot be arranged through the personal mediation of the experimenter. An organism is affected by subtle details of contingencies which are beyond the capacity of the human organism to arrange. Mechanical and electrical devices must be used. Mechanical help is also demanded by the sheer number of contingencies which may be used efficiently in a single experimental session. We have recorded many millions of responses from a single organism during thousands of experimental hours. Personal arrangement of the contingencies and personal observation of the results are quite unthinkable. Now, the human organism is, if anything, more sensitive to precise contingencies than the other organisms we have studied. We have every reason to expect, therefore, that the most effective control of human learning will require instrumental aid. The simple fact is that, as a a mere reinforcing mechanism, the teacher is out of date. This would be true even if a single teacher devoted all her time to a single child, but her inadequacy is multiplied many-fold when she must serve as a reinforcing device to many children at once. If the teacher is to take advantage of recent advances in the study of learning, she must have the help of mechanical devices.

The technical problem of providing the necessary instrumental aid is not particularly difficult. There are many ways in which the necessary contingencies may be arranged, either mechanically or electrically. An inexpensive device which solves most of the principal problems has already been constructed. It is still in the experimental stage, but a description will suggest the kind of instrument which seems to be required. The device consists of a small box about the size of a small record player. On the top surface is a window through which a question or problem printed on a paper tape may be seen. The child answers the question by moving one or more sliders upon which the digits 0 through 9 are printed. The answer appears in square holes punched in the paper upon which the question is printed. When the answer has been set, the child turns a knob. The operation is as simple as adjusting a television set. If the answer is right, the knob turns freely and can be made to ring a bell or provide some other conditioned reinforcement. If the answer is wrong, the knob will not turn. A counter may be added to tally wrong answers. The knob must then be reversed slightly and a second attempt at a right answer made. (Unlike the flash-card, the device reports a wrong answer without giving the right answer.) When the answer is right, a further turn of the knob engages

a clutch which moves the next problem into place in the window. This movement cannot be completed, however, until the sliders have been returned to zero.

The important features of the device are these: Reinforcement for the right answer is immediate. The mere manipulation of the device will probably be reinforcing enough to keep the average pupil at work for a suitable period each day, provided traces of earlier aversive control can be wiped out. A teacher may supervise an entire class at work on such devices at the same time, yet each child may progress at his own rate, completing as many problems as possible within the class period. If forced to be away from school, he may return to pick up where he left off. The gifted child will advance rapidly, but can be kept from getting too far ahead either by being excused from arithmetic for a time or by being given special sets of problems which take him into some of the interesting bypaths of mathematics.

The device makes it possible to present carefully designed material in which one problem can depend upon the answer to the preceding and where, therefore, the most efficient progress to an eventually complex repertoire can be made. Provision has been made for recording the commonest mistakes so that the tapes can be modified as experience dictates. Additional steps can be inserted where pupils tend to have trouble, and ultimately the material will reach a point at which the answers of the average child will almost always be right.

If the material itself proves not to be sufficiently reinforcing, other reinforcers in the possession of the teacher or school may be made contingent upon the operation of the device or upon progress through a series of problems. Supplemental reinforcement would not sacrifice the advantages gained from immediate reinforcement and from the possibility of constructing an optimal series of steps which approach the complex repertoire of mathematical behavior most efficiently.

A similar device in which the sliders carry

the letters of the alphabet has been designed to teach spelling. In addition to the advantages which can be gained from precise reinforcement and careful programming, the device will teach reading at the same time. It can also be used to establish the large and important repertoire of verbal relationships encountered in logic and science. In short, it can teach verbal thinking. As to content instruction, the device can be operated as a multiple-choice self-rater.

Some objections to the use of such devices in the classroom can easily be foreseen. The cry will be raised that the child is being treated as a mere animal and that an essentially human intellectual achievement is being analyzed in unduly mechanistic terms. Mathematical behavior is usually regarded, not as a repertoire of responses involving numbers and numerical operations, but as evidences of mathematical ability or the exercise of the power of reason. It is true that the techniques which are emerging from the experimental study of learning are not designed to "develop the mind" or to further some vague "understanding" of mathematical relationships. They are designed, on the contrary, to establish the very behaviors which are taken to be the evidences of such mental states or processes. This is only a special case of the general change which is under way in the interpretation of human affairs. An advancing science continues to offer more and more convincing alternatives to traditional formulations. The behavior in terms of which human thinking must eventually be defined is worth treating in its own right as the substantial goal of education.

Of course the teacher has a more important function than to say right or wrong. The changes proposed would free her for the effective exercise of that function. Marking a set of papers in arithmetic—"Yes, nine and six *are* fifteen; no, nine and seven *are not* eighteen"—is beneath the dignity of any intelligent individual. There is more important work to be done—in which the teacher's relations to the pupil cannot be duplicated by a mechanical device. Instrumental help would merely improve these relations. One might say that the main trouble with education in the lower grades today is that the child is obviously not competent and *knows it* and that the teacher is unable to do anything about it and *knows that too*. If the advances which have recently been made in our control of behavior can give the child a genuine competence in reading, writing, spelling, and arithmetic, then the teacher may begin to function, not in lieu of a cheap machine, but through intellectual, cultural, and emotional contacts of that distinctive sort which testify to her status as a human being.

Another possible objection is that mechanized instruction will mean technological unemployment. We need not worry about this until there are enough teachers to go around and until the hours and energy demanded of the teacher are comparable to those in other fields of employment. Mechanical devices will eliminate the more tiresome labors of the teacher but they will not necessarily shorten the time during which she remains in contact with the pupil.

A more practical objection: Can we afford to mechanize our schools? The answer is clearly yes. The device I have just described could be produced as cheaply as a small radio or phonograph. There would need to be far fewer devices than pupils, for they could be used in rotation. But even if we suppose that the instrument eventually found to be most effective would cost several hundred dollars and that large numbers of them would be required, our economy should be able to stand the strain. Once we have accepted the possibility and the necessity of mechanical help in the classroom, the economic problem can easily be surmounted. There is no reason why the school room should be any less mechanized than, for example, the kitchen. A country which annually produces millions of refrigerators, dish-washers, automatic washing-machines, automatic clothes-driers, and automatic garbage disposers can certainly afford the equipment necessary to educate its citizens to high standards of competence in the most effective way.

There is a simple job to be done. The task can be stated in concrete terms. The necessary techniques are known. The equipment needed can easily be provided. Nothing stands in the way but cultural inertia. But what is more characteristic of America than an unwillingness to accept the traditional as inevitable? We are on the threshold of an exciting and revolutionary period, in which the scientific study of man will be put to work in man's best interests. Education must play its part. It must accept the fact that a sweeping revision of educational practices is possible and inevitable. When it has done this, we may look forward with confidence to a school system which is aware of the nature of its tasks, secure in its methods, and generously supported by the informed and effective citizens whom education itself will create.

CHARLES E. SILBERMAN
"Technology Is Knocking at the Schoolhouse Door" (1966) *

"Public education is the last great stronghold of the manual trades," John Henry Martin, superintendent of schools in Mount Vernon, New York, recently told a congressional committee. "In education, the industrial revolution has scarcely begun."

But begun it has—slowly, to be sure, but irresistibly, and with the most profound consequences for both education and industry. The past year has seen an explosion of interest in the application of electronic technology to education and training. Hardly a week or month goes by without an announcement from some electronics manufacturer or publishing firm that it is entering the "education market" via merger, acquisition, joint venture, or working arrangement. And

* Charles E. Silberman, "Technology Is Knocking at the Schoolhouse Door." Reprinted from the August, 1966, issue of *Fortune Magazine* by special permission; © 1966 Time Inc.

a number of electronics firms have been building substantial capabilities of their own in the education field.

Business has discovered the schools, and neither is likely to be the same again. It may be a bit premature to suggest, as Superintendent Martin does, that "the center of gravity for educational change is moving from the teachers' college and the superintendent's office to the corporation executive suite." But there can be no doubt about the long-term significance of business' new interest in the education market. The companies now coming into the market have resources —of manpower and talent as well as of capital—far greater than the education market has ever seen before. They have, in addition, a commitment to innovation and an experience in management that is also new to the field. The romance between business and the schools began when the federal government took on the role of matchmaker. Indeed, the new business interest in education is a prime example of Lyndon Johnson's "creative federalism" at work. Federal purchasing power is being used to create— indeed, almost to invent—a sizable market for new educational materials and technologies. Until now, the stimulus has come mainly from the Department of Defense and the Office of Economic Opportunity. But the Elementary and Secondary Education Act of 1965 provided large federal grants to the schools for the purchase of textbooks, library books, audio-visual equipment, etc. It also greatly expanded the Office of Education's research-and-development activities and gave it the prerogative, for the first time, to contract with profit-making as well as nonprofit institutions.

The most remarkable characteristic of industry's invasion of the education market is that it has been accompanied by the affiliation of otherwise unrelated businesses. The electronics companies have felt the need for "software," i.e., organized informational and educational material, to put into their equipment and have gone in search of such publishing companies as possessed it. Some of

THE EDUCATION MARKET'S NEW
FAMILY TREE

Mergers, Acquisitions, and Joint Ventures
since 1962

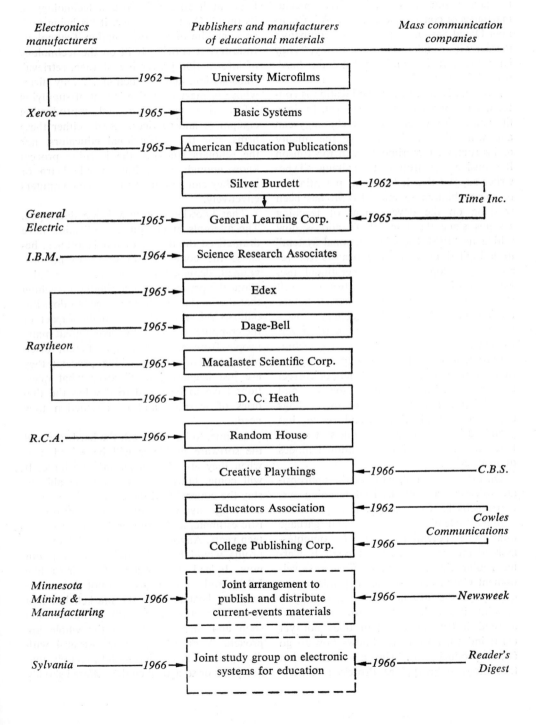

the publishing companies, in turn, particularly textbook publishers, have been apprehensive about the long-range future of their media and willingly joined in such auspicious marriages of convenience. As R.C.A.'s Chairman David Sarnoff explained his company's merger with Random House last May, "They have the software and we have the hardware."

The fact is that, as far as education is concerned, neither side has either—yet. In time, the application of electronic technology can and will substantially improve the quality of instruction. Experiments with the Edison Responsive Environment Talking Typewriter suggest that it has great potential for teaching children to read. I.B.M. has been working on the development of teaching systems since the late 1950's and is now selling its "IBM 1500 instructional system" to a limited number of educators for research, development, and operational use. But a lot of problems—in hardware as well as software—will have to be solved before the computer finds wide acceptance as a teaching device. No computer manufacturer, for example, has begun to solve the technical problems inherent in building a computer that can respond to spoken orders or correct an essay written in natural language and containing a normal quota of misspellings and grammatical errors—and none has promised it can produce machines at a cost that can compete with conventional modes of instruction.

On the other hand, without the appropriate software, a computerized teaching system results in what computer people call a "GIGO system"—garbage in and garbage out. "The potential value of computer-assisted instruction," as Dr. Launor F. Carter, senior vice president of System Development Corp., flatly states, "depends on the quality of the instructional material" that goes into it. But the software for a computer-assisted instructional system does not yet exist; indeed, no one yet knows how to go about producing it. The new "education technology industry," as Professor J. Ster-

ling Livingston of Harvard Business School pointed out at a Defense Department–Office of Education conference in June, "is not being built on any important technology of its own." On the contrary, it "is being built as a satellite of the Information Technology Industry. It is being built on the technology of information processing, storage, retrieval, transmission, and reduction . . . by firms whose primary objective is that of supplying information processing and reproduction equipment and services." And neither these firms, nor the professional educators, nor the scholars studying the learning process know enough about how people learn or how they can be taught to use the computers effectively.

That knowledge is now being developed. The attempts at computer application have dramatized the degree of our ignorance, because the computer, in order to be programed, demands a precision of knowledge about the processes of learning and teaching that the human teacher manages to do without. So far, therefore, the main impact of the computer has been to force a great many people from a great many different disciplines to study the teaching process; they are just beginning to discover what questions have to be asked to develop the theories of learning and of instruction they need.

In time, to be sure, both the hardware and the software problems will be solved, and when they are, the payoff may be large. It will come, however, only to those able to stay the course. And the course will be hard and long—five years, under the most optimistic estimate, and more probably ten or fifteen years. Anyone looking for quick or easy profits would be well advised to drop out now. Indeed, the greatest fear firms like I.B.M. and Xerox express is not that someone may beat them to the market, but that some competitor may rush to market too soon and thereby discredit the whole approach. A number of firms—several with distinguished reputations—did precisely that five years or so ago when they offered shoddy programs to the schools and peddled educationally worthless "teaching machines" and texts door to door.

A lot more is at stake, needless to say, than the fortunes of a few dozen corporations, however large. The new business-government thrust in education, with its apparent commitment to the application of new technologies, is already changing the terms of the debate about the future of American education, creating new options and with them, new priorities. "We have been dealt a new set of cards," Theodore R. Sizer, dean of Harvard's Graduate School of Education, has remarked, "and we must learn how to play with them."

Rarely have U.S. corporations assumed a role so fraught with danger for the society, as well as for themselves, or so filled with responsibility and opportunity. For over the long run, the new business-government thrust is likely to transform both the organization and the content of education, and through it, the character and shape of American society itself. . . .

Most of the experimentation with computer-assisted instruction now going on is based, one way or another, on the technique of "programed instruction" developed in the 1950's by a number of behavioral psychologists, most notably B. F. Skinner of Harvard. Professor Skinner defines learning as a change in behavior, and the essence of his approach is his conviction that any behavior can be produced in any person by "reinforcing," i.e., rewarding closer and closer approximations to it. It is immaterial what reward is used: food (corn for a pigeon, on which most of Skinner's experiments have been conducted, or candy for a child), praise, or simply the satisfaction a human being derives from knowing he is right. What is crucial is simply that the desired behavior be appropriately rewarded—and that it be rewarded right away. By using frequent reinforcement of small steps, the theory holds, one can shape any student's behavior toward any predetermined goal.

To teach a body of material in this way, it is necessary first to define the goal in precise and measurable terms—a task educators normally duck. Then the material must be broken down into a series of small steps— thirty to 100 frames per hour of instruction —and presented in sequence. As a rule, each sequence, or frame, consists of one or more statements, followed by a question the student must answer correctly before proceeding to the next frame. Since the student checks his own answer, the questions necessarily are in a form that can be answered briefly, e.g., by filling in a word, indicating whether a statement is true or false, or by choosing which of, say, four answers is correct. (Most programers have abandoned the use of "teaching machines," which were simply devices for uncovering the answer and advancing to the next frame. Programs are now usually presented in book form, with answers in a separate column in the margin; the student covers the answers with a ruler or similar device, which he slides down the page as needed.) If the material has been programed correctly—so the theory holds— every student will be able to master it, though some will master it faster than others. If anyone fails to learn, it is the fault of the program, not of the student. Programed instruction, in short, is a teaching technology that purports to be able to teach every student, and at his own pace.

But teach him what? That's the rub. Most of the applications of programed instruction have been in training courses for industry and the armed forces, where it is relatively easy to define the knowledge or skills to be taught in precise behavioral terms, and where the motivation to learn is quite strong. (One survey of industry's use of programed instruction indicated that 69 percent of the programs used were "job-oriented.") It's a lot harder to specify the "behavior" to be produced, say, by a course in Shakespeare or in American history, and a lot more difficult to sustain the interest of a student whose job or rank does not depend directly on how well he learns the material at hand. And the small steps and the rigidity of the form of presentation and the limitation of response make a degree of boredom inevitable, at least for students with some imagination and creativity.

If programing is used too extensively, moreover, it may prevent the development of intuitive and creative thinking or destroy such thinking when it appears. For one thing, programing instruction seems to force a student into a relatively passive role, whereas most learning theorists agree that no one can really master a concept unless he is forced to express it in his own words or actions and to construct his own applications and examples. It is not yet clear, however, whether this defect is inherent in the concept of programing or is simply a function of its present primitive state of development. . . .

Computers and their associated electronic gadgetry offer ways of remedying some of the obvious defects of programed instruction. For example, programs generally involve only one sense—sight—whereas most learning theorists believe that students learn faster and more easily if *several* senses are brought into play. Electronic technology makes it possible to do just that. When a youngster presses one of the keys on the Edison Responsive Environment's Talking Typewriter, the letter appears in print in front of him, while a voice tells him the name of it. When he has learned the alphabet, the machine will tell him—aurally—to type a word; the machine can be programed so that the student can depress only the correct keys, in correct order. And at Patrick Suppes' Computer-Based Mathematics Laboratory at Stanford University, students using earlier versions of I.B.M.'s new 1500 Computer-Assisted Instructional System receive instructions or information aurally (through prerecorded sound messages) or visually (through photographs, diagrams, or words and sentences that are either projected on a cathode-ray tube or presented in conventional typewritten form). Students may respond by typing the answer, by writing on the cathode-ray tube with an electronic "light

pen," or by pushing one of several multiple-choice buttons.

To be sure, the 1500 system is still experimental—wide commercial application is five years away—and much richer and far more flexible "environments" are necessary to make the computer a useful teaching device. But computer manufacturers are confident that they can come up with wholly new kinds of input and output devices.

What makes the computer so exciting— and potentially so significant—is its most characteristic attribute, feedback, i.e., its ability to modify its own operation on the basis of the information fed into it. It is this that opens up the possibility of responding to each student's performance by modifying the curriculum as he goes along. This couldn't be done now. Programed instruction currently deals with individual differences in a crude way, chiefly by permitting students to move along as slowly or as rapidly as they can; they still all deal essentially with the same material. But speed of learning is only one relevant dimension of individual differences, and not necessarily the most important. Suppes, among others, is convinced that the best way to improve learning is through "an almost single-minded concentration on individual differences" in the way material is presented to the student.

What this means, in practice, is that a teacher should have a number of different programs at his disposal, since no single strategy of instruction or mode of presentation is likely to work for every student. Second, he should be able to select the most appropriate program for each student on the basis of that student's current knowledge, past performance, and personality. Third and most important, he should be able to modify the program for each student as he goes along in accordance with what the student knows and doesn't know, the kinds of materials he finds difficult and the kinds he learns easily. In time it should be practicable to program a computer to assist in all of these functions. . . .

The biggest obstacle to the introduction of

computer-assisted instruction is not technological; it is our ignorance about the process of instruction. Significant progress has been made, however, in identifying what needs to be known before a theory of instruction can be developed. It is clear, for example, that any useful theory must explain the role of language in learning and teaching— including its role in *preventing* learning. It is language, more than anything else, that distinguishes human from animal learning; only man can deal with the world symbolically and linguistically. But verbalization is not the only way people learn or know, as Jerome Bruner of Harvard emphasizes. We know things "enactively," which is to say, in our muscles. Children can be very skillful on a seesaw without having any concept of what it is and without being able to represent it by drawing a balance beam (the use of imagery) or by writing Newton's law of moments (symbolic representation). Present teaching methods, Bruner argues, place too much emphasis on the verbal—a fact he likes to illustrate by quoting these magnificent lines from Yeats:

> *God guard me from those thoughts men think*
> *In the mind alone;*
> *He that sings a lasting song*
> *Thinks in a marrow-bone*

The result is that youngsters too often display great skill in using words that describe words that describe words, with no real feel for, or image of, the concrete phenomenon itself. . . .

We need to know more about how the way material is presented—for example, the sequence, size of steps, order of words— affects learning. And we need to understand how to make children—all children—*want* to learn. . . .

Interestingly enough, one of the greatest advantages the computer possesses may well be its impersonality—the fact that it can exhibit infinite patience in the face of error without registering disappointment or disapproval—something no human teacher can

ever manage. These qualities may make a machine superior to a teacher in dealing with students who have had a record of academic failure, whether through organic retardation, emotional disturbance, or garden-variety learning blocks. The impersonality of the machine may be useful for average or above-average children as well, since it increases the likelihood that a youngster may decide to learn to please himself rather than to please his parents or teachers. And motivation must become "intrinsic" rather than "extrinsic" if children are to develop their full intellectual capacity.

There is reason to think that we may need a number of theories of learning and instruction. For one thing, the process of learning probably differs according to what it is that is being learned. As the Physical Science Study Committee put it in one of its annual reports, "We have all but forgotten, in recent years, that the verb 'to learn' is transitive; there must be some thing or things that the student learns." Unless that thing seems relevant to a student, he will have little interest in learning it (and he will derive little or no reward from its mastery). In any case, different subjects—or different kinds of students—may require different methods of instruction; a method that works wonderfully well in teaching physics may not work in teaching the social sciences.

More important, perhaps, different kinds of students may require different teaching strategies. It is only too evident that methods that work well with brighter-than-average upper-middle-class families fail dismally when used with children, bright or dull, from a city or rural slum. And differences in income and class are not the only variables; a student's age, sex, ethnic group, and cultural background all affect the way his mind operates as well as his attitude toward learning. Differences in "cognitive style" may also have to be taken into account— for example, the fact that some people have to see something to understand it, while others seem to learn more easily if they hear it.

When adequate theories of instruction have been developed, the new educational-system designers will still have to decide what it is that they want to teach. That decision cannot be made apart from the most fundamental decisions about values and purpose—the values of the society as well as the purpose of education. What we teach reflects, consciously or unconsciously, our concept of the good life, the good man, and the good society.

MARGARET CHISHOLM
"Educational Technology: How Humane Can It Be?" (1967) *

"I had a problem. My problem was that I didn't like being for sale." These were the words of ten-year-old Barry Rudd in *The Child Buyer* as his potential purchaser explained that he had developed an interest in Barry because, "I buy brains. When a commodity that you need falls in short supply you have to get out and hustle." [1]

Will Barry's statement of his problem represent the problems of all coming generations of students? Will educational technology inexorably dehumanize education?

What factors have combined to focus attention on this currently challenging question?

First: The past decade has brought unprecedented pressures to bear upon our schools. These pressures include the population expansion, advances in science and technology, the knowledge explosion, competition in space, and urbanization.

Second: In order to attempt to meet these current pressures on the schools, cataclysmic changes are being implemented in school cur-

* Margaret Chisholm, "Educational Technology: How Humane Can It Be?" *Educational Leadership*, Vol. 25, No. 3 (December, 1967), pp. 225–228. Reprinted with permission of the Association for Supervision and Curriculum Development and Margaret Chisholm. Copyright © 1967 by the Association for Supervision and Curriculum Development.
[1] John Hersey. *The Child Buyer*. New York: Alfred A. Knopf, Inc., 1960, pp. 216, 33.

riculum, in school organization, in teacher education, and in educational materials and media.

Third: At the same time, developments in technology have emerged which hopefully may possess the potential of meeting many of the needs of the changing American education program.

In the past, superior teachers were faced with the constant problem of attempting to acquire a diversity of instructional materials to meet the needs, interests, and abilities of individual students. Today, advances in technology have made the following available to most teachers: film projectors, 8mm single concept projectors, filmstrip projectors, slide projectors, overhead projectors, opaque projectors, television cameras and receivers, micro-projectors, record players, tape recorders, video-tape recorders, radio, 8mm and 35mm cameras, dial access consoles, electronically equipped carrels, teaching machines, and computer assisted instruction equipment. Each type of hardware comes with its appropriate software, the viewing and/or listening materials.

Ostensibly it would seem that technology should be the answer to the prayers of every educator. What, then, are the fears—and what are the potential blessings inherent in educational technology?

The universal claim of the supporters of technology appears to be that through this multitudinous collection of materials and media it is possible to teach every child according to his own ability. If this is true, why should there be any concern about extensive and continuous utilization of all technology in education to a maximum degree?

The concern is twofold: First, will this utilization of technology in education mean that the control of education will pass from the hands of educators to the hands of programmers, and to giant industrial concerns which manufacture the materials and the media? Second, what is meant by quality in education? Can it be achieved through technology alone?

Current research is being done by William

S. Vincent of Teachers College, Columbia University, on determining the dimensions of quality in education. His research has identified four categories of educational procedures exemplifying school quality as follows:

Individualization: procedures that reflect an attempt to deal with individual differences among pupils according to rate of growth, capacities, background, goals, requirements, and the like.

Interpersonal regard: behavior that reflects warmth and respect among pupils and between pupils and teachers.

Creative expression and divergency of thinking: opportunity for the expression of intelligence in many different ways, for the realization of varieties of talent, and the encouragement of intellectual pioneering.

Group activity: group interaction and interpersonal facilitation as instruments to aid learning and the accomplishment of social goals.[2]

If research identifies these four categories of procedure as indicators of quality education in schools, it is obvious that educational technology meets the demands of only one of these categories. Presumably educators would agree that, if used judiciously, educational technology can be utilized to meet the need of individualizing the learning procedure. However, the integral feature of three of these factors, other than individualization, is dependent on the human regard for the student and interpersonal relationships. This cannot depend on technology; it can be achieved only through the human factor, the involvement of people. The major concern must be that the learning-teaching processes involving interpersonal regard, creative expression, divergency of thinking, and group activity will not be neglected or completely disregarded.

Thus far, consideration has been given to the general, overall advantages and concerns with respect to educational technology. Let

[2] William S. Vincent. "Indicators of Quality." *IAR Research Bulletin* 7(3):2; May, 1967.

us give brief consideration to the more specific problems and questions they raise.

Of the developments in educational technology, the computer is undoubtedly the most arcane, yet most viable, and has the greatest potential for encouraging egalitarianism in education. Computers offer unequaled potential in the field of programmed instruction. The advantages over teaching machines or programmed textbooks are that the computers can accept and evaluate responses constructed by the student, can provide almost unlimited branching capabilities, and can branch based on a variety of criteria. The computer can do what amounts to continuous testing to determine student progress, and the program can be changed readily in accordance with student needs. All of these factors increase the capacity for providing individualization of instruction.

Computer assisted instruction appears to be invaluable in the area of educational research. Because the learning process is so complex, researchers are confronted with a dilemma. Experiments can be carefully controlled only if they are restricted to minute portions of the learning process. When studies are made in schools, there is insufficient control of experimental conditions. Computer assisted instruction may provide a means of presenting material under controlled conditions, with a means of including records and analysis. Such data collected under actual learning conditions may lead to enlightenment regarding the learning process.

In addition, the myriads of ways in which the computer can be utilized in solving educational problems stagger the imagination. The computer handles information by collecting, communicating, storing, and retrieving. Each of the pressures and problems of change in education involves analysis through these processes which the computer can provide.

For such purposes as gathering data on the effectiveness of curriculum changes, for providing information for making decisions on organizational patterns, for organizing data collected in research on student characteristics, the computer is limited only by the ingeniousness of the designer of the program.

A basic factor to be considered in the field of technology is the financing of research for development. Endless numbers of philosophical questions arise related to this aspect of the field. One personal experience will serve as an illustration. The writer served on a panel for the federal government for the purpose of determining the funding of proposals submitted by universities which were involved in training and research in the area of educational technology. Much careful consideration was given to the problem of the relative amounts of grants to be appropriated to the so-called deprived areas for training personnel in basic media programs contrasted with the possibility of awarding grants to universities extremely well equipped with computers and having staffs of skilled personnel which were requesting grants for developing highly sophisticated programs of computer assisted instruction. This question arose: How can a fair balance in federal assistance and foundation support be maintained between the needs of the disadvantaged and the equally pressing need for advanced research? The plea is that consideration constantly be given to both needs and that some balance be achieved in providing assistance to both.

Another matter of concern is that provision be made for coordinating the findings of "far-out" research in technology with everyday on-the-job application of the findings. For example, optical scanners are already in common use for the scoring of tests in order to get results back to teachers with extreme rapidity. An overall plan for the training of teachers must be developed which would encompass preservice and in-service training. Teachers must be trained to utilize this vast amount of vital information obtained through computers and be able to translate it into meaningful data which will affect student behavior.

Another aspect of technology closely related to teacher training is that there must be an involvement of more educators in developing materials and programs. Computer technicians must be involved because of their technical knowledge, but educators must be trained in order to develop meaningful curricula. There must be an overlapping and interweaving of the skills of the educators and the technicians in order to achieve acceptable goals. Computers can provide the information; educators must provide the wisdom.[3]

All persons involved in developing educational technology must constantly realize that even complete mastery of technology can in no way guarantee the understanding of the complex human organism. Along with the technological developments there must be a continuous evaluation of the effects of this method of learning on the whole child. Students must first and always be considered as human beings and treated with sensitivity and a maximum of personal attention and understanding.

Thus, if we are to move forward in education let us strive for a considered balance among the following:

Research and intelligent application

Financial support of both fundamental media programs and sophisticated technological research

Maximum utilization of the computer for educational development with maximum translation through training of educational personnel

Utilization of educational technology and humanistic consideration of individual students.

All of these factors must be combined to provide optimum opportunity for developing each child's finest potentials.

When these factors have been considered, the question is not how humane can educational technology be, but rather how humane *must* technology be.

[3] John I. Goodlad and others. *Application of Electronic Processing Methods in Education.* Los Angeles: University of California, 1965, p. 10.

CHAPTER ELEVEN

Conceptions of Higher Education

HISTORICAL ANTECEDENTS

JOHN HENRY CARDINAL NEWMAN
The Idea of a University [1852] *

DISCOURSE VI

*"Knowledge Viewed in Relation
to Learning"*

I will tell you, Gentlemen, what has been the practical error of the last twenty years, —not to load the memory of the student with a mass of undigested knowledge, but to force upon him so much that he has rejected all. It has been the error of distracting and enfeebling the mind by an unmeaning profusion of subjects; of implying that a smattering in a dozen branches of study is not shallowness, which it really is, but enlargement, which it is not; of considering an acquaintance with the learned names of things and persons, and the possession of clever duodecimos, and attendance on eloquent lecturers, and membership with scientific institutions, and the sight of the experiments of a platform and the specimens of a museum, that all this was not dissipation of mind, but progress. All things now are to be learned at once, not first one thing, then another, not one well, but many badly. Learning is to be without exertion, without

* John Henry Cardinal Newman, *The Idea of a University* (London: Longmans, Green, 1891; New Edition; Part I, University Teaching considered in Nine Discourses), Discourse VI, "Knowledge Viewed in Relation to Learning," pp. 142–145, 147–149; and Discourse VII, "Knowledge Viewed in Relation to Professional Skill," pp. 151–153, 163–164, 166–167, 177–178.

attention, without toil; without grounding, without advance, without finishing. There is to be nothing individual in it; and this, forsooth, is the wonder of the age. What the steam engine does with matter, the printing press is to do with mind; it is to act mechanically, and the population is to be passively, almost unconsciously enlightened, by the mere multiplication and dissemination of volumes. Whether it be the school boy, or the school girl, or the youth at college, or the mechanic in the town, or the politician in the senate, all have been the victims in one way or other of this most preposterous and pernicious of delusions. Wise men have lifted up their voices in vain; and at length, lest their own institutions should be outshone and should disappear in the folly of the hour, they have been obliged, as far as they could with a good conscience, to humour a spirit which they could not withstand, and make temporizing concessions at which they could not but inwardly smile.

It must not be supposed that, because I so speak, therefore I have some sort of fear of the education of the people: on the contrary, the more education they have, the better, so that it is really education. Nor am I an enemy to the cheap publication of scientific and literary works, which is now in vogue: on the contrary, I consider it a great advantage, convenience, and gain; that is, to those to whom education has given a capacity for using them. Further, I consider such innocent recreations as science and literature are able to furnish will be a very fit occupation of the thoughts and the leisure of young persons, and may be made the means of keeping them from bad employments and bad companions. Moreover, as to that superficial acquaintance with chemistry, and geology, and astronomy, and political economy, and modern history, and biography, and other branches of knowledge, which periodical literature and occasional lectures and scientific institutions diffuse through the community, I think it a graceful accomplishment, and a suitable, nay, in this day a necessary accomplishment, in the case of educated men. Nor, lastly, am I disparaging or discouraging the thorough acquisition of any one of these studies, or denying that, as far as it goes, such thorough acquisition is a real education of the mind. All I say is, call things by their right names, and do not confuse together ideas which are essentially different. A thorough knowledge of one science and a superficial acquaintance with many, are not the same thing; a smattering of a hundred things or a memory for detail, is not a philosophical or comprehensive view. Recreations are not education; accomplishments are not education. Do not say, the people must be educated, when, after all, you only mean, amused, refreshed, soothed, put into good spirits and good humour, or kept from vicious excesses. I do not say that such amusements, such occupations of mind, are not a great gain; but they are not education. You may as well call drawing and fencing education, as a general knowledge of botany or conchology. Stuffing birds or playing stringed instruments is an elegant pastime, and a resource to the idle, but it is not education; it does not form or cultivate the intellect. Education is a high word; it is the preparation for knowledge, and it is the imparting of knowledge in proportion to that preparation. We require intellectual eyes to know withal, as bodily eyes for sight. We need both objects and organs intellectual; we cannot gain them without setting about it; we cannot gain them in our sleep, or by hap-hazard. The best telescope does not dispense with eyes; the printing press or the lecture room will assist us greatly, but we must be true to ourselves, we must be parties in the work. A University is, according to the usual designation, an Alma Mater, knowing her children one by one, not a foundry or a mint, or a treadmill.

I protest to you, Gentlemen, that if I had to choose between a so-called University, which dispensed with residence and tutorial superintendence, and gave its degrees to any person who passed an examination in a wide range of subjects, and a University which had no professors or examinations at all, but merely brought a number of young men together for three or four years, and then sent them away as the University of Oxford is said to have done some sixty years since, if I were asked which of these two methods was the better discipline of the intellect,—mind, I do not say which is *morally* the better, for it is plain that compulsory study must be a good and idleness an intolerable mischief,—but if I must determine which of the two courses was the more successful in training, moulding, enlarging the mind, which sent out men the more fitted for their secular duties, which produced better public men, men of the world, men whose names would descend to posterity, I have no hesitation in giving the preference to that University which did nothing, over that which exacted of its members an acquaintance with every science under the sun. . . .

Let it be clearly understood, I repeat it, that I am not taking into account moral or religious considerations; I am but saying that that youthful community will constitute a whole, it will embody a specific idea, it will represent a doctrine, it will administer a code of conduct, and it will furnish principles of thought and action. It will give birth to a living teaching, which in course of time will take the shape of a self-perpetuating tradition, or a *genius loci,* as it is sometimes called; which haunts the home where it has been born, and which imbues and forms, more or less, and one by one, every individual who is successively brought under its shadow,

Here then is a real teaching, whatever be its standards and principles, true or false; and it at least tends towards cultivation of the intellect; it at least recognizes that knowledge is something more than a sort of passive reception of scraps and details; it is a something, and it does a something, which never will issue from the most strenuous efforts of a set of teachers, with no mutual sympathies and no intercommunion, of a set of examiners with no opinions which they dare profess, and with no common principles, who are teaching or questioning a set of youths who do not know them, and do not know each other, on a large number of subjects, different in kind, and connected by no wide philosophy, three times a week, or three times a year, or once in three years, in chill lecture-rooms or on a pompous anniversary.

Nay, self-education in any shape, in the most restricted sense, is preferable to a system of teaching which, professing so much, really does so little for the mind. Shut your College gates against the votary of knowledge, throw him back upon the searchings and the efforts of his own mind; he will gain by being spared an entrance into your Babel. Few indeed there are who can dispense with the stimulus and support of instructors, or will do any thing at all, if left to themselves. And fewer still (though such great minds are to be found), who will not, from such unassisted attempts, contract a self-reliance and a self-esteem, which are not only moral evils, but serious hindrances to the attainment of truth. And next to none, perhaps, or none, who will not be reminded from time to time of the disadvantage under which they lie, by their imperfect grounding, by the breaks, deficiencies, and irregularities of their knowledge, by the eccentricity of opinion and the confusion of principle which they exhibit. They will be too often ignorant of what every one knows and takes for granted, of that multitude of small truths which fall upon the mind like dust, impalpable and ever accumulating; they may be unable to converse, they may argue per-

versely, they may pride themselves on their worst paradoxes or their grossest truisms, they may be full of their own mode of viewing things, unwilling to be put out of their way, slow to enter into the minds of others; —but, with these and whatever other liabilities upon their heads, they are likely to have more thought, more mind, more philosophy, more true enlargement, than those earnest but ill-used persons, who are forced to load their minds with a score of subjects against an examination, who have too much on their hands to indulge themselves in thinking or investigation, who devour premiss and conclusion together with indiscriminate greediness, who hold whole sciences on faith, and commit demonstrations to memory, and who too often, as might be expected, when their period of education is passed, throw up all they have learned in disgust, having gained nothing really by their anxious labours, except perhaps the habit of application. . . .

DISCOURSE VII

"Knowledge Viewed in Relation to Professional Skill"

I have been insisting, in my two preceding Discourses, first, on the cultivation of the intellect, as an end which may reasonably be pursued for its own sake; and next, on the nature of that cultivation, or what that cultivation consists in. Truth of whatever kind is the proper object of the intellect; its cultivation then lies in fitting it to apprehend and contemplate truth. Now the intellect in its present state, with exceptions which need not here be specified, does not discern truth intuitively, or as a whole. We know, not by a direct and simple vision, not at a glance, but, as it were, by piecemeal and accumulation, by a mental process, by going round an object, by the comparison, the combination, the mutual correction, the continual adaptation, of many partial notions, by the employment, concentration, and joint action of many faculties and exercises of mind. Such a union and concert of the intellectual powers, such an enlargement and development, such a comprehensiveness, is necessarily a matter of training. . . .

This process of training, by which the intellect, instead of being formed or sacrificed to some particular or accidental purpose, some specific trade or profession, or study or science, is disciplined for its own sake, for the perception of its own proper object, and for its own highest culture, is called Liberal Education; and though there is no one in whom it is carried as far as is conceivable, or whose intellect would be a pattern of what intellects should be made, yet there is scarcely any one but may gain an idea of what real training is, and at least look towards it, and make its true scope and result, not something else, his standard of excellence; and numbers there are who may submit themselves to it, and secure it to themselves in good measure. And to set forth the right standard, and to train according to it, and to help forward all students towards it according to their various capacities, this I conceive to be the business of a University.

Now this is what some great men are very slow to allow; they insist that Education should be confined to some particular and narrow end, and should issue in some definite work, which can be weighed and measured. They argue as if every thing, as well as every person, had its price; and that where there has been a great outlay, they have a right to expect a return in kind. This they call making Education and Instruction "useful," and "Utility" becomes their watchword. With a fundamental principle of this nature, they very naturally go on to ask, what there is to show for the expense of a University; what is the real worth in the market of the article called "a Liberal Education," on the supposition that it does not teach us definitely how to advance our manufactures, or to improve our lands, or to better our civil economy; or again, if it does not at once make this man a lawyer, that an engineer, and that a surgeon; or at least if it does not lead to discoveries in

chemistry, astronomy, geology, magnetism, and science of every kind.

This question, as might have been expected, has been keenly debated in the present age. . . .

Let us take "useful," as Locke takes it, in its proper and popular sense, and then we enter upon a large field of thought, to which I cannot do justice in one Discourse, though to-day's is all the space that I can give to it. I say, let us take "useful" to mean, not what is simply good, but what *tends* to good, or is the *instrument* of good; and in this sense also, Gentlemen, I will show you how a liberal education is truly and fully a useful, though it be not a professional, education. "Good" indeed means one thing, and "useful" means another; but I lay it down as a principle, which will save us a great deal of anxiety, that, though the useful is not always good, the good is always useful. Good is not only good, but reproductive of good; this is one of its attributes; nothing is excellent, beautiful, perfect, desirable for its own sake, but it overflows, and spreads the likeness of itself all around it. Good is prolific; it is not only good to the eye, but to the taste; it not only attracts us, but it communicates itself; it excites first our admiration and love, then our desire and our gratitude, and that, in proportion to its intenseness and fulness in particular instances. A great good will impart great good. If then the intellect is so excellent a portion of us, and its cultivation so excellent, it is not only beautiful, perfect, admirable, and noble in itself, but in a true and high sense it must be useful to the possessor and to all around him; not useful in any low, mechanical, mercantile sense, but as diffusing good, or as a blessing, or a gift, or power, or a treasure, first to the owner, then through him to the world. I say then, if a liberal education be good, it must necessarily be useful too. . . .

If then I am arguing, and shall argue, against Professional or Scientific knowledge as the sufficient end of a University Education, let me not be supposed, Gentlemen, to be disrespectful towards particular studies, or arts, or vocations, and those who are engaged in them. In saying that Law or Medicine is not the end of a University course, I do not mean to imply that the University does not teach Law or Medicine. What indeed can it teach at all, if it does not teach something particular? It teaches *all* knowledge by teaching all *branches* of knowledge, and in no other way. I do but say that there will be this distinction as regards a Professor of Law, or of Medicine, or of Geology, or of Political Economy, in a University and out of it, that out of a University he is in danger of being absorbed and narrowed by his pursuit, and of giving Lectures which are the Lectures of nothing more than a lawyer, physician, geologist, or political economist; whereas in a University he will just know where he and his science stand, he has come to it, as it were, from a height, he has taken a survey of all knowledge, he is kept from extravagance by the very rivalry of other studies, he has gained from them a special illumination and largeness of mind and freedom and self-possession, and he treats his own in consequence with a philosophy and a resource, which belongs not to the study itself, but to his liberal education.

This then is how I should solve the fallacy, for so I must call it, by which Locke and his disciples would frighten us from cultivating the intellect, under the notion that no education is useful which does not teach us some temporal calling, or some mechanical art, or some physical secret. I say that a cultivated intellect, because it is a good in itself, brings with it a power and a grace to every work and occupation which it undertakes, and enables us to be more useful, and to a greater number. There is a duty we owe to human society as such, to the state to which we belong, to the sphere in which we move, to the individuals towards whom we are variously related, and whom we successively encounter in life; and that philosophical or liberal education, as I have called it, which is the proper function of a University, if it refuses the foremost place

to professional interests, does but postpone them to the formation of the citizen, and, while it subserves the larger interests of philanthropy, prepares also for the successful prosecution of those merely personal objects, which at first sight it seems to disparage. . . .

But I must bring these extracts to an end. To-day I have confined myself to saying that that training of the intellect, which is best for the individual himself, best enables him to discharge his duties to society. The Philosopher, indeed, and the man of the world differ in their very notion, but the methods, by which they are respectively formed, are pretty much the same. The Philosopher has the same command of matters of thought, which the true citizen and gentleman has of matters of business and conduct. If then a practical end must be assigned to a University course, I say it is that of training good members of society. Its art is the art of social life, and its end is fitness for the world. It neither confines its views to particular professions on the one hand, nor creates heroes or inspires genius on the other. Works indeed of genius fall under no art; heroic minds come under no rule; a University is not a birthplace of poets or of immortal authors, of founders of schools, leaders of colonies, or conquerors of nations. It does not promise a generation of Aristotles or Newtons, of Napoleons or Washingtons, of Raphaels or Shakespeares, though such miracles of nature it has before now contained within its precincts. Nor is it content on the other hand with forming the critic or the experimentalist, the economist or the engineer, though such too it includes within its scope. But a University training is the great ordinary means to a great but ordinary end; it aims at raising the intellectual tone of society, at cultivating the public mind, at purifying the national taste, at supplying true principles to popular enthusiasm and fixed aims to popular aspiration, at giving enlargement and sobriety to the ideas of the age, at facilitating the exercise of political power, and refining the intercourse of private life.

It is the education which gives a man a clear conscious view of his own opinions and judgments, a truth in developing them, an eloquence in expressing them, and a force in urging them. It teaches him to see things as they are, to go right to the point, to disentangle a skein of thought, to detect what is sophistical, and to discard what is irrelevant. It prepares him to fill any post with credit, and to master any subject with facility. It shows him how to accommodate himself to others, how to throw himself into their state of mind, how to bring before them his own, how to influence them, how to come to an understanding with them, how to bear with them. He is at home in any society, he has common ground with every class; he knows when to speak and when to be silent; he is able to converse, he is able to listen; he can ask a question pertinently, and gain a lesson seasonably, when he has nothing to impart himself; he is ever ready, yet never in the way; he is a pleasant companion, and a comrade you can depend upon; he knows when to be serious and when to trifle, and he has a sure tact which enables him to trifle with gracefulness and to be serious with effect. He has the repose of a mind which lives in itself, while it lives in the world, and which has resources for its happiness at home when it cannot go abroad. He has a gift which serves him in public, and supports him in retirement, without which good fortune is but vulgar, and with which failure and disappointment have a charm. The art which tends to make a man all this, is in the object which it pursues as useful as the the art of wealth or the art of health, though it is less susceptible of method, and less tangible, less certain, less complete in its result.

THE "LAND-GRANT" CONCEPT: THE MORRILL ACT (July 2, 1862) *

An Act donating Public Lands to the several States and Territories which may pro-

* The Statutes at Large, Treaties, and Proclamations, of the United States of America (Boston: Little, Brown, 1863; edited by George P. Sanger), XII, 503–505.

vide Colleges for the Benefit of Agriculture and the Mechanic Arts.

Be it enacted by the Senate and House of Representatives of the United States of America in Congress assembled, That there be granted to the several States, for the purposes hereinafter mentioned, an amount of public land, to be apportioned to each State a quantity equal to thirty thousand acres for each senator and representative in Congress to which the States are respectively entitled by the apportionment under the census of eighteen hundred and sixty: *Provided,* That no mineral lands shall be selected or purchased under the provisions of this act. . . .

SEC. 4. *And be it further enacted,* That all moneys derived from the sale of the lands aforesaid by the States to which the lands are apportioned, and from the sales of land scrip hereinbefore provided for, shall be invested in stocks of the United States, or of the States, or some other safe stocks, yielding not less than five per centum upon the par value of said stocks; and that the moneys so invested shall constitute a perpetual fund, the capital of which shall remain forever undiminished, (except so far as may be provided in section fifth of this act,) and the interest of which shall be inviolably appropriated, by each State which may take and claim the benefit of this act, to the endowment, support, and maintenance of at least one college where the leading object shall be, without excluding other scientific and classical studies, and including military tactics, to teach such branches of learning as are related to agriculture and the mechanic arts, in such manner as the legislatures of the States may respectively prescribe, in order to promote the liberal and practical education of the industrial classes in the several pursuits and professions in life.

SEC. 5. *And be it further enacted,* That the grant of land and land scrip hereby authorized shall be made on the following conditions, to which, as well as to the provisions hereinbefore contained, the previous assent of the several States shall be signified by legislative acts:

First. If any portion of the fund invested, as provided by the foregoing section, or any portion of the interest thereon, shall, by any action or contingency, be diminished or lost, it shall be replaced by the State to which it belongs, so that the capital of the fund shall remain forever undiminished; and the annual interest shall be regularly applied without diminution to the purposes mentioned in the fourth section of this act, except that a sum, not exceeding ten per centum upon the amount received by any State under the provisions of this act, may be expended for the purchase of lands for sites or experimental farms, whenever authorized by the respective legislatures of said States.

Second. No portion of said fund, nor the interest thereon, shall be applied, directly or indirectly, under any pretence whatever, to the purchase, erection, preservation, or repair of any building or buildings.

Third. Any State which may take and claim the benefit of the provisions of this act shall provide, within five years, at least not less than one college, as described in the fourth section of this act, or the grant to such State shall cease; and said State shall be bound to pay the United States the amount received of any lands previously sold, and that the title to purchasers under the State shall be valid.

Fourth. An annual report shall be made regarding the progress of each college, recording any improvements and experiments made, with their cost and results, and such other matters, including State industrial and economical statistics, as may be supposed useful; one copy of which shall be transmitted by mail free, by each, to all the other colleges which may be endowed under the provisions of this act, and also one copy to the Secretary of the Interior. . . .

APPROVED, July 2, 1862.

JUSTIN S. MORRILL
State Aid to the U.S. Land-Grant Colleges
(October 10, 1888) *

* Justin S. Morrill, *State Aid to the U.S. Land-Grant Colleges* (Montpelier, Vt.: Argus and Patriot Printing House, 1888; an address on

Mr. Chairman and Fellow-Citizens,—

It may be remembered that the first proposition, made by me in 1858, for Land-Grant Colleges, was vetoed by President Buchanan, —rather discouraging to a young member of Congress—and it was not until 1862, under President Lincoln, that I was able to secure the consent of all branches of the Government to such a measure. We were then in the first stages of the great war of the rebellion, with daily resounding battles, and the College Land Scrip issued at this unhappy moment, when union men only wanted guns and not land, was often sold for less per acre than half its value. The national bounty to the several States was thus sadly curtailed. Since then I have attempted, and, as far as the action of the Senate has been concerned, not wholly unsuccessfully, to bring forward a measure that would reinforce the Land-Grant Colleges with a supplementary national fund. Let me add that I have not yet abandoned the idea, nor given up all hope of ultimate success, although my further public service is rapidly nearing the end. Of course the fate of such a measure must be regarded as uncertain, and, if favorable action should be had, many years must elapse before the income to be derived from it would be of substantial value.

Under the College Land Grant of 1862 forty-seven institutions have been organized, and they are nearly all now doing excellent educational work. They have over five thousand students and nearly five hundred professors. In every State scientific knowledge is being more or less diffused, and the science of agriculture is especially receiving profounder attention and is more respected and honored.

The bounty of the National Government formed a nucleus in the several States, around which buildings, libraries, laboratories, museums, workshops, gymnasiums, military halls and other educational appli-

behalf of the University of Vermont and the State Agricultural College, delivered in the Hall of Representatives at Montpelier, October 10, 1888), pp. 3–5, 11, 15–16.

ances were expected to be assembled, from funds derived from other and independent sources. It will be remembered that no portion of the national fund can be expended for such purposes, however indispensable— that is to say, for the erection or purchase of buildings, or for keeping them in repair. It was expected that State and individual spontaneous assistance, to the extent of these minor and varying wants, would serve to maintain the bounty of the National Government intact, and that sufficient local consideration and State interest in behalf of the colleges would be enlisted to secure their prosperity and proper management.

I am glad to say that this expectation was well-grounded, and that the generosity of the American people and the liberality of States, with hardly an exception, was not over-estimated. I will not tempt the sleep of any one by a protracted chapter of statistics. . . .

The fundamental idea was to offer an opportunity in every State for a liberal and larger education to larger numbers, not merely to those destined to sedentary professions, but to those much needing higher instruction for the world's business, for the industrial pursuits and professions of life.

In our country there is abundant room for the tireless and inventive activities of a great people, as no Americans appear to have been created only to "swing on a gate," and idleness finds no place of honor. The possessor of a little learning, however, may have, as an unfortunate attachment, great disgust for labor, and where this occurs it is to be feared that one more recruit has joined the inglorious company of the world's incapables. The Land-Grant Colleges are thoroughly in harmony with American character, with republican institutions; and theoretical instruction in the various branches of sound learning that will prepare men for the active uses of life—wanted here more than anywhere else—cannot fail to inspire respect for labor, to give it a profounder meaning than that of mere drudgery, whether that labor be of the hand or head. We can-

not too soon learn that respect for labor is the most effectual means to make it flourish. . . .

Why should not men of equal mental calibre, though destined to different pursuits, when seeking a liberal education, in the broad and ample language of the founder of the Cornell University, "find instruction in any study"? In our republic we want to educate men as men, to make them intellectual freemen. . . .

There is no assumed heredity in the vocation of the farmer, and his son has all the world before him where to choose his calling as much as the son of the mi[n]ister or the lawyer. It does not follow that whoever goes to an agricultural college must be a farmer, any more than that "whoever drives fat oxen must himself be fat." All who wish to be equipped for agriculture, or for some mechanic art, will naturally devote more time to the related fundamental sciences. Those proposing to follow a professional life will be more industrious and thorough in the direction of ancient as well as of modern classical lore. But it will do the latter no harm to observe something of the wide extent of that instruction which must guide and lead the industrial forces of a great nation, and it will do the former good to witness the persistent appreciation accorded to literary culture. In the aggregate all may obtain a liberal and generous education, and will be nobler men from having been associated together. If there is any friction, it will have served to polish both.

NOAH PORTER

A Critique of the Elective System (1870) *

The modification of the college system, which we shall next consider, is that which does not abandon a prescribed curriculum, but makes the college studies *largely elective*. . . .

The objections to the scheme are many;

* Noah Porter, *The American Colleges and the American Public* (New Haven, Conn.: Charles C. Chatfield and Co., 1870), pp. 101, 103–105, 117–118, 271.

some of them seem to us to be insuperable. They may be expressed briefly thus: . . . College students, at the end of the Freshman year, are usually incapable of selecting between any two proposed studies or courses of study. They do not know themselves well enough to be able to decide in what they are best fitted to excel, nor even what will please them best. Their future occupation is ordinarily not so far determined as to deserve to be seriously considered. Their tastes are either unformed or capricious and prejudiced; if they are decided and strong, they often require correction. The study which is the farthest removed from that which strikes his fancy may be the study which is most needed for the student. The preferences are also likely to be fickle. The real but unanticipated difficulties which are revealed by trial will occasion discontent and vexation, or some new discovery concerning the value of a study that has been rejected, will lead to ennui and discontent. So far as the studies presented for selection are disciplinary, the reasons for preferring one above another are not so decisive as to warrant any great liberty of election. So far as they are professional or practical, it is not desirable that these should be entered upon at so early a period of the education. What might seem to be gained in proficiency or in time, is lost many times over in mental breadth and power by a neglect of the studies which are disciplinary and general. . . .

Other objections might be named, as that the introduction of elective studies tends to weaken the class feeling, which may be so efficient for intellectual incitement and culture, and to interfere with that common life which is so powerful in most of the American colleges. It must necessarily be complicated in its arrangements and operose in its working. It must also require greater energy than can be exacted of any single administrator who acts as the driving wheel of the class or the college; or greater united and conspiring activity in the heads of separate departments than can be presumed in ordinary institutions or under the conditions of our imper-

fect humanity. It may further be urged that the existence of a prescribed, rather than an elective curriculum in the preparatory or the professional school, was originally the result of circumstances and the product of experience. The same circumstances that compelled and the same experience which taught it at first, will, we believe, require that it be resumed as often as the attempt is made to abandon it in any institution which is designed for general culture. The inconvenience will be found to be so great and the advantages so inconsiderable—if, indeed, the disadvantages are not so manifold and overwhelming—as to compel a return to what is substantially a uniform and prescribed course. . . .

Harvard has had for a long time the name of a university, with very much of the reality, in that one of its departments which has followed the methods hitherto characteristic of the college. It would be a public loss and a pity if she should cease to be a college, and fail to be any thing more than the mere semblance of a university. We venture to predict that if the new system is persevered in, Harvard College will contain three or four sets of students among its undergraduates: 1st. The devotees of classical learning or of mathematical research, who, in their "small and lively classes" and with the aid of accomplished and earnest teachers, will prosecute their studies with excited enthusiasm and make brilliant acquisitions; 2d. The devotees of some special branch of Physical Science who will pursue their studies either from the excitement of love, or the interest which is derived from their intimate relation to future professional success; 3d. A higher class than either, viz.: those who by reason of early youthful advantages or precocious genius have the capacity and taste for properly university studies, a great number of which they will select and master; 4th. A large, inferior, and heterogeneous class, who will select their "electives" with the keenest appreciation of what will yield a living standing at the least expense of labor—camp-followers and stragglers, who will require a vigorous Provost Marshal to look after and to connect them in reputable relations with the principal battalions. The connection between these several divisions must be loose and uninteresting, the sense of interest in, and responsibility for, the institution as a whole must be weak in the instructors, the common life of the college must be relaxed and feeble in its tone, and the degree with which all the members of these ill assorted classes are to be honored at the close must signify a frightful inequality of opportunities enjoyed, if not of acquisitions actually made. . . .

To introduce the option of the university, or the lectures of the university, to pupils who are grounded in nothing but in a conceit of their adequacy to grapple with any subject, and who are impelled by aspirations to arrive speedily at the goal without travelling over the intervening space, tends only to destroy the college by substituting the show of a university, and to sink the so-called university into a special school of technology.

CHARLES WILLIAM ELIOT
"Liberty in Education" (1885) *

How to transform a college with one uniform curriculum into a university without any prescribed course of study at all is a problem which more and more claims the attention of all thoughtful friends of American learning and education. To-night I hope to convince you that a university of liberal arts and sciences must give its students three things:

I. Freedom in choice of studies.

II. Opportunity to win academic distinction in single subjects or special lines of study.

III. A discipline which distinctly imposes on each individual the responsibility of form-

* Charles William Eliot, *Educational Reform: Essays and Addresses* (New York: Century, 1901), "Liberty in Education" (an address before the Nineteenth Century Club of New York in 1885), pp. 125, 134–148.

ing his own habits and guiding his own conduct.

These three subjects I shall take up in succession, the first of them taking the greater part of the time allotted me.

I. Of freedom in choice of studies.

. . . The individual enjoys most that intellectual labor for which he is most fit; and society is best served when every man's peculiar skill, faculty, or aptitude is developed and utilized to the highest possible degree. The presumption is, therefore, against uniformity in education, and in favor of diversity at the earliest possible moment. What determines that moment? To my thinking, the limit of compulsory uniform instruction should be determined by the elementary quality and recognized universal utility of the subjects of such instruction. For instance, it is unquestionable that every child needs to know how to read, write, and, to a moderate extent, cipher. Therefore primary schools may have a uniform programme. One might naturally suppose that careful study of the mother-tongue and its literature would be considered a uniform need for all youth; but as a matter of fact there is no agreement to this effect. The English language and literature have hardly yet won a place for themselves in American schools. Only the elements of two foreign languages and the elements of algebra and geometry can be said to be generally recognized as indispensable to the proper training of all young people who are privileged to study beyond their seventeenth year. There is no consent as to the uniform desirableness of the elements of natural science, and there is much difference of opinion about the selection of the two foreign languages, the majority of educated people supposing two dead languages to be preferable, a minority thinking that living languages are permissible. The limit of that elementary knowledge, of which by common consent all persons who are to be highly educated stand in need, is therefore a narrow one, easily to be reached and passed, under respectable instruction, by any youth of fair ability before he is eighteen years old. There, at least, ceases justifiable uniformity in education. There, at least, election of studies should begin; and the safest guides to a wise choice will be the taste, inclination, and special capacity of each individual. When it comes to the choice of a profession, everybody knows that the only wisdom is to follow inclination. In my view, the only wisdom in determining those liberal studies which may be most profitably pursued after eighteen is to follow inclination. Hence it is only the individual youth who can select that course of study which will most profit him, because it will most interest him. The very fact of choice goes far to secure the coöperation of his will.

I have already intimated that there exist certain natural guides and safeguards for every youth who is called upon in a free university to choose his own studies. Let us see what these natural aids are. In the first place, he cannot help taking up a subject which he has already studied about where he left it off, and every new subject at the beginning and not at the middle. Secondly, many subjects taught at a university involve other subjects, which must therefore be studied first. Thus, no one can get far in physics without being familiar with trigonometry and analytic geometry; chemical analysis presupposes acquaintance with general chemistry, and paleontology acquaintance with botany and zoölogy; no one can study German philosophy to advantage unless he can read German, and no student can profitably discuss practical economic problems until he has mastered the elementary principles of political economy. Every advanced course, whether in language, philosophy, history, mathematics, or science, presupposes acquaintance with some elementary course or courses. Thirdly, there is a prevailing tendency on the part of every competent student to carry far any congenial subject once entered upon. To repress this most fortunate tendency is to make real scholarship impossible. So effective are these natural safeguards against fickleness and in-

consecutiveness in the choice of studies, that artificial regulation is superfluous. . . .

Under an elective system the great majority of students use their liberty to pursue some subject or subjects with a reasonable degree of thoroughness. This concentration upon single lines develops advanced teaching, and results in a general raising of the level of instruction. Students who have decided taste for any particular subject wisely devote a large part of their time to that subject and its congeners. Those who have already decided upon their profession wisely choose subjects which are related to, or underlie, their future professional studies; thus, the future physician will advantageously give a large share of his college course to French, German, chemistry, physics, and biology; while the future lawyer will study logic, ethics, history, political economy, and the use of English in argumentative writing and speaking. Among the thousands of individual college courses determined by the choice of the student in four successive years, which the records of Harvard College now preserve, it is rare to find one which does not exhibit an intelligible sequence of studies. It should be understood in this connection that all the studies which are allowed to count toward the A. B. at Harvard are liberal or pure, no technical or professional studies being admissible.

Having said thus much about the way in which an American student will use freedom in the choice of studies, I desire to point out that a young American must enjoy the privileges of university life between eighteen and twenty-two, if at all. From two thirds to three fourths of college graduates go into professions or employments which require of them elaborate special preparation. The medical student needs four years of professional training, the law student at least three, the good teacher and the skilful architect quite as much. Those who enter the service of business corporations, or go into business for themselves, have the business to learn—a process which ordinarily takes several years. If a young man takes his A. B. at twenty-two, he can hardly hope to begin the practice of his profession before he is twenty-six. That is quite late enough. It is clearly impossible, therefore, that the American university should be constructed on top of the old-fashioned American college. The average Freshman at Harvard is eighteen and two thirds years old when he enters, and at the majority of colleges he is older still. For the next three or four years he must have freedom to choose among liberal studies, if he is ever to enjoy that inestimable privilege.

Two common objections to an elective system shall next have our attention. The first is often put in the form of a query. Election of studies may be all very well for conscientious or ambitious students, or for those who have a strong taste for certain studies; but what becomes, under such a system, of the careless, indifferent, lazy boys who have no bent or intellectual ambition of any sort? I answer with a similar query: What became of such boys under the uniform compulsory system? Did they get any profit to speak of under that régime? Not within my observation. It really does not make much difference what these unawakened minds dawdle with. There is, however, much more chance that such young men will get roused from their lethargy under an elective system than under a required. When they follow such faint promptings of desire as they feel, they at least escape the sense of grievance and repugnance which an arbitrary assignment to certain teachers and certain studies often creates. An elective system does not mean liberty to do nothing. The most indifferent student must pass a certain number of examinations every year. He selects perhaps those subjects in which he thinks he can pass the best examinations with the smallest amount of labor; but in those very subjects the instruction will be on a higher plane than it can ever reach under a compulsory system, and he will get more benefit from them than he would from other subjects upon which he put the same amount of labor but attained less success.

It is an important principle in education, from primary school to university, that the greater the visible attainment for a given amount of labor the better; and this rule applies quite as forcibly to a weak student as to a strong one. Feeble or inert students are considerably influenced in choosing their studies by the supposed quality of the teachers whom they will meet. As a rule they select the very teachers who are likely to have the most influence with them, being guided by traditions received from older students of their sort. It is the unanimous opinion of the teachers at Cambridge that more and better work is got from this class of students under the elective system than was under the required.

Having said thus much about the effects of free choice of studies upon the unpromising student, I must add that the policy of an institution of education, of whatever grade, ought never to be determined by the needs of the least capable students; and that a university should aim at meeting the wants of the best students at any rate, and the wants of inferior students only so far as it can meet them without impairing the privileges of the best. A uniform curriculum, by enacting superficiality and prohibiting thoroughness, distinctly sacrifices the best scholars to the average. Free choice of studies gives the young genius the fullest scope without impairing the chances of the drone and the dullard.

The second objection with which I wish to deal is this: free choice implies that there are no studies which are recognized as of supreme merit, so that every young man unquestionably ought to pursue them. Can this be? Is it possible that the accumulated wisdom of the race cannot prescribe with certainty the studies which will best develop the human mind in general between the ages of eighteen and twenty-two? At first it certainly seems strange that we have to answer no; but when we reflect how very brief the acquaintance of the race has been with the great majority of the subjects which are now taught in a university the negative answer seems less surprising. Out of the two hundred courses of instruction which stand on the list of Harvard University this year it would be difficult to select twenty which could have been given at the beginning of this century with the illustrations, materials, and methods now considered essential to the educational quality of the courses. One realizes more easily this absence of accumulated experience on considering that all the natural sciences, with comparative philology, political economy, and history, are practically new subjects, that all mathematics is new except the elements of arithmetic, algebra, and geometry, that the recent additions to ethics and metaphysics are of vast extent, and that the literatures of the eighteenth and nineteenth centuries have great importance in several European languages. The materials and methods of university education always have been, and always will be, changing from generation to generation. We think, perhaps with truth, that the nineteenth century has been a period of unprecedented growth and progress; but every century has probably witnessed an unprecedented advance in civilization, simply because the process is cumulative, if no catastrophes arrest it. It is one of the most important functions of universities to store up the accumulated knowledge of the race, and so to use these stores that each successive generation of youth shall start with all the advantages which their predecessors have won. Therefore a university, while not neglecting the ancient treasures of learning, has to keep a watchful eye upon the new fields of discovery, and has to invite its students to walk in new-made as well as in long-trodden paths. Concerning the direct educational influence of all these new subjects the race cannot be said to have much accumulated wisdom.

One presumption of considerable scope may, however, be said to be established by experience. In every new field of knowledge the mental powers of the adventurers and discoverers found full play and fruitful exercise. Some rare human mind or minds must have laboriously developed each new subject of study. It may fairly be presumed that the youth will find some strenuous exercise of his faculties in following the masters into any field which it taxed their utmost powers to explore and describe. To study the conquests of great minds in any field of knowledge must be good training for young minds of kindred tastes and powers. That all branches of sound knowledge are of equal dignity and equal educational value for mature students is the only hopeful and tenable view in our day. Long ago it became quite impossible for one mind to compass more than an insignificant fraction of the great sum of acquired knowledge.

Before I leave the subject of election of studies, let me point out that there is not a university of competent resources upon the continent of Europe in which complete freedom of studies has not long prevailed; and that Oxford and Cambridge have recently provided an almost complete liberty for their students. In our own country respectable colleges now offer a considerable proportion of elective studies, and as a rule the greater their resources in teachers, collections, and money, the more liberal their application of the elective principle. Many colleges, however, still seem to have but a halting faith in the efficacy of the principle, and our educated public has but just begun to appreciate its importance. So fast as American institutions acquire the resources and powers of European universities, they will adopt the methods proper to universities wherever situate. At present our best colleges fall very far short of European standards in respect to number of teachers, and consequently in respect to amplitude of teaching.

As yet we have no university in America —only aspirants to that eminence. All the more important is it that we should understand the conditions under which a university can be developed—the most indispensable of which is freedom in choice of studies.

II. A university must give its students opportunity to win distinction in special subjects or lines of study. The uniform curriculum led to a uniform degree, the first scholar and the last receiving the same diploma. A university cannot be developed on that plan. It must provide academic honors at graduation for distinguished attainments in single subjects. These honors encourage students to push far on single lines; whence arises a demand for advanced instruction in all departments in which honors can be won, and this demand, taken in connection with the competition which naturally springs up between different departments, stimulates the teachers, who in turn stimulate their pupils. . . . The Harvard faculty announced their system of honors in 1866–67, and they certainly never passed a more effective piece of legislation. In 1879 they devised a lesser distinction at graduation called honorable mention, which has also worked very well. To get honors in any department ordinarily requires a solid year and a half's work; to get honorable mention requires about half that time. The important function of all such devices is to promote specialization of work and therefore to develop advanced instruction. It is unnecessary to point out how absolutely opposed to such a policy the uniform prescription of a considerable body of elementary studies must be.

III. A university must permit its students, in the main, to govern themselves. It must have a large body of students, else many of its numerous courses of highly specialized instruction will find no hearers, and the students themselves will not feel that very wholesome influence which comes from observation of and contact with large numbers of young men from different nations, States, schools, families, sects, parties, and conditions of life. In these days a university is best placed in or near the seat of a considerable population; so that its officers and students can always enjoy the various refined pleasures, and feel alike the incitements and the restraints, of a highly cultivated society. The universities of Rome, Paris, Vienna, Berlin, Leipsic, Christiania, Madrid, and Edinburgh forcibly illustrate both of these advantages. These conditions make it practically impossible for a university to deal with its students on any principle of seclusion, either in a village or behind walls and bars. Fifteen hundred able-bodied young men living in buildings whose doors stand open night and day, or in scattered lodging-houses, cannot be mechanically protected from temptation at the university any more than at the homes from which they came. Their protection must be within them. They must find it in memory of home, in pure companionship, in hard work, in intellectual ambition, religious sentiment, and moral purpose. A sense of personal freedom and responsibility reinforces these protecting influences, while the existence of a supervising authority claiming large powers which it has no effective means of exercising weakens them. The *in loco parentis* theory is an ancient fiction which ought no longer to deceive anybody. No American college, wherever situated, possesses any method of discipline which avails for the suppression or exclusion of vice. The vicious student can find all means of indulgence in the smallest village, and the worst vices are the stillest. It is a distinct advantage of the genuine university method that it does not pretend to maintain any parental or monastic discipline over its students, but frankly tells them that they must govern themselves. The moral purpose of a university's policy should be to train young men to self-control and self-reliance through liberty. It is not the business of a university to train men for those functions in which implicit obedience is of the first importance. On the contrary, it should train men for those occupations in which self-government, independence, and originating power are preëminently needed. Let no one imagine that a young man is in peculiar moral danger at an active and interesting university. Far from it. Such a university is the safest place in the world for young men who have anything in them—far safer than counting-room, shop, factory, farm, barrack, forecastle, or ranch. The student lives in a bracing atmosphere; books engage him; good companionships invite him; good occupations defend him; helpful friends surround him; pure ideals are held up before him; ambition spurs him; honor beckons him.

DANIEL COIT GILMAN
The Launching of a University (1906) *

REMINISCENCES OF THIRTY YEARS IN BALTIMORE, 1875–1905

During the last half century American universities have grown up with surprising rapidity. It is not necessary to fix an exact date for the beginning of this progress. Some would like to say that the foundation of the Lawrence Scientific School in Harvard University, and, almost simultaneously, the foundation of the Sheffield School of Science in New Haven were initial undertakings. These events indicated that the two oldest colleges of New England were ready to introduce instruction of an advanced character, far more special than ever before, in the various branches of natural and physical science. An impulse was given by the passage of the Morrill Act, by which a large amount of scrip, representing public lands, was offered to any State that would maintain a college devoted to agriculture and the mechanic arts, without the exclusion of other scientific and literary studies. The foundation of Cornell University was of the highest significance, for it fortunately came under the guidance of one who was equally devoted to historical and scientific research, one whose plans showed an independence of thought and a power of organisation then without precedent in the field of higher education. The changes introduced in Harvard, under masterful leadership, when the modern era of progress began, had profound influence. The subsequent gifts of Johns Hopkins, of

* Daniel Coit Gilman, *The Launching of a University and Other Papers: A Sheaf of Remembrances* (New York: Dodd, Mead, 1906), I, "Reminiscences of Thirty Years in Baltimore (1875–1905)," 3–5, 7, 9–10, 12–16, 19–24; III, "Fundamental Principles," 41–43.

Rockefeller, of Stanford, of Tulane, promoted the establishment of new institutions, in sympathy with the older colleges, yet freer to introduce new subjects and new methods. The State universities of the Northwest and of the Pacific coast, as population and wealth increased, became an important factor. These multiform agencies must all be carefully considered when an estimate is made up of the progress of the last half-century. . . .

In looking over this period, remarkable changes are manifest. In the first place, science receives an amount of support unknown before. This is a natural consequence of the wonderful discoveries which have been made in respect to the phenomena and laws of nature and the improvements made in scientific instruments and researches. Educational leaders perceived the importance of the work carried on in laboratories and observatories under the impulse of such men as Liebig and Faraday. With this increased attention to science, the old-fashioned curriculum disappeared, of necessity, and many combinations of studies were permitted in the most conservative institutions. Absolute freedom of choice is now allowed in many places. . . . Medicine is no longer taught by lectures only, but the better schools require continued practice in biological laboratories and the subsequent observation of patients in hospitals and dispensaries. The admission of women to the advantages of higher education is also one of the most noteworthy advances of the period we are considering.

The historian who takes up these and allied indications of the progress of American universities will have a difficult and an inspiring theme. It has been a delightful and exhilarating time in which to live and to work, to observe and to try. All the obstacles have not been overcome, some mistakes have been made, much remains for improvement, but on the whole the record of the last forty or fifty years exhibits substantial and satisfactory gains. The efforts of scholars have been sustained by the munificence of donors, and more than one institution now has an endowment larger than that of all the institutions which were in existence in 1850. . . .

When the announcement was made to the public, at the end of 1873, that a wealthy merchant of Baltimore had provided by his will for the establishment of a new university, a good deal of latent regret was felt because the country seemed to have already more higher seminaries than it could supply with teachers, students, or funds. Another "college" was expected to join the crowded column, and impoverish its neighbours by its superior attractions. Fortunately, the founder was wise as well as generous. . . . Let me tell some of the conditions which brought the Johns Hopkins foundations into close relations with these upward and onward movements.

Before a university can be launched there are six requisites: An idea; capital, to make the ideal feasible; a definite plan; an able staff of coadjutors; books and apparatus; students. On each of these points I shall briefly dwell, conscious of one advantage as a writer—conscious, also, of a disadvantage. I have the advantage of knowing more than anyone else of an unwritten chapter of history; the disadvantage of not being able or disposed to tell the half that I remember.

"The idea of the university" was a phrase to which Cardinal Newman had given currency in a remarkable series of letters in which he advocated the establishment of a Catholic foundation in Dublin. At a time when ecclesiastical or denominational colleges were at the front, and were considered by many people the only defensible places for the education of young men, his utterances for academic freedom were emancipating; at a time when early specialisation was advocated, his defence of liberal culture was reassuring. The evidence elicited by the British university commissions was instructive, and the writings of Mark Pattison, Dr. Appleton, Matthew Arnold, and others were full of suggestions. Innumerable essays and pamphlets had appeared in Germany discussing the improvements which were called for in that land of research. The endeavours

of the new men at Cambridge and New Haven, and the instructive success of the University of Virginia, were all brought under consideration. Under these favourable circumstances, *Zeit-geist* they may be called, the Johns Hopkins was founded upon the idea of a university as distinct from a college.

The capital was provided by a single individual. No public meeting was ever held to promote subscriptions or to advocate higher education; no speculation in land was proposed; no financial gains were expected; no religious body was involved, not even the Society of orthodox Friends, in which the founder had been trained, and from which he selected several of his confidential advisers. He gave what seemed at the time a princely gift; he supplemented it with an equal gift for a hospital. It was natural that he should also give his name. That was then the fashion. John Harvard and Elihu Yale had lived long ago, and they never sought the remembrance which their contemporaries insured; but in late years Girard, Smithson, Lawrence, Cornell, and Cooper, had all regarded their foundations as children entitled to bear the parental name. Their follower in Maryland did likewise.

It is always interesting to know the genesis of great gifts. Johns Hopkins, who had never married, was in doubt, when he grew old, respecting the bestowal of his acquisitions. The story is current that a sagacious friend said to him, "There are two things which are sure to live—a university, for there will always be the youth to train; and a hospital, for there will always be the suffering to relieve." This germ, implanted in a large brain, soon bore fruit. . . .

Given the idea and the funds, the next requisite was a plan. In my first interviews with the trustees, I was strongly impressed by their desire to do the very best that was possible under the circumstances in which they were placed. We quickly reached concurrence. Without dissent, it was agreed

that we were to develop, if possible, something more than a local institution, and were at least to aim at national influence; that we should try to supplement, and not supplant, existing colleges, and should endeavour to bring to Baltimore, as teachers and as students, the ablest minds that we could attract. It was understood that we should postpone all questions of building, dormitories, commons, discipline, and degrees; that we should hire or buy in the heart of the city a temporary perch, and remain on it until we could determine what wants should be revealed, and until we could decide upon future buildings. We were to await the choice of a faculty before we matured any schemes of examination, instruction, and graduation.

I was encouraged to travel freely at home and abroad. . . . On the Continent I visited Paris, Berlin, Heidelberg, Strasburg, Freiburg, Leipsic, Munich, and Vienna. In all these places the laboratories were new and were even more impressive than the libraries. Everywhere the problems of higher education were under discussion; everywhere, readiness to be helpful and suggestive was apparent. One Sunday afternoon I sat for a long while on the vine-clad hill of Freiburg, looking at the beautiful spire of the cathedral and talking with the historian, Professor Von Holst—already well acquainted with American conditions. He became one of our lecturers, and afterward took part in the development of the University of Chicago. He gave me an inside view of the workings of the German University system. Professor James Bryce was a most serviceable interpreter of the intricacies of Oxford and Cambridge. Through a college classmate who had become an *agrégé* in the University of France, I had a similar introduction to the methods of the French. Among my note-books I think there is one in which, while at Oxford, in the autumn of 1875, I drew up an outline of the possible organisation of our work in Baltimore. It was brief, but it was also comprehensive.

The first real difficulty was the selection of a faculty. . . . The announcement was boldly made that the best men who could be found would be first appointed without respect to the place from which they came, the college wherein they were trained, or the religious body to which they belonged. The effort would be made to secure the best men who were free to accept positions in a new, uncertain, and, it must be acknowledged, somewhat risky organisation. I will not recall the overtures made to men of mark, nor the overtures received from men of no mark. Nor can I say whether it was harder to eliminate from the list of candidates the second best, or to secure the best.

All this it is well to forget. When I die, the memory of those anxieties and perplexities will forever disappear. It is enough to remember that Sylvester, Gildersleeve, Remsen, Rowland, Morris, and Martin were the first professors. As a faculty "we were seven." Our education, our antecedents, our peculiarities were very different, but we were full of enthusiasm, and we got on together without a discordant note. Four of the six are dead; one is still as vigorous and incisive as ever; one is now President. An able corps of associates, lecturers, and fellows was appointed with the professors, and they were admirable helpers in the inception of the work. . . .

The purchase of books and apparatus is of but little interest to the public, so I pass that subject by, and will proceed at once to the sixth requisite. After plans had been formed and teachers installed, the question was still open, Where are the students? We were very fortunate in those that came to us. They were not many at first, and it was comparatively easy to become acquainted with every one. Among the pleasantest recollections of my life are the relations which I have held with the young men among whom my lot has been cast. In later years the numbers have been large, the helpers many, so that I have not been quite as fortunate, but for a long while I was brought into close acquaintance with every student. . . . Whatever service we have rendered them is largely due to the freedom of our methods, and to the close contact which has prevailed between the leading scholars and those that have come under their guidance, and above all to the brilliant and learned men whose influence, often unconscious, has been the most potent factor in the university at Baltimore. Thus with the six requisites, an idea, a plan, an endowment, a faculty, apparatus, and students, we proceeded to launch our bark upon the Patapsco.

As the day drew near for the opening of our doors and the beginning of instruction the word reached us that Professor Huxley of London was coming to this country. We had already decided that, in view of the attention which was to be given to medicine, biology should receive a large amount of attention, more than ever before in America. That meant the study, in the laboratory, of vegetable and animal forms and functions, so that the eyes and hands and brains of the students might become prepared for the study of the human body in health and in disease. Huxley, among English-speaking people, was the leader in these studies. His repute as an investigator was very high, and as the popular interpreter and defender of biological investigations he was without a peer. His acquaintance with the problems of medical education was also well known. As a public speaker upon scientific subjects there was no superior. He had rendered us a service by nominating Dr. Martin to the professorship of biology. The moment was opportune for informing the public, through the speech of this master, in respect to the requirements of modern medicine and the value of biological research. I do not suppose that anyone connected with the university had thought of the popular hostility toward biology. We did not know that to many persons this mysterious term was like a red flag of warning. The fact that some naturalists were considered irreligious filled the air with suspicions that the new foundation would be handed over to the

Evil One. The sequel will show what happened. Professor Huxley was invited; he accepted, he came to Baltimore, he addressed a crowded assembly—then came a storm.

An amusing incident in this visit has been told by his biographer; but as my recollections differ in slight details, I will tell the story in my own way.

On his arrival in Baltimore, Professor Huxley was driven to the country seat of Mr. Garrett, who had offered him hospitality and had invited a large company to meet him in an afternoon party. There was but one intervening day between his arrival, tired out by a long journey in the interior, and his delivery of the address. He had hardly reached the residence of his host before the reporters discovered him and asked for the manuscript of his speech. "Manuscript?" he said, "I have none. I shall speak freely on a theme with which I am quite familiar." "Well, professor," said the interlocutor, "that is all right, but our instructions are to send the speech to the papers in New York, and if you cannot give us the copy, we must take it down as well as we can and telegraph it, for the Associated Press is bound to print it the morning after it is spoken." This was appalling, for in view of the possible inaccuracy of the short-hand, and the possible condensation of the wire-hand, the lecturer was afraid that technical and scientific terms might not be rightly reproduced. "You can have your choice, professor," said the urbane reporter, "to give us the copy or to let us do the best we can; for report the speech we shall." The professor yielded, and the next day he walked up and down in his room at Mr. Garrett's, dictating to a stenographer, in cold and irresponsive seclusion, the speech which he expected to make before a receptive and hospitable assembly.

I sat very near the orator as he delivered the address in the Academy of Music, and noticed that, although he kept looking at the pile of manuscript on the desk before him, he did not turn the pages over. The speech was appropriate and well received, but it had no glow, and the orator did not equal his reputation for charm and persuasiveness. When the applause was over, I said to Mr. Huxley, "I noticed that you did not read your address; I am afraid the light was insufficient." "Oh," said he, "that was not the matter. I have been in distress. The reporters brought me, according to their promise, the copy of their notes. It was on thin translucent paper, and to make it legible, they put clean white sheets between the leaves. That made such bulk that I removed the intermediate leaves, and when I stood up at the desk I found I could not read a sentence. So I have been in a dilemma—not daring to speak freely, and trying to recall what I dictated yesterday and allowed the reporters to send to New York." If he used an epithet before the word "reporters" I am sure he was justified, but I forget what it was.

Those of us who wanted guidance and encouragement from a leading advocate of biological studies were rewarded and gratified by the address, and have often referred to it as it was printed in his American discourses and afterward in his collected works.

We had sowed the wind and were to reap the whirlwind. The address had not been accompanied by any accessories except the presentation of the speaker, no other speech, no music, no opening prayer, no benediction. I had proposed to two of the most religious trustees that there should be an introductory prayer, and they had said no, preferring that the discourse should be given as popular lectures are given at the Peabody Institute and elsewhere, without note or comment.

It happened that a correspondent of one of the religious weeklies in New York was present, and he wrote a sensational letter to his paper, calling attention to the fact that there was no prayer. This was the storm-signal. Many people who thought that a university, like a college, could not succeed unless it was under some denominational control, were sure that this opening discourse was but an overture to the play of irreligious and anti-religious actors. Vain it was to mention the unquestioned orthodoxy

of the trustees, and the ecclesiastical ties of those who had been selected to be the professors. Huxley was bad enough; Huxley without a prayer was intolerable. . . .

The truth is that the public had been so wonted to regard colleges as religious foundations, and so used to their control by ministers, that it was not easy to accept at once the idea of an undenominational foundation controlled by laymen. Harvard and Cornell have both encountered the like animosity. At length the prejudice wore away without any manifesto or explanation from the authorities. From the beginning there was a voluntary assembly daily held for Christian worship; soon the Young Men's Christian Association was engrafted; the students became active in the churches and Sunday-schools and charities of Baltimore; some graduates entered the ministry, and one became a bishop, while the advanced courses in Hebrew, Greek, history, and philosophy, were followed by ministers of many Protestant denominations, Catholic priests and Jewish rabbis. It is also gratifying to remember that many of the ministers of Baltimore, Presbyterian, Episcopalian, Methodist, and Baptist, have intrusted their sons to the guidance of the local seminary whose influence and instructions they could readily watch and carefully estimate. As I consider the situation, I wish it were possible for religious people to agree upon what should be taught to the young, in respect to religious doctrine, or at least to unite in religious worship, yet I cannot forget that, in ages and in countries where one authority has been recognised and obeyed, neither intellect nor morals have attained their highest development.

. . . . .

FUNDAMENTAL PRINCIPLES

The public were naturally impatient to know what sort of an institution was to be established in Baltimore, and accordingly on the 1st of January, 1876, the following announcement was made of fundamental principles by which it was proposed that the new institution should be governed. It is of interest to enquire how closely these positions have been maintained, but the answer I leave for others.

It is the desire of the authorities, I said at that time (speaking in the name of the Trustees), that the institution now taking shape should forever be free from the influences of ecclesiasticism or partisanship, as those terms are used in narrow and controversial senses; that all departments of learning—mathematical, scientific, literary, historical, philosophical,—should be promoted, as far as the funds at command will permit, the new departments of research receiving full attention, while the traditional are not slighted; that the instructions should be as thorough, as advanced and as special as the intellectual condition of the country will permit; that the glory of the University should rest upon the character of the teachers and scholars here brought together, and not upon their number, nor upon the buildings constructed for their use; that its sphere of influence should be national, while at the same time all the local institutions of education and science should be quickened by its power; and finally that among the professional departments, special attention should be first given to the sciences bearing upon medicine, surgery, and hygiene, for which some provision has been made by the munificent gift of our founder to establish The Johns Hopkins Hospital.

The selection of professors and teachers upon whom will devolve the instruction of youth, the chief work of the University, is peculiarly difficult because there are here no traditions for guidance, no usages in respect to the distribution of subjects, and none in respect to the kind of instruction to be given; and also because the plans of the Trustees must depend very much upon the character of the teachers whom they bring together.

A very large number of candidates have been suggested to the Trustees; but among them all there are but a few who have attained distinction as investigators or as teachers. Most of those whose names have been thus presented are young men, usually of much promise, who have not yet had an opportunity to show their intellectual power in any department of higher instruction; and yet among this very class a discerning choice will doubtless discover those who are soon to be the men of scientific and literary renown. The Trustees promise to open freely the doors of promotion to those young men who seem to be capable of the highest work, —appointing them at first for restricted and definite periods. Moreover they hope for a while to gain much of the influence and cooperation of older and more distinguished men by inviting one and another to come here from time to time with courses of lectures. But the idea is not lost sight of that the power of the University will depend upon the character of its resident staff of permanent professors. It is their researches in the library and the laboratory; their utterances in the classroom and in private; their example as students and investigators, and as champions of the truth; their publications, through the journals and the scientific treatises, which will make the University of Baltimore an attraction to the best students, and serviceable to the intellectual growth of the land.

In selecting a staff of teachers, the Trustees have determined to consider especially the devotion of the candidate to some particular line of study and the certainty of his eminence in that specialty; the power to pursue independent and original investigation, and to inspire the young with enthusiasm for study and research; the willingness to cooperate in building up a new institution; and the freedom from tendencies toward ecclesiastical or sectional controversies. The Trustees will not be governed by denominational or geographical considerations in the appointment of any teacher; but will endeavour to select the best person whose services they can secure in the position to be filled, irrespective of the place where he was born, or the college in which he was trained, or the religious body with which he has been enrolled.

THE UNIVERSITY IN AN AGE OF UPHEAVAL

CARL L. BECKER
On Academic Freedom and Responsibility
(April 27, 1940) *

Seventy-five years ago today Reuben E. Fenton, the Governor of the State of New York, signed a charter for Cornell University. The founding of the university was made possible, in great part, by the generosity of Ezra Cornell, a citizen of Ithaca. The first faculty was assembled, the university was organized, and instruction was begun under the farsighted leadership of the first president, Andrew D. White; and in a relatively short time, as such things go, the new institution, as a result of the distinguished achievements of its faculty and the high quality of instruction offered to its students, acquired a reputation which placed it among the leading universities of the country.

In the process of acquiring a reputation Cornell acquired something better than a reputation, or rather it acquired something which is the better part of its reputation. It acquired a character. Corporations are not necessarily soulless; and of all corporations universities are the most likely to have, if not souls, at least personalities. Perhaps the reason is that universities are, after all, largely shaped by presidents and professors, and presidents and professors, especially if they are good ones, are fairly certain to be men of distinctive, not to say eccentric, minds and temperaments. A professor, as the German saying has it, is a man who thinks otherwise. Now an able and otherwise-thinking president, surrounded by able and otherwise-thinking professors, each reso-

* "The Cornell Tradition: Freedom and Responsibility" (an address delivered by Professor Becker on April 27, 1940, in recognition of the seventy-fifth anniversary of the signing of the charter of Cornell University), from Carl L. Becker, *Cornell University: Founders and the Founding* (Ithaca: Cornell University Press, 1943). Copyright, 1943, by Cornell University. Used by permission of Cornell University Press.

lutely thinking otherwise in his own manner, each astounded to find that the others, excellent fellows as he knows them in the main to be, so often refuse in matters of the highest import to be informed by knowledge or guided by reason—this is indeed always an arresting spectacle and may sometimes seem to be a futile performance. Yet it is not futile unless great universities are futile. For the essential quality of a great university d[e]rives from the corporate activities of such a community of otherwise-thinking men. By virtue of a divergence as well as of a community of interests, by the sharp impress of their minds and temperaments and eccentricities upon each other and upon their pupils, there is created a continuing tradition of ideas and attitudes and habitual responses that has a life of its own. It is this continuing tradition that gives to a university its corporate character or personality, that intangible but living and dynamic influence which is the richest and most durable gift any university can confer upon those who come to it for instruction and guidance.

Cornell has a character, a corporate personality, in this sense, an intellectual tradition by which it can be identified. The word which best symbolizes this tradition is freedom. There is freedom in all universities, of course—a great deal in some, much less in others; but it is less the amount than the distinctive quality and flavor of the freedom that flourishes at Cornell that is worth noting. The quality and flavor of this freedom is easier to appreciate than to define. Academic is not the word that properly denotes it. It includes academic freedom, of course, but it is something more, and at the same time something less, than that—something less formal, something less self-regarding, something more worldly, something, I will venture to say, a bit more impudent. It is, in short, too little schoolmasterish to be defined by a formula or identified with a professional code. And I think the reason is that Cornell was not founded by schoolmasters or designed strictly according to existing educational models. The founders, being both in their different ways rebels against convention, wished to establish not merely another university but a somewhat novel kind of university. Mr. Cornell desired to found an institution in which any person could study any subject. Mr. White wished to found a center of learning where mature scholars and men of the world, emancipated from the clerical tradition and inspired by the scientific idea, could pursue their studies uninhibited by the cluttered routine or the petty preoccupations of the conventional cloistered academic life. In Mr. White's view the character and quality of the university would depend upon the men selected for its faculty: devoted to the general aim of learning and teaching, they could be depended upon to devise their own ways and means of achieving that aim. The emphasis was, therefore, always on men rather than on methods; and during Mr. White's administration and that of his immediate successors there was assembled at Cornell, from the academic and the non-academic world, a group of extraordinary men—erudite or not as the case might be, but at all events as highly individualized, as colorful, as disconcertingly original and amiably eccentric a group of men as was ever got together for the launching of a new educational venture. It is in the main to the first president and this early group of otherwise-thinking men that Cornell is indebted for its tradition of freedom.

Many of those distinguished scholars and colorful personalities were before my time. Many of those whom I was privileged to know are now gone. A few only are still with us—worthy bearers of the tradition, indefatigable in the pursuit of knowledge, in the service of Cornell, in the promotion of the public good, young men still, barely eighty or a little more. Present or absent, the influence of this original group persists, and is attested by stories of their sayings and exploits that still circulate, a body of ancient

but still living folklore. It is a pity that some one has not collected and set down these stories; properly arranged they would constitute a significant mythology, a Cornell epic which, whether literally true or only characteristic, would convey far better than official records in deans' offices the real significance of this institution. Some of these stories I have heard, and for their illustrative value will venture to recall a few of them. Like Herodotus, I give them as they were related to me without vouching for their truth, and like Herodotus, I hope no god or hero will take offense at what I say.

There is the story of the famous professor of history, passionate defender of majority rule, who, foreseeing that he would be outvoted in the faculty on the question of the location of Risley Hall, declared with emotion that he felt so strongly on the subject that he thought he ought to have two votes. The story of another professor of history who, in reply to a colleague who moved as the sense of the faculty that during war time professors should exercise great discretion in discussing public questions, declared that for his part he could not understand how any one could have the Prussian arrogance to suppose that every one could be made to think alike, or the Pomeranian stupidity to suppose that it would be a good thing if they could. The story of the eccentric and lovable professor of English who suggested that it would be a good thing, during the winter months when the wind sweeps across the hill, if the university would tether a shorn lamb on the slope south of the library building; who gave all of his students a grade of eighty-five, on the theory that they deserved at least that for patiently listening to him while he amused himself reading his favorite authors aloud, and for so amiably submitting to the ironical and sarcastic comments —too highly wrought and sophistically phrased in latinized English to be easily understood by them—with which he berated their indifference to good literature. There is the story of the professor who reluctantly agreed to serve as dean of a school on condition that he be relieved of the irksome task at a certain date; who, as the date approached with no successor appointed, repeatedly reminded the president that he would retire on the date fixed; and who, on that date, although no successor had meantime been appointed, cleared out his desk and departed; so that, on the day following, students and heads of departments found the door locked and no dean to affix the necessary signature to the necessary papers. A school without a dean—strange interlude indeed, rarely occurring in more decorous institutions, I should think; but one of those things that could happen in Cornell. And there is the story of the professor of entomology, abruptly leaving a faculty meeting. It seems that the discussion of a serious matter was being sidetracked by the rambling, irrelevant, and would-be facetious remarks of a dean who was somewhat of a wag, when the professor of entomology, not being a wag and being quite fed up, suddenly reached for his hat and as he moved to the door delivered himself thus: "Mr. President, I beg to be excused; I refuse to waste my valuable time any longer listening to this damned nonsense." And even more characteristic of the Cornell tradition is a story told of the first president, Andrew D. White. It is related that the lecture committee had brought to Cornell an eminent authority to give, in a certain lecture series, an impartial presentation of the Free-Silver question. Afterwards Mr. White, who had strong convictions on the subject, approached the chairman of the committee and asked permission to give a lecture in that series in reply to the eminent authority. But the chairman refused, saying in substance: "Mr. President, the committee obtained the best man it could find to discuss this question. It is of the opinion that the discussion was a fair and impartial presentation of the arguments on both sides. The committee would welcome an address by you on any other subject, or on this subject on some other occasion, but not on this subject in this series in reply to the lecture just

given." It is related that Mr. White did not give a lecture on that subject in that series; it is also related that Mr. White became a better friend and more ardent admirer of the chairman of the committee than he had been. It seems that Mr. White really liked to have on his faculty men of that degree of independence and resolution.

These stories are in the nature of little flash lights illuminating the Cornell temper. A little wild, at times, the Cornell temper; riding, not infrequently, as one may say, high, wide, and handsome. Some quality in it that is native to these states, some pungent tang of the soil, some acrid smell of the frontier and the open spaces—something of the genuine American be-damned-to-you attitude. But I should like to exhibit the Cornell tradition in relation to a more general and at the same time a more concrete situation; and I will venture to do this, even risking a lapse from good taste, by relating briefly my own experience in coming to Cornell and in adjusting myself to its peculiar climate of opinion.

My first contact with the Cornell tradition occurred in December 1916, at the meeting of the American Historical Association at Cincinnati, where Professor Charles Hull invited me to come to his room in the hotel to meet his colleagues of the history group. Intimations had reached me that I was, as the saying is, being considered at Cornell for a position in European history, so that I was rather expecting to be offered a job, at a certain salary, on condition that I should teach a certain number of courses, assume certain administrative duties, and the like. I took it for granted that Cornell would handle these matters in the same businesslike way that other universities did. But I found that Professor Hull had a manner and a method all his own. He did not offer me a job—nothing as crude as that; he invited me, on behalf of his colleagues, to join the faculty of Cornell University. The difference may be subtle, but I found it appreciable. On the chance that I might have formed a too favorable opinion of Cornell, Professor

Hull hastened to set me right by itemizing, in great detail, the disadvantages which, from a disinterested point of view, there might be in being associated with the institution, as well as, more doubtfully, certain possible advantages. Among the disadvantages, according to Professor Hull, was the salary; but he mentioned, somewhat apologetically, a certain sum which I could surely count on, and intimated that more might be forthcoming if my decision really depended upon it. By and large, from Professor Hull's elaborate accounting, I gathered that Cornell, as an educational institution, was well over in the red, but that, such as it was, with all its sins of omission heavy upon it, it would be highly honored if I could so far condescend to its needs as to associate myself with it.

There apparently, so far as Professor Hull was concerned, the matter rested. Nothing was said of courses to be taught, minimum hours of instruction, or the like mundane matters. In the end I had to inquire what the home work would be—how many hours and what courses I would be required to teach. Professor Hull seemed mildly surprised at the question. "Why," he said, "I don't know that anything is *required* exactly. It has been customary for the Professor of Modern History to give to the undergraduates a general survey course in modern history, and sometimes if he deems it advisable, a more advanced course in some part of it in which he is especially interested, and in addition to supervise, to whatever extent may seem to him desirable, the work of such graduate students as may come to him. We had rather hoped that you would be disposed to do something of this sort, but I don't know that I can say that anything specific in the way of courses is really *required*. We have assumed that whatever you found convenient and profitable to do would be sufficiently advantageous to the university and satisfactory to the students." Well, there it was. Such a magnification of the professor, such a depreciation of the university, had never before, in similar circumstances,

come my way. After a decent interval I condescended to join the faculty of Cornell University. And why not? To receive a good salary for doing as I pleased—what could be better? The very chance I had been looking for all my life.

And so in the summer of 1917 I came to Cornell, prepared to do as I pleased, wondering what the catch was, supposing that Professor Hull's amiable attitude must be either an eccentric form of ironic understatement or else a super-subtle species of bargaining technique. Anyway I proposed to try it out. I began to do as I pleased, expecting some one would stop me. No one did. I went on and on and still no one paid any attention. Personally I was cordially received, but officially no one made any plans to entertain me, to give me the right steer, to tell me what I would perhaps find it wise to do or to refrain from doing. Professor Hull's attitude did seem after all to represent, in some idealized fashion, the attitude of Cornell University. There was about the place a refreshing sense of liberation from the prescribed and the insistent, an atmosphere of casual urbanity, a sense of leisurely activity going on, with time enough to admire the view, and another day coming. No one seemed to be in a hurry, except Mr. Burr of course, and sometimes perhaps Mr. Ranum. But that was their affair—a response, no doubt, to the compulsion of some inner daemon. At least I saw no indication that deans or heads of departments were exerting pressure or pushing any one around. Certainly no head of the history department was incommoding me, for the simple reason, if for no other, that there didn't seem to be any history department, much less a head. There were seven professors of history, and when we met we called ourselves the "History Group," but no one of us had any more authority than any other. On these occasions Professor Hull presided, for no reason I could discover except that we met in his office because it was the largest and most convenient. Whatever the History Group was it was not a department. If there was any department of history, then there were six; in which case I was the sole member, and presumably the head, of the department of Modern European History. The only evidence of this was that twice a year I received a communication from the president: one requesting me to prepare the budget, which consisted chiefly in setting down the amount of my own salary, an item which the president presumably already knew more about than I did; the other a request for a list of the courses given and the number of students, male and female, enrolled during the year. I always supposed, therefore, that there were six departments of history, each manned by one professor, except the department of American history, which ran to the extraordinary number of two. I always supposed so, that is, until one day Professor Hull said he wasn't sure there were, officially speaking, any departments of history at all; the only thing he was sure of was that there were seven professors of history. The inner truth of the matter I never discovered. But the seven professors were certainly members of the Faculty of Arts, the Graduate Faculty, and the University Faculty since they were often present at the meetings of these faculties. They were also, I think, members of the Faculty of Political Science, a body that seemed to have no corporeal existence since it never met, but that nevertheless seemed to be something—a rumor perhaps, a disembodied tradition or vestigial remainder never seen, but lurking about somewhere in the more obscure recesses of Goldwin Smith Hall. I never had the courage to ask Professor Hull about the university— about its corporate administrative existence, I mean—for fear he might say that he wasn't sure it had any: it was on the cards that the university might turn out to be nothing more than forty or fifty professors.

At all events, the administration (I assumed on general principles that there was one somewhere) wasn't much in evidence and exerted little pressure. There was a president (distinguished scholar and emi-

nent public figure) who presided at faculty meetings and the meeting of the Board of Trustees, and always delivered the Commencement address. But the president, so far as I could judge, was an umpire rather than a captain, and a Gallup poll would have disclosed the fact that some members of the community regarded him as an agreeable but purely decorative feature, his chief function being, as one of my colleagues said, "to obviate the difficulties created by his office." I never shared this view. I have a notion that the president obviated many difficulties, especially for the faculty, that were in no sense created by his office. There were also deans, but not many or much looked up to for any authority they had or were disposed to exercise. Even so, the general opinion seemed to be that the appointment of professors to the office was a useless waste of talent. "Why is it," asked Professor Nichols, "that as soon as a man has demonstrated that he has an unusual knowledge of books, some one immediately insists on making him a bookkeeper?" In those days the dean of the College, at all events, was scarcely more than a bookkeeper—a secretary elected by the faculty to keep its records and administer the rules enacted by it.

The rules were not many or much displayed or very oppressive—the less so since in so many cases they were conflicting, so that one could choose the one which seemed most suitable. The rules seemed often in the nature of miscellaneous conveniences lying about for a professor to use if he needed something of the sort. An efficient administrator, if there had been one, would no doubt have found much that was ill-defined and haphazard in the rules. Even to a haphazard professor, like myself, it often seemed so, for if I inquired what the authority for this or that rule was, the answer would perhaps be that it wasn't a rule but only a custom; and upon further investigation the custom, as like as not, would turn out to be two other customs, varying according to the time and the professor. Even in the broad distribution of powers the efficient administrator might have found much to discontent his orderly soul. I was told that according to the Cornell statutes the university is subject to the control of the Board of Trustees, but that according to the laws of the state it is subject to the Board of Regents. It may or may not be so. I never pressed the matter. I was advised not to, on the theory that at Cornell it always creates trouble when any one looks up the statutes. The general attitude, round and round about, seemed to be that the university would go on very well indeed so long as no one paid too much attention to the formal authority with which any one was invested. And, in fact, in no other university that I am acquainted with does formal authority count for so little in deciding what shall or shall not be done.

In this easy-going, loose-jointed institution the chances seemed very good indeed for me to do as I pleased. Still there was an obvious limit. The blest principle of doing as one pleased presumably did not reach to the point of permitting me to do nothing. Presumably, the general expectation would be that I would at least be pleased to do something, and the condition of doing something was that I alone had to decide what that something should be. This was for me something of a novelty. Hitherto many of the main points—the courses to be given, the minimum hours of instruction, the administrative duties to be assumed—had mostly been decided for me. I had only to do as I was told. This might be sometimes annoying, but it was never difficult. Mine not to question why, mine not to ask whether what I was doing was worth while or the right thing to do. It was bound to be the right thing to do since some one else, some one in authority, so decided. But now, owing to the great freedom at Cornell, I was in authority and had to decide what was right and worth while for me to do. This was not so easy, and I sometimes tried to shift the responsibility to Professor Burr, by asking him whether what I proposed to do

was the right thing to do. But Professor Burr wasn't having any. He would spin me a long history, the upshot of which was that what I proposed to do had sometimes been done and sometimes not, so that whatever I did I was sure to have plenty of precedents on my side. And if I tried to shift the responsibility to Professor Hull I had no better luck. He too would spin me a history, not longer than that of Professor Burr, but only taking longer to relate, and the conclusion which he reached was always the same: the conclusion always was, "and so, my dear boy, you can do as you please."

In these devious ways I discovered that I could do as I pleased all right. But in the process of discovering this I also discovered something else. I discovered what the catch was. The catch was that, since I was free to do as I pleased, I was responsible for what it was that I pleased to do. The catch was that, with all my great freedom, I was in some mysterious way still very much bound. Not bound by orders imposed upon me from above or outside, but bound by some inner sense of responsibility, by some elemental sense of decency or fair play or mere selfish impulse to justify myself; bound to all that comprised Cornell University, to the faculty that had so politely invited me to join it without imposing any obligations, to the amiable deans who never raised their voices or employed the imperative mood, to the distinguished president and the Board of Trustees in the offing who every year guaranteed my salary without knowing precisely what, if anything, I might be doing to earn it—to all these I was bound to justify myself by doing, upon request and in every contingency, the best I was capable of doing. And thus I found myself working, although without interference and under no outside compulsion, with more concentration, with greater satisfaction, and, I dare say, with better effect, than I could otherwise have done. I relate my own experience, well aware that it cannot be in all respects typical, since it is characteristic of Cornell to permit a wide diversity in departmental organization and procedure. Yet this very diversity derives from the Cornell tradition which allows a maximum of freedom and relies so confidently upon the sense of personal responsibility for making a good use of it.

I should like to preserve intact the loose-jointed administrative system and the casual freedoms of the old days. But I am aware that it is difficult to do so in the present-day world in which the complex and impersonal forces of a technological society tend to diminish the importance of the individual and to standardize his conduct and thinking, a society in which life often seems impoverished by the overhead charges required to maintain it. Universities cannot remain wholly unaffected by this dominant trend in society. As they become larger and more complicated a more reticulated organization is called for, rules multiply and become more uniform, and the members of the instructing staff, turned out as a standardized article in mass production by our graduate schools, are more subdued to a common model. Somewhat less than formerly, it seems, is the professor a man who thinks otherwise. More than formerly the professor and the promoter are in costume and deportment if not of imagination all compact; and every year it becomes more difficult, in the market place or on the campus, to distinguish the one from the other at ninety yards by the naked eye. On the whole we all deplore this trend towards standardization, but in the particular instance the reasons for it are often too compelling to be denied. Nevertheless, let us yield to this trend only as a necessity and not as something good in itself. Let us hold, in so far as may be, to the old ways, to the tradition in which Cornell was founded and by which it has lived.

But after all, one may ask, and it is a pertinent question, why is so much freedom desirable? Do we not pay too high a price for it in loss of what is called efficiency? Why should any university pay its professors a good salary, and then guarantee them so much freedom to follow their own devices? Surely not because professors deserve, more than other men, to have their way of life made easy. Not for any such trivial reason. Universities are social institutions, and should perform a social service. There is indeed no reason for the existence of Cornell, or of any university, or for maintaining the freedom of learning and teaching which they insist upon, except in so far as they serve to maintain and promote the humane and rational values which are essential to the preservation of democratic society, and of civilization as we understand it. Democratic society, like any other society, rests upon certain assumptions as to what is supremely worth while. It assumes the worth and dignity and creative capacity of the human personality as an end in itself. It assumes that it is better to be governed by persuasion than by compulsion, and that good will and humane dealing are better than a selfish and a contentious spirit. It assumes that man is a rational creature, and that to know what is true is a primary value upon which in the long run all other values depend. It assumes that knowledge and the power it confers should be employed for promoting the welfare of the many rather than for safeguarding the interests of the few.

These are the rational and the humane values which are inseparable from democracy if democracy is to be of any worth. Yet they are older than democracy and are not dependent upon it. They have a life of their own apart from any form of government or type of civilization. They are the values which, since the time of Buddha and Confucius, Solomon and Zoroaster, Socrates and Plato and Jesus, men have commonly recognized as good even when they have denied them in practice, the values which men have commonly celebrated in the saints and martyrs they have agreed to canonize. They are the values which readily lend themselves to rational justification, but need no justification. No man ever yet found it necessary to justify a humane act by saying that it was really a form of oppression, or a true statement by swearing that it was a sacred lie. But every departure from the rational and the humane, every resort to force and deception, whether in civil government, in war, in the systematic oppression of the many or the liquidation of the few, calls for justification, at best by saying that the lesser evil is necessary for the greater good, at worst by resorting to that hypocrisy which, it has been well said, is the tribute that vice customarily pays to virtue.

In the long history of civilization the rational and humane values have sometimes been denied in theory, and persistently and widely betrayed in fact; but not for many centuries has the denial in theory or the betrayal in fact been more general, more ominous, or more disheartening than in our own day. Half the world is now controlled by self-inspired autocratic leaders who frankly accept the principle that might makes right, that justice is the interest of the stronger; leaders who regard the individual as of no importance except as an instrument to be used, with whatever degree of brutality may be necessary, for the realization of their shifting and irresponsible purposes; leaders who subordinate reason to will, identify law and morality with naked force as an instrument of will, and accord value to the disinterested search for truth only in so far as it may be temporarily useful in attaining immediate political ends. If these are indeed the values we cherish, then we too should abandon democracy, we too should close our universities or degrade them, as in many countries whose most distinguished scholars now live in exile they have been degraded, to the level of servile instruments in the support of state policy. But if we still cherish the democratic way of life, and the rational and humane values which are inseparable from it, then it is of supreme importance that we should preserve the tradition of freedom of learning and teaching without which our universities must cease to be institutions devoted to the dis-

interested search for truth and the increase of knowledge as ends in themselves desirable.

These considerations make it seem to me appropriate, on this memorial occasion, to recall the salient qualities which have given Cornell University its peculiar character and its high distinction; and, in conclusion, to express the hope that Cornell in the future, whatever its gains, whatever its losses, may hold fast to its ancient tradition of freedom and responsibility—freedom for the scholar to perform his proper function, restrained and guided by the only thing that makes such freedom worth while, the scholar's intellectual integrity, the scholar's devotion to the truth of things as they are and to good will and humane dealing among men.

HARVARD UNIVERSITY COMMITTEE
General Education in a Free Society (1945) *

In order to pass judgment on the actualities of education and to make reasonable proposals for revising the present system, it is necessary to have an insight, however tentative, into the ideal aims of education in our society. [We shall] accordingly consider what can, perhaps overformally, be called a philosophy of American education, and especially that part of it which is general education. . . .

A supreme need of American education is for a unifying purpose and idea. As recently as a century ago, no doubt existed about such a purpose: it was to train the Christian citizen. Nor was there doubt how this training was to be accomplished. The student's logical powers were to be formed by mathematics, his taste by the Greek and Latin classics, his speech by rhetoric, and his ideals by Christian ethics. College catalogues commonly began with a specific statement about the influence of such a

* Reprinted by permission of the publishers from *General Education in a Free Society: Report of the Harvard Committee* (Cambridge, Mass.: Harvard University Press, 1945), pp. 42–58. Copyright, 1945, by the President and Fellows of Harvard College.

training on the mind and character. The reasons why this enviable certainty both of goal and of means has largely disappeared have already been set forth. For some decades the mere excitement of enlarging the curriculum and making place for new subjects, new methods, and masses of new students seems quite pardonably to have absorbed the energies of schools and colleges. It is fashionable now to criticize the leading figures of that expansive time for failing to replace, or even to see the need of replacing, the unity which they destroyed. But such criticisms, if just in themselves, are hardly just historically. A great and necessary task of modernizing and broadening education waited to be done, and there is credit enough in its accomplishment. In recent times, however, the question of unity has become insistent. We are faced with a diversity of education which, if it has many virtues, nevertheless works against the good of society by helping to destroy the common ground of training and outlook on which any society depends.

It seems that a common ground between some, though not all, of the ideas underlying our educational practice is the sense of heritage. The word heritage is not here taken to mean mere retrospection. The purpose of all education is to help students live their own lives. The appeal to heritage is partly to the authority, partly to the clarification of the past about what is important in the present. All Catholic and many Protestant institutions thus appeal to the Christian view of man and history as providing both final meaning and immediate standards for life. As observed at the outset, it is less than a century since such was the common practice of American education generally, and certainly this impulse to mold students to a pattern sanctioned by the past can, in one form or another, never be absent from education. If it were, society would become discontinuous.

In this concern for heritage lies a close similarity between religious education and education in the great classic books. Ex-

ponents of the latter have, to be sure, described it as primarily a process of intellectual discipline in the joint arts of word and number, the so-called *trivium* (grammar, logic, rhetoric) and *quadrivium* (arithmetic, geometry, astronomy, music). But, since the very idea of this discipline goes back to antiquity and since the actual books by which it is carried out are in fact the great books of the Western tradition, it seems fairer, without denying the disciplinary value of such a curriculum, to think of it as primarily a process of opening before students the intellectual forces that have shaped the Western mind. There is a sense in which education in the great books can be looked at as a secular continuation of the spirit of Protestantism. As early Protestantism, rejecting the authority and philosophy of the medieval church, placed reliance on each man's personal reading of the Scriptures, so this present movement, rejecting the unique authority of the Scriptures, places reliance on the reading of those books which are taken to represent the fullest revelation of the Western mind. But be this as it may, it is certain that, like religious education, education in the great books is essentially an introduction of students to their heritage.

Nor is the sense of heritage less important, though it may be less obvious, a part of education for modern democratic life. To the degree that the implications of democracy are drawn forth and expounded, to that degree the long-standing impulse of education toward shaping students to a received ideal is still pursued. Consider the teaching of American history and of modern democratic life. However ostensibly factual such teaching may be, it commonly carries with it a presupposition which is not subject to scientific proof: namely, the presupposition that democracy is meaningful and right. Moreover, since contemporary life is itself a product of history, to study it is to tread unconsciously, in the words of the hymn, where the saints have trod. To know modern democracy is to know something at least of Jefferson, though you have not read him; to learn to respect freedom of speech or the rights of the private conscience is not to be wholly ignorant of the *Areopagitica* or the *Antigone,* though you know nothing about them. Whether, as philosophers of history argue, being conditioned by the present we inevitably judge the past by what we know in the present (since otherwise the past would be unintelligible) or whether human motives and choices do not in reality greatly change with time, the fact remains that the past and the present are parts of the same unrolling scene and, whether you enter early or late, you see for the most part the still-unfinished progress of the same issues.

Here, then, in so far as our culture is adequately reflected in current ideas on education, one point about it is clear: it depends in part on an inherited view of man and society which it is the function, though not the only function, of education to pass on. It is not and cannot be true that all possible choices are open to us individually or collectively. We are part of an organic process, which is the American and, more broadly, the Western evolution. Our standards of judgment, ways of life, and form of government all bear the marks of this evolution, which would accordingly influence us, though confusedly, even if it were not understood. Ideally it should be understood at several degrees of depth which complement rather than exclude each other. To study the American present is to discern at best the aims and purposes of a free society animating its imperfections. To study the past is immensely to enrich the meaning of the present and at the same time to clarify it by the simplification of the writings and the issues which have been winnowed from history. To study either past or present is to confront, in some form or another, the philosophic and religious fact of man in history and to recognize the huge continuing influence alike on past and present of the stream of Jewish and Greek thought in Christianity. There is doubtless a sense in

which religious education, education in the great books, and education in modern democracy may be mutually exclusive. But there is a far more important sense in which they work together to the same end, which is belief in the idea of man and society that we inherit, adapt, and pass on.

This idea is described in many ways, perhaps most commonly in recent times, as that of the dignity of man. To the belief in man's dignity must be added the recognition of his duty to his fellow men. Dignity does not rest on any man as a being separate from all other beings, which he in any case cannot be, but springs from his common humanity and exists positively as he makes the common good his own. This concept is essentially that of the Western tradition: the view of man as free and not as slave, an end in himself and not a means. It may have what many believe to be the limitations of humanism, which are those of pride and arise from making man the measure of all things. But it need not have these limitations, since it is equally compatible with a religious view of life. Thus it is similar to the position described [in a previous section of this report] as coöperation without uniformity, agreement on the good of man at the level of performance without the necessity of agreement on ultimates. But two points have now been added. First, thus stated, the goal of education is not in conflict with but largely includes the goals of religious education, education in the Western tradition, and education in modern democracy. For these in turn have been seen to involve necessary elements in our common tradition, each to a great extent implied in the others as levels at which it can be understood. Certainly no fruitful way of stating the belief in the dignity and mutual obligation of man can present it as other than, at one and the same time, effective in the present, emerging from the past, and partaking of the nature not of fact but of faith. Second, it has become clear that the common ground between these various views—namely, the impulse to rear students to a received idea of the good—is in fact necessary to education. It is impossible to escape the realization that our society, like any society, rests on common beliefs and that a major task of education is to perpetuate them.

This conclusion raises one of the most fundamental problems of education, indeed of society itself: how to reconcile this necessity for common belief with the equally obvious necessity for new and independent insights leading to change. We approach here the one previously mentioned concept of education which was not included under the idea of heritage: namely, the views associated with the names of James and Dewey and having to do with science, the scientific attitude, and pragmatism. This is hardly the place to try to summarize this body of thought or even to set forth in detail its application by Mr. Dewey to education. To do so would be virtually to retrace the educational controversies of the last forty years. But, at the risk of some injustice to Mr. Dewey's thought as a whole, a few points can be made about it. It puts trust in the scientific method of thought, the method which demands that you reach conclusions from tested data only, but that, since the data may be enlarged or the conclusions themselves combined with still other conclusions, you must hold them only tentatively. It emphasizes that full truth is not known and that we must be forever led by facts to revise our approximations of it. As a feeling of commitment and of allegiance marks the sense of heritage, so a tone of tough-mindedness and curiosity and a readiness for change mark this pragmatic attitude.

Here, then, is a concept of education, founded on obedience to fact and well disposed, even hospitable, to change, which appears at first sight the antithesis of any view based on the importance of heritage. Such hostility to tradition well reflects one side of the modern mind. It is impossible to contemplate the changes even of the last decades, much less the major groundswell of change since the Renaissance, without feeling that we face largely new conditions which call for new qualities of mind and outlook. Moreover, it is obviously no accident that this pragmatic philosophy has been worked out most fully in the United States. Yet, in spite of its seeming conflict with views of education based on heritage, strong doubt exists whether the questioning, innovating, experimental attitude of pragmatism is in fact something alien to the Western heritage or whether it is not, in the broadest sense of the word, a part of it.

The rest of the present [discussion] would hardly suffice for this sweeping subject. But it can be observed even here that we look back on antiquity not simply out of curiosity but because ancient thought is sympathetic to us. The Greek idea of an orderly universe, of political freedom under rationally constructed laws, and of the inner life itself as subject to the sway of reason, was certainly not achieved without skepticism, observation, or the test of experience. The ancient atomists and medical writers and, to a large extent, Socrates himself relied precisely on induction from observed facts. Socrates, the teacher and the gadfly of the Athenian city, impressed on his pupils and the public at large the duty of man to reflect on his beliefs and to criticize his presuppositions. Socrates was an individualist proclaiming that man should form his opinions by his own reasoning and not receive them by social indoctrination. And yet, it was this same Socrates who died in obedience to the judgment of the state, even though he believed this judgment to be wrong. Again, historical Christianity has been expressly and consistently concerned with the importance of this life on earth. The doctrine of the Incarnation, that God took the form of man and inhabited the earth, declares this concern. While perhaps for Greek thought, only the timeless realm had importance, in Christian thought the process of history is vested with absolute significance. If the ideal of democracy was rightly described above in the interwoven ideas of the dignity of man (that is, his existence as an independent moral agent) and his duty to his fellow men (that is, his testing by outward performance), the debt of these two ideas to the similarly interwoven commandments of the love of God and the love of neighbor is obvious.

These evidences of a consistent and characteristic appeal throughout Western history to the test of reason and experience are not adduced for the purpose of minimizing the huge creativeness of the modern scientific age or of glozing over its actual break from the past. In the well-known opening chapters of his *Science and the Modern World* in which he inquires into the origin of modern science, Mr. Whitehead pictures it as inspired by a revolt against abstract reasoning and a respect for unique fact. So considered, the first impulse of modern science was antirational or, better, antitheoretical, in the sense that it was a reaction against the most towering intellectual system which the West has known, namely, scholasticism. But be this question of origin as it may, there is no doubt that the modern mind received one of its characteristic bents in the empiricism, the passion for observation, and the distrust of abstract reasoning which have attended the origin and growth of science.

But there also seems no doubt that what happened was a shift, perhaps to some degree a restoration, of emphasis within the Western tradition itself rather than a complete change in its nature. It is a mistake to identify the older Western culture with traditionalism. Classical antiquity handed on a working system of truth which relied on both reason and experience and was designed to provide a norm for civilized life. Its import was heightened and vastly intensified by its confluence with Christianity. But when, in its rigid systematization in the late Middle Ages, it lost touch with experience and individual inquiry, it violated its own nature and provoked the modernist revolt. The seeming opposition that resulted between traditionalism and modernism has been a tragedy for Western thought. Mod-

ernism rightly affirms the importance of inquiry and of relevance to experience. But as scholasticism ran the danger of becoming a system without vitality, so modernism runs the danger of achieving vitality without pattern.

While, then, there are discontinuities between the classical and the modern components of our Western culture, there are also continuities. For instance, it would be wrong to construe the scientific outlook as inimical to human values. Even if it were true that science is concerned with means only, it would not follow that science ignores the intrinsic worth of man. For the values of human life cannot be achieved within a physical vacuum; they require for their fulfillment the existence of material conditions. To the extent that classical civilization failed to mitigate the evils of poverty, disease, squalor, and a generally low level of living among the masses, to that extent it failed to liberate man. Conversely, to the extent that science, especially in its medical and technological applications, has succeeded in dealing with these evils, it has contributed to the realization of human values. Thus science has implemented the humanism which classicism and Christianity have proclaimed.

Science has done more than provide the material basis of the good life; it has directly fostered the spiritual values of humanism. To explain, science is both the outcome and the source of the habit of forming objective, disinterested judgments based upon exact evidence. Such a habit is of particular value in the formation of citizens for a free society. It opposes to the arbitrariness of authority and "first principles" the direct and continuing appeal to things as they are. Thus it develops the qualities of the free man. It is no accident that John Locke, who set forth the political doctrine of the natural rights of man against established authority, should have been also the man who rejected the authority of innate ideas.

Students of antiquity and of the Middle

Ages can therefore rightly affirm that decisive truths about the human mind and its relation to the world were laid hold of then, and yet agree that, when new application of these truths was made through a more scrupulous attention to fact, their whole implication and meaning were immensely enlarged. Modern civilization has seen this enlargement of meaning and possibility; yet it is not a new civilization but the organic development of an earlier civilization. The true task of education is therefore so to reconcile the sense of pattern and direction deriving from heritage with the sense of experiment and innovation deriving from science that they may exist fruitfully together, as in varying degrees they have never ceased to do throughout Western history.

Belief in the dignity and mutual obligation of man is the common ground between these contrasting but mutually necessary forces in our culture. As was pointed out earlier, this belief is the fruit at once of religion, of the Western tradition, and of the American tradition. It equally inspires the faith in human reason which is the basis for trust in the future of democracy. And if it is not, strictly speaking, implied in all statements of the scientific method, there is no doubt that science has become its powerful instrument. In this tension between the opposite forces of heritage and change poised only in the faith in man, lies something like the old philosophic problem of the knowledge of the good. If you know the good, why do you seek it? If you are ignorant of the good, how do you recognize it when you find it? You must evidently at one and the same time both know it and be ignorant of it. Just so, the tradition which has come down to us regarding the nature of man and the good society must inevitably provide our standard of good. Yet an axiom of that tradition itself is the belief that no current form of the received ideal is final but that every generation, indeed every individual, must discover it in a fresh form. Education can therefore be wholly devoted neither to tra-

dition nor to experiment, neither to the belief that the ideal in itself is enough nor to the view that means are valuable apart from the ideal. It must uphold at the same time tradition and experiment, the ideal and the means, subserving, like our culture itself, change within commitment.

GENERAL AND SPECIAL EDUCATION

In the previous section we have attempted to outline the unifying elements of our culture and therefore of American education as well. In the present section we shall take the next step of indicating in what ways these cultural strands may be woven into the fabric of education. Education is broadly divided into general and special education; our topic now is the difference and the relationship between the two. The term, general education, is somewhat vague and colorless; it does not mean some airy education in knowledge in general (if there be such knowledge), nor does it mean education for all in the sense of universal education. It is used to indicate that part of a student's whole education which looks first of all to his life as a responsible human being and citizen; while the term, special education, indicates that part which looks to the student's competence in some occupation. These two sides of life are not entirely separable, and it would be false to imagine education for the one as quite distinct from education for the other—more will be said on this point presently. Clearly, general education has somewhat the meaning of liberal education, except that, by applying to high school as well as to college, it envisages immensely greater numbers of students and thus escapes the invidium which, rightly or wrongly, attaches to liberal education in the minds of some people. But if one cling to the root meaning liberal as that which befits or helps to make free men, then general and liberal education have identical goals. The one may be thought of as an earlier stage of the other, similar in nature but less advanced in degree.

The opposition to liberal education—both

to the phrase and to the fact—stems largely from historical causes. The concept of liberal education first appeared in a slave-owning society, like that of Athens, in which the community was divided into free-men and slaves, rulers and subjects. While the slaves carried on the specialized occupations of menial work, the freemen were primarily concerned with the rights and duties of citizenship. The training of the former was purely vocational; but as the freemen were not only a ruling but also a leisure class, their education was exclusively in the liberal arts, without any utilitarian tinge. The freemen were trained in the reflective pursuit of the good life; their education was unspecialized as well as unvocational; its aim was to produce a rounded person with a full understanding of himself and of his place in society and in the cosmos.

Modern democratic society clearly does not regard labor as odious or disgraceful; on the contrary, in this country at least, it regards leisure with suspicion and expects its "gentlemen" to engage in work. Thus we attach no odium to vocational instruction. Moreover, in so far as we surely reject the idea of freemen who are free in so far as they have slaves or subjects, we are apt strongly to deprecate the liberal education which went with the structure of the aristocratic ideal. Herein our society runs the risk of committing a serious fallacy. Democracy is the view that not only the few but that all are free, in that everyone governs his own life and shares in the responsibility for the management of the community. This being the case, it follows that all human beings stand in need of an ampler and rounded education. The task of modern democracy is to preserve the ancient ideal of liberal education and to extend it as far as possible to all the members of the community. In short, we have been apt to confuse accidental with fundamental factors, in our suspicion of the classical ideal. To believe in the equality of human beings is to believe that the good life, and the education which trains the citizen for the good life, are equally the privilege of all. And these are the touchstones of the liberated man: first, is he free; that is to say, is he able to judge and plan for himself, so that he can truly govern himself? In order to do this, his must be a mind capable of self-criticism; he must lead that self-examined life which according to Socrates is alone worthy of a free man. Thus he will possess inner freedom, as well as social freedom. Second, is he universal in his motives and sympathies? For the civilized man is a citizen of the entire universe; he has overcome provincialism, he is objective, and is a "spectator of all time and all existence." Surely these two are the very aims of democracy itself.

But the opposition to general education does not stem from causes located in the past alone. We are living in an age of specialism, in which the avenue to success for the student often lies in his choice of a specialized career, whether as a chemist, or an engineer, or a doctor, or a specialist in some form of business or of manual or technical work. Each of these specialties makes an increasing demand on the time and on the interest of the student. Specialism is the means for advancement in our mobile social structure; yet we must envisage the fact that a society controlled wholly by specialists is not a wisely ordered society. We cannot, however, turn away from specialism. The problem is how to save general education and its values within a system where specialism is necessary.

The very prevalence and power of the demand for special training makes doubly clear the need for a concurrent, balancing force in general education. Specialism enhances the centrifugal forces in society. The business of providing for the needs of society breeds a great diversity of special occupations; and a given specialist does not speak the language of the other specialists. In order to discharge his duties as a citizen adequately, a person must somehow be able to grasp the complexities of life as a whole. Even from the point of view of economic success, specialism has its peculiar limitations. Specializing in a vocation makes for inflexibility in a world of fluid possibilities. Business demands minds capable of adjusting themselves to varying situations and of managing complex human institutions. Given the pace of economic progress, techniques alter speedily; and even the work in which the student has been trained may no longer be useful when he is ready to earn a living or soon after. Our conclusion, then, is that the aim of education should be to prepare an individual to become an expert both in some particular vocation or art and in the general art of the free man and the citizen. Thus the two kinds of education once given separately to different social classes must be given together to all alike.

In this epoch in which almost all of us must be experts in some field in order to make a living, general education therefore assumes a peculiar importance. Since no one can become an expert in all fields, everyone is compelled to trust the judgment of other people pretty thoroughly in most areas of activity. I must trust the advice of my doctor, my plumber, my lawyer, my radio repairman, and so on. Therefore I am in peculiar need of a kind of sagacity by which to distinguish the expert from the quack, and the better from the worse expert. From this point of view, the aim of general education may be defined as that of providing the broad critical sense by which to recognize competence in any field. William James said that an educated person knows a good man when he sees one. There are standards and a style for every type of activity—manual, athletic, intellectual, or artistic; and the educated man should be one who can tell sound from shoddy work in a field outside his own. General education is especially required in a democracy where the public elects its leaders and officials; the ordinary citizen must be discerning enough so that he will not be deceived by appearances and will elect the candidate who is wise in his field.

Both kinds of education—special as well as general—contribute to the task of implementing the pervasive forces of our culture. Here we revert to what was said at the start of this [discussion] on the aims of education in our society. It was argued there that two complementary forces are at the root of our culture: on the one hand, an ideal of man and society distilled from the past but at the same time transcending the past as a standard of judgment valid in itself, and, on the other hand, the belief that no existent expressions of this ideal are final but that all alike call for perpetual scrutiny and change in the light of new knowledge. Specialism is usually the vehicle of this second force. It fosters the open-mindedness and love of investigation which are the wellspring of change, and it devotes itself to the means by which change is brought about. The fact may not always be obvious. There is a sterile specialism which hugs accepted knowledge and ends in the bleakest conservatism. Modern life also calls for many skills which, though specialized, are repetitive and certainly do not conduce to inquiry. These minister to change but unconsciously. Nevertheless, the previous statement is true in the sense that specialism is concerned primarily with knowledge in action, as it advances into new fields and into further applications.

Special education comprises a wider field than vocationalism; and correspondingly, general education extends beyond the limits of merely literary preoccupation. An example will make our point clearer. A scholar— let us say a scientist (whether student or teacher)—will, in the laudable aim of saving himself from narrowness, take a course in English literature, or perhaps read poetry and novels, or perhaps listen to good music and generally occupy himself with the fine arts. All this, while eminently fine and good, reveals a misapprehension. In his altogether unjustified humility, the scientist wrongly interprets the distinction between liberal and illiberal in terms of the distinction between the humanities and the sciences. Plato and Cicero would have been very much surprised to hear that geometry, astronomy, and the sciences of nature in general, are excluded from the humanities. There is also implied a more serious contempt for the liberal arts, harking back to the fallacy which identifies liberal education with the aristocratic ideal. The implication is that liberal education is something only genteel. A similar error is evident in the student's attitude toward his required courses outside his major field as something to "get over with," so that he may engage in the business of serious education, identified in his mind with the field of concentration.

Now, a general education is distinguished from special education, not by subject matter, but in terms of method and outlook, no matter what the field. Literature, when studied in a technical fashion, gives rise to the special science of philology; there is also the highly specialized historical approach to painting. Specialism is interchangeable, not with natural science, but with the method of science, the method which abstracts material from its context and handles it in complete isolation. The reward of scientific method is the utmost degree of precision and exactness. But, as we have seen, specialism as an educational force has its own limitations; it does not usually provide an insight into general relationships.

A further point is worth noting. The impact of specialism has been felt not only in those phases of education which are necessarily and rightly specialistic; it has affected also the whole structure of higher and even of secondary education. Teachers, themselves products of highly technical disciplines, tend to reproduce their knowledge in class. The result is that each subject, being taught by an expert, tends to be so presented as to attract potential experts. This complaint is perhaps more keenly felt in colleges and universities, which naturally look to scholarship. The undergraduate in a college receives his teaching from professors who, in their turn, have been trained in graduate schools. And the latter are dominated by the ideal of specialization. Learn-

ing now is diversified and parceled into a myriad of specialties. Correspondingly, colleges and universities are divided into large numbers of departments, with further specialization within the departments. As a result, a student in search of a general course is commonly frustrated. Even an elementary course is devised as an introduction to a specialism within a department; it is significant only as the beginning of a series of courses of advancing complexity. In short, such introductory courses are planned for the specialist, not for the student seeking a general education. The young chemist in the course in literature and the young writer in the course in chemistry find themselves in thoroughly uncomfortable positions so long as the purpose of these courses is primarily to train experts who will go on to higher courses rather than to give some basic understanding of science as it is revealed in chemistry or of the arts as they are revealed in literature.

It is most unfortunate if we envisage general education as something formless—that is to say, the taking of one course after another; and as something negative, namely, the study of what is not in a field of concentration. Just as we regard the courses in concentration as having definite relations to one another, so should we envisage general education as an organic whole whose parts join in expounding a ruling idea and in serving a common aim. And to do so means to abandon the view that all fields and all departments are equally valuable vehicles of general education. It also implies some prescription. At the least it means abandoning the usual attitude of regarding "distribution" as a sphere in which the student exercises a virtually untrammeled freedom of choice. It may be objected that we are proposing to limit the liberty of the student in the very name of liberal education. Such an objection would only indicate an ambiguity in the conception of liberal education. We must distinguish between liberalism in education and education in liberalism. The former, based as it is on the doctrine of individualism, expresses the view that the student should be free in his choice of courses. But education in liberalism is an altogether different matter; it is education which has a pattern of its own, namely, the pattern associated with the liberal outlook. In this view, there are truths which none can be free to ignore, if one is to have that wisdom through which life can become useful. These are the truths concerning the structure of the good life and concerning the factual conditions by which it may be achieved, truths comprising the goals of the free society.

Finally, the problem of general education is one of combining fixity of aim with diversity in application. It is not a question of providing a general education which will be uniform through the same classes of all schools and colleges all over the country, even were such a thing possible in our decentralized system. It is rather to adapt general education to the needs and intentions of different groups and, so far as possible, to carry its spirit into special education. The effectiveness of teaching has always largely depended on this willingness to adapt a central unvarying purpose to varying outlooks. Such adaptation is as much in the interest of the quick as of the slow, of the bookish as of the unbookish, and is the necessary protection of each. What is wanted, then, is a general education capable at once of taking on many different forms and yet of representing in all its forms the common knowledge and the common values on which a free society depends.

RICHARD C. RICHARDSON, JR., AND PAUL A. ELSNER
A New Role for the Community Junior College (1965) *

A distinguishing feature of the community junior college has been its open door

* Richard C. Richardson, Jr., and Paul A. Elsner, "General Education for the Disadvantaged," *Junior College Journal*, Vol. 36, No. 4 (December, 1965), pp. 18–21. Used by permission.

admission policy. The popularization of higher education has resulted in an influx of marginal students who increasingly view the junior college as a logical extension of the secondary school. The junior college, consequently, is torn between the necessity of maintaining standards to guarantee the employability and transferability of its graduates, and the knowledge that it constitutes the last opportunity for formal education some of its students will ever have.

The problem of the marginal student is particularly acute in urban areas where poverty and de facto segregation generate discouraging numbers of educationally disadvantaged students who lack preparation for even the least rigorous technical programs offered by the junior college. Moreover, substantial numbers of these students fail to recognize their limitations and persist in enrolling in college transfer courses for status reasons to the mutual confoundment of themselves and their instructors.

Junior college educators have coined such phrases as the "revolving door" in criticizing existing programs for failing to meet the needs of from one-third to one-half of the total student population. . . .

The educationally disadvantaged student is coming to the open door community college in ever-increasing numbers. The recent trend toward increased college attendance by students falling below predetermined indexes of success criteria has probably resulted from (1) colleges and universities reaching into a wider range of social class structures for its students, (2) the need for higher level vocational and professional training on the part of an expanding future working force, and (3) the emerging of more comprehensive strata of collegiate institutions, such as the public junior college.

More recently, belated consideration is being given to the ethics of using the community college as a one-semester sieve. It appears likely that disadvantaged students will be present at least one semester and in many instances a full year. The question, then, becomes not whether such students will be educated but rather how they can best be educated.

Forest Park Community College of the Junior College District of St. Louis–St. Louis County has devoted extensive study to the problem of the educationally disadvantaged. A faculty committee reviewing the results of the college program for the fall session, 1964, found that of a total on-campus enrollment of 1,510, academic difficulty was experienced by 691 or 46 per cent. A total of 278 students were placed on enforced withdrawal, 318 were placed on academic probation, ninety-five withdrew officially, while an additional eighty-five simply stopped coming. The faculty committee recommended that an experimental program be established to attempt to meet the needs of the disadvantaged student. Specifically, the committee spelled out the following goals:

1. Meeting the needs of students in the lower range of the ability spectrum.

2. Improving standards in transfer courses by removing students incapable of making a contribution or of achieving significant benefit.

3. Providing educationally disadvantaged students with intensive counseling on an individual and group basis to: (a) minimize emotional factors inhibiting success; (b) aid students to assess realistically their potential and to relate this to vocational goals; and (c) identify students incapable of benefiting from any college program and refer them to community resources through accurate and complete knowledge of apprenticeship requirements, job openings, training courses such as those sponsored by the Manpower Development and Training Act, as well as other community resources.

4. Salvaging the academically able students from this group who might be upgraded to the point where they could be successful in regular technical or transfer programs.

It was not by accident that the salvage function of this program was placed last.

The committee was determined that the program should be viewed as an end in and of itself, so that a student who never progressed beyond might nonetheless experience a feeling of success. Further, the committee determined that the emphasis of the program would be neither remedial nor vocational. Rather, an attempt would be made to structure a stimulating and challenging one-year program of general education on the students' level.

Since the salvage function was to be downgraded rather than excluded, some provision had to be made for providing students with the basic skills necessary for success in more demanding programs. The answer to this problem was found in the development of a programed materials learning laboratory. Programed materials and tutorial assistance would be provided in a learning center where the responsibility for mastery of the materials would rest primarily with the student. This center would supplement the organized general education classes.

Concurrent with curriculum planning, intensive efforts were begun to study the characteristics of the student. Social workers, members of the Human Development Corporation, high school curriculum workers, and others met with the committee to convey the benefits of their experience.

It was agreed at an early point in the discussions that instructors must volunteer for the program and would have to be willing to accept full-time assignment.

Students would be grouped in divisions of 100, to which a five-person team would be assigned. Each team was to consist of one counselor, a learning laboratory coordinator (reading specialist backgrounds), and three representatives of academic divisions. The basic approach would involve an attempt to create a core curriculum organized around the social science area. In general, these considerations were central to planning the program:

1. A curriculum for the educationally disadvantaged should be concerned with the broader development of the person—this de-

velopment would include his personal and emotional well-being as well as his intellectual development.

2. The program should assist the student in coping with his environment—his more immediate pressures would come from his academic environment but his ability to adjust to pressures of collegiate life would take on greater implication for total personal development as a citizen.

3. The program should not be delineated in terms of a specific curriculum or in terms of logically arranged course content; the courses should be wider in scope, less fixed —their content should be drawn from many more facets of human problems and they

should emphasize the individual student's needs.

The model presented in Figure I suggests the areas from which the general education content of the program was drawn. It provides also some idea of how the program relates to traditional curriculum patterns.

While students would take their course offerings as a part of a special group, every attempt would be made to include them in other activities common to the college experience. They would be permitted to enroll in standard physical education courses or sing in the college chorus. The entire range of student activities would be open and they would be encouraged to participate. By such

FIGURE I
GENERAL EDUCATION FOR THE
EDUCATIONALLY DISADVANTAGED

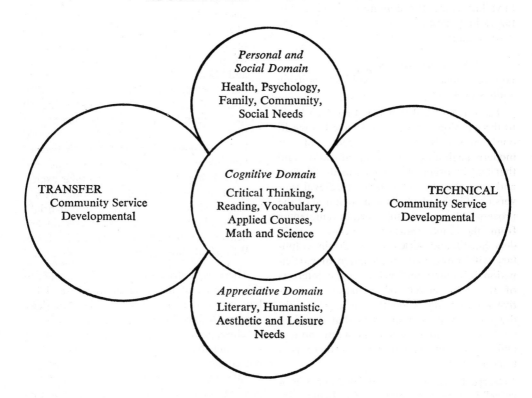

attempts it was hoped that any negative concomitants of enrollment in a special program might be minimized. It was assumed that the above provision would assist the educationally disadvantaged student in widening his social radius, in exploring other possible enriching relationships with students, and in modifying his own self-concept as he related to and became accepted by others. . . .

It is possible that this program, while differing radically from those common to most junior colleges, may represent a trend of thought that will become increasingly evident in the next few years. There is evidence that other community colleges across the nation are becoming ever more cognizant of the need for a new approach to coping with the problems of the disadvantaged. Previous attempts have left much to be desired. The time has come for community colleges to take a long hard look at the education of the disadvantaged.

GEORGE F. KENNAN
Higher Education in a World of Shifting Values (1968)*

There is an ideal that has long been basic to the learning process as we have known it, one that stands at the very center of our modern institutions of higher education and that had its origin, I suppose, in the clerical and monastic character of the medieval university. It is the ideal of the association of the process of learning with a certain remoteness from the contemporary scene—a certain detachment and seclusion, a certain voluntary withdrawal and renunciation of participation in contemporary life in the interests of the achievement of a better perspective on that life when the period of withdrawal is over. It is an ideal that does not predicate any total conflict between thought and action, but recognizes that there is a time for each.

* George F. Kennan, "Rebels Without a Program," *New York Times Magazine,* January 21, 1968, pp. 22–23 ff. © 1968 by The New York Times Company. Reprinted by permission.

No more striking, or moving, description of this ideal has ever come to my attention than that which was given by Woodrow Wilson in 1896 at the time of the Princeton Sesquicentennial.

I have had sight [Wilson said] of the perfect place of learning in my thought: a free place, and a various, where no man could be and not know with how great a destiny knowledge had come into the world—itself a little world; but not perplexed, living with a singleness of aim not known without; the home of sagacious men, hardheaded and with a will to know, debaters of the world's questions every day and used to the rough ways of democracy; and yet a place removed—calm Science seated there, recluse, ascetic, like a nun; not knowing that the world passes, not caring, if the truth but come in answer to her prayer. . . . A place where ideals are kept in heart in an air they can breathe; but no fool's paradise. A place where to hear the truth about the past and hold debate about the affairs of the present, with knowledge and without passion; like the world in having all men's life at heart, a place for men and all that concerns them; but unlike the world in its self-possession, its thorough way of talk, its care to know more than the moment brings to light; slow to take excitement, its air pure and wholesome with a breath of faith; every eye within it bright in the clear day and quick to look toward heaven for the confirmation of its hope. Who shall show us the way to this place?

There is a dreadful incongruity between this vision and the state of mind—and behavior—of the radical left on the American campus today. In place of a calm science, "recluse, ascetic, like a nun," not knowing or caring that the world passes "if the truth but come in answer to her prayer," we have people utterly absorbed in the affairs of this passing world. And instead of these affairs being discussed with knowledge and without passion, we find them treated with transports of passion and with a minimum, I fear, of knowledge. In place of slowness to take excitement, we have a readiness to react emotionally, and at once, to a great variety of issues. In place of self-possession, we have screaming tantrums and brawling in the streets. In place of the "thorough way of talk" that Wilson envisaged, we have banners and epithets and obscenities and virtually meaningless slogans. And in place of bright eyes "looking to heaven for the confirmation of their hope," we have eyes glazed with anger and passion, too often dimmed as well by artificial abuse of the psychic structure that lies behind them, and looking almost everywhere else but to heaven for the satisfaction of their aspirations.

I quite understand that those who espouse this flagrant repudiation of the Wilsonian ideal constitute only a minority on any campus. But tendencies that represent the obsession of only a few may not be without partial appeal, at certain times, and within certain limits, to many others. If my own analysis is correct, there are a great many students who may resist any complete surrender to these tendencies, but who nevertheless find them intensely interesting, are to some extent attracted or morally bewildered by them, find themselves driven, in confrontation with them, either into various forms of pleasing temptation, on the one hand, or into crises of conscience, on the other.

If I see them correctly (and I have no pretensions to authority on this subject), there are two dominant tendencies among the people I have here in mind, and superficially they would seem to be in conflict one with the other. On the one side there is angry militancy, full of hatred and intolerance and often quite prepared to embrace violence as a source of change. On the other side there is gentleness, passivity, quietism—ostensibly a yearning for detachment from the affairs of the world, not the detachment Woodrow Wilson had in mind, for that was one intimately and sternly related to the real world, the objective, external world, whereas this

one takes the form of an attempt to escape into a world which is altogether illusory and subjective.

What strikes one first about the angry militancy is the extraordinary degree of certainty by which it is inspired: certainty of one's own rectitude, certainty of the correctness of one's own answers, certainty of the accuracy and profundity of one's own analysis of the problems of contemporary society, certainty as to the iniquity of those who disagree. Of course, vehemence of feeling and a conviction that right is on one's side have seldom been absent from the feelings of politically excited youth. But somehow or other they seem particularly out of place at just this time. Never has there been an era when the problems of public policy even approached in their complexity those by which our society is confronted today, in this age of technical innovation and the explosion of knowledge. The understanding of these problems is something to which one could well give years of disciplined and restrained study, years of the scholar's detachment, years of readiness to reserve judgment while evidence is being accumulated. And this being so, one is struck to see such massive certainties already present in the minds of people who not only *have not* studied very much but presumably *are not* studying a great deal, because it is hard to imagine that the activities to which this aroused portion of our student population gives itself are ones readily compatible with quiet and successful study.

The world seems to be full, today, of embattled students. The public prints are seldom devoid of the record of their activities. Photographs of them may be seen daily: screaming, throwing stones, breaking windows, overturning cars, being beaten or dragged about by police and, in the case of those on other continents, burning libraries. That these people are embattled is unquestionable. That they are really students, I must be permitted to doubt. I have heard it freely confessed by members of the revolutionary student generation of Tsarist Russia that, proud as they were of the revolutionary exploits of their youth, they never really learned anything in their university years; they were too busy with politics. The fact of the matter is that the state of being *enragé* is simply incompatible with fruitful study. It implies a degree of existing emotional and intellectual commitment which leaves little room for open-minded curiosity.

I am not saying that students should not be concerned, should not have views, should not question what goes on in the field of national policy and should not voice their questions about it. Some of us, who are older, share many of their misgivings, many of their impulses. Some of us have no less lively a sense of the dangers of the time, and are no happier than they are about a great many things that are now going on. But it lies within the power as well as the duty of all of us to recognize not only the possibility that we might be wrong but the virtual certainty that on some occasions we are bound to be. The fact that this is so does not absolve us from the duty of having views and putting them forward. But it does make it incumbent upon us to recognize the element of doubt that still surrounds the correctness of these views. And if we do that, we will not be able to lose ourselves in transports of moral indignation against those who are of opposite opinion and follow a different line; we will put our views forward only with a prayer for forgiveness for the event that we prove to be mistaken.

I am aware that inhibitions and restraints of this sort on the part of us older people would be attributed by many members of the student left to a sweeping corruption of our moral integrity. Life, they would hold, has impelled us to the making of compromises; and these compromises have destroyed the usefulness of our contribution. Crippled by our own cowardice, prisoners of the seamy adjustments we have made in order to be successfully a part of the American establishment, we are regarded as no longer capable of looking steadily into the strong clear light of truth.

In this, as in most of the reproaches with which our children shower us, there is of course an element of justification. There is a point somewhere along the way in most of our adult lives, admittedly, when enthusiasms flag, when idealism becomes tempered, when responsibility to others, and even affection for others, compels greater attention to the mundane demands of private life. There is a point when we are even impelled to place the needs of children ahead of the dictates of a defiant idealism, and to devote ourselves, pusillanimously, if you will, to the support and rearing of these same children—precisely in order that at some future date they may have the privilege of turning upon us and despising us for the materialistic faint-heartedness that made their maturity possible. This, no doubt, is the nature of the compromise that millions of us make with the imperfections of government and society in our time. Many of us could wish that it might have been otherwise—that the idealistic pursuit of public causes might have remained our exclusive dedication down into later life.

But for the fact that this is not so I cannot shower myself or others with reproaches. I have seen more harm done in this world by those who tried to storm the bastions of society in the name of utopian beliefs, who were determined to achieve the elimination of all evil and the realization of the millennium within their own time, than by all the humble efforts of those who have tried to create a little order and civility and affection within their own intimate entourage, even at the cost of tolerating a great deal of evil in the public domain. Behind this modesty, after all, there has been the recognition of a vitally important truth—a truth that the Marxists, among others, have never brought themselves to recognize; namely, that the decisive seat of evil in this world is not in social and political institutions, and not even, as a rule, in the ill will or iniquities of statesmen, but simply in the weakness and imperfection of the human soul itself, and by that I mean literally every soul, including my own and that of the student militant at the gates. For this reason, as Tocqueville so clearly perceived when he visited this country 130 years ago, the success of a society may be said, like charity, to begin at home.

So much, then, for the angry ones. Now, a word about the others: the quiescent ones, the hippies and the flower people.

In one sense, my feeling for these people is one of pity, not unmixed, in some instances, with horror. I am sure that they want none of this pity. They would feel that it comes to them for the wrong reasons. If they feel sorry for themselves, it is because they see themselves as the victims of a harsh, hypocritical and unworthy adult society. If I feel sorry for them, it is because I see them as the victims of certain great and destructive philosophic errors.

One of these errors—and it is one that affects particularly those who take drugs, but not those alone—is the belief that the human being has marvelous resources within himself that can be released and made available to him merely by the passive submission to certain sorts of stimuli: by letting esthetic impressions of one sort or another roll over him or by letting his psychic equilibrium be disoriented by chemical agencies that give him the sensation of experiencing tremendous things. Well, it is true that human beings sometimes have marvelous resources within themselves. It is also true that these resources are capable, ideally, of being released and made available to the man that harbors them and through him to others, and sometimes are so released. But it is not true that they can be released by hippie means.

It is only through effort, through doing, through action—never through passive experience—that man grows creatively. It is only by volition and effort that he becomes fully aware of what he has in him of creativity and becomes capable of embodying it, of making it a part of himself, of communicating it to others. There is no pose more fraudulent—and students would do well to remember this when they look at each other—than that of the individual who pretends to have been exalted and rendered more impressive by his communion with some sort of inner voice whose revelations he is unable to describe or to enact. And particularly is this pose fraudulent when the means he has chosen to render himself susceptible to this alleged revelation is the deliberate disorientation of his own psychic system; for it may be said with surety that any artificial intervention of this sort—into the infinitely delicate balance that nature created in the form of man's psychic make-up—produces its own revenge, takes its own toll, proceeds at the cost of the true creative faculties and weakens rather than strengthens.

The second error I see in the outlook of these people is the belief in the possibility and validity of a total personal permissiveness. They are misjudging, here, the innermost nature of man's estate. There is not, and cannot be, such a thing as total freedom. The normal needs and frailties of the body, not to mention the elementary demands of the soul itself, would rule that out if nothing else did. But beyond that, any freedom *from* something implies a freedom *to* something. And because our reality is a complex one, in which conflicts of values are never absent, there can be no advance toward any particular objective, not even the pursuit of pleasure, that does not imply the sacrifice of other possible objectives. Freedom, for this reason, is definable only in terms of the obligations and restraints and sacrifices it accepts. It exists, as a concept, only in relationship to something else which is by definition its opposite; and that means commitment, duty, self-restraint.

Every great artist has known this. Every great philosopher has recognized it. It has lain at the basis of Judaic-Christian teaching. Tell me what framework of discipline you are prepared to accept, and I will attempt to tell you what freedom might mean for you. But if you tell me that you are prepared to accept no framework of discipline at all, then I will tell you, as Dostoevski told his readers, that you are destined to become the most unfree of men; for freedom begins only with the humble acceptance of membership in, and subordination to, a natural order of things, and it grows only with struggle, and self-discipline, and faith.

To shun the cruelty and corruption of this world is one thing. It is not always unjustifiable. Not everyone is made to endure these things. There is something to be said for the cultivation, by the right people, and in the right way, of the virtues of detachment, of withdrawal, of unworldliness, of innocence and purity, if you will. That, as a phase of life, is just what Wilson was talking about. In an earlier age, those who are now the flower children and the hippies would perhaps have entered monastic life or scholarly life or both. But there, be it noted, they would very definitely have accepted a framework of discipline, and it would normally have been a very strict one. If it was a monastic order, their lives would have been devoted to the service of God and of other men, not of themselves and their senses. If it was the world of scholarship, their lives would have been devoted to the pursuit of truth, which never comes easily or without discipline and sacrifice. They would have accepted an obligation to cultivate order, not chaos; cleanliness, not filth; self-abnegation, not self-indulgence; health, not demoralization.

Now I have indicated that I pity these people, and in general I do. But sometimes I find it hard to pity them, because they themselves are sometimes so pitiless. There is, in this cultivation of an absolute freedom, and above all in the very self-destructiveness with which it often expresses itself, a selfishness, a hardheartedness, a callousness, an irresponsibility, an indifference to the feelings of others, that is its own condemnation. No one ever destroys just himself alone. Such is the network of intimacy in which every one of us is somehow embraced, that whoever destroys himself destroys to some extent others as well. Many of these people prattle about the principle of love; but their behavior betrays this principle in the most elementary way. Love—and by that I mean the receiving of love as well as the bestowal of it—is itself an obligation, and as such is incompatible with the quest for a perfect freedom. Just the cruelty to parents alone, which is implicit in much of this behavior, is destructive of the purest and most creative form of love that does exist or could exist in this mortal state.

And one would like to warn these young people that in distancing themselves so recklessly not only from the wisdom but from the feelings of parents, they are hacking at their own underpinnings—and even those of people as yet unborn. There could be no greater illusion than the belief that one can treat one's parents unfeelingly and with contempt and yet expect that one's own children will some day treat one otherwise; for such people break the golden chain of affection that binds the generations and gives continuity and meaning to life.

One cannot, therefore, on looking at these young people in all the glory of their defiant rags and hairdos, always just say, with tears in one's eyes: "There goes a tragically wayward youth, striving romantically to document his rebellion against the hypocrisies of the age." One has sometimes to say, and not without indignation: "There goes a perverted and willful and stony-hearted youth by whose destructiveness we are all, in the end, to be damaged and diminished."

These people also pose a problem in the quality of their citizenship. One thing they all seem to have in common—the angry ones as well as the quiet ones—is a complete rejection of, or indifference to, the political system of this country. The quiet ones turn their backs upon it, as though it did not concern them. The angry ones reject it by implication, insofar as they refuse to recognize the validity of its workings or to respect the discipline which, as a system of authority, it unavoidably entails.

I think there is a real error or misunderstanding here. If you accept a democratic system, this means that you are prepared to put up with those of its workings, legislative or administrative, with which you do not agree as well as with those that meet with your concurrence. This willingness to accept, in principle, the workings of a system based on the will of the majority, even when you yourself are in the minority, is simply the essence of democracy. Without it there could be no system of representative self-government at all. When you attempt to alter the workings of the system by means of violence or civil disobedience, this, it seems to me, can have only one of two implications: either you do not believe in democracy at all and consider that society ought to be governed by enlightened minorities such as the one to which you, of course, belong; or you consider that the present system is so imperfect that it is not truly representative, that it no longer serves adequately as a vehicle for the will of the majority, and that this leaves to the unsatisfied no adequate means of self-expression other than the primitive one of calling attention to themselves and their emotions by mass demonstrations and mass defiance of established authority. It is surely the latter of these two implications which we must read from the overwhelming majority of the demonstrations that have recently taken place.

I would submit that if you find a system inadequate, it is not enough simply to demonstrate indignation and anger over individual workings of it, such as the persistence of the Vietnam war, or individual situations it tolerates or fails to correct, such as the condition of the Negroes in our great cities. If one finds these conditions intolerable, and if one considers that they reflect no adequate expression either of the will of the majority or of that respect for the rights of minorities which is no less essential to the success of any democratic system, then one places upon one's self, it seems to me, the obligation of saying in what way this political system should be modified, or what should be established in the place of it, to assure that its workings would bear a better relationship to people's needs and people's feelings.

If the student left had a program of constitutional amendment or political reform—if it had proposals for the constructive adaptation of this political system to the needs of our age—if it was *this* that it was agitating for, and if its agitation took the form of reasoned argument and discussion, or even peaceful demonstration accompanied by reasoned argument and discussion—then many of us, I am sure, could view its protests with respect, and we would not shirk the obligation, either to speak up in defense of institutions and national practices which we have tolerated all our lives, or to join these young people in the quest for better ones.

But when we are confronted only with violence for violence's sake, and with attempts to frighten or intimidate an administration into doing things for which it can itself see neither the rationale nor the electoral mandate; when we are offered, as the only argument for change, the fact that a number of people are themselves very angry and excited; and when we are presented with a violent objection to what exists, unaccompanied by any constructive concept of what, ideally, ought to exist in its place—then we of my generation can only recognize that such behavior bears a disconcerting resemblance to phenomena we have witnessed within our own time in the origins of totalitarianism in other countries, and then we have no choice but to rally to the defense of a public authority with which we may not be in agreement but which is the only one we've got and with which, in some form or another, we cannot conceivably dispense. People should bear in mind that if this—namely noise, violence and lawlessness—is the way they are going to put their case, then many of us who are no happier than they are about some of the policies that arouse their indignation will have no choice but to place ourselves on the other side of the barricades.

These observations reflect a serious doubt whether civil disobedience has any place in a democratic society. But there is one objection I know will be offered to this view.

Some people, who accept our political system, believe that they have a right to disregard it and to violate the laws that have flowed from it so long as they are prepared, as a matter of conscience, to accept the penalties established for such behavior.

I am sorry; I cannot agree. The violation of law is not, in the moral and philosophic sense, a privilege that lies offered for sale with a given price tag, like an object in a supermarket, available to anyone who has the price and is willing to pay for it. It is not like the privilege of breaking crockery in a tent at the county fair for a quarter a shot. Respect for the law is not an obligation which is exhausted or obliterated by willingness to accept the penalty for breaking it.

To hold otherwise would be to place the privilege of lawbreaking preferentially in the hands of the affluent, to make respect for law a commercial proposition rather than a civic duty and to deny any authority of law independent of the sanctions established against its violation. It would then be all right for a man to create false fire alarms or frivolously to pull the emergency cord on the train, or to do any number of other things that endangered or inconvenienced other people, provided only he was prepared to accept the penalties of so doing. Surely, lawlessness and civil disobedience cannot be condoned or tolerated on this ground; and those of us who care for the good order of society have no choice but to resist attempts at its violation, when this is their only justification.

Now, being myself a father, I am only too well aware that people of my generation cannot absolve ourselves of a heavy responsibility for the state of mind in which these young people find themselves. We are obliged to recognize here, in the myopia and the crudities of *their* extremism, the reflection of our own failings: our smugness, our timidity, our faintheartedness and in some instances our weariness, our apathy in the face of great and obvious evils.

I am also aware that, while their methods may not be the right ones, and while their discontent may suffer in its effectiveness from the concentration on negative goals, the degree of their concern over the present state of our country and the dangers implicit in certain of its involvements is by no means exaggerated. This is a time in our national life more serious, more menacing, more crucial, than any I have ever experienced or ever hoped to experience. Not since the civil conflict of a century ago has this country, as I see it, been in such great danger; and the most excruciating aspect of this tragic state of affairs is that so much of this danger comes so largely from within, where we are giving it relatively little official attention, and so little of it comes, relatively speaking, from the swamps and jungles of Southeast Asia into which we are pouring our treasure of young blood and physical resources.

For these reasons, I do not mean to make light of the intensity of feeling by which this student left is seized. Nor do I mean to imply that people like myself can view this discontent from some sort of smug Olympian detachment, as though it were not our responsibility, as though it were not in part our own ugly and decadent face that we see in this distorted mirror. None of us could have any justification for attempting to enter into communication with these people if we did not recognize, along with the justification for their unhappiness, our own responsibility in the creation of it, and if we did not accompany our appeal to them with a profession of readiness to join them, where they want us to, in the attempt to find better answers to many of these problems.

I am well aware that in approaching them in this way and in taking issue as I have with elements of their outlook and their behavior, it is primarily myself that I have committed, not them. I know that behind all the extremisms—all the philosophical errors, all the egocentricities and all the oddities of dress and deportment—we have to do here with troubled and often pathetically appealing people, acting, however wisely or unwisely, out of sincerity and idealism, out of the unwillingness to accept a meaningless life and a purposeless society.

Well, this is not the life, and not the sort of society, that many of us would like to leave behind us in this country when our work is done. How wonderful it would be, I sometimes think to myself, if we and they —experience on the one hand, strength and enthusiasm on the other—could join forces.

CHAPTER TWELVE

Dialogues in a Changing World

THE CONTEMPORARY SCENE

JOHN H. BUNZEL
The Influence of Organized Interest Groups
(1964) *

One of the fascinations of the American political system, at least for the political scientist, is that there is no precise explanation for the way it operates. Countless theories have been advanced which claim to account for the institutional arrangements and procedures we have devised to conduct our political affairs. They range all the way from the normative natural rights theory at the heart of our Bill of Rights to the most recent adventures in behaviorism which would make a "science" out of politics. Each in its own way doubtless has a truth by the tail and has contributed substantially to our knowledge. But one inescapable fact emerges: all tightfisted, ironclad assumptions of determinism must be rejected in trying to understand the American political process. Politics is still the art of the second best, which is to say the art of the possible.

As a matter of fact, both American and foreign observers are constantly struck by the incomprehensibility of our politics. As a people, we are so casual about what we believe that we seem to lack any convictions at all. We are so apathetic about what our

government does, or who runs it, that we rarely turn out more than half of our eligible voters for an election. We assume the role of the leading democratic power of the world, but often do not seem to act like one. And as for our two political parties—well, there is just no accounting for them.

Daniel Bell has suggested that there are roughly three ways of looking at American politics. In his view, attention should be paid to 1) the role of the electoral structure, 2) the democratic tradition in the United States, and 3) the role and place of interest groups in the American political system. My major concern here, at least at the outset, is with the third area, but a few words should be said about the other two.

One of the basic and decisive facts of American political life is our two party system. For better or for worse, this constitutes the mainstream of American politics. All of the protest organizations and movements in American history have learned the hard way that a rigid electoral structure delimits their role. They have learned that to be effective and successful, they must work within our two major parties. What stands out in our democratic tradition is that American politics has lacked an aristocratic bias and elitism, at least since the days of Andrew Jackson when American democracy took on a populist look and "the people" emerged as the ultimate source of power and appeal. Politics became the arena of the common man, and politicians learned that they had to speak to the people in democratic terms.

But it is the role of interest groups in the United States that is of special importance. I would offer the following proposition in making this point: The role of interest groups in American society, coupled with the identification of that role with the public good, provides the framework for understanding American politics. The Madisonian tradition is the dominant political tradition in the United States. It was Madison who first spoke of the inevitability of "factions" in society and pointed out that there could be no liberty without them. Madison's contribution is significant because he advanced a theory that would insure a free society in a large territory. (Theretofore, democracy had been identified with small states and communities.) There would be more people from whom to choose able men and a wider variety of interests, and it would be possible to check and balance these social and economic interests so no one interest or faction could become tyrannical over the rest of the community. Faction was the basis of freedom, but the effects of factions must be controlled. Therefore, he said, the government was to act as a broker in settling conflicting interests.

Whatever the weaknesses and inconsistencies of Madison's theory, much of the story of American politics can largely be told in terms of the constant factional struggles which have made up our political history and the way in which our two political parties have combined these conflicting interests, strange alliances, and heterogeneous groups into their own fold.

A central point stands out today as it did in 1789: politics is a process of interaction among groups as well as individuals. This deserves emphasis because many of us still cling to eighteenth century illusions about the nature of political power. We still focus on the individual and neglect his group identifications. We tend to sing the praises of the "independent" voter and the "independent" congressman as ideal types in exercising political power. But when we exalt the individual and the "independent," we ignore

a blunt fact of political life—that power in present-day politics springs from organization. In a large part of our life today, the individual—the average citizen—is almost an innocent bystander and frequently a bewildered one. He feels that his vote is futile because he does not see how it can influence public policy. "Organization represents concentrated power," someone has said, "and concentrated power can exercise a dominating influence when it encounters power which is diffuse and not concentrated, and therefore weaker."

In our modern industrial society, there has been a proliferation of groups to the point that no aspect of our lives is left untouched. Family, schools, churches, street gangs, fraternities, labor unions, cultural groups, professional associations: one need only name a cause and he will quickly discover a group actively promoting it—or, in the case of Los Angeles, a movement about to start one. This vast multiplication of interest groups, it should be stressed, has resulted in the breaking up of considerable unobstructed power that formerly resided for the most part in certain social and economic classes. It is in this sense that we can now refer to our government as the broker state, in the same way that we can evaluate the American political system against the backdrop of modern-day democratic pluralism.

Nowhere is the politics of pluralism more manifest than in education. In every community throughout the country, the schools are on the receiving end of turbulent pressures from groups on every side. Consider for a moment the demands one would be expected to heed if he sat on the local school board. If he lived in a community where there were farmers, he would hear their cries for courses which would benefit rural children. The trade unions, if there were any, would want consumer economics and more shop courses. Another group would argue strongly for vocational courses at the expense of general education. The churches would press for more released time; others would insist that every member of the school board stand up for the right to have God and prayers in the classroom. A taxpayers' group would want to cut educational costs to the bone, while a newly formed group of parents would want to issue bonds for school expansion.

The board member would quickly discover, if he did not already know, that education is inextricably involved with politics and that politics pervades education. It is in the midst of such force and counterforce that superintendents, principals, and boards of education must make their important and complex decisions. All of these pressures for special content in the curriculum, for economy or expansion, or for particular benefits for business or other interests—are part of the daily routine of those who administer to the needs of our schools.

It is no secret that schools are also decisive in forming attitudes. To this end, widely assorted groups expend their energy in trying to control what is taught in the classroom and what is allowed on the library shelves. James McCamy of the University of Wisconsin makes the important observation that most American schools remain free to be sensible only because there is a competition of pressures upon them. When self-appointed guardians of God, Country, and the Flag take out after a "subversive" textbook, other citizens come forward to defend the right and need of students to explore every side of a question. The forces upholding the free pursuit of ideas are not always successful, but then neither are the extremists always victorious in their shrill demands to dictate what the schools should teach.

For better or for worse, as Professor McCamy says, the graduates of public education are "Democrats and Republicans, businessmen and workingmen, churchgoers and non-churchgoers, almost unanimously believers in private enterprise, mostly democratic in their attitudes toward others, most of them, by far, decent, hard-working, patriotic Americans who will do their duty." They are the products of a school system that is on the whole free to discuss whatever comes up, a school system which, in turn, reflects the plural forms and arrangements of American society and the continuous interaction of multiple and diverse political forces.

One of the myths that die hard is the notion that most of the important political decisions in the United States are made by so-called powerful and influential members of a ruling clique. This general idea lies behind the elitist bias and implications of C. Wright Mills' provocative book, *The Power Elite*. In it, he professes to describe the pyramidal structure of American society, headed by a triumvirate of military, business, and political influentials who are in command of the country's major decision-making centers. Floyd Hunter presents the same picture in miniature form in his study of the power structure of Regional City (Atlanta, Georgia) where again a ruling group is said to make the important decisions. Hunter discovered some forty members of the community who, in effect, ran the city. Not surprisingly, they were the economic notables, the leading members of the business community. They exercised their power more in private than in public and in a way which came close to a kind of benevolent manipulation. The point is that these economic interests in Regional City—and, for C. Wright Mills, throughout the United States—were seen to be the real determinants of political action. Like the proverbial iceberg which is nine-tenths submerged, the major economic forces of the community are somewhere behind the scenes, mysteriously pulling strings and making the community hum to their own self-interested tune.

I have overdrawn the picture to make a central point. In the view just outlined, the pluralism of our political institutions and decision-making procedures is denied and in its place is substituted a monolithic structure of power and influence. Put another way, politics is reduced to economics. Political decisions, far from being regarded as the outcome of a complex interaction of competing demands on responsible political leaders by an assortment of claimants, are seen instead as the virtual conditioned reflex of a power structure run by some economic group or groups.

The earliest investigations of American communities were done by sociologists. One thinks of the classic and pioneering *Middletown* studies by the Lynds. Only recently have political scientists discovered, or rediscovered, what is fast becoming a major field of teaching and research—urban politics. They are following in the sociologists' footsteps but are making important corrections to several sociological assumptions and conclusions. Their increasing attention to the distribution rather than the concentration of political influence has resulted in a reevaluation of the meaning and location of power in American society.

It has been remarked that we may say about power in general only what St. Augustine said about time—that we all know perfectly well what it is until someone asks us. Current research in the politics of community decision making is examining the notion of power in the context of actual community behavior. Stated another way, the political scientist is now concerned with putting the concept of power to a variety of empirical tests. Many observers of American society have long entertained the idea that power—for example, the power to "run the city"—is concentrated in a small ruling clique because of the enormous inequalities in the distribution of the resources of influence such as property, income, and social status. According to this view, an economic and social elite decides things behind the scenes—in effect, filling the political vacuum. This explanation fits nicely the general theory of elite control. But the prior question that is now increasingly being asked is this: Given the existence of these inequalities, who in fact actually makes the important community-wide decisions? The answers, it is now clear, must come from knowledge based on observation.

The politics of education in all of our communities is a case in point. It has often been convenient if not fashionable to talk of a given community as "business dominated," meaning that the businessmen in town are the only organized group with effective power and influence. Few would deny, of course, that there are communities which approximate this business-dominated model. The difficulty is that in too many cases the very assumption of business influence and domination precedes any hard investigation of what, in fact, the community power situation really is. There is a tendency, epitomized by the inside dopester style and savvy of newspapermen who cover City Hall, to ask, "Who runs things around here?" The more pertinent question is, "How do things get done around here?" The former almost invites a response suggestive of some kind of ruling elite; the latter has the merit of at least allowing for a wider range of possible replies.

Professor Robert Dahl's recent study of New Haven is illuminating in this regard.[1] He and his associates began their explorations with one essential question in mind: who governs the city? Before long, they realized that this question had to be broken down into many others. They discovered, for example, that the members of the community who played a decisive role in, say, urban redevelopment were not those who participated in the process of decision making in education. Through an exhaustive analysis of carefully obtained interview data, Professor Dahl showed that there are important differences among participants with respect to both the *frequency* with which they participate and the *range* of issue-areas in which they participate. But only a small group of citizens—the professional politicians—participate steadily. "These are citizens to whom politics is a career, or at least an alternate career. They use their political resources at a high rate, acquire superior skills and exert a very high degree

[1] Dahl, Robert A. *Who Governs?* New Haven: Yale University Press, 1961. 355 pp.

of influence. These citizens, the professionals, are sources of both stability and instability in the political system." [2] Perhaps the major conclusion of Dahl's study is that politics cannot be viewed as the slave of economics, that political decisions are not the inevitable outgrowth of economic position and social standing. . . .

Before World War II, American labor had neither the resources nor the time to become actively engaged in local civic affairs. Today, however, the picture is radically changed; community agencies are now seeking the support of labor, and the unions, in turn, are gaining a new understanding of community problems.

In any American community, the school system is one of the major social institutions. The stake of business in the educational process is well known. The schools are regarded as the training ground for future business leadership, and to this end business interests, as well as other groups from the middle and upper classes, stress the advantages of our free enterprise system and expect teachers to uphold its principles. Labor, on the other hand, looks upon the schools as an avenue of occupational and social mobility for its members and particularly their children. Labor feels that education must train young people to be citizens in a democratic community. Education is seen as another step by which the union member can improve his chances to compete in our economic system. Labor believes adequate vocational courses should be provided for those who are interested and that all students should be encouraged to have contact with vocational subjects. It tends to place less emphasis on the traditional, academic type of education. It is opposed to special classes for the gifted and is against removing them from contact with other students.

Thus in the major educational controversy which erupted in San Francisco two years ago, labor exerted its influence to change Lowell High School from an aca-
[2] *Ibid.,* p. 301.

demic to a comprehensive school. Labor was joined by the principals and teachers of the comprehensive schools in the city who understandably resented the fact that Lowell enjoyed a reputation for higher standards than did their own high schools. The teachers at Lowell and the school's alumni association were among the groups influential in support of the academic program.

A prominent union leader offered the following more or less random observations on labor's educational goals and responsibilities:

We have trouble all the time with various taxpayers groups that want to whittle down on vocational schools, apprenticeship programs and the like. We are always having to answer back to attacks on such things as Adult Education. We think these are very necessary and should be continued. Also Child Care Centers. We have always felt deeply about these. We need a decent and a rich Child Care program. Our Women's Organizations support these. Waitresses, for example. They are strong supporters because they have a concern about having their kids taken care of.

Education is a continuing process. You have all the large taxpaying groups continually checking and analyzing the activities of the Board of Education, cutting down and chopping away. In the structure of the Board of Education you have one labor man and six other people. Generally over the years these six are predominantly wealthy or people with business or insurance interests, and by its very nature is bound to be a conservative Board. Thus when it comes to school house construction you will likely see a lot of whittling away. We feel a new school should be a modern complete school. We don't like a school being just specifically an academic school. The basic motive for this kind of academic school is tax-conscious purposes, in our opinion. It's going to cost more money to have a comprehensive high school. An academic high school is the cheapest school. Of course we think it will cost them more in the long run when they eventually have to meet these needs. Our people pay a helluva lot of the taxes, and indirectly probably pay them all.

In San Francisco or any place else, labor's efforts to implement its educational objectives have not always been successful. But in recent years, the involvement of organized labor in these matters has developed to the point where its voice, if not equal to that of the business community, is certainly increasingly important. Of even more interest to the political scientist, however, is the mounting evidence that neither power nor politics in American society is as closely wed to business and financial interests as the varying elitist theories have regularly insisted.

It is undeniable that economics and politics cannot be separated in any strict way. It is also a safe presumption that business leaders and groups not only have more pervasive influence in the general community but also have far greater access to the "tension points" of the decision-making process. This is not to say, however, that these groups and individuals exercise such power and influence so continuously that there are no opportunities for others to participate. In our large metropolitan areas, social change takes many forms and is a response to a variety of different pressures. Local boards of supervisors, for example, are sensitive not only to the ballot box but also to a wide range of influence, persuasion, bargaining, and power in which a multitude of private groups and organizations play a decisive part from one day to the next. It is in this gray area that a disproportionate amount of power may be wielded by some groups and individuals rather than by others. To talk of community decision making, therefore, is to recognize that some of the most crucial "public" decisions are neither public nor private.

If one takes such a pressing problem as the school system, it is clear that the shape and direction of a community's educational program is not simply the result of an electoral choice or even of a public administrative decision. It is also the result of intricate relations between public officials, the board of education, minority racial organizations, teachers groups, neighborhood groups, and many others.

Given the impact of multiple groups on the schools as instruments of the whole community, there is an urgent need for school administrators, along with all other responsible community leaders, to recognize the legitimate role of these groups in our political system and to find ways of dealing with them constructively and democratically.

ROBERT J. HAVIGHURST
Urban Education: The Impact of Metropolitanism (1967)*

One way to look at a big city is to see it as a populous area in which a number of social institutions such as governments, businesses, churches, schools, welfare agencies, and cultural agencies operate to serve human purposes. Each of these kinds of institutions is a social system made up of individuals whose prescribed behaviors or roles are designed to carry on the function or set of functions the social system is organized to achieve. Thus an educational system in this sense consists of a distinctive set of roles which are devised to teach children and adults some things they are not likely to learn outside the system.

In a relatively unchanging society in which social systems can attain their goals without depending a great deal on the actions of other systems, an institution develops a stable set of roles to accomplish the purposes it exists to carry out. In a society undergoing rapid change toward increased interdependence, however, it is more difficult

* Robert J. Havighurst, "Big-City Education: A Cooperative Endeavor," *Phi Delta Kappan*, Vol. XLVIII, No. 7 (March, 1967), pp. 320–322. Used by permission.

for a social system to achieve its goals if it attempts to maintain traditional roles and functions in continuing isolation from other social systems. Our own society has evolved so rapidly toward increased interdependence that it is no longer possible to conceive solutions for the problems faced by a major social system without reference to the functioning of other systems, as has been pointed out by three scholars who recently examined the implications of this change for social planning:

> The problems posed by an advanced industrial society are not only unfamiliar but sufficiently strange in kind and degree of complexity to constitute almost a new genus of problem. We are reaching a stage in the development of thought and action in which problems and goals which we formerly comprehended in relative isolation are perceived in complex, interdependent relationships. Unemployment is currently seen, for example, as in some degree a function of tax rates, interest rates, consumption, savings, investment, the wage-spiral, balance of trade, education and training, segregaton, immigration and automation. In turn, unemployment is viewed as a factor that affects each of these.[1]

Education, in particular, has become a complex function carried out by many kinds of social systems; as a result, the school system does not operate best if left to itself in a way that is more proper to a fire department, a water department, or other systems that carry out more discrete functions.

It is true that in certain areas there is a long and admirable record of close and mutually beneficial cooperation between the schools and other social systems in some of the big cities. The story of school and library cooperation in the city of Chicago is a good

example. In 1910 there were no school libraries in Chicago, so the Chicago Public Library provided a large number of 50-book collections on long-term loan to classrooms in the schools. During 1916–17 the library set up six high school stations which it maintained for five or six years. In 1923 a formal agreement was reached according to which the Chicago Public Library provided books, magazines, and supplies; selected librarians and supervised them; and the Chicago School Board paid the salaries of the librarians. This agreement continued until 1937, when 38 high schools and two junior college branches had libraries under this plan. There were no elementary school libraries during this period, but the classroom loan collections were continued.

Although neither side was completely satisfied, the cooperative agreement was a useful one which lasted more than a decade. After 1937, the Board of Education assumed the cost of books and magazines and later took over the selection and supervision of librarians. A complete library system was established in the Chicago Schools during subsequent years, including almost all of the elementary schools. Thus the school libraries became integral parts of the school system, though the long-term loan collections from the Public Library continued in the elementary schools on a declining basis. In this case a new function (school libraries) was introduced into the school system through inter-system cooperation, and then the cooperation was gradually discontinued as it became less useful.

Today, as in the past, it is possible to find exemplary instances of cooperation between the school system and other social systems. The Oakland, California, schools, for example, recently joined with health and welfare agencies to establish a special school for girls who drop out of school because of pregnancy. Two hundred girls at this school not only will be able to continue their education throughout their pregnancies but also will receive guidance and instruction to prepare them for motherhood. Neither the

[1] Robert Morris and Robert H. Binstock, and Martin Rein (collab.), *Feasible Planning for Social Change*. New York: Columbia University Press, 1966, p. 11.

schools nor the other agencies have the initial capacity to supply this range of services by themselves. If the program succeeds, each party as well as the city as a whole will benefit greatly as the number of poorly cared-for children raised by alienated and dependent mothers declines in future years.

Despite the fact that the school system sometimes has worked well with other social systems, cooperation is a hit-or-miss affair which is all too frequently honored more in the word than the deed. Perhaps the primary reason is that there are still many barriers to cooperation which educators have not made a conscious and systematic attempt to overcome. Although rapid social change undermines the established relationships between formerly independent social systems, institutions tend to keep operating at cross purposes from one another even though they can no longer achieve their original goals unless they complement and reinforce one another. In some cases new functions taken on by one system in response to social change put it in competition with other social systems, as has happened with the educational system's preschool programs which until recently were sponsored on a much smaller scale by the nursery schools and the child-care agencies in the social welfare system. Similarly, many recreation agencies fear they may be put out of operation by the growing number of recreational and leisure-time functions which are being assigned to the educational system because of the latter's more convenient access to large numbers of youth and adults.

In other cases the existing social systems do not perform important new functions because explicit attention has not been given to identifying and filling the gaps between them. For example, the business system and the school system do not work well together in a contemporary society in serving a group of "marginal youth" who are misfits in school and therefore drop out of school as early as possible. These boys and girls, about 15 percent of the age group, find it hard to get jobs when they leave school because the business and industrial systems have few places for unskilled youth aged 14 to 18, on farms, in offices, shops, and factories. Now there is a big gap between the opportunity provided by the business system and the effectiveness of the schools in holding youth and preparing them adequately for jobs.

Many contemporary educators are more ready to acknowledge the value of cooperation with other agencies than their counterparts were some years ago, but in general only a small beginning has been made in actually bringing about the close cooperation we need to achieve in the big cities. In part this is because it is both natural and comfortable to maintain a detached pattern of operation which served fairly well in a previous era. In addition, cooperation between the schools and other institutions has been inhibited by the established administrative principle that the school system should be protected from invasion by other social systems. George Strayer of Columbia University, the most influential leader among school administrators during the period from 1920 to about 1945, said frequently what he wrote in his 1932 report on the Chicago schools: "It is always a mistake for the schools to be organized so that agencies other than a board of education are responsible for the administration of vital and indispensable services in the schools." This principle of school administration tends to be interpreted to mean that the schools should control the administration of all services they perform—even the new and marginal ones such as the school lunch program, recreational services in city parks, job placement of students taking part in work-experience programs, delinquency-prevention projects, and transportation of pupils. The result is that other social systems may see the schools as too aggressive and uncooperative. Thus in practice there may be little actual cooperation between school systems on the one hand and social welfare agencies, recreation agencies, youth-serving agencies, and transportation systems on the other.

The obstacles to cooperation often are particularly serious when it is local city government which is responsible for the social systems which might cooperate with a school system. Such city government services as the police department, the public housing authority, the department of human relations, and the park department may be seen as sources of trouble by the school administrator, because he feels that to cooperate with them might involve him in "local politics." Yet city government is increasingly responsible for a comprehensive program of physical and social urban renewal which brings it very close to the activities of the school system. The mayor or the city manager who understands the dynamics of the big city may take much more of an interest in cooperating with the schools than did his predecessor of 30 years ago, as seems to be happening in New York City, where one observer recently noted signs that:

[Mayor John Lindsay] may be an unprecedentedly active mayor in educational affairs. Already the Board of Education and the hierarchy have been receiving calls from Lindsay aides who ask pointed questions on educational policies and how they are being carried out. Lindsay's staff is also interviewing candidates for the permanent position of educational assistant to the Mayor, and a committee formed by Lindsay is working on recommendations for major revisions throughout the entire school system.[2]

Because the subject is so central to the future of the city, government agencies in the big cities necessarily will be taking an ever greater interest and initiative in the quality and effectiveness of the education made available to disadvantaged youth and adults. For understandable reasons, the school system has not been very successful

in educating the disadvantaged, and as a result it is only to be expected that school officials often will react defensively or negatively when the system's efforts in this critical area come under the scrutiny of other political jurisdictions and the general public. Serious disagreements between the school system and other government systems with whom it should be cooperating to maintain the quality of life in the city can be expected to become even more open and heated to the extent that new semi-official agencies such as the community action boards contain a built-in commitment to reform traditional patterns of control and operation of the schools and other government functions: "*By their very nature* community action programs . . . are designed to push hard and fast for many diverse social changes. In many ways schools tend to look to them like old-fashioned, standpattish organizations that are to be assaulted in the name of social reform." [3]

This brief analysis of the school system in the larger social system of the big city indicates that educators must make a special effort to live up to what until now has been a rhetorical commitment to cooperation with other social systems. In the face of traditional differences in orientation and status between the school system and other governmental institutions, the general imperatives of an interdependent society and the challenge of urban renewal have been forcing the schools to work out cooperative relationships with other government agencies. This striving for cooperation between city government and school government became pronounced in the early 1950's, with the advent of urban renewal legislation, and received additional impetus in the 1960's as a variety of federal acts began to pump money from Washington into local school programs aimed at improving the quality

[2] Nat Hentoff, "Educators as Dropouts," *Evergreen Review*, November, 1966, p. 21.

[3] Lewis J. McGuiness, "The Role of the Public School in Organizing, Coordinating, and Financing Community Action Programs," in *Partnership in School Finance*. Washington, D.C.: National Education Association, 1966, p. 140.

of urban life. Funds made available under the Manpower Development and Training Act, the Vocational Education Act, the Economic Opportunity Act, the Civil Rights Act, the Elementary and Secondary Education Act, and the Higher Education Act are stretching the functions of the school system into forms of more direct service to the city. Education is seen increasingly by civic leaders as serving to improve the city, not only through its effects on the mind and character of the pupil, but also through its effects on the economic system and the social structure of the city. The school system is being seen as an instrument for attracting and holding desirable population elements in the central city, for stabilizing racially integrated neighborhoods, and for solving or holding in check the problems of an alienated and economically marginal minority of slum dwellers. These are socially significant functions for the educational system in the big city, and they all require a good deal of cooperation with other social systems. It is no exaggeration to say that the wisdom and vigor with which administrators work to overcome the barriers to such cooperation will have an important bearing on the future of the cities and the nation.

FRANK RIESSMAN
The Culture of Poverty: Educating Children of the Poor (1967)*

There are numerous paths to improved education of the educationally deprived, culturally different child: the curriculum, parent involvement, school administration. The teacher and his approach stand at a central point; moreover, in the present hopeful atmosphere, the teacher is more open to change than ever before. However, it would be naïve to suppose that teacher change can occur independently of other relevant variables, particularly administration. Presented below is a fivefold plan for the training of

*Frank Riessman, "Teachers of the Poor: A Five-Point Plan," *Journal of Teacher Education,* Vol. XVIII, No. 3 (Fall, 1967), pp. 326–336. Used by permission.

both preservice and in-service teachers of urban disadvantaged children:

1. Building teacher respect for disadvantaged children and their families. This involves attitude change and a proposed method of producing it.
2. Supplying teacher experiences with the disadvantaged.
3. Some general do's and don't's in teaching the urban poor.
4. A teaching technology appropriate for low-income youngsters.
5. The development of a variety of teacher styles through integrating other parts of the plan with the idosyncratic potential of each teacher. This concerns the *art of teaching* and how it can be developed and organized.

1. *Attitude Change Through Interest*

Many people stress the importance of respecting disadvantaged children as the key to their education, but the secret of respect for someone is to know his positives, his strengths. Unfortunately, too many who talk of respecting these children really see nothing to respect. Hence, it is crucial for teachers to know such positives in the culture, behavior, and style of the disadvantaged as the cooperativeness and mutual aid that mark the extended family; the avoidance of the strain accompanying competitiveness and individualism; the equalitarianism, informality, and humor; the freedom from self-blame and parental overprotection; the children's enjoyment of each other's company and lessened sibling rivalry; the security and traditional outlook found in an extended family; the enjoyment of music, games, sports, and cards; the ability to express anger; the freedom from being word bound; and finally, the physical style involved in learning.

These positives must be spelled out in detail lest they become vague, romantic, sentimental, and demagogic. We need clear vision regarding the positives in people who cope with a difficult environment, who can express their anger toward the school, and who are disturbed at being discriminated against. The point is that you cannot have respect in a general way. To have genuine respect, you must know the culture and its positives, you must appreciate how these people cope with their environment, and how in coping with it, they have built their culture.

However, it is not enough to build respect and knowledge; teacher attitudes must also be changed. This is not so difficult as may be imagined; the most important element is to *interest* the teacher in disadvantaged people and their culture. Generally, school personnel have not been especially interested in the make-up of the disadvantaged; the poor, for the most part, are seen as an undifferentiated, drab mass. Surprisingly, providing teachers with sociological analyses of disadvantaged groups, though valuable, is not sufficient to develop deep interest and excitement. Oscar Lewis's literary anthropology is more useful, but it is still not enough; the time has come for teacher preparation to include the novels, films, art, dance, and music of low-income groups, particularly Negro and Spanish. Discussions around books such as *The Cool World*[1] and the movie made from it are more helpful and stimulating than any anthropological text.

Contrasts and issues can be stimulated by books and movies about the disadvantaged elsewhere, such as the British *The Sporting Life* and *Saturday Night and Sunday Morning.*[2] Such films and literature offer prospective teachers a different perspective and a closer feeling for these cultures. Valuable, too, is the study of Negro history and Negro contributions in science, art, and engineering.[3] Discussion of "hip" language may help overcome the stereotype of the nonverbal, inarticulate poor! A look through *Hiption-*

ary[4] is especially valuable in creating a feeling for the language of certain disadvantaged groups; it reveals their wonderful ability to verbalize and destroys the absurd illusion that they lack verbal ability. They have a highly imaginative language, though they are limited in its formal structure, and the school should certainly work on this need. The first area in the proposed program, then, is to build teacher respect for these people by developing interest and excitement in their psychology and culture.

2. Prepared Exposure

The second area considers appropriate laboratory experiences for teachers. Several programs are emerging in this area: one is the Hunter College preservice program described in *The Culturally Deprived Child;*[5] another is the Mobilization for Youth in-service program in New York City. Such programs stress visiting the homes and neighborhoods of the poor. Many people think that this *exposure* will prove positive in and of itself; actually, simple exposure may only reinforce existing stereotypes. Teachers, like everyone else, see selectively what they want and expect to see; consequently, what is needed is a carefully directed, prepared exposure showing *what* to look at and *how* to look at the culture. Instead of merely a broken home, they see an extended female-based family which may be highly organized, although in ways very different from the traditional nuclear family. They learn to see how functions are delegated and organized, how child rearing is handled, how cooking is assigned, how members of the family care for the house, how some go to work, and how responsibility is divided.

Teachers can learn not to confuse the normal with the pathological. The normal

---

[1] Miller, Warren. *The Cool World.* Boston, Mass.: Little, 1959.

[2] Sillitoe, Alan. *Saturday Night and Sunday Morning.* New York: Knopf, 1959.

[3] See *Negro Heritage,* published monthly in Chicago.

[4] Horne, Elliot. *The Hiptionary: A Hipster's View of the World Scene.* New York: Simon & Schuster, 1963.

[5] Riessman, Frank. *The Culturally Deprived Child.* New York: Harper, 1962, pp. 118–119.

female-based family is not pathological, although pathology may occur in some families. The difference may be clarified by a look at the middle-class family. In some middle-class strata, child rearing includes parental overprotection and overindulgence. This is the norm, just as less intensive loving is normative in lower socioeconomic groups. But neither pattern by itself is abnormal, even though pathologies in both classes may well be related to the norm, reflecting it in an extreme form or expressing the constitutional reactions of particular children. What teachers need is an emphasis on the understanding of the basic culture (the norm) rather than on pathology. They should not focus on the environment as such (the crowdedness, the lack of privacy, the lack of economic security) but upon how these people struggle with their environment, how they have thereby forged a culture, and how this culture can be utilized in the school. It is clear, then, that we cannot simply call for tours and home visits. Teachers must be carefully prepared to look beyond the environment and the surface behavior in comprehending the meaning of the life and behavior of the poor.

3. *Some General Do's and Don't's*

The third area briefly considers some do's and don't's in teaching educationally deprived children. Consistency, structure, and order are fundamental. *Informality and authority are not seen as contradictions, and the poor like both.* Extrinsic rewards and punishments are understood, but brutality is strongly rejected. The teacher should be straightforward, direct, and should clearly define what is to be done. *Values related to order, tardiness, or aggression should be strictly oriented toward their usefulness in learning.* (We can't conduct a class if children fight, come late, walk around, etc. This does not mean that fighting is "bad.")

Goldberg states:

The successful teacher meets the disadvantaged child on equal terms, as person to person, individual to individual. But while he *accepts, he doesn't condone.* He sets clearly defined limits for his pupils and will brook few transgressions. He is aware that, unlike middle-class children, they rarely respond to exhortations intended to control behavior through invoking feelings of guilt and shame. He, therefore, sets the rules, fixes the boundaries, establishes the routines with a minimum of discussion. Here he is impersonal, undeviating, strict, but never punitive. Within these boundaries, the successful teacher is business-like and orderly, knowing that he is there to do a job. But he is also warm and outgoing, adapting his behavior to the individual pupils in his class. He shows his respect and liking for his pupils and makes known his belief in their latent abilities.[6]

Different stages of the teaching process should also be considered. There are two crucial stages: first, achieving contact; and second, developing educational power. In the contact stage, comes the special "breaking through" to the child, winning his attention, etc.; although this problem is sometimes exaggerated, it is nevertheless a definite issue in preparing teachers who must develop effective techniques. Unfortunately, a good many teachers who succeed at the contact stage (maintaining orderly, attentive classes) are unable to move on to the next stage and develop educational power. They have done well to achieve the contact stage, but to stop short of the next and most crucial stage is indeed unfortunate.[7]

4. *Appropriate Teaching Technology*

Listed below are a number of approaches that may have special value for low-income children:

[6] Goldberg, Miriam. "Adapting Teacher Style to Pupil Differences." A paper delivered at Teachers College Conference on Disadvantaged *Children,* July 1963, p. 9.

[7] For a fuller discussion of these stages, see Riessman, *op. cit.,* pp. 94–95.

(1) The "organics" approach of Sylvia Ashton-Warner [8] should be especially valuable in utilizing the interests and strengths of the youngsters and should guard against their being "acted upon." (The latter is the current trend in many programs designed for the disadvantaged, who are supposedly deficit-ridden.)

(2) The Montessori System, which envisions a 35 to 1 ratio of children to teacher, may provide valuable leads. The stress on sensory materials and on order in this approach should be particularly congenial to low-income children.[9] (Dr. Ronald Kregler, a neuropsychiatrist at the University of California, Los Angeles, is experimenting with a Montessori nursery program for disadvantaged children.)

(3) Various game techniques may be valuable: In the Manner of the Adverb, Robbins Auditory Set Game, etc.[10]

(4) Senesch's techniques for teaching economics to first- and second-graders seem promising.[11]

(5) Scope, the new magazine published by Scholastic Magazines, is particularly attuned to teaching the disadvantaged.

The Special Significance of Role Playing.[12] Role-playing techniques have long been popular with blue-collar workers in labor unions and industry. Experiences at Mobilization for Youth and various community organizations also indicate an exceptionally positive response to role-play technology by low-income people. Although more systematic research is needed regarding these observations, it would appear that this technology is very congenial to the low-income person's style—physical (action-oriented, doing rather than talking); down to earth, concrete, problem-directed; externally oriented rather than introspective; group-centered; gamelike rather than test-oriented, easy, informal in tempo.

Miller and others,[13] on the basis of investigations, concluded that an outstanding characteristic of the low-income person's style is an emphasis on the physical, especially the motoric (the large muscles involved in voluntary action). They prefer to do rather than to talk. It is not simply that the poor *are* physical: that their labor is characterized by working with things, that their child rearing typically utilizes physical punishment, that their religious expressions more often include physical manifestations of emotion such as handclapping, that when they become mentally ill they appear more likely to develop motoric symptoms such as conversion hysteria and catatonia (disorders involving malfunctions of the voluntary muscles), that they are strongly interested in sports, that they are especially responsive to extraverbal forms of communication such as gestures;[14] the significant factor from the point of view of style is that low-income people tend to *work out mental problems best when they can do things physically.* This is their *habit* or style of work, and it appears when they work on academic problems, personal problems, or whatever.

Role playing appears admirably suited to this physical, action-centered, motoric style that requires a wholistic doing or acting out of situations, a mode of problem solving that low-income males, and young males in particular, find attractive. They frequently

[8] Ashton-Warner, Sylvia. *The Teacher.* New York: Simon & Schuster, 1963.
[9] See Mayer, Martin. "Schools, Slums, and Montessori." *Commentary* 37: 33–39; June 1964.
[10] Riessman, *op. cit.,* pp. 84–85.
[11] Senesch, Lawrence. "The Organic Curriculum: A New Experiment in Economic Education." Reprint Series No. 22. Lafayette, Indiana: Purdue University, School of Industrial Management.
[12] The following discussion of role playing is taken from Riessman, Frank, and Goldfarb, Jean. "Role Playing and the Poor." *Group Psychotherapy,* Vol. 17, No. 1, 1964.
[13] Miller, D. R., and others. *Inner Conflict and Defense.* New York: Holt, 1960, p. 24.
[14] For a discussion of many of these items see Miller and others, *op. cit.*

have a strong dislike for talk, especially talk that is isolated from experience; they want action and prefer talk that is related to action. They also like vivid (e.g., hip slang), down-to-earth, situationally rooted talk; and this, too, is more likely to emerge in the role-play format. Role playing is much more lively, physical, and active than the typical interview.

There are numerous other dimensions of role playing which are congruent with various aspects of the low-income person's style: Low-income groups typically do not like the traditional test format, and this limits diagnostic work with them. The requirements of their style seem to be better met by gamelike atmospheres and situational measures, both of which are found more readily in role-play technology.[15] They are generally less introspective, less introverted, and less concerned with self. They respond more to the external, to the outside, to action. They are more likely to see the causes of their problems in external forces; they project more and tend to externalize their guilt.[16] Kohn notes that their child-rearing patterns center on conformity to external prescriptions in contrast to the self-direction focus of the middle class.[17] He relates this, in part, to the fact that working-class occupations require that one follow explicit rules set down by an authority; middle-class positions are more subject to self-direction.[18]

Although the style of the poor probably includes a strong emphasis on informality, humor, and warmth, the disadvantaged also like a content that is structured, definite, and specific. It is often assumed that role playing is highly unstructured, open, and free. In part, this is true, particularly in the early phase of setting the problem and mood; but in the middle and later phases (especially the role-*training* stage), where the effort is made to teach very specific behaviors, role playing can be highly structured, reviewing in minute detail the various operations to be learned (such as how to run a meeting, organize a conference, talk to a housing manager). Educationally disadvantaged people appear to prefer a mood or feeling tone that is informal and easy but a *content* that is more structured and task-centered. Role-playing may suit both needs.

A Route to Verbalization. In role-playing sessions we have had occasion to observe that the verbal performance of deprived children is markedly improved in the discussion period following the session. When talking about some action they have seen, deprived children are apparently able to verbalize much more fully. Typically, they do not verbalize well in response to words alone. They express themselves more readily when reacting to things they can see and do. Words as stimuli are not sufficient for them as a rule. Ask a juvenile delinquent who comes from a disadvantaged background what he doesn't like about school or the teacher and you will get an abbreviated, inarticulate reply. But have a group of these youngsters act out a school scene in which someone plays the teacher, and you will discover a stream of verbal consciousness that is almost impossible to shut off.[19]

Role playing can have various beneficial results in the teaching of academic material in the school. Considerable excitement is added to a lecture when the instructor illustrates a point this way; for example, if an inquiring student should wonder what Abraham Lincoln would think of our present civil rights policy, let Lincoln and Johnson stage a debate enacted by two students! The im-

[15] Becker, Jerome, and others. "Situational Testing of Social Psychological Variables in Personality." *Mental Health of the Poor: New Treatment Approaches for Low-Income People.* (Edited by Frank Riessman and others.) New York: The Free Press, 1964.

[16] Miller and others, *op. cit.,* p. 396.

[17] Kohn, Melvin L. "Social Class and Parent-Child Relationships: An Interpretation." *American Journal of Sociology* 68: 471–480; January 1963.

[18] *Ibid.*

[19] Riessman, *op. cit.,* p. 77.

possibilities of time and space are eliminated, and the civics lesson will be well remembered.

The Use of Hip Language. A description of the use of hip language (combined with role playing) in teaching disadvantaged children in the Madison Area Project in Syracuse was given in the *Syracuse Herald-Journal* of November 11, 1963.[20]

A teacher had complained to Gerald Weinstein, curriculum coordinator of the Madison Area Project, that her students "practically fell asleep" while she was reading poems from a standard anthology. He responded by distributing to the class copies of "Motto," a poem by the Negro author Langston Hughes:

I play it cool and dig all jive.
That's the reason I stay alive.
My motto, as I live and learn,
Is: Dig and Be Dug in Return

After the students had read the poem, there was a long silence, followed by exclamations, such as, "Hey this is tough"; "Hey, Mr. Weinstein, this cat is pretty cool"; "It's written in our talk." However, when asked the meaning of "playing it cool," the students had difficulty in verbalizing the idea, but a boy volunteered to act it out, with Mr. Weinstein taking the part of the teacher.

During the discussion of the phrase "dig all jive," Weinstein was able to impress upon the class that, in addition to understanding their own jive, their chances of "staying alive" would be infinitely increased if they also understood the school jive.

The enthusiasm of the students for "Motto" led them into more of Hughes' poetry. Later they moved into other kinds of literature, written in more conventional language. But the students were not the only ones to learn from that exciting class. Weinstein learned too: he learned the advantage of being familiar with the language

of the children you are teaching and establishing a rapport with them. If a teacher doesn't "start where the child is," Weinstein says, he only reinforces the failures and frustration that have become the normal pattern for disadvantaged students.

Exposure to the best cultural works produces no magical results, and the phony literature that often characterizes school readers, especially in the lower grades, is even less effective. Exposure must begin "where the child is" and proceed to other varieties of art forms. The method applies to all kinds of students, Weinstein says; for the student who has read Shakespeare but has not read Langston Hughes, for example, is also disadvantaged.

It should be clear that we are *not* suggesting that teachers employ hip language in normal conversation with underprivileged youngsters. It is not intended as a device for attempting to be friendly with the child through imitating his culture; this would indeed be patronizing and dangerous. Rather the use of hip materials in a formal lesson plan can become an excellent avenue to the style and interests of the disadvantaged and contribute to the development of their verbalization.

Recently in tutoring a disadvantaged high school student in English, I employed a hiptionary in a completely systematic and formal fashion. The first and rather immediate result was that the student learned a great many new English word definitions for the hip words with which she had been familiar:

Hip Word[21]	*Definition*
"bug"	to disturb, bother, annoy
"cop out"	to avoid conflict by running away, not considered admirable or honorably accepted
"cool it"	to be quiet, peaceful, tranquil
"far out"	not comprehendible
"weak"	inadequate, inappropriate

[20] Kanasola, Robert. "Students Dig Jive When It's Played Cool." *Syracuse Herald-Journal,* November 11, 1963.

[21] The words in this list were taken from a hiptionary entitled "The Other Language" developed by Anthony Romeo at Mobilization for Youth, January 1962.

Words such as "tranquil," "inappropriate," etc., were unknown to this youngster, but through use of the hip word game, she quickly became familiar with them and derived great pleasure from a new-found use of various "big" words. I then used the hiptionary to clarify the meaning and significance of the metaphor (e.g., the hip phrases for bisexual are "AC-DC," "switch hitter," and "swings from both sides of the fence"). Similarly, many other linguistic concepts can be introduced by utilizing hip language in this word game.

In addition to teaching technology, there is great need for curriculum materials that appear to promise success with disadvantaged youngsters. Both the Bank Street College of Education, through its proposed Educational Resources Center, and Mobilization for Youth have been developing such curriculum laboratories, which should be closely related to the teacher institutes and should contain not only materials but also reports (and films) [22] of positive experiments in the teaching of the disadvantaged, functional illiterates, etc.[23]

5. Effective Teacher Styles

There is some tendency to develop a hypothetical model of the ideal teacher. We

[22] The Lincoln Filene Center of Tufts University and McGraw-Hill Publishing Company are jointly preparing three films related to the teaching of disadvantaged children.

[23] An illustration would be the Bank Street experiment conducted in the summer of 1963 where disadvantaged youngsters showed marked academic and emotional improvement as a result of a special one-month program. Shepard's project in the Banneker District of St. Louis is another illustration. Shepard's program is especially noteworthy because he has demonstrated that disadvantaged youngsters at the elementary and junior high school levels can be quickly improved to grade level. Much more comprehensive efforts than Shepard's might very well produce even more startling results. It is time to put an end to the tendency toward educational surrender on all but preschool disadvantaged children.

tend to assume that effective teachers must be healthy and well adjusted. I seriously question this idea. I am not suggesting, of course, that we look for sick people and make them teachers; what I am suggesting is that we think about the development of individual teacher styles, and some of these may have significant nonhealthy components. There appear to be many styles that function well with low-income youngsters; teachers succeed in different ways. In visits to schools in low-income areas in over thirty-five cities, I have always found at least one teacher in a school who, it was agreed by everyone (children, parents, colleagues, and administrators), was an effective teacher, but the personality of each of these teachers, the manner of approach, and point of view were vastly different.[24]

For example, there is the fussy, compulsive type, whom I find it difficult to query, who teaches things over and over, is very concerned that I understand him, and treats me like a child. But, actually, in the classroom the behavior that annoys me can be quite effective. This kind of person might well be called a "sublimated compulsive"; he directs his compulsivity into the functional order and structure which disadvantaged children like.

Another type of teacher is the "boomer." He shouts out in a loud, strong voice: "You're going to learn. I'm here to teach you, and there is no nonsense in this classroom." He lays the ground rules early, and the kids know immediately that there is a point beyond which they cannot go. They may not like him, but they learn. Some psychologists and educators might call this person hostile; yet he has learned to use this quality effectively in the classroom.

Another kind of teacher might be called the maverick. Everybody loves him but the boss. He upsets everything because he's always raising difficult questions and present-

[24] The discussion of teacher types that follows is based on a joint unpublished paper with Arlene Hannah entitled "Teachers of the Poor," 1964.

ing ideas that disturb. This teacher is convinced that ideas are meant to stir people up, and consequently he develops a close link with his young and eager students. He is as surprised and curious as they at each turn of mind, each new discovery, and it is this fresh quality that comes through to them.

Then there is the coach. He is informal, earthy, and may be an athlete, but in any case, he is physically expressive in conducting his dialogue with the world. Many low-income youngsters like this. Coming from homes characterized by activity and motion, they connect with this quality quickly and naturally.

In sharp contrast is the quiet one. This teacher accomplishes much the same goal by sincerity, calmness, and definitiveness. His essential dignity pervades the situation and commands both respect and attention.

We also have the entertainer, colorful, melodramatic, and most importantly, not afraid to have fun with the children. He may make mistakes through his sheer flair for the comic, but he is free enough to laugh with the children at his own blunders. His inventiveness may furrow his supervisor's brow, as when he has children make western hats from a paper-reading assignment about cowboys. But they learn more about cowboys than if a traditional method had been applied. This teacher actively involves the children—their opinions count, and they know it.

A striking example of another teacher style is the secular. This fellow is relaxed and informal with the kids, may have lunch with them, or use their bathroom. You would be amazed at how many children do not *really* believe that teachers eat and sleep and go to the bathroom like other people! This fellow is comfortable talking turkey with the kids.

There are many other styles, but I will cite just one more—the secular intellectual. He is not academic, but he is interested in knowledge and its transmission to youngsters. He is really interested in the substance

and not just the academic correctness of the material. He doesn't like classical music because he is supposed to but because he likes all types of music; and it so happens that he also likes blues, jazz, and popular music. He really has *broader* horizons. One such person I met was especially interested in hip language, which he was learning from the youngsters—a normally unwise action against which I would warn most people. However, this teacher, because of his deep interest in all language, could show a genuine interest in hip language without being false or condescending.

Teacher preparation should include learning about these types of teachers, with films and observation of them in action, but above all, with an opportunity for student teachers to play each type. Each student should develop his repertoire by trying out the roles in permissive, unthreatening situations in his own group; he should play the classroom and the different problems that arise. Out of this role play, he develops his own repertoire. No matter what is talked about in general, he must formulate these things in his own individual way for his own specific personality. He needs more than practice teaching for this, since the actual classroom cannot allow full experimentation. He needs a practice situation—experimental and permissive—in which he can actually try out various techniques and approaches, experiment with different styles, see which ones fit, blend them to his personality, and develop his own strengths.

Organization of the Teacher Institutes

Without detailing the methods whereby teachers would receive the training proposed in the five-point plan, a number of general principles can be outlined:

Where possible, teachers themselves (master teachers, consulting teachers) should do the teaching or group leading. It may be necessary first to hold master institutes where teachers who would later train other teachers would be exposed to the five-point program. At a later point, these master teachers would be supervised as they translated the program for their local schools. The master institute could call on all kinds of specialists, including sociologists, psychologists, Montessori specialists, role-playing leaders, etc. The institutes could be introduced as special courses in preservice training (in regular sessions or summer sessions) as well as for in-service programs.

Training that is provided close to the operations in which it will be utilized will be most effective.[25] Teachers, for example, should be worked with around their specific school and classroom problems and the trainers should visit the classrooms, observe the teachers closely, and discuss problems and suggestions with them in considerable detail. The ideas embodied in the five-point plan would thus be selectively applied in relation to on-the-job problems experienced by the teacher trainees. An interesting variant of this approach is to be found in the Bank Street College proposal for an Educational Resources Center which will be devoted to "development, collection and dissemination of new instructional materials, new teaching methods, and curriculum innovations specifically designed to raise the achievement of the educationally handicapped minority group child."

Teachers and their pupils selected for demonstration will actually move into the Center for a designated period—say three weeks—where they will receive special instruction from master teachers and other specialists. When the class returns to its home school following the instruction period at the Center, the teacher will continue to use methods and skills acquired at the ERC and will also consult frequently with specialists from the Center who will visit the school. Eventually it is

hoped that each school will boast a number of teachers who, with their classes, have had instructional periods at the Center.[26]

A group or team approach should be a central feature in the training, with a strong emphasis on building esprit de corps in the groups. The group experience would be examined and utilized for the development of concepts, understanding of group process, etc. (T[training]-group approach).

Full participation of the trainees should be intensively solicited with regard to encouraging them to formulate their needs, the way they see their problems, and their suggestions for meeting these problems. Hence, small teacher meetings should be organized to discuss (and role play) ways of meeting classroom difficulties, teaching techniques, and approaches. In this context, the trainers would offer for discussion techniques that have evolved elsewhere.

In order to have the training become a part of the neuromuscular make-up of the trainees, a variety of techniques should be instituted: supervisory conferences, role-playing films, demonstrations, quizzes, intensive brief reading, small group discussions, lectures, debates, and the writing of a paper. This methodology is based on two principles: (a) People learn through a variety of styles—some learn best from doing (e.g., role playing), others from lectures, still others from films, etc. (b) In order to internalize material taught over a relatively short period of time, it is necessary to provide as much active practice and involvement as possible, along with corrective feedback from the supervisory staff; hence the emphasis on role playing and supervisor's sessions. In addition, having the learner teach the material to other trainees appears to be an excellent device for the development of deep learning.

There is constant criticism today of education in the United States—the school system, the curriculum, the teachers, and the

---

[25] This proposal, called site training, as well as a number of other proposals in this section were developed for the Rutgers University Training Center, a grant for which has been requested from the President's Committee on Juvenile Delinquency.

[26] *Bank Street Reporting,* Vol. 1, No. 1, 1964.

administration. There are constant attacks by authors such as Paul Goodman, Edward Friedenberg, and others upon the conformity of the system and the lack of any real learning. There is also constant, powerful criticism of the middle class in our country by authors like Erich Fromm and Paul Goodman, who see the middle class as conformists who have lost their spontaneity and inner convictions. Yet, although this criticism is very widespread, it is rarely applied to the teaching of disadvantaged children, who, apparently, are to adapt to the oft-criticized school and be made into middle-class people by its culture. When we talk about disadvantaged children, we seem suddenly to acquire an idealized picture of the school and the middle-class life for which these children are to be prepared, even though many of us might agree with the David Riesmans, Paul Goodmans, and Erich Fromms that a great deal must be done to change both the middle class and the school. Disadvantaged children have much to contribute to this needed change; their culture, their style, and their positives can aid greatly in the remaking of our middle-class society.[27]

[27] For an excellent discussion of the Negro contributions to our age, see Killens, John Oliver. "Explanation of the 'Black Psyche.'" *New York Times* Magazine Section; June 7, 1964. p. 37.

THE DAWN OF A NEW ERA

FRANCIS KEPPEL
"The Business Interest in Education"
(1967) *

A picture seems to be forming in the mind of the American educator: Knocking at the door of the little red schoolhouse is the giant fist of American business—big business: International Business Machines, Xerox, General Learning Corporation (the affiliate of General Electric and Time, Inc.), Radio Corporation of America, Raytheon, merchants of hardware, makers of electronic computers, of copying machines that can make a million sheets of paper look exactly like the original, and above all, makers of money. On the other side of the door is the classroom teacher, facing something unknown and frightening, and protecting children huddled in a corner. In a seeming competition for the mind of the school child, America's tycoons appear pitted against a lonely, underequipped, underpaid classroom teacher. It is a modern picture of Goliath and David, and it is the result far more of fear than fact.

* Francis Keppel, "The Business Interest in Education," *Phi Delta Kappan*, Vol. XLVIII, No. 5 (January, 1967), pp. 187–190. Used by permission.

Yet the fear is a fact, and must be faced. All of us in education need a calm and rational idea of what the entry of "big" business into education means and what it does not mean; what capabilities business now has for helping education and what it does not have; what capabilities it hopes to develop and those it has no expectation of trying to develop.

In order to understand the so-called confrontation with Goliath, let us examine the situation of David as a teacher in a one-room schoolhouse whose employers are a school board consisting of a farmer, a lawyer, and a housewife. Although this is obviously far from a typical picture of an American school, it may be a useful picture because it represents in ultimate simplicity the basic American idea of locally controlled, citizen-operated education. And it is a good idea. For all the criticism leveled against the idea of control by local school districts, no system of education has operated so successfully and democratically in the history of mankind. And no one should underestimate the power of the local board today.

Our classroom teacher David is harassed by the responsibility of too many children, all making demands from different direc-

r of the team and not as its director. The
t pounding at the schoolhouse door is the
rong picture. The clasped hands of fellow-
ip would be more appropriate.

Americans live in an era when research
nd development are greatly esteemed in
dustry, in technology, in medicine—in
lmost every major enterprise but education,
here research has long been undervalued
nd underfinanced. A few American indus-
ries spend up to 10 percent of their gross
evenues on research and development. In
1965, the federal government alone spent
almost a billion dollars on medical research
and nearly $200 million on agricultural re-
search.

But where did the nation stand in regard
to public schools, an enterprise which stood
at the base of research for knowledge and
the development of human talent? In an
enterprise costing over $40 billion a year at
all levels, the nation spent less than one-half
of one percent of its educational funds on
research to improve the educational process
itself.

This figure—one-half of one percent—
was not a figure from the distant past but an
improvement on the recent past. It included
the new research funds voted by the "Education Congress" in 1965. But it did not
include the promise of new private investment, much of which will probably fall in
the category of "development" rather than
pure "research," if those words are given an
academic definition.

In the middle 1960's, for the first time,
supplies of private capital have become potentially available for the development of
new ways of developing scientific aids to
learning and for making them widely available to a decentralized educational system.
One observer of the scene, Dean Theodore
Sizer of Harvard, regards the development
as comparable in importance to the expanding role of the federal government in education.

But what new contribution can private
corporations make in research and development that educators have not already dis-

covered on their own, or will discover as
a result of research now being undertaken?
My own guess is that industry's contribution will be far less in the area of creating
new ideas or reshaping the content of the
curriculum, and far more in making such
contributions widely available. The decisions
on what should be taught and to whom will
rest where they belong, in the hands of the
educators and scholars supervised by boards
of education and trustees or others representing the public interest. Industry's role
is not to set objectives for American education. It is to help to meet those objectives.

The innovations of recent years, supported
by foundations as well as government, have
shown that change is possible. Yet these
innovations, although many seem promising,
have not yet produced substantial alterations
in the educational picture. This may be because projects have been separately conceived, while major change can be brought
about only if many projects are organized
together with the goal of developing new
systems of education. New curricula influence the preparation of teachers; scientific
aids to learning are inextricably related to
the organization of schools. The scattered
bits of innovation have to be drawn together,
organized by a philosophy, tested and revised by research, and implemented by
methods that lend themselves to reproduction. This is a task for which the research
community in education, and the educational community itself, has not been prepared by habit or experience, and for which
it needs all the help it can get. Business and
technology can provide some of that help,
but can not do more than help. The public
and the educational community realize that
there is need for change. The question is
not whether to change, but how.

What has industry traditionally done in
the face of a demonstrated need, a market
ready and able to buy needed goods, and the
demand for new offerings? By tradition,
American industry sets about to create them.
It is a further tradition of industry to develop competing products to vie against each

tions. (In the country school, David's children may be of different grades. His colleague in an urban school is hardly better off; while his pupils may be all of the same grade, they are stimulated by dissimilar experiences, spurred by disparate curiosities, and they learn at different rates.) David is charged with an almost Godlike task of nurturing the minds of these children toward lives as independent, knowledgeable, ambitious, productive adults. What tools does he have? Indeed, like David of the myth, hardly more than a slingshot. His school board has equipped him with a room, a blackboard, and a few textbooks; now and then a movie, a trip to a museum, a peek through a microscope. With so little, David has succeeded in accomplishing so much. Give him more—a more up-to-date textbook, new scientific aids to learning, a new movie projector, an extra microscope—and it is reasonable to think that he would do even better. For the truth is that David's greatest classroom asset is himself—his warmth, his genuine interest in children, and his ingenuity in somehow managing time for giving individual care to so many.

But what might happen to this all-important personal touch if a computer is rolled in? What can David, backed by his country school board, do against the combined might of America's largest corporations who have declared their intention of moving into the schoolhouse, as some believe, to erase the blackboard and take over the teaching?

By oversimplifying this picture, I am by no means trying to draw a ludicrous one. The fear is real and understandable. As my friend and competitor, Lyle M. Spencer, president of IBM's Science Research Associates, has observed, "There are those who fear that new educational systems involving technology such as computers, video communication systems, and facsimile printing systems will destroy the diversity of our education. Such concern is natural. It is healthy. It is unfounded."

To understand why such concern is unfounded, we have to turn our picture around

and see the same schoolhouse sit   be
the view of modern industry.   fi

Needless to say, one of the t   w
attracted the eye of industry was   st
dollar-size of the present and pot
tional school expenditure. Average   a
ture per year per student has riser   ir
since the war, and it is not unreas   a
assume that the figure in the $300   v
the mid-1950's will double in the mic   a
This possibility is not made less attra   t
the recent addition of more than a
dollars a year of federal aid, an anr
ure that can also be expected to grow
this newly added amount is hardly mo
a small percent of the total local exper
for public schools. But it is a partic
interesting percent. For one thing,
the funds invested by states and local s
districts, the new money is not neces
claimed by commitments to teacher sal
bonded debts for school buildings, or
by old ways of buying textbooks and
strips. On the contrary, a chief purpos
the money is to encourage innovation,
ways of useful educational investment.
billion dollars looking for a good, new v
to be spent does not ordinarily turn
American businessman into a shrinking v
let. Nor should it, for industry has tale
and production facilities and distributic
systems that can contribute to the cause c
education.

But what good, new ways for spending
this money are there? Education, which in
a sense is America's largest industry, lacks
the sound research and the knowledge of
the results of its own experience and tested
ideas on how to meet the demands that will
confront it in the almost immediate future.
It is unequipped with such research because
until very recently no one has been charged
with a large-scale undertaking of it. The
federal government has now entered the
field, but it can only provide the funds and
leadership. Education itself will have to provide the ideas and programs, and it will need
help in their development. This is where the
"new" industry will play its part, as a mem-

other on various levels of performance and price to satisfy various levels of demand in the market. This process leads not only to sales and profits, but to great diversity of choice and great differences in the ways of serving the public. It also describes a basic factor in the relation of industry and education: The latter chooses from the products of the former. If the products do not meet the need, they will not be purchased. Industry must then seek ways to find out what educators need and want (not always an easy task, incidentally), or else go out of business. There seems little doubt that needs and wants exist.

As American industry viewed this need, it was natural to think in familiar terms. Some companies were makers of machines. A few who knew nothing but how to make machines were hasty in rushing new-fangled wares to market, without adequate analysis of what the educator really needed or wanted. They sold "teaching machines" before anyone really knew what the machines could or should teach. And for every sophisticated machine that a manufacturer was impatient to sell, there were some unsophisticated buyers impatient to purchase whatever was new, flashy, and prestigious. As Harold Howe II, the Commissioner of Education, has aptly put it, "Like the drug for which there is as yet no disease, we now have some machines that can talk but have nothing to say."

By now, it is generally understood that any "teaching machine" is simply a piece of equipment. It has no more inherent value than a blackboard or a piece of chalk. What gives it force is the written program that goes *into* the machine and the use to which it is put. Therefore, much speculation about teaching machines would be more relevant if it were speculation about "programmed instruction" and the learning process itself. If by programmed instruction we mean a way to bring the student into the development of an idea step by step, giving him a way to check his own progress, then we come closer to the basic need of helping to make a student realize his successes and errors as soon as he makes them—not days later when the quizzes are returned.

This example is worth our attention in considering the topic of the relation of business, technology, and education. The idea of programmed instruction was not invented by makers of machines but by psychologists and educators. The contribution of a manufacturer to programmed instruction has to be like the contribution of an editor and publisher to a good manuscript of a textbook. He is an agent of transmittal. If he goes beyond his role, he risks failure. The lesson to be learned is that the new offerings of business and technology to the educator have to be developed with the needs of education as a basis, and the cooperation of education as the means.

Creating a better connection between educational content and the equipment that makes it available to learner and teacher can contribute to the improvement of educational methods. It seems obvious that one can hardly move ahead without the other. Neither the authors of instruction nor the makers of machines know precisely in what direction they should move. This is why the nation has recently seen a pooling of interests in the form of corporate mergers between manufacturers of electronics and publishers of the printed word. Understandably, the large number of dollars involved in these mergers have caught public and professional attention, even though they are small compared to the national budget for the schools and colleges. What has received less attention is in reality more important: that these mergers are an attempt to merge talent and professional skill for the support of education, talents that before operated largely in isolation from each other. They include the talents of the editor and publisher, the systems analyst and the engineer, the market analyst and the distributor—all of these as teams to serve the teacher and the school. It is this effort to pool a variety of skills to work on a common task that will prove more significant than the pooling of dollars.

Yet the ultimate test will rest with whether

the services and products that result from these combinations actually serve education's needs and wants. This depends, it seems to me, even more on the educators than it does on industry. The objectives to be met, the organization of schools and colleges to meet these objectives, the content of the curriculum, all rest with the educational institutions. If there is to be effective action, the world of education will have to put these new resources to work. This implies both a desire for change and a willingness to work together. . . .

The real problem of the relation of education and the "new" industry is not whether the American pattern of educational policy and practice will be shifted from present hands to the hands of industry, but rather whether the "new" industry can adapt its offerings to the needs of education and whether education can develop ways of defining those needs and providing the ways for developing and testing the new offerings. As one who has spent his professional life in education, I have become a strong believer in the constant need of bringing fresh points of view and new skills to solving education's problems. The "new" industry offers such a possibility.

But I have also learned through sometimes bitter experience that the pooling of talents and energies is far easier said than done. New vocabularies have to be learned. New techniques have to be developed. Faith in the good intentions of the collaborators has to be built up. All of this takes time and patience. The "new" industry has to accept, as I believe it has already, that this is a business where quick profits are not necessarily good policy; that long development time, in close collaboration with educators and schools, is essential; and that pluralism is "the name of the game." Education will in turn need to be willing to use talents and points of view that are not easy to assimilate, and will have to state its needs and wants both more precisely and perhaps in different language. It will have to bear major responsibility for deciding, through ever more so-

phisticated purchasing techniques, what to choose from industry's new offerings. Both groups have much to learn, and the only safe assumption is that the road to effective collaboration is long and probably rocky. But one point is already clear: It is not a picture of David and Goliath. It is a picture of a team at work on a common task.

PATRICK SUPPES
"The Computer and Excellence" (1967) *

Probably no one doubts the proposition that children are capable of learning more than they actually do in school. Probably no one doubts, either, that the structure of courses and the curriculum can be improved. The hard problem is to become clear about how we can reorganize our schools and the curriculum in order to provide our children an opportunity to learn more. Perhaps the most important point to emphasize about this search for improvement is that we should not anticipate that it will come to an end.

The problem of adjusting the pace of curriculum in any subject area to the background knowledge and motivation of students is a deep and complicated one. I don't pretend to be able to offer a general solution. But some of our experiences at Stanford in elementary-school mathematics, I think, represent a feasible approach to the problem.

Let me begin with two examples from my own experience. The first concerns the teaching of geometrical constructions in the first grade. Starting in 1958, Newton Hawley and I taught a first-grade class daily, two weeks at a time, in the special subject of geometry. We tried to go through as many of the constructions in Book 1 of Euclid's *Elements* as we could. The students we were teaching were bright and able, but we were working with an entire class, not with some

* Patrick Suppes, "The Computer and Excellence," *Saturday Review*, L (January 14, 1967), 46, 48, 50. Published in cooperation with the Committee for Economic Development. Used by permission.

specially selected subgroup. Rather than try to summarize what we did, I will quote from my diary entry for May 2, 1958:

The entire session was spent on review of the things we have done during the past two weeks. The main part of the review was to elicit from the students a list of the eight constructions we have considered which are, namely,

1) draw a circle with given radius;
2) draw a circle with given center and one point on the circle;
3) construct an equilateral triangle with given base;
4) find the midpoint of a line segment;
5) draw an acute angle;
6) draw an obtuse angle;
7) bisect a given angle;
8) given three line segments, construct a triangle.

We then had some discussion of which of these eight constructions was the most difficult. We took a vote and the class results were: No. 8 was the hardest, and No. 4 followed. The students enjoyed this procedure of voting on the most difficult very much.

Almost ten years later, talk about these constructions in the primary grades is not as surprising as it was then. But at the time there was scarcely an elementary school in the country in which such matters were being taught.

The second example concerns the teaching of mathematical logic to bright fifth and sixth graders. We have done this for ten years, with the important practical result that we have found that the elements of logic, as ordinarily taught in introductory college courses, can be mastered without great difficulty by able elementary-school students. Indeed, in the summer of 1964 we even taught a substantial body of material to some very bright children who were about to enter the second grade. These examples suggest that if we can train teachers and provide the appropriate circumstances, it is a relatively simple matter to teach a good

deal more of mathematics and also of other subjects to the abler students in our schools.

There are at least two major obstacles to this straightforward approach. One is a complicated matter of policy, illustrated by the remark of a mother of one of the students I was teaching several years ago: "I don't see any reason for teaching so much mathematics to our children. What they need is a great deal more poetry." Practical decisions must be made about the amount of time devoted to poetry and the amount of time devoted to mathematics, or to social studies, or to English, but it is absolutely essential for all of us to realize that as yet we have scarcely the beginnings of a serious, rational method for making these relative determinations.

A kind of feudal-fiefdom concept dominates the organization of curriculum. Each subject area is allocated a certain percentage of time; for example, elementary-school mathematics ordinarily amounts to about 15 to 16 per cent of the curriculum. It is relatively easy within this 15 or 16 per cent to discuss the advantages and disadvantages of increasing the amount of geometry or giving some exposure to logic. It is quite another thing to discuss whether or not another 1 per cent should be added to the mathematics portion of the curriculum at the expense of literature, elementary science, or social studies, or whether the mathematics curriculum should be reduced in order to provide more time for poetry and belles-lettres. I can't begin here to discuss the complexities of the issues. We are far from having a clear approach to them, let alone a way to resolve them.

The second difficulty results from one of the best substantiated facts in psychology and education: the existence of significant individual differences in learning ability. In 1963 at Stanford we began an accelerated program in mathematics with a group of bright children selected from the first grades in four culturally advantaged schools. Their IQ range is from 122 to 160, with a mean of about 137. Strikingly large individual differences exist even within this relatively homogeneous group of children.

During the first year, for example, the fastest student did 400 per cent more work than the slowest student, as measured by the number of problems completed, which is indicative of the relative speed with which they progressed through the curriculum. To take a slightly different measure for comparison, during the second grade the top four students in the group did about 170 per cent more work than the bottom four students, again as measured by the number of problems completed during the year. We are just completing the analysis of the data for their third-grade work, and the results appear to be comparable to the second grade, although the difference between the top four students and the bottom four students is greater. These differences in learning rate, it is important to emphasize, were not well correlated with IQ, but are due to factors we cannot at present identify.

Examples of significant individual differences in learning ability, even among relatively homogeneous students, are in no sense restricted to mathematics. In experiments with Stanford undergraduates over several years on various aspects of learning Russian, we have been struck by the highly significant differences in ability to learn a second language. In a controlled experiment on the learning of a spoken vocabulary of 300 Russian words, the difference in learning rate, as measured by the number of items successfully mastered in ten sessions, was more than 300 per cent between the slowest and the fastest student in the group. In this case we did not have IQ measures, but we may assume that all the students were highly motivated since they volunteered for the experiment. The data on the slowest and fastest student were not unusual; the other students in the experiment spread out between the two bounds in a relatively uniform fashion.

What can we do to accelerate learning in the schools, especially in a way that is sensitive to the large individual differences in learning rate? . . . For the foreseeable future computer-assisted instruction provides the only practical and economically feasible solution to these problems. Here I would like to describe further how content is handled in computer-assisted instruction—the character of the curriculum and, in particular, the impact of individualization.

Research showing the desirability of regular drill-and-practice in basic mathematical skills, particularly those in arithmetic, goes back for over forty years and is well documented in the literature on mathematics education. Clearly, the computer can offer a regular and standardized program on an individualized basis in this area. During the academic year 1965–66 we wrote and tested such a program of individualized instruction. We divided curriculum for each of the grades three to six into concept blocks and each of these concept blocks was presented for between four and ten days. All students began each concept block at the middle level of difficulty. On subsequent days they moved up or down, depending upon their performance levels. Drills on five different levels of difficulty were available. The student found his own level of difficulty, which could vary over the course of the concept block, depending upon his performance. A very considerable advantage of such an approach is that students are not put in tracks at the beginning of the school year and thereby fixed once and for all at the level at which they should work. We know far too little about evaluation of ability and achievement to make such decisions on a permanent basis.

Consider what would be required of a classroom teacher to conduct such a program of individualized review and practice in arithmetic. At the beginning or end of each day, she would need to assign each student to a level of difficulty based upon his past performance. Upon completion of the exercises she would have to grade and evaluate the student almost immediately to avoid a lag in assignment to the next level.

During the current academic year we are

striving for a still deeper level of individualization. In addition to the five levels of difficulty on a concept block, approximately 30 per cent of the work is devoted to review of past concept blocks. We keep a running score of the student's work for the entire year and continually review his weakest areas of competence. The same five levels of difficulty are used in the review of the concept block on which the student's past performance was the worst. For example, if the student exited from a concept block with a score corresponding to a level-two performance, he enters review work on this block at the same level. The student is branched upward or downward in levels of difficulty, depending upon his daily performance. With a score of 80 per cent or better he branches upward, unless he is already at the top level; with a score running between 60 and 79 per cent, he remains at the same level; and with a score below 59 per cent, he is branched downward.

The preliminary evidence from 1965–66 is that such a program leads to specific improvements in performance on arithmetic-achievement tests as compared to the performance of control groups. This is no surprise. It only confirms research, running back many years, that regular exercises to provide practice on basic skills and concepts will improve long-term performance in arithmetic. The computer provides a standardized and regular way of doing this on an individual basis, tailored to the needs of each student. In principle, such a program could be put into practice by a teacher. But in fact, the elementary-school teacher already has too many responsibilities in too many areas to provide such a daily individualized program.

A common criticism of programed instruction is that the answers required of students are too simple and too stereotyped, and that not enough individual freedom and diversity is permitted. These criticisms do not necessarily apply to properly organized computer-assisted instruction, as shown by the subject of logic, which we have been

teaching at computer consoles for several years.

We initially give children work with "sentential inferences" of the following sort: *If John is here, then Mary is at school. If John is here, where is Mary?* We move on to examples in simple mathematical contexts of the rules of inference that most readers have encountered in secondary-school geometry. We want to provide an environment in which they may make conceptual progress as rapidly as possible. We want to avoid giving the children restricted multiple choices; on the other hand, we do not want to ask them to write out constructed answers, which is tedious for children, particularly at the elementary-school age level. In such a case, we can simply ask the child to input the rule of inference he wishes to apply to the given premises or to the given lines in the proof. Usually, the child needs only three or four characters on the keyboard of the console, which in almost all circumstances is like a standard typewriter keyboard. We use two letters to abbreviate the rule, and in most cases, the rule applies to two previous lines of premises or proof.

In the example about John and Mary given above, the student would use what we call the IF rule. He would input on the keyboard, "IF 1 2," which indicates that the IF rule is to be applied to the lines 1 and 2. The program then would automatically type out the result of applying this rule to those two lines. This is a very simple example. Actually, the student has a large number of opportunities for different types of responses, even essentially different proofs, as he learns an ever larger body of rules of inference and is exposed to larger bodies of laws and facts to be used as premises in inference.

During the current academic year elementary algebra also is being included in this program. We are recording all the different proofs that students give in order to collect objective data on how much genuine diversity students exhibit in coming to grips with a subject—a question that has been of continual concern in discussions of new mathematics and social science curricula. (One of the most positive aspects of computer-assisted instruction is the possibility of gathering complex objective data on student reactions to a given curriculum.)

The presentation of special topics to able students, the provision for selected topics in smaller rural schools, and patient and intensive work with some of the very slow students—all can be handled by computer-assisted instruction, and at present there is no feasible alternative method in sight. Soon, for example, it will be possible to offer an essentially self-contained computer-assisted instruction course in elementary Russian in many high schools throughout the country, without supervisory personnel who are trained in Russian or themselves are prepared to teach Russian. Soon it also will be practical to offer a calculus course in rural high schools by use of computer-assisted terminals connected by telephone lines to a central computer located several hundred miles away.

Today, to equip every elementary-school classroom with a console connected by telephone lines to a computer located at the school district office or some nearby central point would cost approximately $2,000 per terminal, but mass production probably could reduce the cost to not more than $1,000 per terminal, including the cost of curriculum development and preparation. There are approximately 1,000,000 elementary-school classrooms in the country. Thus over a ten-year period the total investment to install a minimum of one terminal per classroom would be approximately $1 billion. This is a great deal of money, but during this same ten-year period the country will spend approximately $500 billion on education, and this $500 billion will itself represent only approximately 5 per cent of the gross national product.

We are all aware of how rapid the spread of television has been in the twenty years from 1946 to 1966. It would be foolish to predict that the spread of computer-assisted

instruction will follow the same rapid course, but it is fair to forecast that in the next ten years the impact of computer-assisted instruction will be felt in a very large number of school systems in this country. The technology alone is not important. What is important is that by the use of computers we can realize the goals of individualized instruction that have been discussed in American education since the beginning of this century. And we can take another significant step toward realizing the full learning potential of our children.

EDWARD JOSEPH SHOBEN, JR.
"Education in Megalopolis" (1967) *

Between 1880 and 1890, the United States committed itself irrevocably to a shift from an agricultural to an industrial economy and from a rural to an urban society. It was not until the decade of the 'fifties, however, that we committed ourselves to the megalopolis. Before this second change, there tended to be a sharp break between the city, with its blocks of houses and shops and its gridiron of streets, and the surrounding countryside, with its fields and woods and farms. Now, in place of the compact, ordered, and intensively used space within the clear boundaries of the city, there is a vastly larger, more diffuse, and more disorderly appearing community. For want of a better term, we call it a metropolitan area, comprising a core city and its abutting suburbs and exurban satellites. And the metropolitan areas themselves are beginning to fuse and grow into each other, forming the great megalopolitan [1] regions of the near future. The American northeast is already

* Edward Joseph Shoben, Jr., "Education in Megalopolis," *Educational Forum,* Vol. XXXI, No. 4 (May, 1967), pp. 431–439. Used by permission of Kappa Delta Pi, An Honor Society in Education, owners of the copyright.
[1] The classic study here—and the one giving currency to the term "megalopolis"—is Jean Gottman, *Megalopolis: The Urbanized Northeastern Seaboard of the United States* (Cambridge, Mass.: M.I.T. Press, 1961).

a functional example—in effect, one great supercity stretching from Boston to Washington. The California coastal belt from San Francisco to San Diego is not far behind in its process of urbanization. The Great Lakes industrial strip, centered in Chicago and reaching from Cleveland to Milwaukee, is another illustration. The Gulf Coast complex that extends from New Orleans through Houston into Dallas is still another. As our modes of transportation become faster and more efficient, it seems virtually inevitable that these nebulous megalopolitan agglomerates will provide the social and economic bases of life for almost all of us.

What makes megalopolis possible, of course, is applied science under the regulation of conventional economics. Medical advances and improved public health measures contribute to the huge populations of the urbanized world. The mechanical and chemical revolutions in agriculture allow us to set ever more sumptuous tables although fewer than ten percent of America's people now live on farms. The radio, telephone, and teletype, together with the jet plane, the fast car, and the superhighway, shrink great spans of space into manageable packages. Because new techniques of production make it more efficient for a manufacturer to organize work on a single floor rather than in multi-storied buildings, he moves from the core city to the urban periphery, where he constructs a plant that rambles like a country club through huge parking lots for employees and customers. Similarly, good roads, automobiles, and extended public utilities permit individual families, striving for always higher standards of living, to search for a balance between the richer offerings of cosmopolitan centers and the more open *Lebensraum* that lies on their fringes. Both retail business and many forms of industry, anticipating new foci of buying power and adjusting to new cost factors in a constantly changing technology, also migrate out of quite comparable motives. Megalopolis, then, is not a static state but a dynamic and gigantic pattern of growth, stimulated by technologized science and by an expansionist economy.

If megalopolis is to be understood not as a thing but a process, not as an end product but as an extremely rapid flowing of people and enterprises, then our urban problems take on a new cast. Our way of life is profoundly in flux; and our difficulties are those of instability, a constant confrontation by novelty, and a perpetual confusion because the immediate past no longer predicts more than the barest lineaments of the immediate future. We are always on the edge of an unfamiliar tomorrow; and this state of affairs, exciting and challenging though it may be, is disquieting to the human heart and mind. One of the central responses this disquiet has evoked has been a major, if somewhat ambivalent, investment of faith in education.

But if education is to prepare children for responsible adulthood in a world of change, for a tomorrow that has less and less in common with yesterday—in short, for the megalopolis—then it cannot simply transmit to a new generation the traditional culture. It is by no means true that the traditional culture has entirely lost its viability and worth. But it is profoundly true that the conditions have radically altered that once made the passing on of our cultural heritage the fundament of effective schooling.

In the last ten years, the family of man has increased by over 600 million people. The entire history of flight, from the first minutes aloft over the sand dunes of North Carolina to the latest traffic in outer space, comprises only sixty-four years, less than the lifetime of a man not yet ready for retirement. The television set was invented only in 1928 and did not become commercially feasible until after the end of World War II. We have not yet lived a quarter of a century with atomic energy; automated industry is an awesome novelty; and the cardiac pacemaker, the electronic gadget that can be surgically inserted into human hearts that otherwise would cease to beat, may indeed be the harbinger of a new

race of androids, beings who are part organism and part machine but far more
clever and efficient than *homo sapiens,* as
we now know him. Given our new computers and cybernetic mechanisms, can we
really say with confidence that the day will
never come when men not only control but
actually *become* a spaceship, a submarine,
or a communications network? Irrespective
of the answer, that such a question can be
seriously asked defines the enormous difference between the world of our fathers
and the world of our children and the reduced (which is *not* a synonym for "eliminated") relevance of our traditional heritage
for the megalopolitan society.

It is within this framework, then, that the
structure of a genuinely modern education
must be developed. The issues here are
numerous and complex, and if education is
truly to contribute to the humanization of
megalopolitan life, then they need to be
thought about and debated. One illustrative
problem has to do with how schools shall
be supported in megalopolis.

As we have seen, megalopolis is characterized by a high degree of mobility; people
and businesses move with considerable frequency as they attempt to alter their economic and social position. When, in favor
of a new plant in a new location, a long-
established industry closes down, it tends to
draw away with it (a) certain of its employees and (b) some of the auxiliary
enterprises—restaurants and bars, super-
markets and neighborhood shops, etc.—that
it supported. Typically, the result is a decline in the tax base that finances schools,
and the people who remain are usually
those whose cultural experience least dis-
poses them to regard education as a capital
investment rather than as a current expense.[2]

[2] The conception of education as a form of
capital investment is a centrally important one.
The basic discussion is that by T. W. Schultz,
The Economic Value of Education (New York:
Columbia University Press, 1963). A compara-
ble, British-based view is developed by John
Vaizey, *The Economics of Education* (New

Large enclaves of our metropolitan areas
therefore are more concerned with tax bills
than with the quality of educational services.
Ironically, these enclaves are not infrequently
places where educational services are most
urgently needed and the sources from which
ignorance, irresponsibility, and violence
creep into the more privileged segments of
the city. Such problems are compounded
when one remembers that a large proportion
of the housing in these areas, both residential and commercial, is owned by absentee
landlords whose local interest is essentially
economic and who understandably but
shortsightedly resent increased property
levies. When communities were relatively
small and stable, when people tended to remain in the same areas in which they grew
up, and when property owners tended to
live in close proximity to their real estate,
then the property tax as the chief source of
educational revenues was sound and sensible. If our faith in education is to be realized
under megalopolitan conditions, however,
we need to think hard about how wise it is
to continue to rely on property taxes as the
primary basis for school support.

But vitally important as problems such as
those of school finance are, they are likely
to be resolved wisely only as we achieve a
viable concept of education in megalopolis.
What must we do if we are to serve our
youngsters and our changing society well?
Any attempt to cope with this question may
be an instance of a fool's rushing in where
angels fear to tread. Yet H. G. Wells's old
characterization of civilization as a race between education and catastrophe was never
more on target.

The basis for one answer to our question
is the concept of megalopolitan education
as being lifelong. A modern education can
have no terminal point, marked by a high

York: Free Press, 1962). Another important
analysis is that by B. A. Weisbrod, *External
Benefits of Public Education* (Princeton, N.J.:
Industrial Relations Section, Dept. of Economics, 1964).

school diploma or a university degree; it must be continued systematically throughout the rapidly changing circumstances with which one must deal in the course of his life span. In the current educational stratosphere, the half-life of scientific knowledge is roughly ten years.[3] That is, only about half of what a new scientist knows at the time he receives his Ph.D. degree will probably be regarded as true ten years later. As a result, many universities and even more industries are finding it both desirable and necessary to send their scientists and engineers back to school to prevent their becoming walking analogues of the hour glass or abacus. The establishment of the new University of California at La Jolla from the top down—beginning with doctoral and postdoctoral work in the sciences, leaving to later the founding of less advanced programs of study—is only one large-scale response to this situation.

But one need not fly so high to make the point about the necessity of lifelong education. In the spring of 1962, President Kennedy was wrestling with the problem of whether to stop atomic testing in the atmosphere. James Reston, the *New York Times* columnist, pointed out that the President's scientific advisers were split into two camps.[4] Some were arguing that nuclear fallout would make genetic monsters out of untold numbers of unborn children for many generations to come. Others, equally illustrious and equally well qualified, were arguing that such claims grossly and luridly overstated the case. On Kennedy's shoulders sat the heavy burden of making a decision, and many of us were not unsympathetic to the lonely load he carried. But sooner or later, Reston reminded us, the average American citizens would have to make some judgment about the wisdom of that presidential decision. The faith on which any democracy

rests is compactly summarized in that little drama. That faith holds that any man, properly educated, can indeed judge wisely in such circumstances. With applied science at the very base of megalopolis, there can be no doubt that comparable issues will frequently recur, and if the understanding of citizens is not constantly renewed at the fount of education, then they will surrender their power and their rights to oligarchs or despots whose benevolence can never be trusted.

Nor need we stay with science. Ours is a world in which place-names like Viet Nam, Tibet, Cuba, Egypt, and the Congo have a familiarity once reserved for Kansas and California. No spot on the globe is more than a day's journey by jet from any other, and the supersonic missiles now trained on us from Russia are soon to be duplicated in China and, regardless of how they may be aimed, other parts of the planet's surface. Because events in Africa or central Asia can quite literally mean life or death for us in North America, they can hardly be of merely exotic interest. The same factors that have given rise to megalopolis have shrunk the earth. But if the earth has shrunk, it has become more complex rather than less. If we are to survive and prosper, we must understand the backgrounds and aspirations of Tanzanians, Japanese, Pakistanis, Argentinians, Laotians, Israelis, Algerians, and many others, as well as Chinese, Russians, Spanish, Scandinavians, the incomprehensible French, and the too often forgotten Canadians! If less theatrical, the requirements of meaningful citizenship are more pervasive with respect to world politics and social development than with respect to the control of atomic energy. Influential debate and informed judgment about world affairs have never been so urgently called for, and their achievement makes it impossible to specify a point in our education at which we "completed" our study of international relations.

What has been said about science and technical knowledge, the public policies reg-

[3] For one useful discussion of the rate and character of scientific expansion, see Derek J. de S. Price, *Science since Babylon* (New Haven: Yale University Press, 1961).

[4] *New York Times*, 7 March, 1962, p. 34.

ulating weaponry (or space programs or automation), and international politics can be modified to fit a host of other important topics: economics and the operations of the business establishment, population growth and the thorny questions associated with its control, conservation and recreational resources, race relations and the embarrassment of grinding poverty in the context of affluence, etc. The range of vital topics is huge, and in the world of the megalopolis it is virtually endless. Obviously, no one can become a master of such a diversity of complex problems, so our principle of lifelong education must be elaborated in two directions.

In the first place, modern education must concentrate less on subject matter and more on learning how to learn and on cultivating the habit of independent inquiry. This notion puts a heavy premium on increasing indvidual senstivity to human issues, on the techniques for acquiring reliable information, and on the processes of thinking about the moral and political, as well as the scientific questions that cut through the affairs of citizenship. Part of the apparatus for further learning is a background of knowledge against which new data and new ideas can be assimilated. But a great deal of our schooling has been built on a curious sequence: Facts and principles, defined as appropriate to particular grades by curriculum committees, have been learned by teachers, who then poured their own learning into pupils; tests were then administered to determine the degree to which youngsters had soaked up this material, not as a background for further learning, but as a kind of end in itself and a ticket to the next grade level.

The point is not to carp about past procedures, but to indicate that films and kinescopes, taped lectures, programed materials, and a rich array of inexpensive and easily accessible books make the amassing of background easy for an individual to manage on his own. What he needs from classroom and teacher is help in the perception of significant problems, a chance to organize his thoughts on paper and to have them rigorously criticized, and the discipline of responsible discussion in which he learns that one of his most crucial auditors is himself. Under these conditions, he is consistently pressed to check his sources, attend to his reasoning, and re-examine his ideas in order both to clarify them in his own mind and to give them some more articulate and public shape. When these circumstances obtain, the student is not preparing for his role of citizen; he is playing it. The teacher, while centrally important, is no longer the source of information and principles. Rather, he is another citizen collaborating in the designing of relevant learning opportunities and serving as a critic of a student's responses to them.

That this conception of education as a systematic and continuing dialogue among citizens is more appropriate to the older ages is, of course, correct. Two qualifiers, however, must be entered into the record. First, as any attentive parent knows, the capacity for meaningful if limited discussion on the part of quite small children is considerable. In our haste to give youngsters the "right" answers to their questions, and in our tendency to regard them as passive receptacles for information and moral values, we have done far too little toward encouraging their becoming self-propelling learners and toward converting their inherent curiosity into the blend of informed criticism and commitment that defines thoughtful citizenship in a world of change. Active dialogue should certainly increase and become more disciplined by logic and knowledge as the educational process continues, but it can be begun much earlier than we have characteristically believed.[5]

[5] Useful technical discussions of this point can be found in the chapter on "Research on Teaching in the Nursery School" by Pauline S. Sears and Edith Dowley (and in their useful bibliography) in N. L. Gage (ed.), *Handbook of Research in Teaching.* (Chicago: Rand McNally, 1963), pp. 814–864. A representative and re-

Our second qualifier is of a somewhat different order. Megalopolis teems with information. The urban world is flooded with news and commentary, material on science and international affairs, statements by public officials, and a thousand varieties of similar stimuli. For this reason, today's generation is demonstrably better informed than yesterday's for all the worries and disappointments of its older compatriots. And it is for this reason that one can travel from Baltimore to Seattle, from Duluth to Biloxi, and never have trouble recognizing one's fellow Americans. Formed and informed by a national press, national radio and television networks, and national movies, all of us share in a common culture whatever the particular wrinkles we bring to it from family or region. This commonality, born of *Time* and the *Saturday Evening Post* (including their highly persuasive advertising) and of TV and the film, is a major source of our sense of community and our unapologetic patriotism. The term "mass civilization," part of the vocabulary of megalopolis, is by no means entirely an insult, implying as it does a body of knowledge and a set of values which are deeply shared and which serve to bind large numbers of people together in mutual loyalties and reasonable respect if not in friendliness.[6]

On the other hand, our common culture is also marked by a worrisome tenuousness. Despite the obvious lessons of American history, mistrust and tension still run high, for example, among our various ethnic and racial groups.[7] The current crimes and disruptions associated with the too long delayed inclusion of Negroes into full citizenship are only virulent symptoms of a long illness in our basic pattern of social life. In spite of these tears in our cultural fabric, the mass civilization of megalopolis threatens the individuality and pluralism that are our historic and fundamental values. As a prominent economist[8] has noted, "It is in the very nature of a scientific technology (the basis of megalopolis) that it steadily contracts the boundaries of the self-sufficient person while expanding those of the public particle." "Conformity," another term in megalopolis' lexicon of danger, means precisely this debasing of the person into the public particle.

And it is here that education finds its greatest significance. Schools have traditionally meant the enhancement of individual lives, the encouragement of intellectual, moral, and aesthetic growth in *persons,* not "public particles." For this reason lifelong education for citizenship in megalopolis must put a new stress on expression, criticism, and the discipline of dialogue. It is worth repeating that expression, criticism, and dialogue are worthless unless they are informed and rational. But our technology now bombards us with information; the wise use of that technology makes much of it easier than ever to acquire; and rationality for most of us is an endless quest, best pursued through honest interaction with one's fellows in important issues. For the foreseeable future, the extension of our educational

---

sponsible popular treatment is by Maya Pines, "How Three-Year-Olds Teach Themselves to Read—and Love It," *Harper's Magazine,* May, 1963. Jerome Bruner's influential *The Process of Education* (Cambridge, Mass.: Harvard University Press, 1960), is also relevant here.

[6] The problem of a common culture that is unifying but not stultifying is discussed provocatively by a number of the essayists in Philip Olson's anthology, *America as a Mass Society* (New York: Free Press, 1963). See also L. A. Cremin, *The Transformation of the School* (New York: Alfred A. Knopf, 1961).

[7] Perhaps the most comprehensive and authoritative analysis is Nathan Glazer's and Daniel Moynihan's *Beyond the Melting Pot* (Cambridge, Mass.: M.I.T. Press and Harvard University Press, 1963).

[8] Robert L. Heilbroner. See his *The Making of Economic Society* (Englewood Cliffs, N.J.: Prentice-Hall, 1962). The issue is also dealt with provocatively by David Riesman in *Abundance for What?* (Garden City, N.Y.: Doubleday, 1964), and it is analyzed in depth by Jacques Ellul, *The Technological Society* (New York: Alfred Knopf, 1964).

establishment (with a small "e") represents the best device for insuring the individuality that we rightfully prize, as well as for making it possible for men to stay responsibly and zestfully abreast of the changes that are the megalopolitan hallmark.

But it is time to return to our second elaboration of the theme of lifelong education. If education must reach up in the age-scale, it must also reach down. Universal and compulsory education has been well established for children between the ages of six and sixteen. It is now being extended, in a preliminary and *de facto* sort of way, into the post-secondary years through community colleges and technical schools. It seems odd that the most plastic and formative period of life has been exempted from formal educational influences.[9] Until very recently, our official doctrine was that the child from birth to six belonged at home. Aside from a few nursery schools, sometimes regarded as baby-sitting operations, we have seldom considered openly the possibility that this policy may be inappropriate to our times.

With the beginnings of Project Head Start, we have learned that, in the case of the culturally underprivileged, waiting until a child is of kindergarten or first-grade age to begin his systematic education may entirely vitiate the opportunity for personal growth that the school represents. Such a youngster tends to bring with him a strong pattern of attitudes toward language and communication, toward print and film, and toward relationships with both adults and other children that are inimical to his launching himself successfully toward the role of citizen-learner. A great deal of such a boy's or girl's school experience for a long time must be remedial, an arrangement that is both less effective and less economical than we can afford. Head Start is funda-

mentally an effort to draw children into the orbit of critical citizenship before they have developed serious inhibitions against it.

To the extent that Head Start and comparable programs prove useful for disadvantaged children, they may also be highly desirable for those from other segments of our society. It has become evident that children can learn a great deal more at earlier ages than we have previously thought. Even good parents are not necessarily skillful teachers. If we can make the distinction between parenthood and the role of the teacher for the first six years of life, just as we have learned to make it for the elementary-school years, then we may be able to register exciting gains, otherwise unobtainable, in the quality of American personhood and citizenship. Rapid reading and good comprehension, for instance, require not only the mastery of some basic skills, but also a friendly and curious attitude toward print as a source of interesting and useful information. Further, growth in reading is broadly linked to growth in written expression. Recent work strongly suggests that the pencil point has been a clumsy obstruction to a child's discovery of how to put his thoughts and observations on paper; a typewriter, on the other hand, is much more manipulable for young hands, more fun, and a greater facilitator of interest and pride in learning to write. An earlier introduction to language functions, using the pedagogical techniques relevant to three- to five-year-olds, could markedly raise the level of cognitive competence in our society in a single generation.[10]

Similarly, we know that early childhood is far freer from the ravages of prejudice

[9] The balance of this discussion leans heavily on the important study by Benjamin Bloom, *Stability and Change in Human Characteristics* (New York: John Wiley & Sons, 1964).

[10] A great deal of useful material here has been collected by Alfred de Grazia and D. A. Sohn (eds.), *Revolution in Teaching: New Theory, Technology, and Curricula* (New York: Bantam Books, 1964). Despite its technicalities, an invaluable paper is Eleanor J. Gibson's "Learning to Read," *Science* (May 21, 1965), 148: 1066–1072.

than are later ages.[11] An earlier school experience, where youngsters become familiar with each other directly, could materially reduce the fear, the disrespect, and the feelings of hierarchy—of inferiority and superiority—that are not irrelevant to urban violence and vandalism.

In any case, we now know that not only arithmetic and language ability, but aggression and personal autonomy are much more amenable to change at earlier ages than later. The longer one waits to develop these traits along socially constructive lines, the more difficult it is to do so. In the static society before the urban revolution, ignorance and eccentricity were not major causes for concern. One of the humane features of megalopolis is that it makes aberrant development an object of shared worry. The school dropout, the delinquent, and the poisonously prejudiced can be neither hidden nor tolerated. If education is indeed the hinge on which a democratic civilization swings, then its effectiveness as a pivot depends in large part on its accessibility to children during their most responsive and pliable years.

Megalopolis means more than big cities. It means a way of life for dense populations. That way of life will remain marked by an increasing rate of change; change not only in our gadgets, but change in our habits, institutions, relationships, and understandings. The megalopolitan way of life is not without its extensive and expensive strains; but it also implies opportunities for humane and gracious living that have never before been imagined for such a vast proportion of society's members. If those opportunities are to be realized, then education, beginning early in childhood, must play a lifelong part in the creation and maintenance of megalopolitan citizens, capable of both enjoying

[11] A sound and nontechnical discussion can be found in Boyd McCandless, *Children and Adolescents: Behavior and Development* (New York: Holt, Rinehart, & Winston, 1961), pp. 355-404.

and directing the rapid currents of contemporary culture.

NORMAN COUSINS
"The End of the Social Contract" (1967) *

The telltale words of contemporary civilization are mobility, power, electronic intelligence. Man can visit the moon; he can move mountains or expunge cities; he can delegate his complications to mechanical brains. But beyond all the swirlings and the shouting is a stark and ultimate fact: The whole concept of natural law is not a workable reality in a nuclear age.

Natural law is one of the oldest ideas in the political and philosophical evolution of man. The idea is uncomplicated: Man acquires basic rights just in the act of being born. Government cannot ignore or obliterate these rights, which have to do with justice, protection, personal dignity, and which are felt by conscience even when they are not in codes. The Magna Carta, the English Bill of Rights, the French Declaration of the Rights of Man, and the U.S. Bill of Rights are attempts to give legal reality to natural law. The moral of Sophocles's *Antigone* was that the law of kings is subordinate to a higher justice based on sensitivity and common sense. Aristotle, Cicero, St. Thomas Aquinas, Sir Edward Coke, Hugo Grotius, John Locke, John Stuart Mill, John Milton, and Thomas Jefferson are only a few names in the long procession of thinkers who recognized the existence of natural rights and the natural obligations of governments with respect to them.

The major obligation of national governments, as John Locke saw it, was to respect and protect the lives, properties, and culture of their peoples. This was a major aspect of the social contract. But this contract is now beyond the means of any government to fulfill. For no state today can protect its people. At a time when the fingertip of a

* Norman Cousins, "The End of the Social Contract," *Saturday Review*, L (October 28, 1967), 24. Used by permission.

desperate man can activate a whole switchboard of annihilation, and when defense is represented by retaliatory holocaust, the historical social contract between man and the state has ceased to exist. For the world has been catapulted into an open and exposed single arena. The national governments are incapable of safeguarding the people inside that arena.

Just as it has been essential, periodically throughout history, to redefine man's basic rights in the context of changing conditions, so it is imperative for modern man to have a new social contract or a human manifesto, one that can serve as a rallying point for meaningful survival in a nuclear age. Herewith some notes for such a manifesto:

We, the peoples of this earth, bear the ultimate responsibility for what happens to our world.

We hold life to be infinitely precious. It must be cherished, nurtured, respected.

If these beliefs are to have reality, we must accept duties to each other and to the generations of men to come.

We have the duty to ennoble life on earth and to protect it against assault, indignity, injustice, discrimination, hunger, disease, and abuse.

We have the duty to safeguard the conditions of existence, to develop and use the world's resources for the human good, to protect and preserve the soil so that it will yield ample food, to keep air and water free of poisons.

Above all, we have the duty to save our world and everything in it from the consequences of senseless violence in a nuclear age.

We have the duty to create the conditions of durable peace on earth, so that man neither has to kill nor to be killed.

We have the duty to use our intelligence and knowledge in the making of a bountiful life on earth for all men, and to encourage the full development of individual man.

In order to carry out these duties, we must assert the primary allegiance of man to man in the family of man. Human sovereignty precedes and transcends national sovereignty.

As citizens of the human commonwealth, we have the right to demand an end to anarchy in the dealings among nations. World anarchy produces untold horror and anguish and can lead only to the disintegration of man's society and to the pulverization of life itself.

We have the right to demand that nations submit to law among themselves, just as they require that citizens submit to law inside nations.

We have the right to demand that the United Nations become the source of world law, replacing the irrational, irresponsible, and violent behavior of nations with orderly and workable methods for insuring a creative and just peace.

In making known these duties and rights, and in asserting a higher allegiance, we pledge ourselves to the goal of a world made safe and fit for man.

Suggestions for Further Reading

The literature dealing with the history of educational thought is quite extensive. The following list presents a brief cross section of some significant works in the field. The reader should also consult my bibliographical essay in *Education in a Free Society: An American History* (New York: David McKay, 1967), pp. 343–355.

PART ONE

EDUCATIONAL THOUGHT

The Formative Years

* BAILYN, BERNARD. *Education in the Forming of American Society: Needs and Opportunities for Study* (Chapel Hill: University of North Carolina Press, 1960), "A Bibliographical Essay," pp. 53–114.

* BECKER, CARL L. *The Heavenly City of the Eighteenth-Century Philosophers* (New Haven, Conn.: Yale University Press, 1932).

BOAS, RALPH and LOUISE. *Cotton Mather: Keeper of the Puritan Conscience* (Hamden, Conn.: Archon Books, 1964; originally published in 1928).

BODE, CARL. *The American Lyceum: Town Meeting of the Mind* (New York: Oxford University Press, 1956).

BOKSER, BEN ZION. *The Legacy of Maimonides* (New York: Philosophical Library, 1950).

* BOORSTIN, DANIEL J. *The Americans: The Colonial Experience* (New York: Random House, 1958).

* BOYD, WILLIAM, ed. and trans. *The Emile of Jean Jacques Rousseau* (New York: Teachers College, Columbia University, 1962; Classics in Education No. 10).

* Starred items refer to titles available in paperbound editions.

* CRANE, VERNER W. *Benjamin Franklin and a Rising People* (Boston: Little, Brown, 1954).

CREMIN, LAWRENCE A. *The American Common School: An Historic Conception* (New York: Teachers College, Columbia University, 1951).

* CURTI, MERLE. *The Social Ideas of American Educators, with New Chapter on the Last Twenty-five Years* (Paterson, N.J.: Littlefield, Adams, 1959; originally published in 1935), Chapter 3, "Education and Social Reform: Horace Mann," pp. 101–138.

* DILLENBERGER, JOHN, ed. *Martin Luther: Selections From His Writings* (Garden City, N.Y.: Doubleday, 1961), "Secular Authority: To What Extent It Should Be Obeyed," pp. 363–402.

* EATON, CLEMENT. *The Mind of the Old South* (Baton Rouge: Louisiana State University Press, 1964), Chapter 12, "The Dynamics of the Southern Mind," pp. 222–244.

* EGGLESTON, EDWARD. *The Transit of Civilization from England to America in the Seventeenth Century* (New York: Appleton, 1901; reissued in 1961 by the Beacon Press).

ELKINS, STANLEY M. *Slavery, A Problem in American Institutional and Intellectual Life* (Chicago: University of Chicago Press, 1959).

ELSON, RUTH MILLER. *Guardians of Tradition: American Schoolbooks of the Nineteenth Century* (Lincoln: University of Nebraska Press, 1964).

ERASMUS, DESIDERIUS. *In Praise of Folly* (Chicago: Pascal Covici, 1924; edited, with an introductory essay, by Horace Bridges).

FRANKLIN, BENJAMIN. *Poor Richard's Al-*

manack: Being the Choicest Morsels of Wisdom, written during the Years of the Almanack's Publication (New York: Peter Pauper Press, n.d.; a facsimile edition).

GAY, PETER. *The Enlightenment: An Interpretation* (New York: Knopf, 1966).

GENOVESE, EUGENE D. *The Political Economy of Slavery: Studies in the Economy and Society of the Slave South* (New York: Pantheon, 1965), Part I, "The Slave South: An Interpretation," pp. 13–39.

HOLLIDAY, CARL. *Woman's Life in Colonial Days* (New York: Frederick Ungar, 1960; originally published in 1922), Chapter 2, "Colonial Woman and Education," pp. 70–94.

* JONES, HOWARD MUMFORD. *O Strange New World; American Culture: The Formative Years* (New York: Viking, 1967).

KLEIN, HERBERT S. *Slavery in the Americas: A Comparative Study of Virginia and Cuba* (Chicago: University of Chicago Press, 1967), Part II, "The Legal Structure," pp. 37–85.

KOCH, ADRIENNE, ed. *The American Enlightenment: The Shaping of the American Experiment and a Free Society* (New York: George Braziller, 1965).

LABAREE, LEONARD W., *et al.*, eds. *The Autobiography of Benjamin Franklin* (New Haven and London: Yale University Press, 1964).

MCNEILL, JOHN, ed. *John Calvin on the Christian Faith: Selections from the Institutes, Commentaries, and Tracts* (New York: Liberal Arts Press, 1957).

MALONE, DUMAS. *Jefferson and His Time* (Boston: Little, Brown, 1948–1962; 3 vols.).

MIDDLEKAUFF, ROBERT. *Ancients and Axioms: Secondary Education in Eighteenth-Century New England* (New Haven, Conn.: Yale University Press, 1963; Yale Historical Publications, *Miscellany* 77).

* MILLER, PERRY, ed. *The American Puritans: Their Prose and Poetry* (Garden City, N.Y.: Doubleday, 1956).

——— and THOMAS H. JOHNSON, eds. *The Puritans* (New York: American Book, 1938).

MINKIN, JACOB S. *The World of Moses Maimonides, with Selections from His Writings* (New York: Thomas Yoseloff, 1957).

MINNICH, HARVEY C., ed. *Old Favorites from the McGuffey Readers* (New York: American Book, 1936).

* DE MONTAIGNE, MICHEL. *Selections from the Essays of Montaigne* (New York: Crofts, 1948; trans. and ed. by Donald M. Frame).

* MORGAN, EDMUND S. *The Puritan Dilemma: The Story of John Winthrop* (Boston: Little, Brown, 1958).

MORISON, SAMUEL ELIOT. *The Intellectual Life of Colonial New England* (New York: New York University Press, 1956; 2d ed.; originally published as *The Puritan Pronaos*).

* *Noah Webster's American Spelling Book* (New York: Teachers College, Columbia University, 1962; a reprint of the 1831 edition).

* NOTESTEIN, WALLACE. *The English People on the Eve of Colonization* (New York: Harper and Row, 1954), Chapters 11, "The Schools," and 12, "The Universities," pp. 116–145.

PAINTER, F. V. N. *Luther on Education, including a Historical Introduction and a Translation of the Reformer's Two Most Important Educational Treatises* (Philadelphia: Lutheran Publication Society, 1889).

PETERSON, MERRILL D. *The Jefferson Image in the American Mind* (New York: Oxford University Press, 1960).

POUNDS, RALPH L. *The Development of Education in Western Culture* (New York: Appleton-Century-Crofts, 1968), Chapter 8, "Education and the Enlightenment (1700–1830)," pp. 166–190.

PRICE, KINGSLEY. *Education and Philosophical Thought* (Boston: Allyn and Bacon, 1967; 2d ed.), Chapters 7, "Locke," and 8, "Rousseau," pp. 251–392.

ROCKWOOD, RAYMOND O., ed. *Carl Becker's Heavenly City Revisited* (Ithaca: Cornell University Press, 1958).

RUDOLPH, FREDERICK, ed. *Essays on Edu-*

cation in the Early Republic (Cambridge, Mass.: Harvard University Press, 1965).

RUNES, DAGOBERT D., ed. *The Selected Writings of Benjamin Rush* (New York: Philosophical Library, 1947).

* SIMPSON, ALAN. *Puritanism in Old and New England* (Chicago: University of Chicago Press, 1955).

* SIZER, THEODORE R., ed. *Religion and Public Education* (Boston: Houghton Mifflin, 1967).

VAN DOREN, CARL. *Benjamin Franklin* (New York: Viking, 1938).

VER STEEG, CLARENCE L. *The Formative Years, 1607–1763* (New York: Hill and Wang, 1964), Chapter 10, "The Provincial Mind: Its American Characteristics," pp. 230–249.

* WOODWARD, WILLIAM HARRISON. *Studies in Education during the Age of the Renaissance, 1400–1600* (New York: Teachers College Press, 1967; Classics in Education No. 32; originally published in 1906).

PART TWO

AN ERA OF TRANSITION
1865–1919

ADDAMS, JANE. *Twenty Years at Hull-House, with Autobiographical Notes* (New York: Macmillan, 1911), Chapter 18, "Socialized Education," pp. 427–453.

ANDERSON, C. ARNOLD. "Southern Education: A New Research Frontier," in *Perspectives on the South: Agenda for Research* (Durham: Duke University Press, 1967; edited by Edgar T. Thompson), pp. 159–194.

ANDERSON, RICHARD C., and DAVID P. AUSUBEL, eds. *Readings in the Psychology of Cognition* (New York: Holt, Rinehart, and Winston, 1965).

ANTIN, MARY. *The Promised Land* (Boston: Houghton Mifflin, 1912).

* ARCHAMBAULT, REGINALD D., ed. *Dewey on Education: Appraisals* (New York: Random House, 1966).

* BAKER, MELVIN C. *Foundations of*

John Dewey's Educational Theory (New York: King's Crown Press, 1955).

* BAYLES, ERNEST E. *Pragmatism in Education* (New York: Harper and Row, 1966).

* BROUDY, HARRY S., and JOHN R. PALMER. *Exemplars of Teaching Method* (Chicago: Rand McNally, 1965), Chapters 9 and 10, "Dialectical Gardening: Froebel," and "Instruction as Construction: Herbart," pp. 117–141.

BRUBACHER, JOHN S. *Henry Barnard on Education* (New York: McGraw-Hill, 1931; reissued in 1965 by Russell and Russell).

CALISTA, DONALD J. "Booker T. Washington: Another Look," *Journal of Negro History*, Vol. XLIX, No. 4 (October, 1964), pp. 240–255.

* CALLAHAN, RAYMOND E. *Education and the Cult of Efficiency: A Study of the Social Forces that Have Shaped the Administration of the Public Schools* (Chicago: University of Chicago Press, 1962).

CHILDS, JOHN. *American Pragmatism and Education: An Interpretation and Criticism* (New York: Holt, 1956).

* CREMIN, LAWRENCE A. *The Transformation of the School: Progressivism in American Education, 1876–1957* (New York: Knopf, 1961).

CURTI, MERLE. *The Growth of American Thought* (New York: Harper and Row, 1964; 3d ed.), Chapter 22, "Impact of Evolutionary Thought on Society," pp. 540–563.

* DEWEY, JOHN. *Democracy and Education: An Introduction to the Philosophy of Education* (New York: Macmillan, 1916).

———. *Lectures in the Philosophy of Education: 1899* (New York: Random House, 1966; edited by Reginald D. Archambault).

DU BOIS, W. E. BURGHARDT. *Darkwater: Voices from Within the Veil* (New York: Harcourt, Brace, and Howe, 1920).

ELKIND, DAVID. "Piaget and Montessori," *Harvard Educational Review*, XXXVII (Fall, 1967), 535–545.

FLAVELL, JOHN H. *The Developmental Psychology of Jean Piaget* (Princeton: Van Nostrand, 1963).

* HANDLIN, OSCAR, ed. *Immigration as a*

Factor in American History (Englewood Cliffs, N.J.: Prentice-Hall, 1959), "Conceptions of Americanization," pp. 146–166.

* HOFSTADTER, RICHARD. *Social Darwinism in American Thought* (Boston: Beacon, 1955).

JAMES, WILLIAM. *The Principles of Psychology* (New York: Holt, 1890; 2 vols.).

* JONES, MALDWYN ALLEN. *American Immigration* (Chicago: University of Chicago Press, 1960).

KALLEN, HORACE M. *Cultural Pluralism and the American Idea: An Essay in Social Philosophy* (Philadelphia: University of Pennsylvania Press, 1956).

* KAZAMIAS, ANDREAS, ed. *Herbert Spencer on Education* (New York: Teachers College Press, 1966; Classics in Education No. 30).

KOFFKA, KURT. *Principles of Gestalt Psychology* (New York: Harcourt, Brace, 1935).

KÖHLER, WOLFGANG. *Gestalt Psychology: An Introduction to New Concepts in Modern Psychology* (New York: Liveright, 1947).

KOLESNIK, WALTER B. *Mental Discipline in Modern Education* (Madison: University of Wisconsin Press, 1958).

LEIDECKER, KURT F. *Yankee Teacher: The Life of William Torrey Harris* (New York: Philosophical Library, 1946).

* MAYHEW, KATHERINE CAMP, and ANNA CAMP EDWARDS. *The Dewey School: The University Laboratory School of the University of Chicago, 1896–1903* (New York: Appleton-Century, 1936).

* MEIER, AUGUST. *Negro Thought in America, 1880–1915; Racial Ideologies in the Age of Booker T. Washington* (Ann Arbor: University of Michigan Press, 1963).

MONTESSORI, MARIA. *Spontaneous Activity in Education: The Advanced Montessori Method* (New York: Stokes, 1917; trans. from the Italian by Florence Simmonds; reissued in 1965 by Schocken Books).

PATRI, ANGELO. *A Schoolmaster of the Great City* (New York: Macmillan, 1923).

PERSONS, STOW, ed. *Evolutionary Thought in America* (New Haven, Conn.: Yale University Press, 1950).

PIAGET, JEAN. *The Origins of Intelligence in the Child* (New York: International Universities Press, 1952; trans. by Margaret Cook).

RAVAGE, MARCUS E. *An American in the Making: The Life Story of an Immigrant* (New York: Harper, 1917).

* ROSE, WILLIE LEE. *Rehearsal for Reconstruction: The Port Royal Experiment* (Indianapolis: Bobbs-Merrill, 1964).

RUDWICK, ELLIOTT M. *W. E. B. Du Bois: A Study in Minority Group Leadership* (Philadelphia: University of Pennsylvania Press, 1960).

SIGEL, IRVING E., and FRANK H. HOOPER, eds. *Logical Thinking in Children: Research Based on Piaget's Theory* (New York: Holt, Rinehart, and Winston, 1968).

SPENCER, SAMUEL R., JR. *Booker T. Washington and the Negro's Place in American Life* (Boston: Little, Brown, 1955).

STEVENS, ELLEN YALE. *A Guide to the Montessori Method* (New York: Stokes, 1913).

THOMAS, ALAN M., JR. "American Education and the Immigrant," *Teachers College Record,* LV (February, 1954), 253–267.

THOMAS, MILTON HALSEY. *John Dewey: A Centennial Bibliography* (Chicago: University of Chicago Press, 1962).

THORNDIKE, EDWARD L. *Educational Psychology* (New York: Teachers College, Columbia University, 1913–1914; 3 vols.).

* WATSON, JOHN B. *Behaviorism* (Chicago: University of Chicago Press, 1958; originally published in 1925).

* WELTER, RUSH. *Popular Education and Democratic Thought in America* (New York: Columbia University Press, 1962), Chapter 14, "Democratic Education in an Evolutionary Society," pp. 228–242.

WERTHEIMER, MAX. *Productive Thinking* (New York: Harper, 1959; enlarged ed., edited by Michael Wertheimer).

* WISH, HARVEY, ed. *The Negro Since Emancipation* (Englewood Cliffs, N.J.: Prentice-Hall, 1964).

* WOODWARD, C. VANN. *The Strange Career of Jim Crow* (New York: Oxford University Press, 1966; 2d ed.), Chapter 3, "Capitulation to Racism," pp. 67–109.

PART THREE

EDUCATION IN MODERN SOCIETY

1919 to the Present

BALLOWE, JAMES, ed. *George Santayana's America: Essays in Literature and Culture* (Urbana: University of Illinois Press, 1967).

BEGGS, DAVID W., III, ed. *Team Teaching: Bold New Venture* (Indianapolis: Unified College Press, 1964).

* BERNSTEIN, ABRAHAM. *The Education of Urban Populations* (New York: Random House, 1967).

* BRUNER, JEROME S. *The Process of Education* (Cambridge, Mass.: Harvard University Press, 1960).

* BUSHNELL, DON D., and DWIGHT W. ALLEN, eds. *The Computer in American Education* (New York: Wiley, 1967).

* CHAMBERLAIN, JOHN. *The Enterprising Americans: A Business History of the United States* (New York: Harper and Row, 1963), Chapter 13, "The Modern World of Enterprise," pp. 243–263.

COLEMAN, JAMES S. "The Concept of Equality of Educational Opportunity," *Harvard Educational Review*, Vol. XXXVIII, No. 1 (Winter, 1968), pp. 7–22.

CORDASCO, FRANCESCO. *Daniel Coit Gilman and the Protean Ph.D.: The Shaping of American Graduate Education* (Leiden, Netherlands: E. J. Brill, 1960).

DAVID, OPAL D., *The Education of Women: Signs for the Future* (Washington, D.C.: American Council on Education, 1959).

EDDY, EDWARD D., JR. *Colleges for Our Land and Time: The Land-Grant Idea in American Education* (New York: Harper, 1956).

* FORD, G. W., and LAWRENCE PUGNO, eds. *The Structure of Knowledge and the Curriculum* (Chicago: Rand McNally, 1964).

* Four Case Studies of Programed Instruction* (New York: Fund for the Advancement of Education, June, 1964).

GARDNER, JOHN W. *Self-Renewal: The Individual and the Innovative Society* (New York: Harper and Row, 1963).

GERARD, R. W., ed. *Computers and Education* (New York: McGraw-Hill, 1967).

GROSS, NEAL. "Who Controls the Schools?" in *Education and Public Policy* (Berkeley, Calif.: McCutchan Publishing Corp., 1965; edited by Seymour E. Harris and Alan Lewensohn), pp. 19–37.

* HAGAN, WILLIAM T. *American Indians* (Chicago: University of Chicago Press, 1961).

* HAVIGHURST, ROBERT J. *Education in Metropolitan Areas* (Boston: Allyn and Bacon, 1966).

HODGKINSON, HAROLD L. *Education, Interaction, and Social Change* (Englewood Cliffs, N.J.: Prentice-Hall, 1967), Chapter 6, "The Quest for Community," pp. 139–160.

* HOFSTADTER, RICHARD. *Anti-intellectualism in American Life* (New York: Knopf, 1963), Part V, "Education in a Democracy," pp. 299–390.

———— and WILSON SMITH, eds. *American Higher Education: A Documentary History* (Chicago: University of Chicago Press, 1961), Vol. II, Part 10, "Academic Freedom in the University," pp. 841–892.

JENCKS, CHRISTOPHER, and DAVID RIESMAN. *The Academic Revolution* (Garden City, N.Y.: Doubleday, 1968).

* KIMBALL, SOLON T., and JAMES E. MCCLELLAN, JR. *Education and the New America* (New York: Random House, 1962), Part I, "The Reality and the Promise," pp. 3–215.

KING, MARTIN LUTHER, JR. *Where Do We Go from Here: Chaos or Community?* (New York: Harper and Row, 1967), Chapter 4, "The Dilemma of Negro Americans," pp. 102–134.

KOHL, HERBERT. *36 Children* (New York: New American Library, 1967).

KRUG, EDWARD A. *The Shaping of the*

American High School (New York: Harper and Row, 1964).

* KVARACEUS, WILLIAM C., *et al.*, eds. *Poverty, Education and Race Relations: Studies and Proposals* (Boston: Allyn and Bacon, 1967).

LIFTON, ROBERT J., ed. *The Woman in America* (Boston: Houghton Mifflin, 1965).

METCALF, LEE and VIC REINEMER. *Overcharge* (New York: David McKay, 1967), Chapter 12, "The Schools—Guess Who Teacher Is," pp. 152–164.

MICHAELIS, JOHN U., *et al. New Designs for the Elementary School Curriculum* (New York: McGraw-Hill, 1967).

MILLER, RICHARD I., *The Nongraded School: Analysis and Study* (New York: Harper and Row, 1967).

MOYNIHAN, DANIEL P. "Sources of Resistance to the Coleman Report," *Harvard Educational Review,* Vol. XXXVIII, No. 1 (Winter, 1968), pp. 23–36.

PERKINS, JAMES A. *The University in Transition* (Princeton: Princeton University Press, 1966).

PRICE, KINGSLEY. "The Problem of the Culturally Deprived," *Record,* Vol. LXIX, No. 2 (November, 1967), pp. 123–131.

* PUSEY, NATHAN M. *The Age of the Scholar: Observations on Education in a Troubled Decade* (Cambridge, Mass.: Harvard University Press, 1963; Harper Torchbook Edition).

ROSS, EARLE D. *Democracy's College: The Land-Grant Movement in the Formative Stage* (Ames: Iowa State College Press, 1942).

* RUDOLPH, FREDERICK. *The American College and University: A History* (New York: Knopf, 1962), Chapters 13 and 14, "The Emerging University" and "The Elective Principle," pp. 264–306.

SAETTLER, PAUL. *A History of Instructional Technology* (New York: McGraw-Hill, 1968), Part II, "Toward a Technology of Instruction," pp. 78–282.

SHULMAN, LEE S., and EVAN R. KEISLAR, eds. *Learning by Discovery: A Critical Ap-praisal* (Chicago: Rand McNally, 1966).

* SILBERMAN, CHARLES E., and the Editors of *Fortune. The Myths of Automation* (New York: Harper and Row, 1966), Chapter 6, "Is Technology Taking Over?" pp. 97–114.

* SKINNER, B. F. *The Technology of Teaching* (New York: Appleton-Century-Crofts, 1968).

* SMILEY, MARJORIE B., and HARRY L. MILLER, eds. *Policy Issues in Urban Education* (New York: The Free Press, 1968), Part III, "Redressing the Imbalance of the Urban School," pp. 275–442.

* STARKEY, MARGARET M., ed. *The Education of Modern Man: Some Differences of Opinion* (New York: Pitman, 1966), Part II, "The Nature of a Liberal Education—A Study in Contrasts," pp. 113–143.

SUPPES, PATRICK. "Computer Technology and the Future of Education," *Phi Delta Kappan,* Vol. XLIX, No. 8 (April, 1968), pp. 420–423.

* TROW, WILLIAM CLARK. *Teacher and Technology* (New York: Appleton-Century-Crofts, 1963).

* TRUMP, J. LLOYD, and DORSEY BAYNHAM. *Focus on Change: Guide to Better Schools* (Chicago: Rand McNally, 1961).

———, and DELMAS F. MILLER. *Secondary School Curriculum Improvement: Proposals and Procedures* (Boston: Allyn and Bacon, 1968), Part II, "Issues and Action in the Subject Areas," pp. 43–222.

VEBLEN, THORSTEIN. *The Higher Learning in America: A Memorandum on the Conduct of Universities by Business Men* (New York: B. W. Huebsch, 1918).

* WASHBURN, WILCOMB E., ed. *The Indian and the White Man* (Garden City, N.Y.: Doubleday, 1964).

WOODWARD, C. VANN. "Equality: America's Deferred Commitment," *American Scholar,* Vol. XXVII, No. 4 (Autumn, 1958), pp. 459–472.

* ZIEGLER, BENJAMIN MUNN, ed. *Desegregation and the Supreme Court* (Boston: Heath, 1958).

INDEX OF DOCUMENTS

INDEX OF NAMES *

* Italicized numbers refer to pages of documentary selections.